Dear NFT User,

Urgh. 2009: you wouldn't want to d
we've decanted our desk drawers ir
sweat on 40° tubes; when we awl
the O2 was a bit much; and when
wielding scallywag (how we miss
hoods).

D1197930

But hey, this is London. Plague didn't get us; fire didn't get us; the Blitz didn't get us; and whilst some oinky sneezes and dodgy MP expenses may have given us a bit of a wobble, the city has still thrived this year.

In fact, so much so that we've had our work cut out bringing you this fully updated NFT. We've packed in hundreds of new listings, gone back to eat, drink, dance and shop our way through last year's listings to check they're still worth knowing, and we've revised the – can we say it? Oh, go on then – hiLARious guide sections the back.

And we've loved all the feedback you've sent in to us. Yes, even the whiney and poorly-punctuated stuff, because we want to make sure that NFT does everything we've set out to do for you. You told us that you love the clear maps, the cut-to-the-chase blurbs for when you're on the go, and the detailed overviews to make you laugh when your bus is stuck in roadworks. But you gave us the tutting of a lifetime over the lack of choice in coffee shops – and hands up, you were right. So we've included 40 extra independent coffee houses, and while we were at it we also made six new regional overview maps, so you know a bit better how our mapping system fits in with your London (whatever that might be).

But that's the least you'd expect right? So we're not just giving you that. We're always looking to make your life easier, and we know there'll be times when you curse yourself for leaving home without your NFT. Well curse no more. We're also launching our brand new city-by-city iPhone apps, crammed with thousands of listings. With geo-location to tell you everything you need to know about wherever you are, it's a brilliant way to get up to the minute tips, the minute you want them.

So here's to 2010, and to hoping that the NFT introduces you to places which help make your London days your best days.

Cheers,

Jane, Rob, Anne, Michael & all the London editors

Central London

Central London Overview Map 6
Map 1 • Marylebone (West) 8
Map 2 • Marylebone (East) 10
Map 3 • Fitzrovia 12
Map 4 • Bloomsbury (West) 14
Map 5 • Bloomsbury (East) 16
Map 6 • Clerkenwell 18
Map 7 • Barbican / City Road (South) 20
Map 8 • Liverpool Street / Broadgate 22
Map 9 • Mayfair / Green Park 24
Map 10 • Piccadilly / Soho (West) 26
Map 11 • Soho (Central) 28
Map 12 • Soho (East) 30
Map 13 • Covent Garden 32
Map 14 • Holborn / Temple 34
Map 15 • Blackfriars / Farrington 36
Map 16 • Square Mile (West) 38
Map 17 • Square Mile (East) 40
Map 18 • Tower Hill / Aldgate 42
Map 19 • Belgravia 44
Map 20 • Victoria / Pimlico (West) 46
Map 21 • Pimlico (East) 48
Map 22 • Westminster 50
Map 23 • St. James's 52
Map 24 • Trafalgar Square 54

West London

West London Overview Map 56
Map 25 • Kensal Town 58
Map 26 • Maida Hill 60
Map 27 • Maida Vale 62
Map 28 • Ladbroke Grove / Notting Hill (West) 64
Map 29 • Notting Hill Gate 66
Map 30 • Bayswater 68
Map 31 • Paddington 70
Map 32 • Shepherd's Bush (West) 72
Map 33 • Shepherd's Bush 74
Map 34 • West Kensington / Olympia 76
Map 35 • Kensington 78
Map 36 • South Kensington / Gloucester Rd 80
Map 37 • Knightsbridge 82
Map 38 • Chiswick 84
Map 39 • Stamford Brook 86
Map 40 • Goldhawk Rd / Ravenscourt Park 88
Map 41 • Hammersmith 90
Map 42 • Barons Court 92
Map 43 • West Brompton / Fulham Broadway / Earl's Court 94
Map 44 • Chelsea 96
Map 45 • Chelsea (East) 98
Map 46 • Sloane Square 100
Map 47 • Fulham (West) 102
Map 48 • Fulham 104
Map 49 • Parson's Green 106
Map 50 • Sands End 108

North London

North London Overview Map 110
Map 51 • Highgate 112
Map 52 • Archway (North) 114
Map 53 • Crouch End 116
Map 54 • Hornsey 118
Map 55 • Harringay Ladder 120
Map 56 • Hampstead Village 122
Map 57 • Hampstead Heath 124
Map 58 • Parliament Hill / Dartmouth Park 126
Map 59 • Tufnell Park 128
Map 60 • Archway 130
Map 61 • Holloway (North) 132
Map 62 • Finsbury Park 134
Map 63 • Manor House 136
Map 64 • Stoke Newington 138
Map 65 • West Hampstead 140
Map 66 • Finchley Road / Swiss Cottage 142
Map 67 • Belsize Park 144
Map 68 • Kilburn High Road / Abbey Road 146
Map 69 • St. John's Wood 148
Map 70 • Primrose Hill 150
Map 71 • Camden Town / Chalk Farm / Kentish Town (West) 152
Map 72 • Kentish Town 154
Map 73 • Holloway 156
Map 74 • Holloway Road / Arsenal 158
Map 75 • Highbury 160
Map 76 • Edgeware Road / Marylebone (North) 162
Map 77 • Mornington Crescent / Regent's Park 164
Map 78 • Euston 166
Map 79 • King's Cross 168
Map 80 • Angel / Upper St 170
Map 81 • Canonbury 172
Map 82 • De Beauvoir Town / Kingsland 174
Map 83 • Angel (East) / City Rd (North) 176
Map 84 • Hoxton 178

East London

East London Overview Map 180
Map 85 • Stoke Newington (East) 182
Map 86 • Dalston / Kingsland 184
Map 87 • Hackney Downs / Lower Clapton 186
Map 88 • Haggerston / Queensbridge Rd 188
Map 89 • London Fields / Hackney Central 190
Map 90 • Homerton / Victoria Park North 192
Map 91 • Shoreditch / Brick Lane / Spitalfields 194
Map 92 • Bethnal Green 196
Map 93 • Globe Town / Mile End (North) 198
Map 94 • Bow 200
Map 95 • Whitechapel (West) / St Katharine's Dock 202
Map 96 • Whitechapel (East) / Shadwell (West) / Wapping 204
Map 97 • Stepney / Shadwell (East) 206
Map 98 • Mile End (South) / Limehouse 208
Map 99 • Bow Common 210
Map 100 • Poplar (West) / Canary Wharf (West) 212
Map 101 • Poplar (East) / Canary Wharf (East) 214
Map 102 • Millwall 216
Map 103 • Cubitt Town / Mudchute 218

Southeast London

Southeast London Overview Map 220
Map 104 • South Bank / Waterloo / Lambeth North 222
Map 105 • Southwark / Bankside (West) 224
Map 106 • Bankside (East) / Borough / Newington 226
Map 107 • Shad Thames 228
Map 108 • Bermondsey 230
Map 109 • Southwark Park 232
Map 110 • Rotherhithe (West) / Canada Waters 234
Map 111 • Rotherhithe (East) / Surrey Quays 236
Map 112 • Kennington / Elephant and Castle 238
Map 113 • Walworth 240
Map 114 • Old Kent Road (West) / Burgess Park 242
Map 115 • Old Kent Road (East) 244
Map 116 • South Bermondsey 246
Map 117 • Deptford (West) 248
Map 118 • Deptford (Central) 250
Map 119 • Deptford (East) 252
Map 120 • Greenwich 254
Map 121 • Camberwell (West) 256
Map 122 • Camberwell (East) 258
Map 123 • Peckham 260
Map 124 • Peckham East (Queen's Road) 262
Map 125 • New Cross Gate 264
Map 126 • New Cross 266
Map 127 • Coldharbour Lane / Herne Hill (West) 268
Map 128 • Denmark Hill / Herne Hill (East) 270
Map 129 • East Dulwich 272
Map 130 • Peckham Rye 274

Southwest London

Southwest London Overview Map....276
Map 131 • Vauxhall / Albert Embankment....278
Map 132 • Battersea (West)....280
Map 133 • Battersea (East)....282
Map 134 • South Lambeth....284
Map 135 • Oval....286
Map 136 • Putney....288
Map 137 • Wandsworth (West)....290
Map 138 • Wandsworth (Central)....292
Map 139 • Wandsworth (East)....294
Map 140 • Clapham Junction / Northcote Rd....296
Map 141 • Battersea (South)....298
Map 142 • Clapham Old Town....300
Map 143 • Clapham High Street....302
Map 144 • Stockwell / Brixton (West)....304
Map 145 • Stockwell / Brixton (East)....306
Map 146 • Earlsfield....308
Map 147 • Balham (West)....310
Map 148 • Balham (East)....312
Map 149 • Clapham Park....314
Map 150 • Brixton....316
Map 151 • Tooting Bec....318
Map 152 • Tooting Broadway....320

Parks & Places

Alexandra Palace Park....322
Barbican Centre....324
Battersea Park....326
Brockwell Park....328
Clapham Common....330
Clissold Park....332
Finsbury Park....334
Greenwich Park....336
Hampstead Heath....338
Highgate Cemetery & Waterlow Park....340
Hyde Park....342
London Fields....344
Mile End Park....346
Regent's Park & Primrose Hill....348
Richmond Park & Kew Gardens....350
The South Bank....352
St James's & Green Park....354
Victoria Park....356
Wimbledon Commom....358
The Markets....360

Colleges & Universities

Central St Martins....362
City University....364
Imperial College....365
King's College....366
London School of Economics....368
University College London....370
SOAS....372
University of London Students Union....373
Continuing Education....374

Sports

Arsenal....376
Charlton....377
Chelsea....378
Fulham....379
Lord's....380
The Oval....381
QPR....382
Tottenham....383
Twickenham....384
West Ham....385
Wembley Stadium....386
Wimbledon....388
Bowling....390
Golf....391
Pool & Snooker....392
Racquet Sports....393
Yoga....394
Sports Leagues....395

Transport

Gatwick Airport....396
Heathrow Airport....398
London City Airport....400
Luton Airport....402
Stansted Airport....404
Underground....406
The DLR....408
Overground Trains....409
Train Stations....410
Buses....417
Coaches....419
Biking in London....420
Taxis....422
Helicopters....423
River Services....424
Driving....426
Car Hire....428
Petrol Stations....429

General Information

Calendar of Events....430
Flat Hunting....432
For the Kids....434
Internet & WiFi....439
LGBT....440
Timeline....444
Media....446
Toilets....449
Hospitals....450
Libraries....452
Police....453
London Postcodes Map....454
Hotels....455
Landmarks....463

Arts & Entertainment

The V & A....472
The British Museum....474
The Natural History Museum....476
The Science Museum....478
The Tates....480
The National Gallery....482
The 02....484
Cinemas....485
Bookshops....487
Theatre....490
Museums & Galleries....494
Nightlife....497
Restaurants....516
Shopping....540

Street Index....565

Underground Map and **Bus Map**
foldout, last page

Regent's Park
REGENT'S PARK
SOMERS TO
ST. JOHN'S WOOD
LISSON GREEN ESTATE
EUSTON
Euston Rd
Tavistock Sq
Gower St
Marylebone Rd
MARYLEBONE
Portland Pl
Great Portland St
Tottenham Court Rd
Montague Pl
Bloomsbury St
FITZROVIA
Goodge St
York St
Gloucester Pl
Baker St
Marylebone High St
James St
Wimpole St
Chapel St
Cavendish Pl
Cavendish Sq Garden
Oxford St
St. Giles
LISSON GROVE
Portman Sq
Soho Square Garden
SOHO
PADDINGTON
Seymour St
New Bond St
Conduit St
Shaftesbury Ave
Charing Cross Rd
Marble Arch
WEST END
Bond St
Haymarket
Piccadilly Pl
PICCADILLY
MAYFAIR
Hyde Park
Park Ln
Piccadilly
St. James's St
Pall Mall
ST. JAMES'S
Green Park
St. James's Park
Kensington Gardens
Hyde Park Corner
Buckingham Palace Gardens
Grosvenor Pl
KNIGHTSBRIDGE
Broad Sanctuary
Great Smith St
SOUTH KENSINGTON
Pont St
Belgrave Kings Rd
Victoria St
Rochester Row
BELGRAVIA
WESTMINS
Sloane St
Eaton Gate
Buckingham Palace Rd
Vauxhall Bridge Rd
BROMPTON
Belgrave Rd
Pimlico Rd
SLOANE SQUARE
PIMLICO
CHELSEA
Grosvenor Rd
1
2
3
4
9
10
11
12
19
20
21
22
23

ANGEL
PENTONVILLE
Pentonville Rd
King's Cross Rd
Caldwell Rd
City Rd
HOXTON
SHOREDITCH
FINSBURY
Lever St
OLD STREET
SPITALFIELDS
Percival St
Catherine St
Farringdon Rd
Rosebery Ave
St. John's St
Old St
ST. LUKE'S
Bath St
Bunhill Row
City Rd
Shoreditch High St
CLERKENWELL
Clerkenwell Rd
Hatton Gdn
Aldersgate St
Beech St
Chiswell St
Finsbury Ave
BROADGATE
BRICK LANE
Theobald's Rd
Gray's Inn Gardens
FARRINGDON
BARBICAN
Moorgate
Bishopsgate
Commercial St
Holborn
Charterhouse St
London Wall
Wormwood St
High Holborn
HOLBORN
Chancery Ln
Fetter Ln
Farringdon St
Newgate St
Kingsway
Strand
Fleet St
New Bridge St
BLACKFRIARS
Gracechurch St
CITY
Minories
COVENT GARDEN
Temple Gardens
TEMPLE
Upr Thames St
Lwr Thames St
Tower Hill
Tower Gardens
Tower of London Park
Thames River
Waterloo Br
Blackfriars Br
Southwark Br
London Br
Tower Br
SOUTH BANK
SOUTHWARK
BOROUGH
Jubilee Gardens
NEWINGTON
BERMONDSEY
WATERLOO
Lambeth Palace Gardens
ELEPHANT & CASTLE
LAMBETH
WALWORTH
Surrey Square Park
KENNINGTON
Spring Gardens
VAUXHALL
Burgess Park
5
6
7
8
14
15
16
17
18

Map 1 • Marylebone (West)

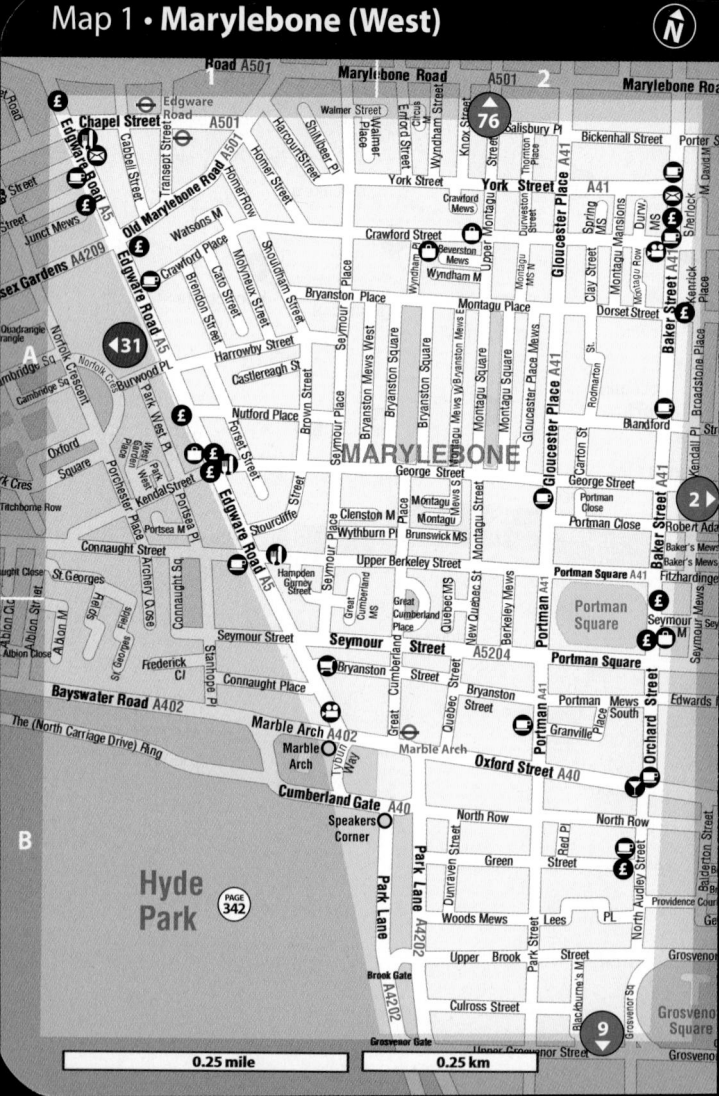
Marylebone Road A501
Edgware Road A501
Chapel Street
Edgware Road
Old Marylebone Road
Transept Street
Cabbell Street
Harcourt Street
Shillibeer Pl
Homer Row
Homer Street
Watsons M
Crawford Place
Brendon Street
Cato Street
Shouldham Street
Bryanston Place
Harrowby Street
Castlereagh St
Burwood Pl
Park West Pl
Norfolk Crescent
Cambridge Sq
Nutford Place
Forset Street
Brown Street
Seymour Place
Bryanston Mews West
Bryanston Square
Montagu Square
Gloucester Place Mews
Gloucester Place A41
Baker Street A41
Dorset Street
Blandford
Broadstone Place
Kendal Pl
Carton St
George Street
Portman Close
Portman Square A41
Portman Square
Baker's Mews
Fitzhardinge
Robert Adam
Seymour Mews
Montagu Mews
Montagu Street
Montagu Place
Montagu Mews W
Montagu Mews E
Clenston Mews
Wythburn Pl
Stourcliffe Street
Portsea Pl
Portsea M
Kendal Street
Porchester Place
Oxford Square
Titchborne Row
Connaught Street
Connaught Place
Connaught M
Bayswater Road A402
Seymour Street
Seymour Place
Upper Berkeley Street
Berkeley Mews
New Quebec St
Quebec MS
Great Cumberland Place
Great Cumberland MS
Cumberland Street
Bryanston Street
Portman Mews South
Granville Place
Orchard Street
Marble Arch A402
Marble Arch
Oxford Street A40
Cumberland Gate A40
Speakers Corner
The (North Carriage Drive) Ring
Hyde Park
PAGE 342
Park Lane
Park Lane A4202
North Row
Green Street
Dunraven Street
Woods Mews
Upper Brook Street
Brook Gate
Culross Street
Grosvenor Gate
Upper Grosvenor Street
Grosvenor Square
Bickenhall Street
Salisbury Pl
Wyndham Street
Knox Street
Walmer Street
Walmer Mews
Circus M
York Street
Crawford Street
Crawford Mews
Beverston Mews
Wyndham M
Montagu Mews N
Montagu Mews S
Montagu Mews W
Montagu Mews E
Montagu Mews
Montagu Mews S
Montagu Square
Montagu Place
Clay Street
Spring MS
Montagu Mansions
Durw
Montagu Row
Sherlock
Kenrick Place
Rodmarton St
Portman Close
Brunswick MS
Bryanston Square
Bryanston Mews W
Bryanston Mews E
Gloucester Place Mews
Providence Court
North Audley Street
Lees PL
Grosvenor St
Blackburne's M
Brook Street
Culross Street
Grosvenor Square
Grosvenor Street
Hyde Park
Marylebone
Edgware Road
Marylebone Road
Oxford Street
Bayswater Road
Park Lane
Baker Street
Portman Square
Orchard Street
Marble Arch
Cumberland Gate
Seymour Street
Connaught Street
Bryanston Street
Upper Berkeley Street
Portman Square
Portman Mews South
Granville Place
Quebec Street
Great Cumberland Place
Great Cumberland MS
Quebec MS
New Quebec St
Berkeley Mews
Portman Square
Portman Square
Seymour Mews
Seymour M
Bryanston
Frederick Cl
Fields
Albion Mews
Albion Close
Albion Sq
Albion St
Albion M
Hyde Park
St Georges
Archery Close
Hampden Gurney Street
Great Cumberland MS
Quebec MS
Montagu Mews W
Montagu Mews E
Montagu Mews
Montagu Mews S
Montagu Square
Montagu Place
Montagu Street
Montagu Mews N
Montagu Mews S
Montagu Square
Montagu Place
Montagu Mews W
Montagu Mews E
Montagu Mews

Where the mulah meets the hookah, a stroll down Edgware Road is soundtracked by gurgling shisha pipes and bangin' Arabic pop music. To the east, ostentatiously bejewelled madams patrol Montague Square. They'd turn their noses up at a Shawarma at Beirut Express on the way to the Sequoia Ruby Lounge, and probably wouldn't deign to shop at Maroush Deli. Good, more for the rest of us.

Banks

- **Abbey** • 388 Edgware Rd
- **Barclays** • 9 Portman St
- **Barclays** • 93 Baker St
- **Barclays** • 127 Edgware Rd
- **Halifax** • 200 Edgware Rd
- **Halifax** • 20 N Audley St
- **Lloyds** • 195 Edgware Rd
- **NatWest** • 508 Edgware Rd
- **NatWest** • 81 Edgware Rd
- **NatWest** • 69 Baker St
- **NatWest** • 1 Portman Sq

Cinemas

- **Odeon Marble Arch** • 10 Edgware Rd
- **Screen on Baker Street** • 96 Baker St

Coffee

- **Apostrophe** • 19 Baker St
- **Bagel Factory** • 39 Paddington St
- **Caffe Nero** • 184 Edgware Rd
- **Coffee Republic** • 1 George St
- **Eat.** • 400 Oxford St
- **Eat.** • 114 Baker St
- **Kings Café** • 177 Edgware Rd
- **Pret A Manger** • 556 Oxford St
- **Starbucks** • 29 N Audley St
- **Starbucks** • 34 Edgware Rd

Landmarks

- **Marble Arch** • Oxford St
- **Speakers Corner** • Cumberland Gate

Nightlife

- **Sequoia Ruby Lounge** • 23 Orchard St

Post Offices

- **Baker St** • 111 Baker St
- **Edgware Rd** • 354 Edgware Rd

Restaurants

- **Beirut Express** • 112 Edgware Rd
- **Maroush IV** • 68 Edgware Rd
- **Nippon Tuk** • 225 Edgware Rd

Shopping

- **Maroush Deli** • 45 Edgware Rd
- **Phil Parker** • 106 Crawford St
- **Spymaster** • 3 Portman Sq
- **Totally Swedish** • 32 Crawford St

Supermarkets

- **Sainsbury's** • 55 Bryanston St

Map 2 • Marylebo :)

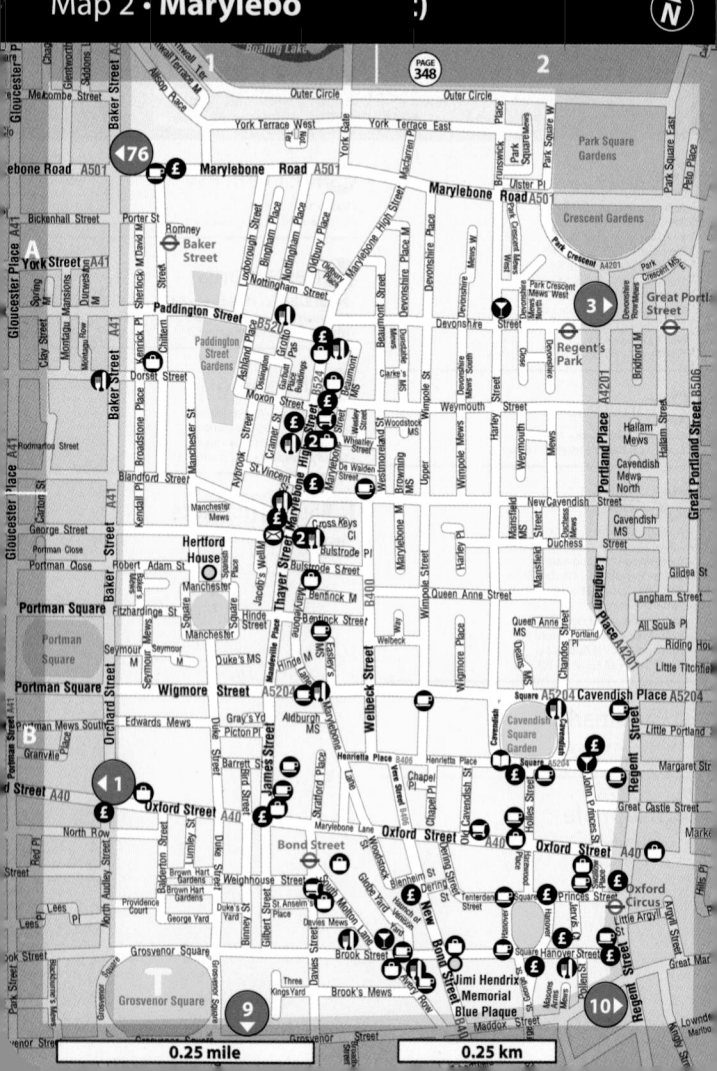

Granted, the plush boutiques and old moneyisms of Marylebone are far removed from most Londoners' lives but there's real thrills to be had in Holmesian London. Start by sauntering into Claridge's to tell Gordon Ramsay to fuck off in an appropriate fashion, or browse books in Daunt if you're not feeling louty. French sweetness and cheesiness can by had at Patisserie Valerie and La Fromagerie repectively.

Banks

- **Abbey** • 14 Hanover Sq
- **Abbey** • 27 Marylebone High St
- **Barclays** • 8 Hanover St
- **Barclays** • 5 Marylebone High St
- **Halifax** • 5 Hanover St
- **Halifax** • 116 Marylebone High St
- **HSBC** • 90 Baker St
- **HSBC** • 19 St George St
- **HSBC** • 431 Oxford St
- **HSBC** • 19 Marylebone High St
- **Lloyds** • 399 Oxford St
- **Lloyds** • 10 Hanover Sq
- **NatWest** • 1 Cavendish Sq
- **NatWest** • 10 Marylebone High St
- **Royal Bank of Scotland** • 97 New Bond St
- **Royal Bank of Scotland** • 28 Cavendish Sq

Coffee

- **Apostrophe** • 23 Barrett St
- **Caffe Nero** • 273 Regent St
- **Caffe Nero** • Marylebone Rd
- **Coffee Republic** • 2 S Molton St
- **Costa** • 69 Wigmore St
- **Eat.** • 9 Avery Row
- **Eat.** • 319 Regent St
- **Eat.** • 25 Hanover Sq
- **Eat.** • 92 Wimpole St
- **Eat.** • 214 Oxford St
- **Paul Rothe & Son** • 35 Marylebone Ln
- **Pret A Manger** • 31 Cavendish
- **Pret A Manger** • 1 Tenterden St
- **Pret A Manger** • 18 Hanover St
- **Starbucks** • 22 Princes St
- **Starbucks** • 14 James St
- **Starbucks** • 63 S Molton St

Landmarks

- **Hertford House** • Manchester Sq
- **Jimi Hendrix Memorial Blue Plaque** • 23 Brook St

Libraries

- **Royal College of Nursing Library** • 20 Cavendish Sq

Nightlife

- **Claridge's Bar** • 55 Brook St
- **Inn 1888** • 21 Devonshire St
- **The Phoenix** • 37 Cavendish Sq

Post Offices

- **Marylebone** • 24 Thayer St

Restaurants

- **Comptoir Libanais** • 65 Wigmore St
- **Diwan** • 31 Thayer St
- **Eat and Two Veg** • 50 Marylebone High St
- **The Golden Hind** • 73 Marylebone Ln
- **Galvin Bistrot de Luxe** • 66 Baker St
- **Gordon Ramsay at Claridge's** • Brook St
- **Hush Brasserie** • 8 Lancashire Ct
- **La Galette** • 56 Paddington St
- **No. 5 Cavendish Square** • 5 Cavendish Sq
- **Patisserie Valerie** • 105 Marylebone High St
- **The Providores** • 109 Marylebone High St
- **Sakura** • 9 Hanover St

Shopping

- **Browns South Molton Street** • 24 S Molton St
- **The Button Queen** • 76 Marylebone Ln
- **Daunt Books** • 83 Marylebone High St
- **Divertimenti** • 33 Maryelbone High St
- **Fenwick** • 63 New Bond St
- **Gray's Antique Market** • 58 Davies St
- **John Lewis** • 278 Oxford St
- **La Fromagerie** • 2 Moxon St
- **Marimekko** • 16 St Christopher's Pl
- **Niketown** • 236 Oxford St
- **Noa Noa** • 14 Gees Ct
- **Paul Smith Sale Shop** • 23 Avery Row
- **Selfridges & Co** • 400 Oxford St
- **The Widescreen Center** • 47 Dorset St
- **Zara** • 242 Oxford St

Supermarkets

- **Marks & Spencer** • Bond St Station
- **Tesco** • 311 Oxford St
- **Waitrose** • 98 Marylebone High St

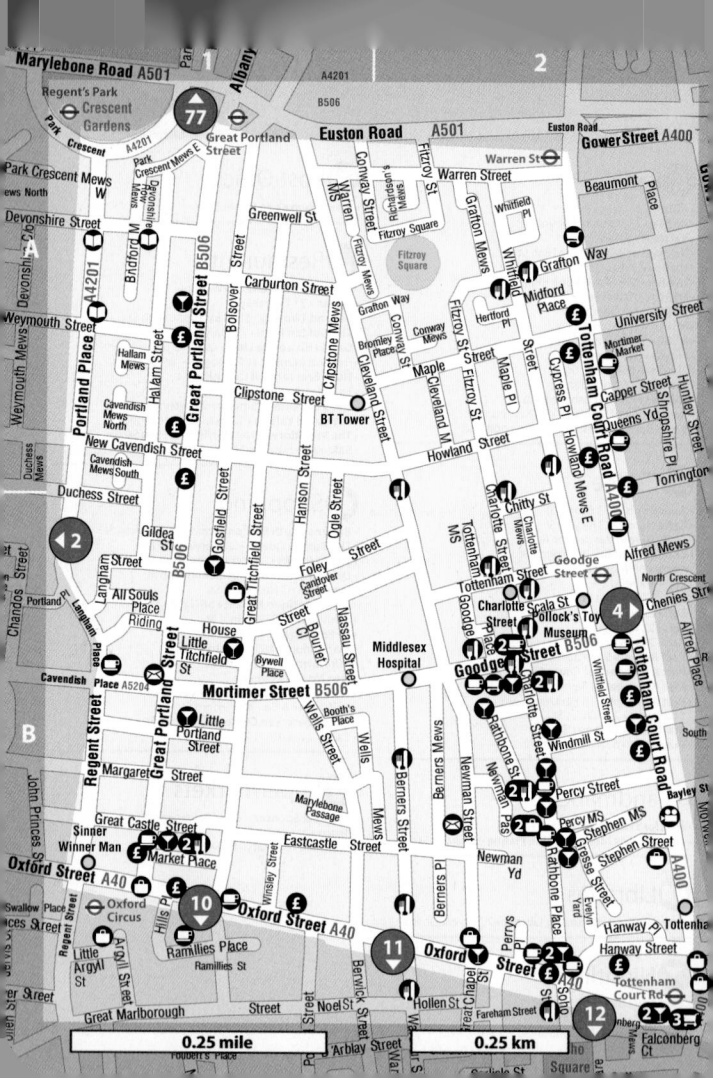
Marylebone Road A501
Regent's Park
Crescent Gardens
Park Crescent
Park Crescent Mews E
Park Crescent Mews W
Albany
A4201
B506
Great Portland Street
Euston Road A501
Euston Road
Gower Street A400
Warren St
Warren Street
Beaumont Place
Devonshire Street
Greenwell St
Fitzroy Square
Fitzroy Mews
Conway Street
Warren MS
Fitzroy St
Grafton Mews
Whitfield Pl
Grafton Way
Midford Place
Tottenham Court Road A400
University Street
Mortimer Market
Capper Street
Shropshire Pl
Huntley Street
Queens Yd
Torrington
Bedford M
Bolsover Street
Carburton Street
Great Portland Street B506
Portland Place
Weymouth Street
Weymouth Mews
Hallam Street
Hallam Mews
Cavendish Mews North
Cavendish Mews South
New Cavendish Street
Duchess Street
Duchess Mews
Clipstone Street
Cleveland Street
Cleveland M
Clipstone Mews
BT Tower
Bromley Place
Conway Mews
Conway St
Maple Street
Maple Pl
Fitzroy St
Cyprus Pl
Howland Street
Howland Mews E
Chitty St
Charlotte Street
Charlotte Mews
Tottenham MS
Tottenham Street
Goodge Street
Alfred Mews
North Crescent
Chenies Street
Alfred Place
Gilsea St
Gosfield Street
Great Titchfield Street
Hanson Street
Ogle Street
Foley Street
Candover Street
Langham Street
Langham Pl
All Souls Place
Riding House
Little Titchfield St
Portland Pl
Chandos Street
Cavendish Place A5204
Mortimer Street B506
Bywell Place
Rouret Cr
Nassau Street
Middlesex Hospital
Charlotte Street
Scala St
Pollock's Toy Museum
Goodge Street
Tottenham Court Road
Whitfield Street
Regent Street
Great Portland Street
Little Portland Street
Margaret Street
Wells Street
Booth's Place
Wells
Berners Mews
Berners Street
Newman Street
Newman Pas
Rathbone St
Rathbone Place
Windmill St
Percy Street
Percy MS
Stephen MS
Stephen Street
Greek Street
Bayley St
Great Castle Street
Sinner
Winner Man
Market Place
Eastcastle Street
Marylebone Passage
Newman Yd
Oxford Street A40
Oxford Circus
Swallow Place
Regent Street
Hills Pl
Winsley Street
Oxford Street A40
Berners Pl
Perrys Pl
Oxford Street
Hanway Street
Tottenham Court Rd
Little Argyll St
Argyll St
Ramillies Place
Ramillies St
Great Marlborough Street
Noel Street
Berwick Street
Hollen St
Great Chapel St
Fareham Street
Soho Square
Falconberg Ct
Arblay Street
Foubert's Place
0.25 mile
0.25 km

Fitzrovia

While the Charlotte Street Ad men piss their expense accounts up the wall in the Fitzroy Tavern, the rest of us can perhaps lament the changing face of a historical chunk of town. Everyone from Karl Marx to the Sex Pistols have slumped drunk in these streets, shouting out slogans for revolutions that never came. Tottenham Court Road is for Hi-Fi heads, while after hours at Bradleys retains its boho sleaze.

Banks

- **Abbey** • 165 Oxford St
- **Barclays** • 15 Great Portland St
- **Barclays** • 190 Tottenham Ct Rd
- **Halifax** • 60 Oxford St
- **Halifax** • 110 Tottenham Ct Rd
- **HSBC** • 39 Tottenham Ct Rd
- **HSBC** • 117 Great Portland St
- **HSBC** • 156 Tottenham Ct Rd
- **HSBC** • 196 Oxford St
- **Lloyds** • 190 Great Portland St
- **Lloyds** • 88 Tottenham Ct Rd
- **Lloyds** • 32 Oxford St
- **NatWest** • 125 Great Portland St
- **Royal Bank of Scotland** • 171 Tottenham Ct Rd

Cinemas

- **Odeon Tottenham Court** • 30 Tottenham Ct Rd

Coffee

- **Apostrophe** • 40 Great Castle St
- **Apostrophe** • 216 Tottenham Ct Rd
- **Caffe Nero** • 79 Tottenham Ct Rd
- **Caffe Nero** • 187 Tottenham Ct Rd
- **Caffe Nero** • 2 Charlotte St
- **Caffe Nero** • 48 Oxford St
- **Coffee Republic** • 23 Rathbone Pl
- **Coffee Republic** • 99 Tottenham Ct Rd
- **Costa** • 213 Tottenham Ct Rd
- **Eat.** • 44 Goodge St
- **Eat.** • 68 Oxford St
- **Eat.** • 94 Tottenham Ct Rd
- **Lantana** • 13 Charlotte Pl
- **Starbucks** • 1 Langham Pl
- **Starbucks** • 203 Oxford St
- **Starbucks** • 51 Goodge St

Landmarks

- **BT Tower** • 60 Cleveland St
- **Charlotte Street** • Charlotte St
- **Middlesex Hospital** • Mortimer St
- **Pollock's Toy Museum** • 1 Scala St
- **Sinner Winner Man** • 216 Oxford St
- **Tottenham Court Road** • Tottenham Ct Rd

Libraries

- **British Architectural Library** • 66 Portland Pl
- **Institute of Contemporary History and Wiener Library** • 4 Devonshire St
- **Royal Institute of British Architects** • 66 Portland Pl

Nightlife

- **100 Club** • 100 Oxford St
- **The Albany** • 240 Great Portland St
- **Bourne & Hollingsworth** • 28 Rathbone Pl
- **Bradleys Spanish Bar** • 42 Hanway St
- **Bricklayers Arms** • 31 Gresse St
- **Charlotte Street Hotel** • 15 Charlotte St
- **The Fitzroy Tavern** • 16 Charlotte St
- **Ghetto** • 1 Falconberg Ct
- **The Jerusalem Tavern** • 55 Britton St
- **Market Place** • 11 Market Pl
- **The Metro Club** • 19 Oxford St
- **Northumberland Arms** • 43 Goodge St
- **Punk** • 14 Soho St
- **The Rising Sun** • 46 Tottenham Ct Rd
- **The Roxy** • 3 Rathbone Pl
- **The Social** • 5 Little Portland St
- **The Yorkshire Grey** • 46 Langham St

Post Offices

- **Great Portland St** • 55 Great Portland St
- **Newman St** • 19 Newman St

Restaurants

- **Archipelago** • 110 Whitfield St
- **Busaba Eathai** • 110 Wardour St
- **Carluccio's Caffe** • 8 Market Pl
- **Crazy Bear** • 26 Whitfield St
- **Eagle Bar Diner** • 3 Rathbone Pl
- **Elena's L'Etoile** • 30 Charlotte St
- **Govinda's** • 9 Soho St
- **Icco Pizza** • 46 Goodge St
- **Latium** • 21 Berners St
- **Market Place** • 11 Market Pl
- **Navarro's** • 67 Charlotte St
- **Neel Akash** • 93 Charlotte St
- **Ragam** • 57 Cleveland St
- **Rasa Express** • 5 Rathbone St
- **Roka** • 37 Charlotte St
- **Salt Yard** • 54 Goodge St
- **Sardo** • 45 Grafton Way
- **Squat & Gobble** • 69 Charlotte St
- **Stef's** • 3 Berners St
- **Thai Metro** • 36 Charlotte St

Shopping

- **Computer Exchange** • 32 Rathbone Pl
- **Harmony** • 103 Oxford St
- **Hobgoblin Shop** • 24 Rathbone Pl
- **Mango** • 225 Oxford St
- **Maplin** • 218 Tottenham Ct Rd
- **Paperchase** • 213 Tottenham Ct Rd
- **Scandinavian Kitchen** • 61 Great Titchfield St
- **Stargreen Box Office** • 20 Argyll St
- **Topshop** • 216 Oxford St

Supermarkets

- **Marks & Spencer** • 55 Tottenham Ct Rd
- **Sainsbury's** • 35 Mortimer St
- **Sainsbury's** • 17 Tottenham Ct Rd
- **Sainsbury's** • 145 Tottenham Ct Rd
- **Tesco** • 10 Goodge St

Map 4 • Bloomsbury (West)

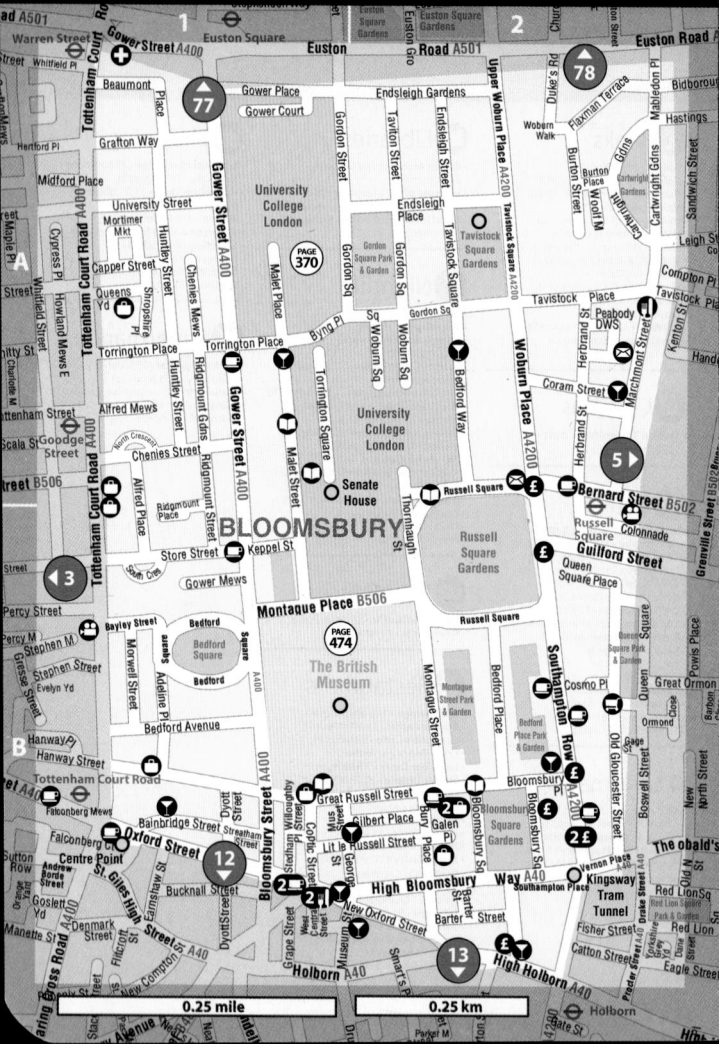
N
BLOOMSBURY
University College London
University College London
The British Museum
Russell Square Gardens
Bedford Square
Senate House
Euston Square Gardens
Euston Square Gardens
Gordon Square Park & Garden
Tavistock Square Gardens
Montague Street Park & Garden
Bedford Place Park & Garden
Queen Square Park & Garden
Bloomsbury Square Gardens
Gower Street A400
Euston Road A501
Euston Road A501
Tottenham Court Road A400
Upper Woburn Place A4200
Woburn Place A4200
Bloomsbury Street A400
Oxford Street A40
High Holborn A40
Holborn A40
High Holborn A40
Kingsway Tram Tunnel
Bernard Street B502
Montague Place B506
Tavistock Place
Tavistock Square
Torrington Place
Gower Place
Endsleigh Gardens
Endsleigh Place
Endsleigh Street
Gordon Square
Woburn Sq
Bedford Way
Russell Square
Thornhaugh St
Guilford Street
Coram Street
Herbrand St
Marchmont Street
Malet Place
Malet Street
Torrington Square
Gower Court
Gower Mews
Keppel St
Store Street
Chenies Street
Alfred Place
Alfred Mews
Ridgmount Gdns
Ridgmount Street
Huntley Street
Cheneies Mews
Capper Street
Mortimer Mkt
University Street
Grafton Way
Hertford Pl
Whitfield Pl
Warren Street
Euston Square
Euston Gro
Euston Street
Churton Street
Duke's Rd
Mabledon Pl
Bidborough St
Hastings St
Sandwich Street
Cartwright Gdns
Burton Street
Burton Place
Woburn Walk
Tavistock Place
Tavistock Pl
Kenton St
Compton Pl
Leigh St
Grenville Street
Goodge Street
Scala St
Charlotte St
Percy Street
Percy M
Stephen M
Stephen Street
Evelyn Yd
Bayley Street
Bedford Square
Bedford
Morwell Street
Adeline Pl
Bedford Avenue
Hanway Pl
Hanway Street
Tottenham Court Road
Falconberg Mews
Falconberg Ct
Centre Point
Andrew Borde Street
St. Giles High Street
Earnshaw St
Bainbridge Street
Streatham Street
Bucknall Street
Dyott Street
Goslett Yd
Denmark Street
Manette St
New Compton St
Grape Street
Stedham Street
Willoughby Pl
Coptic Street
Great Russell Street
Gilbert Place
Lit le Russell St
Museum St
Galen Pl
Bury Place
Bloomsbury Sq
Bloomsbury Square
Southampton Row
Southampton Place
Vernon Place
Barter Street
New Oxford St
Bloomsbury Way
Fisher Street
Catton Street
Eagle Street
Red Lion Sq
Red Lion Square
Red Lion
Drake Street
Boswell Street
Old Gloucester Street
Queen Square
Great Ormond
Ormond Close
Powis Place
Cosmo Pl
Colonnade
Russell Square
Queen Square Place
Mabledon Pl
Hastings
Bidborough
Euston Road
Gower Street
Euston Square
Whitfield Pl
Tottenham Court
Beaumont Place
Gower Place
Gower Court
Grafton Way
Midford Place
University Street
Mortimer Mkt
Cyprus Pl
Capper Street
Queens Yd
Shropshire Pl
Huntley Street
Cheneies Mews
Torrington Place
Alfred Mews
Ridgmount Gdns
Ridgmount Street
Chenies Street
Goodge Street
Tottenham Court Road A400
Gower Street A400
Malet Street
Torrington Square
Woburn Sq
Bedford Way
Russell Square
Thornhaugh St
Bernard Street B502
Russell Square
Colonnade
Guilford Street
Queen Square Place
Coram Street
Herbrand St
Marchmont Street
Tavistock Place
Tavistock Square

Bloomsbury offers a chaotic throng of academics, belligerent tourists and Scientologists. The Virginia Woolf Effect is in its leafy squares, UCL, and the British Museum (blue plaques galore!). Go posh bowling (All Star Lanes), booze at a Victoria gin palace (Princess Louise) and marvel at Britain's colonial loot at the British Museum. Get into rubber at Blade Rubber. Rubber stamps, that is, silly!

Banks

- **Barclays** • 58 Southampton Row
- **Barclays** • 73 Russell Sq
- **Co-Operative** • 64 Southampton Row
- **HSBC** • 210 High Holborn
- **HSBC** • 1 Woburn Pl
- **Lloyds** • Southampton Row
- **Royal Bank of Scotland** • High Holborn

Cinemas

- **Horse Hospital** • 30 Colonnade
- **Odeon Tottenham Court** • 30 Tottenham Ct Rd

Coffee

- **Café Deco** • 43 Store St
- **Costa** • 44 New Oxford St
- **Costa** • 82 Gower St
- **London Review Cake Shop** • 14 Bury Pl
- **Pret A Manger** • 40 Bernard St
- **Pret A Manger** • 23 Southampton Row
- **Pret A Manger** • 44 New Oxford St
- **Pret A Manger** • 102 Southampton Row
- **Starbucks** • 124 Southampton Row
- **Starbucks** • 112 New Oxford
- **Starbucks** • 425 Oxford St

Emergency Rooms

- **University College Hospital** • 235 Euston Rd

Landmarks

- **The British Museum** • Great Russell St
- **Centre Point** • 101 New Oxford St
- **Kingsway Tram Tunnel** •
- **Senate House** • University of London, Malet St
- **Tavistock Square** • Tavistock Sq

Libraries

- **Anthropology Library** • Great Russell St
- **Birkbeck College Library** • Malet St
- **German Historical Institute Library London** • 17 Bloomsbury Sq
- **Institute of Advanced Legal Studies Library** • 17 Russell Square
- **University of London, Senate House Library** • Malet St

Nightlife

- **All Star Lanes** • Victoria House, Bloomsbury Pl
- **Bloomsbury Bowling Lanes** • Bedford Way
- **The Fly** • 36 New Oxford
- **Marquis of Cornwallis** • 31 Marchmont St
- **Old Crown** • 33 New Oxford St
- **The Plough** • 27 Museum St
- **Point 101** • 101 New Oxford St
- **The Princess Louise** • 208 High Holborn
- **ULU** • 1 Malet St

Post Offices

- **Marchmont St** • 33 Marchmont St
- **Russell Square** • 9 Russell Sq

Restaurants

- **Alara** • 58 Marchmont St
- **Bi Won** • 24 Coptic St
- **Savoir Faire** • 42 New Oxford St

Shopping

- **Blade Rubber** • 12 Bury Pl
- **British Museum shop** • Great Russell St
- **Cinema Bookshop** • 13 Great Russell St
- **Gosh! Comics** • 39 Great Russell St
- **London Review Bookshop** • 14 Bury Pl
- **Maplin** • 218 Tottenham Ct Rd
- **Paperchase** • 213 Tottenham Ct Rd
- **York Cameras** • 18 Bury Pl

Supermarkets

- **Waitrose** • Old Gloucester St & Gage St

Map 5 • Bloomsbu

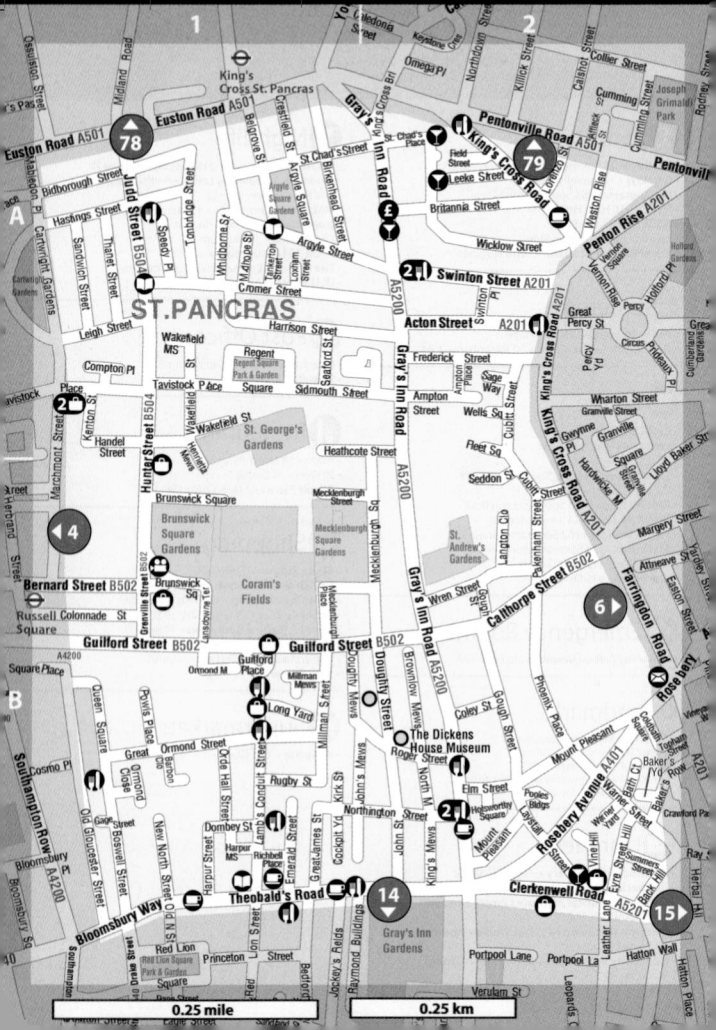

Bloomsbury (East)

A-swarm with agog students, this tract of Bloomsbury is a bustling cultural playground. The brilliant Renoir Cinema resides in the belly of the Brunswick Centre, a Brutalist masterpiece with some posh shops thrown in for good measure. Cavernous student bellies can be filled for very little at The Food Bazaar or the Mary Ward Centre. Blissful, traditional heart failure-a-plenty lurks at Fryer's Delight.

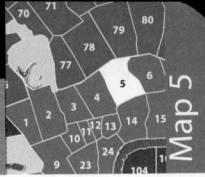

Banks

- **Lloyds** • 344 Gray's Inn Rd

Cinemas

- **Renoir Cinema** • 1 Brunswick Sq

Coffee

- **Caffe Nero** • 54 Theobald's Rd
- **Costa** • 118 King's Cross Rd
- **Pret A Manger** • 15 Theobald's Rd
- **Starbucks** • 57 Theobald's Rd
- **T-HQ** • 55 Gray's Inn Rd

Landmarks

- **The Dickens House Museum** • 48 Doughty St
- **Doughty Street** • Doughty St

Libraries

- **Holborn Library** • 32 Theobald's Rd
- **Royal National Institute of the Blind Research Library** • 105 Judd St
- **St Pancras Library** • Argyle St

Nightlife

- **06 St Chad's Place** • 6 St Chad's Pl
- **The Duke of York** • 156 Clerkenwell Rd
- **Monto Water Rats** • 328 Gray's Inn Rd
- **Smithy's** • 15 Leeke St

Post Offices

- **Mount Pleasant** • Farringdon Rd & Rosebery Ave

Restaurants

- **Acorn House** • 69 Swinton St
- **Aki Bistro** • 182 Gray's Inn Rd
- **Beas of Bloomsbury** • 44 Theobald's Rd
- **Bread and Butter Sandwich Bar** • 100 Judd St
- **Ciao Bella** • 86 Lamb's Conduit St
- **Cigala** • 54 Lamb's Conduit St
- **The Food Bazaar** • 59 Gray's Inn Rd
- **Fryer's Delight** • 19 Theobald's Rd
- **Konstam** • 2 Acton St
- **La Provence** • 63 Gray's Inn Rd
- **Mary Ward Centre** • 42 Queen Sq
- **Paolina Thai Snack Bar** • 181 King's Cross Rd
- **Swintons** • 61 Swinton St
- **Thai Candle** • 38 Lamb's Conduit St

Shopping

- **Biba's Hair and Beauty** • 72 Marchmont St
- **Bobbin Bicycles** • 19 Arlington Way
- **Brunswick Centre** • Hunter St
- **The Flash Centre** • Marchmont St
- **International Magic** • 89 Clerkenwell Rd
- **Joy** • The Brunswick
- **Magma Concept Store** • 117 Clerkenwell Rd
- **Romanian Charity Shop** • Lamb's Conduit St

Map 6 • Clerkenwell

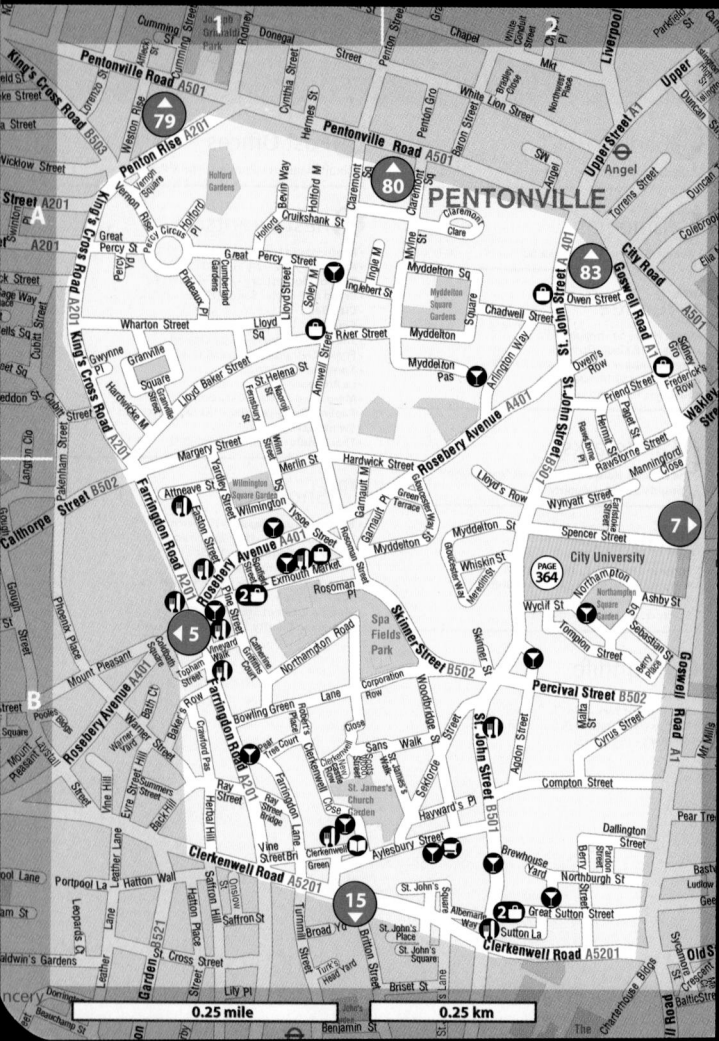
N
PENTONVILLE
Pentonville Road A501
King's Cross Road B503
Penton Rise A201
King's Cross Road A201
Upper Street A1
Angel
Liverpool Rd
Chapel
Donegal
Rodney
Cumming Street
Penton Street
Cynthia Street
Hermes St
Bevin Way
Holford M
Claremont St
Cruikshank St
Great Percy Street
Percy Circus
Vernon Rise
Holford Gardens
Cumberland Gardens
Prideaux Pl
Lloyd Sq
Lloyd Street
Sebley M
Inglebert St
Myddelton Sq
Myddelton Square Gardens
Myddelton Pas
Myddelton Square
Clarkenwell Rd
Clare
Myddelton St
Chadwell Street
Owen Street
City Road
Goswell Road A1
St John's Street A401
Islington Way
River Street
Amwell Street
Wharton Street
Lloyd Baker Street
Granville Pl
Gwynne Pl
Hardwicke M
Cubitt Street
Rosebery Avenue A401
Margery Street
Merlin St
Hardwick Street
Lloyd's Row
Wynyatt Street
Spencer Street
Myddelton St
Whiskin St
Farringdon Road A201
Calthorpe Street B502
Attneave St
Wilmington Square Garden
Wilmington
Garnault M
Green Terrace
Exmouth Market
Rosoman Pl
Spa Fields Park
Skinner Street B502
Skinner St
Northampton Road
Corporation Row
Woodbridge St
Percival Street B502
Mount Pleasant
Phoenix Place
Roseberry Avenue A401
Farringdon Road A201
Bowling Green Lane
Baker's Row
Rosebery Avenue
Farringdon Lane
Clerkenwell Close
St. James's Church Garden
Sans Walk
Sekforde St
St John Street B501
Aylesbury Street
Compton Street
Hayward's Pl
Ray Street
Vine Street Bri
Clerkenwell Green
Clerkenwell Road A5201
Portpool La
Hatton Wall
Saffron Hill
Saffron St
Cross Street
Leather Lane
Brewhouse Yard
Northburgh St
Great Sutton Street
Sutton La
St. John's Square
St. John's Place
Briset St
Benjamin St
Lilly Pl
Dorrington St
Turk's Head Yard
Charterhouse Bldgs
Old St
Farringdon Rd
Pakenham Street
Langton Clo
Gough St
Cubitt Street
Vine Hill
Eyre Street Hill
Back Hill
Herbal Hill
Summers Street
Bowling Green Lane
Rosebery Avenue
Farringdon Lane
Clerkenwell Road
Leapers Ct
Garden Ct
Baldwin's Gardens
Cancery
Dorrington St
Lilly Pl
Briset St
Benjamin St
Charterhouse Bldgs

Clerkenwell is London's own little village, only without the cricket team and middle-class wife swapping. At its heart is Clerkenwell Green, an old-time square that pops up in Dickens (only the nice bits of his books, mind; the grim workhouse stuff he must have got from elsewhere). Grab a free grope in Dans Le Noir, and laugh about it afterward with a bunch of artsy eccentrics in the Betsey Trotwood.

Libraries

- **Marx Memorial Library** • 37 Clerkenwell Green

Nightlife

- **The Bandstand** • Northampton Sq
- **Betsey Trotwood** • 56 Farringdon Rd
- **Café Kick** • 43 Exmouth Market
- **Cicada** • 132 St John St
- **Dollar Grills and Martinis** • 2 Exmouth Market
- **The Dovetail** • 9 Jerusalem Passage
- **Filthy McNasty's** • 68 Amwell St
- **The Harlequin** • 27 Arlington Way
- **Queen Boadicea** • 292 St John St
- **The Slaughtered Lamb** • 34-35 Great Sutton St
- **The Three Kings** • 7 Clerkenwell Close
- **Wilmington Arms** • 69 Rosebery Ave

Restaurants

- **Bada Bing!** • 120 St John St
- **Clarks Pie and Mash** • 46 Exmouth Market
- **Dans Le Noir** • 30 Clerkenwell Green
- **The Eagle** • 159 Farringdon Rd
- **Little Bay** • 171 Farringdon Rd
- **Moro** • 34 Exmouth Market
- **The Quality Chop House** • 94 Farringdon Rd
- **Sandwichman** • 23 Easton St
- **Vic Naylor's** • 38 St John St

Shopping

- **The Black Tulip** • 28 Exmouth Market
- **Brindisa Retail** • 32 Exmouth Market
- **The Family Business Tattoo Shop** • 58 Exmouth Market
- **London Tattoo** • 332 Goswell Rd
- **M and R Meats** • 399 St John St
- **Metro Imaging Ltd** • 32 Great Sutton St
- **Timorous Beasties** • 46 Amwell St
- **Wyvern Bindery** • 56 Clerkenwell Rd

Supermarkets

- **Waitrose** • Ayelsbury St & St John St

N
City Road A501
Goswell Road A1
Lever Street B502
Bath Street B144
Old Street A501
Old Street A5201
Bunhill Row B144
Chiswell Street
Beech Street B100
Aldersgate Street A1
London Wall A1211
Moorgate A501
Finsbury Pl
Finsbury St
Moor Lane
Milton St
Silk Street
Barbican Centre
BARBICAN
St. Giles's Cripplegate
Church of St. Bartholomew the Great
Barbican
Smithfield
Hosier Lane
Cock Lane
Charterhouse Square
Charterhouse St
Clerkenwell Road A5201
Farringdon Rd
Rosebery Ave
Gray's Inn Rd
Kings Square Garden
St. Luke's Garden
LSO St. Luke's
ST.LUKE'S
Bunhill Fields Burial Grounds
Bunhill Fields
Old Street
Moorgate
Finsbury Square
Sebastian St
Percival Street
Compton Street
Brewhouse Yard
Great Sutton Street
Albemarle Way
St. John's Sq
St. John's Lane
Albion Pl
Eagle Court
Smithfield Rd
Little Britain
Aldersgate St
Goswell Road
Central St
Lever Street
Bunhill Row
Chiswell Street
Beech Street
Barbican
Moorgate
Finsbury Pl
Finsbury St
Moor Lane
Milton St
Silk Street
Barbican Centre
BARBICAN
St. Giles's Cripplegate
Church of St. Bartholomew the Great

Barbican / City Road (South)

You may feel like an extra from Bladerunner weaving awe-struck through the towering steel and concrete Brutalism, but this area is ringing with history. The Nazis flattened the place, leaving St-Giles's Cripplegate Church standing alone. God has also favoured the finance and media sectors, who now overrun the area. The Barbican's lake and events are a cultural mecca, while Ironmonger Row Baths provides the sweats.

Banks

- **Barclays** • 128 Moorgate
- **HSBC** • 74 Goswell Rd
- **Lloyds** • 69 Old St

Cinemas

- **Barbican Centre Cinema** • Silk St & Whitecross St

Coffee

- **Caffe Nero** • 40 City Rd
- **Coffee Republic** • City Rd
- **Costa** • 68 Goswell Rd
- **Costa** • Ropemaker St
- **Eat.** • 143 Moorgate
- **Popular Cafe** • 85 Lever St
- **Pret A Manger** • 9 Goswell Rd
- **Pret A Manger** • 1 Long Ln
- **Pret A Manger** • Ropemaker St

Landmarks

- **Barbican Centre** • Silk St
- **Church of St Bartholomew the Great** • 6 Kinghorn St
- **LSO St Luke's** • 161 Old St
- **St Giles's Cripplegate** • Fore St

Libraries

- **Barbican Library** • Silk St

Post Offices

- **Old Street** • 205 Old St

Restaurants

- **Bavarian Beerhouse** • 190 City Rd
- **Carnevale** • 135 Whitecross St
- **De Santis** • Old St
- **NUSA Kitchen** • 9 Old St
- **Warrin Thai Kitchen Stall** • 77 Whitecross St

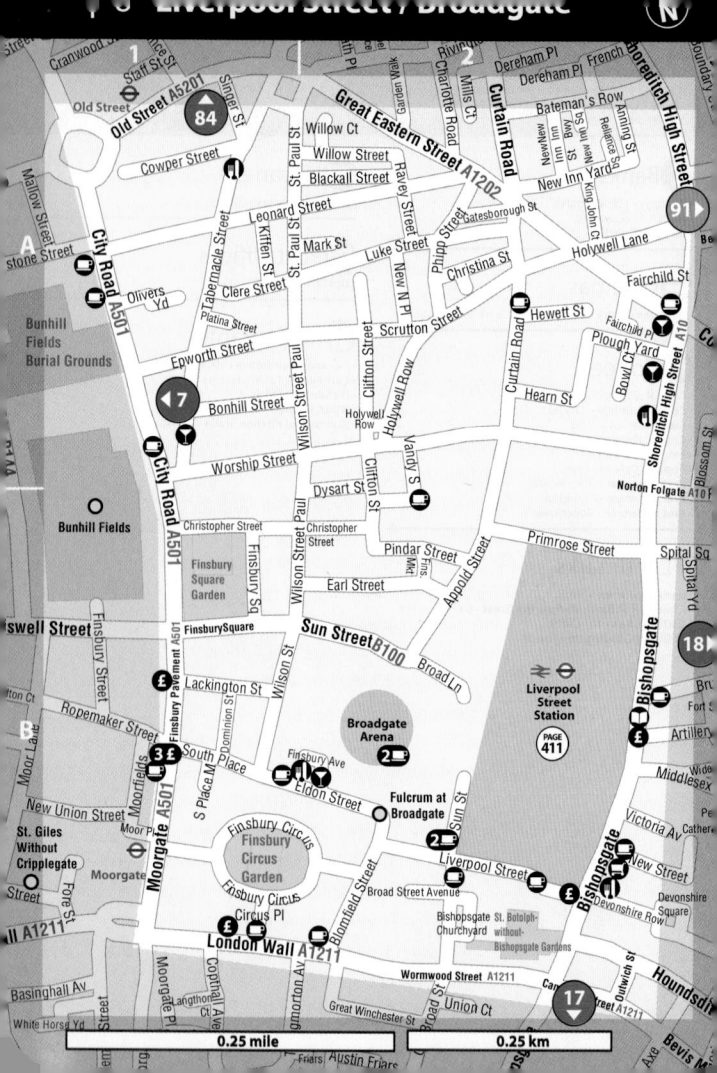
Cranwood St
Staff St
Old Street
Old Street A5201
Singer St
Great Eastern Street A1202
Willow Ct
Willow Street
Cowper Street
Blackall Street
St. Paul St
Ravey Street
Leonard Street
Mark St
Luke Street
Kiffen St
Tabernacle Street
Clere Street
Olivers Yd
Platina Street
City Road A501
Bunhill Fields Burial Grounds
Epworth Street
Bonhill Street
Wilson Street
Paul
Clifton Street
Holywell Row
Worship Street
Dysart St
Vandy St
Christopher Street
Finsbury Square Garden
Finsbury Sq
Finsbury Pavement A501
Finsbury Street
Earl Street
Pindar Street
Appold Street
Primrose Street
Spital Sq
Spital Yd
Sun Street B100
Broad Ln
Lackington St
Ropemaker Street
South Place
Broadgate Arena
Finsbury Ave
Eldon Street
Fulcrum at Broadgate
Sun St
Finsbury Circus
Finsbury Circus Garden
Moorgate A501
Moorgate
New Union Street
Moorfields
St. Giles Without Cripplegate
Liverpool Street Station
PAGE 411
Bishopsgate
Liverpool Street
New Street
Broad Street Avenue
Bishopsgate Churchyard
St. Botolph-without-Bishopsgate Gardens
Devonshire Square
Devonshire Row
Bloomfield Street
London Wall A1211
Wormwood Street A1211
Great Winchester St
Union Ct
Houndsditch
Basinghall Av
White Horse Yd
Austin Friars
Curtain Road
Charlotte Road
Mills Ct
Dereham Pl
French Pl
Bateman's Row
Rivington Pl
Shoreditch High Street
Shoreditch High Street A10
Norton Folgate A10
Hewett St
Fairchild St
Plough Yard
Bowl Ct
Hearn St
Holywell Lane
Christina St
Scrutton Street
Gatesborough St
Philip St
New Inn Yard
New Inn Pl
New Inn St
Rivington St
Bay
Reliance Sq
Anning St
King John Ct
Mallow Street
Stone Street
0.25 mile
0.25 km

Liverpool Street / Broadgate

A grimy maw that spews trendos onto Bishopsgate, Liverpool Street is the gateway to the nowness of Brick Lane and Shoreditch. Its arse-end lets out suits and money into the borders of the City. Avoid a 'flash-mob' in the Light after a grease-up in Damascu Bite, but c'mon, you know you're really on your way to an all night rave in Hoxton, so cut the crap and vamoose.

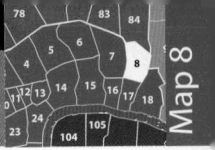

Banks

- **Abbey** • 59 London Wall
- **Abbey** • 224 Bishopsgate
- **Barclays** • 128 Moorgate
- **Halifax** • 136 Bishopsgate
- **HSBC** • 1 South Pl
- **Lloyds** • 109 Finsbury Pavement

Coffee

- **AMT** • Liverpool St & Broadgate Circle
- **Benugo** • 82 City Rd
- **Caffe Nero** • 2 Bishopsgate
- **Caffe Nero** • 40 City Rd
- **Caffe Nero** • 75 London Wall
- **Coffee Republic** • City Rd
- **Coffee Republic** • 25 Exchange Sq
- **Costa** • 1 Ropemaker St
- **Costa** • 18 Liverpool St
- **Eat.** • 1 City Rd
- **Eat.** • 143 Moorgate
- **Eat.** • 176 Bishopsgate
- **Eat.** • 34 Broadgate Circle
- **Eat.** • 62 London Wall
- **Eat.** • 80 Old Broad St
- **Fab Food Patisserie** • 26 Curtain Rd
- **Starbucks** • Liverpool St Station
- **Starbucks** • 8 Charterhouse Buildings
- **Starbucks** • 28 Broadgate Circle

Landmarks

- **Bunhill Fields** • City Rd
- **Fulcrum at Broadgate** • Broadgate
- **St Giles Without Cripplegate** • Fore St

Libraries

- **Bishopsgate Library** • 230 Bishopsgate

Nightlife

- **The Light** • 233 Shoreditch High St
- **Lounge Bohemia** • 1 Great Eastern St
- **The Red Lion** • 1 Eldon St
- **Sosho** • 2 Tabernacle Street

Restaurants

- **Damascu Bite Kebab** • 21 Shoreditch High St
- **Eyre Brothers** • 70 Leonard St
- **Gaucho Grill** • 5 Finsbury Ave
- **Ponti's Caffe** • 176 Bishopsgate

Supermarkets

- **Tesco** • 160 Bishopsgate

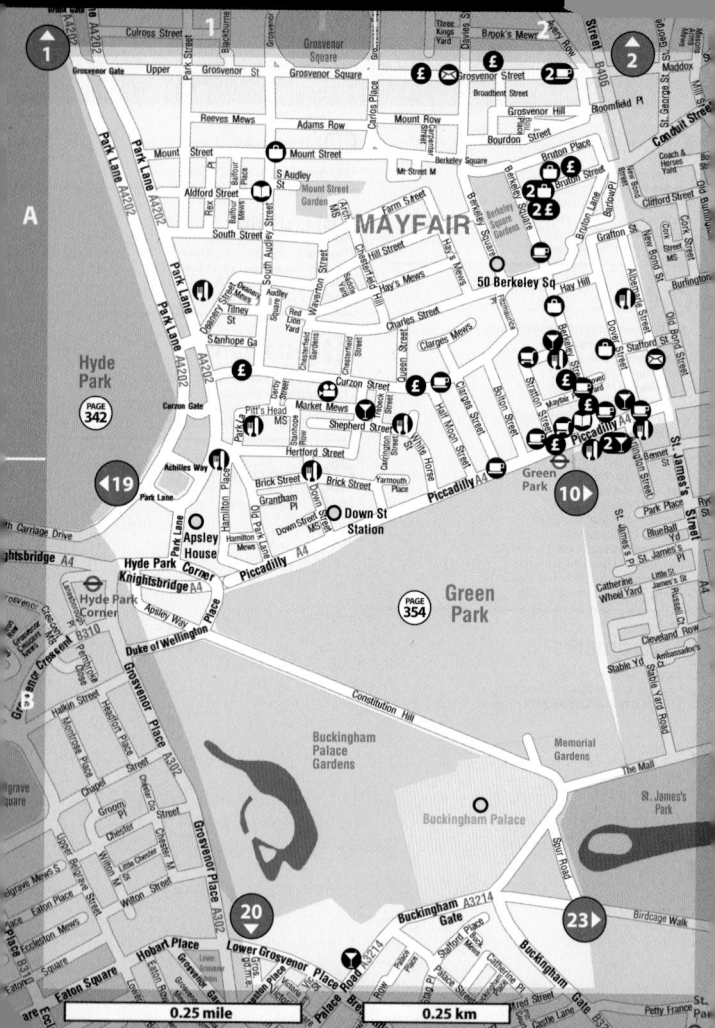
MAYFAIR
Hyde Park
Green Park
Buckingham Palace Gardens
Memorial Gardens
Buckingham Palace
St. James's Park
Hyde Park Corner
Knightsbridge
Down St Station
Apsley House
50 Berkeley Sq
Grosvenor Square
Mount Street Garden
Berkeley Square Gardens
Park Lane A4202
Piccadilly A4
Constitution Hill
Grosvenor Place A302
Buckingham Gate A3214
Lower Grosvenor Place A3214
Hobart Place
Eaton Square
Culross Street
Grosvenor Gate
Upper Grosvenor St
Grosvenor Square
Grosvenor Street
Brook's Mews
Three Kings Yard
Davies St
Avery Row
Brook Street
Broadwell Street
Grosvenor Hill
Bloomfield Pl
Reeves Mews
Adams Row
Mount Row
Bourdon Street
Mount Street
Mt Street M
Berkeley Square
Brutton Place
Brutton Street
Aldford Street
Farm Street
Clifford Street
South Street
Grafton St
Hay's Mews
Hay Hill
Charles Street
Clarges Mews
Curzon Street
Curzon Gate
Market Mews
Shepherd Street
Hertford Street
Brick Street
Grantham Pl
Down Street
Hamilton Place
Hamilton Mews
Old Park Lane
Piccadilly A4
Stratton Street
Berkeley St
Dover Street
Albemarle Street
Bond St
Old Bond Street
Burlington
Stafford St
Bennet St
St James's Street
Park Place
Blue Ball Yd
St James's Pl
Catherine Wheel Yard
Little St James's St
Cleveland Row
Ambassador's Court
Stable Yd
Stable Yard Road
The Mall
Birdcage Walk
Petty France
Buckingham Gate
Palace Street
Stafford Place
Catherine Place
Castle Lane
Victoria Sta
Victoria St
Victoria Road
Palace Road
Eaton Place
Eccleston Place
Eccleston Mews
Wilton Crescent
Wilton Place
Wilton Row
Wilton St
Belgrave Sq
Belgrave Mews S
Belgrave Square
Chester Sq
Chester Row
Chester St
Chester Cl
Chester M
Little Chester St
Groom Pl
Chapel
Chapel Place
Halkin Street
Halkin Place
Hereford Street
Grosvenor Crescent
Grosvenor Gardens
Grosvenor Place
Duke of Wellington Place
Apsley Way
Knightsbridge A4
Hyde Park Corner
Lanesborough Hotel
Wellington Arch
Park Lane
Achilles Way
Carriage Drive
Eaton Square
Eaton Row
Eaton Place
Lower Belgrave St
Belgrave Place
Belgrave Road
Belgrave Mews S
Belgrave Square
Wilton Crescent
Wilton Place
Wilton Row
Wilton St

Mayfair / Green Park

In Monopoly, you can buy both Mayfair and Park Lane, build hotels, and end up really screwing everyone else. In real life you may struggle to afford a t-shirt here, though avant-boutique Dover Street Market is definitely worth a timid visit, and empty the rest of your pockets at the Ritz for afternoon tea. Stake out Mahiki to freak out some minor royals, or test the security at the Palace to freak out some major ones.

Banks

- **Barclays** • 11 Bruton St
- **Halifax** • 51 Berkeley St
- **HSBC** • 18 Curzon St
- **HSBC** • 79 Piccadilly
- **Lloyds** • 14 Berkeley Sq
- **Lloyds** • 50 Grosvenor St
- **NatWest** • 4 Berkeley Sq
- **NatWest** • 94 Moorgate
- **Royal Bank of Scotland** • 43 Curzon St
- **Royal Bank of Scotland** • 24 Grosvenor Pl

Cinemas

- **Curzon Mayfair** • 38 Curzon St

Coffee

- **Apostrophe** • 10 Grosvenor St
- **Caffe Nero** • 50 Curzon St
- **Caffe Nero** • 70 Piccadilly
- **Costa** • 4 Grosvenor St
- **Costa** • 9 Eldon St
- **Eat.** • 8 Berkeley Sq
- **Eat.** • 55 Stratton St
- **Starbucks** • 52 Berkeley St
- **Starbucks** • 84 Piccadilly

Landmarks

- **50 Berkeley Square** • 50 Berkeley Sq
- **Apsley House** • Hyde Park Corner
- **Buckingham Palace** • The Mall
- **Down Street Station** • Down St

Libraries

- **Mayfair Library** • 25 South Audley St
- **Royal Society of Chemistry Library and Information Centre** • Piccadilly

Nightlife

- **1707** • 181 Piccadilly
- **5th View** • 203 Piccadilly
- **bbar** • 43 Buckingham Palace Rd
- **Funky Buddah** • 15 Berkeley St
- **Mahiki** • 1 Dover St
- **Shepherd's Tavern** • 50 Hertford St

Post Offices

- **Albemarle St** • 44 Albemarle St
- **Mayfair** • 32 Grosvenor St

Restaurants

- **Alain Ducasse at The Dorchester** • Park Ln
- **El Pirata of Mayfair** • 5 Down St
- **The English Tea Room at Browns** • Albemarle St
- **Galvin at Windows** • 28th Floor, Hilton Park Lane
- **L'Autre** • 5 Shepherd St
- **Nobu** • 15 Berkeley St
- **The Ritz** • 150 Piccadilly
- **Theo Randall at the InterContinental** • 1 Hamilton Pl
- **The Wolseley** • 161 Piccadilly

Shopping

- **Diane Von Furstenberg** • 25 Bruton St
- **Dover Street Market** • 17 Dover St
- **Green Valley** • Berkeley St
- **Marc Jacobs** • 24 Mount St
- **Matthew Williamson** • 28 Bruton St
- **Stella McCartney** • 30 Bruton St

Supermarkets

- **Marks & Spencer** • 78 Piccadilly
- **Sainsbury's** • 50 Stratton St

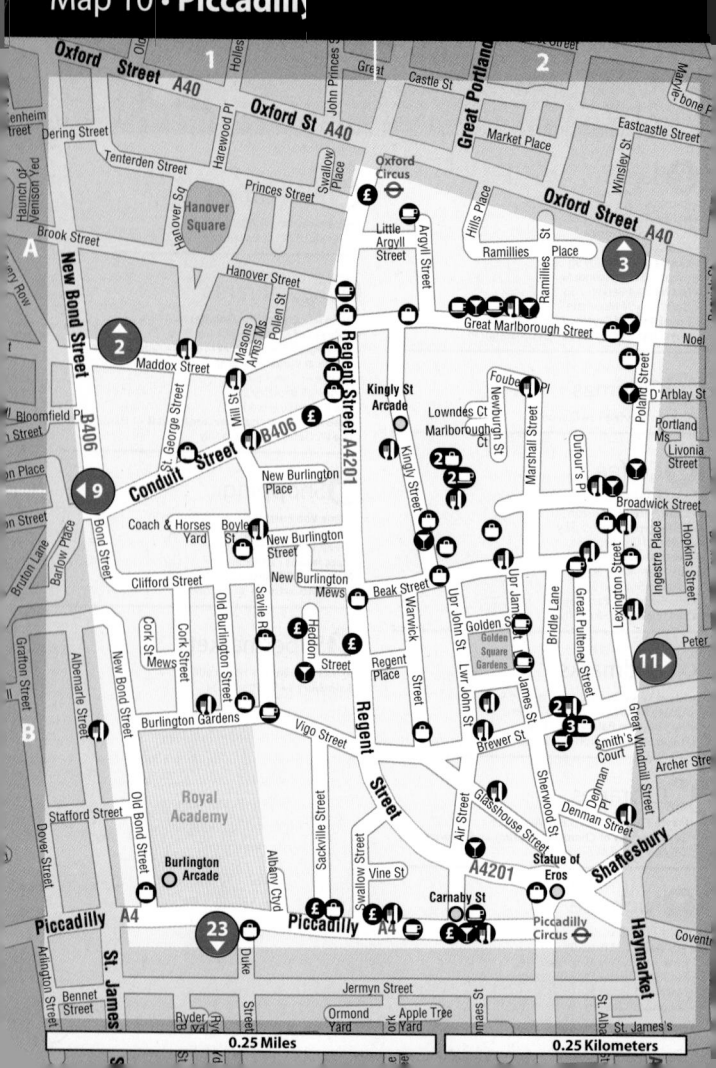
Oxford Street A40
Oxford St A40
Great Portland Street
Great Castle St
Oxford Circus
Oxford Street A40
Dering Street
Tenterden Street
Harewood Pl
Hollies
John Princes St
Market Place
Eastcastle Street
Winsley St
Princes Street
Hanover Sq
Hanover Square
Swallow Place
Hills Place
Brook Street
Little Argyll Street
Argyll Street
Ramillies Place
Ramillies St
Hanover Street
Pollen St
Masons Arms Ms
Great Marlborough Street
Noel
New Bond Street
Regent Street A4201
Maddox Street
Kingly St Arcade
Lowndes Ct
Marlborough Ct
Foubert's Pl
Marshall Street
Poland Street
D'Arblay St
Bloomfield Pl
Mill St
St. George Street
B406
Conduit Street
New Burlington Place
Kingly Street
Dufour's Pl
Portland Ms
Livonia Street
Broadwick Street
Coach & Horses Yard
Boyle St
New Burlington Street
Bond Street
Barlow Place
Brutton Lane
Clifford Street
New Burlington Mews
Beak Street
Upr James St
Upr John St
Lwr John St
Warwick Street
Golden Sq
Golden Square Gardens
Bridle Lane
Great Pulteney Street
Lexington Street
Ingestre Place
Hopkins Street
Peter
Savile Row
Heddon Street
Regent Place
James St
Cork St Mews
Cork Street
Old Burlington Street
Albemarle Street
New Bond Street
Grafton Street
Burlington Gardens
Vigo Street
Brewer St
Great Windmill Street
Smith's Court
Archer Street
Royal Academy
Stafford Street
Old Bond Street
Dover Street
Burlington Arcade
Sackville Street
Albany Cyd
Swallow Street
Air Street
Chasehouse Street
Sherwood St
Denman Street
Denman Pl
Shaftesbury
Vine St
A4201
Statue of Eros
Carnaby St
Piccadilly A4
Piccadilly Circus
Haymarket
Arlington Street
St. James's
Bennet Street
Duke Street
Jermyn Street
Ryder Yard
Ormond Yard
Apple Tree Yard
St. James's
0.25 Miles
0.25 Kilometers

Piccadilly / Soho (West)

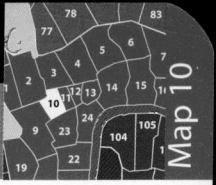

This is where 60's swinging London melts into the present day. It's not a place for budgets or morals though. Carnaby Street has long lost its modishness and is now a temple to boutique vintage, while you can carry on the retro sleaze vibe at the Pigalle Club. John Snow offers economic respite, and Mrs. Kibbles will fatten you up for an encounter with a 'model' down a dirty alley.

Banks

- **Abbey** • 34 Piccadilly
- **Barclays** • 48 Regent St
- **HSBC** • 133 Regent St
- **Lloyds** • 39 Picadilly
- **NatWest** • 208 Piccadilly Circus
- **NatWest** • 250 Regent St
- **Royal Bank of Scotland** • 60 Conduit St

Coffee

- **Caffe Nero** • 62 Brewer St
- **Caffe Nero** • 26 Piccadilly
- **Caffe Nero** • 225 Regent St
- **Coffee Republic** • 39 Great Marlborough St
- **Costa** • 11 Argyll St
- **Eat.** • 19 Golden Sq
- **Eat.** • 8 Vigo St
- **Fernandez & Wells** • 73 Beak St
- **Pret A Manger** • 298 Regent St
- **Pret A Manger** • 27 Great Marlborough
- **Sacred Cafe** • 13 Ganton St
- **Starbucks** • 16 Picadilly

Landmarks

- **Burlington Arcade** • Burlington Arcade
- **Carnaby Street** • Carnaby St
- **Kingly Street Arcade** • Kingly St
- **Statue of Eros** • Piccadilly Circus

Nightlife

- **22 Below** • 22 Great Marlborough St
- **Ain't Nothing But The Blues Bar** • 20 Kingly St
- **Bar Red** • 5 Kingly St
- **Beyond Retro** • 58 Great Marlborough St
- **Cheers Bar** • 72 Regent St
- **Courthouse Bar** • 19 Great Marlborough St
- **John Snow** • 39 Broadwick St
- **Milk & Honey** • 61 Poland St
- **Pigalle Club** • 215 Piccadilly
- **Strawberry Moons** • 15 Heddon St

Supermarkets

- **Fresh & Wild** • 73 Brewer St

Restaurants

- **Atlantic Bar & Grill** • 20 Glasshouse St
- **Cecconi's** • 5 Burlington Gardens
- **Cha Cha Moon** • 15 Ganton St
- **Chowki** • 2 Denman St
- **Dehesa** • 25 Ganton St
- **Fernandez and Wells Coffee Bar** • 73 Beak St
- **Kulu Kulu** • 76 Brewer St
- **Mildred's** • 45 Lexington St
- **Mosaico** • 13 Albermale St
- **Nordic Bakery** • 14 Golden Sq
- **Ping Pong** • 45 Great Marlborough St
- **Pure California** • 39 Beak St
- **Sartoria** • 20 Saville Row
- **Sketch** • 9 Conduit St
- **Taro** • 61 Brewer St
- **Ten Ten Tei** • 56 Brewer St
- **Tentazioni Restaurant** • 2 Mill St
- **Thanks for Franks** • 26 Fouberts Pl
- **Toku @ The Japan Centre** • 212 Piccadilly
- **Wagamama** • 10 Lexington St
- **Wild Honey** • 12 St George St
- **Yauatcha** • 15 Broadwick St
- **Yoshino** • 3 Piccadilly Pl

Shopping

- **Abercrombie & Fitch** • 7 Burlington Gardens
- **American Apparel** • 3 Carnaby St
- **Arigato** • 48 Brewer St
- **b store** • 24 Savile Row
- **Banana Republic** • 224 Regent St
- **Behave** • 48 Lexington Sreet
- **The Black Pearl** • 10 Kingly Ct
- **Burlington Arcade** • Burlington Arcade
- **Cos** • 222 Regent St
- **Deal Real** • 3 Great Marlborough St
- **The European Bookshop** • 5 Warwick St
- **Fortnum And Mason** • 181 Piccadilly
- **Georgina Goodman** • 44 Old Bond St
- **Hamley's** • 188 Regent St
- **Hatchard's** • 187 Piccadilly
- **Hoss Intropia** • 211 Regent St
- **Liberty** • 214 Regent St
- **Lillywhites** • 24-36 Lower Regent St
- **Lucky Voice** • 52 Poland St
- **Mrs Kibble's Olde Sweet Shoppe** • 57 Brewer St
- **Muji** • 41 Carnaby St
- **Phonica** • 51 Poland St
- **Playlounge** • 19 Beak St
- **Richard James** • 29 Savile Row
- **Rigby & Peller** • 22 Conduit St
- **SKK (Lighting)** • 34 Lexington St
- **Twinkled** • 1 Kingly Ct
- **The Vintage Magazine Shop** • 39 Brewer St

Map 11 • Soho (Central)

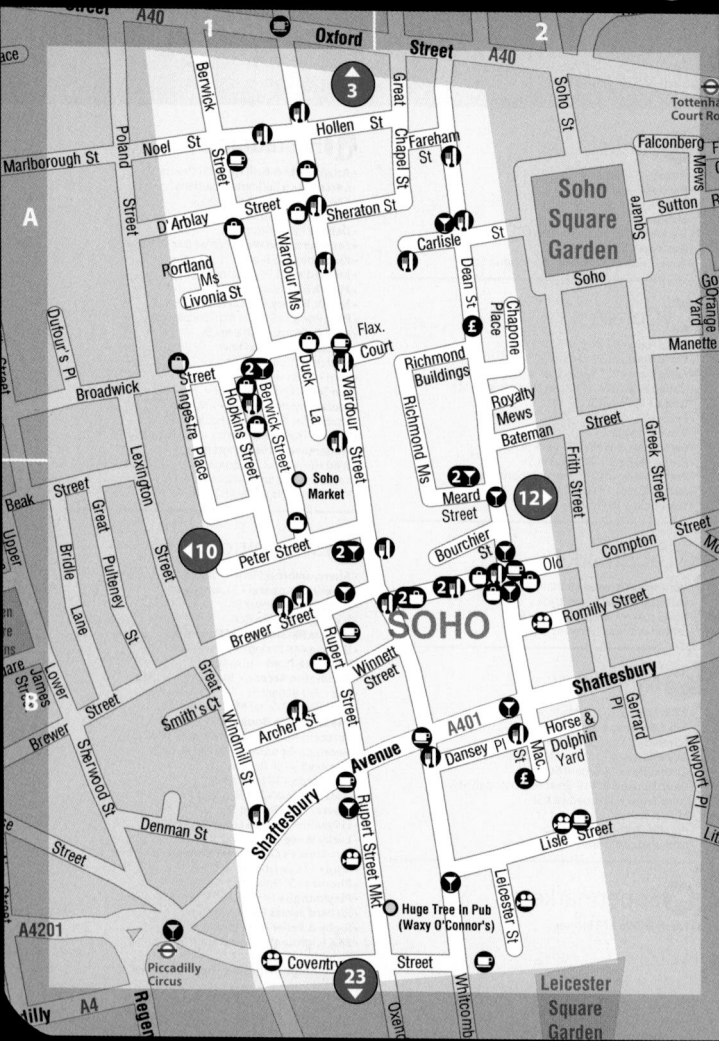

Soho is no longer a bohemian gangster's paradise but a sprawling gay-friendly party zone. The area's old whorehouses and street markets have the sword of Thanatos swinging above them, as places like Berwick street face re-development. It's still Jerk-Off City though. Old soho vibes can still be felt at Bar Bruno or I Camisa, while Bang Bang and Sounds of the Universe do cool threads and tunes respectively.

Banks

- **HSBC** • 17 Gerrard St
- **NatWest** • 20 Dean St

Cinemas

- **Cineworld Shaftesbury Avenue** • 13 Coventry St
- **Curzon Soho** • 99 Shaftesbury Ave
- **Empire Cinemas** • 5 Leicester Square
- **Prince Charles Cinema** • 7 Leicester Pl
- **Rex Cinema and Bar** • 21 Rupert St

Coffee

- **BB's Coffee and Muffins** • Oxford St & Berners St
- **Coffee Republic** • 7 Coventry St
- **Coffee Republic** • 38 Berwick St
- **Costa** • 39 Old Compton St
- **Costa** • 62 Shaftesbury Ave
- **LJ Coffee House** • 3 Winnett St
- **Prince Charles Cinema** • 7 Leicester Pl
- **Starbucks** • 7 Leicester Sq
- **Starbucks** • 60 Wardour St

Landmarks

- **Huge Tree In Pub (Waxy O'Connor's)** • 14 Rupert St
- **Soho Market** • Berwick St

Nightlife

- **Blue Posts** • 22 Berwick St
- **The Blue Posts** • 28 Rupert St
- **Candy Bar** • 4 Carlisle St
- **The Colony Room** • 41 Dean St
- **The Comedy Store** • 1 Oxendon St
- **De Hems** • 11 Macclesfield St
- **The Endurance** • 90 Berwick St
- **Freedom** • 66 Wardour St
- **The French House** • 49 Dean St
- **LUPO** • 50 Dean St
- **Madame Jojo's** • 8 Brewer St
- **Rex Cinema and Bar** • 21 Rupert St
- **Shadow Lounge** • 5 Brewer St
- **Soho Revue Bar** • 11 Walkers Ct
- **Trash Palace** • 11 Wardour St
- **The Village** • 81 Wardour St

Restaurants

- **Balans** • 60 Old Compton St
- **Bar Bruno** • 101 Wardour St
- **Beetroot** • 92 Berwick St
- **Bocca di Lupo** • 12 Archer St
- **Cafe Espana** • 63 Old Compton St
- **Hummus Bros** • 88 Wardour St
- **Imli** • 167 Wardour St
- **Italian Graffiti** • 163 Wardour St
- **Leong's Legends** • 4 Macclesfield St
- **Jerk City** • 189 Wardour St
- **Malletti** • 26 Noel St
- **Maoz** • 43 Old Compton St
- **Paul** • 49 Old Compton St
- **Pizza Express Jazz Club** • 10 Dean St
- **Randall & Aubin** • 16 Brewer St
- **Red Veg** • 95 Dean St
- **Snog** • 9 Brewer St
- **Soho Thai** • 27 St. Annes Ct
- **St Moritz** • 161 Wardour St
- **Sugar Reef** • 42 Great Windmill St
- **Won Kei** • 41 Wardour St

Shopping

- **Algerian Coffee Store** • 52 Old Compton St
- **American Retro** • 35 Old Compton St
- **Bang Bang** • 9 Berwick St
- **Calumet Trading** • 175 Wardour St
- **Chappel of Bond Street** • 152 Wardour St
- **Cheapo Cheapo Records** • 53 Rupert St
- **Cowling & Wilcox** • 26 Broadwick St
- **Gerry's** • 74 Old Compton St
- **I Camisa & Son** • 61 Old Compton St
- **Paradiso** • 60 Dean St
- **Revival Records** • 30 Berwick St
- **Sister Ray** • 34 Berwick St
- **Sounds of the Universe** • 7 Broadwick St
- **Vinyl Junkies** • 94 Berwick St

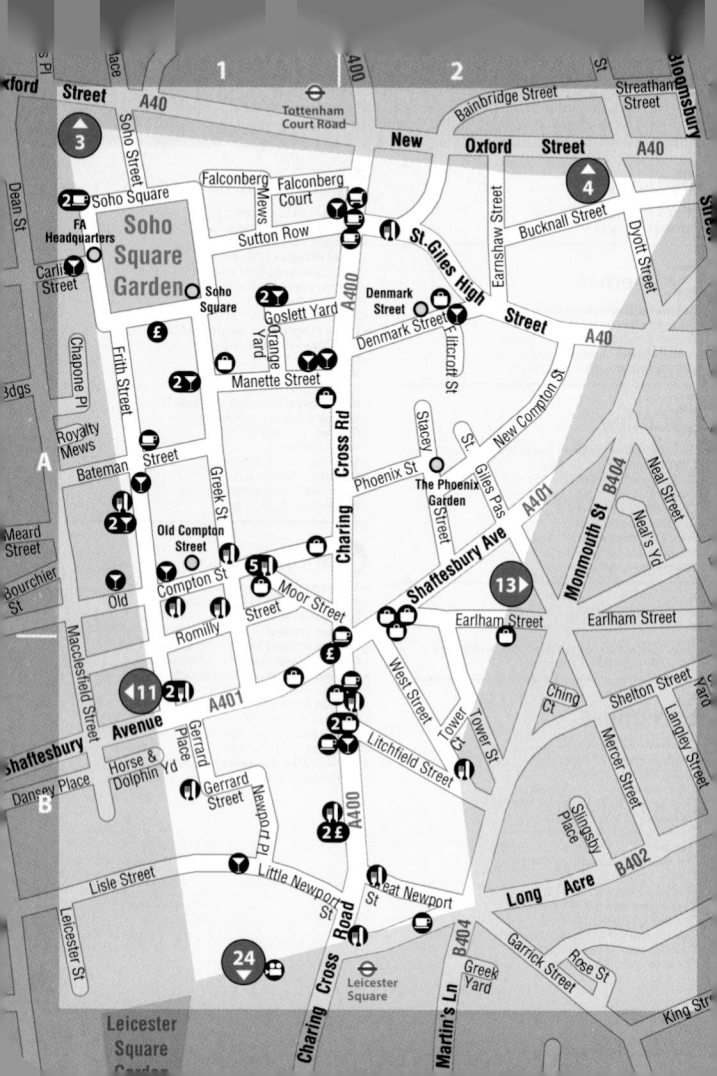
1
2
A
B
Oxford Street
A40
Tottenham Court Road
Bainbridge Street
Streatham Street
Bloomsbury
New Oxford Street
A40
Soho Street
Soho Square
FA Headquarters
Soho Square Garden
Falconberg Mews
Falconberg Court
Sutton Row
St. Giles High Street
Earnshaw Street
Bucknall Street
Dyott Street
Dean St
Carlisle Street
Soho Square
Goslett Yard
Orange Yard
A400
Denmark Street
Denmark Street
Fitzroff St
A40
Chapone Pl
Frith Street
Manette Street
Royalty Mews
Stacey St.
New Compton St
Bateman Street
Greek St
Charing Cross Rd
Phoenix St
The Phoenix Garden
Giles Pas
A401
Neal Street
Neal's Yd
Meard Street
Old Compton Street
Compton St
Moor Street
Shaftesbury Ave
Monmouth St
B404
Bourchier St
Old
Romilly
Earlham Street
Earlham Street
Macclesfield Street
West Street
Tower Ct
Tower St
Ching Ct
Shelton Street
Langley Street
Shaftesbury Avenue
A401
Gerrard Place
Litchfield Street
Mercer Street
Horse & Dolphin Yd
Gerrard Street
Newport Pl
A400
Slingsby Place
Dansey Place
Lisle Street
Little Newport St
Great Newport St
Long Acre
B402
Leicester St
Charing Cross Road
Leicester Square
B404
Garrick Street
Rose St
Greek Yard
Martin's Ln
King Str
Leicester Square Garden

It can be difficult containing one's enthusiasm for London while partying with some traditional unsavoury characters at 57 Greek Street, or gorging on pastries at Maison Bertaux. Inbetween another blast of poppers at G-A-Y and shredding on Denmark Street you might notice that greedy landlordism has forced many independent businesses to shut down (bye bye Shipley's Books). Hopefully the recession will curb the tide of redevolpment…

Banks

- **Barclays** • 27 Soho Sq
- **Barclays** • 25 Charing Cross
- **HSBC** • 138 Shaftesbury Ave
- **Royal Bank of Scotland** • 49 Charing Cross Rd

Cinemas

- **Vue West End Cinema** • 3 Cranbourn St

Coffee

- **Caffe Nero** • 32 Cranbourn St
- **Caffe Nero** • 43 Frith St
- **Caffe Nero** • 155 Charing Cross Rd
- **Coffee Republic** • 19 Soho Sq
- **Costa** • 140 Shaftesbury Ave
- **Eat.** • 16 Soho Sq
- **Eat.** • 155 Charing Cross Rd
- **Foyles** • 113 Charing Cross Rd

Landmarks

- **Denmark Street** • Denmark St
- **FA Headquarters** • 25 Soho Sq
- **Old Compton Street** • Old Compton St
- **The Phoenix Garden** • 21 Stacey St
- **Soho Square** • Soho Sq

Nightlife

- **12 Bar Club** • 22 Denmark St
- **The Astoria** • 157 Charing Cross Rd
- **The Borderline** • 16 Manette St
- **Comptons** • 53 Old Compton St
- **Crobar** • 17 Manette St
- **G-A-Y Bar** • 30 Old Compton St
- **G-A-Y Late** • 5 Goslett Yard
- **Garlic & Shots** • 14 Frith St
- **Green Carnation** • 5 Greek St
- **Jazz After Dark** • 9 Greek St
- **Karaoke Box** • 18 Frith St
- **Ku Bar** • 30 Lisle St
- **Montagu Pyke** • 105 Charing Cross Rd
- **Ronnie Scott's Jazz Club** • 47 Frith St
- **Royal George** • 133 Charing Cross Rd, Goslett Yard
- **The Toucan** • 19 Carlisle St

Restaurants

- **Abeno Too** • 17 Great Newport St
- **Arbutus** • 63 Frith St
- **Assa** • 53 St Giles High St
- **Bar Italia** • 22 Frith St
- **Barrafina** • 54 Frith St
- **Bincho Soho** • 16 Old Compton St
- **Boheme Kitchen and Bar** • 19 Old Compton St
- **Café Emm** • 17 Frith St
- **Chinese Experience** • 118 Shaftesbury Ave
- **Corean Chilli** • 51 Charing Cross Rd
- **Ed's Easy Diner** • 12 Moor St
- **Friendly Inn** • 47 Gerrard St
- **Gaby's** • 30 Charing Cross Rd
- **Garlic & Shots** • 14 Frith St
- **Gay Hussar** • 2 Greek St
- **Haozhan** • 8 Gerrard St
- **Kettners** • 29 Romilly St
- **La Porchetta Pollo Bar** • 20 Old Compton St
- **Le Beaujolais** • 25 Litchfield St
- **Maison Bertaux** • 27 Greek St
- **Malaysia Kopi Tiam** • 67 Charing Cross Rd
- **New World** • 1 Gerrard Pl
- **Stockpot** • 18 Old Compton St
- **Taro** • 10 Old Compton St

Shopping

- **Angels** • 119 Shaftesbury Ave
- **Fopp** • 1 Earlham St
- **Forbidden Planet** • 179 Shaftesbury Ave
- **Kokon to Zai** • 57 Greek St
- **Macaris** • 92 Charing Cross Rd
- **Magma** • 8 Earlham St
- **Maison Bertaux** • 27 Greek St
- **Porselli** • 9 West St
- **Ray's Jazz** • 113 Charing Cross Rd
- **Rockers** • Denmark St
- **Turnkey** • 114 Charing Cross Rd
- **Wunjo Guitars** • 20 Denmark St

Supermarkets

- **Sainsbury's** • 137 Charing Cross Rd

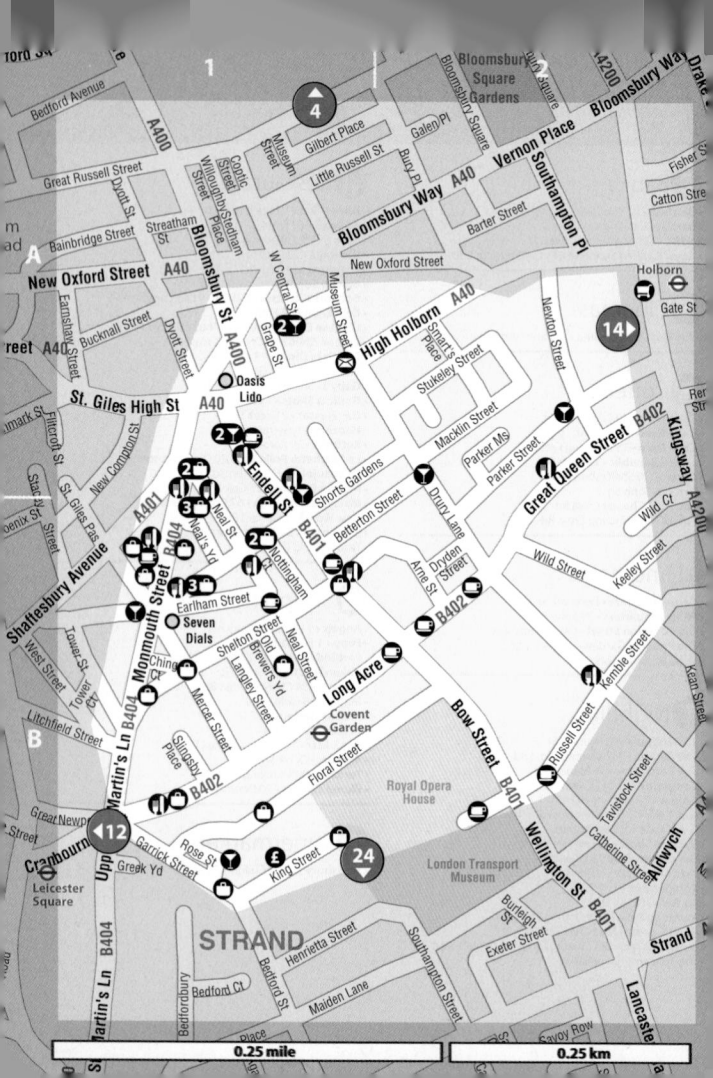
Bedford Avenue
Bloomsbury Square Gardens
Bloomsbury Square
Bloomsbury Way
Drake
Great Russell Street
Gilbert Place
Galen Pl
Museum Street
Little Russell St
Vernon Place
Southampton Pl
Fisher St
Catton Stre
Bainbridge Street
Streatham St
Willoughby Street
Sidmam Place
Bloomsbury Way A40
Barter Street
New Oxford Street A40
New Oxford Street
Holborn
Gate St
Earnshaw Street
Bucknall Street
Drury Street
Bloomsbury St A400
W Central St
Museum Street
High Holborn A40
Newton Street
Stukeley Street
Macklin Street
Parker MS
Parker Street
Great Queen Street B402
Kingsway A4200
St. Giles High St A40
Oasis Lido
Endell St
Shorts Gardens
Drury Lane
Betterton Street
Neal St
Neal's Yd
Wild Ct
Wild Street
Keeley Street
Shaftesbury Avenue
Earlham Street
Seven Dials
Shelton Street
Old Brewers Yd
Langley Street
Long Acre
Covent Garden
Bow Street B401
Russell Street
Kemble Street
Litchfield Street
Floral Street
Royal Opera House
Tavistock Street
Catherine Street
Wellington St B401
Aldwych
Garrick Street
Rose St
King Street
London Transport Museum
Leicester Square
STRAND
Henrietta Street
Southampton Street
Bedford Ct
Maiden Lane
Burleigh St
Exeter Street
Strand
Savoy Row
0.25 mile
0.25 km

Ostensibly a big set from a crap film, pacing around Covent Garden behind tourist sloths, being thwacked by jugglers' clubs and listening to Royal Opera rejects is the quickest way to psychosis. Cool off in a council estate swimming pool at Oasis, and then get musty with the moths at Blackout II. If Bernard Shaw were still alive and drinkin' you'd find him at the Lamb & Flag.

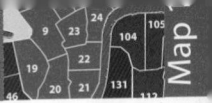

Banks

- **Abbey** • 36 King St

Coffee

- **AMT** • 14 Neal St
- **Bagel Factory** • 18 Endell St
- **Café Metro** • 33 Catherine St
- **Caffe Nero** • 30 Monmouth St
- **Caffe Nero** • 83 Long Acre
- **Coffee, Cake & Kink** • 61 Endell St
- **Pret A Manger** • 65 Long Acre
- **Starbucks** • 10 Russell St
- **Starbucks** • 55 Long Acre

Landmarks

- **Oasis Lido** • 32 Endell St
- **Seven Dials** •
  Junction of Monmouth St, Mercer St and five others

Nightlife

- **AKA Bar** • 18 W Central St
- **Bunker** • 41 Earlham St
- **The Cross Keys** • 31 Endell St
- **The End** • 18 W Central St
- **Freud** • 198 Shaftesbury Ave
- **Guanabara** • Parker St
- **Lamb & Flag** • 33 Rose St
- **Octave** • 27 Endell St
- **Poetry Society Cafe** • 22 Betterton St

Post Offices

- **High Holborn** • 181 High Holborn

Restaurants

- **Café Mode** • 57 Endell St
- **Candy Cakes** • 36 Monmouth St
- **Food for Thought** • 31 Neal St
- **Great Queen Street** • 32 Great Queen St
- **Kulu Kulu** • 51 Shelton St
- **Mon Plaisir** • 21 Monmouth St
- **The Photographers' Gallery** • Great Newport St
- **The Punjab** • 80 Neal St
- **Rock & Sole Place** • 47 Endell St
- **Sarastro** • 126 Drury Ln
- **Souk Medina** • 1 Shorts Gardens

Shopping

- **Blackout II** • 51 Endell St
- **Cath Kidston** • 28 Shelton St
- **Cyber Candy** • 3 Garrick St
- **David and Goliath** • 4 The Market Pl
- **Duffer of St George** • 34 Shorts Gardens
- **Kiehls** • 29 Monmouth St
- **Koh Samui** • 65 Monmouth St
- **Libidex** • 49 Shelton St
- **The Loft** • 35 Monmouth St
- **London Graphic Centre** • 16 Shelton St
- **Neal's Yard Dairy** • 17 Shorts Gardens
- **Nigel Hall** • 18 Floral St
- **Octopus** • 54 Neal St
- **Orla Kiely** • 31 Monmouth St
- **Pop Boutique** • 6 Monmouth St
- **Scoop** • 40 Shorts Gardens
- **Screenface** • 48 Monmouth St
- **Slam City Skates** • 16 Neal's Yard
- **Stanford's** • Long Acre
- **Superdry** • 35 Earlham St (Thomas Neal Centre)
- **Twosee** • 17 Monmouth St
- **Urban Outfitters** • 42 Earlham St

Supermarkets

- **Sainsbury's** • 129 Kingsway

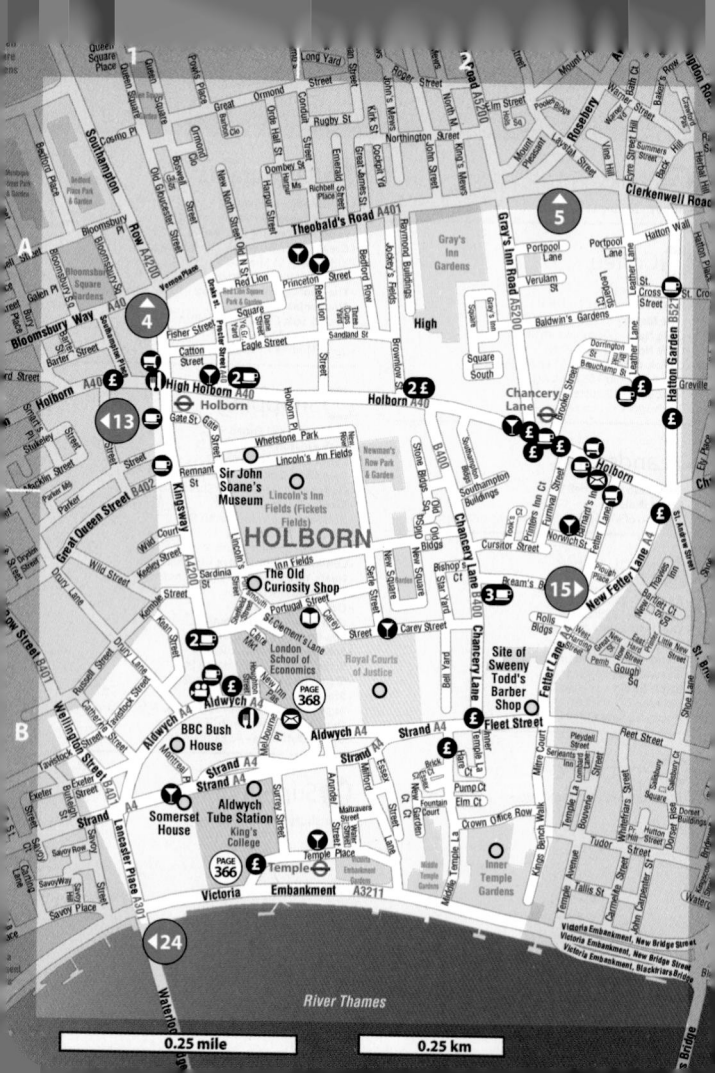
HOLBORN
Theobald's Road A401
Gray's Inn Road A5200
Clerkenwell Road
Rosebery
Southampton Row A4200
Bloomsbury Way A40
Holborn A40
Great Queen Street A402
Kingsway
Chancery Lane A4200
New Fetter Lane A4
Fetter Lane
Fleet Street
Strand A4
Aldwych A4
Wellington Street A4400
Lancaster Place A3211
Victoria Embankment A3211
Waterloo Bridge
Victoria Embankment, New Bridge Street
Victoria Embankment, Blackfriars Bridge
River Thames
Queen Square Place
Queen Square
Great Ormond Street
Ormond Yard
Long Yard
Rugby St
Northington Street
Kirk St
Roger Street
Emerald Street
Great James St
Cockpit Yd
Dombey St
Harpur Street
Richbell Place
Bedford Place
Southampton Place
Bloomsbury Pl
Bloomsbury Square Gardens
Bloomsbury St
Galen Pl
Barter Street
Red Lion Square
Red Lion Street
Princeton Street
Red Lion Row
Sandland St
Fisher Street
Catton Street
Eagle Street
Gate St
Holborn Pl
High Holborn A40
Holborn
Whetstone Park
Lincoln's Inn Fields
Lincoln's Inn Fields (Fickets Fields)
Sir John Soane's Museum
Remnant St
Newman's Row Park & Garden
Gray's Inn Gardens
Raymond Buildings
Jockey's Fields
Bedford Row
Brownlow Mews
High
Portpool Lane
Verulam St
Gray's Inn Square
Baldwin's Gardens
Square South
Leather Lane
Hatton Garden B52
Doddington Place
Beaucham St
Greville St
Chancery Lane
Brooke Street
Holborn
Furnival Street
Southampton Buildings
Staple Inn
Staple Inn Bldgs
Cursitor Street
Norwich St
Fetter Lane
Bishop Ct
Stone Buildings
Lincoln's Inn
Serle Street
New Square
Carey Street
Bell Yard
Chancery Lane
Bream's Bldgs
Rolls Bldgs
Wild Court
Kemble Street
Kean Street
Sardinia St
Portugal Street
Lincoln's Inn Fields
The Old Curiosity Shop
Clement's Lane
London School of Economics
Royal Courts of Justice
Site of Sweeny Todd's Barber Shop
Fleet Street
Gough Sq
Pemb. Sq
Wellington Street
Russell Street
Drury Lane
Catherine St
Tavistock Street
Aldwych
Aldwych A4
BBC Bush House
Strand A4
Somerset House
Aldwych Tube Station
King's College
Temple Place
Temple
Victoria Embankment
Savoy Place
Savoy Row
Savoy St
Lancaster Place
Waterloo Bridge
Essex St
Milford St
Arundel
Maltravers Street
Fountain Court
Middle Temple La
Inner Temple Gardens
Temple Avenue
Tallis St
Carmelite Street
Whitefriars St
Tudor Street
Bouverie
Shoe Lane
Bride Lane
Fleet Street
Pleydell Street
Serjeants' Inn
Fleet Street
Mitre Court
Crown Office Row
Pump Ct
Elm Ct
Brick Ct
Inner Temple La
Middle Temple La
Essex St
Milford St
Arundel
Maltravers Street
Fountain Court

Holborn / Temple

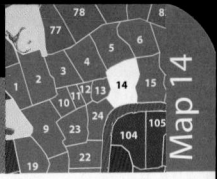

An essential cog in London's machine, this area is resplendent with curios (Old Curiosity Shop, Sweeney Todd's), public squares full of depressed lawyers and legions of serious-looking people being integrated into The System. The ghosts of Londons past hover around Temple and the Strand, where you'll also find the Aldwych Cinema for brunch and a flick. 50 types of vodka shaped escapism can be found at Na Zdrowie.

Banks

- **Abbey** • 10 Leather Ln
- **Abbey** • 306 High Holborn
- **Barclays** • 99 Hatton Garden
- **Barclays** • 147 Holborn
- **Barclays** • 19 Fleet St
- **HSBC** • 31 High Holborn
- **Lloyds** • 6 Holborn Circus
- **Lloyds** • 296 High Holborn
- **NatWest** • 65 Aldwych
- **NatWest** • 214 High Holborn
- **NatWest** • 332 High Holborn
- **NatWest** • King's College Student Union-Macadam Bldg
- **Royal Bank of Scotland** • 1 Fleet St

Cinemas

- **One Aldwych Cinema** • 1 Aldwych

Coffee

- **Caffe Nero** • 333 High Holborn
- **Costa** • 15 Chichester Rents
- **Eat.** • 105 Kingsway
- **Eat.** • 239 High Holborn
- **Eat.** • 34 High Holborn
- **Eat.** • 7 Kingsway
- **Eat.** • 77 Chancery Lane
- **Eat.** • 78 Hatton Garden
- **Pret A Manger** • 10 Leather Ln
- **Pret A Manger** • 240 High Holborn
- **Pret A Manger** • 29 Kingsway
- **Starbucks** • 10 Kingsway
- **Starbucks** • 28 Chancery Ln
- **Starbucks** • 99 Kingsway

Landmarks

- **Aldwych Tube Station** • The Strand
- **BBC Bush House** • The Strand
- **Inner Temple Garden** • Inner Temple
- **Lincoln's Inn Fields** • Lincoln's Inn Fields
- **The Old Curiosity Shop** • 13 Portsmouth St
- **Royal Courts of Justice** • The Strand
- **Sir John Soane's Museum** • 13 Lincoln's Inn Fields
- **Site of Sweeny Todd's Barber Shop** • 186 Fleet St
- **Somerset House** • Somerset House Trust, The Strand

Libraries

- **British Library of Political and Economic Science** • 10 Portugal Street

Nightlife

- **Cittie of Yorke** • 22 High Holborn
- **Enterprise** • 38 Red Lion St
- **The Lamb** • 92 Lamb's Conduit St
- **Na Zdrowie The Polish Bar** • 11 Little Turnstile
- **The Seven Stars** • 53 Carey St
- **Swissotel The Howard Hotel Bar** • Temple Pl
- **Tutu's** • Surrey St
- **Volupte** • 9 Norwich St

Post Offices

- **Aldwych** • 95 Aldwych
- **Grays Inn** • 19 High Holborn
- **Holborn Circus** • 124 High Holborn

Restaurants

- **Asadal** • 227 High Holborn
- **Indigo @ OneAldwych** • 1 Aldwych

Supermarkets

- **Sainsbury's** • 129 Kingsway
- **Sainsbury's** • 60 Fetter Ln
- **Sainsbury's** • 69 High Holborn

Map 15 • Blackfriars / Farringdon

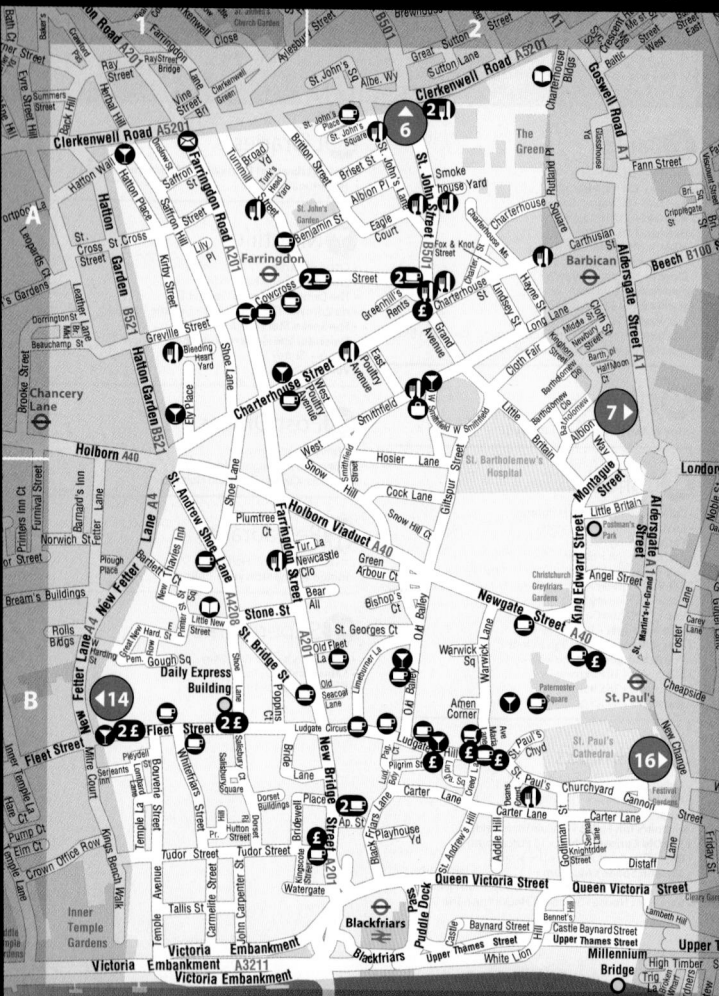

Blackfriars / Farringdon

Blackfriars Bridge opens into the commerical district, which is overrun with bankers fighting for survival. While picturesque, the river bank and Fleet Street are barren in things for us lot. Northwards, Farringdon is cooler: Flaneur may have gone, Deux Beers may have faded, but Beppe's is as Italian as concrete shoes, and Fabric continues to smash out provocatively programmed all-nighters. Come down in the brilliant Postman's Park.

Banks

- **Abbey** • 11 Ludgate Hill
- **Barclays** • 89 Charterhouse St
- **Barclays** • 81 Fleet St
- **Halifax** • 71 Fleet St
- **HSBC** • 165 Fleet St
- **HSBC** • 1 St Paul's Churchyard
- **Lloyds** • 33 Ludgate Hill
- **NatWest** • 156 Fleet St
- **Royal Bank of Scotland** • 9 Paternoster Row
- **Royal Bank of Scotland** • 36 New Bridge St

Coffee

- **Apostrophe** • 3 St Bride St
- **Apostrophe** • 10 St Pauls Churchyard
- **Bagel Factory** • 54 Cowcross St
- **Café Deco** • Charterhouse St & E Poultry Ave
- **Caffe Nero** • Shoe Lane
- **Caffe Nero** • 118 Newgate St
- **Caffe Nero** • Paternoster Sq
- **Costa** • 13 New Bridge St
- **Costa** • 46 Cowcross St
- **Eat.** • 88 Cowcross St
- **Farm Collective** • 91 Cowcross St
- **Meze Meze** • 95 Turnmill St
- **Pret A Manger** • 101 Turnmill St
- **Pret A Manger** • 5 St John's Sq
- **Pret A Manger** • 19 Ludgate Hill
- **Pret A Manger** • 10 Pasternoster Sq
- **Pret A Manger** • 101 New Bridge St
- **Pret A Manger** • 143 Fleet St
- **Starbucks** • 1 Paternoster Sq
- **Starbucks** • 32 Fleet St
- **Starbucks** • 3 Fleet Pl
- **Starbucks** • 30 New Bridge St
- **Starbucks** • 50 Cowcross St
- **Starbucks** • 55 Ludgate Hill
- **Starbucks** • 150 Fleet St

Landmarks

- **Daily Express Building** • 121 Fleet St
- **Millennium Bridge** • Millennium Bridge
- **Postman's Park** • King Edward St

Libraries

- **Shoe Lane Library** • Little New St
- **Society of Genealogists Library** • 14 Charterhouse Buildings (Goswell Road)

Nightlife

- **Corney & Barrow** • 10 Paternoster Sq
- **The Deux Beers** • 3 Hatton Wall
- **Fabric** • 77 Charterhouse St
- **Hat & Tun** • 3 Hatton Wall
- **Smithfield Bar & Grill** • 2 West Smithfield
- **Ye Old Mitre** • 1 Ely Ct
- **Ye Olde Cheshire Cheese** • 154 Fleet St
- **Ye Olde London** • 42 Ludgate Hill

Post Offices

- **Farringdon Road** • 89 Farringdon Rd

Restaurants

- **Beppe's** • 23 West Smithfield
- **The Bleeding Heart** • Bleeding Heart Yard, off Greville St
- **Cafe du Marche** • 22 Charterhouse Sq
- **Gaucho Smithfield** • 93 Charterhouse St
- **Kurz + Lang** • 1 St John St
- **The Larder** • 91 St John St
- **Pho** • 86 St John St
- **Portal** • 88 St John St
- **Smiths of Smithfield** • 67 Charterhouse St
- **St Germain** • 89 Turnmill St
- **St John's Smithfield** • 26 St John St
- **Tinseltown** • 44 St. John St
- **Vivat Bacchus** • 47 Farringdon St
- **Yo! Sushi** • 14 St Paul's

Shopping

- **Pure Groove Records** • 6 West Smithfield

Supermarkets

- **Marks & Spencer** • Ave Maria Lane
- **Sainsbury's** • 23 Farringdon Rd

Map 16 • Square Mile (West)

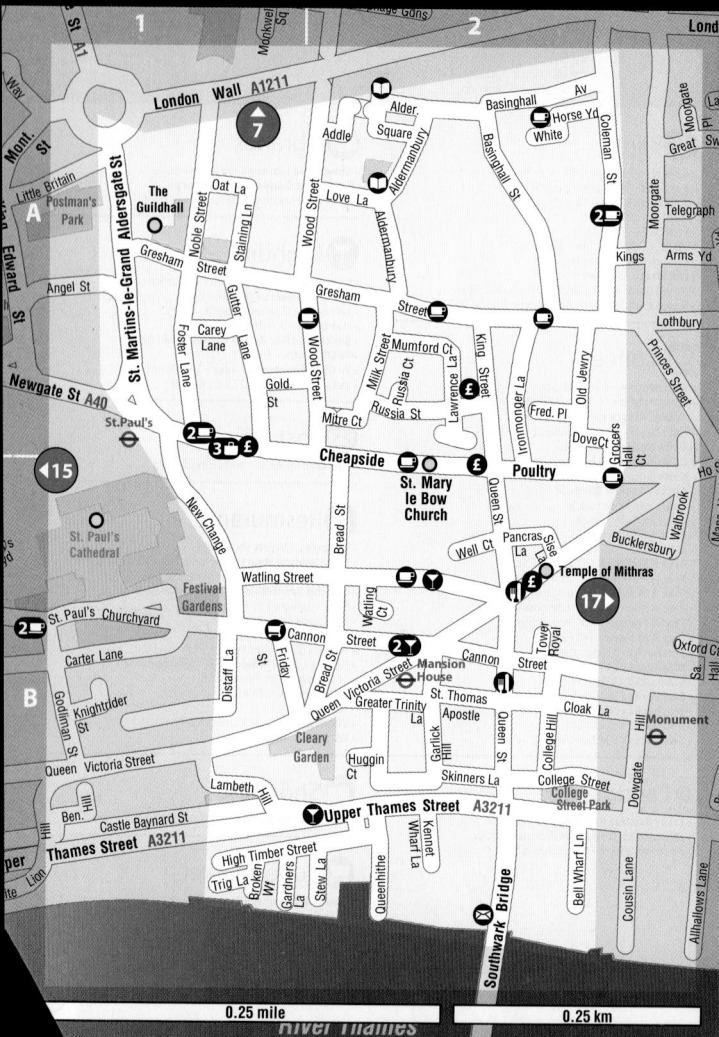

Square Mile (West)

Those bastards. Here's us, slaving away in our McJobs, presuming our financial future to be in capable hands and then the shit hits the fan. The recession has turned the City into more of a ghost town, especially at weekends, but you can still see furrowed brows and great river views at the Samuel Pepys. St. Paul's facelift may bring devotional thoughts to those in need of solace.

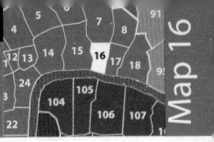

Banks

- **Barclays** • 1 King St
- **Halifax** • 134 Cheapside
- **HSBC** • 60 Queen Victoria St
- **Lloyds** • 70 Cheapside

Coffee

- **Coffee Republic** • 32 Coleman St
- **Costa** • 3 Ludgate Hill
- **Costa** • 9 Bow Ln
- **Costa** • 65 Ludgate Hill
- **Costa** • 99 Gresham St
- **Eat.** • 15 Basinghall St
- **Eat.** • 88 Wood St
- **Eat.** • 143 Cheapside
- **Fab Food Patisserie** • 19 Watling St
- **Fresco Café Bar** • 21 Masons Ave
- **Pret A Manger** • 30 Gresham St
- **Starbucks** • 1 Poultry
- **Starbucks** • 143 Cheapside

Landmarks

- **The Guildhall** • Gresham St
- **St Mary le Bow Church** • Cheapside
- **St. Paul's Cathedral** • St. Paul's Churchyard
- **Temple of Mithras** • Queen Victoria St

Post Offices

- **Southwark** • 136 Southwark Bridge Rd

Libraries

- **City Business Library** • 1 Brewers Hall Garden [off Aldermanbury Square]
- **Guildhall Library** • Aldermanbury

Nightlife

- **Hatchet** • 28 Garlick Hill
- **The Mansion House** • 44 Cannon Street
- **The Samuel Pepys** • 48 Upper Thames Street
- **Ye Olde Watling** • 29 Watling Street

Restaurants

- **Bar Bourse** • 67 Queen Street
- **Sweetings** • 39 Queen Victoria St

Shopping

- **Church's Shoes** • 90 Cheapside
- **Manucci** • 5 Cheapside
- **Space NK Apothecary** • 145 Cheapside

Supermarkets

- **Marks & Spencer** • Cannon St Station

London Wall A1211
Wormwood St
Bishopsgate Gdns
Bishopsgate A10
Union Court
Great Winchester St
Austin Friars Passage
Throgmorton Ave
Copthall Ave
Langthorn Court
Moorgate Pl
Moorgate
Great Swan Al
Basinghall Ave
White Horse Yard
Coleman Street
Telegraph Street
Tokenhouse Yd
Kings Arms Yd
Adams Court
Throgmorton Street
Threadneedle St
Bank of England
Gresham Street
Lothbury
Bartholomew Lane
Capel Ct
Princes St
Threadneedle Street
Royal Exchange Ave
Finch Lane
Mercers' Court
White Lion Court
Sun Ct
Old Jewry
Ironmonger Lane
Frederick's Place
St Mildred's Court
Dove Ct
Cornhill
Cheapside
Poultry
Mansion House St
Bank
Mansion House Pl
Post Office Ct
Birchin Lane
Corbet Ct
Bell Inn Yard
Leadenhall Place
Walbrook
Queen Victoria Street
Bucklersbury
Pancras La
George Yard
Lombard Street
Gracechurch Street
Plough Court
Nicholas Lane
Clements Lane
Abchurch Lane
Abchurch La
King William Street
Sherborne La
St. Swithin's Lane
Brabant Court
St. Benet's Place
Philpot Lane
Rood Lane
Tower Royal
Oxford Ct
Salters Hall Ct
Talbot Ct
Cannon Street
London Stone
Monument
Eastcheap
Cloak Lane
College Hill
College St
Dowgate Hill
Cannon Street Station
Bush Lane
Godliman St
Suffolk La
Laurence Pountney Hill
Laurence Pountney La
Martin Lane
King William St
Monument St
Fish Street Hill
Pudding La
Botolph Lane
St. Mary at Hill
Upper Thames Street A3211
Lower Thames St A3211
Southwark Bridge
Bell Wharf Lane
Cousin Lane
Allhallows Lane
Angel Pas
Swan Lane
CITY
London Bridge A3
0.25 mile
0.25 km
River

London's most Jekyll and Hyde-like hood. By day, the Banking district throbs with worried suits losing fortunes. They still dig steaks at Gaucho City, though perhaps Rhodes 24's Michelin stars are out of their price range now. Well, probably not, but they're not as opulent as the original occupants of The Counting House, now a grandiose pub. By night, well, just don't go there.

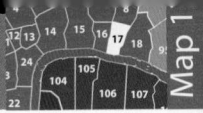

Banks

- **Abbey** • 48 Moorgate
- **Abbey** • 51 Gracechurch St
- **Barclays** • 29 Wormwood St
- **Co-Operative** • 80 Cornhill
- **Halifax** • 33 Old Broad St
- **Halifax** • 58 Moorgate
- **HSBC** • 95 Gracechurch St
- **HSBC** • 100 Old Broad St
- **Lloyds** • 34 Moorgate
- **Lloyds** • 39 Threadneedle St
- **NatWest** • 1 Prince's St
- **NatWest** • 15 Bishopsgate
- **Royal Bank of Scotland** • 62 Threadneedle St

Coffee

- **Bagel** • Cannon's Health Club, Cousins Ln
- **Bagel Factory** • 59 Moorgate
- **Caffe Nero** • 22 Wormwood Stree
- **Costa** • 51 Gracechurch St
- **Eat.** • 54 Cornhill
- **Eat.** • 123 Cannon St
- **Oi Bagel** • 27 Throgmorton St
- **Pret A Manger** • 43 King William St
- **Starbucks** • 5 Camomile St
- **Starbucks** • 13 Old Broad St
- **Starbucks** • 48 Gracechurch St
- **Starbucks** • 74 Cornhill
- **Starbucks** • 90 Old Broad St

Landmarks

- **Bank of England** • Threadneedle St
- **London Stone** • 105 Cannon St
- **Threadneedle Street** • Threadneedle St

Nightlife

- **The Counting House** • 50 Cornhill
- **Grand Cafe & Bar** • The Ctyard, Royal Exchange

Post Offices

- **Moorgate** • 53 Moorgate

Restaurants

- **Gaucho City** • 1 Bell Inn Yard
- **The Mercer** • 34 Threadneedle St
- **Rhodes 24** • 25 Old Broad St
- **Wasabi** • 52 Old Broad St

Shopping

- **Sweatshop (City branch - at Cannon's Gym)** • Cousin Lane

Supermarkets

- **Marks & Spencer** • Cannon St Station
- **Sainsbury's** • 14 Lombard St

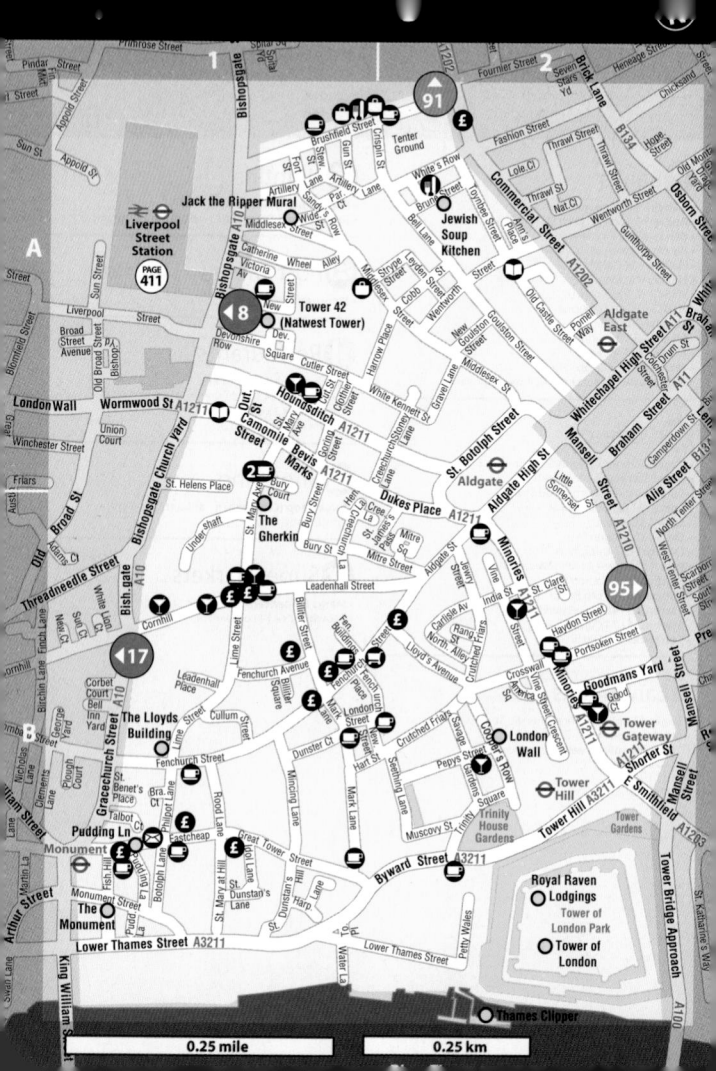
Jack the Ripper Mural
Jewish Soup Kitchen
Liverpool Street Station
PAGE 411
Tower 42 (Natwest Tower)
Aldgate East
Aldgate
The Gherkin
The Lloyds Building
Pudding Ln
The Monument
Monument
London Wall
Tower Hill
Tower Gateway
Goodmans Yard
Royal Raven Lodgings
Tower of London Park
Tower of London
Thames Clipper
0.25 mile
0.25 km

Though on the fringe of the financial cesspit, Aldgate is brilliant to walk and gawp around in. A. Gold's British deli (Yes…ça exist!) is fabulous, as is the atmospheric neighbourhood around Petticoat Lane, where Jack The Ripper used to stalk prozzers. After stodge at Jeff's head South, pass the Erotic Gherkin (ahem), and go seige the London Wall alongside the tourists. Alternatively go become one yourself at Pudding Lane.

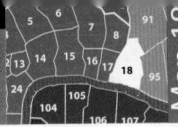

Banks

- **Barclays** • 114 Fenchurch St
- **Barclays** • 99 Commercial St
- **HSBC** • 20 Eastcheap
- **HSBC** • 60 Fenchurch St
- **Lloyds** • 72 Fenchurch St
- **Lloyds** • 113 Leadenhall St
- **NatWest** • 116 Fenchurch St
- **NatWest** • 2 Eastcheap
- **Royal Bank of Scotland** • 5 Great Tower St
- **Royal Bank of Scotland** • 54 Lime St

Coffee

- **Caffe Nero** • 1 Fenchurch Pl [Coopers Row]
- **Caffe Nero** • 23 Eastcheap
- **Caffe Nero** • 88 Leadenhall St
- **Costa** • 74 Mark Ln
- **Eat.** • 28 Brushfield St
- **Eat.** • 84 Aldgate High St
- **Eat.** • 2 Eastcheap
- **Eat.** • 155 Fenchurch St
- **Eat.** • 26 Leadenhall St
- **Eat.** • 122 Minories
- **Eat.** • 48 Mark Ln
- **Eat.** • 2 Tower Hill
- **Eat.** • 33 St Mary Axe
- **Pret A Manger** • 3 Cutler St
- **Starbucks** • 8 Brushfield St
- **Starbucks** • 14 New St
- **Starbucks** • 20 Eastcheap
- **Starbucks** • 65 Fenchurch St
- **Starbucks** • 48 Minories
- **Starbucks** • 66 St Mary Axe

Landmarks

- **The Gherkin** • 30 St Mary Axe
- **Jack the Ripper Mural** • Widegate St
- **Jewish Soup Kitchen** • Brune St
- **The Lloyds Building** • 1 Lime St
- **London Wall** • Cooper's Row
- **The Monument** • Monument St
- **Pudding Lane** • Pudding Lane
- **Royal Raven Lodgings** • Wakefield Tower (Tower of London)
- **Thames Clipper** • Tower Pier
- **Tower 42 (Natwest Tower)** • 25 Old Broad St
- **Tower of London** • The Tower of London

Libraries

- **Camomile Street** • 15 Camomile St
- **The Women's Library** • 25 Old Castle St

Nightlife

- **Dion City** • 52 Leadenhall St
- **Kenza** • 10 Devonshire Sq
- **Mary Janes** • 124 Minories
- **The Minories** • 64-73 Minories
- **Pepys Bar at the Novotel Hotel** • 10 Pepys St
- **Prism** • 147 Leadenhall St
- **Revolution in the City** • 140 Leadenhall St

Post Offices

- **The City of London BO** • 12 Eastcheap

Restaurants

- **Jeff's Cafe** • 14 Brune St
- **S & M Cafe** • 48 Brushfield St

Shopping

- **A. Gold** • 42 Brushfield St
- **Montezuma's** • 51 Brushfield St
- **Petticoat Lane** • Middlesex St

Supermarkets

- **Sainsbury's** • 45 Fenchurch St

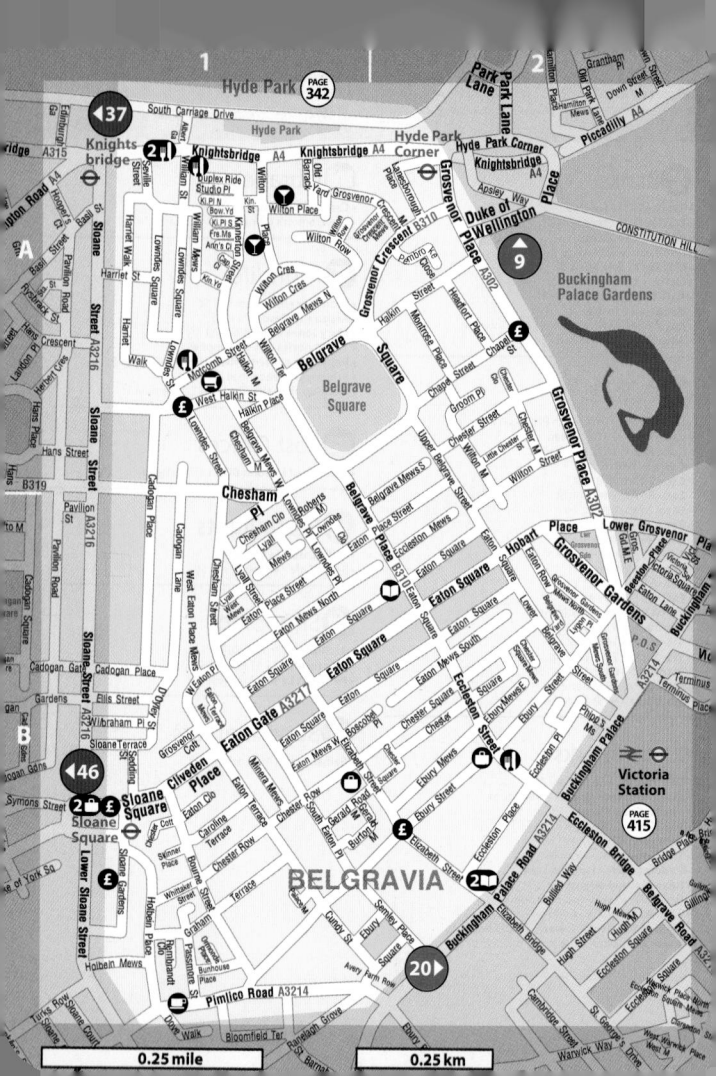
1
2
A
B
Hyde Park
PAGE 342
37
Knightsbridge
Hyde Park Corner
Park Lane
Piccadilly A4
Knightsbridge A4
Knightsbridge A315
South Carriage Drive
Grosvenor Crescent
Grosvenor Place A302
Duke of Wellington Place
Wilton Place
Wilton Row
Belgrave Square
Belgrave Mews N
Belgrave Mews W
Belgrave Place A3212
Belgrave Road A3214
Grosvenor Place A302
Grosvenor Gardens
Hobart Place
Lower Grosvenor Place
Chesham Pl
Chesham Cloose
Eaton Square
Eaton Place
Eaton Mews North
Eaton Mews South
Eaton Gate A3217
Eccleston Street
Eccleston Place
Eccleston Bridge
Buckingham Palace Road A3214
Buckingham Palace
Victoria Station
PAGE 415
9
Buckingham Palace Gardens
CONSTITUTION HILL
Sloane Street A3216
Sloane Square
Cliveden Place
Cadogan Place
Cadogan Gate
Ellis Street
Wilbraham Pl
Sloane Terrace
Lower Sloane Street
Holbein Mews
Pimlico Road A3214
Bloomfield Ter
Ebury Street
Ebury Mews
Chester Square
Chester Row
Elizabeth Street
Elizabeth Bridge
Victoria St
Knightsbridge A4
Harriet Walk
Harriet St
Lowndes Square
Lowndes St
Wilton Crescent
Belgrave Mews N
Belgrave Mews W
Belgrave Mews S
Halkin St
Halkin Place
Chapel St
Groom Pl
Chester Street
Hobart Place
Hobart Mews
Eaton Square
Eaton Place
Eaton Mews North
Eaton Mews South
Eccleston Square
Eccleston Place
Eccleston Bridge
Buckingham Palace Rd
Belgrave Road
Hugh Street
Hugh Mews
Bulleid Way
Ebury Bridge

Ugg and Range Rover fetishists are in a constant state of climax around here. It sure is pretty when the sun isn't being blocked by expensively coiffuered bouffants, but one suspects the plummy accents and tastless richness would dent anyone's enthusiasm for chic dog clothes (Mungo & Maud) or curry (Amaya). Victoria's Red Cross Charity shop provides opportunities for us to pick over upper class leftovers.

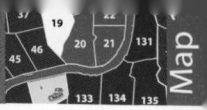

Banks

- **Barclays** • 8 W Halkin St
- **HSBC** • 19 Grosvenor Pl
- **HSBC** • 13 Sloane Sq
- **NatWest** • 141 Ebury St
- **NatWest** • 2 Sloane Gardens

Coffee

- **Starbucks** • 53 Pimlico Rd

Libraries

- **Instituto Cervantes** • 102 Eaton Square
- **Victoria Library** • 160 Buckingham Palace Rd
- **Westminster Music Library** • 160 Buckingham Palace Rd

Nightlife

- **The Blue Bar** • Wilton Pl
- **Nag's Head** • 53 Kinnerton St

Restaurants

- **Amaya** • Halkin Arcade, Motcomb St
- **Boisdale, Victoria** • 15 Eccleston St
- **Noura** • 12 William St
- **One-O-One** • 101 Knightsbridge
- **Yo! Sushi** • 102 Knightsbridge

Shopping

- **British Red Cross Victoria** • 85 Ebury St
- **Moyses Flowers** • Sloane Sq
- **Mungo & Maud** • 79 Elizabeth St
- **Peter Jones** •Sloan Sq

Supermarkets

- **Waitrose** • 27 Motcomb St

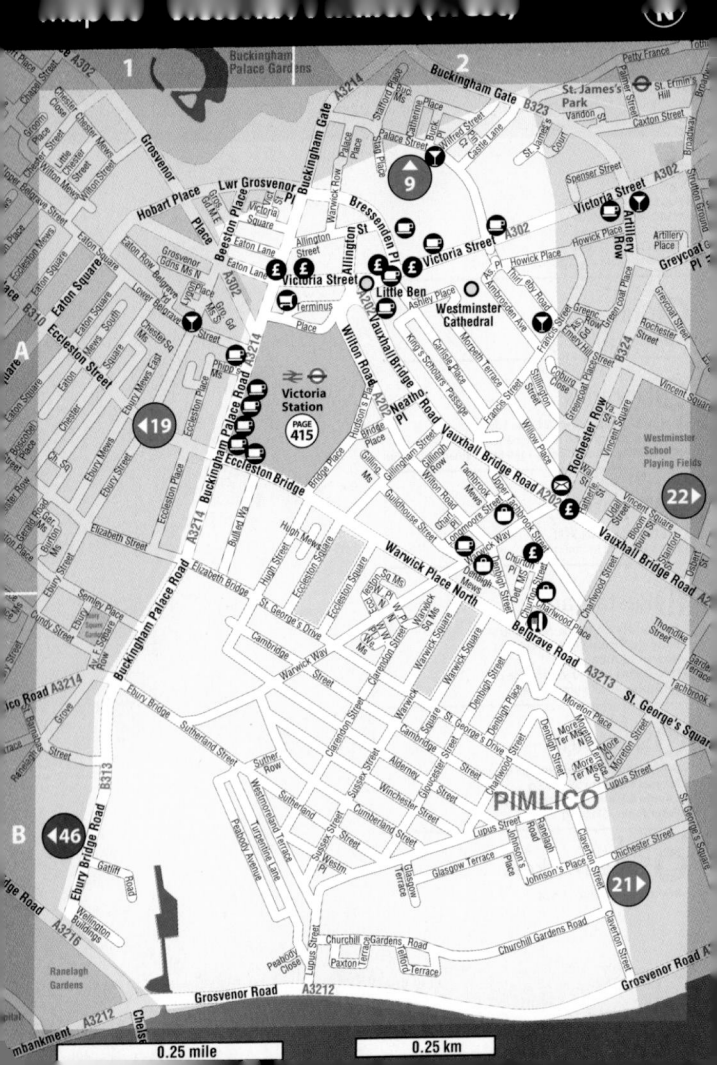
Buckingham Palace Gardens
Buckingham Gate
St. James's Park
Victoria Street
Artillery Row
Grosvenor Place
Hobart Place
Lwr Grosvenor Pl
Beeston Place
Bressenden Pl
Allington St
Eaton Square
Eccleston Street
Little Ben
Westminster Cathedral
Vauxhall Bridge Pl
Neathe Road
Vauxhall Bridge Road
Victoria Station
PAGE 415
Eccleston Bridge
Buckingham Palace Road
Wilton Road
Rochester Row
Westminster School Playing Fields
Warwick Place North
Belgrave Road
St. George's Square
PIMLICO
Ebury Bridge Road
Grosvenor Road
Ranelagh Gardens
Chelsea Embankment
0.25 mile
0.25 km

Victoria / Pimlico (West)

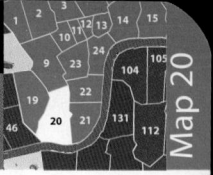

Since the Tower of London closed for business, prisoners have been routinely tortured at weekends in Victoria Station. Surrounding the transit hubs is a dignified 'hood Churchill and Mozart called home. Do a late-night tramp photoshoot on the steps of the magnificent houses of Lupus Street (with a camera from Grays) before heading to the Cask & Glass for a knees up with your new pals.

Banks

- **Barclays** • 1 Churton St
- **Halifax** • 62 Victoria St
- **HSBC** • 89 Buckingham Palace Rd
- **HSBC** • 166 Vauxhall Bridge Rd
- **Lloyds** • 98 Victoria St
- **NatWest** • 169 Victoria St

Coffee

- **Bagel Factory** • Victoria Station
- **Bagel Factory** • 115 Buckingham Palace Rd
- **Caffe Nero** • 31 Warwick Way
- **Costa** • 3 Cardinal Walk
- **Costa** • 115 Buckingham Palace Rd
- **Costa** • 324 Vauxhall Bridge Rd
- **Eat.** • Cardinal Pl
- **Pret A Manger** • 12 Victoria St
- **Pret A Manger** • 173 Victoria St
- **Pret A Manger** • Victoria Station
- **Pret A Manger** • 92 Buckingham Palace Rd
- **Starbucks** • 137 Victoria St
- **Starbucks** • Buckingham Palace Rd & Lower Belgrave St

Post Offices

- **Vauxhall Bridge Road** • 167 Vauxhall Bridge Rd

Landmarks

- **Little Ben** • Victoria St/Vauxhall Bridge Rd intersection
- **Westminster Cathedral** • 42 Francis St

Nightlife

- **The Albert** • 52 Victoria St
- **The Cardinal** • 23 Francis St
- **Cask & Glass** • 39 Palace St
- **The Plumber's Arms** • 14 Lower Belgrave St

Restaurants

- **Grumbles** • 35 Churton St

Shopping

- **Grays of Westminster** • 40 Churton St
- **La Bella Sicilia** • 33 Warwick Way
- **Rippon Cheese Stores** • 26 Upper Tachbrook St

Supermarkets

- **Marks & Spencer** • Victoria Mainline Station

Map 21 • Pimlico (East)

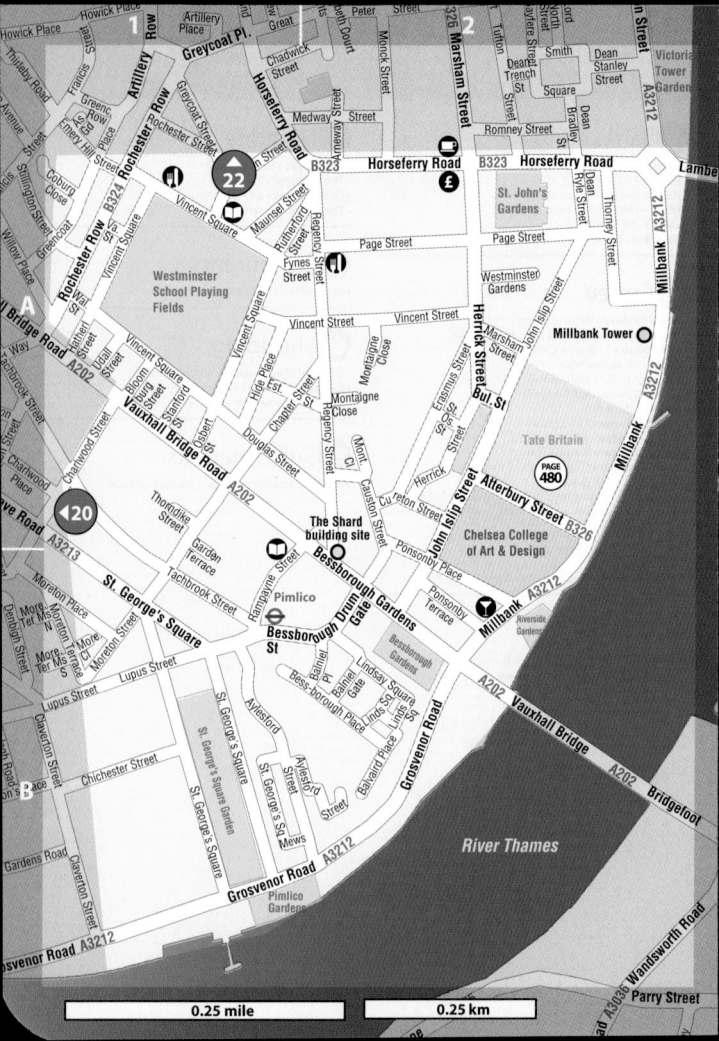

Hugging the curve of the Thames, this princely patch of Pimlico combines the stately Tate with imposing embankment architecture and ancient houses. Check out the old-money splendour of Vincent Street before grabbing lunch at the Regency, a true gem of a caf. Much fun can be had by pretending you acutally live around here, so in this spirit head to the Morpeth as your local.

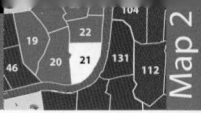

Banks

- **NatWest** • 27 Horseferry Rd

Coffee

- **Starbucks** • 35 Horseferry Rd

Landmarks

- **Millbank Tower** • Millbank
- **The Shard building site** • 32 Vauxhall Bridge Rd

Libraries

- **Pimlico Library** • Rampayne St
- **Royal Horticultural Society Library** • 80 Vincent Sq

Nightlife

- **Morpeth Arms** • 58 Millibank

Restaurants

- **The Regency Cafe** • 17 Regency St
- **Vincent Rooms** • 1 The Victoria Centre, Vincent Sq

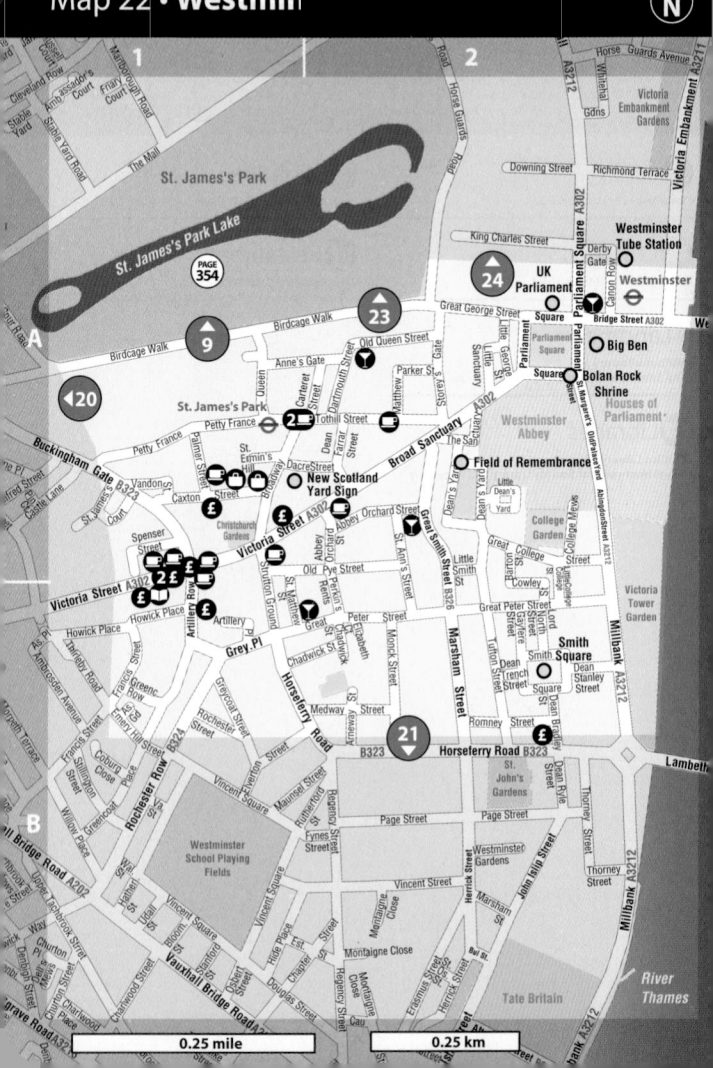
N
1
2
A
B
St. James's Park
St. James's Park Lake
PAGE 354
Cleveland Row
Stable Yard
Stable Yard Road
The Mall
Ambassador's Court
Friary Court
Marlborough Road
Horse Guards Road
Horse Guards Avenue
Whitehall
Gdns
Victoria Embankment Gardens
Victoria Embankment A3211
Downing Street
Richmond Terrace
King Charles Street
Parliament Square A302
Westminster Tube Station
Derby Gate
Canon Row
Westminster
Bridge Street A302
UK Parliament
Square
Great George Street
Birdcage Walk
Old Queen Street
Anne's Gate
Parliament Street
Parliament Square
Big Ben
Bolan Rock Shrine
Parker St
Queen Anne's Gate
Carteret Street
Dartmouth Street
Matthew Parker St
Tothill Street
Petty France
Buckingham Gate B3
Vandon Court
Caxton Street
Palmer Street
St. Ermin's Hill
Broadway
Dacre Street
New Scotland Yard Sign
Broad Sanctuary
Westminster Abbey
Field of Remembrance
Dean's Yard
Little Dean's Yard
College Garden
Great College Street
Little Smith St
Cowley St
Victoria Street A302
Christchurch Gardens
Spenser Street
Abbey Orchard St
Orchard Street
Great Smith Street B326
St. Ann's Street
Old Pye Street
Stratton Ground
Artillery Row
Howick Place
Artillery Pl
Grey Pl
Great Peter Street
Peter Street
Marsham Street
Millbank A3212
Victoria Tower Garden
Smith Square
Dean Stanley Street
Horseferry Road
Chadwick St
Medway Street
Romney Street
Horseferry Road B323
St. John's Gardens
Lambeth
Greencoat Place
Greencoat Row
Rochester Row B324
Vincent Square
Maunsel Street
Page Street
Westminster School Playing Fields
Westminster Gardens
Vincent Street
Herrick Street
John Islip Street
Millbank A3212
Thorney Street
Montagne Close
Vauxhall Bridge Road A202
Tate Britain
River Thames
0.25 mile
0.25 km

Westminster

The long shadow of government falls over these parts, beautiful as they are. Protesters, T-Rex fans and amatuer Guy Fawkeses head to Parliament Square, where they can harangue whichever bunch of jokers are ensconed in the Houses of Parliament. Get away from tourists at the tiny St Stephen's Tavern, or grab a classy cocktail at the Cinnamon Club. If you must shop head to Victoria Street.

Banks

- **Abbey** • 115 Victoria St
- **Barclays** • 13 Artillery Row
- **Barclays** • 2 Victoria St
- **HSBC** • 8 Victoria St
- **Lloyds** • 1 Butler Pl
- **Lloyds** • 4 Dean Stanley St
- **NatWest** • 57 Victoria St
- **Royal Bank of Scotland** • 119 Victoria St

Coffee

- **Caffe Nero** • 1 Bridge St
- **Caffe Nero** • 105 Victoria St
- **Eat.** • 37 Tothill St
- **Eat.** • 3 Strutton Ground
- **Fresco Cafe Bar** • 11 Tothill St
- **Pret A Manger** • 75 Victoria St
- **Pret A Manger** • 49 Tothill St
- **Puccino's** • 6 Victoria St
- **Starbucks** • 17 Palmer St
- **Starbucks** • 27 Victoria St

Landmarks

- **Big Ben** • House of Commons
- **Bolan Rock Shrine** • Queen's Ride, Putney
- **Field of Remembrance** • Victoria St & Dean's Yard
- **New Scotland Yard sign** • 8 Broadway
- **Smith Square** • Smith Sq
- **UK Parliament** • House of Commons
- **Westminster Tube Station** • Bridge St

Libraries

- **St James's Library** • 62 Victoria St

Nightlife

- **The Cinnamon Club** • 30 Great Smith St
- **The Speaker** • 46 Great Peter Street
- **The Two Chairmen** • 39 Dartmouth St
- **St Stephen's Tavern** • 10 Bridge Street

Shopping

- **Haelen Centre** • 41 Broadway
- **National Map Centre** • 22-24 Caxton St

Map 23 • St. James's

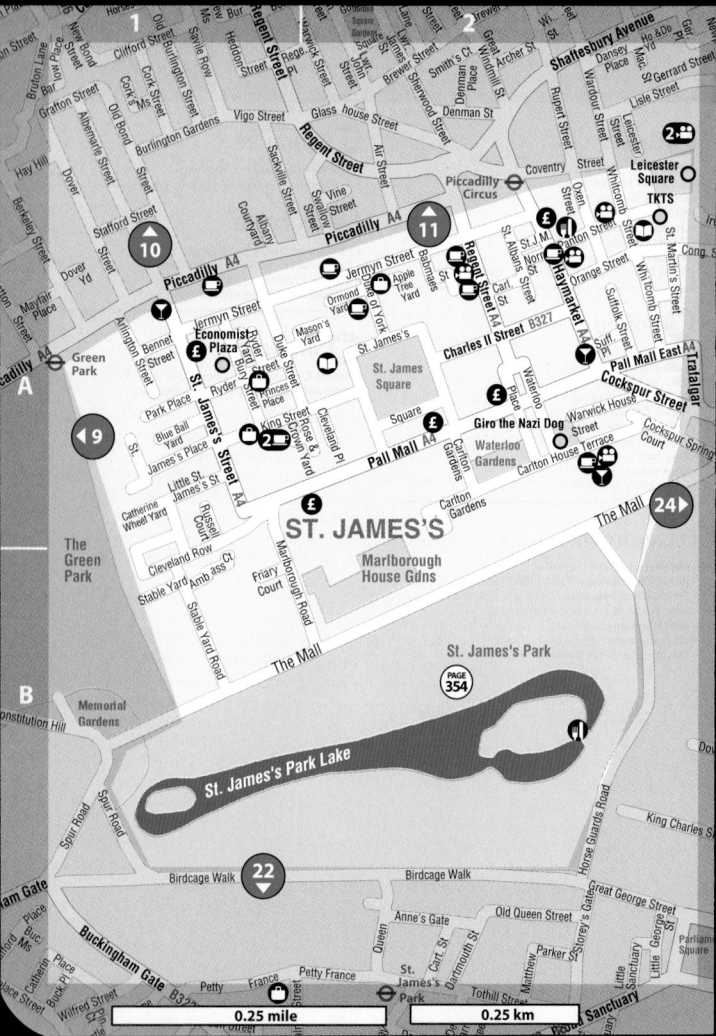

Dignified, decadent, exclusive, Pall Mall and St. James's Street are where the aristobrats come out to play. With stuffy gentlemen's clubs, bespoke tailors and the stale scent of a cigar-fuelled colonialist past pervading you'll want to sweeten up with a macaroon at Laduree. Giro the Nazi dog observes the liberals who get culture fixes at the ICA, but he can't come for scraps at Inn The Park.

Banks

- **Barclays** • 31 St James's St
- **HSBC** • 69 Pall Mall
- **Lloyds** • 7 Pall Mall
- **Lloyds** • 8 Waterloo Pl
- **Royal Bank of Scotland** • 48 Haymarket

Cinemas

- **Apollo West End** • 19 Regent St
- **Cineworld Haymarket** • 63 Haymarket
- **ICA Cinema** • The Mall & Horse Guards Rd
- **Odeon Leicester Square Cinema** • 24 Leicester Sq
- **Odeon Panton Street** • 11 Panton St
- **Odeon West End Cinema** • 40 Leicester Sq

Coffee

- **Apostrophe** • 16 Regent St
- **Caffe Nero** • 35 Jermyn St
- **Coffee Republic** • 63 Haymarket
- **Eat.** • 18 Regent St
- **Eat.** • 3 Duke of York St
- **Eat.** • 9 Crown Passage
- **ICA Cafe** • The Mall
- **Pret A Manger** • 8 King St
- **Starbucks** • 171 Picadilly

Landmarks

- **Economist Plaza** • 25 St James's St
- **Giro the Nazi Dog** • 9 Carlton House Terrace
- **Leicester Square** • Leicester Sq
- **TKTS** • Leicester Sq

Libraries

- **London Library** • 14 St James's Sq
- **Westminster Reference Library** • 35 St Martin's St

Nightlife

- **Aura** • 48 St James's St
- **ICA** • The Mall
- **The Sports Cafe** • 80 Haymarket

Restaurants

- **Inn The Park** • St James' Park
- **Stockpot** • 38 Panton St

Shopping

- **Partridges Deli** • 2 Duke of York St
- **National Map Centre** • 22-24 Caxton St
- **Richard Caplan** • 25 Bury St
- **Thai Smile** • King St

N
1
2
A
B
Moor St
Charing Cross Road
West Street
Tower Street
Monmouth
Shelton Street
Langley Street
Yard
East
B402
Sidney Pl
Long Acre
Floral Street
Russell St
Aldwych
Catherine Street
Wellington Street B401
Montreal Pl
Strand
Avenue A401
Gerrard
Dolphin Yard
Newport Pl
Litchfield Street
Upper St. Martin's Lane
B404
Great Newport St
Little Newport St
Cranbourn Street
Garrick Street
Rose Street
King Street
The Actors Church
Henrietta Street
Southampton St
Tavistock Street
Exeter Street
Bedfordbury
Leicester Square
Charing Cross Rd
St. Martin's Lane B404
New Row
Jane Austen Residence
Bedford Ct
Bedford Street
Lindsey St
Charles Place
Agar St
Maiden Lane
Right-hand drive seat
Duncannon St
Buckingham St
Savoy
Sewer Lamp
Savoy Row
Savoy Place
Savoy Way
Savoyhill
Lancaster Place A301
Waterloo
Irving Street
William IV Street
Adelaide St
Adam Street
Durham Ho St
Cleopatra's Needle
Orange Street
St. Martin's Street
National Gallery & National Portrait Gallery
Eleanor Cross
St. Martin-in-the-Fields
Strand
Victoria Embankment Gardens
Whitcomb St
Suffolk Street
Pall Mall East
Trafalgar Square
Cockspur Street
Corner House Street
Hungerford Lane
Villiers Street
Charing Cross Station
Embankment
Northumberland Ave
Northumberland St
Green Street
Warwick Ho St
Cockspur Court
Spring Gardens
Top Secret Tunnels
Craigs Ct
Great Scotland Yard
Whitehall Place
The Banqueting House
Whitehall Court
Victoria Embankment
River Thames
The Mall
Horse Guards Rd
Whitehall A3212
Horse Guards Avenue
Whitehall Gdns
St. James's Park
10 Downing St
Downing Street
Richmond Terrace
Parliament Street A3212
King Charles Street
Derby Gate
Westminster
PAGE 482
PAGE 410
12
13
14
22
23
0.25 mile
0.25 km

Trafalgar Square / The Strand

If you'd been strolling along here 150 years ago the Thames would have been lapping your ankles. Then they built the Embankment so the tourists could dry out in the louche Gordon's Winebar on their way to scare flying rats at Trafalgar Square. In the event of nuclear armageddon head to the secret tunnels and meet up with the PM for a post-apocalypse pint of bitter.

Banks

- **Abbey** • 406 Strand
- **Barclays** • 366 Strand
- **HSBC** • 455 Strand
- **Lloyds** • 48 Strand
- **Lloyds** • 222 Strand
- **NatWest** • 38 Strand
- **NatWest** • 34 Henrietta St
- **NatWest** • 217 Strand

Coffee

- **Apostrophe** • 215 Strand
- **Bagel Factory** • 45 Villiers St
- **Café Express** • 372 Strand
- **Caffe Nero** • 10 Bedford St
- **Caffe Nero** • 181 Strand
- **Caffe Nero** • 125 Strand
- **Caffe Nero** • 36 St Martin's Ln
- **Caffe Nero** • 20 Southampton St
- **Coffee Republic** • 79 Strand
- **Costa** • 17 Embankment Pl
- **Eat.** • 41 Bedford St
- **Eat.** • 39 Villiers St
- **Pret A Manger** • 135 Strand
- **Pret A Manger** • 421 Strand
- **Pret A Manger** • 78 St Martin's Ln
- **Starbucks** • 355 Strand
- **Starbucks** • 442 Strand
- **Starbucks** • 14 Villiers St
- **Starbucks** • 1 Villiers St

Landmarks

- **10 Downing Street** • 10 Downing St
- **The Actors' Church** • St. Paul's Church, Bedford St
- **The Banqueting House** • Whitehall
- **Cleopatra's Needle** • Embankment
- **Eleanor Cross** • Charing Cross Station, The Strand
- **Jane Austen Residence** • 10 Henrietta St
- **Right-hand Drive Street** • Savoy Ct
- **Sewer Lamp** • Carting Lane
- **St Martin-in-the-Fields** • Trafalgar Sq
- **Top Secret Tunnels** • 6 Craig's Ct (entrance)
- **Trafalgar Square** • Trafalgar Sqaure

Libraries

- **Charing Cross Library** • 4 Charing Cross Rd
- **CILT Resources Library** • 20 Bedfordbury
- **Royal United Services Institute Library** • Whitehall

Nightlife

- **Asia de Cuba** • 45 St. Martin's Lane
- **The Chandos** • 29 St Martins Lane
- **The Coal Hole** • 91 Strand
- **Covent Garden Comedy Club** • The Arches, Off Villiers St
- **Gordon's Wine Bar** • 47 Villiers St
- **Heaven** • Under the Arches, off Villiers St
- **Maple Leaf** • 41 Maiden Ln
- **Punch & Judy** • The Covent Garden Piazza
- **Retro Bar** • 2 George Ct
- **Roadhouse** • 35 The Piazza
- **The Sherlock Homes** • 10 Northumberland St
- **The Ship and Shovel** • 2 Craven Passage
- **Zoo Bar** • 13 Bear St

Post Offices

- **Trafalgar Square** • 24 William IV St

Restaurants

- **Bistro 1** • 33 Southampton St
- **Cafe in the Crypt** • Trafalgar Sq
- **Covent Garden Market Cafe** • Covent Garden
- **Farmer Brown** • 4 New Row
- **Gourmet Burger Kitchen** • 13 Maiden Ln
- **India Club** •
  143 Strand (Second floor, Strand Continental Hotel)
- **J Sheekey** • 28 St Martins Ct
- **RS Hispaniola** • Victoria Embankment
- **Rules** • 35 Maiden Ln
- **Thai Pot** • 1 Bedfordbury
- **Wahaca** • 66 Chandos Pl

Shopping

- **Austin Kaye** • 425 The Strand
- **Australia Shop** • 27 Maiden Ln
- **The Italian Bookshop** • 5 Cecil Ct
- **London Camera Exchange** • 98 Strand
- **Motor Books** • 13 Cecil Ct
- **Rohan** • 10 Henrietta St
- **Stanley Gibbons** • 399 Strand

Supermarkets

- **Marks & Spencer** • Charing Cross Station

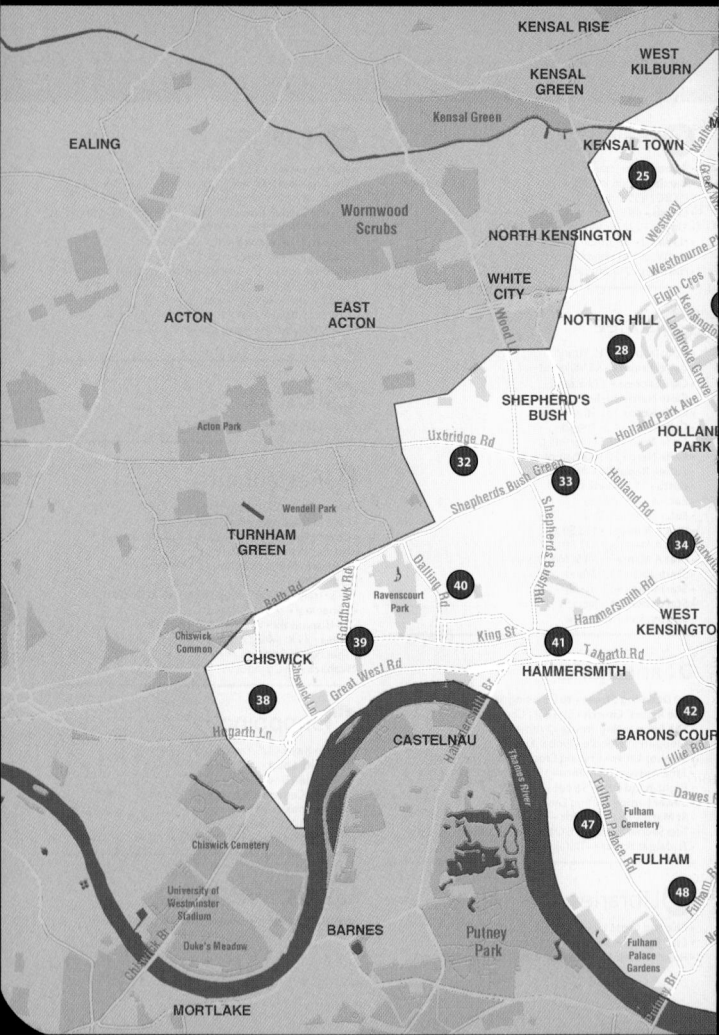
KENSAL RISE
WEST KILBURN
KENSAL GREEN
Kensal Green
EALING
KENSAL TOWN
25
Wormwood Scrubs
NORTH KENSINGTON
Westway
Westbourne Pk
WHITE CITY
Elgin Cres
ACTON
EAST ACTON
Wood Ln
NOTTING HILL
Ladbroke Grove
28
SHEPHERD'S BUSH
Holland Park Ave
Acton Park
Uxbridge Rd
32
33
Holland Rd
Shepherds Bush Green
Wendell Park
TURNHAM GREEN
Shepherds Bush Rd
34
Goldhawk Rd
Datling Rd
40
Ravenscourt Park
Hammersmith Rd
WEST KENSINGTO
Chiswick Common
King St
39
41
Tabarth Rd
CHISWICK
Great West Rd
HAMMERSMITH
38
Chiswick Ln
Hogarth Ln
CASTELNAU
Hammersmith Br
42
BARONS COUR
Lillie Rd
Thames River
Dawes
Fulham Palace Rd
47
Fulham Cemetery
Chiswick Cemetery
FULHAM
48
University of Westminster Stadium
Duke's Meadow
BARNES
Putney Park
Fulham Palace Gardens
Chiswick Br
Putney Br
MORTLAKE

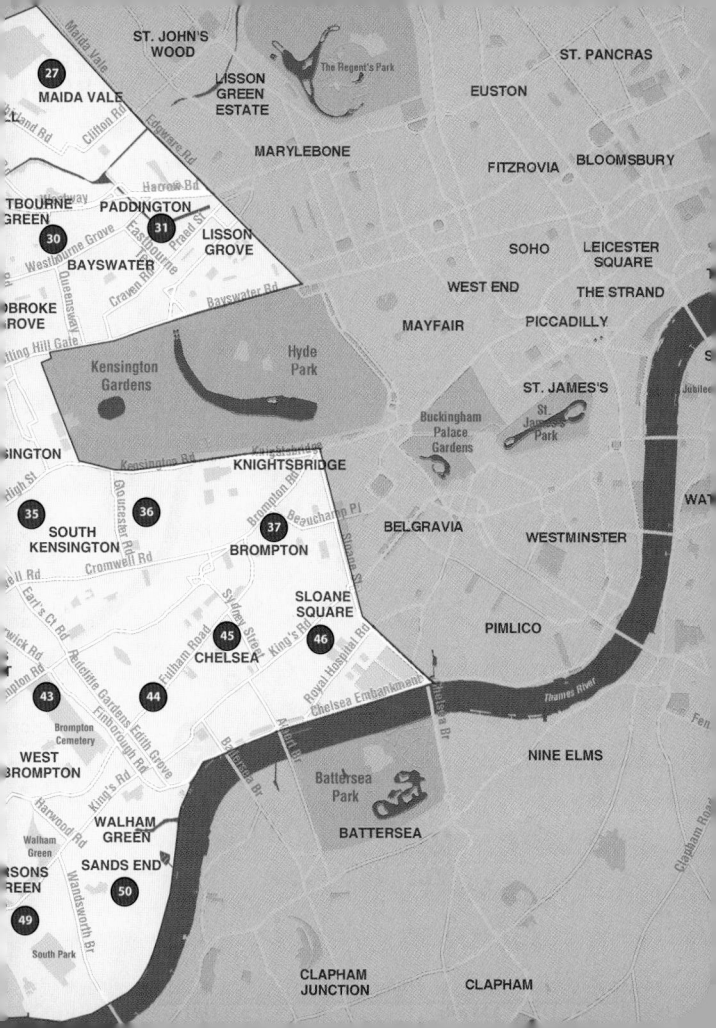
ST. JOHN'S WOOD
The Regent's Park
ST. PANCRAS
27
MAIDA VALE
LISSON GREEN ESTATE
EUSTON
MARYLEBONE
FITZROVIA
BLOOMSBURY
PADDINGTON
31
LISSON GROVE
30
BAYSWATER
SOHO
LEICESTER SQUARE
WEST END
THE STRAND
MAYFAIR
PICCADILLY
Hyde Park
Kensington Gardens
ST. JAMES'S
Buckingham Palace Gardens
St. James's Park
KNIGHTSBRIDGE
35
SOUTH KENSINGTON
36
37
BROMPTON
BELGRAVIA
WESTMINSTER
SLOANE SQUARE
45
CHELSEA
46
PIMLICO
43
44
Brompton Cemetery
WEST BROMPTON
Thames River
NINE ELMS
Battersea Park
WALHAM GREEN
BATTERSEA
SANDS END
50
49
South Park
CLAPHAM JUNCTION
CLAPHAM

Map 25 • Kensal Town

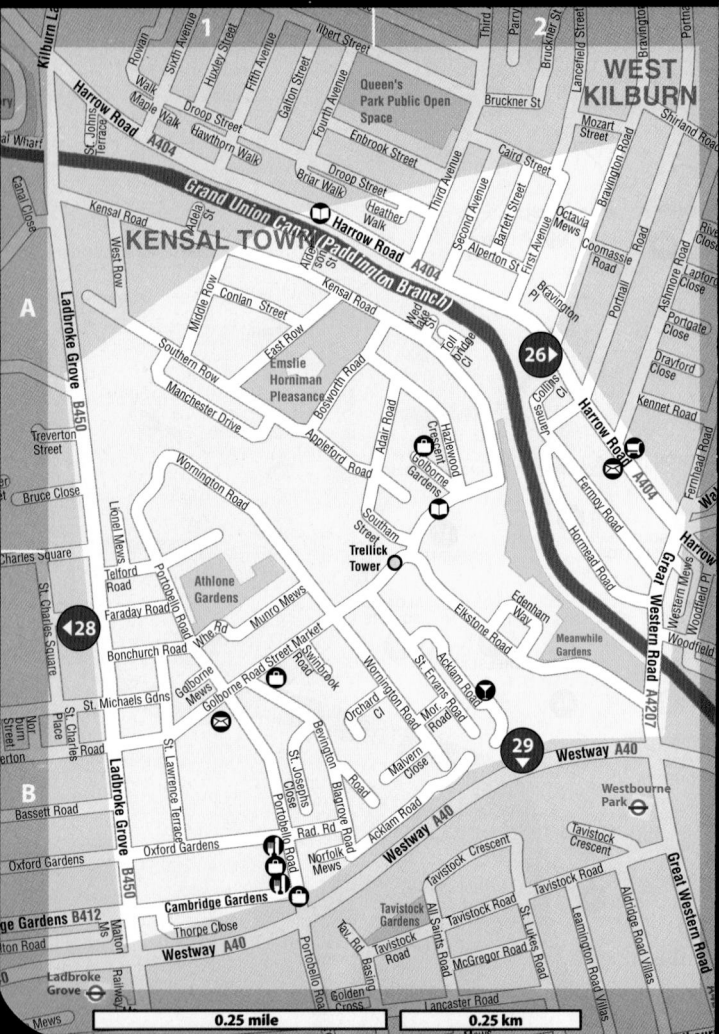

The "new Notting Hill" label weighs heavily on the Kensals. They look east for inspiration, ignoring the Harlesden yardies at their backs. Thai Rice serves eastern food, while Book Slam try to ship a little Shoreditch sauce to the manor Westbourne. Prepare for Carnival by visiting What Katie Did for exhibitionist outfits, while Trellick Tower is perfect for real—"I mean it, I'll jump"—attention-seekers.

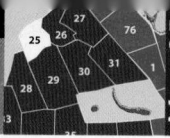

Landmarks

- **Trellick Tower** • 5 Golborne Rd

Libraries

- **Kensal Library** • 20 Golborne Rd
- **Queen's Park Library** • 666 Harrow Rd

Nightlife

- **Book Slam** • 12 Acklam Rd

Post Offices

- **Maida Hill** • 377 Harrow Rd
- **Portobello Road** • 325 Portobello Rd

Restaurants

- **Santo** • 299 Portobello Rd
- **Thai Rice** • 303 Portobello Rd

Shopping

- **Honest Jon's** • 278 Portobello Rd
- **Rellik** • 8 Golborne Rd
- **Sol's Gents Hairdressing** • 87 Goldborne Rd
- **What Katie Did** • 281 Portobello Rd

Supermarkets

- **Iceland** • 512 Harrow Rd

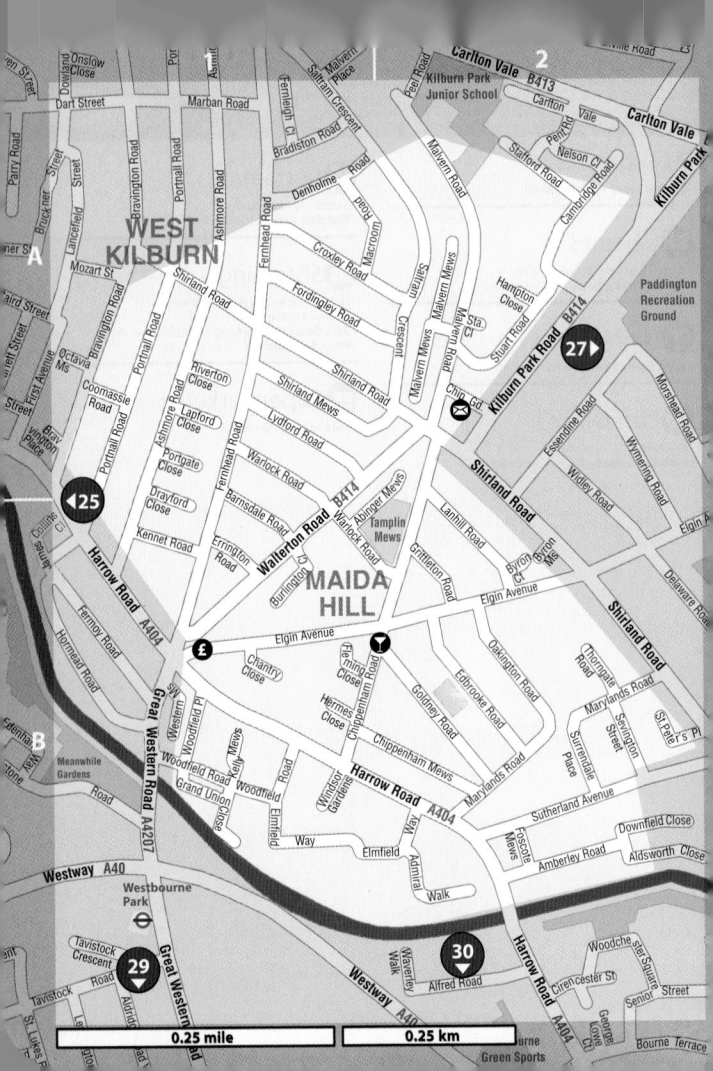
WEST KILBURN
MAIDA HILL
Carlton Vale
Kilburn Park Junior School
Kilburn Park Road
Paddington Recreation Ground
Shirland Road
Walterton Road
Harrow Road
Great Western Road
Westway
Westbourne Park
Meanwhile Gardens
Green Sports
Tamplin Mews
Chippenham Mews
Marylands Road
Sutherland Avenue
Elgin Avenue
Kilburn Park
Dart Street
Marban Road
Bravington Road
Portnall Road
Ashmore Road
Fernhead Road
Malvern Road
Cambridge Road
Stuart Road
Essendine Road
Widley Road
Wymering Road
Maida Vale
Westbourne Terrace
Alfred Road
Amberley Road
Aldsworth Close
Downfield Close
Elmfield Way
Admiral Walk
Tavistock Crescent
Tavistock Road
Woodchester Square
Senior Street
Bourne Terrace
0.25 mile
0.25 km
A
B
1
2
25
27
29
30

Not as posh as Maida Vale or as cool as Ladbroke Grove, Maida Hill is slightly grubby to the south, not helped by the distinctly unlovely Harrow Road. Things get more upmarket heading north where those who can't afford Notting Hill have settled. Hang out at cosy yet lively Victorian pub The Skiddaw for a round of Aspalls and a board game or two.

Banks

• **Royal Bank of Scotland** • 2 Elgin ave

Nightlife

• **The Skiddaw** • 46 Chippenham Rd

Post Offices

• **Kilburn Park** • 5 Chippenham Gardens

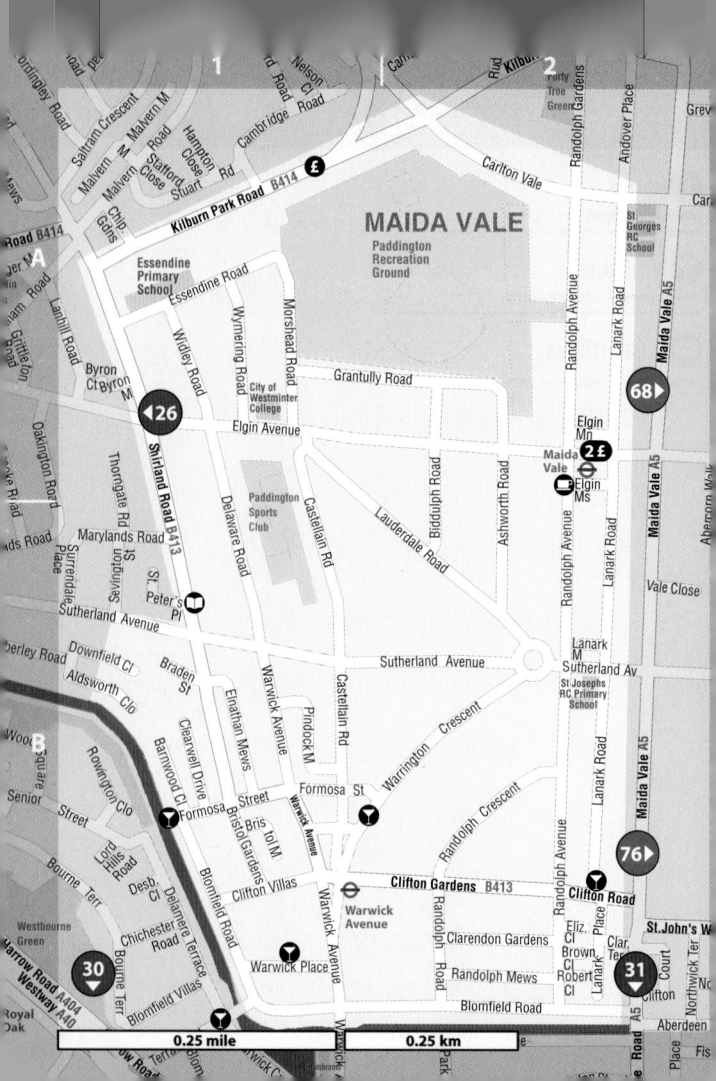
MAIDA VALE
Paddington Recreation Ground
Essendine Primary School
Essendine Road
Kilburn Park Road B414
Carlton Vale
Randolph Gardens
Andover Place
Tarty Tree Green
St Georges RC School
Randolph Avenue
Lanark Road
Maida Vale A5
Grantully Road
Morshead Road
Wymering Road
Widley Road
City of Westminter College
Elgin Avenue
Elgin Mn
Elgin Ms
Maida Vale
Byron Ct
Byron M
Lanhill Road
Oakington Road
Thorngate Rd
Shirland Road B413
Delaware Road
Paddington Sports Club
Castellain Rd
Lauderdale Road
Biddulph Road
Ashworth Road
Marylands Road
Surrendale Place
Sevington St
St. Peter's Pl
Sutherland Avenue
Vale Close
Lanark M
Sutherland Av
St Josephs RC Primary School
Downfield Cl
Aldsworth Clo
Braden St
Warwick Avenue
Elnathan Mews
Pindock M
Warrington Crescent
Clearwell Drive
Barnwood Cl
Formosa St
Formosa Street
Rowington Clo
Senior Street
Bristol Gardens
Bristol M
Warwick Avenue
Randolph Crescent
Lord Hills Road
Bourne Terr
Desb. Cl
Delamere Terrace
Blomfield Road
Clifton Villas
Clifton Gardens B413
Clifton Road
Warwick Avenue
Randolph Road
Clarendon Gardens
Chichester Road
Westbourne Green
Warwick Place
Randolph Mews
Blomfield Villas
Blomfield Road
Harrow Road A404
Westway A40
Royal Oak
St.John's W
Northwick Ter
Aberdeen
0.25 mile
0.25 km
26
68
76
30
31
A
B
1
2

Maida Vale is a posh residential area and that's pretty much all there is to it. Immaculately trimmed trees line street after street of nearly identical Edwardian mansion houses. It's clean, peaceful, and nice (translation: quite dull).Locals frequent the cafés and eateries around the Maida Vale tube station and on Clifton Road. Head to The Robert Browning for cheap Sam Smith's beer by a roasting fire or the E Bar for basement schmoozing and Spanish tapas.

Banks

- **Abbey** • 131 Kilburn Park Rd
- **Barclays** • 320 Elgin ave
- **NatWest** • 298 Elgin ave

Coffee

- **Starbucks** • 160 Randolph Ave

Libraries

- **Maida Vale Library** • Sutherland Ave

Nightlife

- **Bridge House** • 13 Westbourne Terrace Rd
- **E Bar** • 2 Warrington Crescent
- **The Robert Browning** • 15 Clifton Rd
- **The Warwick Castle** • 6 Warwick Pl
- **Waterway** • 54 Formosa St

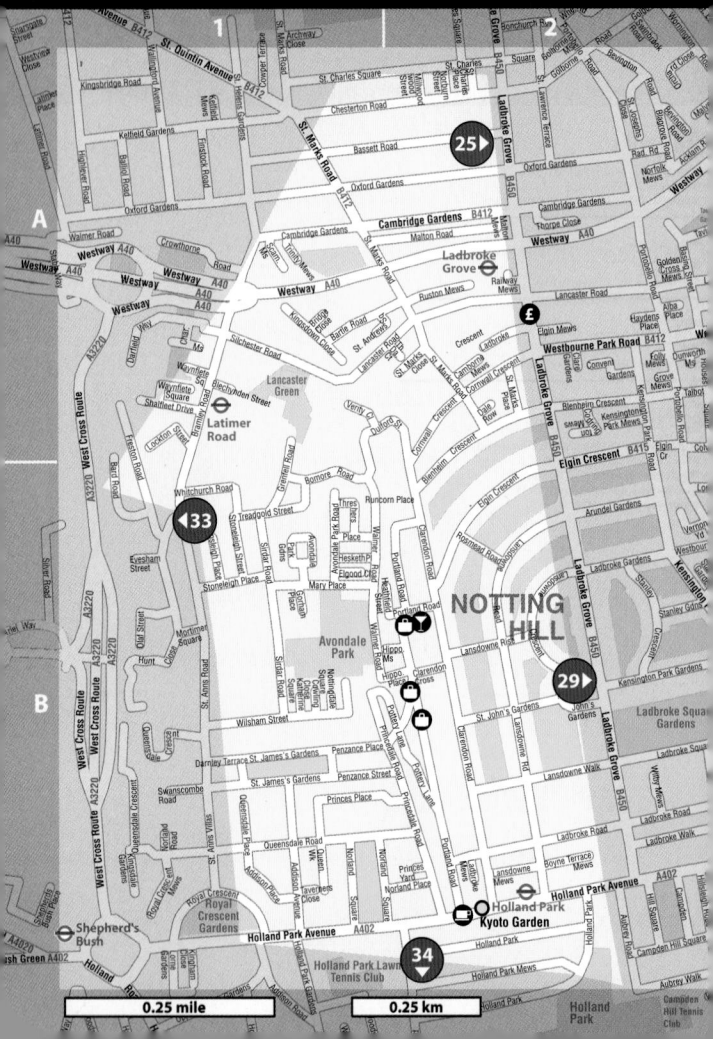
N
1
2
A
B
St Quintin Avenue
Kingsbridge Road
Kelfield Gardens
St Marks Road
Chesterton Road
Bassett Road
Oxford Gardens
Cambridge Gardens
Mailton Road
Ladbroke Grove
Westway A40
Walmer Road
Crowthorne Road
Ruston Mews
Lancaster Road
Elgin Mews
Westbourne Park Road
Lancaster Green
Latimer Road
Chichester Road
Kensington Park Road
Blenheim Crescent
Elgin Crescent
Whitchurch Road
Treadgold Street
Bomore Road
Runcorn Place
Stoneleigh Place
Mary Place
Eversham Street
Silver Road
Cambridge Road
Portland Road
Avondale Park
NOTTING HILL
Lansdowne Rise
Lansdowne Walk
St John's Gardens
Ladbroke Square Gardens
Wilsham Street
Darnley Terrace
St James's Gardens
Penzance Place
Penzance Street
Princes Place
Swanscombe Road
Queensdale Road
Ladbroke Road
Holland Park Avenue
Holland Park
Kyoto Garden
Holland Park Mews
Holland Park Lawn Tennis Club
Royal Crescent Gardens
Shepherd's Bush
West Cross Route
A3220
A402
Camden Hill Tennis Club
0.25 mile
0.25 km
25
29
33
34

Ladbroke Grove / Notting Hill (West)

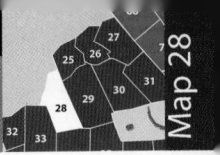

Look at that Westway and tell us you can't hear the opening chords of "London Calling." Maybe Rudie didn't fail but he moved up and moved out. This is leafy Notting Hill away from the Hugh Grant-hungry tourists scouring Portobello and there's not much doing. Around Portland Road try The Cross for expensive knick-knacks and Julie's for a bite. For other shopping and eating options head to Clarendon Cross.

Banks

- **Barclays** • 137 Ladbroke Grove

Coffee

- **Starbucks** • 76 Holland Park Ave

Landmarks

- **Kyoto Garden (Holland Park)** • 100 Holland Park Ave

Nightlife

- **Julie's Wine Bar** • 135 Portland Rd

Shopping

- **Cowshed** • 119 Portland Rd
- **The Cross** • 141 Portland Rd
- **Virginia** • 98 Portland Road

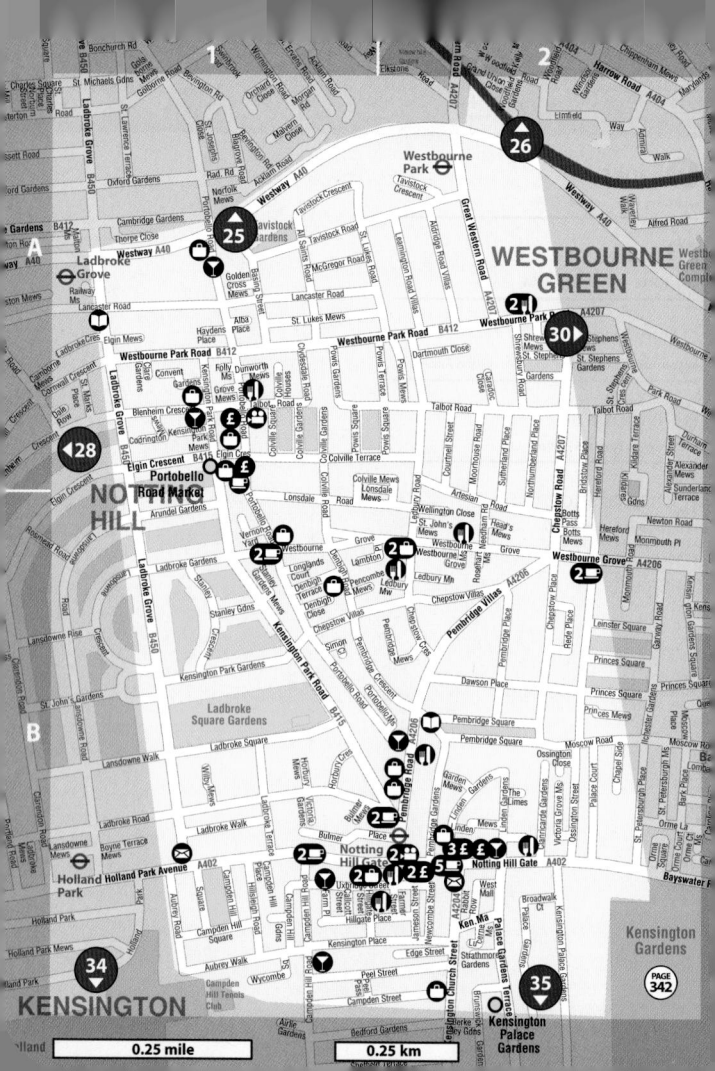
WESTBOURNE GREEN
NOTTING HILL
KENSINGTON
Ladbroke Grove
Westbourne Park
Portobello Road Market
Notting Hill Gate
Holland Park Avenue
Ladbroke Square Gardens
Kensington Gardens
Kensington Palace Gardens
Westbourne Grove
Westbourne Park Road
Kensington Park Road
Pembridge Villas
Chepstow Villas
Westbourne Park Villas
Westway A40
Great Western Road A4207
Bayswater Rd
Ken. Ma
Church St
Palace Gardens Terrace
Kensington Church Street
Holland Park
Campden Hill Square
Kensington Place
Edge Street
Peel Street
Campden Street
Aubrey Walk
Wycombe
Bedford Gardens
Airlie Gardens
Campden Hill Tennis Club
Sussex Gardens
Bonchurch Rd
Charles Square
St Michaels Gdns
Gillborne Road
Bevington Rd
Oxford Gardens
Cambridge Gardens
Therpe Close
Lancaster Road
Elgin Mews
Ladbroke Cres.
Westbourne Park Road B412
Chepstow Road A4207
Bridstow Place
Hereford Road
Kildare Terrace
Alexander Mews
Sunderland Terrace
Newton Road
Monmouth Pl
Westbourne Grove A4206
Leinster Square
Princes Square
Dawson Place
Pembridge Square
Moscow Road
Bayswater Rd
Lansdowne Walk
Ladbroke Walk
Ladbroke Grove B450
Holland Park Mews
Campden Hill Gdns
Kensington Church Street
Bedford Gardens
Sussex Gardens
Hillgate Place
Palace Court
Ossington Close
Chepstow Place
Pembridge Mews
Pembridge Crescent
Princes Mews
Ladbroke Square
Ladbroke Gardens
Kensington Park Gardens
Lansdowne Rise
Lansdowne Mews
Holland Park Avenue
Notting Hill Gate
Westbourne Grove
Westbourne Park
Westbourne Park Villas
Westbourne Park Road
Westway A40
Great Western Road A4207
Ladbroke Grove
Kensington Park Road
Pembridge Villas
Chepstow Villas
Chepstow Road A4207
Bayswater Rd
Ken. Ma
Church St
Palace Gardens Terrace
Kensington Church Street
Holland Park
Campden Hill Square
Kensington Place
Edge Street
Peel Street
Campden Street
Aubrey Walk
Wycombe
Bedford Gardens
Airlie Gardens
Campden Hill Tennis Club
Sussex Gardens
Bonchurch Rd
Charles Square
St Michaels Gdns
Gillborne Road
Bevington Rd
Oxford Gardens
Cambridge Gardens
Therpe Close
Lancaster Road
Elgin Mews
Ladbroke Cres.
Westbourne Park Road B412
Chepstow Road A4207
Bridstow Place
Hereford Road
Kildare Terrace
Alexander Mews
Sunderland Terrace
Newton Road
Monmouth Pl
Westbourne Grove A4206
Leinster Square
Princes Square
Dawson Place
Pembridge Square
Moscow Road
Bayswater Rd
Lansdowne Walk
Ladbroke Walk
Ladbroke Grove B450
Holland Park Mews
Campden Hill Gdns
Kensington Church Street
Bedford Gardens
Sussex Gardens
Hillgate Place
Palace Court
Ossington Close
Chepstow Place
Pembridge Mews
Pembridge Crescent
Princes Mews
Ladbroke Square
Ladbroke Gardens
Kensington Park Gardens
Lansdowne Rise
Lansdowne Mews
Holland Park Avenue
Notting Hill Gate
Westbourne Grove
Westbourne Park
Westbourne Park Villas
Westbourne Park Road
Kensington Park Road
Pembridge Villas
Chepstow Villas
Westway A40
Great Western Road A4207
Ladbroke Grove

Unbelievably, it's only recently that the mega-rich, minor gentry have conquered the Gate like posh rats (mink?). Traces of the area's counter- and multi-cultural past are in the wrinkles of the old eccentrics in the Uxbridge Arms or at the lively Portobello Road Market. Pig out on some of London's best fish n' chips at Costas or to feel old and bitter, go scowl at skinny jeans clad teenagers in the Notting Hill Arts Club. Don't forget The Electric Cinema for movie-going in style.

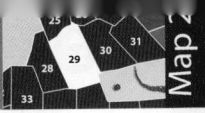

Banks

- **Abbey** • 174 Portobello Rd
- **Abbey** • 88 Notting Hill Gate
- **Barclays** • 35 Notting Hill Gate
- **HSBC** • 152 Portobello Rd
- **HSBC** • 25 Notting Hill Gate
- **Lloyds** • 50 Notting Hill Gate
- **NatWest** • 46 Notting Hill Gate
- **Royal Bank of Scotland** • 78 Notting Hill Gate

Cinemas

- **The Electric Cinema** • 191 Portobello Rd
- **Gate Notting Hill** • 87 Notting Hill Gate
- **Notting Hill Coronet** • 103 Notting Hill Gate

Coffee

- **Apostrophe** • 138 Notting Hill Gate
- **Bagel Factory** • 61 Notting Hill Gate
- **Caffe Nero** • 113 Westbourne Grove
- **Caffe Nero** • 53 Notting Hill Gate
- **Caffe Nero** • 168 Portobello Rd
- **Coffee Republic** • 8 Pembridge Rd
- **Coffee Republic** • 214 Portobello Rd
- **Eat.** • 68 Notting Hill Gate
- **Pret A Manger** • 65 Notting Hill Gate
- **Starbucks** • 96 Westbourne Grove
- **Starbucks** • 227 Portobello Rd
- **Starbucks** • 26 Pembridge Rd
- **Starbucks** • 140 Notting Hill Gate
- **Starbucks** • 64 Notting Hill Gate

Landmarks

- **Kensington Palace Gardens** • Palace Gardens Terrace
- **Portobello Road Market** • Portobello Rd

Libraries

- **North Kensington Library** • 108 Ladbroke Grove
- **Notting Hill Library** • 1 Pembridge Sq

Nightlife

- **Mau Mau** • 265 Portobello Rd
- **Montgomery Place** • 31 Kensington Park Rd
- **Notting Hill Arts Club** • 21 Notting Hill Gate
- **The Sun in Splendour** • 7 Portobello Rd
- **Uxbridge Arms** • 13 Uxbridge St
- **Windsor Castle** • 114 Campden Hill Rd

Post Offices

- **Kensington Church St** • 190 Kensington Church St
- **Ladbroke Grove** • 2 Ladbroke Grove

Restaurants

- **Beach Blanket Babylon** • 45 Ledbury Rd
- **Cafe Diana** • 5 Wellington Terrace
- **Costas Fish Restaurant** • 18 Hillgate St
- **Crazy Homies** • 125 Westbourne Park Rd
- **The Electric Brasserie** • 191 Portobello Rd
- **Geales** • 2 Farmer St
- **Lucky 7** • 127 Westbourne Park Rd
- **Manzara** • 24 Pembridge Rd
- **Taqueria** • 139 Westbourne Grove

Shopping

- **& Clarke's Bread** • 124 Kensington Church St
- **Bodas** • 38 Ledbury Rd
- **The Grocer on Elgin** • 6 Elgin Crescent
- **The Hummingbird Bakery** • 133 Portobello Rd
- **James Knight of Mayfair** • 67 Notting Hill Gate
- **Melt** • 59 Ledbury Rd
- **Music & Video Exchange** • 38 Notting Hill Gate
- **Negozio Classica** • 283 Westbourne Grove
- **Portobello Road Market** • Portobello Rd
- **R Garcia and Sons** • 248 Portobello Rd
- **Retro Man** • 34 Pembridge Rd
- **Retro Woman** • 32 Pembridge Rd
- **Rough Trade Talbot West** • 130 Talbot Rd
- **Travel Bookshop** • 13 Blenheim Crescent

Map 30 • Bayswater

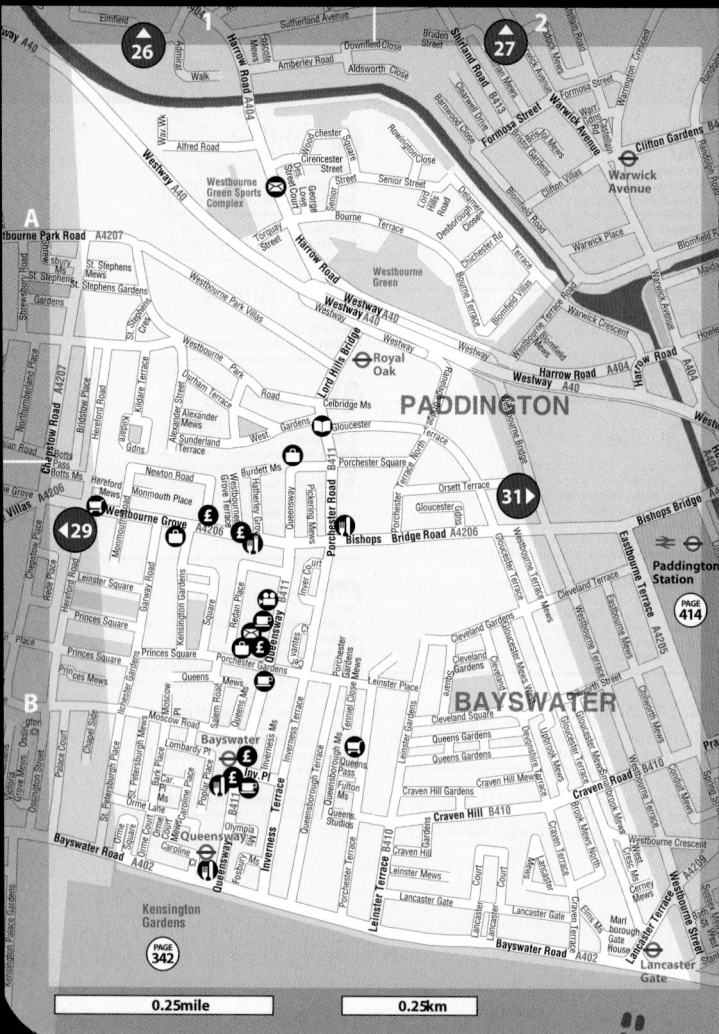

Bayswater is notable for being next to other places that are far more interesting: Hyde Park, Marble Arch, Portobello Road. It's also a xenophobe's nightmare, with billions of camera-clad tourists swarming like flies around buffet pizza joints. The rest of us can go smoke shisha at Berdees or grab some Indo/Malay over a Tsingtao at Kiasu. The adventurous head to All Star Lanes for 50s style bowling.

Banks

- **Barclays** • 93 Queensway
- **Halifax** • 23 Whiteleys Of Bayswater
- **HSBC** • 43 Queensway
- **Lloyds** • 30 Westbourne Grove
- **NatWest** • 16 Westbourne Grove

Cinemas

- **Odeon Whiteleys** • Queensway & Porchester Gardens

Coffee

- **Coffee Republic** • 126 Queensway
- **Pret A Manger** • 127 Queensway
- **Starbucks** • 49 Queensway

Libraries

- **Paddington Library** • Porchester Rd

Post Offices

- **Harrow Rd** • 272 Harrow Rd
- **Queensway** • 118 Queensway

Restaurants

- **Berdees Coffee Shop** • 84 Bishop's Bridge Rd
- **Kiasu** • 48 Queensway
- **Royal China** • 13 Queensway
- **Tiroler Hut** • 27 Westbourne Grove

Shopping

- **Planet Organic** • 42 Westbourne Grove
- **Porchester Gate Spa** • Queensway & Porchester Rd
- **Whiteleys Shopping Centre** • Queensway

Supermarkets

- **Sainsbury's** • 88 Westbourne Grove
- **Waitrose** • 38 Porchester Sq

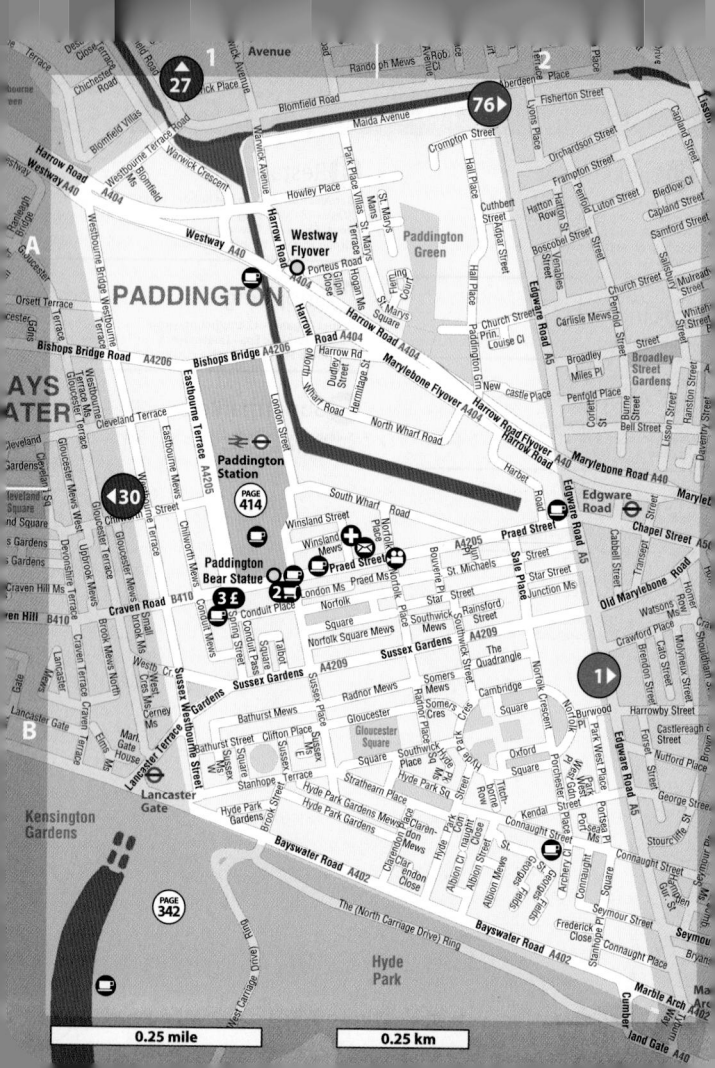
PADDINGTON
Westway Flyover
Paddington Green
Paddington Station
Paddington Bear Statue
Edgware Road
Praed Street
Sussex Gardens
Gloucester Square
Lancaster Gate
Kensington Gardens
Hyde Park
Bayswater Road A402
Bishops Bridge Road A4206
Eastbourne Terrace A4206
Marylebone Flyover A401
Harrow Road A404
Westway A40
Edgware Road A5
Marylebone Road A40
Chapel Street A5
Old Marylebone Road
Craven Road B410
Sussex Gardens A4209
Lancaster Terrace
Bayswater Road A402
The (North Carriage Drive) Ring
West Carriage Drive Ring
Harrow Road
Westway A40
Blomfield Road
Maida Avenue
Fisherton Street
Lisson Grove
Marylebone Road A40
Edgware Road A5
Chapel Street A5
Old Marylebone Road
Bayswater Road A402
Sussex Gardens A4209
Lancaster Terrace
Craven Road B410
Bishops Bridge Road A4206
Eastbourne Terrace A4206
Marylebone Flyover A401
Harrow Road A404
Westway A40
Edgware Road A5
Praed Street
Paddington Station
Paddington Bear Statue
Paddington Green
Westway Flyover
Kensington Gardens
Hyde Park
Lancaster Gate
Gloucester Square
Sussex Gardens

Mainly peopled by Little Venetians, B&B owners, and harassed commuters ("Go west young man, but avoid Reading") Paddington has that Oxford Street cosmopolitan-yet-bland vibe. Grab an anonymous meal with other transients in a café as you fill time before the Heathrow flight. If gazing at a statue of a bear in Wellington's doesn't appeal, banish evening boredom by listening to famous war correspondents' sordid stories over a meal at the Frontline Club.

Banks

- **Barclays** • 17 Spring St
- **HSBC** • 2 Craven Rd
- **NatWest** • 26 Spring St

Cinemas

- **Frontline Club** • 13 Norfolk Pl

Coffee

- **Bagel Factory** • 141 Praed St
- **Caffe Nero** • 14 Spring St
- **Caffe Nero** • Paddington Station
- **Costa** • 254 Edgware Rd
- **Eat.** • Paddington Station
- **Markus Coffee Company** • 13 Connaught St
- **Pret A Manger** • 9 Sheldon Sq
- **Serpentine Bar & Kitchen** • Serpentine Rd

Emergency Rooms

- **St Mary's Hospital** • Praed St

Landmarks

- **Paddington Bear Statue** • Paddington Station
- **Westway Flyover** •

Post Offices

- **Paddington** • 128 Praed St

Supermarkets

- **Sainsbury's** • Paddington Station
- **Sainsbury's** • 12 Sheldon Sq

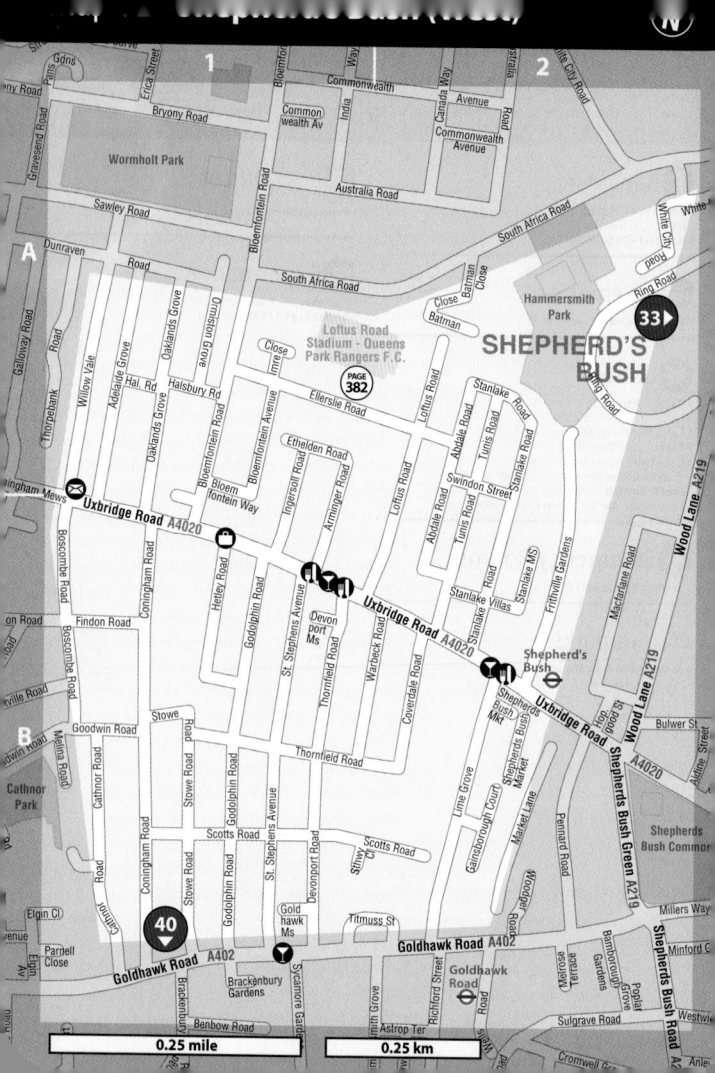
Shepherd's Bush (West)
N
1
2
A
B
Commonwealth Avenue
Commonwealth Av
Canada Way
India Way
Bloemfontein Road
Erica Street
Palm Gdns
Bryony Road
Gravesend Road
Wormholt Park
Australia Road
Sawley Road
Dunraven Road
South Africa Road
White City Road
Ring Road
Hammersmith Park
33
Loftus Road Stadium - Queens Park Rangers F.C.
SHEPHERD'S BUSH
PAGE 382
Batman Close
Galloway Road
Thorpebank Road
Willow Vale
Adelaide Grove
Oaklands Grove
Ormiston Grove
Hal Rd
Halsbury Rd
Ellerslie Road
Loftus Road
Stanlake Road
Abdale Road
Tunis Road
Swindon Street
Ethelden Road
Ingersoll Road
Arminger Road
Bloemfontein Avenue
Bloemfontein Way
Uxbridge Road A4020
Boscombe Road
Coningham Road
Hetley Road
Godolphin Road
St. Stephens Avenue
Devon Ave Ms
Thornfield Road
Warbeck Road
Coverdale Road
Stanlake Villas
Stanlake MS
Frithville Gardens
Macfarlane Road
Wood Lane A219
Shepherd's Bush
Shepherds Bush Mkt
Shepherds Bush Market
Shepherds Bush Green A219
Findon Road
Goodwin Road
Stowe Road
Bulwer St
Millig Road
Cathnor Road
Cathnor Park
Lime Grove
Gamborough Court
Market Lane
Pennard Road
Shepherds Bush Common
Scotts Road
Devonport Road
Wooler Road
Millers Way
Elgin Cl
Parbell Close
Goldhawk Road A402
Brackenbury Gardens
Sycamore Gardens
Goldhawk Ms
Titmuss St
Richford Street
Goldhawk Road
Bamborough Gardens
Poplar Grove
Minford Cl
Shepherds Bush Road A2
Benbow Road
Astrop Ter
Sulgrave Road
Westwi
Cromwell
0.25 mile
0.25 km

Shepherd's Bush (West)

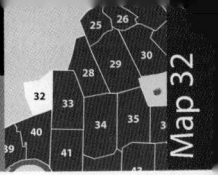

Infamous for shoot outs in Nando's and grim, locals-only boozers. Depending on your viewpoint, this bit of London is either pleasingly unpretentious or a bit of a dump. Pubs here are best avoided but foodies on a budget will be in heaven. For cheap, tasty, and totally authentic grub try Abu Zaad (Syrian), Esarn Kheaw (Thai), or Vine Leaves Taverna (Greek).

Nightlife

- **Bush Hall** • 310 Uxbridge Rd
- **The Goldhawk** • 122 Goldhawk Rd
- **The White Horse** • 31 Uxbridge Rd

Post Offices

- **Uxbridge Road** • 420 Uxbridge Rd

Restaurants

- **Abu Zaad** • 29 Uxbridge Rd
- **Esarn Kheaw** • 314 Uxbridge Road
- **Vine Leaves Taverna** • 71 Uxbridge Rd

Shopping

- **Nut Case** • 352 Uxbridge Rd

Map 33 • Shepherd's Bush

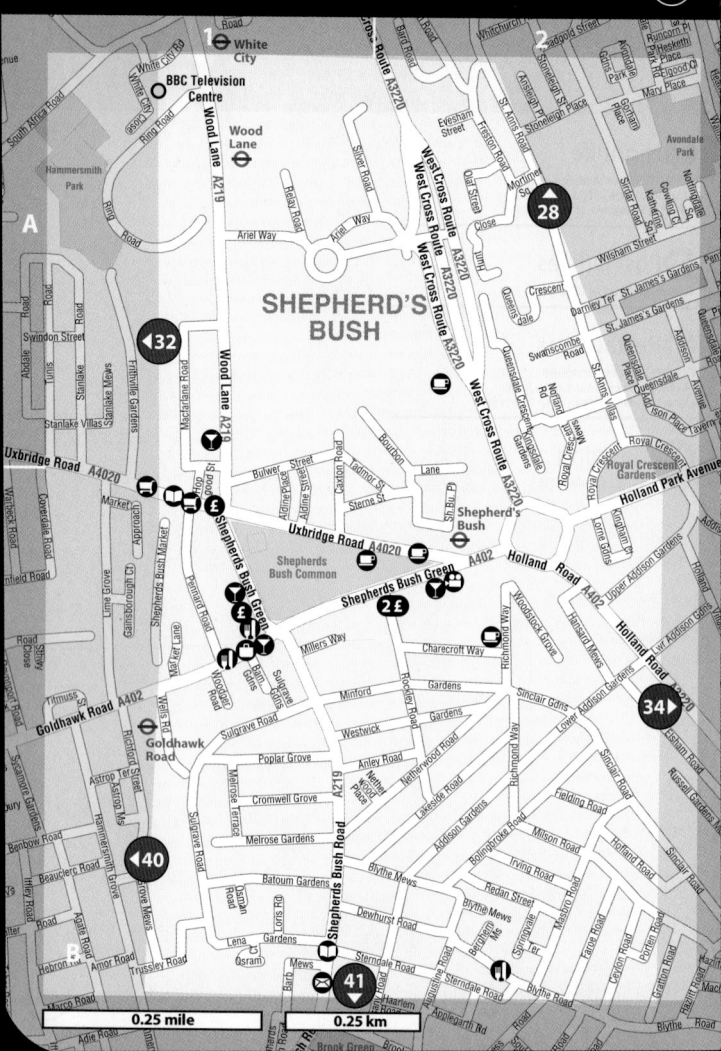
N
SHEPHERD'S BUSH
White City
BBC Television Centre
Wood Lane
Hammersmith Park
Wood Lane A219
West Cross Route A3220
Ariel Way
Uxbridge Road A4020
Shepherds Bush Green
Shepherds Bush Common
Shepherd's Bush
Holland Park Avenue
Holland Road A402
Goldhawk Road A402
Goldhawk Road
Shepherds Bush Road
Stanlake Villas
Stanlake Mews
Frithville Gardens
Macfarlane Road
Bulwer Street
Bourbon Lane
Sterne St
Adine Place
Adine Street
Caxton Road
Tadmor St
St Ann's Rd
Market
Uxbridge Rd
Shepherds Bush Market
Pennard Road
Lime Grove
Millers Way
Charecroft Way
Richmond Way
Hammersmith Grove
Minford Gardens
Rockley Road
Sulgrave Road
Westwick Gardens
Poplar Grove
Aneley Road
Melrose Terrace
Cromwell Grove
Melrose Gardens
Batoum Gardens
Dewhurst Road
Blythe Mews
Sterndale Road
Blythe Road
Lena Gardens
Trussley Road
Amor Road
Hebron Rd
Aldine Street
Lakeside Road
Addison Gardens
Bolingbroke Road
Milson Road
Fielding Road
Sinclair Road
Holland Road
Aldine Place
Avondale Park
Avondale Park Gardens
Avondale Park Mews
Avondale Park Place
Avondale Park Road
Avondale Road
Avondale Place
Avondale Mews
Avondale Crescent
Avondale Gardens
Avondale Terrace
Avondale Avenue
Avondale Place
Avondale Road

The Bush has had a bit of a shake-up recently. The arrival of the enormous Westfield Centre has brought high end fashion and a shit load more people to the former grimy hub of West London—even the tube station and market have been spruced up. Off the Green the O2 Shepherd's Bush Empire continues to attract the most up and coming bands while Jumbucks serves bonza Aussie pies and the BBC kids drown their sorrows at Albertine.

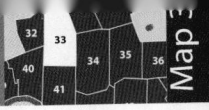

Banks

- **Abbey** • 23 Shepherd's Bush Green
- **Barclays** • 74 Shepherd's Bush Green
- **HSBC** • 16 Shepherd's Bush Green
- **NatWest** • 25 Shepherd's Bush Green

Cinemas

- **Vue Shepherds Bush** • Shepherds Bush Green & Rockley Rd

Coffee

- **BB's Coffee & Muffins** • Richmond Way & Charecroft Way
- **BB's Coffee & Muffins** • 2117 Westfield London Shopping Center
- **Costa** • 72 Uxbridge Rd
- **Starbucks** • 62 Uxbridge Rd

Landmarks

- **BBC Television Centre** • Wood Lane

Libraries

- **Hammersmith Library** • Shepherds Bush Rd
- **Shepherds Bush Library** • 7 Uxbridge Rd

Nightlife

- **Albertine** • 1 Wood Lane
- **Bush Bar & Grill** • 45 Goldhawk Rd
- **Ginglik** • 1 Shepherd's Bush Green
- **Shepherd's Bush Empire** • Shepherd's Bush Green

Post Offices

- **Shepherds Bush Road** • 146 Shepherd's Bush Rd

Restaurants

- **Jasmine** • 16 Goldhawk Rd
- **Jumbucks** • 24 Shepherd's Bush Green
- **Popeseye** • 108 Blythe Rd

Shopping

- **Whole Foods Market** • 63 Kensington High St

Supermarkets

- **Co-Op** • 187 Uxbridge Rd
- **Sainsbury's** • 164 Uxbridge Rd

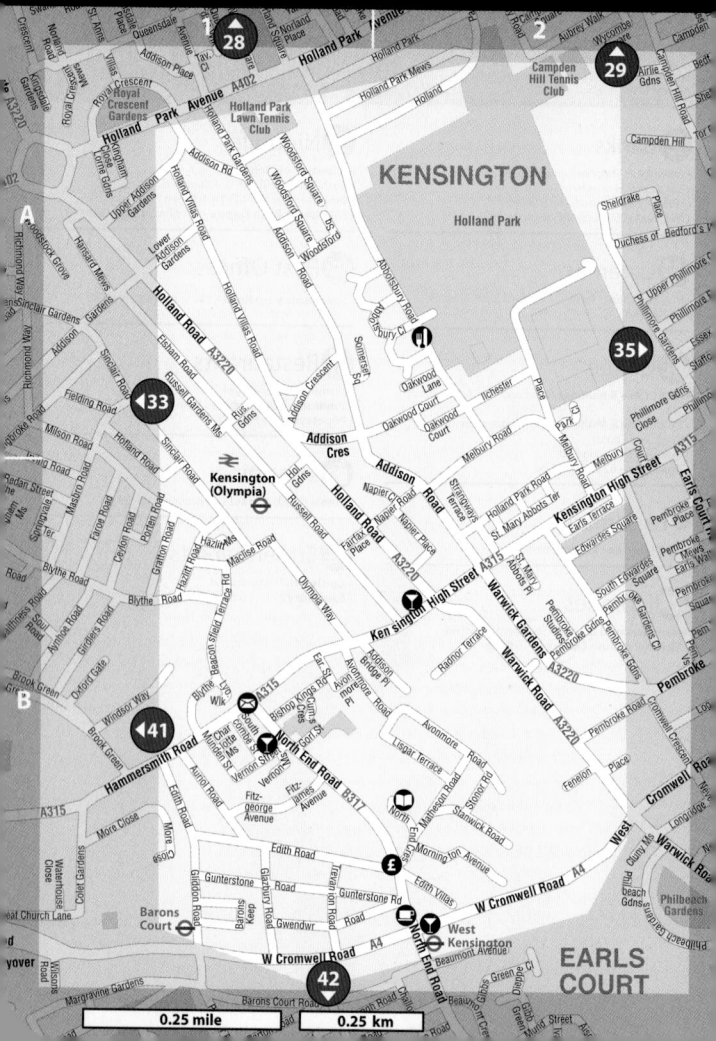
N
1
2
A
B
28
29
35
33
41
42
KENSINGTON
Holland Park
Holland Park Avenue
Holland Park Mews
Holland Park Lawn Tennis Club
Campden Hill Tennis Club
Campden Hill
Royal Crescent Gardens
Addison Place
Holland Park Gardens
Holland Villas Road
Woodsford Square
Addison Road
Lower Addison Gardens
Upper Addison Gardens
Hansard Mews
Holland Road A3220
Sinclair Gardens
Russell Gardens Ms
Fielding Road
Milson Road
Sinclair Road
Kensington (Olympia)
Addison Cres
Addison Road
Holland Road A3220
Napier Road
Napier Place
Russell Road
Olympia Way
Ken sington High Street A315
Kensington High Street
Earls Court Rd
Warwick Gardens A3220
Pembroke
Pembroke Road
Cromwell Road
Hammersmith Road
North End Road B317
Edith Road
Gunterstone Road
Gwendwr Road
Barons Court
West Kensington
North End Road
W Cromwell Road A4
West Cromwell Road
EARLS COURT
Philbeach Gardens
Barons Court Road
Margravine Gardens
Church Lane
Wilsons Road
Waterhouse Close
Bishop's Park
Richmond Way
Sinclair Gardens
Addison Crescent
Somerset Sq
Melbury Ct
Oakwood Lane
Oakwood Court
Melbury Road
Ilchester Place
Phillimore Gdns
Phillimore Close
Duchess of Bedford's W
Upper Phillimore
Campden Hill Road
Sheldrake Place
Earls Terrace
Edwardes Square
Pembroke Place
Pembroke Gdns
Pembroke Gdns Cl
Pembroke Studios
Pembroke Square
Pembroke Mews
Pembroke Villas
Kensington Square
St Mary Abbots Ter
Holland Park Road
Stratfordway Terrace
Napier Place
Fairfax Place
Ken sington High Street A315
Radnor Terrace
Addison Pl
Avondale Pl
Avondale Rd
Lisgar Terrace
Avonmore Road
Matheson Road
Stanwick Road
Stokyn Rd
Fenelon Place
Morning ton Avenue
Edith Villas
Gunterstone Rd
Gwendwr Road
Beaumont Avenue
Beaumont Crescent
Globe Green
Blythe Road
Hazlitt Ms
Hazlitt Road
Maclise Road
Beacon Shield Terrace Rd
Lyte Wlk
Bishop Kings Rd
Earl St
Vernon Ms
Vernon Sq
Fitz-james Avenue
Fitz-george Avenue
Aurel Road
Edith Road
More Close
Brook Green
Windsor Way
Oxford Gate
Gliddon Road
Blythe Road
Gliddon Road
Bury Ms
Bury Pl
Cromwell Crescent
Longridge Road
Warwick Road
Pembroke Road
Fenelon Place
Cromwell Road
Bishop's Park
Richmond Way
Sinclair Gardens
Addison Crescent
Somerset Sq
Melbury Ct
Oakwood Lane
Oakwood Court
Melbury Road
Ilchester Place
Phillimore Gdns
Phillimore Close
Duchess of Bedford's W
Upper Phillimore
Campden Hill Road
Sheldrake Place
Earls Terrace
Edwardes Square
Pembroke Place
Pembroke Gdns
Pembroke Gdns Cl
Pembroke Studios
Pembroke Square
Pembroke Mews
Pembroke Villas
Kensington Square
St Mary Abbots Ter
Holland Park Road
Stratfordway Terrace
Napier Place
Fairfax Place
Ken sington High Street A315
Radnor Terrace
Addison Pl
Avondale Pl
Avondale Rd
Lisgar Terrace
Avonmore Road
Matheson Road
Stanwick Road
Stokyn Rd
Fenelon Place
Morning ton Avenue
Edith Villas
Gunterstone Rd
Gwendwr Road
Beaumont Avenue
Beaumont Crescent
Globe Green
Blythe Road
Hazlitt Ms
Hazlitt Road
Maclise Road
Beacon Shield Terrace Rd
Lyte Wlk
Bishop Kings Rd
Earl St
Vernon Ms
Vernon Sq
Fitz-james Avenue
Fitz-george Avenue
Aurel Road
Edith Road
More Close
Brook Green
Windsor Way
Oxford Gate
Gliddon Road
Blythe Road
Gliddon Road
Bury Ms
Bury Pl
Cromwell Crescent
Longridge Road
Warwick Road
Pembroke Road
Fenelon Place
Cromwell Road
Bishop's Park
Richmond Way
Sinclair Gardens
Addison Crescent
Somerset Sq
Melbury Ct
Oakwood Lane
Oakwood Court
Melbury Road
Ilchester Place
Phillimore Gdns
Phillimore Close
Duchess of Bedford's W
Upper Phillimore
Campden Hill Road
Sheldrake Place
Earls Terrace
Edwardes Square
Pembroke Place
Pembroke Gdns
Pembroke Gdns Cl
Pembroke Studios
Pembroke Square
Pembroke Mews
Pembroke Villas
Kensington Square
St Mary Abbots Ter
Holland Park Road
Stratfordway Terrace
Napier Place
Fairfax Place
Ken sington High Street A315
Radnor Terrace
Addison Pl
Avondale Pl
Avondale Rd
Lisgar Terrace
Avonmore Road
Matheson Road
Stanwick Road
Stokyn Rd
Fenelon Place
Morning ton Avenue
Edith Villas
Gunterstone Rd
Gwendwr Road
Beaumont Avenue
Beaumont Crescent
Globe Green
Blythe Road
Hazlitt Ms
Hazlitt Road
Maclise Road
Beacon Shield Terrace Rd
Lyte Wlk
Bishop Kings Rd
Earl St
Vernon Ms
Vernon Sq
Fitz-james Avenue
Fitz-george Avenue
Aurel Road
Edith Road
More Close
Brook Green
Windsor Way
Oxford Gate
Gliddon Road
Blythe Road
Gliddon Road
Bury Ms
Bury Pl
Cromwell Crescent
Longridge Road
Warwick Road
Pembroke Road
Fenelon Place
Cromwell Road
0.25 mile
0.25 km

West Kensington / Olympia

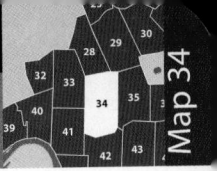

The stretch between Holland Park and the A4 is home to well-shod extras from a Richard Curtis film (oh sorry, they don't really exist) as well as Kensington Olympia which houses exhibitions such as Erotica ("look we're so chilled about sex we've got a whole hangar of this naughty shit!"). For lazy Sunday brunch head to Café Continente or for top nosh try The Beldevere.

Banks

- **Barclays** • 137 N End Rd

Coffee

- **Cafe Continente** • 62 N End Rd

Libraries

- **Barons Court** • North End Crescent

Nightlife

- **Cumberland Arms** • 29 N End Rd
- **Famous 3 Kings** • 171 North End Road
- **Plum Bar** • 380 Kensington High St

Post Offices

- **Olympia** • 87 Hammersmith Rd

Restaurants

- **The Belvedere Restaurant** • Abbotsbury Road

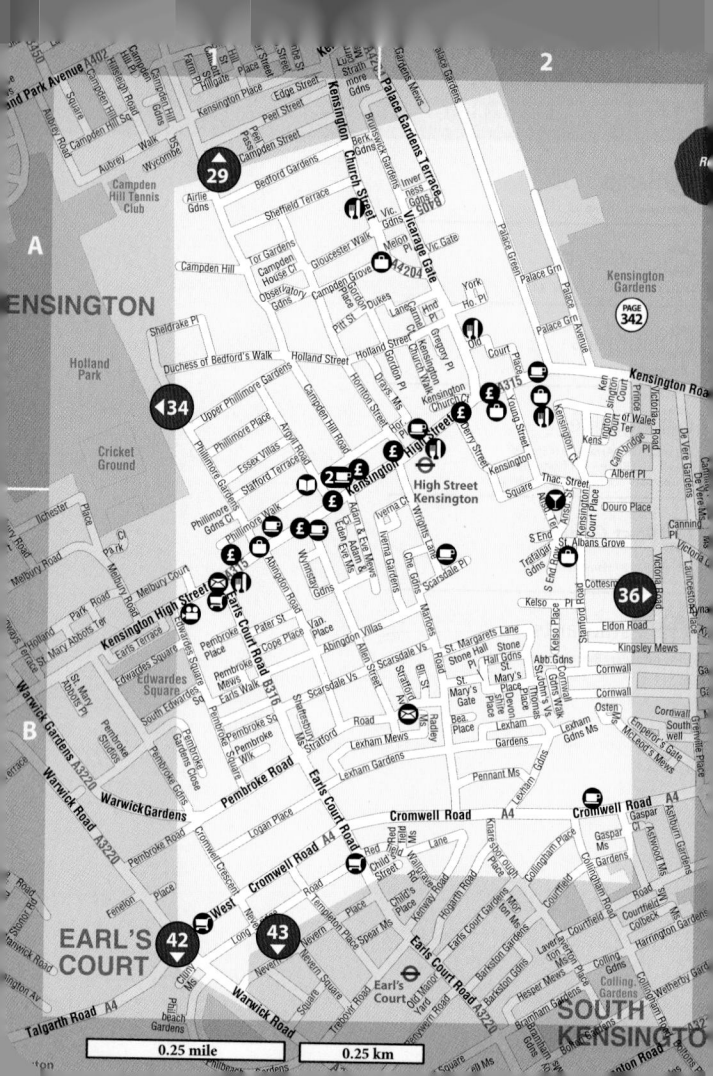
1
2
A
B
ENSINGTON
Kensington Gardens
PAGE 342
Holland Park
Cricket Ground
Campden Hill Tennis Club
EARL'S COURT
SOUTH KENSINGTO
Kensington Church Street
Palace Gardens Terrace
Vicarage Gate
Kensington High Street
Earls Court Road
Pembroke Road
Warwick Road
Cromwell Road
Kensington Road
Talgarth Road
Edwardes Square
High Street Kensington
Earl's Court
West Kensington
Campden Hill Road
Holland Street
Duchess of Bedford's Walk
Bedford Gardens
Sheffield Terrace
Campden Hill
Gloucester Walk
Palace Grn
Palace Gardens
Albert Pl
Kensington Ct
Thac. Street
Douro Place
St Albans Grove
Victoria Road
Cottesmore
Kelso Pl
Eldon Road
Kingsley Mews
Cornwall
Cromwell Place
Lexham Gardens
Pennant Ms
Logan Place
Cromwell Crescent
Warwick Gardens
Pembroke Sq
Pembroke Villas
Abingdon Villas
Scarsdale Vs
Lexham Mews
Talgarth Road
0.25 mile
0.25 km
29
34
36
42
43
342
A4204
A315
A3220
A4
A402
A316
A2126

Witness the endangered Sloane ranger species in their natural habitat. Kensington reeks of money but shows that that doesn't necessarily translate into style. It's not a cool place to hang out but draws hordes of shoppers by day. After dark, try The Builders Arms for a good pint or chow down on arguably London's best burger at Byron, washed down with a thick shake before you waddle away.

Banks

- **Abbey** • 144 Kensington High St
- **Barclays** • 208 Kensington High St
- **Halifax** • 180 Kensington High St
- **HSBC** • 92 Kensington High St
- **Lloyds** • 112 Kensington High St
- **NatWest** • 55 Kensington High St
- **Royal Bank of Scotland** • 175 Kensington High St

Cinemas

- **Odeon Kensington** • Kensington High St & Edwards Sq

Coffee

- **Caffe Nero** • 160 Kensington High St
- **Caffe Nero** • 1 Wrights Lane
- **Costa** • 144 Kensington High St
- **Costa** • 149 Cromwell Rd
- **Pret A Manger** • 149 Kensington High St
- **Pret A Manger** • 123 Kensington High St
- **Starbucks** • 25 Kensington High St
- **Starbucks** • 197 Kensington High St

Libraries

- **Kensington Central Library** • Phillimore Walk

Nightlife

- **Builders Arms** • 1 Kensington Ct Pl

Post Offices

- **Kensington High St** • 257 Kensington High St
- **Startford Road** • 11 Stratford Rd

Restaurants

- **Byron** • 222 Kensington High St
- **Clarke's** • 124 Kensington Church St
- **Kensington Roof Gardens** • 99 Kensington High St
- **Maggie Jones's** • 6 Old Court Pl
- **Zaika** • 1 Kensington High St

Shopping

- **Ben's Cookies** • 12 Kensington High St
- **Buttercup** • 16 St Albans Grove
- **Notting Hill Housing Trust** • 57 Kensington Church St
- **Trailfinders** • 194 Kensington High St
- **Whole Foods Market** • 63 Kensington High St

Supermarkets

- **Sainsbury's** • 160 Earl's Ct Rd
- **Tesco** • 100 W Cromwell Rd
- **Waitrose** • 243 Kensington High St

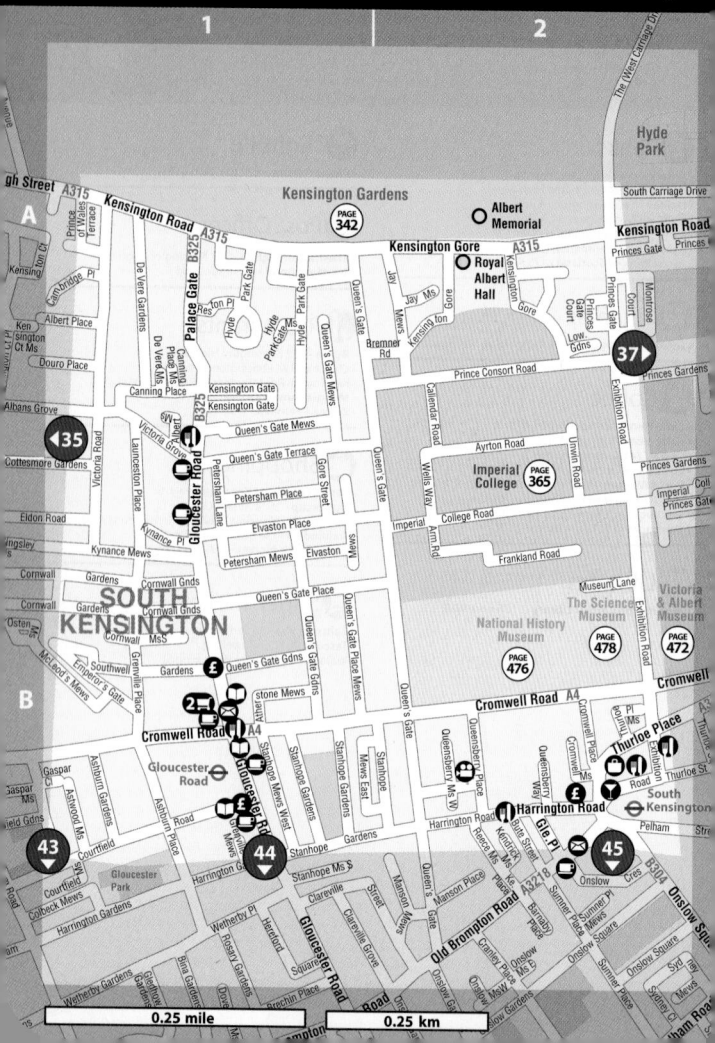
1
2
A
B
Hyde Park
Kensington Gardens
PAGE 342
Albert Memorial
Royal Albert Hall
Kensington Gore A315
Kensington Road A315
Palace Gate B325
Kensington Road
South Carriage Drive
The West Carriage Dr
Princes Gate
Princes Gate Court
Low Gdns
Montrose Court
Prince Consort Road
Exhibition Road
Princes Gardens
Imperial College
PAGE 365
Ayrton Road
Wells Way
Queen's Gate
Queen's Gate Mews
Queen's Gate Place
Queen's Gate Place Mews
Queen's Gate Terrace
Queen's Gate Gdns
Queen's Gate Place Gdns
Gloucester Road
Cromwell Road A4
Cromwell Road
Cromwell Place
Thurloe Place
Thurloe St
South Kensington
Harrington Road
Gloucester Road
Gloucester Gate
Stanhope Gardens
Stanhope Mews West
Stanhope Mews East
Stanhope Gardens
Stanhope Mews
Stanhope Gardens
Stanhope Gardens
Harrington Gardens
Courtfield Gdns
Courtfield
Gloucester Park
Old Brompton Road
Onslow Square
Onslow Gdns
Onslow Ms E
Onslow Ms W
Onslow Gate
Onslow Place
Onslow Square
Summer Pl
Summer Place
Summer Mews
Cranley Pl
Cranley Gdns
Cranley Ms
Bina Gardens
Bina Gardens
Wetherby Pl
Wetherby Gardens
Rosary Gardens
Hereford Square
Clareville Street
Clareville Grove
Manson Place
Queen's Gate
Queen's Gate Place
Queen's Gate Place Mews
Queen's Gate Gdns
Queen's Gate Gdns
Queen's Gate Mews
Queen's Gate Terrace
Petersham Place
Petersham Mews
Petersham Lane
Elvaston Place
Elvaston Mews
Gore Street
Kynance Mews
Kynance Pl
Cornwall Gdns
Cornwall Mews
Cornwall Gardens
Cornwall Ms
Southwell Gdns
Southwell Gardens
Emperor's Gate
Grenville Place
Ashburn Gardens
Ashburn Place
Ashburn Road
Ashbrook Ms
Gaspar Cl
Gaspar Ms
Courtfield
Colbeck Mews
Harrington Gardens
Stone Mews
Alitner
Queensberry Place
Queensberry Ms W
Queensberry Way
Cromwell Place
Cromwell Ms
Pl Ms
Thurloe Place
Exhibition Road
Pelham Street
Onslow
Onslow Cres
Onslow Ms E
Onslow Ms W
Onslow Gdns
Onslow Square
Sydney Mews
Sydney Cl
Sydney Ms
Sydney Pl
Sydney Place
Cranley Pl
Cranley Gdns
Cranley Ms

South Kensington / Gloucester Rd

Befriend a millionaire and you can hang out here all the time, perhaps house-sitting his London 'base' while he unwinds in the countreh. This part of town is museum central and for musos there's the Royal Albert Hall. If all that's made you hungry head to Jacob's for a wholesome lunch and Snog for some frozen yoghurt madness.

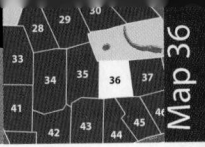

Banks

- **Barclays** • 114 Gloucester Rd
- **HSBC** • 95 Gloucester Rd
- **NatWest** • 18 Cromwell Pl

Cinemas

- **Cine Lumiere** • 17 Queensberry Pl

Coffee

- **Café Deco** • 62 Gloucester Rd
- **Coffee Republic** • 121 Gloucester Rd
- **Pret A Manger** • 99 Gloucester Rd
- **Pret A Manger** • 15 Old Brompton Rd
- **Starbucks** • 17 Gloucester Rd
- **Starbucks** • 83 Gloucester Rd

Landmarks

- **Albert Memorial** • Kensington Gardens
- **Royal Albert Hall** • Kensington Gore

Libraries

- **French Institute Library** • 17 Queensberry Pl
- **National Art Library** • Cromwell Rd
- **Natural History Museum** • Cromwell Rd

Nightlife

- **Boujis** • 43 Thurloe St

Post Offices

- **Gloucester Road** • 118 Gloucester Rd
- **South Kensington Station** • 41 Old Brompton St

Restaurants

- **Cafe Forum** • 145 Gloucester Rd
- **Jacob's** • 20 Gloucester Rd
- **The Kensington Creperie** • 2 Exhibition Rd
- **Little Japan** • 32 Thurloe St
- **Odonno's** • 14 Bute St

Shopping

- **Snog** • 32 Thurloe Pl

Supermarkets

- **Sainsbury's** • 158 Cromwell Rd
- **Waitrose** • 128 Gloucester Rd

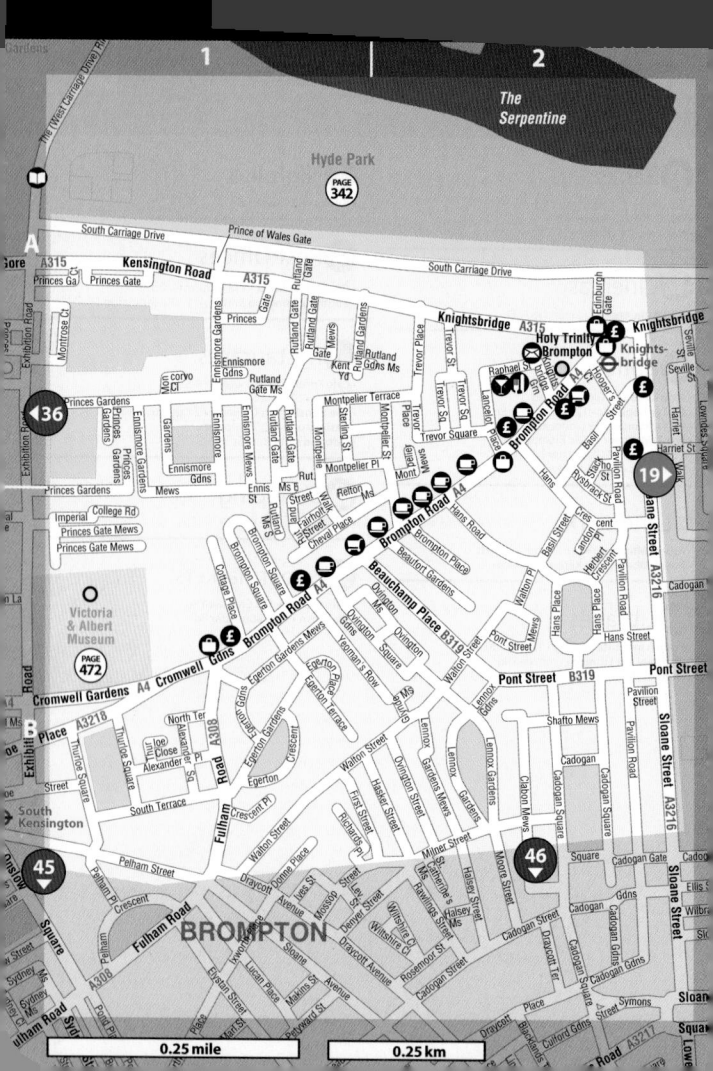
1
2
The Serpentine
Hyde Park
PAGE 342
South Carriage Drive
Prince of Wales Gate
Kensington Road
A315
Princes Gate
Knightsbridge
Holy Trinity Brompton
Knightsbridge
Brompton Road
A4
Beauchamp Place
B319
Cromwell Gardens
A4 Cromwell
Pont Street
B319
Victoria & Albert Museum
PAGE 472
South Kensington
Fulham Road
A308
Sloane Street
A3216
Cadogan
Cadogan Square
Cadogan Gardens
Cadogan Gate
Sloane Square
Pelham Street
Pelham Pl
Pelham Crescent
Draycott Avenue
Draycott Pl
Draycott Place
Cadogan Street
Sloane Street
Symons Street
Fulham Road
A3217
BROMPTON
36
19
45
46
0.25 mile
0.25 km

Knightsbridge

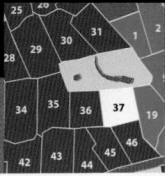

The perfect place to go to get that must-have item at a much higher price than anywhere else. Rammed Brompton Road features Harrods, Harvey Nichols, the flagship Burberry store, and a host of other credit crunchers, populated by hordes of aggressive tourists. Behind that: behold! Luxury apartments worth way more than the lives of your entire family.

Banks

- **Barclays** • 137 Brompton Rd
- **Halifax** • 110 Brompton Rd
- **HSBC** • 237 Brompton Rd
- **HSBC** • 202 Sloane St
- **Lloyds** • 9 Brompton Rd
- **NatWest** • 186 Brompton Rd
- **NatWest** • 185 Sloane St

Coffee

- **Bagel Factory** • 88 Brompton Rd
- **Bagel Factory** • 102 Brompton Rd
- **Caffe Nero** • 124 Brompton Rd
- **Costa** • 197 Brompton Rd
- **Eat.** • 106 Brompton Rd
- **Pret A Manger** • 132 Brompton Rd
- **Starbucks** • 58 Brompton Rd

Landmarks

- **Holy Trinity Brompton** • Brompton Rd
- **Victoria & Albert Museum** • Cromwell Rd

Libraries

- **Goethe-Institut Library** • Exhibition Rd

Nightlife

- **Knightsbridge BO** • 6 Raphael St

Restaurants

- **Zuma** • 5 Raphael St

Shopping

- **Burberry** • 2 Brompton Road
- **Harrods** • 87 Brompton Rd
- **Harvey Nichols** • 109 Knightsbridge
- **Skandium** • 247 Brompton Rd

Supermarkets

- **Marks & Spencer** • 179 Brompton Rd
- **Sainsbury's** • 112 Brompton Rd

Map 38 • Chiswick

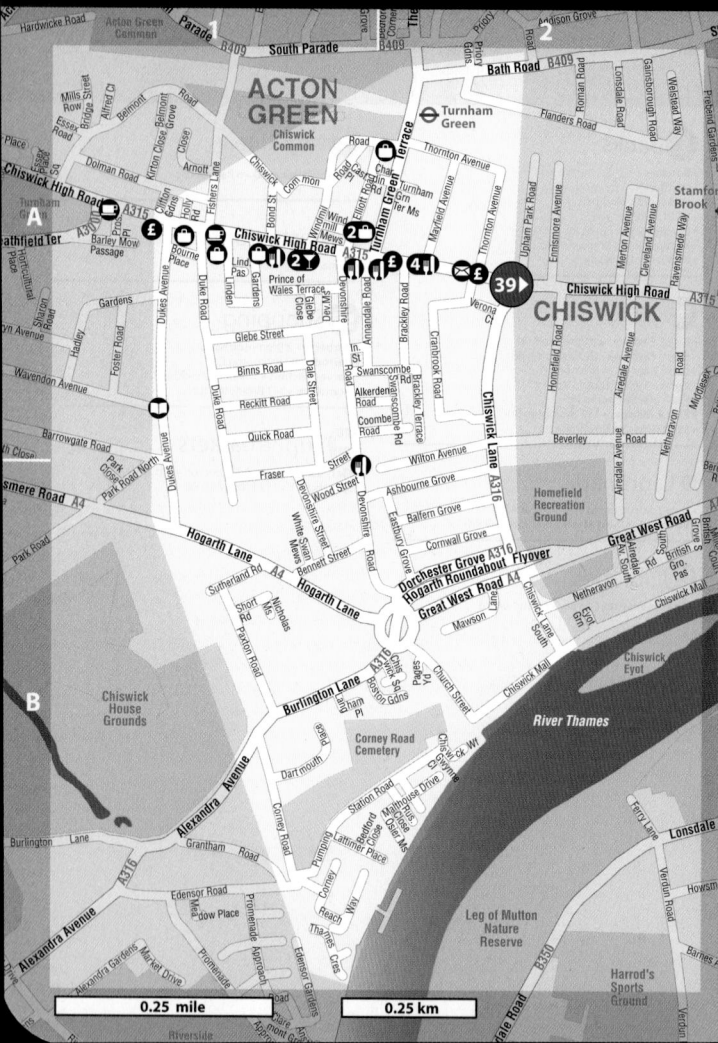
ACTON GREEN
Chiswick Common
Turnham Green
CHISWICK
Chiswick High Road
Bath Road B409
South Parade
Turnham Green Terrace
Thornton Avenue
Flanders Road
Chiswick Lane A316
Great West Road
Dorchester Grove A316
Hogarth Roundabout Flyover
Great West Road A4
Hogarth Lane
Burlington Lane A315
Alexandra Avenue
Lonsdale
Chiswick Mall
River Thames
Chiswick Eyot
Chiswick House Grounds
Corney Road Cemetery
Leg of Mutton Nature Reserve
Homefield Recreation Ground
Harrod's Sports Ground
Prince of Wales Terrace
Barley Mow Passage
Bath Field Ter
Hardwick Road
Acton Green Common
Dukes Avenue
Duke Road
Bond St
Chiswick
Brackley Road
Crabtrook Road
Homefield Road
Airedale Avenue
Beverley Road
Netheravon Road
Burlington Lane
Grantham Road
Edensor Road
Meadow Place
Promenade
Alexandra Gardens
Market Drive
Riverside
Ferry Lane
Verdun Road
Howsman
Barnes
Chiswick Lane South
Church Street
Corney Road
Station Road
Bedford Close
Latimer Place
Pumping Station
Mathouse Drive
Bolton Gdns
Priory Gdns
Prebend Gardens
Stamford Brook
Turnham Green
Hogarth Lane
Sutherland Rd
Short Rd
Paxton Road
Nicholas Ms
Devonshire Street
White Street
Bennett Street
Devonshire Road
Wood Street
Fraser Street
Wilton Avenue
Ashbourne Grove
Balfern Grove
Eastbury Grove
Cornwall Grove
Chiswick Lane South
Netheravon Road
Chiswick Mall
Grove Park
Airedale Avenue
Beverley Road
Verona Cl
Upham Park Road
Erimsmore Avenue
Merton Avenue
Cleveland Avenue
Flaxensmede Way
Roman Road
Lonsdale Road
Gainsborough Road
Wakehurst Way
Madison Grove
Priory Gdns
Bath Road B409
Turnham Green Terrace
Thornton Avenue
Meyrick Avenue
Chiswick Lane A316
Brackley Road
Crabtrook Road
Homefield Road
Airedale Avenue
Beverley Road
Netheravon Road
Chiswick Mall

Chiswick

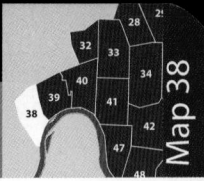

Lean, green, and thankfully not so mean, Chiswick's leafy, cosmopolitan pavement dining is the epitome of what makes west London, well, west London. Hit the High Road for café culture and Turnham Green Terrace for boutique shopping and chocolate to die for at Theobroma Cacao. Sunny days can be spent chilling on Acton Green. Off the High Road The Devonshire is a more affordable Gordon Ramsey venture but the High Road Brasserie still remains the place to be seen.

Banks

- **Halifax** • 91 King St
- **Lloyds** • 308 Chiswick High Rd

Coffee

- **Carluccio's** • 314 Chiswick High Rd
- **Starbucks** • 280 Chiswick High Rd

Libraries

- **Chiswick Library** • Duke's Ave

Nightlife

- **Carvossos** • 210 Chiswick High Rd
- **George IV** • 185 Chiswick High Rd

Post Offices

- **Chiswick High Road** • 110 Chiswick High Rd

Restaurants

- **Boys Authentic Thai** • 95 Chiswick High Rd
- **Chez Gerard** • 163 Chiswck High Rd
- **Chris' Fish and Chips** • 19 Turnham Green Terrace
- **The Devonshire** • 126 Devonshire Rd
- **Fouberts** • 2 Turnham Green Terrace
- **High Road Brasserie** • 162 Chiswick High Rd
- **Kalamari** • 4 Chiswick High Rd
- **Zizzi** • 231 Chiswick High Rd

Shopping

- **As Nature Intended** • 201 Chiswick High Rd
- **The Bread Shop** • 296 Chiswick Rd
- **Eco-Age** • 213 Chiswick High Rd
- **Oxfam Books** • 90 Turnham Green Terrace
- **Theobroma Cacao** • 43 Turnham Green Terrace
- **Something Nice** • 40 Turnham Green Terrace

Map 39 • Stamford Brook

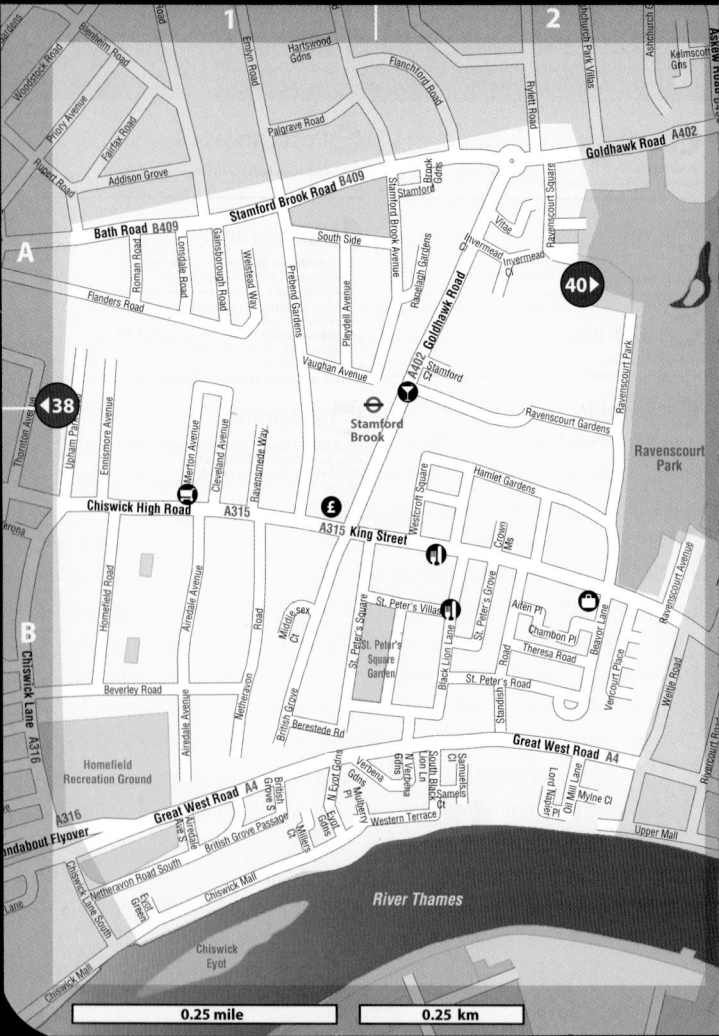

Stamford Brook

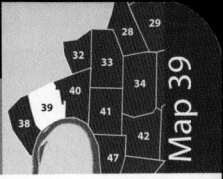

Wedged between Chiswick and Hammersmith, with the actual brook now a sewer, there's not much more to Stamford Brook than a tube station and some very expensive houses. However there are a few gems. On King Street, Tosa serves up some great, authentic Japanese yakitori while thirsty Brookites head to The Carpenter's Arms.

Banks

- **HSBC** • 2 Chiswick High Rd

Nightlife

- **The Raven** • 375 Goldhawk Rd

Restaurants

- **Carpenter's Arms** • 91 Black Lion Ln
- **Tosa** • 332 Kings St

Supermarkets

- **Sainsbury's** • 120 Chiswick High Rd

Shopping

- **Mac's Cameras** • 262 Kings St

Map 40 • Goldhawk Rd / Ravenscourt Park

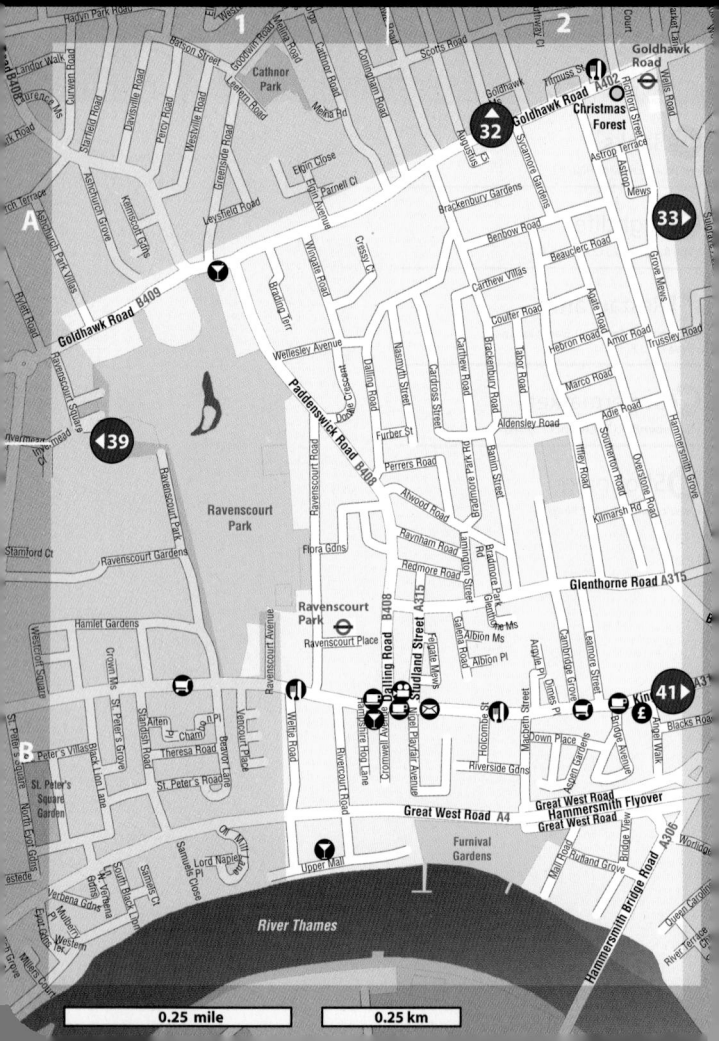
N
1
2
A
B
Cathnor Park
Goldhawk Road
Goldhawk Road B409
Goldhawk Road A402
Christmas Forest
Paddenswick Road B408
Ravenscourt Park
Ravenscourt Park Place
Dalling Road B408
Studland Street A315
Glenthorne Road A315
Great West Road A4
Great West Road
Hammersmith Flyover
Great West Road
Hammersmith Bridge Road A306
Furnival Gardens
River Thames
St. Peter's Square Garden
Lord Napier
Upper Mall
Riverside Gdns
Blacks Road
Hamilton Gardens
Ravenscourt Gardens
Stamford Ct
Flora Gdns
Redmore Road
Reynham Road
Albion Pl
Albion Ms
Furnival Gdns
Aldensley Road
Furber St
Perrers Road
Atwood Road
Wellesley Avenue
Brackenbury Gardens
Benbow Road
Cartview Villas
Coulter Road
Hebron Road
Amor Road
Trusley Road
Marco Road
Adie Road
Hammersmith Grove
Southerton Road
Overstone Road
Tilley Road
Kilmarsh Rd
Aldensley Road
Brackenbury Road
Dalling Road
Nasmith Street
Ravenscourt Road
Ravenscourt Avenue
Ravenscourt Square
Rivercourt Road
Weltje Road
Cromwell Avenue
Crown Pl
St. Peter's Grove
Black Lion Lane
Theresa Road
St. Peter's Road
Beaver Lane
Ashchurch Grove
Ashchurch Park Villas
Kenscott Gdns
Leysfield Road
Greenside Road
Westville Road
Perry Road
Starfield Road
Bridge Avenue
Bridge Terrace
Burland Grove
Mall Road
Cambridge Grove
Leamore Street
Aquila Pl
Macbeth Street
Holcombe St
Bridge Avenue
Angel Walk
Kin
Glenthorne Road
Hammersmith Grove
Bridge Terrace
Rivercourt Road
Cromwell Avenue
Weltje Road
Ravenscourt Avenue
Ravenscourt Square
Ravenscourt Park
Ravenscourt Place
Hamilton Gardens
Stamford Ct
Ravenscourt Gardens
Flora Gdns
Redmore Road
Reynham Road
Atwood Road
Furber St
Perrers Road
Wellesley Avenue
Aldensley Road

Goldhawk Rd / Ravenscourt Park

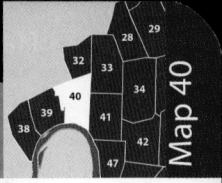

Far enough on the tube to scare the tourists, this area is a haven for locals who want it all on their doorstep. International flavours? Please, it's like a Benetton ad here: try Lowiczanka, Sagar, or Blah Blah Blah. Pretty Thames walk? Check!—along with The Dove, one of the city's most picturesque pubs. There's even a Christmas Tree forest. Life's good in these parts.

Banks

- **Barclays** • 75 King St

Cinemas

- **Cineworld Hammersmith** • 207 King St

Coffee

- **Caffe Nero** • 1 King St
- **Coffee Republic** • 207 King St
- **Starbucks** • 38 King St

Landmarks

- **Christmas Forest** • 83 Goldhawk Road

Nightlife

- **The Dove** • 19 Upper Mall
- **The Mulberry** • 243 Goldhawk Rd
- **Ruby Grand** • 225 King St

Post Offices

- **King St** • 168 King St

Restaurants

- **Blah Blah Blah** • 78 Goldhawk Rd
- **Lowiczanka Polish Cultural Centre** • 238 King Street
- **Sagar** • 157 King St

Supermarkets

- **Iceland** • 111 King St
- **Tesco** • 327 King St

Map 41 • Hammersmith

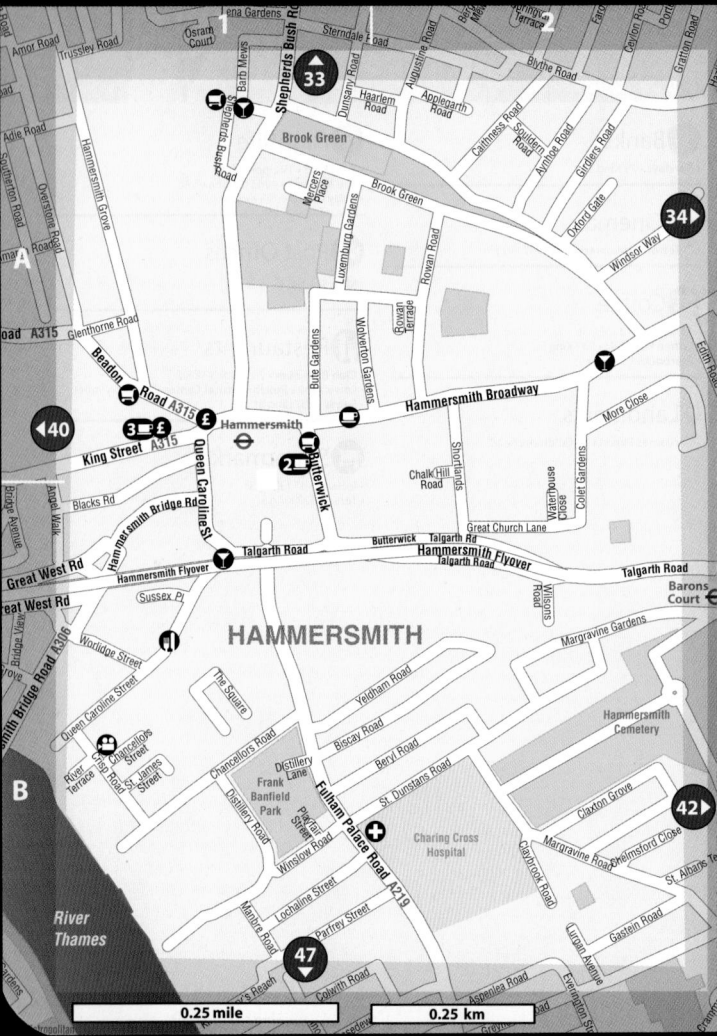

Hammersmith

So the shops and pubs on offer are all pretty drab, but Hammersmith has three great venues for the more culturally inclined. Check out The Apollo for mainstream bands and big-name comedians, The Lyric for the latest in modern theatre, and The Riverside for an awesome selection of foreign/art house films. London's vegetarians flock to The Gate, with its seriously original and inventive menu.

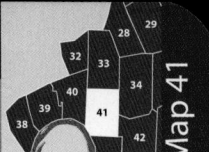

Banks

- **HSBC** • 1 Beadon Rd
- **Lloyds** • 21 King St

Cinemas

- **Riverside Studios** • Crisp Rd & Queen Caroline St

Coffee

- **Cafe Brera** • Hammersmith Foyer & Roof Garden
- **Cafe Brera** • King St & Angel Walk
- **Costa** • Butterwick
- **Costa** • King St
- **Pret A Manger** • Butterwick
- **Starbucks** • 200 Hammersmith Rd

Emergency Rooms

- **Charing Cross Hospital** • Fulham Palace Rd

Nightlife

- **Brook Green Hotel** • 170 Shepherd's Bush Rd
- **Hammersmith Apollo** • 45 Queen Caroline St
- **Lyric Hammersmith** • King St

Restaurants

- **The Gate** • 51 Queen Caroline St

Supermarkets

- **Sainsbury's** • Beadon Rd
- **Tesco** • 180 Shepherd's Bush Rd
- **Tesco** • Butterwick

Map 42 • Barons Court

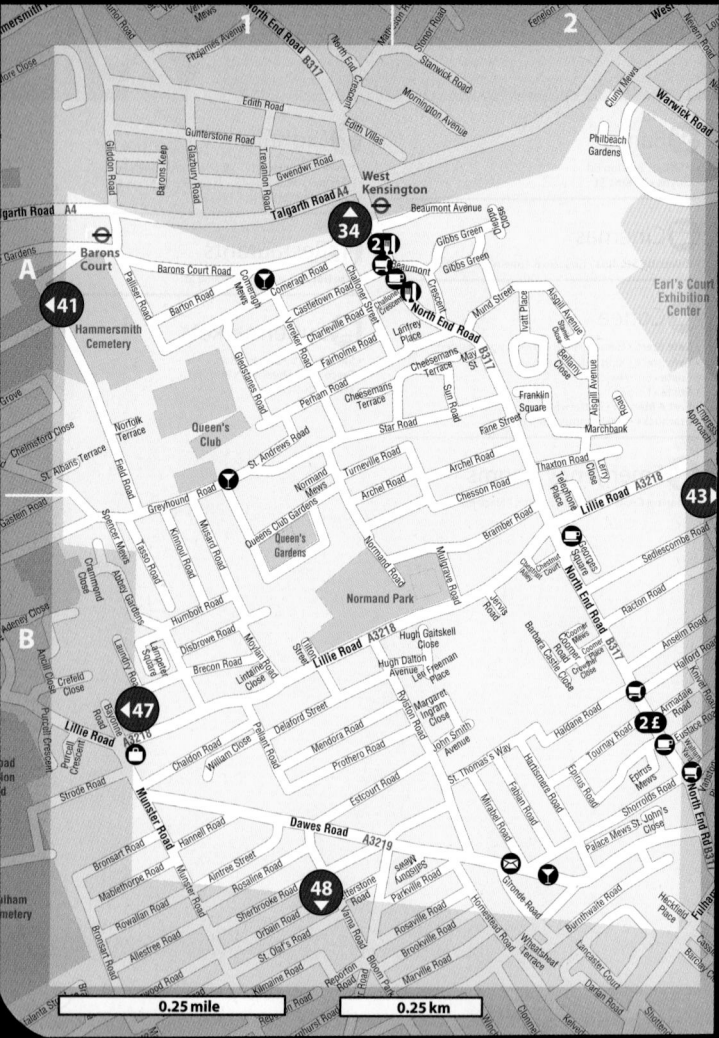
1
2
A
B
Barons Court
West Kensington
Hammersmith Cemetery
Queen's Club
Queen's Gardens
Normand Park
Earl's Court Exhibition Center
Philbeach Gardens
Franklin Square
Talgarth Road A4
Barons Court Road
North End Road B317
Lillie Road A3218
Dawes Road A3219
Munster Road
Fulham Road
Warwick Road
Beaumont Avenue
Gibbs Green
Edith Road
Gunterstone Road
Mornington Avenue
Stanwick Road
Edith Villas
Gliddon Road
Barons Keep
Glazbury Road
Trevanion Road
Palliser Road
Barton Road
Comeragh Road
Castletown Road
Charleville Road
Fairholme Road
Perham Road
Vereker Road
Lantrey Place
Munro Street
Ivatt Place
Aisgill Avenue
Ballantry Close
Cheisemans Terrace
Star Road
Fane Street
Marchbank Road
Thaxton Road
Larry Close
Telephone Place
Norfolk Terrace
Field Road
St Albans Terrace
Chelmsford Close
St Andrews Road
Turneville Road
Archel Road
Chesson Road
Brambler Road
Greyhound Road
Kimnel Road
Musard Road
Tasso Road
Humbolt Road
Brecon Road
Lintaine Road
Lillie Road
Hugh Gaitskell Close
Hugh Dalton Avenue
Lisa Freeman Place
Margaret Ingram Close
John Smith Avenue
Delaford Street
Mendora Road
Frothero Road
Eskmont Road
Chalton Road
William Close
Hannell Road
Bromart Road
Maltlethorpe Road
Rowallan Road
Allestree Road
Airtree Street
Rosaline Road
Sherbrooke Road
Orbain Road
St Olaf's Road
Kilmaine Road
Marville Road
Brookville Road
Rosaville Road
Parkville Road
Lillestone Road
Varna Road
Drewes Road
Wesleyan Terrace
Burdhwaite Road
Lancaster Court
Durdan Road
Hesketh Place
Eyelmo Mews
Shorrolds Road
Tourney Road
Haldane Road
Harlesmere Road
Falham Road
Minchel Road
Eyelmo Road
St. Thomas's Way
Palace Mews
St. John's Close
Ansdell Road
Halford Road
Ansleigh Road
Racton Road
Sedlescombe Road
Barbara Castle Close
Jerrys Road
Mulgrave Road
Normand Road
Queens Club Gardens
Sycamore Mews
Abacus Gardens
Larkhall Square
Crefeld Close
Lillie Road
Purcell Crescent
Aintree Close
Addney Close
Crummond Close
Gliddon Road
Vereker Road
Charleville Road
Cheisemans Terrace
Sun Road
Aisgill Avenue
Gliddon Road
Gwendwr Road
Trevanion Road
Talgarth Road
Beaumont Avenue
Gibbs Green
Comeragh Road
Castletown Road
Charleville Road
Fairholme Road
Perham Road
Star Road
Fane Street
Marchbank Road
Thaxton Road
Larry Close
Telephone Place
Lillie Road
Brambler Road
Chesson Road
Archel Road
Turneville Road
St Andrews Road
Greyhound Road
Kimnel Road
Musard Road
Tasso Road
Humbolt Road
Brecon Road
Lintaine

Barons Court doesn't have a scene as such, unless you're a yummy mummy or a Chihuahua. But it is elegantly lovely. Except North End Road—a fried-chicken blot among Edwardian mansions. Check out Lillie Road's antique stores, particularly Curious Science for the weirdest stock in London. If you need a change from polished chic, seek the Colton Arms for a jug-pint in its cottage-style garden.

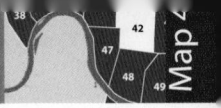

Banks

- **Abbey** • 421 N End Rd
- **Lloyds** • 417 N End Rd

Coffee

- **Café La Cigale** • 353 N End Rd
- **Coffee Republic** • 92 N End Rd
- **Costa** • 431 North End Rd

Nightlife

- **Colton Arms** • 187 Greyhound Road
- **Curtains Up** • 28 Comeragh Rd
- **The Fulham Mitre** • 81 Dawes Rd

Post Offices

- **Dawes Road** • 108 Dawes Rd

Restaurants

- **Best Mangal** • 104 N End Rd
- **Bombay Bicycle Club** • 352 N End Rd
- **Ta Khai** • 100 North End Rd

Shopping

- **Curious Science** • 319 Lillie Road

Supermarkets

- **Co-Op** • 88 N End Rd
- **Iceland** • 290 North End Rd
- **Sainsbury's** • 342 North End Rd

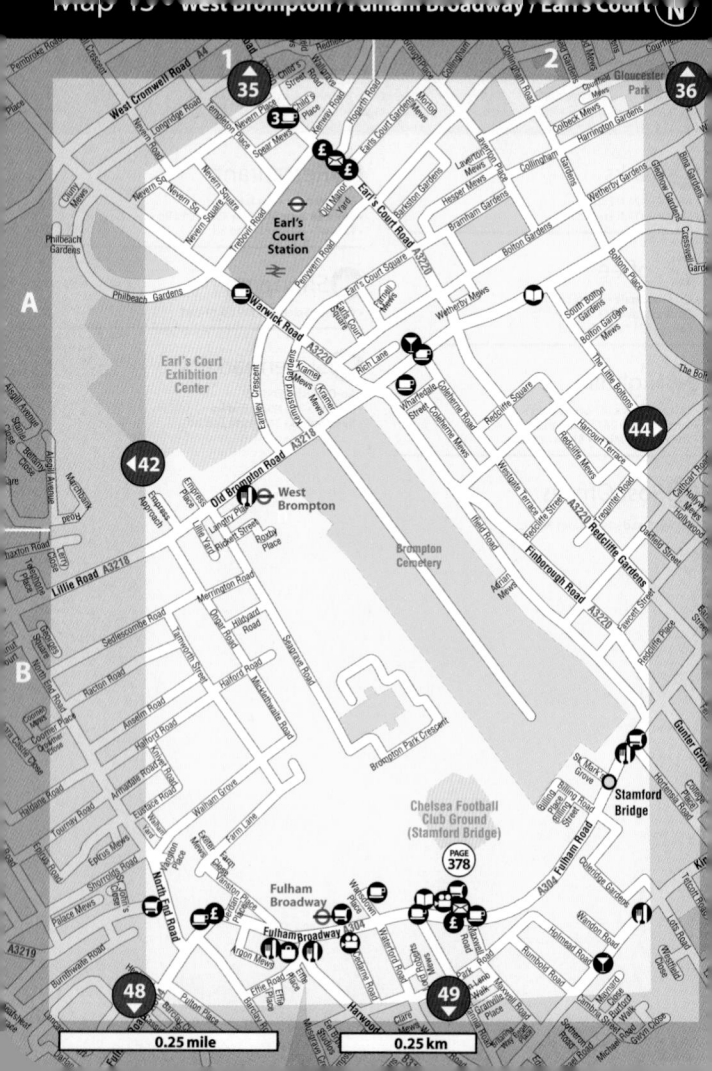
N
1
2
A
B
35
36
42
44
48
49
West Cromwell Road A4
Earl's Court Road A3220
Earl's Court Station
Warwick Road A3220
Earl's Court Exhibition Center
Old Brompton Road A3218
West Brompton
Lillie Road A3218
Brompton Cemetery
Finborough Road
Redcliffe Gardens A3224
Fulham Broadway
Fulham Broadway
Chelsea Football Club Ground (Stamford Bridge)
Stamford Bridge
A304 Fulham Road
North End Road
Harwood
Gloucester Park
PAGE 378
0.25 mile
0.25 km

West Brompton / Fulham Broadway / Earl's Court

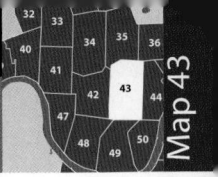

A lively mix of Aussie's, Saffa's, rich kids, and sweaty Chelsea fans occupy these neighbourhoods. Fulham Broadway is the focus of the action offering heaving bars and clubs. Earl's Court is slightly more sedate while West Brompton is positively sleepy in comparison. On Brompton Road '60s boho café The Troubadour is still a happening spot for live music and a coffee while Vingt Quatre is a 24-hour institution serving fry ups to clubbers in the early hours.

Banks

- **Barclays** • 191 Earl's Ct Rd
- **Barclays** • 20 Fulham Broadway
- **HSBC** • 315 Fulham Rd
- **Lloyds** • 179 Earl's Ct Rd

Cinemas

- **Cineworld Fulham Road** • 142 Fulham Rd
- **Vue Fulham** • Fulham Rd & Cedarne Rd

Coffee

- **Caffe Nero** • 480 Fulham Rd
- **Caffe Nero** • 174 Fulham Rd
- **Coffee Republic** • 198 Earl's Ct Rd
- **Coffee Republic** • 142 Fulham Rd
- **Costa** • Warwick Rd
- **Costa** • 153 Earl's Ct Rd
- **Pret A Manger** • Fulham Broadway Retail Centre
- **Starbucks** • 259 Old Brompton Rd
- **Starbucks** • 186 Earl's Ct Rd
- **The Troubadour** • 263 Old Brompton Rd

Landmarks

- **Stamford Bridge** • Fulham Road

Libraries

- **Brompton Library** • 210 Old Brompton Rd
- **Institute of Cancer Research Library** • 237 Fulham Rd

Nightlife

- **The Coleherne** • 261 Old Brompton Rd
- **Nectar** • 562 King's Rd

Post Offices

- **Earls Court** • 185 Earl's Ct Rd
- **Fulham Road** • 369 Fulham Rd

Restaurants

- **The Blue Elephant** • 3 Fulham Broadway
- **Bodean's** • 4 Broadway Chambers
- **Chutney Mary** • 535 King's Rd
- **Vingt Quatre** • 325 Fulham Rd
- **Yo! Sushi** • Fulham Road

Shopping

- **Fulham Broadway Centre** • Fulham Road

Supermarkets

- **Sainsbury's** • 295 Fulham Rd
- **Sainsbury's** • Fulham Rd
- **Tesco** • 459 Fulham Rd
- **Waitrose** • 380 North End Rd

Map 44 • Chelsea

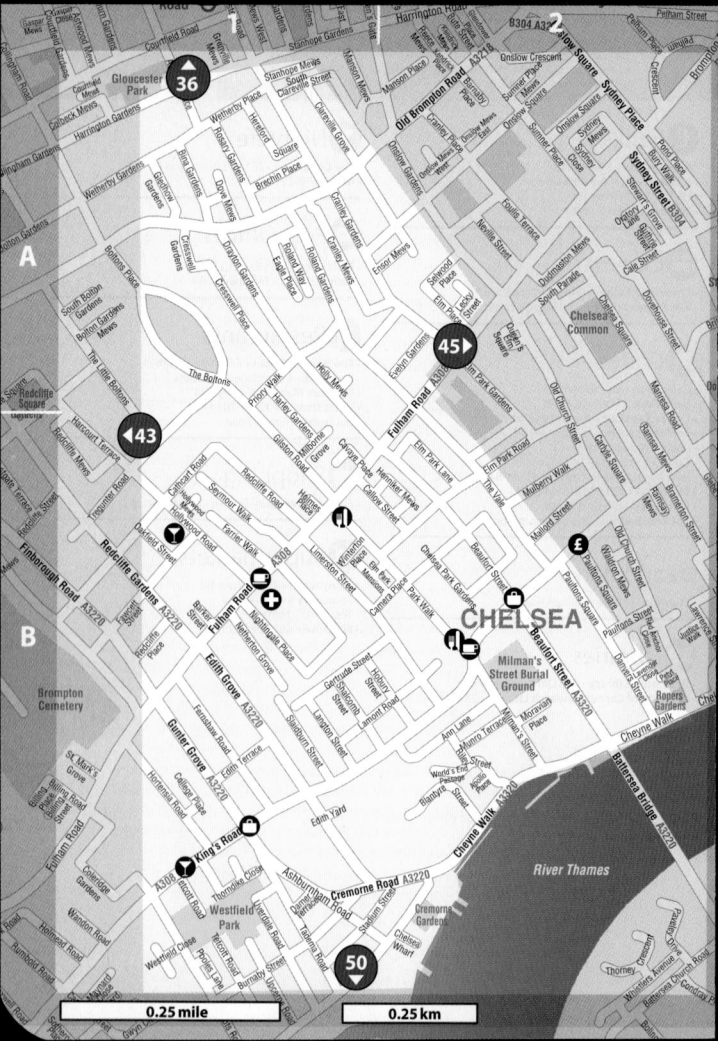

This area drips old money, 4x4s, and people who own rather large things, like, say, Devon. The only way to do Chelsea is to be seen doing it—and if you're paying all that money at least make it worthwhile. Drink one of Eight Over Eight's innovative cocktails, taste Michelin-starred food at Aubergine, and blow a week's wage on a designer sock from The Shop At Bluebird.

Banks

- **Barclays** • 348 King's Rd

Coffee

- **Starbucks** • 388 King's Rd
- **Starbucks** • 369 Fulham Rd

Emergency Rooms

- **Chelsea and Westminster Hospital** • 369 Fulham Rd

Nightlife

- **Brinkleys** • 47 Hollywood Rd
- **Rumi** • 531 King's Rd

Restaurants

- **Aubergine** • 11 Park Walk
- **Eight Over Eight** • 392 King's Rd

Shopping

- **Furniture Cave** • 533 Kings Rd
- **The Shop At Bluebird** • 350 King's Rd

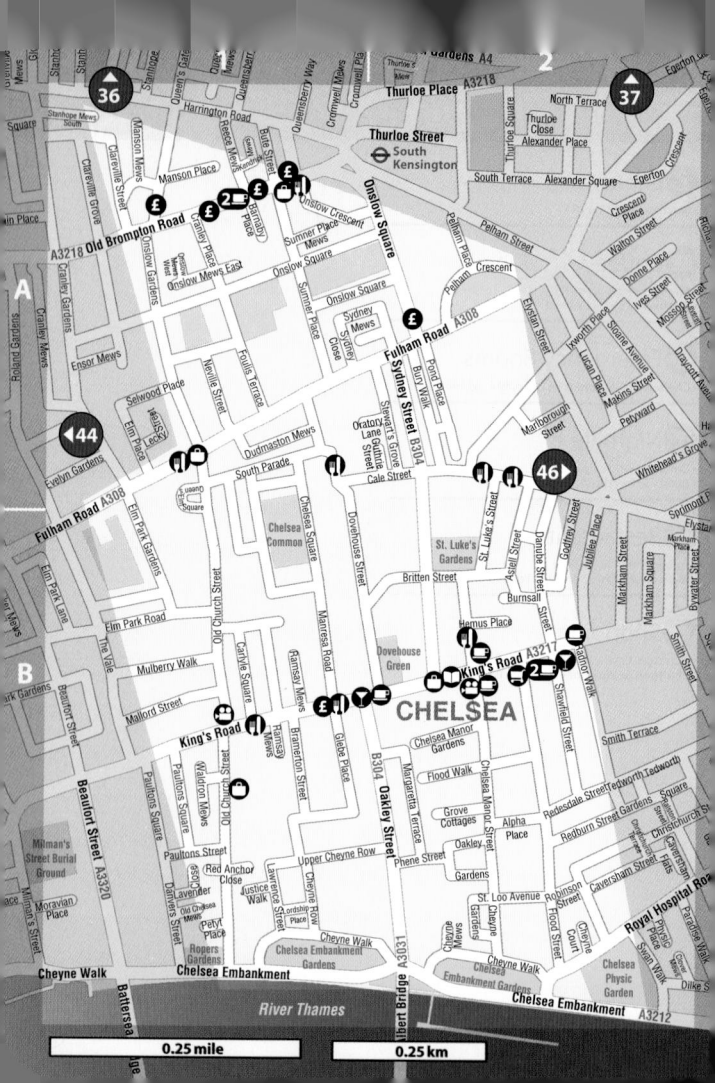
Thurloe Place A3218
Thurloe Street
South Kensington
Harrington Road
Queen's Gate
Queensberry Way
Cromwell Mews
Cromwell Pl
Thurloe Square
Thurloe Close
North Terrace
Alexander Place
South Terrace
Alexander Square
Egerton Crescent
Crescent Place
Walton Street
Pelham Street
Pelham Place
Pelham Crescent
Onslow Square
Onslow Crescent
Sumner Place
Sumner Place Mews
Onslow Mews East
Onslow Mews West
Onslow Gardens
Manson Place
Manson Mews
Clareville Street
Clareville Grove
Bute Street
Cranley Place
Cranley Mews
Cranley Gardens
A3218 Old Brompton Road
Ensor Mews
Selwood Place
Elm Place
Elm Park Gardens
Elm Park Lane
Fulham Road A308
Evelyn Gardens
Queen's Gate Place
Neville Street
Foulis Terrace
Dudmaston Mews
South Parade
Sydney Mews
Sydney Close
Fulham Road A308
Sydney Street B304
Bury Walk
Pond Place
Oratory Lane
Cathcart Street
Stewart's Grove
Cale Street
Chelsea Square
Chelsea Common
Dovehouse Street
St. Luke's Gardens
St. Luke's Street
Astell Street
Danvers Street
Godfrey Street
Jubilee Place
Marlborough Street
Britten Street
Burnsall
Hemus Place
Dovehouse Green
Manresa Road
Ramsay Mews
Carlyle Square
Old Church Street
The Vale
Mulberry Walk
Milford Street
King's Road A3217
Hortus Mews
Brompton Street
Glebe Place
Jekyll's Mews
Old Church Street
Paulton's Square
Waldron Mews
Beaufort Street A3320
Beaufort Street
Milman's Street Burial Ground
Moravian Place
Milman's Street
Lavender Close
Justice Walk
Lawrence Street
Cheyne Row
Cheyne Walk
Chelsea Embankment Gardens
Ropers Gardens
Petyt Place
Old Church Mews
Upper Cheyne Row
Phene Street
Oakley Gardens
B304 Oakley Street
Margaretta Terrace
Chelsea Manor Gardens
Flood Walk
Grove Cottages
Alpha Place
Chelsea Manor Street
Redesdale Street
Fedworth Tedworth Square
Redburn Street
Gardens
Chiltern Street
Christchurch Sq
Caversham Street
Robinson Street
St. Loo Avenue
Flood Street
Chelsea Court
Chelsea Manor Gardens
Chelsea Embankment Gardens
Chelsea Physic Garden
Royal Hospital Road
Paradise Walk
Dilke S
Chelsea Embankment A3212
Chelsea Embankment
Cheyne Walk
Battersea Bridge
Chelsea Bridge A3031
River Thames
0.25 mile
0.25 km
CHELSEA
36
37
44
46
A
B
1
2

Chelsea East is what Hollywood thinks all of London is like, full of dapper English chaps and potential princesses (who, incidentally, donate their clothes to the Red Cross shop: rummage here for London's best bargains). King's Road buzzes as it did when it spawned the Swinging '60s, and foodies are spoiled around Cale Street. Tom's Kitchen is your place for Sloaney eating without the Sloaney allowance. For a cheaper and sweeter taste of the area get to The Hummingbird Bakery for addictive oh-so-good cupcakes.

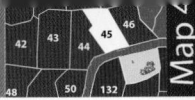

Banks

- **Abbey** • 90 Old Brompton Rd
- **Barclays** • 108 Queen's Gate
- **HSBC** • 1 Sydney Pl
- **Lloyds** • 67 Old Brompton Rd
- **NatWest** • 224 King's Rd
- **Royal Bank of Scotland** • 29 Old Brompton Rd

Cinemas

- **Chelsea Cinema** • 206 King's Rd
- **Cineworld Chelsea** • 279 King's Rd

Coffee

- **Cafe de la Paix** • 159 King's Rd
- **Caffe Nero** • 115 King's Rd
- **Caffe Nero** • 201 King's Rd
- **Caffe Nero** • 66 Old Brompton Rd
- **Coffee Republic** • 157 King's Rd
- **Picasso Cafe** • 127 King's Rd
- **Starbucks** • 123 King's Rd
- **Starbucks** • 72 Old Brompton Rd

Libraries

- **Chelsea Library** • King's Rd

Nightlife

- **Apartment 195** • 195 Kings Rd
- **Chelsea Potter** • 119 Kings Rd

Restaurants

- **Chelsea Kitchen** • 451 Fulham Rd
- **Four o nine** • 409 Clapham Rd
- **Le Columbier** • 145 Dovehouse St
- **The Hummingbird Bakery** • 47 Old Brompton Rd
- **Made In Italy** • 243 King's Rd
- **My Old Dutch Pancake House** • 221 King's Rd
- **Tom's Kitchen** • 27 Cale St
- **Tom's Place** • 1 Cale St

Shopping

- **British Red Cross Chelsea** • 67 Old Church St
- **Frock Me! Vintage Fashion Fair** • Chelsea Town Hall, Kings Rd
- **Kate Kuba** • 24 Duke of York Sq
- **Nomad Books** • 243 Fulham Rd

Supermarkets

- **Waitrose** • 196 Kings Rd

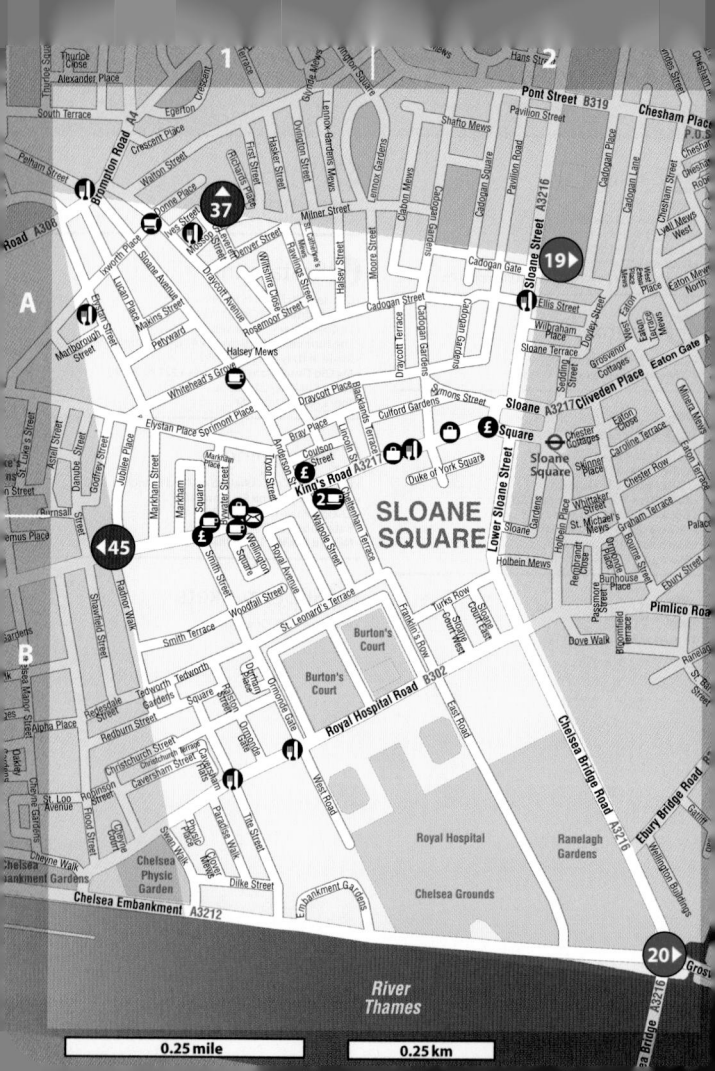
SLOANE SQUARE
Sloane Square
Sloane Square
Kings Road A3217
Sloane Street
Lower Sloane Street
Cliveden Place
Eaton Gate
Pont Street B319
Chesham Place
Sloane Terrace
Ellis Street
Cadogan Gate
Cadogan Street
Cadogan Square
Cadogan Place
Cadogan Lane
Pavilion Road
Sloane Avenue A3216
Hans Place
Hans Street
Milner Street
Moore Street
Halsey Street
Draycott Avenue
Draycott Place
Draycott Terrace
Cadogan Terrace
Sumner Street
Fulham Road
Brompton Road A4
Sloane Square
Sloane Gardens
Holbein Mews
Holbein Place
Pimlico Road
Dove Walk
Royal Hospital Road B302
Burton's Court
Chelsea Bridge Road A3216
Ebury Bridge Road
Royal Hospital
Ranelagh Gardens
Chelsea Grounds
Chelsea Physic Garden
Chelsea Embankment A3212
Embankment Gardens
Dilke Street
Tite Street
Cheyne Walk
Cheyne Row
Flood Street
Oakley Street
Smith Street
Smith Terrace
Woodfall Street
St Leonard's Terrace
Rainer Walk
Shalfleet Street
Tedworth Gardens
Redburn Street
Alpha Place
Christchurch Street
Cavendish Street
Cale Street
Markham Street
Jubilee Place
Elystan Place
Symons Street
Whitehead's Grove
Halsey Mews
Lower Cheyne Row
Oakley Gardens
Chelsea Bridge Road A3216
Ebury Bridge Road
Grosvenor Road

You've got to love a place that spawns an adjective. If you've never met any 'Sloaney' types and are curious as to why the whole of London gets so riled about them, take a walk along the King's Road and observe. Peter Jones stands tall over the square and offers everything you didn't know you wanted. Other attractions in this rather beautiful nabe include a clutch of bank-breaking, but rather good, eateries such as Gordon Ramsay and many lovely (but pricey) boutiques.

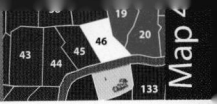

Banks

- **Abbey** • 138 King's Rd
- **Barclays** • 30 Sloane Sq
- **Lloyds** • 33 King's Rd

Coffee

- **Costa** • 138 King's Rd
- **Eat.** • 82 King's Rd
- **Pret A Manger** • 80 King's Rd
- **Starbucks** • 35 Sloane Ave
- **Starbucks** • 128 King's Rd

Post Offices

- **Kings Walk** • 122 King's Rd

Restaurants

- **The Admiral Codrington** • 17 Mossop St
- **Bibendum Restaurant & Oyster Bar** • 81 Fulham Rd
- **Blushes Cafe** • 52 King's Rd
- **Foxtrot Oscar** • 79 Royal Hospital Rd
- **Gordon Ramsay** • 68 Royal Hospital Rd
- **Le Cercle** • 1 Wilbraham Pl
- **Tom Aikens** • 43 Elystan St

Shopping

- **Fresh Line** • 55 King's Rd
- **Peter Jones** • Sloan Sq
- **Space NK Apothecary** • 307 King's Rd

Supermarkets

- **Sainsbury's** • 75 Sloane Ave

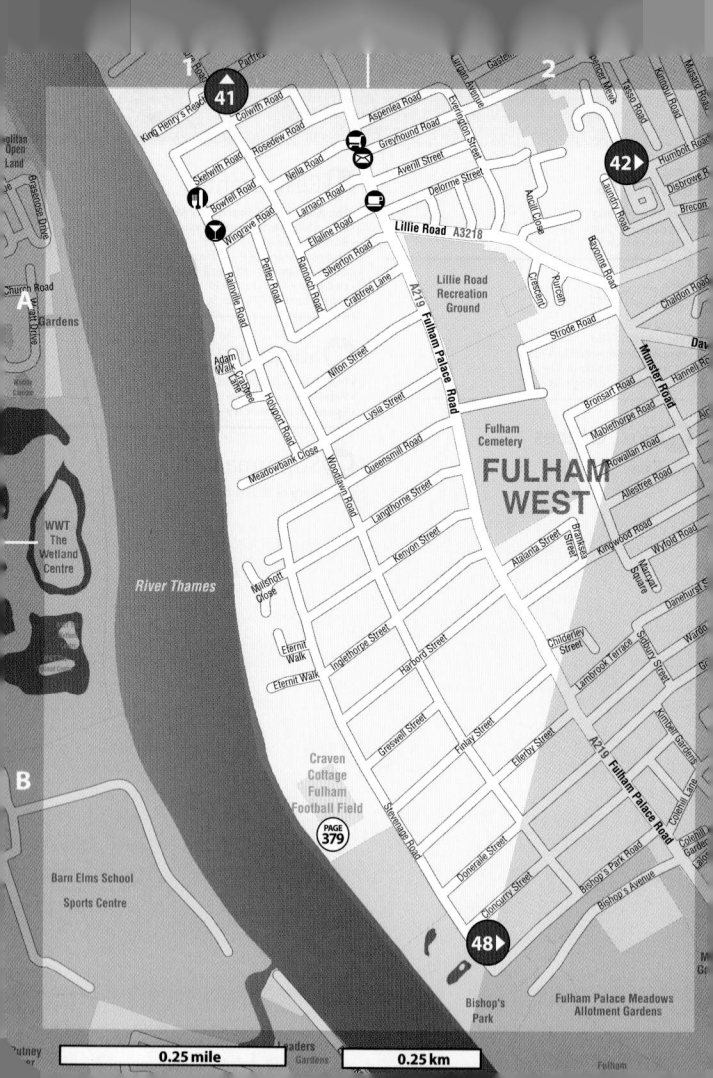
1
2
A
B
41
42
48
King Henry's Road
Colinth Road
Aspenlea Road
Everington Street
Greyhound Road
Rosedew Road
Nella Road
Averill Street
Delorme Street
Skelemth Road
Bosfell Road
Lanhach Road
Elaine Road
Lillie Road A3218
Bainville Road
Crabtree Lane
Lillie Road Recreation Ground
A219 Fulham Palace Road
Adam Walk
Niton Street
Lysia Street
Hoopert Road
Meadowbank Close
Queensmill Road
Langthorne Street
Kenyon Street
Fulham Cemetery
FULHAM WEST
Munster Road
Mabethorpe Road
Alleastree Road
Kingwood Road
Wyfold Road
Alabama Street
Bishop's Street
Marcel Square
Childerley Street
Lambrook Terrace
Salbury Street
Kimber Gardens
Colehill Lane
Eternit Walk
Ingelthorpe Street
Harbord Street
Greswell Street
Finlay Street
Elerby Street
Craven Cottage Fulham Football Field
PAGE 379
Stevenage Road
Donnelle Street
Bishop's Park Road
Bishop's Avenue
Bishop's Park
Fulham Palace Meadows Allotment Gardens
WWT The Wetland Centre
River Thames
Barn Elms School Sports Centre
Putney
Leaders Gardens
Fulham
0.25 mile
0.25 km

This area is an estate agent's wet dream. Leafy, well-heeled, on the river, the thing is, you can't afford to move here so dream on. Instead, live the lie—make the most of the riverside and grab a pint at The Crabtree Tavern. Now you're tipsy, head to The River Café where you'll feel less pained shelling out for top-notch, dead-posh grub.

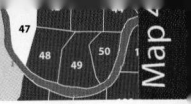

Coffee

• **Starbucks** • 220 Fulham Palace Rd

Nightlife

• **The Crabtree Tavern** • Rainville Rd

Post Offices

• **Fulham Palace Road** • 185 Fulham Palace Rd

Restaurants

• **The River Café** • Thames Wharf, Rainville Rd

Supermarkets

• **Sainsbury's** • 179 Fulham Palace Rd

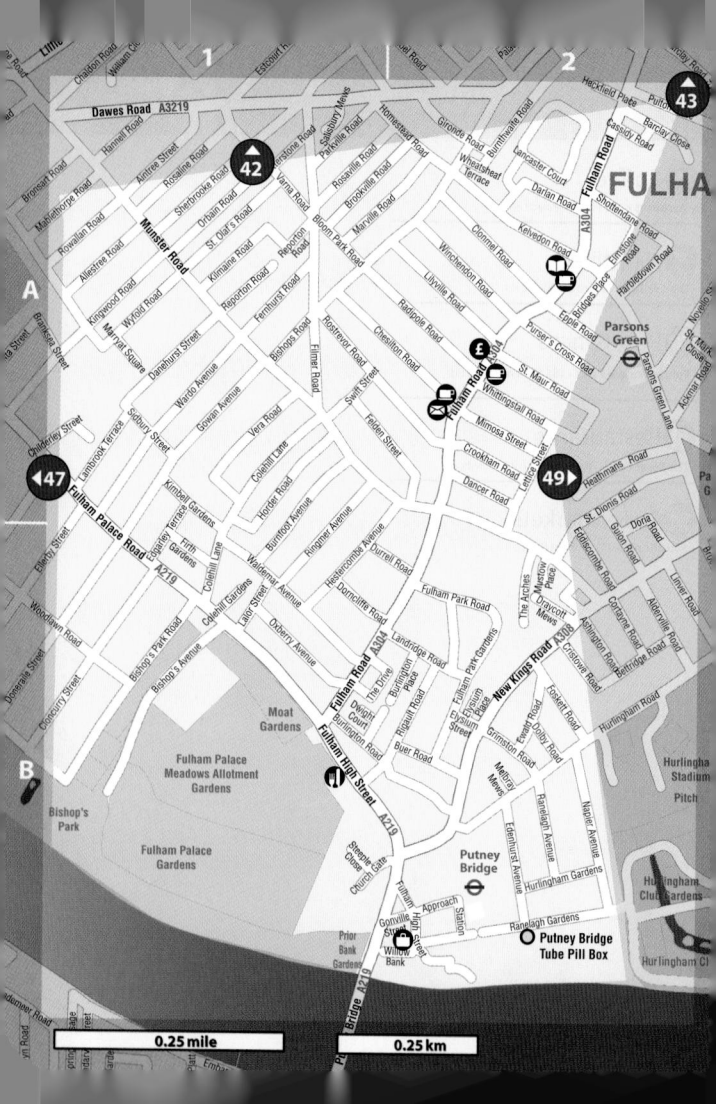
1
2
A
B
Dawes Road A3219
Munster Road
Fulham Palace Road A219
Fulham Road A304
Fulham High Street A219
New Kings Road A308
Putney Bridge Approach
Putney Bridge
Putney Bridge Tube Pill Box
Parsons Green
Moat Gardens
Fulham Palace Meadows Allotment Gardens
Fulham Palace Gardens
Bishop's Park
Hurlingham Stadium Pitch
Hurlingham Club Gardens
Hurlingham Cl
Prior Bank Gardens
Window Bank
Fulham Park Gardens
Fulham Park Road
Lillie Road
Eccleston Road
Hackfield Place
Cassidy Road
Barclay Close
Burnthwaite Road
Lancaster Court
Whitehead Terrace
Homestead Road
Girondie Road
Salisbury Mews
Parkville Road
Rosaville Road
Brookville Road
Minville Road
Bloom Park Road
Lama Road
Sherbrooke Road
Orbain Road
St. Olaf's Road
Rosaville Road
Antrim Street
Bronsart Road
Mallinckrodt Road
Rowallan Road
Alestree Road
Kingwood Road
Wyfold Road
Munster Square
Canalhurst Street
Wardlo Avenue
Gonzin Avenue
Vera Road
Sudbury Street
Lanbrook Terrace
Chilthing Street
Kimbell Gardens
Lightley Terrace
Farm Gardens
Coleridge Lane
Burnthwaite Road
Horder Road
Waldemar Avenue
Lalor Street
Coleridge Gardens
Odberry Avenue
Bishop's Park Road
Bishop's Avenue
Woodlawn Road
Donovan's Street
Doncaster Street
Elmer Road
Bishops Road
Fernhurst Road
Klimaine Road
Raporton Road
Chesilton Road
Swift Street
Felden Street
Ringmer Avenue
Heathcombe Avenue
Durrell Road
Dormcliffe Road
Landridge Road
Burlington Road
Burlington Place
The Drive
Dwight Court
Rigault Road
Buer Road
Church Gate
Sheepcote Close
Gonville Street
Lillie Road
Kelvedon Road
Oldermel Road
Winchendon Road
Lisville Road
Randpole Road
Bridges Place
Epple Road
Purser's Cross Road
St. Maur Road
Whitangstall Road
Mimosa Street
Crookham Road
Dancer Road
Lettis Street
Heathmans Road
St. Dionis Road
Doris Road
Eldon Road
Edithcombe Road
Coftarne Road
Aldensile Road
Limer Road
Ashington Road
Bettridge Road
Crisdown Road
Everard Road
Hurlingham Road
Mahony Mews
Ranelagh Avenue
Edenhurst Avenue
Hurlingham Gardens
Napier Avenue
Ranelagh Gardens
Station
The Arches
Marlow Place
Drycott Mews
Fulham Park Gardens
Lillie Road
Hackfield Place
Cassidy Road
Barclay Close
Burnthwaite Road
Lancaster Court
Whitehead Terrace
Girondie Road
Homestead

Expensive home to rivals Fulham and Chelsea FC with a strong possibility of encountering some Chanel-clad WAGS. Fulham Road is where the good stuff is, but mostly on Map 43. Be a dreamer and stare out at The Thames in Fulham Palace Gardens or next time you're at the tube station soak up some WWII history and look out for The Putney Bridge Tube Pill Box.

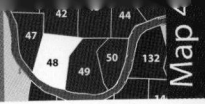

Banks

- **HSBC** • 593 Fulham

Coffee

- **Caffe Nero** • 717 Fulham Rd
- **Local Hero** • 640 Fulham Rd
- **Starbucks** • 809 Fulham Rd

Landmarks

- **Putney Bridge Tube Pill Box** • Putney Bridge Station

Libraries

- **Fulham Library** • 598 Fulham Rd

Post Offices

- **Fulham** • 815 Fulham Rd

Restaurants

- **Fisher's Chips** • 19 Fulham High St

Shopping

- **Hurlingham Books** • 91 Fulham High St

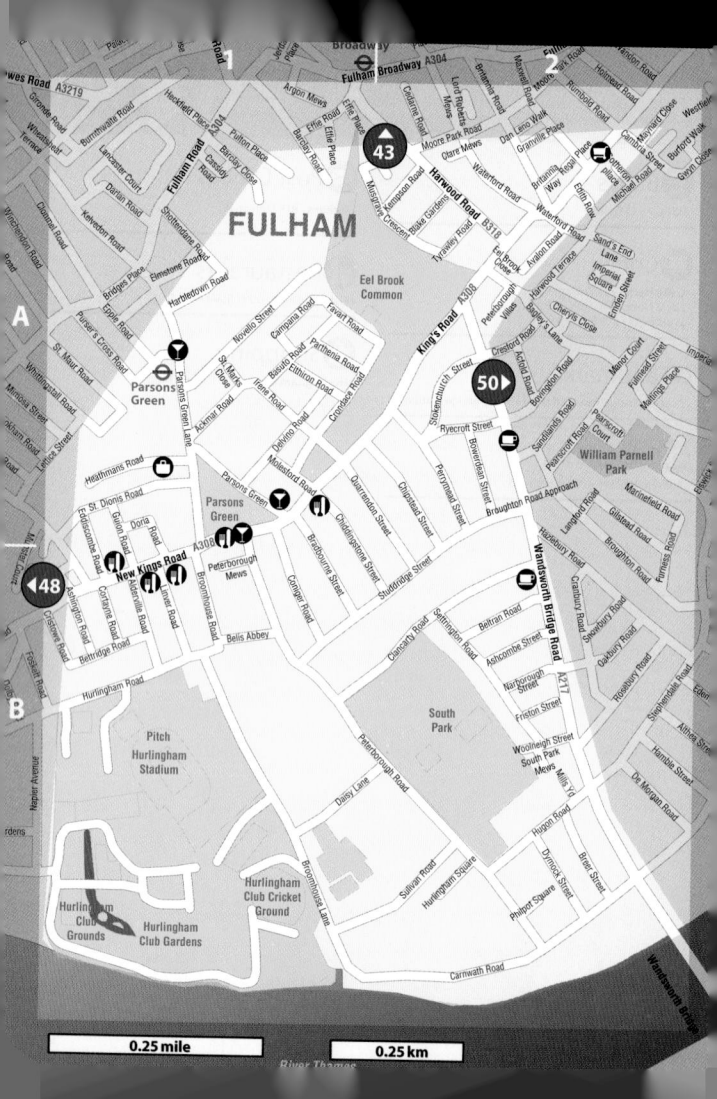
FULHAM
Eel Brook Common
Parsons Green
Parsons Green
New Kings Road
Peterborough Mews
Pitch Hurlingham Stadium
South Park
Hurlingham Club Grounds
Hurlingham Club Gardens
Hurlingham Club Cricket Ground
William Parnell Park
Fulham Broadway
Fulham Broadway A304
Harwood Road A318
King's Road A308
Fulham Road A304
Wandsworth Bridge Road A217
Broadway
Wandsworth Bridge
Carnwath Road
Broomhouse Lane
Peterborough Road
Hurlingham Road
Bishop's Lane
Broughton Road Approach
Broughton Road
Rivercroft Street
Sisterchurch Street
Bowerman Street
Peryminal Street
Chipstead Street
Dwarmouth Street
Chadlington Street
Studridge Street
Bradbourne Street
Broomhouse Road
Belis Abbey
Clancarty Road
St Dionis Road
Heathmans Road
Parsons Green Lane
Dalrymple Road
Moasford Road
Ackmar Road
Crombeck Road
Ethiston Road
Basilis Road
Parthenia Road
Campana Road
Farart Road
Novello Street
St Mark's Close
Bridges Place
Eyphil Road
Purser's Cross Road
St. Maur Road
Whittingstall Road
Munster Road
Lettice Street
Dalling Road
Dorna Road
Edbrooke Road
Cortland Road
Aldensle Road
Abbington Road
Bettridge Road
Crisdee Road
Fasbet Road
Napier Avenue
Argon Mews
Barclay Close
Pulton Place
Effie Place

You know you're in a classy neighbourhood when the kebab house (Kebab Kid) gets people travelling across London. Things here aren't cheap and you may be unnerved by all the people saying "terrific!" with their collars up. But they don't bite (despite their formidable buck teeth) so relax and enjoy a beer in The White Horse, known as the Sloaney Pony, or heavenly Sunday brunch at Duke on the Green.

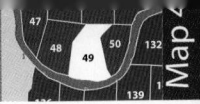

Coffee

- **Caffe Nero** • 142 Wandsworth Bridge Rd
- **Starbucks** • 95 Wandsworth Bridge Rd

Nightlife

- **Amuse Bouche** • 51 Parson's Green Ln
- **The Establishment** • Parson's Green Ln
- **The White Horse** • Parson's Green

Restaurants

- **De Cecco** • 189 New King's Rd
- **Duke on the Green** • 235 New Kings Rd
- **Ghillies** • 271 New King's Rd
- **Kebab Kid** • 90 New Kings Rd
- **Mao Tai** • New King's Rd

Shopping

- **Calumet Trading** • 10 Heathman's Rd

Supermarkets

- **Tesco** • 601 King's Rd

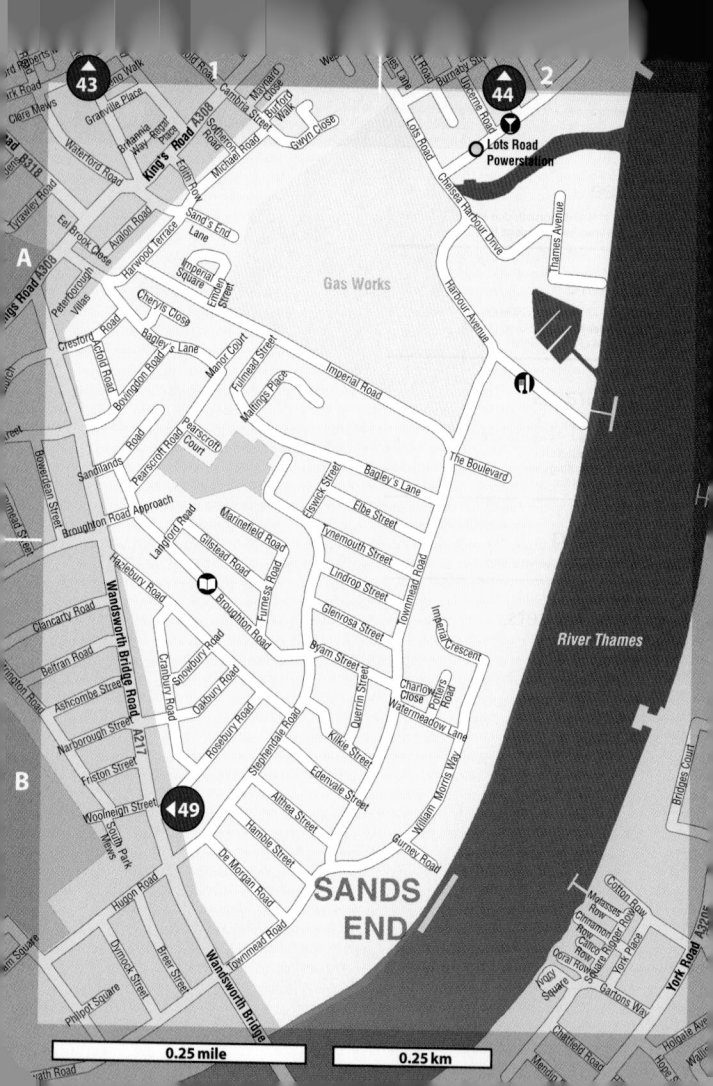
43
44
49
1
2
A
B
Granville Place
Cleve Mews
Waterford Road
King's Road A308
Britannia Way
Roper Place
Cambria Street
Mainard Close
Burford Walk
Garth Close
Michael Road
Lots Road
Burnley Street
Lacorne Road
Lots Road Powerstation
Chelsea Harbour Drive
Thames Avenue
Sand's End Lane
Avalon Road
Harwood Terrace
Ear Brook Close
Imperial Square
Gas Works
Harbour Avenue
Peterborough Villas
Cheryl's Close
Crestord Road
Bagley's Lane
Mayor Court
Fulmeat Street
Imperial Road
Maltings Place
Bowington Road
Pearscroft Road
Pearscroft Court
Sandilands Road
The Boulevard
Bowerdean Street
Broughton Road Approach
Lesvick Street
Elbe Street
Landford Road
Marmefield Road
Glistead Road
Tynemouth Street
Lindrop Street
Townmead Road
Hazlebury Road
Broughton Road
Furness Road
Glenrosa Street
Imperial Crescent
Clancarty Road
Wandsworth Bridge Road
Byam Street
Beltran Road
Ashcombe Street
Cranbury Road
Snowsbury Road
Cranbury Road
Watermeadow Lane
River Thames
Narborough Street
A217
Rosebury Road
Stephendale Road
Quarrin Street
Kilkie Street
Friston Street
Edenvale Street
William Morris Way
Woolneigh Street
Sulm Park Mews
Althea Street
Hamble Street
Burnley Road
Bridges Court
De Morgan Road
SANDS END
Hudson Road
Townmead Road
Cotton Row
Mossop's Row
Cinnamon Row
Ogram Row
York Place
Dymock Street
Brest Street
Wandsworth Bridge
Philpot Square
Holy Square
Gartons Way
York Road A3036
Chatfield Road
0.25 mile
0.25 km

Ask any Londoner where Sand's End resides and you will get blank looks or possibly a bemused 'you wot?' Go on, try it now, stop the nearest person and ask for Sand's End. The reason they don't know is because there's sod all there. Perhaps it's a cartographer's idea of a joke. Hilarious. One for fans of Industrial estates and Gas works only.

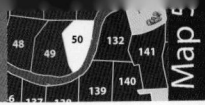

Landmarks

• **Lots Road Power Station** • Lots Rd

Libraries

• **Sands End Library** • 59 Broughton Rd

Nightlife

• **606 Club** • 90 Lots Rd

Restaurants

• **Deep** • The Boulevard, Imperial Wharf

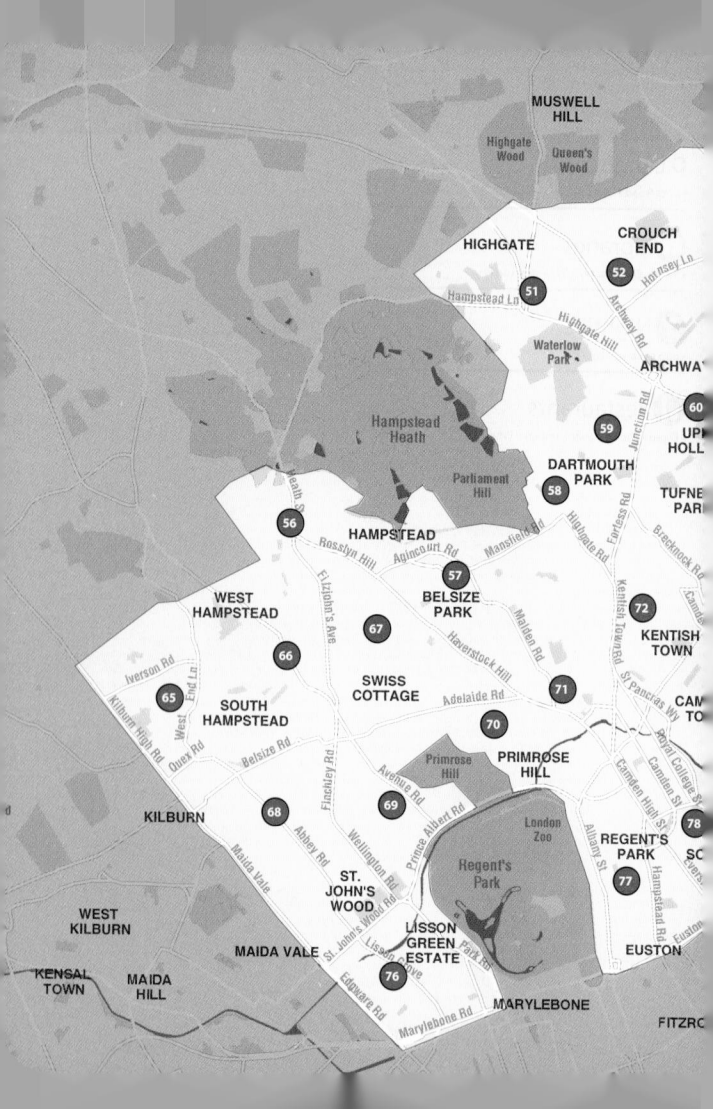
MUSWELL HILL
Highgate Wood
Queen's Wood
HIGHGATE
CROUCH END
Hornsey Ln
Hampstead Ln
Highgate Hill
Archway Rd
Waterlow Park
ARCHWA
Junction Rd
Hampstead Heath
Parliament Hill
DARTMOUTH PARK
TUFNE PARI
Fortess Rd
Highgate Rd
Brecknock Rd
Mansfield Rd
Agincourt Rd
Rosslyn Hill
HAMPSTEAD
Heath St
WEST HAMPSTEAD
Fitzjohn's Ave
BELSIZE PARK
Kentish Town Rd
KENTISH TOWN
Maiden Rd
Haverstock Hill
Iverson Rd
West End Ln
SOUTH HAMPSTEAD
SWISS COTTAGE
Adelaide Rd
St Pancras Wy
Kilburn High Rd
Ques Rd
Belsize Rd
Finchley Rd
Avenue Rd
Primrose Hill
PRIMROSE HILL
Royal Collège St
Camden Rd
Camden High St
KILBURN
Abbey Rd
Wellington Rd
Prince Albert Rd
London Zoo
Albany St
REGENT'S PARK
Maida Vale
ST. JOHN'S WOOD
Regent's Park
Hampstead Rd
WEST KILBURN
St. John's Wood Rd
LISSON GREEN ESTATE
Lisson Grove
Park Rd
MAIDA VALE
EUSTON
KENSAL TOWN
MAIDA HILL
Edgware Rd
Marylebone Rd
MARYLEBONE
FITZRO
51
52
56
57
58
59
60
65
66
67
68
69
70
71
72
76
77
78

HORNSEY
HARRINGAY
54
55
Wightman Rd
Green Lns
Finsbury Park
MANOR HOUSE
Seven Sisters Rd
Stroud Green Rd
BROWNSWOOD PARK
STOKE NEWINGTON
62
FINSBURY PARK
Blackstock Rd
Brownswood Rd
Clissold Park
61
63
Hornsey Rd
Tollington Rd
ARSENAL
Highbury Pk
64
Newington Green
Stoke Newington Rd
SHACKLEWELL
74
HOLLOWAY
HIGHBURY
75
LOWER HOLLOWAY
Highbury Grove
St. Paul's Rd
Balls Pond Rd
Caledonian Road
CANONBURY
KINGSLAND
BARNSBURY
Liverpool Rd
81
82
Canonbury Rd
Southgate Rd
DE BEAUVOIR TOWN
DALSTON
80
Essex Rd
Upper St
Boring St
79
Copenhagen St
ISLINGTON
Kingsland Rd
83
84
ANGEL
Shepherdess Walk
HOXTON
Pentonville Rd
City Rd
PENTONVILLE
FINSBURY
OLD STREET
SHOREDITCH
ST. LUKE'S
ST. PANCRAS
CLERKENWELL
FARRINGDON
BARBICAN
BROADGATE
BLOOMSBURY
HOLBORN
Springfield Park
Lee Valley Park
UPPER CLAPTON
LEA BRIDGE
Hackney Downs
LOWER CLAPTON
HACKNEY
LONDON FIELDS
SOUTH HACKNEY
HAGGERSTON
BETHNAL GREEN
SPITALFIELDS
BRICK LANE
WHITECHAPEL

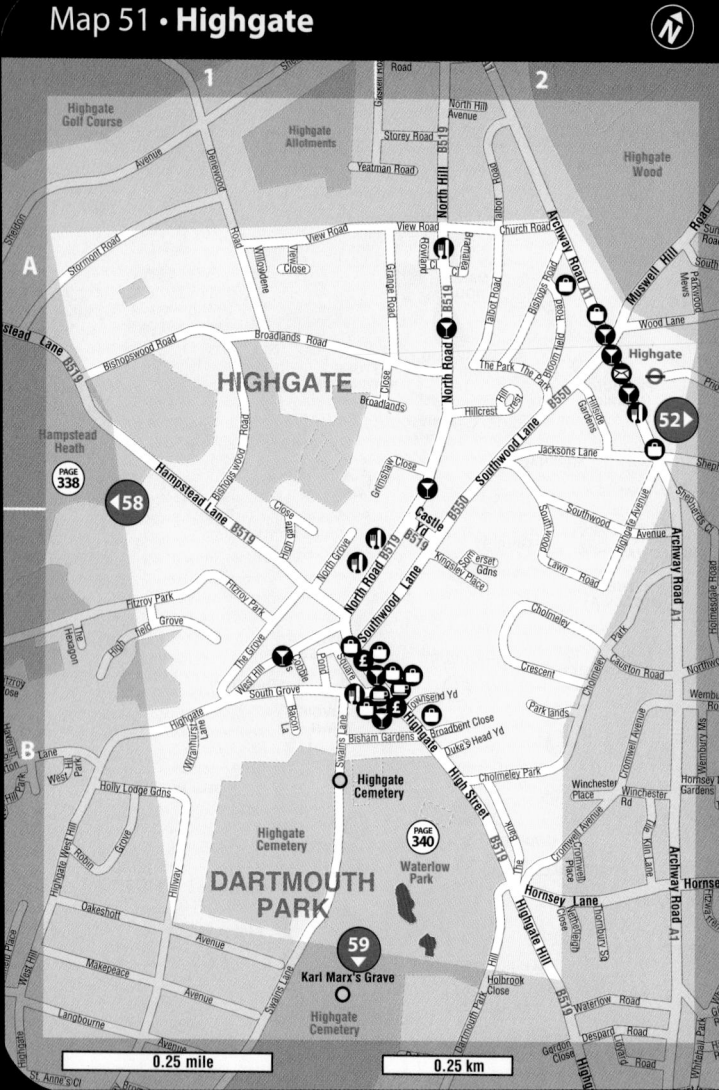
1
2
A
B
Highgate Golf Course
Highgate Allotments
Highgate Wood
North Hill Avenue
Storey Road
Yeatman Road
North Hill B519
Talbot Road
Church Road
View Road
Stormont Road
Willoughby Way
Close
Grange Road
Bertram Pl
Fortnam Pl
Bishop's Road
Archway Road A1
Muswell Hill Road
Wood Lane
Highgate
Broadlands Road
Bishopswood Road
HIGHGATE
North Road B519
The Park
Broom Hall
Hillcrest
Hillcrest Close
Southwood Lane B550
Hillside Gardens
52
Hampstead Heath
PAGE 338
58
Hampstead Lane B519
Bishopswood Road
Jacksons Lane
Grimshaw Close
Castle Rd B519
Kingsley Place
Southwood Avenue
Highgate Avenue
Lawn Road
Fitzroy Park
The Hexagon
High Gate
North Grove
The Grove
Southwood Lane
Cholmeley Park
Crescent
Cauton Road
West Hill
South Grove
Highgate Lane
Wrightsbury Lane
Bishop's Road
Swains Lane
Townsend Yd
Broadbent Close
Bisham Gardens
Duke's Head Yd
Highgate High Street B519
Park Lands
Holly Lodge Gdns
Highgate Cemetery
Winchester Place
Winchester Rd
Cromwell Avenue
Highgate West Hill
Robin Grove
Hillway
Oakeshott Avenue
Makepeace Avenue
Langbourne Avenue
PAGE 340
Waterlow Park
DARTMOUTH PARK
59
Karl Marx's Grave
Highgate Cemetery
Hornsey Lane
Hornsey Lane Gdns
Highgate Hill B519
Holbrook Close
Dartmouth Park Hill
Waterlow Road
Despard Road
Gordon Close
Archway Road A1
St Anne's Cl
0.25 mile
0.25 km

Get your fix of village life here. Sample quaint local shops (The Corner Shop) on the High Street or a selection of book, music, and charity shops on the grittier Archway Road side. There's plenty of food options, but for the true Highgate experience head to The Flask for great modern pub grub and drinks. The Boogaloo is still the local hipster venue of choice.

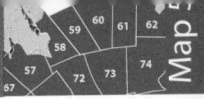

Banks

- **Barclays** • 56 Highgate High St
- **Lloyds** • 51 Highgate High St

Coffee

- **Caffe Nero** • 62 Highgate High St
- **Costa** • 66 Highgate High St

Landmarks

- **Highgate Cemetery** • 1 Swain's Lane
- **Karl Marx's grave** • Highgate Cemetry

Nightlife

- **The Angel Inn** • Highgate High St
- **The Boogaloo** • 312 Archway Rd
- **The Flask** • 77 Highgate West Hill
- **Highgate Inn** • 385 Archway Rd
- **Prince Of Wales** • 53 Highgate High St
- **The Victoria** • 28 N Hill
- **The Woodman** • 414 Archway Rd
- **The Wrestlers** • 98 North Rd

Post Offices

- **Highgate Near Station** • 361 Archway Rd

Restaurants

- **The Bull** • 13 North Hill Ave
- **Cafe Rouge** • 6 South Grove
- **Kiplings** • 100 North Rd
- **Papa Del's** • 347 Archway Rd
- **Red Lion And Sun** • 25 N Rd

Shopping

- **The Corner Shop** • 88 Highgate High St
- **Dragonfly Wholefoods** • 24 Highgate High Street
- **Highgate Butchers** • 76 Highgate High St
- **Hops N Pops** • 389 Archway Rd
- **Le Chocolatier** • 78 Highgate High St
- **Oxfam Bookshop, Highgate** • 47 Highgate High St
- **Second Layer Records** • 323 Archway Rd
- **Walter Castellazzo Design** • 84 Highgate High St
- **Wild Guitar** • 393 Archway Road

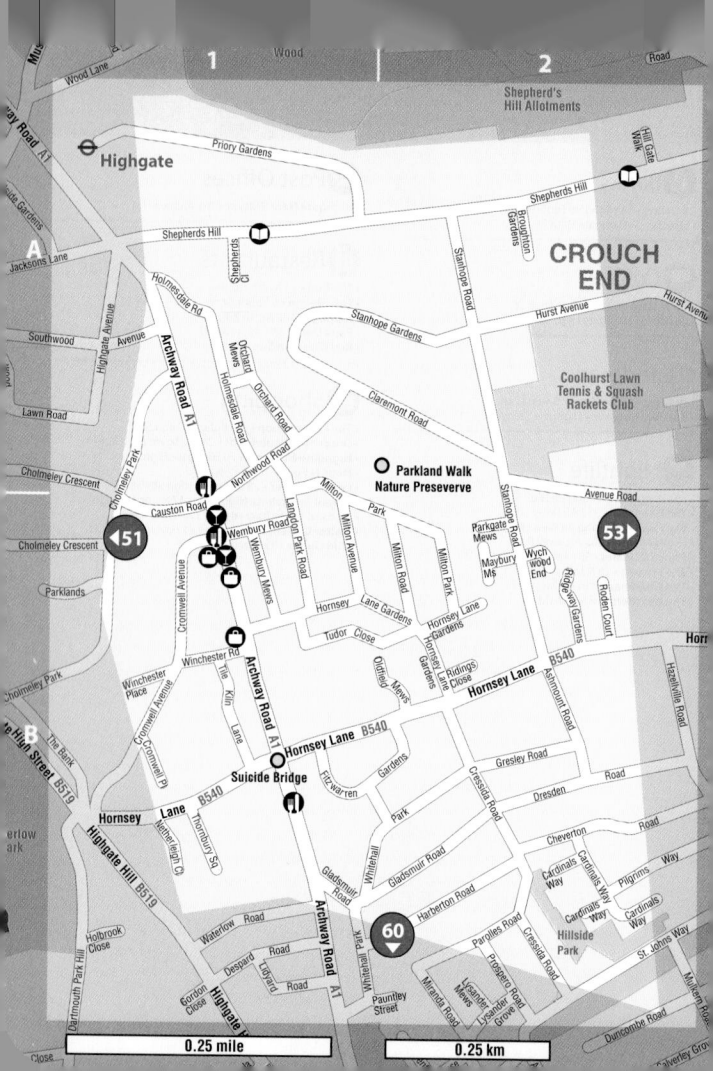
1
2
A
B
Wood
Wood Lane
Road
Shepherd's Hill Allotments
Highgate
Priory Gardens
Hill Gate Walk
Shepherds Hill
Broughton Gardens
CROUCH END
Jacksons Lane
Shepherds Cl
Stanhope Road
Holmesdale Rd
Hurst Avenue
Stanhope Gardens
Southwood Avenue
Highgate Avenue
Archway Road A1
Orchard Mews
Orchard Road
Coolhurst Lawn Tennis & Squash Rackets Club
Lawn Road
Claremont Road
Northwood Road
Parkland Walk Nature Preseverve
Cholmeley Crescent
Cholmeley Park
Causton Road
Milton Park
Avenue Road
51
Wembury Road
Langton Park Road
Milton Avenue
Milton Road
Milton Park
Parkgate Mews
Maybury Ms
Wychwood End
53
Parklands
Wembury Mews
Cromwell Avenue
Hornsey Lane Gardens
Hornsey Lane
Ridgeway Gardens
Roden Court
Tudor Close
Horn
Winchester Rd
Winchester Place
The Kiln Lane
Clifford Mews
Hornsey Lane Gardens
Ridings Close
Hornsey Lane B540
Hainault Hill Road
Cromwell Pl
The Bank
Hornsey Lane B540
Suicide Bridge
Fitzwarren Gardens
Gresley Road
Crescent Road
Dresden Road
Hornsey Lane B540
Thornburn Sq
Park
Cheverton Road
Highgate Hill B519
Whitehall
Gladsmuir Road
Cardinals Way
Pilgrims Way
Harberton Road
Waterlow Road
Gladsmuir Road
60
Hillside Park
St Johns Way
Holbrook Close
Desnard Road
Lorrard Road
Pangbourne Road
Crescent Road
Leander Mews
Leander Grove
Dartmouth Park Hill
Gordon Close
Highgate
Pauntley Street
Miranda Road
Duncombe Road
0.25 mile
0.25 km

Estate agents will hate the fact that we've dubbed the area between posh Highgate and Crouch End/Archway North and Archway Road is a grimy, gritty thoroughfare for an area with so much cash sloshing on either side. Nevertheless it's dotted with jewels like no-nonsense pub The Winchester, the odd Caipirinha Jazz Bar and the incredibly strange charity shop, The Green Room.

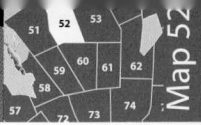

Landmarks

- **Parkland Walk Nature Reserve** • Parkland Walk
- **Suicide Bridge** • Hornsey Lane

Libraries

- **London Mennonite Centre Library** • 14 Shepherds Hill Heights

Nightlife

- **Caipirinha Jazz Bar** • 177 Archway Rd
- **The Winchester Pub Hotel** • 206 Archway Rd

Restaurants

- **Bengal Berties** • 172 Archway Rd
- **Fahrenheit** • 230 Archway Rd
- **The Lighthouse** • 179 Archway Rd

Shopping

- **Archway Video** • 220 Archway Rd
- **The Green Room** • 192 Archway Rd
- **Pax Guns** • 166 Archway Rd

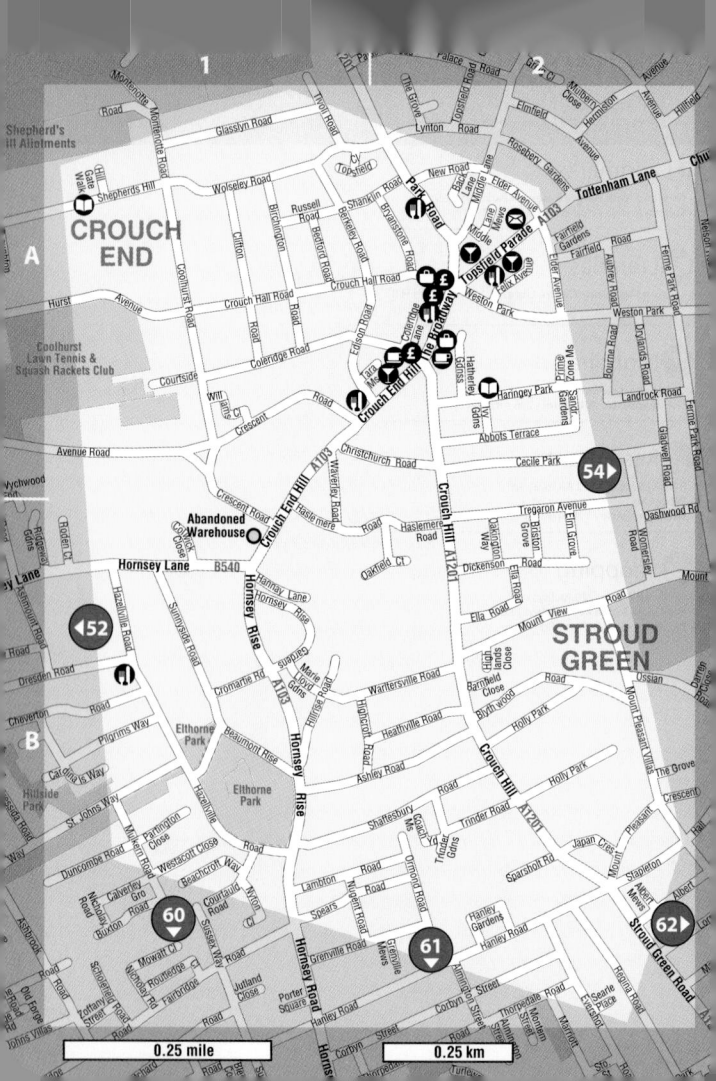
1
2
A
B
CROUCH END
STROUD GREEN
Shepherd's Hill Allotments
Coolhurst Lawn Tennis & Squash Rackets Club
Abandoned Warehouse
Elthorne Park
Tottenham Lane
Park Road
Tonsfield Parade
Crouch End Hill
The Broadway
Crouch End Hill A103
Crouch Hill A1201
Hornsey Rise
Hornsey Lane B540
Stroud Green Road
Hornsey Road
Haringey Park
Abbots Terrace
Cecile Park
Christchurch Road
Weston Park
Crouch Hall Road
Coleridge Road
Avenue Road
Hurst Avenue
Courtside
Wolseley Road
Shepherds Hill
Glasslyn Road
Lynton Road
Elmfield
Rosebery Gardens
Fairfield Road
Ferme Park Road
Landrock Road
Dashwood Rd
Tregaron Avenue
Dickenson Road
Ella Road
Mount View Road
Barnfield Close
Holly Park
Ashley Road
Heathville Road
Warntersville Road
Cromartie Rd
Dresden Road
Pilgrims Way
Beaumont Rise
Sunnyside Road
Hazelville Road
Hillfield Road
Hornsey Rise
Shaftesbury Road
Trinder Road
Japan Cres
Sparsholt Rd
Stapleton
Lambton Road
Ormond Road
Stroud Green Road
Harley Road
Grenville Road
Corbyn Street
Porter Square
Juttland Close
Sussex Way
Courtauld Road
Beachcroft Way
Westcroft Close
Dunromite Road
Parkington Close
St Johns Way
Hillside Park
Chevington Road
Cathcart Way
Ashbrook Road
Old Farm Rd
Johns Villas
Mowan Cl
Nicholas Rd
Fairbridge Rd
Schoolfield Street
Zafiary Street
Nicholson Road
Buxton Road
Galveley Gro
Montenotte Road
Hillfield Avenue
Mulberry Close
Hermiston Avenue
Palace Road
Tonsfield Road
The Grove
Elder Avenue
Aubrey Road
Bounce Road
Dorlands Road
Gladwell Road
Haringey Park
Hatherley Gdns
Tara Mews
Crouch End Hill
Hasleme Road
Briston Grove
Elm Grove
Mount Pleasant Villas
Ossian Road
Highlands Close
Trinder Gdns
Harley Gardens
Eminville Mews
Thorpedale Road
Albert Mews
Mount Pleasant Cres
Coach Yd
Coolhurst Road

Crouch End was nominated in the famous "Crap Towns" book a few years ago under the heading "The Tyranny Of Pesto." Which is a neat way of saying that it's a nice, middle class place with baby-buggies jack-knifing along the crowded streets. Banners does a mean breakfast, if you can live with the hordes of screaming brats.

Banks

- **Abbey** • 5 The Broadway
- **Barclays** • 8 The Broadway
- **Lloyds** • 34 The Broadway

Coffee

- **Spiazzo** • 26 The Broadway
- **Starbucks** • 7 The Broadway

Landmarks

- **Abandoned Warehouse** • Parkland Walk

Libraries

- **Highgate Library** • Shepherds Hill
- **Hornsey Library** • Haringey Park

Nightlife

- **Harringay Arms** • 153 Crouch Hill
- **Queens Pub & Dining Rooms** • 26 Broadway Parade
- **The Wishing Well** • 22 Topsfield Parade, Tottenham Lane

Post Offices

- **Crouch End** • 28 Topsfield Parade

Restaurants

- **Banners** • 21 Park Rd
- **Hot Pepper Jelly** • 11 Broadway Parade
- **Milou's on the Hill** • 83 Hazellville Rd
- **Piya Cafe** • 59 The Broadway
- **Thaitanic** • 66 Crouch End Hill

Shopping

- **Haelen Centre** • 41 The Broadway
- **Walter Purkis And Sons** • 17 The Broadway

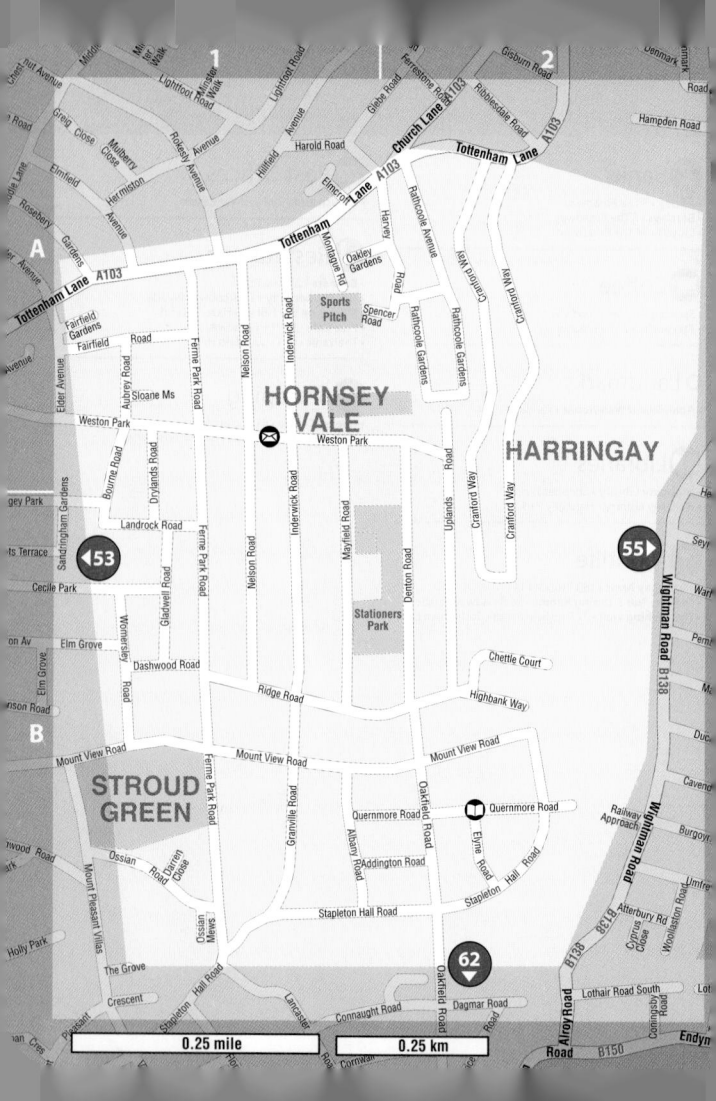
HORNSEY VALE
HARRINGAY
STROUD GREEN
Sports Pitch
Stationers Park
Tottenham Lane A103
Church Lane A103
Wightman Road B138
Alroy Road B150
Lightfoot Road
Harold Road
Hillfield Avenue
Rosebery Avenue
Mulberry Close
Greig Close
Elmfield Avenue
Hermiston Avenue
Gisburn Road
Hampden Road
Rhiblesdale Road
Glebe Road
Perrestone Road
Elmcroft Avenue
Harvey Road
Rathcoole Avenue
Rathcoole Gardens
Cranford Way
Oakley Gardens
Spencer Road
Fairfield Road
Fairfield Gardens
Nelson Road
Inderwick Road
Ferme Park Road
Aubrey Road
Sloane Ms
Weston Park
Bourne Road
Drylands Road
Elder Avenue
Sandringham Gardens
Landrock Road
Cecile Park
Gladwell Road
Womersley Road
Elm Grove
Dashwood Road
Ridge Road
Mayfield Road
Denton Road
Chettle Court
Highbank Way
Mount View Road
Granville Road
Oakfield Road
Quernmore Road
Albany Road
Elyne Road
Addington Road
Stapleton Hall Road
Ossian Road
Ossian Close
Mount Pleasant Villas
The Grove
Crescent
Lancaster Road
Connaught Road
Dagmar Road
Lothair Road South
Coningsby Road
Cornwallis Road
Endymion Road
Railway Approach
Burgoyne Road
Afterbury Rd
Cyprus Close
Seymour Road
Warham Road
Permit
Duck
Cavendish
Holly Park
Terrace
Avenue
Road
Lane
Gardens
Middle
Lightfoot Road
Greig Close
Mulberry Close
Elmfield Avenue
Hermiston Avenue
Rosebery Avenue
Hillfield Avenue
Harold Road
Glebe Road
Perrestone Road
Rhiblesdale Road
Gisburn Road
Denmark Road
Hampden

People who live here will probably say they live in Crouch End or Stroud Green. Partly because it sounds better and partly because most people have no idea where Hornsey is. It's an area bullied on all sides by bigger, brasher neighbourhoods like middle class Crouch End and gritty Green Lanes with the locals taking refuge in ferociously unpretentious pubs like The Wishing Well (Map 53).

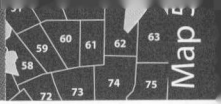

Libraries

• **Stroud Green Library** • Quernmore Rd

Post Offices

• **Weston Park** • 89 Weston Park

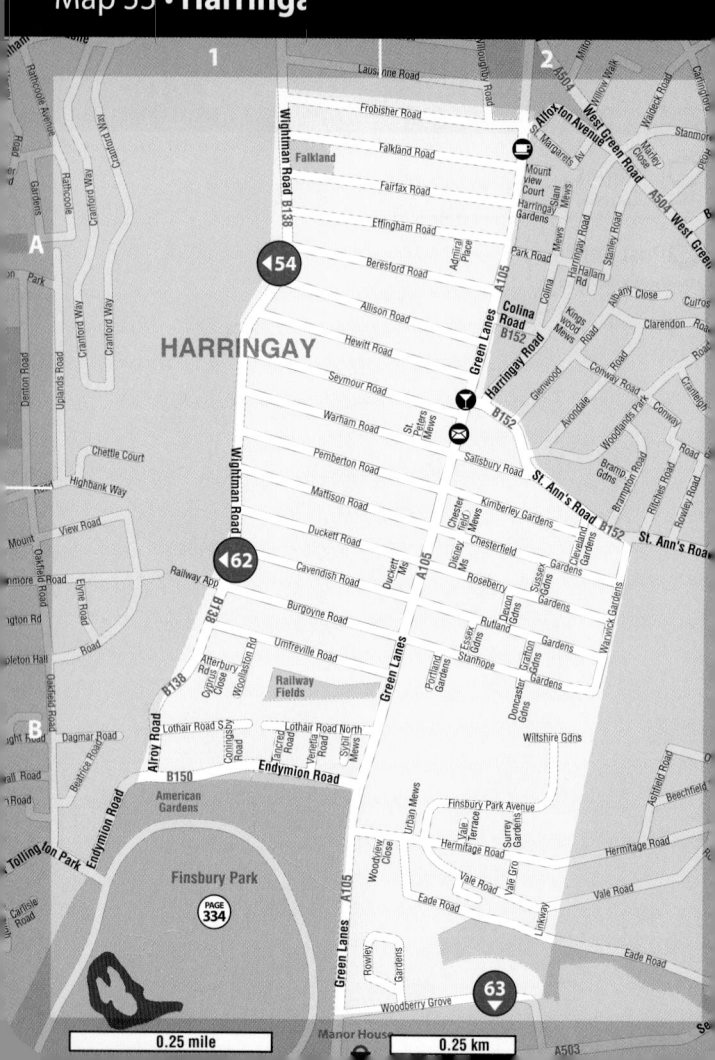
1
2
A
B
Lauderdale Road
Frobisher Road
Falkland Road
Fairfax Road
Effingham Road
Beresford Road
Allison Road
Hewitt Road
Seymour Road
Warham Road
Pemberton Road
Mattison Road
Duckett Road
Cavendish Road
Burgoyne Road
Umfreville Road
Railway App
Wightman Road B138
Falkland
154
162
HARRINGAY
Green Lanes A105
Colina Road B152
Harringay Road
B152
St. Ann's Road
St. Ann's Road B152
Salisbury Road
Kimberley Gardens
Chesterfield
Roseberry
Rutland Gdns
Starnhope
Portland Gardens
Doncaster Gdns
Wiltshire Gdns
Grafton Gdns
Warwick Gardens
Sussex Gdns
Essex Gdns
Devon Gdns
Cleveland Gardens
Duckett Rd
Disney Rd
Chester Mews
St Davids Mews
Park Road
Admiral Place
Mount View Court
Harringay Gardens
Stuart Mews
Stanley Road
Harringay Road
Hallam Rd
Albany Close
Curros
Clarendon Road
Knox Wood Mews
Conway Road
Glenwood
Avondale
Woodlands Park
Bramp Gdns
Brampton Road
Ritches Road
Rowley Road
Cranleigh
Alloxton Avenue
West Green Road
A504 West Green
St Margarets Av
Willow Walk
Waldeck Road
Darlington
Stanmore
Manley Close
Railway Fields
Alroy Road
Lothair Road S
Lothair Road North
Endymion Road
B150
B138
Coningsby Road
Dancrad Road
Venetia Road
Sylvia Mews
Afterbury Close
Ronald Close
Woolleston Rd
Dagmar Road
Beatrice Road
American Gardens
Finsbury Park
PAGE 334
Tollington Park
Finsbury Park Avenue
Urban Mews
Hermitage Road
Vale Terrace
Surrey Gardens
Vale Gro
Vale Road
Eade Road
Linkway
Woodville Close
Rowley Gardens
Woodberry Grove
63
Manor House
A503
Ashfield Road
Beachfield
Cranford Way
Rathcoole Avenue
Rathcoole Way
Uplands Road
Denton Road
Chettle Court
Highbank Way
View Road
Oakfield Road
Elyne Road
Mount
Carlisle Road
0.25 mile
0.25 km

One of the only places in the world where Turks, Turkish Cypriots and Greek Cypriots live together happily, a stroll up Green Lanes means two things: eating and drinking. Any of the little Cypriot or Turkish restaurants will fill you handsomely. Alcoholic respite can be found in the grand Salisbury.

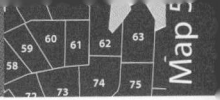

Coffee

• **Cafe Delight** • 351 Green Lanes

Nightlife

• **The Salisbury** • 1 Grand Parade, Green Lanes

Post Offices

• **Harringay** • 509 Green Lanes

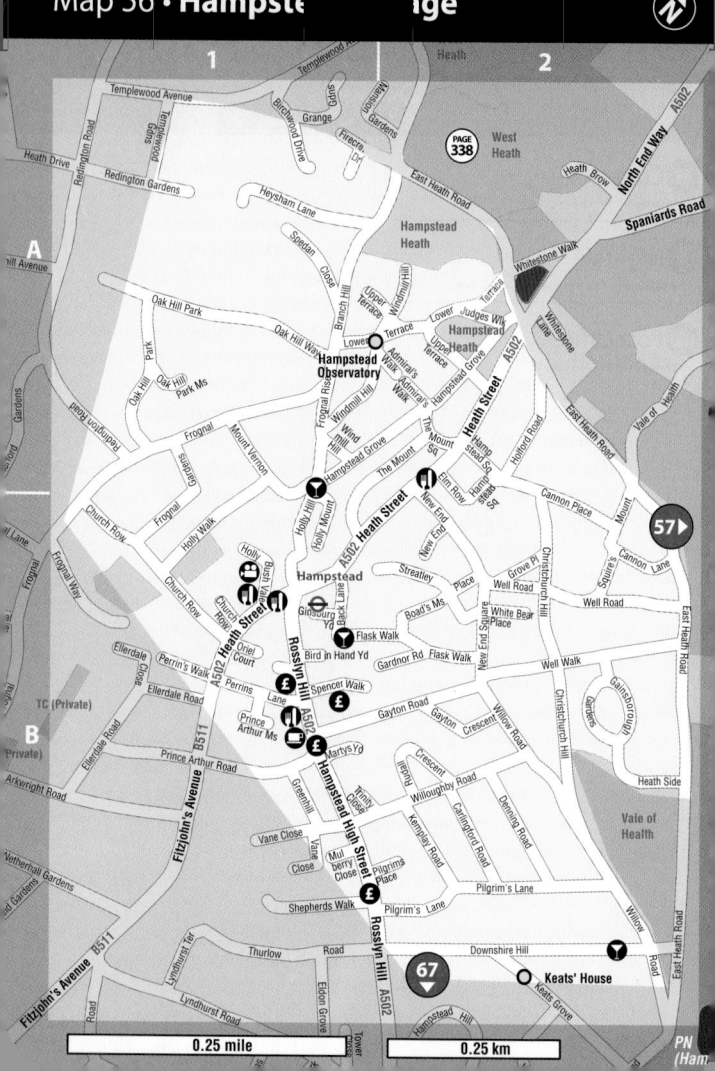
1
2
A
B
Heath
Templewood Avenue
Templewood Gdns
Birchwood Drive
Grange
Grange Gdns
Harmood Gardens
Fitzroy Dr
PAGE 338
West Heath
Heath Drive
Redington Road
Redington Gardens
Heysham Lane
East Heath Road
Heath Brow
North End Way
A502
Spaniards Road
Hampstead Heath
Sandan Close
Branch Hill
Upper Terrace
Windmill Hill
Whitestone Walk
Whitestone Lane
Oak Hill Park
Oak Hill Wk
Oak Hill Park Ms
Oak Hill Pk
Lower Terrace
Hampstead Observatory
Admiral's Walk
Admiral's Walk
Hampstead Grove
Judges Wk
Hampstead Heath
Heath Street
Frognal Rise
Windmill Hill
Wind Hill
Hampstead Grove
The Mount
The Mount Sq
Hampstead Sq
Holford Road
East Heath Road
Vale of Health
Redington Road
Frognal
Mount Vernon
Gardens
Church Row
Holly Walk
Holly Mount
Holly Hill
Cannon Place
Mount
57
Frognal Way
Hampstead
Streatley Place
Grove Pk
Well Road
Square's
Cannon Lane
Church Row
Church Hill
Oriel Court
Ginsburg Yd
Back Lane
Board's Ms
White Bear Place
Well Road
Flask Walk
Bird in Hand Yd
Gardnor Rd
Flask Walk
New End Square
Well Walk
Ellerdale Close
Perrin's Walk
Perrins Lane
Spencer Walk
Ellerdale Road
Prince Arthur Ms
Gayton Road
Gayton Crescent
Willow Road
Christchurch Hill
Gainsborough Gdns
TC (Private)
Ellerdale Road
Prince Arthur Road
B511
Martys Yd
Crescent
Willoughby Road
Heath Side
Arkwright Road
Fitzjohn's Avenue
Greenhill
Hampstead High Street
Holly Close
Kemplay Road
Carlingford Road
Downshire Road
Vale of Health
Vane Close
Vane Close
Mulberry Close
Pilgrims Place
Vetherhall Gardens
Shepherds Walk
Pilgrim's Lane
Willow Road
Lyndhurst Ter
Thurlow Road
Downshire Hill
67
Keats' House
Keats Grove
Lyndhurst Road
Elton Grove
Hampstead Hill
Tower
Rossyln Hill
A502
0.25 mile
0.25 km

Leafy Hampstead Village is as genteel and calm as you're going to get. It's a literary, suburban place where Ye Olde England has been commodified and sold back to the yuppies, but there's still quiet pleasures to be had. Louis Patisserie is great for cakes and the Holly Bush is a quaint 17th Century oaky heaven. Keats wrote Ode To a Nightingale about some bird around here.

Banks

- **Barclays** • 28 Hampstead High St
- **HSBC** • 12 Hampstead High St
- **Lloyds** • 40 Rosslyn Hill
- **NatWest** • 25 Hampstead High St

Cinemas

- **Everyman Cinema Club** • 5 Hollybush Vale

Coffee

- **Caffe Nero** • 1 Hampstead High St

Landmarks

- **Hampstead Observatory** • Lower Terrace
- **Keats' House** • Keats Grove

Nightlife

- **The Flask** • 14 Flask Walk
- **The Freemasons Arms** • 32 Downshire Hill
- **Holly Bush** • 22 Holly Mount

Restaurants

- **Bacchus Greek Taverna** • 37 Heath St
- **La Creperie De Hampstead** • 77 Hampstead High St
- **The Louis Patisserie** • 32 Heath St
- **Tinseltown** • 104 Heath St

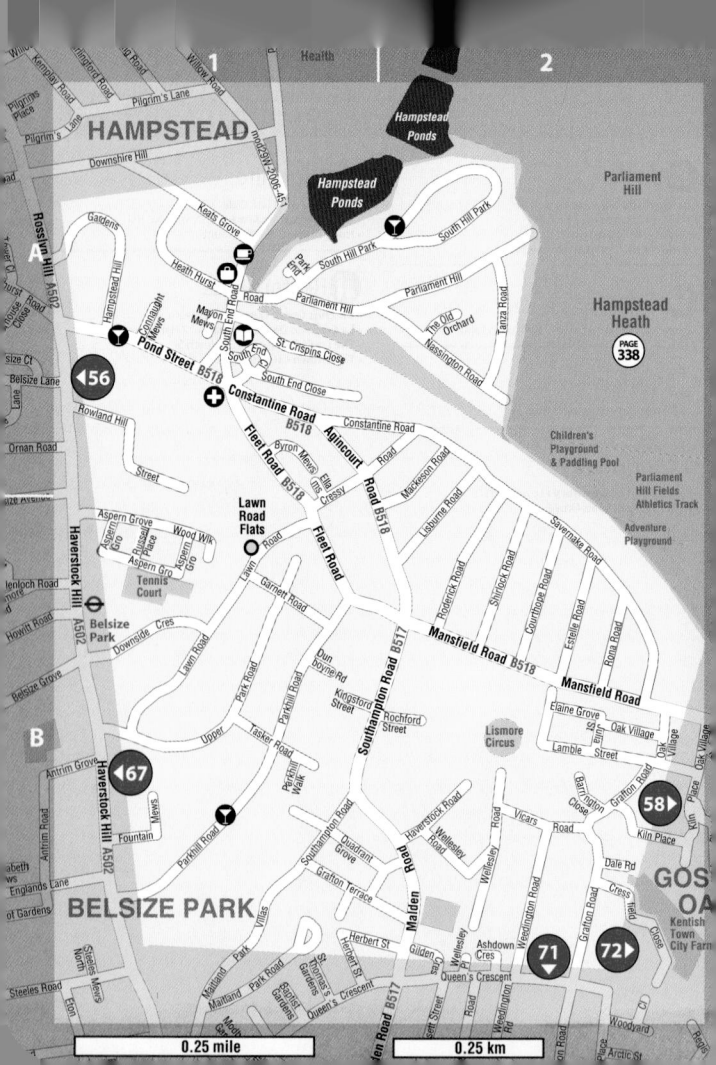
1
2
A
B
Health
HAMPSTEAD
Hampstead Ponds
Hampstead Ponds
Parliament Hill
Hampstead Heath
PAGE 338
Pilgrim's Place
Pilgrim's Lane
Downshire Hill
Rosslyn Hill A502
Gardens
Keats Grove
Heath Hurst
Hampstead Hill
Heath Hurst Road
Parliament Hill
South Hill Park
Mayor Mews
Kenwarden Mews
South End Road
South End
St Crispins Close
Pond Street B518
Constantine Road B518
South End Close
Rowland Hill
Belsize Lane
Ornan Road
Street
Fleet Road B518
Agincourt Road B518
Byron Mews
Ella Cressy
Mckeson Road
Lisburne Road
Tanza Road
The Old Orchard
Nassington Road
Children's Playground & Paddling Pool
Parliament Hill Fields Athletics Track
Adventure Playground
Lawn Road Flats
Fleet Road
Aspern Grove
Wood Wlk
Aspern Gro
Prince Place
Tennis Court
Haverstock Hill A502
Belsize Park
Downside Cres
Lawn Road
Garnett Road
Howitt Road
Belsize Grove
Mansfield Road B518
Mansfield Road
Rodenrick Road
Shirlock Road
Courthope Road
Estelle Road
Rona Road
Sawmake Road
Elaine Grove
Oak Village
Lamble Street
Lismore Circus
Dunboyne Rd
Kingsford Street
Rochford Street
Southampton Road B517
Park Road
Parkhill Road
Upper Tasker Road
Parkhill Walk
Antrim Grove
Fountain Mews
Parkhill Road
Haverstock Hill A502
Ashland Place
Barrington Close
Grafton Road
Kiln Place
Vicars Road
Dale Rd
Cresset Field Close
Haverstock Road
Wellesley Road
Quadrant Grove
Grafton Terrace
Malden Road
Herbert St
Gilden Cres
Ashdown Cres
Queen's Crescent
Mattland Park Villas
Mattland Park Road
St Thomas's Gardens
Belsize Gardens
Steeles Mews North
Steeles Road
Eton
Woodwarde Road
Woodyard
Arctic St
GOSPEL OAK
Kentish Town City Farm
58
67
71
72
156
0.25 mile
0.25 km

It might not be quite as posh as Hampstead Village but the streets to the south of the wonderful heath still have all the advantages of the area—the chance to nip into the woods and have sex with George Michael if one wishes (always ask first), browse in Daunt Books or hang out in nice pubs like The Magdala or Monkey Chews.

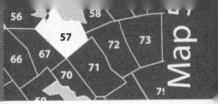

Coffee

- **Starbucks** • 5 South End Rd

Emergency Rooms

- **Royal Free Hospital** • Pond St

Landmarks

- **Lawn Road Flats** • Lawn Rd

Libraries

- **Heath Library** • Keats Grove

Nightlife

- **The Magdala** • 2 South Hill Park
- **Monkey Chews** • 2 Queen's Crescent
- **Roebuck** • 15 Pond St

Shopping

- **Daunt Books** • 51 S End Rd

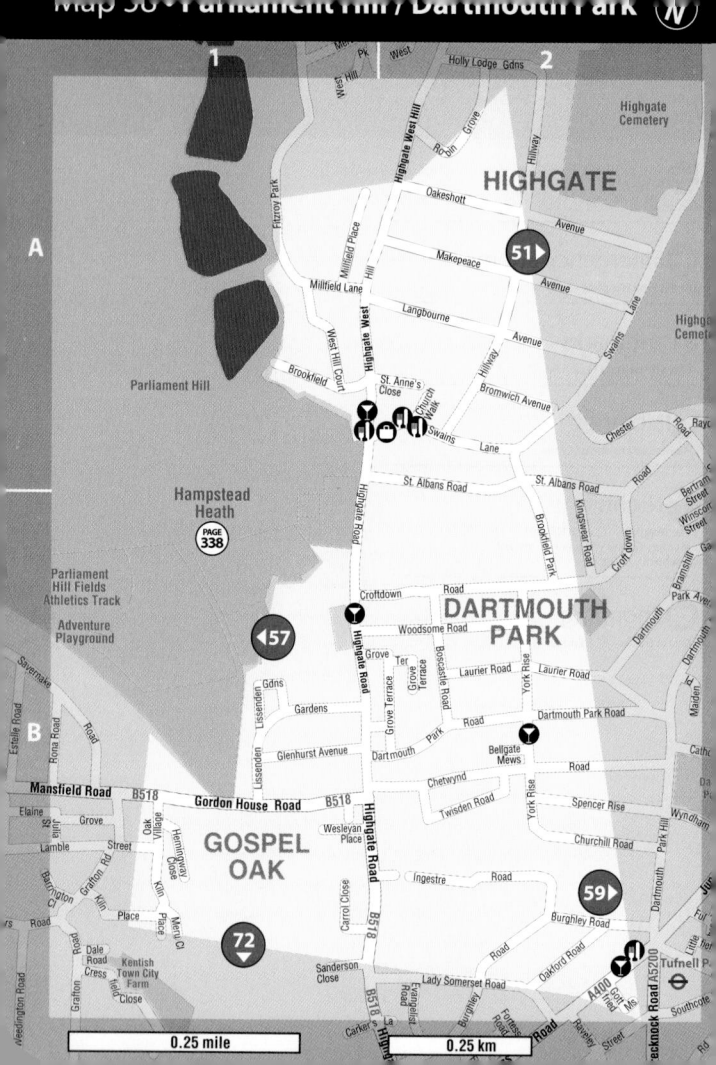
1
2
A
B
Holly Lodge Gdns
Highgate Cemetery
HIGHGATE
Highgate West Hill
Oakeshott
Avenue
Makepeace
Avenue
Millfield Lane
Langbourne
Avenue
Swains
Lane
Fitzroy Park
Millfield Place
Hill
West Hill Court
Brookfield
St. Anne's Close
Church Walk
Bromwich Avenue
Hillway
Parliament Hill
Hampstead Heath
PAGE 338
Parliament Hill Fields Athletics Track
Adventure Playground
Chester Road
St. Albans Road
Kingsmeat Road
Croftdown Road
Brookfield Park
Highgate Road
Croftdown Road
DARTMOUTH PARK
Woodsome Road
Grove Terrace
Boscastle Road
Laurier Road
York Rise
Dartmouth Park Road
Gardens
Lissenden
Glenhurst Avenue
Dartmouth Park Road
Belligate Mews
Chetwynd Road
Twisden Road
Spencer Rise
Churchill Road
Mansfield Road B518
Gordon House Road B518
Elaine Grove
Lamble Street
Oak Village
Hemingway Close
GOSPEL OAK
Wesleyan Place
Ingestre Road
Carol Close
Burghley Road
Dartmouth Park Hill
Grafton Rd
Kiln Place
Mercy Cl
Dale Road
Cress Field Close
Kentish Town City Farm
Sanderson Close
Lady Somerset Road
Oakford Road
Tufnell Park
Weedington Road
Carker's La
Burghley Road
Fortess Road
Navelley Road
Southcote Rd
Rona Road
Estelle Road
Swinnerton Rd
Grafton
Elaine
Dartmouth
Dartmouth Park Avenue
Bromshill
Winscombe Street
Bertram Street
Highgate West Hill
Highgate Cemetery
51
57
59
72
0.25 mile
0.25 km

Parliament Hill / Dartmouth Park

Mainly a leafy residential area, but there's a bunch of good eateries around Swain's Lane/Highgate West Hill. Try Kalendar for a variety of all-day brekkies or Al Parco for their excellent pizzas. Stock up with food and obscure but oh-so-tasty beers from Corks, then head for a celeb-spotting picnic on the heath.

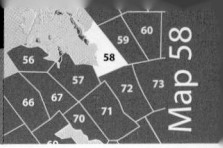

Nightlife

- **Bar Lorca** • 156 Fortress Rd
- **The Bull and Last** • 168 Highgate Rd
- **The Dartmouth Arms** • 35 York Rise
- **Duke of St. Albans** • Highgate Road

Restaurants

- **Al Parco** • 2 Highgate West Hill
- **Cafe Mozart** • 17 Swain's Ln
- **Kalendar** • 15 Swains Lane
- **Stingray Cafe** • 135 Fortess Rd

Shopping

- **Corks** • 9 Swain's Ln

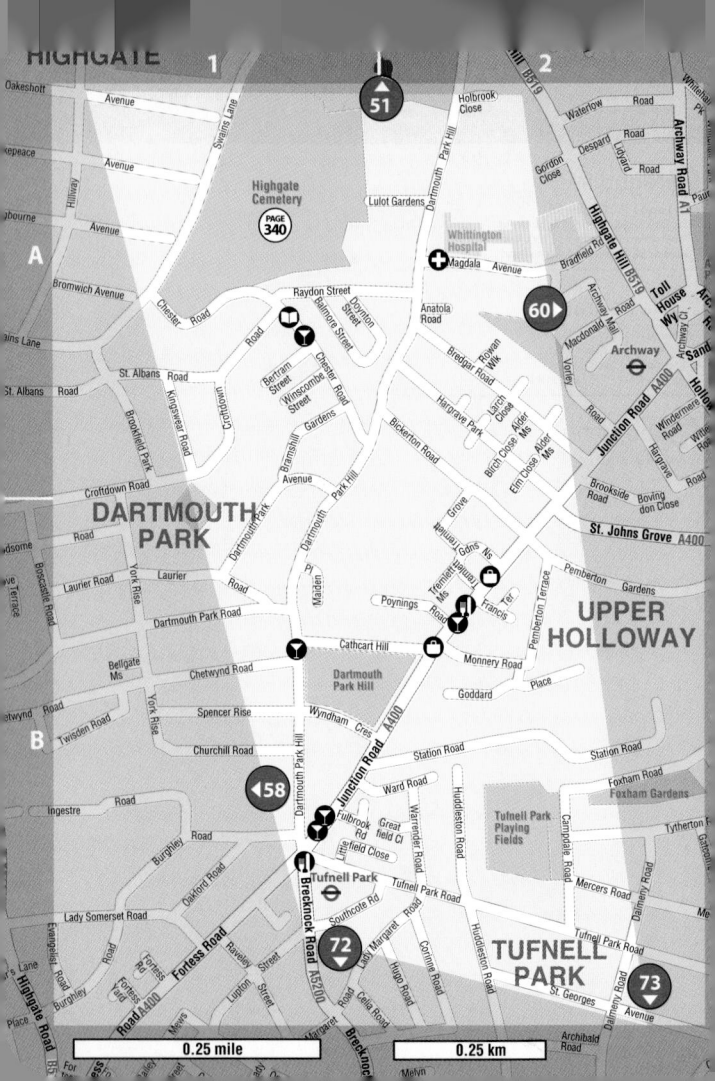
HIGHGATE
1
2
A
B
51
60
58
72
73
Highgate Cemetery
PAGE 340
Whittington Hospital
Magdala Avenue
Holbrook Close
Lulot Gardens
Dartmouth Park Hill
Swains Lane
Hillway
Oakeshott Avenue
Bromwich Avenue
Chester Road
Raydon Street
Belmore Street
Doyenton Street
Anatola Road
Bertram Street
Winscombe Street
Chester Road
St. Albans Road
Kingswear Road
Brookfield Park
Cholmeley Gardens
Bredgar Road
Rowan Wlk
Hargrave Park
Larch Close
Alder Ms
Birch Close
Elm Close
Bickerton Road
Brimsmill Avenue
Dartmouth Park Hill
Croftdown Road
DARTMOUTH PARK
Dartmouth Park
Dartmouth Park Pl
Maiden
Grove
Sons Ms
Trinity
Tremlett Ms
Poynings Road
Ter
Francis
Laurier Road
York Rise
Boscastle Road
Dartmouth Park Road
Cathcart Hill
Monnery Road
Chetwynd Road
Belgate Ms
Dartmouth Park Hill
Goddard Place
Spencer Rise
Wyndham Cres
Junction Road A400
Twisden Road
Churchill Road
Station Road
Ward Road
Fulbrook Rd
Great field Cl
Little field Close
Warmister Road
Huddleston Road
Tufnell Park Playing Fields
Campdale Road
Foxham Road
Foxham Gardens
Tytherton Rd
Ingestre Road
Burghley Road
Oakford Road
Tufnell Park
Breckenock Road A5200
Tufnell Park Road
Mercers Road
Dalmeny Road
Lady Somerset Road
Southcote Rd
Evangelina Road
Fortess Rd
Fortess Road
Ravelay Street
Lupton Street
St Margaret Road
Corinne Road
Huggin Road
Celia Road
Huddleston Road
TUFNELL PARK
St. Georges Avenue
Highgate Road B5
Mews
Fortnam Road
Breckenock
Melvin
Archibald Road
Waterlow Road
Despard Road
Lubard Road
Gordon Close
Archway Road A1
Highgate Hill B519
Toll House Wk
Archway Cl
Macdonald Ave
Archway
Junction Road A400
Vorley Road
Wildermere Road
Hargrave Road
Brookside Road
Boyding don Close
St. Johns Grove A400
Pemberton Terrace
Pemberton Gardens
UPPER HOLLOWAY
0.25 mile
0.25 km

Surrounded by the rougher Archway, Kentish Town, and Holloway—and immortalised by Simon Pegg in cult comedies Spaced and Shaun of the Dead–unassuming Tufnell Park has been quietly fashionable for years. Go for some posh pub grub at The Star or relax with a book and some homemade cake in Rustique.

Emergency Rooms

- **Whittington Hospital** • Magdala Ave

Libraries

- **Highgate Library** • Chester Rd

Nightlife

- **Boston Arms** • 178 Junction Rd
- **The Dome** • 178 Junction Rd
- **The Hideaway** • 114 Junction Rd
- **The Lord Palmerston** • 33 Dartmouth Park Hill
- **The Star** • 47 Chester Rd

Restaurants

- **Charuwan** • 110 Junction Rd
- **Rustique Cafe** • 142 Fortess Rd

Shopping

- **The Blue Carbuncle** • 130 Junction Rd
- **North London Adoption Centre** • 135 Junction Rd

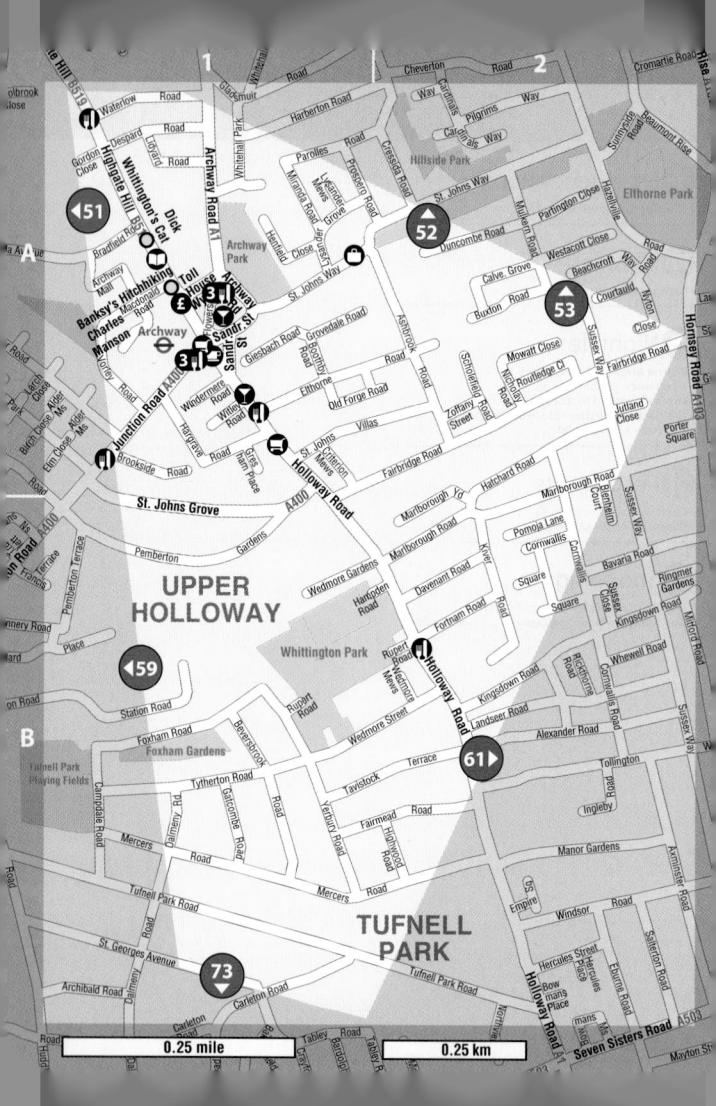
1
2
A
B
Cheverton Road
Cromartie Road
Waterlow Road
Harberton Road
Hillside Park
Elthorne Park
St. Johns Way
Partington Close
Duncombe Road
Westcott Close
Beachcroft Way
Calve Grove
Buxton Road
Courtauld Close
Archway Park
Archway Road A1
Whittington's Cat
Dick
Highgate Hill
Toll House
Banksy's Hitchhiking Charles Manson
Archway
Sandr. St.
Griesbach Road
Grovedale Road
Ethorne Road
Old Forge Road
Wordsmith Road
Mowatt Close
Routledge Cl.
Fairbridge Road
Hornsey Road A103
Junction Road A1
Brookside Road
Holloway Road
St. Johns Grove
A400
Hatchard Road
Marborough Rd.
Marborough Road
Pemberton Gardens
Pomoja Lane
Cornwallis Square
Bavaria Road
Westmore Gardens
Davenant Road
Hargrave Road
Fortnam Road
Kingsdown Road
Whitehall Road
UPPER HOLLOWAY
Whittington Park
Station Road
Foxham Road
Foxham Gardens
Tufnell Park Playing Fields
Westmore Street
Landseer Road
Alexander Road
Tollington Road
Tavistock Terrace
Tytherton Road
Fairmead Road
Manor Gardens
Mercers Road
Tufnell Park Road
TUFNELL PARK
St. Georges Avenue
Archibald Road
Carleton Road
Hercules Street
Seven Sisters Road A503
0.25 mile
0.25 km
51
52
53
59
61
73

Dirty and more than a little rough around the edges, Archway is generally pretty low on the fun scale. Most of the pubs are of the 'old man' variety and not terribly exciting. Head to La Voute for French-style café food and their funky inhouse art exhibitions. Charuwan (Map 59) and RRC are fighting (probably literally) for the local awesome-Thai-for-very-little-money crown.

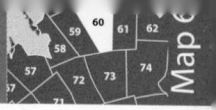

Banks

- **Lloyds** • 19 Highgate Hill

Coffee

- **Cafe Metro** • 4 Junction Rd

Landmarks

- **Banksy's Hitchhiking Charles Manson** • Tally Ho Corner (off Highgate Hill)
- **Dick Whittington's Cat** • Highgate Hill

Libraries

- **Archway Library** • Highgate Hill

Nightlife

- **Archway Tavern** • 1 Archway Close
- **The Mother Red Cap** • 665 Holloway Rd

Restaurants

- **Archgate Café** • 5 Junction Rd
- **Iceland Fish Bar** • 11 Archway Rd
- **Junction Café** • 61 Junction Rd
- **Kingfisher** • 657 Holloway Rd
- **La Voute** • 10 Archway Rd
- **Mosaic Café** • 24 Junction Rd
- **Nid Ting** • 533 Holloway Rd
- **RRC Thai Café** • 36 Highgate Hill
- **St Johns** • 91 Junction Rd
- **The Toll Gate** • 6 Archway Close

Shopping

- **Second Chance** • 79 St John's Way

Supermarkets

- **Co-Op** • 11 Junction Rd
- **Sainsbury's** • 643 Holloway Rd

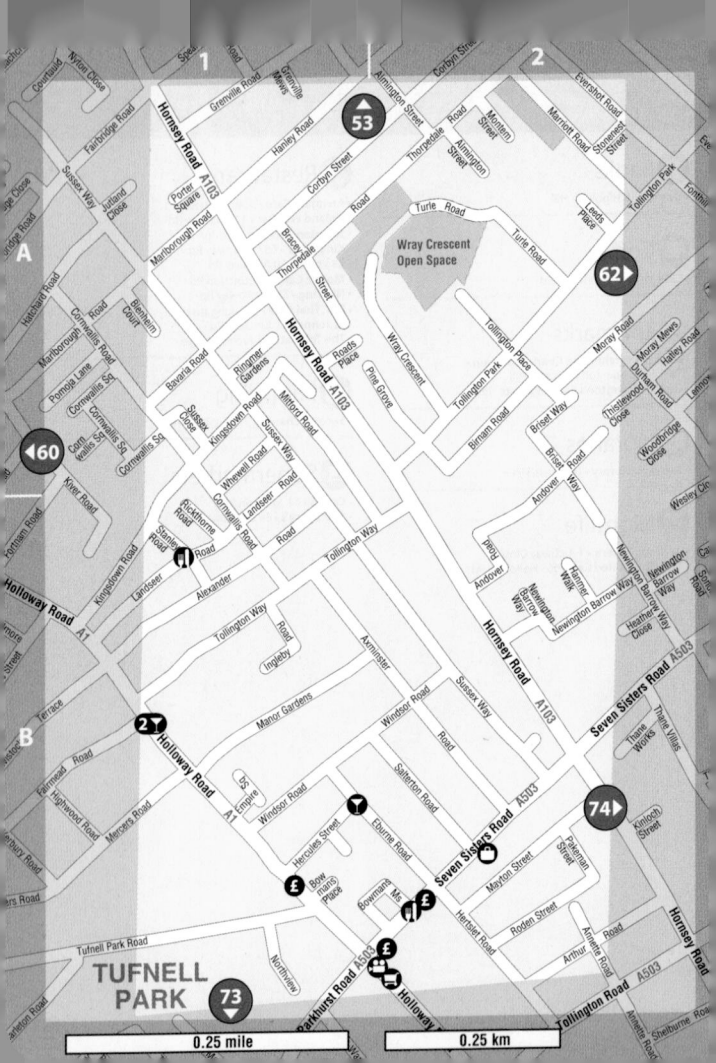
1
2
A
B
53
62
60
74
73
Wray Crescent Open Space
Hornsey Road A103
Holloway Road A1
Seven Sisters Road A503
Tollington Road A503
Holloway Road
Hornsey Road
Tufnell Park Road
Northview
Grenville Road
Grenville Mews
Hanley Road
Corbyn Street
Corbyn Road
Almington Street
Thorpedale Road
Monsam Street
Marriott Road
Everslied Road
Stroud Green Road
Tollington Park
Fairbridge Road
Sussex Way
Porter Square
Marlborough Road
Turle Road
Leeds Place
Thorpedale Street
Wray Crescent
Pine Grove
Tollington Place
Moray Road
Moray Mews
Hatley Road
Durham Road
Thistlewood Close
Woodbridge Close
Cornwallis Road
Cornwallis Sq.
Pomona Lane
Banaria Road
Roads Place
Burnham Road
Briset Way
Bridge Road
Andover Way
Andover
Newington Barrow Way
Newington Barrow Walk
Hammer
Heathcote Close
Kingsdown Road
Sussex Way
Milford Road
Wheelwell Road
Landseer Road
Rickthorne Road
Stanley Road
Kiver Road
Tufnell Park Road
Alexander
Tollington Way
Ingleby
Manor Gardens
Windsor Road
Salterton Road
Hercules Street
Bourne Road
Mayton Street
Rodney Street
Arthur Road
Annette Road
Shelburne Road
Kinloch Street
Thane Works
Fairmead Road
Highwood Road
Mercers Road
Terrace
Bowmans Mews
Bowmans Place
Empire
Tufnell Park
0.25 mile
0.25 km

Holloway (North)

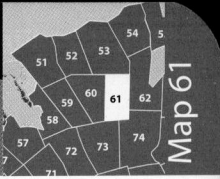

The borough of Islington, in which north Holloway sits, is supposed to be either a byword for liberal middle class cosiness or else grim inner city deprivation, depending on who you talk to. This bit has neither, just lots of very ordinary residential streets. The Swimmer, with its rather splendid jukebox, is still the best pub in the area.

Banks

- **Barclays** • 403 Holloway Rd
- **Halifax** • 19 Seven Sisters Rd
- **NatWest** • 490 Holloway Rd

Cinemas

- **Odeon Holloway** • 419 Holloway Rd

Nightlife

- **Nambucca** • 596 Holloway Rd
- **The Quays** • 471 Holloway Rd
- **The Swimmer** • 13 Eburne Rd

Restaurants

- **The Landseer** • 37 Landseer Rd
- **Pasteleiro** • 22 Seven Sisters Rd

Shopping

- **Michael's Fruiterers** • 56 Seven Sisters Rd

Supermarkets

- **Iceland** • 442 Holloway Rd

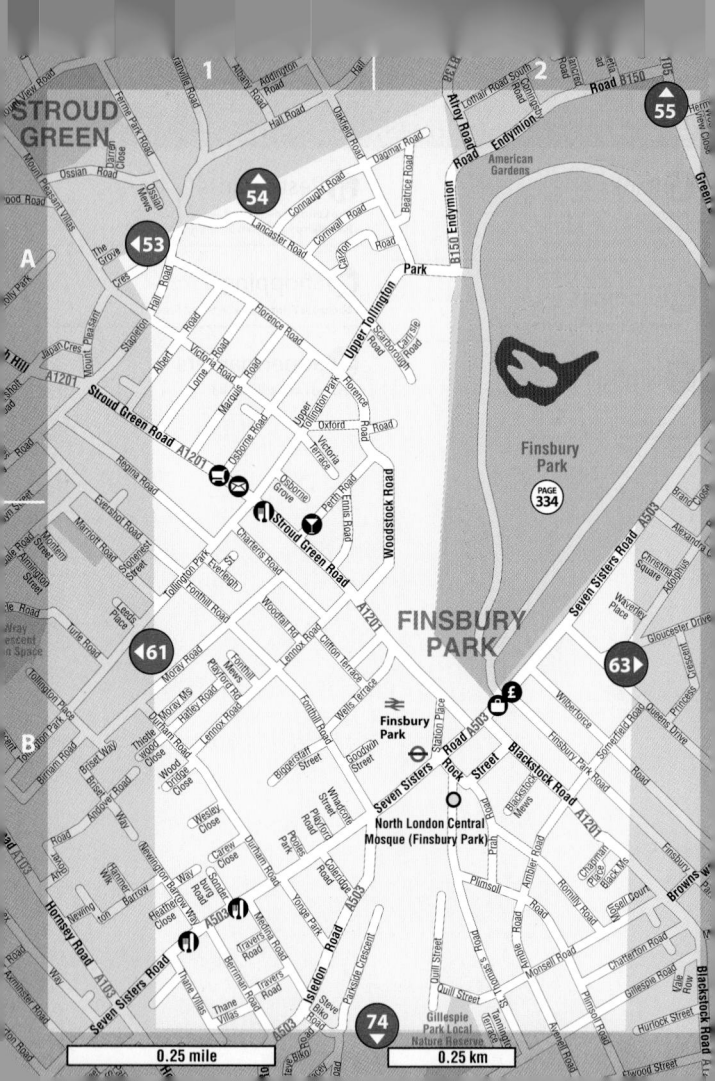
STROUD GREEN
FINSBURY PARK
Finsbury Park
PAGE 334
American Gardens
Upper Tollington Park
Stroud Green Road
Woodstock Road
Seven Sisters Road
Blackstock Road
Finsbury Park Station
Seven Sisters Station
North London Central Mosque (Finsbury Park)
Gillespie Park Local Nature Reserve
Endymion Road
Hornsey Road
Isleden Road
Park
0.25 mile
0.25 km

Finsbury Park

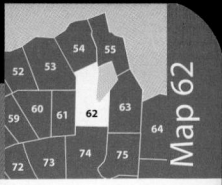

'Let's move to Finsbury Park,' newcomers say, 'why it's so near a park, a tube, AND a station.' Then they get here. But there are twinkles---the park café, and the infamous mosque now doing community outreach. Head to the Faltering Fullback for a pint, Petek for Turkish, the Happening Bagel Bakery for---well you know---or run the gauntlet of Blackstock Road for bundles of mint and tasty lamachun.

Banks

- **NatWest** • 298 Seven Sisters Rd

Landmarks

- **North London Central Mosque (Finsbury Park)** • 7 St Thomas's Rd

Nightlife

- **Faultering Fullback** • 19 Perth Rd

Post Offices

- **Stroud Green Rd** • 97 Stroud Green Rd

Restaurants

- **Fassika** • 152 Seven Sisters Rd
- **Le Rif** • 172 Seven Sisters Rd
- **Petek** • 96 Stroud Green Rd

Shopping

- **The Happening Bagel Bakery** • 284 Seven Sisters Rd

Supermarkets

- **Tesco** • 105 Stroud Green Rd

Map 63 • Manor House

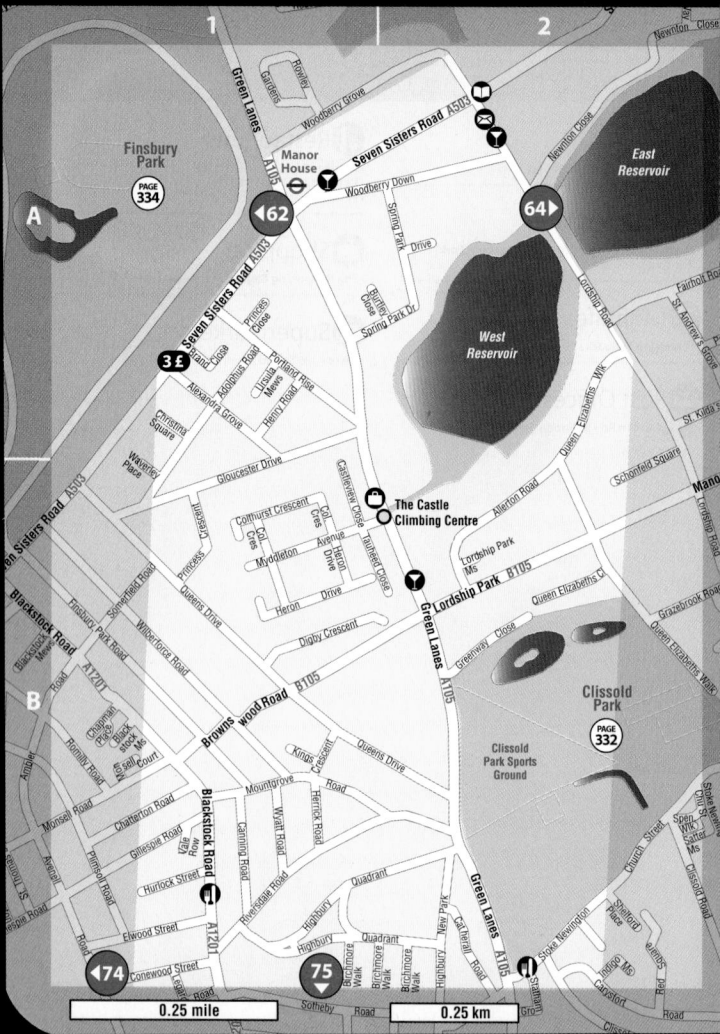

Manor House

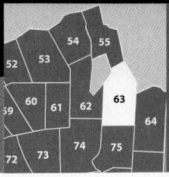

Don't hang out near the 'scummy round the edges' station as it can get pretty gruesome at night, particularly round the horrific Manor Club. You might chance upon a warehouse party round here, but walk south, dodge the rats around the reservoir, admire the faux turrets of the Castle Climbing Centre and head to the New River Café for great fry ups with views over the leafy oasis of Clissold Park.

Banks

- **Abbey** • 304 7 Sisters Rd
- **Barclays** • 254 7 Sisters Rd
- **HSBC** • 312 7 Sisters Rd

Landmarks

- **The Castle Climbing Centre** • Green Lanes

Libraries

- **Woodberry Down Library** • 440 7 Sisters Rd

Nightlife

- **The Blarney Stone** • 89 Woodberry Grove
- **The Brownswood Park Tavern** • 271 Green Lanes
- **Manor Club** • 277 Seven Sisters Rd

Post Offices

- **Woodberry Grove** • 107 Woodberry Grove

Restaurants

- **Il Bacio** • 178 Blackstock Rd
- **New River Café** • 271 Stoke Newington Church St

Shopping

- **Trehantiri Music**• 365 Green Lanes

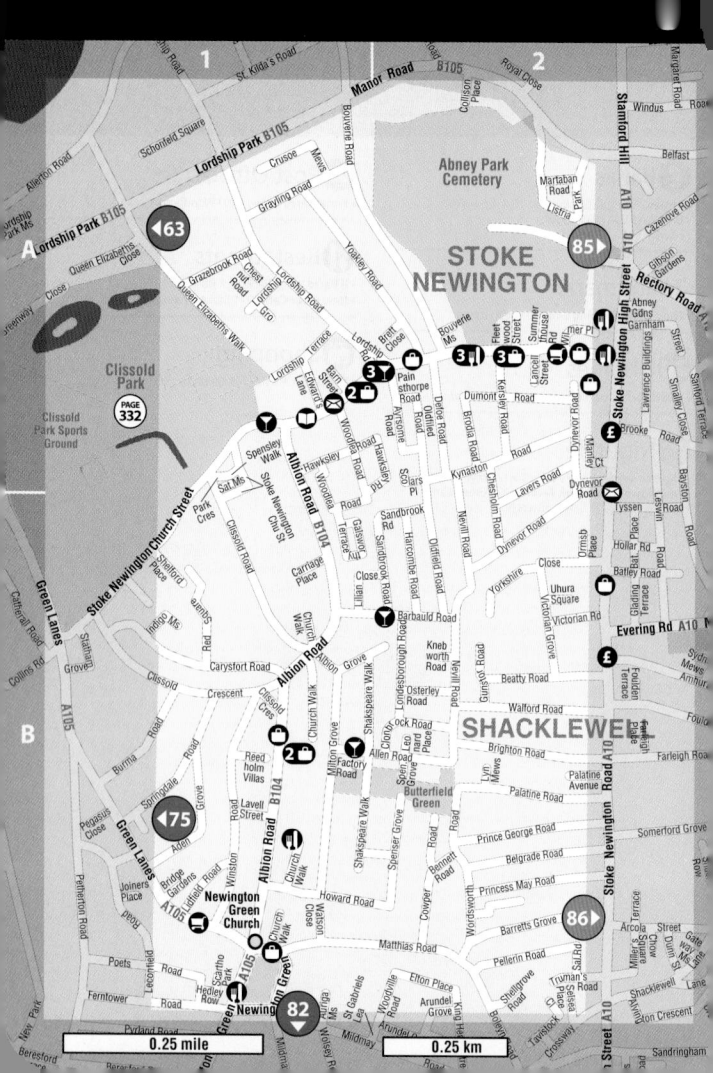
1
2
A
B
STOKE NEWINGTON
SHACKLEWELL
Abney Park Cemetery
Clissold Park
Clissold Park Sports Ground
PAGE 332
Manor Road
Lordship Park B105
Lordship Park
Albion Road B104
Stoke Newington Church Street
Green Lanes
Stoke Newington High Street
Rectory Road
Stoke Newington Road A10
Evering Rd A10
Newington Green Church
Newington Green
Butterfield Green
Pain sthorpe Road
Uhura Square
Victorian Rd
Barbauld Road
Carysfort Road
Church Walk
Shakspeare Walk
Howard Road
Matthias Road
Pellerin Road
Barretts Grove
Prince George Road
Belgrade Road
Princess May Road
Somerford Grove
Palatine Road
Brighton Road
Walford Road
Beatty Road
Farleigh Road
Clissold Crescent
Howard Road
Poets Road
Ferntower Road
Pyrland Road
Mildmay Road
Sandringham
Shacklewell Lane
Arcola Street
Dunn St
Milton Grove
Reed holm Villas
Lavell Street
Springfield Grove
Pegasus Close
Joiners Place
Bridge Gardens
Lufford Road
Winston Road
Pathurton Road
Lecomfield Road
Scarlho Walk
Hedley Row
Wordsworth Road
Cowper Road
Bennett Road
Spenser Grove
Shakspeare Walk
Allen Road
Lock Road
Clorion Road
Lea Bridge Road
Lynn Mews
Palatine Avenue
Victoria Grove
Victorian Grove
Gladding Terrace
Dynevor Road
Kynaston Road
Cheshunt Road
Levers Road
Lyssen Road
Lawrence Buildings
Smaller Close
Sanford Terrace
Bayston Road
Lebrun Road
Ormsb Place
Holler Rd
Battley Road
Yorkshire Road
Newill Road
Osterley Road
Londesborough Road
Sandbrook Road
Harcombe Road
Oldfield Road
Kenley Road
Brooke Road
Dumont Road
Fleet wood Street
Bouverie Ms
Bouverie Road
Yoakley Road
Lordship Terrace
Lordship Road
Grazebrook Road
Queen Elizabeths Walk
Queen Elizabeths Close
Grayling Road
Crusoe Mews
Schonfield Square
Alkerton Road
St. Kilda's Road
Royal Close
Margaret Road
Windus Road
Belfast Road
Cazenove Road
Gibson Gardens
Abney Gdns
Garnham Street
Lordship Park Ms
Sat Ms
Stoke Newington Chu St
Park Cres
Clissold Road
Carriage Place
Shelford Place
Cathcart Road
Collins Rd
Stamford Grove
Hedge Ms
Red Square
Burma Road
Albion Grove
Church Walk
Albion Road
Gaswork Terrace
Lillian Close
Sandbrook Road
Gungate Road
Beatty Road
Dynevor Road
Dynevor Road
Dynevor Ct

Stoke Newington

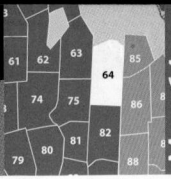

Famed for its high square footage of creative types and three-wheeled buggies, this buzzing villagey 'hood has lost a lot of its Hackney edge but still has the odd shooting to keep locals on their toes. Perfect Guinness (Auld Shillelagh), curry (Rasa N16), Sunday roast (Rose and Crown), and silver jewelry (Metal Crumble) to be found along mainly chain-free Stoke Newington Church Street.

Banks

- **Abbey** • 139 Stoke Newington Rd
- **Lloyds** • 133 Stoke Newington High St

Landmarks

- **Newington Green Church** • 39 Newington Green

Libraries

- **Stoke Newington Library** • Stoke Newington Church St

Nightlife

- **Auld Shillelagh** • 105 Stoke Newington Church St
- **The Lion** • 132 Stoke Newington Church St
- **Londesborough** • 36 Barbauld Rd
- **Rose and Crown** • 199 Stoke Newington Church St
- **Ryan's Bar** • 181 Church St
- **The Shakespeare** • 57 Allen Rd

Post Offices

- **Church Street** • 170 Stoke Newington Church St
- **Stoke Newington** • Stoke Newington High St

Restaurants

- **56** • 56 Newington Green
- **Alistair's Brasserie** • 35 Church Walk
- **Anglo Asian** • 60 Stoke Newington Church St
- **Blue Legume** • 101 Stoke Newington Church St
- **Rasa N16** • 55 Stoke Newington Church St
- **Three Crowns** • 175 Stoke Newington Church St
- **Yum Yum** • 187 Stoke Newington High St

Shopping

- **Ark** • 161 Stoke Newington High St
- **The Beaucatcher Salon** • 44 Stoke Newington Church Street
- **Belle Epoque Boulangerie** • 37 Newington Green
- **Bridgewood & Neitzert** • 146 Stoke Newington Church St
- **Metal Crumble** • 13 Stoke Newington Church St
- **Ocean Books** • 127 Church Walk
- **Ribbons and Taylor** • 157 Stoke Newington Church St
- **Rosa Lingerie** • 3 Church Walk
- **Route 73 Kids** • 92 Stoke Newington Church St
- **S'graffiti** • 172 Stoke Newington Church St
- **Sacred Art** • 148 Albion Rd
- **The Spence** • 161 Stoke Newington Church St
- **Stoke Newington Farmers Market** • Stoke Newington Church St & Stoke Newington High St

Supermarkets

- **Fresh & Wild** • 32 Stoke Newington Church St
- **Iceland** • 17 Green Lanes

1
2
A
B
St. Cuthberts Road
Dornfell Street
Gastonbury Street
Broomsleigh Street
Ravenshare Street
Meyers Ms
Adrian Road
Lyncroft Gardens
Mill Lane
Exeter Road
Garlinge Road
Shoot Up Hill A5
Kilburn
Church Avenue
Fordwych Road
Barlow Road
Brassey Road
Brassey Road
Sumatra Road
Glenbrook Road
Solent Road
Narcissus Road
Hormdale Road
West Cottages
Maygrove Road
Maygrove Peace Park
Pandora Road
Inglewood Road
66
Loveridge Mews
Loveridge Road
Lodiel Road
Sumatra Road
Dennington Park Road
Kingdon Road
Fawley Road
Honeybourne Road
Ariel Road
Maygrove Road
Iverson Road B520
Sandwell Cres
Athlone Mews
Netherwood Street
Medley Road
West End Lane B510
Lymington Road
Palmerston Road
Palmerston Road
Lindsay Road
Rowan Tree Close
Lowfield Road
Kilburn Grange Park
Drakes Court
Kilburn High Road A5
Kilburn Grange Walk
Kilburn Ms
Kilburn Pl
Kilburn Vale
Kilburn Ms
Kilburn Pl
Kilburn Vale
Kilburn Ms
Kilburn Pl
Kilburn Vale

West Hampstead

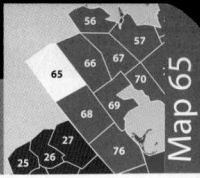

Hampstead's ugly sister, West Hampstead is a leafy suburb that has absorbed some of Kilburn's grittiness. Young urban nomads make up much of the population, as rent is moderate by London standards. The Green Room provides a much-needed alternative to all the dodgy fried chicken joints. Just the right size and with great line-ups most days of the week, the Luminaire is one of London's best alternative music venues.

Banks

- **Barclays** • 83 Kilburn High Rd
- **Barclays** • 208 W End Ln
- **Halifax** • 149 Kilburn High Rd
- **Lloyds** • 106 Kilburn High Rd
- **NatWest** • 74 Kilburn High Rd

Coffee

- **Caffe Nero** • 101 Kilburn High Rd
- **Costa** • 203 W End Ln
- **Starbucks** • 201 W End Ln

Libraries

- **West Hampstead Library** • Dennington Park Rd

Nightlife

- **The Czech and Slovak Club** • 74 West End Lane
- **The Good Ship** • 289 Kilburn High Rd
- **The Luminaire** • 311 High Rd

Post Offices

- **West Hampstead** • 128 W End Ln

Restaurants

- **The Green Room** • 182 Broadhurst Gardens

Supermarkets

- **Sainsbury's** • 88 Kilburn High Rd
- **Sainsbury's** • 377 Kilburn High Rd

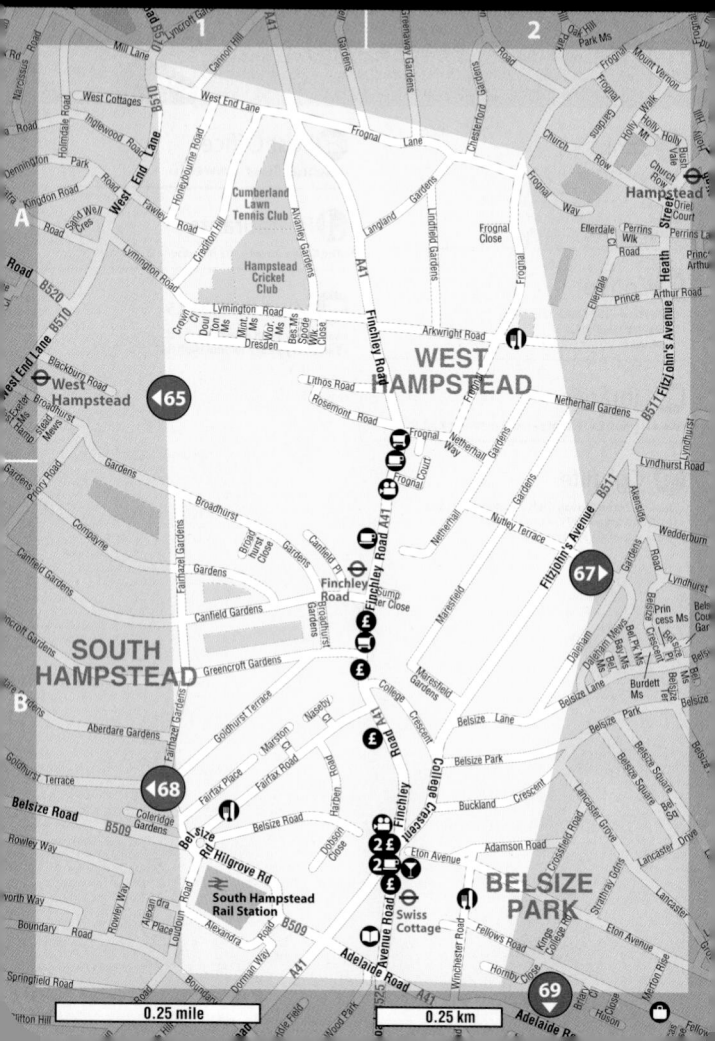
1
2
A
B
West End Lane
Mill Lane
Cannon Hill
West Cottages
West End Lane
Inglewood Road
Dennington Park Road
Kingdon Road
Holmdale Road
Fawley Road
Honeybourne Road
Creedon Hill
Lymington Road
Cumberland Lawn Tennis Club
Hampstead Cricket Club
Alvanley Gardens
Langland Gardens
Lindfield Gardens
Frognal Lane
Frognal Way
Frognal Close
Chesterford Gardens
Greenaway Gardens
Hampstead
Oriel Court
Perrins Wlk
Ellerdale Road
Princess Arthur
Prince Arthur Road
Heath Street
Fitzjohn's Avenue
Finchley Road
Arkwright Road
WEST HAMPSTEAD
Lithos Road
Rosemont Road
Netherhall Gardens
Netherhall Way
Frognal Court
Lyndhurst Road
Wedderburn
Nutley Terrace
Aldenham
West Hampstead
Blackburn Road
Broadhurst Gardens
Priory Road
Compayne Gardens
Canfield Gardens
Finchley Road
Sumpter Close
Maresfield Gardens
Fairhazel Gardens
Broadhurst Gardens
Greencroft Gardens
SOUTH HAMPSTEAD
Goldhurst Terrace
Aberdare Gardens
College Crescent
Belsize Lane
Belsize Park
Belsize Square
Belsize Road
Fairfax Place
Fairfax Road
Marsden Road
Harben Road
Dobson Close
Coleridge Gardens
Buckland Crescent
Eton Avenue
Adamson Road
Hilgrove Rd
South Hampstead Rail Station
Swiss Cottage
BELSIZE PARK
Rowley Way
Boundary Road
Alexandra Place
Alexandra Road
Loudoun Road
Dornan Way
Springfield Road
Adelaide Road
Avenue Road
Winchester Road
Fellows Road
Hornby Close
Merton Rise
Crossfield Road
Lancaster Grove
Lancaster Drive
Strathray Gdns
Princess Ms
Belsize Park Gardens
Belsize Crescent
Belsize Grove
Belsize Avenue
Burdett Ms
Dalehan Mews
Bel Pk Ms
Bel Gr Ms
Bel Cr Ms
Bel Sq Ms
Bel Av Ms
Bel Ln Ms
Bel Pl Ms
Bel Ct Ms
Bel Ex Ms
Bel Ga Ms
Bel Ho Ms
Bel Ri Ms
Bel Vi Ms
Bel Wk Ms
Bel Ma Ms
Bel Ch Ms
Bel Ch Ms
Bel Ch

Finchley Road / Swiss Cottage

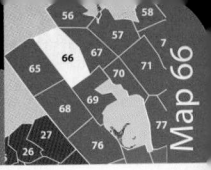

Although it is sandwiched between West Hampstead and Primrose Hill, this is simply not a great spot unless you're seeking bargains in the local pound shop. Finchley Road has a range of mediocre restaurants. Swiss Cottage has a good library and sports centre. The Camden Arts Centre and Freud Museum are jewels in this battered crown—it's worth braving the traffic to see them.

Banks

- **Abbey** • 8 Finchley Rd
- **Barclays** • 131 Finchley Rd
- **Halifax** • 169 Finchley Rd
- **HSBC** • 122 Finchley Rd
- **Lloyds** • 145 Finchley Rd
- **NatWest** • 106 Finchley Rd

Cinemas

- **Odeon Swiss Cottage** • 96 Finchley Rd
- **Vue Finchley Road** • Finchley Rd & Blackburn Rd

Coffee

- **Cafe Express** • 25 Finchley Rd
- **Costa** • 149 Finchley Rd
- **Costa** • 255 Finchley Rd
- **Starbucks** • 255 Finchley Rd

Libraries

- **Swiss Cottage Library** • 88 Avenue Rd

Nightlife

- **Ye Olde Swiss Cottage** • 98 Finchley Rd

Restaurants

- **Bradleys** • 25 Winchester Rd
- **Camden Arts Centre** • Arkwright Rd
- **Singapore Garden** • 83 Fairfax Rd

Shopping

- **Yeomans Grocers** • 152 Regent's Park Rd

Supermarkets

- **Sainsbury's** • 241 Finchley Rd
- **Waitrose** • 199 Finchley Rd

HAMPSTEAD
BELSIZE PARK
Freud Statue
Hampstead
Swiss Cottage
Belsize Park
Finchley Road
Fitzjohn's Avenue
Heath Street
Hampstead High Street
Rosslyn Hill
Haverstock Hill
Pond Street
Adelaide Road
Belsize Avenue
Belsize Lane
Belsize Park
Belsize Grove
Belsize Square
Belsize Park Gardens
Belsize Court Garages
Princess Ms
Burdett Ms
Lancaster Grove
Lancaster Drive
Lambolle Road
Lambolle Place
Eton Avenue
Eton Garages
Adamson Road
Antrim Grove
Antrim Road
Primrose Gardens
Elizabeth Mews
England's Lane
Chalcot Gdns
Fitzjohn's Avenue B511
Rosslyn Hill A502
Haverstock Hill A502
Pond Street B518
Finchley Road A41
Adelaide Road B509
Constantine Road
Fleet Road
Frognal Lane
Frognal Way
Frognal Close
Lindfield Gardens
Langland Gardens
Church Row
Holly Mt
Holly Walk
Streatley
Back Lane
Heath Ms
Hampstead Ms
Perrins Walk
Perrins Lane
Ellerdale Road
Prince Arthur Ms
Prince Arthur Road
Arkwright Road
Netherhall Gardens
Netherhall Way
Mutley Gardens
Lyndhurst Terrace
Lyndhurst Road
Lyndhurst Gdns
Wedderburn Road
Belsize Ct
Belsize Lane
Belsize Avenue
Belsize Park
Belsize Square
Belsize Park Gardens
Belsize Court Garages
Princess Ms
Burdett Ms
Belsize Ms
Belsize Grove
Belsize Crescent
Belsize Lane
Belsize Park
Buckland Crescent
Eton Avenue
Adamson Road
Lancaster Grove
Lancaster Drive
Lambolle Road
Lambolle Place
Eton Garages
Antrim Grove
Antrim Road
Primrose Gardens
Elizabeth Mews
England's Lane
Chalcot Gdns
Haverstock Hill
Rowland Hill Street
Aspern Grove
Glenloch Road
Glenmore Road
Howitt Road
Downshire Cres
Upper Park Road
Tasker Rd
Willow Road
Heath Side
Downshire Hill
Hurst Road
Hampstead Hill
Gardens
Fitzjohn's Avenue B511
Finchley Road A41
Adelaide Road B509
Haverstock Hill A502
Pond Street B518
Constantine Road
Fleet Road
Frognal Lane
Frognal Way
Frognal Close
Lindfield Gardens
Langland Gardens
Church Row
Holly Mt
Holly Walk
Streatley
Back Lane
Heath Ms
Hampstead Ms
Perrins Walk
Perrins Lane
Ellerdale Road
Prince Arthur Ms
Prince Arthur Road
Arkwright Road
Netherhall Gardens
Netherhall Way
Mutley Gardens
Lyndhurst Terrace
Lyndhurst Road
Lyndhurst Gdns
Wedderburn Road
Belsize Ct
Belsize Lane
Belsize Avenue
Belsize Park
Belsize Square
Belsize Park Gardens
Belsize Court Garages
Princess Ms
Burdett Ms
Belsize Ms
Belsize Grove
Belsize Crescent
Belsize Lane
Belsize Park
Buckland Crescent
Eton Avenue
Adamson Road
Lancaster Grove
Lancaster Drive
Lambolle Road
Lambolle Place
Eton Garages
Antrim Grove
Antrim Road
Primrose Gardens
Elizabeth Mews
England's Lane
Chalcot Gdns
Haverstock Hill
Rowland Hill Street
Aspern Grove
Glenloch Road
Glenmore Road
Howitt Road
Downshire Cres
Upper Park Road
Tasker Rd
Willow Road
Heath Side
Downshire Hill
Hurst Road
Hampstead Hill
Gardens
Fitzjohn's Avenue B511
Finchley Road A41
Adelaide Road B509
Haverstock Hill A502
Pond Street B518
Constantine Road
Fleet Road
0.25 mile
0.25 km

Aggressively affluent, Belsize Park is awash with celebrities and salaries bigger than the budgets of small countries. Quaint old streets and the poshness of Finchley Road make this a nice place to stalk Gwyneth Paltrow, but you probably wouldn't want to live here. Check out Freud's statue or drink yourself into an upper-middle class stupor in The Washington.

Banks

- **HSBC** • 147 Haverstock Hill
- **NatWest** • 185 Haverstock Hill

Cinemas

- **Screen on the Hill** • 203 Haverstock Hill

Coffee

- **Starbucks** • 57 England's Lane
- **Starbucks** • 202 Haverstock Hill

Landmarks

- **Freud Statue** •
  Fitzjohn's Ave, opposite Maresfield Gardens Junction

Libraries

- **Belsize Library** • Antrim Rd

Nightlife

- **The Washington** • 50 England's Lane

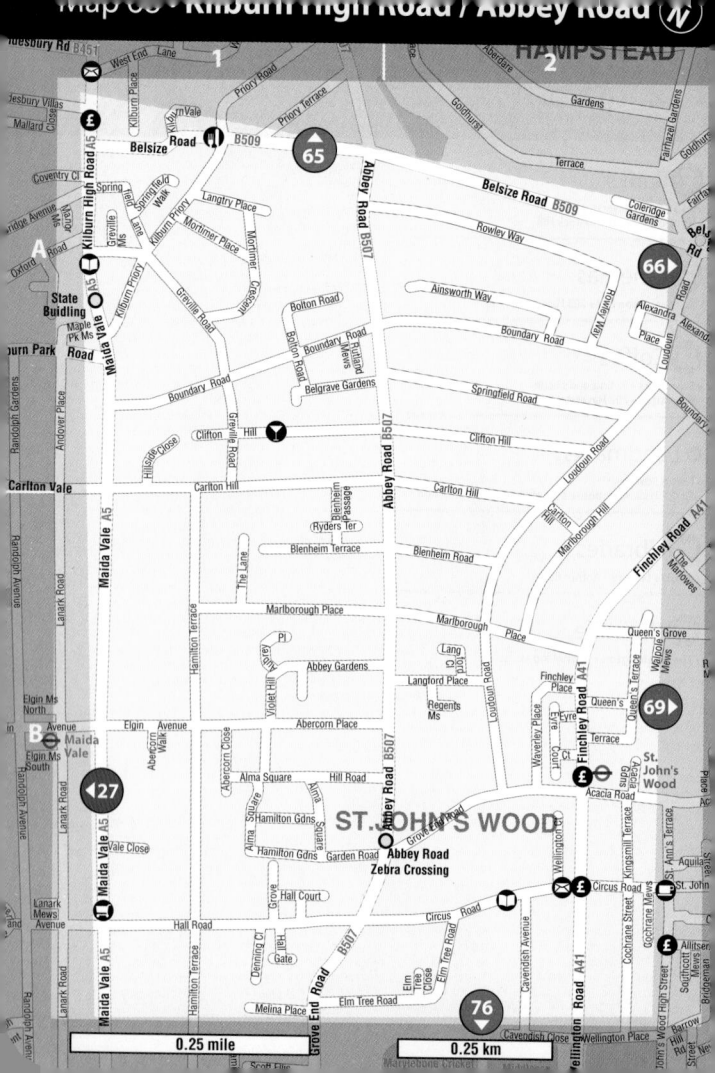
HAMPSTEAD
ST. JOHN'S WOOD
Abbey Road Zebra Crossing
Belsize Road B509
Kilburn High Road A5
Abbey Road B507
Maida Vale A5
Finchley Road A41
Wellington Road A41
Grove End Road B507
Carlton Vale
Boundary Road
Springfield Road
Clifton Hill
Loudoun Road
Marlborough Hill
Blenheim Road
Blenheim Terrace
Marlborough Place
Abbey Gardens
Langford Place
Abercorn Place
Alma Square
Hill Road
Hamilton Gdns
Garden Road
Hall Court
Hall Road
Circus Road
Elm Tree Road
Melina Place
Wellington Place
Acacia Road
Queen's Grove
Finchley Place
Queen's Terrace
Kingsmill Terrace
Cochrane Mews
Cochrane Street
Cavendish Avenue
Cavendish Close
Belsize Avenue
Belsize Park
State Building
Maida Vale
Kilburn Park
St. John's Wood
St. John
Circus Road
Allitsen Rd
Bridgeman Rd
Barrow Hill
Priory Road
Priory Terrace
Goldhurst Terrace
Fairhazel Gardens
Coleridge Gardens
Rowley Way
Ainsworth Way
Alexandra Place
Belgrave Gardens
Ryders Ter
Blenheim Passage
Violet Hill
Regents Ms
Lang Ct
Finchley Place
Waverley Place
Eyre Ct
Elgin Avenue
Elgin Ms North
Elgin Ms South
Abercorn Close
Abercorn Walk
Alma Square
Alma Sq Ms
Hamilton Gdns
Vale Close
Grove Hall Rd
Denning Cl
Gate
Elm Tree Close
Melina Place
Lanark Road
Lanark Mews
Hamilton Terrace
The Lane
Mortimer Place
Langtry Place
Kilburn Priory
Kilburn Vale
Kilburn Place
Spring Field Walk
Greville Ms
Greville Road
Bolton Road
Boundary Road
Rutland Mews
Belgrave Gardens
Clifton Hill
Hillside Close
Carlton Hill
Andover Place
Randolph Gardens
Randolph Avenue
Maida Vale
Maida Vale Ms
Maple Pk Ms
Oxford Road
Coventry Cl
Mallard Close
Jesbury Rd
West End Lane
Belsize Avenue
Belsize Ms
Belsize Gdns
Belsize Park
Fairfax Rd
Fairhazel Gdns
Finchley Rd
Loudoun Rd
Queen's Ms
Wellington Rd
Wellington Ms
Wellington Place
Cavendish Close
Cavendish Avenue
Cochrane Street
Cochrane Mews
Kingsmill Terrace
Queen's Terrace
Finchley Place
Acacia Road
Circus Road
Hall Road
Melina Place
Elm Tree Road
Grove End Road
Hamilton Terrace
Lanark Road
Lanark Mews
Maida Vale
Elgin Avenue
Abercorn Place
Abercorn Close
Abercorn Walk
Alma Square
Hill Road
Hamilton Gdns
Garden Road
Hall Court
Hall Road
Circus Road
Elm Tree Road
Melina Place
Wellington Place
Cavendish Close
Cochrane Street
Cochrane Mews
Kingsmill Terrace
Queen's Terrace
Finchley Place
Acacia Road
Queen's Grove
Finchley Rd
Wellington Rd
Wellington Ms
Wellington Place
Cavendish Close
Cavendish Avenue
Cochrane Street
Cochrane Mews
Kingsmill Terrace
Queen's Terrace
Finchley Place
Acacia Road
Circus Road
St. John's Wood High Street
Allitsen Rd
Bridgeman Rd
Barrow Hill
Lanark Road
Lanark Mews
Hamilton Terrace
Maida Vale A5
Grove End Road B507
Melina Place
Elm Tree Road
Elm Tree Close
Denning Cl
Gate
Hall Court
Grove Hall Rd
Vale Close
Alma Sq Ms
Alma Square
Hill Road
Abercorn Close
Abercorn Walk
Abercorn Place
Elgin Avenue
Elgin Ms South
Elgin Ms North
Maida Vale
Violet Hill
Abbey Gardens
Langford Place
Regents Ms
Lang Ct
Finchley Place
Waverley Place
Eyre Ct
Queen's Terrace
Queen's Grove
Finchley Place
Acacia Road
Circus Road
Cochrane Street
Cochrane Mews
Kingsmill Terrace
Cavendish Avenue
Cavendish Close
Wellington Place
Wellington Ms
Wellington Rd
Finchley Rd
Loudoun Rd
Queen's Ms
Fairhazel Gdns
Fairfax Rd
Belsize Gdns
Belsize Park
Belsize Avenue
Belsize Ms
Coleridge Gdns
Fairhazel Gdns
Goldhurst Terrace
Priory Terrace
Priory Road
Kilburn Vale
Kilburn Place
Spring Field Walk
Greville Ms
Greville Road
Mortimer Place
Langtry Place
Kilburn Priory
Bolton Road
Boundary Road
Rutland Mews
Belgrave Gardens
Clifton Hill
Hillside Close
Carlton Hill
Andover Place
Randolph Gardens
Randolph Avenue
Maida Vale
Maple Pk Ms
Oxford Road
Coventry Cl
Mallard Close
Jesbury Rd
West End Lane
Belsize Avenue
Belsize Ms
Belsize Gdns
Belsize Park
Fairfax Rd
Fairhazel Gdns
Finchley Rd
Loudoun Rd
Queen's Ms
Wellington Rd
Wellington Ms
Wellington Place
Cavendish Close
Cavendish Avenue

Kilburn High Road / Abbey Road

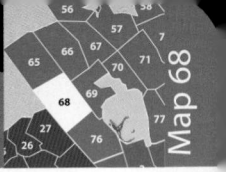

Opposites attract: to the east Abbey Road and dull suburbia beckon, while the west is dominated by grime and urban decay. For pockets of somethin' somethin' try The Clifton for drinkies or pig out at the delightful Little Bay. Better still, look up to the faded Art Deco grandeur of the State Building. Oh yeah, and remember it's just another bloody zebra crossing.

Banks

- **Barclays** • 40 Wellington Rd
- **HSBC** • 50 Kilburn High Rd
- **HSBC** • 1 Finchley Rd
- **NatWest** • 102 St John's Wood High St

Coffee

- **Starbucks** • 79 St John's Wood High St

Landmarks

- **Abbey Road Zebra Crossing** • 3 Abbey Rd
- **State Buidling** • 195 Kilburn High Road

Libraries

- **Kilburn Library** • 12 Kilburn High Rd
- **St John's Wood Library TEMPORARY LOCATION!** • 20 Circus Rd

Nightlife

- **The Clifton** • 96 Clifton Hill

Post Offices

- **Kilburn** • 79 Kilburn High Rd
- **St Johns Wood** • 32 Circus Rd

Restaurants

- **Little Bay** • 228 Belsize Rd

Supermarkets

- **Tesco** • 115 Maida Vale

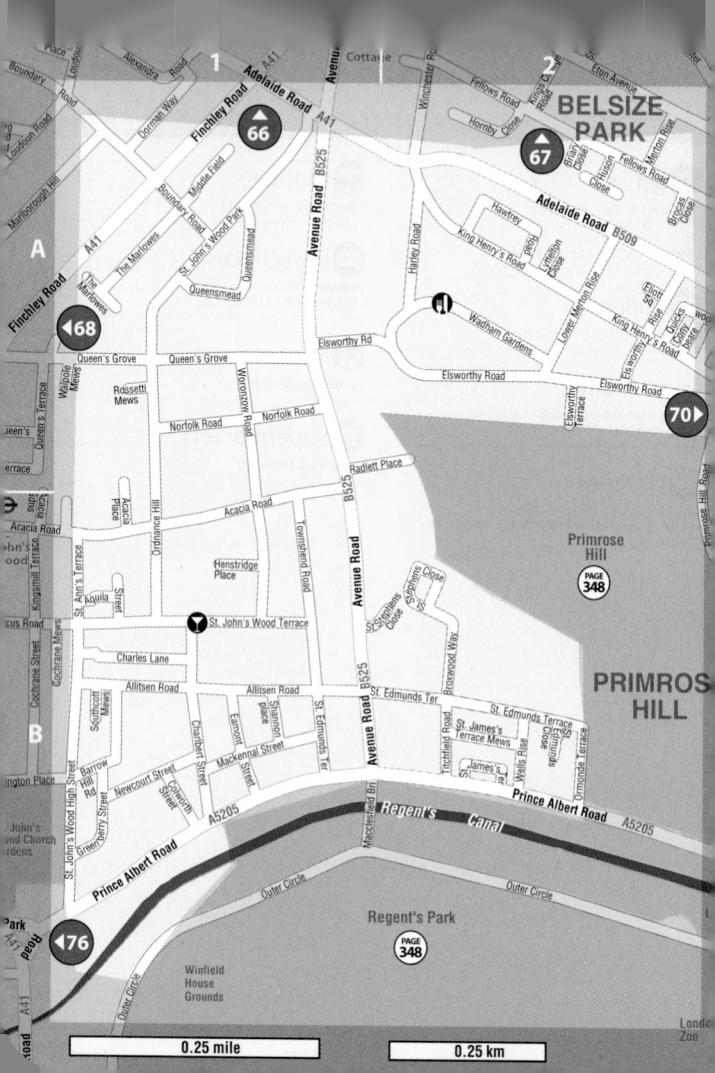
BELSIZE PARK
PRIMROS HILL
Primrose Hill
PAGE 348
Regent's Park
PAGE 348
Regent's Canal
Winfield House Grounds
Adelaide Road
Finchley Road
Avenue Road
Prince Albert Road
Elsworthy Road
Elsworthy Rd
Queen's Grove
Norfolk Road
Radlett Place
Acacia Road
St. John's Wood Terrace
Charles Lane
Allitsen Road
St. Edmunds Ter
St. Edmunds Terrace
Mackenrot Street
Newcourt Street
Outer Circle
Hornby Close
Fellows Road
Hayfrey
King Henry's Road
Wadham Gardens
Lower Merton Rise
Queensmead
St. John's Wood Park
The Marlowes
Boundary Road
Middle Field
Dorman Way
Marlborough Hill
Loudoun Road
Boundary Road
Alexandra Road
Cottage
Winchester Rd
Eton Avenue
Harley Road
Ordnance Hill
Townshend Road
Henstridge Place
Rossetti Mews
Wormholt Road
Walpole Mews
Queen's Terrace
Kingsmill Terrace
St. Ann's Terrace
Aquila Street
Cochrane Mews
Cochrane Street
Acacia Place
Eamont Street
Shannon Place
Southcott Mews
Barrow Hill Rd
St. John's Wood High Street
Maccleslfield Bri
Titchfield Road
St. James's Terrace Mews
St. James's Place
Wells Rise
Wells Mews
Ormonde Terrace
Brookwood Way
St. Stephens Close
St. Stephens Close
Boundary Road
Finchley Road
Adelaide Road
Avenue Road
Prince Albert Road
Outer Circle
A41
A5205
B525
B509
0.25 mile
0.25 km

A leafy suburb for shy, retiring super-rich types. There's not much to do here (especially if you discount spotting hungover celebrities), but the leisure centre on Adelaide road is pretty swish with its climbing wall. To the west, Primrose Hill (and its hyper-bourgeois shops) is like Valhalla in North London and should be flocked to as soon as the sun shines.

Nightlife

• **The Star** • 38 St. Johns Wood Terrace

Restaurants

• **Tupelo Honey** • 27 Parkway, Camden [Arlington Road]

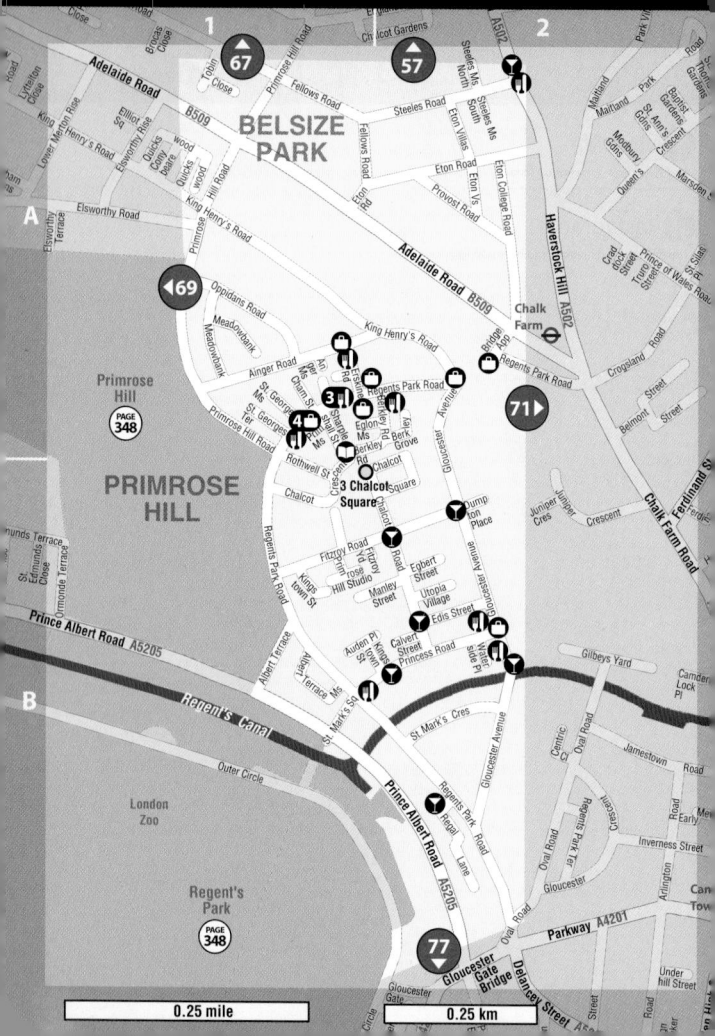
1
2
A
B
67
57
69
71
77
BELSIZE PARK
PRIMROSE HILL
Primrose Hill
PAGE 348
Regent's Park
PAGE 348
London Zoo
Adelaide Road
B509
Elsworthy Road
Elsworthy Terrace
Primrose Hill Road
Fellows Road
Steeles Road
Steeles Ms North
Steeles Ms South
Eton Villas
Eton Road
Eton College Road
Provost Road
King Henry's Road
Haverstock Hill A502
Chalk Farm
Chalk Farm Road
Ferdinand St
Regents Park Road
Croggan Road
Belmont Street
Oppidans Road
Meadowbank
Ainger Road
St Georges Ter
Rothwell St
Chalcot
3 Chalcot Square
Gloucester Avenue
Dumpton Place
Juniper Crescent
Fitzroy Road
Hill Studios
Kings Town St
Manley Street
Utopia Village
Edis Street
Calvert Street
Princess Road
Auden Pl
Wadeside Pl
Albert Terrace
Prince Albert Road A5205
Regent's Canal
St Mark's Sq
St Mark's Cres
Gilbeys Yard
Camden Lock Pl
Outer Circle
Regent's Park Road
Regal Lane
Jamestown Road
Inverness Street
Oval Road
Gloucester
Parkway A4201
Gloucester Gate Bridge
Delancey Street
Gloucester Gate
Under hill Street
Ormonde Terrace
St Edmunds Close
Lyttelton Close
Lewis Merton Rise
Henry's Road
Elliott Sq
Elsworthy Rise
Quicks Corner
Quicks wood
Hill Road
Primrose Hill Road
Fellows Road
Eton Rise
Eton Vs
Maitland Park
Maitland Park Crescent
St Ken's Gardens
Modbury Gdns
Queen's Crescent
Marsden St
Prince of Wales Road
Princes Street
Gloucester Crescent
Regents Park Rd
Berkeley Rd
Egerton Ms
Berkeley Grove
Gloucester Ave
Fellows Road
Eton Rd
Eton Vs
Steeles Ms North
Steeles Ms South
Maitland Park
Bartlett Gardens
Thorney Gdns
Park Vil
Lyttelton Close
Bracken Close
Tobin Close
Primrose Hill Road
Regents Park Rd
Chalcot Gardens
Chalcot Rd
Fitzroy Rd
Fitzroy Close
Fitzroy Rd
Eton Rd
Eton Vs
Eton Rd
Eton Vs
Eton College Rd
Provost Road
Haverstock Hill
Chalk Farm Rd
Ferdinand St
Regents Park Rd
Croggan Road
Belmont Street
Chalcot Rd
Chalcot Sq
Gloucester Ave
Princess Road
Gilbeys Yard
Camden Lock Pl
Jamestown Road
Inverness Street
Oval Road
Gloucester
Parkway A4201
Gloucester Gate Bridge
Delancey Street
Gloucester Gate
Under hill Street
Ormonde Terrace
St Edmunds Close
Lyttelton Close
Lewis Merton Rise
Henry's Road
Elliott Sq
Elsworthy Rise
Quicks Corner
Quicks wood
Hill Road
Primrose Hill Road
Fellows Road
Eton Rise
Eton Vs
Maitland Park
Maitland Park Crescent
St Ken's Gardens
Modbury Gdns
Queen's Crescent
Marsden St
Prince of Wales Road
Princes Street
Gloucester Crescent
Regents Park Rd
Berkeley Rd
Egerton Ms
Berkeley Grove
Gloucester Ave
Fellows Road
Eton Rd
Eton Vs
Steeles Ms North
Steeles Ms South
Maitland Park
Bartlett Gardens
Thorney Gdns
Park Vil
Lyttelton Close
Bracken Close
Tobin Close
Primrose Hill Road
Regents Park Rd
Chalcot Gardens
Chalcot Rd
Fitzroy Rd
Fitzroy Close
Fitzroy Rd
Eton Rd
Eton Vs
Eton Rd
Eton Vs
Eton College Rd
Provost Road
Haverstock Hill
Chalk Farm Rd
Ferdinand St
Regents Park Rd
Croggan Road
Belmont Street
Chalcot Rd
Chalcot Sq
Gloucester Ave
Princess Road
Gilbeys Yard
Camden Lock Pl
Jamestown Road
Inverness Street
Oval Road
Gloucester
Parkway A4201
Gloucester Gate Bridge
Delancey Street
Gloucester Gate
Under hill Street
0.25 mile
0.25 km

Primrose Hill

The debauched Primrose Hill set, a gang of famous drug-taking, booze-swilling, partner-swapping models and actors, has upped sticks for St. John's Wood, but Primrose Hill retains a trendy appeal. Home of yummy mummies and their spouses and a few (older) artistic types, it has an excess of wonderful and expensive shops (Miss Lala's Boudoir, Shikasuki), restaurants (Odette's) and coffee shops (Cafe Seventy Nine, Primrose Bakery).

Landmarks

- **3 Chalcot Square** • 3 Chalcot Sq

Libraries

- **Chalk Farm Library** • 11 Sharples Hall St

Nightlife

- **The Albert** • 11 Princess Rd
- **Cecil Sharp House** • 2 Regents Park Rd
- **The Engineer** • 65 Gloucester Ave [Princess Road]
- **The Lansdowne** • 90 Gloucester Ave [Regent's Park Road]
- **Princess of Wales** • 22 Chalcot Rd
- **Queens No. 1** • 1 Edis St
- **Sir Richard Steele** • 97 Haverstock Hill

Restaurants

- **Cafe Seventy Nine** • 79 Regents Park Rd
- **J restaurant** • 148 Regents Park Rd
- **Legal Cafe** • 81 Haverstock Hill
- **Lemonia** • 89 Regents Park Rd
- **Manna** • 4 Erskine Rd [Regent's Park Road]
- **Melrose and Morgan** • 42 Gloucester Ave
- **Odette's** • 130 Regents Park Rd
- **Primrose Bakery** • 69 Gloucester Ave [Edis Street]
- **Trojka** • 101 Regents Park Rd
- **Two Brothers** • 297 Regents Park Rd

Shopping

- **J Michael & Daughter** • 73 Regents Park Rd
- **Miss Lala's Boudoir** • 148 Gloucester Ave
- **Nicolas (off licence)** • 67 Regents Park Rd
- **Press** • 3 Erskine Rd
- **Primerose Hill Books** • 134 Regent's Park Rd
- **Primrose Newsagent** • 91 Regents Park Rd
- **Richard Dare** • 93 Regents Park Rd
- **Shepherd Foods** • 59 Regents Park Rd
- **Shikasuki** • 67 Gloucester Ave
- **Tann Rokka** • 123 Regent's Park Rd

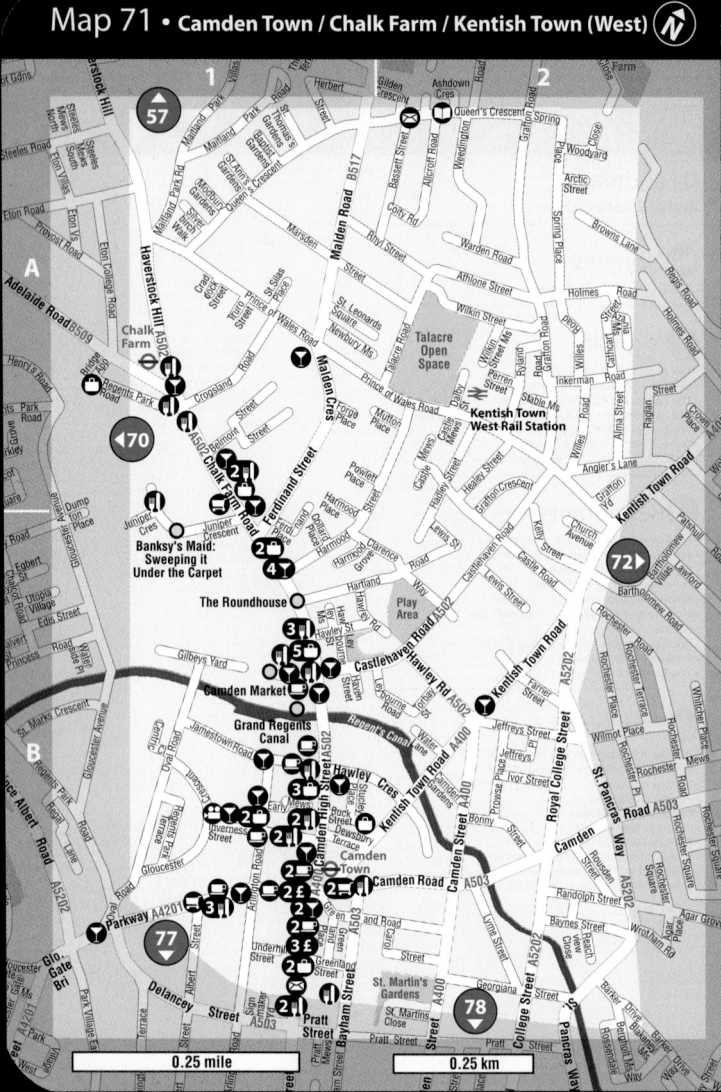
57
70
72
77
78
A
B
1
2
Chalk Farm
Regents Park
Camden Market
Grand Regents Canal
Camden Town
Kentish Town West Rail Station
Talacre Open Space
Play Area
The Roundhouse
Banksy's Maid: Sweeping it Under the Carpet
Haverstock Hill A502
Adelaide Road B509
Malden Road B517
Chalk Farm Road
Ferdinand Street
Castlehaven Road A502
Hawley Rd A502
Kentish Town Road
Kentish Town Road A400
Hawley Cres
Camden High Street A502
Camden Road A503
Camden Street A400
Royal College Street
St. Pancras Way A503
Parkway A4201
Delancey Street
Bayham Street
Pratt Street
College Street
St. Martin's Gardens
0.25 mile
0.25 km

Camden Council might be intent on cleaning up (read destroying) this area, but it's still a place heaving with character. A complete tourist-hell hole during the day, come nighttime it's still all about the music. Barfly and the Electric Ballroom for guitar angst. The Underworld for metal and punk and the Lock Tav for more funky tunes and eye-candy. Weekends are insanely busy, but where else are you gonna get that yellow bootleg Buzzcocks t-shirt? In order to annoy residents and confuse tourists, TFL makes the tube station "exit only" on Sundays.

Banks

- **Abbey** • 121 Camden High St
- **Barclays** • 193 Camden High St
- **HSBC** • 176 Camden High St
- **Lloyds** • 140 Camden High St
- **Royal Bank of Scotland** • 189 Camden High St

Cinemas

- **Odeon Camden Town** • 14 Parkway

Coffee

- **Cafe La Cigale** • 47 Parkway
- **Cafe Metro** • 180 Camden High St
- **Caffe Nero** • 7 Jamestown Rd
- **Caffe Nero** • 11 Parkway
- **Costa** • 181 Camden High St
- **Eat.** • 185 Camden High St
- **Inhabition** • 15 Chalk Farm Rd
- **Pret A Manger** • 157 Camden High St
- **Pret A Manger** • 261 Camden High St
- **Starbucks** • Parkway Camden & Arlington Rd

Landmarks

- **Banksy's Maid: Sweeping it Under the Carpet** • Chalk Farm Rd
- **Camden Market** • Camden Lock Pl
- **Grand Regents Canal** • Grand Regents Canal
- **The Roundhouse** • Chalk Farm Rd

Libraries

- **Queen's Crescent Library** • 165 Queen's Crescent

Nightlife

- **At Proud** • Chalk Farm Rd
- **Bar Vinyl** • 6 Inverness St
- **Barfly** • 49 Chalk Farm Rd
- **Bartok** • 78 Chalk Farm Rd
- **The Camden Tup** • 2 Greenland Pl
- **Dingwalls** • Middle Yard
- **The Dublin Castle** • 94 Parkway
- **Electric Ballroom** • 184 Camden High St
- **The Enterprise** • 2 Haverstock Hill
- **Fiddlers Arms** • 1 Malden Rd
- **Good Mixer** • 30 Inverness St
- **The Hawley Arms** • 2 Castlehaven Rd
- **Jazz Cafe** • 5 Parkway
- **Koko** • 1 Camden High St
- **Lock Tavern** • 35 Chalk Farm Rd
- **Oxford Arms** • 265 Camden High St
- **Quinn's** • 65 Kentish Town Rd
- **The Underworld** • 174 Camden High St
- **The World's End** • 31 Jamestown Rd

Post Offices

- **Camden High Street** • 112 Camden High St
- **Queen's Crescent** • 139 Queen's Crescent

Restaurants

- **Andy's Taverna** • 81 Bayham St
- **Bar Gansa** • 2 Inverness St
- **Bar Solo** • 20 Inverness St
- **Bento Cafe** • 9 Parkway
- **Camden Bar And Kitchen** • 102 Camden High St
- **Camden Kitchen** • 102 Camden High St
- **Cotton's** • 55 Chalk Farm Rd
- **Gilgamesh** • The Stables Market, Chalk Farm Rd
- **HachÉ** • 24 Inverness St
- **Kim's Vietnamese Food Hut** • Unit D, Camden Lock Palace
- **Limani** • 154 Regents Park Rd
- **Marathon Cafe** • 87 Chalk Farm Rd
- **Marine Ices** • 8 Haverstock Hill
- **Market** • 438 Parkway
- **Muang Thai** • 71 Chalk Farm Rd
- **My Village** • 37 Chalk Farm Rd
- **Than Binh** • 14 Chalk Farm Rd
- **Viet-anh Cafe** • 41 Parkway
- **Woody Grill** • 1 Camden Rd
- **Yumchaa Tea Space** • 91 Upper Walkway, West Yard, Camden Lock Market
- **Zorya Imperial Vodka Room** •

Shopping

- **Acumedic** • 101 Camden High St
- **Black Rose** • The Stables Market, Chalk Farm Rd
- **Cyberdog** • Stables Market, Chalk Farm Rd
- **Episode** • 26 Chalk Farm Rd
- **Escapade** • 45 Chalk Farm Rd
- **Eye Contacts** • 10 Chalk Farm Rd
- **Graham and Green** • 164 Regents Park Rd
- **Know How Records** • 3 Buck St
- **Metal Militia** • 259 Camden High St
- **Music & Video Exchange** • 208 Camden High St
- **Ray Man Music** • 54 Chalk Farm Rd
- **Rokit** • 225 Camden High St
- **Sounds That Swing** • 46 Inverness St
- **Up The Video Junction** • Middle Yard, Camden Lock Pl
- **Village Games** • 65 The West Yard

Supermarkets

- **Fresh and Wild** • 49 Parkway
- **Sainsbury's** • 77 Chalk Farm Rd
- **Sainsbury's** • 17 Camden Rd
- **Sainsbury's** • 10 Camden Rd

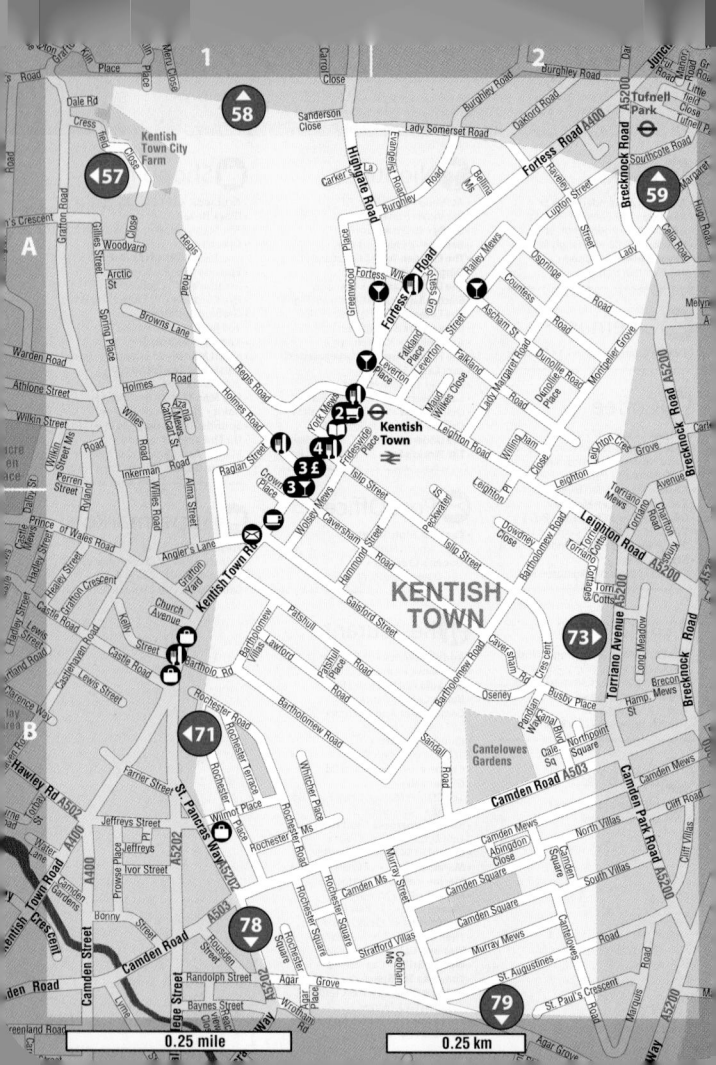
KENTISH TOWN
Kentish Town
Kentish Town City Farm
Tufnell Park
Highgate Road
Fortess Road A400
Brecknock Road A5200
Kentish Town Rd
Leighton Road A5200
Torrians Avenue A5200
Camden Road A503
St. Pancras Way A5202
Hawley Rd A502
Camden Park Road A5200
Camden Street
Cantelowes Gardens
0.25 mile
0.25 km

Sitting contentedly between the mad scrum of Camden and genteel Hampstead, Kentish Town is a usually amicable mix of all day drinkers, winos, and junkies all being politely ignored by Guardian-reading media types. The high street is grubby, but with a bunch of good charity shops for bargain hunters. Make sure no one follows you to the superb Pineapple pub, one of London's quirky hidden gems.

Banks

- **Abbey** • 233 Kentish Town Rd
- **Barclays** • 230 Kentish Town Rd
- **HSBC** • 246 Kentish Town Rd

Coffee

- **Cafe Metro** • 180 Camden High St

Libraries

- **Kentish Town Library** • 262 Kentish Town Rd

Nightlife

- **The Abbey Tavern** • 124 Kentish Town Rd
- **Bull & Gate** • 389 Kentish Town Rd
- **The Forum** • Highgate Rd
- **Monkey Business** • 289 Kentish Town Rd
- **The Pineapple** • 51 Leverton St
- **Rio's Health Spa** • 239 Kentish Town Rd

Restaurants

- **Bintang Cafe** • 93 Kentish Town Rd
- **Café Euro Med** • 225 Kentish Town Rd
- **Eat Zone** • 18 Fortess Rd
- **Le Petit Prince** • 5 Holmes Rd
- **Mario's Cafe** • 6 Kelly St
- **The Oxford** • 256 Kentish Town Rd
- **Pane Vino** • 323 Kentish Town Rd
- **Phoenicia** • 186 Kentish Town Rd

Shopping

- **Dots** • 132 St Pancras Way
- **Fish** • 161 Kentish Town Rd
- **Phoenicia** • 186 Kentish Town Rd

Supermarkets

- **Co-Op** • 250 Kentish Town Rd
- **Iceland** • 301 Kentish Town Rd

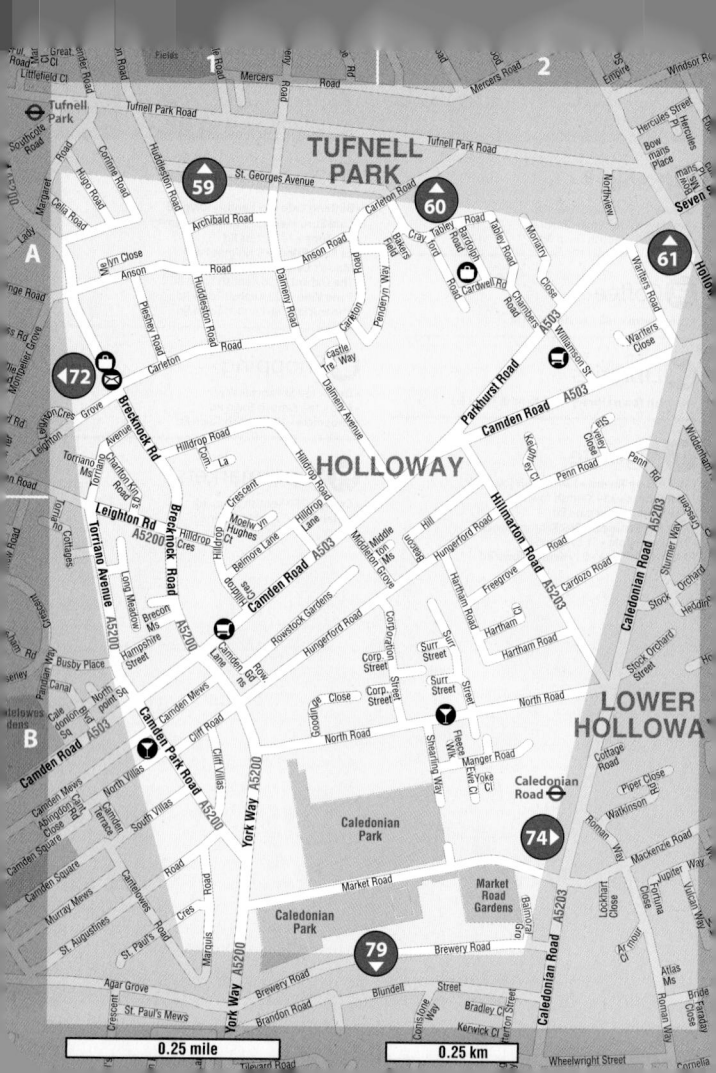
TUFNELL PARK
HOLLOWAY
LOWER HOLLOWA
Tufnell Park
Tufnell Park Road
Mercers Road
Mercers
Road
Fields
Littlefield Cl
Southcote Road
Carmen Road
Hugo Road
Celia Road
Margaret Road
Huddleston Road
Archibald Road
St. Georges Avenue
Carleton Road
Tabley Road
Bakers Field
Cray Ford
Tabley Road
Cardwell Rd
Moriatty Close
Northview
Seven S
Hercules Street
Bow mans Place
Mellin Close
Anson
Anson Road
Dalmeny Road
Carleton
Penderyn Way
Chamberlain Road
A503
Willmarson St
Warters Road
Warters Close
Holloway
Pleasley Road
Carleton
Road
Castle Tre Way
Dalmeny Avenue
Parkhurst Road
Camden Road A503
Brecknock Rd
Grove
Leighton
Avenue
Torriano Mews
Torriano Cres
Chapel Kno Road
Hilldrop Road
Hilldrop Com. La
Hilldrop Road
Crescent
Hilldrop Lane
Hilldrop Cres
Hilldrop Cl
Belmore Lane
Mcelle Ue Hughes
Leighton Rd A5200
Brecknock Road
Torriano Avenue A5200
Long Meadow
Brecon Ms
Hampshire Street
Camden Road A503
Middle Row
Middleton Grove
Hungerford Road
Hillmarton Road A5203
Caledonian Road A5203
Sturmer Way
Cardozo Road
Freegrove
Harham Road
Harham Cl
Hartham Road
Stock Orchard Street
Orchard
Rowstock Gardens
Hungerford Road
Corp Street
Corp. Street
Surr Street
Surr Street
Street
North Road
Goodinge Close
North Road
Busby Place
Canal
North point Sq
Cale donian Rd
Camden Mews
Cliff Road
Cliff Villas
Camden Park Road A5200
Camden Road A503
Camden Mews
Camden Terrace
North Villas
South Villas
Camden Square
Road
Murray Mews
St. Augustines
St. Paul's Road
Marquis
York Way A5200
Smealing Way
Manger Road
Eve Cl
Yoke Cl
Caledonian Road
Cottage Road
Piper Close
Rd
Watkinson
Romen Way
Mackenzie Road
Caledonian Park
Market Road
Market Road Gardens
Lockhart Close
Fortuna Close
Jupiter Way
Vulcan Way
Armour Cl
Atlas Ms
Brewery Road
Agar Grove
Crescent
St. Paul's Mews
Brandon Road
Blundell Street
Bradley Cl
Kenwick Cl
Caledonian Road A5203
Roman Way
Bride Cl
Wheelwright Street
Cornelia
Tileyard Road
0.25 mile
0.25 km
59
60
61
72
74
79
A
B
1
2

Holloway is best known for its women's prison and not much else. To the west of Holloway Road it feels a bit like a sprawling backyard to gentrified Camden, Islington, and King's Cross. Nevertheless bars like The Lord Stanley and Shillibeers have gone all gastro, so it doesn't quite have the gritty vibe that it once had.

Nightlife

- **The Lord Stanley** • 51 Camden Park Rd
- **Shilibeers** • 1 Carpenter's Mews, North Rd

Post Offices

- **Brecknock Rd** • 20 Brecknock Rd

Shopping

- **Bumblebee Natural Foods** • 33 Brecknock Rd
- **DOC Records** • 5 Cardwell Terrace, Cardwell Rd

Supermarkets

- **Sainsbury's** • 4 Williamson St
- **Tesco/Esso** • 196 Camden Rd

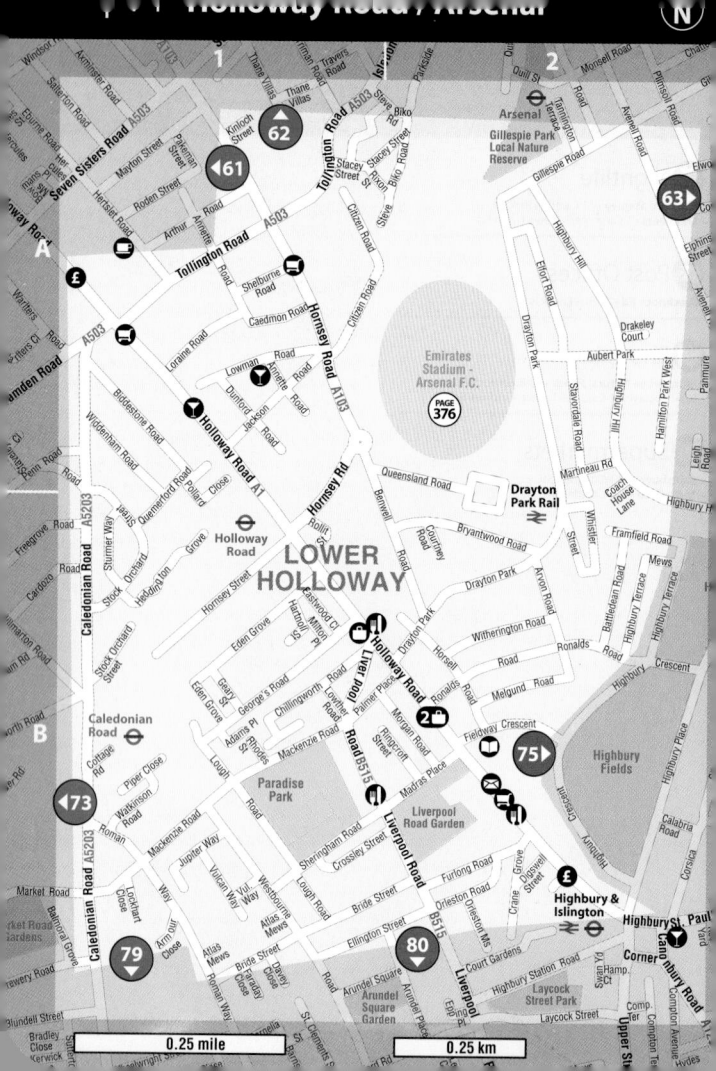
Holloway Road / Arsenal
N
1
2
A
B
Seven Sisters Road A503
Tollington Road A503
Hornsey Road A1103
Holloway Road A1
Caledonian Road A5203
Liverpool Road B5515
Arsenal
Gillespie Park Local Nature Reserve
Emirates Stadium - Arsenal F.C.
PAGE 376
Drayton Park Rail
Holloway Road
LOWER HOLLOWAY
Caledonian Road
Paradise Park
Liverpool Road Garden
Highbury Fields
Highbury & Islington
Highbury St. Paul
Corner
Laycock Street Park
Arundel Square Garden
Hornsey Rd
Queensland Road
Drayton Park
Aubert Park
Gillespie Road
Holloway Road
Caledonian Road
Market Road
Liverpool Road
Highbury Hill
Upper St
Lamb
62
61
63
73
79
80
75
0.25 mile
0.25 km

Holloway Road / Arsenal

One of the universe's biggest football stadiums has been shoe-horned into this area of tidy terraces---red guttering anyone?---and on match days the streets make a sardine tin look roomy. This area also includes the first grotty stretch of Holloway Road. For something different try House of Harlot for fetish fashion, El Comandante for drinks, and Tblisi for cheap eastern European eats.

Banks

- **Abbey** • 408 Holloway Rd
- **Lloyds** • 31 Holloway Rd

Coffee

- **Cafe Nero** • 348 Holloway Rd

Libraries

- **Central Library** • 1 Fieldway Crescent

Nightlife

- **The Coronet** • 338 Holloway Rd
- **El Comandante** • 10 Annette Rd
- **Hen and Chicken Theatre Pub** • 109 St Paul's Rd

Post Offices

- **Holloway Rd** • 118 Holloway Rd

Restaurants

- **Dastarkhan** • 203 Holloway Rd
- **Morgan M** • 489 Liverpool Rd
- **Tbilisi** • 91 Holloway Rd

Shopping

- **21st Century Retro** • 162 Holloway Rd
- **Fettered Pleasures** • 90 Holloway Rd
- **House of Harlot** • 90 Holloway Rd

Supermarkets

- **Sainsbury's** • 104 Holloway Rd
- **Sainsbury's** • 89 Hornsey Rd
- **Waitrose** • 366 Holloway Rd

Map 75 • Highbury

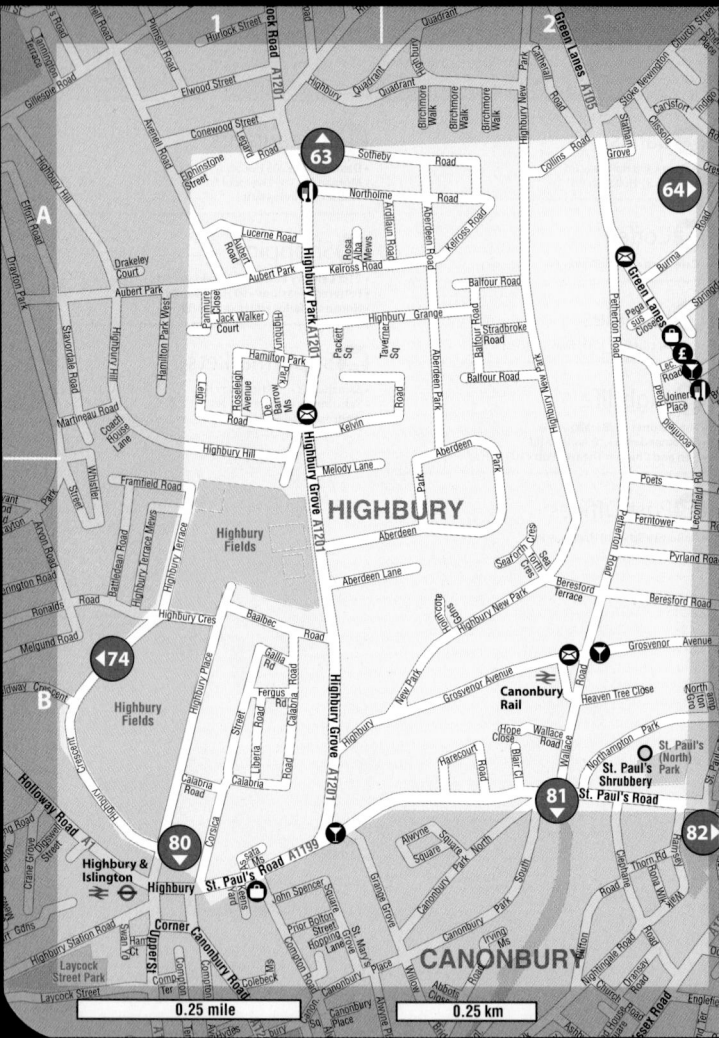

A quiet residential area in the main, blessed with the marvellous Highbury Fields for a hit of green and a thriving gay bar (Oak Bar). Bordered by busy St Paul's Road and bustling Green Lanes—great for Turkish seafood (Sariyer Balik) and the best auto parts shop in the world (Cabbies Delight). All gets packed on match day, but try the Snooty Fox for a quiet drink or San Daniele Del Friuli for classic Italian.

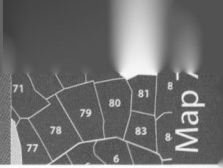

Banks

- **Abbey** • 517 Green Lanes

Landmarks

- **St Paul's Shrubbery** • St Paul's Rd

Nightlife

- **Alwyne Castle** • 83 St. Pauls Road
- **Oak Bar** • 79 Green Lanes
- **Snooty Fox** • 75 Grosvenor Avenue

Post Offices

- **Green Lanes** • 137 Green Lanes
- **Grosvenor Avenue** • 91 Grosvenor Ave
- **Highbury Park** • 12 Highbury Park

Restaurants

- **San Daniele Del Friuli** • 72 Highbury Park
- **Sariyer Balik** • 56 Green Lanes

Shopping

- **Cabbies Delight Auto Parts** • 9 Green Lanes
- **Mother Earth** • 282 St Paul's Rd

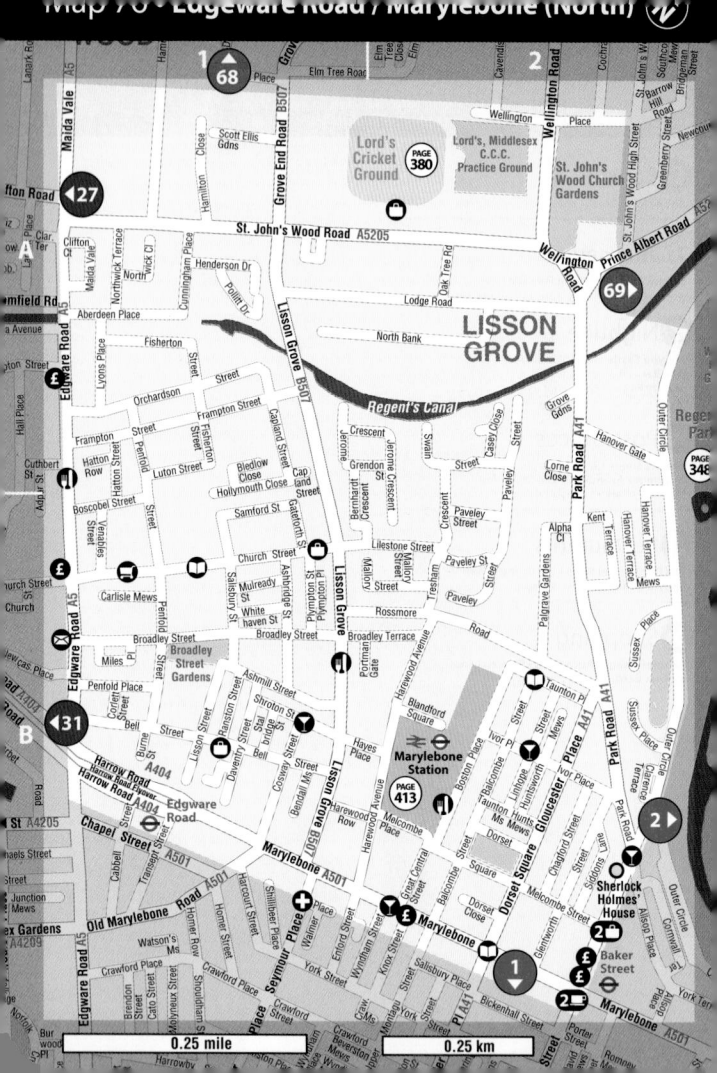
Lord's Cricket Ground
PAGE 380
Lord's, Middlesex C.C.C. Practice Ground
St. John's Wood Church Gardens
LISSON GROVE
Regent's Canal
Marylebone Station
PAGE 413
Sherlock Holmes' House
Baker Street
Edgware Road
Marylebone
Wellington Road
Prince Albert Road
St. John's Wood Road A5205
Grove End Road B507
Lisson Grove B507
Marylebone Road A501
Old Marylebone Road A501
Chapel Street A501
Harrow Road A404
Edgware Road A5
Maida Vale A5
Park Road A41
Gloucester Place A41
Dorset Square
Seymour Place
Baker Street A41
Bickenhall Street
Salisbury Place
Melcombe Street
Dorset Street
Chagford Street
Blandford Square
Harewood Avenue
Broadley Terrace
Broadley Street
Rossmore Road
Lisson Grove
Penfold Place
Ashmill Street
Shroton St
Bell Street
Church Street
Lisson Street
Paveley Street
Lilestone Street
Boscobel Street
Hollymouth Close
Luton Street
Frampton Street
Orchardson Street
Fisherton Street
Aberdeen Place
Lodge Road
North Bank
Elm Tree Road
Wellington Place
Hanover Gate
Outer Circle
Regent's Park
0.25 mile
0.25 km

Edgeware Road / Marylebone (North)

Marylebone Road is noisy enough to have you running for the taps of the Cellars Bar straight away. Things get calmer (meaning duller) further north, but Mandalay's inexpensive Burmese treats save the north end of Edgeware Road, while the Sea Shell of Lisson Grove does fine fish. And did we mention the great detective? Baker Street, dear Watson, Baker Street.

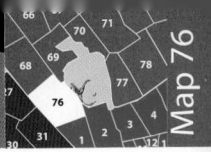

Banks

- **Abbey** • 388 Edgware Rd
- **HSBC** • 186 Baker St
- **Lloyds** • 185 Baker St
- **NatWest** • 508 Edgware Rd
- **Royal Bank of Scotland** • 119 Marylebone Rd

Coffee

- **Costa** • 124 Baker St
- **Pret A Manger** • 120 Baker St

Emergency Rooms

- **Western Eye Hospital** • 173 Marylebone Rd

Landmarks

- **Sherlock Holmes' House** • 221 Baker St

Libraries

- **Church Street Library** • Church St
- **London Business School Library** • 25 Taunton Pl
- **Marylebone Library** • 109 Marylebone Rd

Nightlife

- **Cellars Bar** • 222 Marylebone Road
- **The Feathers** • 43 Linhope Street
- **The Perseverance** • 11 Shroton Street
- **Volunteer** • 245 Baker St

Post Offices

- **Edgware Rd** • 354 Edgware Rd

Restaurants

- **Mandalay** • 444 Edgware Rd
- **Sea Shell of Lisson Grove** • 49 Lisson Grove
- **Zen Spice Market** • Melcombe Place

Shopping

- **Alfie's Antiques Market** • 25 Church St
- **Archive Secondhand Books & Music** • 83 Bell St
- **Beatles London Store** • 231 Baker St
- **Elvisly Yours** • 233 Baker St
- **Lord's Cricket Shop** • Lord's Cricket Ground, Lisson Grove

Supermarkets

- **Tesco** • 94 Church St

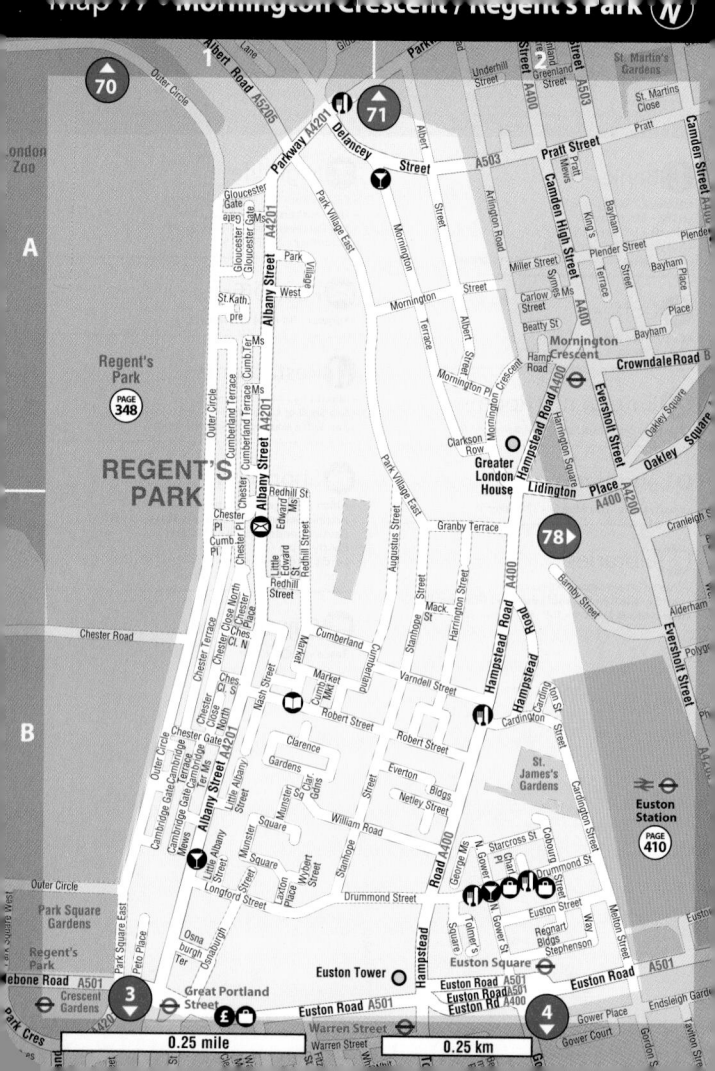
N
A
B
1
2
3
4
70
71
78
Albert Road A5205
Outer Circle
Parkway A4201
Delancey Street
Pratt Street
Camden High Street A400
Camden Street A400
Albany Street A4201
Mornington Crescent
Crowndale Road
Eversholt Street
Hampstead Road A400
Lidington Place
Oakley Square
Greater London House
Regent's Park
PAGE 348
REGENT'S PARK
Chester Road
Euston Station
PAGE 410
St. James's Gardens
Park Square Gardens
Regent's Park
Euston Tower
Euston Square
Euston Road A501
Great Portland Street
Warren Street
Gower Place
Gower Court
Endsleigh Gardens
Euston Road A501
Euston Rd A400
Hampstead Road A400
Crescent Gardens
Park Cres
0.25 mile
0.25 km

Mornington Crescent / Regent's Park

Hemmed in by Regent's Park and Euston, this patch combines pretty streets with tower-block thoroughfares. Skip the din of Euston underpass for Drummond Street, Camden's 'little India'—decent dosas in Bhel Poori, Chutneys for veggies, the Crown & Anchor for mugs of Black Sheep ale. Chow on tofu cheesecake with beatnik slam poets in Green Note. Mingle al fresco with Edinboro Castle's yuppier folk.

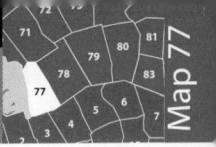

Banks

- **NatWest** • 350 Euston Rd

Landmarks

- **Euston Tower** • 286 Euston Rd
- **Greater London House** • Hampstead Rd

Libraries

- **Regents Park Library** • Robert St [Compton Close]

Nightlife

- **Crown & Anchor** • 137 Drummond St
- **Edinboro Castle** • 57 Mornington Terrace
- **Queen's Head and Artichoke** • 30 Albany St

Post Offices

- **Albany Street** • 6 Chester Ct

Restaurants

- **Chutneys** • 124 Drummond St
- **Diwana Bhel Poori** • 121 Drummond St
- **The Green Note** • 106 Parkway
- **Mestizo** • 103 Hampstead Rd

Shopping

- **Calumet Trading** • 93 Drummond St
- **Chess & Bridge** • 369 Euston Rd
- **Greens and Beans** • 131 Drummond St

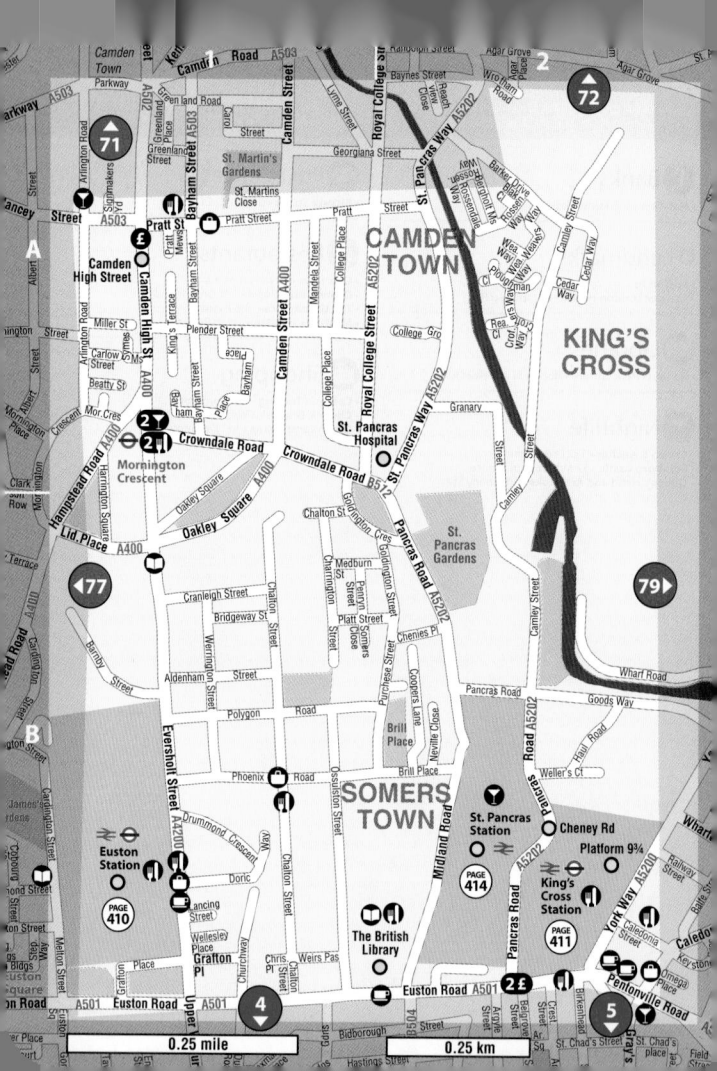
Camden Town
Camden Road A503
Parkway
Kentish Town Road
Agar Grove
Agar Grove
Baynes Street
Royal College St
Camden Street
Pratt Street
Pratt Street
Georgiana Street
St. Martin's Gardens
St. Martins Close
Bayham Street
Greenland Street
Pratt St
Camden High Street
Camden High St.
Miller St
Plender Street
Arlington Road
Carlow Mews
Beatty St
Mor Cres
Mornington Crescent
Crowndale Road
Hampstead Road A400
Oakley Square A400
Lid Place A400
Cranleigh Street
Bridgeway St
Aldenham Street
Polygon Road
Eversholt Street A4200
Phoenix Road
Euston Station
Euston Road A501
Upper Euston Road A501
Grafton Pl
Wellesley Place
Drummond Crescent
Doric
Dancing Street
Chalton Street
Churchway
Chris Pl
Weirs Pas
Bidborough Street
Hastings Street
Euston Road A501
The British Library
Brill Place
Brill Place
Phoenix Road
Clarendon Street
Purchese Street
Goodes Walk
Neville Close
Cranleigh Street
Medburn St
Chalton St
Granary
St. Pancras Hospital
Crowndale Road B512
Pancras Road A5202
St. Pancras Gardens
Camley Street
Wharf Road
Pancras Road
Goods Way
Midland Road
Royal College Street A5202
St. Pancras Way A5202
Camden Road A5202
Weller's Ct
Hall Road
St. Pancras Station
Cheney Rd
Platform 9¾
King's Cross Station
York Way A5202
Pentonville Road
Caledonian Road
Wharf
Caledonian Road
Omega Place
Balfour Street
Argyle Street
Bagnigge Place
Birkenhead Street
St. Chad's Place
St. Chad's Street
Gray's Inn Road
Field Street
Camden Town
CAMDEN TOWN
KING'S CROSS
SOMERS TOWN
71
72
77
79
PAGE 410
PAGE 414
PAGE 411
0.25 mile
0.25 km

Euston's the first port of call for thousands of people each day, be it city workers from the Shires or pilgrims to the many erotic bookshops by the railway. Look beyond the station—an ugly grey cube that dominates the area—and you find few gems. Students and bookish types head to the outstanding library (British that is), hipsters to the Rock'n'Roll Jumble Sale, and nobody to the in-station barber.

Banks

- **Barclays** • 23 Euston Rd
- **Halifax** • 96 Camden High St
- **HSBC** • 31 Euston Rd

Coffee

- **Bagel Factory** • Euston Station
- **Pret A Manger** • 296 Pentonville Rd
- **Pret A Manger** • 117 Euston Rd
- **Starbucks** • 296 Pentonville Rd

Landmarks

- **The British Library** • 96 Euston Rd
- **Camden High Street** • Camden High St
- **Cheney Road** • Cheney Rd
- **Euston Station** • Euston Rd
- **Platform 9¾** • King's Cross Station
- **St Pancras Hospital** • 4 St Pancras Way

Libraries

- **The British Library** • 96 Euston Rd
- **Camden Town Library** • 218 Eversholt St
- **Wellcome Library** • 183 Euston Rd

Nightlife

- **The Champagne Bar at St Pancras** • Pancras Rd
- **The Crown & Goose** • 100 Arlington Rd
- **Purple Turtle** • 61 Crowndale Rd
- **Scala** • 275 Pentonville Rd

Restaurants

- **Asakusa** • 265 Eversholt St
- **Banger Bros.** • Euston Station
- **Camino** • 3 Varnisher's Yard
- **Chop Chop Noodle Bar** • 1 Euston Rd
- **El Parador** • 245 Eversholt St
- **Great Nepalese** • 48 Eversholt St
- **Kitchin** • 8 Caledonia St
- **Last Word Cafe** • 96 Euston Rd, St. Pancras
- **Rodon Live** • 7 Pratt St
- **The Somerstown Coffee House** • 60 Chalton St

Shopping

- **All Ages Records** • 27 Pratt St
- **Housmans** • 5 Caledonian Rd
- **Rock'n'Roll Jumble Sale** • 15 Phoenix Road
- **Transformation** • 52 Eversholt St

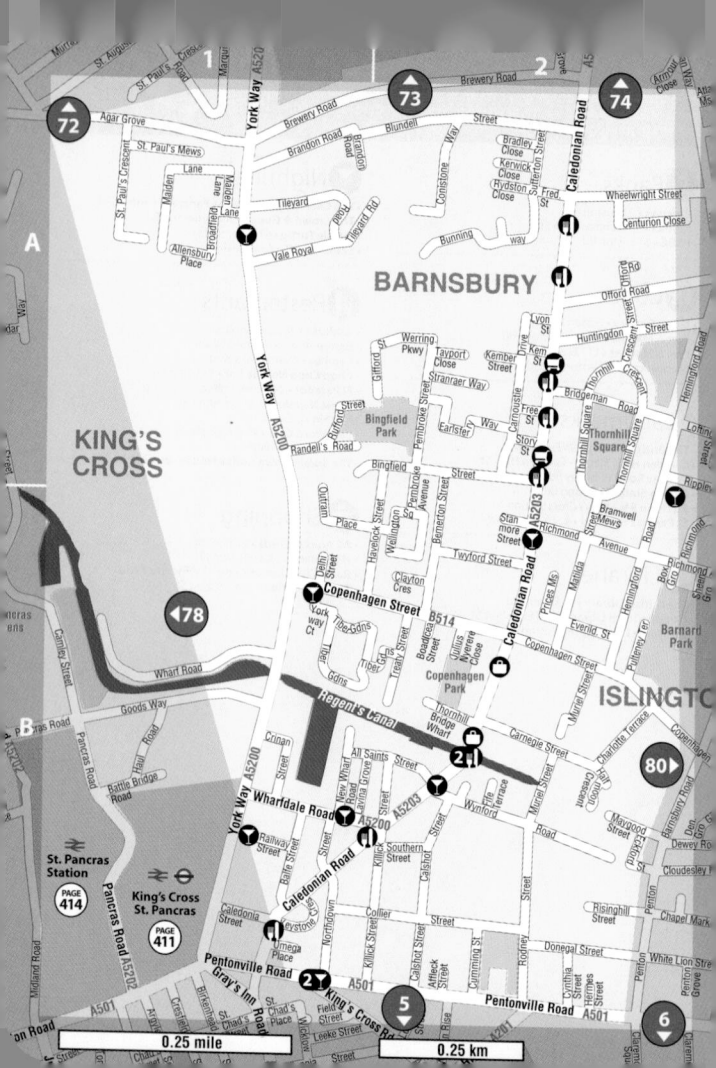
BARNSBURY
KING'S CROSS
ISLINGTO
Bingfield Park
Thornhill Square
Copenhagen Park
Barnard Park
Regent's Canal
York Way A520
York Way A5200
Caledonian Road
Caledonian Road A5203
Copenhagen Street
Wharfdale Road
Pentonville Road
Pentonville Road A501
King's Cross Road
Gray's Inn Road
Pancras Road A5202
St. Pancras Station
PAGE 414
King's Cross St. Pancras
PAGE 411
Brewery Road
Agar Grove
St. Paul's Mews
St. Paul's Crescent
Maiden Lane
Tileyard Road
Vale Royal
Allensbury Place
Brandon Road
Blundell Street
Wheelwright Street
Centurion Close
Offord Road
Huntingdon Street
Hemingford Road
Bridgeman Road
Thornhill Square
Bingfield Street
Pembroke Street
Barnsbury Road
Copenhagen Street
Wharf Road
Goods Way
Camley Street
Pancras Road
Battle Bridge Road
Crinan
Carnegie Street
Charlotte Terrace
Dewey Road
Cloudesley Pl
Chapel Mark
Donegal Street
White Lion Street
Penton Street
Caledonia Street
Collier Street
Northdown Street
Leeke Street
Chalton Street
Euston Road
Midland Road
0.25 mile
0.25 km
72
73
74
78
80
5
6
A
B
1
2

King's Cross

From St Pancras Station, restored to its full former glory, to the futuristic new campus of Central St Martins—this wasteland-turned-construction site-turning-super hub is changing so fast it's hard to keep track. For now, most things worth your while still centre on Caledonian Road (for eating and shopping) and York Way (for the slowing nightlife). As for tomorrow, we'll see.

Nightlife

- **Big Chill House** • 257 Pentonville Rd
- **Canal 125** • 125 Caledonian Rd
- **Central Station** • 37 Wharfdale Rd
- **Cross Kings** • 126 York Way
- **EGG** • 200 York Way
- **Hemingford Arms** • 128 Hemingford Rd
- **The Lexington** • 243 Pentonville Rd
- **Lincoln Lounge** • 52 York Way
- **The Tarmon** • 270 Caledonian Rd

Restaurants

- **Addis** • 42 Caledonian Rd
- **Dallas Burger Bar** • 257 Caledonian Rd
- **Euro Café** • 299 Caledonian Rd
- **Marathon** • 196 Caledonian Rd
- **Menelik** • 277 Caledonian Rd
- **The New Didar** • 347 Caledonian Rd
- **Oz** • 53 Caledonian Rd
- **Tony's Natural Foods** • 10 Caledonian Rd
- **Yum Yum** • 48 Caledonian Rd

Shopping

- **Continental Stores** • 26 Caledonian Rd
- **Cosmo Cornelio** • 182 Caledonian Rd

Supermarkets

- **Co-Op** • 303 Caledonian Rd
- **Iceland** • 259 Caledonian Rd

Map 80 • Angel / Upper St

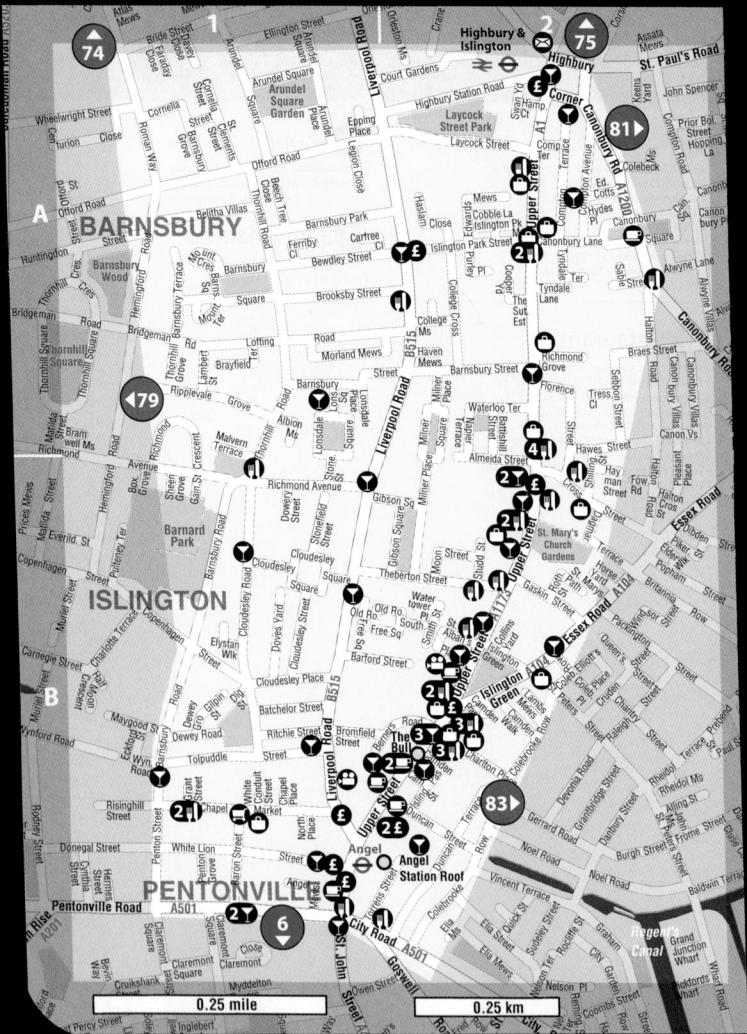

Angel / Upper St

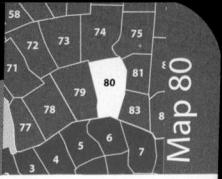

This area has everything. Welcoming bars full of lovely young things (Upper Street), dingy music venues (Buffalo Bar), antique shops full of lovely old things (Camden Passage), romance (Mem & Laz), passion (Cuba Libre), chilled Sunday mornings (The Breakfast Club), and a great mix of shops. And if that all sounds a little too cheerful, Feeling Gloomy at Carling Academy is still the place to dance and be miserable. Awesome!

Banks

- **Abbey** • 15 Islington Park St
- **Barclays** • 38 Islington Green
- **Barclays** • 2 Highbury Corner
- **Barclays** • 14 Upper St
- **Halifax** • 1 Liverpool Rd
- **HSBC** • 25 Islington High St
- **Lloyds** • 19 Upper St
- **NatWest** • 218 Upper St
- **Royal Bank of Scotland** • 40 Islington High St

Cinemas

- **Screen on the Green** • 83 Islington Green
- **Vue Islington** • 36 Parkfield St

Coffee

- **Estorick Gallery** • 39 Canonbury Sq
- **Euphorium Bakery** • 202 Upper St
- **Pret A Manger** • 27 Islington High St
- **Starbucks** • 71 Upper St
- **Starbucks** • 30 Upper St
- **Starbucks** • 7 High St
- **Tinderbox** • 21 Upper St

Landmarks

- **Angel Station Roof**
- **The Bull** •100 Upper St

Nightlife

- **25 Canonbury** • 25 Canonbury Lane
- **The Albert & Pearl** • 181 Upper St
- **The Angel** • 3 Islington High St
- **The Angelic** • 57 Liverpool Rd
- **Barrio North** • 45 Essex Rd
- **Buffalo Bar** • 259 Upper St
- **Camden Head** • 2 Camden Walk
- **Carling Academy** • 16 Parkfield St
- **The Castle** • 54 Pentonville Rd
- **The Cedar Room** • 235 Upper St
- **Compton Arms** • 4 Compton Ave
- **The Crown** • 116 Cloudesley Rd
- **Cuba Libre** • 72 Upper St
- **The Drapers Arms** • 44 Barnsbury St
- **Electrowerkz** • 7 Torrens St
- **Famous Cock** • 259 Upper St
- **The Florence** • 50 Florence St
- **The Garage** • 20 Highbury Corner
- **Hope And Anchor** • 207 Upper St
- **Islington Tap** • 80 Liverpool Rd
- **Jury's Inn** • 60 Pentonville Rd
- **Keston Lodge** • 131 Upper St
- **King's Head Theatre Pub** • 115 Upper St
- **Lucky Voice Private Karaoke** • 173 Upper St
- **Old Red Lion** • 418 St John St
- **The Regent** • 201 Liverpool Rd
- **Salmon & Compass** • 58 Penton St
- **Union Chapel** • Compton Terrace

Post Offices

- **Highbury** • 5 Highbury Corner

Restaurants

- **Afghan Kitchen** • 35 Islington Green
- **The Albion** • 10 Thornhill Rd
- **Alpino** • 97 Chapel Market
- **The Breakfast Club** • 31 Camden Passage
- **Candid Café** • 3 Torrens St
- **Desperados** • 127 Upper St
- **Elk in the Woods** • 39 Camden Passage
- **Fig and Olive** • 151 Upper St
- **Fine Burger Co** • 330 Upper St
- **Gem** • 265 Upper St
- **House** • 63 Canonbury Rd
- **Indian Veg Bhelpoori House** • 93 Chapel Market
- **Isarn** • 119 Upper St
- **Itsuka** • 54 Islington Park St
- **La Forchetta** • 73 Upper St
- **La Porchetta** • 141 Upper St
- **Le Mercury** • 140 Upper St
- **Masala Zone** • 80 Upper St
- **Mem & Laz** • 8 Theberton St
- **Metrogusto** • 13 Theberton St
- **Olive Grill** • 61 Upper St
- **Ottolenghi** • 287 Upper St
- **Pizzeria Oregano** • 19 St Alban's Pl
- **Pomegranate** • 139 Upper St
- **Rodizo Rico** • 77 Upper St
- **Tortilla** • 13 Islington High St
- **The Trawlerman Fish Shop** • 205 Upper St
- **Vigata Ristorante** • Liverpool Rd
- **Zaffrani** • 47 Cross St

Shopping

- **A Ferrari Deli** • 48 Cross St
- **After Noah** • 121 Upper St
- **Annie's** • 12 Camden Passage
- **Camden Passage** • Camden Passage
- **Cass Art** • 66 Colebrooke Row
- **Gill Wing Kitchen Shop** • 194 Upper St
- **Monte's Deli** • 23 Canonbury Lane
- **Palette London** • 21 Canonbury Ln
- **Paul A Young chocolate shop** • 33 Camden Passage
- **Raymond Roe Fishmonger** • Chapel Market
- **Salvation Army Islington** • 284 Upper St
- **Twentytwentyone** • 274 Upper St

Supermarkets

- **Iceland** • 62 Chapel Market

Map 81 • Canonbury

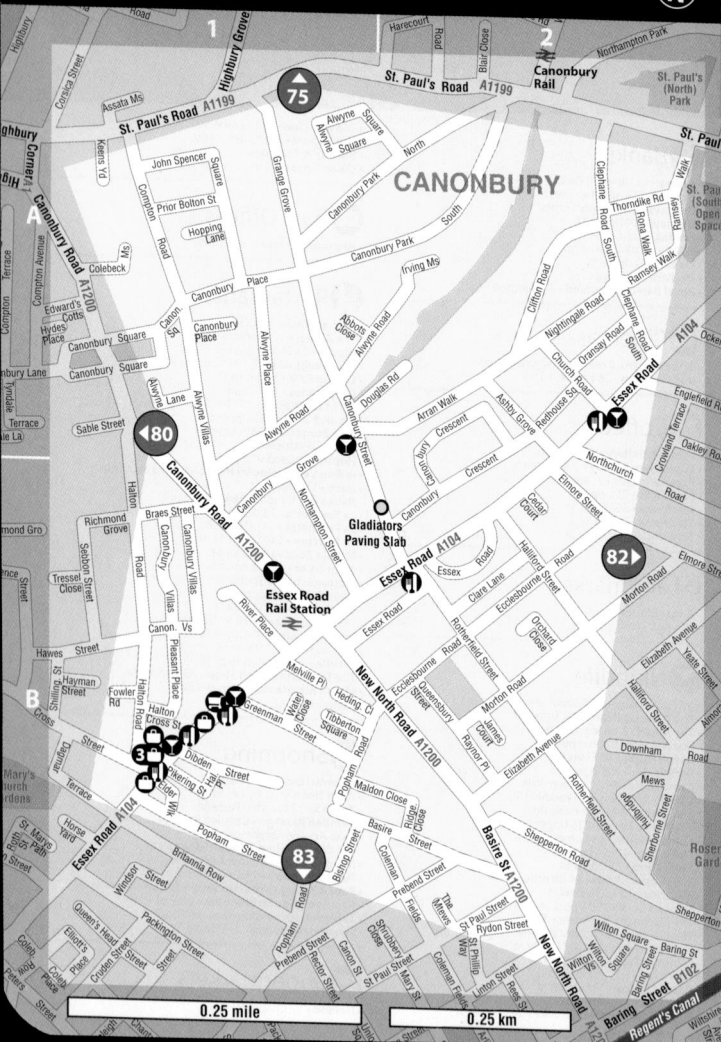
N
CANONBURY
Canonbury Rail
St. Paul's Road A1199
Highbury Grove
Northampton Park
St. Paul's (North) Park
Canonbury Road A1200
Essex Road A104
Essex Road Rail Station
Gladiators Paving Slab
New North Road A1200
Basire St A1200
Baring Street B102
Regent's Canal
Canonbury Square
Canonbury Place
Canonbury Park South
Canonbury Park North
Alwyne Square
Alwyne Place
Alwyne Villas
Alwyne Road
Alwyne Lane
Grange Grove
Compton Road
Compton Terrace
Compton Avenue
Prior Bolton St
Hopping Lane
John Spencer Square
Colebeck Ms
Edward's Cotts
Hydes Place
Sable Street
Halton Road
Braes Street
Richmond Grove
Canonbury Villas
Tressel Close
Selton Street
Hawes Street
Hayman Street
Fowler Rd
Halton Cross St
Pleasant Place
Canon. Vs
River Place
Essex Road
Northampton Street
Douglas Rd
Arran Walk
Canonbury Street
Crescent
Ashby Grove
Redhouse Sq
Church Road
Oransay Road
Nightingale Road
Clifton Road
Clapham Road South
Thorndike Rd
Rona Walk
Ransey Walk
Ramsey Walk
Harecourt Road
Blair Close
Assata Ms
Highbury Corner
Highbury Terrace
Tyndale Terrace
Cedar Court
Elmore Street
Hallford Road
Ecclesbourne Road
Clare Lane
Orchard Close
Morton Road
Elizabeth Avenue
Yeate Street
Hallford Street
Rotherfield Street
Queensbury Street
Raynor Pl
Melville Pl
Water Close
Greenman Street
Troberton Square
Dibden Street
Elder Wk
Popham Road
Maldon Close
Ridge Close
Basire Street
Coleman Street
Prebend Street
Bishop Street
Shepperton Road
Sherborne Street
Downham Road
Mews
Horse Yard
Britannia Row
Windsor Street
Packington Street
Queen's Head Yard
Elliott's Place
Crouden Street
Prebend Street
Penton Street
Canon St
St Paul Street
St Mary's Close
St Mary's Path
Rydon Street
The Mews
Fields
Shrubbery Close
Coleman Fields
St Philip's Way
Linton Street
Wilton Square
Wilton Ms
Baring St
Wilton Way
Hoxton Street
Hoxton Street
Essex Road
Essex Road
Essex Road

Heady mix of leafy spacious streets with multi-million pound mansions, right next to some of London's poorest estates—London in a nutshell. Essex Road has cracking shops including the eccentric Get Stuffed for all your taxidermy needs. Foodies are well catered for with real butchers (James Elliot), bakers (Raab's), and great ethnic eateries (Zigni House and Sabor).

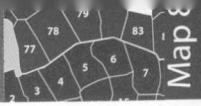

Landmarks

- **Gladiators Paving Slab** • 10 Canonbury St

Nightlife

- **Embassy Bar** • 119 Essex Rd
- **Marquess Tavern** • 32 Canonbury St
- **Myddleton Arms** • 52 Canonbury Rd
- **The Green Man** • 144 Essex Rd
- **The Lord Clyde** • 342 Essex Rd

Restaurants

- **Angel Cafe** • 100 Essex Rd
- **People's Choice Cafe** • 236 Essex Rd
- **Raab's Bakery** • 136 Essex Rd
- **Sabor** • 108 Essex Rd
- **Zigni House** • 330 Essex Rd

Shopping

- **Get Stuffed** • 105 Essex Rd
- **Handmade and Found** • 109 Essex Rd
- **HG Lockey & Sons** • 8 Halton Cross St
- **James Elliot Master Butcher** • 96 Essex Rd
- **Raab's The Baker's** • 136 Essex Rd
- **Sew Fantastic** • 107 Essex Rd

Supermarkets

- **Co-Op** • 132 Essex Rd

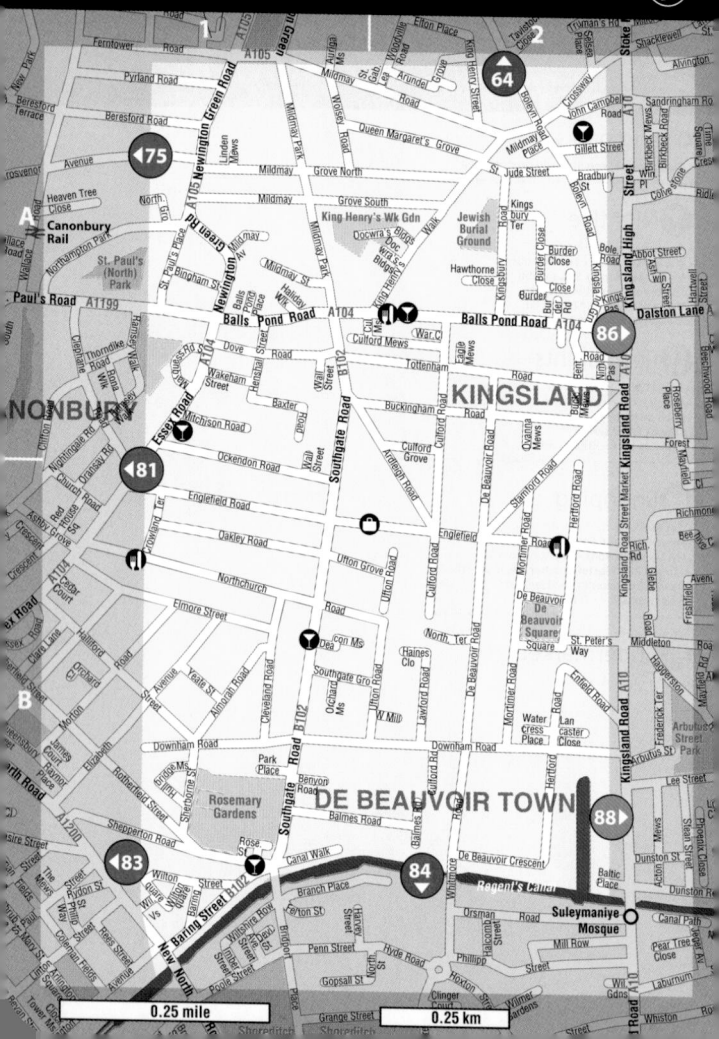
N
1
2
A
B
64
175
81
86
88
83
84
Canonbury Rail
Paul's Road A1199
Balls Pond Road A104
Balls Pond Road A104
Dalston Lane
KINGSLAND
NONBURY
DE BEAUVOIR TOWN
Rosemary Gardens
Suleymaniye Mosque
Regent's Canal
Baring Street B107
New North Rd
Essex Road
Southgate Road
Kingsland Road A10
Kingsland High Street
Newington Green Road
Green Rd
Stoke Newington Church St
Queen Margaret's Grove
Grove North
Grove South
Mildmay Grove
Mildmay Park
Mildmay Road
St Jude Street
Bradbury St
Kingsland Road Street Market
Kingsland Road A10
Kingsland Road A10
Kingsland Road A10

De Beauvoir Town / Kingsland

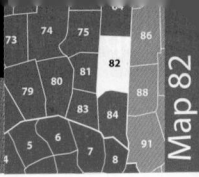

De Beauvoir is the buffer zone where swanky Islington merges into manic Hackney. As such it's the best of both worlds. To the west, there's quiet squares and gastropubs. But turn to the eastern edge for up-till-dawn boozing sessions. Bizarrely, it's also home to thousands of palm trees—so sit in de Beauvoir Square and pretend you're on a tropical holiday.

Landmarks

- **Suleymaniye Mosque** • 212 Kingsland Rd

Nightlife

- **The Northgate** • 113 Southgate Rd
- **The Orwell** • 382 Essex Rd
- **The Rosemary Branch** • 2 Shepperton Rd
- **Vortex** • 11 Gillett Sq
- **The Wellington** • 119 Balls Pond Rd

Restaurants

- **Casaba** • 162 Essex Rd
- **Huong Viet** • 12 Englefield Rd
- **Puji Puji** • 122 Balls Pond Rd

Shopping

- **North One Garden Centre** • 25 Englefield Rd

Map 83 • Angel (East) / City Rd (North)

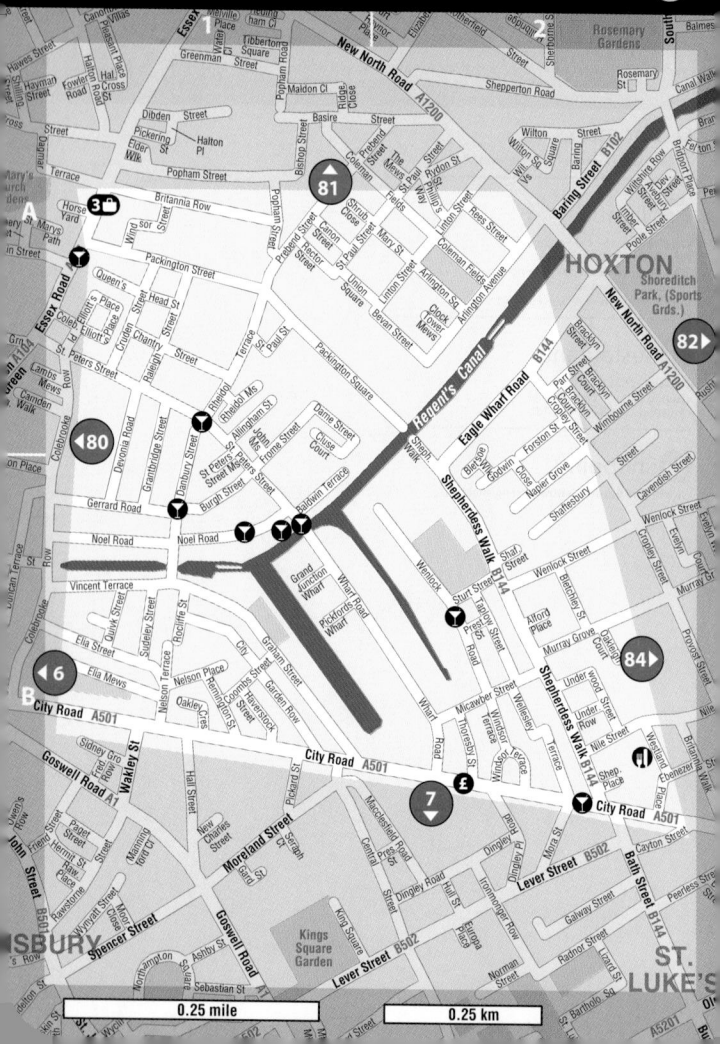
N
New North Road A1200
Essex Road
Baring Street B102
HOXTON
Shoreditch Park, (Sports Grds.)
Rosemary Gardens
Shepherdess Walk B144
Eagle Wharf Road B144
Regent's Canal
City Road A501
Goswell Road A1
Wakley St
Moreland Street
Spencer Street
Lever Street B502
Kings Square Garden
Bath Street B144
ST. LUKE'S
ISBURY
Britannia Row
Packington Street
Popham Street
Basire Street
Shepperton Road
Canal Walk
Wilton Way
Wilton Sq
Pickering St
Halton Pl
Dibden Street
Greenman Street
Tibberton Square
Maldon Cl
Ridge Close
Bishop Street
Popham Road
Horse Yard
Quen's Head St
Colebrooke Row
Camden Walk
Camden Mews
St Peters Street
Chapel Market
Rheidol Ms
Rheidol St
Allingham St
Frome Street
Chase Court
Baldwin Terrace
Burgh Street
Gerrard Road
Noel Road
Vincent Terrace
Elia Street
Elia Mews
Nelson Place
Oakley Cres
Sidney Grove
Hall Street
Pickard St
Dingley Road
Dingley Pl
Hull St
Ironmonger Row
Galway Street
Radnor Street
Bartholo Sq
Sebastian St
Ashby St
Northampton Sq
King Square
Central St
Mora St
Cayton Street
Wynyatt Street
Sidney Grove
Vincent Terrace
Colebrooke Row

For anyone bored of the bars of Upper Street or the ironic chic of Hoxton, the streets in between (along Essex Road or by the canal) are a better bet, with a more laidback atmosphere. NFT writers still remember The Island Queen as the birthplace of NFT London and the site of the now infamous "should Chiswick be in the book?" battle.

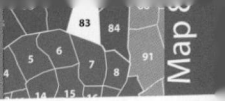

Banks

- **Barclays** • 146 City Rd

Nightlife

- **The Duke of Cambridge** • 30 St Peter's St
- **Earl of Essex** • 25 Danbury St
- **The Island Queen** • 87 Noel Rd
- **The Mucky Pup** • 39 Queen's Head St
- **The Narrow Boat** • 119 St.Peters St
- **Offside Bar and Gallery** • 273 City Rd
- **Old Queenis Head** • 44 Essex Rd
- **The Wenlock Arms** • 26 Wenlock Rd

Restaurants

- **Fifteen** • 15 Westland Pl

Shopping

- **Flashback** • 50 Essex Rd
- **Haggle Vinyl** • 114 Essex Rd
- **Past Caring** • 76 Essex Rd

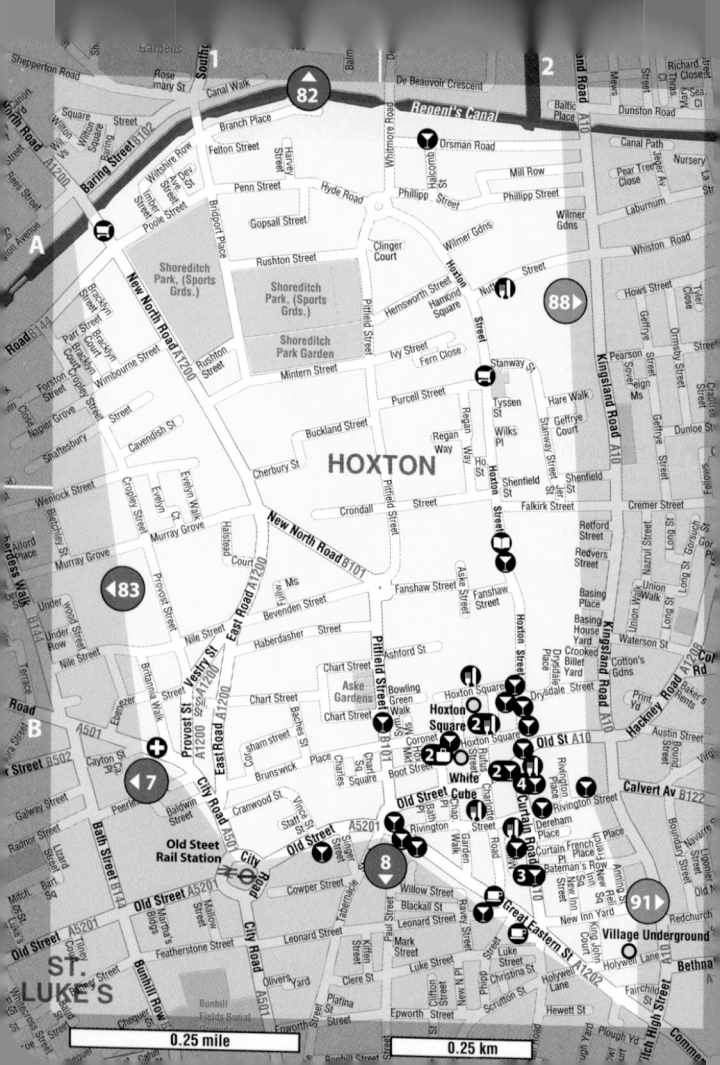
HOXTON
Regent's Canal
Shepperton Road
Canal Walk
Branch Place
Felton Street
Penn Street
Hyde Road
Gopsall Street
Bridport Place
Rushton Street
Shoreditch Park, (Sports Grds.)
Shoreditch Park Garden
Mintern Street
Clinger Court
Hemsworth Street
Hoxton Street
Pitfield Street
Ivy Street
Fern Close
Purcell Street
Buckland Street
Cherbury St
Crondall Street
Falkirk Street
Cremer Street
Fanshaw Street
Bevenden Street
Haberdasher Street
Ashford St
Chart Street
Aske Gardens
Bowling Green Walk
Hoxton Square
Old St A10
Old Street Cube
Old Street Rail Station
Old Street A5201
City Road A501
Bath Street B174
Bath Street B502
Baring Street B102
New North Road A1200
New North Road B101
East Road A1200
Provost St A1200
Kingsland Road A10
Hackney Road A1208
Calvert Av B122
Great Eastern St A1202
Village Underground
Bethnal Green
Bunhill Row
Leonard Street
Featherstone Street
Cowper Street
Willow Street
Blackall St
Leonard Street
Mark Street
Luke Street
Epworth Street
Hewett St
Holywell Lane
Scrutton St
Clere St
Platina
Bunhill Fields Burial
ST. LUKE'S
Rivington Street
Curtain Road
Shoreditch High Street
Commercial St
Dunston Road
Richard Closet
Whiston Road
Laburnum
Hows Street
Geffrye Street
Ormsby Street
Pearson Street
Hare Walk
Geffrye Court
Dunloe Street
Shenfield St
Redford Street
Redvers Street
Basing Place
Basing House Yard
Union Walk
Waterson St
Cotton's Gdns
Crooked Billet Yard
Drysdale Street
Drysdale Place
Print Yd
Austin Street
Bounds Green Road
Boundary Street
Navarre Street
Redchurch
Old Nt
Bethna
Fairchild St
Plough Yd
Hoxton Square
Coronet
Charles Square
Boot Street
Chapel Market
Curtain Road
Dereham Place
Curtain French Pl
Bateman's Row
Great Eastern St
New Inn Yard
King John Court
Holywell Lane
Willow Street
Cowper Street
Rivington
Old Street
Cranwood St
Baldwin Street
Galway Street
Pearson
Radnor Street
Cayton St
Calshamm Street
Bruns wick
Charles
Chap. Sq.
Staff St
Vince St
Bath Street
Bath Sq
Mitch. Bldgs
Morris's Bldgs
Mallow Street
Tabernacle
Leonard Street
Clifton Street
Philip
Scrutton St
Epworth Street
Hewett St
Holywell Lane
Fairchild St
Plough Yd
Bethna
Commercial St
Hackney Road
Austin Street
Bounds Green Road
Boundary Street
Navarre Street
Redchurch
Old Nt
Bethna
Fairchild St
Plough Yd
Commercial St
Shepperton Road
Canal Walk
Branch Place
Felton Street
Penn Street
Hyde Road
Gopsall Street
Bridport Place
Rushton Street
Clinger Court
Hemsworth Street
Hoxton Street
Pitfield Street
Ivy Street
Fern Close
Purcell Street
Buckland Street
Cherbury St
Crondall Street
Falkirk Street
Cremer Street
Fanshaw Street
Bevenden Street
Haberdasher Street
Ashford St
Chart Street
Aske Gardens
Bowling Green Walk
Hoxton Square
Old St A10
Old Street Cube
Old Street Rail Station
Old Street A5201
City Road A501
Bath Street B174
Bath Street B502
Baring Street B102
New North Road A1200
New North Road B101
East Road A1200
Provost St A1200
Kingsland Road A10
Hackney Road A1208
Calvert Av B122
Great Eastern St A1202
Village Underground
Bethnal Green
Bunhill Row
Leonard Street
Featherstone Street
Cowper Street
Willow Street
Blackall St
Leonard Street
Mark Street
Luke Street
Epworth Street
Hewett St
Holywell Lane
Scrutton St
Clere St
Platina
Bunhill Fields Burial
ST. LUKE'S
Rivington Street
Curtain Road
Shoreditch High Street
Commercial St
Dunston Road
Richard Closet
Whiston Road
Laburnum
Hows Street
Geffrye Street
Ormsby Street
Pearson Street
Hare Walk
Geffrye Court
Dunloe Street
Shenfield St
Redford Street
Redvers Street
Basing Place
Basing House Yard
Union Walk
Waterson St
Cotton's Gdns
Crooked Billet Yard
Drysdale Street
Drysdale Place
Print Yd
Austin Street
Bounds Green Road
Boundary Street
Navarre Street
Redchurch
Old Nt
Bethna
Fairchild St
Plough Yd
Commercial St
0.25 mile
0.25 km

With more bars than Brixton prison, Hoxton is so happening anything we say here will probably be out of date within the next two minutes. Most of the good stuff radiates out from Hoxton Square and Curtain Road—follow the trail of hipsters (you can't miss them). Find modern art (White Cube), cheap Thai (Yelo), live music (Cargo, Macbeth), and bars (The Foundry, Old Blue Last).

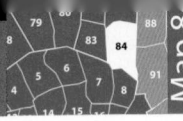

Coffee

- **Apostrophe** • 42 Great Eastern St
- **Eat.** • 59 Great Eastern St

Emergency Rooms

- **Moorfields Eye Hospital** • 162 City Rd

Landmarks

- **Hoxton Square** • Hoxton Sq
- **Village Underground** • 54 Holywell Ln
- **White Cube** • 48 Hoxton Square

Libraries

- **Shoreditch Library** • 80 Hoxton St

Nightlife

- **333** • 333 Old St
- **Bar Music Hall** • 134 Curtain Rd
- **Bedroom Bar** • 62 Rivington St
- **The Bricklayers Arms** • 63 Charlotte Rd
- **The Cantaloupe** • 35 Charlotte Rd
- **Cargo** • 83 Rivington St
- **Charlie Wright's International Bar** • 45 Pitfield St
- **Club Aquarium** • 256 Old St
- **Cocomo** • 323 Old St
- **Comedy Cafe** • 66 Rivington St
- **Cordy House** • Curtain Rd
- **East Village** • 89 Great Eastern St
- **The Elbow Room** • 97 Curtain Rd
- **Electricity Showroom** • 39 Hoxton Sq
- **Favela Chic** • 91 Great Eastern St
- **The Foundry** • 84 Great Eastern St
- **The Griffin** • 93 Leonard St
- **Hoxton Square Bar and Kitchen** • Hoxton Sq
- **The Legion** • 348 Old St
- **The Macbeth** • 60 70 Hoxton St
- **The Old Blue Last** • 39 Great Eastern St
- **Plastic People** • 147 Curtain Rd
- **The Red Lion** • 41 Hoxton St
- **The Stag's Head** • 55 Orsman Rd
- **Strongroom Bar** • 120 Curtain Rd
- **Troy Bar** • 10 Hoxton St

Restaurants

- **The Bean** • 126 Curtain Rd
- **The Diner** • 128 Curtain Rd
- **F. Cooke** • 150 Hoxton St
- **Macondo** • 8 Hoxton Sq
- **Rivington Bar and Grill** • 28 Rivington St
- **Shish** • 313 Old St
- **Yelo** • 8 Hoxton Sq

Shopping

- **Good Hood** • 41 Coronet St
- **Sh!** • 57 Hoxton Sq

Supermarkets

- **Co-Op** • 136 New North Rd
- **Iceland** • 209 Hoxton St

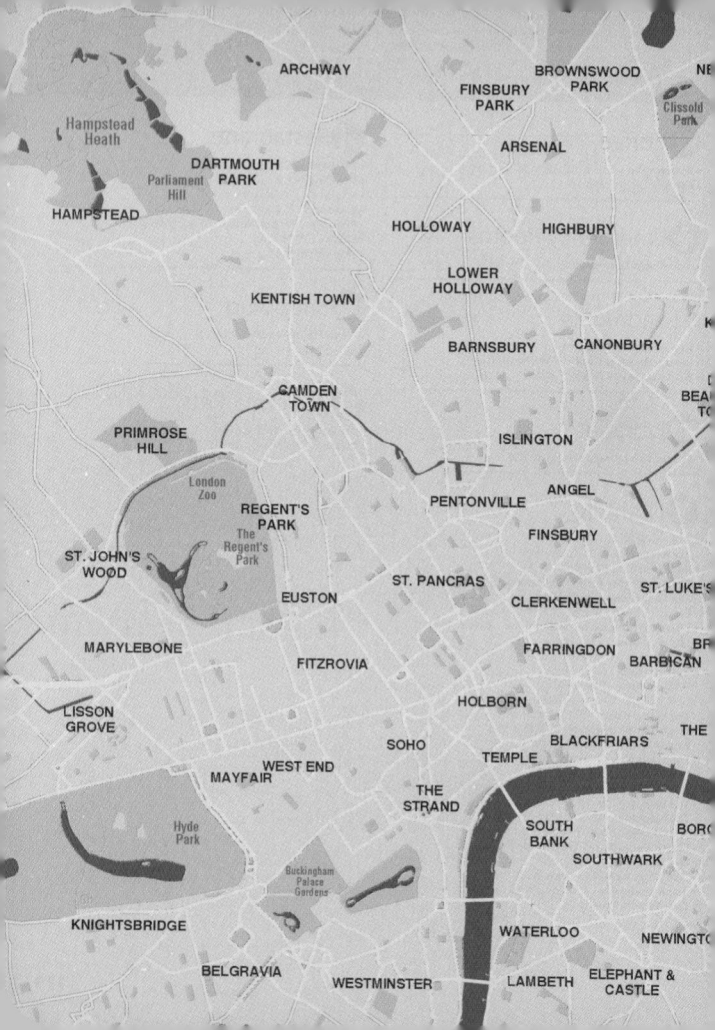
ARCHWAY
BROWNSWOOD PARK
FINSBURY PARK
Clissold Park
Hampstead Heath
ARSENAL
DARTMOUTH PARK
Parliament Hill
HAMPSTEAD
HOLLOWAY
HIGHBURY
LOWER HOLLOWAY
KENTISH TOWN
BARNSBURY
CANONBURY
CAMDEN TOWN
PRIMROSE HILL
ISLINGTON
London Zoo
REGENT'S PARK
The Regent's Park
PENTONVILLE
ANGEL
FINSBURY
ST. JOHN'S WOOD
ST. PANCRAS
EUSTON
CLERKENWELL
MARYLEBONE
FITZROVIA
FARRINGDON
BARBICAN
HOLBORN
LISSON GROVE
SOHO
BLACKFRIARS
TEMPLE
WEST END
MAYFAIR
THE STRAND
Hyde Park
SOUTH BANK
SOUTHWARK
Buckingham Palace Gardens
KNIGHTSBRIDGE
WATERLOO
BELGRAVIA
WESTMINSTER
LAMBETH
ELEPHANT & CASTLE

UPPER CLAPTON
LEA BRIDGE
Lee Valley Park
LOWER CLAPTON
Hackney Downs
CKLEWELL
HOMERTON
Hackney Marsh
HACKNEY WICK
Victoria Park
HACKNEY
DALSTON
LONDON FIELDS
SOUTH HACKNEY
OLD FORD
HAGGERSTON
Haggerston Park
GLOBE TOWN
BOW
SHOREDITCH
BETHNAL GREEN
MILE END
BROMLEY
SPITALFIELDS
BRICK LANE
BOW COMMON
STEPNEY
WHITECHAPEL
RATCLIFF
SHADWELL
POPLAR
LIMEHOUSE
CANARY WHARF
WAPPING
DOCKLANDS
ISLE OF DOGS
ROTHERHITHE
CUBITT TOWN
MILLWALL
Millwall Park
BERMONDSEY
Southwark Park
Tower of London Park
Thames River
Stamford Hill
Stoke Newington High St
Kingsland Rd
Queensbridge Rd
Mare St
Kingsland High St
Dalston Ln
Graham Rd
Amhurst Rd
Pandora Rd
L Clapton Rd
Upswick Rd
Nick Rd
Cassland Rd
Well St
Victoria Park Rd
Old Ford Rd
Bishop's Rd
Hackney Rd
Cambridge Heath Rd
Roman Road
Grove Rd
Mile End Rd
Globe Rd
Dunbridge St
Cheshire St
Brick Ln
Vallance Rd
Whitechapel Rd
Mile End Park
Ben Jonson Rd
St. Pauls Way
Burdett Rd
Commercial St
New Rd
Commercial Rd
Cable St
The Highway
Westferry Rd
Aspen Way
Manchester Rd
85
86
87
88
89
90
91
92
93
94
95
96
97
98
99
100
101
102
103

Map 85 • Stoke Newington (East)

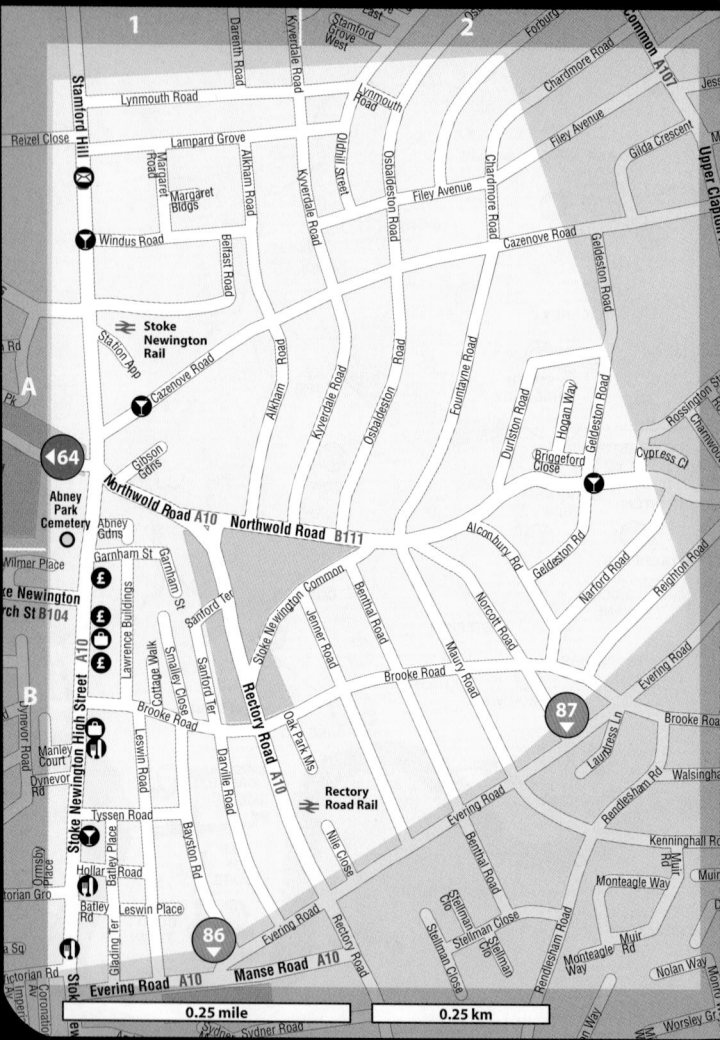

A thriving mosque in the heart of the Orthodox Jewish community, a cemetery-cum-nature reserve-cum-cruising zone (Abney Park Cemetery) and a lesbian bar (Blush) thrown in for extra measure – this is Hackney at its best. Touchdown at Stoke Newington Airport, scoff great bagels at Bagel House and, if cans on the common aren't your style, try the world's biggest beer garden at the White Hart.

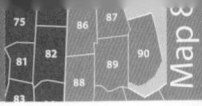

Banks

- **Halifax** • 173 Stoke Newington High St
- **HSBC** • 150 Stoke Newington High St
- **NatWest** • 196 Stoke Newington High St

Landmarks

- **Abney Park Cemetery** • Stoke Newington High St

Nightlife

- **The Birdcage** • 58 Stamford Hill
- **Blush** • 8 Cazenove Rd
- **The Royal Sovereign** • 64 Northwold Rd
- **White Hart** • 69 Stoke Newington High St

Post Offices

- **Stamford Hill** • 82 Stamford Hill

Restaurants

- **Bagel House** • 2 Stoke Newington High St
- **Café Z Bar** • 58 Stoke Newington High St
- **Testi** • 38 Stoke Newington High St

Shopping

- **Hamdys** • 167 Stoke Newington High St
- **Stoke Newington Bookshop** • 167 Stoke Newington High St

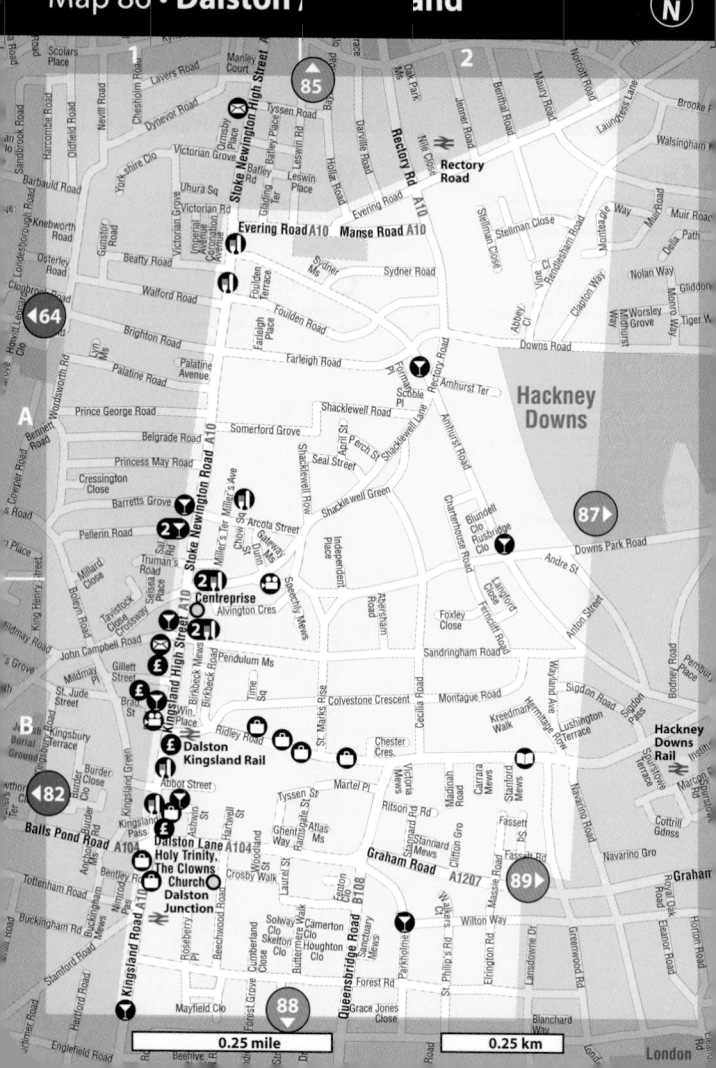
N
1
2
A
B
85
86
87
88
89
Scolars Place
Layers Road
Marley Court
Chesholm Road
Nevill Road
Didfield Road
Dynevor Road
Stoke Newington High Street A10
Tyssen Road
Victorian Grove
Bailey Place
Leswin Rd
Holiss Road
Darvill Road
Rectory Rd A10
Mile Close
Oak Park Mews
Jenner Road
Benthal Road
Maury Road
Norcott Road
Launceston Lane
Brooke Rd
Walsingham
Rectory Road
Dynevor Road
Victorian Grove
Uhura Sq
Victorian Rd
Bailey Place
Glading Ter
Leswin Place
Evening Road A10
Manse Road A10
Stellman Close
Montague Way
Muir Road
Barbauld Road
Knebworth Road
Gunstor Road
Osterley Road
Beatty Road
Sydner Mews
Sydner Road
Nolan Way
Gliddon Road
Walford Road
Foulden Terrace
Foulden Road
Clapton Way
Worsley Grove
Morris Way
Brighton Road
Farleigh Place
Farleigh Road
Downs Road
Palatine Road
Palatine Avenue
Formosa Pl
Scoble Pl
Amhurst Ter
Hackney Downs
Prince George Road
Shacklewell Road
Somerford Grove
Belgrade Road
Princess May Road
Cressington Close
Barretts Grove
Shacklewell Lane
Amhurst Road
April St
Parsons St
Seal Street
Shacklewell Row
Shacklewell Green
Pellerin Road
Arcola Street
Millar's Ave
Millar's Ter
Stoke Newington Road A10
Independent Place
Charnwood Road
Blundell Clo
Rustridge Clo
Downs Park Road
Andre St
Millard Close
Truman's Road
Selsea Place
Tavistock Close
Crossway
Balsam Rd
Centreprise
Alvington Cres
Speedbird Mews
Abersham Road
Foxley Close
Lakeford Close
Ferncliff Road
Arlton Street
John Campbell Road
Sandringham Road
Pendulum Ms
Birkbeck Mews
Birkbeck Road
Gillett Street
Kingsland High Street A10
Colvestone Crescent
Montague Road
Cecilia Road
Kreedman Walk
Kermington Rd
Wyndham Ave
Sigdon Road
Sigdon Pass
Bodney Road
Pembury Place
Hackney Downs Rail
Lushington Terrace
Mildmay Road
St. Jude Street
Kingsbury Terrace
Burial Ground
Ridley Road
St. Martin Rise
Chester Cres.
Dalston Kingsland Rail
Abbot Street
Kingsland Green
Burder Clo
Burder Close
Tyssen St
Martel Pl
Victoria Mews
Madinah Road
Carrara Mews
Stanford Mews
Navarino Road
Balls Pond Road A104
Kingsland Pass
Ashwin St
Hartwell St
Ghent Way
Hamsgate St
Atlas Ms
Ritson Rd
Mannard Mews
Fassett Rd
Cottrill Gdnss
Dalston Lane A104
Holy Trinity, The Clowns Church
Dalston Junction
Woodland St
Crosby Walk
Laurel St
Graham Road A1207
Clinton Gro
Massie Road
Navarino Gro
Graham
Tottenham Road
Bentley Rd
Kingsland Road A10
Rosebery Pl
Beechwood Road
Cumberland Close
Solway Clo
Skelton Clo
Butterfield Walk
Camerton Clo
Houghton Clo
Queensbridge Road
Parkholme
Wilton Way
Etrington Rd
Lansdowne Dr
Greenwood Rd
Eleanor Road
Royal Oak Road
Horton Road
Buckingham Road
Stamford Road
Hertford Road
Forest Grove
Mayfield Clo
Forest Rd
Grace Jones Close
Blanchard Way
Englefield Road
Beehive Pl
0.25 mile
0.25 km
London

Dalston / Kingsland

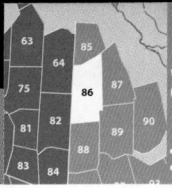

The length of Kingsland Road provides a catwalk for London's bright young creative things sporting the latest 'dos (and, frankly referee, don'ts). Head to The Haggerston for London's best £3-a-pint house party and squeeze into the Jazz Bar for the night's glorious final throes. And, if you're that way inclined, The Clowns Church proves religion really is one big joke.

Banks

- **Abbey** • 86 Kingsland High St
- **Barclays** • 3 Kingsland High St
- **Halifax** • 81 Kingsland High St
- **NatWest** • 74 Kingsland High St

Cinemas

- **Lux Salon** • 18 Shacklewell Ln
- **Rio Cinema** • 107 Kingsland High St

Landmarks

- **Centreprise** • 136 Kingsland High St
- **Holy Trinity, The Clowns Church** • Beechwood Rd & Kirkland Walk

Libraries

- **CLR James Library** • 30 Dalston Ln

Nightlife

- **Bar 23** • 23 Stoke Newington Rd
- **Barden's Boudoir** • 38 Stoke Newington Rd
- **Café Oto** • 18 Ashwin St
- **Dalston Superstore** • 117 Kingsland High St
- **The Haggerston** • 438 Kingsland Rd
- **Jazz Bar** • 4 Bradbury St
- **Marquis of Lansdowne** • 48 Stoke Newington Rd
- **Passion** • 251 Amhurst Rd
- **Pembury Tavern** • 90 Amhurst Rd
- **The Prince George** • 40 Parkholme Rd

Post Offices

- **Kingsland High Street** • 118 Kingsland High St
- **Stoke Newington** • 138 Stoke Newington High St

Restaurants

- **The Best Turkish Kebab** • 125 Stoke Newington Rd
- **Evin Bar and Café** • 115 Kingsland High St
- **Mangal 1** • 10 Arcola St
- **Mangal 2** • 4 Stoke Newington Rd
- **Peppers and Spice** • 20 Kingsland High St
- **Shanghai** • 41 Kingsland High St
- **Somine** • 131 Kingsland High St
- **Stone Cave** • 111 Kingsland High St
- **The Tea Rooms** • 155 Stoke Newington Rd

Shopping

- **Centre Supermarket** • 588 Kingsland Rd
- **Dalston Mill Fabrics** • 69 Ridley Rd
- **Oxfam Dalston** • 570 Kingsland Rd
- **Party Party** • 9 Ridley Rd
- **Ridley Road Market** • Ridley Rd
- **Sound 323 @ Cafe Oto** • 18 Ashwin St
- **Turkish Food Centre** • 89 Ridley Rd

Map 87 • Hackney Downs / Lower Clapton

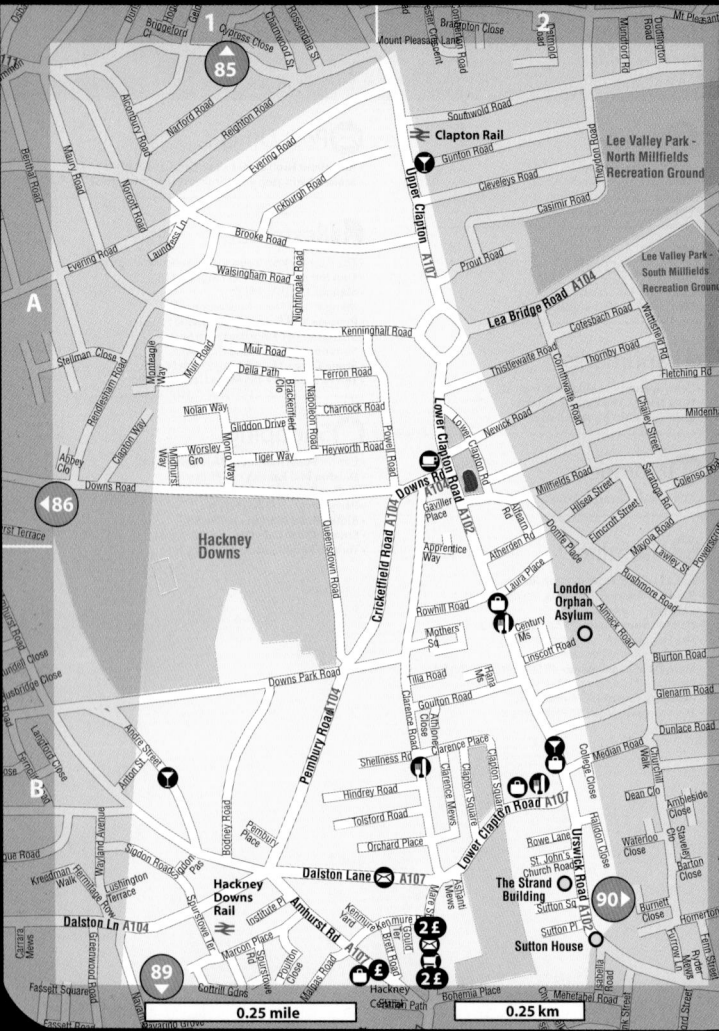

Hackney Downs / Lower Clapton

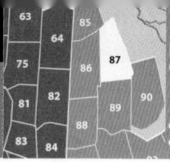

Ok, the place looks like a foul dump, but it's pretty happening. As Dalston's budget brother the Downs are a breeding ground for secret gigs (see Hugo's), warehouse raves, and the occasional blud with a shank. Lower Clapton is an eccentric area in mid-boom; check out the grand Orphan Asylum before a pint with the pissheads in Biddle Brothers. *Then* try and talk sense with Umit.

Banks

- **Abbey** • 392 Mare St
- **Barclays** • 298 Mare St
- **Halifax** • 402 Mare St
- **HSBC** • 283 Mare St
- **NatWest** • 20 Amhurst Rd

Coffee

- **Organic & Natural** • 191 Lower Clapton Rd

Landmarks

- **London Orphan Asylum** • Linscott Rd
- **The Strand Building** • 29 Urswick Rd
- **Sutton House** • 2 Homerton High St

Nightlife

- **Biddle Brothers** • 88 Lower Clapton Rd
- **Crooked Billet** • 84 Upper Clapton Rd
- **Hugo's Speaker Palace** • 14 Andre St

Post Offices

- **Dalston Lane** • 244 Dalston Ln
- **Hackney** • 382 Mare St

Restaurants

- **India Gate** • 75 Lower Clapton Rd
- **Parioli** • 90 Lower Clapton Rd
- **Pogo Café** • 76 Clarence Rd

Shopping

- **The Pet Shop** • 40 Amhurst Rd
- **Salvation Army Clapton** • 122-124 Lower Clapton Rd
- **Second Time Around** • 60 Lower Clapton Rd
- **Umit & Son** • 35 Lower Clapton Rd

Supermarkets

- **Iceland** • 150 Mare St

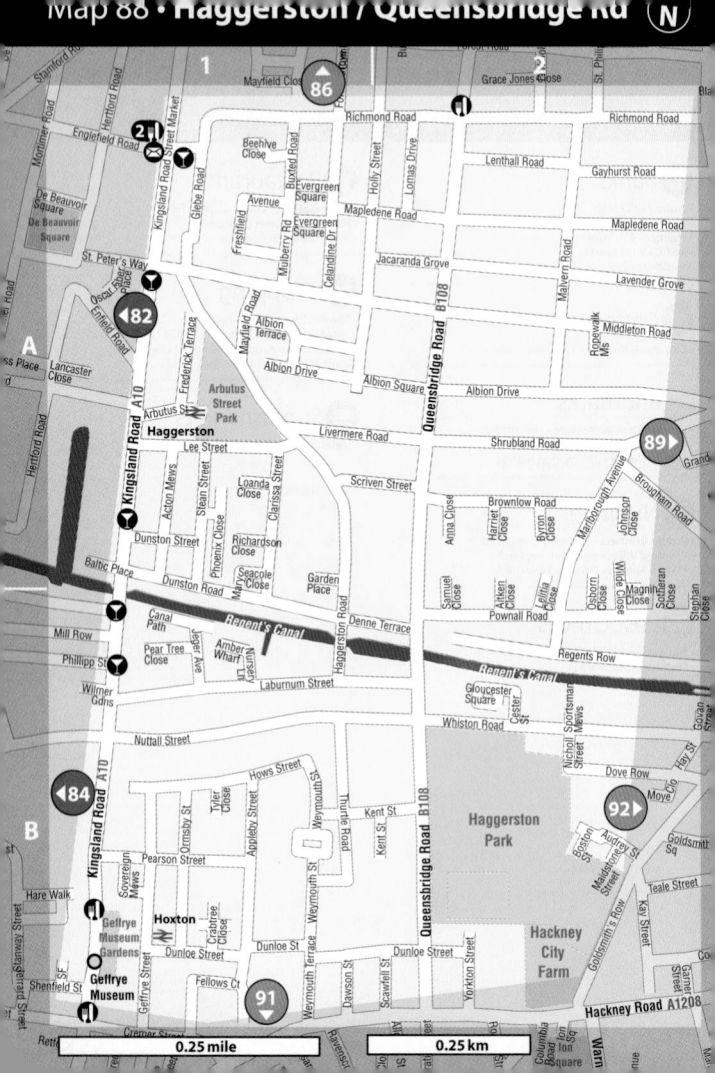
N
1
2
A
B
Mayfield Close
Grace Jones Close
Richmond Road
Englefield Road
Montmer Road
Hertford Road
Kingsland Road Street Market
Beehive Close
Buxted Road
Evergreen Square
Holly Street
Lomas Drive
Lenthall Road
Gayhurst Road
Mapledene Road
Avenue
Glebe Road
Freshfield
Mulberry Rd
Celandine Dr
Jacaranda Grove
Malvern Road
Lavender Grove
De Beauvoir Square
St. Peter's Way
Enfield Road
Frederick Terrace
Maylield Road
Albion Terrace
Albion Drive
Albion Square
Ropewalk Ms
Middleton Road
Lancaster Close
Arbutus Street Park
Arbutus St
Haggerston
Kingsland Road A10
Queensbridge Road B108
Livermere Road
Shrubland Road
Lee Street
Acton Mews
Stean Street
Loanda Close
Clarissa Street
Scriven Street
Brownlow Road
Anna Close
Harriet Close
Byron Close
Mainbrough Avenue
Brougham Road
Johnson Close
Dunston Street
Richardson Close
Phoenix Close
Baltic Place
Seacole Close
Dunston Road
Garden Place
Samuel Close
Aitken Close
Lillia Close
Pownall Road
Osborn Close
Wilde Close
Magnin Close
Scottaran Close
Stephan Close
Canal Path
Regent's Canal
Denne Terrace
Haggerston Road
Mill Row
Pear Tree Close
Amber Wharf
Phillipp St
Wilmer Gdns
Laburnum Street
Regents Row
Gloucester Square
Whiston Road
Nicholl Sportsman Mews
Nuttall Street
Hows Street
Tyler Close
Appleby Street
Weymouth St
Thurlow Road
Kent St
Dove Row
Hay St
Moye St
Haggerston Park
Ormsby St
Pearson Street
Sovereign Mews
Hare Walk
Geffrye Museum Gardens
Hoxton
Crabtree Close
Dunloe Street
Dunloe St
Weymouth Terrace
Dawson St
Scawfell St
Yorkton Street
Boston St
Audrey St
Mackenzie Street
Goldsmith's Row
Teale Street
Kay Street
Goldsmith Sq
Hackney City Farm
Geffrye Street
Fellows Ct
Shenfield St
Geffrye Museum
Hackney Road A1208
Cremer Street
Columbia Road Flower Market
Columbia Road
Ion Square
0.25 mile
0.25 km
86
21
82
89
84
92
91

Haggerston / Queensbridge Rd

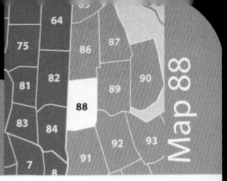

Subsumed by the Hackney/Dalston/Stokey axis of cool, this area is a fashionable rash on a dirty backside. There are delicate highs in the Geffrye Museum but the place belongs to seedy, trendy joints like Melange and the Russian Bar. You can really be 'artistic' round Kingsland Road or at least get pissed with a bunch of people you're going to despise come daylight.

Landmarks

- **Geffrye Museum** • 136 Kingsland Rd

Nightlife

- **A10 (aka The Russian Bar)** • 267 Kingsland Rd
- **The Fox** • 372 Kingsland Rd
- **Melange** • 281 Kingsland Rd
- **Passing Clouds** • 440 Kingsland Rd
- **Plaza** • 161 Kingsland Rd

Post Offices

- **Kingsland Road** • 416 Kingsland Rd

Restaurants

- **Faulkner's** • 424 Kingsland Rd
- **LMNT** • 316 Queensbridge Rd
- **That Vietnamese Place** • 134 Kingsland Rd
- **Usha** • 428 Kingsland Rd
- **Viet Hoa Café** • 70 Kingsland Rd

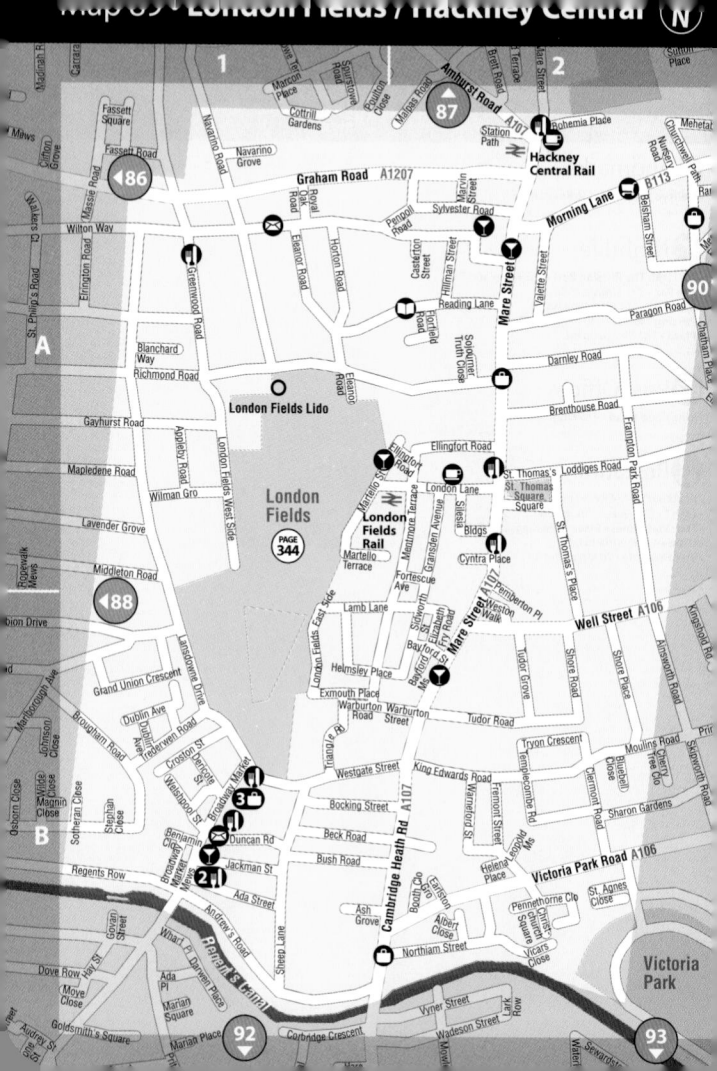
1
2
A
B
Marcon Place
Cottrill Gardens
Southwold Road
Poulton Close
Malmas Road
Ambrust Road A107
87
Brett Road
Station Path
Bohemia Place
Hackney Central Rail
Mehetat
Fassett Square
Fassett Road
Navarino Road
Navarino Grove
Graham Road A1207
86
Royal Oak Road
Sylvester Road
Morning Lane
B113
Wilton Way
Eleanor Road
Horton Road
Hillman Street
Mare Street
Valette Street
Reading Lane
Paragon Road
90
Greenwood Road
Blanchard Way
Richmond Road
Darnley Road
Brentwood Road
London Fields Lido
Gayhurst Road
Ellingfort Road
Mapledene Road
Wilman Gro
Lavender Grove
London Fields
PAGE 344
London Fields Rail
Martello Terrace
Cyntra Place
St. Thomas's Square
Loddiges Road
Frampton Park Road
St. Thomas's Place
Middleton Road
88
Lamb Lane
Well Street A106
Mare Street A107
Weston Walk
Bayford St
Helmsley Place
Exmouth Place
Warburton Road
Tudor Road
Tudor Grove
Short Road
Grand Union Crescent
Broadway Road
Dublin Ave
Trederwen Road
Croston St
Westgate Street
King Edwards Road
Tryon Crescent
Moulins Road
Bocking Street
Sharon Gardens
Beck Road
Bush Road
Jackman St
Regents Row
Ada Street
Cambridge Heath Rd A107
Victoria Park Road A106
Northiam Street
Victoria Park
Vyner Street
Wadeson Street
Corbridge Crescent
92
93
Mare Street
Hackney Central

London Fields / Hackney Central

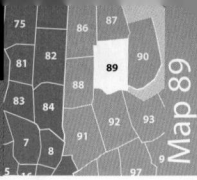

London Fields is Hackney showing off. Join the area's arty warehouse residents and VW van-driving young families in their cracking park, before browsing Broadway Market's cute delicatessen and quirky shops. Hackney Central is either annoyingly busy or refreshingly vibrant. Up to you. Thirsty? The Dove for Belgian brews, The Pub on the Park for its sunny terrace, The Dolphin for debauched late-nighters.

Coffee

- **Caffe Nero** • 22 London Lane
- **The Corner Deli** • 121 Mare St

Landmarks

- **London Fields Lido** • London Fields Westside

Libraries

- **Hackney Central Library** • 1 Reading Lane

Nightlife

- **Baxter's Court** • 282 Mare St
- **The Dolphin** • 165 Mare St
- **The Dove** • 24 Broadway Market
- **The Old Ship** • 2 Sylvester Path
- **Pub on the Park** • 19 Martello St

Post Offices

- **London Fields** • 39 Broadway Market
- **Wilton Way** • 67 Wilton Way

Restaurants

- **Buen Ayre** • 50 Broadway Market
- **Cafe Bohemia** • 2 Bohemia Pl
- **Cat and Mutton** • 76 Broadway Market
- **Corner Deli** • 121 Mare St
- **F. Cooke** • 9 Broadway Market
- **Hai Ha** • 206 Mare St
- **R Cooke and Sons** • 9 Broadway Market
- **The Spurstowe Arms** • 68 Greenwood Rd

Shopping

- **Artvinyl** • 13 Broadway Market
- **Broadway Market** • Broadway Market
- **Burberry Factory Shop** • 29 Chatham Pl
- **Candle Factory** • 184 Mare St
- **L'eau a la Bouche** • 49 Broadway Market London
- **Lazy Days** • 21 Mare St

Supermarkets

- **Tesco** • 55 Morning Ln

Map 90 • Homerton / Victoria Park North

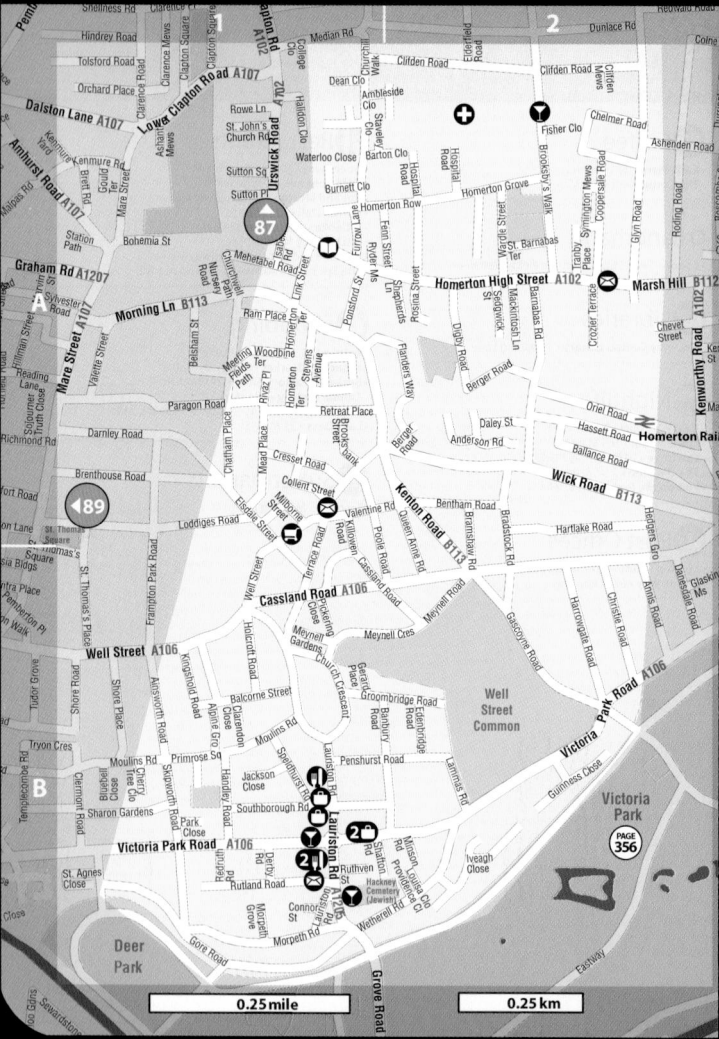

Homerton / Victoria Park North

Hackney heartlands with rows of terraces that get posher the nearer Vicky Park you go. The gentrification fairy has sprinkled lots of magic dust on villagey Lauriston Road – head to Sublime if you get a mega raise, Empress of India on payday and Royal Inn on the Park or The Ginger Pig if you find a tenner on the floor.

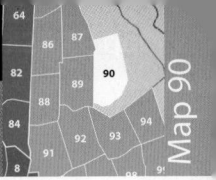

Emergency Rooms

- **Homerton University Hospital** • Homerton Row

Libraries

- **Homerton Library** • Homerton High St

Nightlife

- **Chats Palace Arts Centre** • 42 Brooksby Walk
- **The Lauriston** • 162 Victoria Park Rd
- **Royal Inn on the Park** • 111 Lauriston Rd

Post Offices

- **High Street** • 226 Homerton High St
- **Victoria Park** • 112 Lauriston Rd
- **Well Street** • 188 Well St

Restaurants

- **Blueberries** • 87 Lauriston Rd
- **The Empress of India** • 130 Lauriston Rd
- **The Fish House** • 126 Lauriston Rd

Shopping

- **Cheech Miller** • 227 Victoria Park Rd
- **The Ginger Pig** • 99 Lauriston Rd
- **Sublime** • 225 Victoria Park Rd
- **Work Shop** • 77 Lauriston Rd

Supermarkets

- **Tesco** • 180 Well St

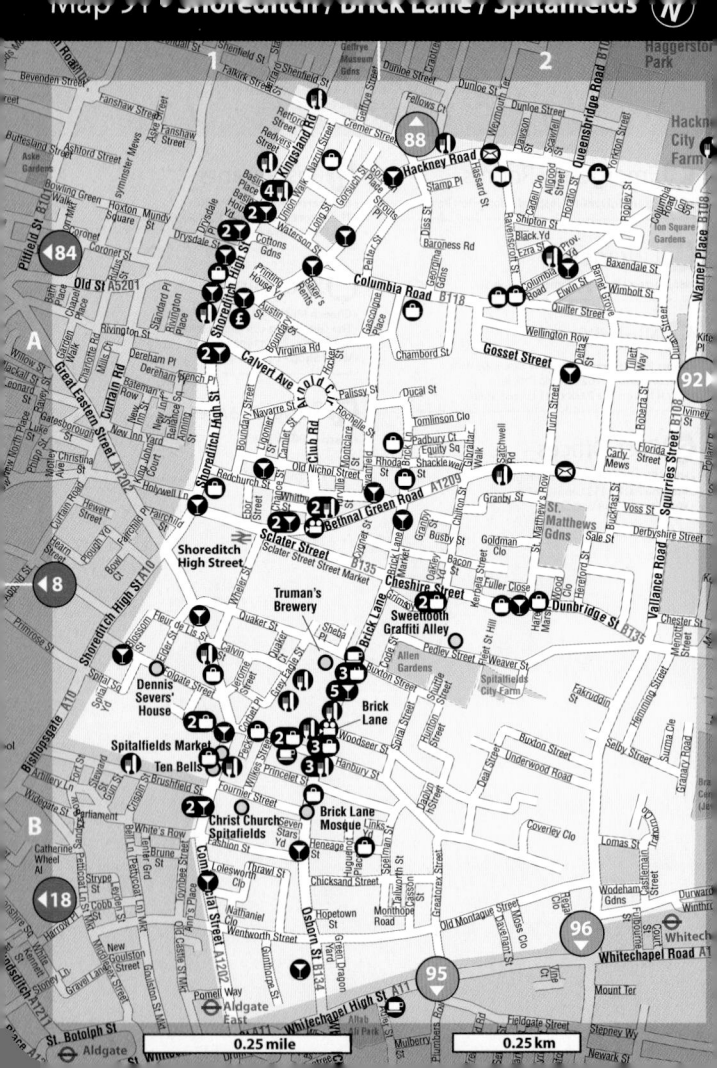
N
1
2
A
B
Haggerston Park
Hackney City Farm
Hackney Road
Kingsland Rd
Queensbridge Road B110
Pitfield St B110
Old St A5201
Shoreditch High St
Columbia Road B118
Gosset Street
Calvert Ave
Great Eastern Street A1202
Curtain Rd
Shoreditch High St
Club Rd
Bethnal Green Road A1209
Sclater Street
Shoreditch High Street
Squirries Street B1068
Vallance Road
Cheshire Street
Dunbridge St B135
Truman's Brewery
Sweetooth Graffiti Alley
Brick Lane
Dennis Severs' House
Spitalfields Market
Ten Bells
Brick Lane Mosque
Christ Church Spitalfields
Commercial Street A1202
Whitechapel Road A11
Whitechapel High St A11
Bishopsgate A11
St Botolph St
Aldgate
Aldgate East
Warner Place B1068
0.25 mile
0.25 km

horeditch / Brick Lane / Spitalfields

So achingly hip you wonder why this golden triangle of neighbourhoods doesn't get itself off to the doctors for some ointment. Brick Lane for curries (Le Taj), bars (Vibe or Loungelover), clubs (93 Feet East), and leather by the yard. Shoreditch for more boozers (Bar Kick or Anda De Bridge) and Spitalfields for the spangley tarted-up market and the best lunch stalls in the City.

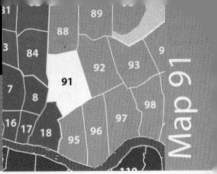

Banks

- **NatWest** • 180 Shoreditch High St

Cinemas

- **Rich Mix Centre** • 34 Bethnal Green Rd
- **Short & Sweet** • 91 Brick Ln

Coffee

- **Coffee @** • 154 Brick Ln
- **Nude Espresso** • 26 Hanbury St
- **Starbucks** • 45 Whitechapel Rd

Landmarks

- **Brick Lane Mosque** • 59 Brick Lane
- **Christ Church Spitalfields** • 2 Fournier St
- **Dennis Severs' House** • 18 Folgate St
- **Spitalfields Market** • 105 Commercial St
- **Sweettooth Graffiti Alley** • Pedley St
- **Ten Bells** • 84 Commercial St
- **Truman's Brewery** • Brick Lane

Libraries

- **Dorset Library** • Ravenscroft St

Nightlife

- **93 Feet East** • 150 Brick Ln
- **Anda De Bridge** • 42 Kingsland Rd
- **The Archers** • 42 Osborn St
- **Bar Kick** • 127 Shoreditch High St
- **Bethnal Green Working Men's Club** • 44 Pollard Row
- **The Big Chill Bar** • Dray Walk off Brick Lane
- **Café 1001** • 91 Brick Lane
- **The Carpenter's Arms** • 73 Cheshire St
- **Casa Blue** • 228 Brick Lane
- **Catch** • 22 Kingsland Rd
- **Club In a Toilet!** • 82 Commercial St
- **The Commercial Tavern** • 142 Commercial St
- **Ditch Bar** • 145 Shoreditch High St
- **Exit** • 174 Brick Lane
- **The George & Dragon** • Hackney Rd
- **The Golden Heart** • 110 Commercial St
- **The Gramaphone Bar** • 60 Commercial St
- **Green and Red** • 51 Bethnal Green Rd
- **Herbal** • 10 Kingsland Rd
- **Jaguar Shoes** • 32 Kingsland Rd
- **Joiners Arms** • 116 Hackney Rd
- **Loungelover** • 1 Whiteby St
- **On the Rocks** • 25 Kingsland Rd
- **Owl And The Pussycat** • 34 Redchurch St
- **Prague** • 6 Kingsland Rd
- **Pride of Spitalfields** • 3 Heneage St
- **Public Life** • 82 Commercial St
- **Redchurch** • 107 Redchurch St
- **The Royal Oak** • 73 Columbia Rd
- **Shoreditch House** • Ebor St
- **T Bar** • 56 Shoreditch High St
- **Vibe Bar** • 91 Brick Ln
- **The Water Poet** • 9 Folgate St
- **Ye Olde Axe** • 69 Hackney Rd

Post Offices

- **Bethnal Green** • 223 Bethnal Green Rd
- **Hackney Road** • 198 Hackney Rd

Restaurants

- **Beigel Bakery** • 159 Brick Lane
- **Brick Lane Clipper Restaurant** • 104 Brick Ln
- **Café Bangla** • 128 Brick Lane
- **Drunken Monkey** • 222 Shoreditch High St
- **Ethiopian Food Stall** • Sunday Upmarket, Truman's Brewery, Brick Lane
- **Green and Red** • 51 Bethnal Green Rd
- **Hackney City Farm** • 1 Goldsmiths Row
- **Hanoi Cafe** • 98 Kingsland Rd
- **Hawksmoor** • 157 Commercial St
- **Jones Dairy Cafe** • 23 Ezra St
- **Le Taj** • 96 Brick Ln
- **Les Trois Garcons** • 1 Club Row
- **Noodle King** • 185 Bethnal Green Rd
- **Ping Pong** • 3 Steward St
- **The Premises** • 201 Hackney Rd
- **Que Viet** • 102 Kingsland Rd
- **Rootmaster** • Elys Yard
- **Song Que** • 134 Kingsland Rd
- **St John Bread and Wine** • 94 Commercial St
- **Story Deli** • 91 Brick Ln
- **Tay Do** • 60 Kingsland Rd
- **Tay Do Cafe** • 65 Kingsland Rd
- **Viet Grill** • 58 Kingsland Rd

Shopping

- **A Butcher of Distinction** • 91 Brick Ln
- **Absolute Vintage** • 15 Hanbury St
- **Arckiv** • 37 Heneage St
- **Bangla City** • 86 Brick Lane
- **Bernstock Speirs** • 234 Brick Lane
- **Beyond Retro** • 112 Cheshire St
- **Blackman's Shoes** • 42 Cheshire St
- **Brick Lane** • Brick Lane
- **Caravan** • 3 Redchurch St
- **Columbia Road Flower Market** • Columbia Rd
- **Columbia Road Market** • Columbia Rd
- **Comfort Station** • 22 Cheshire St
- **Duke of Uke** • 22 Hanbury St
- **FairyGothMother** • 15 Lamb St
- **The Grocery** • 54 Kingsland Rd
- **Hurwundeki** • 98 Commerical St
- **The Laden Showrooms** • 103 Brick Lane
- **Labour & Wait** • 18 Cheshire St
- **Luna and Curious** • 198 Brick Lane
- **No One** • 1 Kingsland Rd
- **Nudge Records** • 20 Hanbury St
- **Rough Trade East** • 91 Brick Ln
- **Scooter Emporium** • 10 Dray Walk, Brick Lane,
- **Second Tread** • 261 Hackney Rd
- **Taj Stores** • 112 Brick Lane
- **Tatty Devine** • 236 Brick Ln
- **Taylor Taylor** • 137 Commercial St
- **Treacle** • 160 Columbia Rd

Map 92 • Bethnal Green

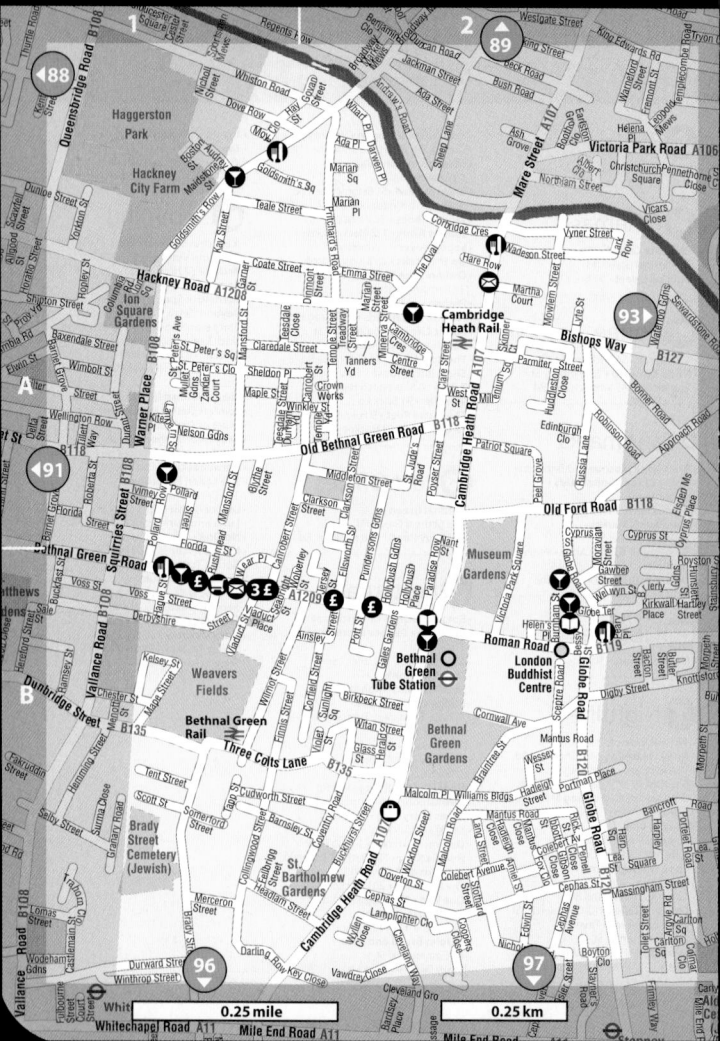

Ah, you've got to love it. Blossoming from a caricature inner-city ghetto into glorious yummy-mummy media-worker land, you can sate pretty much any desire here, dark or quaint. The Columbia Road Flower Market is genuinely 'nice,' with retro shops lining its fringes, and the Working Men's Club is full of ideas. Drink in The Camel and then go on a pissed psychogeographical meander.

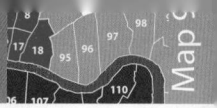

Banks

- **Abbey** • 450 Bethnal Green Rd
- **Barclays** • 412 Bethnal Green Rd
- **Halifax** • 376 Bethnal Green Rd
- **HSBC** • 465 Bethnal Green Rd
- **Lloyds** • 404 Bethnal Green Rd
- **NatWest** • 403 Bethnal Green Rd

Landmarks

- **Bethnal Green Tube Station** • Bethnal Green Tube Station
- **London Buddhist Centre** • 51 Roman Rd

Libraries

- **Bethnal Green Library** • Cambridge Heath Rd
- **Idea Store Bow** • Roman Rd

Nightlife

- **The Albion** • 94 Goldsmiths Row
- **Backyard Comedy** • 231 Cambridge Heath Rd
- **Bethnal Green's Working Men's Club** • 44 Pollard Row
- **The Camel** • 277 Globe Rd
- **Florist** • 255 Globe Rd
- **Images** • 483 Hackney Rd
- **The Star of Bethnal Green (DUP)** • 359 Bethnal Green Rd

Post Offices

- **Bethnal Green Road** • 365 Bethnal Green Rd
- **Cambridge Heath** • 481 Cambridge Heath Rd

Restaurants

- **Bistrotheque** • 23 Wadeson St
- **E Pellicci** • 332 Bethnal Green Rd
- **Little Georgia** • 87 Goldsmiths Row
- **Wild Cherry** • 241 Globe Rd

Shopping

- **AP Fitzpatrick** • 142 Cambridge Heath Rd

Supermarkets

- **Tesco** • 361 Bethnal Green Rd

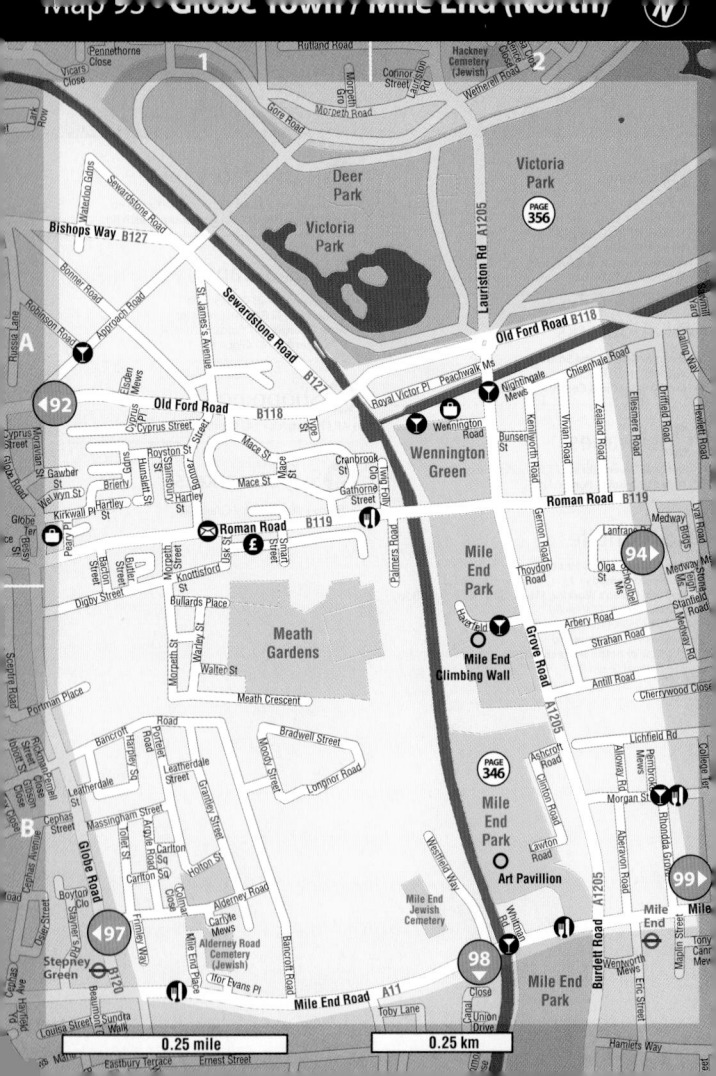
1
2
A
B
Pennethorne Close
Vicars Close
Rutland Road
Morpeth Gro
Connor Street
Lauriston Rd
Hackney Cemetery (Jewish)
Wetherell Road
Morpeth Road
Gore Road
Deer Park
Victoria Park
Victoria Park
PAGE 356
Lauriston Rd A1205
Sewardstone Road
Waterton Gdns
Bishops Way B127
Bonner Road
Approach Road
Robinson Road
St. James's Avenue
Sewardstone Road B127
Old Ford Road B118
Royal Victor Pl
Peachwalk Ms
Nightingale Mews
Chisenhale Road
Dalling Way
Hewlett Road
Eldon Mews
Old Ford Road
B118
Cyprus Street
Cyprus Pl
Tope St
Mace St
Wennington Road
Wennington Green
Bunsen St
Kenworth Road
Vivian Road
Zealand Road
Ellesmere Road
Driffield Road
Cranbrook St
Twig Folly
Gathorne Street
Roman Road B119
Royston St
Humbert St
Hartley St
Brierly
Gawber St
Wallwyn St
Kirkwall Pl
Globe Ter
Roman Road
B119
Palmers Road
Mile End Park
Thoydon Road
Olga St
Lanfranc Rd
Medway
Medway Ms
Stanfield Road
Mentmore Rd
Lyn Road
Knottisford St
Digby Street
Bullards Place
Meath Gardens
Walter St
Meath Crescent
Portman Place
Mile End Climbing Wall
Grove Road
A1205
Arbery Road
Strahan Road
Antill Road
Cherrywood Close
Bradwell Street
Longnor Road
Woody Street
Bancroft Road
Pioneer Road
Leamerdale Street
Granaby Street
Leatherdale St
Cephas Street
Massingham Street
Toilet St
Carlton Sq
Holton St
Globe Road
Boyton Cl
Stepney Green
B120
Firmin Way
Aldenby Road
Carlyle Mews
Aldenby Road Cemetery (Jewish)
Mile End Place
Bancroft Road
Mile End Jewish Cemetery
Westfield Way
Mile End Park
Art Pavillion
PAGE 346
Ashcroft Road
Clinton Road
Lawton Road
Lichfield Rd
Pembroke Mews
Allaway Rd
Morgan St
Rhondda Grove
Aberavon Road
Burdett Road
A1205
Mile End
Westworth Mews
Eric Street
Maplin St
Mile End Park
Mile End Road A11
Toby Lane
Union Drive
Hamlets Way
Eastbury Terrace
Ernest Street
Louisa Street
Sundta Walk
Beaumont Sq
Tower Hamlets Cemetery
Tony Cam Mew
492
497
98
94
99
0.25 mile
0.25 km

Globe Town / Mile End (North)

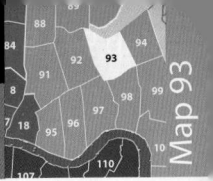

Victoria Park in the north might get all the attention but, friends, there are some pleasant surprises in this unassuming stretch of east London. And, no, we don't mean Mile End Hospital. We mean the up-for-it vibe at The Approach Tavern, the pizza-and-cocktail menu of The Fat Cat, the glorious seafood at Winkles, and the purple-coloured dance hole that is Club E3.

Banks

- **NatWest** • 154 Roman Rd

Landmarks

- **Art Pavilllion** • 221 Grove Rd
- **Mile End Climbing Wall** • Haverfield Rd

Nightlife

- **The Approach Tavern** • 47 Approach Rd
- **Club E3** • 562 Mile End Rd
- **The Fat Cat** • 221 Grove Rd
- **Jongleurs (Bow Wharf)** • 221 Grove Rd
- **The Morgan Arms** • 43 Morgan St
- **Palm Tree** • 1 Haverfield Rd

Post Offices

- **Roman Road** • 138 Roman Rd

Restaurants

- **L'Oasis** • 237 Mile End Rd
- **Matsu** • 558 Mile End Rd
- **The Morgan Arms** • 43 Morgan St
- **Winkles** • 238 Roman Rd

Shopping

- **Massage Table Store** • Bow Wharf, Grove Rd
- **Paul Mark Hatton** • 65 Roman Rd

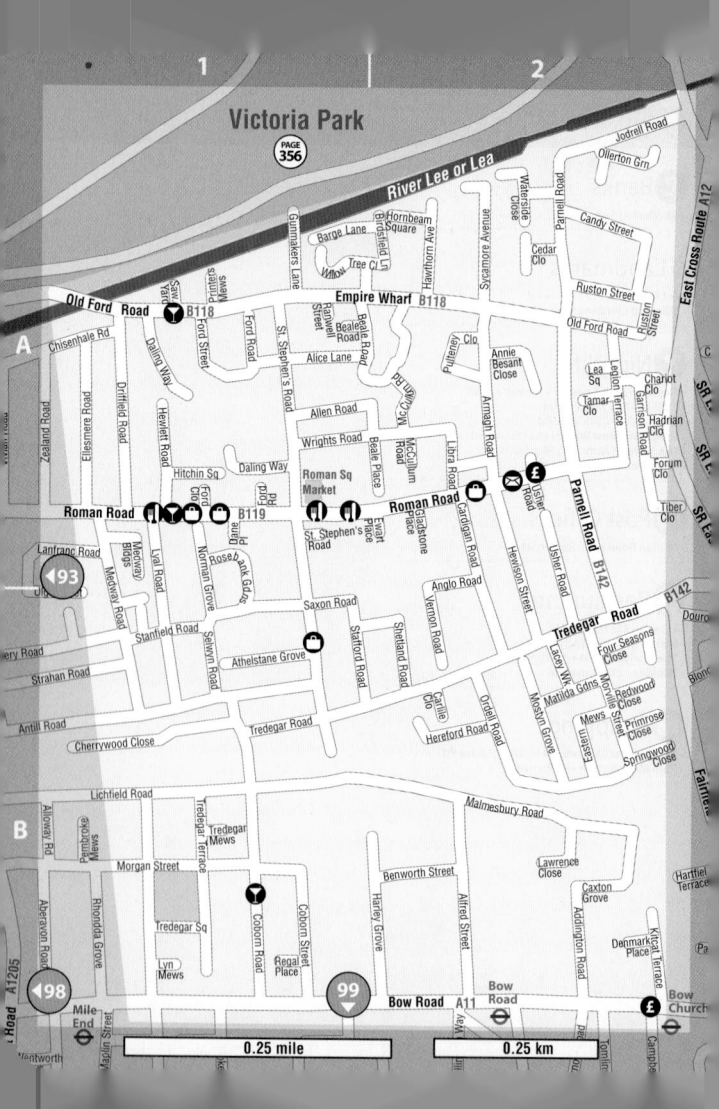
1
2
A
B
Victoria Park
PAGE 356
River Lee or Lea
Jodrell Road
Ollerton Grn
Waterside Close
Parnell Road
Candy Street
Cedar Clo
Ruston Street
Old Ford Road
Hornbeam Square
Barge Lane
Tree Ct
Hawthorn Ave
Sycamore Avenue
Gunmakers Lane
Empire Wharf
B118
Old Ford Road
B118
Chisenhale Rd
Dalling Way
Ford Street
Ford Road
St. Stephen's Road
Alice Lane
Beale Road
Ranwell Street
Pulteney Clo
Annie Besant Close
Lea Sq
Lagon Terrace
Chariot Clo
Tamar Clo
Garrison Road
Hadrian Clo
Forum Clo
Tiber Clo
Zealand Road
Ellesmere Road
Driffield Road
Hewlett Road
Allen Road
Wrights Road
Beale Place
McCullum Road
Armagh Road
Libra Road
Hitchin Sq
Dalling Way
Roman Sq Market
Roman Road
B119
Roman Road
St. Stephen's Road
Fright Place
Gladstone Place
Cardigan Road
Fisher Road
Parnell Road
B142
Lanfranc Road
Lyal Road
Medway Bldgs
Medway Road
Norman Grove
Rose Gdns
Selwyn Road
Henson Street
Usher Road
Anglo Road
Vernon Road
Saxon Road
Stanfield Road
Stafford Road
Shetland Road
Tredegar Road
B142
Athelstane Grove
Strahan Road
Antill Road
Tredegar Road
Cherrywood Close
Carlile Clo
Ordell Road
Hereford Road
Mostyn Grove
Larey Wk
Matilda Gdns
Morville Street
Four Seasons Close
Redwood Close
Mews
Primrose Close
Springwood Close
Lichfield Road
Malmesbury Road
Alloway Rd
Bethnal Green Mews
Tredegar Terrace
Tredegar Mews
Morgan Street
Benworth Street
Lawrence Close
Caxton Grove
Addington Road
Denmark Place
Kirkland Terrace
Aberavon Road
Rhondda Grove
Tredegar Sq
Lyn Mews
Coborn Road
Coborn Street
Regal Place
Hatley Grove
Alfred Street
Bow Road
A11
Bow Road
Mile End
Bow Church
Hartfiel Terrace
East Cross Route A12
A205
A198
99
93
0.25 mile
0.25 km

Bow

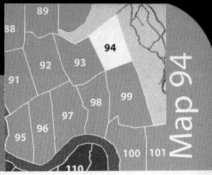

What have the Romans ever done for us? Not much, you might think, walking down Roman Road. But look closer and you'll find not only one of the oldest, most authentically East End jellied eels and mash eateries of the city, but also a market so cheap it'll knock even the most die-hard bargain hunters right out of their Centurion sandals. Pint? The haughty-sounding combo of The Young Prince or The Lord Mopeth.

Banks

- **Barclays** • 92 Bow Rd
- **Barclays** • 611 Roman Rd

Nightlife

- **The Coborn Arms** • 8 Coborn Road
- **The Lord Morpeth** • 402 Old Ford Road
- **The Young Prince** • 448 Roman Road

Post Offices

- **Roman Road (603)** • 603 Roman Rd

Restaurants

- **Chicchi** • 516 Roman Rd
- **G.Kelly Pie & Mash shop** • 526 Roman Rd
- **The Roman Tandoori** • 432 Roman Road

Shopping

- **Pure** • 430 Roman Rd
- **Roman Road Market** • Roman Rd
- **Sew Amazing** • 80 St Stephens Rd
- **South Molton Drugstore** • 583 Roman Rd

Map 95 • Whitechapel (West) / St Katharine's Dock

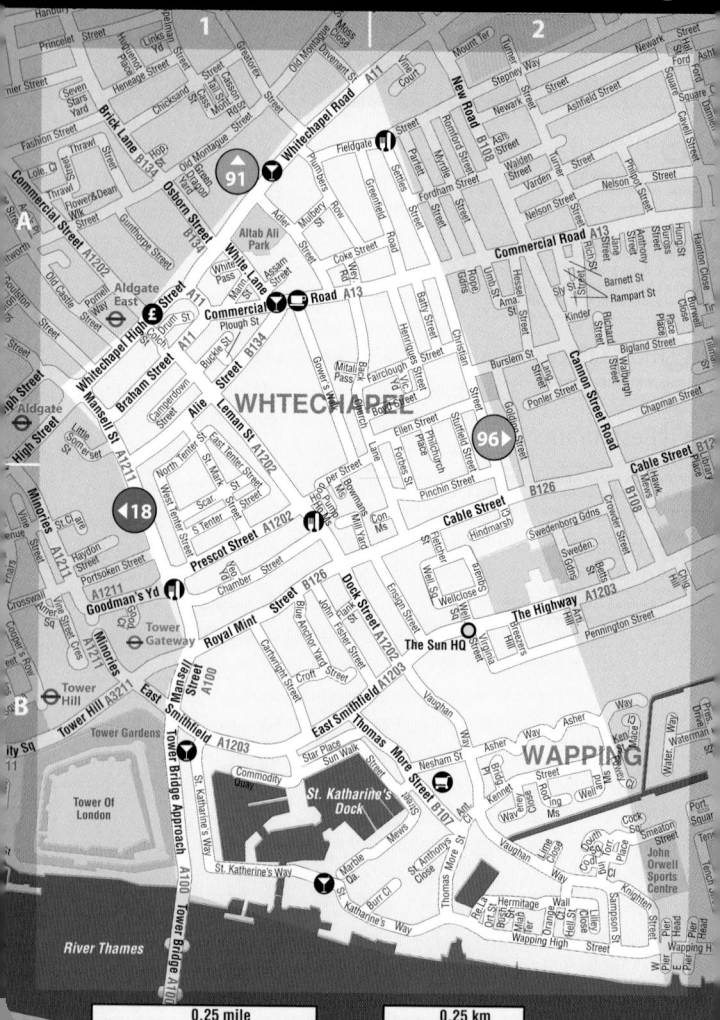
1
2
A
B
WHITECHAPEL
WAPPING
Whitechapel Road
Commercial Road A13
Cable Street
Cable Street B126
Commercial Street A1202
Brick Lane B134
Osborn Street
Whitechapel High Street
Braham Street
Commercial Street
Alie Street
Leman St A1202
Mansell St A1211
Minories A1211
Prescot Street A1202
Goodman's Yd
Tower Gateway
Royal Mint Street B126
Dock Street A1202
The Highway A1203
The Sun HQ
East Smithfield A1203
Tower Hill A3211
Tower Hill
Tower Bridge Approach A100
Tower Bridge A100
Wapping High Street
St. Katharine's Dock
Tower Of London
River Thames
Altab Ali Park
Aldgate East
Aldgate
Tower Gardens
Commodity Quay
Thomas More Street B101
New Road B100
Cannon Street Road
Burbidge Close
John Orwell Sports Centre
Wapping Wall
Hermitage Wall
Knightrider Street
Sampson St
Pier Head
Wapping H
Pennington Street
Swedenborg Gdns
Sweden
Hindmarsh
Cable Street B126
Commercial Road A13
Nelson Street
Burslem St
Chapman Street
Bigland Street
Barnett St
Rampart St
Ashfield Street
Newark Street
Stepney Way
Mount Ter
Turner Street
Varden Street
Philmot Street
Hanbury Street
Princelet Street
Heneage Street
Chicksand St
Brick Lane
Fashion Street
Thrawl Street
Old Montague Street
Fieldgate Street
Plumbers Row
Greenfield Road
Sidney Street
Fordham Street
Mulberry Street
Parfett Street
Romford Street
Ashe Street
Walden Street
Varden Street
Nelson Street
Philmot Street
Hanbury Street
Commercial Street A1202
Old Castle Street
Pomell Way
Pelham Street
Princes Street
Plough Street
Buckle St
Camperdown Street
Little Somerset
Leman Street
Alie Street
Mansell St A1211
Minories A1211
Portsoken Street
Hardon Street
Crosswall
Vine Street Cres
Cooper's Row
Tower Hill A3211
Tower Gardens
Tower Bridge Approach A100
Tower Bridge A100
St. Katharine's Way
Commodity Quay
St. Katharine's Dock
Mews
Marble Quay
Burr Ct
St Anthony's Close
Thomas More St
Vaughan Way
Star Place
Sun Walk
Nesham St
Asher Way
Wapping High Street
Wapping Wall
Hermitage Wall
Knightrider Street
Sampson St
Pier Head
Wapping H
Cannon Street Road
Burbidge Close
Burslem St
Bigland Street
Barnett St
Rampart St
Commercial Road A13
Cable Street B126
Cable Street
Pennington Street
The Highway A1203
Swedenborg Gdns
Sweden
Hindmarsh
Cable Street B126
Commercial Road A13
Nelson Street
Philmot Street
Varden Street
Ashfield Street
Newark Street
Stepney Way
Mount Ter
Turner Street
Hanbury Street
Princelet Street
Heneage Street
Chicksand St
Brick Lane
Fashion Street
Thrawl Street
Old Montague Street
Fieldgate Street
Plumbers Row
Greenfield Road
Sidney Street
Fordham Street
Mulberry Street
Parfett Street
Romford Street
Ashe Street
Walden Street
Varden Street
Nelson Street
Philmot

Whitechapel (West) / St Katharine's Dock

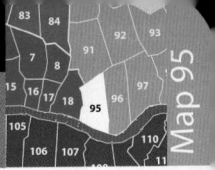

The Whitechapel Gallery, the pumping heart of the manor, has finally come out of a monster two-year bypass. Much like a busty Page 3 girl (see if you can spot one totter out of The Sun's nearby offices) the gallery has burst out of its shackles to reveal something quite magnificent. The Rhythm Factory and The Castle are chaotic boozing dens – or head to Prohibition for drinkers dumb enough to believe it when you claim to captain one of the on-looking yachts.

Banks

- **Lloyds** • 35 Whitechapel High St

Coffee

- **Oi Bagel** • 45 Commercial Rd

Landmarks

- **The Sun HQ** • 1 Pennington St

Nightlife

- **The Castle** • 44 Commercial Rd
- **Dickens Inn** • St Katharine's Way
- **Prohibition** • 1 St. Katherine's dock
- **Rhythm Factory** • 16 Whitechapel Rd

Restaurants

- **Cafe Spice Namaste** • 16 Prescot St
- **The Empress** • 141 Leman St
- **Tayyab's** • 83 Fieldgate St

Supermarkets

- **Waitrose** • Thomas More St & Nesham St

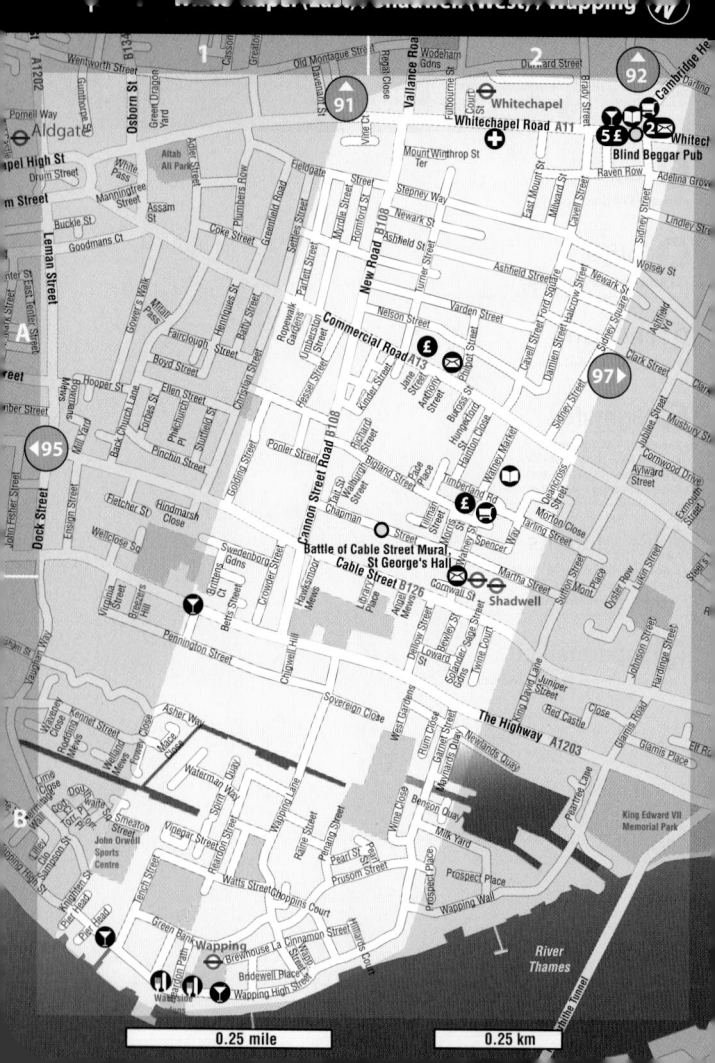
Wentworth Street
Old Montague Street
Regal Close
Wodeham Gdns
Dunard Street
Vallance Road
Fombourne St
Court
Whitechapel
Whitechapel Road A11
Mount Winthrop St Ter
Blind Beggar Pub
Raven Row
Adelina Grove
Cambridge He
Darling
Pomell Way
Aldgate
Osborn St
Green Dragon Yard
Gunthorpe St
Altab Ali Park
Ashby Street
White Pasture
Manningtree Street
Assam St
Drum Street
Buckle St
Goodmans Ct
Leman Street
Fieldgate Street
Plumbers Row
Myrdle Street
Bromford St
New Road B108
Stepney Way
Newark St
Ashfield Street
Turner Street
East Mount St
Milward St
Cavell Street
Sidney Street
Lindley Str
Wolsey St
Ashfield Street
Newark St
Commercial Road A1203
Nelson Street
Varden Street
Cavell Street
Ford Square
Sidney Square
Clark Street
Ashfield Street
Musbury Str
Cornwood Drive
Ayliward Street
Exmouth Street
Fairclough Street
Henriques St
Bath Street
Gower's Walk
Mitre Passage
Boyd Street
Hopper St
Ellen Street
Christian Street
Sutton Street
Ropewalk Gardens
Hessel Street
Kinder Street
Jubilee Street
Antony Street
Burdett St
Hungerford Street
Hanbury Close
Sidney Street
James Street
Mill Yard
Back Church Lane
Forbes St
Sheffield St
Pinchin Street
Dock Street
Leman Street
Cannon Street Road B108
Ponler Street
Richard Street
Boreland Street
Pole Place
Winter Market
Timberland Rd
Hanbury Close
Fletcher St
Hindmarsh Close
Wellclose Sq
Chapman Street
Mansfield Street
Spencer Street
Tarling Street
Murton Close
Swedenborg Gdns
Berts Street
Angel Mews
Battle of Cable Street Mural
St George's Hall
Cable Street B126
Cornwall St
Shadwell
Martha Street
Mont Place
Oyster Row
Lucas Street
Stepney Way
Virginia Street
Brewers Hill
Pennington Street
Chigwell Hill
Dellow Street
Ward Street
Schandorf Sqs Gdns
Swing Court
King David La
Juniper Street
Johnson Street
Harrington Street
Vaughan Way
Kennet Street
Asher Way
Watson Close
Rodney Mews
Wilford Mews
Forest Close
Mace Close
Sovereign Close
West Gardens
Plum Close
Garnet Street
Montague Close
Newlands Quay
Red Castle Close
Gramps Road
Glamis Place
The Highway A1203
Elf Ro
Lime Close
Wilson Close
Waite Close
Smeaton Street
John Orwell Sports Centre
Watermen Quay
Wapping Lane
Vine Close
Benson Quay
Milk Yard
Pearless Lane
King Edward VII Memorial Park
Vinegar Street
Rope Walk
Pearl St
Prusom Street
Prospect Place
Prospect Place
Wapping Wall
Watts Street
Chopins Court
Kinnerton St
Pier Head
Green Bank
Wapping
Brewhouse La
Cinnamon Street
Hermitage Cres
Bridewell Place
Wapping High Street
Wapping
River Thames
Rotherhithe Tunnel
0.25 mile
0.25 km

hitechapel (East) / Shadwell (West) / Wapping

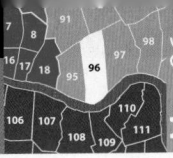

Ex-dockland Wapping now imports yuppies into its converted warehouses, less gleaming Shadwell and Whitechapel keep more of the East End spirit alive. Wapping High Street is mainly residential, Whitechapel Road is more lively. Drink at Indo if you're boho, stick with The Captain Kidd if not. Tayyab's is cracking—stick out the queues, or if curry's not your thing head to Il Bordello.

Banks

- **Abbey** • 40 Watney Warket
- **Barclays** • 240 Whitechapel Rd
- **HSBC** • 75 Whitechapel Rd
- **Lloyds** • 210 Commercial Rd
- **NatWest** • 130 Whitechapel High St
- **NatWest** • 45 Whitechapel Rd
- **NatWest** • 331 Whitechapel Rd

Emergency Rooms

- **Royal London Hospital** • Whitechapel Rd

Landmarks

- **Battle of Cable Street Mural, St George's Hall** • 236 Cable St
- **Blind Beggar Pub** • 337 Whitechapel Rd

Libraries

- **Idea Store Whitechapel** • 321 Whitechapel Rd
- **Watney Market Library** • 30 Watney Market

Nightlife

- **The Captain Kidd** • 108 Wapping High St
- **The Caxtons** • 50 The Highway
- **Indo** • 133 Whitechapel Rd
- **Town of Ramsgate** • 62 Wapping High St

Post Offices

- **Eastern** • 206 Whitechapel Rd
- **Philpot Street** • 12 Philpot St
- **Watney Street** • 81 Watney St
- **Whitechapel** • 75 Whitechapel Rd

Restaurants

- **Il Bordello** • 81 Wapping High Street
- **Tayyabs** • 83 Fieldgate St

Supermarkets

- **Iceland** • Watney St & Tarling St
- **Sainsbury's** • 1 Cambridge Heath Rd

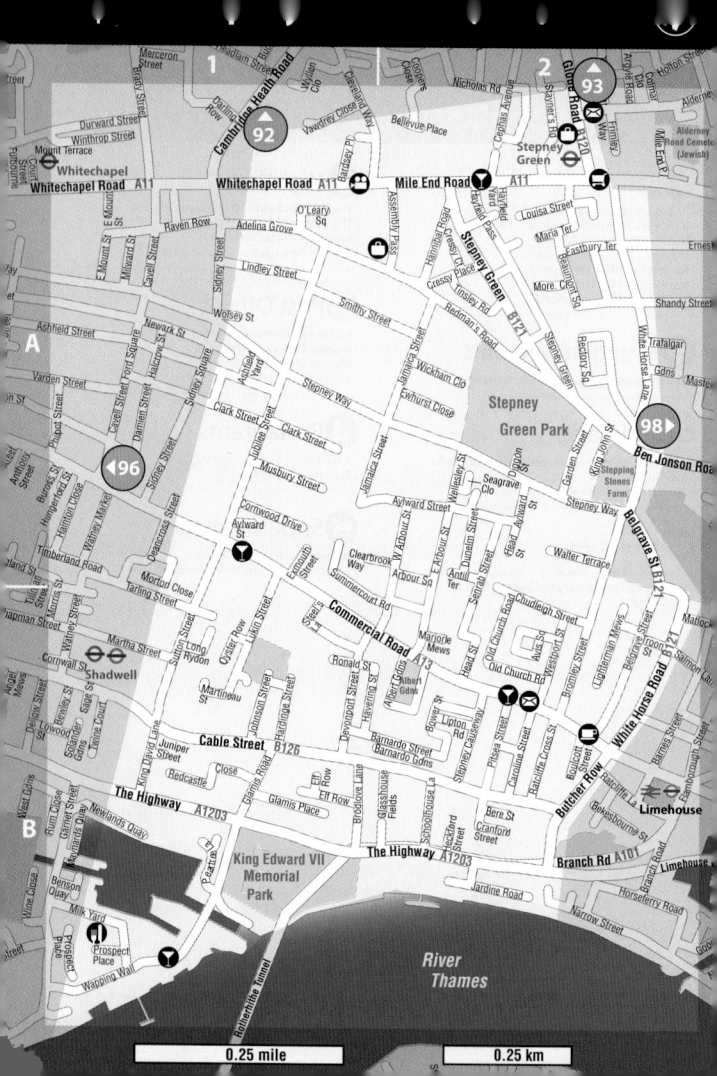
1
2
A
B
92
93
98
196
Cambridge Heath Road
Whitechapel Road A11
Mile End Road A11
Stepney Green
Stepney Green B121
Stepney Green Park
Ben Jonson Road
Commercial Road A13
Shadwell
Cable Street B126
The Highway A1203
King Edward VII Memorial Park
Limehouse
Branch Rd A1D1
Butcher Row
White Horse Road
Belgrave St B121
Globe Road B1 201
Whitechapel
Mount Terrace
Durward Street
Winthrop Street
Mercerton Street
Brady Street
Cardigan Row
Vaudrey Close
Bellevue Place
Nicholas Rd
Cleveland Way
Stepney's Rd
Globe Road
Alderney Road Cemetery (Jewish)
Mile End P
Raven Row
Adelina Grove
O'Leary Sq
Assembly Pas
Cassy Cl
Cassy Place
Tinsley Rd
Radinan's Road
Stepney Green
Louisa Street
Maria Ter
Eastbury Ter
Ernest
Lindley Street
Sidney Street
Wolsey St
Smithy Street
Shandy Street
Ashfield Street
Newark St
Varden Street
Cavell Street
Cavell Street Front Square
Danmer Street
Hancock St
Sidney Square
Ashley Yard
Stepney Way
Wickham Clo
Exhurst Close
Jamaica Street
Clark Street Pl
Clark Street
Musbury Street
Jamaica Street
Wellesley St
Seagrave Clo
Garden Street
King John St
Stepping Stones Farm
Trafalgar
Gdns
White Horse Lane
Cornwood Drive
Ashward St
Ashward Street
Head Ashward St
Walter Terrace
Timberland Road
Mortlod Close
Tarling Street
Commercial Rd
Cleartbrook Way
N Arbour St
E Arbour St
Arbour Sq
Antill Ter
Dunelm Street
Sebrob Street
Chudleigh Street
Old Church Road
Old Church Rd
Westport St
Bromley Street
Lighterman Mews
Belgrave Trade Ctr
Matlock
Salmon Lan
Cornwall St
Martha Street
Sutton Street
Long Hydon
Oxser Row
Martineau St
Johnson Street
Ronald St
Head St
Alfred Gdns
Albert Gdns
Devonport Street
Hilverna St
Bower St
Lipton Rd
Barnardo Street
Barnardo Gdns
Stepney Causeway
Pitsea Street
Carcline Street
Sebolt Cross St
Fairclive La
Limehouse
Bekesbourne St
Juniper Street
Redcastle Close
Grove Road
Elf Row
Glamis Place
Broadview Lamp
Glasshouse Fields
Schoolhouse La
Hickford Street
Bere St
Cranford Street
Jardine Road
Horseferry Road
Narrow Street
Newlands Quay
Benson Quay
Milk Yard
Prospect Place
Wapping Wall
Rotherhithe Tunnel
River Thames
0.25 mile
0.25 km

Stepney / Shadwell (East)

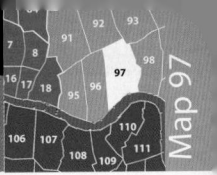

Cockney geezers run into hipsters and smart new developments sit next to run-down estates. No one quite knows where this area is going. We know where we're going, though—to The George Tavern, mainly, for impromptu theatre, blue-collar poetry and other arty madness, or The Prospect of Whitby, if we're feeling nostalgic. Wapping Food, meanwhile, serves great fare inside a century-old power station.

Cinemas

- **Genesis Mile End** • 93 Mile End Rd

Coffee

- **Popular Café** • 536 Commercial Rd

Nightlife

- **The Black Horse** • 168 Mile End Rd
- **The George Tavern** • 373 Commercial Rd
- **The Prospect of Whitby** • 57 Wapping Wall
- **Troxy** • 490 Commerical Rd

Post Offices

- **Globe Road** • 34 Globe Rd
- **Stepney** • 502 Commercial Rd

Restaurants

- **Wapping Food** • Wapping Wall

Shopping

- **John Lester Wigmakers** • 32 Globe Rd
- **East End Thrift Store** • Assembly Passage

Supermarkets

- **Co-Op** • 193 Mile End Rd

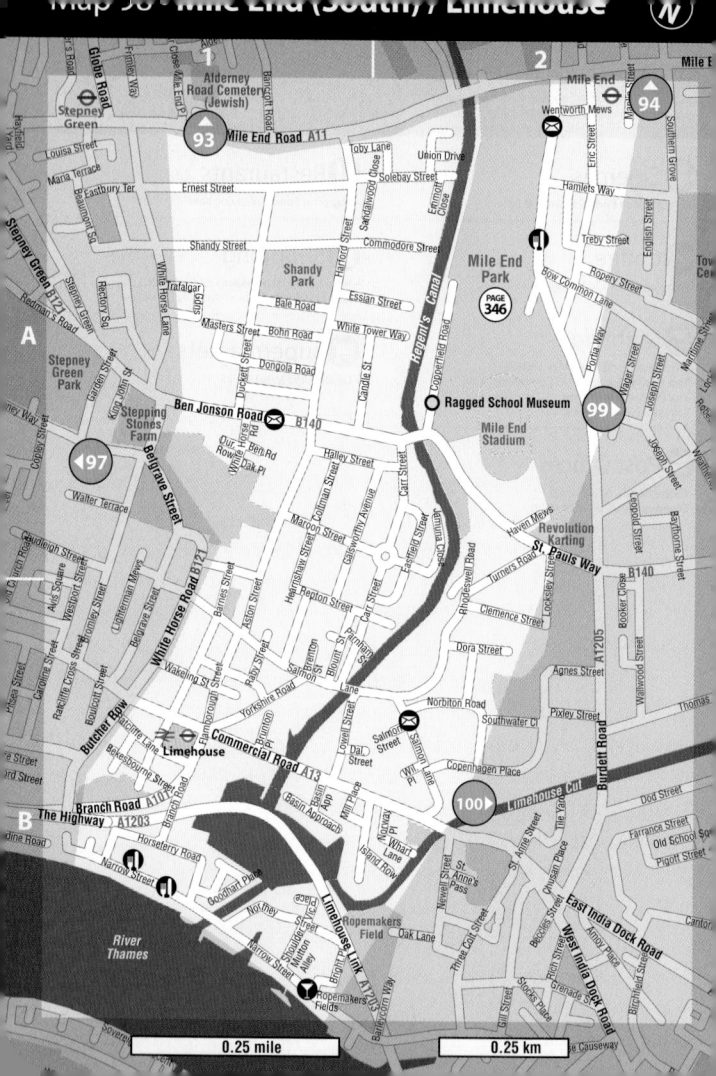
N
1
2
A
B
Mile End Road A11
Globe Road
Stepney Green
Stepney Green B1273
Stepney Green Park
Stepping Stones Farm
Ben Jonson Road
B140
Belgrave Street
White Horse Road B1121
Butcher Row
Commercial Road A13
Limehouse
The Highway A1203
Branch Road A1261
Shandy Park
Mile End Park
Regent's Canal
Ragged School Museum
Mile End Stadium
Mile End
Revolution Karting
St. Pauls Way
B140
Burdett Road
A1205
Limehouse Cut
East India Dock Road
West India Dock Road
Limehouse Link A1203
Rope makers Field
Rope makers Fields
River Thames
Alderney Road Cemetery (Jewish)
Toby Lane
Union Drive
Solebay Street
Ernest Street
Louisa Street
Maria Terrace
Eastbury Ter
Beaumont Sq
Shandy Street
Commodore Street
Harford Street
Essian Street
Bale Road
Masters Street
Bohn Road
White Tower Way
Dongola Road
Candle St
Hamlets Way
Treby Street
English Street
Bow Common Lane
Ropery Street
Southern Grove
Wentworth Mews
Eric Street
Haley Street
Carr Street
Maroon Street
Burdett Street
Haven Mews
Turners Road
Lockesley Street
Rhodeswell Road
Clemence Street
Dora Street
Agnes Street
Pixley Street
Southwater Cl
Norbiton Road
Copenhagen Place
Salmon Street
Salmon Lane
Lowell Street
Dal Street
Mill Place
Basin App
Basin Approach
Wharf Pl
Wharf Lane
Island Row
Newell Street
St. Anne's Pass
Oak Lane
Three Colt Street
Amoy Place
Grenade Street
Birchfield Street
Stepney Green
Redman's Road
Rectory Sq
Trafalgar
White Horse Lane
Garden Street
King John St
Copley Street
Ben Rd
Oak Pl
Walter Terrace
Westport Street
Lightermen Mews
Belgrave Street
Ratcliffe Cross Street
Wakeling St
Yorkshire Road
Burdett Street
Salmon Street
Blount Pl
Ashton Street
Barnes Street
Regent Street
Carr Street
Commercial Street
Belgrave Street
Lightermen Mews
Westport Street

Mile End (South) / Limehouse

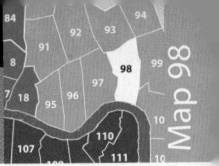

Classic east end with a heady mix of poverty-stricken bleakness around the tail of Mile End park and a Docklands developer's wet dream by the river. But cheer up—great eats and drinks along the Thames on Narrow Street (The Grapes, The Narrow, and La Figa) and the illuminating Ragged School Museum and Lebanese tastiness (Orange Room) near Mile End.

Landmarks

- **Ragged School Museum** • 45 Copperfield Rd

Nightlife

- **The Grapes** • 76 Narrow Street

Post Offices

- **Ben Jonson Road** • 52 Ben Jonson Rd
- **Mile End** • 1 Burdett Rd
- **Salmon Lane** • 127 Salmon Ln

Restaurants

- **La Figa** • 45 Narrow St
- **The Narrow** • 44 Narrow Street
- **Orange Room Café** • 63 Burdett Rd

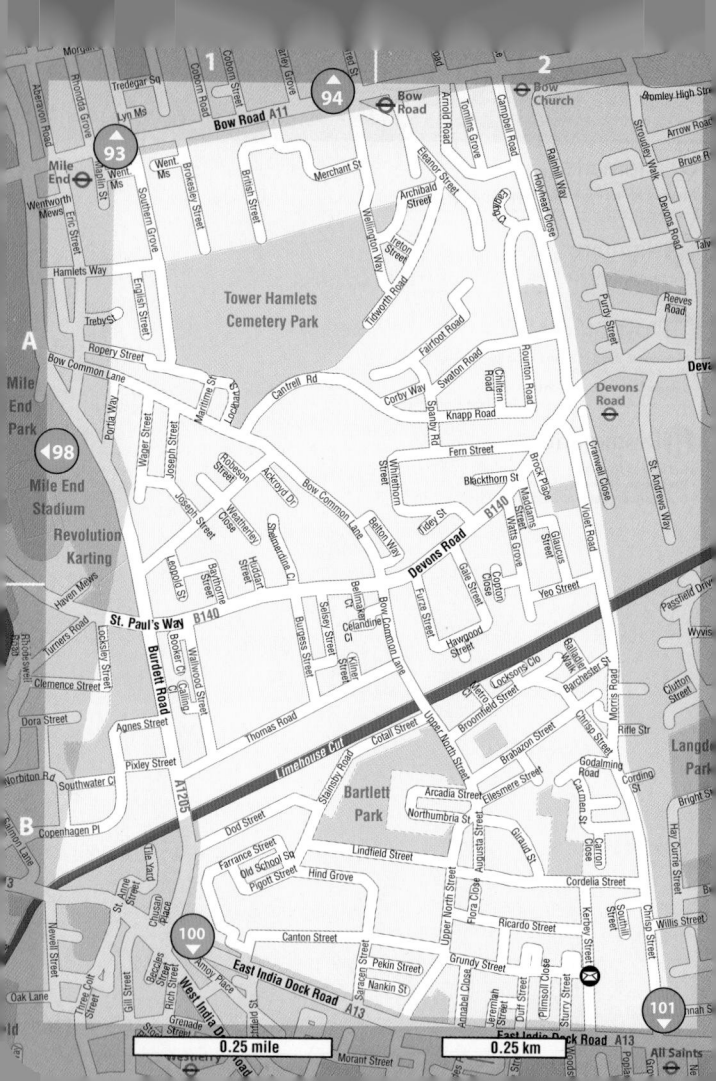
1
2
A
B
3
94
93
98
100
101
Bow Road A11
Bow Road
Bow Church
Mile End
Mile End Park
Mile End Stadium
Revolution Karting
Tower Hamlets Cemetery Park
Devons Road
Devons Road B140
St. Paul's Way B140
Burdett Road
Limehouse Cut
Bartlett Park
East India Dock Road A13
West India Dock Road
A1205
Aberavon Road
Rhondda Grove
Tredegar Sq
Lyn Ms
Cobourn Road
Cobourn Street
Bailey Grove
Tredegar Road
Arnold Road
Tomlins Grove
Campbell Road
Bromley High Str
Arrow Road
Bruce R
Stroudley Walk
Devons Road
Talw
Rainhill Way
Hoyland Close
Eleanor Street
Wellington Way
Tidworth Road
Fairfoot Road
Reeves Road
Wentworth Mews
Eric Street
Southern Grove
Went Ms
Brodesser Street
British Street
Merchant St
Archibald Street
Hamlets Way
English Street
Trebys St
Ropery Street
Bow Common Lane
Portia Way
Maritime St
Lockhart St
Wager Street
Joseph Street
Robeson Street
Ackroyd Dr
Weatherley Close
Leopold St
Haven Mews
Turners Road
Cockley Street
Clementine Street
Dora Street
Agnes Street
Pixley Street
Southwater Cl
Norbiton Rd
Copenhagen Pl
Booker Cl
Collinson Cl
Wallwood Street
Thomas Road
Burgess Street
Selsey Street
Kilner Street
Bellamy Cl
Celandine Cl
Bow Common Lane
Belton Way
Tidey St
Whitethorn Street
Canrell Rd
Corby Way
Swaton Road
Stanby Rd
Knapp Road
Chilham Road
Rounton Road
Fern Street
Blackthorn St
Brook Place
Margaret Watts Grove
Gladiolus Street
Violet Road
Cranwell Close
St Andrews Way
Gale Street
Cordon Close
Yeo Street
Furze Street
Hawgood Street
Pagefield Drive
Wyvis
Bulkeley Walk
Barchester St
Morris Road
Clutton Street
Locksons Clo
Broomfield Street
Cotall Street
Upper North Street
Stanstead Road
Arcadia Street
Chesmere Street
Northumbria St
Augusta Street
Glaucus St
Carmen St
Cordon Close
Brabazon Street
Chrisp Street
Rifle Str
Langdale Park
Godalming Road
Cording St
Bright Sw
Hay Currie Street
Dod Street
Farrance Street
Old School Sq
Pigott Street
Lindfield Street
Hind Grove
Cordelia Street
Ricardo Street
Kerley Walk
Southill Street
Willis Street
Canton Street
Pekin Street
Grundy Street
Nankin St
Saracen Street
Upper North Street
Poplar Close
Annabel Close
Jeremiah Street
Duff Street
Plimsoll Close
Sturry Street
Saxon Street
Morant Street
Newell Street
Gill Street
Three Colt Street
Oak Lane
Rich Street
Beccles Street
Grenade Street
Armoy Place
Chrisian Place
St Anne Street
Poplar
All Saints
0.25 mile
0.25 km

There's not a whole lot to do or see here. Countless old housing estates and boarded up pubs is about as exciting as it gets. If for some reason you need to visit, The Tower Hamlets Cemetery Park is a nice place to spend half an hour. Keep alert after dark in these parts.

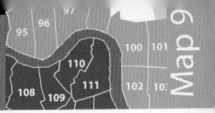

Post Offices

• **Poplar** • 22 Market Sq

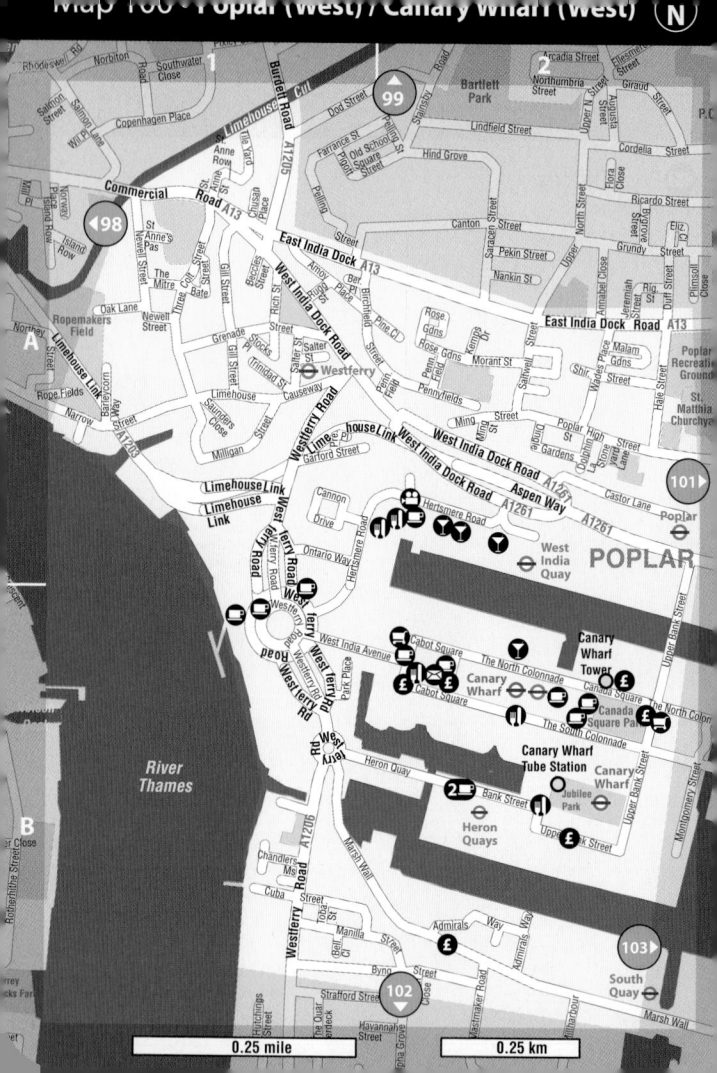
N
Rhodeswell Rd
Norbiton Road
Southwater Close
Salmon Street
Salmon Lane
Copenhagen Place
Wild Pl
Limehouse Cut
Burdett Road
A1205
Dod Street
Bartlett Park
Arcadia Street
Northumbria Street
Upper Lt. Street
Giraud Street
Lindfield Street
Cordelia Street
Hind Grove
Farrance St
Old Schooling Square
Poplar St
Stainsby Road
Commercial Road A13
Anne Row
Tiller Yard
Anne St
Pekina Place
Flora Close
Ricardo Street
Canton Street
North Street
Pekin Street
Upper
Grundy Street
Nankin St
Kimablel Close
Jeremiah Street
Big Ben Street
Durff Street
Climsol Close
Elizabeth Gdns
Island Row
St Anne's Pas
Newell Street
The Mitre
Three Colt Street
Gill Street
West India Dock Road
East India Dock A13
Amoy Place
Rich St
Burchfield Street
Pine Ct
Rose Gdns
Kemp St
East India Dock Road A13
Malam Gdns
Ropemakers Field
Oak Lane
Northey Street
Limehouse Link
Grenade St
Trinidad St
Salter St
Westferry
Morant St
Sahwell Street
Sbir
Warden Place
Poplar Recreation Ground
Rope Fields
Barleycorn Way
A1206
Limehouse
Milligan Street
Causeway
Pennyfields
Penny Field
Ming St
Hale Street
St. Matthias Churchyard
Westferry Road
Limehouse Link
Barford Street
Poplar High St
Chrisp Street
Gardens
Cordelia St
Young Lane
West India Dock Road A1261
Aspen Way A1261
Castor Lane
101
Poplar
Limehouse Link
Limehouse Link
Cannon Drive
Hertsmere Road
West India Quay
POPLAR
Ferry Road
Westferry Road
Ontario Way
Hertsmere Road
Westferry Road
Westferry Rd
West India Avenue
Cabot Square
The North Colonnade
Canary Wharf
Canada Square
Canary Wharf Tower
Canada Square Pk
The South Colonnade
Upper Bank Street
Park Place
Westferry Rd
Westferry Rd
Westferry Rd
River Thames
Heron Quay
Canary Wharf Tube Station
Canary Wharf
Jubilee Park
Bank Street
Heron Quays
Upper Bank Street
Montgomery Street
Rotherhithe Street
Chandler Mews
Westferry Road
A1206
Marsh Wall
Cuba Street
Manilla Street
Admirals Way
Admirals Way
103
South Quay
Byng Street
Marsh Wall
Strafford Street
102
Hutchings Street
The Quay Dock
Havannah Street
0.25 mile
0.25 km

Poplar (West) / Canary Wharf (West)

Finance's faltering engine room. Wander the wharf and marvel at the scrapers (just watch out for ruined brokers tumbling from the windows above). If sterile malls are your thing – madly, for some people they are – waste your cash under Cabot Square and Jubilee Place. Best lunch options are Nicolas or Tiffin Bites. Since the world went belly-up, there's free comedy too – just sit by the tube and chuckle at the latest round of suited tossers to be given their P45.

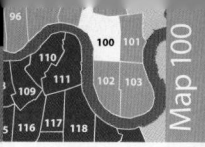

Banks

- **Halifax** • 350 Cabot Pl E
- **HSBC** • Canary Wharf
- **HSBC** • 45 Bank St
- **Lloyds** • 230 Cabot Sq
- **NatWest** • 54 Marsh Wall
- **NatWest** • 20 Canada Sq

Cinemas

- **Cineworld West India Quay** • 11 Hertsmere Rd

Coffee

- **Bagel Factory** • 7 Westferry Circus
- **Café Brera** • 45 Bank St
- **Café Brera** • 12 Cabot Sq
- **Café Brera** • 31 Westferry Circus
- **Coffee Republic** • Canary Wharf
- **Coffee Republic** • Hertsmere Rd
- **Fresco Café Bar** • 15 Cabot Sq
- **Fresco Café Bar** • 22 Canada Sq
- **Starbucks** • 1 Canada Sq
- **Starbucks** • 45 Bank St
- **Starbucks** • 7 Westferry Circus

Landmarks

- **Canary Wharf Tower** • 1 Canada Sq
- **Canary Wharf Tube Station** • Canary Wharf

Nightlife

- **Bar 38** • West India Quay
- **Davy's at Canary Wharf** • 31 Fisherman's Walk
- **Dion Canary Wharf** • Port East Building, West India Quay
- **Via Fossa**• 18 Hertsmere Rd

Post Offices

- **Canary Wharf** • 5 Chancellor Passage

Restaurants

- **1802 Bar** • Hertsmere Rd
- **Browns** • Hertsmere Rd
- **Nicolas** • 480 One Canada Sq
- **Plateau** • Canada Pl
- **Tiffin Bites** • 22 Jubilee Place

Supermarkets

- **Tesco** • 15 Cabot Sq
- **Waitrose** • N Colonnade & Canada Sq

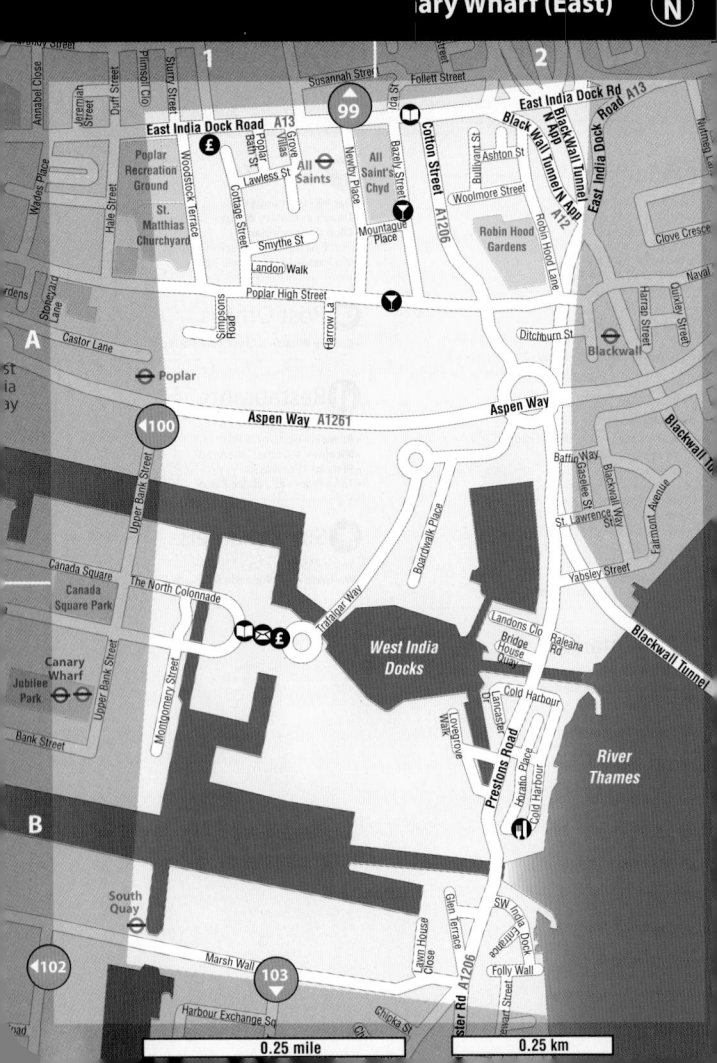
N
1
2
A
B
Susannah Street
Follett Street
East India Dock Road A13
Poplar Recreation Ground
St. Matthias Churchyard
All Saints
All Saint's Chyd
Cotton Street
Ashton St
Woolmore Street
Robin Hood Gardens
Robin Hood Lane
Clove Crescent
Mountague Place
Smythe St
Landon Walk
Poplar High Street
Simpsons Road
Harrow La
Ditchburn St
Blackwall
Harrap Street
Quixley Street
Castor Lane
Poplar
Aspen Way A1261
Aspen Way
Baffin Way
Blackwall Way
St. Lawrence St
Fairmont Avenue
Upper Bank Street
Boardwalk Place
Canada Square
Canada Square Park
The North Colonnade
Trafalgar Way
West India Docks
Landons Clo
Bridge House Quay
Raleana Rd
Yabsley Street
Blackwall Tunnel
Canary Wharf
Jubilee Park
Montgomery Street
Bank Street
Cold Harbour
Lancaster Dr
Lovegrove Walk
Prestons Road
River Thames
South Quay
Marsh Wall
Glen Terrace
Lam House Close
SW India Dock
Folly Wall
Harbour Exchange Sq
Chipka St
Stewart Street
0.25 mile
0.25 km

Poplar (East) / Canary Wharf (East)

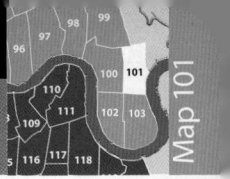

Let's be honest, there's not much to do here unless you like gazing up dull glass towers (and ugly council estates) or enjoy squeezing past investment bankers talking credit derivatives in chain bars. That said, Gun, tucked away on Coldharbour, is an excellent British restaurant-cum-pub that's enjoyed by docklands veterans and office workers alike. After real East End boozing? Try Poplar's Greenwich Pensioner.

Banks

- **Barclays** • 2 Churchill Pl
- **Barclays** • 159 E India Dock Rd

Libraries

- **Idea Store Canary Wharf** • Churchill Pl
- **Idea Store Chrisp Street** • East India Dock Rd

Nightlife

- **The Greenwich Pensioner** • 28 Bazely Street
- **The Resolute** • 210 Poplar High Street

Post Offices

- **Churchill Place** • 2 Churchill Pl

Restaurants

- **Gun** • 27 Coldharbour

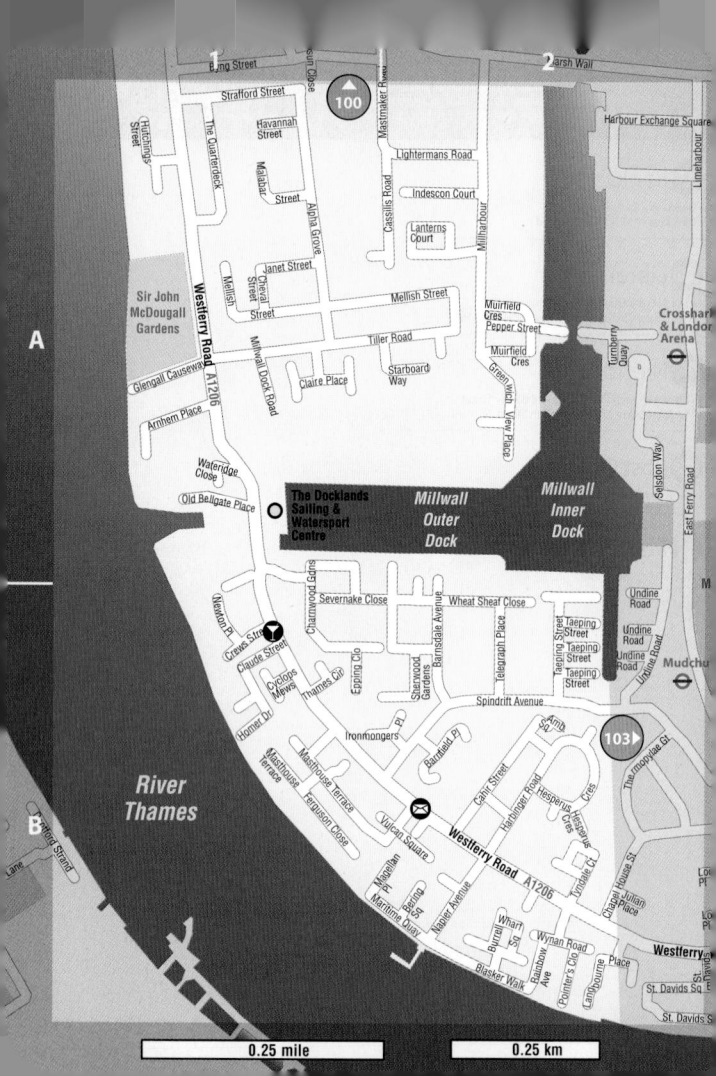
1
2
A
B
Marsh Wall
Strafford Street
Sun Close
Mastmaker Road
Harbour Exchange Square
Hutchings Street
The Quarterdeck
Havannah Street
Millwall Street
Alpha Grove
Lightermans Road
Cassilis Road
Indescon Court
Millharbour
Lanterns Court
Janet Street
Mellish Street
Sir John McDougall Gardens
Westerry Road A1206
Mellish Street
Muirfield Cres
Pepper Street
Muirfield Cres
Crossharb & Londo Arena
Tiller Road
Millwall Dock Road
Glengall Causeway
Claire Place
Starboard Way
Green Mch View Place
Turnberry Quay
Arnhem Place
Wateridge Close
Old Bellgate Place
The Docklands Sailing & Watersport Centre
Millwall Outer Dock
Millwall Inner Dock
Saksion Way
East Ferry Road
Newton Pl
Claude Street
Cyclone Mews
Thames Cir
Epping Clo
Charnwood Gdns
Severnake Close
Barnsdale Avenue
Wheat Sheaf Close
Telegraph Place
Taeping Street
Taeping Street
Taeping Street
Undine Road
Undine Road
Undine Road
Mudchu
Spindrift Avenue
Homer Dr
Ironmongers PL
Barnfield Pl
103
Thermopylae Gt
River Thames
Masthouse Terrace
Masthouse Terrace
Ferguson Close
Vulcan Square
Cahir Street
Hesperus Cres
Hesperus Cres
Westerry Road A1206
Chapel House St
Magellan Pl
Maritime Quay
Napier Avenue
Wharf St
Wyman Road
Blacker Walk
Rainbow Ave
Pointer's Clo
Westferry
St. Davids Sq
St. Davids Sl
Rotherhithe Strand
Lane
0.25 mile
0.25 km

Millwall

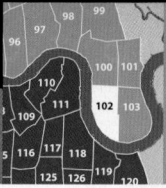

Though Millwall has award winning Docklands Sailing Centre and decent community venue The Space (Hubbub Café and Bar), it doesn't really have much else. Bereft of tube, overground, or DLR, it doesn't even have Millwall FC anymore. Despite the potential of Canary Wharf on the doorstep and flush of luxury riverside apartments, it's still tainted with the whiff of BNP and football hooliganism. Buy now.

Landmarks

• **The Docklands Sailing & Watersport Centre** • 235 Westferry Rd

Nightlife

• **Hubbub** • 269 Westferry Rd

Post Offices

• **Westferry Rd** • 367 Westferry Rd

Map 103 • Cubitt Town / Mudchute

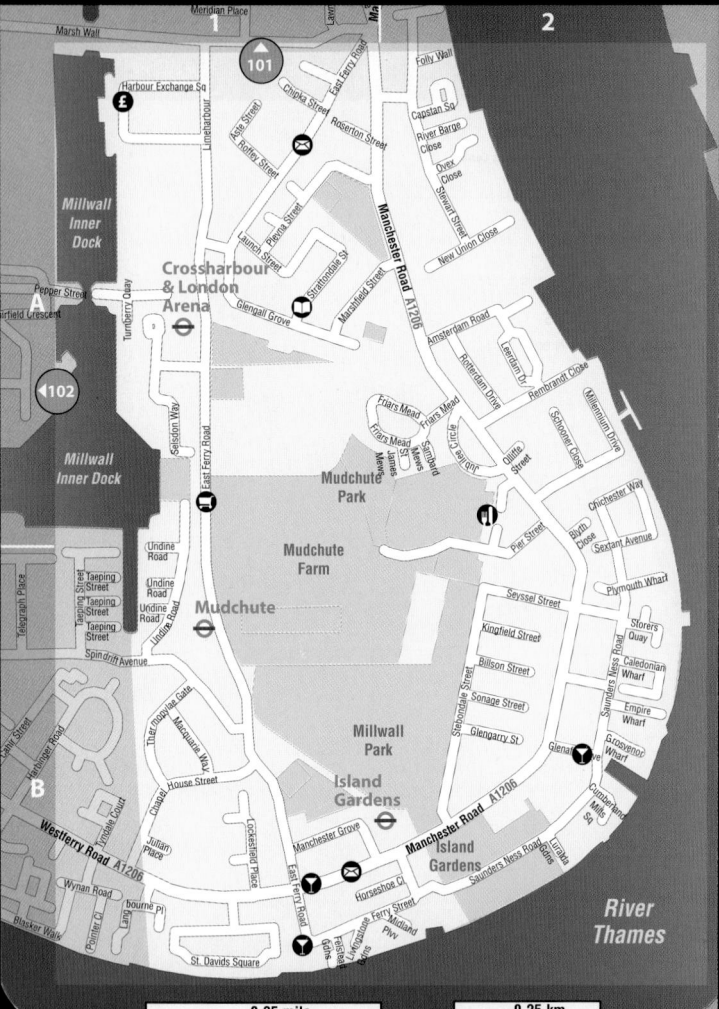

0.25 mile

0.25 km

Though shaded by the skyscrapers of Canary Wharf and a rash of luxury developments, this corner of the Island is blessed by the marvellous Mudchute Farm and Park (with the stand out Mudchute Kitchen and equestrian centre), not one, not two, but three DLR stations, and a number of down-to-earth boozers (Lord Nelson, Waterman's Arms). Who let the Isle of Dogs out?

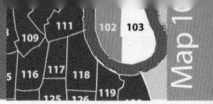

Banks

- **Lloyds** • 24 Harbor Exchange

Libraries

- **Cubitt Town Library** • Strattondale St

Nightlife

- **Ferry House** • 26 Ferry St
- **Lord Nelson** • 1 Manchester Road
- **Waterman's Arms** • 1 Glenaffric Avenue

Post Offices

- **Cubitt Town** • 15 Castalia Sq
- **Isle Of Dogs** • 159 Manchester Rd

Restaurants

- **Mudchute Kitchen** • Pier Street,

Supermarkets

- **ASDA** • 151 E Ferry Rd

THE STRAND
WAPPI
Tower of London Park
SOUTH BANK
SOUTHWARK
BOROUGH
Stamford St
Southwark St
Thrale St
St. Thomas St
Tooley St
Union Street
The Cut
Waterloo Rd
Blackfriars Rd
Borough Rd
Long Ln
Great Dover St
Bermondsey St
Tower Bridge Rd
Druid St
Abbey St
Bermondsey
Strange Rd
Westminster Br
Bayliss Rd
York Rd
WATERLOO
St. Georges Rd
London Rd
Harper Rd
NEWINGTON
New Kent Rd
ELEPHANT & CASTLE
Kennington Rd
Southwark P
LAMBETH
Old Kent Rd
Dunton Rd
WALWORTH
Walworth Rd
Rolls Rd
KENNINGTON
Kennington Park Rd
VAUXHALL
Albany Rd
Burgess Park
Trafalgar Ave
Peckham Park Rd
Kennington Park
CAMBERWELL
Camberwell Rd
Camberwell New Rd
PECKHA
Peckham Rd
Hanover
SOUTH LAMBETH
Denmark Hill
Coldharbour Ln
STOCKWELL
Grove Ln
Dog Kennel Hill
Ruskin Park
Hinton Rd
E Dulwich
BRIXTON
Milkwood Rd
Herne Hill
EAST DULWICH
Railton Rd
E Dulwich Grv
Lordship Ln
HERNE HILL
Dulwich Rd
Half Moon Ln
104
105
106
107
108
112
113
114
115
121
122
123
127
128
129
130

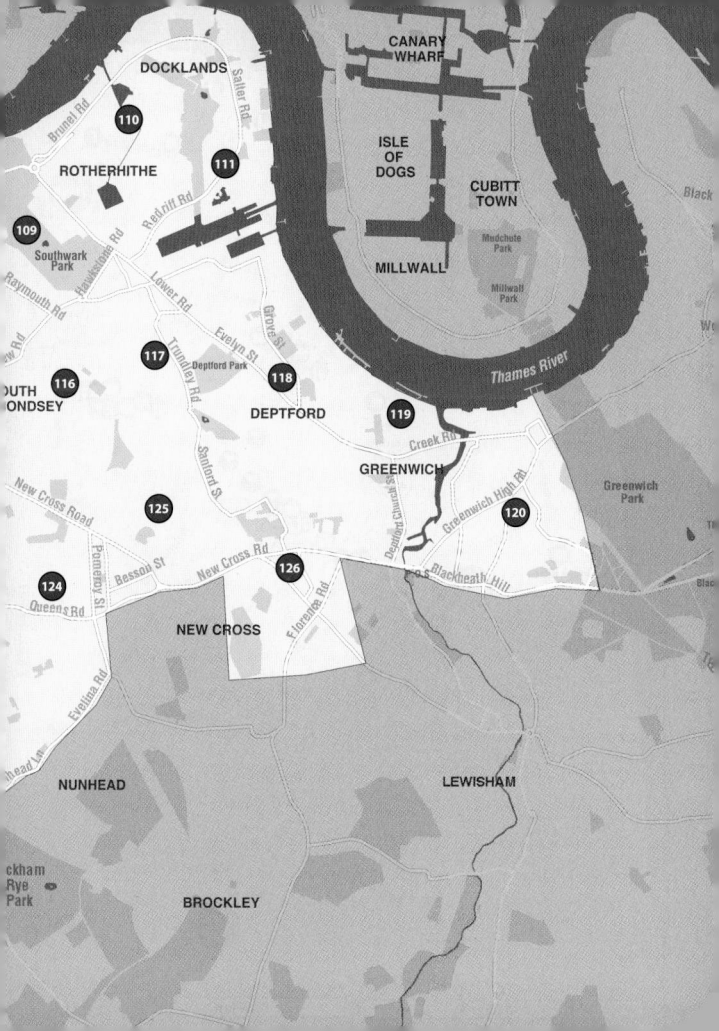
CANARY WHARF
DOCKLANDS
Salter Rd
Brunel Rd
110
ROTHERHITHE
111
ISLE OF DOGS
CUBITT TOWN
Redriff Rd
109
Southwark Park
Hawkstone Rd
Mudchute Park
MILLWALL
Millwall Park
Raymouth Rd
Lower Rd
Grove St
Evelyn St
117
Deptford Park
Trundley Rd
118
116
Thames River
DEPTFORD
119
Creek Rd
Salford St
GREENWICH
New Cross Road
125
Deptford Church St
Greenwich High Rd
120
Greenwich Park
Pepys Rd
Bessou St
New Cross Rd
126
124
Queens Rd
Blackheath Hill
NEW CROSS
Florence Rd
Evelina Rd
NUNHEAD
LEWISHAM
Rye Park
BROCKLEY

Map 104 • South Bank / Waterloo / Lambeth North

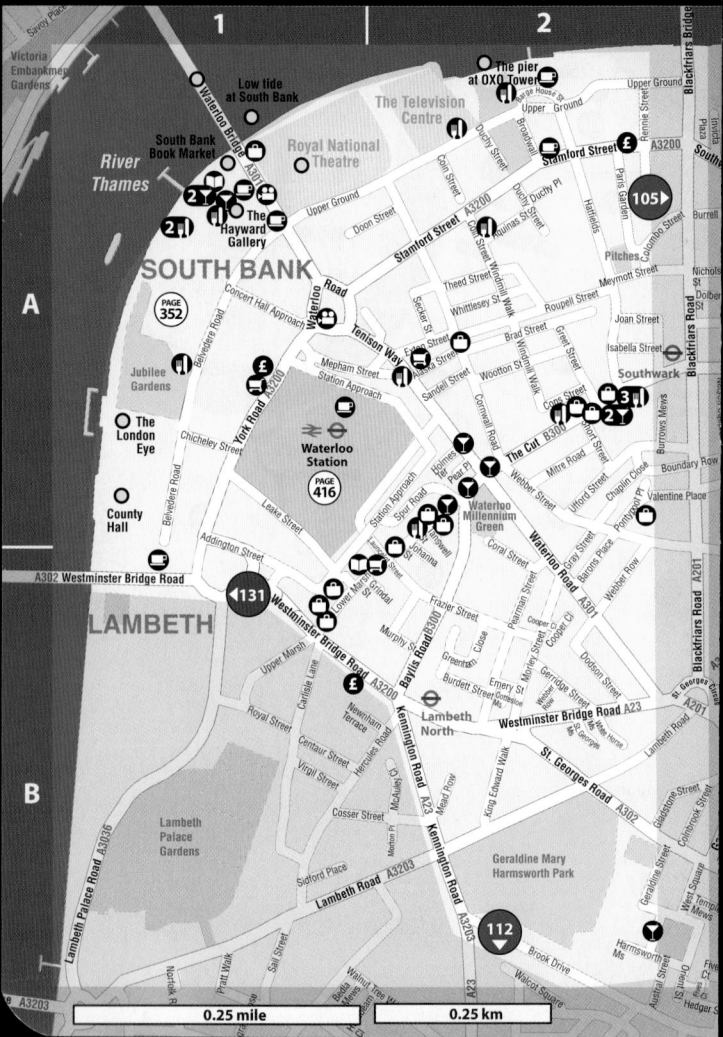
1
2
A
B
Victoria Embankment Gardens
Savoy Place
Low tide at South Bank
The pier at OXO Tower
The Television Centre
Royal National Theatre
South Bank Book Market
River Thames
The Hayward Gallery
SOUTH BANK
PAGE 352
Jubilee Gardens
The London Eye
County Hall
Waterloo Station
PAGE 416
Waterloo Millennium Green
LAMBETH
Lambeth Palace Gardens
Lambeth North
Geraldine Mary Harmsworth Park
Southwark
Pitches
Upper Ground
Stamford Street A3200
Waterloo Road
Tenison Way
Concert Hall Approach
Belvedere Road
York Road A3200
Mepham Street
Station Approach
Chicheley Street
Leake Street
Addington Street
A302 Westminster Bridge Road
Westminster Bridge Road A3200
Baylis Road A3200
Kennington Road A23
Lambeth Palace Road A3036
Lambeth Road A3203
St. Georges Road A302
Blackfriars Road A201
Blackfriars Bridge
The Cut B3086
Webber Street
Waterloo Road A301
Upper Marsh
Royal Street
Centaur Street
Virgil Street
Cosser Street
Sidford Place
Brook Drive
Walcot Square
Harmsworth Ms
Lambeth Road
Westminster Bridge Road A23
Boundary Row
Valentine Place
Mitre Road
Upford Street
Chaplin Close
Burrows Mews
Joan Street
Isabella Street
Roupell Street
Meymott Street
Nicholson Street
Doddson Street
Burdett Street
Emery St
Gerridge Street
Dodson Street
Frazier Street
Murphy St
Coral Street
Baron's Place
Webber Row
Pearman Street
Cooper Cl
Greenham Close
Cut Mews
Lower Marsh
Stamford Street
Upper Ground
Broadwall
Duchy Street
Colombo Street
Burrell
Hatfields
Paris Garden
Blackfriars Road
Southwark Bridge Road
Kennington Road A3203
Meard Row
King Edward Walk
Geraldine Street
Lakeside Street
West Square
Temple Mews
Harmsworth Ms
Brook Drive
Walcot Square
Lambeth Palace Road A3036
Pratt Walk
Sail Street
Norfolk Rd
Wallman Tree Way
Bata Mews
Hedger St
Australia Street
US Street
Lambeth Road
Westminster Bridge Road A23
St. Georges Road A302
Kennington Road A3203
Lambeth Palace Road A3036
Lambeth Road A3203
A302 Westminster Bridge Road
Waterloo Road A301
Blackfriars Road A201
Blackfriars Bridge
Southwark Bridge Road

South Bank / Waterloo / Lambeth North

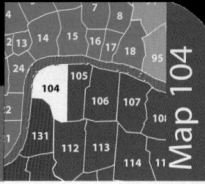

Hug the riverbank and you can culture 'till you puke. But you'll need stamina to survive; with such densely populated institutions your brain will give up long before your body. When it does, head for the cafe by day/bar by night, Concrete, tucked away behind the Southbank Centre, where the most current art installation du jour promises to have you wetting your pants in no time.

Banks

- **HSBC** • 22 Stamford St
- **Lloyds** • 2 York Rd
- **NatWest** • 91 Westminster Bridge Rd

Cinemas

- **BFI London IMAX** • Waterloo Rd & York Rd
- **BFI Southbank** • Belverdere Rd

Coffee

- **Bagel Factory** • Waterloo Station
- **Costa** • Belvedere Rd
- **Eat.** • Belvedere Rd
- **Eat.** • Barge House St
- **Pret A Manger** • 58 Stamford St
- **Starbucks** • 3 Belvedere Rd

Landmarks

- **County Hall** • Riverside Walkway
- **The Hayward Gallery** • Southbank Centre
- **The London Eye** • Westminster Bridge Rd
- **Low tide at South Bank** • South Bank
- **National Theatre** • South Bank
- **The pier at OXO Tower** •
- **South Bank Book Market** • Southbank (under Waterloo Bridge, opposite BFI)
- **Waterloo Bridge** • Waterloo Bridge

Libraries

- **Poetry Library** • Belvedere Rd
- **Waterloo Library** • 114 Lower Marsh

Nightlife

- **Anchor & Hope** • 32 The Cut
- **Barrio** • 14 W Square
- **Concrete** • Southbank Centre
- **Cubana** • 48 Lower Marsh
- **The Cut Bar** • 66 The Cut
- **Da Vinci's** • 6 Baylis Rd
- **The Fire Station** • 150 Waterloo Rd
- **The Pit Bar at the Old Vic** • The Cut
- **Royal Festival Hall** • Belvedere Rd
- **Skylon** • Belvedere Rd

Restaurants

- **Anchor & Hope** • 32 The Cut
- **Canteen** • Royal Festival Hall, Belvedere Rd
- **Concrete** • Southbank Centre
- **The Cut Bar** • 66 The Cut
- **Enis's Cafe** • 79 Waterloo Rd
- **Giraffe** • Riverside Level 1
- **Livebait** • 45 The Cut
- **Marie's Cafe** • 90 Lower Marsh
- **Oxo Tower Wharf** • Barge House St
- **RSJ** • 33 Coin St
- **Skylon** • Belvedere Rd
- **Studio 6** • 56 Upper Ground
- **Tas Cafe** • 33 The Cut

Shopping

- **The Bookshop Theatre** • 51 The Cut
- **Calder Bookshop** • 51 The Cut
- **I Knit London** • 106 Lower Marsh
- **Konditor & Cook** • 22 Cornwall Rd
- **Oasis** • 84 Lower Marsh
- **Radio Days** • 87 Lower Marsh
- **Scooterworks** • 132 Lower Marsh
- **Silverprint** • 12 Valentine Pl
- **Southbank Book Market** • Under Waterloo Bridge
- **Top Wind** • 2 Lower Marsh
- **Waterloo Camping** • 37 The Cut
- **What The Butler Wore** • 131 Lower Marsh

Supermarkets

- **Iceland** • 112 Lower Marsh
- **Marks & Spencer** • Waterloo Station
- **Sainsbury's** • 101 Waterloo Rd

Map 105 • Southwark / Bankside (West)

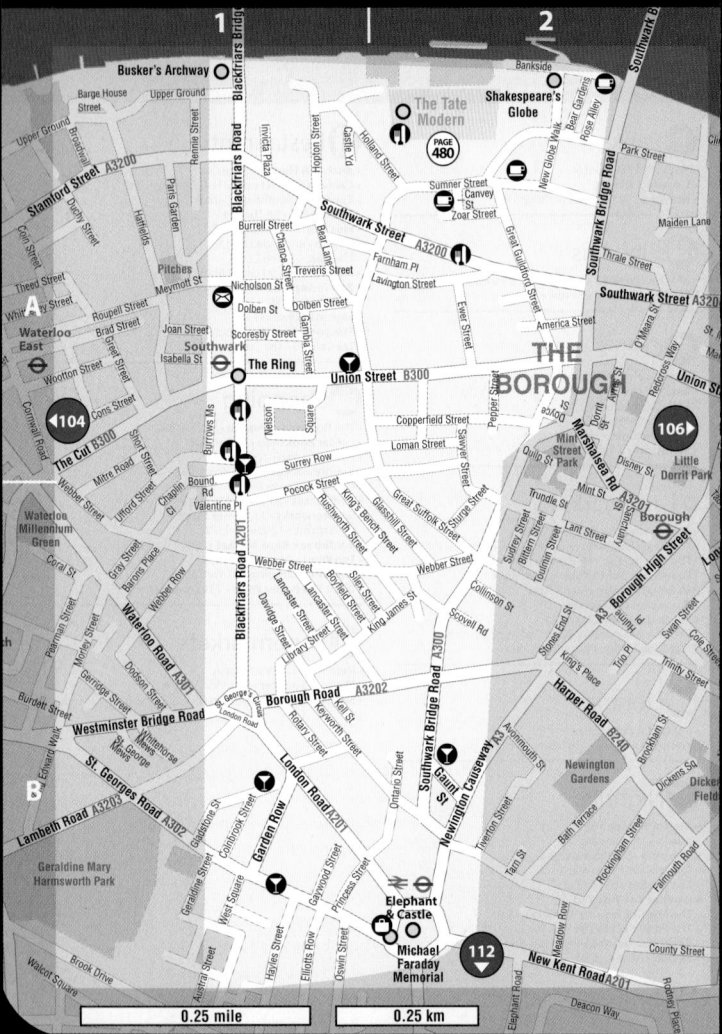

Southwark / Bankside (West)

The Tate Modern, ladies and gents. This is where it is and it deserves all the praise it gets. Next door, there's the reconstruction of Shakespeare's famous playhouse, making this looked-after stretch of the Thames embankment a treasure for those hungry for culture. For those hungry for something else, the area behind the gallery is more than up-and-coming: Baltic for Polish hunter's stew, The Table for fresh salads.

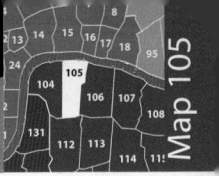

Coffee

- **Eat.** • Bankside
- **Pret A Manger** • 2 Canvey St
- **Starbucks** • Emerson St (Units 1-3 Benbow House)

Landmarks

- **Buskers' Archway** • Southbank
- **Elephant & Castle** • Elephant & Castle
- **Michael Faraday Memorial** • Elephant & Castle
- **The Ring** • 72 Blackfriars Rd
- **Shakespeare's Globe** • 21 New Globe Walk
- **Tate Modern** • Bankside

Nightlife

- **Albert Arms** • 1 Gladstone St
- **Imbibe** • 173 Blackfriars Rd
- **Ministry of Sound** • 103 Gaunt St
- **Prince of Wales** • 51 St George's Rd
- **The Wine Theatre** • 206 Union St

Post Offices

- **Blackfriars Road** • 52 Blackfriars Rd

Restaurants

- **Baltic** • 74 Blackfriars Rd
- **Blackfriars Cafe** • 169 Blackfriars Rd
- **Laughing Gravy** • 154 Blackfriars Rd
- **The Table** • 85 Southwark St
- **Tapas Brindisa** • 18 Southwark St
- **Tate Modern Restaurant** • Bankside

Shopping

- **Elephant & Castle Market** • Elephant & Castle

Map 106 • Bankside (East) / Borough / Newington

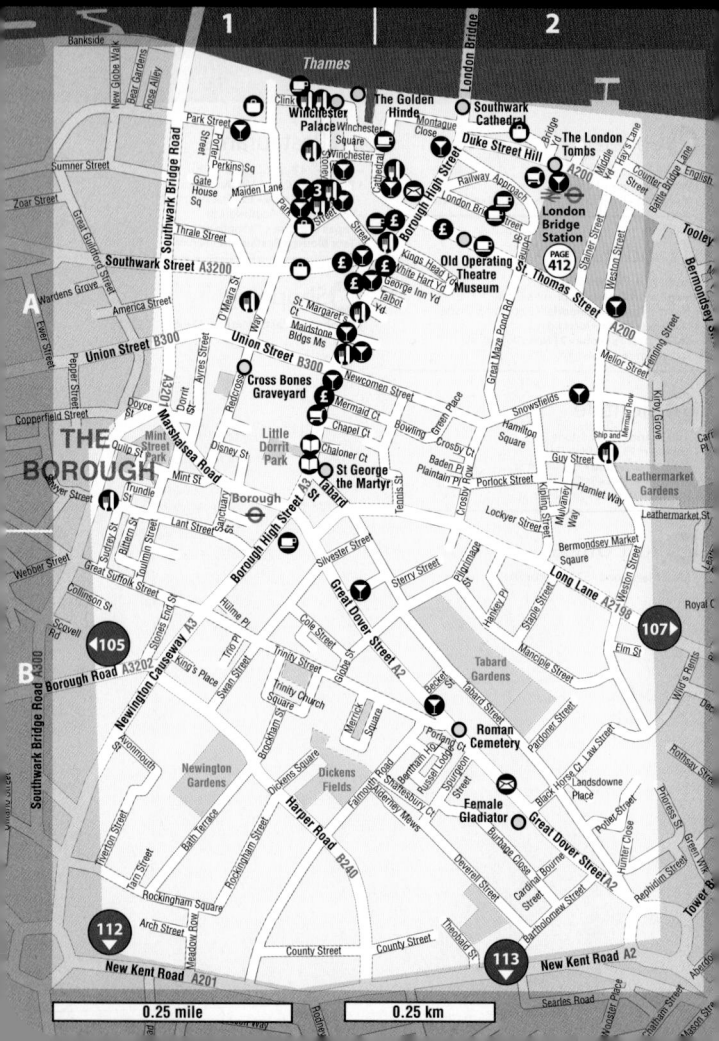
1
2
A
B
Thames
Bankside
New Globe Walk
Bear Gardens
Rose Alley
Winchester Palace
The Golden Hinde
Southwark Cathedral
Winchester Square
Montague Close
Duke Street Hill
The London Tombs
Bridge
Hay's Lane
Counter Street
Better Bridge Lane
English
Park Street
Porter Street
Sumner Street
Perkins Sq
Gate House Sq
Maiden Lane
Southwark Bridge Road
Borough High Street
Cathedral
Railway Approach
London Bridge Street
London Bridge Station
PAGE 412
Tooley
Zoar Street
Great Guildford Street
Thrale Street
Southwark Street A3200
Kings Head Pl
White Hart Yd
George Inn Yd
Talbot Yd
Old Operating Theatre Museum
St Thomas Street
Western Street
Bermondsey St
Wardens Grove
America Street
D Mews St
St Margaret Ct
Maidstone Bldgs Ms
Union Street B300
Great Maze Pond Rd
A200
Mellor Street
Fenning Street
Pepper Street
Cross Bones Graveyard
Newcomer Street
Mermaid Ct
Snowfields
Copperfield Street
Marshalsea Road
Mint Street Park
Little Dorrit Park
Chapel Ct
Bowling Green Place
Crosby Ct
Hamilton Square
Ship and Mermaid Row
Kipling Street
Guy Street
THE BOROUGH
Quilp St
Disney St
Chaloner Ct
St George the Martyr
Baden Pl
Plaintain Pl
Porlock Street
Leathermarket Gardens
Trundle St
Mint St
Borough
Tabard
Tennis St
Crosby Row
Hamlet Way
Lockyer Street
Leathermarket St
Bermondsey Market Sqaure
Lant Street
Southwark St
Southwark Bridge Road A300
Webber Street
Great Suffolk Street
Silvester Street
Sterry Street
Pilgrimage St
Long Lane A2198
Western Street
Royal C
Collinson St
Scovell Rd
Snowes End St
Hulme Pl
Cole Street
Trio Pl
Trinity Street
Globe St
Mancipic Street
Elm St
Newington Causeway A3
King's Place
Swan Street
Borough Road A3202
Trinity Church Square
Tabard Gardens
Becket St
Tabard Street
Merrick Square
Roman Cemetery
Pardoner Street
Newington Gardens
Brookham St
Dickens Square
Dickens Fields
Falmouth Road
Russell Lodge
Sturgeon Street
Black Horse Ct
Law Street
Landsdowne Place
Progress St
Tower Br
Sq
Iverson Street
Bath Terrace
Harper Road B240
Rockingham Street
Rockingham Square
Hain Street
Meadow Row
Arch Street
Female Gladiator
Great Dover Street A2
Burbage Close
Cardinal Bourne Street
Poyler Street
Hunter Close
Rephidim Street
Bartholomew Street
County Street
County Street
New Kent Road A201
New Kent Road A2
Searles Road
Bermondsey St
Chatham Street
Mason Street
Rodney Rd
Kipling Street
Bermondsey Wall
Southwark Bridge
Bus Station

Bankside (East) / Borough / Newington

A Shoreditch for grown-ups, these parts have become a bit suitified lately – and promises to be more so when the area is reborn as "London Bridge Quarter" under The Shard. Still, there's plenty of fun to be had. Gourmet-minded Borough Market draws the crowds on Saturdays, while the railway arches give way to night-time haunts like Shunt Lounge and Vaults for the cool kids and SeOne for the less cool kids. Head to El Vergel to nurse that hangover.

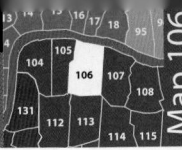

Banks

- **Abbey** • 9 Southwark St
- **Barclays** • 29 Borough High St
- **HSBC** • 28 Borough High St
- **Lloyds** • 69 Borough High St
- **NatWest** • St Thomas St
- **NatWest** • 10 Southwark St

Coffee

- **Bagel Factory** • 12 Joiner St
- **Caffe Nero** • 3 Cathedral St
- **Costa** • 134 Borough High St
- **Patisserie Lila** • 1 Bedale St
- **Pret A Manger** • 8 London Bridge st
- **Starbucks** • Clink Wharf, Clink St
- **Starbucks** • 21 St. Thomas St

Landmarks

- **Cross Bones Graveyard** • Red Cross Way
- **Female Gladiator** • Great Dover St
- **The Golden Hinde** • Clink St
- **The London Tombs** • Tooley St
- **Old Operating Theatre Museum** • 9 St Thomas St
- **Roman Cemetery** • 165 Great Dover St
- **Southwark Cathedral** • London Bridge
- **St George the Martyr** • Borough High St & Tabard St
- **Winchester Palace** • Clink St

Libraries

- **John Harvard Library** • 211 Borough High St
- **Local History Library** • 211 Borough High St

Nightlife

- **The Anchor** • 34 Park St
- **Belushi's** • 161 Borough High St
- **The Blue-Eyed Maid** • 173 Borough High St
- **Brew Wharf** • Brew Wharf Yard, Stoney St
- **The George Inn** • 77 Borough High St
- **The Globe** • 8 Bedale St
- **La Cave** • 6 Borough High St
- **The Market Porter** • 9 Stoney St
- **The Rake** • 14 Winchester Walk
- **The Roebuck** • 50 Great Dover St
- **The Rose** • 123 Snowfields
- **Roxy Bar and Screen** • 128 Borough High St
- **The Royal Oak** • 44 Tabard St
- **SeOne** • Weston St
- **Shunt Lounge and Vaults** • 20 Stainer St
- **Southwark Tavern** • 22 Southwark St
- **Wine Wharf** • Stoney St

Post Offices

- **Great Dover Street** • 159 Great Dover St
- **London Bridge** • 19 Borough High St

Restaurants

- **Amano** • Clink St
- **Boot and Flogger** • 10 Redcross Way
- **Brew Wharf** • Brew Wharf Yard, Stoney St
- **Cantina Vinopolis** • 1 Bank End
- **Champor-Champor** • 62 Weston St
- **El Vergel** • 8 Lant St
- **Feng Sushi** • 13 Stoney St
- **Fish!** • Cathedral St
- **Fusebox** • 12 Stoney St
- **Hing Loon** • 159 Borough High St
- **Roast** • The Floral Hall, Stoney St
- **Silka** • Southwark St
- **Tas EV** • 72 Borough High St
- **Wright Bros Oyster Bar** • 11 Stoney St

Shopping

- **German Deli** • 8 Southwark St
- **Paul Smith** • 13 Park St
- **Richer Sounds** • 2 London Bridge Walk
- **Vinopolis** • 1 Bank End

Supermarkets

- **Marks & Spencer** • London Bridge Station
- **Sainsbury's** • 116 Borough High St

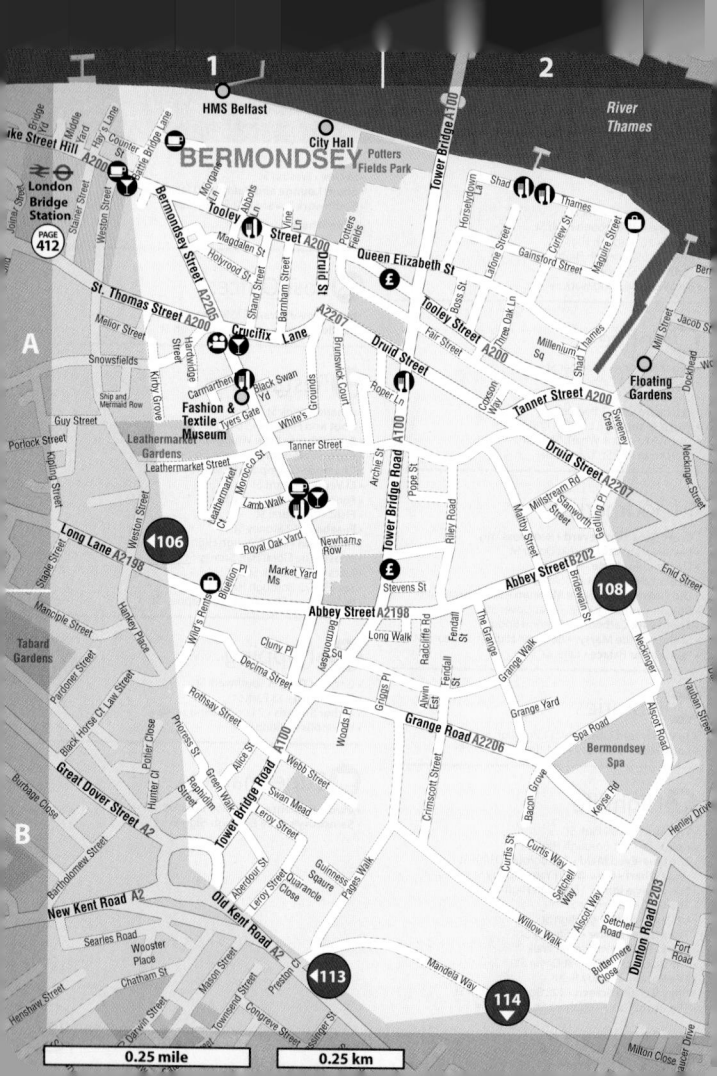
1
2
A
B
HMS Belfast
City Hall
BERMONDSEY
Potters Fields Park
River Thames
Tower Bridge A100
Lake Street Hill A200
London Bridge Station
PAGE 412
Bermondsey Street A2206
Tooley Street A200
Druid St A2207
Queen Elizabeth St
Tooley Street A200
St. Thomas Street A200
Crucifix Lane
Druid Street
Tanner Street A200
Floating Gardens
Fashion & Textile Museum
Leathermarket Gardens
Tanner Street
Druid Street A2207
Tower Bridge Road A100
Long Lane A2198
Abbey Street B202
Abbey Street A2198
Tabard Gardens
Grange Road A2206
Bermondsey Spa
Great Dover Street A2
Tower Bridge Road A100
New Kent Road A2
Old Kent Road A2
Dunton Road B203
106
108
113
114
0.25 mile
0.25 km

The elitist's Bermondsey, Shad Thames is an ultra-hip jumble of glass balconies and converted warehouses, emanating an excited-to-be-in-London buzz. It's heyday has only just begun. Where previously you might have positioned its epicentre under the eaves of The Design Museum, the hubbub seems to have shifted further south to the blossoming Bermondsey Square – with its indie Shortwave cinema and boutique Bermondsey Square Hotel. Venture down the road for perfect Buratta at the Long Lane Deli.

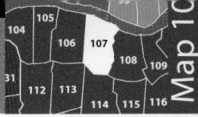

Banks

- **Barclays** • 104 Tower Bridge Rd
- **NatWest** • 201 Tooley St

Cinemas

- **Shortwave** • 10 Bermondsey Sq

Coffee

- **Bermondsey Street Coffee** • 163 Bermondsey St
- **Caffe Nero** • 6 More Pl [Tooley Street]
- **Pret A Manger** • 49 Tooley St

Landmarks

- **City Hall** • Queen's Walk, More London Development
- **Fashion and Textile Museum** • 83 Bermondsey St
- **Floating Gardens** • 31 Mill St
- **HMS Belfast** • Morgan's Lane, Tooley St

Nightlife

- **The Hide** • 39 Bermondsey St
- **Hilton London Tower Bridge** • 5 Tooley St
- **Village East** • 171-173 Bermondsey St

Restaurants

- **Butlers Wharf Chop House** • 36 Shad Thames
- **Delfina** • 50 Bermondsey St
- **Le Pont de la Tour** • 36 Shad Thames
- **M Manze Pie and Mash** • 87 Tower Bridge Rd
- **Magdalen** • 152 Tooley St
- **Village East** • 171-173 Bermondsey St

Shopping

- **The Design Museum Shop** • Shad Thames
- **Long Lane Deli** • 218 Long Ln

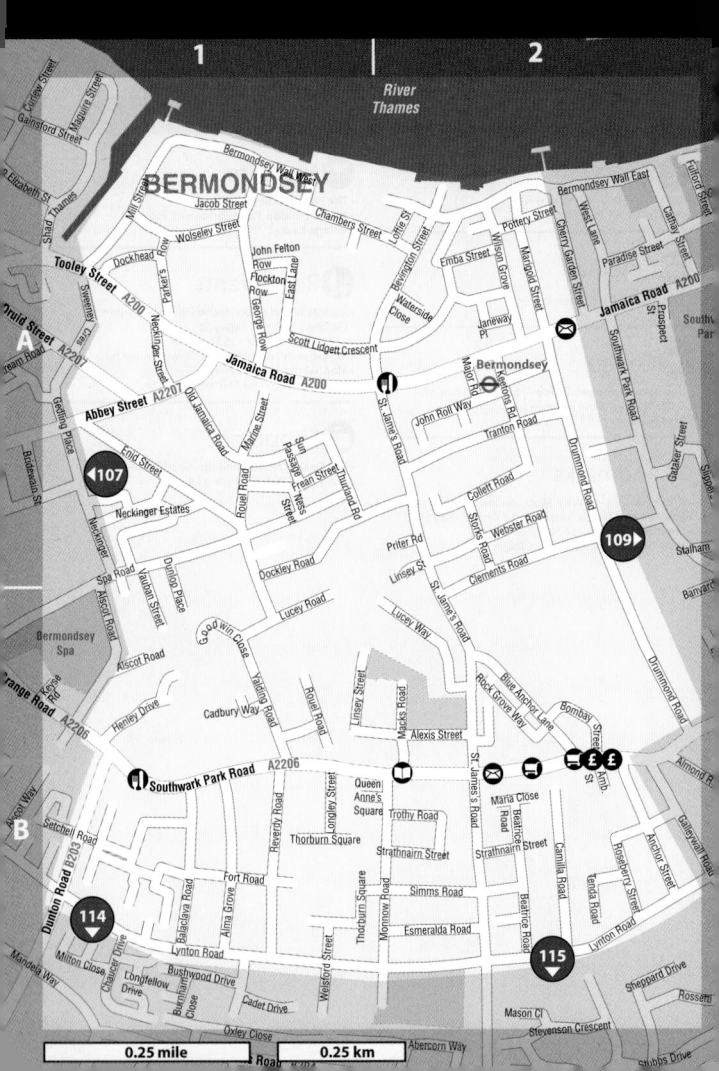
1
2
River Thames
BERMONDSEY
Bermondsey Wall West
Bermondsey Wall East
Jacob Street
Chambers Street
Wolseley Street
Mill Street
Tooley Street A200
Druid Street A2207
Abbey Street A2207
Jamaica Road A200
Scott Lidgett Crescent
John Felton Row
Rockton Row
Dockhead Row
Parker's Row
Neckinger Street
Old Jamaica Road
Marine Street
Sun Passage
Frean Street
Thurland Rd
St. James's Road
Bermondsey
Major Rd
Bermondsey Rd
John Roll Way
Tranton Road
Enid Street
Rouel Road
Neckinger Estates
Collett Road
Webster Road
Stokes Road
Clements Road
Drummond Road
Southwark Park Road
Jamaica Road A200
Prospect St
Gatekeer Street
Stalham
Bermondsey Wall West
Cherry Garden Street
West Lane
Paradise Street
Pottery Street
Wilson Grove
Marguis Street
Emba Street
Waterside Close
Janeway Pl
Bevington Street
Gainsford Street
Curlew Street
Shad Thames
Spa Road
Vauxhall Street
Dunton Place
Ascot Road
Bermondsey Spa
Ascot Road
Lucey Road
Lucey Way
Lucey St
Prter Rd
Good Win Close
Yalding Road
Cadbury Way
Henley Drive
Rouel Road
Linsey Street
Macks Road
Alexis Street
Blue Anchor Lane
Rock Grove Way
Bombay Street
Almond Rd
Southwark Park Road A2206
Queen Anne's Square
Longley Street
Beverly Road
Trothy Road
Thorburn Square
Strathnairn Street
Maria Close
Beatrice Road
Camilla Road
Rosebery Street
Anchor Street
Galleywall Road
Setchell Road
Dunton Road B203
Fort Road
Alma Grove
Balaclava Road
Simms Road
Esmeralda Road
Lynton Road
Bushwood Drive
Milton Close
Longfellow Drive
Cadet Drive
Weisford Street
Mandela Way
Oxley Close
Abercorn Way
Mason Cl
Stevenson Crescent
Sheppard Drive
Rossatti
Stubbs Drive
Tenda Road
Lynton Road
Bermondsey Spa
Druid Street
Tooley Street
Jamaica Road
Southwark Park Road
Abbey Street
Jamaica Road
Bermondsey
A
B
107
109
114
115
0.25 mile
0.25 km

Bermondsey

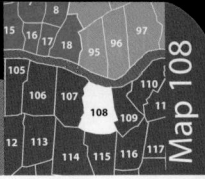

With its mixed bag of winding cobbled streets, council estates and posh new builds, you can imagine the awkwardness when the new-to-the-neighbourhood clean shirt steps into the adamantly local Bermondsey local. The old-timers are sticking to their guns, and there is a definite dirty side to this on-the-cusp part of town. For quaint Japanese try PoppyHana on Jamaica Road.

Banks

- **Barclays** • 264 Southwark Park Rd
- **Lloyds** • 255 Southwark Park Rd

Libraries

- **Blue Anchor Library** • Southwark Park Rd

Post Offices

- **Jamaica Road** • 158 Jamaica Rd
- **Southwark Park Road** • 200 Southwark Park Rd

Restaurants

- **Arancia** • 52 Southwark Park Rd
- **PoppyHana** • 169 Jamaica Rd

Supermarkets

- **Co-Op** • 193 Southwark Park Rd
- **Iceland** • 222 Southwark Park

Map 109 • Southwark Park

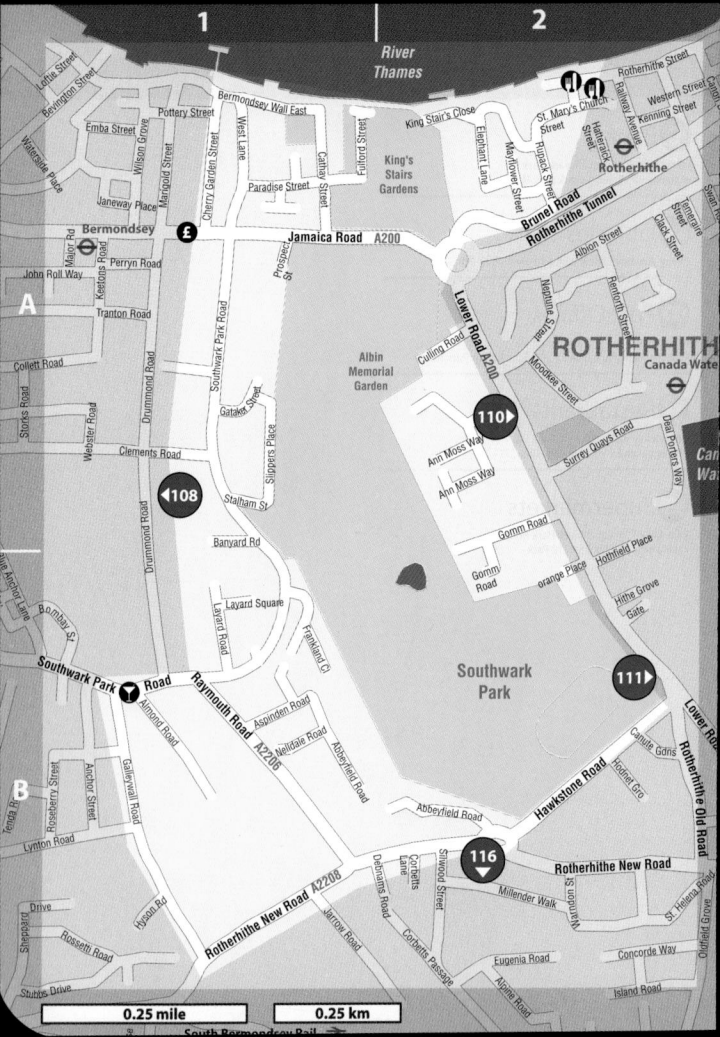

It might look a little runty compared to its Royal Park rivals, but if you want green without getting on a tube then Southwark Park is a lovely option. Well-spent investment has given it a boating lake, wildlife area, an inspiring artist-led café and the Dilston Grove gallery. For drinks, head to the river for an ale in the Mayflower—the pub of dreams.

Banks

- **Abbey** • 210 Southwark

Nightlife

- **Ancient Foresters** • 282 Southwark Park Rd

Restaurants

- **Mayflower** • 117 Rotherhithe St
- **Simplicity** • 1 Tunnel Rd

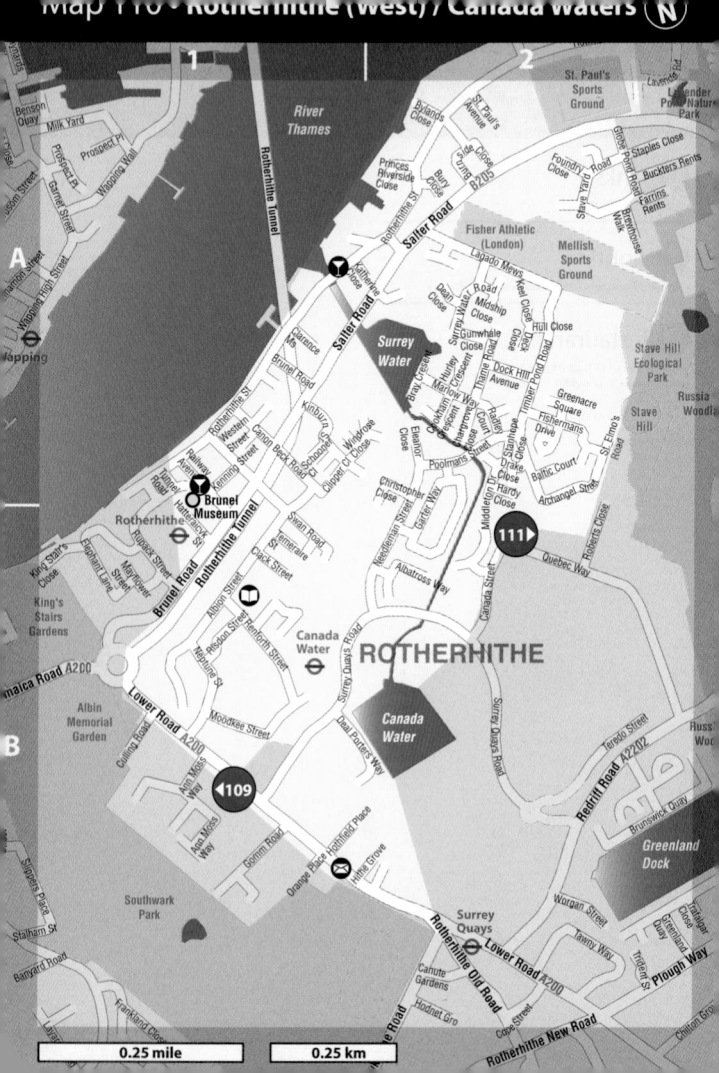
River Thames
Rotherhithe Tunnel
Salter Road
St. Paul's Sports Ground
Lavender Pond Nature Park
Milk Yard
Prospect Pl
Prospect Est
Wagoner Wall
Garnet Street
Mapping
Bylands Close
St. Paul's Avenue
Princes Riverside Close
Burgh Close
Rotherhithe St
Close
B205
Staples Close
Close Pond Road
Buckters Rents
Farmers Rents
Foundry Close
Shaw Yard Road
Warehouse Walk
Fisher Athletic (London)
Mellish Sports Ground
Lagado Mews
Keel Close
Deal Close
Surrey Water Road
Gunwhale Close
Hull Close
Surrey Water
Marlow Way
Thame Road
Dock Hill Avenue
Timber Pond Road
Stave Hill Ecological Park
Russia Wood
Stave Hill
Greenacre Square
Fishermans Drive
St. Elmo's Road
Clarence St
Brunel Road
Rotherhithe St
Kinburn St
Western Street
Kennington Street
Canon Dock Road
Schooner Cl
Clipper Cl
Clipper Close
Elsinor Close
Poolmans Street
Baltic Court
Drake Close
Hardy Close
Archangel Street
Christopher Close
Garter Way
Middleton Dr
Rotherhithe
Brunel Museum
Rotherhithe Tunnel
Brunel Road
Rotherhithe Tunnel
Swan Road
St Emerance
Clack Street
Albion Street
Albion St
Albatross Way
Needleman Street
Quebec Way
Roberts Close
Canada Street
King Stairs Close
Elephant Lane
Rennick Street
King's Stairs Gardens
Canada Water
ROTHERHITHE
Surrey Quays Road
Canada Water
Jamaica Road A200
Albion Memorial Garden
Lower Road A200
Cuming Road
Moodkee Street
Deal Porters Way
Surrey Quays Road
Tenedo Street
Redriff Road A2202
Brunswick Quay
Greenland Dock
Ann Moss Way
Gomm Road
Orange Place
Hothfield Place
Hatcliffe Grove
Southwark Park
Surrey Quays
Worgan Street
Tawny Way
Trogen St
Prough Way
Rotherhithe Old Road
Lower Road A200
Canute Gardens
Hodnet Grove
Cole Street
Rotherhithe New Road
Chilton Grove
Stratham St
Barnard Road
Frankland Close
0.25 mile
0.25 km

Rotherhithe (West) / Canada Waters

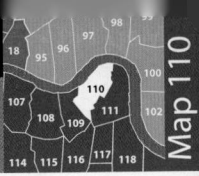

If residential flats are your thing you'll love Rotherhithe West. Not if pubs are your thing though. Or shops. Or life. But among the warren of apartments you can drink on the fabulous Thameside patio at Old Salt Quay, entertain your dad at the Brunel Museum, and stroll the enchantingly serene stretch of the Thames Path (if you can stand the joggers and the snoggers).

Landmarks

- **Brunel Museum** • Railway Ave

Libraries

- **Rotherhithe Library** • Albion St

Nightlife

- **Cable** • Tunnel Rd
- **Old Salt Quay** • 163 Rotherhithe St

Post Offices

- **Lower Road Rotherhithe** • 142 Lower Rd

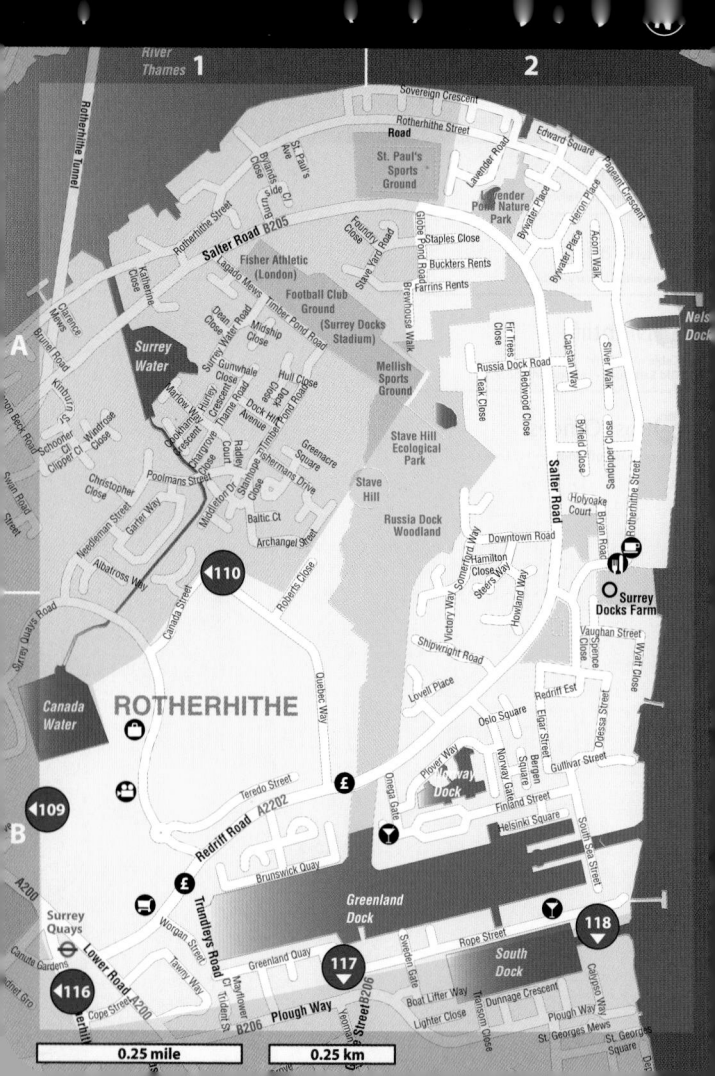
River Thames
1
2
A
B
Rotherhithe Tunnel
Sovereign Crescent
Rotherhithe Street
Road
St. Paul's Sports Ground
Edward Square
Lavender Road
Lavender Pond Nature Park
Heron Place
Acorn Walk
Salter Road B205
Rotherhithe Street
Foundry Close
Globe Pond Road
Staples Close
Buckters Rents
Farrins Rents
Fisher Athletic (London)
Lapado Mews
Football Club Ground (Surrey Docks Stadium)
Timber Pond Road
Brewhouse Walk
Katherine Close
Clarence Mews
Brymer Road
Surrey Water
Dean Close
Surrey Water Road
Midship Close
Gunwhale Close
Hull Close
Mellish Sports Ground
Russia Dock Road
Fir Trees Close
Redwood Close
Teak Close
Capstan Way
Silver Walk
Nels Dock
Kinburn St
Schooner Ct
Clipper Ct
Marlow Way
Hurley Crescent
Thames Road
Dock Hill Avenue
Timber Pond Road
Greenacre Square
Stave Hill Ecological Park
Byfield Close
Sandpiper Close
Christopher Close
Poolmans Street
Fisherman's Drive
Stave Hill
Salter Road
Holyoake Court
Bryan Road
Rotherhithe Street
Needleman Street
Barter Way
Middleton Dr
Baltic Ct
Russia Dock Woodland
Downtown Road
Albatross Way
Archangel Street
Roberts Close
Hamilton Close
Steers Way
Howland Way
Surrey Docks Farm
Canada Street
Surrey Docks Road
Victory Way
Somerford Way
Vaughan Street
Shipwright Road
Wyatt Close
Canada Water
ROTHERHITHE
Quebec Way
Lovell Place
Redriff Est
Oslo Square
Elgar Street
Odessa Street
Norway Gate
Bergen Square
Gullivar Street
Plough Way
Norway Dock
Finland Street
Teredo Street
Omega Gate
Helsinki Square
Redriff Road A2202
Brunswick Quay
South Sea Street
A200
Greenland Dock
Surrey Quays
Trundlers Road
Worgan Street
Canada Gardens
Lower Road A200
Tawny Way
Greenland Quay
Swedenborg Gate
Rope Street
South Dock
Cabpen Way
Cope Street
Plough Way B206
Yeoman Street B206
Boat Lifter Way
Lighter Close
Teesom Close
Dunmage Crescent
Plough Way
St Georges Mews
St Georges Square
110
109
116
117
118
0.25 mile
0.25 km

Rotherhithe (East) / Surrey Quays

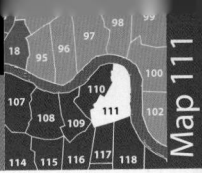

It still has some dodgy estates, but Rotherhithe East is blossoming in a clean-cut city-worker kind of way. The docks are delightful and have resisted the chain bars, instead allowing great little independents like Wibbley Wobbley and Moby Dick to flourish. Trying to be healthy? Enjoy lunch among the goats at wholesome Café Nabo in Surrey Docks Farm, and visit Decathlon for sport equipment paradise.

Banks

- **Halifax** • 28 Redriff Rd
- **HSBC** • Redriff Rd

Cinemas

- **Odeon Surrey Quays** • Redriff Rd & Surrey Quays Rd

Landmarks

- **Surrey Docks Farm** • Rotherhithe St

Nightlife

- **Moby Dick** • 6 Russell Place, off Greenland Dock
- **Wibbley Wobbley** • South Dock Marina, Rope St

Restaurants

- **Café Nabo** • Surrey Docks Farm, Rotherhithe St

Shopping

- **Decathlon** • Surrey Quays Road

Supermarkets

- **Tesco** • Redriff Rd

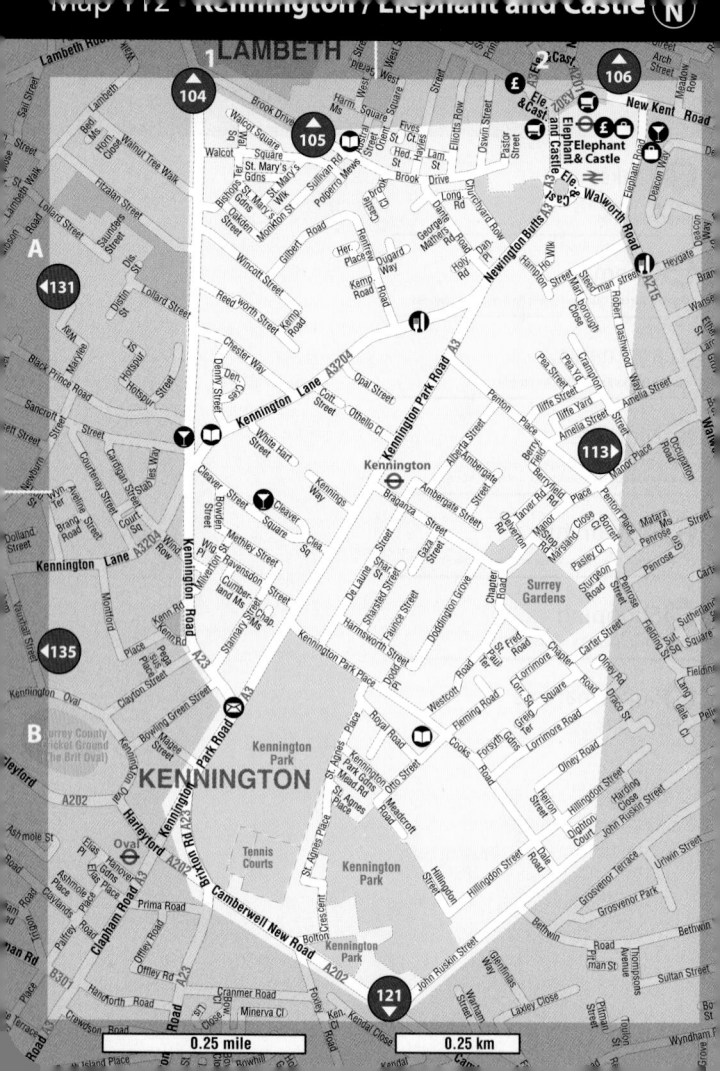
LAMBETH
KENNINGTON
Kennington Park
Kennington Lane A3204
Kennington Park Road A3
Kennington Road A23
Kennington Lane A3204
Newington Butts A3
Walworth Road A3
New Kent Road
Elephant & Castle
Camberwell New Road A202
Clapham Road A3
Brixton Rd A23
Harleyford Rd A202
Surrey Gardens
Tennis Courts
Oval
Lambeth Walk
Lambeth Road
Kennington Oval
Kennington Park Place
Kennington Park Road
Brook Drive
Walcot Square
St Mary's Gdns
Sullivan Rd
Gilbert Road
Wincott Street
Reed Worth Street
Kemp Road
Chester Way
Denny Street
Opal Street
Cott Street
Othello Cl
White Hart Street
Kennington
Braganza Street
Ambergate Street
Cleaver Square
Cleaver Street
Bowden Street
Methley Street
Ravensdale Street
Cumberland Mis
Stannary St
Kennington Park Place
Harmsworth Street
Doddington Grove
Westcott Road
Fleming Road
Roral Road
Cooks Road
Forsyth Gdns
Lorrimore Road
Olney Road
Carter Street
Chapter Road
Hillington Street
Dighton Court
John Ruskin Street
Grosvenor Terrace
Grosvenor Park
Bethwin Road
Sultan Street
Thomlinson Avenue
Wyndham Rd
Ottley Road
Cranmer Road
Minerva Cl
Kendal Close
Foley Road
Bolton Crescent
Wyndham Street
Laxley Close
Glenmilne Way
Kennington Oval
Clayton Street
Bowling Green Street
Kennington Oval
Vauxhall Street
Montford Place
Kennington Oval
Ashmole St
Prima Road
Ottley Road
Palfrey Road
Clayland Road
Ashmole Place
Elias Pl
Harleyford Road
Kennington Oval
Bolton Crescent
Kennington Park Road
Kennington Park Place
Kennington Park Road
Kennington Oval
Kennington Park Road
Kennington Park Place
Kennington Park Road
Kennington Oval
Kennington Park Road
Kennington Oval
Kennington Park Road
Kennington Oval

Kennington / Elephant and Castle

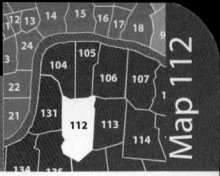

For those that thought it would never happen – change seems well under way at the double roundabouts that make up the infamous Elephant and Castle. The redevelopment budget is something in the realm of £1.5 billion – so whatever happens, it had better be good.

Banks

- **Abbey** • 335 Elephant & Castle
- **Lloyds** • 245 Elephant and Castle

Libraries

- **Brandon Library** • Cooks Rd [Maddock Way]
- **Durning Library** • 167 Kennington Ln
- **Imperial War Museum** • Austral St

Nightlife

- **Corsica Studios** • 5 Elephant Rd
- **Dog House** • 293 Kennington Rd
- **Prince of Wales** • 43 Cleaver Sq

Post Offices

- **Kennington Park** • 410 Kennington Park Rd

Restaurants

- **Dragon Castle** • 114 Walworth Rd
- **Lobster Pot** • 3 Kennington Ln

Shopping

- **Pricebusters Hardware** • 311 Elephant & Castle Shopping Centre
- **Recycling** • 110 Elephant Rd

Supermarkets

- **Iceland** • 300 Elephant & Castle
- **Tesco** • Elephant & Castle

Map 113 • Walworth

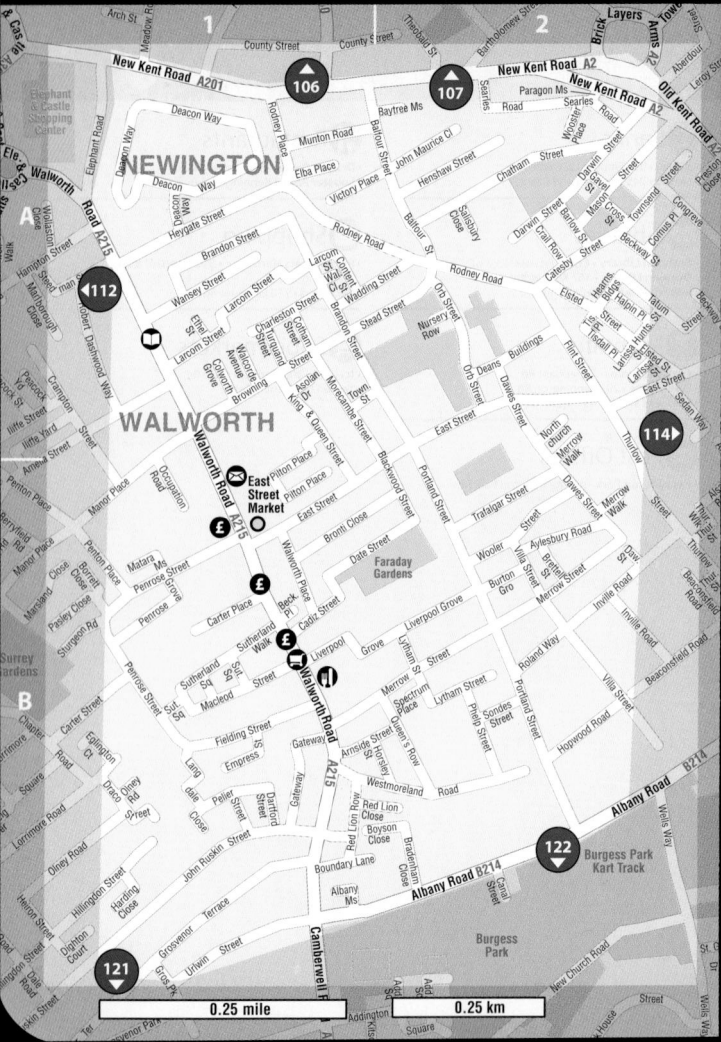
NEWINGTON
WALWORTH
Elephant & Castle Shopping Centre
Walworth Road A215
New Kent Road A201
New Kent Road A2
Old Kent Road A2
Albany Road B214
Camberwell Rd
Burgess Park
Burgess Park Kart Track
Faraday Gardens
East Street Market
Surrey Gardens
County Street
Elephant Road
Deacon Way
Munton Road
Elba Place
Victory Place
Heygate Street
Brandon Street
Wansey Street
Larcom Street
Walworth Place
Carter Place
Sutherland Walk
Liverpool Grove
Westmoreland Road
Red Lion Row
Boundary Lane
Albany Ms
Grosvenor Terrace
Urlwin Street
Addington Square
Walworth Road
Rodney Road
Old Kent Road
Thurlow Street
Penton Place
Manor Place
Penrose Street
Carter Street
Fielding Street
Gateway
Dolphin Court
Harding Close
Hillingdon Street
Olney Road
John Ruskin Street
Lorrimore Road
Chaucer Square
Surrey Gardens
Burgess Park
Nunhead Road
Walworth Road
Camberwell Rd
Addington Square
Kitson Street

Oh, Walworth. With all this about the Elephant and Castle redevelopment, why do we get the funny feeling you will never change? From the excessive amount of Gregg's bakeries along Walworth Road, to the 'who really buys these things?' tat at East Street Market, Walworth's lack of motivation is somehow endearing. La Luna for pizza is a find, as is the Newington Library.

Banks

- **Abbey** • 347 Walworth Rd
- **Barclays** • 260 Walworth Rd
- **NatWest** • 290 Walworth Rd

Landmarks

- **East Street Market** • East Street

Libraries

- **Newington Library** • 157 Walworth Rd

Post Offices

- **Walworth Road** • 234 Walworth Rd

Restaurants

- **La Luna** • 380 Walworth Rd

Supermarkets

- **Iceland** • 332 Walworth Rd

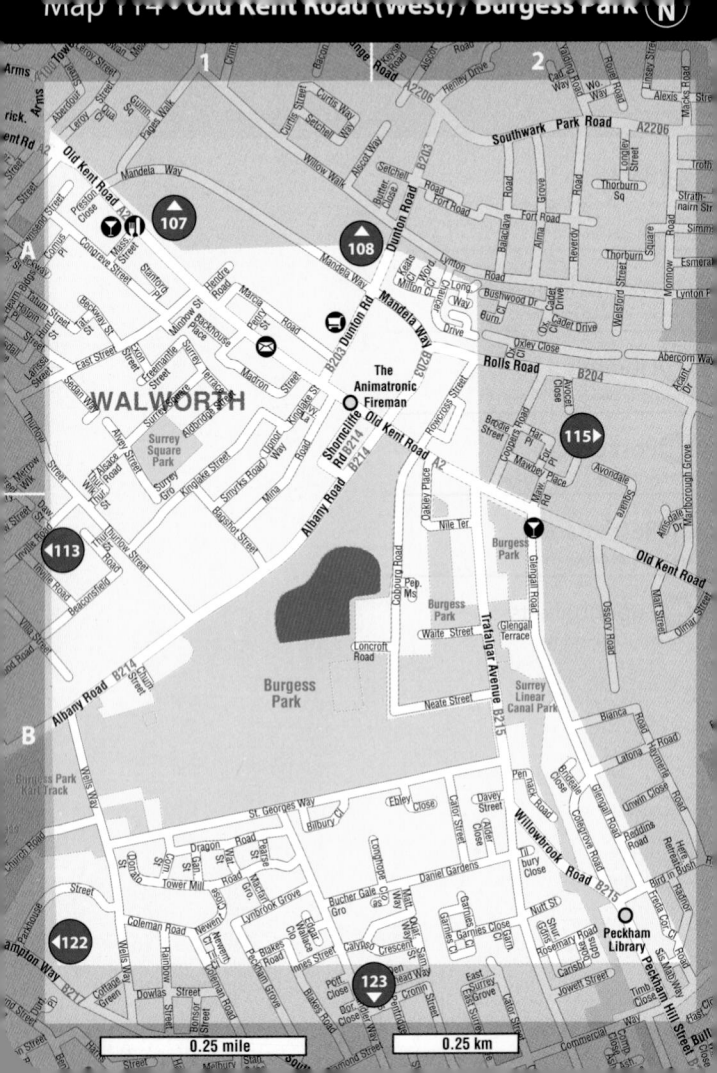
N
1
2
A
B
WALWORTH
The Animatronic Fireman
Surrey Square Park
Burgess Park
Burgess Park Kart Track
Surrey Linear Canal Park
Peckham Library
Old Kent Road A2
Southwark Park Road A2206
Dunton Road
Mandela Way
Rolls Road B204
Albany Road B214
Trafalgar Avenue B215
Willowbrook Road B215
Peckham Hill Street
Shenclifte Rd B214
Commercial
Coleman Road
Dowlas Street
Daniel Gardens
St Georges Way
Tower Mill
Bucher Gale Gro
Calypso
Crescent
Bakers Road
Peckham Grove
Lynton Road
Fort Road
Thorburn Sq
Thorburn Square
Bushwood Dr
Oxley Close
Abercorn Way
Avondale Square
Marlborough Grove
Nile Ter
Oakley Place
Cobourg Road
Pep Ms
Loncroft Road
Waite Street
Glengall Terrace
Glengall Road
Neate Street
Mark Street
Bianca Road
Latona Road
Urwin Close
Bird in Bush Road
Jowett Street
Timber Close
East Surrey Grove
Calton Street
Cronin Street
Peckham Grove
Bakers Road
Calypso
Crescent
Bucher Gale Gro
Daniel Gardens
Tower Mill
Coleman Road
Dowlas Street
Rainbow Street
Walls Way
Cottage Green
Newent Cl
Willowbrook Road
Peckham Hill Street

Old Kent Road (West) / Burgess Park

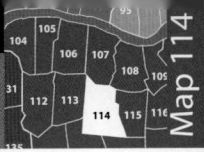

With the actually-not-that-bad Burgess Park at its heart, this bustling bit of Old Kent Road is probably most famous for its Tesco—it's a big one. But oddest of all is the animatronic fireman in the fireplace shop across the way. See the Pearly Kings and Queens' original headquarters at the World Turned Upside Down and take in the strip's one piece of culture at car showroom turned artist space Auto Italia South East.

Landmarks

- **The Animatronic Fireman** • Old Kent Road
- **Peckham Library** • 122 Peckham Hill St

Nightlife

- **Auto Italia South East** • 1 Glengall Rd
- **World Turned Upside Down** • 145 Old Kent Rd

Post Offices

- **Old Kent Road** • 240 Old Kent Rd

Supermarkets

- **Tesco** • 107 Dunton Rd

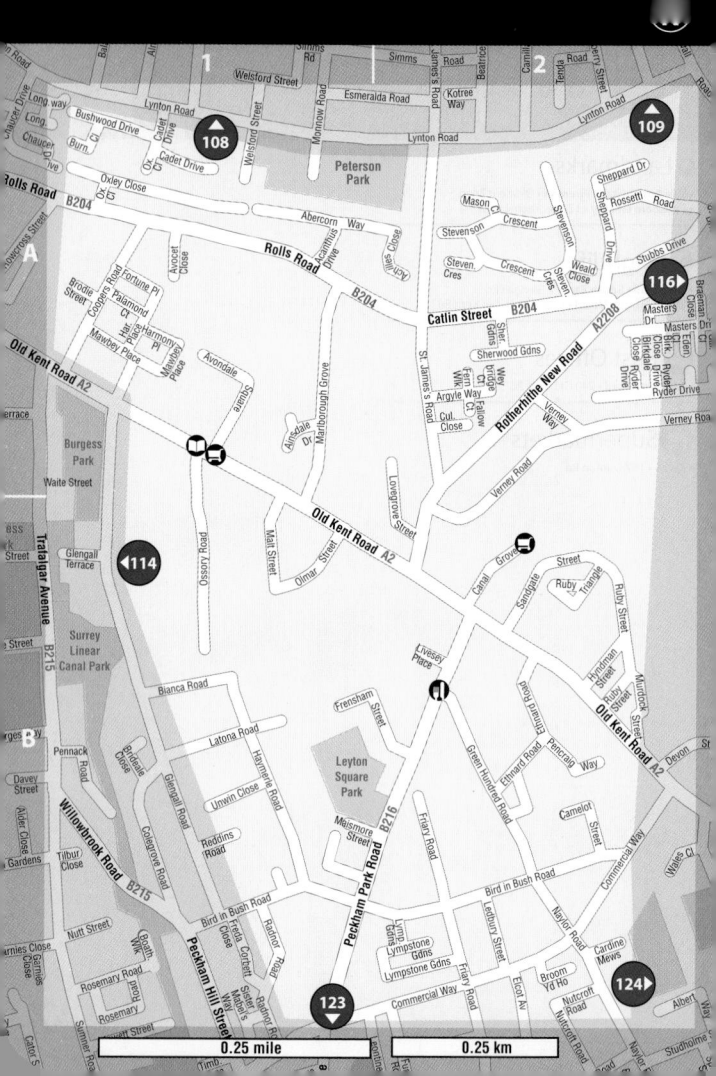
Simms Rd
Simms Road
Beatrice
Camilla
Tenda Road
Welsford Street
Esmeralda Road
Kotree Way
Lynton Road
Long Way
Bushwood Drive
Chaucer Drive
Burn
Cadet Drive
Winsford Street
Monnow Road
108
109
Peterson Park
Oxley Close
Rolls Road
B204
Abercorn Way
Sheppard Dr
Rossett Road
Mason Cr
Stevenson Crescent
Stevenson Drive
Sheppard Drive
Steven Cres
Crescent
Weald Close
Stubbs Drive
Rolls Road
B204
Avocet Close
Fortune Pl
Brodie Street
Coopers Road
Palamond Cl
Harmony Pl
Mawbey Place
Mawbey Place
Avondale Square
Avondale Dr
Marlborough Grove
St James's Road
Catlin Street
B204
Sherwood Gdns
Sherwood Gdns
Way
Farm Wk
Farm Cl
Gallow Cl
Cul. Close
Rotherhithe New Road
A2208
Masters Dr
Masters Dr Cl
Eclan Cl
Brick Close
Brickdale Drive
Ryder Close
Ryder Drive
Ryder Drive
Verney Way
Verney Road
Verney Road
116
Old Kent Road A2
Burgess Park
Waite Street
Trafalgar Avenue
Glengall Terrace
114
Ossory Road
Mall Street
Olmar Street
Old Kent Road A2
Canal Grove
Sandgate Street
Ruby Triangle
Ruby Street
Surrey Linear Canal Park
B215
Bianca Road
Livesey Place
Frensham Street
Bryndman Street
Ruby Street
Murdock Street
Old Kent Road A2
Devon
Latona Road
Pennack Road
Leyton Square Park
Green Hundred Road
Ethward Road
Way
Camelot Street
Davey Street
Glengall Road
Umvin Close
Colegrove Road
Reddins Road
Meismore Street
B216
Friary Road
Willowbrook Road
B215
Tilbur Close
Bird in Bush Road
Commercial Way
Wales Cl
Nutt Street
Bird in Bush Road
Radnor Road
Leabury Street
Naylor Road
Peckham Park Road
Lymington Gdns
Lymington Gdns
Lymington Gdns
Fairy Road
Cardine Mews
Peckham Hill Street
Rosemary Road
Rosemary
Broom Yd Ho
Nutcroft Road
124
123
Commercial Way
Albert Way
Summer Road
0.25 mile
0.25 km
Studholme

Old Kent Road (East)

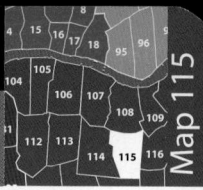

There must be something to this portion of Old Kent Road, as the Pearly Kings and Queens won't shut up about the whole thing. As far as we can tell, it's not that much more than a giant Asda. Walk along Bird In Bush Road to laugh at its name and over to Peckham Park Road for a damn good fry-up at Roma Café.

Libraries

- **East Street Library** • 168 Old Kent Rd

Restaurants

- **Roma Café** • 21 Peckham Park Rd

Supermarkets

- **ASDA** • Old Kent Rd & Ossory Rd
- **Sainsbury's** • 2 Canal Grove

Map 116 • South Bermondsey

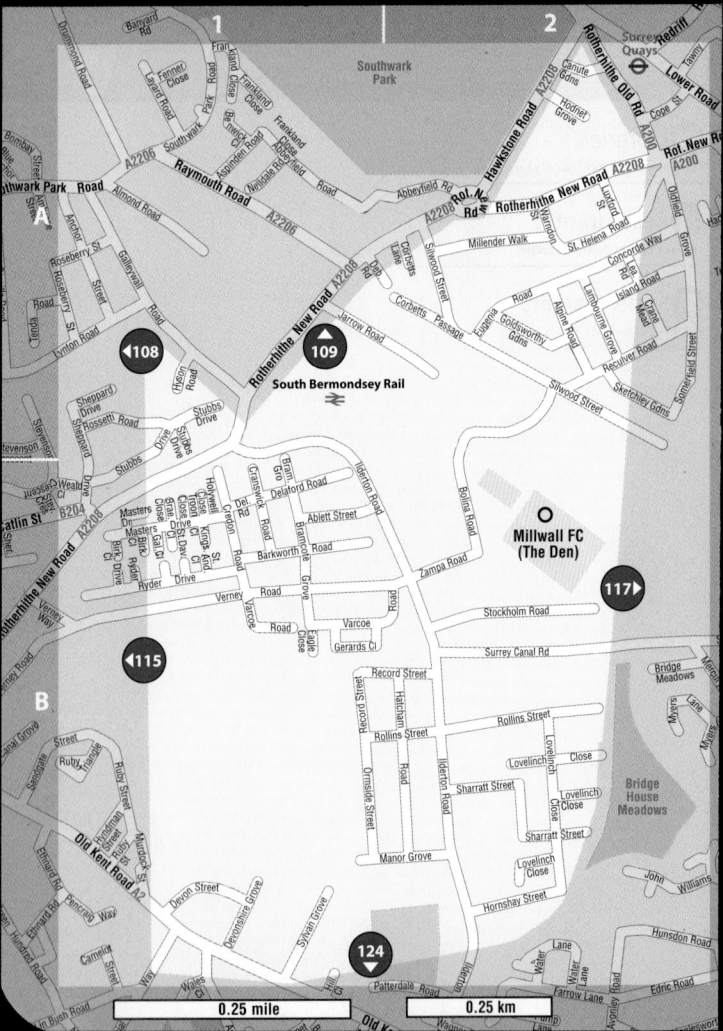

South Bermondsey plays home to one of the more over-looked London football clubs, Millwall FC, and this might be the only landmark. But they are proposing cool cycle lanes on the disused rail bridges, so watch this space. Population-wise, it's an odd slurry of Surrey Quay/Old Kent Road/Rotherhithe overspill but probably home to some of London's last real estate deals.

Landmarks

• **Millwall FC Stadium** • The Den, Zampa Road

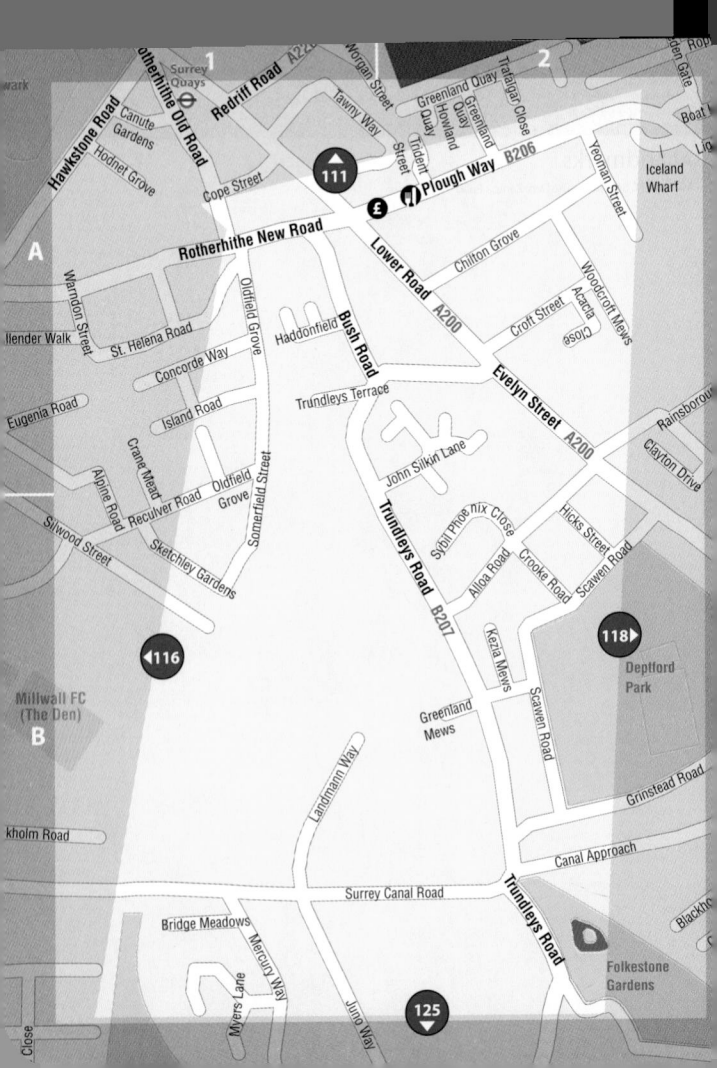
1
2
A
B
Surrey Quays
Rotherhithe Old Road
Redriff Road A2
Morgan Street
Tawny Way
Greenland Quay
Greenland Quay
Trafalgar Close
Trident Street
Howland
Hawkstone Road
Canute Gardens
Hodnet Grove
Cope Street
111
Plough Way B206
Yeoman Street
Iceland Wharf
Rotherhithe New Road
Lower Road A200
Chilton Grove
Woodcroft Mews
Acacia Close
Croft Street
Warndon Street
St. Helena Road
Oldfield Grove
Haddonfield
Bush Road
Concorde Way
Evelyn Street A200
Trundleys Terrace
Island Road
Eugenia Road
Crane Mead
Alpine Road
Reculver Road
Oldfield Grove
Somerfield Street
John Silkin Lane
Clayton Drive
Silwood Street
Sketchley Gardens
Trundleys Road B207
Sybil Phoenix Close
Hicks Street
Alloa Road
Crooke Road
Scawen Road
Kenia Mews
116
118
Deptford Park
Millwall FC (The Den)
Greenland Mews
Scawen Road
Landmann Way
Grinstead Road
Canal Approach
Surrey Canal Road
Trundleys Road
Bridge Meadows
Mercury Way
Myers Lane
Jump Way
125
Folkestone Gardens

Deptford (West)

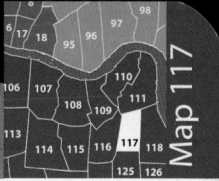

Apparently, developers have their eye on Deptford West. You've really got to hope so. The Blitz did its best, but the area came back with hastily built and charmless '60s tower blocks. Still, like the rest of Deptford it's going through a gradual regeneration as young buyers move in to make their money stretch. The Yellow House offers salvation for eating out.

Banks

• **Barclays** • 1 Plough Way

Restaurants

• **Yellow House** • 37 Plough Way

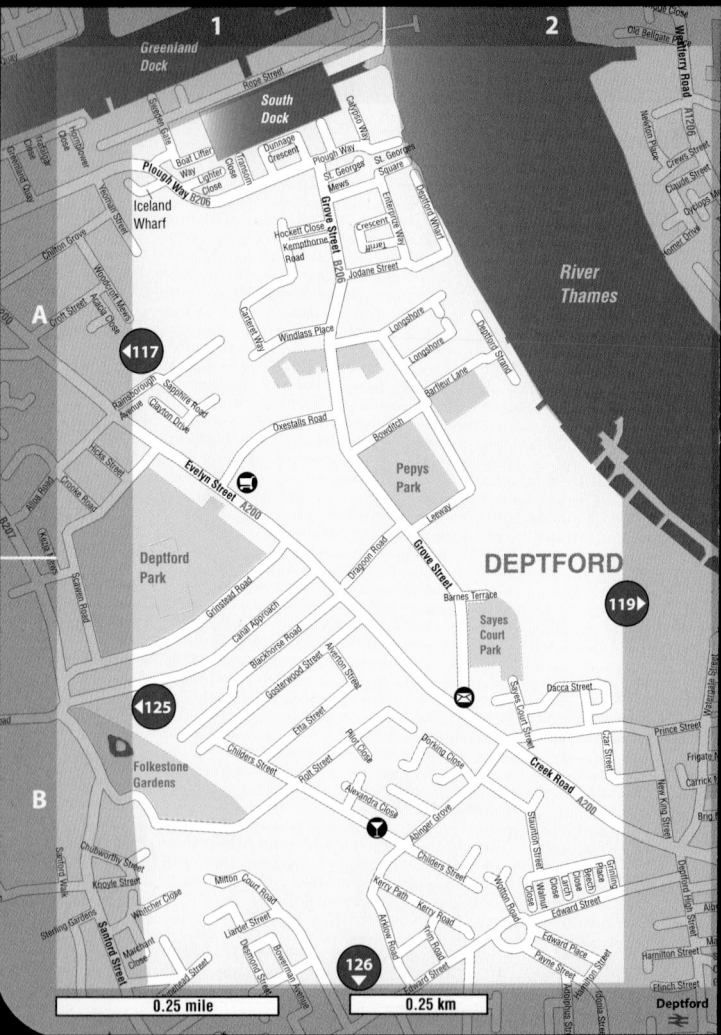
1
2
Greenland Dock
South Dock
Rope Street
Plough Way
St. Georges Square
St. Georges Mews
Dunmage Crescent
Boat Lifter Way
Lighter Close
Transom Close
Plough Way B206
Iceland Wharf
Grove Street B206
Hockett Close
Kempthorne Road
Crescent
Enterprise Way
Jodane Street
Deptford Wharf
River Thames
Old Bellgate Place
Wetherry Road
Newton Place
Crown Street
Claude Street
Cyprus Mews
Yeoman Street
Chilton Grove
Woodcroft Mews
Acacia Close
Croft Street
A
117
Windlass Place
Longshore
Longshore
Deptford Strand
Barfleur Lane
Avenue
Clayton Drive
Oxestalls Road
Bowditch
Pepys Park
Lateway
Evelyn Street A200
Hicks Street
Crooke Road
Alma Road
A207
Kender Arms
Deptford Park
Scovell Road
Grinstead Road
Canal Approach
Blackhorse Road
Goldarwood Street
Aventon Street
Ella Street
Childers Street
Rolt Street
Plevy Close
Pocking Close
Alexandra Close
Abinger Grove
Dragoon Road
Grove Street
Barnes Terrace
DEPTFORD
119
Sayes Court Park
Sayes Court Street
Dacca Street
Prince Street
Car Street
Creek Road A200
Frigate
Carrick
New King Street
Brig
Watergate Street
125
Folkestone Gardens
B
Chubworthy Street
Knoyle Street
Sanford Walk
Whitcher Close
Sterling Gardens
Sanford Street
Marlpant Close
Mitton Court Road
Llanbet Street
Deptford Street
Rosemman Tavern
Childers Street
Kerry Path
Kerry Road
Yorn Road
Archer Road
Woolston Road
Stanton Street
Grining Place
Beech Close
Walnut Close
Larch Close
Edward Street
Edward Place
Payne Street
Hamilton Street
Deptford High Street
Hamilton Street
Finch Street
Idonia Street
126
Edward Street
0.25 mile
0.25 km
Deptford

Deptford (Central)

When Christopher Marlowe was murdered in a Deptford tavern, Deptford hit its nightlife peak. That was 1593. Today, while the rest of London turns everything into a pub, Deptford turns its pubs into churches. Without beer, you may want to drown your sorrows in the Thames, but even that is thwarted: here the Thames path breaks to take you through neglected residential areas instead. Escape!

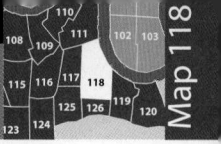

Nightlife

• **The Lord Palmerston** • 81 Childers Street

Post Offices

• **Evelyn Street** • 301 Evelyn St

Supermarkets

• **Sainsbury's** • 101 Evelyn St

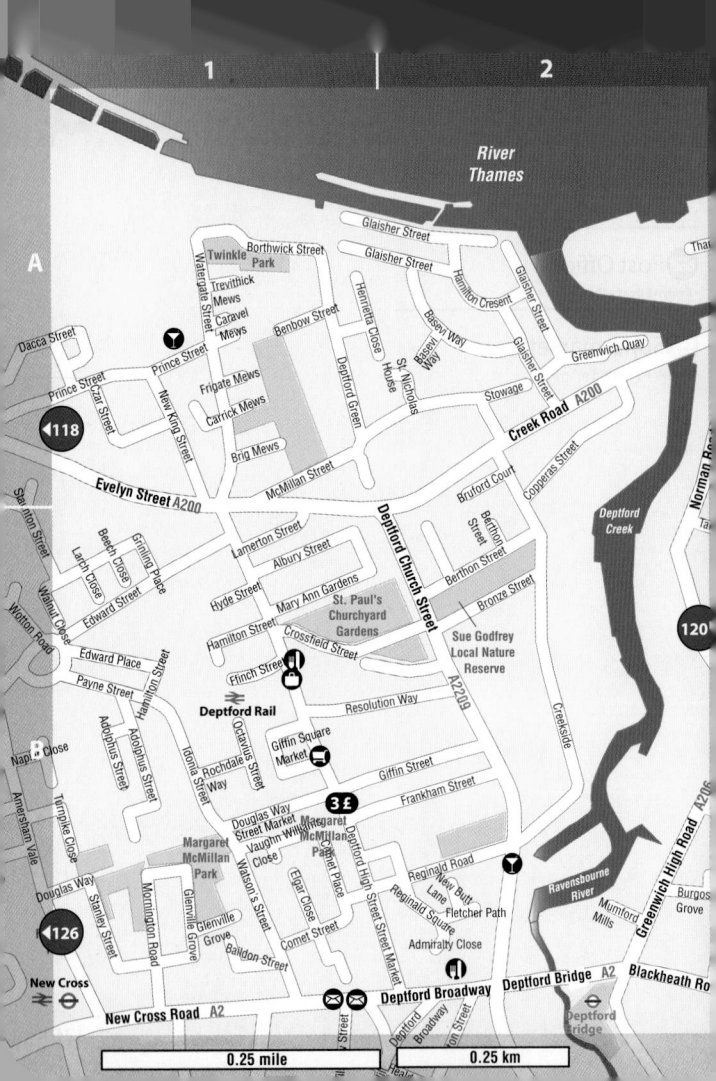
1
2
A
B
River Thames
Glaisher Street
Twinkle Park
Borthwick Street
Trevithick Mews
Caravel Mews
Watergate Street
Benbow Street
Henrietta Close
Hamilton Cresent
Basevi Way
Greenwich Quay
Dacca Street
Prince Street
Frigate Mews
Carrick Mews
Deptford Green
St. Nicholas House
Stowage
Creek Road A200
New King Street
Brig Mews
McMillan Street
Evelyn Street A200
Bruford Court
Coppermas Street
Deptford Church Street
Berthon Street
Deptford Creek
Lamerton Street
Albury Street
Grinling Place
Beech Close
Larch Close
Edward Street
Walnut Close
Hyde Street
Mary Ann Gardens
St. Paul's Churchyard Gardens
Bronze Street
Hamilton Street
Crossfield Street
Sue Godfrey Local Nature Reserve
Edward Place
Flinch Street
Payne Street
Hamilton Street
Deptford Rail
Resolution Way
A2209
Creekside
Adolphus Street
Octavius Street
Rochdale Way
Giffin Square Market
Giffin Street
Frankham Street
Douglas Way Street Market
Vaughn Williams Close
Margaret McMillan Park
Deptford High Street
Reginald Road
Reginald Square
Buff Lane
Fletcher Path
Admiralty Close
Ravensbourne River
Greenwich High Road A206
Burgos Grove
Mumford Mills
Amersham Vale
Turnpike Close
Napier Close
Douglas Way
Stanifer Street
Mornington Road
Glenville Grove
Baildon Street
Comet Street
Elbar Close
Watson's Street
New Cross
New Cross Road A2
Deptford Broadway
Deptford Bridge A2
Blackheath Ro
Deptford Bridge
0.25 mile
0.25 km

As you arrive you may think twice about stepping out the comforting folds of the bendy bus. But toughen up: it's not all bad. Even if the clothes are nicked from your back, you can buy replacements from Deptford Market and still have change for pie & mushy peas from Manzes. The Dog & Bell is a rare local gem for a comforting pint.

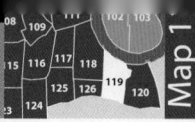

Banks

- **Barclays** • 80 Deptford High St
- **Halifax** • 93 Deptford High St
- **HSBC** • 90 Deptford High St

Nightlife

- **Bird's Nest** • 32 Deptford Church St
- **Dog & Bell** • 116 Prince Street

Post Offices

- **New Cross** • 500 New Cross Rd
- **New Cross Gate** • 500 New Cross Rd

Restaurants

- **Kaya House** • 37 Deptford Broadway
- **Manzes** • 204 Deptford High St

Shopping

- **Deptford Market** • Deptford High St

Supermarkets

- **Iceland** • 112 Deptford High St

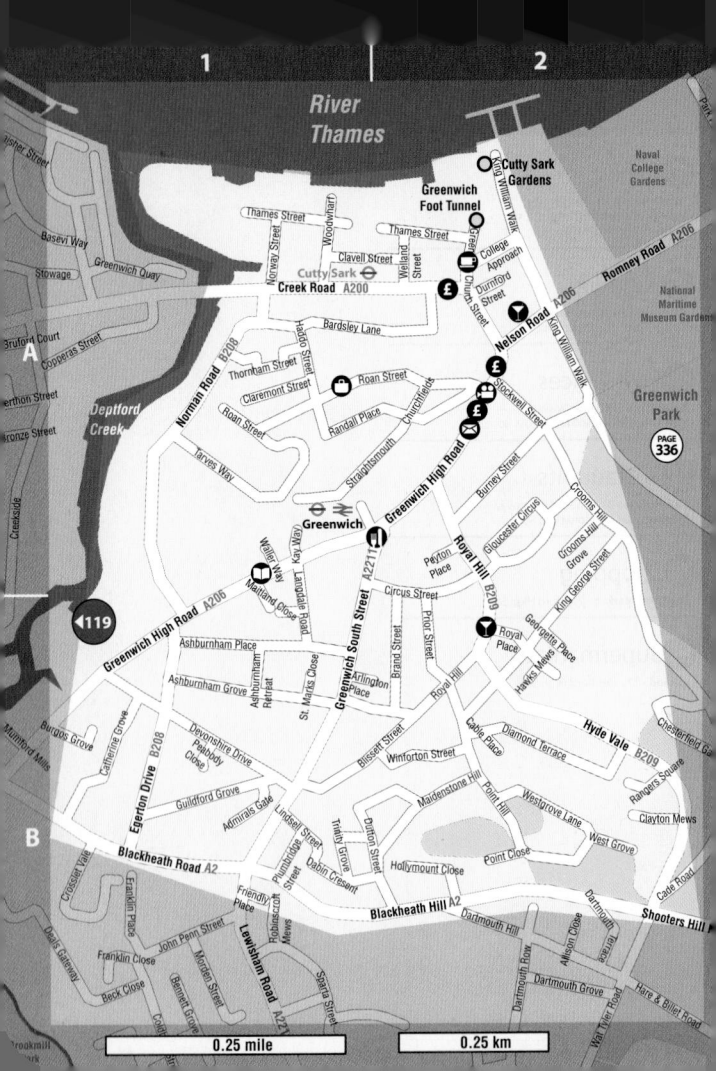
1
2
A
B
River Thames
Cutty Sark Gardens
Greenwich Foot Tunnel
Thames Street
Woodwharf
Norway Street
Clavell Street
Wellard Street
Thames Street
College Approach
Dumford Street
Church Street
King William Walk
Romney Road A206
Nelson Road A206
Cutty Sark
Creek Road A200
Stowage
Greenwich Quay
Basevi Way
Bardsley Lane
Hearn Street
Thornham Street
Claremont Street
Roan Street
Blackwell Street
Randall Place
Churchfields
Norman Road B208
Deptford Creek
Copperas Street
Tarves Way
Straightsmouth
Greenwich High Road
Burney Street
Greenwich
Wellington Way
Kay Way
Maidland Close
Lundale Road
Greenwich South Street A2211
Peyton Place
Gloucester Circus
Royal Hill B209
Croom's Hill
Croom's Hill Grove
King George Street
Circus Street
Greenwich High Road A206
Ashburnham Place
Ashburnham Grove
Ashburnham Retreat
St. Marks Close
Arlington Place
Brand Street
Prior Street
Royal Place
Geoffrey's Place
Hawks Mews
Royal Hill
Blissett Street
Winforton Street
Cadle Place
Diamond Terrace
Hyde Vale B209
Chesterfield Gr
Rangers Square
Burgos Grove
Catherine Grove
Devonshire Drive
Peabody Close
Egerton Drive B208
Guildford Grove
Admirals Gate
Lindsell Street
Maidenstone Hill
Point Hill
Westgrove Lane
West Grove
Clayton Mews
Point Close
Tilney Grove
Dutton Street
Hollymount Close
Dabin Crescent
Plumstead Street
Blackheath Road A2
Crossfell Way
Franklin Place
Friendly Place
Robinscroft Mews
Blackheath Hill A2
Dartmouth Hill
Shooters Hill
Cade Road
Dartmouth Road
Allison Close
Dartmouth Row
Dartmouth Grove
Hare & Billet Road
Wat Tyler Road
Dark Gateway
Franklin Close
John Penn Street
Lewisham Road A2211
Morden Street
Beck Close
Bennett Grove
Spring Street
Noval College Gardens
National Maritime Museum Gardens
Greenwich Park
PAGE 336
119
0.25 mile
0.25 km

Host of the lacklustre O2 Arena and one of the most charming village markets in London, don't forget to set your watch and give thanks to the birthplace of Greenwich Mean Time (GMT). Cure your sweet tooth at Humbug in the now somewhat tat-ified covered market, stroll through Cutty Sark Gardens where the Archbishop of Canterbury met his fate in 1012 and try not to notice the drips in the Greenwich Foot Tunnel.

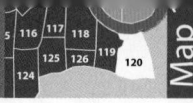

Banks

- **HSBC** • 275 Greenwich High Rd
- **Lloyds** • 6 Crescent Arcade
- **NatWest** • 2 Greenwich Church St

Cinemas

- **Greenwich Picturehouse** • 180 Greenwich High Rd

Coffee

- **Starbucks** • 54 Greenwich Church St

Landmarks

- **Cutty Sark Gardens** • Cutty Sark
- **Greenwich Foot Tunnel** • Greenwich Church St

Libraries

- **West Greenwich Library** • Greenwich High Rd

Nightlife

- **Bar du Musee** • 17 Nelson Rd
- **Greenwich Union** • 56 Royal Hill

Post Offices

- **Greenwich** • 261 Greenwich High Rd

Restaurants

- **Inside** • 19 Greenwich South St

Shopping

- **Mr Humbug** • Greenwich Market

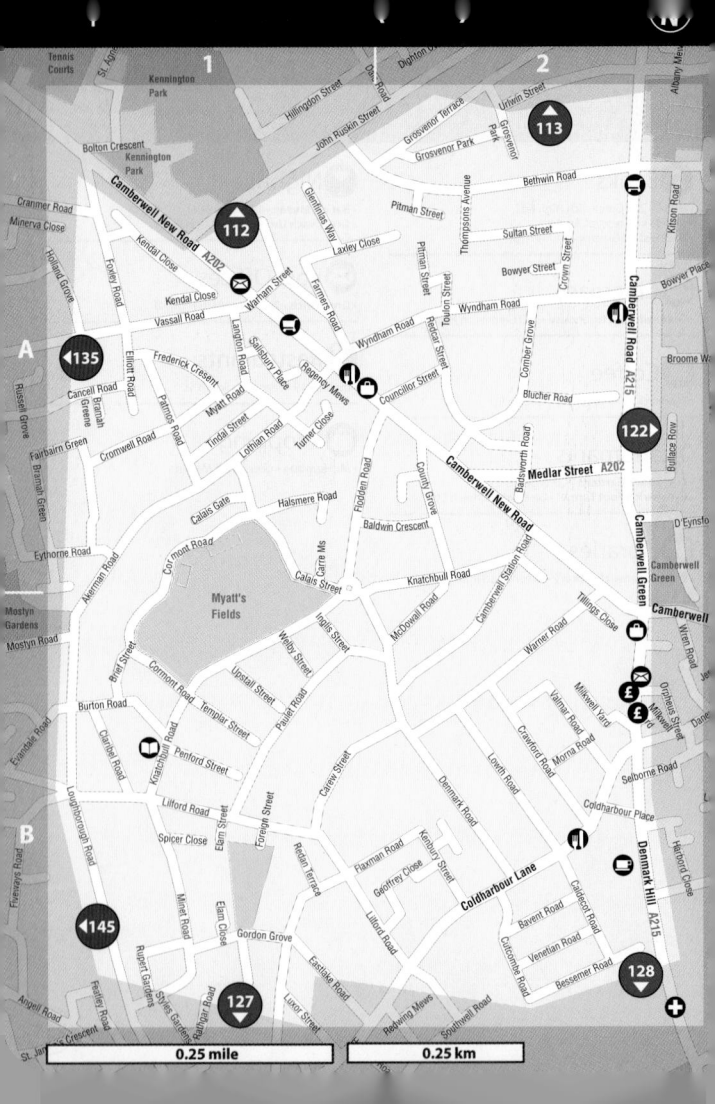
1
2
A
B
Tennis Courts
Kennington Park
Bolton Crescent
Kennington Park
Hillingtion Street
John Ruskin Street
Grosvenor Terrace
Grosvenor Park
Grosvenor Park
Urlwin Street
Albany Mews
Bethwin Road
Cranmer Road
Minerva Close
Camberwell New Road A202
Glenfinlas Way
Laxley Close
Pitman Street
Thompsons Avenue
Sultan Street
Kitson Road
Holland Grove
Kendal Close
Forley Road
Kendal Close
Warham Street
Farmers Road
Pitman Street
Bowyer Street
Crown Street
Bowyer Place
Vassall Road
Wyndham Road
Wyndham Road
Camberwell Road A215
Camberwell Road A215
Camberwell Grove
Broome Way
Salisbury Place
Langton Road
Regency Mews
Councillor Street
Rector Street
Blucher Road
Frederick Crescent
Elliott Road
Cancell Road
Bramah Green
Russell Grove
Fairbairn Green
Bramah Green
Cromwell Road
Patmore Road
Myatt Road
Tindal Street
Lothian Road
Turner Close
Camberwell New Road
Medlar Street A202
Bedwardworth Road
Bullace Row
Calais Gate
Halsmere Road
Rodden Road
Comity Grove
Baldwin Crescent
D'Eynsford
Eythorne Road
Cormont Road
Calais Street
Knatchbull Road
Camberwell Station Road
Camberwell Green
Camberwell Green
Camberwell
Mostyn Gardens
Mostyn Road
Myatt's Fields
Ingelis Street
Webb Street
McDowall Road
Tillings Close
Warner Road
Vernon Road
Bird Street
Cormont Road
Upstall Street
Paulet Road
Burton Road
Templar Street
Penford Street
Knatchbull Road
Chatsfield Road
Evandale Road
Valmar Road
Mulvell Yard
Morna Road
Crawford Road
Orphens Street
Selborne Road
Coldharbour Place
Lilford Road
Spicer Close
Elam Street
Foreign Street
Carey Street
Denmark Road
Lowth Road
Loughborough Road
Fiveways Road
Paxman Road
Kenbury Close
Geoffrey Close
Coldharbour Lane
Denmark Hill A215
Harbord Close
Redan Terrace
Lilford Road
Calecott Road
Bavent Road
Venetian Road
Calcombe Road
Bessemer Road
Mimet Road
Elam Close
Gordon Grove
Rupert Gardens
Styles Gardens
Rathbar Road
Eastlake Road
Luxor Street
Redwing Mews
Southwell Road
Angell Road
Feltham Road
Crescent
0.25 mile
0.25 km
112
113
122
127
128
135
145

This slowly reviving segment of Camberwell brings together a minority of polite arty types in the crumbling yet quaint town houses of Camberwell New Road with take-no-prisoners urbanites as seen in the chaos of Denmark Hill and its pointless Butterfly Shopping Centre (why?). The neighbourhood good stuff includes music bargains (Rat Records), killer Indian (New Dewaniam), and the new and unpronounceable Central Asian eatery at the Pasha Hotel: Kazakh Kyrgyz Restaurant.

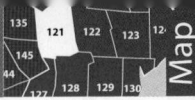

Banks

- **HSBC** • 23 Denmark Hill
- **NatWest** • 70 Denmark Hill

Coffee

- **Kings Cafe** • 120 Denmark Hill

Emergency Rooms

- **King's College Hospital** • Denmark Hill

Libraries

- **Minet Library** • 52 Knatchbull Rd

Post Offices

- **Camberwell Green** • 25 Denmark Hill
- **Camberwell New Road** • 163 Camberwell New Rd

Restaurants

- **Kazakh Kyrgyz Restaurant** • 158 Camberwell Rd
- **New Dewaniam** • 225 Camberwell New Rd
- **Su-Thai** • 16 Coldharbour Ln

Shopping

- **Butterfly Walk Shopping Centre** • Denmark Hill
- **Rat Records** • 348 New Camberwell Rd

Supermarkets

- **Co-Op** • 177 Camberwell New Rd
- **Iceland** • 120 Camberwell Rd

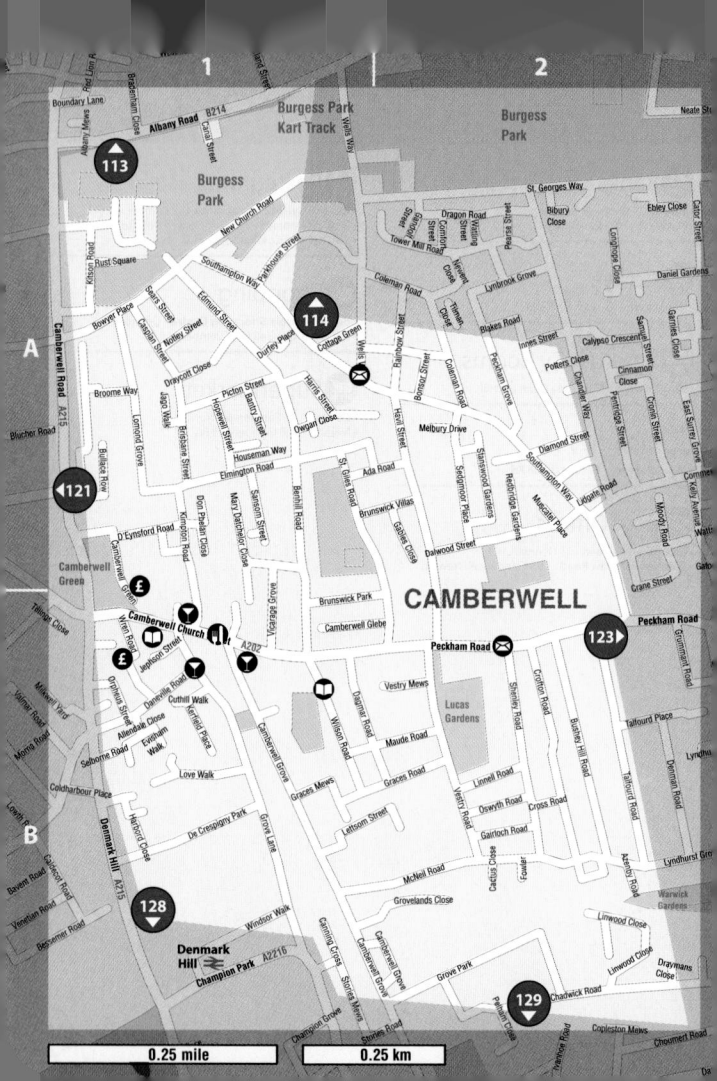
1
2
A
B
Boundary Lane
Albany Road B214
Burgess Park Kart Track
Burgess Park
Burgess Park
Neate Sta
113
114
121
123
128
129
Camberwell Road A215
Camberwell Green
Camberwell Church St A202
Peckham Road
CAMBERWELL
Lucas Gardens
Denmark Hill A215
Denmark Hill
Champion Park A2216
St Georges Way
Bibury Close
Ebley Close
Longhorn Close
Daniel Gardens
Lymbrook Grove
Coleman Road
Blakes Road
Innes Street
Calypso Crescent
Potters Close
Cinnamon Close
Melbury Drive
Diamond Street
Southampton Way
Sedgmoor Place
Stanwood Gardens
Dalwood Street
Brunswick Villas
Brunswick Park
Camberwell Glebe
Vestry Mews
Maude Road
Wilson Road
Graces Mews
Graces Road
Linnell Road
Oswyth Road
Cross Road
Gairloch Road
Lettsom Street
McNeil Road
Grovelands Close
Limwood Close
Grove Park
Chadwick Road
Copleston Mews
Choumert Road
Talfourd Place
Denmark Road
Lyndhurst Grove
Warwick Gardens
Draymans Close
Love Walk
Coldharbour Place
Dr Cresswell Park
Windsor Walk
Champion Grove
Grove Lane
Camberwell Grove
Ada Road
Harris Street
Owsen Close
Houseman Way
Elmington Road
Sr Giles Road
Sampson Street
Mary Datchelor Close
Vicarage Grove
Kimpton Road
Don Phelan Close
D'Eynsford Road
Camberwell Grove
Wren Road
Danemill Road
Cuthill Walk
Orphan Street
Allendale Close
Selborne Road
Herbert Close
Bowyer Place
Broome Way
Picton Street
Hopewell Street
Brisbane Street
Jago Walk
Lomond Grove
Bullace Row
Blucher Road
Tillson Close
Morris Road
Bevern Road
Venetian Road
Bessemer Road
Kibson Road
Rust Square
Southampton Way
Peckham Street
New Church Road
Edmund Street
Sears Street
Calypso Street
Motley Street
Drayton Close
Dudley Place
Cottage Green
Rainbow Street
Bonsolo Street
Coleman Road
Harris Street
Peckham Grove
Commercial Way
Penrose Street
Garnies Close
East Surrey Grove
Kelly Avenue
Moody Road
Grove Park
Grove Lane
Camberwell Grove
Champion Grove
Choumert Road
Grove Lane
Camberwell Grove
Grove Park
Chadwick Road
Limwood Close
Lyndhurst Grove
Talfourd Road
Bushey Hill Road
Crofton Road
Shenley Road
Grommet Road
Denman Road
Peckham Road
Tower Mill Road
Dragon Road
Commercial Way
Penrose Street
Tower Close
Southampton Way
Peckham Street
Bibury Close
Longhorn Close
Calypso Crescent
Cromer Street
Penrose Street
Commercial Way
Potters Close
Innes Street
Blakes Road
Lymbrook Grove
Coleman Road
Melbury Drive
Diamond Street
Southampton Way
Redcross Gardens
Sedgmoor Place
Stanwood Gardens
Dalwood Street
Brunswick Villas
Brunswick Park
Camberwell Glebe
Vestry Mews
Maude Road
Wilson Road
Graces Mews
Graces Road
Linnell Road
Oswyth Road
Cross Road
Gairloch Road
Lettsom Street
McNeil Road
Grovelands Close
Limwood Close
Grove Park
Chadwick Road
Copleston Mews
Choumert Road
Talfourd Place
Denmark Road
Lyndhurst Grove
Warwick Gardens
Draymans Close
Love Walk
Coldharbour Place
Dr Cresswell Park
Windsor Walk
Champion Grove
Grove Lane
Camberwell Grove
Ada Road
Harris Street
Owsen Close
Houseman Way
Elmington Road
Sr Giles Road
Sampson Street
Mary Datchelor Close
Vicarage Grove
Kimpton Road
Don Phelan Close
D'Eynsford Road
Camberwell Grove
Wren Road
Danemill Road
Cuthill Walk
Orphan Street
Allendale Close
Eastman Walk
Selborne Road
Herbert Close
Bowyer Place
Broome Way
Picton Street
Barrett Street
Hopewell Street
Brisbane Street
Jago Walk
Lomond Grove
Bullace Row
Blucher Road
Tillson Close
Morris Road
Bevern Road
Venetian Road
Bessemer Road
Kibson Road
Rust Square
Southampton Way
Peckham Street
New Church Road
Edmund Street
Sears Street
Calypso Street
Motley Street
Drayton Close
Dudley Place
Cottage Green
Rainbow Street
Bonsolo Street
Coleman Road
Harris Street
Peckham Grove
Commercial Way
Penrose Street
Cromer Street
Garnies Close
East Surrey Grove
Kelly Avenue
Moody Road
Grove Park
Grove Lane
Camberwell Grove
Champion Grove
Choumert Road
Grove Lane
Camberwell Grove
Grove Park
Chadwick Road
Limwood Close
Lyndhurst Grove
Talfourd Road
Bushey Hill Road
Crofton Road
Shenley Road
Grommet Road
Denman Road
Peckham Road
Tower Mill Road
Dragon Road
Penrose Street
Tower Close
Southampton Way
Peckham Street
Bibury Close
Longhorn Close
Calypso Crescent

This lucky dip of a neighbourhood is home to a few gangs, art students, and the occasional Time Out editor. Anyone who wrinkles their nose at Camberwell has never experienced the bohemian opulence of Camberwell Grove (which does fade rather quickly into the familiar dodginess of Camberwell Church Street). For posh, sip cocktails at the Dark Horse, for nosh, try Carravaggio.

Banks

- **Barclays** • 1 Butterfly Walk
- **Lloyds** • 25 Camberwell Green

Libraries

- **Camberwell Library** • 17 Camberwell Church St
- **Education Library Service** • Wilson Rd

Nightlife

- **The Castle** • 65 Camberwell Church St
- **Dark Horse** • 16 Grove Lane
- **Funky Munky** • 25 Camberwell Church St

Post Offices

- **Peckham Road** • 46 Peckham Rd
- **Southampton Way** • 156 Southampton Way

Restaurants

- **Caravaggio** • 47 Camberwell Church St

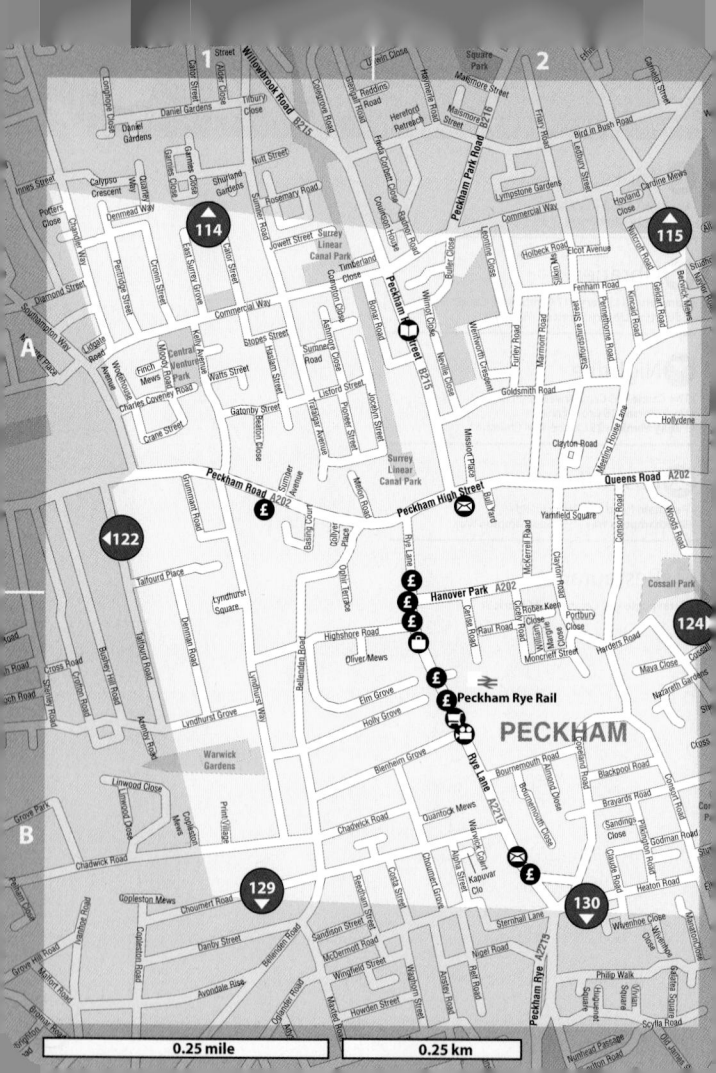
1
2
A
B
Willowbrook Road B215
Peckham Park Road
Peckham Road A202
Peckham High Street
Queens Road A202
Hanover Park A202
Rye Lane A2215
Peckham Rye A2215
Peckham Rye Rail
PECKHAM
Daniel Gardens
Calypso Crescent
Commercial Way
Surrey Linear Canal Park
Central Venture Park
Camberwell Road
Walworth Road
Lordship Lane
Dulwich Road
Choumert Road
Bellenden Road
Warwick Gardens
Cossall Park
Peckham Rye Station
Kapuvar Clo
114
115
122
124
129
130
0.25 mile
0.25 km

Peckham: so many gang wars, so little time. Though it tries hard with such overly-enthusiastic delights as the cheery Peckham Library set on spindly post-modern stilts or those palm trees planted down Queen's Road to 'reflect the multi-cultural diversity of Peckham'. Not that anyone notices. Rye Lane's the real hub, with its disconcertingly affordable Peckham Multiplex cinema and classic Primark.

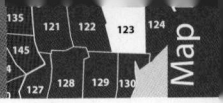

Banks

- **Abbey** • 97 Rye Ln
- **Barclays** • 28 Rye Ln
- **Barclays** • 223 Rye Ln
- **Halifax** • 24 Rye Ln
- **HSBC** • 47 Rye Ln
- **Lloyds** • 76 Rye Ln
- **NatWest** • 65 Peckham High St

Libraries

- **Peckham Library** • 122 Peckham Hill St

Movie Theaters

- **Peckham Multiplex** • 95 Rye Ln

Post Offices

- **Peckham** • 121 Peckham High St
- **Rye Lane** • 199 Rye Ln

Shopping

- **Primark** • 51 Rye Lane

Supermarkets

- **Iceland** • 74 Rye Lane

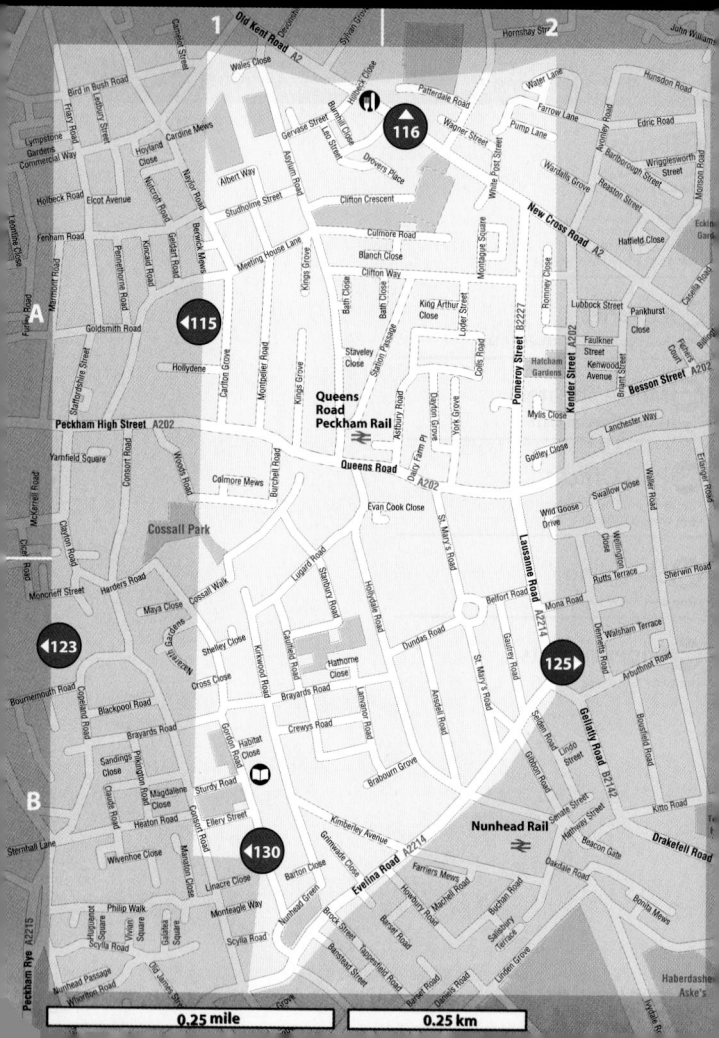
N
1
2
A
B
Old Kent Road A2
Hornshay Street
John Williams
Wales Close
Bird in Bush Road
Friary Road
Camelot Street
Sylvan Grove
Patteredale Road
Water Lane
Humsdon Road
Farrow Lane
Edric Road
Pump Lane
Wagner Street
Lea Street
Gerrase Street
Ashburn Road
Drovers Place
White Post Street
Avonley Road
Barlborough Street
Wriggleswort Street
Wordsells Grove
Reaston Street
Monson Road
Limestone Gardens Commercial Way
Hoyland Close
Cardine Mews
Holbeck Road
Elcot Avenue
Nunscroft Road
Naylor Road
Albert Way
Studholme Street
Clifton Crescent
New Cross Road A2
Hatfield Close
Lanchester Close
Fenham Road
Kincaid Road
Godart Road
Berkeley Mews
Meeting House Lane
Kings Grove
Culmore Road
Blanch Close
Clifton Way
Montague Square
Romney Close
Clarella Road
Mimmont Road
Goldsmith Road
Bath Close
King Arthur Close
Lodge Street
Lubbock Street
Pankhurst Close
Staveley Close
Sallust Passage
Collis Road
Pomeroy Street B2227
Hatchard Gardens
Faulkner Street
Kenwood Avenue
Kender Street A202
Besson Street A202
Hollydene
Carlton Grove
Montpelier Road
Queens Road Peckham Rail
Ashburn Road
Bryan Street
Mylis Close
Lanchester Way
Gadley Close
Peckham High Street A202
Yarnfield Square
Consort Road
Vivian Road
Culmore Mews
Burchell Road
Queens Road A202
Evan Cook Close
Wild Goose Drive
Swallow Close
Wilder Road
Eastanger Road
Cossall Park
Monckton Street
Harders Road
Maya Close
Cossall Walk
Lugard Road
Stanton Road
Holmdale Road
St. Mary's Road
Lausanne Road A2214
Belfort Road
Mona Road
Rutts Terrace
Sherwin Road
Wellington Close
Dermott Road
Walsham Terrace
Aroughton Road
Shelley Close
Kirkwood Road
Cranfield Road
Hathorne Close
Dundas Road
Gaurey Road
Bournemouth Road
Blackpool Road
Cross Close
Bravards Road
Lamprior Road
Aisdell Road
Selden Road
Geldart Road
Linda Street
Bonfield Road
Bravards Road
Crewys Road
Habitat Close
Gordon Road
Sandringham Close
Pennington Road
Magdalene Close
Sturdy Road
Brabourn Grove
Kitto Road
Heaton Road
Ellery Street
Sternhall Lane
Wivenhoe Close
Marston Close
Kimberley Avenue
Grimsdyke Close
Barton Close
Evelina Road A2214
Farriers Mews
Nunhead Rail
Hathaway Street
Beacon Gate
Drakefell Road
Linacre Close
Nunhead Green
Kinnaird Road
Marchel Road
Bichan Road
Bonits Mews
Philip Walk
Monteagle Way
Brock Street
Barnet Road
Salisbury Terrace
Scylla Road
Gaskin Square
Vivian Square
Scylla Road
Burnstead Street
Tapestry Road
Linden Grove
Peckham Rye A2215
Nunhead Passage
Wheatton Road
Old James Street
Haberdasher Aske's
Cross Road
0.25 mile
0.25 km
116
115
123
125
130

Peckham East (Queen's Road)

Never one to be cheery, the eastern side of Peckham surrounding the Queen's Road is a rather bleak landscape of monolithic tower blocks and sprawling council estates. But there is something refreshingly gritty and nonplussed about the area and its dedicated locals. For instance, the 805 Bar Restaurant has excellent African food and is a culinary oasis in an urban desert.

Libraries

- **Nunhead Library** • Gordon Rd

Restaurants

- **805 Bar Restaurant** • 805 Old Kent Rd

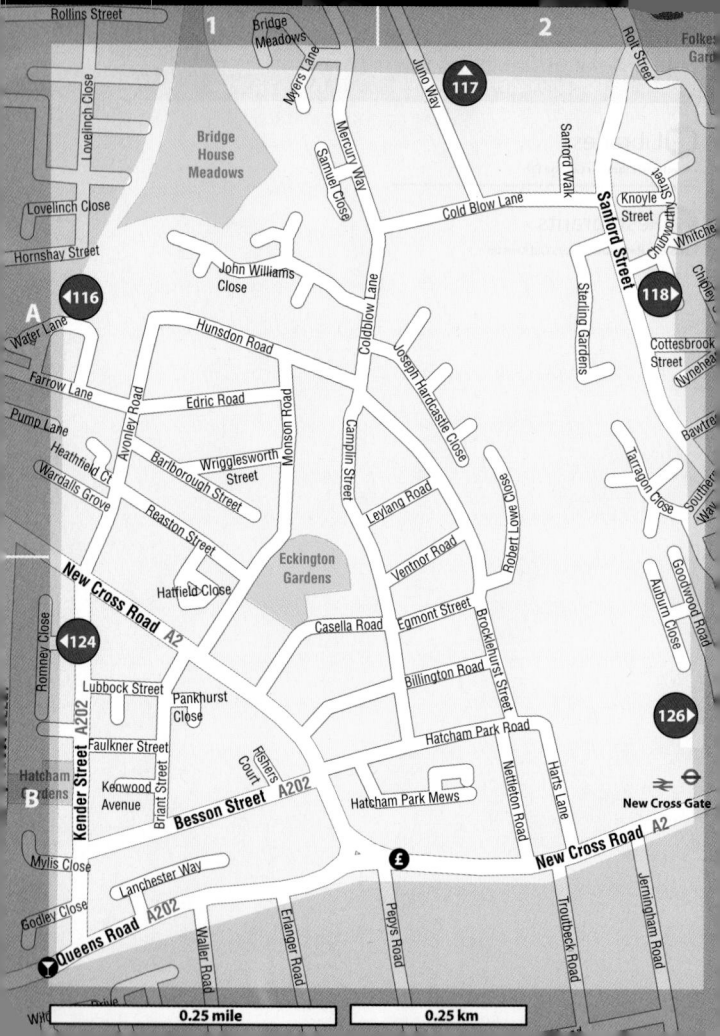
1
2
A
B
Rollins Street
Bridge Meadows
Myers Lane
Juno Way
Rolt Street
Folkes Gard
117
Lovelinch Close
Bridge House Meadows
Mercury Way
Samuel Close
Sanford Walk
Knoyle Street
Cold Blow Lane
Sanford Street
Chichworth Street
Whitche
Hornshay Street
John Williams Close
116
118
Water Lane
Coldblow Lane
Sterling Gardens
Cottesbrook Street
Hunsdon Road
Farrow Lane
Edric Road
Joseph Hardcastle Close
Pump Lane
Avonley Road
Monson Road
Campion Street
Heathfield Cl
Barborough Street
Wrigglesworth Street
Wardalls Grove
Reaston Street
Leylang Road
Robert Lowe Close
Tarragon Close
Eckington Gardens
Ventnor Road
New Cross Road A2
Hatfield Close
Goodwood Road
Auburn Close
124
Romney Close
Casella Road
Egmont Street
Brockhurst Street
Lubbock Street
Billington Road
Pankhurst Close
126
Hatcham Park Road
Faulkner Street
Fishers Court
Kender Street A202
Briant Street
Kenwood Avenue
Besson Street A202
Hatcham Park Mews
Nettleton Road
Harts Lane
New Cross Gate
New Cross Road A2
Mylis Close
Lanchester Way
Jermingham Road
Godley Close
Queens Road A202
Waller Road
Erlanger Road
Pepys Road
Troubeck Road
0.25 mile
0.25 km

There used to be an urban myth that there are no cash machines in New Cross because of the muggings. Since then it's gone all art-student-cool but this bit is still quite rugged. Its biggest claim to fame is the fantastic Montague Arms, which looks like it was furnished by a drunken sailor-turned-taxidermist waking up and bellowing "bring me…stuff!"

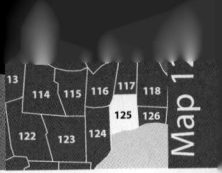

Banks

• **Barclays** • 197 New Cross Rd

Nightlife

• **The Montague Arms** • 289 Queen's Rd

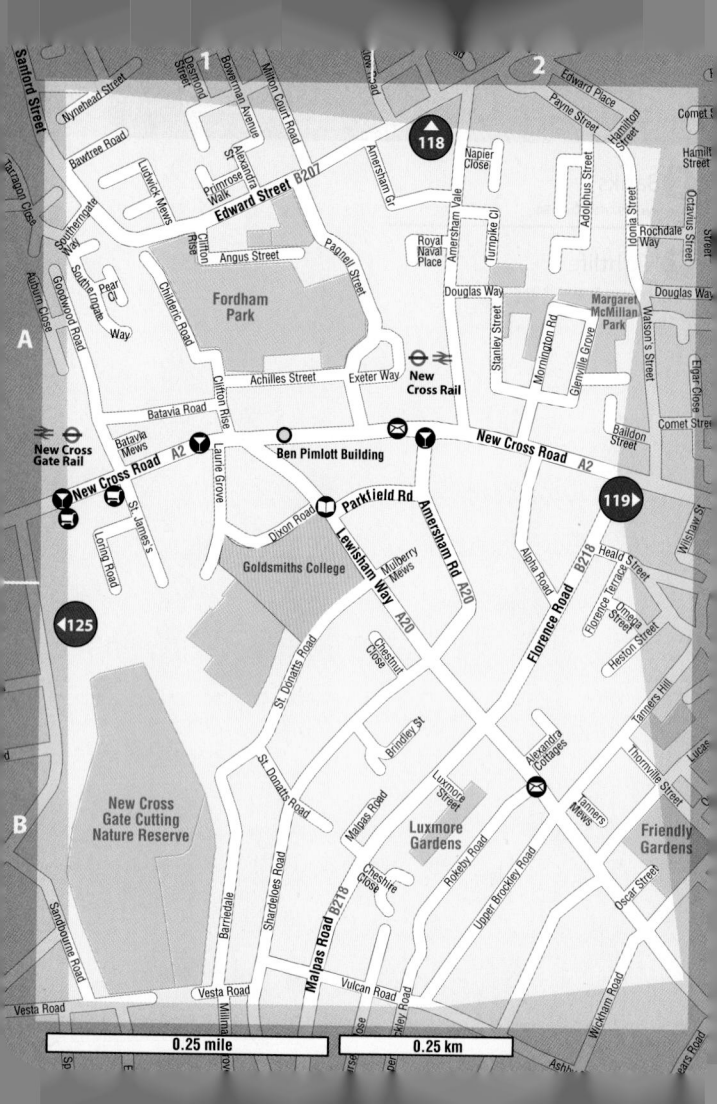
Sanford Street
Nymehead Street
Bawtree Road
Tarapon Close
Southernhay Way
Saxone Crate
Pear Tree Way
Auburn Close
Goodwood Road
Ludlow Mews
Edward Street B207
Primrose Walk
Alexandra St
Bowerman Avenue
Milton Court Road
Denmond Street
Clifton Rise
Angus Street
Childeric Road
Fordham Park
Paignell Street
Amersham Gr
Amersham Vale
Napier Close
Royal Naval Place
Turnpike Cl
Adolphus Street
Iona Street
Rochdale Way
Octavius Street
Hamilton Street
Hamilton Street
Payne Street
Edward Place
Comet Street
Douglas Way
Douglas Way
Margaret McMillan Park
Watson's Street
Elgar Close
Comet Street
Bailldon Street
Stanley Street
Mornington Rd
Glenville Grove
Achilles Street
Exeter Way
New Cross Rail
Batavia Road
Batavia Mews
New Cross Gate Rail
New Cross Road A2
Laurie Grove
Clifton Rise
Ben Pimlott Building
New Cross Road A2
Parkfield Rd
Amersham Rd A20
Lewisham Way A20
Dixon Road
St James's
Loring Road
Goldsmiths College
Mulberry Mews
Alpha Road
Florence Road B218
Florence Terrace
Omega Street
Heald Street
Heston Street
Willisham St
Tanners Hill
Thornville Street
Lucas
Chestnut Close
St Donatts Road
Brindley St
Alexandra Cottages
Luxmore Street
Tanners Mews
Luxmore Gardens
Friendly Gardens
Oscar Street
New Cross Gate Cutting Nature Reserve
St Donatts Road
Malpas Road
Rokeby Road
Upper Brockley Road
Cheshire Close
Shardeloes Road
Barriedale
Malpas Road B218
Vulcan Road
Vesta Road
Vesta Road
Sandbourne Road
Wickham Road
Ashby Road
118
119
125
A
B
1
2
0.25 mile
0.25 km

Around here, the art student is king. In the shadow of the rather ugly Goldsmiths College Ben Pimlott Building, trendy young students enthralled to debauchery live out their art-school fantasies. Join them in the Hobgoblin for booze or try the decrepit New Cross Inn for your mate's band. Since its establishment in 2007 Amersham Arms is well on its way to becoming one of London's best music venues – leading the way to this neighbourhood's well-deserved revival.

Landmarks

- **Ben Pimlott Building** • University of London, New Cross

Libraries

- **Goldsmiths Library** • Lewisham Wy

Nightlife

- **Amersham Arms** • 388 New Cross Rd
- **Hobgoblin** • 272 New Cross Rd
- **New Cross Inn** • 323 New Cross Rd

Post Offices

- **Lewisham Way** • 150 Lewisham Way
- **New Cross Road** • 405 New Cross Rd

Supermarkets

- **Iceland** • 277 New Cross Rd
- **Sainsbury's** • 263 New Cross Rd

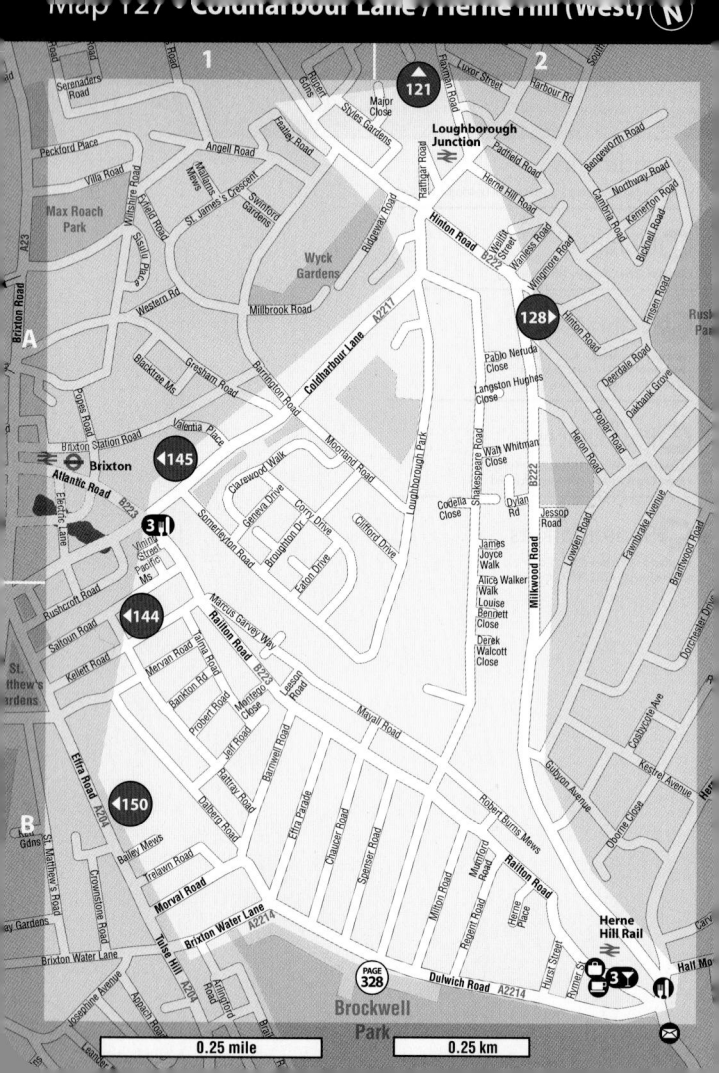
N
1
2
A
B
121
128
145
144
150
Loughborough Junction
Herne Hill Rail
Brixton
Brixton Station Road
Atlantic Road
Brockwell Park
Max Roach Park
Wyck Gardens
Coldharbour Lane
Brixton Road
Rushcroft Road
Saltoun Road
Effra Road
Morval Road
Brixton Water Lane
Tulse Hill
Dulwich Road
Herne Hill
Milkwood Road
Railton Road
Mayall Road
Loughborough Park
Hinton Road
Rathnan Road
Harbour Rd
Lucerne Street
Farmer Road
Angell Road
Peckford Place
Villa Road
Wilmore Road
Mailing Mews
St James's Crescent
Swinford Gardens
Millbrook Road
Western Rd
Brixton Station Road
Valentia Place
Barrington Road
Mayall Road
Clifford Drive
Corri Drive
Brighton Dr
Eaton Drive
Marcus Garvey Way
Mervan Road
Talma Road
Bankton Rd
Probert Road
Barnwell Road
Lessar Road
Effra Parade
Chaucer Road
Spenser Road
Milton Road
Regent Road
Herne Place
Robert Burns Mews
Gladson Avenue
Crosbie Ave
Keslet Avenue
Divorne Close
Lowden Road
Favershale Avenue
Brankwood Road
Dorchester Drive
Poplar Road
Heron Road
Oakbank Grove
Oberdale Road
Trinsen Road
Pablo Neruda Close
Langston Hughes Close
Walt Whitman Close
Codella Close
Dylan Rd
Jessop Road
James Joyce Walk
Alice Walker Walk
Louise Bennett Close
Derek Walcott Close
Cavewood Walk
Genera Drive
Bailey Mews
Trelawn Road
Croxstone Road
Josephine Avenue
Ruskin Park
Rushcroft Road
Hurst Street
Rumes St
Halt Mo
Herne Hill Road
Dulwich Road A2214
Brixton Water Lane A2214
Tulse Hill A214
Effra Road A214
Brixton Road A23
Coldharbour Lane A2217
Hinton Road B2352
Milkwood Road B222
Railton Road B223
Atlantic Road B223
Loughborough Park
Rathnan Road
Farmer Road
Lucerne Street
Harbour Rd

Coldharbour Lane / Herne Hill (West)

There don't seem to be as many shootings on Coldharbour Lane as there used to be. Maybe the crack dealers are just quietly selling the stuff, as somebody on The Wire once sensibly advised. Or maybe they've all left the buzzing bars of Brixton, like the infamous Dogstar, and their favourite KFC haunt for the laid back Herne Hill with its famous Brockwell Lido and quaint Blackbird Bakery.

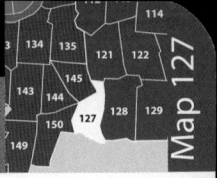

Nightlife

- **The Commercial** • 210 Railton Rd
- **Escape Bar and Art** • 214 Railton Rd
- **The Florence** • 133 Dulwich Rd

Post Offices

- **Herne Hill** • 31 Norwood Rd

Restaurants

- **Café Prov** • 2 Half Moon Ln
- **Ichiban Sushi** • 58 Atlantic Rd
- **The Lounge** • 56 Atlantic Rd
- **New Fujiyama** • 5 Vining St

Shopping

- **Blackbird Bakery** • 208 Railton Rd

Coffee

- **Pullens** • 293 Railton Rd

Map 128 • Denmark Hill / Herne Hill (East)

Denmark Hill / Herne Hill (East)

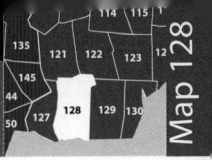

There's something quaintly grounded about the leafy Victorian suburb of Herne Hill where funky neo-hippies settle into dreadlocked nuclear families. Denmark Hill sits at its top, with its imposing Salvation Army training grounds, following on to Ruskin Park for ornamental ponds and Edwardian ruins. Half Moon Lane plays main drag—get lost in a book at Tales on Moon Lane and lost in a bowl of noodles at Lombok.

Libraries

- **Carnegie Library** • 188 Herne Hill Rd

Post Offices

- **Crossthwaite Avenue** • 6 Crossthwaite Ave

Restaurants

- **Lombok** • 17 Half Moon Ln
- **Number 22** • 22 Half Moon Ln
- **Olley's Fish and Chips** • 65 Norwood Rd

Supermarkets

- **Sainsbury's** • 132 Herne Hill

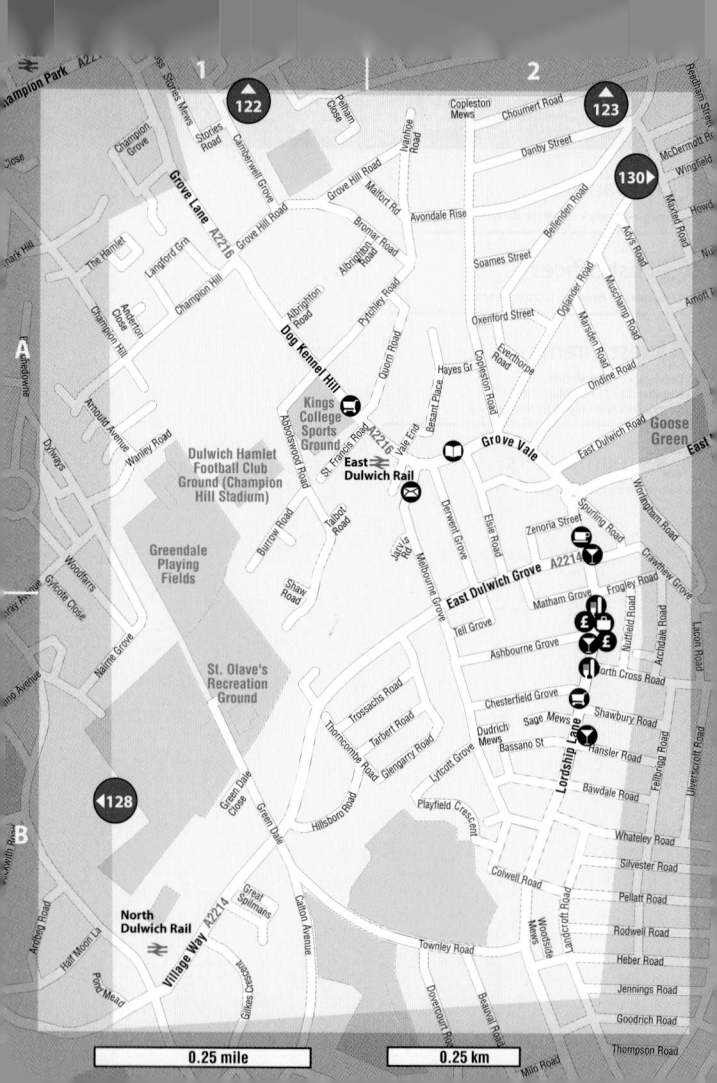
1
2
A
B
122
123
130
128
Champion Park
Stories Mews
Stories Road
Pelham Close
Copleston Mews
Choumert Road
Danby Street
Champion Grove
Grove Lane A2216
Camberwell Grove
Grove Hill Road
Madfort Rd
Ivanhoe Road
Avondale Rise
Bromar Road
Albrighton Road
Bellenden Road
Mantel Road
McDermott Pl
Wingfield
The Hamlet
Langford Grn
Champion Hill
Soames Street
Adys Road
Muscharne Road
Oglander Road
Oxenford Street
Pytchley Road
Dog Kennel Hill
Quorn Road
Hayes Gr
Copleston Road
Earthorpe Road
Marsden Road
Ondine Road
Anderton Close
Armould Avenue
Wanley Road
Kings College Sports Ground
Abbotswood Road
St Francis Road
A2216
Vale End
Belsant Place
Grove Vale
East Dulwich Road
Goose Green
East Dulwich Rail
Dulwich Hamlet Football Club Ground (Champion Hill Stadium)
Burrow Road
Talbot Road
Derwent Grove
Elsie Road
Zenoria Street
Sturling Road
Wentworth Road
Crawthew Grove
Greendale Playing Fields
Shaw Road
Melbourne Grove
East Dulwich Grove A2214
Matham Grove
Frogley Road
Nutfield Road
Archdale Road
Lason Road
Woodfarns
Gyrcote Close
Tell Grove
Ashbourne Grove
Nairne Grove
St. Olave's Recreation Ground
North Cross Road
Chesterfield Grove
Trossachs Road
Tarbert Road
Thorncombe Road
Glengarry Road
Sage Mews
Shawbury Road
Dudrich Mews
Bassano St
Lyncott Grove
Lordship Lane
Hansler Road
Fellbridge Road
Ulverscroft Road
Bawdale Road
Green Dale Close
Green Dale
Hillsboro Road
Playfield Crescent
Whateley Road
Silvester Road
Colwell Road
Pellatt Road
Great Spilmans
Calton Avenue
Rodwell Road
North Dulwich Rail
Village Way A2214
Half Moon La
Ferndale Road
Gilkes Crescent
Townley Road
Dovercourt Road
Beauval Road
Landcroft Road
Westgate Mews
Heber Road
Jennings Road
Goodrich Road
Thompson Road
Milo Road
0.25 mile
0.25 km

East Dulwich is where your ex-flatmate finally settled down and now won't shut up about taramasalata, babies, and how he's only fifteen minutes from London Bridge by train over perfect cocktails at Black Cherry. Dodge baguettes, pushchairs, and delis along Lordship Lane, just don't get sucked in. Try the Sea Cow for fish & chips, a pint at the Palmerston, and a night out at Inside 72.

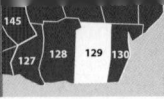

Banks

- **Barclays** • 68 Lordship Ln
- **HSBC** • 66 Lordship Ln

Coffee

- **Caffe Nero** • 8 Lordship Ln

Libraries

- **Grove Vale library** • 25 Grove Vale

Nightlife

- **Black Cherry** • 21 Lordship Ln
- **Inside 72** • 72 Lordship Ln
- **liquorish** • 123 Lordship Ln

Post Offices

- **Melbourne Grove** • 7 Melbourne Grove

Restaurants

- **The Palmerston** • 91 Lordship Ln
- **Sea Cow** • 37 Lordship Ln

Shopping

- **The Cheeseblock** • 69 Lordship Ln

Supermarkets

- **Iceland** • 84 Lordship Ln
- **Sainsbury's** • 80 Dog Kennel Hill

Map 130 • Peckham

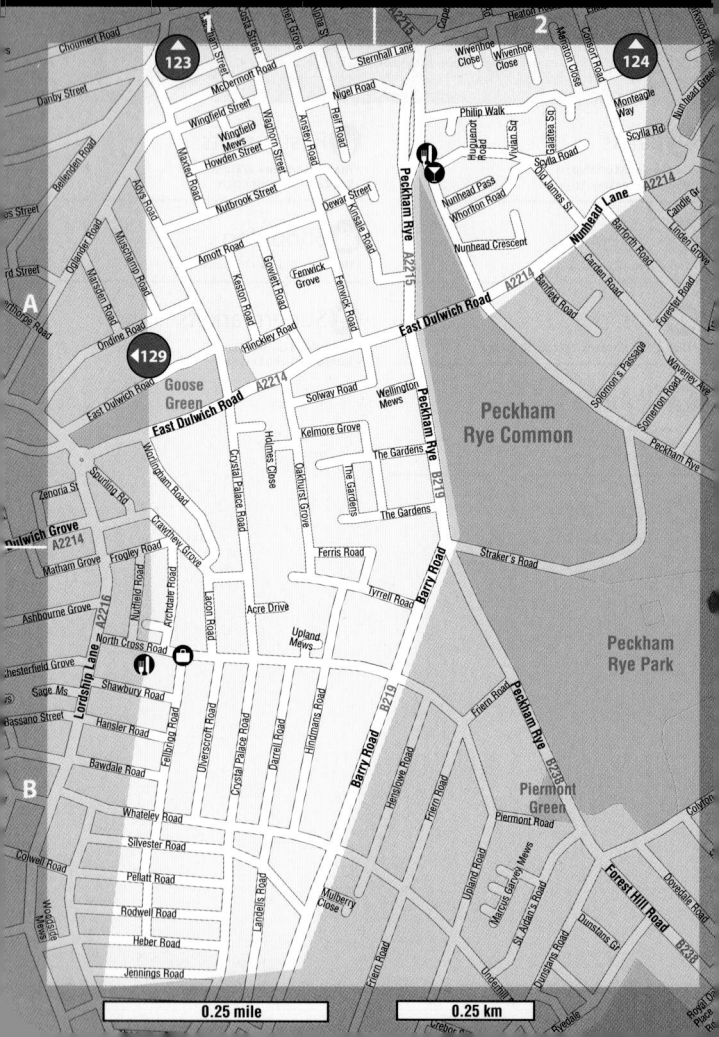

Peckham Rye

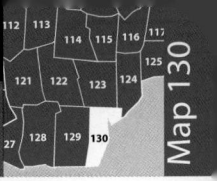

A noticeboard on Peckham Rye Common alleges that ancient British Queen Boudicca was finally defeated by the Romans here. Anyone suggesting that the very middle class streets around North Cross Road—with its market, twee sweets at Hope and Greenwood, and lazy Sunday lunches at The Rye—have anything to do with Peckham as we know it might get the same treatment.

Nightlife

- **The Rye** • 31 Peckham Rye

Restaurants

- **Thai Corner Cafe** • 44 Northcross Rd
- **The Rye** • 31 Peckham Rye

Shopping

- **Hope And Greenwood** • 20 North Cross Rd

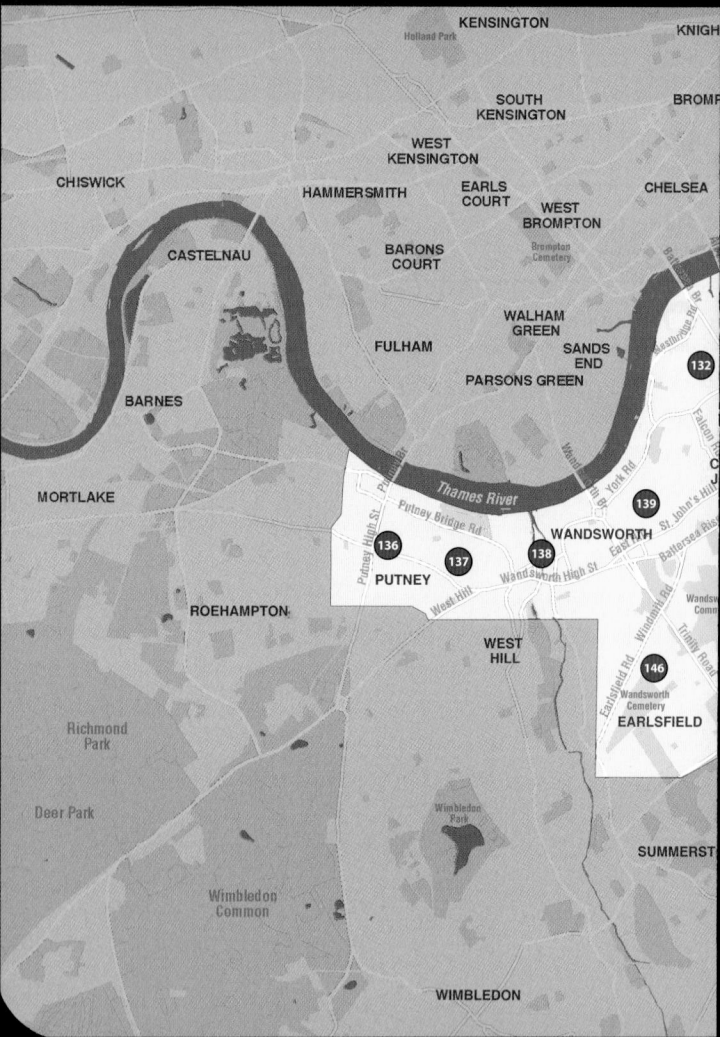
KENSINGTON
Holland Park
KNIGH
SOUTH KENSINGTON
BROMP
WEST KENSINGTON
CHISWICK
HAMMERSMITH
EARLS COURT
CHELSEA
WEST BROMPTON
Brompton Cemetery
CASTELNAU
BARONS COURT
WALHAM GREEN
FULHAM
SANDS END
PARSONS GREEN
132
BARNES
Thames River
York Rd
139
MORTLAKE
Putney Bridge Rd
WANDSWORTH
136
138
137
PUTNEY
Putney High St
Wandsworth High St
West Hill
ROEHAMPTON
WEST HILL
146
Wandsworth Cemetery
EARLSFIELD
Richmond Park
Deer Park
Wimbledon Park
SUMMERST
Wimbledon Common
WIMBLEDON

WATERLOO
NEWINGTON
BERMONDSEY
BELGRAVIA
ELEPHANT & CASTLE
WESTMINSTER
LAMBETH
131
WALWORTH
PIMLICO
KENNINGTON
Kennington Ln
Party St
VAUXHALL
Burgess Park
Tenthman Rd
Hadleyford Rd
CAMBERWELL
NINE ELMS
134
135
133
SOUTH LAMBETH
South Lambeth Rd
Brixton Rd
Wandsworth Rd
Clapham Rd
Stockwell Rd
STOCKWELL
145
141
142
143
144
CLAPHAM
Cedars Rd
Silverthorne Rd
Queenstown Rd
Lavender Hill
Long Road
Bedford Rd
Acre Ln
BRIXTON
Brixton Hill
Milkwood Rd
EAST DULWICH
Clapham Common
The Avenue
CLAPHAM PARK
150
HERNE HILL
Cavendish Rd
149
Poyanders Rd
King's Ave
Brockwell Park
Nightingale Ln
Balham Hill
Dulwich Park
147
148
BALHAM
DULWICH
Balham High Rd
TULSE HILL
STREATHAM HILL
TOOTING BEC
Tooting Bec Common
WEST NORWOOD
151
Factory Ln
Mitcham Rd
STREATHAM
NORWOOD
152

Map 131 • Vauxhall / Albert Embankment

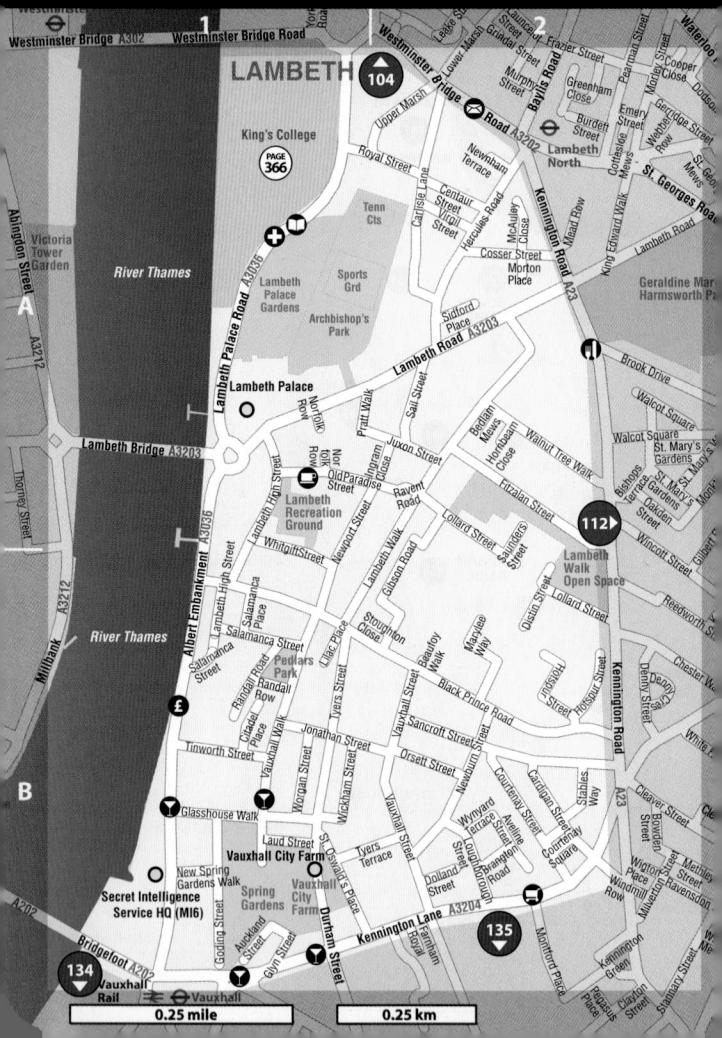

Vauxhall / Albert Embankment

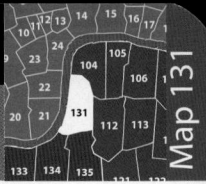

Despite being sliced up by busy roads, major rail tracks and infested with millionaire riverside apartments, there is life to be found here. Around Spring Gardens, where the IRA allegedly fired a rocket at the MI6 building, is a great local (The Lavender) and the ponies of Vauxhall City Farm. Hunt down tasty Thai (Thai Pavillion East) and trashy cabaret (The Royal Vauxhall Tavern).

Banks

- **HSBC** • 20 Albert Embankment

Coffee

- **Costa** • 34 Old Paradise St

Emergency Rooms

- **St Thomas' Hospital** • Lambeth Palace Rd

Landmarks

- **Lambeth Palace Rd** • Lambeth Palace Rd
- **Secret Intelligence Service HQ (MI6)** • Vauxhall Cross
- **Vauxhall City Farm** • 165 Tyers St

Libraries

- **Lambeth Palace Library** • Lambeth Palace Rd

Nightlife

- **Area** • 67 Albert Embankment
- **The Lavender** • 112 Vauxhall Walk
- **The Royal Vauxhall Tavern** • 372 Kennington Ln
- **South Central** • 349 Kennington Ln

Post Offices

- **Westminster Bridge Road** • 125 Westminster Bridge Rd

Restaurants

- **Thai Pavillion East** • 78 Kennington Rd

Supermarkets

- **Tesco** • Kennington Ln

Map 132 • **Battersea (West)**

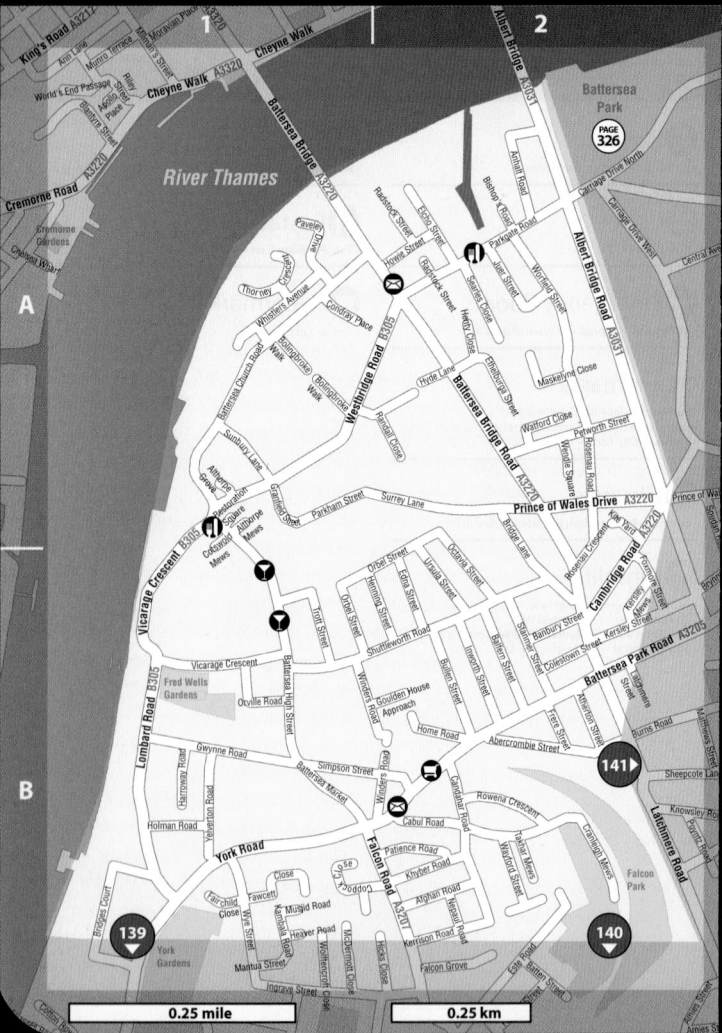
1
2
A
B
River Thames
Battersea Park
PAGE 326
King's Road A3217
Cheyne Walk A3220
Cheyne Walk A3220
Cremorne Road A3220
Cremorne Gardens
Chelsea Wharf
Battersea Bridge A3220
Albert Bridge A3031
Albert Bridge Road A3031
Carriage Drive North
Carriage Drive West
Battersea Bridge Road A3220
Westbridge Road B3015
Prince of Wales Drive A3220
Cambridge Road A3220
Vicarage Crescent B3015
Lombard Road B3015
Battersea Park Road A3205
Falcon Road A3211
York Road
Latchmere Road
Fred Wells Gardens
York Gardens
Falcon Park
Gouden House Approach
Home Road
Abercrombie Street
Simpson Street
Gwynne Road
Holman Road
Cabul Road
Rowena Crescent
Sheepcote Lane
Knowsley Road
Burns Road
Coldstown Street
Kersley Street
Bridge Lane
Prince of Wales Crescent
Kirk Yard
Vicarage Crescent
Battersea High Street
Ottyville Road
Grantham Street
Surrey Lane
Parkham Street
Thorney Crescent
Whistler's Avenue
Thorney Close
Battersea Church Road
Sunbury Lane
Prescottown Square
Coldstream Mews
Aldporne Mews
Trott Street
Orbel Street
Hemming Street
Ursula Street
Linworth Street
Banbury Street
Amerton Street
Burns Road
Matthews Street
Kersley Mews
Grantham Street
Knowsley Road
Latchmere Road
Falcon Road
Khyber Road
Afghan Road
Nepaul Road
Kerrison Road
Falcon Grove
Winner Street
Falcon Grove
Ingrave Street
Mantua Street
Heaver Road
Wolfencroft Close
McDermott Close
Hicks Close
Musjid Road
Kenilworth Road
Wyr Street
Fairchild Close
Tawcett Close
Coppock Close
Yeoman Road
Harmony Road
Bridges Court
Carriage Mews
Riley Square
Ann Lane
World's End Passage
Bishop's Road
Parkgate Road
Henry Close
Elm Park Gardens
Hyde Lane
Maskelyne Close
Watford Close
Petworth Street
Rosenau Road
Rosenau Crescent
Bridge Lane
Orbel Street
Shuttleworth Road
Candahar Road
Cabul Road
Patience Road
Khyber Road
Afghan Road
Nepaul Road
Kerrison Road
Falcon Grove
Ingrave Street
Mantua Street
Heaver Road
Wolfencroft Close
McDermott Close
Hicks Close
Musjid Road
Kenilworth Road
Wyr Street
Fairchild Close
Tawcett Close
Coppock Close
Yeoman Road
Harmony Road
Bridges Court
Carriage Mews

Battersea (West)

With no tubes or trains to attract the Hoi Polloi, Battersea West is a slightly smug area, happily cut off from the rest of London. But its spacious apartments with enviable river views shame the city's shoeboxes, so Londoners are increasingly choosing the commute. Top up your air of sophistication at Le QuecumBar, go al fresco in Battersea Square, or head to The Woodman for a nice pint of Badger.

Nightlife

- **Le QuecumBar** • 42 Battersea High St
- **The Woodman** • 60 Battersea High St

Post Offices

- **Battersea Bridge Road** • 72 Battersea Bridge Rd
- **York Road** • 583 Battersea Park Rd

Restaurants

- **Ransom's Dock** • 35 Parkgate Rd
- **La Tosca** • 31 Battersea Square

Supermarkets

- **Sainsbury's** • 326 Battersea Park Rd

Map 133 • **Battersea (East)**

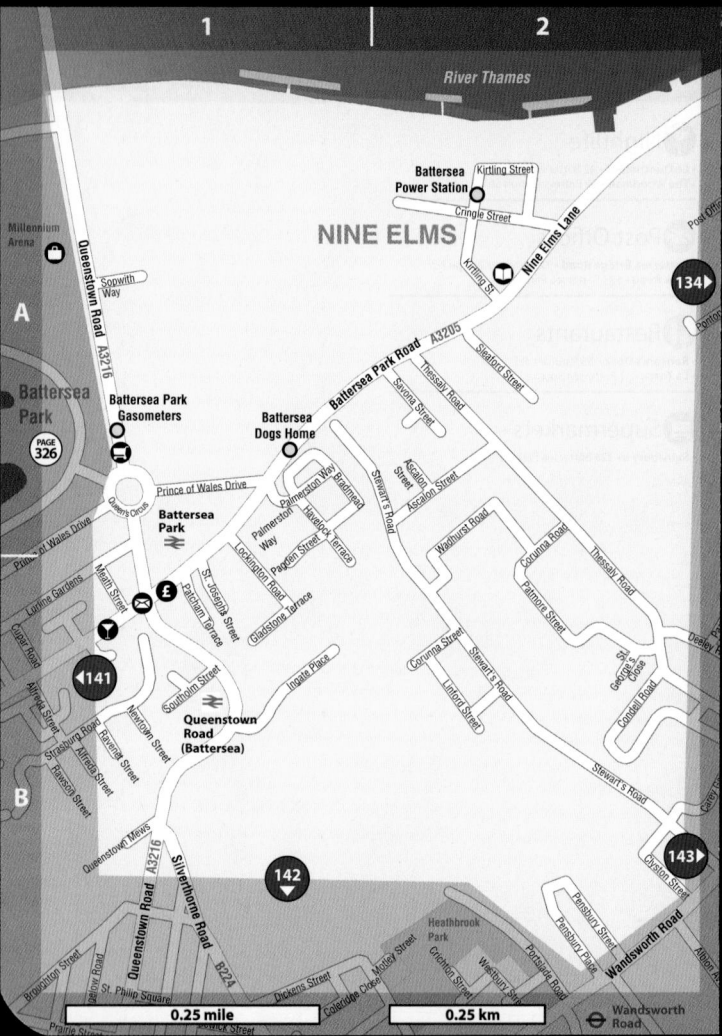

Battersea (East)

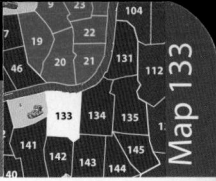

An odd slice of post-industrial London dominated by the derelict Battersea Power Station, there's naff all here until someone decides what to do with the old hulk and its surrounding domain. In the meantime, try registering for a new pooch at the Dogs' Home or cycling around nearby Battersea Park from where you can rue the slow death of the crumbling giant.

Banks

- **Barclays** • 278 Queenstown Rd

Landmarks

- **Battersea Dogs' Home** • 4 Battersea Park Rd
- **Battersea Park Gasometers** • Queenstown Rd
- **Battersea Power Station** • 188 Kirtling St

Libraries

- **Battersea Park Library** • 309 Battersea Park Rd

Nightlife

- **The Chelsea Reach** • 181 Battersea Park Rd

Post Offices

- **Battersea Park Road** • 20 Battersea Park Rd

Shopping

- **London Recumbents** • Battersea Park

Supermarkets

- **Sainsbury's** • 326 Queenstown Rd

Map 134 • South Lambeth

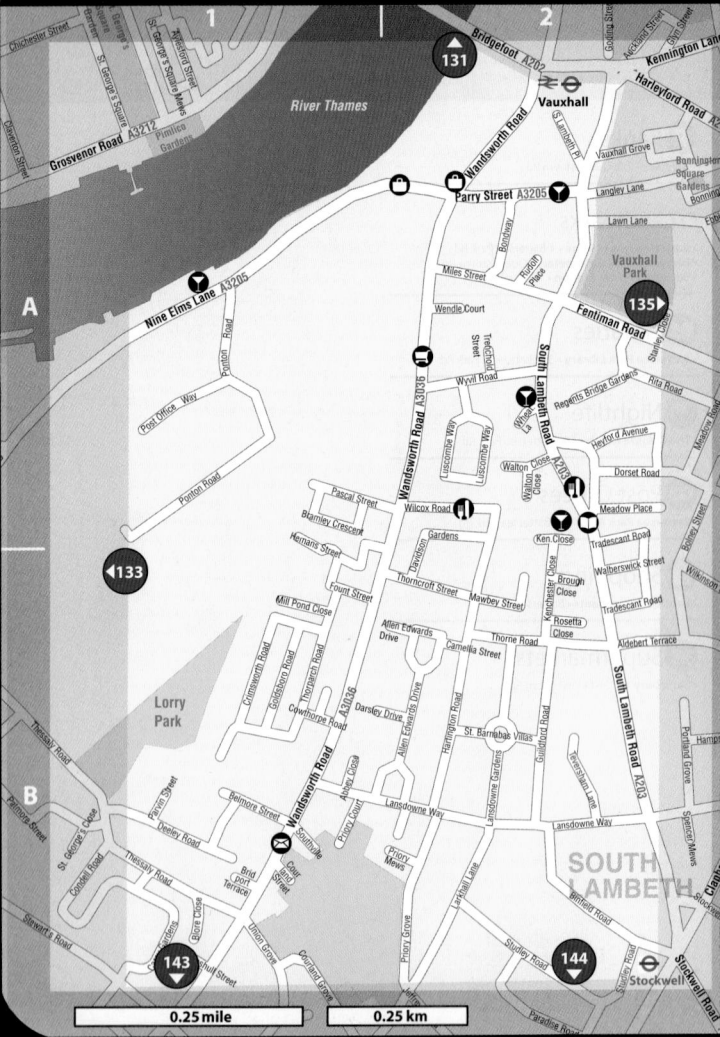

This neighbourhood ain't glamorous but it still has a lot to offer. The area around Vauxhall has a buzzing gay scene – not for the faint hearted. 'Little Portugal' around South Lambeth Road boasts a number of great traditional tapas bars and restaurants; try Estrella for an authentic Mediterranean vibe. Join the traders and head to New Covent Garden Market for fresh flowers, fruit and veg but you'll need to be early!

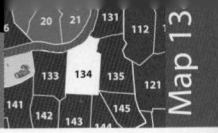

Libraries

- **South Lambeth Library** • 180 S Lambeth Rd

Nightlife

- **Bar Estrella** • 115 Old South Lambeth Rd
- **The Battersea Barge** • Nine Elms Ln
- **Fire** • 38 Parry St
- **Roller Disco @ Renaissance Rooms** • 126 S Lambeth Rd

Post Offices

- **South Lambeth** • 347 Wandsworth Rd

Restaurants

- **Bar Estrella** • 115 Old South Lambeth Rd
- **Hot Stuff** • 19 Wilcox Rd

Shopping

- **Lassco House & Garden** • 30 Wandsworth Rd
- **New Covent Garden Market** • Nine Elms Lane

Supermarkets

- **Sainsbury's** • 62 Wandsworth Rd

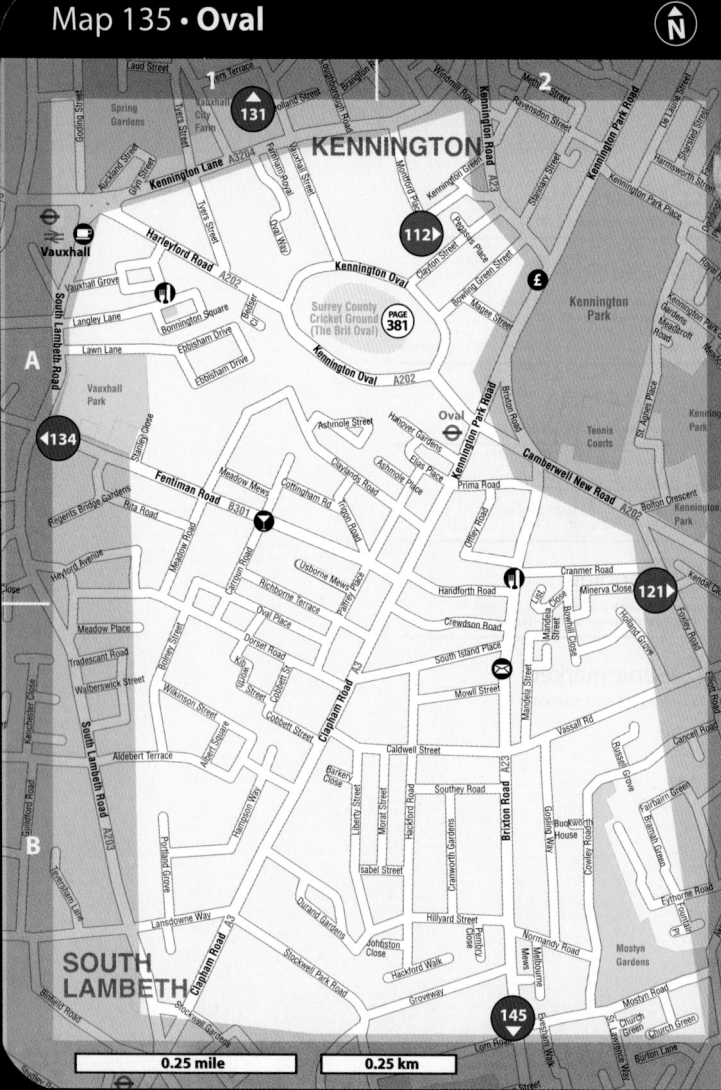
KENNINGTON
SOUTH LAMBETH
Vauxhall
Oval
Kennington Lane A204
Harleyford Road A202
Kennington Oval A202
Kennington Oval A202
Kennington Road A23
Kennington Park Road
Camberwell New Road A202
Fentiman Road B301
South Lambeth Road A203
Clapham Road A3
Brixton Road A23
Surrey County Cricket Ground (The Brit Oval)
PAGE 381
Kennington Park
Vauxhall Park
Spring Gardens
Vauxhall City Farm
Bonnington Square
Ebbisham Drive
Tennis Courts
Meadow Place
Tradescant Road
Walberswick Street
Aldebert Terrace
Albert Square
Lansdowne Way
Stockwell Park Road
Groveway
Hackford Walk
Hillyard Street
Southey Road
Caldwell Street
Mowll Street
Handforth Road
Crewdson Road
South Island Place
Cranmer Road
Minerva Close
Prima Road
Ashmole Street
Mostyn Gardens
Mostyn Road
Church Green
Burton Lane
Lorn Road
Lawrence Way
Normandy Road
Pembury Close
Johnston Close
Durand Gardens
Isabel Street
Cranworth Gardens
Hackford Road
Mont Street
Liberty Street
Barkery Close
Portland Grove
Wilkinson Street
Dorset Road
Oval Place
Richborne Terrace
Lisburne Mews
Meadow Road
Meadow Mews
Cottingham Rd
Tyson Road
Claylands Road
Ashmole Place
Elgin Place
Hardover Gardens
Mandela Way
Mandela Street
Bowhill Close
Howland Grove
Vassall Rd
Cancell Road
Cancell Grove
Brixton Road
Buckworth House
Cowley Road
Eythorne Road
Mowlem Street
Kennington Park Place
Harmsworth Street
Stansfeld Street
Rivenscroft Street
Kennington Road
Clayton Street
Boyling Green Street
Mayes Street
Montford Place
Kennington Oval
Vauxhall Grove
Langley Lane
Lawn Lane
Ebbisham Drive
Stockwell Gardens
Clapham Road
Kennington Park Place
Kennington Park Road
Bolton Crescent
Kennington Park
St Agnes Place
Kennington Park Gardens
Meadcroft Road
Tyers Street
Kennington Road
Harleyford Road
Vauxhall Grove
Vauxhall Street
Laud Street
Tyers Terrace
Spring Gardens
Goding Street
Kennington Lane
Auckland Street
Fentiman Road
Kennington Road
Kennington Oval
Kennington Park Road
Camberwell New Road
Fentiman Road
South Lambeth Road
Clapham Road
Brixton Road
Kennington Park Road
Kennington Park Place
Kennington Park Road
Kennington Road
Kennington Oval
Kennington Lane
Kennington Road
Kennington Oval
Kennington Oval
Kennington Road
Kennington Park Road
Kennington Park Road
Kennington Road
Kennington Oval
Kennington Oval
Kennington

Oval

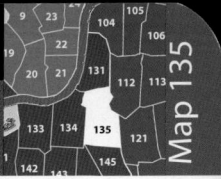

Posh mansions rub shoulders uneasily with housing estates. The Oval cricket ground draws the crowds but usually people just pass through here en route to somewhere more interesting. It's the kind of place where the best nightlife tip we can give you is "go elsewhere". Make of that what you will. Hippy loving veggies will love The Bonnington Café but meat eaters head to Adulis for Eritrean delicacies.

Banks

- **Barclays** • 414 Kennington Rd

Coffee

- **Starbucks** • 2 South Lambeth Rd

Post Offices

- **Brixton Road** • 82 Brixton Rd

Restaurants

- **Adulis** • 44 Brixton Rd
- **The Bonnington Café** • 11 Vauxhall Grove

Nightlife

- **Fentiman Arms** • 64 Fentiman Rd

Map 136 • Putney

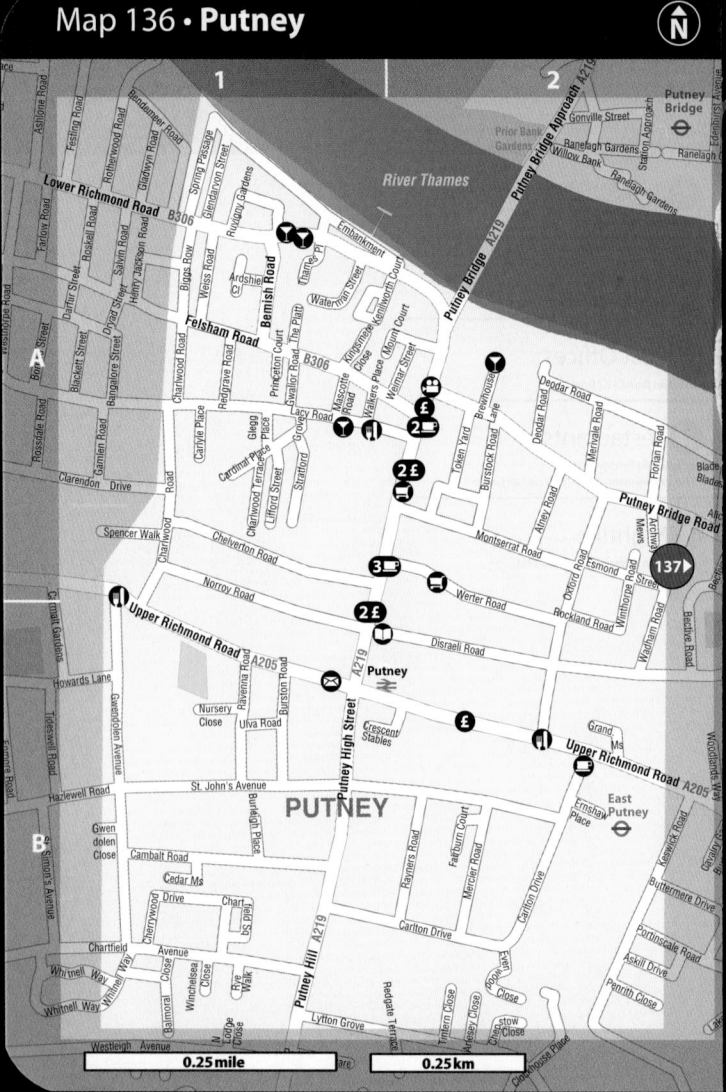

Ah, Putney—a bi-polar place with an air of suburban middle England. Maybe it's all the Rugby and Rowing types. The high street is bland and genteel but by night a generally young, up-for-it crowd descend. Chakalaka offers up a taste of home to hordes of South Africans and the Jolly Gardeners is a great spot for beer tasting and funky tunes.

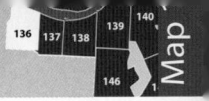

Banks

- **Abbey** • 88 Putney High St
- **Barclays** • 159 Putney High St
- **Barclays** • 60 Putney High St
- **Halifax** • 171 Putney High St
- **HSBC** • 172 Upper Richmond Rd
- **Lloyds** • 110 Putney High St

Coffee

- **BB's Coffee and Muffins** • Putney High St & Chelverton Rd
- **Caffe Nero** • 95 Putney High St
- **Caffe Nero** • 112 Upper Richmond Rd
- **Costa** • 86 Putney High St
- **Pret A Manger** • 121 Putney High St
- **Starbucks** • 117 Putney High St

Libraries

- **Putney Library** • 5 Disraeli Rd

Movie Theaters

- **Odeon Putney** • 26 Putney High St

Nightlife

- **The Boathouse** • Brewhouse Lane
- **Duke's Head** • 8 Lower Richmond Rd
- **Jolly Gardeners** • 61 Lacey Rd
- **Star & Garter** • 4 Lower Richmond Rd

Post Offices

- **Putney** • 214 Upper Richmond Rd

Restaurants

- **Chakalaka** • 136 Upper Richmond Rd
- **Moomba Bar & Kitchen** • 5 Lacy Rd
- **Talad Thai** • 320 Upper Richmond Rd

Supermarkets

- **Sainsbury's** • 2 Werter Rd
- **Waitrose** • Putney High St & Lacy Rd

Map 137 • Wandsworth (West)

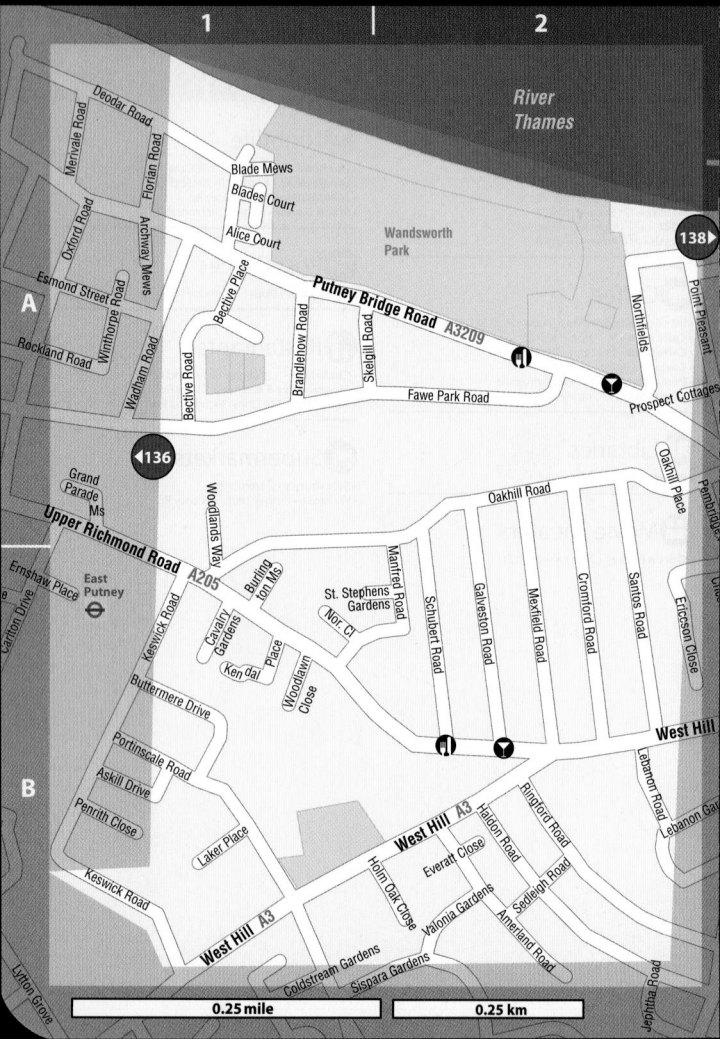

Dissected by the busy Upper and Lower Richmond Roads, this bit of Wandsworth is a bit lifeless though pleasant enough. The pretty, riverside Wandsworth Park is a huge plus and heaves with locals with the first sniff of sunshine. Head to The Queen Adelaide or the Upper Lounge for a spot of liquid refreshment after a hard day's Frisbee chucking.

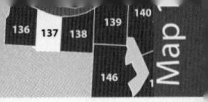

Nightlife

- **The Queen Adelaide** • 35 Putney Bridge Rd
- **Upper Lounge** • 26 Upper Richmond Rd

Restaurants

- **Miraj** • 123 Putney Bridge Road
- **Yia Mas** • 40 Upper Richmond Rd

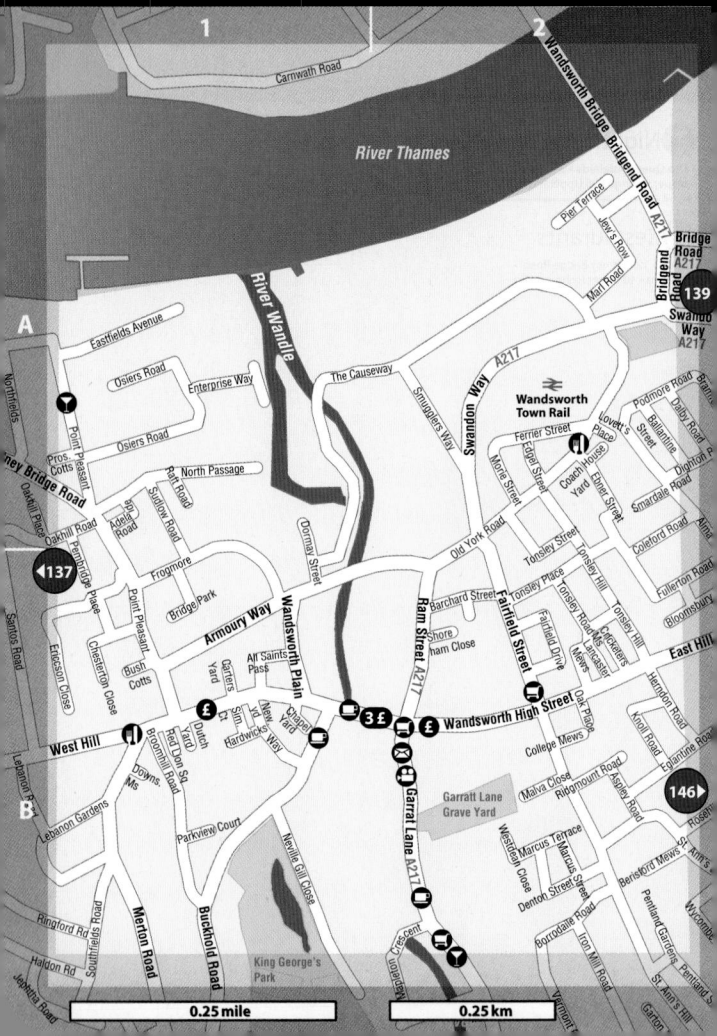
1
2
A
B
River Thames
Carnwath Road
Wandsworth Bridge Bridgend Road A217
Bridge Road A217
Bridgend Road
Pier Terrace
Jew's Row
Mart Road
139
Swandon Way A217
River Wandle
Eastfields Avenue
Osiers Road
Enterprise Way
The Causeway
Smugglers Way
Swandon Way A217
Wandsworth Town Rail
Ferrier Street
Edgar Street
Elmer Street
Coach House Yard
Lovett's Place
Podmore Road
Ballantine Street
Smardale Road
Coleford Road
Fullerton Road
Bloomsbury
Point Pleasant
Pros Cotts
North Passage
Putt Road
Sydlow Road
Adelia Road
Oakhill Road
Pembridge Place
Frogmore
Bridge Park
Dormay Street
Old York Road
Torsley Street
Torsley Place
Torsley Hill
Torsley Road
Fairfield Drive
Fairfield Street
Barchard Street
Ram Street A217
Ham Close
Armoury Way
Wandsworth Plain
Chesterton Close
Bush Cotts
Carters Yard
All Saints Pass
Cockpit Yard
Hardwicks Way
Dutch Yard
Bromhill Road
Road Dun Sq
Wandsworth High Street
Oak Place
College Mews
Harmon Road
Knoll Road
Edgarture Road
East Hill
West Hill
Downs Ms
Lebanon Gardens
Parkview Court
Garratt Lane Grave Yard
Garratt Lane A217
Malva Close
Ringmount Road
Ashley Road
146
Rosen
Marcus Terrace
Marcus Street
Westdean Close
Denton Street
Borrodaile Road
Iron Mill Road
Bensford Mews
St Ann's
Pentland Gardens
Wycombe
Merton Road
Buckhold Road
Southfields Road
Ringford Rd
Haldon Rd
Nevill Gill Close
King George's Park
Magdalen Crescent
Vermont
St Ann's Hill
Garton
Jephtha Road
Sarina Road
Ericsson Close
Northfields
Oakhill Place
137
0.25 mile
0.25 km

Wandsworth (Central)

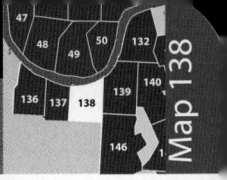

Pity poor Wandsworth Central. Not only is it lumbered with an ugly shopping centre but a four lane gyratory system brings constant traffic and pollution. On the plus side, plenty of chain stores (GAP, Uniqlo etc) and a multi-screen cinema make life a little easier. Old York Road offers a pleasant escape from the madness—try the retro Brady's for great fish and chips.

Banks

- **Abbey** • 81 Wandsworth High St
- **Barclays** • 83 Wandsworth High St
- **Halifax** • 87 Wandsworth High St
- **HSBC** • 73 Wandsworth High St
- **Lloyds** • 159 Wandsworth High St

Cinemas

- **Cineworld Wandsworth** • Wandsworth High St & Ram St

Coffee

- **BB's Coffee and Muffins** • Buckhold Rd & Wandsworth High St
- **Caffe Nero** • Southside Shopping Centre
- **Coffee Republic** • Wandsworth High St

Nightlife

- **The Cat's Back** • 88 Point Pleasant
- **GJ's** • 89 Garratt Lane

Post Offices

- **Wandsworth** • 1 Arndale Walk

Restaurants

- **Brady's** • 513 Old York Rd
- **Kathmandu Valley** • 5 West Hill

Supermarkets

- **Iceland** • Wandsworth High St & Buckhold Rd
- **Sainsbury's** • 45 Garratt Ln
- **Waitrose** • 66 Wandsworth High St

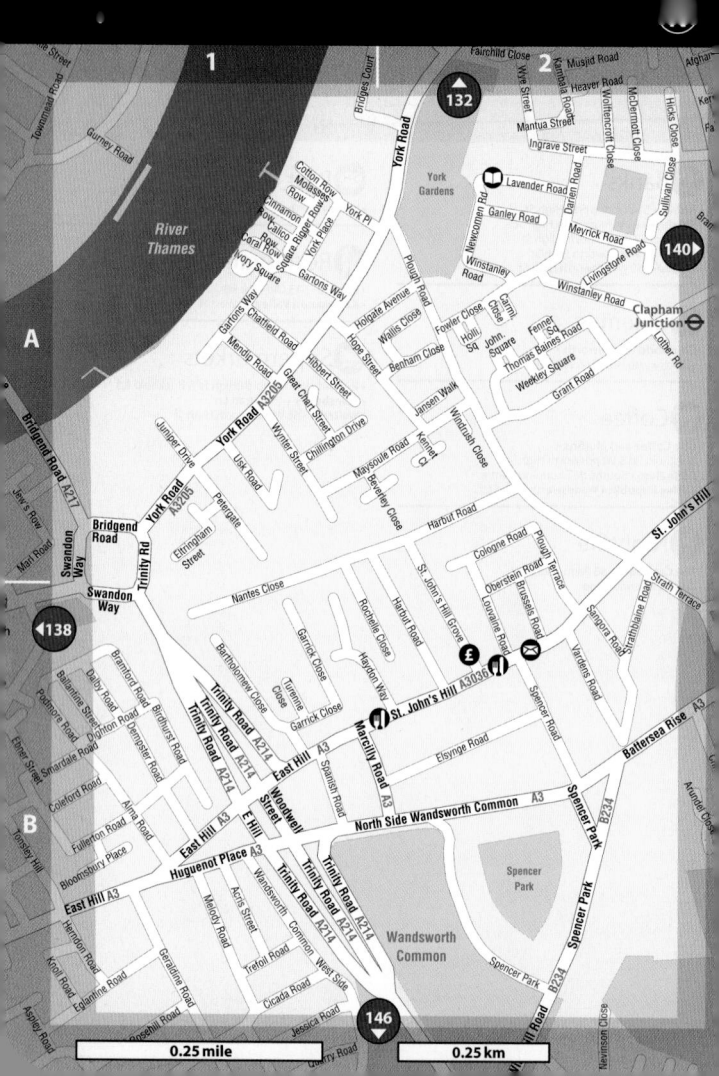
1
2
A
B
River Thames
York Gardens
Wandsworth Common
Spencer Park
Clapham Junction
Bridgend Road
Swandon Way
Trinity Rd
York Road A3205
Trinity Road A214
East Hill A3
Wandsworth Common West Side
Spencer Park B234
Battersea Rise A3
St. John's Hill
St. John's Hill A3036
Marcilly Road A3
Elsynge Road
Spencer Road
North Side Wandsworth Common A3
Huguenot Place A3
Woodwell Street
Lavender Road
Ganley Road
Meyrick Road
Winstanley Road
Winstanley Road
Clapham Junction
Gartons Way
Plough Road
Hibbert Street
Chillington Drive
Harbut Road
Nantes Close
Cologne Road
Plough Terrace
Oberstein Road
Brussels Road
Louisine Road
Sangora Road
Strathbaine Road
Verdeins Road
Garrick Close
Rochelle Close
Hardon Way
Bartholomew Close
Turenne Close
Brambord Road
Dalby Road
Dighton Road
Dempster Road
Coleford Road
Alma Road
Fullerton Road
Bloomsbury Place
Hemdon Road
Knol Road
Edgarmine Road
Geraldine Road
Acris Street
Trefoil Road
Cicada Road
Jessica Road
Rosehill Road
Asciey Road
Gurney Road
Townmead Road
Bridges Court
Fairchild Close
Muslid Road
Kambala Road
Heaver Road
Mantua Street
Ingrave Street
Wye Street
Wolfencroft Close
McDermott Close
Hicks Close
Sullivan Close
Newcomen Rd
Livingstone Road
Carmi Close
Fenner Sq
Thomas Baines Road
Weekly Square
Grant Road
Lother Rd
Cotton Row
Molasses Row
Cinnamon Row
Calico Row
Square Rigger Row
York Place
Coral Row
Ivory Square
Chatfield Road
Mendip Road
Great Chert Street
Wynter Street
Usk Road
Petergate
Ethringham Street
Juniper Drive
Jew's Row
Mall Road
Hogate Avenue
Wallis Close
Hope Street
Benham Close
Fowler Close
Holly Sq
John Square
Jansen Walk
Mayscule Road
Berkeley Close
Kennet Cl
Bridges Street
Townmead Road
Gurney Road
Afghan
Kerr
Fa
Brae
Arundel Close
Newinson Close
Quarry Road
Tinsley Hill
Ashley Road
Ferner Street
Smartdale Road
Potomora Road
Bridges Street
Afghan
Kerr
Fa
Arundel Close
Newinson Close
Quarry Road
Tinsley Hill
Ashley Road
Ferner Street
Smartdale Road
Potomora Road
Bridges Street
132
140
138
146
0.25 mile
0.25 km

Superstores, gas works, swanky apartment blocks, some of London's most deprived housing estates; Wandsworth East has it all! St John's Hill to the south is more promising, offering a bustling strip of boutique shops, bars, and restaurants. Grab a great curry at the Spice of Life and work it off with a brisk Frisbee session on Wandsworth Common.

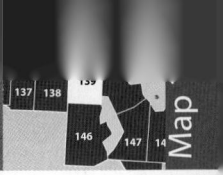

Banks

• **Halifax** • 6 St John's Hill Grove

Libraries

• **York Gardens Library** • 34 Lavender Rd

Post Offices

• **St Johns Hill** • 7 St John's Hill

Restaurants

• **The Fish Club** • 189 St John's Hill
• **Spice of Life** • 147 St. Johns Hill

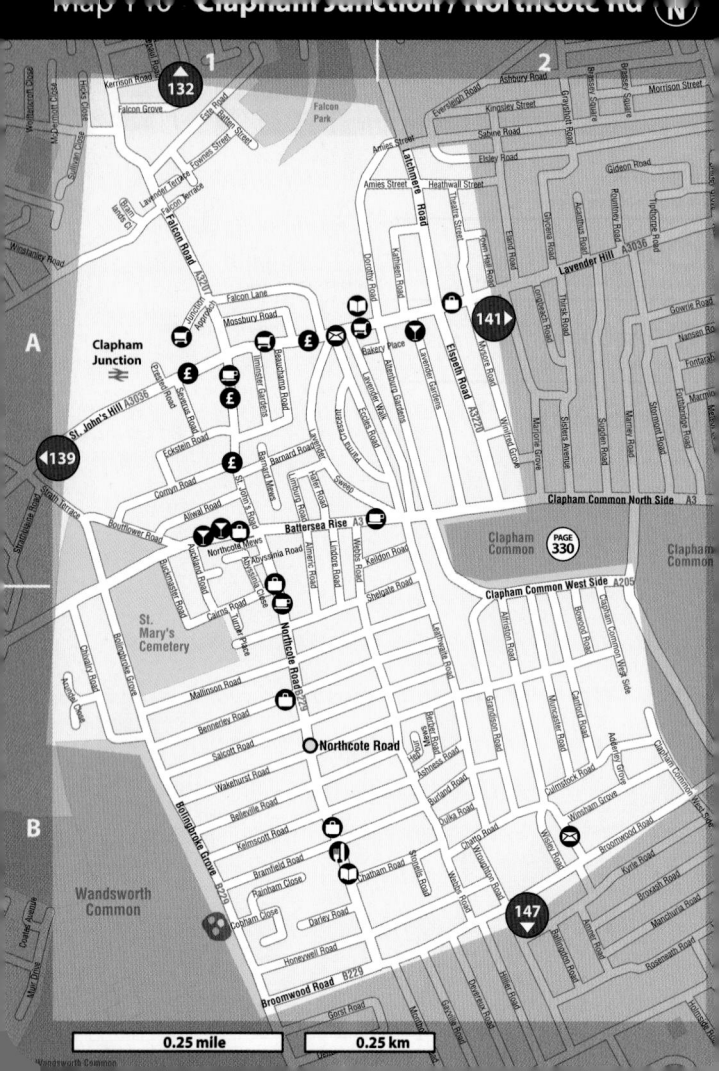
N
1
2
A
B
132
141
139
147
Falcon Park
Clapham Junction
St. John's Hill A3036
Falcon Road A3207
Lavender Hill A3036
Clapham Common North Side A3
Battersea Rise A3
Clapham Common West Side A205
Clapham Common
PAGE 330
St. Mary's Cemetery
Northcote Road
Northcote Road B275
Bellevue Road
Bellingham Grove B275
Wandsworth Common
Broomwood Road B229
Falcon Grove
Falcon Terrace
Falcon Lane
Mossbury Road
Eckstein Road
Common Road
Alwyl Road
Southflower Road
Northcote Mews
Bolingbroke Grove
Mallinson Road
Bennerley Road
Sabcott Road
Wakehurst Road
Kelmscott Road
Branfield Road
Pantham Close
Clapham Close
Darley Road
Honeywell Road
Gorst Road
Espeth Road A3207

Clapham Junction / Northcote Rd

Yummy mummies rule by day when fancy pushchairs, laden with organic groceries from Fresh & Wild, cram the pavement. Hedonistic party people invade at night. With direct rail links to 'the provinces,' Clapham Junction buzzes with out-of-towners while locals hang at the bars on Northcote Road. Try B@1 for drinks, tunes, and bright young things.

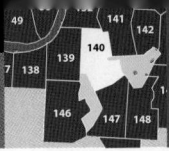

Banks

- **Abbey** • 24 St John's Rd
- **Barclays** • 7 St John's Hill
- **HSBC** • 240 Lavender Hill
- **NatWest** • 66 St John's Rd

Coffee

- **Caffe Nero** • 20 St John's Rd
- **Caffe Nero** • 21 Battersea Rise
- **Starbucks** • 33 Northcote Rd

Landmarks

- **Northcote Road** • Northcote Rd

Libraries

- **Battersea Library** • 265 Lavender Hill
- **Northcote Library** • 155 Northcote Rd

Nightlife

- **adventure bar and lounge** • 91 Battersea Rise
- **B@1** • 85 Battersea Rise
- **Jongleurs (Battersea)** • 49 Lavender Gardens

Post Offices

- **Alfriston Road** • 99 Alfriston Rd
- **Battersea** • 202 Lavender Hill

Restaurants

- **I Sapori di Stefano Cavallini** • 146 Northcote Rd

Shopping

- **Anita's Vintage Fashion Fair** • Battersea Arts Centre, Lavender Hill
- **Huttons** • 29 Northcote Rd
- **QT Toys and Games** • 90 Northcote Rd
- **Russ** • 101 Battersea Rise
- **Sweaty Betty** • 136 Northcote Rd

Supermarkets

- **ASDA** • 204 Lavender Hill
- **Fresh & Wild** • 305 Lavender Hill
- **Sainsbury's** • Clapham Junction

Battersea Park
PAGE 326
Carriage Drive South
Prince of Wales Drive A3220
Albert Bridge Road A3031
Maskelyne Close
Watford Close
Petworth Street
Wycliffe Square
Rosenau Road
Cambridge Road
Kenyer Mews
Kersley Street
Coachtower Street
Battersea Park Road
Fred Street
Burns Road
Joubert Street
Matthews Street
Freedom Street
Reform Street
Sheepcote Lane
Knowsley Road
Falcon Park
Lavender Hill A3036
Lavender Gardens
Lavender Walk
Aldenham Gardens
Bakery
Elspeth Road A3220
Myrtle Road
Wisteria Gro
Clapham Common North Side
Battersea Rise A3

No one goes to Battersea South. You either live there, congratulating yourself on your nice Victorian conversion, or, you pass through on the way to Clapham or one of the lively bits of Battersea. Any of the 'action' happens around Lavender Hill. Lost Angel is an eccentrically fabulous boozer that would rather be a mile east or west.

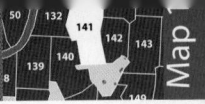

Coffee

- **Captain Corelli** • 132 Battersea Park Rd

Nightlife

- **Halo** • 317 Battersea Park Rd
- **The Lost Angel** • 339 Battersea Park Rd

Shopping

- **Battersea Car Boot Sale** • 401 Battersea Park Rd

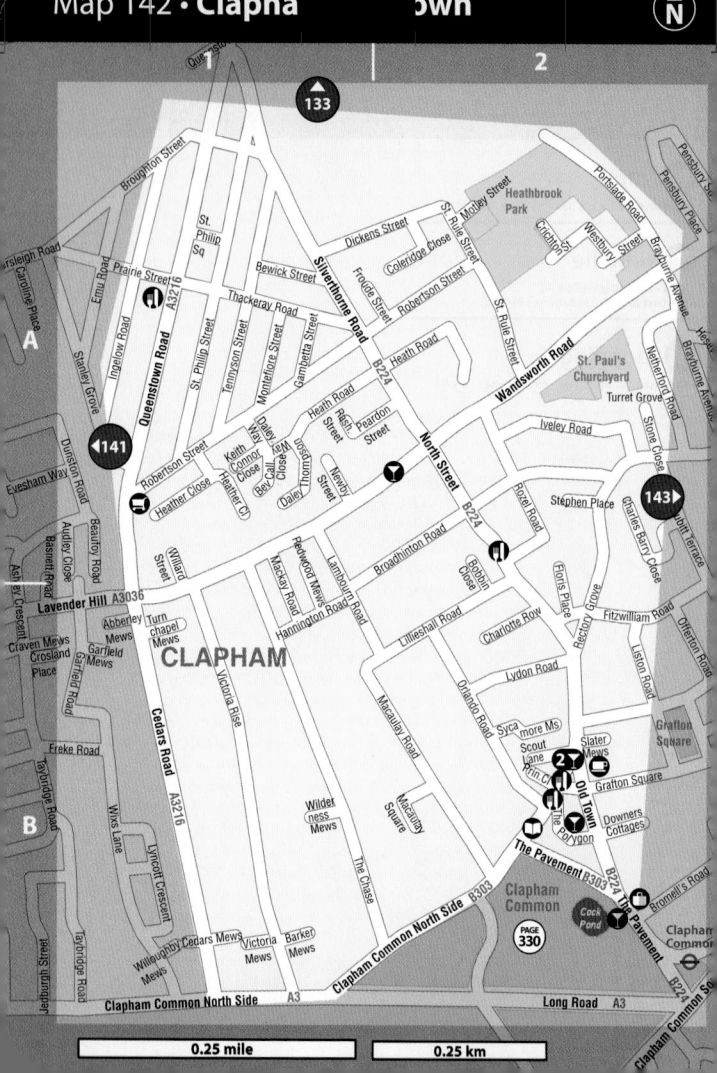
N
1
2
A
B
133
141
143
Queenstown Road
Silverthorne Road
Wandsworth Road
North Street
Cedars Road
Old Town
The Pavement
Clapham Common North Side
Clapham Common South Side
Long Road
Lavender Hill A3036
Broughton Street
Prairie Street
Dickens Street
Bewick Street
Thackeray Road
Heath Road
Robertson Street
Broadhurst Road
Lilleshall Road
Lydon Road
Fitzwilliam Road
Stephen Place
Iveley Road
Turret Grove
Freke Road
Grafton Square
Heathbrook Park
St. Paul's Churchyard
Clapham Common
Cock Pond
Clapham Common
Clapham
PAGE 330
0.25 mile
0.25 km

The more genteel side of Clapham, Old Town hosts some fine restaurants (Trinity, Mooli), good watering-holes (The Prince of Wales, Frog, and Forget-Me-Not) and one of London's best butchers (Moen's), all bordered by the green of Clapham Common. If you need more, and can resist Fish & Chips with free banter (Benny's), head to Queenstown Road for further fine dining establishments.

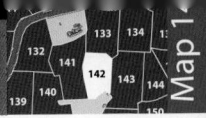

Coffee

- **Starbucks** • 40 Old Town

Libraries

- **Clapham Library** • 1 Clapham Common North Side

Nightlife

- **Frog and Forget-Me-Not** • 32 The Pavement
- **Lost Society** • 697 Wandsworth Rd
- **Prince of Wales** • 38 Old Town
- **Rose and Crown** • 2 The Polygon
- **The Sun** • 47 Clapham Old Town

Restaurants

- **Benny's** • 30 North St
- **Mooli** • 36 Old Town
- **Tom Ilic** • 123 Queenstown Rd
- **Trinity** • 4 The Polygon

Shopping

- **M. Moen & Sons** • 24 The Pavement

Supermarkets

- **Sainsbury's** • 646 Wandsworth Rd

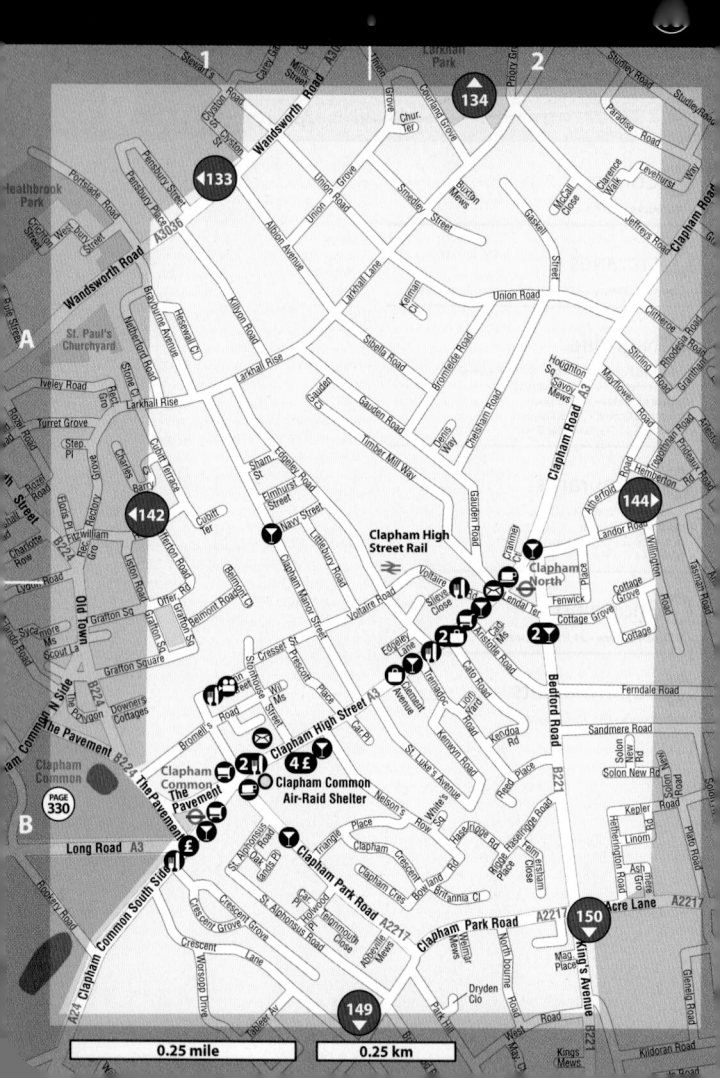
Clapham High Street Rail
Clapham North
Clapham Common Air-Raid Shelter
Clapham Common
Clapham High Street
Clapham Park Road
Clapham Road
Wandsworth Road
Bedford Road
Acre Lane
Kings Avenue
Long Road
The Pavement
Clapham Common South Side
Clapham Common N Side
Old Town
Kildoran Road
Kings Mews
Dryden Clo
Mag Place
Kepler Rd
Linom
Solon New Rd
Ferndale Road
Sandmere Road
Cedars Road
Studley Road
Paradise Road
Clarence Walk
Levehurst Way
Jeffreys Road
Clapham Road
Grantham Rd
Stirling Road
Mayflower Road
Prideaux Rd
Henherton Rd
Landor Road
Wilmington Road
Tasman Road
Cottage Grove
Cottage
Fenwick
Cedars Road
Union Grove
Church Ter
Stewart's Grove
Priory Gr
Portsack Road
Peabury Street
Peabury Place
Clapham Common West Side
Heathbrook Park
Stone Cl
Iveley Road
Turret Grove
Steed Pl
Charlotte Rowe
Fitzwilliam Rd
Lydon Road
Grafton Sq
Grafton Square
Scout La
Downing Cottages
The Polygon
Clapham Common
Bromell's Road
Wd Ms
Cresset Sq
Prescott Place
Clapham Manor Street
Voltaire Road
Voltaire Close
Cato Road
Kenworth Road
Kendoa Rd
Car Pl
St Luke's Avenue
Nelson's Hdn
Wilfred's Sq
Triangle Place
Clapham Crescent
Bow Lond Rd
Britannia Cl
Hasslinge Rd
Hasslinge Close
Ferrersham Place
Clapham Cres
St Alphonsus Road
Grove Pl
Crescent Grove
Crescent Lane
Worsopp Drive
Tabner Av
Park Hill
Mayfair Mews
Tenterden Close
Holmewood Gdns
Cedar Pl
Rosery Road
Gauden Rd
Gauden Road
Timber Mill Way
Clapham Manor Street
Elmhurst Street
Navy Street
Cobbit Ter
Cobbit Terrace
Hurlton Road
Union Road
Grafton Sq
Dfer Rd
Grantham Rd
Belmont Cl
Tremadoc Road
Ferndale Road
Sandmere Road
Solon New Rd
Kepler Rd
Linom
Plato Road
Acre Lane
Kings Avenue
Mag Place
Dryden Clo
Kings Mews
Kildoran Road
Clemig Road

Filled with young pros spending too much on rent, look past the nobs on the main drag, Clapham High Street, to enjoy decent drinking (Bread & Roses) and even better eating (Tsunami, Pepper Tree, Café Wanda). Alternatively, if you are a nob, try one of the High Street's brash bars or The Falcon, where everyone else will be talking too loudly and wearing shades.

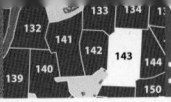

Banks

- **Abbey** • 164 Clapham High St
- **Barclays** • 188 Clapham High St
- **HSBC** • 154 Clapham High St
- **Lloyds** • 12 Clapham Common South Side
- **NatWest** • 145 Clapham High St

Cinemas

- **Clapham Picturehouse** • 76 Venn St

Coffee

- **Café Delight** • 19 Clapham High St
- **Caffe Nero** • 186 Clapham High St

Landmarks

- **Clapham Common Air-Raid Shelter** • Clapham High St

Nightlife

- **The Alexandra** • 14 Clapham Common South Side
- **Bread & Roses** • 68 Clapham Manor St
- **The Clapham North** • 409 Clapham Rd
- **The Falcon** • 33 Bedford Rd
- **Green & Blue** • 20 Bedford Rd
- **Infernos** • 146 Clapham High St
- **The Railway** • 18 Clapham High St
- **The Two Brewers** • 114 Clapham High St
- **The White House** • 65 Clapham Park Rd

Post Offices

- **Clapham Common** • 161 Clapham High St
- **Clapham High Street** • 16 Clapham High St

Restaurants

- **Café Wanda** • 153 Clapham High St
- **The Fish Club** • 57 Clapham High St
- **The Pepper Tree** • 19 Clapham Common South Side
- **The Rapscallion** • 75 Venn St
- **San Marco Pizzeria** • 126 Clapham High St
- **Tsunami** • 5 Voltaire Rd

Shopping

- **Apex Cycles** • 40 Clapham High St
- **Paws** • 62 Clapham High St
- **Today's Living** • 92 Clapham High St

Supermarkets

- **Iceland** • 4 The Pavement
- **Sainsbury's** • Clapham High St
- **Sainsbury's** • 33 Clapham High St

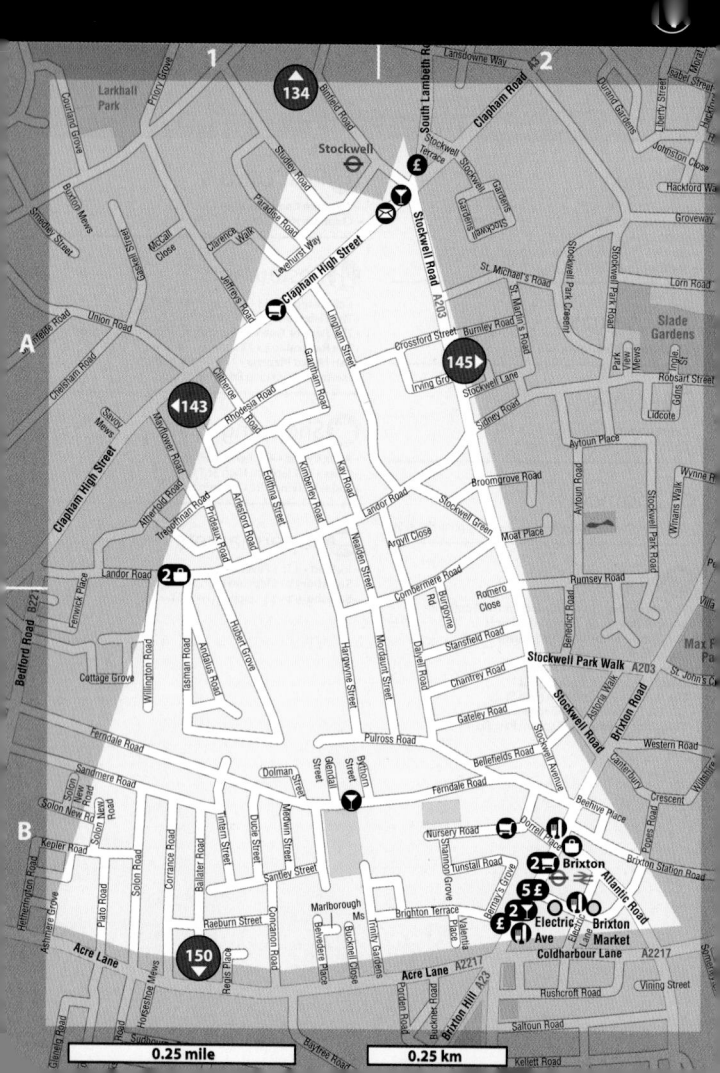
1
2
A
B
Larkhall Park
Stockwell
Clapham Road
South Lambeth Rd
Stockwell Road A203
Clapham High Street
Clapham High Street
Brixton Road
Stockwell Park Walk A203
Bedford Road B22
Acre Lane
Acre Lane A2217
Brixton Hill A23
Atlantic Road
Brixton
Brixton Market
Electric Ave
Coldharbour Lane A2217
Slade Gardens
Brixton Station Road
Ferndale Road
Pulross Road
Landor Road
Lansdowne Way
Stockwell Park Crescent
Stockwell Park Road
Lorn Road
Groveway
Hackford Walk
Johnston Close
Liberty Street
Rabel Street
Courland Grove
Priory Street
Brixton Mews
Studley Road
Paradise Road
Clarence Walk
McCall Close
Jeffrey's Road
Stockwell Terrace
Stockwell Gardens
Lambeth Walk
St. Michael's Road
St. Martin's Road
Crossford Street
Burnley Road
Lingham Street
Clarence Road
Rhodrons Road
Kimberley Road
Kat Road
Edithna Street
Atherfold Road
Trevithan Road
Brixton Road
Landor Road
Argyll Close
Stockwell Green
Moat Place
Broomgrove Road
Avlmun Place
Avlmun Road
Wynne Rd
Wilmans Walk
Robsart Street
Lidcote Gdns
Lidcote Gardens
Stockwell Lane
Sidney Road
Irving Grove
Lemrick Place
Cottage Grove
Willington Road
Tasman Road
Andalusia Road
Robert Grove
Hardwyne Street
Mordaunt Street
Darnell Road
Newlands Street
Combermere Road
Burgoyne Rd
Rothero Close
Benedict Road
Rumsey Road
Stansfield Road
Chantrey Road
Gateley Road
Stockwell Avenue
Atlanta Walk
Canterbury Crescent
Western Road
Belfields Road
Beehive Place
Popes Road
Dolman Street
Glendall Street
Brixton Street
Sandmere Road
Solon New Rd
Solon Road
Kepler Road
Plato Road
Hetherington Road
Ashmere Grove
Corrance Road
Ballater Road
Tintern Street
Ducie Street
Merlyn Street
Sanley Street
Nursery Road
Dorrell Place
Shamrock Grove
Tunstall Road
Mariborough Ms
Raeburn Street
Belvedere Place
Buckwell Close
Brighton Terrace
Trinity Gardens
Valentia Place
Porden Road
Rushcroft Road
Vining Street
Saltoun Road
Kellett Road
Sidmouth Road
Hogsesha Mews
0.25 mile
0.25 km

Stockwell has turned from dodgy to lively without losing character. If you can ignore the crack dealers outside KFC then the same can be said of Brixton. Brixton Market is an institution and a great taste of Caribbean flavour. At night, avoid the sweaty, heaving Swan at Stockwell unless desperate. Plan B is a decent option but you might need ear plugs.

Banks

- **Abbey** • 498 Brixton Rd
- **Barclays** • 463 Brixton Rd
- **Halifax** • 393 Brixton Rd
- **HSBC** • 512 Brixton Rd
- **NatWest** • 358 S Lambeth Rd
- **NatWest** • 395 Brixton Rd
- **NatWest** • 504 Brixton Rd

Landmarks

- **Brixton Market** • Electric Ave
- **Electric Avenue** • Electric Ave

Nightlife

- **Duke of Edinburgh** • 204 Ferndale Rd
- **Plan B** • 418 Brixton Rd
- **The Prince** • 469 Brixton Rd
- **The Swan** • 215 Clapham Rd

Post Offices

- **Stockwell** • 225 Clapham Rd

Restaurants

- **Franco Manca** • 4 Electric Ln
- **Speedy Noodle** • 506 Brixton Rd
- **SW9 Bar Cafe** • 11 Dorrell Pl

Shopping

- **A&C Co Grocers** • 3 Atlantic Rd
- **Lisa Stickley London** • 74 Landor Rd
- **The Old Post Office Bakery** • 76 Landor Rd

Supermarkets

- **Iceland** • 441 Brixton Rd
- **Iceland** • 314 Clapham Rd
- **Sainsbury's** • 425 Brixton Rd
- **Tesco** • 330 Brixton Rd

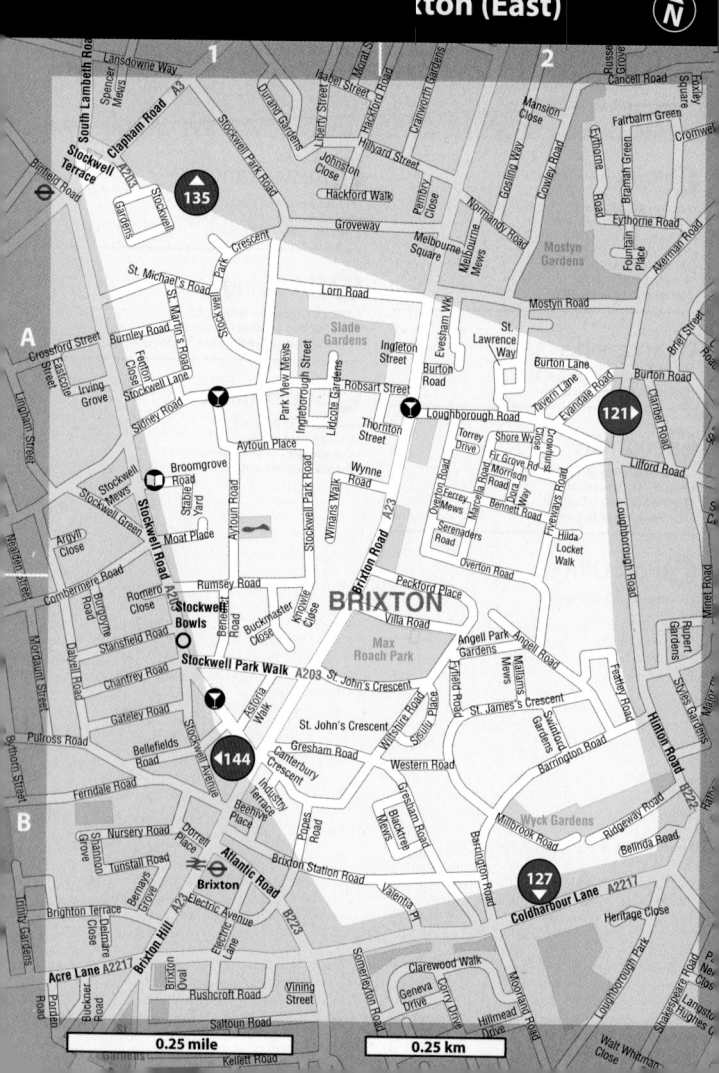
ton (East)
N
1
2
A
B
South Lambeth Road
Lansdowne Way
Spencer Mews
Clapham Road
A3
Stockwell Terrace
Stockwell Gardens
Brixton Road
135
Durand Gardens
Stockwell Park Road
Liberty Street
Isabel Street
Moat S
Hackford Road
Cranworth Gardens
Hillyard Street
Johnson Close
Hackford Walk
Groveway
Penry Close
Normandy Road
Melbourne Square
Melbourne Mews
Mansion Close
Coslima Way
Cowley Road
Russell Grove
Cancell Road
Fairbairn Green
Cromwell
Eythorne Road
Bramah Green
Eythorne Road
Fountain Place
Akerman Road
Mostyn Gardens
Mostyn Road
Lorn Road
St. Michael's Road
St. Martin's Road
Stockwell Park Crescent
Burnley Road
Fenton Close
Stockwell Lane
Sidney Road
Irving Grove
Crossford Street
Eastcote Street
Lingham Street
Slade Gardens
Ingleton Street
Burton Road
Evesham Wk
St. Lawrence Way
Park View Mews
Ingleborough Street
Lidcote Gardens
Robsart Street
Thornton Street
Loughborough Road
Burton Lane
Tavern Lane
121
Brixton Road
Brief Street
Chatham Road
Lilford Road
Aytoun Place
Broomgrove Road
Stockwell Mews
Stockwell Grange
Stockwell Road
Stable Yard
Aytoun Road
Stockwell Park Road
Wynne Road
Wimans Walk
Torrey Drive
Shore Way
Fir Grove Rd
Morrison Road
Bennett Road
Overton Road
Ferrey Mews
Serenders Road
Fivekyars Road
Hilda Locket Walk
Overton Road
Loughborough Road
Moat Place
Argyll Close
Trenton Street
Cornbrook Road
Romero Close
Rumsey Road
Peckford Place
BRIXTON
Stockwell Bowls
Bernell Road
Buckmaster Close
Villa Road
Max Roach Park
Angell Park Gardens
Angell Road
Mornington Street
Stansfield Road
Stockwell Park Walk
A203
St. John's Crescent
Mellanis Mews
Feather Road
Skyes Gardens
Minet Road
Rupert Gardens
Dalvel Road
Chantrey Road
Astoria Walk
Wilshire Road
Sidney Place
St. James's Crescent
Gateley Road
Stockwell Avenue
Hinton Road
Pulross Road
Bethnom Street
Bellefields Road
144
Gresham Road
Canterbury Crescent
Western Road
Sandford Gardens
Barrington Road
Ferndale Road
Industry Terrace
Beehive Place
Copes Road
Gresham Road
Blacktree Mews
Wyck Gardens
Millbrook Road
Ridgeway Road
Belinda Road
Nursery Road
Dorrell Place
Tunstall Road
Atlantic Road
Brixton
Brixton Station Road
Valentia Pl
127
Coldharbour Lane
A2217
Heritage Close
Trinity Gardens
Brighton Terrace
Bernays Grove
Electric Avenue
B223
Brixton Hill
A23
Electric Lane
Clarewood Walk
Acre Lane
A2217
Brixton Oval
Rushcroft Road
Vining Street
Somerleyton Road
Geneva Drive
Corry Drive
Moyland Road
Hillmead Drive
Loughborough Park
Shakespeare Road
Porden Road
Buckner Road
Saltoun Road
Kellett Road
Walt Whitman Close
0.25 mile
0.25 km

Stockwell / Brixton (East)

Things have changed a bit since The Clash sang 'The Guns of Brixton' in '79 and race riots were a regular occurrence. While the middle classes have infiltrated most parts of Brixton, this neighbourhood still retains a defiant edge. Community spirit and close-knit neighbourhoods take precedence over trendy bars and pricey restaurants. Live music rules here; the legendary Brixton Academy still draws the hordes while Jamm offers an eclectic and worthy alternative.

Landmarks

- **Stockwell Bowls** • Stockwell Rd

Libraries

- **Anti-Slavery International Library** • Broomgrove Rd

Nightlife

- **Brixton Academy** • 211 Stockwell Rd
- **The Grosvenor** • 17 Sidney Rd
- **Jamm** • 261 Brixton Rd

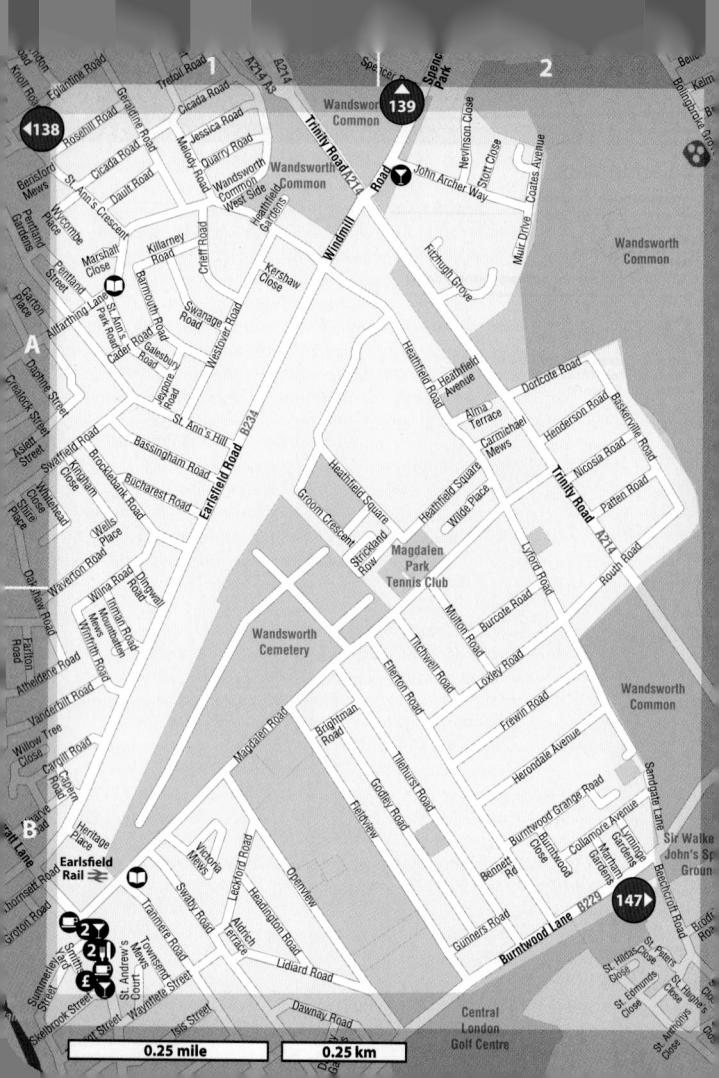
1
2
A
B
138
139
147
Wandsworth Common
Wandsworth Common West Side
Heathfield Gardens
Trinity Road A214
Windmill Road
John Archer Way
Nevinson Close
Stott Close
Coates Avenue
Muir Drive
Richmond Grove
Kershaw Close
Creff Road
Killarney Road
Barmouth Road
Swanage Road
Westover Road
Gatesbury Road
Jessica Road
Quarry Road
Mandy Road
Cicada Road
Rosehill Road
Equitine Road
Trefoil Road
Geraldine Road
St. Ann's Crescent
Dault Road
Bristford Mews
Wycombe Place
Penfland Gardens
Marshall Close
Penfland Street
Allfarthing Lane
St. Ann's Park Road
Cadogan Road
Garton Place
Daphne Street
Greenlock Street
Aslett Street
Swaffield Road
Kingham Close
Brocklebank Road
Bucharest Road
Bassingham Road
St. Ann's Hill
Earlsfield Road B234
Heathfield Road
Heathfield Avenue
Alma Terrace
Carmichael Mews
Dorncote Road
Henderson Road
Baskerville Road
Nicosia Road
Patten Road
Trinity Road A214
Heathfield Square
Willda Place
Groom Crescent
Strickland Row
Magdalen Park Tennis Club
Lyford Road
Routh Road
Burcote Road
Munton Road
Lonley Road
Tidcwell Road
Ellerton Road
Frewin Road
Heronsdale Avenue
Burntwood Grange Road
Burntwood Close
Collamore Avenue
Luminos Gardens
Merton Gardens
Bennett Rd
Semigate Lane
Beechcroft Road
Burntwood Lane B229
Gunners Road
Godley Road
Tilehurst Road
Fitzhugh Road
Brightman Road
Magdalen Road
Wandsworth Cemetery
Waverton Road
Wilna Road
Trinity Road
Mauchan Mews
Wimbrin Road
Athelstone Road
Vanderbilt Road
Willow Tree Close
Cargill Road
Calvern Road
Heritage Place
Earlsfield Rail
Victoria Mews
Leckford Road
Swaby Road
Tranmere Road
Townsend Mews
St. Andrew's Court
Wayfleet Street
Isis Street
Summerley Street
Skelbrook Street
Groton Road
Alderch Terrace
Headmoor Road
Openview
Lidiard Road
Dawnay Road
Central London Golf Centre
St. Hilda's Close
St. Edmunds Close
St. Anthony's Close
St. Hughes's Close
St. Cuthbert's Close
Sir Walter John's Sp Groun
0.25 mile
0.25 km

Sleepy little Earlsfield tends to mind its own business. It's a pretty sedate kind of place, slightly cut off by the lack of a tube stop. The well-heeled locals seem happy enough and make the most of what's on offer. Try Amaranth for great noodles before moving on to Bar 366 a few doors down for some chilled boozing.

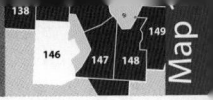

Banks

- **Barclays** • 376 Garratt Ln

Coffee

- **Caffe Nero** • 529 Garratt Ln
- **Refuel** • 515 Garratt Ln

Libraries

- **Alvering Library** • 2 Allfarthing Lane
- **Earlsfield Library** • 276 Magdalen Rd

Nightlife

- **Bar 366** • 366 Garratt Ln
- **Baraza** • 561 Garratt Ln
- **Halfway House** • 521 Garratt Ln
- **Le Gothique** • Windmill Rd & John Archer Wy

Restaurants

- **Amaranth Cafe & Noodle Bar** • 346 Garratt Ln
- **Carluccio's** • 537 Garratt Ln

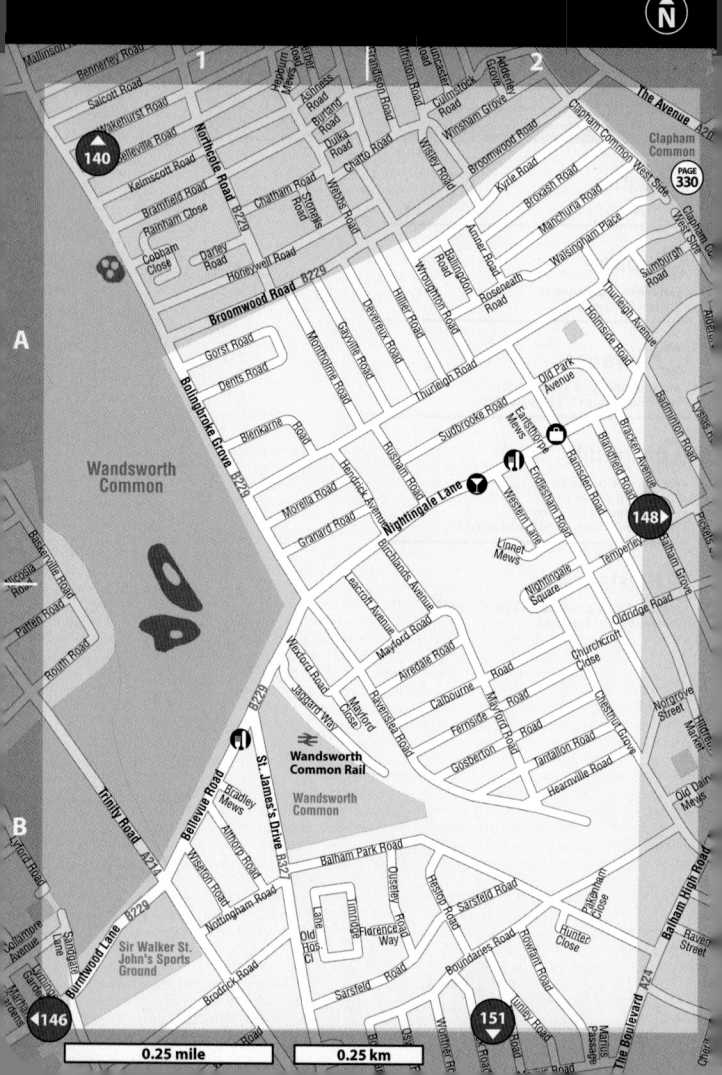
N
1
2
A
B
140
146
148
151
PAGE 330
Bennerley Road
Salcott Road
Keimscott Road
Northside Road B229
Bramfield Road
Rainham Close
Cobham Close
Darley Road
Horneywell Road
Broomwood Road B229
Chatham Road
Wrenbs Road
Ashness Road
Byrland Road
Dolka Road
Chatto Road
Bradlison Road
Wiseley Road
Culmstock Road
Wiltsham Grove
Broomwood Road
Kyle Road
Broxash Road
Manchuria Road
Walsingham Place
Armar Road
Rosenean Road
Wroughton Road
Ballington Road
Hillier Road
Devereux Road
Montcalme Road
Thurleigh Road
Holmside Road
Thurleigh Avenue
Sumburgh Road
Clapham Common West Side
The Avenue A20
Clapham Common
Clapham Co. West Side
Gorst Road
Dents Road
Blenkarne Road
Bolingbroke Grove B229
Wandsworth Common
Southbrooke Road
Old Park Avenue
Earlsmoor Mews
Ramsden Road
Braken Avenue
Morella Road
Granard Road
Henrick Avenue
Rushain Road
Nightingale Lane
Westover Lane
Endlesham Road
Linnet Mews
Tempelhey
Balham Grove
Nightingale Square
Birchlands Avenue
Maybury Road
Airedale Road
Oldridge Road
Churchcroft Close
Chestnut Grove
Norgrove Street
Hillier Market
Old Dairy Mews
Jaggard Way
Mayford Close
Ravenslea Road
Calbourne Road
Fernside Road
Mayford Road
Gosberton Road
Tantallon Road
Hearnville Road
Wandsworth Common Rail
Wandsworth Common
St. James's Drive B27
Bellevue Road
Bradley Mews
Alnford Road
Wiseton Road
Nottingham Road
Balham Park Road
Queeley Road
Hector Road
Sarsfield Road
Paddenham Close
Hunter Close
Florence Way
Tinnock
Old Hospital
Boundaries Road
Rovelent Road
Balham High Road
Balham Street
Trinity Road A214
Burntwood Lane B229
Sir Walker St. John's Sports Ground
Brodrick Road
Sarsfield Road
Tinley Road
Mantus Passage
The Boulevard A214
Worthe Rd
Chelt
0.25 mile
0.25 km

Ensconced between the livelier Clapham and Tooting, this is a gentle slice of residential south west London. Bellevue Road offers a number of places to eat and drink overlooking Wandsworth Common, climaxing with the stupendous Chez Bruce. Nightingale Lane is terribly twee and hosts a few opportunities to shop organically and, you know, locally, or to stuff yourself silly at The Bombay Bicycle Club.

Nightlife

• **The Nightingale** • 97 Nightingale Lane

Restaurants

• **The Bombay Bicycle Club** • 95 Nightingale Lane
• **Chez Bruce** • 2 Bellevue Rd

Shopping

• **Bon Vivant** • 59 Nightingale Lane

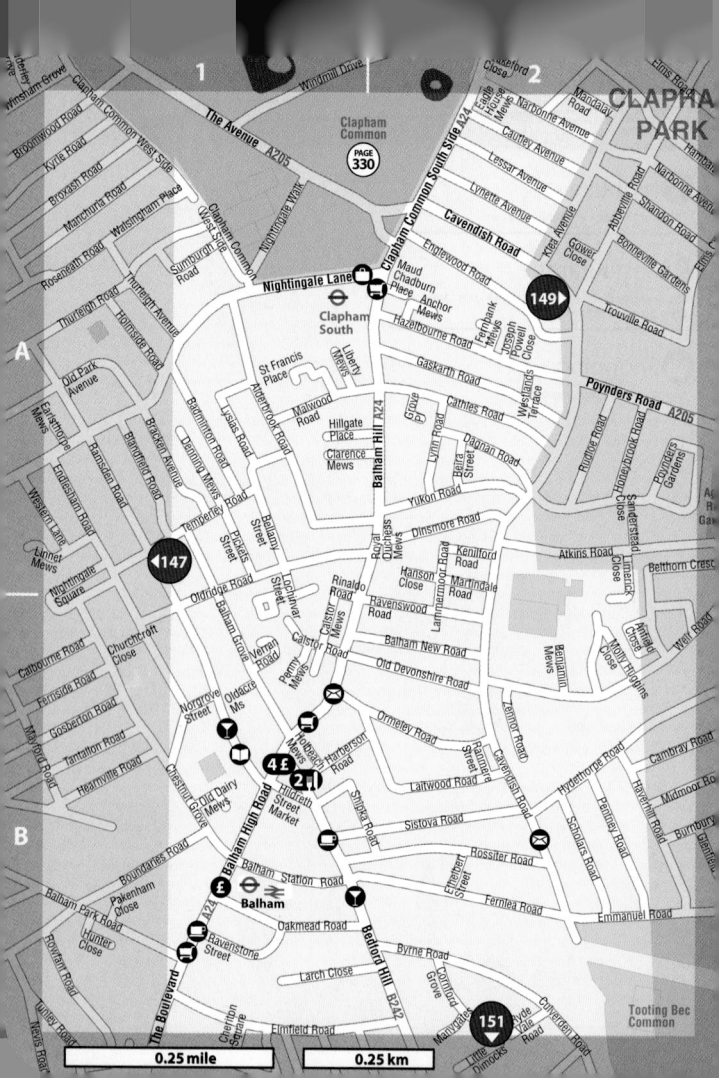
CLAPHA
PARK
1
2
A
B
Windmill Drive
The Avenue A205
Clapham Common
PAGE 330
Clapham Common West Side
Clapham Common South Side A24
Cavendish Road
Nightingale Lane
Clapham South
Balham Hill A24
Poynders Road A205
Balham High Road
Bedford Hill B242
The Boulevard
Balham
Balham Station Road
Balham New Road
Old Devonshire Road
Bedford Road
Tooting Bec Common
Little Dimocks
149
147
151
0.25 mile
0.25 km

The gentrification of Balham proceeds at pace but it hasn't yet killed off its character. Illegal all-nighters are a thing of the past but once the baby buggy crowds have finished their Waitrose run, Balham really comes alive. Diverse eating options (try Dish Dash for Persian treats), great pubs (Balham Bowls Club rules) and swanky bars (Harrison's darhling) all vie for your hard earned nuggets.

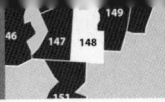

Banks

- **Abbey** • 200 Balham High Rd
- **Barclays** • 169 Balham High Rd
- **Halifax** • 160 Balham High Rd
- **HSBC** • 117 Balham High Rd
- **Lloyds** • 125 Balham High Rd

Coffee

- **Caffe Nero** • 137 Balham High Rd
- **Starbucks** • 41 Bedford Hill

Libraries

- **Balham Library** • 16 Ramsden Rd

Nightlife

- **Balham Bowls Club** • 79 Ramsden Rd
- **The Bedford** • 77 Bedford Hill

Post Offices

- **Balham** • 92 Balham High Rd
- **Cavendish Road** • 273 Cavendish Rd

Restaurants

- **Dish Dash** • 11 Bedford Hill
- **Harrison's** • 15 Bedford Hill

Shopping

- **Moxon's** • Westbury Parade

Supermarkets

- **Sainsbury's** • 149 Balham High Rd
- **Sainsbury's** • 19 Balham Hill
- **Waitrose** • Balham High Rd & Ramsden Rd

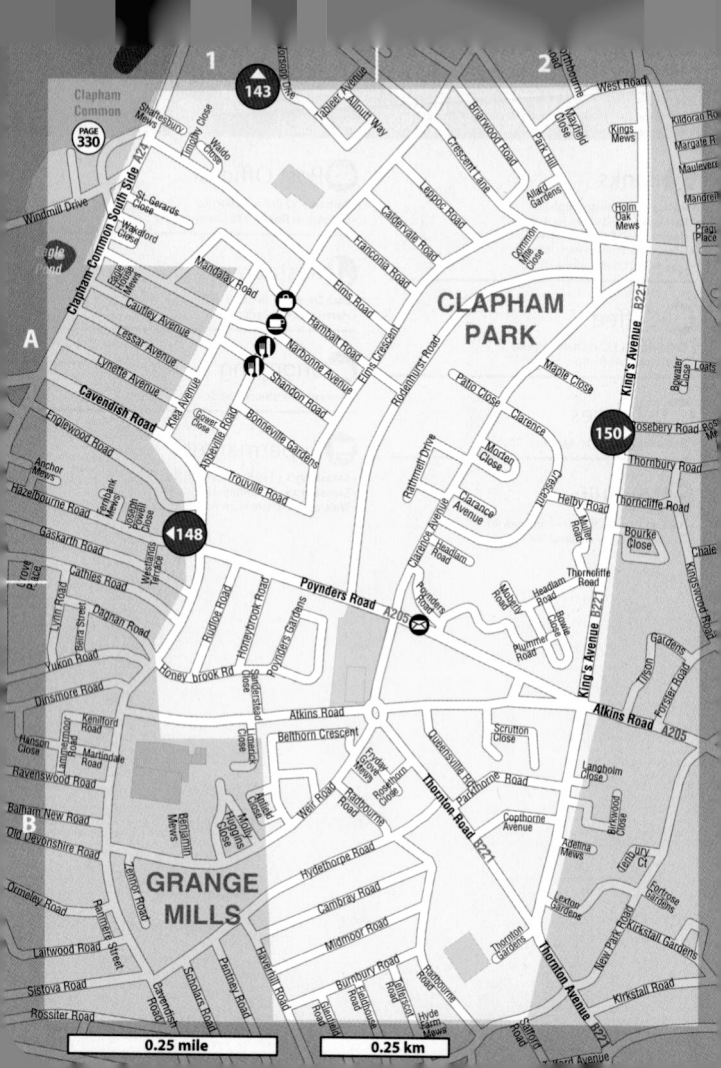
1
2
A
B
143
PAGE 330
148
150
CLAPHAM PARK
GRANGE MILLS
Clapham Common
Clapham Common South Side A24
Windmill Drive
Shrewsbury Mews
Wakefield Close
St. Gerards Close
Mandeville Road
Cantley Avenue
Lessar Avenue
Lynette Avenue
Cavendish Road
Frideswood Road
Anchor Mews
Hazelbourne Road
Gaskarth Road
Cathles Road
Dagnan Road
Yukon Road
Dinsmore Road
Kenilford Road
Hanson Close
Martindale Road
Ravenswood Road
Balham New Road
Old Devonshire Road
Ormeley Road
Latwood Road
Sistova Road
Rossiter Road
Rhymer Street
Tennor Road
Benjamin Mews
Molly Hoggins Close
Wallace Close
Weir Road
Bambourne Road
Rosebourne Close
Hydethorpe Road
Cambray Road
Midmoor Road
Harkehill Road
Pentney Road
Schalders Road
Burbury Road
Cotleigh Road
Hyde Farm Mews
Balham Hill
Balham Road
Tablet Avenue
Almott Way
Caldervale Road
Fauconna Road
Elms Road
Hambalt Road
Narbonne Avenue
Shandon Road
Bonneville Gardens
Trouville Road
Rodbourne Road
Elms Crescent
Rodrigues Road
Honeybrook Road
Poynders Gardens
Poynders Road A205
Honey brook Rd
Sandersteed Close
Lisardick Close
Atkins Road
Belthorn Crescent
Thornton Road B221
Queensville Road
Earlsthorne Road
Scrutton Close
Copthorne Avenue
Langholm Close
Birkwood Close
Aldenna Mews
Lexton Gardens
Thornton Gardens
Thornton Avenue B221
New Park Road
Kirkstall Gardens
Kirkstall Road
Ford Avenue
Clarence Avenue
Clarence Close
Patio Close
Maple Close
Mortlake Close
Rummer Drive
Headlam Road
Headlam Road
Bowie Close
Plummer Road
Thornlifte Road
Helby Road
Crescent
Thorncliffe Road
Thornbury Road
Rosebery Road
King's Avenue B221
Bourke Close
Kingswood Road
Tilson Gardens
Alkins Road A205
Maxfield Close
Park Hill
Briarwood Road
Crescent Lane
Lappoc Road
Allard Gardens
Holm Oak Mews
West Road
Margate Rd
Maulevere
Mandrell
Page Place
Loats
Bowater Close
Bowater Mews
Kidderpore Road

Clapham Park

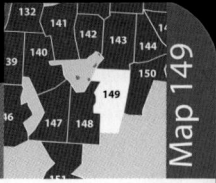

Largely a residential rat run, Clapham Park has its moments. After a day out on Clapham Common it's far less hectic and boozy than its tube served neighbours. Head to Abbeville Road for a wide selection of bars and restaurants. Fill up on hearty Italian at Grissini or head to Dexter's for a lazy brunch.

Coffee

- **Starbucks** • 39 Abbeville Rd

Post Offices

- **Clapham Park** • 49 Poynders Rd

Restaurants

- **Dexter's** • 36 Abbeville Rd
- **Grissini** • 31 Abbeville Rd

Shopping

- **MacFarlanes** • 48 Abbeville Rd

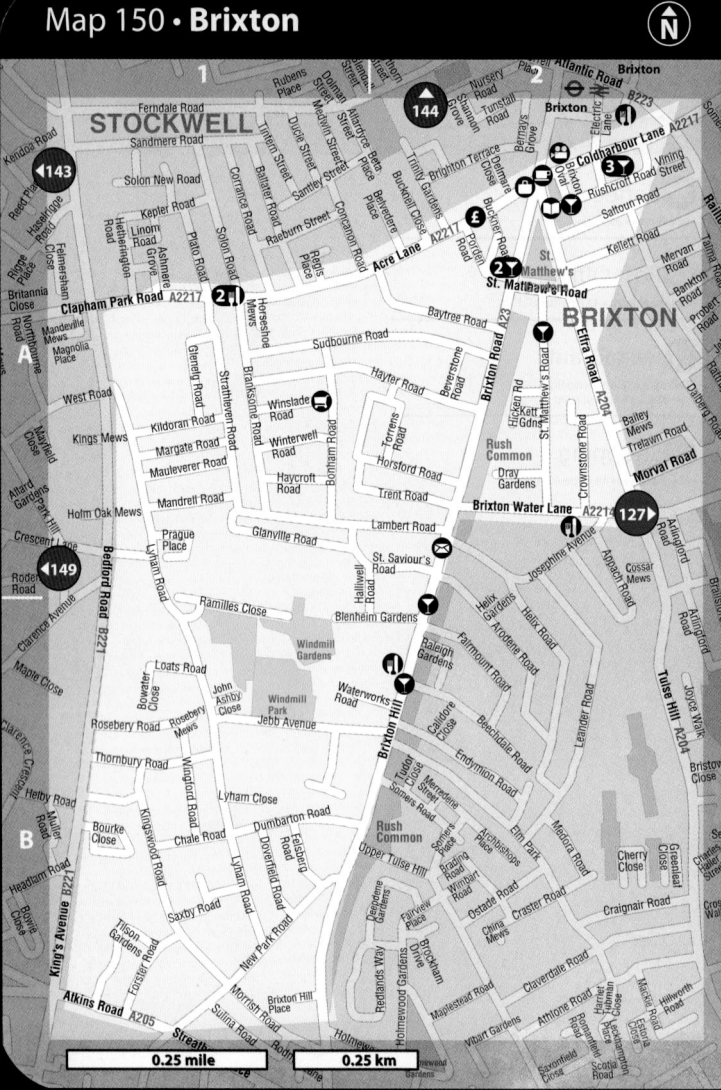
STOCKWELL
BRIXTON
Brixton
Brixton
Ferndale Road
Sandmere Road
Kendoa Road
Solon New Road
Keptel Road
Linom Road
Hetherington Road
Ashmere Grove
Plato Road
Solon Road
Corrance Road
Dulce Street
Atlantic Road
Rubens Place
Donnan Street
Nursery Road
Tunstall Road
Barnays Grove
Electric Lane
Coldharbour Lane A2217
Brixton Hill
Vining Street
Rushcroft Road
Saltoun Road
Kellett Road
Mervan Road
Tulse Hill Road
Talma Road
Bankton Road
Probert Road
Brixton Road A23
Effra Road A204
Morval Road
Brixton Water Lane
Josephine Avenue
Cossar Mews
Atlingford Road
Joyce Walk
Tulse Hill A204
Leander Road
Endymion Road
Beaculade Road
Calidore Close
Fairmount Road
Acadene Road
Helix Gardens
Helix Road
Blenheim Gardens
Raleigh Gardens
Waterworks Road
Brixton Hill
Hallswell Road
St. Saviour's Road
Lambert Road
Glanville Road
Prague Place
Ramilles Close
Windmill Gardens
Windmill Park
Loats Road
Bowater Close
John Ashby Close
Rosebery Road
Rosebery Mews
Jebb Avenue
Thornbury Road
Wingford Road
Lyham Close
Dumbarton Road
Chale Road
Bourke Close
Kingswood Road
Doverfield Road
Lyham Road
Saxby Road
New Park Road
Tulse Hill
Upper Tulse Hill
Somers Road
Mercadine Street
Tudor Close
Rush Common
Dray Gardens
Trent Road
Horsford Road
Haycroft Road
Bonham Road
Winterwell Road
Torrens Road
Winslade Road
Blanksome Road
Strathleven Road
Glenelg Road
Sudbourne Road
Hayter Road
Baytree Road
Acre Lane A2217
Clapham Park Road A2217
Horseshoe Mews
Mandeville Mews
Magnolia Place
Northbourne Road
West Road
Kings Mews
Kildoran Road
Margate Road
Mauleverer Road
Mandrell Road
Holm Oak Mews
Crescent Lane
Bedford Road B221
Clarence Avenue
Maple Close
Hetby Road
Headlam Road
King's Avenue B221
Atkins Road A205
Morrish Road
Sulina Road
Brixton Hill Place
Tisson Gardens
Forster Road
Redlands Way
Holmewood Gardens
Brickham Drive
Fairview Place
Dendrene Gardens
Maplestead Road
Vibart Gardens
Athlone Road
Chaverdale Road
Craster Road
Craignair Road
Ostade Road
Winbart Road
Reading Road
Archbishops Place
Elm Park
Medora Road
Cherry Close
Greenleaf Close
Hillreth Road
Mackie Road
Scotia Road
Harriet Tubman Close
Rosemary Road
Rosemary Mews

Believe the hysteria and Brixton is a nest of gun-toting crack heads. Yes, it has its problems but Brixton is also one of London's most diverse and vibrant neighbourhoods popular with a young, cool crowd. The Brixton Ritzy is a brilliant art house cinema offering bars and interesting food as well as great films. Clubbers gravitate towards The Fridge (sweaty) and Mass (funky), a sprawling multi-purpose venue housed in a church.

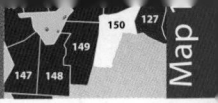

Banks

- **Lloyds** • 18 Acre Ln

Cinemas

- **Ritzy Cinema** • Coldharbour Ln & Brixton Oval

Coffee

- **Rosie's Deli Cafe** • 14 Market Row

Libraries

- **Brixton Library** • Brixton Oval

Nightlife

- **The Dogstar** • 389 Coldharbour Ln
- **The Effra** • 38 Kellet Rd
- **The Fridge** • 1 Town Hall Parade, Brixton Hill
- **Mango Landin'** • 40 St Matthews Rd
- **Mass** • Brixton Hill
- **Prince Albert** • 418 Coldharbour Ln
- **Ritzy Café** • Brixton Oval, Coldharbour Lane (above Ritzy cinema)
- **St Matthews Church** • Brixton Hill
- **The Windmill** • 22 Blenheim Gardens

Post Offices

- **Brixton Hill** • 104 Brixton Hill

Restaurants

- **Asmara** • 386 Coldharbour Ln
- **Khan's** • 24 Brixton Water Lane
- **Negril** • 132 Brixton Hill
- **Opus Café** • 89 Acre Ln
- **Upstairs Bar and Restaurant** • 89 Acre Ln

Shopping

- **Traid** • 2 Acre Ln

Supermarkets

- **Iceland** • 13 Winslade Rd

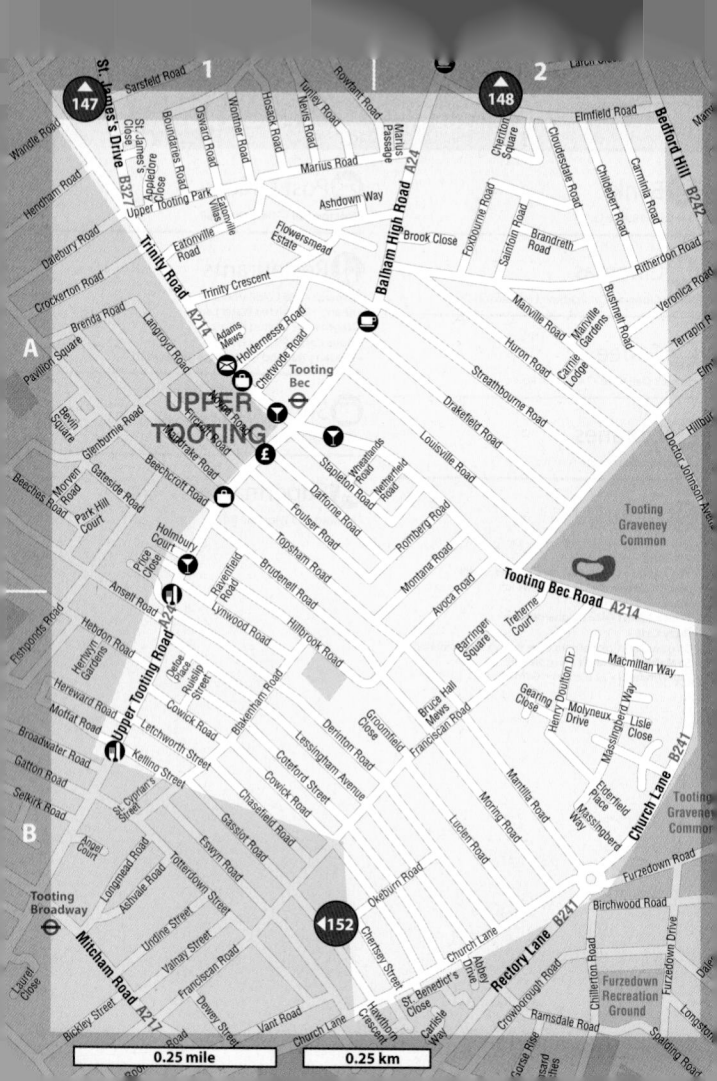
1
2
A
B
147
148
152
St. James's Drive B327
Sarsfield Road
Wandle Road
Hengham Road
Crockerton Road
Brenda Road
Pavilion Square
Langroyd Road
Glenburnie Road
Gatesideroad
Beechcroft Road
Beechas Road
Park Hill Court
Holmbury Court
Price Close
Ansell Road
Fishponds Road
Hebdon Road
Herbwyn Gardens
Hereward Road
Moffat Road
Broadwater Road
Gatton Road
Selkirk Road
Upper Tooting Road A24
Kelling Street
Letchworth Street
Angel Court
Longmead Road
Ashvale Road
Totterdown Street
Eswyn Road
Gassiot Road
Chassfield Road
Cowick Road
Bakenham Road
Boundaries Road
Upper Tooting Park
Appledore Close
Dsward Road
Wolfmer Road
Hosack Road
Nevis Road
Turley Road
Rowfant Road
Marius Road
Marius Passage
Ashdown Way
Flowersmead Estate
Eatonville Road
Eatonville Villas
Trinity Road A214
Trinity Crescent
Adams Mews
Holderness Road
Chetwode Road
Tooting Bec
UPPER TOOTING
Balham High Road A24
Brook Close
Foxbourne Road
Salsilon Road
Brandreth Road
Ritherdon Road
Elmfield Road
Cherrion Square
Chudleigh Road
Chilebert Road
Carming Road
Bedford Hill B242
Veronica Road
Terrapin R
Manville Road
Manville Gardens
Bushnell Road
Huron Road
Carlile Lodge
Streathbourne Road
Drakefield Road
Louisville Road
Doctor Johnson Avenue
Hillbur
Wheatlands Road
Stapleton Road
Netherfield Road
Daffodil Road
Fouiser Road
Romberg Road
Topsham Road
Brudenell Road
Montana Road
Avoca Road
Tooting Bec Road A214
Treherne Court
Barringer Square
Tooting Graveney Common
Lynwood Road
Hillbrook Road
Bruce Hall Mews
Francis Road
Macmillan Way
Gearing Close
Henry Doulton Dr.
Molyneux Drive
Massingberd Way
Lisle Close
Church Lane B241
Elderfield Place
Massingberd Way
Mantlia Road
Morning Road
Lucien Road
Groomfield Close
Derrinton Road
Lessingham Avenue
Cotsford Street
Cowick Road
Furzedown Road
Birchwood Road
Okeburn Road
Tooting Broadway
Mitcham Road A217
Urdine Street
Valnay Street
Franciscan Road
Dewey Street
Vant Road
Church Lane
Chertsey Street
Church Lane
Abbey Drive
St. Benedict's Close
Carlisle Way
Rectory Lane B241
Crowborough Road
Furzedown Recreation Ground
Chilterton Road
Furzedown Drive
Ramsdale Road
Laurel Close
Bickley Street
Spadding Road
Gorse Rise
0.25 mile
0.25 km

Not quite the Bec of beyond, the home of Europe's largest lido has a plethora of Asian snack bars for post-pub munchies. Generally you're going to have to travel to work up that hunger though, maybe trot over the border to Balham. But for midweek (or for the lazy), try daiquiris at the Bec Bar, cocktails at Smoke, or top drawer curry at Mirch Masala.

151
152
Map 1

Banks

- **Barclays** • 29 Upper Tooting Rd

Coffee

- **Bertie and Boo** • 162 Balham High Rd
- **Caffe Moka** • 243 Balham High Rd

Nightlife

- **The Bec Bar** • 26 Tooting Bec Rd
- **King's Head** • 84 Upper Tooting Rd
- **Smoke Bar** • 14 Trinity Rd

Post Offices

- **Upper Tooting** • 63 Trinity Rd

Restaurants

- **Masaledar Kitchen** • 121 Upper Tooting Rd
- **Mirch Masala** • 213 Upper Tooting Rd

Shopping

- **Russell's Hardware & DIY** • 46 Upper Tooting Rd
- **Wandsworth Oasis HIV/AIDs Charity Shop** • 40 Trinity Rd

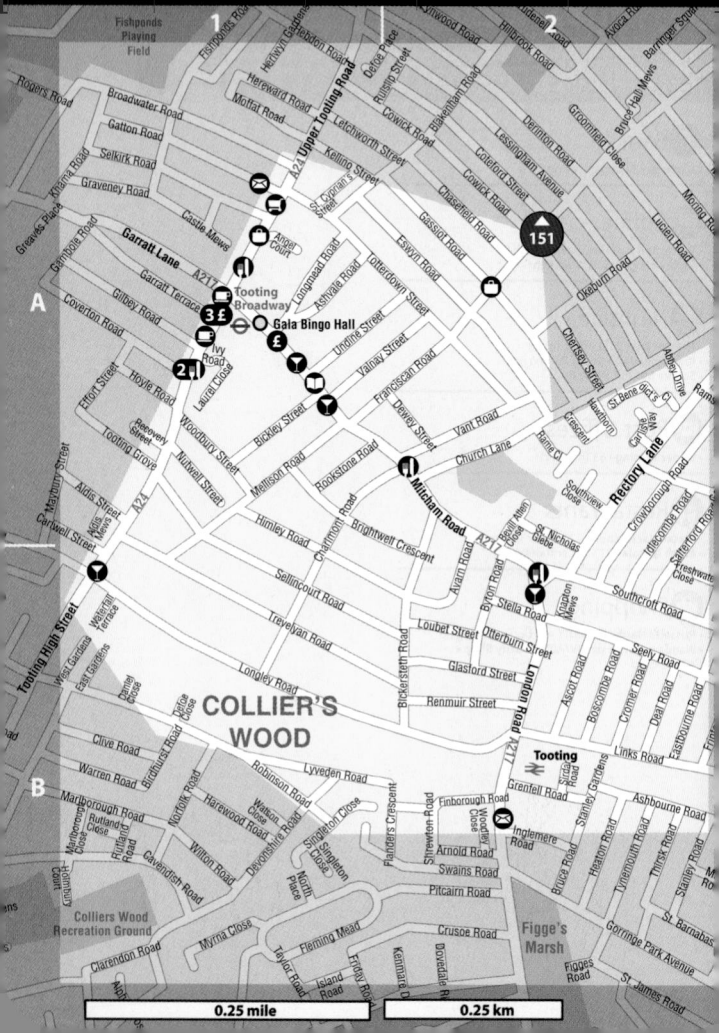
N
1
2
A
B
Fishponds Playing Field
Fishponds Road
Herbert Gardens
Hebden Road
Upper Tooting Road
Sylwood Road
Hillcrest Road
Rogers Road
Broadwater Road
Moffat Road
Hereward Road
Gatton Road
Selkirk Road
Graveney Road
Khartoum Road
Greaves Place
Garratt Lane
Garratt Terrace
Gilbey Road
Coverton Road
Effort Street
Hoyle Road
Tooting Grove
Reservoir Street
Aldis Street
Aldis Mews
Cardwell Street
Tooting High Street
West Gardens
East Gardens
Kelling Street
Cowick Road
Leicworth Street
Cowick Road
Lessingham Avenue
Colliford Street
Chasefield Road
Gassiot Road
Esryn Road
Tottenham Street
Ashvale Road
Longmaat Road
Undine Street
Valiant Street
Francoscan Road
Dewey Street
Yant Road
Church Lane
Harma Ct
Southview Close
Rectory Lane
Crowborough Road
Indesombe Road
Sutterford Road
Southcroft Road
Stella Road
Mitcham Mews
Byfort Road
Avarn Road
Mitcham Road
Brightwell Crescent
Charmouth Road
Rookstone Road
Mellison Road
Nutwell Street
Woodbury Street
Bixley Street
Himley Road
Sellincourt Road
Trevelyan Road
Longley Road
Clive Road
Brighurst Road
Warren Road
Marlborough Road
Norfolk Road
Harewood Road
Wilton Road
Devonshire Road
Cavendish Road
Rutland Close
Rutland Road
Colliers Wood Recreation Ground
Myrna Close
Clarendon Road
Fleming Mead
Taylor Road
Island Road
Friary Road
Broadlake Road
Figge's Marsh
Figges Road
St James Road
Gorringe Park Avenue
St Barnabas
Crusoe Road
Pitcairn Road
Swains Road
Arnold Road
Inglemere Road
Finborough Road
Grenfell Road
Stanley Gardens
Ashbourne Road
Links Road
Eastbourne Road
Deal Road
Cromer Road
Seely Road
Boscombe Road
Ascott Road
Stella Road
Otterburn Street
Loubet Street
Glasford Street
Renmuir Street
Bickerstem Road
London Road
Tooting
Stanley Road
Heaton Road
Tynemouth Road
Thirlex Road
Stanley Road
Bruce Road
Shrewton Road
Flanders Crescent
Singleton Close
Devonshire Road
Robinson Road
Lyveden Road
COLLIER'S WOOD
Tooting Broadway
Gala Bingo Hall
Ivy Road
Laurel Close
Angel Court
Cyprian Street
Castle Mews
Rectory Lane
Church Lane
Mitcham Road
Tooting
Okeburn Road
Chertsey Street
Hawthorn Crescent
Lucien Road
Moring Road
Groomfield Close
Bruce Hall Mews
Dermion Road
Fishponds Road
Hebden Road
Upper Tooting Road
Sylwood Road

Tooting Broadway

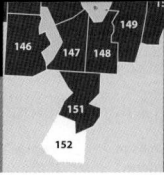

Decent rent, a Northern Line station, and a grade one listed bingo hall, there's not much here not to like. Hit the High Street for curries and halal everything, Mitcham Road should supply you with anything else required. Local eat treats include Radha Krishna Bhavan and Rick's Café, whereas Garden House and Tram & Social show that trendy pubs can survive this far south.

Banks

- **Abbey** • 266 Upper Tooting Rd
- **Barclays** • 14 Mitcham Rd
- **Halifax** • 50 Tooting High St
- **HSBC** • 56 Tooting Broadway

Coffee

- **Cafee Manal** • 984 Garratt Ln
- **Urban Coffee** • 74 Tooting High St

Landmarks

- **Gala Bingo Hall** • 50 Mitcham Road

Libraries

- **Tooting Library** • 75 Mitcham Rd

Nightlife

- **Garden House** • 196 Tooting High St
- **Jack Beard's** • 76 Mitcham Rd
- **The Ramble Inn** • Amen Corner
- **Tram & Social** • 46 Mitcham Rd

Post Offices

- **London Road** • 47 London Rd
- **Tooting** • 2 Gatton Rd

Restaurants

- **Jaffna House** • 90 Tooting High St
- **Kebab and Hamburger Bar** • 64 Tooting High St
- **Radha Krishna Bhavan** • 86 Tooting High St
- **Rick's Cafe** • 122 Mitcham Rd
- **Sette Bello** • 8 Amen Corner

Shopping

- **Tooting Market** • 21 Tooting High St

Supermarkets

- **Iceland** • 27 Tooting High St

General Information

Website: www.alexandrapalace.com
Phone: 020 8365 2121

Overview

If you fancy panoramic London views, exemplary Victorian architecture and an unrelenting stiff breeze to the face, the heights of Alexandra Park could be your cup of tea. With a fraction of the visitors of North London neighbours Hampstead Heath and Primrose Hill, Alexandra Park is nonetheless home to Ally Pally – Alexander Mackenzie's magnificent 1873 exhibition centre once renowned as the home of television after the BBC used it to broadcast the world's first high def transmissions in '36. It also boasts 196 acres of pristine, Green Flag-winning parkland, a two-hectare conservation area, and a fully functioning ice rink to boot.

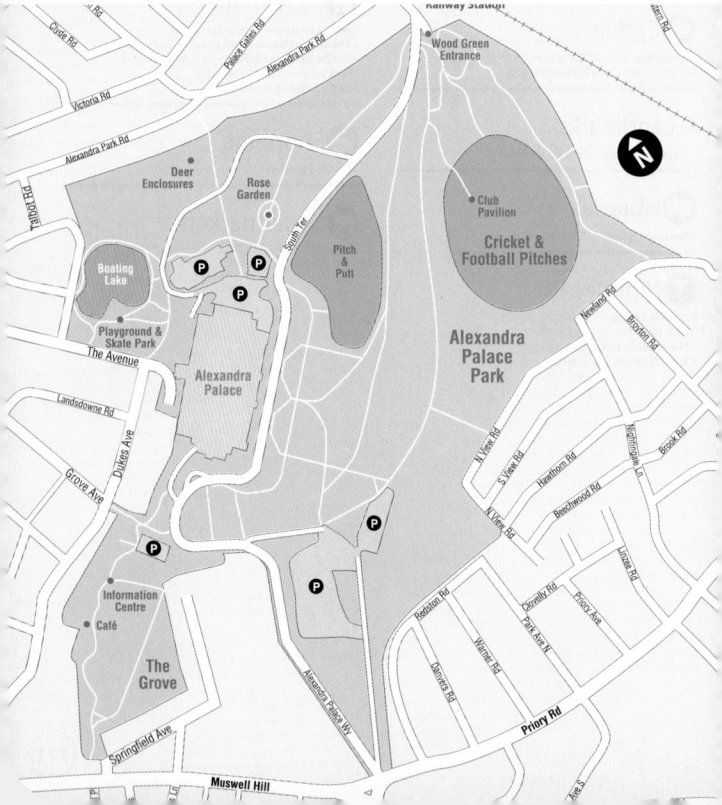

Practicalities

Alexandra Park is well served by public transport: Alexandra Palace railway station is a short ride from King's Cross and Moorgate and sits directly next to the park's Wood Green entrance. You can also take the underground to Wood Green, catch the W3 direct to Ally Pally from just outside. You could also take advantage of the 2000 free parking spaces in the park itself if driving, though it's only a short walk from Muswell Hill town centre.

Nature

No doubt tempted by the reservoirs, 155 species of birds have been spotted in the park over the last 30 years. Nature fetishists should take in the two-hectare conservation area, which includes a wide array of animals including deer, donkeys, foxes and rabbits. In 1998, there was even a rare water vole sighting. There he was, large as life, like he owned the bloody place.

Architecture

For most Alexandra Park visitors it's all about the Palace, these days a thriving hub for exhibitions, concerts, farmer's markets and, uh, world darts tournaments. The Palace building itself was ravaged by fire in the 80s and has since been restored to its former glory, though nearby banqueting venue Blandford Hall succumbed to the same fate in 1971 and was completely destroyed. No matter: Ally Pally remains an impressive, domineering building well worth a nose-around. For the less active, admiring the view from sedentary perspective from the underrated Phoenix Bar (located in the south wing) is just as good.

Open Spaces

It's safe to say that Alexandra Park has more than enough grass to keep Cheech & Chong happy, being typified by the diverse range of landscaped grounds that can be found within. The Grove Garden actually pre-dates the park itself and there's also a good little café here if you fancy a quick bite. The Rose Garden is to the east side of the Palace and is even more aesthetically pleasing. Many newer small woodlands have been developing over the last few decades owing to the planting of large numbers of trees, producing an environment pleasing to both the rambler and runner.

Performance

The park often plays host to funfairs and circuses, but the Palace itself will usually be used at night for concerts. Its revival over recent years as a gig venue has led to the likes of the Arctic Monkeys and Paul Weller playing there, with its capacity being around 8,500, making it ideal for bands who've outgrown the Brixton Academy. Other parts of the Palace, such as the Great Hall, are used for classical music recitals.

The Palace also houses a theatre, which was dormant for over sixty-five years until a performance took place in 2004. It is still being restored and should be re-opened to the public for performances in the near future.

Check out Ally Pally's informative website (listed above) for a full calendar of upcoming events.

Sports

An indoor ice rink is housed within the Palace with a capacity of 1,250, with all manner of ice sports catered for (you can get further information by ringing 020 8365 4386). There is also a large boating lake with its own islands and fishing area (and even a smaller area for kids to boat on their own), with pedalos and rowing boats available for hire; being a seasonal facility, it's best to ring the operators Bluebird Boats Ltd. (020 7262 1330) beforehand. The boating pond is adjacent to a children's playground as well. The popular nine hole pitch and putt golf course was reopened this year after an injection of Heritage Fund money, and price and booking info can be found at www.pitchnputt.co.uk or on 01245 257682. Alexandra Palace Park is also popular with cyclists, with the Parkland Walk a particular favourite, being a disused railway line that links up with Finsbury Park. In summertime the park is also a great place to get embroiled in countless spontaneous games of football and Frisbee, or to gawp/hurl insults at joggers.

General information

NFT Map: 7

Address: Barbican Centre, Silk St, London, EC2Y 8DS.

Phone: Box Office & Membership: 020 7638 8891 (9 am-8 pm daily); Switchboard: 020 7638 4141

Centre opening times:
Mon-Sat: 9 am-11 pm; Sun & Public Holidays: 12 pm-11 pm (although different parts of the centre may open at different times)

Website: www.barbican.org.uk

Overview

As terrifying as it is impressive, the Barbican Centre is a one-stop shop for all things cultural. At its best, the Barbican is utterly brilliant: a rambling collection of cinemas, galleries, bars, theatres, even a housing estate and a school. But stay after dark, when the culture vultures have left, and you can find yourself alone and lost in this city-within-a-city.

That the centre is brutally ugly makes what's inside even more splendid. The gallery space hosts world-class exhibitions and the cinemas show both mainstream and arthouse films. There's a world, classical and jazz music programme catering for everyone from scruffy backpackers to bearded professors. Most are sensible enough to leave before it gets too spooky. But plan your exit route in advance just in case.

Music

The heart of the Barbican monster is its music hall. Its near-2,000 capacity has become a mecca for lovers of cerebral music, hosting major festivals in the thinking genres. Each summer the Barbican holds the Mostly Mozart festival, a celebration of the composer that reaches sci-fi convention levels of fanaticism. In 2006, 250

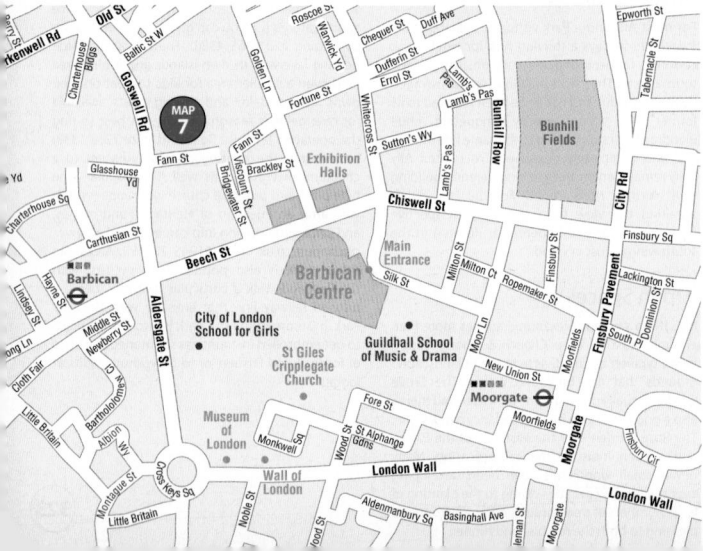

years since he was born, the festival claimed to be the biggest birthday bash held for him in the capital. The music centre's resident band is the London Symphony Orchestra, classical heavyweights who play year-round. Come winter, though, and it's elbow patches that take centre stage as the Barbican hosts the London Jazz Festival. But it's not all polite serenity in the hall—the world music programme delves into the lairiest parts of Africa and Latin America for its own noisy festival.

Film

In keeping with its creed as a cultural hotspot, the Barbican's film programme is suitably arty. The three-screen cinema is home to two permanent showcases—the London Australian and London Children's film festivals—and the centre curates its own programmes. The listings constantly change, but you can generally stick to the following rule: silent films, in; Sly Stallone, out; subtitles, in; J Lo, out; indy award-winners, in; the Mighty Ducks trilogy, out. But they do offer the screens for private hire—so, if you really want to, you can stick it to 'em and have your own showing of Snakes on a Plane.

Theatre and Dance

Don't be fooled by the Barbican's hulking exterior—the centre dabbles in the more delicate arts rather well. Its two theatres cater for both ends of the performance spectrum. The main room, a shared home for acting and dance, seats over 1,000 punters and attracts some of the biggest names in high culture. Deep in the Barbican's bowels the smaller Pit theatre is home to experimental and new acts. But be warned: with just 200 seats the Pit is small enough for anyone dozing off to be highly visible.

Art

Nowhere else at the Barbican is the idea of making culture accessible for all more apparent than their art spaces. The main gallery hosts temporary exhibitions, mixing all types of art into one cultural hot pot. In 2007, under the umbrella of Art and Sex from Antiquity to Now, erotic Roman cutlery—that's right: erotic cutlery—shared a stage with impressionist paintings and an 11-minute film of someone's face as she was, ahem, attended to. Every first Thursday of the month the gallery opens for a nocturnal viewing, with talks, performances—burlesque dancers for the art and sex exhibition—and a themed bar. A second space, The Curve, winds its way round the ground floor where the exhibitions are generally free.

The Library

Libraries often get a bad press. They've got stuck with an image of frumpy, middle-aged women peering down their spectacles and telling youths to be quiet. But this couldn't be further removed from the reality of the Barbican Library. Alongside a decent array of books, there's a dazzling collection of live musical recordings. Some of these tracks are so rare that they can't be heard anywhere else in the world. Put some headphones on and rock out. Just don't get carried away and smash up the children's section.

How To Get There

By car: Parking is pricey with two hours costing £5 and each hour thereafter costing two or three quid more, though there's a flat weekend and evening (post-5.30 pm) fee of just a fiver.

By bus: The 153 (which runs from Liverpool Street to Finsbury Park) stops directly outside the Barbican at Silk Street; the following buses run nearby: 8, 11, 23, 26, 35, 42, 43, 47, 48, 55, 56, 76, 78, 100, 133, 141, 149, 172, 214, 242, 243, 271, 344 (seven days a week); 4, (Mon-Sat); 21, 25, 521 (Mon-Fri). If none of these buses can take you home then consider yourself extremely unlucky.

By tube: Barbican stations runs on the Circle, District and Hammersmith & City lines. Other stations nearby are Moorgate, St Paul's, Bank, Liverpool Street and Mansion House.

By train: The nearest overland stations are Liverpool Street, Farringdon and Blackfriars. City Thameslink services run through Barbican, Moorgate and Cannon Street.

Practical Information

NFT Map: 132, 133, & 141

Official opening time is 8 am, although the gates are usually unlocked a little earlier than this. The park closes at dusk.

Friends of Battersea Park:
www.batterseapark.org

Zoo: www.batterseaparkzoo.co.uk

Local council: www.wandsworth.gov.uk (see also for information on the Pump House Gallery)

Cycle hire:
www.londonrecumbents.co.uk

Blue bird boat hire:
www.wandsworth.gov.uk

Overview

Opened in 1858 with the aim of giving the Victorian working classes something to do other than drinking gin, Battersea Park has developed to become one of London's prettiest, most popular and most usable parks. Squeezing a range of gardens, cafes, animals, walks, sports and cultural facilities into its diminutive 200 acres, the park is popular with everyone from hordes of snotty little kids to wandering dog-walkers. It is also centrally located enough to be easy to get to but still far enough from Central London to retain a local feel.

The park is about two miles southwest from Westminster and occupies the spot on the south bank of the Thames between Albert and Chelsea bridges. Originally used for duelling, the Duke of Wellington famously discharged upon the Earl of Winchelsea on the site in 1829. Rather than the vast open and flat spaces that many London parks offer, Battersea is neatly divided into a number of features and sections, making it feel much larger than it is.

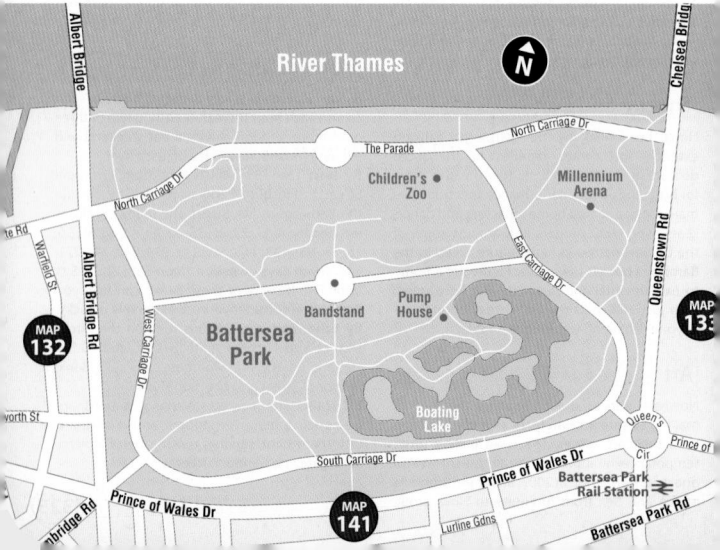

Sporting Activities

Battersea has an incredibly good array of sporting facilities. The 'Millennium Arena' is a 400m 8-lane running track situated in the northeast corner of the park; it hosts athletic meets and training sessions and it benefited from an expensive overhaul in, you guessed it, 1999. Next to the arena are ten tennis courts and an all-weather football pitch whilst there are further all-weather astro-turf pitches in the south east corner of the park marked for both hockey and football. The park also boasts cricket pitches and practice nets, a bowling green, a number of routes for jogging and enough spare open spaces to invite impromptu sessions of pretty much any other sport. If you consider attacking fish a sport, and have a permit and rod licence, the park's lake offers fishing for nine months of the year. Rowing boats and pedaloes can also be taken out on to the lake during July and August (adults £4.50/hour, children £2.50). Bicycles can be hired from the London Recumbents shop, which is next to the Millennium Arena on the park's East Carriage Drive.

Art

Battersea has fostered a creative relationship with the arts and has a number of sculptures dotted about, its own public gallery and a biannual art fair. Taking pride of place next to the lake are two large Henry Moore and Barbara Hepworth sculptures, both of which are well worth rooting out. The Pumphouse Gallery is a grade II-listed building, originally used to power the park's water works, which has been restored and converted into a gallery and information centre with six exhibitions throughout the year. The Gallery, located northeast of the lake, is also available for private hire and even has a licence to hold civil weddings. The park has hosted the Affordable Art Fair since 1999, which has become a leading showcase for art priced under £3,000.

Performance

In summer music aficionados should head down to La Gondola al Parco, the café by the lake, for free live concerts every Tuesday and Friday from 7 pm. Entrance is free and there's also a BBQ and refreshments aplenty.

Nature and Children's Zoo

Battersea's varied landscapes ensure you stand a decent chance of seeing more than a rat or a pigeon while you saunter round. Squirrels, ducks and Canada geese are all too plentiful. More interesting potential sightings include woodpeckers, cormorants, Peregrine falcons, terrapins and, according to the RSPB, Pochards (whatever they are). If you don't come across any interesting wildlife, your only option is to cheat and visit the park's zoo. A five-minute stroll from the Chelsea Gate entrance, the zoo is aimed at children and has a cool collection of small mammals, including lemurs, as well as small farm animals and some excitingly named birds, such as some 'Peach-faced Love birds'. In case you do fall in love with any of the zoo's inhabitants, most are available for adoption. Mice start at £10 for six months, pay-up and claim it's for your kid. The zoo is open throughout the year.

How To Get There

By tube: Sloane Square (on the Circle and District lines) is the nearest Underground station at just under a mile away. From the station walk down Lower Sloane Street, which becomes Chelsea Bridge Road and leads to the Thames. Walk over Chelsea Bridge and you will see the park on your right. Alternatively take bus no 319.

By bus: From central London, buses run to the park from Liverpool Street (number 344), Notting Hill (452), Oxford Circus (137), Sloane Square (319, 137), Victoria Station (44) and Vauxhall (344).

By train: Battersea Park station is within sight of the park, trains run to both Clapham Junction and Victoria at high frequency. Queenstown Road is around 300m from the park. Trains from this station run to Waterloo and Clapham Junction and depart less often than from Battersea Park.

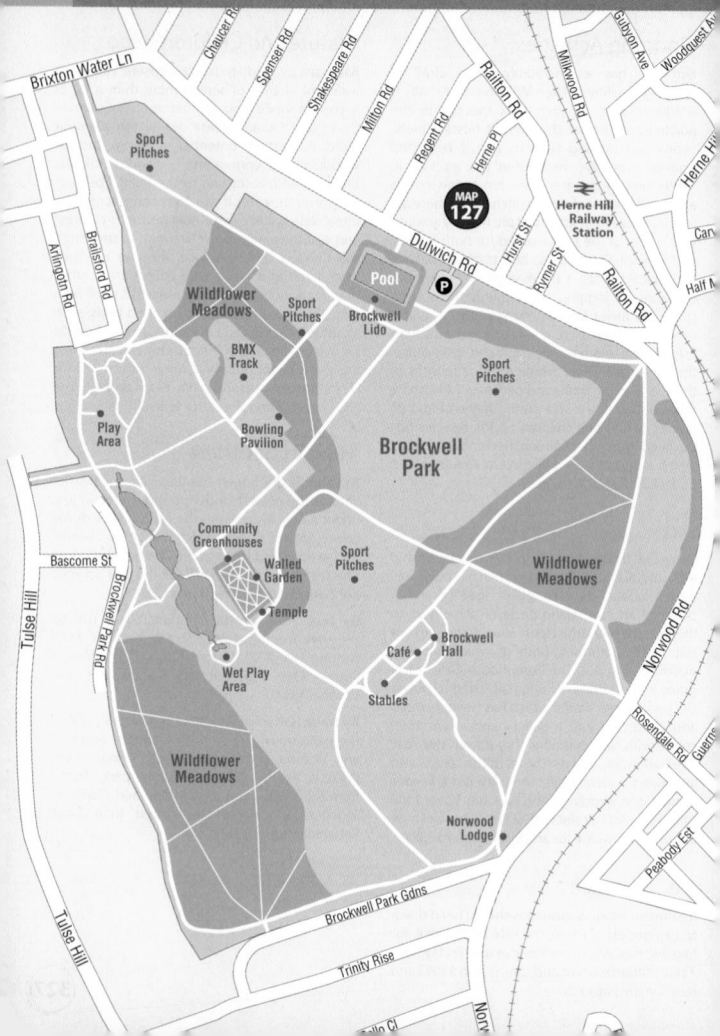
Brixton Water Ln
Chaucer Rd
Spenser Rd
Shakespeare Rd
Milton Rd
Regent Rd
Herne Pl
Railton Rd
Milkwood Rd
Gubyon Ave
Woodquest Av
Herne Hill
Sport Pitches
MAP 127
Herne Hill Railway Station
Dulwich Rd
Hurst St
Rymer St
Railton Rd
Half M
Carn
Pool
P
Wildflower Meadows
Sport Pitches
Brockwell Lido
BMX Track
Sport Pitches
Play Area
Bowling Pavilion
Brockwell Park
Community Greenhouses
Walled Garden
Sport Pitches
Wildflower Meadows
Temple
Brockwell Hall
Café
Wet Play Area
Stables
Norwood Rd
Rosendale Rd
Guerns
Wildflower Meadows
Norwood Lodge
Peabody Est
Brockwell Park Gdns
Trinity Rise
Tulse Hill
Tulse Hill
Brockwell Park Rd
Bascome St
Allingon Rd
Brailsford Rd

General Information

NFT Map: 127
Brockwell Park: www.brockwellpark.com
Brockwell Park Lido: www.brockwelllido.com
020 7274 3088

Overview

Brockwell Park may not be a household name when it comes to London Parks but for many South Londoners – not least residents of neighbouring Herne Hill – it's the pick of the bunch, all the lovelier for its unconventionality, tattiness and relative anonymity. It's eclectic, it's quirky, and it's impossible not to fall in love with.

History

By the end of the 19th century the local population was large, growing and in need of a serious park. Brockwell was secured for use by the public after MP Thomas Bristowe got wind of a private country estate that seemed just the ticket. Still, he might have over-exerted himself in the process: having taken a Bill through Parliament to convert the land, led a committee to negotiate the price, and raised funds from across the community, Bristowe himself promptly collapsed and died on the steps of Brockwell Hall, moments after the opening ceremony in 1892.

Café

If that doesn't put you off your scones, nowadays, the ground floor of Brockwell Hall is a café where refreshments have been served ever since. Located at the top of the hill, it's a great place to stop for inexpensive cake, drinks etc. after some…

Activities!

There's heaps to do. A BMX track, tennis courts, bowling green, football and cricket pitches, basketball courts, outdoor theatre club, a children's play area and a paddling pool. Or you could chill by the ponds, in the walled garden, under the clock tower, at the picnic area, near the flower gardens, etc.

Brockwell Lido and Greenhouses

Built in 1937, Brockwell Lido is essentially an (unattractive) art deco building that replaced an old bathing pond. After experiencing financial difficulty it was restored and reopened in 2007. As well as a large outdoor pool, there is a gym and classes are held in yoga, pilates, tai-chi and meditation. For the under 5s, Whippersnappers have everything from acrobatics to puppets and African drumming. A Miniature Railway runs between Herne Hill Gate and the Lido. Run by a local enthusiast on a not-for-profit basis; it's only £1 for a round trip. May–Sept, Sat–Sun, 11am–5pm.

Brockwell also boasts a superb community greenhouse project open to volunteers. The greenhouses are open Sundays 1 pm – 5 pm and give Londoners a rare chance to get green fingers and grow their own produce. Contact the greenhouse secretary on bpcgsecretary@gmail.com to get involved.

Annual Events

July: Lambeth Country Show in is always good fun and involves medieval jousting, farm animals, live reggae/dub and rides, and there are homemade cake and jam contests too. The Alternative Vegetable Animal Competition requires fruit and veg be crafted into a famous person or building with a very entertaining adult category.
September: The first Urban Green Fair was held in 2007.
November: The big fireworks show on Guy Fawkes Night is worth braving the cold for.

How to Get There

By rail/tube/foot: The park is a short walk from the following overland and underground stations:

Herne Hill Rail Station—5 mins
Tulse Hill Rail Station —15 mins
Brixton Tube —20 mins
Clapham North Tube —30 mins

By bus: The following all stop at Brockwell Park—2, 3, 37, 68, 196, 322, 468, P15

Parks & Places • **Clapham Common**

Overview

Lively and happening; youngish, professional, and trendy (in a safe way). Clapham Common reflects the area well.

Popular all year round, the Common truly comes alive in summer. On a warm weekend you'll find the park overflowing with picnickers sipping champagne and just plain lookin' good. It's a lovely scene made better by the relaxed, friendly atmosphere. And, when the sun finally sets, you're left with a seriously impressive choice of bars close by.

As well as drawing the usual funky sophisticates, the park is also family-friendly with lots of little ones enjoying the space.

Plenty of organised (or not) sport, kite flying, model boating, Ultimate Frisbee, and even fishing happens here too, but while the common is safe as houses during the day, at night-time its leafier enclaves are worth avoiding unless you're particularly keen on paying for a game of grown-up hide the sausage with other gentlemen.

History

Clapham began as a Saxon village. Back then it was called Clopp Ham, meaning the village (ham) by the short hill (clopp). The common was used by villagers to graze their livestock and as a source of firewood.

In the late 17th century the population began to grow as refugees arrived from the Great Plague of London (1665) and the fire of 1666. During this time, the rich gentry of London built a number of fine country houses around the common. When the railways were developed there was a sudden influx of commuters, driving the upper class away to somewhere less, um, common.

Today, the surrounding area is one of the more expensive in South London, partly because of its excellent transport links.

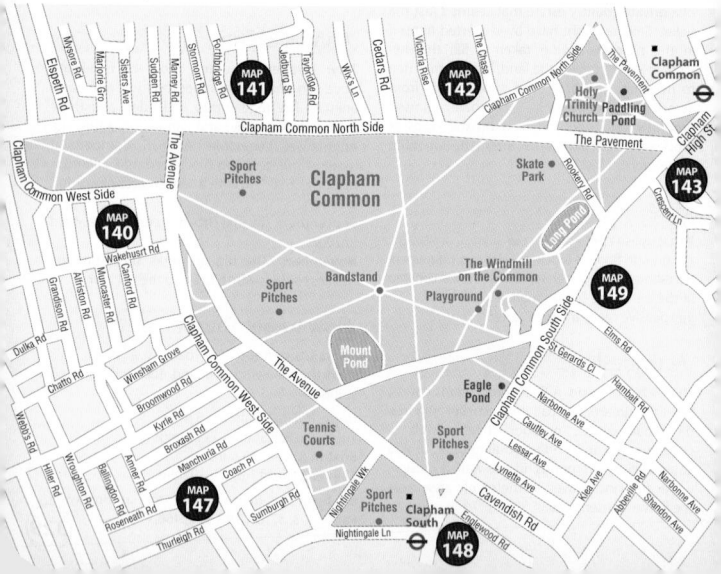

Clapham Sect

On the common is the Holy Trinity Church. This was a meeting place of the Clapham Sect, a group of 19th-century Evangelical Anglicans who fought for social reform. "Ugh" you say, but wait…

The Clapham Sect played a significant part in the abolition of slavery in England. They didn't stop there, going on to campaign for the eradication of slavery worldwide. They also fought for reform in the penal system, focusing on unjust sentencing and the dire prison conditions of the time.

Eateries

Cicero's on the Common (vegetarian)
2 Rookery Road, SW49QN, 020 7498 0770

Cafe Des Res (English/ Carribean)
8 The Pavement, SW4 0HY, 020 7622 6602

The Bowling Green Café (sandwiches, pasta etc)
Clapham Common West Side, SW4 9AN, 020 7801 0904

Three ponds

Mount Pond – is a fishing park pond about three acres in size. It contains carp, roach, gudgeon and eels. Suggested baits include pellet, maggot, meat, and boilies, it says here.

Eagle Pond – is a smaller pond with a little island. This one is also fishable. Stocks include carp, tench, bream, roach, rudd, perch, chub and gudgeon. Best baits are bread, pellet, maggot, hemp and castor, it goes without saying.

Long Pond – has a century-old tradition of use for model boating.

Activities

These days there are still some nice leafy pathways lined by mature trees left for the strollers to enjoy.

Sporty types can go for the football, rugby, cricket, softball, tennis, basketball, Aussie rules football, croquet (!) or bowling.

Events

Some of the annual highlights include:

May: A Country Affair—is kinda interesting. There are rides, bands, Morris dancing and lots of cleaner than usual farm animals.

June/July: The Sprite Urban Games—Showcases pro skateboarding, BMXing and breaking, with (mostly hip hop) DJs providing the beats.

July: Ben 'n Jerry's Sundae On The Common—also goes down well. If it sounds horribly corporate, it's worth noting that a full restoration of the bandstand in '05/'06 was partly funded by proceeds from this festival. Or, just think of the free ice-cream…

August: The Clapham Common Metro Weekender—Two successful, quality festivals have joined forces. South West Four (progressive house, trance, and breaks) and Get Loaded In the Park (indie/dance) now happen side by side at the end of August.

November: The Bonfire Night Fireworks—it's as good as it gets here.

How to Get There

By train: Wandsworth Road Station (12 minutes), Clapham High Street Station (12 minutes)

By tube: Clapham Common (4 minutes), Clapham South (13 minutes)

By bus: 4, 35, 37, 88, 137, 155, 255, 345, 355, 417, G1

Overview

A lot is packed into this 54-acre park—mostly people. On a sunny day Clissold throngs with Stokenewingtonites; yummy mummies and three wheeled buggies; gaggles of youths, with or without hoods; lads playing football; and assorted dog walkers. Visitors can see deer and goats in the animal enclosure, diamond doves and love birds in the aviary, and coots and moorhens in the nature ponds. Parents take little ones to the paddling pool (summer months only), toddlers group at the One O'clock Club or the well-equipped children's playground. The park hosts the usual hodgepodge of circuses and steam fairs as well as the famous arts festival, StokeFest, in the summer. On grey days, chilly days, or in the early hours, peace can be found - in the rose garden perhaps, or underneath one of the ancient trees.

Clissold Park Café

Phone:	0207 923 9797
Email:	info@clissoldparkcafe.com
Website:	www.clissoldparkcafe.com
Hours:	9 am–5.30 pm (winter) 7.30 pm (summer)
Admission:	FREE

Clissold Mansion, the Grade II listed building just visible from Stoke Newington Church Street, is home to a large, child friendly cafe (that is, the cafe is large and child friendly, not friendly only to the larger child). Herbal tea drinkers jostle with dripping ice-cream cone lickers on the sun trap front veranda and circular lawn. The large inside rooms are best avoided if you find children's chatter grating, but otherwise a lively spot to tuck into a plate of egg and chips. The building was constructed in the late 18th century on behalf of a Quaker family whose daughter was courted by a local reverend—Augustus Clissold. He wooed, then married her, and swiftly changed the name

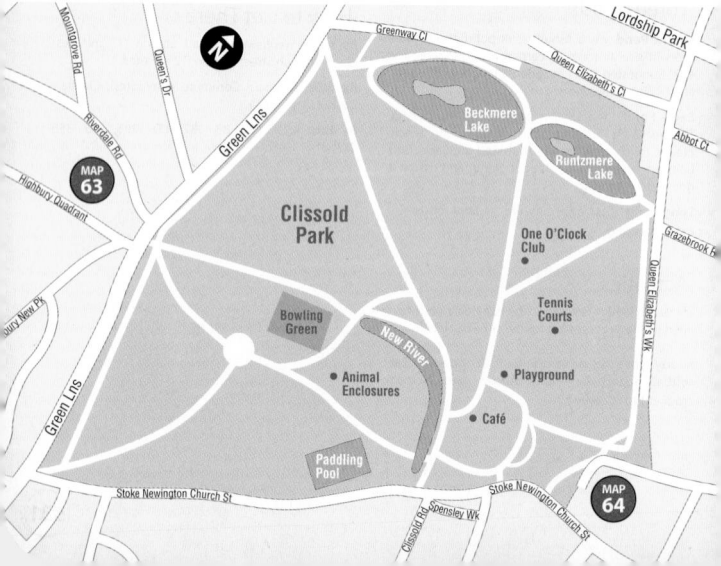

of the estate to Clissold Place. Where is Catherine Cookson when you need her? A hundred years later when the land was up for redevelopment, two influential campaigners persuaded the Metropolitan Board of Works to create a public space, and Clissold Park was born on 24 July 1889. Now run by the London Borough of Hackney, Clissold is kept in check by the Clissold Park User Group, who recently secured a multi-million pound lottery bid to spruce the place up a bit and return it to its former 19th century splendour.

Sport in the Park

Year round you can hear the yells of football players churning up mud, the whine of iPods as joggers run in ever decreasing circles, the thwack of cricket ball against cricket bat, and the crunch of misthrown Frisbees hitting the litter bins. There is a basketball court and 10 tennis courts (two kiddies' sized) which are bookable by contacting the Park rangers (020 7254 4235) though they are impossible to get your hands on around Wimbledon—and they say TV doesn't affect our behaviour.

But one of the delights of this park is the more unusual sport that takes place. On misty mornings you can watch cotton-clad figures practice tai chi, and on warm weekends you can nearly always spot a group of hotties from the London School of Capoeira circling around each other. Then there is the occasional father/ daughter pair practising Taekwondo, or two dreadlocked crusties slinging up a line to get some tightrope practice in. Most recent addition to watchable sports in the park is run by 'Pushy Mothers' - groups of mums exercising with buggies. The buggy, with child on board, is pushed hither and thither by the panting parent. It's the ultimate in resistance training.

Nature and The Ponds

Hackney is one of the greenest inner-city boroughs and though relatively small, Clissold Park is still an important green, shady and watery spot for local wildlife, particularly waterfowl. The two nature ponds are named Beckmere and the Runtzmere in honour of the two principal founders (Beck and Runtz, in case you were wondering). The third pond in front of the cafe is more of a 'canalette' and actually used to be part of the New River built in the early 1600s to supply drinking water to London.

The animal enclosure with its fuzzy-nosed deer, fluffy rabbits and bearded mini-goats are popular with visitors who stand stuffing chips and handfuls of poisonous leaves from nearby bushes through the fence directly under the signs saying: 'Please don't feed the animals—it will make them ill.'

Note: the paddling pool is not a nature pond and though you still can't let your dog in, hours spent gazing at its inhabitants are not looked on kindly.

How to Get There

By car: Don't. There isn't much in the way of parking. But if you really need to, from Newington Green head north along Green Lanes until you see a large green space with trees on your right. Or from the A10 turn left onto Stoke Newington Church St past all the cute shops and inviting pubs, until you get to the large church on your left. The park is on your right.

By tube: From Manor House, take exit 4 and walk south down Green Lanes for 10 minutes. The park is on your left.

By train: From Stoke Newington station, head south down the High St and turn right up Stoke Newington Church St, walk for 10 minutes until you see the park on your left just past Stoke Newington Town Hall.

By bus: The 341, 141, 73, 393, and 476 all stop at various entrances to the park

Additional Information

London Borough of Hackney
www.hackney.gov.uk/cp-community-park.htm

Clissold Park User Group
www.clissoldpark.com

Stokefest
www.stokefest.co.uk

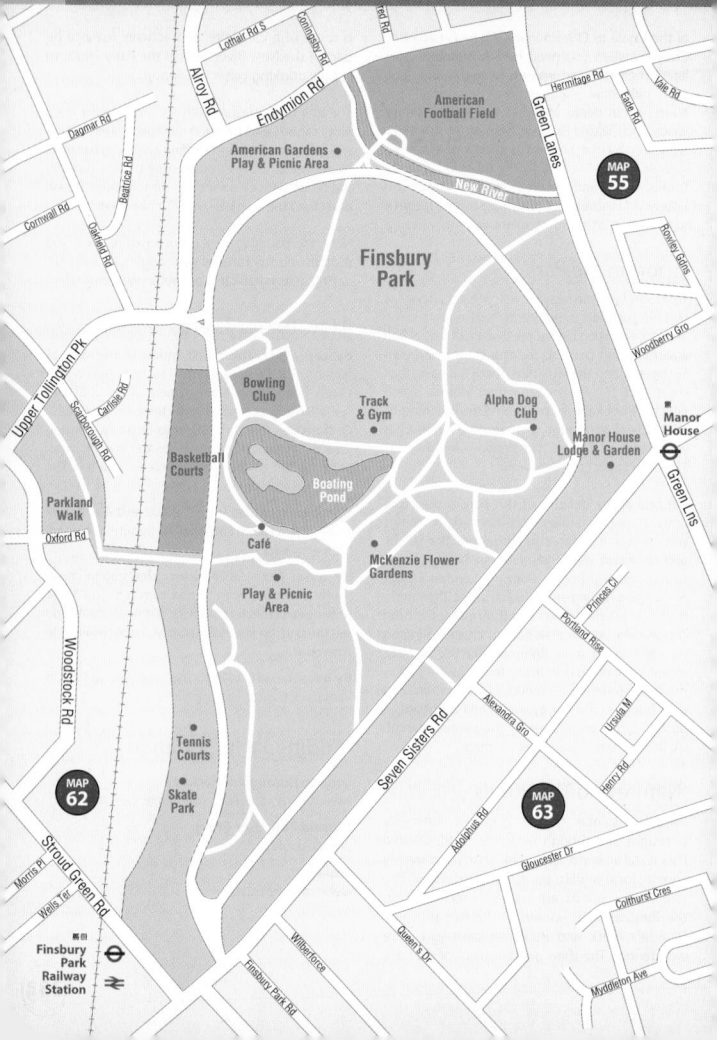
Lothair Rd S
Connaught Rd
Tiel Rd
Alroy Rd
Endymion Rd
American Football Field
Hermitage Rd
Vale Rd
Estcourt Rd
Green Lanes
MAP 55
American Gardens Play & Picnic Area
New River
Tagmar Rd
Beatrice Rd
Cornwall Rd
Oakland Rd
Finsbury Park
Rowley Gdns
Woodberry Grv
Upper Tollington Pk
Carlisle Rd
Scrutton Rd
Bowling Club
Track & Gym
Alpha Dog Club
Manor House
Manor House Lodge & Garden
Basketball Courts
Boating Pond
Green Lns
Parkland Walk
Oxford Rd
Café
McKenzie Flower Gardens
Play & Picnic Area
Princes Cl
Portland Rise
Woodstock Rd
Alexandra Grv
Ursula M
Tennis Courts
Skate Park
Seven Sisters Rd
Henry Rd
MAP 62
MAP 63
Adolphus Rd
Gloucester Dr
Stroud Green Rd
Morris Pl
Wells Ter
Colthurst Cres
Finsbury Park Railway Station
Queen's Dr
Wilberforce
Finsbury Park Rd
Middleton Ave

General Information

NFT Map: 55, 62, & 63
Website: www.haringey.gov.uk/finsbury_park_leaflet.pdf

Overview

Sculpted from what was once a large woodland area on the fringes of London, Finsbury Park was baptized officially in the mid 19th Century as a green escape for increasingly urbanized North Londoners. Today's Finsbury Park has been revamped to the tune of £5 million in an attempt to shake off the cloak of urban grime which descended during the 1970s. Though it certainly has cleaned up its act, the park is still a barren tundra-esque plain compared to Hyde or Regent's Park. More of a green scab on the city landscape that surrounds it, the sparse shrubbery and token trees are more suitable for football or running away from Staffordshire Terriers. Delve a little deeper, however and there are quaint eccentricities and little gems dotted around.

Practicalities

You can enter this veritable urban Oz at Endymion Road, Seven Sisters Road, Green Lanes and Stroud Green Road. Two tube stops serve Finsbury Park: Manor House and the eponymous Finsbury Park. There are also overland trains at Harringey Green Lanes (grab an opulent Turkish meal on the way) and at Finsbury Park Stroud Green Road. Buses 4, 19, N19, 29, N29, 106, N106, 253, N253, 254, N279, W3 and W7 all touch the park at some point. Bear in mind that if you wish to travel in the area during an Arsenal match day you'd better take a stun gun and a red scarf to navigate the crowds!

Attractions

Quaint Englishness and sweaty sporting pursuits abound within the perimeters of Finsbury Park. There are many activities you can partake in from tennis (seven courts are available on a turn up and play basis) to running in the Heathside Athletics Club (020 8802 9139). There are even two American Football pitches. For a more twee time stroll up to the tiny boating pond and spend an hour in a beat-up boat circling the aviary island—home to exotic birds like ducks, some swans and, uh, ducks again. The kidz are catered for in the form of a skate park. Best of all is the amazing Parkland Walk, which snakes out from Finsbury Park to Alexandra Palace via Highgate.

Nature

The Arboretum and the Avenue of Mature Trees are the two main spots for tree watching. Granted, experienced botanists may find little to fire them up here, but on a mild Autumn day there are plenty of rich colours and textures that enrich any stroll through the park. There are no real 'wild' areas in the park, unlike Hampstead Heath, but there are some lovely quiet spots in the American Gardens which have been landscaped according to the original 19th century plans, with added kiddie play areas. There are some shrubs planted around the boating pond which Harringey Council calls the 'McKenzie Flower Garden' with capital letters which are barely merited.

Festivals

Recently the vast open spaces of the park have been used for music festivals and various other fairs. The Rise, Fleadh, and FinFest festivals are all fairly regular events. The park is also a popular venue for one off special music events—both the Sex Pistols and Morrissey have played controversial shows here. The steam and fun fairs are also worth going to for nostalgic or regressive fun.

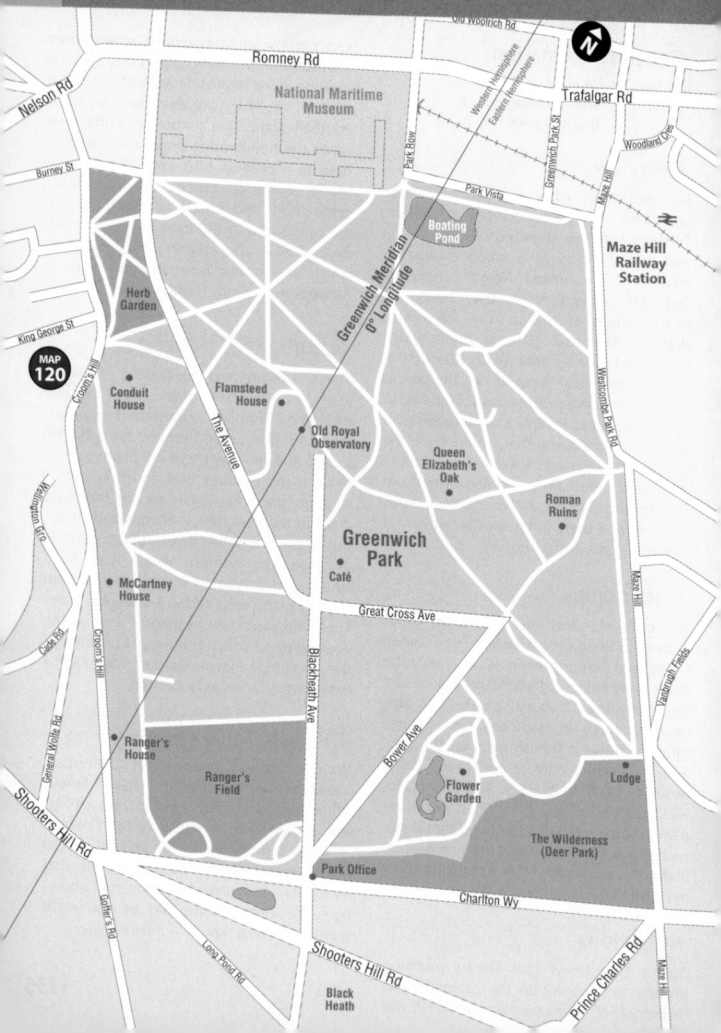
Old Woolwich Rd
Romney Rd
Nelson Rd
National Maritime Museum
Western Hemisphere
Eastern Hemisphere
Trafalgar Rd
Park Row
Greenwich Park St
Woodland Drive
Burney St
Park Vista
Maze Hill
Boating Pond
Maze Hill Railway Station
Greenwich Meridian
0° Longitude
Herb Garden
King George St
MAP 120
Crooms Hill
Conduit House
Flamsteed House
The Avenue
Old Royal Observatory
Westcombe Park Rd
Queen Elizabeth's Oak
Roman Ruins
Old Woolwich Rd
Greenwich Park
Café
McCartney House
Great Cross Ave
Maze Hill
Cade Rd
Crooms Hill
Blackheath Ave
Vanbrugh Fields
General Wolfe Rd
Ranger's House
Ranger's Field
Bower Ave
Flower Garden
Lodge
Shooters Hill Rd
The Wilderness (Deer Park)
Park Office
Charlton Wy
Golfers Rd
Long Pond Rd
Shooters Hill Rd
Prince Charles Rd
Maze Hill
Black Heath

Overview

Greenwich Park is the oldest enclosed Royal Park in Britain and has been an integral part of London life for centuries. Saxons built mounds here; Romans worshipped here; King Henry VIII and Anne Boleyn flirted here, and Charles II even built an observatory here. It's now a playground for ageing eccentrics escaping London, yuppie families with new puppies, and heaps of tourists trekking up the staggeringly steep hill towards the iconic Royal Observatory.

And it's worth the trek. The sweeping views from the highest point are spectacular and beat the London Eye hands down. London is revealed in all its glory, from the jutting skyline of Canary Wharf, to the sinuous turns of the Thames and the seemed-like-a-good-idea-at-the-time Millennium Dome. All in stark contrast with the neoclassical architecture of the Old Royal Observatory, Royal Naval College, National Maritime Museum and the Queen's House in the immediate foreground.

A well sought-after spot throughout history, the park has belonged to the Royal Family since 1427, and in the early 1600s, under James I, the park was given a makeover in the French style, which gave it its well-groomed tree-lined pathways. He then had Inigo Jones build the missus the stately Queen's House.

The Royal Observatory and Flamsteed House

Address: Greenwich Royal Park, Greenwich, London SE10
Phone: 020 8858 4422
Website: www.nmm.ac.uk
Hours: 10 am-5 pm daily
Admission: Free

Time begins, rather arbitrarily, here—on the Prime Meridian of the World, or Longitude 0°. Time all over the earth is based on a place's distance east or west from this imaginary line, outlined in metal so throngs of tourists can gawp at it. Thanks to Charles II's interest in science, Sir Christopher Wren was commissioned to build the Royal Observatory and Flamsteed House, the living quarters for the first Royal Astronomer. It is the imaginary axis of the Meridian, which runs through Greenwich Park from the Royal Observatory, which gives this World Heritage site its fame.

Also notable is the Camera Obscura, which sits in a small building next to Flamsteed House. A predecessor to the modern camera, this small dark room displays a live image of the distant National Maritime Museum, projected using only a small hole in the roof.

National Maritime Museum

Address: Greenwich, London SE10 9NF
Phone: 020 8858 4422
Website: www.nmm.ac.uk
Hours: 10 am-5 pm daily
Admission: Free

Adjacent to the park's boundaries, this is a museum dedicated to all things nautical. It comprises the Royal Observatory, as well as the Queen's House, but its main components are the Maritime Galleries. Highlights include a collection of ships' figureheads, navigational charts, maps, medals, flags and models. They also host relics from Sir John Franklin's ill-fated Northwest Passage expedition (1845-1848) including a pair of his very old-school sunglasses.

Nature

Amongst the well-mowed green are trees of infinite varieties. The scented herb garden is best enjoyed in the summer time. The fallen remains of the 900 year-old Queen Elizabeth Oak can still be viewed and lie as proof of Henry VIII's passion for these grounds, he was said to have danced around the younger tree with Anne Boleyn (before he had her executed, obviously).

How to Get There

You can also take the Greenwich foot tunnel – actually beneath the Thames itself - from the Isle of Dogs, but contrary to received schoolboy wisdom, it is neither clever nor funny to go for a widdle along the way. It's fun too. You can sit in the front and pretend to be the driver. The nearest DLR station is Cutty Sark. By bus, take the 199 or 188 bus. From North Greenwich Station take the 188 or 129. You can also take the Greenwich Foot Tunnel (very cool and quite short, actually) from the Isle of Dogs.

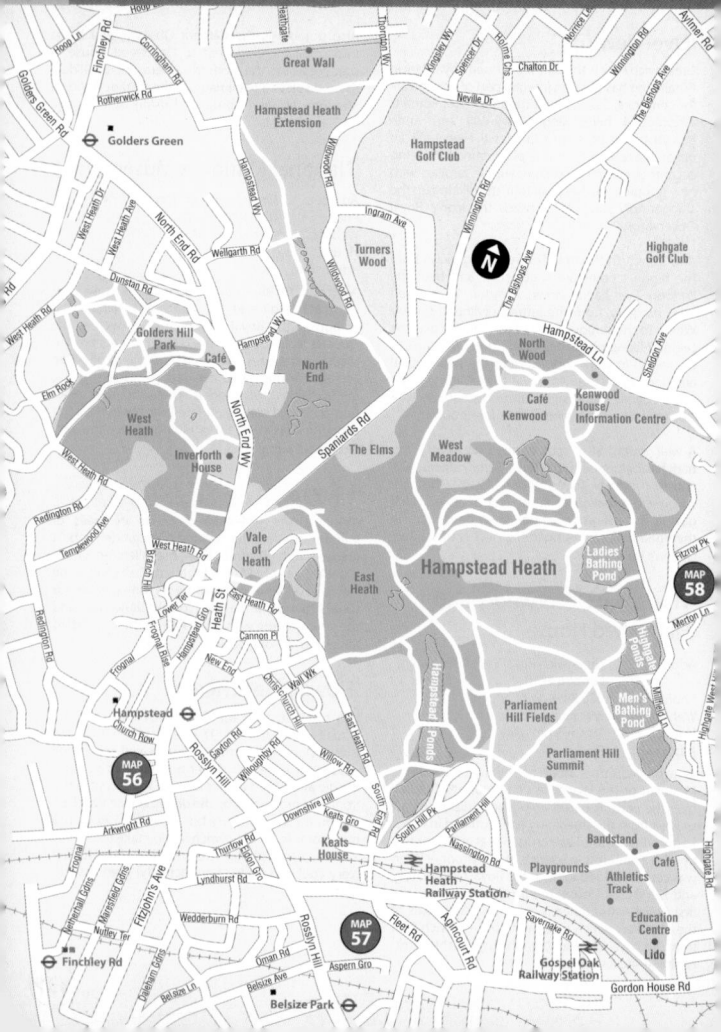
Great Wall
Hampstead Heath Extension
Golders Green
Hampstead Golf Club
Turners Wood
Highgate Golf Club
Golders Hill Park
Café
North End
North Wood
Café Kenwood
Kenwood House/ Information Centre
West Heath
Inverforth House
The Elms
West Meadow
Vale of Heath
East Heath
Hampstead Heath
Ladies' Bathing Pond
MAP 58
Highgate Ponds
Hampstead Ponds
Men's Bathing Pond
Parliament Hill Fields
Parliament Hill Summit
Hampstead
MAP 56
Keats House
Hampstead Heath Railway Station
Bandstand
Café
Playgrounds
Athletics Track
Education Centre
Lido
MAP 57
Finchley Rd
Belsize Park
Gospel Oak Railway Station
Gordon House Rd
Hoop Ln
Golders Green Rd
Finchley Rd
Rotherwick Rd
Heathgate
Thornton Wy
Kingsley Wy
Spencer Dr
Hoop Ln
Chalton Dr
Neville Dr
Willoughby Rd
Wellgarth Rd
Ingram Ave
Wildwood Rd
Hampstead Wy
North End Rd
West Heath Dr
West Heath Ave
Dunstan Rd
West Heath Rd
Elm Rock
Hampstead Wy
North End Wy
Spaniards Rd
Hampstead Ln
Sheldon Ave
The Bishops Ave
Aylmer Rd
Redington Rd
Templewood Ave
West Heath Rd
Heath St
East Heath Rd
Cannon Pl
New End
Hampstead Gro
Frognal Ave
Frognal
Church Row
Willow Rd
South Hill Pk
Parliament Hill
Nassington Rd
Fitzroy Pk
Merton Ln
Highgate West Hill
Rosslyn Hill
Downshire Hill
Keats Gro
Arkwright Rd
Thurlow Rd
Lyndhurst Rd
Fitzjohn's Ave
Wedderburn Rd
Mulley Trr
Maresfield Gdns
Oman Rd
Aspern Gro
Belsize Ave
Belsize Ln
Fleet Rd
Savernake Rd
Highgate Rd

Overview

Hampstead Heath is 791 acres of rambling woods and idyllic meadows worthy of much frolicking. It's the fact that its wilderness seems so, well, wild that makes this London park deceptive. You can be merrily re-enacting the Brothers Grimm, only to be spat out rather rudely onto Parliament Hill and confronted with gob-smacking views of St Paul's and the Gherkin. The Heath is truly nothing short of heaven—until you stumble over George Michael up to no good in the bushes. You can swim naked in its ponds, stroll amongst its tall grasses without seeing another living soul for twenty minutes or more and engage in a little sex scandal amongst the greenery. The park's common theme is one of a hidden countryside retreat right in the middle of it all.

Most likely because it *is* countryside. It's just the rest of London that's gone all urban around it. Long-established hedgerows and ancient trees attest to its lengthy history. The range of wildlife on show is impressive—kingfishers, parakeets, 300 species of fungi and several types of bat, to name a few. All sorts of famous people have enjoyed its leafy company through the years. Boudicca's Mound near the men's bathing pond (hmm... sounds dirty), is said to mark the ancient queen's burial chamber. Karl Marx and his family had a picnic here every Sunday while he lived in London and writer Wilkie Collins used the park as a backdrop for The Woman in White. All in all, the Heath has been a much-loved place of social gathering and strolling for centuries, a place of peace and perspective amongst the greater hustle and bustle of the Big Smoke.

Ponds, Ponds and... Oh Yeah, More Ponds…

It might be argued that losing your Heath virginity consists of swimming in one of its famous outdoor bathing ponds. These are open throughout the year and attract throngs of dedicated swimming fans. On the eastern side—closer to Highgate—are a series of eight 17th and 18th century reservoirs dotted between Parliament Hill Fields and Kenwood House. Amongst these is one swimming pond for guys, another for gals, a toy boat pond, a wildlife reserve pond, and a lake for fishing. On the western side of the Heath are three more, including the 'mixed pond', where you can have some underwater flirtations, should you wish.

Kenwood House

Address:	Hampstead - NW3 7JR
Phone:	0208 348 1286
Website:	www.english-heritage.org.uk/server/show/conProperty.106
Hours:	April-October: 11 am-5 pm, Monday-Sunday, November-March: 11 am-4 pm, Monday-Sunday
Admission:	Free

Kenwood House, a 17th century manor in the middle of the park, adds very nicely to the Heath's countryside effect. Its striking classically white walls and landscaped grounds play backdrop to summer jazz festivals as well as a few scenes in the movie Notting Hill. Purchased by brewing magnate Edward Cecil Guinness in 1925, Kenwood House is more than just a pretty façade. Thanks to Guinness's fortune and interest in art, the manor house is also a very noteworthy art gallery featuring works by the likes of Rembrandt, Turner and Gainsborough.

Golders Hill Park

Golders Hill Park is the younger brother to the bigger Hampstead Heath, adjoining it on the western side. Where the latter is an icon of epic proportions, the former is more of a good ol' neighbourhood park. Its large expanse of grass was created rather suddenly when a house that stood on the grounds was bombed during the Blitz. It has a lot to offer for its size though, with a formal flower garden, a deer park and a small zoo (with alpacas no less). If you're feeling sporty, there are tennis courts, putting greens and plenty of jogging paths.

How to Get There

The closest tube stations are Hampstead, Golder's Green and Archway on the Northern Line. Nearby overland stations include Hampstead Heath and Gospel Oak. Bus numbers running to the park are the 168, 268 and 210, which cuts through on Spaniard's Road (where you may want to stop for a pint at the historic Spaniard's Inn).

Additional Information

City of London
www.cityoflondon.gov.uk

Information and booking tickets for swimming:
020 7485 5757

Heath and Hampstead Society:
www.heathandhampsteadsociety.org.uk

Highgate Cemetery General Info

NFT Map: 51 & 59
Web: www.highgate-cemetery.org
Phone: 020 8340 1834

West Cemetery

The West Cemetery opened in 1839 and most of the original pathways and structures still exist. On weekdays, tours take place daily at 2 pm from March to November. There's a limit of 15 people so you'll need to book in advance on the number above. The weekends are a free-for-all with tours taking place hourly from 11 am until 4 pm April to November and until 3 pm December to March.

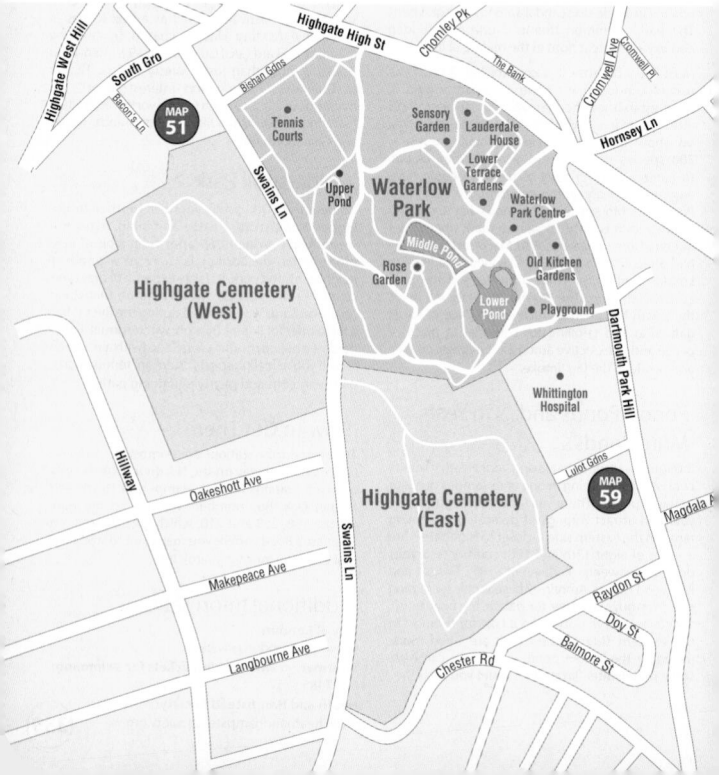

East Cemetery

The newer East Cemetery is located on the opposite side of the road to the West entrance. This side is open daily and for three pounds you get to roam unsupervised for as long as you please. It may not be as impressive as the West side, but it's still a place of breathtaking beauty. Although there are some well-trodden paths and proper walkways, large parts of the cemetery are almost completely overgrown, making it a wonderful place to go for a stroll.

Opening Hours
1st April to 31st October
Mon-Fri: 10 am-5 pm
Sat-Sun: 11 am-5 pm

1st November to 31st March
Mon-Fri: 10 am-4 pm
Sat-Sun: 11 am-4 pm

Famous Occupants

Quite a few notable people are buried here. The caretakers will be more than willing to inform you of the whereabouts of the following graves and plenty of others.

Douglas Adams, author. Most famous for the *Hitchhiker's Guide To The Galaxy* series of books.

George Eliot, English author and poet; also actually a woman.

Christina Rossetti, English poet.

Karl Marx. Philosopher; considered the father of communism.

Alexander Litvinenko, Russian ex-spy, famously murdered by radiation poisoning in a Soho sushi restaurant in 2006.

The Highgate Vampire

There have been numerous accounts of shapes, ghosts and supernatural figures seen on the cemetery grounds, and in the early 70s the media picked up on a theory involving a vampire and the legend of The Highgate Vampire was born. It caused quite a stir and soon mobs of 'vampire hunters' descended on the place (imagine something like the Thriller video, but with flares and tank tops). Finally, Sean Manchester, president and founder of the Vampire Research Society, claimed to have killed the fiend in 1973, when he tracked it to a nearby house. Manchester was also, in his spare time, patron of the Yorkshire Robin Hood society, and remains, in this publication's estimation, the single most compelling reason not to wander around Highgate Cemetery after dark.

Waterlow Park Overview

Waterlow Park is a beautifully landscaped park located just next to the cemetery, making it a perfect spot for a pre or post-gravespotting picnic. Often overlooked and overshadowed by nearby Hampstead Heath it is a charming and peaceful alternative. You can feed the ducks in one of the three ponds, hire tennis courts by the hour, admire the awesome view of London, wander in the rose garden, or just go and look at the cool hollow tree at the bottom of the park.

Lauderdale House

Address: Highgate Hill, Waterlow Park
London N6 5HG
Tel: 020 8348 8716
Web: www.lauderdalehouse.co.uk

Lauderdale House operates independently from the park, but is located on its grounds. The original house was built in 1582, but has gone through major alterations and restorations since then. In 1963 a major fire destroyed much of the old building and it was left untouched and unoccupied for 15 years. In 1978 it was finally repaired and reopened in its current incarnation. The house runs classes, concerts and exhibitions by local artists. There's also a small café. The House and the galleries are usually open Tue-Fri 11 am-4 pm, Sat 1.30 pm-5 pm & Sun 12 pm-5 pm, but you can always phone in advance to avoid disappointment.

How to Get There

Nearest tube station is Archway. Exit the station and turn left up Highgate Hill. Waterlow Park is about five minutes walk on your left hand side. To get to the cemetery, cross the park down to the Swain's Lane exit, which is adjacent to the East Cemetery gates.

General Information

Website: www.royalparks.org.uk/parks/hyde_park
Phone: 020 7298 2000

Overview

Hyde Park serves as the 'lungs of London'. For over 370 years it has been *the* place to go for oxygen-starved Londoners to take a breath of fresh air. As the city's grown, so has the desire to preserve this 350-acre mass of parkland and thankfully, Hyde Park has never been in better shape.

Eating

Perambulating through the park is bound to get that metabolism going, so stop off at one of the numerous food stalls to quench your thirst or down a plasticky hot-dog. Yum. For a more civilised affair check out one of the park's seated joints - **Lido** (which also has a paddling pool), **Dell Restaurant** or the **Cumberland Café**.

Nature, Architecture & Sculpture

The Serpentine Lake attracts the usual assortment of ducks and insects as well as some exotic additions, such as Egyptian Geese. **The Lookout Education Centre** holds informative talks about the park's wildlife. **The Grand Entrance** at Hyde Park Corner is an awe-inspiring arched construction of Greek influence, whilst the **Albert Memorial**, erected by Queen Victoria after her husband's death, is a true show of love. The **Diana, Princess of Wales Memorial Fountain**, remains one of the most visited areas in Hyde Park and is worth a look to satisfy curiosity, as is the **Peter Pan Memorial**.

Performance

The park attracts big musical events, and by big we mean Live 8 big. It's only the musical deities that get their own special Hyde Park treatment—The Stones, Queen, The Police, but

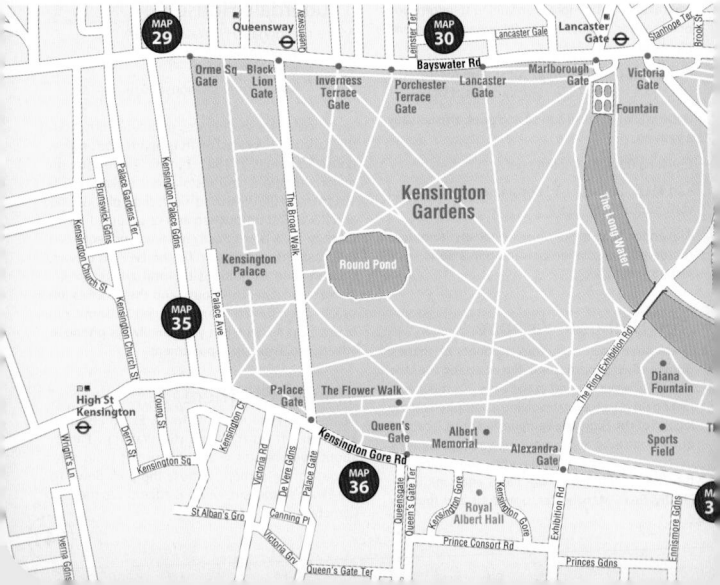

Summer means festival time and the annual 02 Wireless Festival and Capital FM Party In The Park. Brass band concerts are held throughout the summer at **The Bandstand**. **Speakers' Corner** is guaranteed to entertain. Since 1872 it's been the site of a verbal free-for-all stemming from the activities of the Reform League who marched for manhood suffrage in 1866. These days the topics aren't quite as revolutionary. Heather Mills sounded off here recently…ah, the injustice of having too much cash.

Sports

There are ample jogging paths, designated bike routes (see www.companioncycling.org.uk) and great paths for roller-blading and walking. Even more fun is boating on **The Serpentine Lake** from March to October. Informal games of rugby, football or cricket can be played on the **'Sports Field'** while **Hyde Park Tennis & Sports Centre** does exactly what it says on the tin. There's also a bowling green and horse riding at the **Manege.**

Kensington Gardens

The 111 hectares west of the Western Carriage Drive are known as Kensington Gardens. Annexed from the main park in 1689, the area retains a slightly more formal air, with regular tree-lined avenues to stroll down and less spaces for rambunctious sporting displays. This makes the Gardens an ideal spot for a picnic or a quiet ponder. Kensington Gardens also boasts the **Serpentine Gallery** (in between the Diana Fountain and the Albert Memorial), a toy-sized venue for renowned modern and contemporary art exhibitions, and the rather stunning **Kensington Palace**. Still a royal residence, the palace majestically overlooks some of the most well ordered green spaces London has to offer.

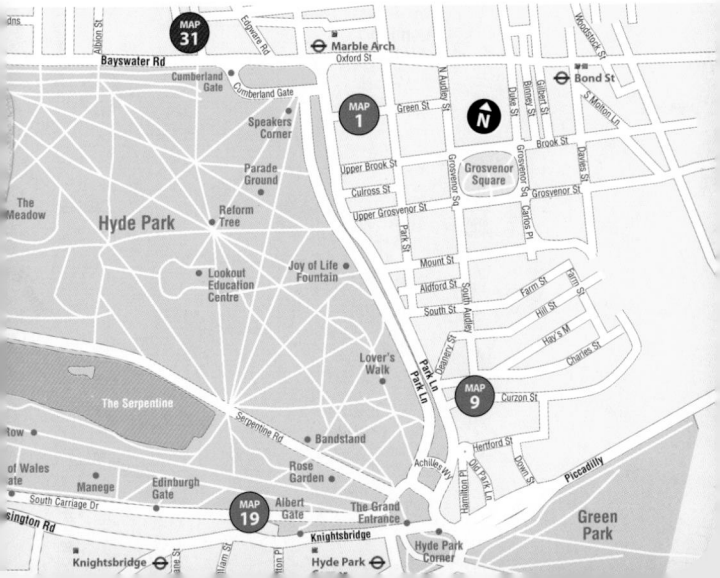

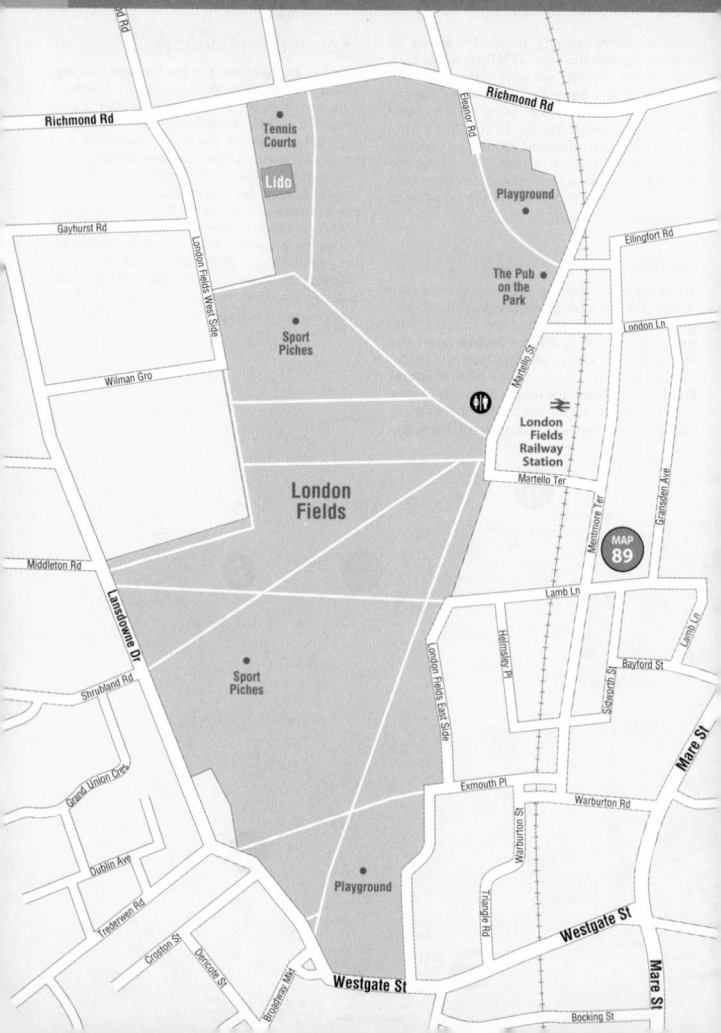
Richmond Rd
Richmond Rd
Tennis Courts
Lido
Eleanor Rd
Playground
Gayhurst Rd
Ellingfort Rd
The Pub on the Park
London Fields West Side
Sport Piches
London Ln
Wilman Gro
Martello St
London Fields Railway Station
Martello Ter
London Fields
Mentmore Ter
Grangden Ave
MAP 89
Middleton Rd
Lamb Ln
Lansdowne Dr
Helmsley Pl
Lamb Ln
Bayford St
Sport Piches
London Fields East Side
Sidworth St
Shrubland Rd
Mare St
Grand Union Cres
Exmouth Pl
Warburton Rd
Warburton St
Dublin Ave
Playground
Triangle Rd
Tredevwen Rd
Westgate St
Crostton St
Dericote St
Broadway Mkt
Westgate St
Mare St
Bocking St

Overview

Best green space of the northeast? Victoria Park might still bag the accolade, but this relaxed, mid-sized park in the middle of Hackney is catching up. And quickly. It's lush and it's spacious and its latest addition, a smashing 50-metres Lido (see below), is hard to beat. Just off busy Mare Street and minutes from Regent's Canal, the park is easily reachable and easily manageable. There are two tennis courts, football, basketball and cricket pitches, and two well-equipped and well-maintained playgrounds, if you have kids in tow. London Fields does a nice job of attracting a pleasantly diverse mix of people, from Hoxton-refugee artists and rollie-smoking would-be philosophers, to pram-pushing mums and East End geezers with no teeth and big dogs. The architecture framing the tree-studded space is just as varied: bland high rises, pretty Victorians, depressing brick estates and fancy new developments, all modern Hackney is there.

The park's own drinking spot, imaginatively called Pub on the Park, is good for a relaxed outside pint, simple pub food or the footie. If you're after a slightly more refined meal, check the gastropub-ish Cat and Mutton at the park's bottom. This is also where Broadway Market begins, a traditional East End market street, now brimming with nice little shops, several pubs and original eateries. If the red wine you shared with your painter friends on their picnic blanket got you into serious party mood, head to the close-by (and late-night) Dolphin on Mare Street. Or just fall asleep in the shadows of those massive oak trees. Chances are, one of the dogs will lick you back to reality.

London Fields Lido

Address: London Fields Westside, London E8 3EU
Phone: 020 7254 9038
Website: http://www.hackney.gov.uk/c-londonfields-lido.htm
Hours: Mon-Fri 6.45 am-6 pm; Sat-Sun 8 am-5 pm
Admission: £4 for adults, £2.40 for kids

You might say that in a city where, essentially, you have the choice between stomach-turningly grotty leisure centre pools and hopelessly overpriced member gym versions, any new public swimming basin would be a winner. Fair enough. But WHAT a winner. Having mouldered closed for almost two decades, a £2.5m effort has restored this art deco gem to its former glory. In fact, it's probably better than ever: the 50-metre basin is nicely heated all year round (25C when we last checked), the changing rooms are modern and clean, admission's okay. Come during the week for a few pre-work lanes, when steam mysteriously hangs over the water, or jump in on the weekend, followed by a Sunday roast in one of the pubs close-by or a picnic in the park. Sounds nice? We know.

Sports

There's no shortage of things to do. The park's two tennis courts can be booked for hourly slots (open 8.30 am-dusk; £5.50/h during peak times, £2.50/h off-peak; call 020 7254 4235 for more info). The Hackney Tennis Club (www.hackneycotytennisclub.co.uk) also offers classes and joint sessions. The football pitch (just come and play) is located in the middle, the basketball space (ditto) towards the south. Follow the sound of children for the playgrounds, one in the north, one in the south. If cricket is your cup of tea, get in touch with the London Fields Cricket Club (londonfieldscc@gmail.com), who keep the park's long-standing tradition as a cricket pitch alive (which, incidentally, is said to go back to 1800).

How to Get There

By bus: Most buses stop on Mare Street (get off at the London Fields stop), a few minutes walk from the actual park. From Liverpool Street Station, take 48 and 55, from Mile End or Bethnal Green grab the D6. The 106 takes you here from Finsbury Park, the 277 from Highbury & Islington. Two buses stop directly at the bottom of the park: the 236 (connecting to Dalston, Newington Green, Finsbury Park) and the 394 (Hackney Central, Homerton Hospital, Hoxton, Angel).

By train: The train is a great option, since London Fields station is located right next to the park. Train operator National Express East Anglia (formerly known as One Railway) serves the central Liverpool Street Station (via Cambridge Heath and Bethnal Green) and connects the Victoria Line tube stations Seven Sisters and Tottenham Hale further north. You can travel using your Oyster Card, for timetables check www.nationalexpresseastanglia.com.

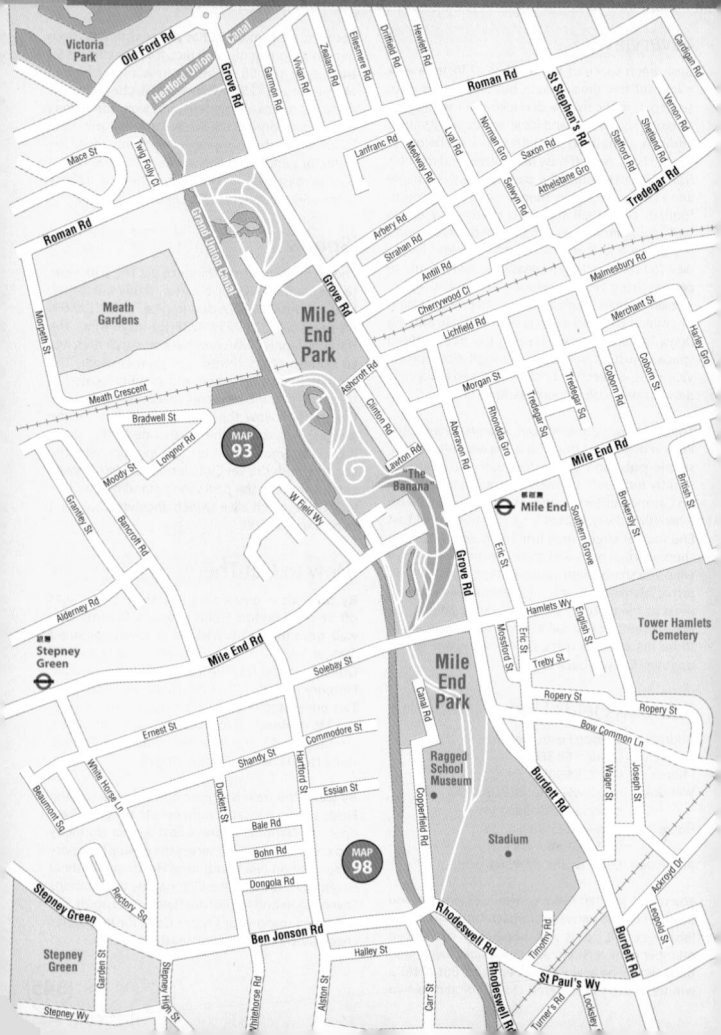
Victoria Park
Old Ford Rd
Hertford Union Canal
Grove Rd
Garmet Rd
Vivian Rd
Zealand Rd
Ellesmere Rd
Drimfield Rd
Hewlett Rd
Roman Rd
St Stephen's Rd
Cardigan Rd
Vernon Rd
Shetland Rd
Stanford Rd
Tredegar Rd
Mace St
Twig Folly Cl
Lanfranc Rd
Medway Rd
Leal Rd
Norman Gro
Saxon Rd
Athelstane Gro
Saberry Rd
Roman Rd
Canal Union Canal
Meath Gardens
Morpeth St
Meath Crescent
Bradwell St
Longnor Rd
MAP 93
Moody St
Grantley St
Bancroft Rd
Alderney Rd
Stepney Green
Mile End Rd
Arbery Rd
Strahan Rd
Antill Rd
Cherrywood Cl
Lichfield Rd
Grove Rd
Mile End Park
Ashcroft Rd
Clinton Rd
Laxton Rd
The Banana
W Ferry Wy
Malmesbury Rd
Merchant St
Harley Gro
Cobourn St
Cobourn Rd
Morgan St
Tredegar Sq
Tredegar St
Rhondda Gro
Aberaron Rd
Mile End Rd
Mile End
Southern Grove
Braxfield St
British St
Eric St
Grove Rd
Hamlets Wy
Mostard St
Eric St
English St
Treby St
Tower Hamlets Cemetery
Solebay St
Mile End Park
Ropery St
Ropery St
Bow Common Ln
Ernest St
Commodore St
Shandy St
Harford St
Essian St
Ragged School Museum
Copperfield Rd
Canal Rd
Burdett Rd
Wager St
Joseph St
White Horse Ln
Beaumont Sq
Dickett St
Bale Rd
Bohn Rd
Dongola Rd
MAP 98
Stadium
Ackroyd Dr
Leopold St
Stepney Green
Rectory Sq
Ben Jonson Rd
Rhodeswell Rd
Timothy Rd
Burdett Rd
Stepney Green
Garden St
Halley St
St Paul's Wy
Stepney High St
Whitehorse Rd
Alston St
Cyprus St
Rhodeswell Rd
Turner's Rd
Lockesley
Stepney Wy

Overview

Bordered at the north by the chain-ridden fake-a-rama, Bow Wharf, to the east and south by rat runs, and to the west by the dank waters of the Regent's Canal, this strange elongated park doesn't appear to have a lot going for it. However, this 32-hectare wiggle of green is more a string of mini parks—divided up by roads and railway lines—and each segment has hidden treasures worth digging for. There is an adventure playground, an arts pavilion with weird orange-and-white sculptural seats by Leona Matuszczak, an ecology park with moths and all sorts, a terraced garden and a sheltered children's playground. Clever landscaping and inventive use of space creates pockets of peace, and when the sun comes out, sparkling on the canal, bouncing off of the reflective jackets of the cyclists bombing past or laying its beams on giggling young couples, the park of many parks comes into its own.

It was created following the Second World War after the area was destroyed in the Blitz. The idea of Lord Abercombie, who envisioned a creepy-sounding 'finger of green' in amongst the rubble, Mile End really came into being in 1999 with Millennium Commission funding providing new areas, strange metal cross signage and an amazing green bridge—known by locals as the Banana. It actually has grass and shrubs taking walkers and cyclists over Mile End Road.

The remains of the Victorian terraces sit on the west side of the park, and one resilient pub, The Palm Tree, squats alone in the middle of a grey car park, a testament to the rows of two-up-two-downs which no longer flank the pub. This great local boozer is filled most nights with a mix of climbers and locals tucking into doorstep sandwiches and draft beer.

For those who want a bit more local history, The Ragged School Museum (www.raggedschoolmuseum.org.uk) on Copperfield St overlooks the southern tip of the park: a canal side slum that was transformed into a school for the local urchins by philanthropist Dr Barnado. It now has a mocked-up Victorian classroom and clunky little cafe. Only open Wednesday and Thursday and the occassional Sunday—check before you go.

Sports in the Park

The southern end of the park is a haven for sporty types with a refurbished stadium and 10 all weather pitches made from recycled car tyres, a go-kart track and the large Ikea-like Mile End Leisure Centre with all the usual sauna, gym, pool and verruca infested changing rooms.
Mile End Climbing Wall is housed in an old pipe engineering works in the middle of the park, and is one of London's 'big three' (The Castle and the Westway are the others). It was opened in the 80s and some of its users seem unaware of time's passage, judging by their fetching leggings.

How to Get There

By tube: Turn left out of Mile End station, cross Grove Rd and you'll find yourself at one of the entrances to the middle section of the park.

By car: The park can be easily accessed from Bow Road, Grove Rd, or Mile End Rd, though according to London Borough of Tower Hamlets, 'The local streets operate a resident's parking permit system and are regularly patrolled by traffic wardens. Limited parking is available at Bow Wharf.'

By bus: The, D6, D7, 25, 205, 277, 323, 339 and all take you to various entrances around the park.

Additional Information

London Borough of Tower Hamlets
www.towerhamlets.gov.uk/data/discover/data/parks/mile-end/the-park-map.cfm

Mile End Climbing Wall
www.mileendwall.org.uk

General Information

Website:	www.royalparks.org.uk/parks/regents_park
Park Tel:	020 7486 7905
London Zoo:	www.zsl.org
Open Air Theatre:	www.openairtheatre.org

Overview

Whenever your quaint and backward country-dwelling friends are telling you the virtues of rural life, you can silence them with two words: Regent's Park. Let the yokels have their cleaner lungs, their maypoles and their children running barefoot and feral, because London may have its city drawbacks but it knows how to do a good park. When you stroll in Regent's Park, you're strolling on nothing less than Property of the Crown—you can see tigers and gorillas, play on the largest outdoor sports area in London, take in some Shakespeare, or, on a very good day, watch girls playing volleyball in bikinis. With 410 acres of parkland, you will always find a spot away from the (many thousands of) fellow visitors. It is the perfect space to take stock, step back and refresh, to sit in a deckchair with a good book, picnic with friends, breathe better air. Moreover, the same obnoxious people who wouldn't move down the tube to let you on or

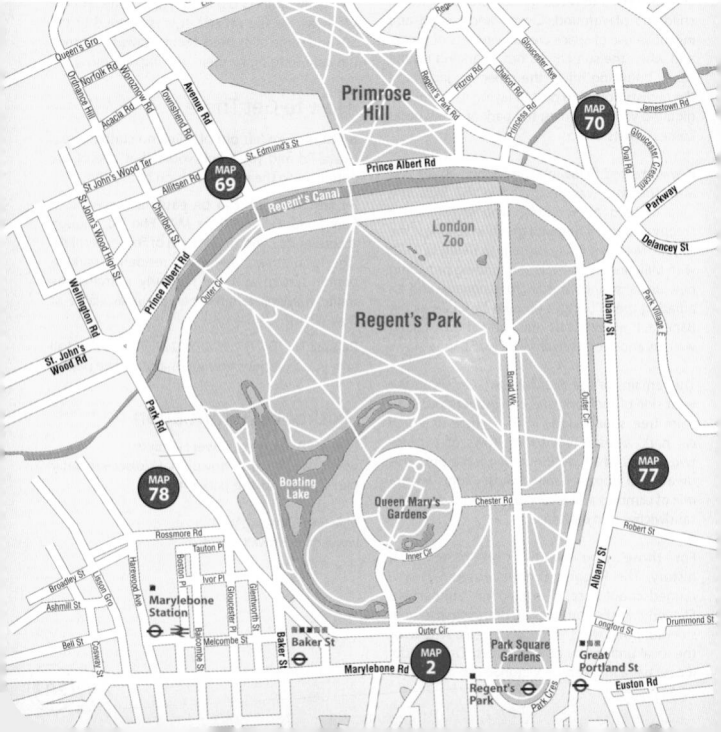

who pushed in the sandwich queue, are here relaxing with their families, lazing over a paper in a patch of sun, falling in love, throwing a Frisbee: it can be just what you need to re-bond with London when you're becoming jaded, and to get away from it all without leaving Zone One.

How to Get There

By tube:
Regent's Park – Bakerloo.
Great Portland St – Hammersmith & City, Circle, Metropolitan.
Baker St – Hammersmith & City, Jubilee, Metropolitan, Bakerloo.
St John's Wood – Jubilee.
Camden Town – Northern.

The Park is served by bus routes 2, 13, 18, 27, 30, 74, 82, 113, 139, 189, 274, 453 and C2.

Nature

The Park is a haven for the city's wildlife, thanks to a biodiversity which includes grassland, woodland, wetland, lakes and scrubs, as well as beautifully-tended and fragrant gardens. Over 200 species of birds have been spotted in the Park, along with favourite garden mammals such as hedgehogs, squirrels and foxes. But if that's all just a bit too Beatrix Potter, you can get your fix of the more badass species at London Zoo in the Park's north-east end, where in addition to the normal enclosures, visitors can get closer to some of the animals with events like "Meet the Monkeys" or even help as a volunteer.

The Park's size and calm makes it a choice hangout for celebrities (not strictly nature, but dandelion schmandelion: spotting A-Listers doing Tai Chi in oversized sunglasses will impress more down the pub, and can there be a nobler calling?).

Performances and Events

The Park's permanent outdoor theatre is an absolute treat. The shows have a Shakespearian bias, but the venue also puts on non-bard performances, comedy nights and concerts. It is the experience more than the performance which will likely stay in your memory. Among the atmospheric trees of the park in the evening, with a bottle of wine and a blanket to snuggle up in (it is Britain after all—how many other theatres have an official "weather policy"?), it is a magical way to spend an evening. Outdoor does not mean free however: prices range from £10–£42 (Saturdays are the most expensive), and you pay theatre prices for food and drink. Cheaper to bring a picnic to enjoy in front of the theatre before the performance.

Regent's Park also hosts a number of big outdoor events. Notable regulars include Taste of London, the Innocent Smoothies Festival, and the Frieze art show. Check the website for one-off listings.

Primrose Hill

To the north of Regent's Park sits Primrose Hill, boasting corking views of much of Central and East London.

The former hunting ground for playboy king Henry VIII has a murky history, becoming the scene of a political feud in 1678, when magistrate Edmund Berry Godfrey was found dead there after being implicated in a plot to kill Charles II. In later generations Primrose Hill became the setting for duels: London lovers fought there over their ladies, while fops found it a good place to settle literary disagreements ("I say Dryden is naught but a one-trick satirist sir!" "Well then I say you are a cad and a scoundrel! Die you maggot!").

Celebrity voyeurs should keep 'em peeled for the likes of Kates Moss and, uh, writer Alan Bennett, while Primrose Hill in winter is the ideal spot to check out panoramic views of fireworks across the city on Guy Fawkes' night (5 November).

High St
Dawes Rd
Kew Palace
Café
Princess of Wales Conservatory
Chiswick Railway Station
London Rd
Kew Gardens
Kew Gardens
River Thames
Syon Park
Palm House
Great Chertsey Rd
Lonsdale Rd
Temperate House
Kew Rd
Mortlake Rd
Barnes Bridge Railway Station
Restaurant
Sandycombe Rd
Clifford Ave
Queen Charlotte's Cottage
Pagoda
Mortlake High St
Barnes Railway Station
Japanese Landscape
Royal Mid-Surrey Golf Course
Mortlake Railway Station
North Sheen Railway Station
Upper Richmond Rd W
Richmond Railway Station
Twickenham Rd
Sheen Rd
Roehampton Ln
Roehampton Golf Course
Kings Rd
Richmond Hill
Queen's Rd
Park Office
Sawyer's Hill
Roehampton Café
Richmond Park
Sidmouth Wood
King Henry's Mound
White Lodge
Pen Ponds
Richmond Park Golf Course (Public)
Pembroke Lodge
Petersham Rd
Roehampton Vale
Ham Gate Ave
Isabella Plantation
Kingston Vale
Robin Hood Wy (Kingston Bypass)
Wimbledon Common
Richmond Rd
Queen's Rd
Kingston Hill

Overview

In 1625 Charles I brought his court to Richmond. He subsequently, with quite heroic selfishness, built a wall 'round a large expanse of open grassland, and created Richmond Park. These days the park is thankfully accessible to the public, opening at 7 am (or 7.30 in the winter) and closing at dusk every day. It's the biggest of the Royal Parks in London, and is an obvious choice for long bike rides, picnics, informal sports and other wholesome pursuits for your golden, happy days of youth.

Attractions

The park has a number of gardens and wooded areas, the most beautiful of which is probably the Isabella Plantation, an organic woodland garden that blooms with azaleas and rhododendrons. The Pen Ponds is another popular feature, as is Pembroke Lodge, the park's Georgian mansion, which can be rented out for weddings and conferences (www.pembroke-lodge.co.uk or call 020 8940 8207). The adjacent café also does a mean cream tea, if that's not a contradiction in terms.

Sports

There are three rugby pitches near the Roehampton Gate that are available for rental on weekdays during winter (contact the Rosslyn Park Rugby Club at 020 8948 3209), and two eighteen hole, pay and play golf courses (call 020 8876 1795 for info. and booking). Between 16 June and 14 March you can purchase a fishing permit for the Pen Ponds (call 020 8948 3209 for information) and for more extreme park-goers there is the option of Power Kiting, whatever the hell that is (www.kitevibe.com).

Kew

The Royal Botanic Gardens at Kew, begun in 1660, are not only easy on the eyes but an important centre for horticultural research and a UNESCO world heritage site. The gardens are still going strong, with record amounts of visitors. The Gardens are a hugely popular day trip destination for schoolchildren and adults alike and contain such a surplus of sights and attractions that repeat visits are always surprising.

Attractions

Of course the main attractions here are the Gardens themselves. Between the formal gardens, smaller themed collections of plants and wildlife and conservation areas, there is enough walking and cooing to be done to justify any length of cake and sandwich sessions at one of the Gardens' eateries. There are also 39 Grade I and II listed buildings, all of which have some kind of historic significance. The 17th century Kew Palace (www.hrp.org.uk), is one of the most interesting of these, having previously been home to the notoriously 'mad' King George III. Other buildings in the gardens include the Chinese Pagoda of 1762, a traditional Japanese 'Minka' house and a number of museums. Decimus Burton's glasshouses (The Palm House and the Temperate) are iconic examples of this quintessentially Victorian architectural theme, and an essential part of any visit to Kew.

Events

Kew Gardens is run with great enthusiasm and has a packed programme of events throughout the year. These occur and change frequently so it's best to check the Kew website, which has comprehensive listings of everything that is going on in the Gardens, down to the blooming or blossoming of individual plant species: www.kew.org.

Several of the historic buildings, most spectacularly the Temperate Glasshouse, are available to rent for corporate and private parties.

How to Get There

Richmond station (overland trains, District Line) is a 20 minute walk from Richmond Park, or buses 371 and 65 both go from the station to the pedestrian gate at Petersham. Kew Gardens is (surprisingly) the closest station for Kew Gardens, London Overground trains stop here from across North and North West London. Trains from Waterloo stop at Kew Bridge station, a ten- minute walk from the gardens.

A large number of buses go from Hammersmith, Fulham, Clapham Junction, Wandsworth and Ealing to Richmond Park and to Kew Gardens.

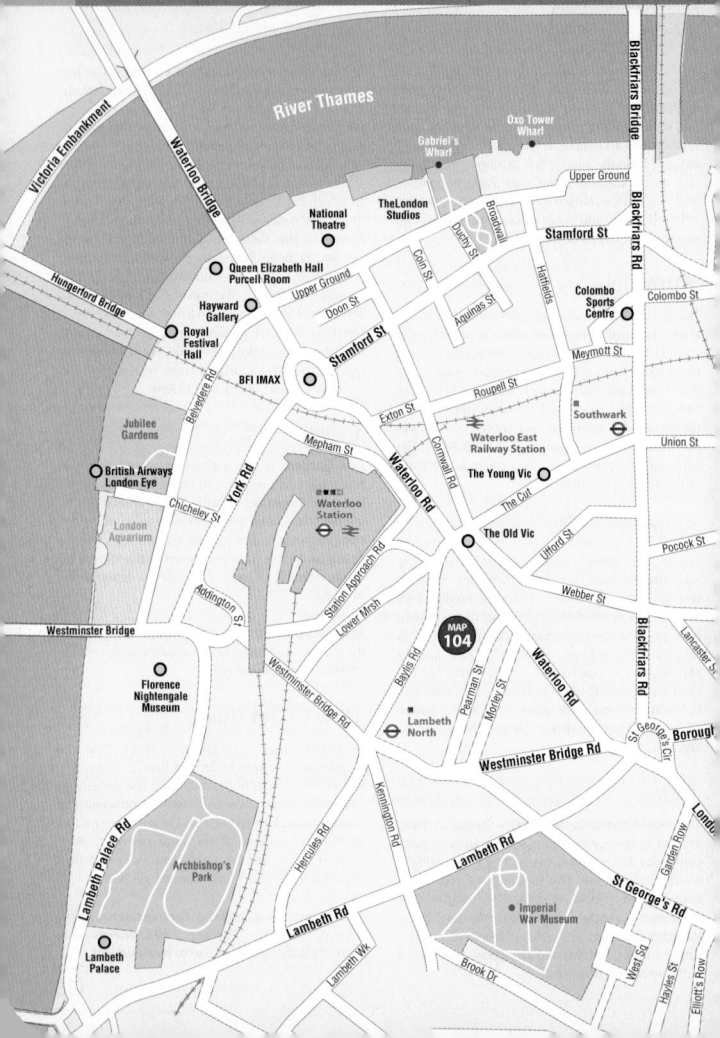
River Thames
Victoria Embankment
Waterloo Bridge
Blackfriars Bridge
Oxo Tower Wharf
Gabriel's Wharf
Upper Ground
National Theatre
TheLondon Studios
Broadwall
Derby St
Stamford St
Blackfriars Rd
Colin St
Hatfields
Queen Elizabeth Hall
Purcell Room
Hungerford Bridge
Upper Ground
Hayward Gallery
Doon St
Aquinas St
Colombo Sports Centre
Colombo St
Royal Festival Hall
Stamford St
Meymott St
BFI IMAX
Belvedere Rd
Roupell St
Exton St
Southwark
Jubilee Gardens
Mepham St
Cornwall Rd
Waterloo East Railway Station
Union St
British Airways London Eye
Waterloo Rd
The Young Vic
York Rd
Chicheley St
The Cut
Waterloo Station
London Aquarium
The Old Vic
Ufford St
Pocock St
Station Approach Rd
Webber St
Addington St
Lower Mrsh
Westminster Bridge
MAP 104
Lancaster St
Florence Nightengale Museum
Bagnigge Rd
Pearman St
Morley St
Waterloo Rd
Blackfriars Rd
Westminster Bridge Rd
Lambeth North
St George's Cir
Borough
Westminster Bridge Rd
Kennington Rd
Lambeth Palace Rd
Hercules Rd
Lambeth Rd
Garden Row
St George's Rd
Archbishop's Park
Imperial War Museum
Lambeth Rd
Lambeth Mk
Brook Dr
Lambeth Palace
Lower St
Hayles St
Elliott's Row

Overview

A pedestrianised quarter formed of venues for theatre, music, cinema, art and various other artistically orientated entities, the South Bank is the realisation of a post-war dream of an arts-for-all hub in London. The area has its roots in 1951's Festival of Britain, a technicoloured marvel designed to showcase an optimistic future for Britons used to coal, Spitfires and fake mashed potato. The legacy of the Festival ensured that the surrounding area went on to grow into the playground that it has become today.

The South Bank Centre

The actual 'South Bank Centre' is officially formed of the Royal Festival Hall, the Queen Elizabeth Hall, the Purcell Room, the Hayward Gallery and the Saison Poetry Library, which are all concentrated in the centre of the South Bank. The Royal Festival Hall hosts a variety of musical and dance performances from its auditorium, whilst the Hall's foyer is an enormous and relaxed open-plan area with a bar, performance spaces and shop. The Queen Elizabeth Hall and Purcell Room offer further stages for musical recitals whilst the Saison Poetry Library houses a vast collection of poetry dating from 1912 onwards. The Hayward Gallery has an exterior of frightening ugliness, which shields a surprisingly spacious interior, devoted to exhibitions of the visual arts.

The National Theatre

The National Theatre is next-door to the South Bank Centre complex and is another gaping example of uncompromising architecture. Opened in 1963, it still looks slightly unhinged. The building consists of three theatres and puts on a range of productions from the established to the experimental. It also features an inviting foyer, and in the open spirit of the South Bank, offers back-stage tours, workshops, talks and costume and prop hire to Joe Schmo.

British Film Institute and IMAX

Nestling under Waterloo Bridge, the BFI promotes film and television through its archives, cinema screens, talks and festivals. It's a great alternative to the disgustingly over-priced and sticky-floored chain cinemas of central London and promotes an all-encompassing program from its three screens. The Film Café and Benugo Bar & Kitchen do good pre and post-flick munch. The BFI IMAX is the separate, rotund glass building situated around 200m south of the BFI. It shows films on Britain's biggest cinema screen accompanied by sound pumped from a gargantuan 11,600 watt sound system.

Everything Else

Beyond its theatres, music halls, galleries and cinemas, the South Bank has spawned a number of other attractions. The London Eye is an enormous Ferris wheel built in 2000 on the banks of the Thames adjacent to Westminster Bridge, it revolves at a leisurely 0.5 mph and offers brilliant views from its 135m high peak. The London Aquarium is just opposite but with ticket prices roughly similar to the Eye, seeing big fish in small tanks starts to look a distinctly lame option. Less expensive attractions around South Bank include the open-air book market tucked under Waterloo Bridge and Gabriel's Wharf, a dinky enclave of small shops, bars and restaurants that offer succour to those cultured-out.

Getting There

By tube: Nearest stations are Waterloo (Northern, Bakerloo, Jubilee and Waterloo & City lines) and Embankment (Circle, District, Northern & Bakerloo lines). From Waterloo, head 50m towards the river. Embankment station is at the foot of Hungerford footbridge.

By train: Nearest stations are Waterloo & Charing Cross. For directions from Waterloo, see 'By Tube'. From Charing Cross, walk 100m down Villiers Street towards the river and then walk across the Hungerford footbridge.

By bus: The South Bank is on numerous bus routes. Buses stop on nearby Waterloo Bridge, York Road, Belvedere Road, Stamford Street and Waterloo Station. Most coming from the North get to South Bank via Holborn, The Strand or Victoria. From the South they come via Elephant and Castle or Lambeth North.

By boat: Festival Pier is adjacent to the London Eye. Pleasure boats dock here on cruises, as do riverboat services which sail west as far as Tate Britain and east as far as Woolwich Arsenal.

General Information

NFT Maps: 9 & 23
Website: www.royalparks.org.uk/parks/st_james_park
www.royalparks.org.uk/parks/green_park
Free guided walks: 020 7930 1793
Inn the Park Café and Restaurant (St. James's Park): 020 7451 9999

Overview

With Trafalgar Square at one end and Buck Palace at the other, both St. James's and Green Park are slap-bang in the heart of picture-postcard London. When the belching fumes of bendy buses and hordes of Oxford Street shoppers threaten both health and sanity, there's only one place to go. Zip past the crowds and pigeons in Trafalgar Square and head under the grand curve of Admiralty Arch into the stately calm of St. James's Park. Stand yourself on the bridge that crosses the lake, take a deep breath and marvel at the history surrounding you in the city's oldest Royal Park, dating back to the days of Henry VIII.

The views: fairytale Buckingham Palace to the west, Downing Street, the seat of Parliament and Big Ben jutting out over Horse Guards' Parade to the east and the towers of Westminster Abbey to the south. There ain't nowhere else in London where you can view the icons of Church, State and Monarchy in one quick spin on your heels. Impressive. And when you're done marvelling, join the families, office workers, joggers and tourists in taking a stroll round the lake for pelican-spotting, duck-feeding, lunching and romancing.

A hop across the Mall and you'll find yourself in the rolling green of, yup, Green Park. Flowerbed free, this 53-acre patch of park with its aged plane trees is the more meditative of the two. A refuge from the noisy thoroughfare of Piccadilly and Hyde Park corner, its grounds soon fill with picnicking office-workers at the slightest suggestion of sun while the tree-lined Mall is the nearest you'll get to a Parisian boulevard.

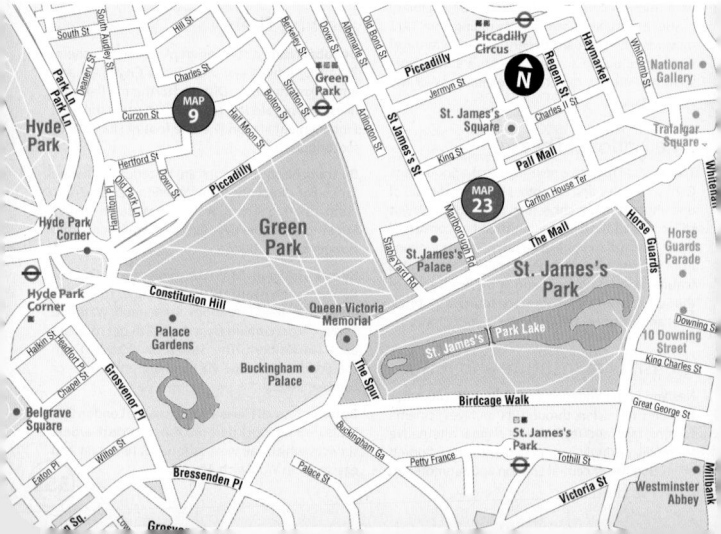

Nature

The curving lake of St. James's park runs the length of the grounds and is perfect for indulging in some casual bird-spotting. Ever since the days of James I, the park has been home to an exotic menagerie, once including elephants, camels and even crocs.

While the crocs and ellies might be long gone, both Duck Island and the smaller West Island remain home to an impressive array of water birds. Beyond the humble duck and gulls, there are suitably stately black swans, rare golden eyes and the rather less-illustrious sounding shovelers, a close relative of the time-starved office-worker on lunch, we believe. But, with their gentlemanly swagger and mighty beaks, the five resident pelicans unquestionably steal the show. A gift from the Russian Ambassador in 1664, feeding time is worth a gander at 3pm daily. Known for their entertaining antics—like flying to Regent's Park Zoo on fish-stealing sprees—one caused a media storm when, clearly lusting after a menu change, it swallowed a live pigeon whole, flapping feathers 'n' all.

Take some old bread and the park's tame, tubby squirrels will feast from your hand. Hang around 'til dusk and the bats come out to play.

Architecture & Sculpture

As if housing ol' Queenie's Buckingham Palace wasn't enough, the parks are surrounded by two more palaces—Westminster, now the Houses of Parliament, and St. James's. From the Regency elegance of the Mall's Carlton House, home to the Institute of Contemporary Arts (ICA), to the impressive frontage of Horse Guard's Parade, the parks are hemmed in by grandeur.

Once a swampy wasteland for grazing pigs, it's a tale with humble beginnings for London's most royal park. While each passing King and Queen slowly improved St. James's Park, it was Charles II that really put the work in, getting trees planted, lawns laid and then opening it up for the first time to us commoners.

Sobering war memorials in St. James's Park abound, including world war icons Mountbatten and Kitchener in Horse Guards' Parade, and an overblown marble statue of Queen Victoria complete with glitter and gates. Oh, and that grand old Duke of York, best-known for marching his men up and down some hill? He's here too, in bronze atop a mighty pillar by the ICA.

The Parks in Season

St. James's in spring is carpeted with crocuses and daffodils. Come summer, they're quickly replaced with a carpet of sun-starved Tom, Dick and Sallys, laid bare as they dare to catch some rays. For an instant upgrade from the rabble, head to Green Park by the tube and hire a stripy deck-chair at £1.50 a pop from April to September.

Between May and August, add a dash of high-brow culture to your day with free concerts at the bandstand every lunchtime and early evening.

Autumn days might be chilly but clear skies make for impressive sunsets while wintry strolls are all the more head-clearing, especially after a night on the Soho tiles.

Sports

With cycling and ball-games banned—*entirely* inappropriate in such stately surrounds!—jogging, morning tai chi, leisurely strolls and pigeon chasing are as energetic as it gets. Sundays are best for strolling when Constitution Hill is closed to traffic.

The Mall and Constitution Hill are cycle-friendly and make a pleasant cut through the West End. Join the Serpentine running club for regular jaunts through St. James's. (www.serpentine.org.uk).

Enjoy the sedate pace with free lunch-time guided walks twice a month, discussing anything from horticulture to royalty (booking line: 020 7930 1793).

General info

NFT Map: 90, 93, & 94
Website: http://www.towerhamlets.gov.uk/lgsl/451-500/461_parks_and_open_spaces/victoria_park.aspx
Information: 020 8985 1957

Overview

Look at all the joggers, skaters, cricketers and picnickers swarming in Victoria Park on any given weekend, and it seems hard to continue calling this 218-acres green space one of London's best-kept secrets. Yet, to many Londoners not living east, it still is. Lined by Regent's Canal in the south, London's third-largest cultivated green space is a nice blend of Regent's Park's beauty and the wilderness found in Hampstead Heath. It's also far enough off the Central London map to stay virtually tourist-free, while, at the same time, feeling reassuringly inner city urban, with the Gherkin and Canary Wharf's skyscrapers all in sight.

Divided into two handy bits by Grove Road, Victoria Park has much of what makes a park more than just grass and trees: excellent sporting facilities, ranging from athletics to rugby, several lakes, a deer enclosure, a secret garden—and plenty of decent drinking holes nearby. Designed in the 1840s to bring much needed greenery and breathing space to a soul-destroyingly grim East End, the "people's park" can also look back on an intriguing past of dissent, non-conformist rallying and all sorts of political mischief-making. And it's home to the oldest model boat racing club in the country. Come now, before the Olympics do. Once the squirrels start digging out amphetamines, the secret will be gone forever.

Nature

Ducks, swans, birds and god knows what else live around The Lake in the west, while deer and goats graze slightly further north. You're allowed to fish in the Old Lake, although we're not at all sure that there are really many fish in there. Pretty oak trees and hawthorns stud the whole place; colourful flowers and perfectly-groomed shrubs grow in the Old English Garden. It's a beautifully landscaped gem of a garden and one of this city's most peaceful spots—if you don't mind the odd greying philosopher, mumbling to himself.

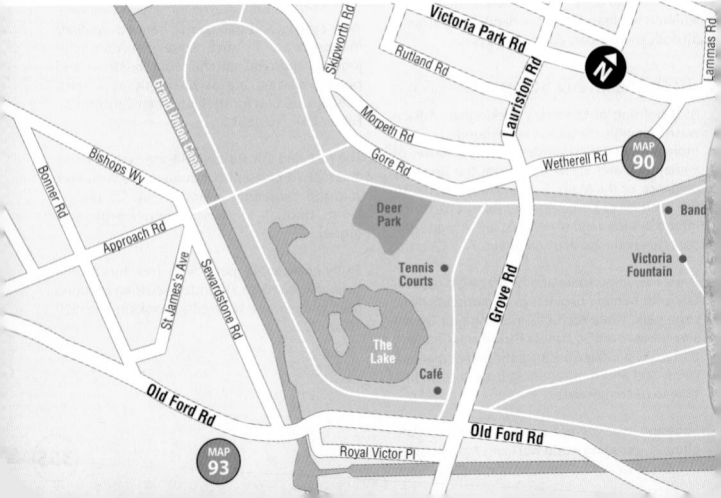

Sports

Jogging and skating are popular and, thanks to wide pathways, possible throughout the park. There's a rugby pitch, a large dedicated football area, four tennis courts (call 020 8986 5182) and three all-weather cricket pitches, run by the esteemed Victoria Park Community Cricket League (www.vpccl.co.uk). The children's playgrounds are decent enough, and the athletic field is excellent. Get in touch with the park's own athletics association (www.vphthac.org.uk) for access to changing rooms, showers and its indoor training hall.

Architecture & sculpture

Rising in the middle of the park is a Grade-II listed drinking fountain erected by Baroness Angela Burdett-Coutts (England's wealthiest woman at some point, we're told), adorned by several half-naked marble boys, smiling cheekily. The Hackney Wick Great War Memorial, in the east part of the park, is a reminder that this part of London was hit especially hard by the bombings of the Second World War. Close-by, you'll find two alcove-type fragments that survived the demolition of the old London Bridge Station. Fairly unremarkable, but good shelter when it's raining. Let's face it, no one comes here for architecture.

Festivals

The hazy days when The Clash whipped up a beer-can-throwing frenzy in the park—heralding a new area called punk along the way—might be over, but Victoria Park has kept its musical tradition alive. Slightly more tamed and organised, the festivals taking place these days range from the trendy, village-feel Fields Day to the indie-and-electro-blending Lovebox Weekender, while big names (Radiohead for one) have also discovered a liking for the park's scenery and music-appreciating attitude.

Eat & drink

The park's café, next to The Lake, is tiny, but the organic cakes are a tasty lot. That aside, you have to venture to the park's fringes for food and drink, but fear not: a tap is never far. Leave behind the bog-standard, soulless pub that is The Victoria and opt for the East End earthiness of the Top of the Morning instead, near the Cadogan Gate. Good Ales, a real fireplace, and up-marketish pub food make The Royal Inn on the Park, near the Royal Gates, the usually busy favourite. The Fat Cat, a few minutes south of the park along Grove Road, is more restaurant than pub, a bit pricey but a good choice for high-quality pasta, burgers and steaks.

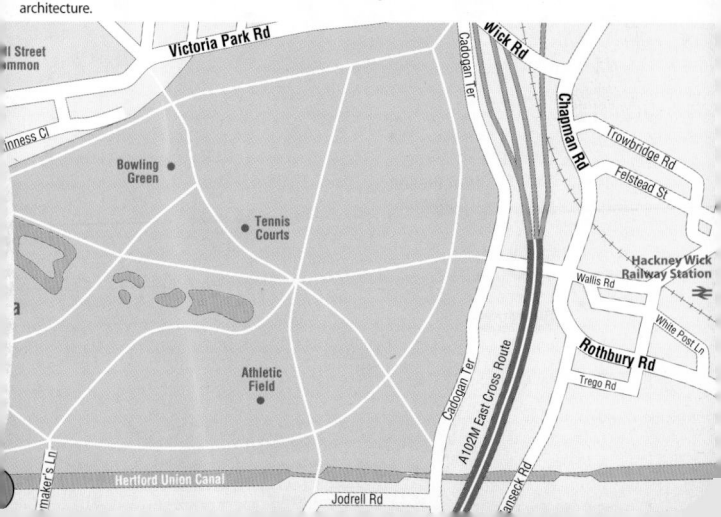

Parks & Places • **Wimbledon Common**

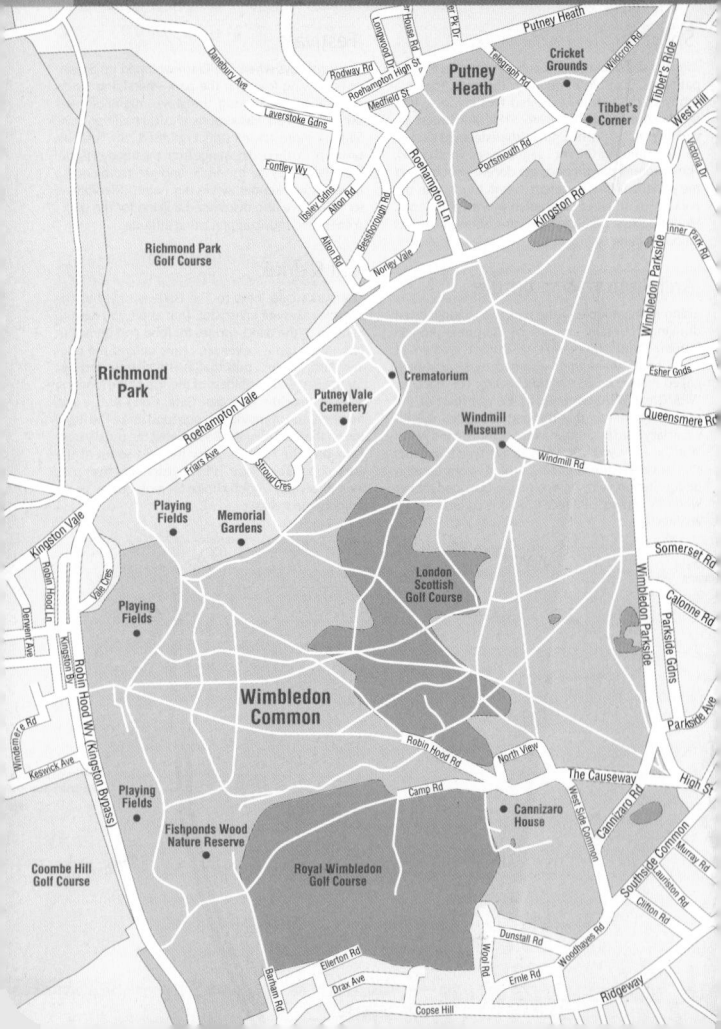

General Information

www.wpcc.org.uk

Overview

If London life starts to get you down, but trekking to the countryside is too much hassle, then Wimbledon Common provides the best of both worlds. Incorporating Putney Heath to the north, Wimbledon Common offers over 1000 acres of wild woodland, scrubland, heathland, ponds and well-tended, mown areas for sports and recreation. Bordered by the urban sprawls of Wimbledon, Putney and Richmond, the common has offered Londoners an escape from city life for centuries. Although thousands visit every weekend, the scale of the place is so vast that you can easily find a private haven for reading a book or a romantic picnic.

Unlike the micro-managed and perfectly structured central London parks, Wimbledon feels much more natural and random. Paths are unpaved and often little more than a muddy track leading off in unlikely directions. The untamed beauty of the common and the lack of traffic noise, or any noise for that matter, make it hard to believe you are still in London.

After a hard day of outdoor activity, or sunbathing, there are plenty of historic pubs to retire to in Wimbledon village. If you prefer your nature tamed or don't want to get your shoes dirty, head to the southeast corner of the common for Cannizaro House and gardens, a grand mansion converted into a boutique hotel and restaurant, with elegantly manicured gardens open to the public. In the summer, the friendly hotel bar opens onto a patio overlooking the grounds and makes a good spot for a sun-downer as you imagine being Lord or Lady of the Manor for the day.

Nature

The common is home to many animals including bats, badgers, and muntjac deer. It's also an important breeding ground for dragonflies and damselflies. For anyone wanting to find out more about the flora and fauna, the London bat group organises 'bat walks' while the London Wildlife Trust organises guided walks. You can also take a self-guided wander along The Windmill Nature Trail. 800 metres long, the trail has been created with accessibility in mind and begins right next to the Windmill car park. The visitors' centre behind the Windmill has wildlife exhibits and also tells the history of the common. It also sells maps and booklets giving the low down on the nature on offer.

Recreation

There is loads of space on the common for pick-up games of rugby, football, Frisbee and cricket. If you fancy a 'real game', you can hire tennis courts by the hour, cricket pitches by the day (from as little as £100) or enjoy a round of golf on the two available courses. The common is very popular with runners and steeplechase events have been held here since 1867. Various running clubs such as the South London Harriers and Hercules Wimbledon use the Common. If you've ever fancied trying horse riding, there are a number of stables that make use of the 16 miles of trails—or bring your own nag with you.

Golf
www.wcgc.co.uk
www.londonscottishgolfclub.co.uk

Horse Riding
Wimbledon Village Stables: 020 8946 8579
Ridgway Stables: 020 8946 7400

Rugby, Football and Cricket Pitch Hire
020 8788 7655

How to Get There

By public transport:
The Northern Line goes to South Wimbledon where you can take a bus to central Wimbledon then change or walk to the village and common. Wimbledon station is much closer. Take the District Line from central London or over ground trains from Waterloo or London Bridge. If you are feeling fit, a ten-minute walk up Wimbledon Hill takes you to Wimbledon village and beyond that, the edge of the common. Regular buses serve the village. Alternatively, you can access Putney Heath which joins up with Wimbledon Common. To do this, take the District Line to Putney Bridge or East Putney overground to Putney mainline station and take a bus up Putney Hill.

It's likely that at some point during your London residence, you've been seized with the romantic notion of floating your way round a London market—savouring the smells, laughing with a vendor, flirting your way to some freebies. If you have, then your attempts to live that dream almost certainly resulted in you silently fuming as you crawled among a crowd of thousands, trekking for a cashpoint because you forgot that stalls don't accept cards, and getting crapped on by a pigeon. Don't be put off!

At the markets you can buy some of the most unique, quirky, fresh, stylish, grungy, exquisite, unusual items in London. Sometimes you'll get brilliant bargains, sometimes you'll pay high for something you fall in love with. And sometimes, yes, you'll be driven near to homicidal rampage. But they're one of London's great strengths: use them while you can, because the developers have their evil, dollar-signed eyes on them.

For groceries

The food in markets isn't necessarily locally grown, but you get a much more tempting choice than in most supermarkets. Expect fruit, veg, breads, cheeses, meats, spices and pastries, as well as stalls concocting irresistible snacks from around the world.

Borough (Map 106)

You don't come here for bargains: you come for ambiance, exquisite international foods, and to impress the person you woke up with. If you're rich and like the finer things in life, then here your weekly shop can consist of some of the freshest vegetables, plumpest fruit, sweetest patisseries and sockiest cheeses in London. If you're poor and just fancy a change from Saturday morning repeats of *Friends*, then head here for a hearty hog roast sandwich and to snaffle some free samples.

Broadway (Map 89)

As gorgeous as Borough, for a third of the price and a fifth of the crowds. It's a pain to get to, stuck in one of the city's remaining quaintly retro spots not closely served by the tube (London Fields), but you'll want to move here by the end of your visit.

Ridley Road (Map 86)

If the gourmet markets are too poncey for you, with their Bavarian organic rye bread and Malaysian honey from breast-fed bees, then get down the Ridley Road. Here, in a market which is bright, chaotic, grubby and bouncing to reggae, you can pick up an incredible array of Jamaican, Turkish, African, Indian and Chinese foodstuffs (and possibly e-coli).

For market-chic

You won't necessarily pay less than at the high street, but you will have a choice of original and irresistible items sold with passion and knowledge. Expect to leave these markets with a lighter pocket (though try to make sure it's not because of the pickpockets…).

Spitalfields (Map 91)

Mecca for anyone looking for ethnic-hip and well-priced clothes, bags and jewellery. Here you can often chat to the maker of the clothes you're eyeing up and learn the story behind their designs. Which is all very inspiring, until you try on their beloved creations, realise you're too fat for it, and reject it having slightly stretched it. Because then it's just awkward.

Greenwich (Map 120)

Craft-tastic: a great place to go for beautiful handmade gifts which people love to receive and then put in a cupboard for the rest of their useful life. Here you'll find a gorgeous range of items for home and lifestyle: pictures, antiques, candles, pottery, soft furnishings and clothes, as well as some great food stalls, and an above-average number of beautiful rich people than at most markets.

Portobello Road (Map 29)

Although famed for being the World's Largest Antique's Market, Portobello Road seems to sell *everything*. You'll need patience to work around its sprawling size and the crowds, but just about anything you're looking for is there somewhere or can be sourced by speaking to the right vendor. Stalls include clothes (from classy-vintage to student-cheap), jewellery, fabric, food, as well as 1500 antique stalls selling maps, medals, silverware, and things you never thought you needed (and which, after you've got them home, you realise you didn't).

Camden (Map 71)

Camden is actually home to six markets, though "chic" doesn't do any of them justice. Here you'll find a purse-emptying range of alternative fashions, vintage clothes, accessories, gifts, t-shirts, comedy hot water bottle covers, tie-dyed hippies, teeny-punks and chaps asking if you'd care for a nice bit of crack. Anything goes, and this open, free atmosphere makes it a major and exciting draw. Hit Camden Stables for brilliant international food stalls.

Fer findin a bit o Laaandon prop'a.

If you're a Londoner who "just adores the city! But oh dear *no*, wouldn't *dream* of bringing kids up here", then chances are you don't mingle much with the Prop'a Laandoner. This hardy breed whose family history is a Dickensian yarn of blitzes, TB and chimney sweeps are the core of this city, and the gradual nudging out of their jellied eels and pub sing-songs is tantamount to ethnic cleansing. Find them at London's Propa Markets before they vanish.

Smithfield (Map 15)

Smithfield Market is in full swing at 4 am, which makes it the perfect place to stumble into on your way home from clubbing. Unless you're vegetarian, because while frying bacon may have you yearning for looser morals, the smell of this 800 year old meat market will have you retching over your recycled sandals. It's the best place in London to pick up any meat you could hope for, including, in the 1500s, a barbecued Protestant or a topside of William Wallace, this being the site of hundreds of executions in its time. Some of the local pubs hold special early licenses, so on your way to the office you can swing in for breakfast over a pint with some of the meat porters: they'd just *love* it if you did.

Columbia Road (Map 91)

There's something deeply touching about an exquisite flower market being manned by some of the burliest Cockneys you'll see outside a Guy Ritchie film. Get there first thing on Sundays for the best choice, or in a low-cut top for the best bargains. And if the crowds and cries of the "daffs, dahlin'?" become too much, just slip into the enchanting boutiques lining Columbia Road.

Billingsgate (Map 101)

For the largest selection of fish in London, outside the London Aquarium (where they frown on you if you try to fry the fish. Bloody bureaucracy.), head to Billingsgate. People were buying their fish here long before London went all yuppie, and much the same stock is available—winkles, cockles, potted shrimp and things which smell ungodly. Today you'll find alongside them almost any fish you could hope for (though don't ask for goldfish), as well as poultry, oils and snacks.

General info

Address: Southampton Row, London, WC1B 4AP
Phone: 020 7514 7022
Website: www.csm.arts.ac.uk

Overview

Though hyped to infinity, and often lazily editorialised as the one vital source of all things up-and-coming in London, Central St Martins nevertheless has an undeniable history of producing graduates that tend to rocket to international fame upon leaving. The frequently-cited list of alumni reads like a Who's Who of European art-and-design talent, and includes past superstars such as Alexander McQueen, Gilbert and George, and Anthony Gormley, as well as recent fashion darlings Christopher Kane, Gareth Pugh and Kim Jones, to name a few.

The school as it is today was formed in 1989 through the amalgamation of two prestigious 19th century institutions, the Central School of Arts and Crafts and St Martins School of Art. Since then it has annexed the Drama Center and the Byam Shaw School of Art in Archway, and as a result offers a huge range of courses covering most areas of the visual and performing arts. St Martins has a particularly formidable reputation for fashion design—it is the only university to show student collections as part of London Fashion Week—but it is well-respected in all departments for its hyper-progressive ethos (expect to hear words like 'challenging,' and 'risk-taking' liberally thrown around on open days). The college has recently revealed plans to move to a swish new building in King's Cross in 2011, where student activity will be centralised and everyone will no doubt be even more fabulous than before. Consequently, whether you find the whole thing pretentious and overrated or are waiting in breathless anticipation for the next St Martins wunderkind, it's going to be very difficult to ignore the place in the coming years.

Campuses

Central St Martins

The majority of teaching for fine art, fashion and design students takes place in the very centre of London, with one building on Southampton Row (nearest tube Holborn) and one on Charing Cross Road (near Tottenham Court Road). This means many of sensitive creative souls find themselves struggling against tides of tourists, but on the plus side they also get to inflict their frequently baffling artwork upon a large section of the general public, who, on their way to Wetherspoons, are treated to installations of varying quality in the front windows of the Charing Cross site. Of course, being in the heart of Soho, most St Martins students are a moment away from a cornucopia of incredibly trashy bars where they can lubricate their inner muses.

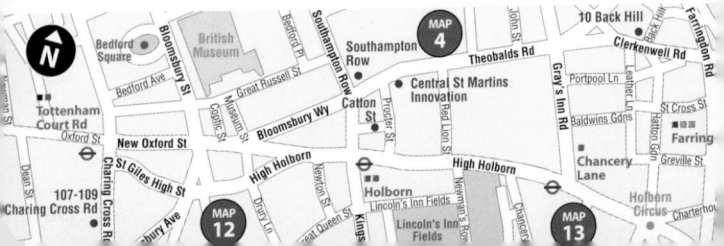

Drama Centre
The theatre types are based in Clerkenwell, home of Sadler's Wells and the Barbican, and mount public performances at the university-owned Cochrane Theatre in Holborn. The Drama Centre runs courses ranging from set design to classical acting, but also has a programme specifically designed for those wanting to act, direct or write in the film and television industries, and to this end is equipped with various studio and recording facilities. Pierce Brosnan went there but there's no need to let that put you off.

Byam Shaw
The Byam Shaw School of Art in Archway is a fairly recent addition (2003) to Central St Martins, the 'Central' tag here being somewhat misleading as it's a good 20 minutes by tube from the other sites. Devoted solely to fine art, it runs a BA and a more skills-based 2 year FdA as well as a variety of short and post-graduate courses.

College Culture

As is the case with most London institutions, the university community is massively subsumed by the bright lights of the city itself, but this is no bad thing. Though the college puts on frequent exhibitions, talks and events, there is no independent bar or central hub—students will instead inevitably find themselves taking advantage of the central location (which is, after all, a short walk from the National Gallery and ICA). The Student Union is not particular to Central St Martins but provides services for and represents all the art colleges in London (University of the Arts London) as a whole, and various services and societies (such as sports clubs) are run at this level. As far as the education part goes, it's not always easy being in the midst of the constant search for the next-big-thing, but at the same time the idiosyncratic slant of the teaching makes for a unique experience, and the generally high talent level of the students fosters a fantastic creative and social atmosphere.

Tuition

Fees vary between courses and change all the time, but most BA degrees cost in the region of £3,000 a year for home students and run for three years, though you may pay less if you receive support from your local authority. Fees for international students are about three times as much.

Short Courses

Central St Martins also runs a large number of short courses for all aspirational (and rich) non-students wanting a piece of the action. Prices are high but the courses very popular, partly because of the college's reputation and partly because there are many interesting options to choose from. The courses run in evenings, weekends, or can be taken intensively as a Summer, Easter or Christmas school. Information: www.csm.arts.ac.uk or call 020 7514 7015.

Phone Numbers:

Charing Cross Road site: 020 7514 7190

Southampton Row site: 020 7514 7037

Drama Centre: 020 7514 8778

Byam Shaw School of Art: 020 7281 4111

Admissions—degree courses: 020 7514 7023

Admissions—short courses: 020 7514 7015

International Office: 020 7514 7027

Charing Cross Road Shop: 020 7514 7612

Southampton Row Shop: 020 7514 7017

Back Hill Shop: 020 7514 6851

University of the Arts Students' Union: 020 7514 6270

General info

Address: Northampton Square, London, EC1V 0HB
Phone: 020 7040 5060
Website: www.city.ac.uk

Overview

In London, a place rich with academia, City University often gets overlooked. Unlike King's or LSE it has no grand halls, secret-handshakes or old-boys' networks. Its facilities are modest and its library short on fusty books. But it's carved out a reputation as a supplier of professionals, cementing its place in the top five for graduate employment in recent years.

Located on a pretty park on the edge of the City of London—the 'Square Mile' that's fast becoming the centre of the global economy—the university is overwhelmingly diverse. Ethnicities make up over half the student body, with young Chinese and wealthy Russians flocking to the business school. It's that section of the university that churns out workers for the finance industry—students who are so hell-bent on business success that they go to school in suits.

The university's first incarnation came in 1894 as an industrial college for the working classes. The on-site swimming pool was used when London hosted the 1908 Olympics, although it wasn't until 1966 that it gained full university status. It's maintained strong links with industry, with alumni including the founding father of budget Euro-travel, easyJet's Stelios (like Sting and Madonna he chooses to use only one name). Students at City may be lined up for good jobs when they graduate; but it comes at the cost of having to explain what their less well-known university is whenever they mention it.

Tuition

In line with most British universities, undergraduate fees for EU students were £3,070 in the 2007-2008 academic year. International fees range from £7,750 (law) to £9,850 (informatics). There are three undergraduate-only uni digs, starting at £3,497.

Culture

Culture in the traditional sense is a little thin on the ground. There are no museums or galleries to speak of, although one department did exhibit photos of prisoners at work last year. But as it included a con making sandwiches for 16p an hour this could've just been to get the wayward students to knuckle down.

Instead, the uni hosts some heavyweight lectures. Although it sounds a little dull, some top speakers in the uni's specialised fields—like journalism, or business—address City pretty frequently. If you're lucky enough to love asset management or food policy then congratulations! You'll be thoroughly entertained.

Departments

Admissions office (undergrad and postgrad): 020 7040 8716
Library..... 020 7040 8191
Saddler's Sports Centre..... 020 7040 5656
Student Union 020 7040 5600

1 Gloucester Building
2 Innovation Centre
3 School of Social Sciences
4 College Building
5 Centenary Building
6 Drysdale Building
7 Refectory Building
8 University Building
9 Tait Building
10 Goswell Place
11 Myddelton Building
12 Parkes Building
13 Health Centre
14 Walmsley Building
15 Paramount House
16 Saddlers Sports Centre
17 Finsbury Residence Hall
18 Heyworth Residence Hall
19 Peartree Court Residence Hall

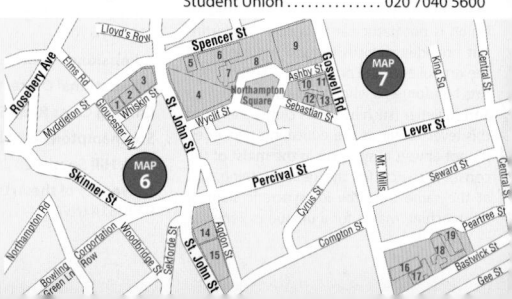

General info

Address: Imperial College London
South Kensington Campus
London SW7 2AZ
Phone: 020 7589 5111
Website: www3.imperial.ac.uk

Overview

Imperial College is London's specialist college of science, engineering and medicine. It consistently ranks in the top five British universities; usually third, although a few years ago it beat Oxford to come in second. Students come from far and wide and it is super-selective; undergraduate applications to admissions are approximately 7:1. Formerly a constituent college of the University of London, Imperial became independent in 2007 (the 100th anniversary of its founding). Students now receive Imperial College degrees awarded by the university.

Departments

The pride and soul of the college are three faculties, each headed by a principal: engineering, medicine and natural sciences. The Tanaka Business School doesn't offer undergraduate degrees, but does allow undergraduate students to study management modules towards their degrees. The main purpose of the Humanities department is to provide elective subjects and language courses for the science students.

Campus Culture

Students come here to study. There are many clubs and societies, but it's hardly a party place. Live! is an online student news source and forum run by the City and Guilds College Union. (http://live.cgcu.net/). Felix is a free weekly student newspaper which aims to be independent of both the College itself and also the Student Union. Stoic TV (Student Television of Imperial College) is Imperial College Union's TV station: Programmes are available to watch on their website. ICRadio broadcasts on www.icradio.com and on 1134 AM.

Facilities

The main campus in South Kensington is surrounded by museums and other lovely cultural institutions, there are also smaller campuses and in Berkshire and Kent. The college is associated with various hospitals in Greater London, including St. Mary's Hospital, Charing Cross Hospital, Northwick Park & St. Mark's Hospital, and Hammersmith Hospital.

The main campus has impressive facilities. The sports centre has a boathouse, 60-acre athletic ground and a swimming pool. There is a large central library and several smaller departmental libraries for specialisation. There is also a language laboratory. The College has a range of on-campus shops, including a bookshop, restaurants, a newsagent, a shop for general provisions, a travel agent and a bank.

Tuition

£3,070 per year for full-time UK and EU undergraduate students in (2007).

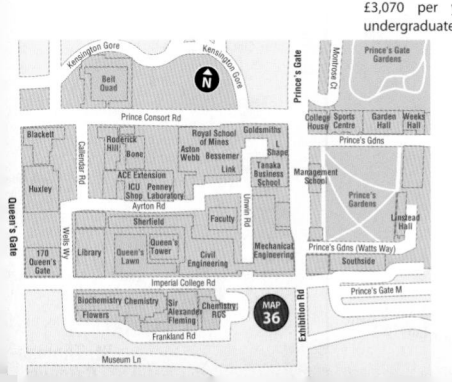

General Information

Address: Too many campuses to list!
Phone: 020 7836 5454
Website: www. kcl.ac.uk

Overview

The University of London, with its 19 colleges, sprawls over the city. King's College London is part of it. King's (or KCL, as otherwise known) has nearly 20,000 students and five campuses—the Strand, Guy's, Waterloo, St. Thomas' and Denmark Hill. It has an excellent academic reputation and ranks in the top ten UK universities. Unlike some of the other University of London colleges, King's is equally well known for its arts and science courses.

Its religious affiliation is now less central, but back in 1829 King's was founded as a Church of England institution to counter University College London, or "the godless college in Gower Street." The beautifully designed chapel at the Strand campus testifies to its pious beginnings, though few students would consider it a motivation for attending the college. The student body is diverse, as the societies list reflects—it includes a Catholic society, a Christian Union, a Krishna Consciousness group, and a Nomads society, amongst a myriad others.

King's boasts a number of famous alumni. Keats studied apothecary there (he didn't like it much), and Florence Nightingale set up the world's first school of nursing at St. Thomas' Hospital, now the Florence Nightingale School of Nursing and Midwifery. In the 1960s, Archbishop Desmond Tutu spent time in its halls. The KCL student union nightclub, Tutu's—a pretty grungy place but one of the few open past 2 am in the Strand on a Saturday—is named after him.

London prices may take their toll on the student purse, but King's students at least benefit from a prime location. As well as the nightclub, the college has two bars, one at Guy's Campus and one at the Strand. The Waterfront bar at the Strand looks directly onto the Thames, giving a view of everything from Westminster to the

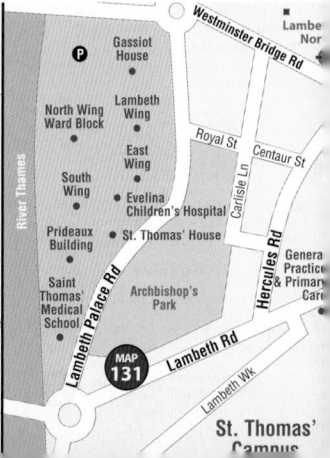

Oxo Tower. It's also a great gig venue—Alanis Morissette, Richard Ashcroft, and Beth Orton have all played there.

Sports

The college's sports facilities are impressive. It caters to almost anything—it has a swimming pool, gym, and even rifle range. Although King's cannot rival the Oxbridge rowing tradition, its sports do have a history—two of the men's rugby clubs, Guy's and St. Thomas', are the oldest in the world. To access the sports grounds students must leave Zone 1; the grounds are in Dulwich, Surrey, and South London.

Culture

King's has numerous dramatic societies where amateur thesps can hone their skills. More unusually, its classics department stages a play in ancient Greek every year, and is the only classics department in the UK to do so. The college's religious origins are evident in its wonderful choral music. 25 choral scholars uphold this tradition.

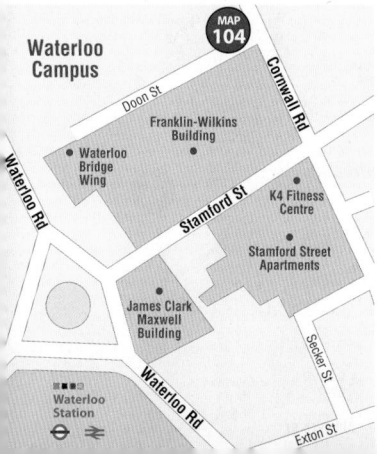

Tuition

Fees were controversially introduced in the UK in 1997 and increased in 2001. King's undergrads can expect to pay £3,070 a year, though overseas students pay between £10,980 and a whopping £25,600 (for clinical programs). Postgraduate study is at around the £3,500 mark for most courses (about £11,000 for overseas students).

Contact details

General Enquiries 020 7836 5454
Social Science and Public Policy . 020 7848 1495
Physical Sciences and Engineering 020 7848 2267/2268
Nursing and Midwifery 020 7848 4698
Medicine 020 7848 6501
Law..... 020 7836 5454
Institute of Psychiatry 020 7836 5454
Humanities 020 7848 2350
Dental Institute .... 020 7848 6512 (undergrad), ... 020 7848 6703 (postgrad)
Biomedical and Health Sciences .... 020 7848 6400 (Guy's) ..... 020 7848 4172 (Waterloo)

Libraries:
Maughan Chancery Lane 020 7848 2430
Waterloo..... 020 7848 3000
St. Thomas..... 020 7188 3740
Guy's 020 7848 6900
Denmark Hill 020 7848 5740
Student Union 020 7848 1588

General Information

Address: Houghton Street, London WC2A 2AE
Phone: 020 7405 7686
Website: www.lse.ac.uk

Overview

The London School of Economics and Political Science, or LSE as it is commonly known, is a single faculty college focused on the social sciences; world-renowned for its highly prestigious programmes and distinguished alumni. Located amidst a hub of academic activity with UCL, Kings College, SOAS and Birkbeck nearby, the college is affiliated with the University of London and stands apart due to its high proportion of postgraduate students. LSE was founded in 1895 by the intellectual socialist movement, the Fabian Society, with the aim of bettering society through the education of Britain's business and political elite. Today it remains a strongly political institution, with considerable influence in government through both its research programmes and campaigns. Its alumni are also highly represented in business and law spheres. While best known for its economics and politics degrees, the broad range of social science programmes offered complements the international ethos of the school and it remains at the cutting edge in terms of research.

The college enrolls around 8,000 students who represent over 140 different countries; over half of these are postgraduates who

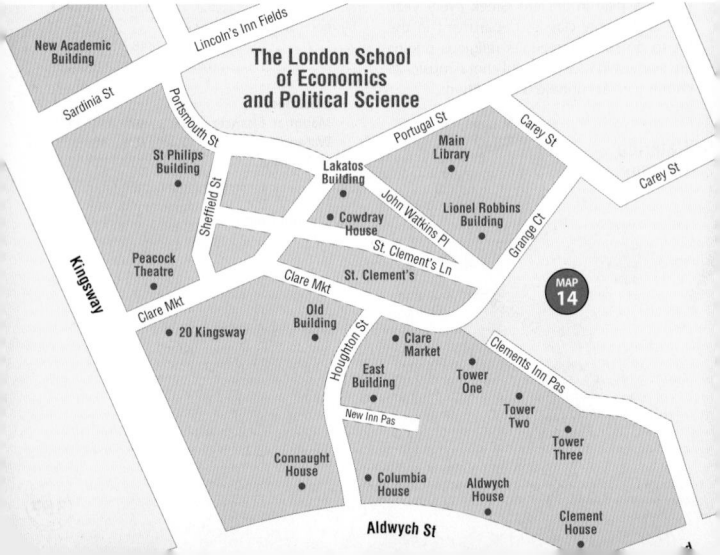

rarely leave the library unless attending high-brow seminars on globalization and inequality. Its starry alumni includes Nobel laureates, international Heads of State, outstanding academics, and a notable proportion of British MP's. And of course Mick Jagger.

Culture On Campus

Despite its reputation for academic excellence, LSE's social activities are mainly fuelled by a lively undergraduate population who also know how to enjoy themselves. With over 170 eclectic student societies, ranging from 'Catalan' to 'Taiwanese'; from 'United Nations' to 'Anti-Authoritarian' and from 'Maths&Stats' to good old fashioned 'Lager&Real Ale', the broad international and diverse facets of the student population is encompassed. An atmosphere of work hard/play hard prevails and nightly events lure the undergraduates from the libraries and keep the campus buzzing. The large postgraduate population tends to shuffle by however, books in hand; the days of cheesy music, luminous drinks in shot glasses and ill-conceived experimental fashions behind them while they actually do some work.

Sports

Not to be let down by its central, and somewhat geographically limited campus, LSE manages to maintain a thriving sports culture through the Athletics Union. Football and rugby seem to top the bill, with provision for some of the less mainstream athletic pursuits such as capoeira and ultimate Frisbee. The college makes use of its affiliation with the University of London Union, which broadens the scope for sports participation alongside students of other universities.

Tuition

2008-2009 undergraduate fees are £3,145 for home students and £12,360 for international students. Graduate fees are varying from around £3,000 to £17,000. Add on books, accommodation and personal expenses.

Departments

Undergraduate Admissions Office 020 7955 7125
..... 020 7955 7757
Graduate Admissions Office 020 7955 7160
Library..... 020 7955 6733
Students' Union..... 020 7955 7158

General Information

Address: Gower Street
London WC1E 6BT
Phone: 020 7679 2000
Website: www.ucl.ac.uk

Overview

UCL, a constituent college of the University of London, has been a place of diversity from the word go—living very much up to its status as London's Global University. University College London was founded in 1826 by Jeremy Bentham as a progressive alternative to Oxford and Cambridge's social exclusivity and religious restrictions. Thus, it was the first university in England to admit students of any race, class or religion and welcome women on equal standing with men. International students have been a part of the college's fabric since day one and it was the first English university to offer the systematic teaching of law, architecture and medicine. Bentham even requested in his will that his body be preserved in the name of science and stored in a wooden cabinet, which is on display to this day in the main building of the College. Creepy.

UCL consistently ranks among the top five universities in Britain and is currently in the top ten universities globally. To this day, the science, law and medical departments are still some of its strongest. 20 Nobel prizes have been awarded to UCL academics and students, ten of which were in Physiology & Medicine alone. However, UCL degrees in anthropology, history and the arts are also very highly regarded in their fields.

UCL's many networks of libraries are impressive and an easy place to get lost. The Main Library, designed by William Wilkins, who also

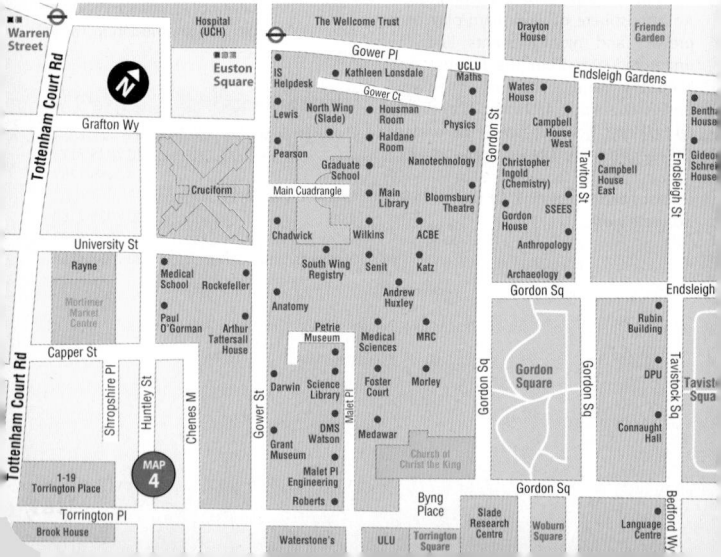

designed the similar National Gallery building, focuses on arts and humanities, history, economics, public policy and law. The Special Collections include medieval manuscripts and first editions of works by George Orwell, James Joyce's *Ulysses*, Newton's *Principia* and Darwin's *Origin of the Species*.

There's no such thing as a typical UCL student, as it's such a diverse place. The only thing students have in common is their intelligence and London. Because it's a university with great academics right in the heart of Bloomsbury, it makes for some pretty interesting alums. Where else can you have such diverse graduates as Alexander Graham Bell, Mahatma Gandhi, Ricky Gervaise, and all four members of Coldplay?

Tuition

Fees vary, but for a resident of the EU, the maximum fee payable is £3,145 per year. If you're an international student who is not a resident of the EU, fees are quite a bit more expensive at £11,360 - £22,170. You should expect to pay between £90-£95 a week for accommodation. Other costs to consider are entertainment, travel, books, TV licence and clothes. Remember that you'll be living in London, where everything is that much more expensive generally.

Sports

UCL's sports are as diverse as its students—everything from hockey, rowing and women's rugby to Kung Fu, skateboarding and water polo. The UCLU (University College London Union) is your one-stop shop for campus sports teams and clubs. If you're looking for football, The 90-acre UCL sports ground at Shenley, Hertfordshire, has very high quality pitches. Watford football club even train there. The Union gym (Bloomsbury Fitness) offers facilities for activities such as basketball and personal fitness programmes.

Culture

Being right in the centre of London means that you're never short of something cultural to do. However, UCL stands up quite well. It even has its own museum—the Petrie Museum of Egyptian Archaeology—accessible from the Science Library. Here you're even given your own torch to explore the collection of over 80,000 rare objects DIY (or Indiana Jones) style. UCL also has its own West End theatre, the UCL Bloomsbury, wedged into the maze of main buildings. It's a must-stop for top comedian tours. Jimmy Carr and Ricky Gervaise have been known to shoot their stand-up DVDs there. The UCL Union has access to the theatre for at least ten weeks a year, where it is dedicated to student drama and music society performances. Although neither drama, music nor dance are formally taught at UCL, this does not stop the Union's drama club from making it to the Edinburgh Fringe Festival. At UCL, despite the fact that students can really go out just about anywhere in London, many stay loyal to the bars within the Union, and it's usually a great place to meet before a bigger night out.

Departments

Undergraduate & Postgraduate Admissions 020 7679 7742
Student Information Centre . 020 7679 3000
UCL Union 020 7387 3611
UCL Bloomsbury Theatre 020 7388 8822
Petrie Museum..... 020 7679 2884

General Information

Address: Thornhaugh Street, Russell Square, London WC1H 0XG
Phone: 020 7637 2388
Website: www.soas.ac.uk

Overview

The School of African and Oriental Studies is a specialist college which focuses on the languages, cultures, law and social studies of Africa, Asia, and the Near and Middle East. SOAS, as it is commonly known, is part of the University of London and is the only institution of its kind in the United Kingdom. It has an excellent reputation as one of the leading authorities on African and Asian studies in the world and ranks highly in university charts on the strength of its programmes Originally founded in 1916 to educate and inform British citizens bound for overseas postings, the school began with an Oriental studies' focus and later incorporated African studies. SOAS is nestled in the corner of Russell Square, with another campus up close to King's Cross; its diversity complements the hotbed of academic activity that makes up this part of London.

The college enrolls over 4,000 students and nearly half of the postgraduates are from countries outside of the UK or the EU. They are often seen sitting in Russell Square eating their organic lunch, and chatting (in Swahili or Taiwanese) about their UNICEF internships. SOAS's alumni include members of parliament and royalty of a range of countries from Ghana to Burma. The Crown Princess of Norway went here. Well of course she did. The Norwegians are so PC. Except for whale hunting.

Culture On Campus

One thing to be said about SOAS students is: they are serious. The Students Union has a reputation of leaning heavily to the left and is very politically active. SOAS students have been a notable presence at anti-war protests, and they are also now rather concerned with environmental causes—campaigning for the reduction of carbon footprints, among other issues. Societies at the college, unsurprisingly, have a very international, 'right-on' flavour, and include the obvious 'Amnesty International Society', 'Campaign for Human Rights in the Philippines Society', 'Model United Nations' and of course the 'Natural Remedies Society' for when these guys need to let their hair down and knock back an entire bottle of Echinacea.

Tuition

2008-2009 undergraduate fees are £3,145 for home students and £11,460 for international students. Graduate fees vary from around £4,090 to around £12,000. Add on books, accommodation and personal expenses.

Departments

Undergraduate Admissions Office
020 7898 4301/ 4306

Graduate Admissions office
020 7898 4300/ 4311/ 4322/ 4361

Library
020 7898 4197

Students Welfare Office
020 7074 5014

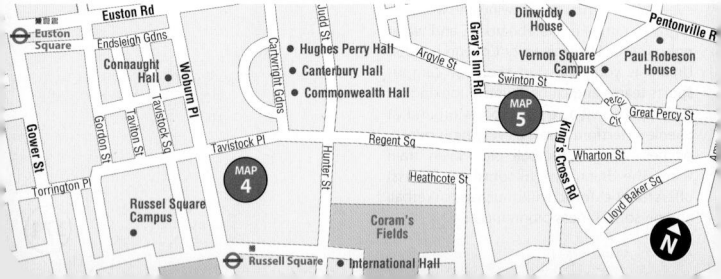

General Information

University of London Students Union (ULU),
Malet Street, WC1E 7HY
www.ulu.co.uk
www.thebarflyclub.com/ulu (The Venue)

Overview

Students are the same the world over and in London they ain't no different. In amongst the banter over Bronte and misunderstandings about Marx stands beer, boogying and burgers. Luckily, for over 100,000 of the University of London's students there's a central place to go to make your university years active and sociable—ULU.

You will need to be a member of ULU to get into some of the events, although grabbing a cheeky cheap sarnie in the café shouldn't pose too much of a problem for clued-up Londoners. There are 20 University of London colleges that are eligible for ULU membership, so if you're a student at one of these then you've got it made. If not, use your powers of persuasion to get the gold dust of cheap beer and food.

Practicalities

There's a plethora of nearby tube stations on various lines:

Piccadilly Line – Russell Square

Central Line/Northern Line (Charing Cross Branch) – Tottenham Court Road.

Victoria Line – Euston or Warren Street

Circle Line/Metropolitan Line/Hammersmith & City Line – Euston Square

ULU is also a 5 minute stroll from the numerous buses of Oxford Street.

Clubs & Societies (non-sport)

ULU offers more extra-curricular activities than Micky J's had nose jobs. What's on offer is somewhat subject to annual change which is more reason to get down there and sign up. Now. Yes, there's the usual suspects such as Drama Club et al but it's easy to be tempted by some of ULU's more obscure offerings such as the Revelation Rock Gospel Choir. Hell, yeah.

Sports

Sports are big at ULU. Again, there's the usual—tennis, football, cricket, and swimming clubs etc. There are also opportunities to master a martial art at Shorinji Kempo (may come in handy for students living in Seven Sisters). Amongst other things you can also participate in Salsa, Break Dancing, Mountaineering, Fencing, Lifesaving or Rifle Club. Now there's one for the CV…

Food & Bars

Lunch Box is ULU's coffee shop, perfectly located on the ground floor for those who want to grab a quick (Fair Trade) coffee or a bargain meal deal—you even get fruit—how healthy. The aptly named **Duck 'n Dive** bar is, erm, a bit of a dive in that usual charming student way, but does have a lively atmosphere and loads of events. There's also **The Gallery Bar** which, despite the rather odd sheets hanging from the ceiling, serves up some wallet and taste bud satisfying treats until 11pm.

Facilities

The **Student Print Centre** will resolve all your reprographics and binding troubles. Wander into the **Student Union Shop** with a clear conscience to grab a Fair Trade snack or a recycled notepad. Open until 7pm on weekdays.

Events

You'll never be without events at ULU. You've got the **Duck 'n Dive** for regular events but there's also live music at **The Venue** hosting up and coming unsigned bands as well as the odd better-known act. For gigs enter ULU on Byng Place.

Learning in the capital has a long and venerable history. University College London (UCL) was the third university founded in England after Cambridge and Oxford and the first to admit students of any race or religion. It even let women in, showing scant regard for their swooning nature and feeble minds. Now there are hundreds of universities, colleges and adult education centres offering a mind-boggling array of courses.

The first port of call for those with a lust for learning or even an empty Tuesday night to fill is Floodlight (www.floodlight.co.uk), which lists 40,000 courses. Fancy brushing up your motorbike maintenance skills at Hackney Community College, getting an NVQ in sugar modelling at the National Bakery School, learning how to create the ultimate kitchen garden at the English Gardening School or studying the nonsense verse of Lear and Carroll at City Lit? The sky is your oyster.

Continuing Education and Professional Development

University College London
Gower Street, WC1E 6BT
020 7679 2000
www.ucl.ac.uk

City University
Northampton Square, EC1V 0HB
020 7040 5060
www.city.ac.uk

London South Bank University
103 Borough Road, SE22 0HU
020 7815 7815
www.lsbu.ac.uk

London Metropolitan University
31 Jewry Street, EC3N 2EY
020 7423 0000
www.londonmet.ac.uk

University of East London
4 University Way, E16 2RD
020 8223 2420
www.uel.ac.uk

University of Greenwich
Park Row, SE10 9LS
020 8331 8000
www.gre.ac.uk

A Little Bit of Everything…

Birkbeck
26 Russell Square, WC1B 5DQ
0845 601 0174
www.bbk.ac.uk/ce/aboutus

Open University
Your home
0845 300 60 90
www.open.ac.uk

Bishopsgate Institute
230 Bishopsgate, EC2M 4QH
020 7392 9200
www.bishopsgate.org.uk

Arts and Lifestyle

University of the Arts London
65 Davies Street, W1K 5DA
020 7514 6000
www.arts.ac.uk

Leiths School of Food and Wine
16-20 Wendell Road, W12 9RT
020 8749 6400
www.leiths.com

The London School of Journalism
126 Shirland Road, W9 2BT
020 7289 7777
www.lsj.org

Glass Blowing Courses
15 Forest Trading Estate, E17 6AL
020 8418 5900
www.glassblowingcourses.co.uk

English Gardening School
66 Royal Hospital Road, SW3 4HS
020 7352 4347
www.englishgardeningschool.co.uk/

London School Of Beauty & Make-Up
47-50 Margaret Street, W1W 8SB
020 7636 1893
www.lond-est.com

Institute Francais
17 Queensbury Place SW7 2DT
020 7073 1350
www.institut-francais.org.uk

London Buddhist Centre
51 Roman Road, E2 0HU
084 5458 4716
www.lbc.org.uk

Athletics and Dance

Circus Space
Coronet Street, London, N1 6HD
020 7613 4141
www.thecircusspace.co.uk

Tokei Martial Arts
28 Magdalen Street, SE1 2EN
020 7403 5979
www.tokeicentre.org

Jump and Dance
400 York Way, N7 9LR
020 7700 7722
www.jumpanddance.com

Regents Canoe Club
Regents Canal, Graham Street, N1
www.regentscanoeclub.co.uk

Docklands Sailing & Watersport Centre
235a Westferry Road, E14 3QS
020 7537 2626
www.dswc.org

London School of Capoerira
1 & 2 Leeds Place, N4 3RF
020 7281 2020
www.londonschoolofcapoeira.co.uk

General Information

NFT Map: 74
Website: www.arsenal.com
Phone: 020 7704 4000
Box office: 020 7704 4040
Location: Highbury House, 75 Drayton Park, London N5 1BU

Overview

On the British sporting landscape, few other institutions continue to dominate proceedings more than Arsenal Football Club. Although skinflint manager Arsene Wenger refuses the board's pleas to splash out on top players – a mad role reversal in these greedy times – he has crafted a side of willing, talented youngsters. The club holds numerous national records and has a trophy room packed with more silver than any other, save Manchester United. T'was not always thus of course. From humble beginnings south of the river, Arsenal built themselves up from roots level, with glory years seeming to come in waves. The mid 80s saw the instatement of George Graham, a hugely popular former player, who begat a powerful, muscular side captained by local hero Tony Adams. Wenger has brought in a continental flavour to the team and an invigorating playing style—once a byword for boring defensive football. Following Arsenal is not always an easy ride. It's surprising that so many people still flock to the new Emirates stadium in Holloway given the stupendous ticket prices (anywhere between £30 and £75), and that's if you can even get one, given the six year Membership waiting list. If you're lucky enough to have the £1000s needed for a decent season ticket then you get to sit in a huge, soulless stadium named after an airline company to watch what are ostensibly a bunch of bloody foreigners. On the plus side, those bloody foreigners play some of the most dazzling football in Europe.

How to Get There

By Car: The Arsenal website states: 'Supporters are strongly advised not to drive to Emirates Stadium. The ground is situated in a mainly residential area with an extensive Event Day Parking Scheme in operation. Only car owners with resident's permits will be allowed to park on-street in the designated areas and any cars parked illegally will be towed away'. In other words, don't bother bringing a car.

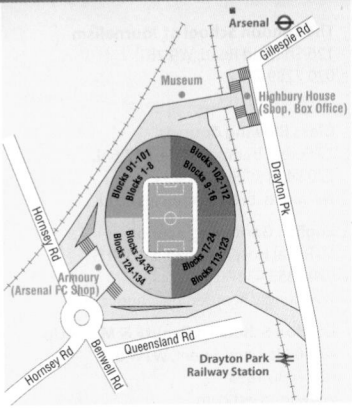

By Public Transport: Arsenal (Piccadilly Line) is the nearest tube station, around three minutes walk from the ground. Finsbury Park (Victoria, Piccadilly Lines and Great Northern rail) and Highbury & Islington (Victoria Line, North London Line and Great Northern rail) stations are around a 10-minute walk - these should be slightly less crowded.

How to Get Tickets

As Arsenal play some damn sexy football, tickets are not easy to come by. However, in the new, swanky Emirates stadium there is always going to be one or two no-shows or corporate tickets that have slipped into the wrong hands. Members have first dibs on tickets and snap them up but the less scrupulous ones sell them on to make a fast buck. Try Gumtree or matchday touts if you really must. To be honest, it's probably one of the rare instances where it really is worth the hassle.

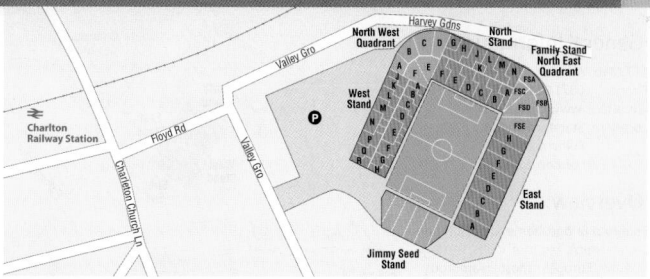

General Information

Phone: 0871 226 1905
Website: www.cafc.co.uk
Location: The Valley, Floyd Road, Charlton, London SE7 8BL

Overview

Thinking of a day out at Charlton? You're a few years late. Back in 2007, The Addicks were mixing it with the big boys. But after several seasons in freefall, Charlton now find themselves in football's third tier. A day out at The Valley isn't even fun for the fans any more.

Where did it all go wrong? It's all gone downhill since Iain Dowie, officially football's ugliest man, took the reigns. He played a brand of football to go with his grotesque looks and got the boot (no, not to his face, that's just how he looks). Inexplicably, Les Reed got the job next – a man with no managerial experience. He lasted a month.

That year they went down to the Championship. And guess what? Last year, they were relegated again.

Charlton used to have a reputation as being a family club. Sadly, these days they're more like that creepy uncle who lives on his own.

How to Get There

By Car: You can leave the M25 at Junction 2 in order to access the A2, heading towards London. When the A2 becomes the A102 (M), take the right hand exit at the roundabout into the A206 Woolwich Road. After passing the major set of traffic lights at the junction of Anchor and Hope Lane and Charlton Church Lane, turn right at the second roundabout into Charlton Lane. Go over the railway crossing then take the first right into Harvey Gardens, with the road leading to the ground. From central London, travel along the A13 until it becomes the East India Dock Road, then take the A102 through the Blackwall Tunnel. Come off at the second junction and take the first exit at the roundabout, then go along the A206 Woolwich Road into Charlton Lane as detailed above. Thanks to the local residents' parking scheme, you'll be hard pushed to find a parking space; try Westmoor Street, Eastmoor Street, Warspite Road and Ruston Road.

By Public Transport: The ground is within walking distance of Charlton railway station, with the Southeastern line running services from mainline stations Charing Cross and London Bridge and services from Cannon Street on Saturdays. You can also take the Jubilee Line to North Greenwich, and then take a short ride on buses 161, 472 or 486 to get to the Valley. Moderate masochists can walk from the tube station.

How to Get Tickets

Unless the unlikely event arises of a successful cup run, getting to see a match shouldn't be an issue. Tickets can be ordered by phone from the Box Office, via the internet at the club's website or in person at The Valley.

General Information

NFT Map: 43
Phone: 0871 984 1905
Website: www.chelseafc.com
Location: Stamford Bridge,
Fulham Road,
London, SW6 1HS

Overview

Stamford Bridge, home to one of the Premiership's 'big four' clubs, is now one of Europe's most glamorous stadiums. However, 'The Bridge' was once an unappealing and daunting shit-hole more used to hosting pitch invasions and fighting hooligans than the well-heeled city types and Russian oligarchs of today. In the '70s and '80s, it was the violent 'headhunters' that made the club unpopular, but as 'The Blues' never won anything, no one took much notice. In recent years, Chelsea have succeeded in wrestling the mantle of most-hated team in England away from Manchester United, largely due to winning things with the never-ending supply of money from Roman Abramovich. The hooligans have all but gone, either priced out or grown up, but the antics of Prima Donna players and managers, who have often been less than graceful in defeat, hasn't exactly helped the club's public profile. With money to burn, Chelsea have attracted some of the world's great names over the years, such as Gianfranco Zola and Marcel Desailly, as well as some big flops (anyone remember Veron?). With the club able to cherry-pick (and steal) the biggest stars, many believe the back-to-back Premiership wins in 04/05 and 05/06 were inevitable, but that would be unfair. Many other clubs have tried to 'buy' success and got nowhere; so Chelsea, under the recently departed manager and larger-than-life 'character' José Mourinho, should be applauded. With regular qualifications for the Champions League, Chelsea often play twice a week, with Premiership fixtures on the weekend and European football mid-week.

How to Get There

By Car: It is possible to drive to Stamford Bridge on match days but it's pretty pointless to do so.

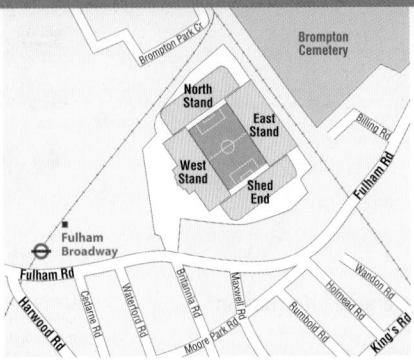

Traffic snarls up badly and the effects are felt throughout South West London. If you do brave the traffic, remember that Fulham Road is closed off on match days. Parking is a nightmare with most zones given over to residents. Gangs of eager traffic wardens are on hand to make your Saturday afternoon miserable.

By Public Transport: Stamford Bridge is a two-minute stroll from Fulham Broadway tube station. Regular district line underground trains deliver the hordes from central London in a matter of minutes. If the idea of a packed train full of sweaty football fans isn't your idea of heaven, many fans descend at Ealing Broadway and take the ten-minute walk to the stadium instead.

How to Get Tickets

With so many competitions and cups, getting tickets is easier than you might think. The 'big' fixtures—London derby's, Man U, Liverpool and the later cup stages are either impossible to get or crazily priced, but tickets for the less glamorous ties can be picked up from the Chelsea website or box office. Otherwise, cheeky geezers will be on hand to fleece you on match day. You will probably end up in the new West Stand alongside Japanese and American tourists, but that might be preferable to a fat skinhead in the 'Shed.'

General Information

NFT Map: 47
Tickets: 0870 442 1222
Website: www.fulhamfc.com
Location: Craven Cottage, Stevenage Road, London SW6 6HH

Overview

Fulham like to think of themselves as a family club. The have a quaint little stadium by the Thames; their manager has a speech impediment; they play in Fulham for God's sake. Overlook their sexually charged nickname – The Cottagers – and all seems hunky dory.

That, in part, is why their recent recovery has been so lovely. When Roy Hodgson took the reigns in 2008 they were doomed. But he rescued The Cottagers – seriously. That is easily the most X-rated nickname in football – from relegation and, in 2009, guided them into Europe. The perfect family feel-good story.

That is, it would be – except the club's sugadaddy is barmy passport-chaser Mohamed Al-Fayed. That's the same Mo who owns Harrods, and whose son died with Princess Diana. The same Mo who tried suing, er, Prince Phillip for killing his boy.

That aside, though, Roy has done a sterling job. Craven Cottage is still one of the nicest grounds in London and tickets are relatively easy to come by. Just be wary of that hole in the gents.

How to Get There

By Car: Craven Cottage sits in a leafy, riverside suburb of Fulham. Parking is relatively easy around the ground with plenty of parking meters, although reaching the ground could be difficult as weekend traffic in London is never fun to negotiate.

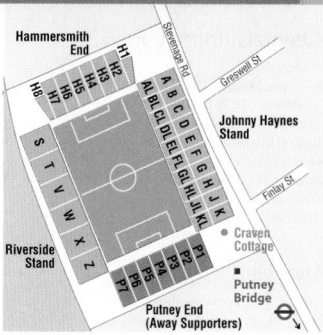

By Public Transport: Putney Bridge on the District Line is your best bet. Putney also has a mainline station with connections from Clapham Junction and direct trains from Waterloo. Cross the road opposite Putney station and hop on any passing bus. Alternatively, a ten minute walk down the high street and over the river will get you to the ground.

How to Get Tickets

One of the 'joys' of watching Fulham is that tickets are easy to get your hands on. Many games are available on general sale through the club website. For the biggest matches, priority is given to members but persevere and you should be rewarded. If you can't get a ticket legitimately, you can always take your chance with a tout on match day. Try haggling; due to Fulham's fortunes, you could get lucky.

General Information

NFT Map: 76
Main switchboard: 020 7616 8500
Ticketline: 020 7616 8700
Lord's website: www.lords.org
England Cricket Board website: www.ecb.co.uk
Middlesex CCC website: www.middlesexccc.com
Location: St John's Wood, London, NW8 8QN.

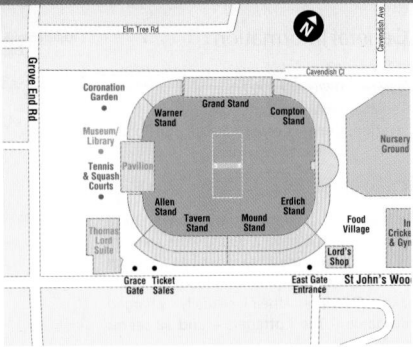

Overview

Even if you know nothing about cricket, don't be put off coming to Lord's. Yes, some games last for five days, and yes, it can still be a draw at the end of it. But as much as anything else Lord's is a fabulous place to come and have a drink. On a hot day the ground is paradise. The sunburnt crowd get slowly boozed up and by the time the players break for tea—yes, tea—few people are concerned at what's going on in the middle. With the polite hum of chatter building up to full-blown drunken singing, it's worth going to Lord's for the atmosphere alone. But when the rabble have calmed down, Lord's is a very genteel place. It's widely seen as the Home of Cricket, and used to house the international governing body. It hosts a heap of England games every year and it's the home ground of county side Middlesex. There's also a year-round gym—you don't even have to be posh to use it—and an indoor training centre. There's even a museum to amuse you when rain stops play. And, rest assured, at some point rain WILL stop play. At the moment Lords holds two Test matches (the marathon international five-dayers) and a handful of England one-day games. These are the ground's showpiece events, where the crowd are at their most boisterous. Middlesex games rarely attract many spectators, and unless you're an old man or a dog you may be in a minority.

How to Get There

By Car: There's little parking around Lord's so, as you'll be parked up all day, public transport will always be cheaper. If you must drive, the ground is off the A4, which turns into the M4.

By Public Transport: The nearest station is St John's Wood (Jubilee Line). Marylebone (Bakerloo) and Baker Street (Bakerloo, Jubilee, Hammersmith and City, Metropolitan and Circle) are both nearby. Marylebone mainline station serves the north and west of the country. London Paddington is a short bus ride away. Dozens of buses run to Baker Street, many of which stop right outside the ground: 13, 82, 113, 139, 189, 755, 757, 758, 768, 771, 772, 773, 797

How to Get Tickets

Getting your hands on England tickets can be tricky. The first few days of a Test match tend to sell out months in advance, though tickets for the last day never go on pre-sale (as the game could be over by then). Similarly, One Day Internationals are normally sell-outs, so it does take a little planning to get in. Check the website over the preceding winter and you might get lucky. If there are less than ten overs in a day due to rain, or if the game's already over, you can claim the full ticket price back. If the weather limits play to between 10.1-24.5 overs (in English, that's up to 149 balls played) you get a 50 per cent refund. Any more than that and you're deemed to have got your money's worth. Middlesex games rarely sell out, however, so you can just rock up on the day, beers in hand, and enjoy the Lord's village.

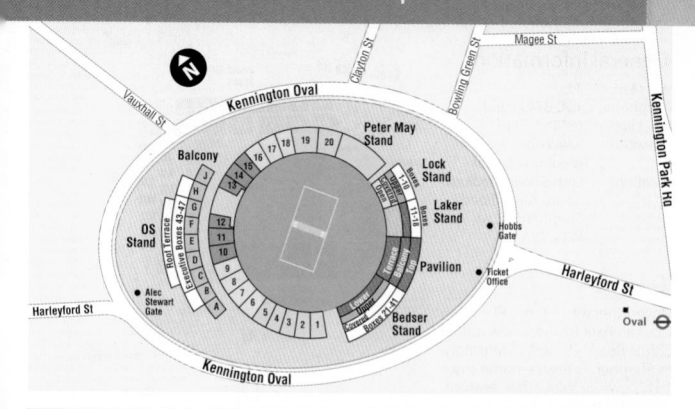

General Information

NFT Map: 135
Telephone: 020 7582 6660
Website: www.surreycricket.com the-brit-oval
Location: The Brit Oval, Kennington, London, SE11 5SS

Overview

What better way to while away a sunny summer's day than at The Oval cricket ground, typically alongside hundreds of other shirkers who also called in sick? The Oval is one of London's twin icons of the game, alongside Lord's in North London, and boasts a rich history stretching all the way back to 1846, when it was converted from cabbage patch to cricket pitch. It now plays host to Surrey County and international test matches, including the biennial England-Australia slugfest "The Ashes." Live international cricket remains a boozy, good natured affair with English fanbase 'The Barmy Army' typically belting out salty chants and cheering occasional streakers. County cricket is a mellower, no less enjoyable event, with readily available tickets and a good portion of the crowd more interested in today's paper than the action in front of them. Taxing it ain't.

How to Get There

By Car: Driving to the Oval is not ideal, because parking is near impossible. Should you be willing to risk it, it's situated on the A202, near the junction with the A3 and A24, south of Vauxhall Bridge. As ever with London driving, you'll need your A to Z and nerves of steel.

By Public Transport: The Oval boasts its own, eponymous tube stop on the Northern Line, from which the stadium is a few hundred yards walk. Determinedly overground travellers should alight at Vauxhall, from which Oval is a ten minute jaunt, tops. Buses 36, 185 and 436 stop right outside the ground too.

How to Get Tickets

Tickets for Surrey county matches are relatively easy to get hold of, though seats for some fixtures can only be bought on site on the day of the match. Check www.surreycricket.com/tickets/domestic for a list of fixtures and availability. International matches tend to sell out very quickly indeed—touts or online sales sites like eBay and Gumtree are usually the best option, at a price. Check out www.surreycricket.com/tickets/international for more info. Ticketmaster also offers tickets to all Oval fixtures at www.ticketmaster.co.uk/venue/147862.

General Information

NFT Map: 32
Telephone: 020 8743 0262
Ticket hotline: 08444 777 007
Website: www.qpr.premiumtv.co.uk
Location: Loftus Road Stadium, South Africa Road, Shepherds Bush, W12 7PA

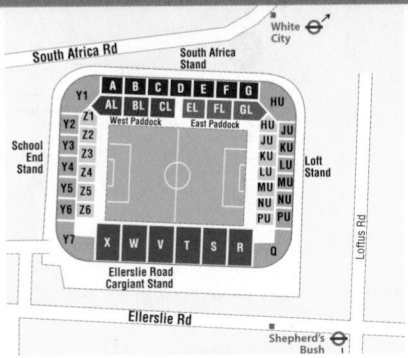

Overview

Once-itinerant football club Queen's Park Rangers have called Loftus Road—based, confusingly, in Shepherd's Bush—home since 1917, give or take a few seasons. Their footballing fortunes have yo-yoed through the decades: once a whisker away from winning Division One in the years before it became the Premiership; they now scuffle about in the Championship (or second division, in layman's terms), with one eye fixed anxiously on the precipitous drop to Football League One (or third division, it says here). New ownership, including pint-sized F1 oligarch Bernie Eccleston, injected some much needed glamour into the club (prior to the takeover, Pete Doherty was the Hoop's most famous fan). But, amid wacky boasts of Euro domination, Bernie was cut down to size. In 2009, Rangers sacked their exotic Italian boss – you don't need to know who he is, no one else did – and appointed Iain Dowie. Dowie – as you may be aware from Charlton's woes – is unrivalled in football for his hard-to-love face. Oh, and they're still in the Championship. Back to cars for you, Bernie.

How to Get There

By Car: Whether you're approaching Loftus Road from the North (from the M1 through the A406 and A40), East (via the A40(M)), South (from the A3 and A219) or West (up the M4 via the A315 and A402 on a wing and a prayer), all routes lead through White City. Once there, turn right off Wood Lane into South Africa Road. Don't even set off without your NFT London, or emergency rations. For the brave, full details of all journeys are available at QPR's official website listed above.

By Public Transport: The majority of QPR fans are local and rely either on nearby tube stops (White City on the Central Line, Shepherd's Bush on the the Hammersmith and City Line), any of buses 72, 95, or 220 to White City Station, or overground train to Acton Central, followed by a quick bus ride.

How to Get Tickets

As long as QPR are knee deep in the Championship, tickets are relatively easy to get hold of, either via the Rangers' ticket website (eticketing.co.uk/qpr) or phone numbers listed above, or by visiting the Loftus Road box office on game days. They're around £25 per person.

General Information

Ticketline: 0844 499 5000
Website: www.spurs.co.uk
Location: Bill Nicholson Way, 748 High Road, London, N17 OAP

Overview

Even the Spurs die-hard would admit that White Hart Lane is a little scruffy. The team moved into the stadium over a century ago, and it's been growing slowly more dog-eared ever since. Few grounds in the capital are located further from a tube stop, and it's in a corner of London where even the police dogs walk in pairs. But that's part of the old ground's charm. More than most fans, the Spurs faithful have a tight grasp of history (which could be because there's been no league title there since 1961). And it shows at the stadium—supporters even chant about what a grand old team Spurs are. But that song only gets sporadic outings. Most of the chants that ring around White Hart Lane are about how much the fans hate Arsenal. It's a rivalry that's as intense as any in football—and as Arsenal started out in the south of the city, only moving across the river in 1913, Spurs claim of being Kings of North London isn't such a wild one. And the division has grown deeper since Arsenal moved into their corporate-branded Emirates Stadium. While Spurs have remained in touch with their Jewish roots—old ladies still sell bagels inside the ground—Arsenal have become the bourgeoisie of football. Their fans may sneer down their lattes at the Spurs supporters who piss in the sinks, but be honest—the queue's huge, the game's kicking off: wouldn't you?

How to Get There

By Car: The area's congested at the best of times; on match days, traffic can grind to a standstill. But if you don't mind a bit of gridlock, White Hart Lane is on the Tottenham High Road (A1010) a mile south of the North Circular (A406). This is easily accessible from junction 25 of the M25, in itself a temple to traffic.

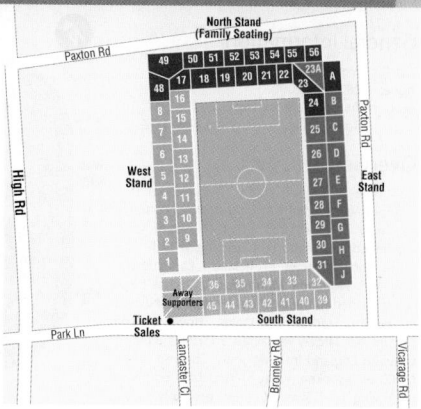

By Public Transport: The nearest tube is Seven Sisters (Victoria Line), which is a 25 minute walk away. But at least if you work up a hunger from all that walking there's hundreds of kebab shops en route. White Hart Lane overland station, which runs from Liverpool Street through Seven Sisters, is a five-minute walk from the ground. Bus routes 279, 349, 149, 259 run closest to the stadium, but many more pass nearby.

How to Get Tickets

Although home games normally sell out, tickets are fairly easy to get hold of. Club members get first refusal at tickets (it costs £32 to join), ten days before going on sale to the public. But few games sell out before this stage, and if you're savvy about the on-sale dates, snapping up tickets is reasonably simple. To get on the season ticket waiting list, you have to become a One Hotspur Bronze Member. This costs £47; but as the club's fortunes are on the rise, the wait could be some time.

General Information

Website: www.rfu.com
Phone: 0870 405 2000
Location: Twickenham Stadium,
Rugby Road, Twickenham, TW1 1DZ

Overview

The home of English rugby, Twickenham is a behemoth of a stadium. An ugly chunk of concrete seemingly dumped from a great height onto a quiet London suburb, Twickenham lacks the charm and character of Ireland's Landsdowne Road and Scotland's Murrayfield, and has been all but pushed to the sidelines by the magnificent Millennium Stadium in Wales. However, the stadium has largely remained a fortress when it comes to England Internationals. Cheered on by 82,000 well-spoken, white-shirted fans booming out 'Swing Low Sweet Chariot' probably helps. Maybe the England players absorb the unfussy and uncompromising nature of their surroundings into their psyche on match days. Critics would argue that their style of rugby is as ugly and bland as the stadium they play in. This would be harsh if England hadn't consistently under-performed after carrying off the Rugby World Cup in 2003. Twickenham also hosts a series of Rugby tournaments and exhibition matches, including the famous 'Sevens', in addition to the occasional Premiership fixture. Outside the Rugby season, the stadium is given over to rock concerts for international bands like Bon Jovi and R.E.M.

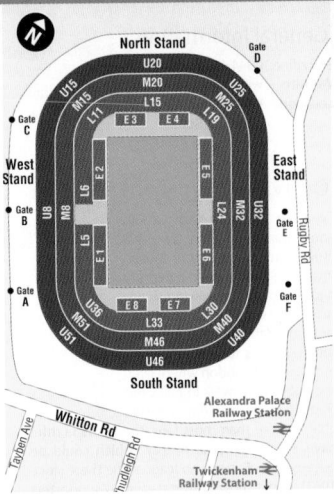

How to Get There

By Car: Twickenham is very accessible by road - if you live in the South. The M3 motorway turns into the A316 that passes the stadium, carrying on into central London. Certain roads get closed down on match days so drivers should allow plenty of time. Parking at the stadium is extremely limited and should be booked in advance. Resident permits are helpfully required for all roads bordering the stadium so the best thing to do is park in the general vicinity and walk the rest of the way.

By Public Transport: Mainline trains run to Twickenham station from Waterloo and Reading. London Underground runs to Richmond on the District Line where shuttle buses will take fans to the stadium (50p outbound. Free return) Hounslow is an alternative Underground station but shuttle buses only run from Twickenham to Hounslow station so you will have to make it to the stadium under your own steam. Bus numbers 281, 267 and H22 all have regular services passing close to the stadium.

How to Get Tickets

England rugby tickets are hot property, commanding higher prices than top football games. As competition games are relatively infrequent, tickets sell out well in advance so keep checking the website for updates on ticket releases. Premiership tickets and friendly matches are easier to come by but will generally sell out. If you don't get lucky in advance, rugby touts (slightly less aggressive than their football cousins) will happily make your wallet lighter for you. Ticketmaster is the best option for concerts or Gumtree and Craigslist for re-sales and swaps.

General Information

Website: www.whufc.com
Phone: 020 8548 2794
Location: Boleyn Ground,
Green Street,
London E13 9AZ

Overview

When bald biscuit king Eggert Magnusson bought the Hammers everything looked rosy. But then the world went tits up. The recession meant Icelander Eggert's companies were suddenly worth nothing. He went bankrupt – and West Ham became a Scandinavian IOU. While boss Gianfranco Zola was leading a revolution on the pitch – shepherding a young team to the brinks of Europe – there were real dangers the club would fold.

Currently, West Ham is owned by a consortium that seized the club off Magnusson – made up of, er, Icelandic banks. Not really where you want your money right now. But if they survive, the Irons are on the way up. If you can find the ground in deepest East London they're well worth a look.

Over the years, West Ham has been unfairly tainted by association with the ICF hooligan firm. Largely active in the '70s and '80s, a 2005 film, 'Green Street' did its best to rekindle unwanted memories. The drama was undermined slightly by giving the lead role to a hobbit. These days, thanks to CCTV and high ticket prices, the Premiership is a largely peaceful affair. Under the stewardship of current manager Alan Curbishley, it should only be a matter of time before West Ham find their feet again and start a serious league challenge.

How to Get There

By Car: Driving in London is a waste of time even on the best of days, but try it on match days and you are asking for trouble. East London is a warren of one way streets, dead ends and no through roads. You are likely to either miss kick-off or get a parking ticket or both.

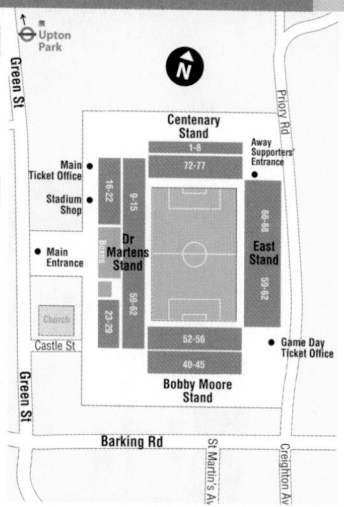

By Public Transport: The district line will 'whisk' you from central London to Upton Park in half an hour or so. The Boleyn Ground is 5 minutes walk from the underground station.

How to Get Tickets

Unless you want to pay through the nose for tickets against the big clubs, you should be able to find spares for the smaller fixtures. West Ham is a relatively small ground with a dedicated, hardcore following. Being less glamorous than Chelsea et al means that casual fans have a better chance of watching a game for a decent price.

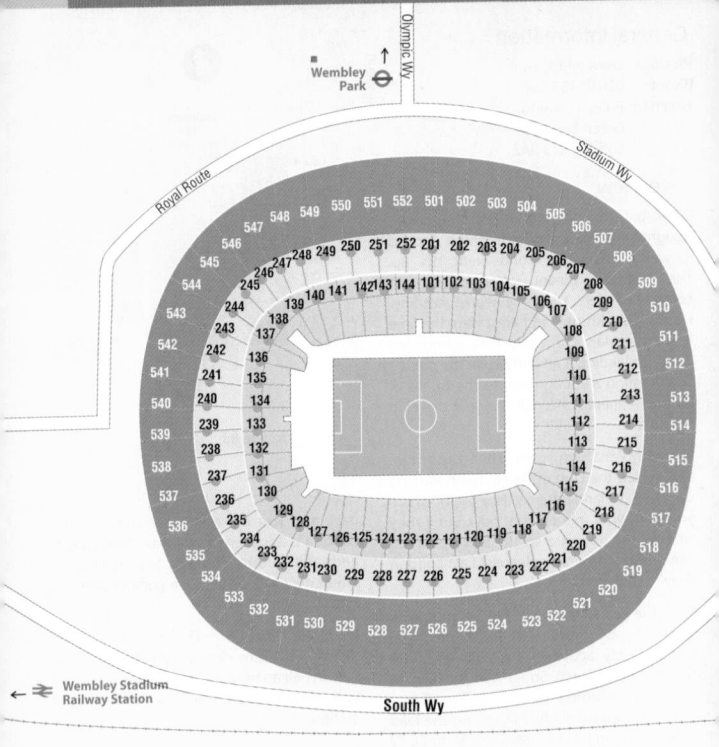

General Information

Phone: 0844 980 8001
Website: www.wembleystadium.com
Location: Wembley Stadium, Wembley HA9 0WS

Overview

Wembley Stadium enjoys a strange position in the British psyche. For football fans it's most significant as the scene of England's only World Cup win back in 1966, as well as numerous pitch invasions by angry / jubilant Scottish fans whenever their national team came down to play. Plus, a generation of British bands have

grown up dreaming of the day they'd bellow: "hello Wem-ber-ley, are you ready to rock?!!" to tens of thousands of people who've just paid a fiver for a chewy patty of minced spleen 'n' testicles in a dry bun. For these sentimental reasons, then, very few people complained that the National Stadium was a bit of a crap-hole stuck in an inaccessible suburb of West London. By the late '90s the place was looking a bit battered, so they knocked it down and then very, very slowly, and at tremendous, tabloid-scandalising expense, built a replacement on the same site. The result is, just about, worth it. There are none of the blind spots for spectators that the old stadium used to have, plus it has far greater leg-room for 90-thousand-plus people and much more comfortable seating. It also looks fantastically imposing as you walk out of Wembley Park tube with its massive arch curving into the sky. A trip here might not make your knees go "all trembly" as fans used to sing but for football lovers it's one of the world's great venues. They also have a special removable running track for athletics and, to the disgust of "soccer" purists, they've even let American "football" teams play here, too.

How to Get There

By Car: Short of hiring snipers to pick drivers off as they approach the mighty arch, the Stadium could hardly do more to discourage visitors from driving. "Wembley Stadium is a public transport destination. Please leave your car behind," the website primly advises. However, if you are some kind of die-hard, planet-raping petrol-head you'll see signs pointing to the stadium from Great Central Way onwards. There are very few parking spaces at the Stadium itself and these need to be booked in advance for £25 or £12 for disabled users and, despite the prices, they often sell out. On match days, or when there's anything else happening, the local area becomes residents' parking only, too. Yes, they really don't want you to bring your car.

By Public Transport: The nearest Tube is Wembley Park on the Metropolitan and Jubilee line. Wembley Central (on the Bakerloo line) is about 10–15 minutes walk and there's also Wembley Stadium mainline train station with links all over the country. If you're travelling from outside London there are National Express coaches from 43 different towns and cities.

How to Get Tickets

Easier said than done. 'Club Wembley' have kindly created a 'ten year seat licence'—no doubt to re-coup the massive overspend that accompanied completion of the stadium. These licences give owners access to all major events hosted at Wembley and its worth going on the website to laugh at the ridiculous prices. A 'one-off licence fee' costs from £1,650 to £19,226. Annual season tickets are on top of that. Cloud Cuckoo Land. 'Normal' people can buy tickets to England games through the FA (you need to be a member), for football and rugby cup games through the respective clubs and tickets for one off events and shows through Ticketmaster. It's always worth checking Gumtree.com as you never know who might be flogging off a golden ticket to the highest bidder.

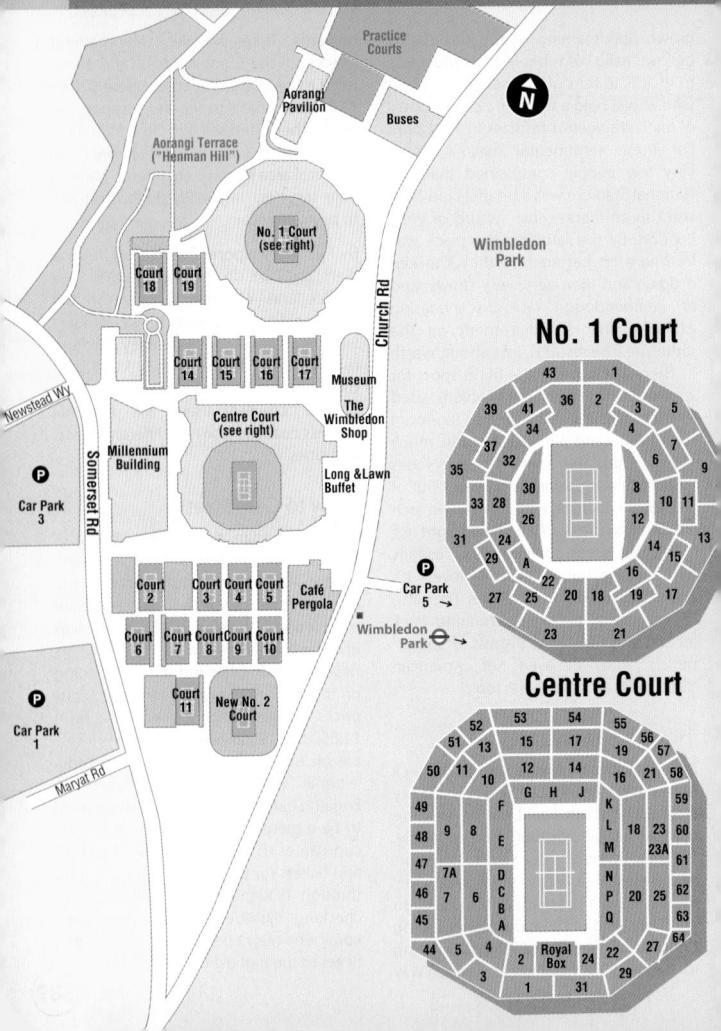
Practice Courts
Aorangi Pavilion
Buses
N
Aorangi Terrace ("Henman Hill")
No. 1 Court (see right)
Wimbledon Park
Court 18
Court 19
Church Rd
Court 14
Court 15
Court 16
Court 17
Museum
The Wimbledon Shop
Newstead Wy
Centre Court (see right)
Millennium Building
Long &Lawn Buffet
Car Park 3
Somerset Rd
Court 2
Court 3
Court 4
Court 5
Café Pergola
Car Park 5
Wimbledon Park
Court 6
Court 7
Court 8
Court 9
Court 10
Court 11
New No. 2 Court
Car Park 1
Maryat Rd
No. 1 Court
Centre Court
Royal Box

General Information

Telephone: 020 8944 1066
Website: www.wimbledon.org
Location: The All England Lawn Tennis and Croquet Club, Church Road, Wimbledon, SW19 5AE

Overview

New balls please! If it's not pissing it down—which is a big if—Wimbledon's All England Tennis and Croquet Club is the place to witness the world's finest tennis players do battle on rye grass courts, home as it is to the oldest major Championship in the game each June/July. But this is also a place to be seen and to be merry—sure, it's about the tennis, but it's also about strawberries and cream (of which 62,000 pounds and 1,540 gallons worth are sold each year respectively), the free flowing champagne, the celebrity crowd, and the Ralph Lauren-designed ballboy and ballgirl outfits. And if you can't actually get a ticket for the tournament—and the All England Club makes approximately 1,500 of them available each day, if you're prepared to camp out overnight in the queue—you can always sit yourself on Henman Hill at the northern end of the complex, where a vast television screen allows you to watch British players systematically eliminated in typically heartbreaking fashion. Really, we should stick to darts.

How to Get There

By Car: During the tournament, traffic and parking are nightmarish propositions, and you're better off using public transport. Nonetheless, the determined will need to take the A219 from the A3, and turn off left onto Church Road once in Wimbledon itself.

By Public Transport: Wimbledon railway station is a short journey from both Waterloo and Clapham Junction, and is otherwise serviced (Vicar!) by trains from towns right across the South of England. From here, board the London General shuttle bus straight to the grounds; they depart every five minutes or so during the tournament. Tube users should head for Southfields on the District Line, from where a London General shuttle also operates. Those who prefer to saunter can mosey on down Wimbledon Park Road heading south for ten minutes or so, and you can also walk it from Wimbledon Park tube station, heading north-west.

How to Get Tickets

You can (legally) come by tickets to Wimbledon in two ways—one, apply in advance to the public 'ballot', via the website above, in the hope you are selected at random to purchase tickets (closing date end of December). Two, join the serpentine, overnight queues for on-the-day tickets, of which five hundred are usually made available for each of Centre, Number One and Number Two Courts. Then, of course, there are all the other methods of which you're already no doubt aware.

Overview

Any bowling buff will tell you that there are two types of bowling in this country. Ten Pin Bowling, the ghastly Americanized import, is by far the most popular among Londoners and the generally disrespectful 'Youth Of Today.' Crown Green Bowling is a far more serene, (elderly) gentlemanly pursuit complete with its own rules and rituals. Of course, bowlers of both persuasions are served in London, ensuring that violent confronations between the two groups are kept to a minimum.

London's Ten Pin bowlers have been spoiled rotten of late. With the opening of new bowling lanes like 'All Star Lanes' (in Bayswater, Holborn and soon Brick Lane) the onset of yuppie money and boho style has transformed this past-time into an aesthetically pleasing but financially painful experience. At a peak time rate of £8.50 per person per game (your average game is a mere 10 minutes!) it's no wonder these shiny palaces of faux vintage design and Americana are populated largely by corporate parties and big spenders. Even cooler and slightly cheaper is the Bloomsbury Bowling Lanes (Holborn) which boasts an American diner and rates of £36 per lane per hour—doable if you have a large posse. It's even become a hip live music venue for indie gigs!

For families and the penniless, London has plenty of more 'traditional' British bowling lanes. By this, of course, we mean cavernous warehouses with pumping chart music, scary underage drinkers and sticky air hockey tables. Try the classic Rowans (Finsbury Park) which at its priciest is a mere £3.70 per person per game or Queens (Bayswater) which has also has an ice rink to cool off those skittle blues.

And what of Green Bowling? Well, being an outdoor pursuit in Britain, it's safe to say it is primarily a Summer affair. When the sun is out you'll find bowling greens in all the major parks; Hyde Park offers a set of woods for £5 (with no time limit) May till October.

After suffering at the hands of boho and cheapo Ten Pin bowling facilities you may find that there can be no better way to waste an afternoon than to sit around a bowling green in Finsbury Park with a beer in hand, laughing at your idiot friends' attempts to hit the 'jack.' Maybe those elderly gentlemen are on to something...

Bowling	*Address*	*Phone*	*Map*
All Star Lanes	Victoria House, Bloomsbury Pl	020 7025 2676	4
All Star Lanes	6 Porchester Gardens	020 7313 8363	30
Bloomsbury Bowling Lanes	Bedford Way	020 7183 1979	4
Hyde Park	Hyde Park	020 7262 3474	n/a
Queens	17 Queensway	020 7229 0172	30
Rowans	10 Stroud Green Rd	020 8800 1950	62

Overview

Nothing combines relaxation and hypertension quite like golf, nor indeed knee-length socks, spats and flat caps. For golfing Londoners, opportunities to play must be sought towards the outskirts of the capital, where the city shore is lapped once more by greenery and open space. You can, of course, take your one wood out onto London's pavements and practise your fade drive there, but you're odds on to be arrested if you do.

You'll be better received moving clockwise around London from the North, at establishments such as the Highgate Golf Club and Muswell Hill Golf Club. Both are highbrow member institutions with epic fairways, open nonetheless to the public, as long as that public is wearing a decent shirt. Eighteen holes at each are in the £30-40 range, which is also the case at the Hampstead Golf Club, home of one of England's toughest front nines. Nearby Finchley Golf Club is similarly priced for visitors but also offers some neat specials such as winter green fees in the £25 range and knockdown prices for twelve holes of 'twilight golf'. A little further north, Mill Hill Golf Club is a shade cheaper though no less satisfying.

In the south-east, the Royal Blackheath Golf Club positions itself as the oldest in the world, which might be why playing eighteen holes as a visitor requires a small trust fund, at £50 during summer weekdays. Moving further west, the Central London Golf Centre is a no-nonsense 'pay-and-play' establishment offering nine full-length holes to golfers of all standards for little more than a tenner. The Wimbledon Park Golf Club is another quality members club open to visitors, while nearby Royal Wimbledon Golf Club terms itself a 'very private' club—visitors are welcome but will be required to apply in writing, prove handicap and, in all likelihood, undergo some kind of permanently scarring initiation ritual. Access to each of these Wimbledon clubs kicks off at a chokingly high £70 for eighteen holes. You could buy a second hand Playstation for that. The London Scottish Golf Club on Wimbledon Common is much more like it, at £20 a round, though a pillar-box red top is compulsory for all. Out west, Dukes Meadows Golf Club in Chiswick offers nine three-par holes, a driving range and function rooms, all at a reasonable price.

For golfers who really are determined not to leave Zone One, there is one option after all. Urban Golf, with venues in Soho (W1) and Smithfield (EC1), is the last word in golf simulation, with the chance to play, virtual-style, some of the world's top courses. It also boasts well-stocked bars and chic lounge areas. You just know the purists will loathe it.

Golf Clubs	*Address*	*Phone*	*Map*
Central London Golf Centre	Burntwood Ln	020 8871 2468	n/a
Dukes Meadows Golf Club	Dukes Meadow	020 8995 0537	n/a
Finchley	Frith Ln	020 8346 1133	n/a
Hampstead Golf Club	82 Winnington Rd	020 8455 0203	n/a
Highgate Golf Club	Denewood Rd	020 8340 3745	n/a
Holland Park	Ilchester Pl	020 7602 2226	34
London Scottish Golf Club	Windmill Rd	020 8788 0135	n/a
Mill Hill Golf Club	100 Barnet Way	020 8959 2339	n/a
Muswell Hill Golf Club	Rhodes Ave	020 8888 1764	n/a
Royal Blackheath Golf Club	Court Rd	020 8550 1795	n/a
Urban Golf	33 Great Pulteney St	020 7434 4300	10
Urban Golf	12 Smithfield St	020 7248 8600	15
Wilbledon Park Golf Club	Home Park Rd	020 8946 1250	n/a

Overview

Remember the Levi's ad in the pool hall? The one which had The Clash's *Should I Stay Or Should I Go?* as the soundtrack? Yeah, that one. It conjured up a pretty cool image, right? Unfortunately London's pool halls have not had the retro revamp (is that an oxymoron?) that bowling is currently enjoying (All Star Lanes, Bloomsbury Bowling) so it's rare to actually find a place where you can stand around looking like James Dean, kissing your teeth, chewing on a tooth pick, and generally inviting any hustler to take you on without like, really being taken on by someone from the Russian/Turkish mafia. Of course, if you just want to chill, have a few beers and play some 8-ball with your buddies there is the ever reliable Elbow Rooms (Shoreditch/ Islington/Westbourne Grove) and the slightly less groovy but no less functional Riley's (Victoria/Clapham/Lewisham). The Islington Elbow Room has experienced a couple of shootings of the gun variety in recent years, so try not to spill your pint on anyone as you go from bar to pool table. The Shoreditch Elbow Room has a ping pong table in the summer. Why it is a seasonal attraction is uncertain but us Brits tend to associate sports according to weather it seems. We also inextricably link shooting some pool with having a drink or two, but it is often the lesser red and yellow-balled "pub" pool table (funnily enough) rather than the greater spotted (and striped) genuine American pool table which is found within the confines of the few remaining non-chain traditional pubs in London.The Westbury Bar in Kilburn however, has three American pool tables in a rather swank environment of leather Chesterfields, parquet flooring and red lampshades. Food is pan-Asian and roasts are served on Sundays, adding to a pub vibe. 19:20 in Clerkenwell has more of a pool hall feel with media types taking their game a little more seriously at the end of the working day. If you do fancy something a little more louche, there are many a pool and snooker hall to be found on the edges of central London which can offer a grittier atmosphere. Bomonti on the Kingsland Road is a Russian Bar where various art "happenings", poetry readings and live music nights occur as well as being a near-open all hours venue to play pool. The fact that Pete Doherty has been known to frequent the premises will either pique your interest or put you right off.

Pool & Snooker	*Address*	*Phone*	*Map*
19:20	20 Great Sutton St	020 7253 1920	6
Bomonti	340 Kingsland Rd	020 7923 1548	88
The Elbow Room	97 Curtain Rd	020 7613 1316	84
The Elbow Room	89 Chapel Market	020 7278 3244	80
The Elbow Room	103 Westbourne Grove	020 7221 5211	30
Riley's	638 Wandsworth Rd	020 7498 0432	142
Riley's	16 Semley Pl	020 7824 8261	19
Rowans	10 Stroud Green Rd	020 8800 1950	62
The Westbury	34 Kilburn High Rd	020 7625 7500	68

Tennis

Ah…the other beautiful game, beloved of park fence jumpers and upper class grunters alike. Like many popular sports, tennis may have originated in Britain, but we're pretty consistent in our ineptitude at it. This is not for the lack of trying: the country's capital is packed full of tennis clubs, outdoor park courts and large sports complexes.

Tennis is certainly not as exclusive as it once was, with an hour's playing a lot cheaper than ten-pin bowling, for example. You can mince about amidst leafy surroundings in Hyde Park (Hyde Park Sports Centre, 020 7262 3474), flail in the dark depths of Finsbury Park on a turn-up-and-play basis, or in the luxury of the historic Queens Club (www.queensclub.co.uk, 020 7386 3429 for membership information). Also commendable are the Paddington Sports Club (020 7286 8448) in Maida Vale and the courts in Regent's Park: go to www.tennisintheparks.co.uk for information on, uh, playing tennis in parks. Indicative of the new equalitarian nature of the game are Tennis London International (www.tennislondon.com) who take pride in being 'the largest gay and lesbian tennis group in the UK.' But it's not all democratic: there's always Wimbledon (www.wimbledon.org, which due to the jaw dropping ticket prices, still is as exclusive as it's always been. If you still want to get caught up in the annual tennis frenzy, head to Henman Hill, or Murray Mound, or whatever it's called these days. Essentially a hill outside Centre Court, here you can sit on the grass and watch the action on video screens with all the other poor proles who don't have any kidneys left to trade for a ticket.

Squash

Like some weird secret society, squash players spend their time locked indoors, organised into little private clubs and engaged in an activity which will eventually mess them up. Squash is hard—just ask your poor knees. The squash court is a high-octane containment tank swimming in adrenalin, which explains why Londoners have taken to it with such gusto. A court at Sobell Center (020 7609 2166) in Finsbury Park for example, is near impossible to book at peak times. In Shepherd's Bush, there's the exclusive squash club New Grampians (020 7603 4255) which is lush, but there are sizeable membership fees to match. Be warned—a lot of sports centres don't have squash facilities, but somewhere like the Oasis Sports Centre (0207 831 1804) in Tottenham Court Road is a church to all things sweaty and squashy…and you can go for an outdoor swim afterwards too. For a quirkier court try Maiden Lane (020-7267 9586)—a community centre in a housing estate, which has one beat-up court for £6 an hour. If there isn't a yoga class in progress, that is.

Badminton/Table Tennis

They may be worlds apart in many ways, but badminton and table tennis are usually offered in the same place, and both are 'genteel' sports in which it is almost acceptable to be beaten by the opposite sex (whichever sex you are). Badminton is especially popular across the board, with almost all sizeable sports centres offering courts and equipment. However, if you've any experience in attempting to book a court at most public sports complexes you'll know of the often depressing amount of phone wrangling and frustration that arises from these exchanges. Chief perpetrator is Kings Hall Sports Centre (020 8985 2158) in Lower Clapton, who will test your patience to inhumane limits. The Brixton Recreation Centre (020 7926 9779) caters for badminton and squash players but always sound like they can't wait to get you off the phone; their rates are around £7 for badminton, which is pretty competitive. The Sobell Centre, as mentioned above, also caters for table tennis (doesn't ping pong sound nicer?) and badminton. The best strategy is to phone your local centre to ascertain which racquet sports they cater for and then prepare yourself to be either double-booked, misinformed or given a free session depending on the ability of the desk assistant!

Overview

As the nascent city of 'Londinium' was being named by the Romans in AD 43, in Asia the practice of yoga was entering its third or fourth millennium. Nineteen hundred years on, at last it found its way out west, and London's yoga establishments have flourished ever since. Essentially, the capital's schools can be divided into those concerned primarily with physical fitness—often the larger institutions offering a range of styles—and those with a more spiritual bent. Of the former, Go Yoga in Shepherd's Bush is a fine example, offering yoga and pilates for adults and kids alike, while the popular Triyoga centres in Primrose Hill and Covent Garden are one-stop holistic shops for the upwardly mobile set. More specialised centres include Bikram Yoga College of India in Kentish Town, and its partner Bikram Yoga City—bring water and a towel for hard wearing, specially heated sessions—and the Iyengar Yoga Institute in Maida Vale, which offers a free introductory class. Special mention also goes to Fulham Yogashala, a newish venture offering all sorts including, unnervingly, 'power yoga'. Still, entering the peaceful surroundings of Yogashala is, according to one client, like getting a hug. Those more spiritual schools include the wonderful Sivanada Yoga Centre, an oasis of serenity in the midst of Putney boasting resident yogi teachers, and the Satyananda Yoga Centre in Clapham with its deep focus on yoga-meditation techniques. Shanti Sadam, out west, is also more concerned with inner stillness than downward dogs. And hidden away in Archway, the Kriya Centre runs a series of kundalini yoga classes in humble but hospitable surroundings—Ohm tastic!

Yoga Centers	*Address*	*Phone*	*Website*	*Map*
Alchemy	Stables Market	020 7267 6188	www.alchemythecentre.co.uk	71
Battersea Yoga	152 Northcote Rd	020 7978 7995	www.batterseayoga.com	140
Bikram Yoga City	6 Vestry St	020 7336 6330	www.bikramyoga.co.uk/studio_city.html	84
Bikram's Yoga College Of India	173 Queen's Crescent	020 7692 6900	www.bikramyoga.co.uk/studio_north.html	71
Fulham Yogashala	11 Lettice St	079 5609 1696	www.fulhamyogashala.co.uk	48
Go Yoga	140 Percy Rd	020 8740 1989	www.go-yoga.co.uk	n/a
The Hidden Space	93 Falkland Rd	020 8347 3400	www.thehiddenspace.co.uk	55
Islington Yoga	357 City Rd	020 7704 6796	www.islingtonyoga.com	83
Iyengar Yoga Institute	223 Randolph Ave	020 7624 3080	www.iyi.org.uk	27
Jamyang Buddhist Centre	43 Renfrew Rd	020 7820 8787	www.jamyang.co.uk	112
The Kriya Centre	25 Bickerton Rd	020 7272 5811	www.karamkriya.co.uk	59
The Lotus Exchange	Black Prince Rd	020 7463 2234	www.lotusexchange.com	131
North London Buddhist Centre	72 Holloway Rd	020 7700 1177	www.northlondonbuddhistcentre.com	74
Satyananda Yoga Centre	70 Thurleigh Rd	020 8673 4869	www.syclondon.com	147
Shanti Sadan Yoga Centre	29 Chepstow Villas	020 7727 7846	www.shantisadan.org	29
Shoreditch Studio	49 Curtain Rd	020 7012 1238	www.shoreditchstudio.co.uk	8
Siddha Yoga Sangham Of Europe	63 Collier St	020 7278 0567		79
Sivananda Yoga	51 Felsham Rd	020 8426 9795	www.sivananda.co.uk	136
Surya Yoga Studio CLOSED TILL JULY 09	9 Park Hill	020 7622 4257	www.suryayoga.co.uk	149
Templeton House Yoga Studio,	34 Chiswell St	020 7074 6000	www.templetonhouse.co.uk	7
Triyoga	6 Erskine Road	020 7483 3344	www.triyoga.co.uk	70
Urban Bikram	24 Shacklewell Ln	020 7254 3060		86
Yoga Place	449 Bethnal Green Rd	020 7739 5195	www.yogaplace.co.uk	92
Yoga Therapy Center	92 Pentonville Rd	020 7689 3040	www.yogatherapy.org	80

There's nothing quite like an obesity epidemic to make a city sporty. We're constantly being told that we're swelling to huge new levels. The message is worrying: buck up fatties, or you won't even fit into your own coffin. But with a London Olympics on the horizon, grassroots sport has been thrust into the spotlight. Part of the package that won the Games was to build a sporting legacy. And in the hope that we won't all be housebound when the Olympics rolls into town, lower-level sport is seeing increased investment. London's sizeable ethnic communities have also brought weird and wonderful games with them (American Football? In London? Not in our lifetimes). Dozens of leagues, in dozens of sports, gather every evening to try and beat the bulge.

General tips

A good starting point is the Gumtree website (www.gumtree.com). Their sports and community section is full of ads trying to fills gaps in sports teams. And as it was started by born-to-sweat Aussies, it never lets up in sheer quantity of athletic opportunities. The local press is also a decent bet. All London boroughs have their own newspapers, who cover amateur sports with as much enthusiasm as the professionals. You may never make it in the big leagues, but at least you can be a hero in Camden. But one area where London struggles is with the concept of pick-up games. Perhaps it's part of our reserved nature, but it's unusual to just rock up at a park and challenge whoever's there. By all means try, but you may get rebuked by a stiff upper lip.

Football

Sunday league football in London used to have a reputation of being rough. For many years it was the preserve of hungover builders, who wanted ninety minutes letting off steam by kicking people around. But it's moved on slightly from those days, with a more general acceptance of skill and less emphasis placed on pain. The spiritual home of recreational football is Hackney Marshes. The east London site has a whopping 87 pitches—so many leagues and teams play there that it's worth just turning up and asking around. If you draw a blank there, then the FA website (www.thefa.com) has a club locator search. Regardless of where you live, you'll get a mammoth list of clubs. The hardest part of finding a team in London is narrowing down who it is you want to play for. Five-a-side football is also booming in London. In the city centre, where space is at a premium, it's often the only way of getting in a game. Powerleague (www.powerleague.co.uk) organise leagues around the capital, though these can be pricey. A cheaper option is to head to a leisure centre with a five-a-side pitch. They often run leagues and are less profit-driven than the private companies. Lists of leisure centres can be found on specific borough's website (such as Islington's www.islington.gov.uk).

Rugby

Don't mind drinking pints of your team-mates' urine? Enjoy a good eye-gouging? Then you must be a rugby fan! The Rugby in London website (www.rugbyinlondon.co.uk) is a Bible for lovers of casual violence, as it lists hundreds of clubs, contact details and even training venues and times. Female fans of egg chasing are also well represented. Most teams play around south-west London, though there's a few more dotted around the city. A full list is on the RFU Women's website (www.rfuwlonse.co.uk). If you don't fancy the full-on ear-biting code of the sport there's a flourishing touch rugby scene in London. In this form of the game tackling is represented by tagging your opponent. It's an altogether less bloody type of rugby, although you're still allowed to indulge in the booze-fuelled rituals that the contact players enjoy. In2Touch (www.in2touch.com) lists a few of these leagues.

Cricket

As a sport that takes up plenty of space, you have to head slightly out of town to play cricket. Most London clubs play in either the Essex, Middlesex or Surrey leagues, in the outskirts of the capital. The Play-Cricket website (www.play-cricket.co.uk) has a full rundown on London clubs.

Athletics and the London Marathon

Every spring, London's runners dust down their gorilla costumes and tackle the London Marathon. If you feel up to it then you have to plan ahead; places are limited and dished out via a ballot. If you need a helping hand in the run up to the race, there's a list of jogging and road-running clubs at www.onesite.co.uk/find/running. As well as getting you in shape, so you don't die after 20 miles, they can help you get a spot in the starting line-up. And if you catch the bug of competitive athletics, there are six clubs who compete in the London Inter Club Challenge (www.licc.co.uk).

Miscellaneous

For fans of all things Irish, there's the London Gaelic Sports Association (www.londongaa.org); American footballers can get their fix with the British American Football League (www.bafl.org.uk); and if tight shorts and sleeveless shirts are your thing there's the British Aussie Rules Association (www.barfl.co.uk; or you could just join the navy).

Transport • **Gatwick Airport**

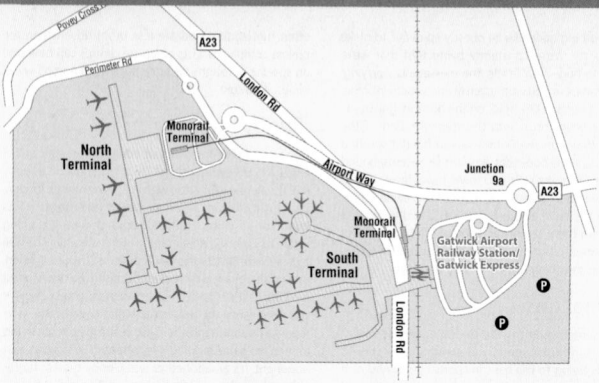

Airline	*Terminal*	*Phone Number*
Adria Airways	North	020 8099 7254
Aer Lingus	South	0871 521 2772
Afriqiyah	South	0870 040 5040
Air Algerie	South	0870 111 1111
Air Baltic	South	0870 190 0737
Air Comet	North	0870 111 1111
Air Europa	South	0844 493 0787
Air Malta	South	0844 493 0787
Air Namibia	North	0870 066 1472
Air Southwest	North	0870 111 1111
Air Transat	South	0870 190 0737
Air Zimbabwe	South	0870 040 5040
Atlas Blue	North	0870 111 1111
Aurigny	South	0870 190 0737
Azerbaijan Airlines	South	0870 190 0737
Belavia Belarusian Airlines	South	
BH Air (Balkan Holidays)	South	0845 600 0950
bmi	South	0870 066 1472
British Airways	North	0870 574 7747
British Jet	South	0800 091 4444
Brussels Airlines	North	0870 190 0737
Bulgaria Air	South	0870 111 1111
Cimber Sterling	South	0870 111 1111
Clickair	North	0870 190 0737
Croatia Airlines	South	0870 066 1472
Cubana	South	0844 493 0787
Daallo Airlines	North	0870 243 2222
Delta Air Lines	North	0870 876 5000
easyJet	North & South	0870 111 1111
Emirates	North	0870 040 5040
Estonian Air	South	0870 111 1111
Eurocypria	South	0870 190 0737
Flybe	South	0870 111 1111
flyglobespan	South	0870 190 0737
flyLAL Lithuanian Airlines	North	01293 579 900

Airline	*Terminal*	*Phone Number*
Flystar Astraeus	North	01293 819 800
Ghana International Airlines	South	0870 60 70 555
Iceland Express	South	0870 066 1472
Karthago	South	0870 111 1111
Kibris Turkish Airlines	North	0870 190 0737
Malev	North	0871 737 8155
Meridiana Airlines	South	01293 596 609
Mexicana	South	0870 574 7747
Monarch Airlines	South	0870 876 5000
Montenegro Airlines	South	0870 040 5040
norwegian.no	South	0870 190 0737
Olympic Airlines	South	0870 111 1111
Onur Air	South	0870 190 0737
Pakistan International Airlines	South	0800 587 1023
Qatar Airways	North	0870 190 0737
Rossiya Airlines	South	0844 493 0787
Ryanair	South	0870 876 5000
SAS	South	020 7393 1201
SATA International	South	0870 066 1472
TAP Air Portugal	South	
Tarom	North	0870 111 1111
Thomas Cook	South	0870 190 0737
Thomson Airways	North	0844 493 0787
Ukraine International Airlines	South	0870 190 0737
US Airways	South	0844 493 0787
Viking Airlines	South	0844 493 0787
Virgin Atlantic Airways	South	0870 876 5000
Virgin Nigeria	North	0844 412 1788
Wizz Air	South	+48 22 351 9499
XL Airways	South	0870 169 0169
Zoom Airlines	South	0870 240 0055

General Information

West Sussex
RH6 0NP
General enquiries: 0870 000 2468
Lost property: 01293 503 162
www.gatwickairport.com

Overview

"Gatwick is the busiest single-runway airport in the world." No shit. And they say that like it's a good thing. Basically if you've ever had to go to Spain in high summer, you know the reasons why you shouldn't go to Gatwick: it's not on the Tube and, more importantly, the check-in zone is a sweat-filled free-for-all. Realistically, if being in an airport really was some kind of holiday, you wouldn't need to fly out of the place. Gatwick, though clunkier than some of the bigger, flashier airports, is not so bad to deal with if you have patience. Just don't be there when all the transatlantic flights arrive at the same time.

As far as amenities go, the usual suspects are all present, with convivial times available at Britain's premier diluting station, J.D. Wetherspoons, and the glamour of Knightsbridge miraculously squeezed into one of those little airport branches of Harrods—just in case you feel the need to inflict one of their god-awful teddy bears on another country. As far as eating's concerned, you could try something apart from McDonald's but then again why pretend to yourself that you're having a nice time when it's clearly not on the cards for the next few hours?

Which Terminal?

Trains arrive at the South Terminal, and there are more shops here – but if your flight is from the North Terminal, a free automated train will take you on the five minute transfer.

Getting There

A refreshingly good train service—the creatively-titled Gatwick Express (www.gatwickexpress.com) —runs from Victoria every 15 minutes 5.20 am–12:50 am; and hourly during the night. It takes 30 minutes and if you're near the rail hubs it is by far the most pleasant way to get there—though a single journey is going to set you back around £16. First Capital Connect run trains to Gatwick from St Pancras International and London Bridge which costs closer to £8 and take only about 45 minutes. Easybus coaches from Victoria Coach Station get to Gatwick in 40 minutes, and cost around £2–6 for a single.

To drive to Gatwick from the M25 you need to leave at Junction 7 and carry on southwards along the M23, following the signs. Leave the M23 at junction 9 and again, follow those handy signs to get to the appropriate terminal.

Parking

The short stay car park is recommended for up to five hours at a time, and is incremented every 15 minutes then every hour, with a maximum charge of £21 per 24 hours. For long stays there are several parks located 5-15 minutes away (via bus transfers) from the airport. These are best booked in advance. For the official Gatwick car park, charges are £8.60 per day 1–5 days and £8.20 for six days and over.This can be done through the BAA Gatwick website.

Car Hire

All the big names are represented, or you can try generic websites such as www.travelsupermarket.com/carhire.

Shops

There is the usual wide range of shops ranging from chemists to food/drink to fashion. Retail stores include Harrods, Monsoon, Nike, Quiksilver, Ray Ban, and Yo! Sushi.

Hotels

Alexander House
Arora International
Cambridge Hotel
Clarion Hotel
Copthorne Hotel
Corner House Hotel
Effingham Park Hotel
Europa Hotel
Express
Felbridge Hotel
George Hotel
Hilton
Holiday Inn
Ibis Hotel
Langshott Manor
Moathouse Hotel
Premier Travel Inn
Ramada Plaza
Renaissance Hotel
Russ Hill
Skylane Hotel
Sofitel Hotel
Thistle
Travelodge
Whitehouse
Worth Hotel

Transport • Heathrow Airport

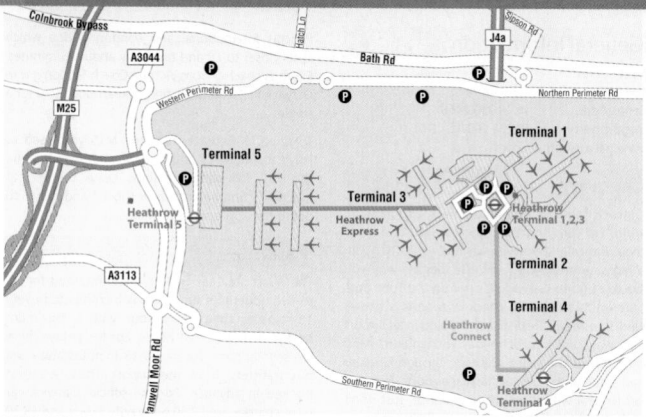

Airline	Terminal	Phone Number
Aer Lingus	1	0870 876 5000
Aeroflot	2	020 7355 2233
Air Algerie	2	020 8750 3300
Air Astana	2	01293 596 622
Air Canada	3	0871 220 1111
Air China	3	020 8745 4624
Air France	2	0870 142 4343
Air India	3	020 8560 9996
Air Malta	4	0906 103 0012
Air Mauritius	3	020 7434 4375
Air New Zealand	1	0800 028 4149
Air Seychelles	2	01293 596 656
Air Transat	2	020 7616 9187
Alitalia	2	0870 544 8259
All Nippon Airways	3	+44 (0)870 837 8811
American Airlines	3	+44 (0)20 7365 0777
Arik Air	2	08444 822324
Asiana Airlines	1	020 7304 9900
Atlas Blue	2	020 7307 5803
Austrian Airlines	2	020 7766 0300
Azerbaijan Airlines	2	0870 760 5757
Bellview Airlines	2	020 7372 3770
Biman Bangladesh Airlines	3	020 7629 0252
Blue1 (SAS Group)	3	
bmi	1	0870 60 70 555
bmi	1	0870 60 70 555
British Airways	3 & 4 but mainly 5	0844 493 0787
Bulgaria Air	2	020 7637 7637
Cathay Pacific Airways	3	020 8834 8888
China Eastern	2	020 7935 2676
Clickair	3	00 800 25425247
Continental Airlines	4	0845 607 6760
Croatia Airlines	2	020 8563 0022
CSA Czech Airlines	2	0870 444 3747
Cyprus Airways	1	020 8359 1333
Delta Air Lines	4	0845 600 0950
Egypt Air	3	020 8759 3635
El Al Israel Airlines	1	020 7957 4100
Emirates	3	0870 243 2222
Ethiopian Airlines	3	020 8745 4235

Airline	Terminal	Phone Number
Etihad Airways	3	0870 241 7121
Eva Air	3	020 7380 8300
Finnair	3	0870 241 4411
Gulf Air	3	0870 777 1717
Iberia	3	0870 609 0500
Icelandair	1	0870 787 4020
Iran Air	3	020 8759 0921
Japan Airlines	3	0845 774 7700
JAT Airways	2	020 8745 0899
Jet Airways	3	0808 101 1199
Kenya Airways	4	020 8283 1818
Kibris Turkish Airlines	3	020 7930 4851
Kingfisher Airlines	4	0800 047 0810
KLM Royal Dutch Airlines	4	0870 507 4074
Korean Air	3	0800 413 000
Kuwait Airways	3	020 8745 7772
Libyan Arab Airlines	2	020 8750 4066
LOT Polish Airlines	1	0845 601 0949
Lufthansa	1	0871 945 9747
Malaysia Airlines System	3	0870 607 9090
MEA Middle East Airlines	3	020 7467 8000
Northwest Airlines	4	0870 507 4074
Pakistan International Airlines		3
0800 587 1023		
Qantas	4	0845 774 7767
Qatar Airways	3	020 7896 3636
Singapore Airlines	3	0844 800 2380
South African Airways	1	0870 747 1111
Sri Lankan Airlines	4	020 8538 2000
Swiss International Airlines	2	0845 601 0956
Syrianair	2	020 7493 2851
Transaero Airlines	1	0870 850 7767
Tunisair	2	020 7734 7644
Turkish Airlines	3	0844 800 6666
Turkmenistan Airlines	3	020 8577 2211
United Airlines	1	0845 844 4777
US Airways	1	0845 600 3300
Uzbekistan Airways	2	020 7935 4775
Virgin Atlantic Airways	3	0870 574 7747
Yemenia Yemen Airways	2	0870 732 3213

General Information

234 Bath Road, Hayes, Middlesex, UB3 5AP
General enquiries: 0870 000 0123
Lost property: 020 8745 7727
www.heathrowairport.com

Overview

We all hate airports—especially Heathrow. It's way overcrowded and has tiresome security checks; delays; queues; overpriced shops; terrible food and a tendency to lose baggage. Even our ex-mayor Ken Livingstone has accused Heathrow of keeping people "prisoner" in its "ghastly shopping mall." There does seem to be slow, gradual improvement but it's still a long way from what it should be, and gives a poor first impression of the UK.

Often said to be busiest in the world, there are a few contenders for this title. Heathrow definitely has the largest number of international passengers.

For years its facilities have been stretched beyond capacity, but Heathrow now has some large-scale and controversial expansion plans. The expansion began with T5 and an unsurprisingly chaotic luggage-losing launch in 2008. T5 will provide capacity for an additional 30 million people, taking the total number of passengers to 90 million annually. Next steps are to replace terminals 1 and 2 with Heathrow East, although this won't be ready until 2012 . A third runway and a sixth terminal are also grinding inexorably through the planning process—to the dismay of local residents. A new high-speed luggage tunnel linking T3 & 5 should avoid another lost luggage debacle.

Which Terminal?

Heathrow is in a seemingly constant state of flux, so confirm before you travel.

Terminal 1 is for domestic flights, most UK airline departures to Europe plus EL AL, South African, and United. **Terminal 2** is for most non-UK carriers' flights to Europe and some long haul destinations.**Terminal 3** is the long haul terminal for Asian and Asia Pacific airlines, US and South American, plus most African and Middle Eastern carriers. **Terminal 4** is for most British Airways long haul flights and some European services. KLM and Qantas also use T4. **Terminal 5** is used exclusively by BA, though at time of press a small number of flights departed from T3 (European) & 4 (long haul).

Terminals 1-3 are within walking distance of each other (up to 15 minutes) so just follow the signs. You can transfer (for free) to T4 on the Heathrow Connect train and T5 on the Heathrow Express. There is also a free bus which connects T4 and T5, every 6 minutes.

Getting There

The London Underground's Piccadilly Line can get you to central London in less than an hour for only about £4. The wait time for a train is generally no more than 10 minutes. Heathrow has three underground stations; one servicing terminal 1, 2 & 3, and one each for terminals 4&5.

Heathrow Express is a non-stop train between the airport and Paddington station, "In 15 minutes—every 15 minutes". It stops at Heathrow Central Station (T1-3) and the new T5. £16.50 one way

Heathrow Connect follows the same route into west London, but serves intermediate stations making its journey time 25 minutes. Trains depart Paddington every 30 minutes from Platform 12, stopping at Heathrow Central (Terminal 1,2,3) and Terminal 4. £7.40 one way. Passengers arriving at T5 may catch the Heathrow Express free of charge to Central station if they wish to use Heathrow Connect into town.

Both these trains run between approx 5 am–12 am. There are also three tube stations—a cheaper and slower option. Roughly £4 for an hour's journey to central London. During rush hour it gets packed with commuters.

National Express run a bargain bus from London Victoria station which only costs £5 one way. It takes anywhere from 45-75 minutes and drops you off at Heathrow Central bus terminal (T1,2,3)

Driving from Central London takes about 45-60 minutes—well anything really—depending on traffic. When leaving Terminals 1–3, follow exit signs to the access/exit tunnel. Then follow signs to the M4 motorway, which will eventually bring you into London. A taxi to central London takes 45-60 minutes and costs £35+.

Car Parking

There are short-term and long-term car parks, both are expensive. An hour at the short stay is £4.10, 48 hours is £90.40. The long stay car park is about 10 minutes away by courtesy bus and the drive-up price is £15.60 per day.

General Information:

Royal Docks,
London, E16 2PX
General Enquiries: 020 7646 0000/88
www.londoncityairport.com

Overview

With its one wee runway squeezed over the water between the old George V and Royal Albert Docks, City is London's smallest and most central airport (6 miles from the City of London). Where once stevedores ate pie and mash, stockbrokers are now whisked off to lunchtime meetings on dinky short take-off jets. Primarily used by business types, its small size and short runway means City only serves European destinations (20 in total, although British Airways do have a flight to New York in the pipeline) from its single terminal and 22 check-in desks. Still, this means much faster check-in times and fewer delays than at the comparative behemoths of Heathrow and Gatwick.

Getting There

In 2005 someone, somewhere, saw the light and extended the DLR (Docklands Light Railway) to City. The airport now couldn't be simpler to get to by public transport: get on the DLR at Bank; make sure you take a train destined for the King George V branch (these are marked "via City Airport"); and you'll arrive at the airport's station in 25 minutes. A slightly quicker route is to take the Jubilee Underground line to Canning Town and take the DLR a mere three stops westbound from there. There is a taxi rank directly outside the terminal exit, expect to pay at least £35 for a black cab to go to or from the West End. Don't expect the journey to be much faster than on the DLR/Underground. Pre-booked cabs should be a little cheaper, try Airport Executive (020 8838 3333) or the trusty Addison Lee (020 7387 8888).

If you're driving—given its central location—there's no obvious route to City. A useful general rule is to point your wheels at the eastern end of Central London and then keep going that way from Tower Hill on the A1203 (East Smithfield/The Highway). The airport is signposted from this road. If you're getting there from the South East, head through the Blackwall tunnel and follow signs once you emerge into the daylight. If you're near the M25 and like traffic jams, crawl your way to junction 30 and take the Thames Gateway to the airport from there.

Parking

Short stay is directly next to the terminal and rates start at £8 for one hour going up to £82 for 48 hours.

You can also have your car valet-parked for no extra cost (apart from having to tip the man entrusted with not scratching your pride and joy).

The long stay carpark is a short walk from the terminal and will relieve you of £14 for up to four hours, £24 for 4-12 hours, £36 from 12-24 hours, or £82 per day if you stay two or more days.

So parking is expensive. If you still feel the need to park and can book in advance, get in touch with BCP airport parking for a (slightly) cheaper option at www.parkbcp.co.uk.

Car Hire

Avis 020 7646 0832
Europcar..... 020 7646 0844
Hertz 020 7476 9646

Hotels

Etap Hotel London City Airport,
North Woolwich Road, Silverstown,
London, E16 2EE
020 7474 9106

Custom House Hotel Excel Docklands,
272-283 Victoria Dock Road, London,
E16 3BY
020 7474 0011

Premier Travel Inn
Excel East, Royal Victoria Docks, Canning
Town, E16 1SL
0870 238 3322

Novotel London Excel
7 Western Gateway Royal Victoria Dock,
London, E16 1AA
020 7540 9700

Ibis London Excel
9 Western Gateway, London, E16 1AB
020 7055 2300

Sunborn Yacht Hotel
1 Royal Victoria Dock, London, E16 1SL
020 70599100

Holiday Inn Express
1 Silvertown Way, Docklands, London,
E16 1EA
020 75404040

Travelodge London City Airport Hotel
Hartmann Road, Silvertown, London
E16 2BZ
0871 9846290

Airlines:

Aer Arann

British Airways

CityJet

KLM

Lufthansa

Luxair

SAS

SunAir

Swiss International Air Lines

VLM Airlines

General Information

London Luton Airport
Navigation House
Airport Way
Luton, Bedfordshire LU2 9LY
General enquiries including lost property: 01582 405100
www.london-luton.co.uk

Overview

To call Luton Airport a 'London' airport is surely one HUGE marketing scam. The same tragedy happens everyday: the unsuspecting traveller smugly enters their credit card details as they book their £2.99 easyJet flight to some godforsaken club 18-30 resort on the Spanish coast, thinking they got the best deal *ever*. One big problem. The flight's from Luton Airport—which should stop any celebrating London traveller dead. Unless you live in North London, getting to and from Luton by public transport is awful. It consists of taking an unreliable half-hour train service from St Pancras or London Bridge to Luton Parkway. After your train journey, if you're lucky, you'll be met at Luton Parkway by a shuttle bus. Be sure to purchase your rail tickets with London Luton Airport as your final destination. If your plane is delayed past midnight, which most budget airlines tend to be, God help you. Where's the Luton Express you might wonder? Ha ha. Good question…

Once you get to the one-terminal airport, your travelling companions will be the kind of people who hunt down the absolute cheapest airfares for their raucous stag or hen nights. Inside security, the few shops and cafés of the Pret a Manger and Dixons variety, will be teeming with these unsavoury characters. So next time you select 'all London airports' when booking your weekend getaway—think carefully!

Getting There

This can be extremely tricky and there's really no easy way. What with a Tube journey to St Pancras or London Bridge station, a train journey, and finally a shuttle bus, you better pack light. Also, you really don't want to get stuck sleeping in the airport when the shuttle bus stops at midnight.

Coach services, such as the 757 Greenline (collaborating with Terravision), easyBus and National Express are good alternatives that will at least get you home if your flight comes in late. Greenline & Terravision are probably your best bet (0990 747 777) with pick-up and drop-off points on Buckingham Palace Road, Marble Arch and Baker Street. Prices are from £13 and it takes about an hour, but it runs pretty regularly through the night. The National Express (08705 80 80 80) service 421 also operates between Luton, Heathrow Airport and London Victoria.

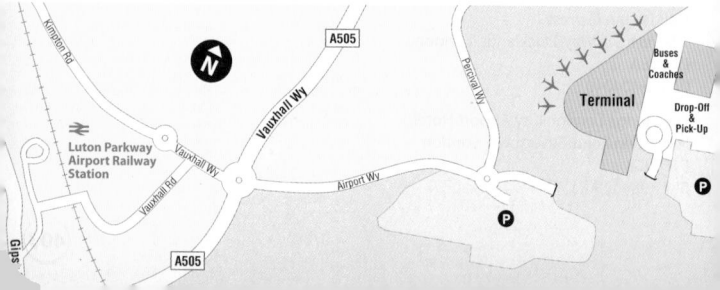

London Luton Airport is somewhat accessible from both the M1 and M25. If you have a choice, go for the M1, as the airport is only about five minutes from junction 10. Without traffic, it can take c. 45 minutes from central London. This can sometimes be longer when there are extensive road works, which tends to be always. When using Sat Nav systems, use the postcode LU2 9QT.

How To Get There – Really

Seriously. You've paid next to nothing for your airfare, splash out on a private cab. If you book a licensed mini-cab ahead of time, the service is often cheaper than the equivalent black cab fare and definitely easier, as they'll meet you at the arrivals hall. A consistently cheap company is Simply Airports (020 7701 4321) which is usually under £55, but you may want to get a quote from your own local company. If you leave it to the last minute, and must take a black cab, get ready to shell out at least £85 (with their meters, this can increase with traffic) plus a meeting fee if you want them to wait for you. Cab rides from central London usually take about an hour.

Parking

Short Term Parking is pricier but situated closest to the terminal, with prices ranging from £3 for 15 minutes, to £480 for 16 days. Mid-term is ideal for stays of around five days and is about a five-minute transfer by bus. Prices can vary from £11.25 to £17.00 per day dependent on length of stay. Long-term parking is about 10 minutes from the terminal by bus, and can be booked ahead of time online (www.ncp.co.uk) to save money. Prices range from £12.50 per day for up to four days to £90 for eight days. NCP can be reached on 01582 395484 (9 am–4 pm) and 07734 595560 in an emergency.

Rental Cars

Hertz Rent A Car 01582 450333
Avis Rent A Car Ltd 01582 454040
Thrifty Car Rental 01582 416222
National Car Rental.....01582 454554

Shops

Luton has a small selection of shops and is slowly getting better, but don't expect too much. There is a Boots (chemist/drugstore), a newsagent, and somewhere to eat/drink.

Hotels

Chiltern Hotel Luton
73 Beechwood Road; 01582 575911

Days Hotel Luton
Regent Street; 01582 878 090

Express by Holiday Inn Hotel
2 Percival Way; 01582 589 100

Holiday Inn Luton South
London Road; 0870 443171

Menzies Strathmore Hotel Luton
The Luton Arndale Centre; 01582 734199

Airlines

Aer Arann

Blue Air

easyJet

El Al

Flybe

Monarch

Ryanair

SkyEurope

Thomson

transavia.com

Wizz Air

General Information

Address: Stansted Airport,
Essex CM24 1QW
General enquiries: 0 870 000 0303
Lost property: 0 1279 663 293
Left luggage: 0 1279 663 213
Police: 0 1245 452 450
Website: www.stanstedairport.com

Overview

It might be tucked away in the middle of the dull Essex countryside, but Stansted Airport has one thing going for it—it's amazingly simple. One terminal (and quite a nice one too, Norman Foster saluted), one check-in area, one security gate. Take that, Heathrow. Around 20 airlines, most of them budget, fly more than 20 million passengers from here to a growing list of mainly domestic and short-haul destinations. If you're budget-crazy enough to fly in the middle of the night, there are several breakfast opportunities. Eating options are generally better before security—unless you like tiny, overpriced ciabatta baguettes or the sugar-drenched fare offered by the big coffee chains. But once through, you can settle for a few surprisingly average-priced pints at Est Bar Est and grab a sandwich on the run once you hear your name being called for the third time. On the downside, the ridiculously long walk to your gate is often obstructed by screaming children or singing hen-night crowds. And the queue at border control is, at most times, long enough to make you reconsider the whole affair and just run back to your plane.

Getting There

Public Transport

Stansted might seem a long way from London, but getting there by public transport is surprisingly easy. All you have to do is choose between the train (fast) and the bus (cheap). Several train operators serve the airport from Liverpool Street Station. But before you start struggling with too many timetables for trains that stop at too many stops, opt for the dedicated Stansted Express (www.stanstedexpress.com; 08456 007 245). The service runs every 15 minutes and takes you to the airport in 45 minutes straight. Tickets start at £18 and can be bought online, from the ticket office or a ticket machine. Buses will take an hour to take you to the airport, and longer if there's a lot of traffic, but single tickets start at £2. A number of operators fight for your custom, the main ones are: Terravision (01279 680 028; www.terravision.eu) leaves from Liverpool Street Station and Victoria Station. The slightly more expensive National Express (08705 747 777; www.nationalexpress.com) connects to the same stations but some buses also stop in Stratford and Golders Green. Easybus (www.easybus.co.uk) gives you the intimacy of a small mini-van, stopping in Baker Street and Victoria

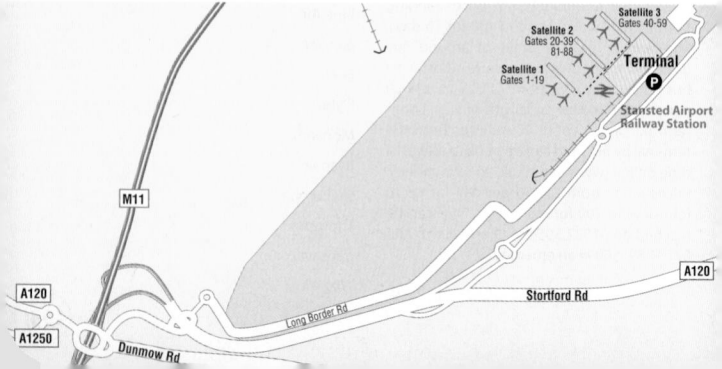

Station. If you're traveling during the rush hour, take a book. Whitechapel Road is one of London's most bustling streets, but it will get boring at some point.

Driving

If you're fortunate enough to have a car, or managed to convince your dad-in-law to lend you his, find your way out of the city via Stratford and hit the M11. It's a straight drive from here and amid Essex' greenery, the airport is hard to miss. Cab drivers will know how to get you to the airport, but will probably charge you a small fortune for it.

Parking

Daily parking rates start at £2.50 for the first half-hour and rise in steps to £26.40 for 24 hours. Long-term parking, in the intriguingly christened Pink Elephant car park, will cost you £9 a day. If you're in for a weekend trip, opt for the mid-stay car park, which is closer to the terminal than the Elephant and charges £12.50/day. The airport recently introduced valet parking, which can be pre-booked on 08708 502 825. Once there, drop your car at the end of Set Down Lane; the pick-up point is next to the Fast Track car park. For discounts on all Stansted parking options, call BAA Advance on 0121 410 5228 and book your parking lot before you head off.

Car Rental

Hertz, Check-In Concourse..... 0 8708 460 005
Budget, Check-In Concourse..... 0 1279 681 396
Avis, Check-In Concourse 0 8706 086 364
Europcar, Check-In Concourse 0 1279 680 240
National, International Arrivals Concourse .....
..... 0 1279 506 534

Shops

Stansted has the usual selection of 'small airport shops', more aimed at passing the time than serious purchases.

Hotels

Hilton National Hotel, Enterprise House, Bassingbourne Road, Essex CM24 1QW , 0 08700 000 303

Radisson SAS Hotel, Waltham Close, London Stansted Airport, Essex CM24 1PP, 0 1279 661 012

Express by Holiday Inn, Thremhall Avenue, Stansted, Essex CM24 1PY, 0 1279 680 015

Airlines

Aegean Airlines
Air Arabia Maroc
Air Berlin
Air Malta
Air Moldova
Air Asia X
Atlantic Airways
Aurigny
Blue Air
Cyprus Airways
easyJet
El Al Israel Airlines
Esprit Ski
Germanwings
Kibris Turkish Airlines
norwegian.no
Pakistan International
Pegasus Airlines
Ryanair
Snowjet
Turkish Airlines
(There's only one terminal)

Overview

If the Underground had a motto it wouldn't be "Mind the gap" but "Sorry for any inconvenience caused." But as we grumble and ponder if anyone is ever actually sorry for squeezing you 30m below the surface, in a sweat-box held together by dust, rust and expensive fares, the magnificence of the 'Tube' network should really be appreciated. Across its 250-odd miles of track the Underground will take you to 275 stations spread the length and breadth of London (although with disproportionately few lines reaching into south London). The system is well integrated with the bus and overground train networks and—with the advent of the Oyster card—most of these share a common ticketing system.

When fully functioning, the Underground will get you across town quicker than the bus and without the complicated timetables and schedules of overground trains. When it is struck by signal failures and breakdowns, which is very often, it can be excruciatingly slow and get very overcrowded, very quickly. In conclusion: the Underground won't necessarily get you anywhere on time, in style or in comfort, but it will (eventually) get you pretty much anywhere.

Fares

The vast majority of the network is divided into concentric fare rings or zones (1-6). Zone 1 covers central London, zone 6 covers the outskirts of London. Fares are dependent on how many zones your journey includes and there's a premium for travelling in zone 1. Peak fares (Monday to Friday from 4.30-9.30 am and 4-7 pm) are from 50p to a few pounds more than off-peak, although journeys limited to zone 1 do not benefit from the off-peak discount. Your best bet is to get an Oyster Card—lowest single fare is £1.60 off-peak (£2 peak) instead of £4 if you pay by cash. Oyster Cards are available for just £3 from vending machines. It's a total no-brainer. The total amount that can be deducted from your Oyster card is also capped over a 24-hour period to match the equivalent cost of a one day travel card.

So the fare system is complicated, but if you take £1.60 (which will get you a single journey within zone 1 with an Oyster card) as a base rate, and add to this the further out of zone 1 you travel, things become clearer. If you feel the need to marvel at the full intricacy of the fares and ticketing system, give yourself eye-strain at Transport for London's website www.tfl.gov.uk.

Frequency and Quality of Service

The vast majority of centrally-located stations will have a train at least every three minutes most of the day. At the very beginning and end of the day service frequency tails-off and can get as low as eight minutes between trains. Trains are also much less frequent at the further reaches of some lines—the Metropolitan line has trains only every 20 minutes from its most north-western stations, even during peak times. Almost all lines have a reduced frequency on Sundays. First trains are 05:00-05:30, last trains are between midnight and 12.30. Last trains are generally safe; expect a slightly raucous mix of pickled after-workers and overly obsequious rough-sleepers rather than any real troublemakers. Mayor Boris Johnson's initially-controversial booze ban seems to have been accepted now. The whole network is currently having £5bn thrown at it to try to get things ship-shape for the 2012 Olympics. As a result, line closures are common at weekends, so check before you travel.

Lines

Bakerloo: (Brown coloured on maps) Runs from Harrow & Wealdstone in the north west to Elephant & Castle in the south east.

Central: (Red) Runs from West Ruislip in the east to Epping in the far north east. The central section is buried under Oxford Street and has four stops on the street, the quietest usually being Bond Street.

Circle: (Yellow) Circles the circumference of the city centre. Shares almost all of its track and stations with other lines so don't necessarily bother waiting specifically for a dedicated Circle Line train. Look out for the 'Platform for Art' as you pass Gloucester Road station.

District: (Green) One of the few lines to serve deepest south London, branches run into Richmond and Wimbledon in the southwest and also to Ealing. The line continues up to Upminster in the northeast. Almost all of the branches of this fragmented line come together at Earls Court station into an infuriating mess, so plan ahead if changing there.

East London: (Orange) Still features on maps but is now closed. Due to re-open in 2010 as part of the London Overground network. Until then you'll have to plump for a limited rail-replacement bus service.

Hammersmith & City: (Pink) Starts at Hammersmith in the west of the city before heading north to Paddington and continuing east to Barking. Take it to Ladbroke Grove if heading to the Portobello market.

Jubilee: (Silver) Silver coloured as it opened in the year of the Queen's Silver Jubilee in 1977, the line serves northwest, central and east London, including the Canary Wharf business district. The section east of Green Park is the most recent addition to the network (it opened in 1999) and has a number of architecturally exemplary stations.

Metropolitan: (Dark Purple) The oldest of all the lines, this granddaddy of metropolitan underground railways strikes far out in the suburbs and countryside northwest of the city from its central root at Aldgate.

Northern: (Black) Presumably given black as its colour to reflect the dark mood of anyone unlucky enough to have to commute on it, the Northern line is the overcrowded spine of London, covering vast swathes of the city centre, the north and the south.

Piccadilly: (Dark Blue) From Cockfosters in the far northeast this line trundles all the way to Heathrow airport, with some of the most popular tourist spots in between. It's a very cheap way to the airport but is also the slowest. Southgate and Arnos Grove stations are both 1930s modernist brilliance.

Victoria: (Light Blue) Runs from Walthamstow in the north to Brixton in the south. This musty line is currently undergoing refurbishment and will feature new trains and track by 2011. In the meantime, check for early closing and shutdowns, particularly during weekends.

Waterloo & City: (Turquoise) No-one has ever met anyone who has been on this line. Erm, it has two stations, Waterloo and Bank, and is designed for suited and booted commuters coming in by train from Waterloo. No trains on Sundays.

London Overground: (Orange) TfL took over part of the overground rail network, notably the somewhat shabby and North London Line which runs from Richmond to Stratford. Just think of it as an extension to the tube network.

Bicycles

Bicycles are generally only allowed on the tube outside peak hours and only from stations outside central London. They are not permitted on the Victoria or Waterloo and City lines at all. Folding bicycles can be taken on all sections of the Tube free of charge.

General Info

Website: www.tfl.gov.uk/dlr
Phone: 020 7363 9700
Lost property: 020 7363 9550

Overview

Not quite a tram, tube or train, it's simply the Docklands Light Railway, a nifty little thing that makes getting to places like Greenwich Village and City Airport easy and cheap. Launched in 1987 with a modest 11 trains and only 15 stations, the regeneration of the Docklands area has seen it grow to 94 trains covering 38 stations and counting. Serving the east and Southeast of the city, it is pretty much as pleasant as London public transport gets. It's reliable, less noisy than the tube, generally less crowded and it's pretty well air-conditioned. The DLR is also fully-automated and most of the time there is no driver, meaning that you can take the front seat and pretend that you're actually driving the thing.

The DLR provides a key service for London's suits, with the Bank to Canary Wharf journey taking just over ten minutes. For normal people, Canary Wharf also makes an interesting/unusual weekend destination. Almost completely deserted, a stroll amongst the abandoned skyscrapers is a strangely satisfying way to spend a Sunday afternoon.

With the Olympic games invading East London in 2012, there's quite a bit of engineering work going on. Stations are being adapted to cope with longer trains and they're also building an extension to the new Stratford International Station and the nearby Olympic Park. Expect some disruptions to service over the next few years and check the website before you travel.

Fares

As on the rest of London's public transport you're best off with an Oyster card. One thing to remember is that there are no barriers at DLR stations and instead Oyster readers are located at station exits and entrances. To avoid getting slapped with a fine and to ensure you're charged the right amount, remember to touch in and out correctly. The prices are similar to the tube, so cash works out more expensive; though not as expensive as the tube with its £4 cash single.

Hours

The DLR runs 5.30 am–12.30 am, with train frequencies depending on the time of day. During peak hours, there's usually a train every three minutes or so, but even on Sundays you shouldn't have to wait more than 10 minutes.

General Information

National Rail Enquiries 08457 48 49 50
Tickets.....www.thetrainline.com;
.....also websites of individual franchisees
Eurostar .....08705 186 186 or
.....0 1233 617 575
.....www.eurostar.com

Overview

The railways are one of the great British inventions but, unfortunately, the Victorians who built the network in this country did slightly too good a job. Every generation since has taken one look at the massively expensive task of modernising them and scuttled back into their Ford Fiestas. So, while France, Germany and Japan got on with building super-speed bullet trains Britain was stuck with an uneasy compromise between the technologies of 1950 and 1850. This doesn't mean that you shouldn't use trains. It just means that it's probably best to avoid them at peak times. That's when London plays a cruel trick on people who choose to live in places with names like 'Gravesend' and 'Slough' by making them lurch home slowly with less personal space than the legal minimum for cattle. During off-peak times train travel can, in contrast, be positively pleasant. It's a great way to see the countryside, every city and major town in the country is connected, and, if you book far enough in advance and shop around on sites like www.megatrain.com it can be less expensive than you'd think. In London itself, the Thameslink improvement programme will help a little; Crossrail will (eventually) arrive; and pay as you go Oyster will be grudgingly accepted by all train operators.

Stations

Broadly speaking, Euston and King's Cross stations serve the north of the country, Liverpool Street the east, Victoria the south, Paddington and Marylebone the west.

Eurostar

The King's Cross area is also home to the splendid St Pancras—the terminal for the Eurostar train service which connects Britain with the rest of Europe. Since November 2007 it's been possible to get from here to Paris or Brussels in around two hours—with connecting trains to Siberia and beyond.

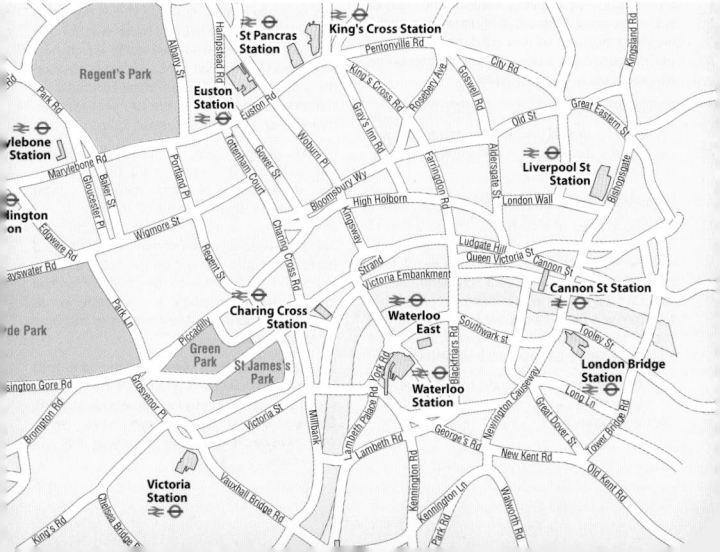

Charing Cross Station

NFT Map:	24
Address:	12-30 The Strand, London WC2N 6RQ
General enquiries:	020 7839 2576
South Eastern Trains:	08706 030405
Southern Trains:	0845 123 7770

Overview

Perched at the top of the Strand amidst popular tourist attractions such as Trafalgar Square and with the majestic 1865 Charing Cross Hotel being part of the station, you may presume that a cornucopia of ornate delights lies within. Well, it's a dump; the chances of "Brief Encounter" being remade here are pretty slim. But your chances of being barged by a curmudgeonly office worker are very good, what with it being the fifth busiest rail terminal in London. Still, can you blame them for wanting to get out of the place so quickly?

With services to south London and Kent, even the pigeons give the concourse here a wide berth. It's also home to possibly the worst station pub in the country; "The Boadicea" excels in the areas of soullessness and morbidity, likely to satisfy only the hardened alcoholic on their third liver and with a preference for pubs that reek of urine. If only Dante had been able to sample this place…

Tickets

There is a small ticket office open some 20 hours per day, and three banks of ticket machines on or around the concourse.

Services

If you're in need of a quick bite, there's a decent variety of food outlets to cater for all tastes, whether burger-lover (Burger King) or health food freak (Cranberry). Indulge your Schadenfreude by watching the beleaguered information guy having to dispense a plethora of poor excuses as to why the 17.34 to Margate was cancelled. And those kinky souls with a tie fetish will love Tie Rack.

Natwest and Bank of Scotland cash machines can be found on the concourse, as well as a Barclays in the front entrance.

Public Transport

The station is easily accessible by Charing Cross station (Northern & Bakerloo lines) and also the adjoining Embankment station (Circle & District lines). The nearby Trafalgar Square is a major hub for buses—especially night buses for post-West End madness—which inch their way out to places as far apart as Harrow and Crystal Palace.

Euston Station

NFT Map:	78
Address:	Euston Road NW1 2RT
General enquiries:	020 7922 6482
Lost property:	020 7247 4297
First Scotrail:	0845 601 5929
London Midland:	0844 811 0133
London Overground:	020 7222 5600
Virgin Trains :	08457 222 333

Overview

Easily the ugliest station in London, Euston creeps up as you nervously edge along Euston Road. The first inter-city terminal built in London, it was originally constructed in 1837, but the lovely original was demolished to make way for the monstrous concrete-and-glass coffin which now squats next to the mail depot. Since privatisation the interior has become an identi-kit British rail station with more chain businesses per head than is morally decent. Thanks Network Rail.

It's not all doom and gloom, however. Within this architectural eyesore you'll find a scarily concise summation of human nature. Like most busy stations, there's plenty of eccentricity and electricity here: abandoned Tube tunnels; stressed-out coffee guzzling power-commuters; fresh-faced backpackers sprawled out on the floor ; and the infamous beggar who — to the delight of football lovers everywhere except in Manchester — was arrested for punching Manchester Utd manager Sir Alex Ferguson.

The station is London's gateway to the north west of England and Scotland, and also North Wales. As such it is the point of entry for Scousers, Mancunians, Glaswegians and more. Virgin trains (www.virgintrains.co.uk) to Glasgow can take as little as 4 hrs 10 mins.

Tickets

The ticket cashiers may have the glazed look of Kafka-esque zombies but the cleaning staff are often more helpful. Just use the Fasttrack machines!

Services

There's plenty of eating and drinking options, all of the 'chain' variety. Of this motley crew Paul and Upper Crust are as good as it gets. If you're determined to hang around, check out the Doric Arch (1 Eversholt St; 020 7388 2221) which is a shoddy little boozer with a cool 'end of the world' vibe. The left luggage office is at the top of the ramp to platforms 16–18 and is open between 7 am–11 pm.

Public Transport

As an actual railway station it is adequate. Served by two Tube lines and nine bus routes, it's nothing if not convenient.

King's Cross Station

NFT Map:	78
Address;	Euston Rd & Pancras Rd N1 9AP
General enquiries:	0207 922 4931
Lost property:	0207 2783310
National Express East Coast	08457 225 225
First Capital Connect	0845 676 9904

Overview

Previously a dingy playground for prostitutes, drug dealers, and all sorts of similarly bad kids, King's Cross Station has scrubbed up a bit in recent years, thanks to lots of chin scratching and typically panicked spending on the government's part. Built in 1852 on the site of a former smallpox hospital, it is one of the busiest and most well-connected stations in the country: running trains to Edinburgh; Newcastle; the East coast; as well as six Tube lines. Zany trivia about the station includes the fact that it is supposedly built on top of legendary Fembot-Queen Boudicea's grave (most probably a total lie) and that it has a tacky little shrine to Harry Potter at what has been designated 'Platform 9 3/4' (oh God).

Nearly all long distance train services leave from the overground platforms under the arches straight ahead of you as you enter from Euston Road. The Tube is also accessible from steps at this entrance and at what used to be the Thameslink station next to the Scala on Pentonville Road. From the main Tube entrance there is a pedestrian subway that comes up on the other side of Euston road just outside Macdonald's. This is handy for crossing the road at busy times, and of course for getting chips. There is a Spartan waiting lounge just outside the entrance.

Tickets

Tube tickets, including Oyster top ups and season tickets, can be purchased from the machines in front of the Tube entry gates, located just at the bottom of both sets of stairs at the station. For railcard discounts and more specific enquiries you'll have to queue at the manned ticket desks next to the machines. For all other tickets go to the upstairs ticket hall which is to the left of the main Euston Road entrance.

Services

Food options are pretty poor, consisting of a small array of chain stores with prices hiked just enough so that people in a rush will not notice they're being ripped off. If you're not one of those people, it's probably best to just pop across the road and get some noodles from Chop Chop, which is fast, cheap and dirty, like the best rail travel.

Public Transport

King's Cross crosses more Tube lines (six) than any other station, and is serviced by at least twice as many buses, many of which run all night. For full details of bus routes look at the bus maps for Camden on the Transport for London website: http://www.tfl.gov.uk/tfl/gettingaround/maps/buses/.

Liverpool Street Station

NFT Map:	8
Address:	EC2M 7QH
General enquiries:	020 7295 2789
Lost property:	020 7247 4297
One Railway:	0845 6007245
Natl Express East Anglia Railway	0845 6007245

Overview

Scene of drunken anarchy at the infamous Facebook party that preceded Boris's booze ban,

it's not that Liverpool Street is is particularly ugly, but if it's architectural beauty you're after, you're much better off heading to Paddington or the newly re-opened St. Pancras International. In comparison to these two icons of British station design, Liverpool Street is extremely modest, boring even. Clean, modern and easy to navigate around, it is simply a good train station. With the markets, bars and restaurants of Spitalfields and Brick Lane just around the corner, the station is the perfect starting point to explore east London. First opened to the public in 1874, it is now the second-busiest station in London (after Waterloo) with an estimated 123m visitors each year. With 18 platforms, the station mainly serves destinations in the east of England, including daytrip favourites such as Cambridge and Southend on Sea.

It is also the home of the Stansted Express, providing easy airport access with departures every 15 minutes. If you're travelling with a group of people a taxi might work out slightly cheaper, but the train is much quicker and more reliable. The Tube station, with its main entrance centrally located on the main concourse, makes all of London easily accessible with the Central, Hammersmith & City, Circle and Metropolitan lines all passing through. Being the fifth busiest station on the underground network, rush hour can get nasty and is best avoided.

Tickets

The ticket office is located on the main concourse, on your left hand side if entering from Bishopsgate. Ticket windows are open for immediate travel 24/7 with advance ticket purchases available between 7.30 am–7.30 pm. There are also several express ticket machines scattered throughout the station. Tickets for the Stansted Express can be purchased from designated ticket machines opposite platforms 5-6. A cluster of cash machines can be found by the stairs leading up to the Old Broad Street exit. There are payphones on both levels and most are located on the Bishopsgate side of the station.

Services

With Brick Lane just around the corner, eating, drinking and shopping here should really be a last resort. The regular big-chain fast food joints are scattered (some of them repeatedly) throughout the station with the usual selection of coffee, burgers, sandwiches and sweets. The main shopping area is on the lower level around the Broadgate and Exchange Square exits, offering everything from toiletries and birthday cards to Italian silk ties and double-glazed windows.

Passengers are invited to wait for their trains in the so-called "food court," which really isn't much more than a few cramped tables between Burger King and The Wren, one of the station's two shitty pubs. There's a small but nicer waiting lounge located adjacent to platform 10. Here you also find the left luggage, a bureau de change, a less-busy cash machine and access to the main taxi rank. Smoking is prohibited at all times throughout the station.

Public Transport

The main bus station is located on the upper level of the station (Broadgate end), and provides a large number of services to destinations throughout London. Plenty of buses also stop on the street just outside the Bishopsgate exit.

London Bridge Station

NFT Map:	106
Address:	Station Approach SE1 9SP
General enquiries:	020 7234 1209
Lost property:	020 7234 1247
Southern Trains	0845 123 7770
South East Trains	0845 000 2211
First Capital Connect	0845 026 4700
South Eastern disabled contact:	0800 783 4524

Overview

Around in one form or other since 1836, when steam trains filled the air with smoke, London Bridge is the city's oldest station. Sounds romantic? It's anything but. Hopelessly overcrowded, with 42 million people elbowing their way through the tunnel-like walkways every year, and crumbling on its grey concrete edges, London Bridge has long been SCREAMING for a makeover. Someone finally heard the call, and £3.5m is earmarked to get this vital commuter hub (connecting south London, Sussex and Kent) up to scratch. The ambitious revamp will also see the construction of one of Europe's highest skyscrapers—a massive arrowhead of a building, hosting 7,000 people once completed.

It's a good starting point for weekend trips to Kent's countryside or days on Brighton's beach. Operators Southeastern and Southern cover the south east, while First Capital Connect operates (little-known) connections to the airports Gatwick and Luton. The station couldn't be better connected to public transport, with two Tube lines and a plethora of buses at the doorstep. The catacombs underneath the station—said to be haunted—have been turned into the museum-cum-gore-fest London Bridge Experience, adding to the spooky entertainment already provided by the London Dungeon next door—just in case a cancelled or delayed train leaves you with too much time on your hands. Does happen, we're told.

Tickets

The main office is located next to the main entrance (London Bridge Street) or there are machines situated throughout the station. Jump the queues by booking online at www.nationalrail.co.uk.

Services

The main concourse is lined with eating and shopping options. Grab Cornish pasties, sandwiches, donuts; and the usual burgers from the usual chains. Bodyshop, M&S and WH Smith lead the list of practical, but terribly unexciting shop names. There are toilets on platforms 1-2 and 5-6.

Public Transport

Connections are excellent. London Bridge Station is served by the Jubilee Line and the Bank branch of the Northern Line. Escalators take you down from the main concourse. Step outside the main entrance for the massive bus station, where buses leave in all directions of the city, except its far western reaches.

Marylebone Train Station

NFT Map;	76
Address:	Great Central House Melcombe Place NW1 6JJ
Central number:	08456 005165

Overview

Despite Monopoly-board notoriety, Marylebone railway station fell into neglect in the mid to late-twentieth century, spurned as a rundown piggy-in-the-middle wedged haplessly between neighbours Paddington and Euston. But it's an aimless drifter no more. A refurb' in the 90s and again in 2006 saw Marylebone reinvigorated, with a thorough sprucing up and two new platforms. Servicing the Midlands, it now threads as far as Birmingham, Shakespeare's Stratford-Upon-Avon, Leamington Spa, Aylesbury, and High Wycombe, amongst others. It remains the runt of the London train station litter, but is a popular location for television filming (Doctor Who; Magnum PI; Green Wing; Peep Show) at a mere £500 per hour—half the price of King's Cross. In its bowels, Bakerloo Line trains rumble through an underground station of the same name.

Tickets

Rail ticket windows are to the north of Marylebone's relatively petite concourse and open Monday-Saturday 06.30–22:10 or Sunday 07.30–21.30. As with all mainline train stations, self-service ticket machines are in abundance should ticket offices be closed or queues too long. Sturdy padded-barriers ensure buying tickets on board the train, or getting away without them, is not an option. Underground tickets can be purchased from windows or machines alike within the Tube station itself.

Services

The usual plethora of railway station chains are on hand: newsagent WH Smith, baguette bakers Upper Crust, supermarket Marks & Spencer, and pasty purveyors the West Cornwall Company among them. More individually, Marylebone also hosts AMT Coffee, a café with a seating area at the centre of the concourse, the nifty Chiltern Flowers on the south wall, and The V&A free house in the west passageway—an old man's boozer in the classic, wood panelled style. Cash points and payphones are in this same walkway, and toilets are situated on the south wall.

Public Transport

Marylebone underground station lies directly beneath Marylebone overground, and is serviced (Matron!) by the Bakerloo Line, while buses 2, 205 and 453 stop directly outside the main entrance. A taxi stand is also situated out front. Baker Street and Edgware tube stations are a short walk away.

Paddington Station

NFT Map:	31
Address:	Paddington, London, W2 1HQ
General enquiries:	020 7922 6793
Lost property:	020 7247 4297
First Great Western:	084 5700 0125
Heathrow Express:	084 5600 1515
Chiltern Railways:	084 5600 5165

Overview

If you're in that small minority of people who love stations, then Paddington's paradise. Designed by engineering legend Isambard Kingdom Brunel—his middle name is Kingdom for God's sake, of course his work's going to be magnificent—this barn-like structure harks back to an era when train travel retained a little glamour. If it wasn't for the on-site Burger King you could easily imagine tearful ladies waving silk handkerchiefs at dapper gents.

The station also occupies a unique place in literary heritage. Every British child in the last half-century knows the tales of Paddington Bear. From "deepest darkest Peru", he was left unattended at the station; but a kind family picked him up, took him in, and named him after it. No other station name can inspire such genuine warmth. It certainly wouldn't have worked if he'd been found at Clapham Junction.

Heathrow Express

The super-fast link to Heathrow runs from Paddington. Be warned, though; it's far from cheap. At £32 return it could end up being more than your flight (and works out at £24 more than taking the tube). Ouch.

Tickets

A ticket office and machines are located near platforms 9-10, and there are other machines and an information point near the Eastbourne Terrace entrance and also underneath the mezzanine.

Services

If you have any money left from your ticket—unlikely at today's prices—there are plenty of sharks who can take it off you. Burger King and Upper Crust will overcharge you for burgers or baguettes and there's an 'offie' (off-license) for expensive booze. There's also a pub that resembles a building site (Portakabin). If you find yourself drinking in there you've got some serious questions to ask yourself.

There are other ways of staying amused; as it's the main portal for commuters entering London from the west and Wales) there's WiFi, a supermarket, a bookshop and curiously, a lingerie shop. Just what sort of a job do you have if you get to the station and realise: "Bollocks! No suspenders!"? Certainly not one compatible with Paddington's place in children's lit, that's for sure.

Public Transport

The Bakerloo, Circle, District, and Hammersmith & City Tube lines all stop at Paddington. Buses serve west and north west London.

St Pancras International

NFT Map;	78
Address:	Pancras Road, London, NW1 2QP
Central number:	020 7843 4250
Eurostar:	08705 186 186
Midland Mainline:	08457 125678

Overview

The newly souped-up St Pancras station has been generating waves of breathless excitement ever since its opening ceremony in 2007, which was by all accounts a pretty histrionic affair. This "Cathedral of Transport" situated next door to King's Cross station, is now home to the Eurostar international train service and has domestic connections (via First Capital Connect's Thameslink trains) to Luton Airport, Bedford and Brighton; as well as Midland Mainline connections to places like Leicester and Sheffield. As the first major project of a huge scheme to redevelop the area, St Pancras has been marketed as so-much-more-than-a-station. Alongside its rail platforms it features Europe's longest Champagne bar, a farmers market, and an arcade of pointedly-classy shops. All this is housed within beautiful listed buildings dating from 1868, with an extension for the long Eurostar trains designed by British starchitect Norman Foster—presumably on time out from his usual business of making pleasure domes for the world's nastiest totalitarian governments.

Tickets

The Eurostar ticket office and travel centre is located at the Euston Road end of the long arcade, while self-

service machines (for collecting pre-booked tickets) can be found outside the Eurostar departure lounge further along the arcade and to the right. Opening times for the Eurostar ticket office are 4.30 am–9 pm (Mon-Fri), 5.30 am–9 pm (Sat) and 6.30 am–9 pm (Sun). For National Rail services, you will need to buy tickets from machines, or a manned ticket desk at the designated area at the far end of the Arcade, next to that horrific kissing statue.

Services

At St Pancras International there are more than 40 places to eat, drink and shop, with a fair number of chain stores as well as some exclusives, such as the Champagne Bar and Gastro Pub. The station has its own dedicated shopping arcade with branches of classic London stores Hamleys and Foyles, as well as a market area and another brace of shops at the north end of the station ('The Circle'). Everything is shiny, new and upmarket, so expect your money to vanish pretty damn quickly. The Betjeman Arms pub – named after the famous poet whose petition saved the listed buildings from the same fate as Euston's arch – hosts beer festivals and music/literature events.

Public Transport

St Pancras can be reached by Tube (via adjacent King's Cross station) on the Victoria, Hammersmith & City, Circle, Piccadilly, Northern and Metropolitan Lines. A large number of buses also stop along Euston Road day and night. For route details check the bus maps for Camden borough at www.tfl.gov.uk/tfl/gettingaround/maps/buses/.

Victoria Station

NFT Map:	20
Address:	Buckingham Palace Road SW1V 1JU
General enquiries:	020 7922 6214
Lost property:	020 7963 0957
Gatwick Express	0845 850 1530
Southern	08451 27 29 20
Southeastern	0845 000 2222

Overview

80 million people use London Victoria per year, making it one of the UK's busiest stations. Hit it at rush hour and it will feel like those 80 million are all there with you. Built a century ago for a less populous, less rushed and less demanding city, it struggles with crowds of commuters who jostle for platform space. Now it enforces crowd-control measures at peak times: prepare to be patient. Nevertheless, it is well laid-out with services clearly sign-posted, and a major upgrade is planned to improve its capacity.

Victoria's main train operators are Southeastern, Southern and Gatwick Express, who between them will whisk you to Brighton, Portsmouth, Hastings and Gatwick, among other south eastern towns. Or if you're looking for a romantic break and the Victoria route to Bognor Regis is just a little too obvious for you, you can earn yourself brownie points and a hefty overdraft by taking the Orient Express from this station.

The building itself is impressive: look above the modern shop fascias to enjoy century-old architecture. But if that is all a little too high-brow, look up anyway, as the entrance to the South East building sports four caryatids: columns shaped like women, whose tunics saucily hang open so a gratuitous nipple can pop out to cheer the commuters. Rule Britannia!

Tickets

If you haven't booked in advance (why? Why?!), then head for the 24 hour ticket office in the central concourse, where you will queue for anything up to a year to buy your journey for much more money than you'd have paid online a week earlier. If you don't require assistance from a ticket officer, use the automated machines dotted round the concourse: their queues always move faster (unless the person in front of you is a newbie who can't figure out the buttons, which is guaranteed if you have less than five minutes to catch your train). Keep your ticket handy as all platforms are guarded by ticket barriers, and add a few extra minutes to reach platforms 15–19.

Services

All the predictable station fare is available in the main concourse for your journey's usual sandwich, loofah and tie needs. Food options have mercifully diversified so in addition to the obligatory artery-cloggers you can now grab sushi from the Wasabi

stand or maintain your body's temple-status at the Camden Food Co. If it's a meal you're after and you must remain at the station, head up to the food court via Victoria Place for a choice of what could charitably be described as restaurants. Victoria Place itself boasts the ubiquitous high street shops to help you kill time or for any last minute gifts (as long as you don't really like the person you're buying for). Station loos are 20p—even up in the food court you can't pee for free—and showers are available if you're getting a bit ripe. Victoria also has a left luggage service, WiFi (charged) and photo booths.

Public Transport

Victoria is on the Victoria, Circle and District lines: entrance to the underground is opposite platform 7. The bus terminus is just outside the main entrance. It is also next door to London's national bus depot for cheapo travel to/from other parts of the UK. The main taxi rank is outside the main entrance, but if it has a heart-sinking queue then head up to the Plaza exit for an alternative rank.

Waterloo Station

NFT Map;	104
Address:	Waterloo, London, SE1 8H
Train company:	South West Trains
General enquiries:	020 7922 2545
Lost property:	0845 330 9882 0845 6000 650
Website:	www.southwesttrains.co.uk

Overview

Until 2007, Waterloo was the first port of call for 'Europeans' arriving by train. Thousands of chic foreigners, clutching manbags and sporting huge sunglasses, would arrive at the station every week. But not any more. Nearly 200 years after the British triumphed in the first battle of Waterloo—a town in Belgium—the French got their revenge. Last November Eurostar gave the two fingers to the British Waterloo and promiscuously buggered off to St Pancras. Rumour has it that ex-PM Margaret Thatcher had specifically ordered that Eurostar terminate at a station named after a famous French defeat; but things have moved on a little since the "Iron Lady" left office. We're all Europeans now…

In truth, perhaps it's not that bad a thing. Even though no other British station covers as much space, Waterloo feels like it's at bursting point. Even without the Eurostar it has a whopping 19 platforms—in almost constant use—and four Tube lines. It's calmed down slightly since the international terminal was put out to stud, but it's still pretty manic.

The station services London's south western suburbs (as can be seen by the swathes of well dressed commuters) and, further afield, the towns south west of the capital.

Waterloo East

NFT Map;	104
Address:	Sandell St, SE8 8H
Central number:	0871 200 49650

Overview

If the south west isn't your bag, you can disappear to England's south east—Kent, Sussex and SE London—from Waterloo East. There's an escalator next to Burger King, opposite platform 12, that makes a trip to the south east look far more alluring than it really is.

Tickets

The main office is opposite platforms 16–17. And it's open 24 hours—so why not charm them into giving you a free ticket after a few drinks? They can't have heard it before, right?

Services

A delay is just unplanned "me time", so make the most of it by buying a newspaper, eating your own weight in overpriced pasties and cookies; then wash it down with a few pints of generic football-sponsor lager in Bonaparte's pub before buying your loved-one a novelty tie/'cute' socks to make for up being late. And drunk. And flatulent. And tasteless. There's a left luggage office between platforms 11-12.

Public Transportation

Waterloo is served by four underground lines: Bakerloo, Jubilee, Northern, Waterloo & City; and approximately 20 bus routes. See tfl.gov.uk for details.

Overview

If there's one thing that screams London, it's big red buses—loads of 'em—preferably passing beneath Big Ben for maximum iconic impact. The furore that greeted the withdrawl of the old style Routemasters continues to rumble on years after their replacement by hi-tech bendy buses.

Whether you view the latter as characterless boxes and a fare-dodger's paradise, or whether you think the Routemaster was a diesel-breathing dinosaur: you're going to spend a lot of time in buses, around them, dodging them or talking about them. As a Londoner, your list of hobbies and interests now includes transport. Deal with it.

Former mayor Ken Livingstone always had a thing for buses and we make 6m journeys every day. There are a variety of different operating companies, but to us they're all the same, all the way out to the frontiers of Zone 6. Get on at the front, get off at the middle.

A big red bus featured in the Beijing Olympics closing ceremony, as the world looked to London 2012. And new(ish) boy Boris has taken up the bus baton with a new design set to enter service in 2011. At procurement stage, a key design requirement was an open platform – so the spirit of the Routemaster looks set to live on after all. A reduction in those nasty diesel particulates has also been specified, as excuses for capital car drivers become ever weaker.

Fares

In an effort to make the city more efficient and to cut down on theft-based attacks on drivers, Transport for London (TfL) introduced the Oyster card. Now people only beat up drivers for fun. The Oyster ("The world's your…"—geddit?) is an electronic swipe card that can be bought at all 275 Tube stations and some 4,000 other outlets such as newsagents.

The card can carry a mixture of travel passes (often referred to as travelcards in a nod to the pre-electronic age of cardboard); and pay-as-you-go cash value. Note that if you choose pay-as-you-go, and you end up making more journeys than you anticipated; once it reaches the equivalent cost of a one-day travelcard, it will cap itself so you don't spend more.

Unless you are making a small number of journeys it usually works out cheaper to get a travelcard. In a further move towards the cashless society, coins are still accepted—but you will pay more for a journey. A single ticket costs £1 with Oyster or £2 with cash. On some bus routes you will not be allowed to purchase a ticket on the bus, but instead there will be a roadside ticket machine. Believe us, Oyster's just easier…

When you get on, don't forget to push your card against the scanner by the drivers' window. Sure, you're on camera 300 times per day, and every journey you make is recorded. But if you're paranoid, try another city, because they *are* watching you here.

You can buy a bus and tram pass (£13.80 p/w), or you can buy a bus/tube travelcard (prices vary by zones). If you don't work or socialise in the centre, and you only buy, let's say a Zone 2-3 bus travelcard, you can still use this on all buses in Zones 1-6. Which is nice. An Oyster card costs £3 to get, but you'll soon recoup that. Concessions are also available for the unemployed and for full-time students.

24-Hour Services

You'll not hear London referred to as "the other city which never sleeps". Partly because it's unwieldy, but mostly because it's not true. After a hard night's binge-drinking and fighting in taxi ranks, we like our kip.

But for those of you that are hardcore no-sleep-till-Brockley types, there is a network of 24-hour services. There are also a large number of night buses. They're just like day buses, except the route number is prefixed by a large 'N' and the view is less interesting.

Information

TfL's website (tfl.gov.uk) is an essential reference. Fare information and travel updates are available, plus PDFs of routes and timetables. As you get closer to central London, many routes operate on a frequency—basis rather than at fixed times.

The main reason to visit TfL's site is the Journey Planner. Enter your start and end points and it will (usually) calculate the best options. A word of warning though, computers are fallible and some route maps are schematics—so do check your own map and use common sense. Like those idiots that follow their GPS even when it tells them to drive into a river, it's frustrating to take three buses in a big circuit then realise you could have walked it in five minutes…

If you do want to live out your 1940s film fantasies, you can still catch the quaint old Routemasters doddering along 'Heritage Routes' 9 and 15. If you're wondering who this guy is that keeps bugging you at the door-less rear step, it's the conductor and he only wants your money. It's the silent guy in the corner who wants your soul that you have to watch out for…

Safety

Like all big cities, London has its fair share of oddballs and criminals. And then a few institution-loads more in case things ever get boring. But CCTV in every bus and the creation of Safer Transport teams is having an effect—and not just on the share price of video camera manufacturers. TfL claimed an 11% reduction in reported crime at the end of 2007 and a ratio of 15 crimes per million journeys. Also, bus crime is concentrated in particular areas on particular routes. And you'll soon get to know the 'usual suspects' so don't worry. Night buses can get a bit lairy, so follow a few tips below to make sure the only stress you suffer is traffic-related. Gangsters may wish to laugh at the following; Mother Theresas may wish to tattoo it on the inside of their eyelids:

Avoid the top deck when possible. Sit on the left so the driver can see you (he has a radio link to base). Don't fall asleep. Use the same stop at night and know your surroundings so you can be confident. Keep your belongings close to you and be switched on. Get to know the 'hot spots' so you can be aware.

For more info, see our fabulous fold out bus map.

Overview

Coaches are traditionally associated with the grimier side of travel. But London's biggest coach company, National Express, are desperately trying to shake their image as a purveyor of seedy transport. They're rebranding themselves as quick, comfortable and green. Their fleet of coaches are shiny and the drivers slightly less grumpy than they used to be.

Then there's the Megabus. In comparison to their coaches, just walking where you wanted to go would be more comfortable. It's no surprise that the repositioning of National Express as a classy operator is linked to the rise of Megabus. Faced with a company who reroute you so your journey takes an extra week, anything else is 'luxury'. But you know what? They're dirt cheap. Literally. With fares from £1 you can ignore the garish buses and the man being sick in the back. They're the cheap version of the cheap version of transport.

The main coach hub is near Victoria train station. You can buy tickets for both Megabus and National Express—the two main operators who run from Victoria Coach Station—from the same booths just inside the station. But, like plane tickets, (only without that last shred of glamour that air travel still has) if you buy in advance, you can get some super-cheap prices. National Express has an office on the road between the train and bus stations.

London's other main hub is Golder's Green. This is the last stop for services heading north (or the first stop for buses coming down into London). If you live in north London, it's worth jumping off here, as it's on the Northern Line and can shave an hour off the trip.

There's also a healthy trade in coaches to Oxford. The Oxford Tube competes with National Express on the route from Victoria; travelling via Marble Arch, Notting Hill and Shepherd's Bush. Tickets normally cost about £13 and you can buy on board. They also run through the night—so if you get drunk and have the urge to go on an impromptu holiday—well, Oxford it is.

Beyond Tooting, Croydon's trams will take you from places like Wimbledon to shop – lemming-like with the locals – at the Ampere Way IKEA. The trams accept Oyster and use a similar charging scale to buses. Once you get back on the map, your flatpacked sideboard will win admiring glances but few friends as you trail home on busy tubes.

National Express

Unit 6/7 Collonades Walk
123 Buckingham Palace Road, SW1W 1SH
08717 818181
www.nationalexpress.com

Megabus
0900 160 0900
www.megabus.co.uk

Oxford Tube
01865 772250
www.oxfordtube.com

There's a war going on out there, one with real casualties and collateral damage. When Tory leader David Cameron was spotted going through a red light on his bicycle, it threw into sharp relief a low level conflict which has been going on for decades. Bikes v. Cars: with hapless pedestrians caught in the middle.

Cycling around London is not for the faint-hearted, but recent improvements—like Ken's Congestion Charge and the hard work of the London Cycling Campaign (www.lcc.org.uk) are encouraging people to drop their Oyster cards and jump on their bikes. Some of the routes highlighted in the brilliant (and free) maps produced by LCC and Transport for London have become so popular, cycling along them is like taking part in the Tour de France (albeit slower and with slightly fewer drugs). There's even a Velib'-style communal bike scheme planned to start in May 2010 and tangle-haired tearaway Boris upset skivers everywhere by leading a mass ride-to-work to beat the tube strike.

But cycling does hold some risks. As well as the nightmare of walking around all day with 'helmet hair' you've got accidents and theft. LCC's website has details of road-confidence training and lists local cycling groups who run social events and cycle maintenance classes. They will sometimes cycle your new route to work with you to help you negotiate the difficult bits. Aren't they nice?

For those new to cycling on London's roads, basic rules include: stay a door length (or stride) away from the pavement or parked cars; watch out for distracted office drones leaping into the road and into black cabs; don't undertake bendy-buses or HGVs; don't use your phone while moving; and if in doubt on a tricky junction, transform yourself into a pedestrian—get off and push your bike wherever you need to go. For debates around riding on pavements, wearing helmets and jumping red lights check out www.cyclechat.co.uk/forums.

Bolt-cutting 'tea-leaves' steal thousands of bikes every year. You have three options to reduce this particular risk. One, buy a rubbish bike that no-one would want to steal and lock it with one lock. Two, get a decent bike, carry around a D-lock and two other locks and spend 20 mins each time you stop. Three, get a shit-hot bike and never take it out.

Where to Ride Bikes

There are plenty of great rides around town and a happy cyclist is one who has been able to incorporate one into their commute. The cycling maps mentioned above give colour-coded help, look for the brown routes (separate from the traffic) or even better the green routes (separate from the traffic and passing through parks, beside canals or rivers.)

Good options are the short but scenic Parkland Walk Nature Reserve, which links Finsbury Park to Highgate via an abandoned railway line; a Saturday morning cycle takes you to one of Highgate's wonderful pubs for lunch and a lazy pint. The City, normally snarled with cabs, buses and kamikaze pedestrians, is a dream on a Sunday morning.

Though not continuous, the path along the Regent's Canal linking Paddington with Canary Wharf takes cyclists away

from traffic and along some surprisingly gorgeous stretches of canal (which also sport some top notch graffiti)—as well as some godawful, festering dumps. A useful section of the canal links the west side of Regent's Park with Paddington via Lisson Grove and Warwick Avenue. Watch out for super-fast cyclists determined to slice a second off their PB, especially where the path narrows under bridges or around ramps. Also recent yellow crime signs around London Fields spoke of a gang of youths pushing cyclists into the canal for fun. Watch out for them too.

A jaunt through any of the capital's great parks seems an obvious choice, but beware, some parks (notably Hampstead Heath) ban bikes on almost all paths, thanks to selfish cyclists of the past who went too fast and frightened the jumpy pedestrians.

The new anarchic FreeWheel Event is a real highlight, where great swathes of normally packed roads along the Embankment and up to St James's Park are closed to all but cyclists every September (we fervently hope this will remain forever). And the London Critical Mass meet at 6 pm on the last Friday of the month by the National Film Theatre, if you can't wait that long.

www.londonfreewheel.com
www.criticalmasslondon.org.uk

Bike Shops	*Address*	*Phone*
Apex Cycles	40-42 Clapham High St, SW4 7UR	020 7622 1334
Bicycle Magic	6 Greatorex St, E1 5NF	020 7375 2993
Bikefix	48 Lamb's Conduit St, WC1N 3LJ	020 7405 1218
Brick Lane Bikes	118 Bethnal Green Rd, E2 6DG	020 7033 9053
Brixton Cycles	145 Stockwell Rd, SW9 9TN	020 7733 6055
Condor Cycles	51 Gray's Inn Rd, WC1X 8PP	020 7269 6820
Evans (Spitalfields)	The Cavern, 1 Market St, E1 6AA	020 7426 0391
Holloway Cycles	290 Holloway Rd, N7 6NJ	020 7700 6611
London Fields Cycles	281 Mare St, E8 1PJ	020 8525 0077
Mosquito	123 Essex Rd, N1 2SN	020 7226 8765
ReCycling	110 Elephant Rd, SE17 1LB	020 7703 7001

To consider taking a taxi in London you either need (a) a trust fund, or (b) to be drunk. If you are both, congratulations: prepare to be taken for a ride in more ways than one.

Dating back to the mid-17th Century (kind of), London's 'black cabs' (www.londonblackcabs.co.uk), or 'Hackneys', are the world's oldest taxi service and are as representative of London as Routemasters, Big Ben and robbery. They are the most visible, the most iconic and probably the most expensive taxi service in London. While this flag-down option is great (they are the only company licensed to pick up on the street) budgeting for a black cab is tricky. Their prices are designed to confuse passengers into parting with huge wads for what often feels like a round-the-block trip. A whole range of metaphysical problems contribute to that huge sum waiting to be paid at jouney's end; all fares start at £2.20 and then go up according to the time of day, speed, and the time spent in the cab. There's also an airport surcharge and the 'puke charge' of £40. Keep it in!

Black cabs are operated by many different companies who are all regulated and licensed by the Public Carriage Office (PCO). Generally speaking, the service you receive doesn't vary much from company to company, though some boast little add-ons to capture your fare. Big, well organized companies like Dial-A-Cab (www.dialacab.co.uk; 020 7253 5000) and Radio Taxis (www.radiotaxis.co.uk; 020 7272 0272) offer online booking, carbon neutral trips, and friendly service. All black cab drivers must pass 'The Knowledge' test to get their license, so every driver will have a labyrinthine understanding of London and most will not be shy in sharing this with you.

Though a cheaper option, going private can be a minefield. Since 2001 all taxi services in London are required by law to be licensed by the PCO: this includes the city's thousands of private-hire minicabs. Private hire companies are everywhere you look and often take the form of nicotine-stained, shoddily-built little offices with lots of bored men milling about. Every neighbourhood has plenty of local services and it's really trial and error to find one that doesn't rip you off or drive barely roadworthy chariots of rust. The drivers of these little companies can be pretty eccentric—you can be regaled by tales of times past, given essential life advice or simply receive the disdainful silent treatment. The website www.taxinumber.com offers a list of local minicabs for every postcode in the UK.

The 'private taxi sector' does do upmarket, however. By far the most efficient and elegant service is that offered by Addison Lee, (www.addisonlee.com; 020 7387 8888) who text you twice, have huge gleaming six-seaters, and perfectly-manicured drivers. Fares are pretty cheap over longer distances but the minimum is around £10. E-london Cars are almost as good (www.elondoncars.co.uk; 020 7494 4004). Of course, you can also sup from the cup of bad taste by ordering a stretch hummer or pink limo at Book A Limo (www.booklimo.co.uk; 020 8965 1724).

A word of warning: London is awash with rogue taxi-drivers who are not licensed and who will attempt to pick you up from outside a club or theatre. These guys will either charge you more than you agreed upon, not know where they are going, or they will be driving beat-up death-traps. There are also many stories of attacks on women, so if in doubt, don't get in!

Helicopter Services

Westland Heliport
020 7228 0181 www.helipad.co.uk

SW11's very own heliport! Aerial tours of London can be made online with Helipad running from Westland Heliport in Battersea, Elstree and London City Airport. The nearest tube is Clapham Junction.

EBG Helicopters
01737 823 282 www.ebghelipcopters.co.uk

Running helicopter tours of London and charter flights from Redhill Airport in Surrey, 10 minutes by car from Gatwick Airport. £140 will get you 35 minutes over London, the only downside is getting to Surrey. Flights are between 10-4pm. Also offers charters for weddings and corporate events. Flying from Heathrow? Take a 20 minute sky ride for a cool £1,200.

Helicopter Days
08704 430 555 www.helicopterdays.co.uk

Operating out of Biggin Hill, 30-minute flights over Canary Wharf and Westminster start at £125 per person and you can cram up to 5 friends in with you. Lessons are available for less than £200. For drivers the helipad's close to M25 or you can be picked up by a helicopter from another location!

Elstree Aerodrome
020 8953 7480 www.egtr.net

A variety of charters operate out of Elstree offering sky tours, as well as flight academies for those who want to take the wheel. On site is The Elstree Bar & Café, plus it's close to M1.

Ferries/Boat Tours, Rentals & Charters

London River Services (LRS)
020 7222 1234
www.tfl.gov.uk/gettingaround

Provides commuter river transportation on the Thames. This runs in the East from Masthouse Terrace Pier to Savoy Pier at Embankment. In peak hours services run to Woolwich Arsenal with a further service from Blackfriars Millenium Pier in the City to Putney Pier in the west costing £15 return. WiFi is available on boats serving Woolwich. Services run every 20 minutes. All are wheelchair friendly.

Thames Clippers
0870 7815049
www.thamesclippers.com

London's answer to the NYC water taxis, primarily serving the O2 stadium from Waterloo, Embankment and Tower Bridge. Conveniently runs later than the Tube meaning you can actually stay right to the end of a show without the worry of being stranded on the south side of the river. Single tickets cost between £3-5 with Oyster Card holders getting 1/3 off. Boats leave every 15 minutes.

Bateux London
020 7925 2215
www.bateuxlondon.com.

Dinner, lunch and charter cruises from Embankment Pier. Yes, there's even a jazz cruise.

Westminster Passenger Services Association
020 7930 2062
www.wpsa.co.uk

One of the only popular charters to offer services upriver to Kew, Richmond and Hampton Court.

City Cruises
020 7740 0400
www.citycruises.com.

Hop on hop off services primarily aimed at tourists and with tourist prices. Tickets start from £11 return for adults from Greenwich to Westminster/Waterloo Pier.

Heritage Boat Charters
01932 224 800
www.heritageboatcharters.com

For something different, try messing about on the river in one of these historic wooden numbers. On offer are skippered cruises down the Thames starting at £825. Formal dinner on board is available.

Silver Fleet Woods River Cruises
020 7481 2711
www.silverfleet.co.uk

Luxury chartered boats. Particularly good at putting on top-notch corporate events.

Thames Cruises
020 7928 9009
www.thamescruises.com

Two words—disco cruise. Hot pants are not required for dinner cruises.

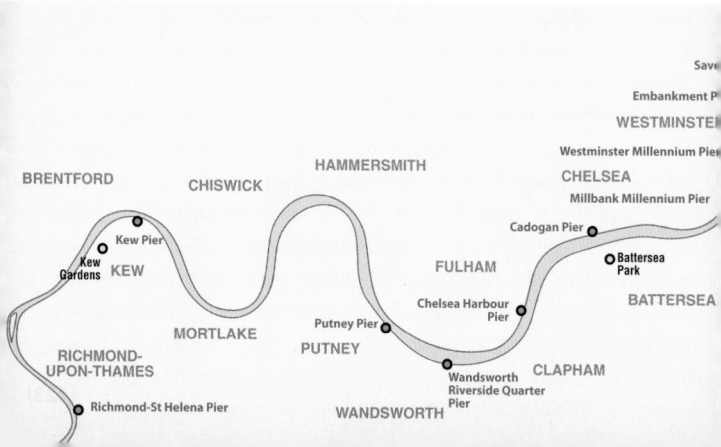

Marinas/Passenger Ship Terminal

Chelsea Marina
07770 542 783
www.chelseaharbourmarina.com

Despite being in upmarket Chelsea, the prices for mooring your boat here are incredibly generous—£2 per metre a night or £300 a year with space for 60 boats. Secure subterranean parking also available.

Chiswick Quay Marina
020 8994 8743
www.chiswickquay.com/marina

Great, secluded spot for West Londoners near Chiswick Bridge. A little far from a tube station, yet Chiswick overland station is within walking distance with services to Waterloo. Prices are on an annual basis at £162 per metre including a resident harbourmaster, shower block, mains water and electricity.

Gallions Point Marina
020 7476 7054
www.gallionspointmarina.co.uk

In London's Docklands and therefore perfect for those working in the city.

St Katharine Haven
020 7481 8350
www.stkaths.co.uk

One of London's best marinas. Great location by Tower Bridge, close to the quayside bars and restaurants and reasonable London prices—£3.60 per metre, per day.

Welcome Floating Terminal in Greenwich
01474 562 200
www.portoflondon.co.uk

Built in 2004 and believed to be the world's first floating terminal. Welcome has on-site immigration and custom services for cruise ship passengers entering or leaving London.

London Cruise Terminal at Tilbury
01375 852 360
www.londoncruiseterminal.com

The most popular regional departure point for passenger liners is 25 miles from Central London in Essex. Its close proximity to the M25 makes it easy for Londoners to get to. Current destinations from here include Scandinavia and continental Europe.

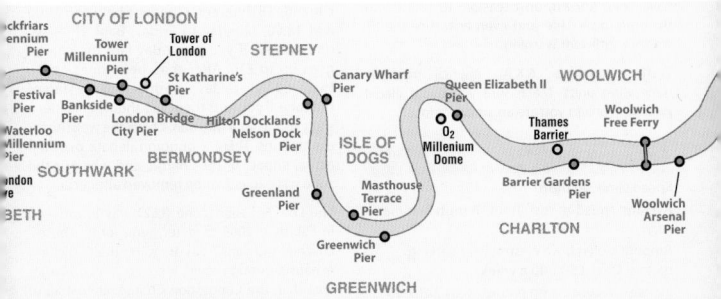

With London's Congestion Charge, Low Emission Zone, pricey parking, kamikaze bus drivers, dreaded speed bumps, speed cameras and a road layout that would give Spock the night terrors—*"it's so illogical Captain"*—driving around town is something to be avoided. Combine this with over 7.5 million people who just want to get from A to B without anyone getting in their frickin' way, and you can see where problems arise.

But, there are times when a four-wheeler is the only option, and for those times here are some things to watch out for:

Pedestrians love to stride purposefully into the road with nary a thought for their safety. Keep a weather eye out, one foot over the brake and one hand over the horn.

Cyclists are ever-increasing in number—give them plenty of space and remember for the one speedhound jumping the lights there are hundreds of law abiders that you just don't notice. Try to focus on them.

Motorbikes and Scooters are not all ridden by leather clad Hells Angels or Jamie Oliver clones; most just want get about and avoid the Congestion Charge. As with cyclists, give plenty of space and check your blind spots.

Black Cabs, these roving London landmarks have been known, on occasion, to pull up to the curb, do a 'U-ie' and even advertise the FT without sufficient warning.

Traffic Wardens A.K.A. 'council revenue generating units'. Make sure you avoid illegal parking—unless you are an ambassador.

Driving Statistics

Speed Limit: **30 mph**

Average speed in rush hour: **6 mph** (estimates vary)

Amount stolen from Westminster parking meters: **Over £50,000 a week**

Increase in congestion predicted by 2015: **25%**

Amount of UK Carbon emissions coming from road traffic: **21%**

Worst day of the week for accidents: **Friday**

Ways to make it bearable

Most of the stress caused by driving in London, apart from the sheer volume of traffic, is caused by lack of consideration for others—usually as drivers are running late. So make sure you leave PLENTY of time for your journey, try not to block junctions, and let people out if you have a chance.

Get a tiny car that you can park sideways. Ha! That'll show 'em.

Join a car club like Street Car or WhizzGo– then you can drive whenever you want at a fraction of the cost of owning a car.

Try and avoid rush hour. Morning rush lasts from 7 am to 10.30 am, lunch rush from 11 am to 2.30 pm, school run rush from 2.45 pm to 4.15 pm and afternoon rush from 4.30 pm to 8.45 pm. Bonne chance…

Driving in the Congestion Charge Zone and the Low Emission Zone

The Congestion Zone, introduced in 2003, meant the centre of town was remarkably less congested—for about twenty minutes if the Daily Mail is to be believed. The charge is currently £8 if you enter the zone between 07:00 and 18:00, Monday to Friday. Bank Holidays don't count. If you pay a day late the charge goes up to £10. After that, hefty fines apply. Huge red Cs in circles alert drivers to the start of the zone, if you miss them you should consider a swift visit to your optician. Check the website for exemptions. There is ongoing debate over the actual impact of the charge, and whether the zone will expand, or be removed altogether.

The Low Emission Zone (LEZ) was introduced in February 2008 to deter large lorries, buses, coaches and vans from dragging their belching exhausts through town. It covers a much larger area than the Congestion Charge: almost all of London within the M25 and applies 24/7. The charge varies between £100 and £200. A DAY.

Key Roads

A1
Running straight north from St Paul's Cathedral in the City through Islington, Archway, Highgate and beyond, this old Roman Road has some freer stretches allowing the frustrated drive to accelerate to 43 mph for 3 seconds, get a speeding ticket and then slam on the brakes. Ends (eventually) in Princes Street, Edinburgh, Scotland.

North Circular/South Circular (A406)
This is the M25's angrier and twisted little brother. Circling Outer London it has some of the busiest stretches of road in London and even includes a ferry across the river at Woolwich. The way dwindles to one exhausted lane in certain sections, causing great clots of traffic every day in rush hour. See left for rush hour times.

Euston Rd/Marylebone Road (A501)
Running east-west past King's Cross and Euston, this wide road skirts the northern edge of the congestion zone. It gets very crowded, because it's a feeder road to the relatively breezy start of the A40 heading out of London.

Embankment
The view as you drive along the Embankment along the north bank of the Thames is breathtaking. It needs to be to keep you occupied as you inch forward for hours. Runs from Chelsea (A4) to Tower Bridge.

Vauxhall Bridge Rd/Grovesnor Place/Park Lane/Edgware Rd (A5)
Running roughly north-west from Vauxhall Bridge Rd, around Victoria, past Hyde Park Corner and Marble Arch and out to join the A40, this route is a free corridor through the Congestion zone – free from charge rather than free from traffic. Be prepared—it's rammed.

Old Kent Rd / New Cross Rd / Lewisham Way / etc. (A2/A20)
Running south-west from The Bricklayers Arms roundabout and eventually down to Dover, where you catch the ferry to France; the Old Kent Rd, despite being the cheapest Monopoly property, is totally free from traffic at all times. No wait—that can't be right.

A3
Starting at London Bridge, this road eventually ends up in Portsmouth, but you have to struggle past Elephant and Castle, Clapham Common and Wimbledon Common along with everyone else trying to get to Guildford.

Traffic Hot Spots
Angel, Elephant and Castle, Hanger Lane Gyratory, Vauxhall Gyratory, Trafalgar Square, Parliament Square, Hammersmith Gyratory, everywhere else.

Useful links

TfL Interactive Traffic Map:
trafficalerts.tfl.gov.uk/microsite

Capital FM for traffic news from the Flying Eye 95.8 FM

Parking for Cars
www.park-up.com

Parking for Motorbikes and Scooters:
www.parkingforbikes.com

Route Planner:
www.theaa.com/travelwatch/planner_main.jsp

Congestion Charge:
www.tfl.gov.uk/roadusers/congestioncharging

Parking Ticket Appeals:
www.ticketbusters.co.uk

The great thing about being a Londoner is there's really no need to have a car. Except on those few occasions where you're cursing yourself for hauling a flat-packed Ikea coffee table on the shitty Croydon tram service. This is where joining a membership-based carsharing company, such as Streetcar (www.streetcar.co.uk; 0845 644 8475), Zipcar (www.zipcar.co.uk; 0800 011 2555), City Car Club (www.citycarclub.co.uk; 0845 330 1234) or fledgling Connect by Hertz (www.connectbyhertz.com; 08708 45 45 45) comes in handy.

Streetcar and Zipcar are your best bet, as they offer self-service cars and vans to members, billable by the hour, day, week or month. The beauty of this service is there's probably either a Zipcar or Streetcar parked around the corner from wherever you are in central London, which means you don't have to hike to a car rental centre, stand in a queue or deal with annoying upselling at a counter. Plus, if you get thrown out of your girlfriend's flat at 2 am and need a ride, you're in luck. Both offer a 24/7, 365 day a year self-service. For a membership fee of £50-60 a year, you have access to a fleet of cars, where all you have to do is enter the PIN, grab the keys from the glovebox and away you go.

On top of the membership fee, prices vary from £3.95 to £7.50 p/h depending on the company. The difference between Streetcar and Zipcar is the car. Streetcar offers only Volkswagens but their prices are pretty standardised. With Zipcar, you can have fun varying the car, with Minis, environmentally-friendly hybrids and BMWs on offer—but this means prices can vary too.

If you must go the conventional route, there are, of course, Hertz, National, and Avis centres aplenty, but for a smart Londoner who only wants a car sometimes—go for a carshare.

Company	*Address*	*Phone*	*Map*
Avis	8 Balderton St	0870 153 9104	002
Avis	88 Eversholt St	0840 010 7967	078
Avis	20 Seagrave Rd	0870 010 7968	043
Avis	86 St Katharines Wy	0207 423 8875	095
Avis	33 York Rd	0870 608 6369	104
Easy Car	Elms Mews	0871 0500 444	030
Easy Car	20 Seagrave Rd	0871 0500 444	043
Easy Car	88 Eversholt St	0871 0500 444	078
Easy Car	77 Britannia Rd	0871 0500 444	043
Easy Car	37 Munster Rd	0871 0500 444	048
Easy Car	68 Clapham Rd	0871 0500 444	135
Easy Car	136 Pentonville Rd	0871 0500 444	079
Easy Car	1 Brewery Rd	0871 0500 444	073
Easy Car	7 Bryanston St	0871 0500 444	001
Easy Car	171 Battersea Park Rd	0871 0500 444	133
Easy Car	43 York Rd	0871 0500 444	104
Easy Car	131 Belsize Rd	0871 0500 444	068
Easy Car	8 Balderton St	0871 0500 444	002
Easy Car	12 Semley Pl	0871 0500 444	019
Easy Car	33 York Rd	0871 0500 444	104
Easy Car	245 Warwick Rd	0871 0500 444	034
Enterprise	145 Bow Rd	02089805600	094
Enterprise	131 Belsize Rd	02073280200	068
Enterprise	200 King St	02085637400	040
Enterprise	59 Royal Mint St	02076809944	095
Enterprise	202 Ilderton Rd	02077323838	116
Enterprise	49 Woburn Pl	02076314700	094
Hertz	156 Southampton Row	087 0850 2664	004
Hertz	200 Buckingham Palace Rd	0870 8460002	020
Hertz	35 Edgware Rd	0870 8460011	001
Hertz	79 Clapham Rd	0207 582 5775	135
Hertz	713 Old Kent Rd	020 76392121	116
National	68 Clapham Rd	44 207 8200202	135
National	150 Pentonville Rd	44 20 72782273	079
National	7 Bryanston St	44 207 4081255	001
National	12 Semley Pl	44 207 2 59 16 00	019
National	43 York Rd	44 207 9282725	104
Thrifty	131 Belsize Rd	44 20 76253556	068
Thrifty	Sloane Ave	44 02072622223	046
Thrifty	178 Tower Bridge Rd	44 02074033458	107

Petrol Stations	*Address*	*Map*
Total	170 Marylebone Rd	002
Jet	30 Clipstone St	003
BP	Russell Ct & Woburn Pl	004
Shell	198 Old St	007
BP	Park Ln & Mount St	009
BP	Vauxhall Bridge Rd & Udall St	021
Esso	115 Sutherland Ave	027
Shell	104 Bayswater Rd	030
Texaco	383 Edgware Rd	031
BP	383 Edgware Rd	031
BP	1 Westwick Gardens	033
BP	Shepherds Bush Green & Rockley Rd	033
Total	137 Chiswick High Rd	038
Total	372 Goldhawk Rd	039
BP	Great West Rd & Oil Mill Ln	039
BP	372 Goldhawk Rd	039
Jet	182 Goldhawk Rd	040
BP	Talgarth Rd & Gliddon Rd	041
Tesco	459 Fulham Rd	043
Shell	49 Tadema Rd	044
Shell	106 Old Brompton Rd	045
Tesco	601 King's Rd	049
Total	31 N Rd	051
Esso	640 Holloway Rd	060
Texaco	73 Stapleton Hall Rd	062
Jet	314 7 Sisters Rd	063
Total	409 Kilburn High Rd	065
BP	Finchley Rd & College Crescent	066
BP	Haverstock Hill & Oman Rd	067
BP	Wellington Rd & Wellington Pl	068
Tesco	115 Maida Vale	068
Esso	33 Chalk Farm Rd	071
BP	142 Camden Rd	072
Tesco	196 Camden Rd	073
Sainsbury's	4 Williamson St	073
Total	109 York Wy	073
Sainsbury's	104 Holloway Rd	074
Sainsbury's	89 Hornsey Rd	074
BP	Hampstead Rd & Cardington St	077
BP	Goodsway & Camley St	078
Shell	276 Upper St	080
Jet	43 Stamford Hill	083
BP	144 Stoke Newington Rd	086
Texaco	168 Shoreditch High St	091

Petrol Stations	*Address*	*Map*
Total	112 Vallance Rd	091
BP	Cambridge Heath Rd & Paradise Row	092
Sainsbury's	1 Cambridge Heath Rd	092
Texaco	51 Grove Rd	093
Texaco	127 Bow Rd	094
Texaco	77 The Highway	095
Texaco	102 The Hwy	096
Shell	139 Whitechapel Rd	096
ASDA	151 E Ferry Rd	103
Shell	101 Southwark Bridge Rd	106
Shell	137 Walworth Rd	113
BP	New Kent Rd & Balfour St	113
Total	234 Old Kent Rd	114
Tesco	107 Dunton Rd	114
Total	272 St James Rd	115
Jet	747 Old Kent Rd	116
Sainsbury's	101 Evelyn St	118
Jet	179 Creek Rd	119
Jet	25 Greenwich High Rd	120
BP	Camberwell Rd & Albany Rd	121
BP	Peckham Rd & Southampton Wy	122
Total	38 Peckham Rd	122
BP	New Cross Rd & Pomeroy St	125
Sainsbury's	263 New Cross Rd	125
Jet	42 Hinton Rd	127
Jet	13 E Dulwich Rd	130
Texaco	213 Kennington Rd	131
BP	238 Kennington Ln	131
Shell	326 Queenstown Rd	133
Sainsbury's	326 Queenstown Rd	133
Esso	2 Battersea Park Rd	133
Esso	54 Wandsworth Rd	134
Sainsbury's	62 Wandsworth Rd	134
Esso	77 Clapham Rd	135
Total	257 Upper Richmond Rd	136
BP	Swandon Wy & Smugglers Wy	138
Texaco	474 Wandsworth Rd	142
Tesco	330 Brixton Rd	144
Esso	243 Brixton Rd	145
Total	39 Nightingale Ln	147
Total	40 Balham Hill	148
BP	124 Brixton Hill	150
BP	Marius Rd & Rowfant Rd	151

January

- **New Year's Day Parade** • Big Ben to Piccadilly Circus • Marching band and thousands of kids. How better to cure a hangover?
- **London Boat Show** • ExCel Exhibition Centre • Like we always say: you can never have too many yachts.
- **Russian Winter Festival** • Trafalgar Square • Magical Russian Winterland replaces the normal Pigeon-Crap Land.
- **London Art Fair** • Business Design Centre • Pick up something to hide that patch of mould.
- **Destinations: Holiday and Travel Show** • Earls Court Exhibition Centre • Chase away the January Blues.
- **Chinese New Year** • West End • Party like it's 4707.
- **London International Mime Festival** • Southbank Centre • Even weirder when you see it for real.
- **Charles I Commemoration Ceremony** • Trafalgar Sq - St James' Palace • Thousands of uniformed Cavaliers confuse the tourists.

February

- **London Fashion Week** • Natural History Museum • Far Too Thin.
- **National Wedding Show** • Olympia • Perfect day out for a first date.
- **Lifted** • Harrods • A bizarre annual exhibition inside Harrod's lifts.
- **The Great Spitalfields Pancake Race** • Old Truman Brewery • Pancake race in wacky clothes. No, London. Just, no.
- **Blessing the Throats** • St Ethelreda's Church, Ely Place • Lemsip not working? Sore throats cured by holy candle.
- **Clowns' Service** • Holy Trinity, Dalston • Because God likes clowns too.

March

- **Affordable Art Fair** • The Marquee, Battersea Park • Now even The Great Unwashed can buy art!
- **Ideal Home Show** • Earls Court Exhibition Centre • Make your home ideal (or a bit less grotty).
- **St Patrick's Day Parade** • Park Lane • Shamrocks, river-dancing, big fluffy Guinness hats: true Irish tradition.
- **East Festival** • East London • Because East London isn't just for muggers.

April

- **Oxford & Cambridge Boat Race** • River Thames • Hole up in a pub by the river and cheer over a beer.
- **Careers and Jobs Live** • ExCel Exhibition Centre • Career ideas and thousands of vacancies.
- **Flora London Marathon** • Greenwich – The Mall • 35,000 pairs of bleeding nipples.
- **London Book Fair** • Earl's Court • The publishing industry's main event. Occasionally stuff for free.
- **Camden Crawl** • Throughout Camden • If you're not crawling by the end, you haven't done it right.
- **Alternative Fashion Week** • Old Spitalfields Market • Huge range of cutting edge fashion. And fetishwear.
- **BAFTAs** • London Palladium • Ten points per autograph.
- **Queen's Birthday Gun Salute** • Hyde Park • Who said the monarchy is archaic?
- **St George's Day** • Covent Garden / Cenotaph / Shakespeare's Globe • Brush up your Morris dancing skills.
- **The Real Food Festival** • Earl's Court Exhibition Centre • Real Food: much nicer than fake food.
- **Hot Cross Bun Service** • St Bartholomew-the-Great, Smithfield • Widows get a free hot cross bun. Worth losing the husband.
- **London Independent Film Festival** • Various West and Central Cinemas • Cool celebration of cinematographic indieness without The Man. Or something.

May

- **Sci-Fi Festival** • London Apollo • The UK's only Sci-Fi Festival. Thank god.
- **Freedom of the City** • Central London • Frequently awesome improv and experimental festival attracting top names.
- **Baishakhi Mela** • Brick Lane • Celebrate the Bengali New Year in the British tradition: vindaloo.
- **Mind, Body, Spirit Festival** • Royal Horticultural Halls • Make up for all the time in the pub.

June

- **City of London Festival** • The City • Bringing High Culture to a bunch of bankers.
- **Start of Open Air Theatre season** • Regent's Park • Ignore the climate and take in an outdoor play.
- **Taste of London** • Regent's Park • The best picnic in the world.
- **O2 Wireless Festival** • Hyde Park • Big names vibrate the Serpentine.
- **Wimbledon** • All England Lawn Tennis and Croquet Club • Short skirts and grunting. Marvellous.
- **Trooping the Colour** • Horse Guard's Parade • Hundreds of chaps in uniforms. Ohhhhh yes.
- **Meltdown Festival** • Southbank Centre • Eclectic music festival curated by major musicians.
- **Chelsea Flower Show** • Royal Hospital Chelsea • You'll go for the flowers. You'll stay for the Pimms.
- **Royal Academy Summer Exhibition** • Royal Academy • Lots and lots and LOTS of art.
- **Arts Festival Chelsea** • Chelsea • The artists formerly known as 'The Chelsea Festival'.
- **Big Sexy Festy Party** • Finsbury Park • So good-natured you'll want to hug a tree. And it's FREE!

July

- **The Big Dance (biennial: even years)** • Various around London • London learns to dance.
- **The Drag Olympics** • The Way Out Club • Drag Queens are put through their pedicured, high-heeled paces.
- **Dogget's Coat & Badge Race** • Thames: London Bridge to Chelsea • Intense boat race to win a badge. Hardly seems worth it.
- **Pimms Urban Regatta** • Finsbury Square • People full of Pimms race on land in bottomless boats. Bloody Ozzies.
- **Pride of London** • Trafalgar Square • One of Britain's biggest, funnest street parties.
- **The British 10k London Run** • Hyde Park - Whitehall • Work off the pies.
- **Hampton Court Palace Show** •

Hampton Court • Stock up your garden / flowerpot / imagination.

- **The Chap Olympics** • Bedford Square Gardens • Olympics for gentleman—no sportswear please.
- **Rise Festival** • Finsbury Park • Celebrating the best of multicultural London, for free.
- **Swan Upping** • River Thames • Census of swans. For goodness sake.
- **Opening of Buckingham Palace** • Buckingham Palace • The Plebeians allowed in to see how their taxes (and steep entrance fees) are spent.

August

- **Innocent Smoothies Festival** • Regent's Park • You wouldn't think fun could be this wholesome.
- **Great British Beer Festival** • Earls Court Exhibition Centre • A festival that puts the Great in Britain.
- **Trafalgar Square Festival** • Trafalgar Square • 3 weeks of music, theatre, dance and art.
- **Carnaval del Pueblo** • Burgess Park • Thousands of Latino lovelies. That's all you need to know, right?
- **London Triathlon** • Docklands • Marathons are for pussies.
- **London Mela** • Gunnersbury Park • Partaaaay, Asia-style.
- **Metro Weekender** • Clapham Common • Dance music Saturday, bands on Sunday, chilled all weekend.
- **Notting Hill Carnival** • Ladbroke Grove • Party till your wallet gets nicked.
- **Kids Week** • West End • West End shows free for kids. Soooo unfaaaaiiiiir.
- **Shoreditch Festival** • Shoreditch. • Because you can never have too many local festivals. Apparently.
- **Bathing the Buddha** • Leicester Square • Buddha gets a birthday bath.

September

- **The Great British Duck Race** • The Thames • Like the Oxbridge boat race. But with 165,000 rubber ducks.
- **Horseman's Sunday** • Hyde Park Crescent • London's horses say their Hail Maries. Yes, really.
- **Oyster & Seafood Fair** • Hays Galleria • The romance of oysters with the unholy stink of kippers.
- **Thames Festival** • Tower Bridge - Westminster • Fireworks, costumes, river races, carnivals. Kids like it.
- **Last Night of the Proms** • Royal Albert Hall • Camp overnight if you want tickets.
- **Spitalfields Show & Green Fair** • Buxton Street • Who has the biggest marrow?
- **Open House Weekend** • Various around London • Over 600 architectural landmarks open for a nosey.

October

- **The Big Draw** • Museum of Childhood • Pencils, not guns. Unfortunately.
- **Cockney Pearly Kings & Queens** • Church of St Martin-in-the-Fields • British eccentricity at its best.
- **London Tattoo Convention** • Old Truman Brewery • Who cares if it looks crap when you're 80?
- **International Halloween Festival** • Queen Mary College • Witches, druids and shamans unite for Europe's biggest Pagan festival.
- **Halloween** • London Dungeon • Trick Or Treating is for pussies.
- **Frieze Art Fair** • Regent's Park • Air kisses all round.
- **London Film Festival** • BFI Southbank • Two weeks of the best new films and lectures from A-Listers.
- **Metro Ski & Snowboard Show** • Olympia • London hosts the world's biggest winter sport show. Naturally.
- **Shell Wildlife Photographer of the Year (exhibition opens, for 6mths)**
- **Natural History Museum** • Puts your arty market photos to shame.
- **The Yoga Show** • Olympia • Bendy people upon bendy people. Literally.

November

- **London's Christmas Ice Rinks** • Venues across London • Much more romantic in your head than in reality.
- **London-Brighton Car Race** • Starts Hyde Park • Century-old bangers potter their way to Brighton.
- **Erotica Show** • Olympia • 31,000 horny adults pretend they're just browsing.
- **Bonfire Night** • Venues across London • Hundreds of thousands of pounds go pop.
- **Royal British Legion Festival of Remembrance** • Royal Albert Hall • Take tissues.
- **Lord Mayor's Show** • Central London • Running for over 800 years and yet still a bit crap.
- **London Jazz Festival** • South Bank Centre • Start practising your jazz hands.

December

- **Satan's Grotto** • London Dungeon • Tortured elves and spit-roasting robins.
- **Trafalgar Square Christmas Tree** • Trafalgar Square • The only thing everyone knows about Oslo.
- **Blackrock Masters Tennis** • Royal Albert Hall • Former World No.1s wheeze their way through a tournament.
- **Peter Pan Cup** • Serpentine Lido, Hyde Park • Freeze your nipples off on Christmas morning.
- **Christmas Pudding Race** • Covent Garden • We're mad, us! What are we like? Crazy!
- **Christmas Carol Sing-along** • Royal Albert Hall • Belt out your favourites and get in the mood.
- **International Horse Show** • Olympia • Not just for posh people. But mostly.
- **Midnight Mass at St Paul's** • St Paul's • Eats the other Midnight Masses for breakfast.
- **New Year's Eve Fireworks** • Jubilee Gardens • Oooooh. And, of course, aaaaaaah.

Tactics

Finding somewhere to live in London is a ruthless and cutthroat business. Make sure you have plenty of red bull, cigarettes and patience. Also take a week off. And hire a driver, maybe.

Ok, so these precautions aren't completely necessary, but you will have to work in mysterious and multifarious ways if you don't want to spend the next six months paying through your gullible nose for mice and verrucas. A good place to start is everywhere you can think of. Estate agents (see below for a list) will invariably try and rip you off but, then again, so will everyone else, so it's worth registering with all the big ones, as well as any whose office you see in the street, or you spot in newspapers, on TV or the internet. After uncovering a fair few completely brazen lies in the property listings on www.gumtree.com you will find that many of the smaller businesses place adverts for (sometimes fake) properties here. Don't be put off by the lies though, because this can be a good way of finding an agent (or getting in direct contact with a landlord) who is keen to make a deal with you, or who will try and match the prices advertised, even if they have nothing that fits the bill at the exact moment of lying. Of course, some of these listings are also genuine, and a good way to find rooms/apartments at lower than usual rates. Just bare in mind that a LOT of people use this site.

General sites

www.gumtree.com
www.findaproperty.co.uk
www.craigslist.org
www.rightmove.co.uk
www.propertyfinder.com

Estate Agents

There are hundreds of Estate Agents and Letting Agents across the city, some of the larger players (good and bad) include:

www.foxtons.co.uk - Offices all over London.
www.keatons.co.uk - Bow, Hackney, Harringey, Kentish Town, Stratford.
www.black-katz.com - Lettings only agency, numerous offices.
www.fjlord.co.uk - Numerous offices, specialise in uncooperative staff.
www.nelsonslettings.com - South and central London.
www.atkinsonmcleod.com - City and Docklands.

If you do end up using an agent, they will of course want to charge you an additional fee beyond any deposits or advance rent required by the landlord. But, as many of the agents in central London are close together, it's possible that they may be competing with each other to sell/rent the same properties. This will enable you to get a better deal. So shop around, be devious, and backstab as much as possible.

Council Tax

Council Tax is an annoying hidden cost that always comes as a bit of a surprise. It is worked out by your local council and is based on the value of your house/flat, which the council will already have placed in to one of 8 tax bands (bands are A–G, G covering the most valuable properties).There are several ways to determine the value of a property, but the easiest is probably to go to the website of the valuation office at www.voa.gov.uk. Having done that, it's possible to weigh up the benefits of different areas by comparing the council tax in equivalent bands charged by different local councils. It's fairly laborious, but worth it in the long run, if you can be bothered.

Because council tax is based on the property,

not the people inside it, the rate is constant no matter how many people live in the house. This means that it's much cheaper to live in a big house with lots of people to split the tax with, than on your own, when you are liable for the full amount. Students do not have to pay council tax at all, but if they are sharing with one or more non-students then there will still be council tax to pay. A single non-student in a house full of students receives a 25% discount on his/her council tax bill, but if there is more than one non-student then all non-students are liable to pay full whack.

Alternative Options

In a city where house prices have been soaring through the roof for some time now (although it's calmed down somewhat recently), of course people do things like squat, have dreadlocks and go vegan. If you're not willing to go the whole way but fancy an adventure, or simply don't have much money, then it might be worth taking a look at being a guardian for Camelot. This company aims to fill vacant properties with responsible people who will prevent them from being abused. You must have good references, a job, and be over eighteen, as well as be ok with sharing with an indeterminate number of strangers, but the benefits are the unusual properties (e.g. schools, disused churches), the often large spaces and the ridiculously cheap rent (£25–60 pw inclusive of all bills). Of course loads of people want to do this and properties in London are not always available, but it's nevertheless a good idea to keep an eye on their site if the idea excites you: www.camelotproperty.co.uk.

WAREHOUSES

As with Starbucks and obesity, us Brits have finally caught on to the American craze for warehouse 'live/work' spaces. Okay we may have had the likes of Tracey Emin and other artists living in old carpet factories since the YBA days, but recently a whole crop of established estate agents have been refurbishing lofts and factories for letting at a premium. Any established warehouser will tell you the way to go is independent, through enthusiastic urban explorers who renovate and convert these old buildings for love and enjoyment. Often the only way into this secret brotherhood of the leaky roof is by simply ending up at a huge party at 4am in one of these spaces and asking the residents politely. The freedom of living in these places can be exhilirating if you've spent years toeing the line with grumpy neighbours and grumpier landlords.

CANAL-BOATS

If all this land lubbing is bringing you down, there's always the option of dropping anchor at Little Venice or the Lea Valley Harbour and sampling London's canal networks. More and more skint artsy fartsy folk are squeezing their possessions into canal boats and living a romantic life on the water. A casual stroll down Regent's Canal may convince you this is the way to live, but bare in mind the hidden cons of London nautical life: mooring fees, fuel, unlit walks down leafy paths frequented by degenerates… Don't say we didn't warn you!

The best of the best

London is full of interactive children's pursuits, and nothing beats discovering all the joys that the city has to offer to the little ones, so we thought we'd give you some inside tips on what there is!

- **Best Rainy Day Activity:** The Science Museum (Exhibition Road, SW7 2DD, 0870 870 4868) is great fun and one of London's most interactive museums. Don't miss the Launchpad gallery, which is full of hands-on exhibits to tinker with, simulators and a face morphing machine. The museum's occasional Science Nights are activity filled, with overnight camping in the building included. Entry is free. Open 7 days a week from 10am to 6pm.
- **Coolest Cinema:** The BFI London IMAX Cinema (1 Charlie Chaplin Walk, SE1 8XR, 020 7902 1234) has the largest screen (20 metres) in the country, as well as an 11,600-watt digital surround sound system with which to deafen your children. With most of the cinema's 3D programming dedicated to children's films, they'll be spoilt rotten by the whole experience; even the entrance to the place is cool, with futuristic blue lighting paving your way through the tunnels.
- **Goriest Tourist Haunt:** The London Dungeon (28-34 Tooley Street, SE1 2SZ, 020 7403 7221) specialises in the darker side of English history and has a preponderance of gruesome waxworks, theme rides and costumed staff to scare the bejesus out of your children, which they'll love (unless you've brought them up to be soft). Open all week from 11am to 5pm.
- **Best Tour For Budding Media Moguls:** The BBC Television Centre Tour (Wood Lane, W12 7RJ, 0870 603 0304) provides a chance for children 9 and over to take a behind the scenes look at the world of TV, as well as a chance to play in an interactive studio. A separate tour (ages 7 and over) entitled "The CBBC Experience" is based on the BBC's kids' channel and offers visitors the chance to roam around the Blue Peter garden, amongst other things. Regular tours are conducted every day except Sunday.
- **Best Ice Cream:** It's no secret that kids love ice cream, but the plethora of dodgy "Mr Whippy" vans selling their frozen wares in London can be improved upon. For outstanding homemade gourmet sorbets and exotic ice cream cones, there is no better place than the kiosk to the side of Golders Hill Park Refreshment House (North End Road, NW3 7HD, 020 8455 8010); prices are very reasonable and the park is a gorgeous setting within which to consume such tasty delights.
- **Best One To Keep The Boys Happy:** The Arsenal Emirates Stadium Tour (Ashburton Grove, N7 7AF, 020 7704 4504). Surely even Spurs fans would appreciate a look behind the scenes at London's newest and most aesthetic football venue. Poke around the first team dressing room, walk down the player's tunnel and sample a unique pitchside view of the stadium; under 5s get in free.
- **Best For Halloween Costumes:** Escapade (150 Camden High Street, NW1 0NE, 020 7485 7384) has been kitting kids out in all manner of costumes since 1982, and offers wigs (maybe one for Dad?), hats, masks, make-up, jokes and magic tricks. Perfect for trick or treat, or for those already bored of their child's ugly face.
- **Best Eatery For Families:** Maxwell's (8-9 James Street, WC2E 8BH) lies deep in the heart of Covent Garden and specialises in burgers (does any child not like burgers?) which won't break parents' banks. A kids' menu is provided, as well as activities and games.

Rainy day activities

Especially for when the infamous London weather puts a dampener on outdoor activities…

- **Cartoon Museum** (35 Little Russell Street, WC1A 2HH, 020 7580 8155) This fascinating place archives the development of cartoon art in Britain, from the 18th century through to the present day; best of all, the Young Artists' Gallery lets children try their hands at animation and claymation.
- **London Aquarium** (County Hall, Westminster Bridge Road, SE1 7PB, 020 7967 8000) One of the largest aquariums in the world, over 400 species of aquatic life (including the only zebra sharks in the U.K.) can be found within this building. With three floors, piranhas, and pools where you can prod things, there's more than enough to keep even the most jaded parent happy.
- **London Eye** (Jubilee Gardens, South Bank, SE1 7PB, 0870 500 0600) This 135-metre high riverside Ferris wheel offers breathtaking views of London in up to 25 miles in each direction, all from the

vantage point of an air-conditioned glass pod. Book online to beat the queues.

- **Natural History Museum** (Cromwell Road, SW7 5BD, 020 7942 5000) Ever wanted to see a replica skeleton of a 26-metre long Diplodocus dinosaur? It's one of the 70 million items housed within this excellent museum, which also includes the Darwin Centre, a must for any budding paleontologists; non-nerds should love it too.
- **Madame Tussaud's** (Marylebone Road, NW1 5LR, 0870 999 0046) Infamous exhibition of waxworks, with recently introduced interactive exhibits giving you the chance to score a goal for England or sing with Britney Spears (she'll be the one lip-syncing). Worth booking online to avoid the often long queues.
- **Museum Of London** (150 London Wall, EC2Y 5HN, 0870 444 3852, some galleries undergoing renovation and due to re-open late 2009) Explains the history of London in vivid detail; the innovative layout consists of a chain of chronological galleries (no skipping to 1945, OK?) Also has fragments of the old London Wall in the grounds.
- **Peter Harrison Planetarium** (Royal Observatory Greenwich, Greenwich Park, SE10 9NF, 020 8312 8565) Open since 2007 and the only planetarium in London seats 120 and uses the latest technology to take you on an armchair tour of the universe. Children aged 4 and under will not be admitted.
- **Queens Ice And Bowl** (17 Queensway, W2 4QP, 020 7229 0172) An ice rink, ten pin bowling alleys and a pizza restaurant, it's the perfect opportunity for kids to stuff their faces whilst watching their Dad break a bone on the rink. Children's skating classes available.
- **Topsy Turvy World** (Brent Cross Shopping Centre, Prince Charles Drive, NW4 3FP, 020 8359 9920) A huge indoor playground in the middle of one of London's busiest shopping centres. There's more to this place than just bouncy things and over-excitement, it also offers baking activities (might as well get your children cooking for you early) and various classes.
- **Tower Of London** (Tower Hill, EC3N 4AB, 0870 756 7070) A cornucopia of royal history and English culture lies within the Tower's ancient walls, with royal jewels aplenty. Good for the whole family, and under 5s get in free. Avoid the queues by booking ahead.
- **The V&A Museum Of Childhood** (Cambridge Heath Road, E2 9PA, 020 8983 5200) This lesser known gem of the Victoria & Albert Museum houses the national childhood collection, which basically means it's full of toys, games, dolls, dollhouses, nursery antiques and children's costumes. There's no shortage of activities and events going on here to keep your kids occupied, and it's free.

Classes

A recent resurgence in the amount of out of school programmes being implemented in the capital means that there's more for your kids to do than ever before.

- **Art Club** (Orleans House Gallery, Riverside, TW1 3DJ, 020 8831 6000) A rare opportunity for 5-10 year olds to work with practicing artists and explore new techniques and materials. Every Wednesday and Thursday from 3.45-5pm.
- **Barnsbury One O'Clock Club** (Barnard Park, Hemingford Road, N1 0JU, 020 7278 9494) Fun and games for the under 5s.
- **Brixton Recreation Centre** (27 Brixton Station Road, SW9 8QQ, 020 7926 9779) Recently refurbished, this centre includes The Energy Zone (ages 5-15) for ball games and The Fitness Zone (ages 8-15) with SHOKK fitness equipment specifically designed for the younger body builder/steroid abuser.
- **Camden Square Play Centre** (Camden Square, NW1 9RE, 020 7485 6827) After school (and school holiday) centre with fun activities for children aged 4-12.
- **Camden Swiss Cottage Swimming Club** (Swiss Cottage Leisure Centre, Winchester Road, NW3 3NR, 020 7974 5440) Swimming lessons for children aged 4 and upward.
- **Chang's Hapkido Academy** (Topnotch Health Club, 3 Tudor Street, EC4Y 0AH, 07951 535876) Martial arts school with classes for ages 12 and upward.
- **The Circus Space** (Coronet Street, N1 6HD, 020 7613 4141) Prepare your children for a life in the circus with The Circus Space's variety of classes and workshops for all ages.

- **Crazee Kids** (Jackson Lane Community Centre, Archway Road, N6 5AA, Tuesdays), (Union Church & Community Centre, Weston Park, N8 9TA, Saturdays) 020 8444 5333, Weekly term-time dance, drama and music classes. Summer workshops.
- **Harringay Club** (Hornsey YMCA, 50 Tottenham Lane, N8 7EE, 020 8348 2124) A range of things to do for those aged up to 15, including a pre-school programme, gymnastics, ballet, street dance and kickboxing.
- **The Kids' Cookery School** (107 Gunnersbury Len W3 8HQ, 020 8992 8882) Get your kids cooking at this fine venue which offers classes and workshops for those aged 3 and upwards.
- **Kite Art Studios** (Priory Mews, 2B Bassein Park Road, W12 9RY, 020 8576 6278) Courses and workshops on painting, pottery and jewellery making amongst other fun activities for kids of all ages. Mother and toddler sessions too.
- **London Irish Centre** (50-52 Camden Square, NW1 9XB, 020 7916 7222) Irish dancing classes for beginners upwards, every Monday at 6pm, courtesy of the Barrett Semple-Morris School.
- **The Little Angel Theatre** (14 Dagmar Passage, Cross Street, N1 2DN, 020 7226 1787) Children's theatre offering after-school courses in puppet making, the art of puppetry performance and a Saturday Puppet Club.
- **The Little Gym** (Compass House, Riverside West, Smugglers Way, SW18 1DB, 020 8874 6567) Gymnastics and skills development within a relaxed environment for children aged up to 12.
- **Music House For Children** (Bush Hall, 310 Uxbridge Road, W12 7LJ, 020 8932 2652) Whether it's instrumental or singing lessons, this wonderful place can provide individual and group tuition and even caters for 1 year olds!
- **Painted Earth** (Arch 65, The Catacombs, Stables Market, NW1 8AH, 020 7424 8983) Ceramic arts classes supervised by staff. Children can make their own mugs and plates.
- **Richmond Junior Chess Club** (ETNA Community Centre, 13 Rosslyn Road, TW1 2AR, 07720 716336) Chess classes with a mixture of instruction and play for those up to the age of 18.
- **Sobell Leisure Centre** (Hornsey Road, N7 7NY, 020 7609 2166) No need to book, just turn up for coached sessions in basketball, badminton, football and ice hockey amongst other sports. Children aged 7 and under must be accompanied by an adult.
- **Tricycle Theatre** (269 Kilburn High Road, NW6 7JR, 020 7328 1000) Not just a theatre/cinema/gallery, the Tricycle also runs term-time workshops in drama, storytelling and music.
- **Triyoga** (6 Erskine Road, NW3 3AJ, 020 7483 3344) Let the kids get their Zen on at after school yoga classes for ages 5 and over.
- **Westway Stables** (20 Stable Way, Latimer Road, W11 6QX, 020 8964 2140) Horse riding lessons for the over 5s in the heart of Notting Hill.

Babysitting/nanny/services,

- **Nannies Unlimited** 11 Chelveton Road, SW15 1RN, 020 8788 9640
- **Nanny Search** 1st Floor, 1 Shepherds Hill, N6 5QJ, 020 8348 4111
- **Sleeptight Nannies** 20 Nursery Road, N14 5QB, 020 8292 2618
- **Top Notch Nannies** 49 Harrington Gardens, SW7 4JU, 020 7259 2626

Where to go for more info

www.kidslovelondon.com

Shopping essentials

- **Baby Dior** 6 Harriet Street, SW1X 9JW, 020 7823 2039 – Encourage label envy as soon as possible.
- **Baby Munchkins** 186 Hoxton Street, N1 5LH, 020 7684 5994 – Baby wear.
- **Balloonland** 12 Hale Lane, NW7 3NX, 020 8906 3302 – Balloons and party supplies.
- **Benjamin Pollock's Toyshop** 44 The Piazza, Covent Garden WC2E 8RF, 020 7379 7866 – Toys.
- **Biff** 43 Dulwich Village, SE21 7BN, 020 8299 0911 – Designer and street brands.
- **Boomerang** 69 Blythe Road, W14 0HP, 020 7610 5232 – Clothes and necessities for tots.
- **Bonpoint** Chic clothes.

  17 Victoria Grove, W8 5RW – 020 7584 5131

  197 Westbourne Grove, W11 2SE – 020 7792 2515

  256 Brompton Road, SW3 2AS – 020 3263 5057

  35B Sloane Street, SW1X 9LP – 020 7235 1441

  38 Old Bond Street, W1S 4QW – 020 7495 1680

- **Burberry** 21-23 New Bond Street, W1S 2RE, 020 7839 5222 – Clothes.
- **Caramel** 291 Brompton Road, SW3 2DY, 020 7589 7001 – Cool clothes.
- **Catamini** – Babies and children's clothes. 33C King's Road, SW3 4LX – 020 7824 8897, 52 South Molton Street, W1Y 1HF – 020 7629 8099
- **Cheeky Monkeys** – Mainly wooden toys. 202 Kensington Park Road, W11 1NR – 020 7792 9022, 94 Kings Road, SW6 4UL – 020 7731 3037
- **Children's Book Centre** 237 Kensington High Street, W8 6SA, 020 7937 7497 – Books.
- **Coco Children's Boutique** 27A Devonshire Street, W1G 6PN, 020 7935 3554 – Children's boutique (fancy that!).
- **D2 Leisure** 201-203 Roman Road, E2 0QY, 020 8980 4966 – Bicycle shop.
- **Daisy & Tom** 181 King's Road, SW3 5EB, 020 7352 5000 – Clothes, toys and a carousel.
- **Davenports Magic Shop** 7 Adelaide Street, WC2N 4HZ, 020 7836 0408 – Magic shop.
- **Early Learning Centre** 36 King's Road, SW3 4UD, 020 7581 5764 – Educational toyshop.
- **Disney Store** – Disney merchandise.,

  Unit 10, The Piazza, WC2E 8HD – 020 7836 5037

  22A & 26 The Broadway Shopping Centre, W6 9YD – 020 8748 8886

  360-366 Oxford Street, W1N 9HA – 020 7491 9136
- **Eric Snook's Toyshop** 32 Covent Garden Market, WC1 8RE, 020 7379 7681 – Toys and teddies.
- **Escapade** 150 Camden High Street, NW1 0NE, 020 7485 7384 – Costumes and masks.
- **The Farmyard** 63 Barnes High Street, SW13 9LF, 020 8878 7338 – Toys for younger children and babies.
- **GapKids/Baby Gap**

  35 Hampstead High Street, NW3 1QE – 020 7794 9182

  146-148 Regent Street, W1B 5SH – 020 7287 5095

  Brent Cross Shopping Centre, NW4 3FB – 020 8203 9696

  122 King's Road, SW3 4TR – 020 7823 7272

  4 Queens Road, SW19 8YE- 020 8947 9074

  101-111 Kensington High Street, W8 5SA – 020 7368 2900

  260-262 Chiswick High Road, W4 1PD – 020 8995 3255

  47-49 St John's Wood High Street, NW8 7NJ – 020 7586 6123

  151 Queensway, W2 4YL – 020 7221 8039

  330-340 Cabot Place East, E14 4QT – 020 7513 0241

  121-123 Long Acre, WC2E 9PA – 020 7836 0646
- **Green Rabbit** 20 Briston Grove, N8 9EX, 020 8348 3770 – Contemporary kids' wear.
- **Hamley's** 188-196 Regent Street, W1B 5BT, 020 7153 9000 – Toys galore, tourists galore.
- **Happy Returns** 36 Rosslyn Hill, NW3 1NH, 020 7435 2431 – Toys again!
- **Honeyjam** 267 Portobello Road, W11 1LR, 020 7243 0449 – Retro and vintage toys and rocking horses.
- **Igloo Kids** Wide range of kids' clothes. 300 Upper Street, N1 2TU – 020 7354 7300, 80 St John's Wood, NW8 7SH – 020 7483 2332
- **Infantasia Unit 103** Wood Green Shopping City, N22 6YA, 020 8889 1494 – Furniture and bedding.
- **International Magic** 89 Clerkenwell Road, EC1R 5BX, 020 7405 7324 – Magic shop.
- **Joujou & Lucy** 32 Clifton Road, W9 1ST, 020 7289 0866 – Children's boutique.
- **Kent & Carey** 154 Wandsworth Bridge Road, SW6 2UH, 020 7736 5554 – Classic children's clothes.
- **Little Stinkies** 15 Victoria Grove, W8 5RW, 020 7052 0077 – Dolls' houses, toys and puppet theatres.
- **Marie Chantal** 148 Walton Street, SW3 2JJ, 020 7838 1111 – Children's fashion.
- **MIMMO** 602 Fulham Road, SW6 5PA, 020 7731 4706 – Designer duds.
- **Mothercare** – The leading chain for baby stuff in the UK; will sell you everything but the baby.

  Brent Cross Shopping Centre, NW4 3FD – 020 8202 5377

  416 Brixton Road, SW9 7AY – 020 7733 1494

  Unit 7, The Waterglade Centre, 1-8 The Broadway, W5 2ND – 0208 579 6181

  Ravenside Retail Park, Angel Road, N18 3HA – 020 8807 5518

  146 High Street, SE9 1BJ – 020 8859 7957

  4 Palace Gardens, EN2 6SN – 020 8367 1188

316 North End Road, SW6 1NG – 020 7381 6387

Kings Mall Shopping Centre, W6 0PZ – 020 8600 2860

448 Holloway Road, N7 6QA – 020 7607 0915

112 High Street, TW3 1NA – 020 8577 1767

Unit 1A, Richmond Retail Park, Mortlake Road, Kew – 020 8878 3758

41 Riverdale High Street, SE13 7EP – 020 8852 2167

526-528 Oxford Street, W1C 1LW – 0845 365 0515

Unit 2, Aylesham Centre, Rye Lane, SE15 5EW – 020 7358 0093

33-34 The Mall, E15 1XD – 020 8534 5714

BHS Surrey Quays Shopping Centre, Redriff Road, SE16 7LL – 020 7237 2025

Unit 59, Southside Shopping Centre, SW18 4TF – 020 8877 4180

Unit Lsu4, Centre Court, SW19 8YA – 020 8944 5296

38-40 High Road, N22 6BX – 020 8888 6920

62 Powis Street, SE18 1LQ – 020 8854 3540

- **Never Never Land** 3 Mildhurst Parade, Fortis Green, N10 3EJ, 020 883 3997 – Toys and dolls.
- **Olive Loves Alfie** 84 Stoke Newington Church Street, N16 0AP, 020 7241 4212 – Children's lifestyle boutique.
- **Patrick's Toys & Models** 107 Lillie Road, SW6 7SX, 020 7385 9864 – Outdoor games and equipment.
- **Patrizia Wigan** 19 Walton Street, SW3 2HX, 020 7823 7080 – Clothing boutique.
- **Petit Bateau** 62 South Molton Street, W1K 5SR, 020 7491 4498 – Luxurious baby wear.
- **Petite Ange** 6 Harriet Street, SW1X 9JW, 020 7235 7737 – Exclusive clothing.
- **Please Mum** 85 Knightsbridge, SW1X 7RB, 020 7486 1380 – Expensive clothing.
- **Pom D'Api** 3 Blenheim Crescent, W11 2EE, 020 7243 0535 – Classy shoes.
- **QT Toys** 90 Northcote Road, SW11 6QN, 020 7223 8637 – Toys, games and gifts.
- **Rachel Riley** 14 Pont Street, SW1X 9EN, 020 7935 7007 – Clothes.
- **Rainbow** 253 Archway Road, N6 5BS, 020 8340 9700 – Toys, games and clothes.
- **Showroom** 64 Titchfield Street, W1W 7QH, 020 7636 2501 – Funky children's clothes.
- **Soup Dragon** 27 Topsfield Parade, Tottenham Lane, N8 8PT, 020 8348 0224 – Toys and clothes.
- **The Shoe Station** 3 Station Approach, Kew Gardens, TW9 3QB, 020 8940 9905 – Shoes and footwear.
- **Their Nibs** 214 Kensington Park Road, W11 1NR, 020 7221 4263 – Designer clothes and bedding.
- **Tots** 39 Turnham Green Terrace, W4 1RG, 020 8995 0520 – Clothes boutique.
- **Toys R Us** - Toys, toys, toys.

  Tilling Road (opposite Brent Cross Shopping Centre), NW2 1LW – 020 8209 0019

  Great Cambridge Road, EN1 3RN – 020 8364 6600

  Hayes Road, UB2 5LN – 020 8561 4681

  760 Old Kent Road, SE15 1NJ – 020 7732 7322
- **Traditional Toys** Chelsea Green, 53 Godfrey Street, SW3 3SX, 020 7352 1718 – Timeless toys.
- **The Little White Company** 261 Pavillion Road, SW1X 0BP, 020 7881 0783 – Clothing, bed linen and furniture.

For many, the Internet is *the* key to the city. Before the dawning of the Internet, we Dickensian scamps had to scurry around in the filth foraging for information in 'books' and by talking to actual 'people'. Now that the future is here, Londoners can navigate their city's streets, explore its dark history, organise a debauched weekend in Chiswick or, as is more likely, peer over the shoulder of men in raincoats in Internet Cafes.

Internet Cafes are *everywhere.* In fact you probably live in one. They can range from the dimly lit 'Money Transfer' shacks that have an air of illegality, to the over-orange **Easyeverything** chain that dominated the market before home internet use skyrocketed in the late 90s. You can escape the grim D.I.Y. flea pits in chic coffee outlets like **Coffee @ (155 Brick Lane 020 7247 6735)** but sharpen your elbows as space is tight. **Cyberia Cafe** near Goodge Street **(39 Whitfield Street Tel No – 020 7209 0984)** claims to have been the first Internet Cafe in the world and is still very plush. To be fair, internet use in these places is usually criminally cheap : as low as 50p per hour in the non-tourist areas. For a large list of London internet cafes check out **http://www.allinlondon.co.uk/directory/1166.php.**

London was recently crowned WiFi capital of the world, owing to its astronomical rate of increase in WiFi networks. It is becoming more and more difficult to move in your local cafe without catching the sharp edge of a laptop. The **Apostrophe Cafe** chain is efficient, expensive and has WiFi as standard. Like many WiFi-compatible eateries, wireless access is limited to an hour and they give out passwords to paying customers only. If you wish to cook your internal organs with your PowerBook you can do so in hundreds of cafes in London; for a decent online map of WiFi locations check out **http://londonist.com/2007/05/free_wifi_in_lo.php**. **Of course there is always the pirate option—dodging the Community Officers and fiendishly stealing a neighbours connection.** Beware however, in 2007 a man was arrested in what was the first case of WiFi theft—he was balancing his laptop on his garden wall!

Useful And/Or Fun London Links:

www.fedbybirds.com
www.royalparks.org.uk
www.tfl.gov.uk
www.londonist.com
www.londonfreelist.com
www.davehill.typepad.com
www.shadyoldlady.com
www.derelictlondon.com
www.walk-london.blogspot.com
www.hiddenlondon.com
www.londonbloggers.iamcal.com
www.london-underground.blogspot.com
www.fancyapint.com
www.dailycandy.com/london
www.gumtree.com
www.timeout.com
www.brickads.blogspot.com
www. wildinlondon.blogspot.com
www. westlondonblogger.blogspot.com
www. dalstonoxfamshop.blogspot.com
www.viewlondon.co.uk
www.lecool.com/cities/london
www.deadcafesociety.org.uk
www.londonreviewofbreakfasts.blogspot.com
www.beerintheevening.com

The doom-sayers have less cause to complain about the decline of Gayhood in London recently, what with **Heaven** (London's self-proclaimed most famous gay club) hanging on and new nights popping up everywhere. Yes, popular indie discos **Popstarz** and **Rebel Rebel** have relocated but **Girl's Action** at Ghetto promises great things and we are so in love with 'polysexual' club **Dalston Supermarket** at the moment. Of course every time one door (read: gay club) closes another one opens, and let's face it, the latter will probably open later and sell you even cheaper Red Bull and vodka.

One of the most exciting developments in the past few years has been the advent of what has been dubbed London's new 'Gay Village'—the cluster of clubs, saunas and after-hours hangover incubators that have sprung up in Vauxhall. Now it's possible, though still just as unadvisable, to party from Thursday through to Tuesday without stopping to reapply deodorant, or think about the consequences of what you're doing—hooray. The small outcrop of gay and 'polysexual' nights in the East End, (which until recently included the notoriously wonderful, but necessarily short-lived 'Boombox') is still thriving, and offers another refreshing alternative to Soho for those in search of an aggressive fashion consciousness and a less cruisy atmosphere. This said, if you can handle bright lights, pop music, tight t-shirts and a lot of hair gel, you'll still have massive amounts of fun around Soho and Old Compton Street, the traditional central London gay epicentre. This area is always buzzing, day and night, and is a great place to sit back and do some people watching as well as to go out and, y'know, go crazy.

For girls there is still room for improvement, with options fewer and less centralised, but **The Minories'** new Girls' night is a blast and the continuing women-only nights at **Village** and **Element** are cause for celebration. Many mixed and polysexual nights (such as Motherfucker at **Barden's Boudoir**) also draw large female crowds, and though dedicated lesbian bars and clubs are few and far between, there is enough going on in the city to make any day of the week a possible night out.

Websites

www.dirtydirtydancing.com - Super-airbrushed photos from many of the trendier Soho and east London nights.

http://scene-out.com - Comprehensive mainstream scene guide.

www.gaylondon.co.uk - Online gay and lesbian community for London.

www.gingerbeer.co.uk - Lesbian guide to London.

www.girlguidelondon.co.uk - Does what it says on the tin.

www.gmfa.org.uk - Gay men's health charity.

www.pinkdate.com - Speed dating events for gay men and women in central London.

Publications

The following are all free listings/scene magazines that can be found in most gay shops and venues (anywhere on Old Compton Street should have some copies lying around):

Boyz Magazine - Weekly scene news and listings, out Thursdays. www.boyz.co.uk

G3 Magazine - Lesbian scene, monthly. www.g3mag.co.uk

Out in the City Mag - Monthly London lifestyle magazine for gay men. www.outmag.co.uk

Qx Magazine - Gay men's mag. www.qxmagazine.com

Shops

Gay's the Word, 66 Marchmont Street, WC1N 1AB, 020 7278 7654, http://freespace.virgin.net/gays.theword/, The only dedicated Gay and Lesbian Bookshop in London, recently threatened by rising rent. Visit whilst it's still there!

Foyles, 113–119 Charing Cross Road, WC2H 0EB, 020 7437 5660, www.foyles.co.uk, Huge bookshop with large gay and lesbian section.

Prowler, 5–7 Brewer Street, W1F 0RF, 020 7734 4031, The ultimate gay men's shop, stocking everything from (skimpy) clothes to sex toys plus mountains of lube, pornography, and the other usual suspects.

Sexual Health

A comprehensive list of London clinics that offer same day HIV testing and PEP treatments for gay/bisexual men is available at www.gmfa.org.uk/londonservices/clinics. CLASH, below, is particularly recommended.

CLASH (Central London Action on Street Health), 11 Warwick Street, W1B 5NA, 020 7734 1794, Friday night clinic for gay men, with incredibly friendly staff who will offer comfort and advice. Same day (often instant) HIV testing, PEP treatment. Fridays, 5 - 8.30pm, call for an appointment.

Support Organizations

Again, a more comprehensive list can be found at the GMFA website: www.gmfa.org.uk/londonservices/support-groups/index

Stonewall, Tower Building, York Road, SE1 7NX, www.stonewall.org.uk, Gay rights charity and lobbying group.

PACE Youthwork Service, 34 Hartham Road, N7 9LJ, 020 7700 1323, www.outzone.org, Support organization for gay and lesbian youths under 25. Organizes regular social events and offers one to one consultations with advisors: phone or visit the website to get involved.

London Friend, 86 Caledonian Road, N1 9DN, 020 7833 1674, www.londonfriend.org.uk, Voluntary organization which runs several helplines, group workshops and social events, as well as offering advice on reporting hate crime.

London Lesbian and Gay Switchboard, 020 7837 7324 (helpline), 020 7689 8501 (Volunteers), Counselling and information service.

Kairos in Soho, Unit 10, 10-11 Archer Street, W1D 7AZ, 020 7437 6063, www.kairosinsoho.org.uk, Gay and lesbian charity which organises a variety of recreational events to promote the health, well being and development of the LGBT community.

Naz Project London, Palingswick House, 241 King Street, W6 9LP, 020 8741 1879 www.naz.org.uk, Charity that organizes support and sexual health services for black and ethnic minority communities in London. Various services, including free one-on-one counselling and support groups are available, phone or check website for details.

GALOP, PO Box 32810, N1 3ZD, 020 7704 6767, www.galop.org.uk, Charity specialising in advice about reporting hate crime.

Annual Events

Pride London, www.pridelondon.org, Large pride festival, takes place every July.

London Lesbian and Gay Film Festival, www.bfi.org.uk/llgff, Film festival at the BFI on South Bank, March–April.

Bistrotheque Annual Drag Ball, www.myspace.com/trannylipsync or www.bistrotheque.com, Annual team-based drag contest. Open entry but fierce competition!

London LGBT History Month, www.lgbthistorymonth.co.uk, Nationwide awareness month, with various talks and events staged in London, every February.

Gay/mixed venues

Soho:

79CXR, 79 Charing Cross Road, WC2H 0NE, 020 7734 0769, Dingy bar with middle aged crowd.

The Admiral Duncan, 54 Old Compton Street, W1D 4UB, 020 7437 5300

Barcode Soho, 3-4 Archer Street W1D 7AT, 020 7734 3342

Box, 32–34 Monmouth Street, WC2H 9HA, 020 7240 5828, Civilised bar and eatery.

Comptons, 53–57 Old Compton Street, W1D 6HN, 020 7479 7961, Crammed gay pub.

Duke of Wellington, 77 Wardour Street, W1D 6QA

The Edge, 11 Soho Square, W1D 3QF, 020 7439 1313

G-A-Y Bar, 30 Old Compton Street, W1D 5JX, 020 7494 2756, Poptastic bunker. Video walls and cheap drinks.

G-A-Y Late, 5 Goslett Yard, WC2H 0ER, 020 7734 9858, Cheap drinks and pop videos wipe out brain functions 'til 3am.

Ghetto, Falconberg Court, W1D 3AB, 020 7287 3726, Loud electro at this busy gay club. Thursday is ladies night.

Halfway to Heaven, 7 Duncannon Street, WC2N 4JF, 020 7321 2791.

Heaven, Under the Arches, Villiers Street, WC2N 6NG, 020 7930 2020, Legendary gay club. An institution.

Ku Bar, 30 Lisle Street, WC2H 7BA, 020 7437 4303, Newly relocated bar for the young and clueless.

Kudos, 10 Adelaide Street, WC2N 4HZ, 020 7379 4573

Profile, 56–57 Frith Street, W1D 3JG, 020 7734 8300

Shadow Lounge, 5 Brewer Street, W1F, 020 7439 4089, Supposed to be a shi-shi cocktail lounge. Hmmmm.

Soho Revue Bar, 11 Walkers Court, Brewer Street, W1F 0ED, Cabaret acts followed by dancing 'til late.

The Village, 81 Wardour Street, W1D 6QD, 020 7434 2124, Tacky, flirtatious bar spread across two floors.
Trash Palace, 11 Wardour Street, W1D 6PG, 020 7734 0522, Bratty queer indie bar.

North:
Cosmo Lounge, 43 Essex Road, N1 2SF, 020 7688 0051, Subdued bar, normally full of regulars.
Central Station, 37 Wharfdale Road, N1 9SD, 020 7278 3294. Pub/club with ominously blacked out windows.
The Green, 74 Upper Street N1 0NY, 0871 971 4097, Innocuous gay bar/restaurant frequented by many unsuspecting straight couples.
King Edward VI Pub, 25 Bromfield Street, N1 0PZ
The Black Cap, 171 Camden High Street, NW1 7JY, 020 7428 2721, Slightly crummy gay pub.

East:
Bistrotheque, 23–27 Wadeson Street, E2 9DR, Jonny Woo's restaurant, great food and drag acts.
The Black Horse, 168 Mile End Road, E1 4LJ, 020 7790 1684
George and Dragon, 2 Hackney Road, E2 7NS, Small, atmospheric pub full of trendy boys and girls.
Joiners Arms, 116–118, Hackney Road, E2 7Q, Late opening free-for-all with a wonderfully mixed crowd. ('til 2/3am most nights)

South:
Area, 67–68 Albert Embankment, SE1 7TP
Barcode Vauxhall, 69 Albert Embankment, 020 7582 4180
The Two Brewers, 114 Clapham High Street, SW4 7UJ, 020 7498 4971
Depot, 66 Albert Embankment, SE11 7TP, Sister club of Area, with a more cruisy vibe.
Fire, South Lambeth Road, SW8 1RT, 020 7434 1113, The quintessential Vauxhall club. Open pretty much forever, bulging muscles everywhere.
The Fort, 131 Grange Road, Bermondsey, SE1 3AL - Themed cruising/fetish/sex bar.
Kazbar Clapham, 50 Clapham High Street, SW4 7UL, 020 7622 0070
Little Apple Bar, 98 Kennington Lane, SE11 4XD Mixed/lesbian bar.
Man Bar, 82 Great Suffolk Street, SE1 OBE, 020 7928 3223, Cruise bar.
The Powder Monkey, 22 King William Walk, SE10 PHU, 020 8293 5928, thepowdermonkey.net
Royal Vauxhall Tavern, 372 Kennington Lane, SE11 5HY, 020 7820 1222
South Central, 349 Kennington Lane, SE11 5QY, 020 7793 0903
Substation South, 9 Brighton Terrace, SW9 8DJ, 020 7737 2095
XXL, 51–53 Southwark Street, SE1 1TE, www.fatsandsmalls.com, Busy bear club.

West:
Bromptons, 294 Old Brompton Road, SW5 9JF, 020 77370 1344
The Coleherne, 261 Old Brompton Road, SW5 9JA020 7244 5951

Recommended Nights

Club Motherfucker, second Saturdays @ Barden's Boudoir, 38 Stoke Newington Road, Dalston, N16 7XJ, Polysexual band night. Sweaty, noisy, very much about the music.
Circus, Fridays @ Soho Revue Bar, 11 Walkers Court, Brewer Street, W1F 0ED, Drag Queen Jodie Harsh's long running night attracts its fair share of celebrities from both on and off the scene. Get there early or be prepared to queue.
DTPM, www.myspace.com/dtpm, Legendary event, no longer with a fixed location. See site for details of upcoming parties.
For3ign, Saturdays @ Bar Music Hall, 134 Curtain Road, EC2A 3AR, 020 7613 5951, Outlandish costumes and, of course, thumping electro.
Horsemeat Disco, Sundays @ South Central, Italo and 70s Disco bring all sorts to this fantastic night, originally a bear love club.
Icon, Sundays @ Essence, 562a Mile End Road, E3 4PH, 0208 980 6427, mob 07843 440 443 (weekly), New night in the East End. Yet to prove itself.
Issue, monthly (check site for details) @ Electricity Showrooms, 39a Hoxton Square, N1 6NN, issueclub.blogspot.com. Polysexual parties to coincide with the launch of this scene/fashion magazine.
Matinee, monthly (check site) @ Fabric, 77a Charterhouse Street, EC1M 3HN, 020 7335 8898, www.matineelondon.com, Irregular gay night at this enormous club in Farringdon.
Popstarz, Fridays @ Sin, 144 Charing Cross Road, WC2H 0LB, 020 7240 1900, Gay indie institution, recently relocated.

Trailer Trash, Fridays @ On the Rocks, 25 Kingsland Road, E2 8AA, 020 7688 0339, The dirtiest electro and the drunkest you've ever been. Crammed with sweating fashionistas.

Wet Yourself, Sundays @ Aquarium, 256–264 Old Street, EC1V 9DD, 020 7251 6136, This used to be the place to be after Boombox. It's lost only a little of its charm since (mixed polysexual crowd).

Lesbian Venues

Blush Bar, 8 Cazenove Road, Stoke Newington N16, 020 7923 9202, www.blushbar.co.uk

Candy Bar, 23-24 Bateman Street, W1V 5HR, 020 7437 1977, The reluctant epicentre of the Lesbian scene in Soho.

First Out Café Bar, Soho - 52 St Giles High St, WC2H 8LH, 020 7240 8042, Cafe with nightly events. All girls on Friday.

Oak Bar, 79 Green Lanes, N16, www.oakbar.co.uk, 020 7354 2791,

The Star At Night, 22 Great Chapel Street, Soho, W1 8FR, 020 7434 3749, Mixed cocktail bar with a predominantly female crowd.

Recommended Nights

100% Babe, Bank Holiday Sundays @ The Roxy, 3 Rathbone Place, W1P 1DA, 020 7636 1598, Irregular party for fans of funky house, R&B, old skool and electropop.

Blue Light, last Saturdays @ Bar Med, Triton Court, 14 Finsbury Square, EC2, 020 7588 3056

Club Wotever, first Saturday of the month @ The Masters Club, 12 Denman Street, Piccadilly, W1D 7HH, 020 7734 4243, Draggy night with a large 'King' quota.

Code, irregular night @ the Enclave, 25–27 Brewer Street, W1F 0RR, www.club-code.net - check website for details.

Girls on Girls, Wednesdays @ Village, 81 Wardour Street, W1D 6QD, 020 7434 2124

Lounge, second Thursdays @ Vertigo, 1 Leicester Square, WC2H 7NA, 020 7734 0900, Relaxed cocktail night at this swish Leicester Square club.

Miss Shapes, Thursdays @ Ghetto, Falconberg Court, W1D 3AB, 020 7287 3726, Popular girls-only indie night.

Pink, Wednesdays @ Element, 4-5 Greek Street, W1D 4DD, 020 7434 3323.

Play, irregular night @ Bar Rumba, 35 Shaftesbury Ave, W1D 7EP, 020 7287 2715, www.myspace.com/_clubplay

Rumours, last Saturday of the month @ 64–73 Minories, EC3, 07949 477 804

Smack, irregular night @ various venues, check website, www.myspace.com/smackclub

Wish, first Saturdays @ Gramophone, 60–62 Commercial Street, E1 6LT, Style conscious night for young techno-heads and indie girls.

Women's Anarchist Nuisance Cafe, Penultimate wednesdays @ the RampART Creative Centre and Social Space, Rampart St, Aldgate, E1 2LA, Social group and cooperative vegan women's cafe.

Stickier Options

Club Fukk, second Fridays @ Central Station, 37 Wharfdale Road, N1 9SD, 020 7278 3294, www.centralstation.co.uk or www.woteverworld.com/id12.html, Predominantly Lesbian fetish/play club. One of many sex/cruising nights at the venue – check site for details.

Chariots, www.gaysauna.co.uk, Popular chain of gay saunas, with branches at the following locations: *Shoreditch*: 1 Fairchild Street, EC2A 3NS, *Waterloo*: 101 Lower Marsh, SE1 7AB, 020 7401 8484, *Limehouse*: 574 Commercial Road, E14 7JD, 020 7791 2808, *Streatham*: 292 [rear of] Streatham High Road, SW16 6HG, 020 8696 0929, *Farringdon*: 57 Cowcross Street, EC1M 6BX, 020 7251 5553, *Vauxhall*: 63-64 Albert Embankment, SE1, 020 7247 5333

The Fort,131 Grange Road, Bermondsey, SE1 3AL , Themed cruising/fetish/sex bar.

Hard On, monthly @ Hidden, 100 Tinworth Street, SE11 5EQ, www.hardonclub.co.uk, Rubber and fetish sex club for gay and bisexual men and women.

The Hoist, Arch 47b & 47c, South Lambeth Road, SW8 1RH, 020 7735 9972, www.thehoist.co.uk, Fetish sex club with strict dress codes, check website for details.

Man Bar, 82 Great Suffolk Street, SE1 OBE, 020 7928 3223, www.manbar.info, Cruise bar.

Nudity, first Fridays @ Hidden, 100 Tinworth Street, SE11 5EQ, Nude men's dance/play club.

Purrrr, 87 Fortess Road, Kentish Town NW5, www.purrrr.co.uk, Monthly S&M play club for Lesbians.

London Timeline

A timeline of significant events in London's history.

50: The Romans found Londinium, building the first London Bridge.

61: Queen Boudicca burns Londinium down.

100: Londinium becomes the capital of Roman Britain.

200: The Romans build the London Wall.

410: Roman occupation ends and Londinium is largely abandoned for many years.

604: King Aethelbert of Kent completes the first St Paul's Cathedral.

700: The Saxons build Lundenwic a mile to the west of old Londinium.

851: The Vikings burn Lundenwic down (starting to see a pattern, here?)

878: Alfred The Great defeats the Vikings and establishes a new settlement within the Roman Walls.

1013: The Viking King Canute besieges London.

1066: William The Conqueror becomes the first king to be crowned at Westminster Abbey.

1088: William The Conqueror builds the Tower Of London.

1097: William Rufus builds Westminster Hall—later part of the Houses Of Parliament.

1176: The wooden London Bridge is replaced by a stone structure.

1343: 'The Canterbury Tales' author Geoffrey Chaucer is born in London.

1348: The Black Death wipes out between a third and half of London's population in 18 months.

1381: Peasants revolt, storming the Tower Of London.

1599: William Shakespeare's theatre company The Chamberlain's Men build the Globe Theatre.

1605: Guy Fawkes' Gunpowder Plot fails to blow up the Palace Of Westminster.

1635: Hyde Park opens to the public.

1649: King Charles I is beheaded at Whitehall.

1665: The Great Plague kills a fifth of London's population (starting to see another pattern, here?)

1666: The Fire of London destroys 60% of the city, including St Paul's Cathedral, but wipes out the plague. This really must have been a great year.

1708: The new St Paul's Cathedral is completed by Sir Christopher Wren.

1732: Downing Street becomes the home of the Prime Minister.

1750: Westminster Bridge is built.

1814: Lord's Cricket Ground is opened.

1829: Robert Peel establishes the Metropolitan Police force, policemen known as 'Bobbies' or 'Peelers'.

1831: London becomes the world's biggest city.

1834: The Houses Of Parliament are built.

1843: Nelson's Column is completed in Trafalgar Square.

1851: Six million people gawp at newfangled technology and design at The Great Exhibition.

1858: The Great Stink inspires the 19th century's biggest civil engineering project—London's sewerage system.

London Timeline

1863: The first London Underground line is built.

1876: The Albert Memorial to Queen Victoria's husband Prince Albert is completed.

1884: An imaginary line through Greenwich Royal Observatory is internationally accepted as the Prime Meridian. Except by the French.

1887: Arthur Conan Doyle publishes the first Sherlock Holmes story 'A Study In Scarlet.'

1888: Jack The Ripper's first victim, Mary Ann Nichols, is murdered.

1908: London hosts the Olympics for the first time.

1915: German Zeppelin airships launch first air raids on London, ultimately killing over 700 people.

1923: Wembley Stadium is built in 300 days, costing £750,000.

1940: The Blitz begins—German bombs kill over 30,000 Londoners by the end of WW2 and destroy large areas of the city.

1946: Heathrow Airport opens for commercial flights.

1948: The second London Olympics is held.

1951: The Royal Festival Hall is built as part of the Festival Of Britain.

1952: The Great Smog, caused by a combination of fog and coal smoke, kills 4000 people in five days.

1956: The Clean Air Act puts an end to London's smog problems.

1965: The Notting Hill Carnival is established by West London's Caribbean community.

1969: The Beatles play their last ever gig on the roof of the Apple building.

1976: The Sex Pistols play at the first 'International Punk Festival' at the 100 Club on Oxford Street.

1981: The first London Marathon.

1983: Six people are killed when the IRA bombs Harrods.

1991: London's tallest building, One Canada Square (better known as Canary Wharf), is completed.

2000: Ken Livingstone becomes London's first directly-elected Mayor.

2005: 52 people are killed by four suicide bombers on Underground trains and a bus.

2007: The rebuilt Wembley Stadium is completed after four years, costing £778 million.

2008: Boris Johnson defeats Red Ken in the London Mayoral Election with a promise to re-instate the Routemaster.

2012: London's third Olympics to be held, expectations of a bumper haul of medals remains low.

London is an egotist—it just *loves* to talk about itself. As you might expect, there's a vast array of print and online publications, not to mention radio stations, designed to let the city do exactly that. Single-handedly forcing the environmental movement back twenty years are freebie dailies **The London Paper, Metro** and **London Lite**. Each a celeb-focused quasi-tabloid, distributed and discarded in the millions. The more substantial, twice-daily **Standard** is the preferred news-roundup du jour of suburbanites and city types alike, if only for the sudoku and quick crossword puzzles. Online, **www.thisislocallondon.co.uk** condenses forty local newspapers into 'one online voice'. On the wireless, **Capital Radio** broadcasts an irksome parade of popular hits and frenetic DJs, whilst **Heart** and **Magic** corner the market on lip-trembling power ballads, mid-paced chart rock and wacky quizzes. All of the British Broadcasting Corporation's national radio stations—including the snazzy, young(ish) **Radio 1** and ovaltine-drinkers' choice **Radio 2**—are based in London, as is (surprisingly) **BBC London**, a decent option for weekend sports coverage. Cooler, urban types are more likely to be tuning into **Kiss FM** (dance, hip hop), **Smooth FM** (jazz, soul) or **Choice** (dancehall, roots), while alternative rockers tune their dials anguishedly to **XFM**, and the talkative indulge in unreserved subjectivity over at **LBC.** Of course, the undisputed king of alternative London broadcasting is **Resonance FM**, a 'community run' station which has just been granted a permanent licence: expect everything from 'Calling All Pensioners' to live psycho-geographic wanders around city's warped dark streets. Un-licensed and illegal pirate radio stations offer a slightly un-hinged ear into the fringes of London's musical society. Twiddle your dials around the extreme ends of the FM spectrum for pirate stalwarts **Rude FM** and **Kool FM**. On the goggle-box, the latest news is spoon-fed to you on ITV's **London Tonight** show and delivered in short slots at the end of the BBC and ITV national news programs. For those actually risking going outside, **Time Out** remains the socialite's sacred text.

Print

The London Paper 1 Pennington Street, E98 1XY, 020 7782 4835, Free, gossipy daily.

The Evening Standard Northcliffe House, 2 Derry Street, W8 5TT, 020 7938 6000, Scaled down Daily Mail, leaning to the right.

London Lite Northcliffe House, 2 Derry Street, W8 5TT, 020 7938 6000, Free, mini Standard.

Metro Northcliffe House, 2 Derry Street, W8 5TT, 020 7651 5200, Free underground daily from same stable.

City AM New London Bridge House, 25 London Bridge St, SE1 9SG, 020 7015 1200, Free morning business bulletin for city-goers.

My Free Sport Third Floor, Courtyard Building, 11 Curtain Road, EC2A 3LT, 0207 375 3175 Free sports overview every Friday.

TimeOut London 251-255 Tottenham Court Road, Universal House, W1T 7AB, 0207 813 3000, Listings & reviews across the city. Pretty damned comprehensive.

London Gazette PO Box 7923, SE1 5ZH, 020 7394 4517, Capital's oldest paper—official journals record of the government.

London Literary Review 44 Lexington Street, W1 0LW, 020 7437 9392, Fortnightly publication for the bookish.

The London Magazine 32 Addison Grove, W4 1ER, 020 8400 5882, Bi-monthly Arts reviews.

TNT London 14-15 Childs Place, Earls Court, SW5 9RX, 020 7373 3377, Info and opinion for the antipodean set.

Loot 31 John Street, WC1N 2AT, 0871 222 5000, Classifieds: flats, bought/sold and lonely hearts.

The Voice GV Media Group Ltd, Northern & Shell Tower, 6th Floor, 4 Selsdon Way, E14 9GL, 020 7510 0340, African-British national.

London Bichitra Bangalink Media, 272 Holton Road, Barry, CF63 4HU, Bengali monthly.

Polish Express 603 Cumberland House, 80 Scrubs Lane, NW10 6RF, 020 8964 4488 , News and info for the Polish community.

Reflect Magazine 130 Stroud Green Road, N4 3RZ, 020 7272 8502, For 'thinking, young Muslims'.

Live Listings Magazine Keith Villa (House), 102 Mallinson Rd, SW11 1BN, 020 7207 2734 Guide to what's on in multicultural London.

Public Radio

FM

89.1 BBC Radio Two: Middle-aged music and chat.
91.3 BBC Radio Three: Classical.
93.5 BBC Radio Four: Current affairs, comfort listening.
94.9 BBC London: Chat, sport.
95.8 Capital FM: Chart, capers.
96.9 Choice FM: Hip Hop, R&B.
97.3 LBC: Phone in, chat.
98.8 BBC Radio 1: Pop, rock, more pop.
100.0 Kiss FM: Dance, urban.
100.9 Classic FM: Classical.
102.2 Smooth FM: Jazz, soul.
102.6 Essex FM: Audible in East London.
103.3 London Greek Radio: Um, Greek.
103.5 BBC Essex: Audible out East.
104.4 Resonance FM: Always bizzare, always brilliant.
104.9 Xfm: Alternative, rock.
105.4 Magic: Pop, slush.
105.8 Virgin Radio: Pop, rock.
106.2 Heart: Chart, pop.
106.6 Time: West London only.
107.3 Time: South East London only.

AM

252 Atlantic: Rock.
558 Spectrum International: Multi-ethnic.
648 BBC World Service: Global.
720 BBC Radio Four: Spoken word.
909 BBC Radio Five Live: Sport, phone in.
963 Liberty Radio: 70s, 80s pop.
1035 Ritz: Country.
1089 talkSPORT: Sports phone in.
1152 LBC News: News, weather.
1215 Virgin Radio: Pop, rock.
1305 Premier Radio: Christian.
1458 Sunrise: Asian.
1548 Capital Gold: Rock 'gold', sport.
1584 London Turkish Radio: Turkish community.

Essential London Books

London – The Biography, and ***Illustrated London***, Peter Ackroyd: definitive, eight hundred page mother lode of remarkable city history, and lavish pictorial version.

The Clerkenwell Tales, Peter Ackroyd: corking murder mystery set in the time of Chaucer.

Oliver Twist; Hard Times; Great Expectations, Charles Dickens: any Dickens novel paints Victorian London at its most exacting.

Intimate Adventures of a London Call Girl, Belle de Jour: steamy, real-life shenanigans ahoy.

Brick Lane, Monica Ali: award winning coming-of-age tale centred on Brick Lane's Muslim community.

The Diary of Samuel Pepys, Samuel Pepys: eyewitness accounts of the Restoration, Great Plague and Fire of London from noted sixteenth century scribbler.

Secret London: Exploring the Hidden City, with Original Walks and Unusual Places to Visit, Andrew Duncan: an explorer's dream.

Around London with Kids – 68 Great Things to See and Do, Eugene Fodor: should keep the little rascals from breaking into cars.

The London Encyclopaedia, Ben Weinreb and Christopher Hibbert: London's history and culture documented in minutest detail

London's Disused Underground Stations, JE Connor: documenting forgotten, ghostly tube stations beneath the pavements.

From Here to Here, Simmons, Taylor, Lynham, Rich: 31 top notch short stories about Circle Line destinations, includes Simon Armitage.

The Adventures of Sherlock Holmes; The Hound of the Baskervilles, Arthur Conan Doyle: classic whodunits featuring Holmes and Watson.

The Strange Case of Dr. Jekyll and Mr. Hyde, Robert Louis Stevenson: the book that enthralled a city unnerved by Jack the Ripper.

The Inimitable Jeeves, P.G. Wodehouse: prewar upper-class tomfoolery in London Town.

London Fields, Martin Amis: post-modern jaunt through London at the end of the millennium.

The London Bombings: An Independent Inquiry, Nafeez Mosadeq Ahmed: balanced, subtle overview of 2005 Underground bombings.

London Orbital and Hackney That Rose Red Empire, Iain Sinclair: London's premier scribe continues to fill our brains with joy despite being ripped off by devotee Peter Ackroyd.

Art Deco London, Colin Michael Hines: Wistful but enjoyable stroll around London's Art Deco heritage.

Derelict London, Paul Talling: The urban explorers' bible!

I Never Knew That About London, Christopher Winn: Well, did you?

V For Vendetta, Alan Moore, The world's greatest comic writer blows up London in a fit of Anarchist fantasies.

Essential London Songs

Lambeth Walk, Noel Gay/Douglas Furber (1937): All together! *Doing the Lambeth Walk! Oi!*

A Nightingale Sang in Berkeley Square, Judy Campbell (1940): Wartime cheer made famous by Vera Lynn.

London Pride, Sir Noel Coward (1941): Written during the Blitz, this sensational ballad gave comfort to Londoners being bombed nightly.

Maybe It's Because I'm a Londoner, Hubert Gregg (1944): Pearly Queen favourite crammed with WWII spirit.

A Foggy Day (In London Town), Ella Fitzgerald (1956): Definitive recording of Gershwin classic.

Waterloo Sunset, The Kinks (1967): Timeless paean to the nation's capital.

Consider Yourself, Lionel Bart (1968): Oliver Twist hoodwinked into a life of crime by the Artful Dodger, the rascal.

Baker Street, Gerry Rafferty (1978): Feel that sax line, air that guitar.

London Calling, The Clash (1979): Joe Strummer paints an apocalyptic vision of a city in post-punk transition.

Electric Avenue, Eddy Grant (1983): Roots-rock champion name checks 80s Brixton scene.

London, The Smiths (1983): Morrissey lugubriously debates a trip south. Miserable shite.

West End Girls, Pet Shop Boys (1986): East London working class meets West London affluence in electro-pop classic.

Parklife, Blur (1994): Home counties-boys get cockney makeover while eyeing London's jogging scene.

Primrose Hill, John and Beverly Martyn (1970). Folk rock's second couple never had to deal with Katie Frost and Kate Moss when they were watching the sun set, did they?

Streets Of London, Ralph McTell (1974). Cool folk dude destroys credibility forever with international monster hit.

Pump Up London, Mr. Lee (1988). Squelchy Chicago House dude makes London sound amazing whilst name checking every British town he can think of: Leeds! Manchester! Scatland!

Essential London Films

The 39 Steps (1935): Hitchcock adaptation of John Buchan novel.

Pygmalion (1938): Leslie Howard as Henry Higgins and Wendy Hiller as Eliza Doolittle prove Shaw's classic comedy does very well without music.

Great Expectations (1946): Rare Richard Attenborough acting outing in classic Dickens adaptation.

The Ladykillers (1955): Superb black comedy from the Ealing canon, with pre-Obi Wan Alec Guinness.

Oliver! (1968): Sprightly musical adaptation of Dickens classic.

One Hundred and One Dalmations (1961): Innocent pelt-seeker tortured by 101 belligerent pups. For shame.

Mary Poppins (1964): Notable for Dick Van Dyke's confounding, lanky turn as cockney chimney sweep.

A Hard Day's Night (1964): Classic, swinging 60s' comedy from the Fab Four.

Alfie (1966): Caine in much-lauded role as audience-addressing lothario.

Carry On Doctor (1967): Critically-panned, guilty-pleasure raunchfest from Pinewood Studios.

The Elephant Man (1980): John Merrick 'accepted' by London's polite Victorian-era society in David Lynch masterpiece.

An American Werewolf in London (1981): US student attacked on moors; gets haunted; romps with Jenny Agutter; becomes werewolf; slaughters innocents; is shot in alley; credits roll.

My Beautiful Launderette (1985): Hanif Kureishi's controversial depiction of cross-culture, same-gender love in the Thatcher-era.

Muppet Christmas Carol (1992): That Michael Caine, he sure can act. But he sure can't sing.

Lock, Stock and Two Smoking Barrels (1998): East End crime capers from Madonna's (not from the East End) husband.

Notting Hill (1999): Hugh Grant as mumbling, bumbling, lovesick fop.

Bridget Jones's Diary (2001): Rene Zellweger goes Sloane in adaptation of Helen Fielding novel.

Love Actually (2003): Expansive Richard Curtis romcom with Grant in slightly-less mumbly, slightly-more bumbly form.

Shaun of the Dead (2003): Fighting off zombies at the local pub. Hilarious.

The London Nobody Knows (1967): The greatest film about London ever. Period.

London (1994): Patrick Kellier's abstract ramble through 'the most unsociable and reactionary of cities.'

28 Days Later (2002): Us Londoners finally erupt in pandemic rage at how slow tourists are on the tube.

There can't be anything worse than the inconvenience of trying to find a convenience when nature takes an unexpected hold of your nether regions; you may choose to follow the lead of many a Saturday evening reveller and use a public doorway, but is it really worth the £80 fine that will be levied if caught in the act (and let's face it, it's hard to conceal the evidence)?

Unfortunately, London has seen a recent decline in the provision of public toilet facilities, as local councils seem to have decided that they are under no obligation to provide such a service; you'll also be hard pushed to find a toilet attendant manning a lavatory these days, and the dubious goings-on in some loos may not be quite what you had in mind, unless your name has a "Michael" in it. Most surviving public toilets seem also to emit their own particular aroma of…well, you don't really have to use your imagination. But don't get down in the dumps!

The most obvious place to go to when in need is McDonald's. Despite what some may say about their food, their outlets are the place to go when caught short and not wishing to pay to pee. Usually maintained and cleaned throughout opening hours, they can also be used inconspicuously and without purchasing anything; and let's face it, you can't move for McDonalds in London. It's also a safe bet to use Starbucks, Caffe Nero and Costa Coffee bars, although they often have a policy of access to toilets by key only, which can be a bit of a bummer (groan).

It may seem like a good idea to visit pubs or bars solely for their toilets, but you might find yourself being hauled out by an irked landlord mid-act. Furthermore, don't expect luxury; pub toilets are usually fairly scummy and often not furnished with toilet paper. It's also unlikely to find a men's cubicle that will have a working lock in it; do you really wish to have an unwanted visitor whilst on the throne? Exceptions are the Wetherspoon's chain, which prides itself on having toilets cleaned on the hour, and the nicest of gastro pubs, which can offer commodious and clean facilities (at least during the day). Otherwise, if desperate, at least go for a pub or bar that's busy.

Also bear in mind that if you find yourself in need in the City of Westminster, you can use a toilet text service from your mobile phone! Known as SatLav, texting the word 'Toilet' to 80097 will result in a message being sent to your phone informing you of the nearest public convenience. It may prove to be the most relieving 25p you'll ever spend in London…

A good and extensive list of London public toilets can be found at www.lastrounds.co.uk/public_toilets.html.

If none of the afore-mentioned places are available, there are other options:

Other street public toilets—yes, those bizarre futuristic looking structures on some of London's central streets are toilets. Known as sanisettes or "superloos", there is a charge to use them and once in, you've got 15 minutes before the door automatically opens (don't get extended stage-fright). They're self-cleaning, which usually means that they're in a right state, and are also quite popular with junkies and prostitutes, so best saved for when extremely desperate.

There are also a few pop-up toilets which, intended for night use, disappear underground during the day. These are only suitable for (drunk) men and rise to the challenge of channelling away an evening's excesses from 7pm to 6am. Located at notorious 'wet spots' in the West End, they are linked to the main sewerage system; taking the piss, indeed…

Stations—including almost all large railway stations and a few central London tube stations. There will usually be a cost for these facilities though (around 20p).

Department Stores—All the large ones, including John Lewis, Selfridges, Debenhams and Harrods. Smaller shops rarely have toilets for public use.

Supermarkets—many larger branches of Sainsbury's and Marks & Spencer.

Museums—the majority of London's large museums and galleries are free to enter (erm, and have toilets).

Libraries—most libraries will have an area of salvation for the needy.

Universities and Colleges—and you get to pass yourself off as a student or lecturer (in need of the loo).

Hospitals—you can also drop in on that relative that you always meant to visit, or maybe leave a stool sample; just try not to leave with a superbug.

Parks—not on the grass, please.

Hotels—larger hotels shouldn't pose a problem.

London has some of the finest hospitals in the world, attracting top-notch specialists who carry-out state-of-the-art procedures—the trick is, getting in to see one of them. An appointment at a specific hospital, or with a specialist, requires a referral from your GP and plenty of patience. In an emergency go to your nearest A&E—bring a book and some earplugs. On the weekends after eleven, waiting times for non-urgent problems can be measured in aeons, but rest assured, if something is seriously wrong you'll be seen very quickly—lucky ol' you. For non serious injuries or illnesses, find your nearest Minor Injuries Unit or Walk-in Centre on www.nhs.uk. You'll spend less time hanging around and free up A&E for critical cases and over-cidered teens needing stomach pumps. The ever-friendly 24 hr NHS Direct 0845 4647 is also always available for advice.

If you have the money, numerous private sector hospitals and clinics are available to cure what ails you, or to pander to your hypochondriacal needs. You won't necessarily get better treatment, but there'll be less waiting, more pampering and more grapes by your bedside. For information, start at www.privatehealth.co.uk.

A & E	*Address*	*Phone*	*Map*
Charing Cross Hospital	Fulham Palace Rd	020 8846 1234	047
Chelsea and Westminster Hospital	369 Fulham Rd	020 8746 8000	043
Homerton University Hospital	Homerton Row	020 8510 5555	090
King's College Hospital	Denmark Hill	020 3299 9000	121
Moorfields Eye Hospital	162 City Rd	020 7253 3411	084
Royal Free Hospital	Pond St	020 7794 0500	057
Royal London Hospital	Whitechapel Rd	020 7377 7000	096
St Mary's Hospital	Praed St	020 78866666	031
St Thomas' Hospital	Lambeth Palace Rd	020 7188 7188	131
University College Hospital	235 Euston Rd	0845 155 5000	004
Western Eye Hospital	173 Marylebone Rd	020 7886 6666	002
Whittington Hospital	Magdala Ave	020 7272 3070	059

Other Hospitals	*Address*	*Phone*	*Map*
Bolingbroke Hospital	Bolingbroke Grove	020 7223 7411	140
Capio Eye	114 Harley St	0800 169 2020	002
Capio Nightingale Hospital	11 Lisson Grove	020 7535 7700	076
Capio Nightingale Hospital	1 Radnor Walk	020 7351 7098	045
Charing Cross Hospital	Fulham Palace Rd	020 8846 1234	047
Chelsea and Westminster Hospital	369 Fulham Rd	020 8746 8000	043
Cromwell Hospital	162 Cromwell Rd	020 7460 2000	035
Eastman Dental Hospital	256 Gray's Inn Rd	020 7915 1000	005
Elizabeth Garrett Anderson Hospital	Huntley St	0845 155 5000	004
Gordon Hospital	Bloomburg St	020 8746 8733	021
Great Ormond St Hospital	Great Ormond St	020 7405 9200	005
Guy's Hospital	Great Maze Pond	020 7188 7188	106
Heart Hospital	16 Westmoreland St	020 7573 8888	002
Highgate Private Hospital	17 View Rd	020 8341 4182	051
Homerton University Hospital	Homerton Row	020 8510 5555	090
Hospital For Tropical Diseases	Martimer Market	0845 155 5000	004
Hospital of St John and St Elizabeth	60 Grove End Rd	020 7806 4000	068
King Edward VII Hospital For Officers	5 Beaumont St	020 7486 4411	002
King's College Hospital	Denmark Hill	020 3299 9000	121
Lambeth Hospital	108 Landor Rd	020 3228 6000	144
Lister Hospital	Chelsea Bridge Rd	020 7730 7733	020

Other Hospitals	*Address*	*Phone*	*Map*
London Bridge Hospital	27 Tooley St	020 7407 3100	106
London Chest Hospital	Bonner Rd	020 7377 7000	093
London Independent Hospital	1 Beaumont Sq	020 7780 2400	097
London Welbeck Hospital	25 Welbeck St	020 7224 2242	002
Mildmay Mission Hospital	Hackney Rd	020 7613 6309	091
Mile End Hospital	Bancroft Rd	020 7377 7000	093
Moorfields Eye Hospital	162 City Rd	020 7253 3411	084
National Hospital for Neorology and Neurosciences	Queen Sq	0845 155 5000	005
Portland Hospital For women and Children	209 Great Portland St	020 7580 4400	003
Princess Grace Hospital	42 Nottingham Pl	020 7486 1234	002
Royal Brompton Hospital	Sydney St	020 7352 8121	045
Royal Free Hospital	Pond St	020 7794 0500	057
Royal London Homeopathic Hospital	60 Great Ormond St	0845 155 5000	005
Royal London Hospital	Whitechapel Rd	020 7377 7000	096
Royal Marsden Hospital	Fulham Rd	020 7352 8171	045
Royal National Orthopaedic Hospital	51 Bolsover St	020 8954 2300	003
Royal National Throat, Nose and Ear Hospital	330 Gray's Inn Rd	020 7915 1300	005
St Bartholomew's	West Smithfield	020 7377 7000	015
St Luke's Hospital For The Clergy	14 Fitzroy Sq	02073884954	003
St Mary's Hospital	Praed St	020 78866666	031
St Pancras Hospital	4 St Pancras Way	020 7530 3500	078
St Thomas' Hospital	Lambeth Palace Rd	020 7188 7188	131
University College Hospital	Grafton Wy	0845 1555 000	004
University College Hospital	235 Euston Rd	0845 155 5000	004
Wellington Hospital	8 Wellington Pl	020 7483 5148	076
Western Eye Hospital	173 Marylebone Rd	020 7886 6666	002
Whittington Hospital	Magdala Ave	020 7272 3070	059

Overview

Librarians love nothing more than a warm cardigan and a complex cataloguing system, nevertheless, they've done themselves proud with London's libraries. London boasts an enormous, if somewhat eccentric and confusing, network of over 360 libraries. NFT have tried to make things a little clearer with a starter guide below, but check www.londonlibraries.org for a great searchable database to match your needs with the right library.

London's libraries vary enormously in subject, range and facilities, with some accessible for free, some for a fee, some with an appointment and some only if you are very very nice and give the curator a chocolate digestive. But the treat of such a large network, apart from the world-class breadth, depth and quality of collections, is that many of the libraries have a unique personality to make them a treasured part of London. For example, £10 will get you a day's membership to the **London Library (Map 23)**, an atmospheric labyrinth where you can browse alongside ghosts of past members including Dickens, Tennyson and Darwin, and feel several IQ points higher than before you went in. In Tower Hamlets, libraries are now **"Ideas Stores" (Map 92, 101, 96)**, because Tower Hamlets is, like, cool. In addition to the books, magazines, music and internet facilities which are available at most public libraries, these superb spaces also offer activities such as free PopLaw legal advice clinics, homework clubs and jazz classes. The borough has built four of these wonders; find them in Bow, Whitechapel, Canary Wharf and on East India Dock Road. London linguists are spoiled with the excellent **French Institute (Map 36)**, **Instituto Cervantes (Map 19)** and the **Goethe Institut (Map 37)**, while more cunning linguists may prefer the eye-opening gynaecological collection among the 2.5 million medical-related works in the **Wellcome Library (Map 4)**. Poets should meander their way to the **Saison Poetry Library (Map 104)**, ensconced within the South Bank Centre, for a little inspiration. Artists will enjoy the **National Art Library (Map 36)**, which nestles within the V&A Museum. You can use many of London's academic and specialist libraries through the Inspire London scheme, which grants one-day reference access to collections throughout London; ask your local library to refer you.

However, the Daddy of them all is the **British Library (Map 78)**. This behemoth receives a copy of every publication printed in the UK and Ireland, and requires 625km of shelving space to accommodate its 150million items. But it's just such a tease. You cannot borrow books, and to even access the collections you need to obtain a Reader Pass, via an introductory discussion to establish why you need it and whether you're likely to doodle on the books. This requires two forms of ID, no compromise: refer to www.bl.uk for the latest guidelines. Once you have your pass you can access the Reading Rooms, albeit with your personal belongings in a clear plastic bag (or stored in a locker). But if you just fancy seeing the Magna Carta, Shakespeare in Quarto or some Beatles manuscripts, you can access the book-free visitor areas without appointment and still gain an impressive look at one of the world's greatest information resources.

General Information

Important phone numbers:
All emergencies: 999
Non-emergencies: 101
Anti-terrorism hotline: 0800 789 321
Crime Stoppers: 0800 555 111
Neighbourhood Watch: 020 79934709
Missing Persons: 0500 700 700
Complaints: 08453 002 002
Websites:
www.met.police.uk
www.cityoflondon.police.uk (Separate police force specifically covering the Square Mile).
www.btp.police.uk (Separate police force specifically covering public transport).

Statistics* (Greater London)

	2007/08	2007/06	2006/05	2005/04
Murder	123	142	142	155
Rapes	1,558	1,977	2,001	2,035
GBH	3,785	4,380	4,702	4,496
Burglary (res)	49,946	50,193	53,939	52,693
Vehicle Crime	100,678	109,436	114,501	114,698

* taken from a report from the Metropolitan Police Performance Directorate

Police Stations

	Address	*Phone*	*Map*
Albany Street Police Station	60 Albany St	020 7404 1212	77
Battersea Police Station	112 Battersea Bridge	020 7350 1122	132
Belgravia Police Station	203 Buckingham Palace Rd	020 7730 1212	20
Brixton Police Station	367 Brixton Rd	020 7326 1212	144
Camberwell Police Station	22 Camberwell Church St	020 7378 1212	122
Cavendish Road Police Station	47 Cavendish Parade	020 7326 1212	149
Charing Cross Police Station	Agar St & Strand	020 7240 1212	24
Chelsea Police Station	2 Lucan Pl	020 7376 1212	46
Chiswick Police Station	209 Chiswick High Rd	020 8577 1212	38
Deptford Police Station	114 Amersham Vale	020 8297 1212	126
East Dulwich Police Station	173 Lordship Ln	020 7378 1212	129
Greenwich Police Station	31 Royal Hill	020 8853 1212	120
Hampstead Police Station	26 Rosslyn Hill	020 7404 1212	56
Harrow Road Police Station	325 Harrow Rd	020 7402 1212	26
Holborn Police Station	10 Lamb's Conduit St	020 7404 1212	5
Holloway Police Station	284 Hornsey Rd	020 7704 1212	61
Hornsey Police Station	98 Tottenham Ln	020 8808 1212	54
Islington Police Station	2 Tolpuddle St	020 7704 1212	80
Kennington Police Station	49 Kennington Rd	020 7326 1212	131
Kensington Police Station	72 Earl's Court Rd	020 7376 1212	35
Kentish Town Police	12 Holmes Rd	020 7404 1212	72
Lavender Hill Police Station	176 Lavender Hill	020 7350 1122	140
Marylebone Police Station	1 Seymour St	020 7486 1212	1
Notting Hill Police Station	100 Ladbroke Grove	020 7376 1212	28
Paddington Green Police Station	2 Harrow Rd	020 7402 1212	31
Peckham Police Station	177 Peckham High St	020 7378 1212	123
Rotherhithe Police Station	99 Lower Rd	020 7378 1212	110
Southwark Police Station	323 Borough High St	020 7378 1212	106
St John's Wood Police Station	20 Newcourt St	020 7486 1212	69
Tooting Police Station	251 Mitcham Rd	020 8807 1212	152
Walworth Police Station	12 Manor Pl	020 7378 1212	113
Wandsworth Police Station	146 Wandsworth High St	020 7350 1122	138
West End Central Police Station	27 Savile Row	020 7437 1212	10

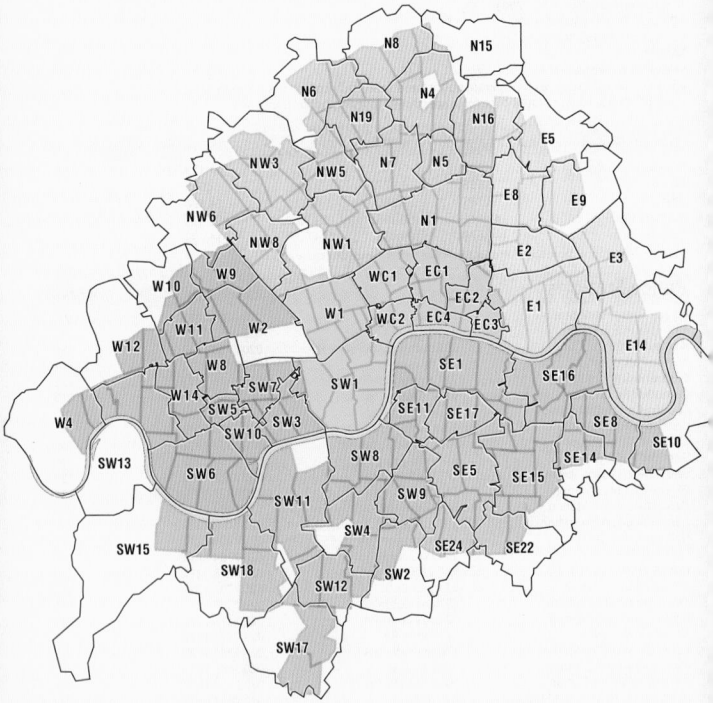
N8
N15
N6
N4
N19
N16
E5
NW3
NW5
N7
N5
E8
E9
NW6
N1
NW8
NW1
E2
E3
W10
W9
WC1
EC1
EC2
E1
W1
WC2
EC4
EC3
W11
W2
W12
E14
W8
SE1
SE16
W14
SW7
SW1
SW5
SE11
SE17
SE8
W4
SW3
SW10
SE10
SW13
SW8
SE14
SW6
SE5
SE15
SW11
SW9
SW4
SW15
SE24
SE22
SW18
SW2
SW12
SW17

Overview

London hotels can be sources of hopelessly romantic creativity. In 1899 Claude Monet painted the Houses of Parliament from his balcony at the Savoy hotel. About 100 years later, Fay Weldon moved in with her typewriter as writer in residence. If you've got visitors in town, fancy giving Claude a run for his money, or just can't face going back to your dump of a flat, you'll need the services of a hotel. When choosing your hotel, think carefully about what kind of London you're looking to experience and whom the room is for. We've identified a few of the usual suspects for whom you may find yourself booking a hotel room, and heartily offer you our best suggestions for each. Just don't expect to emerge from any of them clutching a masterpiece penned overnight.

Only the best, Daah-ling

So you need to find a hotel for a VIP client who will accept nothing but the best. Where to start? Since you don't have to cover the bill yourself, here is where you can really dig into London hospitality at its most deluxe. Start by trying to book **The Ritz (Map 9)**, with its amazing views of Green Park, Rococo detailing and killer high tea. **Brown's (Map 9)** is a stunning five-star and was the first hotel in London to have a lift. There is also the **Dorchester (Map 9)**, and its neighbour the **Hilton Park Lane (Map 9)**, where you may see a celebrity stumbling back to their quarters at four in the morning, if you're very, very lucky. **The Landmark (Map 76)** is a wonderfully Victorian retreat in the centre of ritzy Marylebone and has a rather fine atrium. But the granddaddy of luxury London must be the **Savoy (Map 24)**. This elegant old-timer stunk of old money until its temporary closure in 2007 for a £100 million spruce-up. It was built on the location of the Savoy Palace, which burned down during the Peasants' Revolt in 1381. We say let them eat cake (and tea).

A Dirty Weekend

This can be any weekend where a Londoner decides booze-goggled sex and/or quick-to-bed access after a night of clubbing is worthy of dishing out the dosh on an über-chic central hotel. It's one (giant) step up from splurging on a taxi and is the realm of the London boutique hotel where location is everything. **Hazlitt's (Map 12)** is right in the middle of Soho yet still wonderfully intimate. **Andaz Hotel (Map 8) (formerly Great Eastern Hotel)** is in the heart of the City, with funky Shoreditch on its doorstep, whilst the 'modern English' style of the **Charlotte Street Hotel (Map 3)** is painfully hip and sophisticated.

The Tea-and-Crumpet Tourist

Then there's the hotel for your sweetly naïve cousin that sees London through rose-tinted Ray Bans: full of scones, Mary Poppins and the chimes of Big Ben. You wouldn't want to burst her cute little bubble, would you? Not to worry, there are plenty of hotels to satisfy the Harrods tourist. **San Domenico House London (Map 46)** is a Chelsea boutique hotel that is about as warm and cuddly as a cup of sugary tea. **The Rookery (Map 15)**, built amongst a row of once derelict Georgian townhouses in Clerkenwell, is cluttered with museum-worthy furniture, open fires and ye oldey worldey frippery. Or, if she can't bear to be too far away from Buckingham Palace, there's the nearby **Windermere (Map 20)**.

Parents in Town?

If your parents have spent their nest egg on bailing you out of your London-induced debt, they will probably want to get the most out of London for the least money possible. But if the hotel you pick for their stay is anything short of perfect, you'll never hear the end of it. If they have loyalty cards with any of the bigger hotel chains, now is a good time to use them. **The Sheraton Park Lane (Map 10)** is a glamorous choice; it has an entire floor for its reward cardholders, plus its Art Deco Palm Court is worth a gin and tonic or two. **The London Bridge Hotel (Map 106)** is an independent four-star that usually has good deals and is conveniently close to Borough Market and London Bridge station. Gower Street has a wealth of small family-run hotels

at reasonable prices, including the **Cavendish (Map 23)** and **Jesmond (Map 4)**, both within stumbling distance of the British Museum. There's also the nearby **Crescent Hotel (Map 4)**, next to Russell Square.

In Lieu of a Couch to Crash On

Then you get your university friend still in strong denial of the real world, who refuses to get a real job. The amount of times this sponger has crashed on your sofa has been enough to send your might-be-the-one girl/boyfriend packing. Instead of blaming him/her for your future life of loneliness, banish them from the flat and call in the services of one of London's cheapies. They do exist, you just have to look hard. Sometimes short-term rental companies, like **Best London Rent**, offer shared-facility flats at very cheap prices. This is perfect if it's going to be for a week or more, and although the locations aren't too central, this can be a good alternative to endless weeks of friends imposing on your hospitality. Otherwise, London does have one or two great youth hostels. Decent choices include **St Christopher's Inn (Map 106)** on Borough High Street, the **Alhambra (Map 5)** by King's Cross, and a number of reasonable choices by Paddington Station, such as **Europa House (Map 31)**. If your visitor can't be separated from Camden, escort them to the **Hampstead Britannia Hotel (Map 70)** on Primrose Hill Road.

Where to Stick Your Best Friend From School

(And Her Husband, Two Perfect Kids and a Dog)

Unfortunately, for some people visiting London, a dodgy guesthouse isn't going to cut it. You want to show them how your city can be just as perfect as their countryside home and how not jealous you are of them! Of course, they don't see the point in paying tons either. This is where the few and far between bed and breakfasts come out of the woodwork. Most of these are small, so book in advance. London's best is the warm and welcoming **Bay Tree House and Annex B&B (Out of coverage)**. Great for families or singletons alike, it's in New Southgate (about 25 minutes by tube from central London) but can be a relaxing retreat. **Barclay House (Map 43)** is a hidden gem in Fulham Broadway (make sure you write down the address as it's not signposted and can blend in). **Aster House (Map 45)** is a bit pricier but close enough to posh High Street Kensington to give a glimpse of how the other half live.

With all these hotels, compare prices online, ask for their best rate and/or call for last minute deals, you may be surprised at the reductions available. Good offers mean you can pay less than you'd think for the best, and London does really have the best.

Map 1 • Marylebone (West)	*Address*	*Phone*	*Price in £*
22 York St	22 York St	020 7224 2990	89
Boston Court Hotel	26 Upper Berkeley St	020 7723 1445	89
The Cumberland	Marble Arch	087 1376 9014	110
Edward Lear	28 Seymour St	020 7402 5401	50
Hadleigh Hotel	24 Upper Berkeley St	020 7262 4084	81
Hotel 82	82 Gloucester Pl	020 7486 3679	110
The Leonard	15 Seymour St	020 7935 2010	100
Sherlock Holmes Hotel	108 Baker St	020 7486 6161	117
Thistle Marble Arch	Bryanston St Marble Arch	0871 376 9027	149

Map 2 • Marylebone (East)	*Address*	*Phone*	*Price in £*
Claridges	Brook St	020 7629 8860	167
Hotel La Place	17 Nottingham Pl	020 7486 4335	99
Jury's Clifton Ford	47 Welbeck St	020 7486 6600	120
The Langham	1 Portland Pl	020 7636 1000	198
No. 5 Maddox	5 Maddox St	020 7647 0200	270

Map 3 • Fitzrovia	*Address*	*Phone*	*Price in £*
Grange Fitzrovia Hotel	20 Bolsover St	020 7467 7000	101
Sanderson Hotel	50 Berners St	020 7300 1400	214

Map 4 • Bloomsbury (West)	*Address*	*Phone*	*Price in £*
Academy	19 Gower St	020 7631 4115	200
Ambassadors Hotel	12 Upper Woburn Pl	020 7693 5400	112
Arosfa	83 Gower St	020 7636 2115	55
Bloomsbury Park Hotel	126 Southampton Row	087 1376 9006	99
Crescent Hotel	49 Cartwright Gardens	020 7387 1515	100
Hotel Cavendish	75 Gower St	020 7636 9079	95
Hotel Russell	1 Russell Square	020 7837 6470	119
The Montague	15 Montague St	020 7637 1001	135
Myhotel Bloomsbury	11 Bayley St	020 7667 6000	186
Radisson	97 Great Russell St	020 7637 3477	142
St Giles	Bedford Ave	020 7300 3000	88

Map 5 • Bloomsbury (East)	*Address*	*Phone*	*Price in £*
Comfort Inn	2 St Chad's St	020 7837 1940	98
Generator Hostel	37 Tavistock Pl	020 7388 7666	17

Map 7 • Barbican / City Road (South)		*Phone*	*Price in £*
Barbican Hotel	120 Central St	087 1376 9004	71
Citadines Hotel	7 Goswell Rd	020 7566 8000	99

Map 8 • Liverpool Street / Broadgate		*Phone*	*Price in £*
Andaz Hotel	8 Liverpool St	020 7961 1234	160

Map 9 • Mayfair / Green Park	*Address*	*Phone*	*Price in £*
Athenaeum Hotel	116 Piccadilly	020 7499 3464	153
Brown's Hotel	1 Albemarle St	020 7493 6020	239
Chesterfield	35 Charles St	020 7491 2622	116
The Connaught	Carlos Pl	020 7499 7070	188
Curzon Plaza Hotel	56 Curzon St	020 7499 4121	122
The Dorchester	53 Park Ln	020 7629 8888	245
Flemings Mayfair Hotel	7 Half Moon St	020 7493 2088	134
Grosvenor House	86 Park Ln	020 7499 6363	175
Hilton Park Lane	22 Park Ln	020 7493 8000	226
The Intercontinental	1 Hamilton Pl	020 7409 3131	198
May Fair Hotel	Stratton St	020 7629 7777	173
Metropolitan	Old Park Lane	020 7447 1047	191
Millennium Hotel	44 Grosvenor Square	020 7629 9400	145
The Ritz	150 Piccadilly	020 7493 8181	265

Map 11 • Soho (Central)	*Address*	*Phone*	*Price in £*
The Shaftesbury	65 Shaftesbury Ave	020 7871 6000	164
The Soho Hotel	4 Richmond Mews	020 7559 3000	240

Map 12 • Soho (East)	*Address*	*Phone*	*Price in £*
Hazlitt's Hotel	6 Frith St	020 7099 3190	159

Map 13 • Covent Garden	*Address*	*Phone*	*Price in £*
Covent Garden Hotel	10 Monmouth St	020 7806 1000	235
Fielding	4 Broad Ct	020 7836 8305	85
The Radisson	20 Monmouth St	020 7836 4300	150

Map 14 • Holborn / Temple	*Address*	*Phone*	*Price in £*
Citadines Hotel	94 High Holborn	020 7395 8800	99
One Aldwych	1 Aldwych	020 7300 1000	240
Renaissance Chancery Court	252 High Holborn	020 7829 9888	340

Map 15 • Blackfriars / Farringdon		*Phone*	*Price in £*
Club Quarters	24 Ludgate Hill	020 7451 5800	84
Malmaison	18 Charterhouse Sq	020 7012 3700	225
The Rookery	12 Peter's Ln	020 7336 0931	128

Map 17 • Square Mile (East)	*Address*	*Phone*	*Price in £*
Club Quarters	7 Gracechurch St	020 7451 5800	79
Threadneedles Hotel	5 Threadneedle St	020 7657 8080	153

Map 18 • Tower Hill / Aldgate	*Address*	*Phone*	*Price in £*
Apex Hotel	1 Seething Ln	020 7702 2020	86
Chamberlain	130 Minories	020 7680 1500	94
Novotel Tower Bridge	10 Pepys St	020 7265 6000	145

Map 19 • Belgravia	*Address*	*Phone*	*Price in £*
B&B Belgravia	64 Ebury St	020 7259 8570	99
The Berkeley	Wilton Pl	020 7235 6000	255
The Halkin	Halkin St	020 7333 1000	390
Morgan Guest House	120 Ebury St	020 7730 2384	52
Sheraton Belgravia	20 Chesham Pl	020 7235 6040	178

Map 20 • Victoria / Pimlico (West)		*Phone*	*Price in £*
41	41 Buckingham Palace Rd	020 7300 0041	255
Caswell Hotel	25 Gloucester St	020 7834 6345	63
Central House	39 Belgrave Rd	020 7834 8036	122
Days Hotel	80 Belgrave Rd	020 7828 8661	102
Dover Hotel	42 Belgrave Rd	020 7821 9085	63
Durrants Hotel	26 St George's Dr	020 7935 8131	153
Elizabeth Hotel and Apartments	37 Eccleston Square	020 7828 6812	85
Enrico Hotel	77 Warwick Way	020 7834 9538	56
Goring	Beeston Pl	020 7396 9000	279
Hart House Hotel	51 Gloucester St	020 7935 2288	85
Hesperia London Victoria Hotel	2 Bridge Pl	087 0225 4134	114
Windermere	144 Warwick Way	020 7834 5163	90

Map 21 • Pimlico (East)	*Address*	*Phone*	*Price in £*
Best Western	85 Belgrave Rd	020 7828 9279	76
City Inn Westminster	30 John Islip Street	020 7630 1000	140
Corbigoe Hotel	101 Belgrave Rd	020 7834 9790	46
Dolphin House Hotel	Chichester St	020 7798 8000	52
Wellington	71 Vincent Square	020 7834 4740	62

Map 22 • Westminster	*Address*	*Phone*	*Price in £*
51 Buckingham Gate	51 Buckingham Gate	020 7769 7766	326
London Bridge Hotel	8 Bridge St	020 7855 2200	172
Vandon House Hotel	Vandon St	020 7799 6480	45

Map 23 • St. James's	*Address*	*Phone*	*Price in £*
The Cavendish Hotel	81 Jermyn St	020 7930 2111	142
Dukes Hotel	35 St James's St	020 7491 4840	185
Radisson	3 St Martin's St	020 7930 8641	167
Radisson Edwardian Hampshire	31 Leicester Square	020 7839 9399	160
The Stafford	16 St James's Pl	020 7493 0111	290
Thistle Trafalgar Hotel	Whitcomb St	087 1376 9037	114

Map 24 • Trafalgar Square / The Strand		*Phone*	*Price in £*
Guoman Charing Cross	The Strand	087 0333 9105	111
The Savoy	Strand	020 7420 2405	TBD
The Strand Palace	372 Strand	020 7836 8080	115

Map 27 • Maida Vale	*Address*	*Phone*	*Price in £*
Colonade	2 Warrington Crescent	020 7286 1052	270
The Royal Park	3 Westbourne Terrace Rd	020 7479 6600	140

Map 29 • Notting Hill Gate	*Address*	*Phone*	*Price in £*
Guesthouse West	165 Westbourne Grove	020 7792 9800	155
The Lennox	34 Pembridge Gardens	087 0850 3317	190
The Main House	6 Colville Rd	020 7221 9691	50
Miller's Residence	111 Westbourne Grove	020 7243 1024	150
The Portobello Hotel	22 Stanley Gardens	020 7727 2777	145

Map 30 • Bayswater	*Address*	*Phone*	*Price in £*
Bayswater Inn	8 Princes Square	020 7727 8621	91
Best Western	27 Devonshire Terrace	020 7745 1200	102
Best Western Mornington	12 Lancaster Gate	020 7262 7361	130
Best Western Phoenix Hotel	1 Kensington Gardens Sq	020 7229 2494	91
Blakemore Hotel	30 Leinster Gardens	020 7262 4591	102
Caesar Hotel	26 Queen's Gardens	020 7262 0022	91
Central Park Hotel	49 Queensborough Terrace	020 7229 2424	61
Comfort Inn	19 Craven Hill Gardens	020 7262 6644	72
Commodore Hotel	50 Lancaster Gate	020 7099 3190	102
Craven Gardens Hotel	16 Leinster Terrace	020 7262 3167	56
Duke of Leinster Hotel	20 Leinster Gardens	014 8039 4138	89
Dylan House	14 Devonshire Terrace	020 7723 3280	117
Garden Court	30 Kensington Gardens Square	020 7229 2553	48
Hempel Hotel	31 Craven Hill Gardens	020 7298 9000	173
Henry VIII Hotel	19 Leinster Gardens	020 7262 0117	101
Hyde Park Premier	14 Craven Hill	020 7262 0111	132
Paddington Court Hotel	27 Devonshire Terrace	020 7262 2204	113
Pembridge Palace Hotel	52 Princes Square	020 7229 6262	87
Princes Square Hotel	23 Prince's Sq	020 7229 9876	115
Royal Lancaster Hotel	1 Lancaster Terrace	086 6539 8063	145
Vancouver Studios	30 Prince's Square	020 7221 8678	85
Whites Hotel	90 Lancaster Gate	0871 376 9022	86

Map 31 • Paddington	*Address*	*Phone*	*Price in £*
Castleton	164 Sussex Gardens	020 7706 4666	76
Chrysos Hotel	25 Norfolk Square	020 7262 2417	102
The Delmere	130 Sussex Gardens	020 7262 1863	99
Edward Hotel	1 Spring St	020 7262 2671	95
Hilton	225 Edgware Rd	020 7402 4141	117
Hilton	146 Praed St	020 7850 0500	153
Pavilion Hotel	36 Sussex Gardens	020 7262 0905	60
Queensway Hotel	147 Sussex Gardens	020 7723 7749	61

Map 35 • Kensington	*Address*	*Phone*	*Price in £*
Ambassadors Hotel	16 Collingham Rd	020 7693 5400	104
Best Western	33 Hogarth Rd	020 7370 6831	119
Comfort Inn	22 West Cromwell Rd	020 7373 3300	68
Copthorne Tara Hotel	Scarsdale Place	020 7937 7211	117
Derby Hotel	155 Cromwell Rd	020 7262 0022	103
Exhibition Court Hotel	109 Warwick Rd	020 7244 9750	67
Exhibition Court Hotel	25 Collingham Pl	020 7370 7788	124
Majestic	160 Cromwell Rd	020 7373 3083	57
The Milestone Hotel	1 Kensington Ct Pl	020 7917 1010	265
Radisson	68 W Cromwell Rd	020 7761 9000	98
The Rockwell	181 W Cromwell Rd	020 7244 2000	120

Map 36 • South Kensington / Gloucester Rd		*Phone*	*Price in £*
Baglioni Hotel	60 Hyde Park Gate	020 7368 5700	357
Best Western	4 Queens Gate	020 7808 8400	122
Citadines Hotel	35 Gloucester Rd	0207 543 7878	107
Eden Plaza Hotel	68 Queens Gate	020 7370 6111	74
Fraser Place Hotel	39 Queen's Gate Gardens	020 7969 3555	115
Gainsborough Hotel	7 Queensberry Pl	020 7957 0000	91
Gallery Hotel	8 Queensberry Pl	020 7915 0000	112
The Gore	190 Queen's Gate	020 7584 6601	178
Grange Hotel	41 Queen's Gate Gardens	020 7584 0512	90
Grosvenor Kensington Hotel	2 Harrington Rd	020 8859 3333	119
Holiday Inn	97 Cromwell Rd	870 400 9100	99
Millennium Hotel	140 Gloucester Rd	020 7373 6000	110
Park International Hotel	117 Cromwell Rd	020 7370 5711	101

Map 37 • Knightsbridge	*Address*	*Phone*	*Price in £*
Cadogan Hotel	75 Sloane St	020 7235 7141	178
The Capital Hotel and Apartments	22 Basil St	020 7589 5171	230
Durley House Hotel	115 Sloane St	020 7235 5537	459
The Franklin Hotel	22 Egerton Gardens	020 7584 5533	200
The Knightsbridge	10 Beaufort Gardens	020 7584 6300	170
Knightsbridge Green Hotel	159 Knightsbridge	020 7584 6274	150
The Rembrandt Hotel	11 Thurloe Pl	020 7589 8100	142

Map 42 • Barons Court	*Address*	*Phone*	*Price in £*
Holiday Inn Express	295 North End Rd	020 7384 5151	109

Map 43 • West Brompton / Fulham Broadway / Earl's Court			*Price in £*
Barclay House	21 Barclay Rd	020 7384 3390	66
Best Western	18 Barkston Gardens	020 7373 3151	74
City Continental London	11 Penywern Rd	020 7373 6514	106
Enterprise Hotel	15 Hogarth Rd	020 7373 4502	68
Garden View Hotel	29 Nevern Square	020 7244 6466	68
Mayflower Hotel	26 Trebovir Rd	020 7370 0991	170
Rushmore	11 Trebovir Rd	020 7370 3839	164
Twenty Nevern Square	20 Nevern Square	020 7565 9555	79

Map 44 • Chelsea	*Address*	*Phone*	*Price in £*
Astons Apartments Hotel	31 Rosary Gardens	020 7590 6000	97
Blakes Hotel	33 Roland Gardens	020 7370 6701	175

Map 45 • Chelsea (East)	*Address*	*Phone*	*Price in £*
Aster House	3 Sumner Pl	020 7581 5888	99
Myhotel Chelsea	35 Ixworth Pl	020 7225 7500	222
Regency	100 Queens Gate	020 7373 7878	114
Sydney House	9 Sydney St	020 7376 7711	160

Map 46 • Sloane Square	*Address*	*Phone*	*Price in £*
Draycott Hotel	22 Cadogan Gardens	020 773 06466	306
San Domenico House	29 Draycott Pl	020 7581 5757	210

Map 56 • Hampstead Village	*Address*	*Phone*	*Price in £*
Hampstead Village Guesthouse	2 Kemplay Rd	020 7435 8679	65

Map 69 • St. John's Wood	*Address*	*Phone*	*Price in £*
Marriot	128 King Henry's Rd	020 7722 7711	127

Map 70 • Primrose Hill	*Address*	*Phone*	*Price in £*
Hampstead Britannia Hotel	Primrose Hill Rd	087 1222 0043	76

Map 76 • Edgeware Road / Marylebone (North)		*Phone*	*Price in £*
Danubius Hotel	18 Lodge Rd	0207 722 7722	84
Dorset Square Hotel	39 Dorset Sq	020 7723 7874	160
Four Seasons Hotel	173 Gloucester Pl	020 7723 5978	96
Landmark	222 Marylebone Rd	020 7631 8000	210

Map 77 • Mornington Crescent / Regent's Park		*Phone*	*Price in £*
Melia White House Hotel	Albany St	207 391 3000	109

Map 91 • Shoreditch / Brick Lane / Spitalfields		*Phone*	*Price in £*
City Hotel	12 Osborn St	020 7247 3313	102
Hotel St Gregory	100 Shoreditch High St	020 7613 9800	137

Map 98 • Mile End (South) / Limehouse		*Phone*	*Price in £*
Holiday Inn Express	The Highway	020 7791 3850	133

Map 100 • Poplar (West) / Canary Wharf (West)		*Phone*	*Price in £*
The Hilton	Marsh Wall	020 3002 2350	104
International Hotel	163 Marsh Wall	086 6539 8063	81
Marriot	22 Hertsmere Rd	020 7093 1000	119

Map 104 • South Bank / Waterloo / Lambeth North		*Phone*	*Price in £*
Marriott County Hall	Westminster Bridge Rd	020 7928 5200	189
Travel Inn London County Hall	Belverdere Rd	0870 238 3300	104

105 • Southwark / Bankside (West)		*Phone*	*Price in £*
The Mad Hatter Hotel	3 Stamford St	020 7401 9222	115

Map 106 • Bankside (East) / Borough / Newington		*Phone*	*Price in £*
Novotel London City South	61 Southwark Bridge Rd	020 7089 0400	98

Map 113 • Walworth	*Address*	*Phone*	*Price in £*
Express by Eurotraveller Hotel	18 Amelia St	020 7358 4898	79

Map 120 • Greenwich	*Address*	*Phone*	*Price in £*
Novotel Greenwich	173 Greenwich High Rd	020 8312 6800	145

Map 121 • Camberwell (West)	*Address*	*Phone*	*Price in £*
Park Plaza Hotel	1 Addington Square	020 7021 1800	127

Map 131 • Vauxhall / Albert Embankment		*Phone*	*Price in £*
Days Hotel	54 Kennington Rd	020 7922 1331	97
Park Plaza Hotel	18 Albert Embankment	020 7958 8000	119
Plaza on the River	18 Albert Embankment	020 7769 2525	224

Map 134 • South Lambeth	*Address*	*Phone*	*Price in £*
Comfort Inn	87 S Lambeth Rd	020 7735 9494	74
Hotel 87	87 Old South Lambeth Rd	084 5082 2456	134

Map 137 • Wandsworth (West)	*Address*	*Phone*	*Price in £*
Best Western	52 Upper Richmond Rd	020 8874 1598	97

As you might expect from a site constantly inhabited since the Roman invasion of Britain, and probably before, London has managed to assemble a vast array of good, bad and ugly landmarks. The city is, in fact, stuffed with them, and the following is a slightly subjective rumination on a small proportion of some of the most noteworthy.

Historical

London gracefully bears a massive weight of history, and many of its landmarks reflect this. One of the oldest is the remains of the **Temple of Mithras (Map 16)** on Walbrook, built by the Romans when London was Londinium. Parts of the **London Wall (Map 18)**, also originally built by the Romans, still exist, the best fragments are around Tower Hill station. In Medieval times London became a bustling place; celebrate one of its most beautiful churches by visiting the oddly named **St Giles' Cripplegate (Map 7)**, which is ensconced within the brutal **Barbican Centre**, a landmark itself. By the 1600s, London was bustling so hard it got the plague and then some idiot burnt the entire city down in 1666. Celebrate three days of the Great Fire by climbing to the top of the 202 feet high **Monument (Map 18)**, before visiting post-fire architect Christopher Wren's masterpiece, **St Paul's Cathedral (Map 16)**. Into the 18th century, things became a little more sophisticated and some of London's prettiest domestic architecture bloomed. Stroll down Bloomsbury's **Doughty Street (Map 5)**, stopping at Charles Dickens'House, for perfectly proportioned Georgian elegance. The Victorians had a huge impact on London, with whole tracts of the city bearing the stamp of the starched times of chimney sweeps and empire bashing. For the lighter side of Victorian London, poke about the museums quarter from the **Victoria & Albert Museum (Map 37)** up to the **Albert Memorial (Map 36)**. For the darker, dodge the elderly at the **St Pancras Hospital (Map 78)**, an ex-workhouse.

Tourist Bait

London has a host of over-exposed landmarks that are honey to the swarms of tourist worker-bees but over-rated in the eyes of many Londoners. We don't necessarily share this view, but if you want to venture beyond the crowds at **Big Ben (Map 22)**, try some of the following. The aforementioned **St Paul's Cathedral (Map 16)** is an absolute wonder, although try the smaller **Southwark Cathedral (Map 106)** for a more intimate option. **The British Museum (Map 4)** is a beauty made fairer by its recent courtyard renovation; peruse the library to see where Marx pondered upon 'Das Kapital'. **The Burlington Arcade (Map 10)** is how shopping should be, whilst the **Wallace Collection (Map 2)** is probably the perfect townhouse museum to take your mother-in-law. The crypt under **St Mary-le-Bow Church (Map 16)** is 11th century weirdness complete with its own vegetarian restaurant. The Thames is long enough to provide you with your own spot of riverside tranquillity. If you're scared of bridges, burrow under the river at the **Greenwich Foot Tunnel (Map 120)**, or chug across it on the free Woolwich Ferry. For a weekend mooch, try the **Grand Regent's Canal (Map 71)** around **Little Venice (Map 27)**. For a grimier option, avoid local children as they try to push you in the same canal around **Mile End (Map 98)**.

Modern Landmarks

The 20th century blessed the city with some opinion splitting contributions. **The Hayward Gallery (Map 104)** and **National Theatre (Map 104)** are both concrete frighteners which we are learning to love. Despite originally housing a power station, **Tate Modern (Map 105)** has been more graciously received. Meanwhile, further down the river, disused **Battersea Power Station (Map 133)** continues to crumble. The **BT Tower (Map 60)** is like a 1960s lighthouse for central London drunks. **The Lloyds Building (Map 18)** and **Tower 42 (Map 18)** are both absorbing odes to the banker and glare menacingly at new rival **One Canada Square (or Canary Wharf Tower) (Map 100)**. A more recent contribution to the city is the **Canary Wharf Underground Station (Map 100)**. **The Ark (Map 64)** at Hammersmith is west London's greeting to those driving in from Heathrow. East London is currently revelling in its revamped **V&A Museum of Childhood (Map 92)**.

Lowbrow

In these clean times of starchitects, steel and glass, a few minutes spent gawping at **Elephant and Castle (Map 105)** shopping centre is enough to remind anyone how awry a landmark can go. Even a quick squizz at the nearby **Faraday Memorial (Map 105)** may not lift your gloom, largely as it now forms the body of a clogged roundabout. However, London can do lowbrow with the best of them, starting with the **Westway Flyover (Map 31)**: a noisy, dusty shard of concrete to remind you that the car is still king. The disused **Kingsway Tram Tunnel (Map 4)** is a forgotten piece of prime underground real estate and **Centre Point (Map 4)** and **Millbank Tower (Map 21)** are good examples of dodgy skyscrapers that no-one needed. **Battersea Park Gasometers (Map 133)** are imposing monsters, whereas **Lots Road Power Station (Map 50)** is fast becoming London's trendiest disused power station. If you must jump upon band wagons, keep your eyes peeled around east London for art left on walls by Banksy. Mobile lowbrow starts with a trip on a Routemaster, despite the buses being withdrawn in 2005, two heritage routes are still running. Lowbrow (along with logic, aesthetic quality and planning) finishes with **Euston Station (Map 78)**, which is, simply, disgusting.

Map 1 • Marylebone (West)

Marble Arch	Oxford St	Randomly plonked gateway to nowhere.
Speaker's Corner	Cumberland Gate	It's easy—stand on the corner and listen to the 'speeches.'

Map 2 • Marylebone (East)

Hertford House	Manchester Sq	Terribly twee home of the Wallace Collection.
Jimi Hendrix Memorial Blue Plaque	23 Brook St	Jimi lived here. Some bloke called Handel lived next door.

Map 3 • Fitzrovia

BT Tower	60 Cleveland St	A 574 foot tall official government secret until 1993.
Charlotte Street	Charlotte St	Restaurant strip for the advertising in-crowd.
Middlesex Hospital	Mortimer St	Closed-down and spooky-looking.
Pollock's Toy Museum	1 Scala St	Brimming with delightful, traditional toys and Dickensian atmosphere.
Sinner Winner Man	216 Oxford St	Are you a sinner? Or a winner? London's top preacher's patch.
Tottenham Court Road	Tottenham Ct Rd	Buy your electronics 'ere, innit?

Map 4 • Bloomsbury (West)

The British Museum	Great Russell St	Newly-covered Great Court is architectural manna.
Centre Point	101 New Oxford St	Ugly skyscraper looking kinda out of place.
Kingsway Tram Tunnel		Spooky remnant of London's defunct Tram network.
Senate House	University of London, Malet St	Ominous art deco building; Orwell's Ministry of Truth.
Tavistock Square	Tavistock Sq	Has a statue of Gandhi looking as cool as ever.

Map 5 • Bloomsbury (East)

The Dickens House Museum	48 Doughty St	Unassuming from the outside, mecca for Dickens' fans on the inside.
Doughty Street	Doughty St	Exquisite Georgian street in heart of literary land.

Map 7 • Barbican / City Road (South)

Barbican Centre	Silk St	An architechtual eyesore. Bloody good events though.
Bunhill Fields	City Rd	120 thousand dead people, including William Blake. All buried, luckily.
Church of Saint Bartholomew	6 Kinghorn St	Stroll in for your daily dose of frankincense and choir song.
LSO St Luke's	161 Old St	Home to the London Symphony Orchestra. Peaceful gardens for relaxation.
St. Giles Without Cripplegate	Fore St	Medieval church which defied the Blitz. Catch an organ recital.

Map 8 • Liverpool Street / Broadgate

Fulcrum at Broadgate	Broadgate	Richard Serra's overwhelming steel megalith.

Map 9 • Mayfair / Green Park

50 Berkeley Square	50 Berkeley Sq	The most haunted house in all of London town!
Apsley House	Hyde Park Corner	"Number One, London"—former hip address of Duke of Wellington.
Buckingham Palace	The Mall	Unofficial HQ for Fathers For Justice.
Down Street Station	Down St	Bricked-up Underground station. The Turtles didn't live here.

Map 10 • Piccadilly / Soho (West)

Burlington Arcade	Burlington Arcade	Welcoming shoppers since 1819.
Carnaby Street	Carnaby St	Will anything innovative ever come from here again?
Kingly Street Arcade	Kingly St	Flash the cash to cut a dash.
Statue of Eros	Piccadilly Circus	God of Love, smothered in pigeon crap: a cautionary tale.

Map 11 • Soho (Central)

Huge Tree In Pub (Waxy O'Connor's)	14 Rupert St	No, you're not drunk, it really is a tree.
Soho Market	Berwick St	Arrive early for traditional Cockney trader songs / off-duty hookers.

Map 12 • Soho (East)

Denmark Street	Denmark St	Guitar land. 'Enter Sandman' forbidden in most stores.
FA Headquarters	25 Soho Sq	Home of English football's top brass.
Old Compton Street	Old Compton St	Dubious gay hub.
The Phoenix Garden	21 Stacey St	A beautiful green mini-oasis in the middle of the city.
Soho Square	Soho Sq	Great atmosphere on hot summer days.

Map 13 • Covent Garden

Oasis Lido	32 Endell St	A lido in central London! In a 50s housing estate!
Seven Dials	Junction of Monmouth St, Mercer St and five others	Slum area in the past. Now great for shopping!

Map 14 • Holborn / Temple

Aldwych tube station	The Strand	Creepy abandoned tube station. With a photo booth... of doom?
BBC Bush House	Aldwych	London calling the world, since 1940.
Inner Temple Garden	Inner Temple	So peaceful even the lawyers look relaxed.
Lincoln's Inn Fields	Lincoln's Inn Fields	Largest public square in London.
The Old Curiosity Shop	13 Portsmouth St	The oldest shop in London is truly Dickensesque.
Royal Courts of Justice	Strand	Witness justice meted out to all, even the McCartneys.
Sir John Soane's Museum	13 Lincoln's Inn Fields	Spooky museum dedicated to the great 18th century architect.
Site of Sweeny Todd's Barber Shop	186 Fleet St	Swing by for a demon haircut and lovely pie.
Somerset House	Strand	18th century palace, beautiful fountains; has various modern functions.

Map 15 • Blackfriars / Farringdon

Daily Express Building	121 Fleet St	Art Deco sleeper.
Millennium Bridge	Millennium Bridge	Footbridge famous for wobbling alarmingly when it was opened.
Postman's Park	King Edward St	Tile memorial for 'average' people who did really cool things.

Map 16 • Square Mile (West)

The Guildhall	Gresham St	Big, posh, old... Like Prince Phillip but less entertaining.
St Mary le Bow Church	Cheapside	A historic place for City tycoons to save their souls.
St. Paul's Cathedral	St. Paul's Churchyard	Magnificence since 604AD.
Temple of Mithras	Queen Victoria St	3rd century Roman temple foundations. Discovered 1954 and moved here.

Map 17 • Square Mile (East)

Bank of England	Threadneedle St	The 'Old Lady' still churns out the pounds.
London Stone	105 Cannon St	Possibly used by Romans to measure all distances in Britannia.
Threadneedle Street	Threadneedle St	London's original Grope Cunt Lane. Seriously, it's a true story.

Map 18 • Tower Hill / Aldgate

The Gherkin	30 St Mary Axe	Phwoar.
Jack the Ripper Mural	Widegate St	Spooky mural down a gloomy alley. Good for scaring kids.
Jewish Soup Kitchen	Brune St	The kitchen's gone; the stunning ornate façade is still there.
The Lloyds Building	1 Lime St	Dystopia's nicer side.
London Wall	Cooper's Row	Ruins, should be re-built to keep Northerners out.
The Monument	Monument St	Climb 311 coronary-inducing steps for unique, unsung London views.
Pudding Lane	Pudding Ln	Starting point for Great Fire of 1666. No smoking.
Royal Raven Lodgings	Wakefield Tower	Want to upgrade your pokey flat? Become a raven.
Thames Clipper	Tower Pier	
Tower 42 (Natwest Tower)	25 Old Broad St	One of London's skyscrapers. Great view (and restaurant) at top.
Tower of London	The Tower of London	Kings and Queens. Surprisingly insightful, annoyingly expensive.

Map 20 • Victoria / Pimlico (West)

Little Ben	Victoria St/Vauxhall Bridge Rd intersection	Big Ben's runty kid brother.
Westminster Cathedral	42 Francis St	Yep, impressive.

Map 21 • Pimlico (East)

Millbank Tower	Millbank	Ugly sore thumb. And Labour Party HQ!
The Shard Building	32 Vauxhall Bridge Rd	Site of the super tall skyscraper to be.

Map 22 • Westminster

Big Ben	House of Commons	The world's most famous clock and pretty damn cool.
Bolan Rock Shrine	Queen's Ride, Putney	Memorial shrine where 70s rock star Marc Bolan died.
Field of Remembrance	Victoria St & Dean's Yard	
New Scotland Yard Sign	8 Broadway	It spins!! Just like on the telly!!
Smith Square	Smith Sq	Square with great concert venue--watch out for MPs.
UK Parliament	House of Commons	Parliament buildings where you can watch government debates.
Westminster Tube Station	Bridge St	A daunting, soulless, engineering playground. Good and bad both extinct here...

Map 23 • St. James's

Economist Plaza	25 St James's St	Rotating sculpture installations from bratty young artists.
Giro the Nazi Dog	9 Carlton House Terrace	London's sole Nazi memorial. You'd think there'd be more…
Leicester Square	Leicester Sq	Tragic, tacky, always inexplicably heaving. Avoid.
TKTS	Leicester Sq	

Map 24 • Trafalgar Square / The Strand

10 Downing Street	10 Downing St	The Prime Minister's house.
The Actors' Church	St. Paul's Church, Bedford St	Somewhat hidden and unique church long-associated with thesps.
The Banqueting House	Whitehall	Unsullied Renaissance cum-shot. Still does private parties.
Cleopatra's Needle	Embankment	Ancient-Egyptian Empire esoterica, with additional Luftwaffe-era 'distressed' styling.
Eleanor Cross	Charing Cross Station, The Strand	A mourning King's tribute to his expired Queen.
Jane Austen Residence	10 Henrietta St	The first Bridget Jones' bachelorette crashed here for a time.
Right-hand Drive Street	Savoy Ct	Britain's only right-hand-drive street. Like being on holiday! (Ish)
Sewer Lamp	Carting Ln	Lit by the power of your bowels.

St Martin-in-the-Fields	Trafalgar Sq	Was indeed surrounded by fields once. Just TRY to imagine!
Top Secret Tunnels	6 Craig's Ct (entrance)	Government's WWII tunnels, 100ft below London. But shhh: top secret.
Trafalgar Square	Trafalgar Sq	Hardly an oasis but space to sit, look and think.

Map 25 • Kensal Town

Trellick Tower	5 Golborne Rd	Grade II listed 1960s council estate inspiring love/hate reactions.

Map 28 • Ladbroke Grove/ Notting Hill (West)

Kyoto Garden	100 Holland Park Ave	Traditional Japanese Garden in Holland Park offering peace and tranquility

Map 29 • Notting Hill Gate

Kensington Palace Gardens	Palace Gardens Terrace	Billionaire's Row. Stunning street to amble down and gawp at the mansions.
Portobello Road Market	Portobello Rd	Antiques, clothes, food and more. A London institution.

Map 31 • Paddington

Paddington Bear Statue	Paddington Station	The statue's pleasant. But they're milking it with the crap shop.
Tony Blair's house	Connaught Sq	Promise not to do anything naughty now.
Westway Flyover		Coolest car route into London

Map 33 • Shepherd's Bush

BBC Television Centre	Wood Lane	Treasure it before the BBC moves out in 2013.

Map 36 • South Kensington / Gloucester Rd

Albert Memorial	Kensington Gardens	The shiniest balding head in town.
Royal Albert Hall	Kensington Gore	One stunner of a music hall, inside and out.

Map 37 • Knightsbridge

Holy Trinity Brompton	Brompton Rd	Historic HTB is home to the Alpha course. Even Guy Ritchie's been!
Victoria & Albert Museum	Cromwell Rd	Victorian treasure trove, building a beauty itself.

Map 40 • Goldhawk Rd / Ravenscourt Park

Christmas Forest	83 Goldhawk Rd	Just like Norway, but without the bears or hairy women.

Map 43 • West Brompton / Fulham Broadway / Earl's Court

Stamford Bridge	Fulham Rd	That's not sweat you smell but money at Chelsea FC's HQ.

Map 48 • Fulham

Putney Bridge Tube Pill Box	Putney Bridge Station	"We will fight them on the platforms!"

Map 50 • Sand's End

Lots Road Power Station	Lots Rd	Pint-sized power station, now disused.

Map 51 • Highgate

Highgate Cemetery	1 Swain's Ln	Eerily gothic home to Karl Marx and The Highgate Vampire.
Karl Marx's grave	Highgate Cemetry	Exactly what it says on the tin.

Map 52 • Archway (North)

Parkland Walk Nature Reserve	Parkland Walk	Hedgehogs and graffiti to be spotted along this abandoned railway.
Suicide Bridge	Hornsey Ln	Former London entry point, now very much an exit point.

Map 53 • Crouch End

Abandoned Warehouse	Parkland Walk	Dereliction galore along one of the best walks in London

Map 56 • Hampstead Village

Hampstead Observatory	Lower Terrace	The highest point in London, and open to the public!
Keats' House	Keats Grove	Beautiful buildin' where some bloke wrote some poem. Innit.

Map 57 • Hampstead Heath

Lawn Road Flats	Lawn Rd	c.1934 modern living. Learn to love concrete.

Map 60 • Archway

Banksy's Hitchhiking Charles Manson	Tally Ho Corner (off Highgate Hill)	Early stencil by internationally renowned graff artist.
Dick Whittington's Cat	Highgate Hill	Small stone statue of obscure Mayor's cat.

Map 62 • Finsbury Park

North London Central Mosque (Finsbury Park)	7 St Thomas's Rd	New name, ethos for once controversial, now myth-dispelling, mosque.

Map 63 • Manor House

The Castle Climbing Centre	Green Lanes	Fake castle, real climbers.

Map 64 • Stoke Newington

Newington Green Church	39 Newington Green	'ERECTED 1708, ENLARGED 1860'...well, it made us laugh.

Map 67 • Belsize Park

Freud Statue	Fitzjohn's Ave, opposite Maresfiend Gardens Junction	Statue by Oscar Nemon near the psychoanalyst's Hampstead home.

Map 68 • Kilburn High Road / Abbey Road

Abbey Road Zebra Crossing	3 Abbey Rd	Go on. Take THAT photo. You know you want to.
State Buidling	195 Kilburn High Rd	Awesome Art Deco building now a scary cult center.

Map 70 • Primrose Hill

3 Chalcot Square	3 Chalcot Sq	Home of poet Sylvia Plath, 1960-61.

Map 71 • Camden Town / Chalk Farm / Kentish Town (West)

Banksy's Maid: Sweeping it Under the Carpet	Chalk Farm Rd	Grafitto symbolising response to African Aids crisis.
Camden Market	Camden Lock Pl	Shop, hang, drink, listen, pose, watch, chill, rock, laugh.
Grand Regents Canal	Grand Regents Canal	London's best bike lane. Or canoe to Birmingham.
The Roundhouse	Chalk Farm Rd	Prominent round building and historic performance venue.

Map 75 • Highbury

St Paul's Shrubbery	St Paul's Rd	All Monty Python jokes welcome, in fact, positively encouraged.

Map 76 • Edgeware Road / Marylebone (North)

Sherlock Holmes' House	221 Baker St	It's elementary my dear Watson!

Map 77 • Mornington Crescent / Regent's Park

Euston Tower	286 Euston Rd	Quite an impressive erection.
Greater London House	Hampstead Rd	Crazy Art Deco building.

Map 78 • Euston

The British Library	96 Euston Rd	Prestigious research library with unmatched collection.
Camden High Street	Camden High St	'Alternative' tourist mecca.
Cheney Road	Cheney Rd	"Chaplin, "Alfie" and many more were filmed on these cobbles.
Euston Station	Euston Rd	So ugly it's oogly.
Platform 9¾	King's Cross Station	This Harry Potter thing has gone way too f'ing far.
St Pancras Station	St Pancras Way	Listed Gothic frontage, massive modern Eurostar hangar behind.
St Pancras Hospital	4 St Pancras Way	Ex-Victorian workhouse turned superbug den.

Map 80 • Angel / Upper St

Angel Station Roof	Angel	You can get on the roof here, you epic teens.
The Bull	100 Upper St	Hands up: who loves beer?

Map 81 • Canonbury

Gladiators Paving Slab	10 Canonbury St	Logo of fighty telly show built into pavement. Me neither.

Map 82 • De Beauvoir Town / Kingsland

Suleymaniye Mosque	212 Kingsland Rd	Striking minaret silhouetted against Shoreditch Church spire and Broadgate Tower.

Map 84 • Hoxton

Hoxton Square	Hoxton Sq	Great in summer. Buy some cans and join the hipsters.
Village Underground	54 Holywell Ln	How did they get the trains up there?
White Cube	48 Hoxton Sq	Jay Jopling's homage to modern art

Map 85 • Stoke Newington (East)

Abney Park Cemetery	Stoke Newington High St	Egyptian revival-style, spooky nature reserve.

Map 86 • Dalston / Kingsland

Centreprise	136 Kingsland High St	Multi-cultural art centre, cafe, bookshop and venue.
Holy Trinity, The Clowns Church	Beechwood Rd & Kirkland Walk	Every Feb, clowns mourn Grimaldi. In full costume.

Map 87 • Hackney Downs / Lower Clapton

London Orphan Asylum	Linscott Rd	Grandiose remains of historic site now beloved of enviornmental artists.
The Strand Building	29 Urswick Rd	Beautiful Art Deco building, NOT the subject of Roxy Music song.
Sutton House	2 Homerton High St	Music and arts in the oldest house in East London.

Map 88 • Haggerston / Queensbridge Rd

Geffrye Museum	136 Kingsland Rd	English interior design from 1600 to today.

Map 89 • London Fields / Hackney Central

London Fields Lido	London Fields Westside	Open-air swimming for hardy Hackney folk.

Map 91 • Shoreditch / Brick Lane / Spitalfields

Brick Lane Mosque	59 Brick Ln	The area's changes reflect on the building – once a synagogue, now a mosque.
Christ Church Spitalfields	2 Fournier St	Star architect Nicholas Hawksmoor's pretty masterpiece.
Dennis Severs' House	18 Folgate St	Candle-lit cellar, parlour, smoking room - step 300 years back in time.
Spitalfields Market	105 Commercial St	No bargains but certainly one-of-a-kind fashions.
Sweettooth Graffiti Alley	Pedley St	Signature sweeties and skulls – just off Brick Lane.
Ten Bells	84 Commercial St	Where Jack the Ripper got his victims.
Truman's Brewery	Brick Lane	Beautiful old building now a hip weekend market. That's progress...

Map 92 • Bethnal Green

Bethnal Green Tube Station	Bethnal Green Tube Station	Scene of the worst civilian loss of the Second World War.
London Buddhist Centre	51 Roman Rd	Get your freak om.

Map 93 • Globe Town / Mile End (North)

Art Pavilllion	221 Grove Rd	Arts center seemingly designed by the Teletubbies.
Mile End Climbing Wall	Haverfield Rd	Classic climbing centre - one of London's big three.

Map 95 • De Beauvoir Town / Kingsland

The Sun HQ	1 Pennington St	It's probably not legal to stake out Page 3 girls.

Map 96 • Whitechapel (East) / Shadwell (West) / Wapping

Battle of Cable Street Mural, St George's Hall	236 Cable St	Celebrating an almighty multi-faith bashing of a 1930s fascist march.
Blind Beggar Pub	337 Whitechapel Rd	A killing here finally led to Ronnie Kray doing porridge.

Map 98 • Mile End (South) / Limehouse

Ragged School Museum	45 Copperfield Rd	Barnado's school 'for the deserving poor' turned East End museum.

Map 100 • Poplar (West) / Canary Wharf (West)

Canary Wharf Tower	1 Canada Sq	You can smell the money yards away. Look, don't touch.
Canary Wharf Tube Station	Canary Wharf	Norman Foster's Jewel in the Jubilee Line Extension.

Map 102 • Millwall

The Docklands Sailing & Watersport Centre	235 Westferry Rd	Award-winning sailing centre.

Map 104 • South Bank / Waterloo / Lambeth North

County Hall	Riverside Walkway	One of London's most historical and vast buildings.
The Hayward Gallery	Southbank Centre	Revered and reviled bruiser.
The London Eye	Westminster Bridge Rd	Two words: Tourist. Trap. Nice view though.
Low Tide at South Bank	South Bank	Go for a walk on the exposed riverbed.
National Theatre	South Bank	South Bank centre-piece, looked like it was from 2050 in 1960.
The Pier at OXO Tower	OXO Tower	Screw OXO! Have a picnic on the pier instead.
South Bank Book Market	Southbank (under Waterloo Bridge, opposite BFI)	Little-known outdoor market; heaps of vintage and second-hand reads.
Waterloo Bridge	Waterloo Bridge	When tired with London, come here and watch the sunset.

Map 105 • Southwark / Bankside (West)

Buskers' Archway	Southbank	Excellent acoustics make the decorated tunnel a coveted buskers' spot.
Elephant & Castle	Elephant & Castle	Everything that was wrong with 60s town planning. Concrete hell.
Michael Faraday Memorial	Elephant & Castle	He gave us electromagnetism, we gave him a roundabout.
The Ring	72 Blackfriars Rd	London's first boxing ring was here; now a characterful pub.
Shakespeare's Globe	21 New Globe Walk	The Bard's famous playhouse reconstructed.
Tate Modern	Bankside	Herzog and de Meuron dazzler.

Map 106 • Bankside (East) / Borough / Newington

Cross Bones Graveyard	Red Cross Way	Medieval resting place for London's ladies of the night.
Female Gladiator	Great Dover St	1st centruy AD grave of London's very own Xena.
The Golden Hinde	Clink St	Amazing replica of Francis Drake's Tudor war ship.
The London Tombs	Tooley St	Lesser known Tower experience—beware the plague pits.
Old Operating Theatre Museum	9 St Thomas St	Macabre ancient operating theatre, with gallery for eager spectators.
Southwark Cathedral	London Bridge	Worth the diversion to see Chaucer and Shakespeare's stomping grounds.
St George the Martyr	Borough High St & Tabard St	
Winchester Palace	Clink St	Random 13th century ruins with remarkable rose window.

Map 107 • Shad Thames

City Hall	Queen's Walk, More London	Dubbed 'The Testicle' by Mayor Ken Livingston. Nice.
Fashion and Textile Museum	83 Bermondsey St	DAH-ling, it's just fabulous!
Floating Gardens	31 Mill St	Gardens. Mad tramps. On Boats. What else do you want?
HMS Belfast	Morgan's Lane, Tooley St	Floating WW2 killing machine, much beloved of children.

Map 110 • Rotherhithe (West) / Canada Waters

Brunel Museum	Railway Ave	Where engineering geeks can seek refuge from being picked on.

Map 111 • Rotherhithe (East) Surrey Quays

Surrey Docks Farm	Rotherhithe St	Show the kids what their bacon used to look like.

Map 113 • Walworth

East Street Market	East St	Gloriously useless stuff.

Map 114 • Old Kent Road (West) / Burgess Park

The Animatronic Fireman	Old Kent Rd	Be afraid. Be very afraid.
Peckham Library	122 Peckham Hill St	Groundbreaking modern architecture or huge, carelessly dropped Tetris block?

Map 116 • South Bermondsey

Millwall FC Stadium	The Den, Zampa Road	A football mecca for somebody?

Map 120 • Greenwich

Cutty Sark Gardens	Cutty Sark	Where the Archbishop of Canterbury was murdered in 1012.
Greenwich Foot Tunnel	Greenwich Church St	Walk/crawl/skip/limp under the Thames.

Map 126 • New Cross

Ben Pimlott Building	University of London, New Cross	A building of cheerful, dreary, warped, modern fascist fun.

Map 131 • Vauxhall / Albert Embankment

Lambeth Palace	Lambeth Palace Rd	Where the Archbishop of Canterbury lives; no, not in Canterbury, stupid.
Secret Intelligence Service HQ (MI6)	Vauxhall Cross	Real life James Bonds in a not-so-secret location.
Vauxhall City Farm	165 Tyers St	So that's where an egg comes from.

Map 133 • Battersea (East)

Battersea Dogs' Home	4 Battersea Park Rd	Re-house a pooch. Now does cats too.
Battersea Park Gasometers	Queenstown Rd	Rusting monsters.
Battersea Power Station	188 Kirtling St	The world's most beautiful power station, surely.

Map 140 • Clapham Junction / Northcote Rd

Northcote Road	Northcote Rd	Middle-class marketing-types mecca.

Map 143 • Clapham High Street

Clapham Common Air-Raid Shelter	Clapham High St	The depths of government paranoia.

Map 144 • Stockwell / Brixton (West)

Brixton Market	Electric Ave	Caribbean flavours, smells and sounds.
Electric Avenue	Electric Ave	First shopping area in Britain lit by electricity, in 1880.

Map 145 • Stockwell / Brixton (East)

Stockwell Bowls	Stockwell Rd	70's concrete skatepark, take quads and get beaten-up.

Map 152 • Tooting Broadway

Gala Bingo Hall	50 Mitcham Rd	Bingo hall with Grade One listed interior.

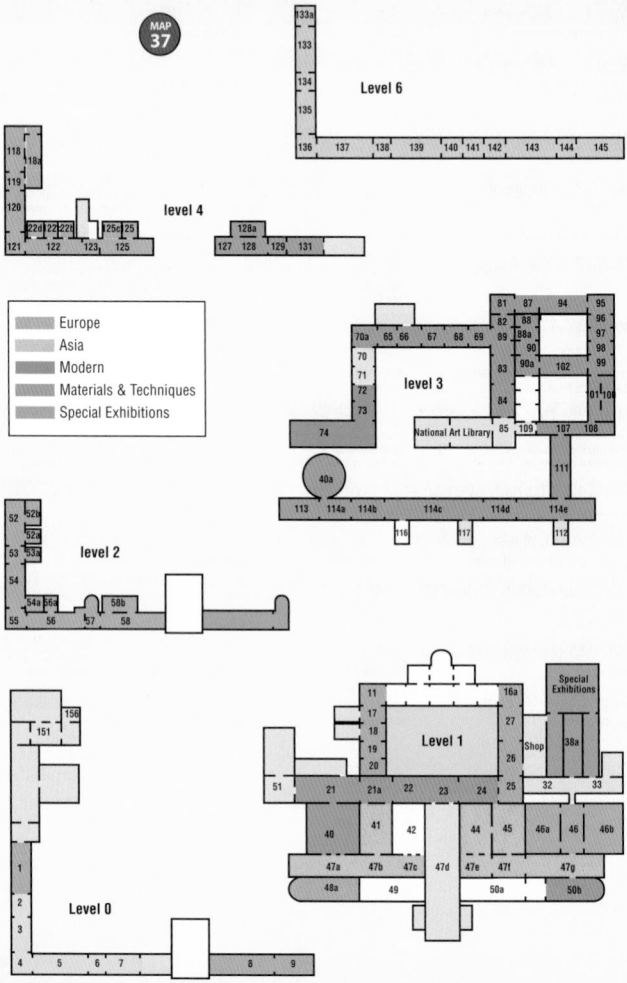
MAP 37
Level 6
133a 133 134 135 136 137 138 139 140 141 142 143 144 145
level 4
118 118a 119 120 121 122 122b 122c 122d 123 125 125e 125
128a 127 128 129 131
Europe
Asia
Modern
Materials & Techniques
Special Exhibitions
level 3
70a 65 66 67 68 69 70 71 72 73 74 81 82 83 84 85 87 88 88a 89 90 90a 94 95 96 97 98 99 102 101 100 109 107 108 111 National Art Library 40a 113 114a 114b 114c 114d 114e 116 117 112
level 2
52 52b 52a 53 53a 54 54a 54b 55 56 57 58 58b
Level 0
150 151 1 2 3 4 5 6 7 8 9
Level 1
11 17 18 19 20 16a 27 26 25 51 21 21a 22 23 24 32 33 Shop 38a Special Exhibitions
40 41 42 44 45 46a 46 46b
47a 47b 47c 47d 47e 47f 47g
48a 49 50a 50b

General Information

NFT Map: 37

Address: Cromwell Road
London SW7 2RL
Phone: 020 7942 2000
Website: www.vam.ac.uk
Hours: 10 am–6 pm daily,
Wednesdays until 9 pm.

Admission: Free to the permanent collection. There is a charge for temporary exhibitions. Tickets have an allotted time slot and although they can be purchased on the day, it is recommended you book ahead of time by phone or online, especially with the more popular exhibitions.

Overview

The Victoria and Albert Museum, or the V&A, calls itself the world's greatest museum of art and design and nowhere has there ever been such an eclectic collection of objects inducing so many 'oooooohs', 'aaaaahs' and 'holy shits!'. With a permanent collection of over 4.5 million objects, pretty much all on display in the 145 galleries, you can go everyday for a lifetime and be blown over by something you hadn't noticed before. For the tourist and non-tourist alike, the V&A is a wonderful maze of cultural ramblings. You'll get lost, overwhelmed and flustered, but we promise you won't get bored.

The V&A is a cabinet of curiosities of gargantuan proportions, boasting 5000 years of art and design, in every medium imaginable (from wax dioramas to a little black dress made of bras), spread over seven levels and organised by five themes—Asia, Europe, Materials & Techniques, Modern and Exhibitions. The trouble is where to start. You'll no doubt spend the first 10 minutes mesmerised by the glass Chihuly chandelier over the information booth, but what you do afterwards depends on how much time you have. Got hours? Avoid structure and just wander. Got an hour? Take a look at the map, see what strikes your fancy and head straight there. Just don't forget to hit up the gift shop afterwards—it's killer.

The Greatest Hits

There's no real method to the V&A's madness. Despite their best efforts to categorise everything, Vivienne Westwood gowns are just a stumble away from 1000 year-old Buddhas. But this is a great thing. The best advice is really to ditch the guidebook and go with your instincts. To make sure you take in the best stuff, start in the basement (having arrived through the Tunnel Entrance from the tube station), where you'll find the 17th century **Cabinet of Curiosities**—predecessors to the modern museum—which will get you in the right mind set. Weaving past bits and pieces of **Versailles**, you emerge onto the ground floor (Level 1) which covers fashion, Asia and both Medieval and Renaissance Europe. Highlights of which include the **cast courts**, which boast a life-size replica of **Trajan's Column** in plaster, then onto ancient **samurai swords** and spectacular **kimonos** in Asia, the **Ardabil Carpet**—the largest and most amazing Islamic carpets in existence dating from 1539 (lit up on the hour and half-hour), an extensive costume room covering everything from **18th century crinolines** to **Juicy Couture** worthy of Paris Hilton, and lastly, **Raphael's cartoons** – massive sketches for a 1515 commission of tapestries that now hang in the Vatican. Before heading on, stop for a tea in the **Morris, Gamble & Poynter Rooms** café for teacakes in 1860s arts and crafts surroundings. Level 2 consists of the tucked away **British Galleries**, including the **Great Bed of Ware** as well as the endearing **Lord and Lady Clapham** dolls bedecked in miniature turn-of-the-18th century outfits. Up again on Level 3, you'll find the Materials & Techniques rooms, with its vast collections of **silver, ironwork and musical instruments**, as well as some dynamite paintings. Don't miss **Rossetti's The Daydream** and then **Ron Arad's Chair** in the modern rooms. This floor also houses the **National Art Library**—an art history student's research dream (you have to get a reading pass to study here though). Level 4 has a wonderfully tactile display of **glasswork**, as well as **architecture** and more **British Galleries from 1760-1900**. If you've made it this far, you deserve a knighthood.

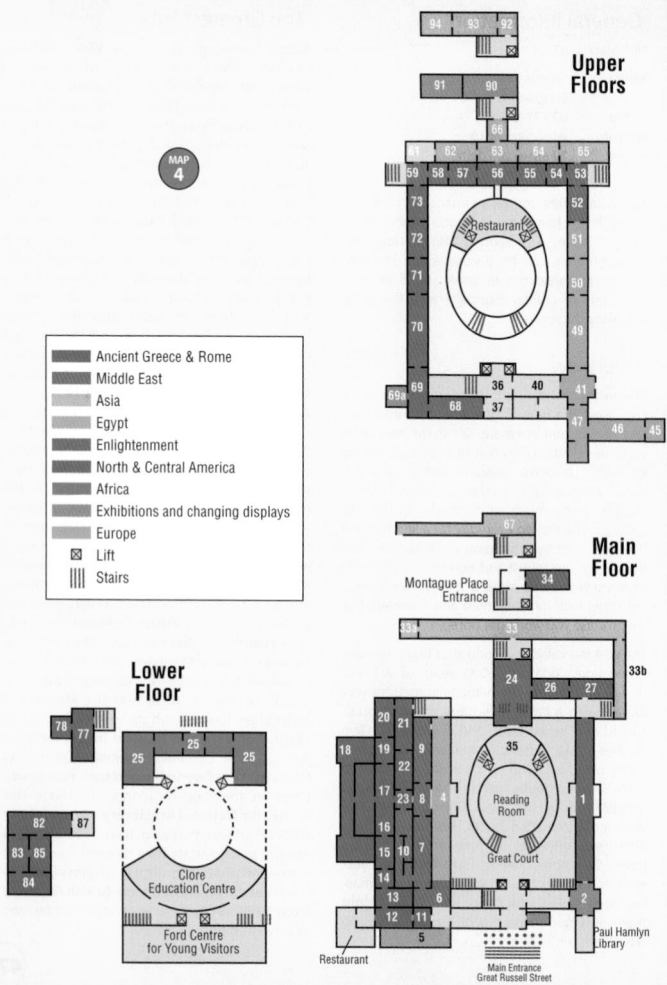
MAP 4
Ancient Greece & Rome
Middle East
Asia
Egypt
Enlightenment
North & Central America
Africa
Exhibitions and changing displays
Europe
Lift
Stairs
Upper Floors
94 93 92
91 90
66
61 62 63 64 65
59 58 57 56 55 54 53
73 72 71 70 69 69a 68
52 51 50 49 41 47 46 45
Restaurant
36 40 37
Main Floor
67
Montague Place Entrance
34
33a 33 33b
24 26 27
20 21 19 9 22 18 17 23 8 4 16 15 10 7 14 13 6 12 11 5
35
Reading Room
Great Court
1 2
Restaurant
Main Entrance Great Russell Street
Paul Hamlyn Library
Lower Floor
78 77
25 25 25
82 87
83 85
84
Clore Education Centre
Ford Centre for Young Visitors

General Information

NFT Map: 4

Address: Great Russell Street, WC1B 3DG

Phone: 020 7323 8299 (information) or 020 7323 8181 (exhibition tickets)

Website: www.britishmuseum.org

Hours: The galleries open daily 10 am–5.30 pm, with selected galleries open until 8.30 pm Thu & Fri (see website for details). The Great Court is open 9 am–6 pm. Jan 1, Good Friday, Dec 24-26: closed.

Admission: Free, with a charge for some special exhibitions.

Overview

Unless you're Indiana Jones, combining archaeological expertise with the swashbuckling energy to defeat obnoxious school groups, then do not attempt to cover the British Museum in a day. With 13 million items covering two million years of human history in almost 100 permanent and temporary galleries, you are better off treating yourself to different sections when the mood takes you—a perk of having one of the world's largest museums on your doorstep and open for free.

At 250 years, it is also the oldest museum in the world, but forget preconceptions of dusty urns and endless Roman coins—they're there if that's your bag, but this is a very modern organisation. The permanent displays include some of the world's most fascinating treasures, while the temporary exhibitions bring London a chance to break and lose artefacts which have seen some of the greatest moments of history, such as the recent Moctezuma: Aztec Ruler display.

However, while preserving artefacts to inspire its visitors, the Museum can also be seen as a testament to the great British pastime of looting. Some of the shining lights of its collection were acquired under the shadiest of circumstances, and the countries which were plundered so that snotty kids could chortle at the genitalia of their sculptures are increasingly vocal about getting the items back. For example the Elgin Marbles, rechristened with their pleasantly playful English name after the earl who helped himself to them, are huge slabs hacked from the 2500 year old Athenian Parthenon (albeit Elgin's entire nose later rotted off due to syphilis: a gratifying example of one-upmanship by nature). The legality of this move is hotly debated, but apart from the damage to the Parthenon, the Marbles undeniably suffered when they were cut into smaller pieces for transport to Britain, and when rowdy schoolboys bopped the leg off a centaur in 1961. The Museum holds firm that returning debated items would empty the museums of the world, but it has extended the occasional olive branch to ease the controversy; compensation was paid for the display of drawings stolen by Nazis, and they returned the Tasmanian Ashes (aboriginal human remains) to Australia after a 20-year battle.

The Greatest Hits

The **Great Court** is not just a Greatest Hit of the Museum, but of London as a whole. Being "the world's largest covered public square" may sound too niche an accolade to be impressive, but it really is stunning. The 150 year old **Reading Room** at its centre is a delight, both for the excellent library and for the wall-mounted list of major historical figures who have sought inspiration within its round walls. Whatever your ethics on plunder, some of the most morally-dubious exhibits are among the absolute must-sees: the **Elgin Marbles** in Room 18 are remarkable, while the **Rosetta Stone** in Room 4 gives you the irresistible buzz of seeing something so legendary up close, or as close at the backpacked hordes will allow, in your own town. A whole **Moai Statue** from Easter Island is in Room 24, the **Lewis Chessmen** set is in Room 42, and the **Mausoleum of Halikarnassos** exhibition displays some of the last remaining fragments of one of the Seven Wonders of the World. However, it is the stories of heartache, adventure, mystery and passion behind the items which bring them to life. Asking the steward of Rooms 62-3 how the **mummies** came to be in the museum, or seeing the pages from **The Book of the Dead** which recorded lives of the deceased, is a fascinating way to gain insight to people around the world and throughout time. And if that's a bit too deep, just head to one of the four **shops** for a mummy-shaped pencil case or replica Rosetta Stone.

General Information

NFT Map: 36
Address: Cromwell Road, SW7 5BD
Phone: 020 7942 5000
Website: www.nhm.ac.uk
Hours: Daily 10 am–5.50 pm (Last admission 17.30) "After Hours" events run on the last Friday of each month during Nov–Apr. 24–26 Dec: closed.
Admission: Free access to most of the Museum. Fee charged for some special exhibitions (free to Members).

Overview

Visiting the Natural History Museum is like reading National Geographic, if it was edited by JK Rowling. As imagination-tingling to adults as it is to kids, you can mull over serious questions about genetic modification and the environmental cost of modern life, while walking inside a termite mound or knocking on a petrified tree.

With more than 70 million specimens in their collection, you simply won't see it all at once, or for most of us—ever. But with free entry, regularly refreshed exhibits and unforgettable special exhibitions, it's worth

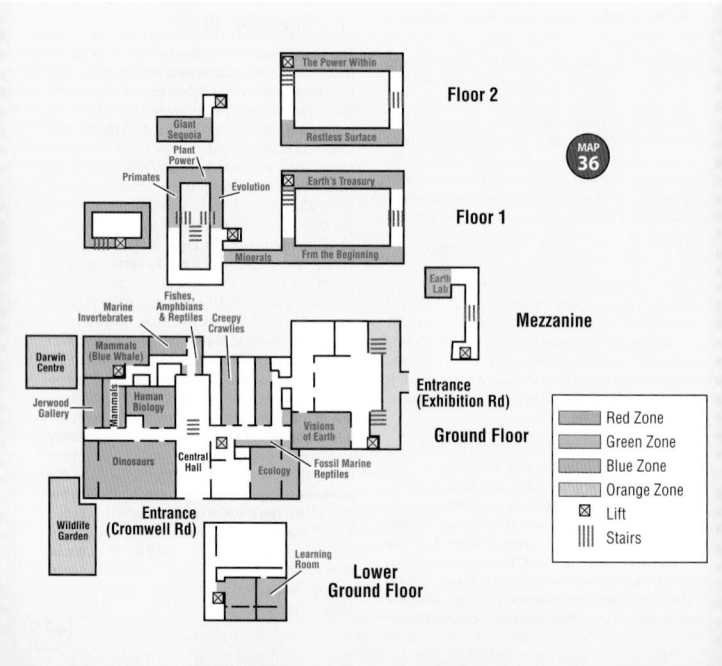

dropping in when you have the opportunity. Grab a free map at the entrance to work out your route, which is colour-coded for a (slightly) easier life: Red Zone for the planet and forces of nature; Green for ecology and the environment; Blue for dinosaurs, mammals and biology; and Orange for the Wildlife Garden and behind-the-scenes peeks.

Weekends are inevitably heaving with hyperactive button-pressing families, spellbound tourists and Londoners trying to rebuild the brain cells they killed off with the night before's drinking; weekdays are amok with school groups. But don't let this put you off. If there's a queue outside the main entrance on Cromwell Road, and you don't fancy killing time by spotting all the different creatures carved around the entrance arch, pop 'round the side to Exhibition Road entrance and you'll fast-track yourself in. You can go early or late for fewer crowds, or stick with the permanent exhibitions, which are superb but not as sexy as the world-class special exhibitions which draw in the masses. Or, if all else fails, just shove the kids out the way: they're smaller than you and the buttons are *so much fun* to press.

The Greatest Hits

Anyone who didn't see the **Dinosaur Exhibition** as a child really missed out: run here and rectify the situation immediately if you haven't been, or revisit and enjoy the modernised exhibits if you have. The **Mammals Exhibition** will get you wondering exactly *how* someone stuffs a giraffe, and gives you a chance to get close to the gaping jaws of a hippo. For a different perspective on this room, go up to the balcony around it: watching people stare agog at the brilliantly-displayed **blue whale** is as entertaining as the exhibits themselves. For proof that even history geeks can make the earth move for you, visit the **Power Within** exhibition which recreates an earthquake (though don't expect a Universal Studios experience. The will is there, bless, but the budget just isn't…). Watch blushing parents introduce their kids to the birds and the bees in the **Human Biology** section, where an 8-times-life sized model of a **foetus** will put you off pregnancy forever. The **Wildlife Garden** is an oasis of serenity open from April–October, or you can impress a date (or not, depending on your coordination) by **ice-skating** next to the stunning Victorian building from November–January.

The Museum's Special Exhibitions are superb—check the website for current information. The annual **Shell Wildlife Photographer of the Year**, October–April, is utterly inspirational, while a varying daily programme of events includes **lectures, behind the scenes tours** of the botany department, and **fossil workshops** for kids.

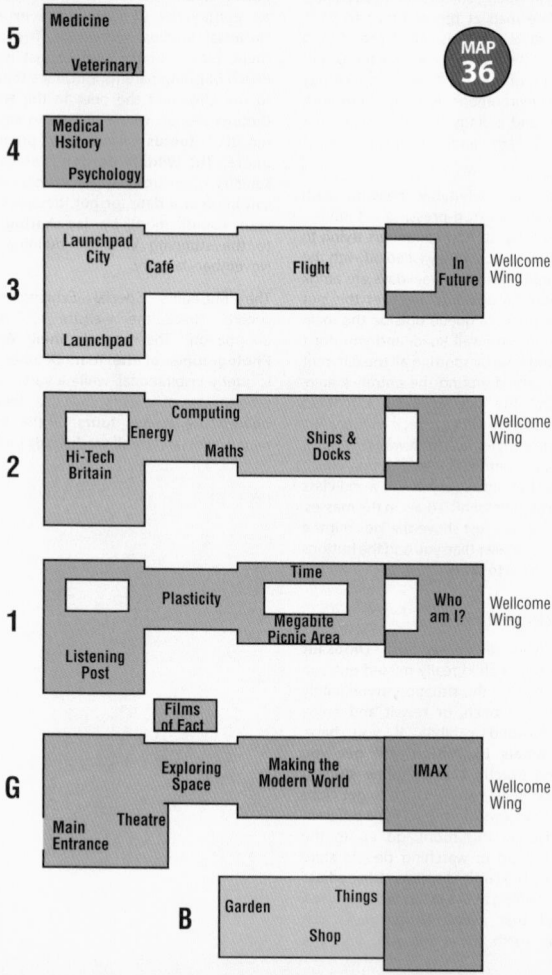
MAP 36
5
Medicine
Veterinary
4
Medical Hsitory
Psychology
3
Launchpad City
Café
Flight
In Future
Wellcome Wing
Launchpad
2
Computing
Energy
Hi-Tech Britain
Maths
Ships & Docks
Wellcome Wing
1
Time
Plasticity
Megabite Picnic Area
Who am I?
Wellcome Wing
Listening Post
Films of Fact
G
Exploring Space
Making the Modern World
IMAX
Wellcome Wing
Main Entrance
Theatre
B
Garden
Things
Shop

General Information

NFT Map:	36
Address:	Exhibition Road, South Kensington, London SW7 2DD.
Phone:	0870 870 4868
Website:	www.sciencemuseum.org.uk
Hours:	Open 10 am–6 pm every day except 24 to 26 December.
Admission:	Free, but charges apply to IMAX 3D Cinema, simulators & a few special exhibitions.

Overview

Museum and Science. Two words known to strike fear into the heart of many a child. And many a grown-up, come to that. But the Science Museum is one of the most visited museums in London. How so? Perhaps it's the heady mix of mildly erotic pistons and shafts; 60s room-sized computers and Bakelite ashtrays; special affects simulators and the mighty IMAX theatre? Or maybe it is the multitude of buttons; red and blue and green actual buttons, as well as Minority Report-style touch screens? We know they're aimed at kids, but we like. Oh and levers, did we mention levers?

The museum has its origins in the popular Great Exhibition of 1851. Prince Albert (no laughing in the back please) suggested the extra cash made by the Exhibition be used to found a number of educational establishments. Following a number of building moves and expansions the Science Museum as we know and love it opened in 1885.

The Greatest Hits

The museum's 300,000 gidgets, gadgets and gizmos attract 2.5 million visitors a minute or something, but venture above the third floor, to the **medical floors**, and you will have the place almost to yourself. The most popular area is the main drag along the ground floor which includes **Exploring Space** hung with real life space probes and other relics that look like they've come from the Doctor Who costume and props department, and **Making of the Modern World** featuring **Stephenson's Rocket**, to titillate your dormant trainspotter.

The third floor's **Launchpad** area has as many interactive displays as an 8-year-old could ever want. Parents hope their little darlings are actually learning something as they race from exhibit to exhibit whirling wheels, spinning liquids in plastic tubes and grimacing through head-sized lenses till tiredness or RSI sets in. For younger kids the tactile **Pattern Pod** on the ground floor makes up for its lack of buttons by its immensely pleasing shape.

Other smaller areas worth a once over include the **Listening Post** that samples and broadcasts words live from blogs and chatrooms – a brain bending experience. Don't even think about going in with a hangover. A huge silver hoop joins the **Energy exhibition** on the second to the ground floor. Answer a question on a nearby monitor, (don't worry they are easy) and watch your initials and age whiz around the inside of the ring. But what's that BUZZ? Like a huge electric fly killer? It's the inspired **'don't touch' display**—irresistible for the naughtiest in the class, one small electric shock later, the rest of the lemmings race over for a turn. Hilarious.

Tate Modern

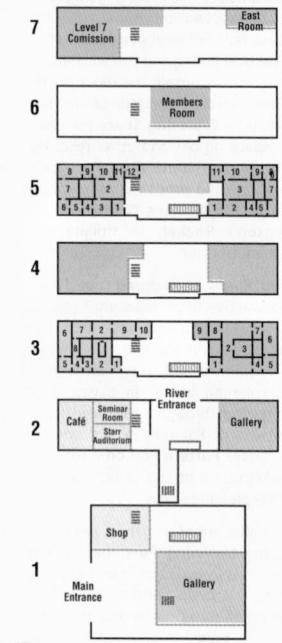

MAP 105

Level 5
- States of Flux
- Idea and Object
- Conceptual Models

Level 4
- Exhibitions

Level 3
- Poetry and Dream
- Material Gestures

Stairs
Escalators

Tate Britain

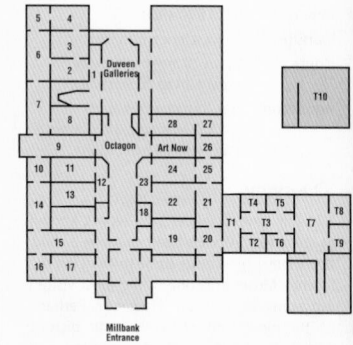

MAP 21

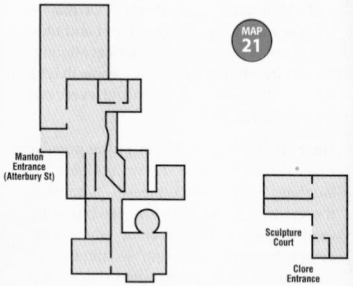

- Level 3
- Level 2
- Level 1

General Information

Tate Britain:

NFT Map:	21
Address:	London SW1P 4RG
Phone:	020 7887 8888
Website:	www.tate.org/uk
Hours:	Daily 10 am–5.50 pm; until 10 pm on the first Friday of each month for Late at Tate Britain.

Tate Modern:

NFT Map:	105
Address:	London SE1 9TG
Phone:	020 7887 8888
Hours:	Sunday–Thursday 10 am–6 pm, Friday and Saturday 10 am–10 pm. Last admission into exhibitions is 5.15 pm (Friday and Saturday 8.15 pm).

Overview

In a city renowned for its galleries and museums, London's Tate galleries shine from the banks of the Thames. The first Tate was founded in 1897 as the National Gallery of British Art, but was renamed soon afterwards after its main patron Henry Tate—he of Tate and Lyle and the sugar cube. Originally on the site of the former Milbank Prison (where Tate Britain remains), the gallery gradually expanded and divided its collection over the four sites, two in London, one in Liverpool and the last in St Ives. In London, Tate Britain houses British art dating from 1500 to the present day, while Tate Modern was created to house—yes you've guessed it—more modern work from 1900 to the present day.

The two Tates carry the same trendy Tate logo and the shops contain much of the same avant-garde merchandise with a great range of children's stuff available in both. But while the more traditional Tate Britain more closely resembles the National Gallery in architectural and artistic flavour, Tate Modern has a very hip feel and draws a slightly broader audience, in part due to its location on the increasingly buzzy South Bank.

Tate Modern

Based in the former Bankside Power Station, Tate Modern has proved to be an extremely popular attraction for tourists and Londoners alike since its opening in 2000. It houses the national collection of modern art, so expect plenty of inspirational and challenging works alongside exhibits that look like your cat sicked them up. The temporary art installations of the five-storey tall Turbine Hall provide much of the draw to the gallery. This huge space displays specially commissioned works from October to April of each year—a programme which was intended to run for only five years, but was extended due to its popularity. Quirky exhibitions fill the vast Turbine Hall, like Olafur Eliasson's 'Weather Project' which encouraged visitors to lie back on the floor in their thousands, gazing at the shadows cast by the synthetic sun. At the time of going to press we await the unveiling of Miroslaw Balka's use of the space. The son of a tombstone carver, his past works include a piece on bed-wetting, a sculpture made with live maggots, and the use of "different qualities of silence". So that's something to look forward to. But if it all seems like you could have created better art yourself, then try one of the gallery's excellent workshops or courses and give it a go.

Tate Britain

The Tate Britain boasts the most comprehensive collection of British art in the world, and is home to the annual and unmissable Turner Prize show. Stone steps lead up to the portico and once inside, the Duveen Galleries' ethereal sculptures lie straight ahead, giving the first taste of a breathtaking collection of artwork. Tate Britain's collection is divided chronologically and dedicates space exclusively to notable artists, such as Turner, Blake and Constable. The gallery also includes significant works by William Hogarth, Stanley Spencer and Francis Bacon. The restaurant and café are popular but to encourage those of us who don't have a subscription to the Tates to sign up, Tate Britain offers a members' room with a café; alluring '*special offers and designated staff*' and probably nicer toilets to those with membership cards. While lacking the hip ambience of its sister gallery down the river, Tate Britain has been attempting to trend-ify itself with 'Late at Tate Britain' between 6pm and 10pm on the first Friday of every month, which aims to lure young'uns from the pub for some after-hours art-appreciation with exhibitions, performances, music, talks and films.

Look out for the themed guides to suit your mood, such as "The I've Just Split Up", "The I'm In A Hurry" and "The I Haven't Been Here For Ages" collections: a highly endearing way ease you through the 500 years of exhibits.

General Information

NFT Map: 24
Address: Trafalgar Square
London WC2N 5DN
Phone: 020 7747 2885
Website: www.nationalgallery.co.uk
Hours: 10 am–6 pm daily,
Wednesdays until 9 pm.

Admission: Free to the permanent collection and temporary exhibitions in the Sunley Room, Room 1 and The Space on Level 2. There is a charge for temporary exhibitions held on Level 2 in the Sainsbury Wing. Tickets have an allotted time slot and although they can be purchased on the day, it is recommended you book them ahead of time online, especially with the more popular exhibitions.

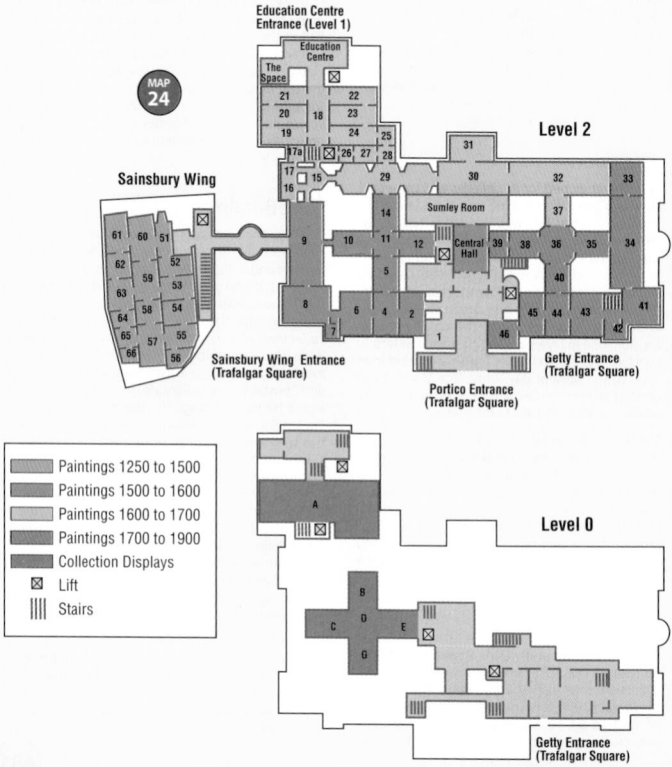

Overview

The National Gallery is home to one of the best and largest collections of Western European painting in the world, coming in at around 2100 paintings on display at any one time. An emphasis on *Western* and *painting* is needed. If you're looking for Roman antiquities or Persian miniatures, head for the British Musuem or the V&A—this is not where you're going to get it. Furthermore, if you're into anything post-Impressionist, make an about face for the Tate Britain. This is a celebration of the arts of Europe in all their old-school occidental glory. Taking the surprisingly manageable tour around the galleries (most of which are on one floor) will leave you wowed by how many works of art you will recognise. This is a collection that has been branded deep into your subconscious – with its oh-yeah-that-one Turners, Hogarths, Rembrandts and Leonardos. Bring a date and even the most culturally-challenged will be able to impress.

The collection came into being in 1824 when the House of Commons paid £57,000 for 38 paintings belonging to a banker, using his Pall Mall home as the exhibition space. Compared to the Louvre, calling a few paintings in some guy's house the National Gallery was a little too embarrassing for the British public. So the great and the good demanded the Government pull their finger out and get to work on a purpose-built gallery worthy of a national art collection. In 1832, architect William Wilkins was given the job, constructing the recognisable porticoed façade in an up-and-coming area known as Trafalgar Square, called by one trustee 'the very gangway of London'. The most recent addition to the gallery is the Sainsbury Wing, designed in 1991 by leading contemporary architects Robert Venturi and Scott Brown after much controversy. Prince Charles, notoriously fussy when it comes to architecture, dismissed one suggested design as "a monstrous carbuncle on the face of a much-loved and elegant friend".

The National Gallery can be tackled in one exhausting afternoon, if you put your mind to it. Take advantage of the fancy benches, as many of the more epic paintings are best viewed from a distance. Be sure to get lost in the many smaller galleries, which house some dynamite, lesser-known, works. If you're feeling hungry, the National Dining Rooms is a critically-acclaimed (read: expensive) restaurant, serving up the best in British fare. If you're feeling like a little culinary nationalism, the more casual National Café serves a very good cream tea.

The Greatest Hits

Starting with the Sainsbury Wing, the collection snakes around, covering European painting in chronological order from 1250 to 1900. There are a lot of paintings and it can get slightly overwhelming, so if you're pressed for time and want to make sure you've 'done' the National Gallery, start in the Sainsbury Wing. Don't miss the **Arnolfini Portrait** (signed with 'Van Eyck was here' above the mirror—hilarious), **Botticelli's Venus and Mars**, **The Wilton Diptych**, and **Uccello's The Battle of San Romano**. Moving onto the 1500-1600 range, you'll recognise **Leonardo's cartoon of The Virgin and Child with St Anne and St John the Baptist**, **'The Ambassadors'** by Hans Holbein the younger (the one where you have to crouch to see the skull), the still-hilarious portrait of **A Grotesque Old Woman** by Quinten Massys (a 1664 example of the classic conundrum—a 64 year-old trying desperately to look 16) and **Titian's Bacchus and Ariadne**. Moving on, the collection houses a rather large collection of Dutch masters, including **Rembrandt, Rubens and van Dyck**. If you're sick of 2-D, a rather cool contraption is **Samuel von Hoogstraten's peepshow**. Peer through the peep hole in this painted box for an eye-popping view of the interior of a Dutch house. Very cool. A trip to the museum is never complete without viewing a **Gainsborough, Turner and Hogarth**, all of which are housed in the 1700-1900 galleries. Do not miss Hogarth's **Marriage a la Mode** a comical rendition of an 18th century arranged marriage—in a series of six paintings. Last but not least, onto the juxtaposition of three epic 19th century history paintings depicting corporal punishment with chilling realism—**Manet's Execution of Maximillian, Delaroche's Lady Jane Gray and Puvis de Chavanne's Beheading of St John the Baptist.** What a way to end it all, quite literally.

General Information

Address:	Peninsula Square, London, SE10 0DX
Website:	www.theO2.co.uk
General Information:	020 8463 2000
Tickets:	0871 984 0002

Overview

Exactly how the Millennium Dome transformed itself from national embarrassment and vortex for millions of taxpayers' money to the slick new home of groovy events is a bit of a mystery. Or maybe it's blindingly obvious—suits are better than politicians at this kind of thing. Anyway, on the outside it looks the same—the oversized lovechild of a jellyfish and hedgehog. Inside, gone are the attractions and concepts of 1999, aimed at celebrating all things British, so visionary that visitors stayed away in droves. Instead, the contents of an above-average high street have been stuffed inside—generic bistro food and wine bars, a multi-screen cinema. Whoope-doo you might think. But hold on—people come for the music. No really, they do.

Enter the O2 Arena or its little sis, the IndigO2 (see what they did there?) and be very impressed. The Arena has been engineered to provide sight lines that older venues can only dream of. The air conditioning—usually a rarity at London gigs, actually works. The acoustics have to be heard to be believed. It might not be a destination venue for mosh-loving purists and those who like the sweat and beer to fly, but if you like your music with a bit of comfort and luxury, you know, like toilets that work and don't stink of piss (548 of them!) then the 02 is well worth a look. Wheelchair users are catered for with fully accessible facilities. London seems to have its first venue that feels like some real thought has gone into its creation. If the organisers get their act together and diversify the bands appearing, including more that veer away from mainstream bands then it could become unstoppable.

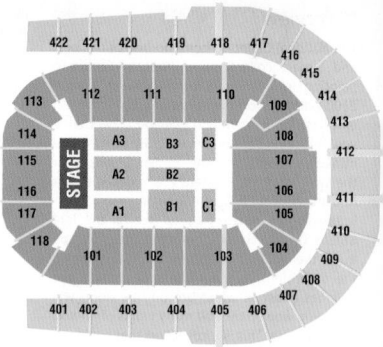

How to Get There – Driving

Driving to the O2 isn't as daft as it might sound considering its location—previously un-chartered industrial wastelands of south east London. 2,000 parking spaces can be reserved in advance. With decent road links, traveling after rush hour should be bearable. The A102 linking north and south London runs through the Blackwall Tunnel, right next to the venue.

How to Get There – Mass Transit

The O2 has excellent transport links no matter how you travel. The Jubilee Underground line stops at North Greenwich and connects directly with Waterloo and London Bridge overland stations. The Docklands Light Railway is one stop away and several bus routes drop off right outside. But the best way to arrive has to be by boat – the high speed Thames Clipper runs every 15 minutes from several piers including Greenwich, Embankment and Waterloo. It's not only relaxing, but you get to see London at its best on the trip.

How to Get Tickets

Ticketmaster. Naturally. Try Gumtree and Craigslist for swaps, unwanted tickets and scum-of-the-earth touts.

Life in London can sometimes seem like one continuous, eventful film, but if you like your plots to take place on screen then the city has a lot to offer. Going to catch a flick in London can often unravel like some kind of Indiana Jones-esque adventure—the Holy Grail being a reasonably-priced ticket in a clean, comfortable theatre, that can only be sought after battling hundreds of tourists and fellow Londoners all with the same thought. Every year 164 million people visit London's cinemas; now that's a fair few ticket stubs.Thankfully, by leaving The Twilight Zone (a.k.a. the tourist trap of the West End) there are plenty of cinematic treasures to be plundered. Whatever genre of film takes your fancy, whatever time of night and whether you want a velour seat and popcorn or a leather chair and glass of champagne, you are sure to find it in the nation's capital.

For those who are desperate to catch Spielberg's latest offering, and are crazy enough to stick it out in the West End, chain cinemas abound. You'll find **Odeon (Maps 1, 4, 23, 30, 35, 61, 66, 71, 111 & 136)**, **Vue (Maps 12, 33, 43, 66 & 80)** and **Cineworld (Maps 11, 23, 40, 43, 45, 100 & 138)** theatres all over London. If you're brave, or just fancy seeing a star or two at one of the regular premiers, **Odeon Leicester Square (Map 23)** (made up of two separate theatres) could be for you. Another monster on the square is the historic **Empire (Map 11)**, seating an impressive 1,300 patrons is a landmark in itself, although she is a slightly faded leading lady these days. Beware though. While the price of a cinema ticket in the big smoke is normally enough to make you choke on your Butterkist , wandering into any of the theatres in Leicester Square may force you to re-mortgage with prices as high as £17.50 a ticket at peak times. **Apollo West End Multiplex (Map 23)** on Lower Regent Street was formerly the home of Paramount Pictures in the UK but now houses five small, luxurious theatres showing the latest flicks on general release.

It's not hard to find cinemas offering art house and independent films in London. Finding a good one, however, can be more of a challenge. We highly recommend the **Curzon Soho (Map 11)** offering not only a wide range of cinematic gems but also a plush bar to loosen you up for that three hour Kurasawa number. Remember if the queue is snaking along the pavement, tickets can be bought at the bar downstairs too. Check out the cinema's cousin in **Mayfair (Map 9)** as well as the slightly shabby **Renoir (Map 5)** in Brunswick Square. **Cineworld Chelsea (Map 45)** on the lustrous King's Road is one of London's premier art houses with two-seaters available for the perfect smooching experience. **The Gate (Map 29)** in Notting Hill was created from a restaurant in 1911 and now offers independent releases in a luxurious setting. **BFI Southbank (Map 104)** specializes in film through the ages as well as hosting frequent events. Who would have thought old Charlie would help us save our pennies? **The Prince Charles Cinema (Map 11)** off Leicester Square sits in a perfect location and offers revivals, cult and foreign language films for as low as £1.50. Now that's a bloody bargain. For those with a penchant for 'le cine' courtesy of our French neighbours visit **Cine Lumiere (Map 36)** in South Kensington. Uber-cool Clapham has an equally trendy art house cinema, the **Clapham Picturehouse (Map 143),** Dalston's Art Deco gem the **Rio Cinema (Map 86)** is worth a look, while Bloomsbury offers up **The Horse Hospital (Map 4)**—the name's almost as avant-garde as the films they show. Just leave Dobbin behind.

There are some wonderful cinematic experiences to be had too. **BFI IMAX (Map 104)** is housed in a curious circular building, south of Waterloo Bridge, with the biggest screen in the UK—the size of five double-decker buses. Then there are those three magic words—**The Electric Cinema (Map 29)** on Portobello Road. Grab a Pinot Grigio, rest your derriere on a soft leather seat and munch away at home-made ice cream all the way from sunny Hampshire while catching the latest Polish release. We now have the first British cinema to be opened in the 21st century: **Shortwave**, in the optimistically chic Bermondsey Square, has among its 50 seats some which were shrewdly rehoused from the Electric Cinema. For those who are lured by bling, bling, bling and the power of exclusivity, get down to Soho's private member's joint**, Rex Cinema and Bar (Map 11),** where miniature hamburgers and reclining leather seats await you for a mere £250 a year.

Remember Londoners! Those on the Orange phone network get 2 for 1 on Wednesday nights—an ideal opportunity to save some precious pounds.

Cinemas	*Address*	*Phone*	*Map*
Apollo West End	19 Regent St	0871 2233 444	23
Barbican Centre Cinema	Silk St & Whitecross St	020 7382 7000	7
BFI London IMAX	Waterloo Rd & York Rd	0870 787 2525	104
BFI Southbank	Belverdere Rd	020 7928 3232	104
Chealsea Cinema	206 King's Rd	020 7351 3742	45
Cine Lumiere	17 Queensberry Pl	020 7073 1350	36
Cineworld Chelsea	279 King's Rd	0871 200 2000	45
Cineworld Fulham Road	142 Fulham Rd	0871 200 2000	43
Cineworld Hammersmith	207 King St	0871 200 2000	40
Cineworld Haymarket	63 Haymarket	0871 200 2000	23
Cineworld Shaftesbury Avenue	13 Coventry St	0871 200 2000	11
Cineworld Wandsworth	Wandsworth High St & Ram St	0871 220 8000	138
Cineworld West India Quay	11 Hertsmere Rd	0871 200 2000	100
Clapham Picturehouse	76 Venn St	020 7498 2242	143
Curzon Mayfair	38 Curzon St	0870 756 4621	9
Curzon Soho	99 Shaftesbury Ave	020 7292 1686	11
The Electric Cinema	191 Portobello Rd	020 7908 9696	29
Empire Cinemas	5 Leicester Square	0871 471 4714	11
Everyman Cinema Club	5 Hollybush Vale	08700 66 4777	56
Frontline Club	13 Norfolk Pl	020 7479 8950	31
Gate Notting Hill	87 Notting Hill Gate	020 7727 4043	29
Genesis Mile End	93 Mile End Rd	020 7780 2000	97
Greenwich Picturehouse	180 Greenwich High Rd	087 0755 0065	120
Horse Hospital	30 Colonnade	020 7833 3644	4
ICA Cinema	The Mall & Horse Guards Rd	020 7930 3647	23
Lux Salon	18 Shacklewell Ln	020 7503 3980	86
Notting Hill Coronet	103 Notting Hill Gate	020 7727 6705	29
Odeon Camden Town	14 Parkway	0871 22 44 007	71
Odeon Holloway	419 Holloway Rd	0871 22 44 007	61
Odeon Kensington	Kensington High St & Edwards Sq	0871 22 44 007	35
Odeon Leicester Square Cinema	24 Leicester Sq	0871 22 44 007	23
Odeon Marble Arch	10 Edgware Rd	0871 22 44 007	1
Odeon Panton Street	11 Panton St	0871 22 44 007	23
Odeon Putney	26 Putney High St	0871 22 44 007	136
Odeon Surrey Quays	Redriff Rd & Surrey Quays Rd	0871 22 44 007	111
Odeon Swiss Cottage	96 Finchley Rd	0871 22 44 007	66
Odeon Tottenham Court	30 Tottenham Ct Rd	0871 22 44 007	4
Odeon West End Cinema	40 Leicester Sq	0871 22 44 007	23
Odeon Whiteleys	Queensway & Porchester Gardens	0871 22 44 007	30
One Aldwych Cinema	1 Aldwych	020 7300 1000	14
Peckham Multiplex	95 Rye Ln	0870 0420 299	123
Phoenix Cinema	52 High Rd	020 8444 6789	na
Prince Charles Cinema	7 Leicester Pl	020 7494 3654	11
Renoir Cinema	1 Brunswick Sq	0871 7033 991	5
Rex Cinema and Bar	21 Rupert St	020 7287 0102	11
Rich Mix Centre	34 Bethnal Green Rd	020 7613 7490	91
Rio Cinema	107 Kingsland High St	020 7241 9410	86
Ritzy Cinema	Coldharbour Ln & Brixton Oval	020 7733 2229	150
Riverside Studios	Crisp Rd & Queen Caroline St	020 8237 1111	41
Screen on Baker Street	96 Baker St	020 7486 0036	1
Screen on the Green	83 Islington Green	020 7226 3520	80
Screen on the Hill	203 Haverstock Hill	020 7435 3366	67
Short & Sweet	91 Brick Ln	07921 822 749	91
Shortwave	10 Bermondsey Square	0207 357 6845	107
Vue Finchley Road	Finchley Rd & Blackburn Rd	08712 240 240	66
Vue Fulham	Fulham Rd & Cedarne Rd	08712 240 240	43
Vue Islington	36 Parkfield St	08712 240 240	80
Vue Shepherds Bush	Shepherds Bush Green & Rockley Rd	08712 240 240	33
Vue West End Cinema	3 Cranbourn St	08712 240 240	12

It seems that every pub, bench and bridge in London has a tale to tell of past literary greats mulling over their troubles, weeping over lovers lost or launching themselves into the Thames. Ours is a city saturated in literary history and literature-lovers, with an abundance of bookshops and diversity of readers. While so many other retailers are homogenising, our independent bookshops—with their knowledgeable staffs and their often narrow focus—remain as eclectic and enthusiastic as ever. As well as a great selection of specialist independent stores, London is also home to dozens of second-hand bookshops, book markets, a literature festival, a major international book trade fair, and Europe's largest bookshop.

General

The **Foyles** flagship store on Charing Cross Road **(Map 12)** is a London institution, with a history as eccentric as its stock. Along with mainstream books and best-sellers, it offers a good range of second hand and out-of-print books, as well as a specialist Antiquarian department and a chilled jazz café. Venerable **Hatchard's (Map 10)** has been hawking books for over 200 years, making it London's oldest bookstore. The **London Review Bookshop (Map 4)** offers a huge range of constantly updated books with an intellectual bent and intellectual staff. **Metropolitan Books (Map 6)** is small but perfectly stocked, and Phil the owner makes time for any customer seeking advice or a friendly chat. Kids can find a bookshop wonderland in **Tales on Moon Lane (Map 128)** while parents can find the books they grew up with at **Ripping Yarns (Map 51).** The excellence of the independent stores has meant the chains have had to up their game—and loath though we are to say it, some, such as **Borders (Maps 10, 12, 43 & 80)** and academic specialists **Blackwells (Maps 4, 12 & 74)** have got it very right indeed. In particular, **Waterstone's** in Piccadilly **(Map 23)** attracts all sorts of excitable superlatives, being the largest bookshop in Europe, running a range of literary activities to complement their stock, and even hosting a bar with some of the finest views of London.

Second Hand

Sadly, the world-renowned status Charing Cross Road used to command as the Mecca of second-hand bookstores is fading, and those who go looking for the genteel expertise immortalised in Helene Hanff's bestseller *84 Charing Cross Road* will find a "Med Kitchen" (shudder) at number 84. Many shops still cling to their ideals however, such as **Any Amount of Books (Map 12)** selling titles from as little £1 and offering a leather-binding service so your books can furnish your room as well as your mind. Good places to start if you are scouting for quality second-hand bookshops are: the tardis-like **The Bookshop (Map 129)** staffed by bookworms who have read *everything* (or so it seems) and can always help you find a gem; **John Sandoe (Map 46)** for true bookshop charm (rickety staircases, passionate staff, enchanting atmosphere); and the **Trinity Hospice (Map 136)** and **Oxfam Bookshops (Maps 38, 51, 86)**—not only an astonishingly cheap and broad collection of works, but all for charidee.

Specialist

Finding a bookshop devoted to your passion is like finding a club of old friends, and London caters for all tastes. Bored of cheese toasties? **Books for Cooks (Map 29)** smells as good as the recipes look, as they're tested in their kitchen first, while in-store cooking workshops teach new skills to avid customers. While Sci-Fi nerds will be in their element at **Forbidden Planet (Map 179)**. **Gekoski (Map 4)** stocks a good range of modern first editions, or for older and rarer first editions try **Henry Sotheran (Map 10)**: a unique, but pricey, treat for any enthusiast. Head to **Atlantis (Map 4)** for all your occult needs (though no doubt the Spirits had already tipped you off on that one). Arty types are extensively catered for: **The Photographers' Gallery**, a treat in itself, has a substantial shop stocking photography titles, artists' monographs and unusual cameras; the **ICA Bookshop (Map 23)** is a great destination for art and film fans, and you can take in an exhibition while you're there; **Travis & Emery (Map 24)** stocks a vast

range of music books and scores; comic geeks can get their fix at **Gosh! (Map 4)**. And for those with a passion for passion, pop along to the book section of **Coco de Mer (Map 13)**. Head to **Artwords** for books on – nope, I'll see if you can guess. Or to **Chappell** to supplement your Abba Hits keyboard book with some of their 50,000 music titles. **Motor Books**, surprisingly London's only shop dedicated to motoring, rail, aviation and military books, is the ideal repository for your menfolk when you need some peace.

Travel

Feeling lethargic? Head to one of the city's superb travel bookshops to have your energy restored. **Stanford's (Map 13)** has been inspiring London for 150 years, with its enormous collection of travel books and maps. A bookshop for travellers who like to read, **Daunt Books (Maps 2, 28, 57 & 67)** arranges all its books by geographical location, so even its fiction, cookbooks and history are shelved by country. Or to learn any of over 150 languages, head to **Grant & Cutler (Map 10),** the UK's largest foreign-language specialist.

Politics

Bookmarks (Map 4) stocks left-leaning works on a huge range of issues and takes a lively role in political activism, giving it a real and infectious sense of purpose. Also hugely right-on, both representing and driving several lefty social movements, is **Housmans (Map 78)**. Or for a more balanced approach with political works across the parties and even the odd Minister browsing for ideas, try **Westminster Bookshop (Map 22).**

Talks and events

Publishing is a cut-throat business, and many writers have to sell their soul to get noticed. For them, it means an endless round of book signings and talks; for us, it means a fabulous chance to hobnob with our favourite authors. Most bookshops host occasional signings, but for regular events from the most celebrated authors, the big boys predictably have all the clout. **Foyles (Maps 12)** and **Waterstone's (Maps 23)** attract huge names: recent guests have included JK Rowling, Louis de Bernières, Salman Rushdie and AS Byatt. **Stanford's (Map 13)** offers opportunities to hear well-known travel editors, writers and photographers for an inspirational and sometimes career-changing evening. For intellectually stimulating debates and literary discussions, check out the **London Review Bookshop (Map 4)** and **Bookmarks (Map 4)**. Some events are free, some as much as a theatre ticket, but all should be booked in advance to ensure a place.

Bookshops	*Address*	*Phone*	*Map*
Any Amount of Books	56 Charing Cross Rd	020 7836 3697	12
Artwords	65 Rivington St	020 7729 2000	84
Atlantis	49 Museum St	020 7405 2120	4
Bargain Bookshop	153 Stoke Newington High Street	020 7249 8983	85
Blackwell	119 London Road	020 7928 5378	105
Blackwell Business + Law Bookshop	243 High Holborn	020 7831 9501	14
Blackwell Medical Bookshop	St Thomas Street	020 7403 5259	106
Blackwell University Bookshop	Kings College	020 7240 9723	14
Blackwells	183 Euston Road	020 7611 2160	4
Blackwells	100 Charing Cross Rd	020 7292 5100	12
Blackwells	158 Holloway Road	020 7700 4786	74
Bookmarks	1 Bloomsbury St	020 7637 1848	4
Books etc.	255 Finchley Road	020 7433 3299	66
Books etc.	176 Fleet St	020 7353 5939	14
Books etc.	28 Broadway shopping centre	020 8764 3912	41
Books etc.	263 High Holborn	020 7404 0261	14
Books etc.	115 Buckingham Plalace Road	020 7630 6244	20
Books etc.	66 Victoria St	020 7931 0677	22
Books etc.	Southside Shopping Centre	020 8874 4597	138
Books etc.	Queensway	020 7229 3865	30
Books etc.	30 Broadgate Circle	020 7628 8944	8

Bookshops	*Address*	*Phone*	*Map*
Books etc.	Cabot Place East	020 7513 0060	100
Books etc.	45 Bank Street	020 7719 0688	100
Books etc.	54 London Wall	020 7628 9708	17
Books for Cooks	4 Blenheim Crescent	020 7221 1992	29
The Bookshop	1 Calton Ave	020 8693 2808	129
Borders	122 Charing Cross Rd	020 7379 8877	12
Borders	Parkfield Street	0207 226 3602	80
Borders	Fulham Broadway	020 7386 5451	43
Borders	203 Oxford Street	020 7292 1600	10
Chappell of Bond St	152 Wardour St	020 7432 4400	11
Coco de Mer	23 Monmouth St	020 7836 8882	13
Daunt Books	83 Marylebone High St	020 7224 2295	2
Daunt Books	193 Haverstock Hill	020 7794 4006	67
Daunt Books	51 S End Rd	020 7794 8206	57
Daunt Books	112 Holland Park Ave	020 7727 7022	28
The Dover Bookshop	18 Earlham St	020 7836 2111	12
Forbidden Planet	179 Shaftesbury Ave	020 7420 3666	12
Foyles	113 Charing Cross Rd	020 7437 5660	12
Foyles	Upper Ground	020 7437 5660	104
Foyles	Pancras Road	020 7437 5660	78
Foyles	400 Oxford Street	0800 123400 ext. 13678	3
Gosh! Comics	39 Great Russell St	020 7636 1011	4
Grant & Cutler	57 Great Marlborough Street	020 7734 2012	10
Hatchard's	187 Piccadilly	020 7439 9921	10
Henry Sotheran	2 Sackville St	020 7439 6151	10
Highgate Bookshop	9 Highgate Highstreet	020 8348 8202	na
Housmans	5 Caledonian Rd	020 7837 4473	78
ICA Bookshop	The Mall	020 7766 1452	23
John Sandoe	10 Blacklands Terrace	020 7589 9473	46
The Lion and Unicorn Bookshop	19 King Street	020 8940 0483	na
London Review Bookshop	14 Bury Pl	020 7269 9030	4
Magma	8 Earlham St	020 7240 8498	12
Metropolitan Books	49 Exmouth Market	020 7278 6900	6
Motor Books	13 Cecil Court	020 7836 5376	24
Oxfam Bookshop, Highgate	47 Highgate High St	020 8347 6704	51
Pages of Hackney	70 Lower Clapton Rd	020 8525 1452	87
The Photographers' Gallery	Great Newport St	020 7831 1772	13
R. A. Gekoski	15 Bloomsbury Square	020 7404 6676	4
Ripping Yarns	355 Archway Rd	020 8341 6111	51
Southbank Book Market	Under Waterloo Bridge	0871 663 2501	104
Stanford's	Long Acre	020 7836 1321	13
Stoke Newington Bookshop	159 Stoke Newington High Street	020 7249 2808	85
Tales on Moon Lane	25 Half Moon Ln	020 7274 5759	128
Travis & Emery	17 Cecil Ct	020 7240 2129	24
Trinity Hospice Bookshop	206 Upper Richmond Rd	020 8780 0737	136
Waterstone's	Trafalgar Square	020 7839 4411	24
Waterstone's	206 Piccadilly	020 7851 2400	23
Waterstone's	9 Garrick St	020 7836 6757	13
Waterstone's	19 Oxford St	020 7434 9759	3
Waterstone's	Ludgate Circus	020 7236 5858	15
Waterstone's	421 Oxford St	020 7495 8507	2
Waterstone's	82 Gower St	020 7636 1577	4
Waterstone's	87 Brompton Rd	020 7730 1234	37
Waterstone's	151 King's Rd	020 7351 2023	45
Waterstone's	Exhibition Rd	020 7942 4481	36
Waterstone's	1 Whittington Ave	020 7220 7882	18
Waterstone's	Spencer Street	020 7608 0706	6
Waterstone's	128 Camden High Street	020 7284 4948	78
Waterstone's Economists' Bookshop	Clare Market	020 7405 5531	14
Westminster Bookshop	8 Artillery Row	020 7802 0018	22

Yep you've heard the news. Theatre in the capital is all commercial. Predictable. Repetitive. Uncontroversial. If you believe the whingers, it's all fucking boring stuff. Don't, because it's not. Yes, the West End, that heartland of commercial theatre around Shaftesbury Avenue, is filled with tourist-grabbing, crowd-pleasing musicals. Yes, there are more star-dominated, tried-and-tested plays than ever. Yes, the Mousetrap is still taking up the space at St Martin's after 54 years of we-bloody-well-know-whodunit.

But all that's only half the story. To find the other half, look beyond the glittering billboard signs to find the daring, small West End theatres, such as the **Donmar Warehouse (Map 13)**, bringing the innovative and unusual to Theatreland. There are the Off-West End theatres that proudly fly the flag for new writers, unafraid of being political, controversial and in-yer-face: **The Royal Court (Map 19)**, **The Soho (Map 11)**, **The Bush (Map 33)**. There are the unconventional, anarchic ensemble companies, such as PunchDrunk, shaking up things all the way from the fringe to the West End, while innovative short-play evenings are popping up at pubs across the city (see below).

But let's not forget the cracking double-whammy of the **National Theatre (Map 104)** and **The Old Vic (Map 104)**, two artistic powerhouses currently going from strength to strength. At the National, the unstoppable Nicholas Hytner brings original works to this Southbank concrete colossus (coupled with a £10-tickets offer), while down the road, Hollywood-star-turned-theatre-connoisseur Kevin Spacey is returning the Old Vic into its former glory. The refurbished **Young Vic (Map 104)**, meanwhile, is one of the best places to see fresh, new theatre (and get drunk afterwards). And, whatever you do, you're never far from a good Shakespeare production.

The (Real) West End

The Donmar Warehouse (Map 13), the West End's smallest theatre, has gained a reputation for being one of Theatreland's most innovative, yet still crowd-pleasing houses (Jude Law as Hamlet, anyone?). It's quite common for good new plays that have successfully kicked off at a fringe or Off-West End venue to transfer to the West End, such as Tom Stoppard's guitars-meet-politics cracker Rock'n'Roll The West End is also a great place to catch up on those classics you always wanted to see but never got round to: from Beckett to Shakespeare. If the thought of being in a theatre at all is too bourgeois for you, then you're still well catered for. London thesps it up wherever it can so you're never too far from a performance and its sometimes unwitting audience. Recent outings have included an opera about domesticity and flatpack furniture in the Wembley Ikea, a play about clashing cultures as the audience are led around the Whitechapel Gallery, and a thriller performed in an office while the audience watch with binoculars and audiophones from the terrace opposite. Or if it's sunny, squeeze among the crowds and their bottles of rosé for the occasional performances at The Scoop.

Off-West End & The Fringe – The Best

The underground-led, breakneck guerrilla heyday might be over, but theatre outside the West End is in rude health. Head to rough-around-the-edges Dalston, where the **Arcola Theatre (Map 86)** continues to thrive in its scruffy ex-factory home, thanks to eclectic programming, an early-fringe-days feel and heaps of creative energy. The tiny **Bush Theatre (Map 33)** has long been a fierce champion of new work, and after being rescued by a star-studded tantrum in the face of funding cuts in 2008 it will doubtless continue to discover exciting new talent. So will **Dean Street's Soho Theatre (Map 11)** and the **Royal Court (Map 19)** on Sloane Square, which remain two of London's finest. For new, innovative work, also keep your eyes on the **Battersea Arts Centre (Map 140)**, to watch what others will pay £50 to see next year (such as its premiere of Jerry Springer The Opera while other theatres nervously wrung their hands).

Theatre can't change society? Try telling that to the conviction-led crew of Kilburn's **The Tricycle (Map 65)**—easily London's most radical and most dedicated, political theatre. Islington's **Almeida (Map 80)** is far more conventional, but

pretty—and that's got to count for something. If you're up for a laugh, check **The Hackney Empire (Map 87)**, a turn-of-the-century music hall, hosting some of London's best variety shows. **The Old Red Lion (Map 80)**, home inside an Islington pub, stubbornly clings to its unconventional, ale-fuelled fringe attitude, while **Battersea's Theatre 503 (Map 132)** is as provocative as ever. Be surprised.

Tickets

If you know what you're after, check the theatre's website—they will either have their own system, a link to a ticket selling site, or provide a phone number. If not, check www.officiallondontheatre.co.uk, which lists shows by name, theatre and genre. The site also displays shows that are just opening, or just closing, and links straight to the appropriate ticketing website, once you have made your mind up. There's a handy map of all West End venues, too.

Fancy a bargain? The iconic TKTS ticket booth on Leicester Square sells on-the-day tickets for most big shows, half-price. The queue can be mind-boggling, so go early. There's a £2.50 booking fee, but it's included in the price shown. Many theatres also have their own discount schemes. If you don't mind standing, you can get Royal Court tickets for as little as 50p. Yes, that's 50p. Just show up between 6 pm and 6.30 pm on the day of the performance. The National has £5 standing tickets for all shows, but the view ain't always great.

Exciting & New

Enter the ensemble. They are multi-skilled, imaginative and are shaking the cosy, venue-obsessed Theatreland with a vengeance. Ensemble companies like PunchDrunk and Kneehigh are touring their way through London's venues in vigorously anarchic fashion. The result is increasingly physical, increasingly unconventional—and increasingly exciting theatre, which you'd be mad to miss.

PunchDrunk (www.punchdrunk.org.uk) have gained a reputation for site-specific productions, inviting the audience to walk around and follow actors and themes as they please. Their 2006 treatment of Goethe's Faust at the National Theatre was widely hailed as one of the best things to have happened to British theatre in years. Kneehigh (www.kneehigh.co.uk) enjoy setting their nightmarish productions in outside mystical locations, but aren't afraid of West End constraints either. The award-winning Cheek by Jowl (www.cheekbyjowl.com), which have been producing Shakespeare and European classics since 1982, keep discovering hot talent—and ways to innovate.

If that's not grassroots enough, visit one of the themed short-play evenings that are popping up across town. Bringing together writers, actors and directors for twenty-minutes-or-so mini-shows, they have become a popular theatre alternative. Take your pick: Established organisers Nabokov (www.nabokov-online.com) have found a West End home at the **Trafalgar Studios (Map 24)**, SourFeast (www.sourfeast.co.uk) are based at **Brixton's Dogstar Pub (Map 150)**, and relative newcomers DryWrite have made Whitechapel's **The George Tavern (Map 97)** their own. The message is spreading. What you thought was a boozer, really is a stage. The possibilities are endless.

Contemporary Dance

From small company shows to big stage spectacles, contemporary dance is having one hell of a ride. **Sadlers Wells (Map 6)** (www.sadlerswells.com), the grand old lady of dance venues, is still doing a fine job bringing some of the world's best dance to London. Check their Sadler's Wells Sampled programme, showcasing dazzling future talent for as little as £10. **The Barbican (Map 7)** (www.barbican.org.uk) has established itself as a reliable source of powerful dance performances, while the **Royal Festival Hall (Map 104)** attracts increasingly bold and interesting works to its refurbished riverside location. For London's most innovative dance performances, check **The Place (Map 4)**, a stylish venue that combines performance, training and dance education (www.theplace.org.uk).

Theatres	*Address*	*Phone*	*Type*	*Map*
Adelphi Theatre	The Strand	0870 403 0303	West End	24
Aldwych Theatre	49 Aldwych	0870 4000 805	West End	14
Almeida Theatre	Almeida St	020 7359 4404	Fringe	80
Ambassadors Theatre	West St	020 7369 1761	West End	12
Apollo Theatre	Shaftesbury Ave	020 7494 5070	West End	11
Apollo Victoria Theatre	17 Wilton Rd	0870 4000 751	West End	20
Arcola Theatre	27 Arcola St	020 7503 1646	Fringe	86
Arts Theatre	Great Newport St	0870 060 1742	West End	12
The Astoria	157 Charing Cross Rd	020 7434 9592	Performing Arts	12
Barbican Centre	Silk St	020 7638 4141	Performing Arts	7
Barons Court Theatre	28 Comeragh Rd	020 8932 4747	Fringe	42
Battersea Arts Centre	Lavender Hill & Theatre St	020 7223 2223	Fringe	140
Bloomsbury Theatre	15 Gordon St	020 7388 8822	Fringe	4
Brixton Academy	211 Stockwell Rd	020 7771 3000	Performing Arts	145
Bush Theatre	2 Shepherd's Bush Rd	020 7610 4224	Fringe	33
Cadogan Hall	5 Sloane Terrace	020 7730 4500	Performing Arts	19
Cambridge Theatre	Earlham St	0844 412 4652	West End	13
Chats Palace Arts Centre	42 Brooksbys Walk	020 8533 0227	Performing Arts	90
Cinema on the Haymarket	65 Haymarket	0871 230 1562	West End	23
Comedy Theatre	Panton St	0870 060 6637	West End	23
Criterion Theatre	Piccadilly Circus	020 7413 1437	West End	10
The Dogstar	389 Coldharbour Ln	020 7733 7515	Fringe	150
Dominion Theatre	Tottenham Court Rd	0870 169 0116	West End	4
Donmar Warehouse Theatre	41 Earlham St	0870 060 6624	West End	13
Drill Hall	16 Chenies St	020 7307 5060	Fringe	4
Duchess Theatre	Catherine St	020 7494 5075	West End	14
Duke of York's Theatre	St Martin's Ln	0870 060 6623	West End	24
Etcetera	265 Camden High St	020 7482 4857	Fringe	71
Fortune Theatre	Russell St	0870 060 6626	West End	13
The Forum	Highgate Rd	020 7428 4099	Performing Arts	72
Garrick Theatre	Charing Cross Rd	0870 890 1104	West End	24
Gate Theatre	11 Pembridge Rd	020 7229 0706	Fringe	29
The George Tavern	373 Commercial Rd	020 7790 1763	Fringe	97
Gielgud Theatre	Shaftesbury Ave	020 7494 5065	West End	11
Greenwich Theatre	Crooms Hill & Nevada St	020 8858 7755	Fringe	120
Hackney Empire	291 Mare St	020 8985 2424	Fringe	87
Hampstead Theatre	Eton Ave	020 7722 9301	Fringe	66
Haymarket Theatre	Haymarket	020 7930 8800	West End	23
Her Majesty's Theatre	Haymarket	0844 412 2707	West End	23
Indigo2	Millenium Way	020 8463 2000	Performing Arts	na
Jermyn Street Theatre	16 Jermyn St	020 7287 2875	Fringe	23
King's Head Theatre Pub	115 Upper St	020 7226 1916	Fringe	80
Koko	1 Camden High St	0870 4325 527	Performing Arts	71
Leicester Square Theatre	5 Leicester Pl	0870 899 3335	West End	11
London Apollo Hammersmith Theatre	Queen Caroline St	0870 606 3400	West End	41
London Palladium	Argyll St	020 7494 5020	West End	10
Lyceum Theatre	Wellington St	0870 243 9000	West End	14
Lyric Theatre	29 Shaftesbury Ave	020 7494 5045	West End	11
National Theatre	South Bank	020 7452 3400	West End	104
New London Theatre	Drury Ln	0870 890 0141	West End	13
Noël Coward Theatre	St Martin's Ln	0870 060 6621	West End	24
Novello Theatre	Aldwych	0870 950 0940	West End	14

Theatres	*Address*	*Phone*	*Type*	*Map*
Old Red Lion	418 St John St	020 7837 7816	Fringe	80
Old Vic Theatre	103 The Cut	0870 060 6628	West End	104
Palace Theatre	Shaftesbury Ave	0870 890 0142	West End	12
Phoenix Theatre	Charing Cross Rd	0870 060 6629	West End	12
Piccadilly Theatre	16 Denman St	0870 060 0123	West End	10
The Place	17 Duke's Rd	020 7121 1000	Performing Arts	4
Playhouse Theatre	Northumberland Ave	0870 060 6631	West End	24
Prince Edward Theatre	28 Old Compton St	020 7447 5400	West End	12
Prince of Wales Theatre	Coventry St	020 7839 5972	West End	11
Queen Elizabeth Hall	South Bank Centre	08703 800 400	Performing Arts	104
Queens Theatre	Shaftesbury Ave	0870 950 0930	West End	11
Riverside Studios	Crisp Rd & Queen Caroline St	020 8237 1111	Fringe	41
Ronnie Scotts	47 Frith St	020 7439 0747	Performing Arts	12
The Roundhouse	Chalk Farm Rd	0844 482 8008	Performing Arts	71
Royal Albert Hall	Kensington Gore	020 7589 8212	Performing Arts	36
Royal Court Theatre	Sloane Sq	020 7565 5000	West End	19
Royal Festival Hall	Belvedere Rd	087 1663 2500	Performing Arts	104
Royal Opera House	Bow St	020 73044000	Performing Arts	13
Sadler's Wells	Rosebery Ave	0844 412 4300	Performing Arts	6
Savoy Theatre	The Strand	0870 164 8787	West End	24
Scala	275 Pentonville Rd	020 7833 2022	Performing Arts	78
The Scoop	The Queen's Walk	020 7403 4866	Performing Arts	107
Shaftesbury Theatre	210 Shaftesbury Ave	020 7379 5399	West End	12
Shakespeare's Globe	21 New Globe Walk	020 7902 1400	West End	105
Shepherds Bush Empire	56 Shepherd's Bush Green	0870 771 2000	Performing Arts	33
Soho Theatre	21 Dean St	0870 429 6883	Fringe	11
The Space	269 Westferry Rd	020 7515 7799	Fringe, Performing Arts	na
St John's	Smith Square	020 7222 1061	Performing Arts	22
St Martin's Theatre	West St	020 7836 1443	West End	12
Sutton House	2 Homerton High St	020 8986 2264	Performing Arts	87
Theatre 503	503 Battersea Park Rd	020 7978 7040	Fringe	132
Theatre Royal Drury Lane	Catherine St	0870 890 6002	West End	13
Toynebee Studios	28 Commercial St	020 7650 2350	Fringe	91
Trafalgar Studios	14 Whitehall	020 7369 1735	West End	24
Tricycle Theatre	259 Kilburn High Rd	020 7372 6611	Fringe	65
Vaudeville Theatre	404 Strand	0870 890 0511	West End	24
Victoria Palace Theatre	Victoria St	020 7834 1317	West End	22
Wembley Stadium	Wembley Hill Rd	0844 980 8001	Performing Arts	na
Wigmore Hall	36 Wigmore St	020 7258 8240	Performing Arts	2
Wilton's Music Hall	Graces Alley & Ensign St	020 7702 2789	Fringe	95
Wyndham's Theatre	Charing Cross Rd	0870 950 0925	West End	12
Young Vic Theatre	66 The Cut	020 7922 2922	West End	104

There are many great things about London's vibrant art world. The best? It's free. Granted, if you want to see some of the big show-stopping exhibitions that pass through the **Tates (Maps 21 & 105)**, **British Museum (Map 4)**, **National Gallery (Map 23)** and **Royal Academy (Map 2)** you'll have to pay quite a hefty sum, but overall, you can experience visual arts throughout the capital without coughing up much dough. This might be a contributing factor to London's sprawling art scene, as it is so easy to duck in and out of the capital's 300+ museums and galleries on a lunch break.

Of course, there are concentrations of art in locations around Piccadilly and Bond Street (check out Cork Street for its galleries, such as **Messum (Map 10)** and the **Adam Gallery (Map 10)**, running parallel with Savile Row), the East End (funkier affair and an artistic hipster breeding ground—check out Vyner Street in Bethnal Green), South Kensington/Chelsea (a major culture scene as a result of the Great Exhibition of 1851—and not much has changed) and various institutions dotted along the Thames (as seen from the Tate to Tate boat service). But great art is all over the this city, so get out your Oyster Card, and get ready to cover a lot of ground.

Starting with London's modern art, the **Tate Modern (Map 105)**, with its massive smoke stack, has become a major London landmark. This is despite it only existing as a separate entity from the **Tate Britain (Map 21)** since 2000. Check out its spacious turbine hall, with often spectacular installations.

It's not surprising that the Tate Modern is often the London tourist's first stop these days, as the city has become well-known for contemporary art. Due in part to the too-cool-for-school London art scene of the 1990s, which saw the establishment of Turner Prizers Tracy Emin, Rachel Whiteread and Damien Hirst, and made a major mark under Saatchi's guiding light. This light has faded somewhat, as the movement's personalities have slowly sold out a little (Emin designing for Longchamp is a case and point). But certain London galleries remain as monuments to this explosion of counter-culture, and, in addition to the **Saatchi Gallery (Map 19)**, these include the **Serpentine Gallery (Map 30)**, **Haunch of Venison (Map 2)**, and **Victoria Miro (Map 31)**. Other inspiring alternatives include the **Riflemaker (Map 10)**, **South London Gallery (Map 122)**, **Camden Arts Centre (Map 66)**, the **White Cube** at **Mason's Yard (Map 23)** and **Hoxton Square (Map 84)**.

London is a city with a lot on offer, and if you're looking for something a bit more traditional, start with the **National Gallery (Map 23)** in Trafalgar Square, moving onto the **National Portrait Gallery (Map 24)** next door, which presents you with a who's who of British culture past and present. Stroll up Charing Cross Road to the awesome **British Museum (Map 4)** with its jaw-dropping two acre roof over the Great Court (yet another example of Norman Foster's obsession with glass and geometry). Be sure to take in the Parthenon Marbles, aka Elgin Marbles, before the Greek government makes any attempt to get them back. Then over to the not-nearly-praised-enough **Wallace Collection (Map 2)** behind Selfridge's for some tea and Watteau action. A traditional art-lover's tour of London is not over without a trip to the **Royal Academy (Map 2)** with its epic exhibitions and finally to the **Tate Britain (Map 21)**, where the Pre-Raphaelites reign supreme.

Feeling a little non-conformist? London has a brilliant array of cultural institutions that offer more than just marble and canvas. From ceramics to dolls houses, kimonos to plaster casts of just about every great sculpture in the world—the V&A has it all (not to mention an awesome gift shop). Other alternatives to the mainstream include **The Photographers' Gallery (Map 13)** by Leicester Square, which not only squeezes in the best photographic exhibitions in town, but also boasts the best bookshop on the subject. Odd in its own way is the **Museum of London (Map 7)**, which walks you through the history of the city from prehistoric times to the present day. Recent London museum gems also include the newly renovated **London Transport Museum (Map 24)**, **Fashion and Textile Museum (Map 107)**, **Museum of Brands**, **Packaging and Advertising (Map 29)** and the **Design Museum**

(Map 107), with cars and video games in case you're stuck entertaining your nephew. The Horniman (*snigger*) Museum is a legacy of Victorian curiosity, starring an overstuffed walrus whose taxidermist didn't realise that walruses are supposed to have wrinkles.

A lot of the capital's best museum and gallery treasures are off the beaten path and may even require a trip in a bendy bus (gasp!). **The Geffreye Museum (Map 88)** is a good one to check out when you're in Shoreditch and tired of being hip. Just up Kingsland Road from **Flowers East (Map 91)** (a good British contemporary art gallery), this museum of domestic interiors runs through the history of Britain one living room at a time. Somewhat forgotten are the weird and wonderful **Sir John Soane's Museum (Map 14)**, **Leighton House (Map 35)** and **Dennis Severs' House (Map 91)**—but we'll let you discover these gems for yourself.

So forget Pret a Manger—feed your soul in one of London's many museums and galleries. They certainly have more to offer than one of those crappy no bread sandwiches, anyway.

Museums & Galleries	*Address*	*Phone*	*Map*
2 Willow Road	2 Willow Road	020 7435 6166	56
Apsley House	Hyde Park Corner	020 7499 5676	9
Arsenal Museum and Stadium Tour	Drayton Park	020 7704 4504	74
Bank of England Museum	Threadneedle Street	020 7601 5491	17
The Banqueting House	Whitehall	0844 482 7777	24
Benjamin Franklin House	36 Craven St	020 7930 6601	24
Bramah Tea & Coffee Museum	40 Southwark Street	020 7403 5650	106
Britain At War Experience	66 Tooley Street	020 7403 3171	107
The British Library	96 Euston Rd	020 7412 7353	78
The British Museum	Great Russell St	020 7323 8000	4
Brunel Museum	Railway Ave	020 7231 3840	110
Brunswick House	30 Wandsworth Rd	020 7394 2100	134
Cartoon Museum	35 Little Russell St	020 7580 8155	4
Chelsea FC Museum and Stadium Tour	Stamford Bridge	087 1984 1955	43
Chelsea Physic Garden	66 Royal Hospital Rd	020 7352 5646	45
Chiswick House	Burlington Lane	020 8995 0508	38
Churchill Museum and Cabinet War Rooms	King Charles Street	020 7930 6961	24
Clink Prison Museum	1 Clink St	020 7378 1558	106
Clockmakers' Museum	Aldermanbury	020 7332 1868	16
Cuming Museum	151 Walworth Rd	020 7525 2332	113
Dennis Severs' House	18 Folgate St	020 7247 4013	91
Design Museum	28 Butlers Wharf	087 0833 9955	107
The Dickens House Museum	48 Doughty St	020 7405 2127	5
Dr Johnson's House	17 Gough Square	020 7353 3745	15
Fan Museum	12 Croom's Hill	020 8305 1441	120
Fashion and Textile Museum	83 Bermondsey St	020 7407 8664	107
Florence Nightingale Museum	2 Lambeth Palace Rd	020 7620 0374	131
Foundling Museum	40 Brunswick Square	020 7841 3600	5
Freud Museum	20 Maresfield Gardens	020 7435 2002	66
Geffrye Museum	136 Kingsland Rd	020 7739 9893	88
Grant Museum of Zoology	Gower Street	020 7679 2647	4
Guards Museum	Birdcage Walk	020 7414 3271	22
Hampstead Museum	New End Square	020 7431 0144	56
Handel House Museum	23 Brook St	020 7495 1685	2
Hayward Gallery	Belvedere Rd	0871 663 2501	
Horniman Museum & Gardens	100 London Rd	020 8699 1872	na
Hunterian Museum	35 Lincoln's Inn Fields	020 7869 6560	14
Imperial War Museum	Austral St	020 7416 5294	112

Museums & Galleries	*Address*	*Phone*	*Map*
Jewish Museum	129 Albert St	020 7284 1997	71
Kinetica	61 Brushfield St	020 7392 9674	18
King's Place Gallery	90 York Way	020 7520 1485	79
Kirkaldy Testing Museum	99 Southwark St	01322 332195	105
Leighton House	18 Stafford Terrace	020 7602 3316	35
The Library and Museum of Freemasonry	60 Great Queen St	020 7395 9257	13
London Canal Museum	12 New Wharf Rd	020 7713 0836	79
London Dungeon	29 Tooley St	020 7403 7221	106
London Fire Brigade Museum	94 Southwark Bridge Rd	020 7587 2894	106
London Sewing Machine Museum	293 Balham High Rd	020 8767 4724	151
London Transport Museum	Covent Garden Piazza	020 7379 6344	24
Marylebone Cricket Club Museum	St John's Wood Rd	020 7289 1611	76
Museum in Docklands	Hertsmere Road	087 0444 3857	100
Museum of Brands, Packaging and Advertising	2 Colville Mews	020 7908 0880	29
Museum Of Childhood	Cambridge Heath Road	020 8983 5200	92
Museum of Fulham Palace	Bishops Avenue	020 7736 3233	48
Museum of Garden History	Lambeth Palace Road	020 7401 8865	131
Museum of Immigration and Diversity	19 Princelet St	020 7247 5352	91
Museum of London	150 London Wall	087 0444 3851	7
Museum of Methodism & Wesley's Chapel	49 City Rd	020 7253 2262	7
Museum of the Order of St John	26 St John's Ln	020 7324 4005	15
Museum of the Royal Pharmaceutical Society	1 Lambeth High St	020 7572 2210	131
National Army Museum	Royal Hospital Road,	020 7730 0717	46
National Maritime Museum	Park Row	020 8312 6565	na
Natural History Museum	Cromwell Rd	020 7942 5685	36
The Old Operating Theatre, Museum & Herb Garret Venue	9 St Thomas St	020 7188 2679	106
Petrie Museum of Egyptian Archaeology	Gower St	020 7679 2884	4
Pollock's Toy Museum	1 Scala St	020 7636 3452	3
Ragged School Museum	45 Copperfield Rd	020 8980 6405.	98
Rootstein Hopkins Parade Ground	16 John Islip St		21
Royal Academy of Music Museum	Marylebone Rd	020 7873 7373	2
Saatchi Gallery	King's Road	020 7823 2332	46
Science Museum	Exhibition Rd	087 0870 4868	36
Sherlock Holmes Museum	221 Baker St	020 7935 8866	76
Sikorski Museum	20 Princes Gate	020 7589 9249	37
Sir John Soane's Museum	13 Lincoln's Inn Fields	020 7440 4263	14
Smythson Stationery Museum	New Bond St	020 7629 8558	10
Spencer House	27 St James's Pl	020 7499 8620	23
St Bartholomew's Hospital Museum	West Smithfield	020 7601 8033	15
Tate Britain	Millbank	020 7887 8888	21
Tate Modern	Bankside	020 7887 8888	105
Tower Bridge Exhibition	Tower Bridge	020 7940 3985	107
Victoria & Albert Museum	Cromwell Rd	020 7942 2000	37
Wallace Collection	Manchester Square	020 7563 9551	2
Westminster Abbey	Parliament Square	020 7222 5152	22

Overview

Where on this crumbling, recession-diseased planet can you still quaff bitter next to a stuffed horse and carriage, or gorge on tapas to wild flamenco at 4 in the morning? Okay, probably a few places, but London remains a capital of capriciousness. Traditional thinking has Soho and the Shoreditch/Hoxton axis as the epicenters of the night, but the exciting truth is that greatness and weirdness is breeding out with these borders. Soho refuses to grow up, with manic clubs and seedy pubs laughing in the face of change, but SoHo is slowly becoming the weekend playground of out-of-towners and tasteless trendy cash-ins. A walk down Brick Lane on a Saturday night is more likely to be interrupted with hen nights than illegal ravers. So where is everyone going? The trendos have creeped up Kingsland Road to Dalston, Hackney and Bethnal Green, the crusties have taken up position in ragged parts of Manor House, Camden and Brixton while the poshos have fortified West London with cocktails. Yes, options are endlessly varied but so are tastes: One Londoner's Camden Town is another Londoner's Brick Lane is another Londoner's Tooting. As far as we're concerned, it's all in the mix. The economy may have crashed around us but to paraphrase Thurston Moore: 'All I know is that we've got no money but that's got nothing to do with a good time!' Amen, sister.

Local Pubs For Local People

Let's start with the traditional. We like getting pissed, or lost, and usually both, in **Ye Olde Cheshire Cheese (Map 15)**, a dark Victorian Dickens was fond of. Borough's **George Inn (Map 106)**, with a dazzling selection of ales, is as ancient as they get, and the clocks stopped ticking a long, long time ago at the **Nag's Head (Map 19)**, where mobile phones are forbidden. We love philosophising with Bloomsbury's grey literary types at **The Lamb (Map 14)** just as much as drinking up and down the Sam Smith range at Holborn's Grade-II-listed **Princess Louise (Map 4)**. In Hampstead, it's the pretty, and pretty hidden, **Holly Bush (Map 56)**. And we still like **The Carpenter's Arms (Map 39)**, even though it's no longer run by the Kray twins' mum. Modern rot has yet to set in at Highgate's old-school **The Winchester (Map 52)**, nor Angel's bastion of oldeness **The Compton Arms (Map 80)**. The old-timers in Rotherhithe's dream-of-your-dad **The Mayflower (Map 109)**, and Brixton's **The Effra (Map 150)** will be thoroughly confused by Facebook, Twitter, computers and other ills of modern life.

Keep it Real Ale

For seasoned ale-lovers, or ale-snobs depending on which side of the ale fence you reside, many corners of London are brimming with choice. Borough's **Market Porter (Map 106)** has a great selection, and is full of market traders counting their cash. **The Dove (Map 89)** is best for Belgian, **Quinn's (Map 71)** for German beers. Too fancy? For great ale selections, there's **The Royal Oak (Map 106)** also in Borough, where the taps come courtesy of the Harveys brewery, or the **Wenlock Arms (Map 83)**, where the frequently changing line-up is so good we can't bloody decide which ale to go for, usually. Pitfield, Freedom and St Peter's, meanwhile, supply Islington's **Duke of Cambridge (Map 83)** with organic beer, if you like that kind of stuff. We definitely like Guinness and there's no better place for drinking it than Stoke Newington's tiny **Auld Shillelagh (Map 64)**.

Good Mixers

London got into mixing in recent years—and big time, with new cocktail bars constantly popping up across the city. Hit **Loungelover (Map 91)** for the kitschiest deco, or **Green and Red (Map 10)** for the best tequila. Martinis? You'll find us at the **Charlotte Street Hotel (Map 3)**. At **5th View (Map 9)**, your Kir Royal comes with amazing views OF Big Ben, while the NYC-style **Milk & Honey (Map 10)** comes with eight handy house rules, including "no star fucking". We like Soho's **22 Below (Map 10)** for its down-to-earth attitude, and the plush art deco heaven that is **Claridge's Bar (Map 2)** for the opposite. **Dusk (Map 141)** serves Battersea, **Montgomery Place (Map 29)** Notting Hill, and both do so extremely well. We would also love to praise **The Cinnamon Club (Map 22)**, inside the Old Westminster Library. If only we could find it.

Weirdos

Let's face it, sometimes the booze just isn't enough to keep you entertained. Destroying your internal organs with the stuff is just sometimes a little boring, right? Well just walk past the New Cross Inn and head to the **Montague Arms (Map 125)** for some pirate-themed taxidermy action. **The Foundry (Map 84)** is pretty weird with an outsider art chic, and **Public Life (Map 91)**, a refurbished toilet, is literally a shithole. **Stoke Newington International Airport (Map 85)** is an artist-run warehouse space and not an actual airport. **The Windmill (Map 150)** of Brixton is a handmade weirdo magnet and **The Battersea Barge (Map 134)** is a friendly old pub. On a very thin barge. **The Coronet (Map 74)** in Holloway has a desolate, nostalgic charm as does perhaps the weirdest pub of them all, the **Palm Tree (Map 93)**, a celebration of British antiquity with crooners of a certain age most nights.

Smoker-Friendly

If the merciless prohibition regime of 2007 hasn't resulted in reluctant surrender, don't despair: from provisionally erected patios to all-year beer gardens to secret backdoors, London's ban-bashing creativity knows no boundaries. Great fag spots include the terrace of **At Proud (Map 71)**, overlooking Camden's roofs, the barbeque-and-beer-can courtyard of **93 Feet East (Map 91)** and the tree-shaded garden of the **Edinboro Castle (Map 77)**. Hang out in front of Highgate favourite **The Flask (Map 51)** or combine a late-night pint with a rollie in the backyard of the **The Dolphin (Map 89)**. For clubbing, consider **Egg (Map 79)**, where you're allowed to smoke in the massive garden. **The Owl & Pussycat (Map 91)** is not just a surprisingly pleasant pub in Shoreditch, it's also got a surprisingly nice garden, where smoking is not just allowed, dear friends, but encouraged.

We're Raving We're Raving

The End may have reached, well, the end, but grandaddy **Fabric (Map 77)** is going strong in the Farringdon club complex. We prefer the slightly more off-beat, mid-sized variety: groovy **Guanabara (Map 13)**, frequently fun **Plastic People (Map 84)**, swanky **Images (Map 92)**. The ever-so-eclectic **Notting Hill Arts Club (Map 29)** continues to come up with good nights, as does Brick Lane's **93 Feet East (Map 91)**. For indie moves we trust **Metro (Map 3)**, but much prefer the madness at Shoreditch's **On the Rocks (Map 91)**. **Madame Jojo's (Map 11)** provides exactly the kind of decadence we demand from Soho clubbing, while Piccadilly's **Pigalle Club (Map 10)** swoops us back to the 40s. As long as lip fuzz is stilll trendy there's always the **Moustache Bar (Map 086)**. in Coolest Place In Britain (copywrite The Guardian)For serious rockabilly, find **Ye Olde Axe (Map 91)** gentlemen's club on Hackney Road, where the rock'n'roll starts as soon as the last naked girl has disappeared behind the big-mirrored wall. Last look at your quiff, and move!

Great Bars

George Orwell's ideal pub was all about 'draught stout, open fires, cheap meals, motherly barmaids and no radio.' These days we'd maybe add music straight from a blog, handmade decor and a dangerous vibe. For some if not all of these try up-beat **Jaguar Shoes (Map 91)** and the hidden **Dragon Bar (Map 8)**. **Freud (Map 13)** or the **French House (Map 11)** in the West End are also solid contenders for boho shlock. But there's so much more: crawl from **Barrio North's (Map 80)** caravan to the country-house of **Lost Society (Map 142)**, from the Island **Queen (Map 84)** to the Moijto-fuelled **Mau Mau (Map 29)**. We like standing next to (would-be) artists at the **ICA Bar (Map 23)** and actor types on the terrace of **The Cut Bar (Map 104)**. Or in front of a movie screen, at **Roxy Bar and Screen (Map 106)**. Later on, you'll find us nibbling cheese in Dalston's **Jazz Bar (Map 86)**, dancing to trashy music at **Da Vinci's (Map 104)**.

Best Of The Rest

Want to feel exclusive? Members-only clubs are not only becoming ever more popular, but also ever more accessible. So there. Escape Shoreditch's terrifying hordes to the rooftop

swimming pool of **Shoreditch House (Map 91)** or the boredom of Shepherd's Bush to the underground ex-toilets that have become **Ginglik (Map 33)**. Get stupidly drunk with the nonsense-talking artists of Soho's **Colony Room (Map 11)**. Of course, most of those in the know will drag you to the various warehouse raves that fire up every weekend. People like **Real Gold (http://wearerealgold.com)** are a good place to start if you fancy some of this awfulness. Remember it's not who you know but, oh wait, it is who you know.

If relying on that notoriously joke-cracking friend of a friend for your evening's amusement sounds a bit risky, consider these alternatives: The standard-setting **Comedy Store (Map 11)** (book in advance), Bethnal Green's **Backyard Comedy (Map 92)** and **Covent Garden Comedy Club (Map 24)**, or, at the pub end of things, the **Monkey Business (Map 72)**, **The Bedford (Map 148)** and the **Camden Head (Map 80)**. If you think that YOU should in fact provide the evening's amusement, well, the **Poetry Café (Map 13)** gives you the stage. Or stay at home and talk to yourself; it's cheaper.

Music, Sweet Music

More than anything else, London's veins are pumped by its rhythms, its licks and axes, by a blow of a horn or a beautiful word sung. From the outisder buskers to the fat cat headliners at the city's stadiums, from Tin Pan Alley to Dalston, the city's music is a thriving beast.

Strummin' Mental

As always London's Rock, Pop and 'Alternative' scenes are in constant flux. This is a healthy state of affairs, but it's hard not to gulp down a tear at the passing of the Astoria, or small indie dives **Nambucca** and the **Horse & Groom**. It was always thus, of course, as the historic music halls of today become the designer yuppie flats of tomorrow. Yes, we've got our share of giant cesspits of corporateness (we're looking at you, O2) but for every Temple to Carling there are 2 or three brilliant dives like the **Grosvenor (Map 145)** or the **Haggerston (Map 88)**.

For the sweatily inclined there are infinite choices. Bethnal Green's **Star of Bethnal Green (Map 92)** (formerly the Pleasure Unit), Highgate's **Buffalo Bar (Map 80)** and **Angel's Lexington (Map 79)** are as pant-wettingly indie as they come but if you like harder or weirder stuff the **Camden Underworld (Map 71)** does all the metals while **Cafe Oto (Map 86)** handles experimental and improv. **The MacBeth (Map 84)**, might have sunk in our estimations of late, but **Monto Water Rats (Map 5)** is an unshakeable legend. Shoreditch's **Old Blue Last (Map 84)** -the puppet venue for trendy/sick rag Vice Magazine - has partied its way to the top of the pub gigging scene: always busy, always up for surprises. Mid-sized venues for mid-fame bands? **Scala (Map 78)** and **The Forum (Map 72)** are good, but **The Dome (Map 59)** is fast becoming our favourite school hall-like venue. The now legal **Barden's Boudoir (Map 86)**is a dingy Dalston basement, while the **ICA (Map 23)** has established itself as an eclectic stage for artistes amid some posh old money surroundings. For a grungier layout and the matching attitude, try New Cross favourite **Amersham Arms (Map 126)**, one of the city's hottest live stages. Easily. The city's electronic music scene generally piggy-backs the guitars, but new places like **Cable (Map 106)** and **Lightbox (Map 131)**.

As for the classics, the **Shepherd's Bush Empire (Map 33)** and the breathtakingly beautiful **Bush Hall (Map 32)** remain west London's finest, while Camden stalwart **Koko (Map 71)** keeps rocking in the free world. The north London show is being stolen by the **Roundhouse (Map 71)**, though, boasts a healthy "I am legend"-attitude and some bloody horrible Anthony Gormley statues waiting to jump from the top. **Brixton Academy (Map 145)** might be slightly overrated, but its sky-like ceiling remains awesome. If you have to do stadium-size, do stadium-size in style and get your seat in the **Royal Albert Hall (Map 36)**, which is increasingly luring good non-classical acts. The refurbishment of the **Royal Festival Hall (Map 104)**, meanwhile, has kick-started more pop-oriented programming on the South Bank.

A World of Jazz And Blues

Camden's intimate **Jazz Café (Map 71)** seems to have no intention of stopping its relentless stream of first-rate jazz performances, getting in more soul, funk and pop at the same time, while **Ronnie Scott's Jazz Club (Map 12)**, London's undisputed jazz original, is equally determined to keep up the good programming. For some of the freshest jazz, alongside great contemporary folk and world music, head to Dalston, where the plush **Vortex (Map 82)** is a-buzz with free-spirited legends. On the other side of town, **Chelsea's 606 Club (Map 50)** is a fine, small jazz venue with crammed, small tables within slobbering distance from the saxes. Catch excellent blues and singer/songwriter stuff every night of the week at **Ain't Nothing But The Blues Bar (Map 10)**, or Denmark Street's **12 Bar Club (Map 12)**. Latin jazz lurks at **Archway's Caipirinha Jazz Bar (Map 52)**. For world music, the **Barbican Centre (Map 7)** leads the pack, but is easily beaten in atmosphere stakes by the **Union Chapel (Map 80)**, an Islington church doubling as one of London's most beautiful venues and in scummy stakes by **Dingwalls (Map 71)** who continue to expand their programming. The home of folk is the brilliant **Cecil Sharp House (Map 70)**. If classical music is your cup of tea, look beyond the obvious venues and settle amid the great acoustics of **Chelsea's Cadogan Hall (Map 19)**, the historical brilliance of **Hackney's Sutton House (Map 87)** or the magnificent **Wigmore Hall (Map 2)**, in Mayfair

Map 1 • Marylebone (West)

Sequoia Ruby Lounge	23 Orchard St	020 7486 3671	Dimly-lit, sexy bar with kick ass Mojitos.

Map 2 • Marylebone (East)

Claridge's Bar	55 Brook St	020 7629 8860	Posh and plush and Art Deco. More champagne!
Inn 1888	21 Devonshire St	020 7486 7420	Quiet pint perfection.
The Phoenix	37 Cavendish Sq	020 7493 8003	A quirky gem amidst an ocean of crappy chain bars.

Map 3 • Fitzrovia

	Address		
100 Club	100 Oxford St	020 7636 0933	Ancient club that's seen off Nazi bombs and Sex Pistols.
The Albany	240 Great Portland St	020 7387 0221	Swanky, but nice. And the music's good.
Bourne & Hollingsworth	28 Rathbone Pl	020 7636 8228	Fine Fitzrovian basement boutique.
Bradleys Spanish Bar	42 Hanway St	020 7636 0359	60's rock joint with awesome jukebox and disgusting toilets.
Bricklayers Arms	31 Gresse St	020 7636 5593	Advertising types fake no-nonsense boozing.
Charlotte Street Hotel	15 Charlotte St	020 7806 2000	Dirty gossip over dirty martinis.
The Fitzroy Tavern	16 Charlotte St	020 7580 3714	Sam Smith's, anyone?
Ghetto	1 Falconberg Ct	020 7287 3726	Loud electro at this busy gay club. Thursdays is ladies night.
The Jerusalem Tavern	55 Britton St	020 7490 4281	A tiny old wooden gem of a pub. And organic ale.
Market Place	11 Market Pl	020 7079 2020	Warm buzz. Hot crowd. Cool prices.
The Metro Club	19 Oxford St	020 7437 0964	Contingency plan for bored indie kids.
Northumberland Arms	43 Goodge St	020 7580 7975	Cosy, old-style bar with a local feel.
Punk	14 Soho St0	871 223 1242	Starf***er central. But kinda fun.
The Rising Sun	46 Tottenham Ct Rd	020 7636 6530	Bordering studentland and Fitzrovia; pretty name, less pretty pub.
The Roxy	3 Rathbone Pl	020 7255 1098	Hip subterranean hangout. More chicks than dicks.
The Social	5 Little Portland St	020 7636 4992	Fab music, nonchalant surroundings and plenty of trendsters.
The Yorkshire Grey	46 Langham St	020 7636 4788	Upstairs is perfect when Oxford Street's pissing you off.

Map 4 • Bloomsbury (West)

All Star Lanes	Victoria House, Bloomsbury Pl	020 7025 2676	You'll be bowled over. Oh yes you will.
Bloomsbury Bowling Lanes	Bedford Way	020 7183 1979	As cool as bowling gets.
The Fly	36 New Oxford	020 7688 8955	For your quick indie fix on New Oxford.
Marquis of Cornwallis	31 Marchmont St	020 7278 8355	Chilled couches.
Old Crown	33 New Oxford St	020 7836 9121	After-work bar that takes itself very seriously.
The Plough	27 Museum St	020 7636 7964	Fancy a bite? Vampyre Society meetings held here monthly.
Point 101	101 New Oxford St	020 7379 3112	Even mass murderers on day-release get in here.
The Princess Louise	208 High Holborn	020 7405 8816	Victorian gin palace now serving cheap but good lager.
ULU	1 Malet St	020 7664 2000	Student union, student prices, student bands.

Map 5 • Bloomsbury (East)

06 St Chad's Place	6 St Chad's Pl	020 7278 3355	Stylish wine bar with plastic chairs? SOOO avant-garde, dahhhling!

The Duke of York	156 Clerkenwell Rd	020 7837 8548	You and a hundred cycle couriers.
Monto Water Rats	328 Gray's Inn Rd	020 7837 4412	No rats here, only the best up-and-coming bands.
Smithy's	15 Leeke St	020 7278 5949	Our lunchtime to late-night-wind-down friend.

Map 6 • Clerkenwell

The Bandstand	Northampton Sq		Free acoustic gigs in summer. Dreamy.
Betsey Trotwood	56 Farringdon Rd	020 7253 4285	Thoroughly likable Shepherd Neame pub renowned for live music.
Café Kick	43 Exmouth Market	020 7837 8077	Creaky, Latin American table football cafe.
Cicada	132 St John St	020 7608 1550	Gorgeous Art Deco interior, original and classic cocktails.
Dollar Grills and Martinis	2 Exmouth Market	020 7278 0077	Forget the grills, go with the martinis.
The Dovetail	9 Jerusalem Passage	020 7490 7321	Small, but perfectly formed Clerkenwell sister to Broadway Market's The Dove.
Filthy McNasty's	68 Amwell St	020 7837 6067	Disappointingly un-filthy or nasty. Sigh.
The Harlequin	27 Arlington Way	020 7837 0090	Livingroom boozer.
Queen Boadicea	292 St John St	020 7354 9993	Full of students paying their lecturers off with pints.
The Slaughtered Lamb	34-35 Great Sutton St	020 7253 1516	Dimly-lit pub that's still packing in the Clerkenwell crowd.
The Three Kings	7 Clerkenwell Close	020 7253 0483	Quirky pub that dies on weekends.
Wilmington Arms	69 Rosebery Ave	020 7837 1384	Rock out with real ale a stone's throw from Exmouth Market.

Map 8 • Liverpool Street / Broadgate

The Light	233 Shoreditch High St	020 7247 8989	Light at the end of the tunnel for city revellers.
Lounge Bohemia	1 Great Eastern St	077 2070 7000	Vintage Martinis make up for neo avant garde pretences.
The Red Lion	1 Eldon St	020 7247 5381	Drinkers near Moorgate can't be choosers. So there.
Sosho	2 Tabernacle St	020 7920 0701	It's so Sosho darhling.

Map 9 • Mayfair / Green Park

1707	181 Piccadilly	084 5602 5694	Empty Fortnum & Mason's wine cellar.
5th View	203 Piccadilly	020 7851 2433	Spill Bloody Marys over books in full view of Big Ben.
bbar	43 Buckingham Palace Rd	020 7958 7000	Get drunk behind Elizabeth's back.
Funky Buddah	15 Berkeley St	020 7495 2596	Overpriced, overrated, tacky Z-list haunt. Apart from that, it's great!
Mahiki	1 Dover St	020 7493 9529	Crushingly tropical cocktail bar. Pineapples a-go-go.
Shepherd's Tavern	50 Hertford St	020 7499 3017	For drinking within Shepherd's Market.

Map 10 • Piccadilly / Soho (West)

22 Below	22 Great Marlborough St	020 7437 4106	Table-service cocktail lounge - without being snooty. We love it.
Ain't Nothing But The Blues Bar	20 Kingly St	020 7287 0514	Bracingly raw music in a tiny frontroom.
Bar Red	5 Kingly St	020 7434 3417	Soho cocktail madness. Plush, sexy and red.
Beyond Retro	58 Great Marlborough St	020 7434 1406	Addictive. An Aladdin's cave of goodies. £250 vintage Nikes anyone?
Cheers Bar	72 Regent St	020 7494 3322	Sitcom-themed Americana; wags shouting 'Norm!' at regular intervals.
Courthouse Bar	19 Great Marlborough St	020 7297 5555	Drink where Oscar Wilde was in the clink.
Green and Red	51 Bethnal Green Rd	020 7749 9670	Tequila bar worth its post-shot salt - you're spoilt for choice.
John Snow	39 Broadwick St	020 7437 1344	Soho drinkers! Sam Smith's full range and a relaxed upstairs!
Lucky Voice	52 Poland St	020 7439 3660	Why is this London's best karaoke bar? The dress up box.
Milk & Honey	61 Poland St	0700 655 463	The promised land of after-hours cocktails. Members club, so join.
Pigalle Club	215 Piccadilly	020 7644 1420	Ladies and gentleman, welcome to the 40s.
Strawberry Moons	15 Heddon St	020 7437 7300	Dig the cheese, with your new squeeze.

Map 11 • Soho (Central)

Blue Posts	22 Berwick St	020 7437 5008	Unreformed, scuzzy boozer.
The Blue Posts	28 Rupert St	020 7437 1415	Hey, a decent pub in Soho.
Candy Bar	4 Carlisle St	020 7494 4041	Soho's premier all-girl venue.
The Colony Room	41 Dean St	020 7437 9179	Arty pisshead private members' hangout; Shane MacGowan virutally lives here.
The Comedy Store	1 Oxendon St	020 7930 2949	It ain't world famous for no reason, chuckles.
De Hems	11 Macclesfield St	020 7437 2494	Dutch bar with brain-cell-annihilatingly strong beer. Hic!
The Endurance	90 Berwick St	020 7437 2944	Hang-out for loud media twats.
Freedom	66 Wardour St	020 7734 0071	Neon green cocktail kitsch.
The French House	49 Dean St	020 7437 2799	Boho Soho hang-out for eccentrics.
LUPO	50 Dean St	020 7434 3399	A labyrinth of candlelit corners and sophisticated conversation.
Madame Jojo's	8 Brewer St	020 7734 3040	Unpretentious club where you won't remain single for too long.
Rex Cinema and Bar	21 Rupert St	020 7287 0102	Rexcellent.
Shadow Lounge	5 Brewer St	020 7439 4089	Gay chi chi lounge.
Soho Revue Bar	11 Walkers Ct	020 7734 0377	For the trashier nighthawk. Cabaret and remorse.

Trash Palace	11 Wardour St	020 7734 0522	Aptly named gay indie bar. Skullz everywhere.
The Village	81 Wardour St	020 7434 2124	Tacky, flirtatious Soho gay bar.

Map 12 • Soho (East)

12 Bar Club	22 Denmark St	020 7240 2622	Ludicrously tiny live club with singer/songwriter focus.
The Astoria	157 Charing Cross Rd	020 7434 9592	Gigging legend. Go before they get serious about tearing it down.
The Borderline	16 Manette St	020 7734 5547	Cool basement club, bizarrely got up in Tex-Mex decor.
Comptons	53 Old Compton St	020 7479 7961	Crammed gay pub.
Crobar	17 Manette St	020 7439 0831	Heavy metal and cheap bourbon. Be a man for once.
G-A-Y Bar	30 Old Compton St	020 7494 2756	Poptastic gay bunker.
G-A-Y Late	5 Goslett Yard	020 7734 9858	Cheap drinks and pop videos wipe out brain functions 'til 3 am.
Garlic & Shots	14 Frith St	020 7734 9505	Drunken vampires beware.
Green Carnation	5 Greek St	020 7434 3323	Sexy, Oscar Wilde-inspired lounge that Oscar would have approved of.
Jazz After Dark	9 Greek St	020 7734 0545	Tunes and cheap drinks, until LATE.
Karaoke Box	18 Frith St	020 7494 3878	A bit gritty but one of London's cheaper karaoke bars.
Ku Bar	30 Lisle St	020 7437 4303	Newly relocated gay bar for the young and clueless.
Montagu Pyke	105 Charing Cross Rd	020 7287 6039	Cheap beer - in the West End.
Ronnie Scott's Jazz Club	47 Frith St	0207 439 0747	Original, and still the best.
Royal George	133 Charing Cross Rd, Goslett Yard	020 7734 8837	Busy, but the crowd's nice. Board games and food.
The Toucan	19 Carlisle St	020 7437 4123	Small and snug central bolthole for Guinness.

Map 13 • Covent Garden

AKA Bar	18 W Central St	020 7836 0110	Proper drinks and proper DJs. And pizza for in-between.
Bunker	41 Earlham St	020 7240 0606	Beer brewed in front of your eyes.
Coffee, Cake & Kink	61 Endell St	020 7419 2996	Does what it says on the tin!
The Cross Keys	31 Endell St	020 7836 5185	Tiny old-school boozer.
The End	18 W Central St	020 7419 9199	The beginning is the end is the beginning. This pioneering club's still rockin' it.
Freud	198 Shaftesbury Ave	020 7240 9933	Intimate basement bar that used to be Alex of Blur's living room. Literally.
Guanabara	Parker St	020 7242 8600	Brasil. But in Holborn.
The Lamb and Flag	33 Rose St	020 7497 9504	Cobbled lane leads to a crowded but gloriously timeless inn.
Octave	27 Endell St	020 7836 4616	Dressy but mellow jazz-cum-cocktail bar for Ally McBeal and friends.
Poetry Society Cafe	22 Betterton St	020 7420 9887	Eat, drink, write, listen or, yes, PERFORM!

Map 14 • Holborn / Temple

Cittie of Yorke	22 High Holborn	020 7242 7670	Soe olde it's name has extra e's. A marvellouse pube.
Enterprise	38 Red Lion St	020 7269 5901	More Captain Cook than Captain Kirk.
The Lamb	92 Lamb's Conduit St	020 7405 0713	Legendary little place with Victorian touches.
Na Zdrowie The Polish Bar	11 Little Turnstile	020 7831 9679	With 50 types of vodka, even beetroot soup tastes good.
The Seven Stars	53 Carey St	020 7242 8521	Tiny, slightly dusty bar frequented by barristers.
Swissotel The Howard Hotel Bar	Temple Pl	020 7836 3555	A touch of Bertie Wooster open to all.
Tutu's	Surrey St	020 7836 7132	King's College students' very own nightclub.
Volupte	9 Norwich St	020 7831 1622	They call it burlesque, we call it strippers with tassles.

Map 15 • Blackfriars / Farringdon

Corney & Barrow	10 Paternoster Sq	020 7618 9520	Champagne breakfast, anyone?
The Deux Beers	3 Hatton Wall	020 7405 9777	Home of the original politically incorrect 100 shooter list.
Fabric	77 Charterhouse St	020 7336 8898	Debauched club mecca for gurners of all persuasions.
Hat & Tun	3 Hatton Wall	020 7242 4747	Home of the original politically incorrect 100 shooter list.
Smithfield Bar & Grill	2 West Smithfield	020 7246 0900	Suits, suits, suits. And chandeliers, jazz and cocktails. And suits.
Ye Olde Cheshire Cheese	154 Fleet St	020 7353 6170	Get tanked up where Dickens used to. Historic.
Ye Olde London	42 Ludgate Hill	020 7248 1852	It ain't Olde, really, but it sells beer.
Ye Olde Mitre	1 Ely Ct	020 7405 4751	Elizabeth I used to dance here, don't you know?!

Map 16 • Square Mile (West)

Hatchet	28 Garlick Hill	020 7236 0720	Lost in the City? Escape here.
The Mansion House	44 Cannon St	020 7248 1700	Out of the tube, into the House.
The Samuel Pepys	48 Upper Thames St	020 7489 1871	Find it and be rewarded with Thames views.
Ye Olde Watling	29 Watling St	020 7653 9971	Squeeze in.

Map 17 • Square Mile (East)

The Counting House	50 Cornhill	020 7283 7123	A truly magnificent (former) bank. That sells beer now.
Grand Cafe & Bar	The Ctyard, Royal Exchange	020 7618 2480	The courtyard of the Royal Exchange. Fancy, eh?

Map 18 • Tower Hill / Aldgate

Dion City	52 Leadenhall St	020 7702 9111	Veuve Clicquot La Grande Dame Rose, anyone?
Kenza	10 Devonshire Sq	020 7929 5533	Belly-dancers, cocktails & couscous.
Mary Janes	124 Minories	020 7481 8195	Inconspicuous perspex floor catches out the knickerless.
The Minories	64-73 Minories	020 7702 1659	Cavernous boozer by day, thumping disco by night.
Pepys Bar at the Novotel Hotel	10 Pepys St	020 7265 6000	Get on the Kir Royales and kiss tomorrow goodbye.
Prism	147 Leadenhall St	020 7256 3873	Cocktails underneath the former Bank of New York.
Revolution in the City	140 Leadenhall St	020 7929 4233	Vodka-drenched, vault-like DJ bar that couldn't care less about the revolution.

Map 19 • Belgravia

The Blue Bar	Wilton Pl	020 7235 6000	It's blue. Mindboggingly so.
Nag's Head	53 Kinnerton St	020 7235 1135	No mobiles allowed. Says it all.

Map 20 • Victoria / Pimlico (West)

The Albert	52 Victoria St	020 7222 5577	Distinguished, well-preserved period pub. Tourist haunt but rightly so.
The Cardinal	23 Francis St	020 7834 7260	Easier to like than to find.
Cask & Glass	39 Palace St	020 7834 7630	Teeny tiny, English country garden-esque drinking hole. Flower-festoned frontage, real ale.
The Plumber's Arms	14 Lower Belgrave St	020 7730 4067	Tradesman's pub from days of yore. Ask about Lord Lucan.

Map 21 • Pimlico (East)

Morpeth Arms	58 Millbank	020 7834 6442	Where Millbank prisoners used to escape to.

Map 22 • Westminster

The Cinnamon Club	30 Great Smith St	020 7222 2555	Cocktail classiness inside the Old Westminster Library. Try finding it.
The Speaker	46 Great Peter St	020 7222 1749	Good after-worker with guest ales.
St. Stephen's Tavern	10 Bridge St	020 7925 2286	Tiny pub with character, despite being on tourist trail.
The Two Chairmen	39 Dartmouth St	020 7222 8694	Public servants galore! Decent pub for this area though.

Map 23 • St. James's

Aura	48 St James's St	020 7499 9999	If you ain't on the list, you ain't coming in. Seriously.
ICA	The Mall	020 7930 3647	Cutting edge arts complex/bar, weirdly stuck on the upper-crust Mall.
The Sports Cafe	80 Haymarket	020 7839 8300	Umpteen screens of international sport distract from appalling service/grub.

Map 24 • Trafalgar Square / The Strand

Asia de Cuba	45 St Martin's Lane	020 7300 5588	For rum-drinking with the jet set.
The Chandos	29 St Martins Lane	020 7836 1401	All Trafalgar Square pubs are tourist traps? Think again.
The Coal Hole	91 Strand	020 7379 9883	Genuine old style.
Covent Garden Comedy Club	The Arches, Off Villiers St	07960 071 340	Good acts play to a friendly crowd drinking awful beer.
Gordon's Wine Bar	47 Villiers St	020 7930 1408	Candle-lit vaults. Romantic perfection.
Heaven	Under the Arches, off Villiers St	020 7930 2020	Epicentre of London's late night gay scene.
Maple Leaf	41 Maiden Ln	020 7240 2843	Just don't ask which State they're from.
Punch & Judy	The Covent Garden Piazza	020 7379 0923	Naff, naff, naff. 'Nuff said?
Retro Bar	2 George Ct	020 78398760	Chilled gay bar, hiding from Charing Cross in a small alley.
Roadhouse	35 The Piazza	020 7240 6001	"You're the one that I want, ooh-ooh-ooh"
The Sherlock Homes	10 Northumberland St	020 7930 2644	Unintentionally sinister, must-see Holmes waxwork upstairs. Expect bad dreams.
The Ship and Shovel	2 Craven Passage	020 7839 1311	A pub made of two pubs, both obsessed with Sherlock Holmes.
Zoo Bar	13 Bear St	020 7839 4188	Wake up with someone new.

Map 25 • Kensal Town

Book Slam	12 Acklam Rd	n/a	Books for clubbers or DJ-night for literary folks – can't decide.

Map 26 • Maida Hill

The Skiddaw	46 Chippenham Rd	020 7432 1341	West London trendy hang out. Great Sunday roast.

Map 27 • Maida Vale

Bridge House	13 Westbourne Terrace Rd	020 7266 4326	Canal views and comedy. Lovely.
E Bar	2 Warrington Crescent	020 7432 8455	Basement lounge for a quiet drink.
Robert Browning	15 Clifton Rd	020 7286 2732	Cheapo boozer in posh surroundings.
The Warwick Castle	6 Warwick Pl	020 7266 0921	Down-to-earth drinking in Maida Vale. Indeed.
Waterway	54 Formosa St	020 7266 3557	Try not to fall into the canal.

Map 28 • Ladbroke Grove / Notting Hill (West)

Julie's Wine Bar	135 Portland Rd	020 7229 8331	Pleasantly posh wine bar full of pleasantly posh ladies.

Map 29 • Notting Hill Gate

Black Cherry	21 Lordship Ln	020 8299 8877	Oh ya, only the boutique-iest of cocktails here.
Mau Mau	265 Portobello Rd	020 7229 8528	Ace mojitos and Thursdays open-mic. Wear your dancing shoes.
Montgomery Place	31 Kensington Park Rd	020 7792 3921	The mixers rock. And they know it.
Notting Hill Arts Club	21 Notting Hill Gate	020 7460 4459	Indie cave with bands, lurid projections and teenagers.
The Sun in Splendour	7 Portobello Rd	020 7792 0914	Notting Hill denizens' choice.
Uxbridge Arms	13 Uxbridge St	020 7727 7326	Warm little place full of eccentric old toffs.
Windsor Castle	114 Campden Hill Rd	020 7243 8797	A wood-panelled piece of pub history.

Map 32 • Shepherd's Bush (West)

Bush Hall	310 Uxbridge Rd	020 8222 6955	The red carpet, the ornate walls…the sheer beauty!
The Goldhawk	122 Goldhawk Rd	020 8576 6921	A pub, ladies and gentleman.
The White Horse	31 Uxbridge Rd	020 8743 0624	Did you call my pint a slag? Outside, now!

Map 33 • Shepherd's Bush

Albertine	1 Wood Lane	020 8743 9593	Drink wine with the Beep set.
Bush Bar & Grill	45 Goldhawk Rd	020 8746 2111	Pre-gig margarita, post-gig wood fired pizza.
Ginglik	1 Shepherd's Bush Green	020 7348 8968	Members-only underground ex-toilets. Join free on the door.
Shepherd's Bush Empire	Shepherd's Bush Green	020 8354 3300	Still among London venueland's finest.

Map 34 • West Kensington / Olympia

Cumberland Arms	29 N End Rd	020 7371 6806	Where long hard days become good again.
Famous 3 Kings	171 North End Rd	020 7603 6071	Brilliant atmosphere for big matches, especially rugby. Pool tables too.
Plum Bar	380 Kensington High St	020 7603 3333	Dying for a drink in Kensington? Well there.

Map 35 • Kensington

Builders Arms	1 Kensington Ct Pl	020 7937 6213	Boozy haven from High Street Kensington's shopping madness.

Map 36 • South Kensington / Gloucester Rd

Boujis	43 Thurloe St	020 7584 2000	If you want to see the two princes drunk. And only then.

Map 38 • Chiswick

Carvossos	210 Chiswick High Rd	020 8995 9121	For a glass of wine before dinner.
George IV	185 Chiswick High Rd	020 8994 4624	Fullers pies, real ale and a comedy club on the High Road? Sweet.

Map 39 • Stamford Brook

The Raven	375 Goldhawk Rd	020 8748 6977	A bit grubby on the outside but £4 handmade pies are part of the appeal.

Map 40 • Goldhawk Rd / Ravenscourt Park

The Dove	19 Upper Mall	020 8748 9474	So perfect for dates that Charles II brought Nell Gwynne here.
The Mulberry	243 Goldhawk Rd	020 8748 0229	Always pretty empty but decent menu and decor.
Ruby Grand	225 King St	020 8748 3391	Self-proclaimed purveyor of elegance.

Map 41 • Hammersmith

Brook Green Hotel	170 Shepherd's Bush Rd	020 7603 2516	Lost between Hammersmith and Shepherd's Bush? Fear not.
Hammersmith Apollo	45 Queen Caroline St	084 4844 4748	Still West London's best music venue
Lyric Hammersmith	King St	087 1221 1729	Hammersmith's hottest home of hentertainment..

Map 42 • Baron's Court

Colton Arms	187 Greyhound Road	020 7385 6956	If you're not already a regular, you'll wish you were.
Curtains Up	28 Comeragh Rd	020 8932 4747	Pub which keeps actors in the basement.
The Fulham Mitre	81 Dawes Rd	020 7386 8877	Young, trendy Fulhamites like it. We don't.

Map 43 • West Brompton / Fulham Broadway / Earls Court

The Coleherne	261 Old Brompton Rd	020 7373 8337	Leather, baby!
Nectar	562 Kings Rd	020 7326 7450	Green lights, red lights, and cocktails.

Map 44 • Chelsea

Brinkleys	47 Hollywood Rd	020 7351 1683	Enter the cougar's lair.
Rumi	531 Kings Rd	020 7823 3362	Fulham's secret, chic and cosy jewel.

Map 45 • Chelsea (East)

Apartment 195	195 Kings Rd	020 7349 4468	Hire your personal Kings Road party apartment.
Chelsea Potter	119 Kings Rd	020 7352 9479	Chelsea old school.

Map 47 • Fulham (West)

The Crabtree Tavern	Rainville Rd	020 7385 3929	Great riverside location. So-so pub.

Map 49 • Parson's Green

Amuse Bouche	51 Parson's Green Lane	020 7371 8517	Fizzy fun.
Duke on the Green	235 New Kings Road	020 7736 2777	If only all pub food was this good (but half the price).
The Establishment	45-47 Parsons Green Ln	020 7384 2418	British favourites meet retro cool. Pie and...Pimms anyone?
The White Horse	Parson's Green	020 7736 2115	Victorian pub and a beer drinker's heaven. Book a table.

Map 50 • Sand's End

606 Club	90 Lots Rd	020 7352 5953	Great jazz venue. If you like ten minute sax solos.

Map 51 • Sand's End

The Angel Inn	Highgate High St	020 8347 2921	Lively local with board games and unusual beers.
The Boogaloo	312 Archway Rd	020 8340 2928	Not as cool as it thinks it is.
The Flask	77 Highgate West Hill	020 8348 7346	Great beers, great food, great place. Really, it is.
Highgate Inn	385 Archway Rd	n/a	Chummy, licensed version of your own front room.
Prince Of Wales	53 Highgate High St	020 8340 0445	Friendly local for posh Highgaters and their even posher dogs.
The Victoria	28 N Hill	020 8340 6091	Try to catch the Sunday sing-along sessions.
The Woodman	414 Archway Rd	020 8340 3016	Reformed fight club with gastropub intentions.
The Wrestlers	98 North Rd	020 8340 4297	Branded "best pub in Highgate" by residents.

Map 52 • Archway (North)

Caipirinha Jazz Bar	177 Archway Rd	020 7287 1269	Cosiness! Cocktails! Latin jazz! Sherpa required to find it!
The Winchester Pub Hotel	206 Archway Rd	020 8374 1690	Wonky-floored palace of boozy delight.

Map 53 • Crouch End

Harringay Arms	153 Crouch Hill	020 8340 4243	No music, plenty of beer.
Queens Pub & Dining Rooms	26 Broadway Parade	020 8340 2031	God save the Queens.
The Wishing Well	22 Topsfield Parade, Tottenham Lane	020 8340 1096	Goodbye Crouch End gastropub, hello Hornsey cheap boozer.

Map 55 • Harringay Ladder

The Salisbury	1 Grand Parade, Green Lanes	020 8800 9617	A local's secret...no longer! Exceptional.

Map 56 • Hampstead Village

The Flask	14 Flask Walk	020 7435 4580	Hampstead allyway classic that's been refitted. But nicely so.

The Freemasons Arms	32 Downshire Hill	020 7433 6811	Lovely beer garden.
Holly Bush	22 Holly Mount	020 7435 2892	It's hidden. It's a gem. Really.

Map 57 • Hampstead Heath

The Magdala	2 South Hill Park	020 7435 2503	Ruth Ellis bullet-holed boozer.
Monkey Chews	2 Queen's Crescent	020 7267 6406	Dark and intimate bar and music venue.
Roebuck	15 Pond St	020 7435 7354	Somewhere between cosy pub and stylish bar. And good at it.

Map 58 • Parliament Hill / Dartmouth Park

Bar Lorca	156 Fortress Rd	020 7485 1314	Spanish beer. Spanish tapas.
The Bull and Last	168 Highgate Rd	020 7267 3641	Good place for a post-Heath pint.
The Dartmouth Arms	35 York Rise	020 7485 3267	A fire. Dogs. Old gits. The perfect local.
Duke of St. Albans	Highgate Road	020 7209 0385	Pretty dodgy at times, but also the only pub around.

Map 59 • Tufnell Park

Boston Arms	178 Junction Rd	020 7272 8153	Ferociously scruffy but friendly Irish pub, with rock pit attached.
The Dome	178 Junction Rd	020 7272 8153	Fast becoming our favourite venue!
The Hideaway	114 Junction Rd	020 7561 0779	Beer, pizza, dancing. What else do you need?
The Lord Palmerston	33 Dartmouth Park Hill	020 7485 1578	Gone a bit plastic, but still worth it.
The Star	47 Chester Rd	020 7263 9067	It's a star.

Map 60 • Archway

Archway Tavern	1 Archway Close	020 7272 2840	Cheap beer, plentiful fisticuffs.
The Mother Red Cap	665 Holloway Rd	020 7263 7082	Begorra! Bejesus! Be better off going to another boozer!

Map 61 • Holloway (North)

Nambucca	596 Holloway Rd	020 7272 7366	Self-proclaimed cult venue.
The Quays	471 Holloway Rd	020 7272 3634	Into bad U2 cover bands? Then you'll love it here.
The Swimmer	13 Eburne Rd	020 7281 4632	No running, diving in the shallow end, or heavy petting.

Map 62 • Finsbury Park

Faultering Fullback	19 Perth Rd	020 7272 5834	Tardis-like local. Avoid match nights unless you're a Gooner.

Map 63 • Manor House

The Blarney Stone	89 Woodberry Grove	n/a	Friendly local.
The Brownswood Park Tavern	271 Green Lanes	020 8809 2846	Enter, before Manor House drives you mad.
Manor Club	277 Seven Sisters Rd	020 8211 0211	Once a historic pub, now a strip club. No brainer.

Map 64 • Stoke Newington

Auld Shillelagh	105 Stoke Newington Church St	020 7923 9256	The best Guinness in London; you won't leave standing up.
The Lion	132 Stoke Newington Church St	020 7249 1318	Nice 'nuff.
Londesborough	36 Barbauld Rd	020 7254 5865	Stokey trendies on leather sofas.
Rose and Crown	199 Stoke Newington Church St	020 7254 7497	Sunday roasts to die for and step-back-in-time décor.
Ryan's Bar	181 Church St	020 7275 7807	Boho cafe and venue with a noise limiter! Pussies.
The Shakespeare	57 Allen Rd	020 7254 4190	The Bard would be proud.

Map 65 • West Hampstead

The Czech and Slovak Club	74 West End Lane	020 7372 5251	Go Czech.
The Good Ship	289 Kilburn High Rd		Where Kilburn takes music seriously.
The Luminaire	311 High Rd	020 7372 7123	Regular winner of "best live venue" awards, despite the weird decor.

Map 66 • Finchley Road / Swiss Cottage

Ye Olde Swiss Cottage	98 Finchley Rd	020 7722 3487	What can we say.

Map 67 • Belsize Park

The Washington	50 England's Lane	020 7722 8842	Monday night is pub quiz night.

Map 68 • Kilburn High Road / Abbey Road

The Clifton	96 Clifton Hill	020 7372 3427	Not as secret as they want you to believe. But very nice.

Map 69 • St. John's Wood

The Star	38 St. Johns Wood Terrace	020 7722 1051	Drink face-to-face with a huge Highland Terrier.

Map 70 • Primrose Hill

The Albert	11 Princess Rd	020 7722 1886	A local. Cosy and relaxed.
Cecil Sharp House	2 Regents Park Rd	020 7485 2206	Sword dancing and Olde Stuffe.
The Engineer	65 Gloucester Ave	020 7722 0950	The classy chandeliers say it all.
The Lansdowne	90 Gloucester Ave	020 7483 0409	Home of the beautiful people.
Princess of Wales	22 Chalcot Rd	020 7722 0354	Traditional pub with occasional jazz performances.
Queens No. 1	1 Edis St	020 7586 3049	Comfy, quiet local.
Sir Richard Steele	97 Haverstock Hill	020 7483 1261	Friendly local with quirky decor.

Map 71 • Camden Town / Chalk Farm / Kentish Town (West)

At Proud	Chalk Farm Rd	020 7482 3867	Oh-so-casual, trendy little bar. Fairy lights and arty types.
Bar Vinyl	6 Inverness St	020 7482 5545	DJ Bar. And good coffee.
Bartok	78 Chalk Farm Rd	020 7916 0595	Hip, late-night bar with chilled-out sofa feel.
The Camden Tup	2 Greenland Pl	020 7482 0399	A-spade's-a-spade drinking spot off the beaten track.
Dingwalls	Middle Yard	019 2082 3098	Camden Lock's guitar-smashing heartland.
The Dublin Castle	94 Parkway	020 7485 1773	Famous, small, LOUD.
Electric Ballroom	184 Camden High St	020 7485 9006	Scruffy but essential rock haunt, perennially threatened by developers.
The Enterprise	2 Haverstock Hill	020 7485 2659	Literary Irish pub with tiny indie venue upstairs.
Fiddlers Arms	1 Malden Rd	020 7485 3269	Live music venue pub sans pretention.
Good Mixer	30 Inverness St	020 7916 7929	Ah, remember those halcyon days of Britpop?
The Hawley Arms	2 Castlehaven Rd	020 7428 5979	The Hawley will rise from the ashes. Camden needs it.
Jazz Cafe	5 Parkway	0207 688 8899	A relentless stream of excellent gigs.
Koko	1 Camden High St	0870 4325 527	From Charlie Chaplin to Lenny Kravitz, playing Koko still kicks ass.
Lock Tavern	35 Chalk Farm Rd	020 7482 7163	Great gigs, Sunday roasts and (unpainfully) hip clientele.
Oxford Arms	265 Camden High St	020 7267 4945	Theatre pub where you may stumble upon Amy Winehouse, stumbling.
Quinn's	65 Kentish Town Rd	020 7267 8240	More German beer than you can pronounce.
The Underworld	174 Camden High St	020 7482 1932	Throbbing pit of angry rock and even angrier metal.
The World's End	31 Jamestown Rd	020 7424 9054	Mammoth rock pub. Bring your eyeliner.

Map 72 • Kentish Town

The Abbey Tavern	124 Kentish Town Rd	020 7267 9449	Fairy-lit, casual beer garden with talented DJs on Saturdays.
Bull & Gate	389 Kentish Town Rd	020 8826 5000	A gigging institution.
The Forum	Highgate Rd	020 7428 4099	Good venue for medium-sized bands.
Monkey Business	289 Kentish Town Rd	07932 338203	Grotty pub, hosting a good comedy club.
The Pineapple	51 Leverton St	020 7284 4631	Backstreet Victorian with good beers and Thai grub.
Rio's Health Spa	239 Kentish Town Rd	020 7485 0607	Bored of your wife? Swap her here.

Map 73 • Holloway

The Lord Stanley	51 Camden Park Rd	020 7428 9488	Dark wood, Edwardian interior, fireplace and secret walled garden.
Shilibeers	1 Carpenter's Mews, North Rd	020 7700 1858	For relaxed drinking on comfy couches.

Map 74 • Holloway Road / Arsenal

The Coronet	338 Holloway Rd	020 7609 5014	The smell of old men's piss is abound, but it's cheap!
El Comandante	10 Annette Rd	020 7607 3961	South American vibe in a Victorian pub.
Hen and Chickens Theatre Pub	109 St. Paul's Rd	020 7704 2001	All the best pubs have theatres. Fact.

Map 75 • Highbury

Alwyne Castle	83 St Pauls Road	020 7288 9861	Alright for a pint.
Oak Bar	79 Green Lanes	0207 354 2791	Eclectic programme of events at this mixed/lesbian venue.
Snooty Fox	75 Grosvenor Avenue	020 7354 9532	Strangely empty - shame for such a great pub.

Map 76 • Edgeware Road / Marylebone (North)

Cellars Bar	222 Marylebone Rd	020 7631 8000	Grand is the word.
The Feathers	43 Linhope St	020 7402 1327	Tiny backstreet den.

The Perseverance	11 Shroton St	020 7723 7469	Perseverance in finding it will be rewarded.
Volunteer	245 Baker St	020 7486 4091	Grand old Victorian taphouse great for a lively post-work pint.

Map 77 • Mornington Crescent / Regent's Park

Crown & Anchor	137 Drummond St	020 7383 2681	A pub makeover masterpiece.
Edinboro Castle	57 Mornington Terrace	020 7255 9651	Huge outdoors bit, great BBQ on summer weekends.
Queen's Head and Artichoke	30 Albany St	020 7916 6206	The pinchos are addictive. We have warned, friends.

Map 78 • Euston

The Champagne Bar at St Pancras	Pancras Rd	020 3006 1552	Miss your train!
The Crown & Goose	100 Arlington Rd	020 7485 8008	Delightfully old-fashioned pub with good grub and an open fire.
Purple Turtle	61 Crowndale Rd	020 7383 4976	Rock club that looks like a wacky goth spaceship.
Scala	275 Pentonville Rd	020 7833 2022	Historic venue with plush edges. If these walls could talk...

Map 79 • King's Cross

Big Chill House	257 Pentonville Rd	020 7427 2540	Allow staff 28 working days to process your drinks order.
Canal 125	125 Caledonian Rd	020 7837 1924	Upmarket local bar that draws a swanky crowd.
Central Station	37 Wharfdale Rd	020 7278 3294	Ominous looking cabaret bar-cum-cruise emporium. Check site first.
Cross Kings	126 York Way	020 7278 83 18	Nice little place that tries but usually fails to be 'edgy.'
EGG	200 York Way	020 7609 8364	Big club, big garden, big night out.
Hemingford Arms	128 Hemingford Rd	020 7607 3303	Full of local aleheads.
The Lexington	243 Pentonville Rd	020 7837 5371	Come and support your boyfriend"s shit band.
Lincoln Lounge	52 York Way	020 7837 9339	Arty, quirky and cool. Does King's Cross proud.
The Tarmon	270 Caledonian Rd	020 7607 3242	Character. Lots of character.

Map 80 • Angel / Upper St

25 Canonbury	25 Canonbury Ln	020 7226 0955	You'll never love it as much as it loves itself.
The Albert and Pearl	181 Upper St	020 7354 9993	Classy when dark. Garish when lit.
The Angel	3 Islington High St	020 7837 2218	Students. The elderly. The unemployed.
The Angelic	57 Liverpool Rd	020 7278 8433	A sophisticated local.
Barrio North	45 Essex Rd	020 7688 2882	Groovy little bar with friendly international vibe. And a caravan!
Buffalo Bar	259 Upper St	020 7359 6191	Sweaty, small venue. You'll see them here first.
Camden Head	2 Camden Walk	020 7359 0851	Comedians debut new gags upstairs. Cheap—and mostly cheerful.
Carling Academy	16 Parkfield St	020 7288 4400	Grubby live music. Slap on some skinny jeans first.
The Castle	54 Pentonville Rd	020 7713 1858	Needs breaking in.
The Cedar Room	235 Upper St	020 7704 6977	Happy-hour cocktails.
Compton Arms	4 Compton Ave	020 7359 6883	Islington's only real pub—or so they say.
The Crown	116 Cloudesley Rd	020 7837 7107	Jovial spot for a quiet pint and Sunday roasts.
Cuba Libre	72 Upper St	020 7354 9998	Tank up with mojitos. Salsa with the barman.
The Drapers Arms	44 Bransbury St	020 7619 0348	Celeb backlash against new CCTV. Big Brother really is watching.
Electrowerkz	7 Torrens St	020 7837 6419	Crumbling rave labyrinth.
Embassy Bar	119 Essex Rd	020 7226 7901	Wannabe DJs' last real hope.
Famous Cock	259 Upper St	020 7226 4627	No sniggering at the back.
The Florence	50 Florence St	020 7354 5633	Refurbed, warm Georgian boozer.
The Garage	20 Highbury Corner		Bad sound and a guaranteed black hole in your evening.
The Green Man	144 Essex Rd	020 7226 2692	Eerie inside, scary punters.
Hope And Anchor	207 Upper St	020 7704 2689	Scuzzy pub with even scuzzier bands in the basement.
Islington Tap	80 Liverpool Rd	020 7354 5111	Vast, ornate ceilings and over-priced beer.
Jury's Inn	60 Pentonville Rd	020 7282 5500	Really? Why did you even buy this book?
Keston Lodge	131 Upper St	020 7354 9535	Just the right side of poncy.
King's Head Theatre Pub	115 Upper St	020 7226 8561	Proper, good-time boozer.
The Lord Clyde	342 Essex Rd	020 7288 9850	Like boozing in Land of Leather.
Lucky Voice Private Karaoke	173 Upper St	020 7354 6280	Singing in private? Like a bathroom with beer.
Marquess Tavern	32 Canonbury St	020 7354 2975	Scruffy locals live on despite gastro revolution.
Myddleton Arms	52 Canonbury Rd	020 7226 4595	Don't those people have, y'know, jobs?
Old Red Lion	418 St John St	020 7837 7816	Theatre pub legend.
The Regent	201 Liverpool Rd	020 7700 2725	Good news: it's finally starting to fray.
Salmon & Compass	58 Penton St	020 7837 3891	The old-boozer exterior belies the hip-hop lovin', all night-dancin' crowd within.
Union Chapel	Compton Terrace	020 7226 3750	God's favourite music venue. Hell, everyone's.

Map 82 • De Beauvoir Town / Kingsland

The Northgate	113 Southgate Rd	020 7359 7392	Reliable local despite being—gasp!—a gastro.
The Orwell	382 Essex Rd	020 7288 1914	Drinking in the day. George would be proud.

The Rosemary Branch	2 Shepperton Rd	020 7704 2730	Theatre pub with great selection of ales and hearty fare.
Vortex	11 Gillett Sq		Dalston's only real jazz bar.
The Wellington	119 Balls Pond Rd	020 7254 4338	Nice little boozer, as they say.

Map 83 • Angel (East) / City Rd (North)

The Duke of Cambridge	30 St Peter's St	020 7359 3066	Feel self-righteous in the world's first organic pub.
Earl of Essex	25 Danbury St	020 7226 3608	For drinking in the day. In the dark.
The Island Queen	87 Noel Rd	020 7354 8741	Where NFT planned the London guide. Sweet.
The Mucky Pup	39 Queen's Head St	020 7226 2572	The dog's bollocks.
The Narrow Boat	119 St Peters St	020 7288 0572	Cheerful canal-side pub for lazy pints and people-watching.
Offside Bar and Gallery	273 City Rd	020 7253 3306	Like a football stadium, but without anyone pissing in the sinks.
Old Queen's Head	44 Essex Rd	020 7354 9993	Trendier than the name suggests.
The Wenlock Arms	26 Wenlock Rd	020 7608 3406	Threadbare, battered old boozer with a magnificent range of real ales.

Map 84 • Hoxton

333	333 Old St	020 7739 5949	The Shoreditch grandfather.
Bar Music Hall	134 Curtain Rd	020 7613 5951	Nice wallpaper, free music. Who's complaining?
Bedroom Bar	62 Rivington St	020 7623 5637	Saturday's DJ 'n' sax players mean dancing til dawn.
The Bricklayers Arms	63 Charlotte Rd	020 7739 5245	Double bypass heart of 90s Britart scene. Barely still beating.
The Cantaloupe	35 Charlotte Rd	020 7729 5566	Of course YOU'RE not a corporate whore.
Cargo	83 Rivington St	020 7749 7844	Cavernous, sterile hole with bad sound but good gigs. Natch.
Charlie Wright's International Bar	45 Pitfield St	020 7490 8345	Does anyone turn up here sober?
Club Aquarium	256 Old St	020 7251 6136	After-hours swimming pool scuzzfest.
Cocomo	323 Old St	020 7613 0315	Cocktail bar with cakes, comfy sofas and scrumptious staff.
Comedy Cafe	66 Rivington St	020 7739 5706	Fun venue, but invariably a dud in the line-up.
Cordy House	Curtain Rd	N/A	Secret warehouse rave place. Authentically at odds with the authorities.
East Village	89 Great Eastern St	020 7739 5173	Shoreditch clubbing novice where the DJ is king.
The Elbow Room	97 Curtain Rd	020 7613 1316	Pricey, mildly funky pool joint.
Electricity Showroom	39 Hoxton Sq	020 7739 3939	Shark-infested waters.
Favela Chic	91 Great Eastern St	020 7613 4228	Caipirinha-lovin', shabby-chic bar full of clothes-swapping kwaziness.
The Foundry	84 Great Eastern St	020 7739 6900	Like a pretentious art student's dream bar. In a good way.
The Griffin	93 Leonard St	020 7739 6719	NOT the strip bar of the same name...
Hoxton Square Bar & Kitchen	Hoxton Sq	020 7613 0709	Snotty bands and doormen. Wear something uber.
The Legion	348 Old St	020 7729 4441	Free jukebox, quality DJs, cheap beer. Happy times.
The Macbeth	60 70 Hoxton St	020 7739 5095	Hot new bands love it. And so do we.
The Old Blue Last	39 Great Eastern St	020 7739 7033	Until the bass drum WILL bring down that pub ceiling.
Plastic People	147 Curtain Rd	020 7739 6471	Tiny, pitch black musical adventure.
Pool Bar	104 Curtain Rd	020 7739 9608	Shiny cocktail dive sympathetic to noise and club gigs.
The Red Lion	41 Hoxton St	020 7729 7920	Stay forever if you bag the chaise lounge...
The Stag's Head	55 Orsman Rd	020 7739 6741	Run down boozer currently being used for hip gigs.
Strongroom Bar	120 Curtain Rd	020 7426 5103	Shoreditch's last stronghold of unpretentiousness?
Troy Bar	10 Hoxton St	020 7739 6695	A semi-hidden gem with soul and funk music most nights.

Map 85 • Stoke Newington (East)

The Birdcage	58 Stamford Hill	020 8806 6740	High-ceilinged pub with squishy sofas and lived-in feel.
Blush	8 Cazenove Rd	020 7923 9202	Pink pint-parlour with poker and personable patrons (oh please!)
The Royal Sovereign	64 Northwold Rd	020 8806 2449	Drink with the locals.
White Hart	69 Stoke Newington High St	020 7254 6626	Huge pub, huge beer garden – really it's huge.

Map 86 • Dalston / Kingsland

Bar 23	23 Stoke Newington Rd	020 7241 2060	A slice of weirdness with wacked out DJing and drinking.
Barden's Boudoir	38 Stoke Newington Rd	020 7249 9557	Anything can happen in this basement. The beating heart of Dalston's music shenanigans.
Cafe Oto	18 Ashwin St	020 7923 1231	Mysterious new venue importing music from the hinterlands of psychedelia.
Dalston Superstore	117 Kingsland High St	020 7254 2273	Uber hip polysexual squelch-a-thon.
The Haggerston	438 Kingsland Rd	020 7923 3206	Artist-run flea pit. Chaotic crowd surfing most nights.
Jazz Bar	4 Bradbury St	020 7254 9728	Funk and free cheese. Until 5. Need we say more?
Marquis of Lansdowne	48 Stoke Newington Rd	020 7254 1104	Pleases long-standing locals and hip Hackneyites alike.
Passion	251 Amhurst Rd		Tiny basement venue that hosts massive all-nighters.
Pembury Tavern	90 Amhurst Rd	020 8986 8597	Large selection of microbrews.
The Prince George	40 Parkholme Rd	020 7254 6060	Buzzing local favourite. Renowned Monday quiz night, great jukebox.

Map 87 • Hackney Downs / Lower Clapton

Biddle Brothers	88 Lower Clapton Rd	N/A	Almost trendy oasis for the trendy in an eccentric neighbourhood.
Crooked Billet	84 Upper Clapton Rd	020 8806 2747	Proof that Clapton can still be f***ing terrifying.
Hugo's Speaker Palace	14 Andre St	020 8968 5704	Clandestine speaker cemetery. Very hush-hush and very cool.

Map 88 • Haggerston / Queensbridge Rd

A10 (aka The Russian Bar)	267 Kingsland Rd	n/a	It's hell and it's heaven and we can't make our f'ing minds up.
The Fox	372 Kingsland Rd	020 7254 4012	Half-way stop for Shoreditch-to-Dalston pub crawls.
Melange	281 Kingsland Rd	078 9635 0086	Like your frontroom. With more parties.
Passing Clouds	440 Kingsland Rd	020 7168 7146	Back alley arts collective and live venue.
Plaza	161 Kingsland Rd	020 7613 1319	Sometime gig venue, all-the-time scary East-end boozer.

Map 89 • London Fields / Hackney Central

Baxter's Court	282 Mare St	020 8525 9010	A chain pub, okay, okay. But check the ladies' toilets!
The Dolphin	165 Mare St	020 8985 3727	Pathos-sodden karaoke occasionally ruined by post-opening art people.
The Dove	24 Broadway Market	020 7275 7617	Belgian beer paradise.
Pub on the Park	19 Martello St	020 7275 9586	Tap for London Fields.
The Old Ship	2 Sylvester Path	020 8986 1641	Nicely refurbed ex-dive.

Map 90 • Homerton / Victoria Park North

Chats Palace Arts Centre	42 Brooksbys Walk	020 8533 0227	Fantastic community arts venue—Hackney classic.
The Lauriston	162 Victoria Park Rd	020 8985 5404	As vamped up as its would-be-village surroundings.
Royal Inn on the Park	111 Lauriston Rd	020 8985 3321	Victoria Park's prime boozer.

Map 91 • Shoreditch / Brick Lane / Spitalfields

93 Feet East	150 Brick Ln	020 7247 3293	Enthusiastic, trendy club (to impress out-of-towners).
Anda De Bridge	42 Kingsland Rd	020 7739 3863	Cocktail party, Caribbean-style.
The Archers	42 Osborn St	020 7247 3826	Nice ole pub that's resisted Shoreditchification. Perfect for pre-curry pints.
Bar Kick	127 Shoreditch High St	020 7739 8700	Lemon-yellow table football gaff.
Bethnal Green Working Men's Club	44 Pollard Row	020 7739 7170	Saucy amateur burlesque that still confuses the resident Working Men.
The Big Chill Bar	Dray Walk off Brick Lane	020 7392 9180	Still among Brick Lane's better drinking spots.
Browns	1 Hackney Rd	020 7739 4653	Now really. What would your mother say?
Café 1001	91 Brick Ln`	020 7247 9679	Like a house party. But one where cans cost £3.
The Carpenter's Arms	73 Cheshire St	020 7739 6342	No longer run by the Kray twins' mother, still felonious fun.
Casa Blue	228 Brick Lane	020 7729 6444	Hookah and bottled beer.
Catch	22 Kingsland Rd	020 7729 6097	Reliably active dance floor, reliably silly hats, reliably good fun.
Club In a Toilet!	82 Commercial St		Yes, a club in a toilet! Tiny. Secret. No longer smelly.
The Commercial Tavern	142 Commercial St	020 7247 1888	Trusty Shoreditch traditional.
Ditch Bar	145 Shoreditch High St	020 7739 4018	Noisy electro bar/scrum.
Exit	174 Brick Lane	020 7377 2088	Sit in a row with fellow Brick Lane trendies.
The George & Dragon	2 Blackheath Hill	020 8691 3764	Witness the E2 gay clique rev up for imminent carnage.
The Golden Heart	110 Commercial St	020 7247 2158	Has it all: fires, pints and a lazy resident dog.
The Gramaphone Bar	60 Commercial St	020 7377 5332	Dark basement venue.
Green and Red	51 Bethnal Green Rd	020 7749 9670	Tequila bar worth its post-shot salt—you're spoilt for choice.
Herbal	10 Kingsland Rd	020 7613 4462	It's small enough to shout at the DJ. And groovy.
Jaguar Shoes	32 Kingsland Rd	020 7729 5830	Happy hipsters behind wide windows.
Joiners Arms	116 Hackney Rd	020 7739 9397	Popular gay pub that knows how to have fun.
Loungelover	1 Whiteby St	020 7012 1234	Kitsch-colonial glitter-ball of a cocktail bar.
On the Rocks	25 Kingsland Rd	020 7688 0339	Come face to face with oblivion every Friday.
Owl And The Pussycat	34 Redchurch St	020 7613 3628	Crooked little place, tucked in the folds of Shoreditch's blubber.
Prague	6 Kingsland Rd	020 7739 9110	The closest you'll ever get to a romantic bar in Shoreditch.
Pride of Spitalfields	3 Heneage St	020 7247 8933	The only East End boozer left on Brick Lane.
Public Life	82 Commercial St	020 7375 1631	Used to be a toilet. Kinda still is. Moronic fun.
Redchurch	107 Redchurch St	020 7729 8333	Late, loud DJ box.
The Royal Oak	73 Columbia Rd	020 7729 2220	Gentrifying, gentrifying... gentrified.
Shoreditch House	Ebor St	020 7739 5040	Last one in the rooftop pool buys the drinks!
T Bar	56 Shoreditch High St	020 7729 2973	Does cool well.
Vibe Bar	91 Brick Ln	020 7426 0491	Bar in a brewery. Feel the vibe?
The Water Poet	9 Folgate St	020 7426 0495	Mismatched chairs, over-stuffed sofas, philosophy and beer.
Ye Olde Axe	69 Hackney Rd	020 7729 5137	Rockabilly-only weekends. That's right: rockabilly-only. Occasional gentleman's club.

Map 92 • Bethnal Green

The Albion	94 Goldsmiths Row	020 7739 0185	Friendly, footy-mad local. All welcome.
Backyard Comedy	231 Cambridge Heath Rd	020 7739 3122	The comedian's comedy house: this one knows what it's doing.
Bethnal Green Working Men's Club	44 Pollard Row	020 7739 7170	Saucy amateur burlesque that still confuses the resident Working Men.
The Camel	277 Globe Rd	020 8983 9888	Bethnal Green's best kept secret... D'oh!
Florist	255 Globe Rd	020 8981 1100	The Camel's naughty little sister.
Images	483 Hackney Rd	020 7739 5213	When the lapdancing's over, the clubbing madness begins.
The Star of Bethnal Green (DUP)	359 Bethnal Green Rd	020 7729 0167	Formerly the Pleasure Unit. Still Bethnal Green's live music best.

Map 93 • Globe Town / Mile End (North)

The Approach Tavern	47 Approach Rd	020 8980 2321	Great if you can tolerate the ironic haircuts crew.
Club E3	562 Mile End Rd	020 8980 6427	Purple everywhere. If Prince lived in Bow, he'd come here.
The Fat Cat	221 Grove Rd	020 8983 1412	No fat cats, but a good mix of locals and trendies.
Jongleurs (Bow Wharf)	221 Grove Rd	0844 499 4062	Blandard comedy chain.
The Morgan Arms	43 Morgan St	020 8980 6389	Grab a pint with some gourmet food.
Palm Tree	1 Haverfield Rd	020 8980 2918	Brass walls and retired crooners! Amazingly old-fashioned boozer.

Map 94 • Bow

The Coborn Arms	8 Coborn Rd	020 8980 3793	Nice ales, nice beer garden.
The Lord Morpeth	402 Old Ford Rd	020 8981 9336	Bow boozing's best.
The Young Prince	448 Roman Rd	020 8980 1292	If on Roman Road...

Map 95 • Whitechapel (West) / St Katharine's Dock

The Castle	44 Commercial Rd	020 7481 2361	East End fortress holding it against the City.
Dickens Inn	St Katharine's Way	020 7488 2208	Proof that an awesome location can conquer all.
Prohibition	1 St. Katherine's Dock	020 7702 4210	Gormless bar.
Rhythm Factory	16 Whitechapel Rd	020 7375 3774	The Libertines' old haunt, with all the grimy 'chic' that implies.

Map 96 • Whitechapel (East) / Shadwell (West) / Wapping

The Captain Kidd	108 Wapping High St	0207 480 5759	Pub with nice Thames-side beer garden.
The Caxton	50 The Highway	020 7481 2961	Opens weekdays at 4am. Depressing, but come here to kick-on.
Indo	133 Whitechapel Rd	020 7247 4926	Very narrow and everything but narrow-minded.
Town of Ramsgate	62 Wapping High St	020 7481 8000	Get nautical.

Map 97 • Stepney / Shadwell (East)

The Black Horse	168 Mile End Rd	020 7790 1684	Recently renovated gay local. Drag acts and gogo boys.
The George Tavern	373 Commercial Rd	020 7790 1763	Old men, hipsters and blue-collar poets in imperfect harmony.
The Prospect of Whitby	57 Wapping Wall	020 7481 1095	Ye olde pub(e) on ye Thames(e).
Troxy	490 Commercial Rd	020 7734 3922	Glorious art deco palace.

Map 98 • Mile End (South) / Limehouse

The Grapes	76 Narrow St	020 7987 4396	True to its roots East End boozer—natural survivor.

Map 100 • Poplar (West) / Canary Wharf (West)

Bar 38	West India Quay	020 7515 8361	Great inside and out.
Davy's at Canary Wharf	31 Fisherman's Walk	020 7363 6633	Traditional-style with fine ales, wine and food.
Dion Canary Wharf	Port East Building, West India Quay	020 7987 0001	Docklands warehouse-turned-champagne heaven.
Via Fossa	18 Hertsmere Rd	0871 971 5240	Three floors of bankers...

Map 101 • Poplar (East) / Canary Wharf (East)

The Greenwich Pensioner	28 Bazely St	020 7987 4414	No pensioners and not in Greenwich.
The Resolute	210 Poplar High St	020 79871429	In Poplar? Desperate for a drink?

Map 102 • Millwall

Hubbub	269 Westferry Rd	020 7515 5577	Oasis in Docklands desert.

Map 103 • Cubitt Town / Mudchute

Ferry House	26 Ferry St	020 7537 9587	Beer-drenched docks time capsule.
Lord Nelson	1 Manchester Rd	020 7987 1970	Can I have a half, Nelson?
Waterman's Arms	1 Glenaffric Ave	020 7093 0837	Proper boozer on the Island.

Map 104 • South Bank / Waterloo / Lambeth North

Anchor & Hope	32 The Cut	020 7928 9898	For that intellectual pre-theatre/dinner chat.
Barrio	14 W Square	020 7801 9548	What balmy Sunday evenings were made for.
Concrete	Southbank Centre	020 7928 4123	Restaurant/bar features Russian beer, food, absinthe.
Cubana	48 Lower Marsh	020 7928 8778	Still riding the mojito trend. But good at them.
The Cut Bar	66 The Cut	020 7928 4400	Enjoy the outdoor terrace with trendy media types and thesps.
Da Vinci's	6 Baylis Rd	020 7928 8099	Cheesy and bizarre late-night fun.
The Fire Station	150 Waterloo Rd	020 7620 2226	Only fun when you're desperate.
The Pit Bar at the Old Vic	The Cut	020 7928 2975	Guzzle champagne with Kevin Spacey and friends.
Royal Festival Hall	Belvedere Rd	087 1663 2500	Increasingly exciting programming amid nicely refurbished surroundings.
Skylon	Belvedere Rd	020 7654 7800	Impress someone with the view, then split the bill.

Map 105 • Southwark / Bankside (West)

Albert Arms	1 Gladstone St	020 7928 6517	Where yuppies meet students meet blow-ins meet locals.
Imbibe	173 Blackfriars Rd	020 7928 3693	Studenty feel, mid-week. Shouty after-workers, otherwise.
Ministry of Sound	103 Gaunt St	020 7740 8728	The sound really IS amazing.
Prince of Wales	51 St George's Rd	020 7582 9696	Cheap local with downright scary karaoke.
The White Theatre	206 Union St	020 7261 0209	Free aperitvo food excuses their 'TWT' abbreviation.

Map 106 • Bankside (East) / Borough / Newington

The Anchor	34 Park St	020 7407 1577	Did Samuel Johnson have to battle this many tourists?
Belushi's	161 Borough High St	020 7939 9700	Drunk Antipodeans. Karaoke. General carnage.
The Blue-Eyed Maid	173 Borough High St	020 7378 8259	It's never too late for a last drink in Borough.
Brew Wharf	Brew Wharf Yard, Stoney St	020 7378 6601	Beer lovers' heaven.
The George Inn	77 Borough High St	020 7407 2056	Grab a home brew in the dazzlingly ancient George Inn.
The Globe	8 Bedale St	020 7407 0043	Bridget Jones' home? Do we care?
La Cave	6 Borough High St	020 7378 0788	So delightful you'll even start liking the French. Briefly.
The Market Porter	9 Stoney St	020 7407 2495	Market traders and suits neck real ale. Smell the testosterone.
The Rake	14 Winchester Walk	020 7407 0557	Tiny place with a hundred different beers. Honestly, a hundred.
The Roebuck	50 Great Dover St	020 7357 7324	Cool but calm drinkerie for a pre-night-out drink.
The Rose	123 Snowfields	020 7378 6660	Superb backstreet boozer full of human oddities.
Roxy Bar and Screen	128 Borough High St	020 7407 4057	Mingle with baby yuppies at the Roxy Bar & Screen.
The Royal Oak	44 Tabard St	020 7357 7173	Possibly the friendliest landlords in London.
SeOne	Weston St	020 7407 1617	Loud music & louder people.
Shunt Lounge and Vaults	20 Stainer St	020 7378 7776	Dusty dancing under the railway arches. Membership required.
Southwark Tavern	22 Southwark St	020 7403 0257	Traditional ambience and ordinary fare in ye olde Southwark Tavern.
Wine Wharf	Stoney St	020 7940 8335	If you're as crazy about wine as they are.

Map 107 • Shad Thames

The Hide	39 Bermondsey St	020 7403 6655	Slightly odd vibe, but cracking drinks.
Hilton London Tower Bridge	5 Tooley St	020 3002 4300	Super-chilled, low-lit relaxation zone for the wealthy.

Map 109 • Southwark Park

Ancient Foresters	282 Southwark Park Rd	020 7394 1633	Surprise charmer in an otherwise grimy area.

Map 110 • Rotherhithe (West) / Canada Waters

Cable	Tunnel Rd	020 7403 7730	Get messed up in a dark tunnel. Again.
Old Salt Quay	163 Rotherhithe St	020 7394 7108	Pub-by-numbers, but the riverside patio of dreams.

Map 111 • Rotherhithe (East) Surrey Quays

Moby Dick	6 Russell Pl, off Greenland Dock	020 7231 6719	Once here, it's hard to leave. Because it's really far from the tube.
Wibbley Wobbley	South Dock Marina, Rope St	020 7232 2320	Great dinky boat-bar, for short people.

Map 112 • Kennington / Elephant and Castle

Corsica Studios	5 Elephant Rd	020 7703 4760	Sweaty music venue with 'home-made' vibe.

Dog House	293 Kennington Rd	020 7820 9310	Like your scruffy, unpretentious younger brother. Made for chill-axing.
Prince of Wales	43 Cleaver Sq	020 7735 9916	Stuart's favourite pub in Kennington.

Map 114 • Old Kent Road (West) / Burgess Park

Auto Italia South East	1 Glengall Rd		Frankly amazing artist-run space in an old car showroom!
World Turned Upside Down	145 Old Kent Rd	020 7237 4181	Original headquarters of the Pearly Kings & Queens.

Map 118 • Deptford (Central)

The Lord Palmerston	81 Childers St	020 8692 1575	Fewer brawls than your average Deptford pub.

Map 119 • Deptford (East)

Bird's Nest	32 Deptford Church St	020 8692 1928	Hilarious 'locals vs. trendies' vibe. Go for monthly Flesh Dunce!
Dog & Bell	116 Prince St	020 8692 5664	Now why can't ALL pubs in Deptford be like this?

Map 120 • Greenwich

Bar du Musee	17 Nelson Rd	020 8858 4710	"You have beautiful eyes, you know that?"
Greenwich Union	56 Royal Hill	020 8692 6258	Beers galore.

Map 122 • Camberwell (East)

The Castle	65 Camberwell Church St	020 7277 2601	Locals, board games and disco.
Dark Horse	16 Grove Lane	020 7703 9990	A wine pub itching to test its cocktail skills.
Funky Munky	25 Camberwell Church St	020 7277 1806	A local, of sorts, for middle class Camberwellites.

Map 125 • New Cross Gate

The Montague Arms	289 Queen's Rd	020 7639 4923	Semi-legendary, bizarrely decorated local, staffed by the world's oldest barmen and women.

Map 126 • New Cross *Address*

Amersham Arms	388 New Cross Rd	020 8469 1499	Art school hipdom in grimy New Cross's coolest venue.
Hobgoblin	272 New Cross Rd	020 8692 3193	Get drunk with the Goldsmiths crowd.
New Cross Inn	323 New Cross Rd	020 8692 1866	Someone's gotta keep "the scene" going.

Map 127 • Coldharbour Lane / Herne Hill (West)

The Commercial	210 Railton Rd	020 7733 8783	Roaring fire and mulled wine in winter. Fits like a glove.
Escape Bar and Art	214 Railton Rd	020 7737 0333	The bar's alright, the art's excellent.
The Florence	133 Dulwich Rd	020 7326 4987	Microbrewery on premises.

Map 129 • East Dulwich

Inside 72	72 Lordship Lane	020 8693 7131	The only bit of cool in Dulwichgastropubland.
liquorish	123 Lordship Ln	020 8693 7744	Good things happen here.

Map 130 • Peckham Rye

The Rye	31 Peckham Rye	020 7639 5397	For lazy lunches on summer Sundays. A pocket of delicious East Dulwich swank Peckham-side.

Map 131 • Vauxhall / Albert Embankment

Area	67 Albert Embankment		Another massive Vauxhall rave hole. Serious gay clientele.
The Lavender	112 Vauxhall Walk	020 7735 4440	Just popping to the Lav
The Royal Vauxhall Tavern	372 Kennington Ln	020 7820 1222	Fun gay pub with trashy cabaret.
South Central	349 Kennington Ln	020 7793 0903	Fur on tap throughout the week. Sundays recommended.

Map 132 • Battersea (West)

Le QuecumBar	42 Battersea High St	020 7787 2227	Gypsy jazz, honkytonk and frogs legs in bygone Parisian chic.
The Woodman	60 Battersea High St	020 7228 2968	A nice fire. Pint of Badger. Luverleee.

Map 133 • Battersea (East)

The Chelsea Reach	181 Battersea Park Rd	020 7627 8434	Rough-around-the-edges local pub for local people.

Map 134 • South Lambeth

Bar Estrella	115 Old South Lambeth Rd	020 7793 1051	Football on telly, tapas in tummy. The heart of Little Portugal.

The Battersea Barge	Nine Elms Ln	020 7498 0004	Bouncy, buoyant, thrilled to see you—the Labrador puppy of venues.
Fire	38 Parry St	020 7820 0550	Legendary gay terrordrome with LED ceiling.
Roller Disco @ Renaissance Rooms	126 S Lambeth Rd	0844 736 5375	Roller skates, alcohol, and a very nervous Health & Safety officer.

Map 135 • Oval

Fentiman Arms	64 Fentiman Rd	020 7793 9796	The staff believe that smiles kill kittens.

Map 136 • Putney

The Boathouse	Brewhouse Ln	020 8789 0476	Riverside pub with loadsa outdoor space.
Duke's Head	8 Lower Richmond Rd	020 8788 2552	Typical gastro pub upstairs. Dark DJ bar downstairs.
Jolly Gardeners	61 Lacey Rd	020 8789 2539	Like all good pubs. And sock monkey classes on Wednesdays.
Star & Garter	4 Lower Richmond Rd	020 8788 0345	Upscale Saturday night hotspot on the Thames.

Map 137 • Wandsworth (West)

The Queen Adelaide	35 Putney Bridge Rd	020 8874 1695	Good beer selection. Mixed crowd. Decent Sunday Roast.
Upper Lounge	26 Upper Richmond Rd	020 8875 0269	Utterly likeable. Except Thursdays when it heaves with excitable Saffas.

Map 138 • Wandsworth (Central)

The Cat's Back	88 Point Pleasant	020 8877 0818	Atmospheric and busy with loadsa obscure decoration.
GJ's	89 Garratt Ln	020 8874 2271	Party with snow bunnies.

Map 139 • Wandsworth (East)

Adventure Bar and Lounge	91 Battersea Rise	020 7223 1700	Laid back lounging. Friendly crowd. Poncey cocktails.

Map 140 • Clapham Junction / Northcote Rd

B@1	85 Battersea Rise	020 7978 6595	Be at one with a cocktail menu the size of a book.
Jongleurs (Battersea)	49 Lavender Gardens	0844 499 4060	Lots and lots of laughs. Turns into a scary club.

Map 141 • Battersea (South)

Halo	317 Battersea Park Rd	020 7801 8683	A halo isn't enough. Give this bar a sainthood.
The Lost Angel	339 Battersea Park Rd	020 7622 2112	Put this in your pipe and smoke it, Shoreditch.

Map 142 • Clapham Old Town

Frog and Forget-Me-Not	32 The Pavement	020 7622 5230	A first floor terrace that's just made for summer.
Lost Society	697 Wandsworth Rd	020 7652 6526	Country-house drinking, in Clapham.
Prince of Wales	38 Old Town	020 7622 3530	Eccentric, friendly. Run by a magpie.
Rose and Crown	2 The Polygon	020 7720 8265	For the CAMRA purists.
The Sun	47 Clapham Old Town	020 7622 4980	Nice pub. Ruined by surfeit of twats.

Map 143 • Clapham High Street

The Alexandra	14 Clapham Common South Side	020 7627 5102	Join an up-for-it crowd as multinational as the sport here.
Bread and Roses	68 Clapham Manor St	020 7498 1779	Surprisingly pleasant socialist boozer. Without Clapham tossers.
The Clapham North	409 Clapham Rd	020 7274 2472	A bit 'Clapham', but pretty likable really.
The Falcon	33 Bedford Rd	020 7274 2428	"I told Daddy, I've nowhere to even PARK a GTi!"
Green & Blue	20 Bedford Rd	020 7498 9648	For the finest wine. Because you're worth it.
Infernos	146 Clapham High St	020 7720 7633	Oh God no.
The Railway	18 Clapham High St	020 7622 4077	Half-trendy, half-local, three-quarters cool.
The Two Brewers	114 Clapham High St	020 7819 9539	Club nights, gay cabaret, lots of fu-un!
The White House	65 Clapham Park Rd	020 7498 3388	Manhattan in Clapham? Erm, O.K.

Map 144 • Stockwell / Brixton (West)

Duke of Edinburgh	204 Ferndale Rd	020 7924 0509	Warm, traditional pub with massive beer garden.
Plan B	418 Brixton Rd	08701 165 421	Has made a name for itself, but pretty lame really.
The Prince	469 Brixton Rd	020 7326 4455	Behind dealers chanting skunk lies a nothin' special pub.
The Swan	215 Clapham Rd	020 7978 9778	Don't worry about spitting on the floor.

Map 145 • Stockwell / Brixton (East)

Brixton Academy	211 Stockwell Rd	020 7771 3000	Overrated, but still a tad awesome.
The Grosvenor	17 Sidney Rd	020 7733 1799	Rough n' ready local with amazing crust/noise/punk gigs.
Jamm	261 Brixton Rd	020 7274 5537	The real deal a little way out.

Map 146 • Earlsfield

Bar 366	366 Garratt Ln	020 8944 9591	Chilled, lounge-type bar.
Baraza	561 Garratt Ln	020 8944 9009	Teeny, funky bar with cocktails-a-go-go.
Halfway House	521 Garratt Ln	020 8946 2788	Slinky, chardonnay-swilling pub with terrific terrace.
Le Gothique	Windmill Rd & John Archer Wy	020 8870 6567	The answer to: "Open a bar! What could go wrong?"

Map 147 • Balham (West)

The Nightingale	97 Nightingale Ln	020 8673 1637	Untrendified local. Long may it stay so.

Map 148 • Balham (East)

Balham Bowls Club	79 Ramsden Rd	020 8673 4700	A pub. In a bowling club circa 1950. Genius.
The Bedford	77 Bedford Hill	020 8682 8940	Music and comedy pub with great bands but crappy beer.

Map 150 • Brixton

The Dogstar	389 Coldharbour Ln	020 7733 7515	The burritos are great, but leave before the tunes get cheesy.
The Effra	38 Kellet Rd	020 7274 4180	A slice of the real Brixton.
The Fridge	1 Town Hall Parade	020 7326 5100	Techno, trance, hardcore venue avec occasional stabbing.
Mango Landin'	40 St Matthews Rd	020 7737 3044	Reggae-tinged alternative bar.
Mass	Brixton Hill	020 7738 7875	Drum and Bass + Hard House + Fetish Nights = Hedonist Heaven
Prince Albert	418 Coldharbour Ln	020 7274 3771	It's charming, trust us. In a not too obvious kindaway.
Ritzy Café	Brixton Oval, Coldharbour Lane (above Ritzy cinema)	020 7733 2229	Where Brixton sparkles. Cinema, bar, café and free live music.
The Windmill	22 Blenheim Gardens	020 8671 0700	Rough-edged weirdo magnet. Unique and brilliant.

Map 151 • Tooting Bec

The Bec Bar	26 Tooting Bec Rd	020 8672 7722	Pleasant enough. Go for sport.
King's Head	84 Upper Tooting Rd	020 8767 6708	Former gin palace brings yesteryear flair to the wasteland.
Smoke Bar	14 Trinity Rd	020 8767 3902	Standard, compact DJ bar.

Map 152 • Tooting Broadway

Garden House	196 Tooting High St	020 8767 6582	Revived Victorian local. Live music and log fire.
Jack Beard's	76 Mitcham Rd	020 8767 8967	Drink. Dance. Drink. Feck—what happened?
The Ramble Inn	Amen Corner	020 8672 2777	Irish/locals bullcrap-free boozer.
Tram and Social	46 Mitcham Rd	020 8767 0278	Cavernous, funky and cool without trying.

It's hard to judge Londoners by their favourite restaurants. We all have a fully-stocked larder of eateries we frequent—adapting to every culinary occasion like cosmopolitan chameleons. We'll rough it over a hangover-challenging fry-up by day **(E Pellicci (Map 92))**, camp it up deluxe style by night **(Ruby & Sequoia (Map 1))** and blow most of our wage on a bottle of champagne over Sunday lunch, just to celebrate pay day in the first place. The truth is—there's so much choice, we can't really help it. We don't pay out extortionate rents just to cook spag bol ourselves, like the rest of the country. No. We choose to live in London, where the disproportionate amount of restaurants per capita leaves us no choice but to accept our fate and embrace the restaurant as foreplay to a damn good night out. After all, we have restaurants to suit every imaginable situation. Everyone has their local Italian; die-hard curry house; girly bistro where rosé becomes acceptable; guaranteed-a-shag-later candlelit brasserie; close-that-deal power lunch spot; greasy caff; and of course, that Sunday lunch gastropub where you can think about all of this over a massive Yorkshire pudding. Probably you don't need us, but we know how fickle London can be. We swear by our local one day, but the minute Jamie O. opens another reasonably over-priced gastropub, there goes that old favourite.

Eating For Britain

From pie shops to posh Sunday lunches, great British food has become our little pièce de résistance in the global restaurant scene. And like everything else, we do it with a bit of a nudge nudge wink wink. We rule the gastropub roost—especially when the likes of the **Eagle (Map 6)**, **Anchor & Hope (Map 104)** and **Great Queen Street (Map 13)** opened their doors, taking a new look at British cuisine and putting it on our tables in ways we'd never seen it before, while other old standards refuse to budge from doing what they do best—partly because there's no one else on earth that can do it like them. The pie and mash at **F. Cooke (Maps 84 & 89)**, for instance, is so good they'd have made Queen Victoria demanding: "Please sir, may I have some more?".

With the onslaught of the recession, leaving us crying for mummy under piles of rejected bank loans, London's appetite for the most comforting of comfort foods on every corner has become more of a necessity than ever. Take the new **Pieminister** wagon, for want of a better word, stationed outside St Mary's Church on Angel's Upper Street or **Banger Bros.** pitching up its stall outside of Euston Station **(Map 78)** – comfort food is everywhere. If you're in need of a gastronomical tribute to ol' Blighty try **Roast (Map 106)** for its native breed Mondays (promising only to use British meat); **Boot and Flogger (Map 104),** for some whiffy, yet delicious, Stilton and Port; and **The Carpenter's Arms (Map 91)** for gastropub fare that's as good as it gets.

For a Sunday lunch to savour try **Annie's Chiswick (Map 107)** for its cheery fare, **The Charles Lamb (Map 83)** for a long-drawn out afternoon and **Blueberries (Map90)** for its bright, eager-to-please atmosphere. Last but not least, London has some of the most sophisticated fish & chips around with über-fresh ingredients like at **Brady's (Map 106)**, **Fisher's Chips (Map 48)**, **Tom's Place (Map 45)**, **Sea Cow (Map 129)**, and **Rock & Sole Place (Map 13)**.

London is still a great place to eat British.

Caffs and Breakfast Joints

Few of us have time to actually eat it during the week, but nothing beats a breakfast when a hangover has descended. From a posh crumpet brunch at the **Wolseley (Map 9)** to the most traditional of caffs like **Alpino (Map 80)** or those that think outside of sausage n' egg box like the **Dalston Lane Cafe (Map 86)** with its french toast, breakfast really has become the most important meal of any Londoner's Saturday morning, anyway. All these are well and good, but if you can discover one of those rarities like the absolutely knock-you-on the floor-delicious Latin breakfast at **El Vergel (Map 106)**, you know you must have rock-hard London karma. If you like people watching, there's **Bar Italia (Map 12)** or **Jones Dairy Café (Map 91)**. For healthier fare try **The Larder (Map 15)**. For a Mediterranean take on a fry-up try **La Voute (Map 60)** or if you like your morning meal more Yank than rank try anything

at **The Breakfast Club (Map 80)**. The best greasy spoons include **Jeff's Café (Map 18)**, **Mario's Café (Map 72)**, and **Marie's Café (Map 104)**.

Credit Crunch Lunches...

...breakfasts, dinners or snacks. There's this nasty rumour—spread mostly by those out-of-towners who resent their commute yet insist on living two hours away—that London is no place for the impoverished restaurant lover, particularly in these economically unstable times. Such slanderers should be stopped at the M25 and made to pay double congestion charge. The truth is, if you know London, you know how to eat out for under £20 (and even under a tenner when particularly skint). We have plenty of true gems where you can boldly shout 'I'll get this one!' all smugly moving ahead in the old restaurant rounds game, with your accompanying party none the wiser. We have to sing the praises of **Cha Cha Moon (Map 10)**, once boasting a price of £3.50 for everything on the menu when it first opened, punters still don't have to reach too deeply in their wallets for spot-on char kway teow. **Comptoir Libanais (Map 2)** has uncompromisingly delicious, yet undeniably affordable mezes. **The Table (Map 105)** has thankfully extended its opening hours slightly, to include weekend brunch, therefore keeping its title as cheap eats supreme. For a less-than-a-tenner bento, try Japanese hideaway **Yoshino (Map 10)**. If you have no qualms re: pretense and just want to eat cheap try **Paul Rothe & Son** for its Austrian Liptauer on Ukrainian rye bread **(Map 2)** and **Tortilla (Map 80)** for a fiver burrito. Stuck in Chelsea without a trust fund? Try **Le Columbier (Map 45)**. Now, go cash in on that overdraft and keep reading...

Eating On Trend

London *du jour* is one of tightening purse strings. Gone are the glory days of "putting it on expenses" ever since the media descended upon Parliament's love of fudging budgets. So while the yummy mummies and Sloane Rangers still roam, fashionable eating has become about being in-the-know over chic, "my little discovery" eateries where how much dosh you dish falls second fiddle to dishing the right nosh.

While Michelin-starred institutions like **Gordon Ramsay at Claridges (Map 2)**, **Alain Ducasse at the Dorchester (Map 9)** and **Rhodes 24 (Map 17)** still matter in this town, celebrities are now seen frequenting holes in the wall, as we hear Marc Jacobs likes slurping noodles at Hackney's **Que Viet (Map 91)**. The real Big Smoke cognoscenti make their way to **Beas of Bloomsbury (Map 5)** for artisan cupcakes, **Negozio Classica (Map 29)** for latenight luxuriating over vino and sharing platters at the newspaper critic's latest fave - **Bocca di Lupo (Map 11)**—with its sophisticated yet somehow affordable Italian fare. We've always been a city that loves a "bargain" alternative—like Matthew Williamson's collection at H&M)—and we're still proud to say that for every celebrity chef hot spot, there's a high street version. If you can't afford the £95 per person price at **Gordon Ramsay (Map 46)** (and that's without splashing out on the £10,000 bottles of wine), you'll love **The Devonshire (Map 38)**. And if you lust over Tom Aikens, try **Tom's Kitchen (Map 45)**, an ever-popular brasserie that still has a lot to write home about. If you've been following Jamie Oliver on Twitter, you'll know one of his affordable chain of tasty Italians – aptly named Jamie's Italian – is due to open up in London's Canary Wharf by the time you read this. So in this sprawling city, you can still eat like a king while the rest of the world moans about its financial woes.

For classically chic and delicious, try **The Bleeding Heart (Map 15)** – the bistro's better than the restaurant - or **Galvin Bistrot de Luxe (Map 2)**. For a view, **Galvin at Windows (Map 9)**, **Skylon (Map 104)** and **Oxo Tower Wharf (Map 104)** still reign supreme over London's skyline. If you're a visiting footballer's wife lurching around in 10-inch heels, try **Balans (Map 11)**, **Deep (Map 50)**, **Eight Over Eight (Map 44)** or **Beach Blanket Babylon (Map 29)**. Hipster deluxe joints include **Village East (Map 108)**, **The Market (Map 106)** and **Bistrotheque (Map 92)**. Take mummy dearest to **Aubergine (Map 44)** or **Morgan M (Map 74)** when she's in town and if you like anything with a label, try **J Sheekey (Map 24)**. But, if you want something worth every penny try **Ubon by Nobu (Map 100)**, **Le Cercle (Map 46)**, and **Wild Honey (Map 10)**. Pretty soon you'll be able to enter your fave fashionable joint and exchange noisy bisoux with the maitre d' (that's when you know you're in).

Going for a... (fill in the blank ethnic food)

In such an ethnically-diverse capital as this one, we savour our wide-range of foreign grub. For Londoners 'going for a curry' is an adventure which can encompass such a wide range of cuisines from Nepalese at **Kathmandu Valley (Map 138)** to Eritrean at **Adulis (Map 150)** and a kebab at **Tayyabs (Map 96)** or **Beirut Express (Map 1)** is more than just an ill-advised stop on the way to the night bus. We choose our indulgences carefully. We know how to avoid the incessant menu hawkers along Brick Lane on our way to the **Beigel Bakery (Map 91)**. After all, the best curry houses are rarely on this over-hyped thoroughfare—if you have to, try **The Clipper (Map 91)** or **Le Taj (Map 91)**—but tucked away on neighbouring streets are places like **The Empress (Map 95)** and **Cafe Spice Namaste (Map 95)** (get yourself dhal-ed up) or those a good tube ride away at **Masaledar Kitchen (Map 151)**, **Mirch Masala (Map 151)**, and **The Punjab (Map 13)**.

The best Chinese food can be found around Chinatown, but you have to hunt. Your first stop should be **Leong's Legends (Map 11)** for to die for Taiwanese. Also try **Pear Liang (Map 86)**, **Royal China (Map X30)**, **Haozhan (Map 12)** or authentic **Gourmet San** – rabbit saddle and all **(Map 91)**. But why settle for Chinese when there are so many other Asian foods to try?: Thai at **Yum Yum (Maps 79 & 64)**, **Charuwan (Map 59)**, **Thai Pavillion East (Map 131)** and **Su-Thai (Map 121)**; cheap and cheerful Malaysian at Malaysia **Kopi Tiam (Map 12)**; greasy spoon Korean at **Assa (Map 12)** and over karaoke at **Corean Chilli (Map 12)**; Singaporese at **Singapore Garden (Map 66)**; Vietnamese at **Hai Ha (Map 89)** and **Que Viet (Map 91)**; favoured Filipino fare at Kusinang Munti (out of coverage area) and Japanese skewers at **Bincho Soho (Map 12)**. And of course, because we're London, for every down-and-out corner spot, there's its posh cousin. Try glamorous Indian at **Amaya (Map 19)**, stylish Thai at **Crazy Bear (Map 3)**, and gourmet Malaysian at **Champor-Champor (Map 106)**.

If you're looking for a neighbourhood Italian, try **Vigata Ristorante (Map 80)** for its lobster linguine, **Il Bordello (Map 96)** and **La Luna (Map 113)**. Mexican is another newcomer that's been thriving lately with **Santo (Map 25)**, **Taqueria (Map 29)** and **Crazy Homies (Map 29)**. In terms of French, if you haven't noticed, this is the cuisine of choice for any Michelin-starred restaurant in this town worth its salt. But for those of us on a smaller budget there's **Le Petit Prince (Map 72)**, **Le Beaujolais (Map 12)** and **Savoir Faire (Map 4)**. For extraordinary Tapas combinations right every time try **The Providores (Map 2)** and **Tapa Room (Map 2)**. One cuisine boom, which reflects that of the population, is of the Eastern European variety. For Hungarian, try **Gay Hussar (Map 12)**; Polish, try **Baltic (Map 105)**; and Russian try **Trojka (Map 70)**.

Eating Meat

Here's where we implore you, begging you on both knees, not to let yourself EVER stumble into one of those steakhouse chains, mainly around Leicester Square, that shall not be named. If we succeed in anything with this guide, it should be at least to give carnivores a decent alternative. If you're stuck on the Aberdeen Angus variety of beef, try the **Popeseye Steakhouse (Map 33)**. But if you're open to other options, Argentinian steakhouses are really where it's at right now, with **Gaucho (Map 8)** at the forefront and **Buen Ayre (Map 89)** not far behind. If you want steak with a heart of gold (read: ethically sourced) try **Hawksmoor (Map 91)**.

If you like your meat on a bun, go for **The Diner's (Map 84)** blue cheese burgers, **Byron (Map 71)** for the best local, and **Haché (Map 71)**. If you'd rather someone else fired up your barbie, go for **Bodean's (Map 43)** or **Rodizo Rico (Map 80)**. If you're into eating things the rest of us see at the zoo, try **Archipelago (Map 3)** and **Chakalaka (Map 136)**.

Eating Veggie

In a town full of yoga bunnies, eco warriors and Madonna, veggie restaurants are pretty prevalent. And lucky for us, they're not just serving up nut roast. There are places that even sworn meat-eaters love. Get your carnivorous best mate to try

the sweet potato curry at **Mildred's (Map 10)**, the home-cooked gluten dishes at Eat and Two **Veg (Map 2)** or the veggie food by the pound at **Tibits (Map 10)**. If you're looking for a place to impress your new vegan girlfriend (you swear she's the one!), try **Rootmaster (Map 91)**. But there are plenty of other goodies like **Beetroot (Map 11)**, **Jacobs (Map 36)** and **Alara (Map 4)**. Also, remember Indian is always a good bet, like **Rasa N16 (Map 64)**, **Diwana Bhel Poori (Map 77)** or **Indian Veg Bhelpoori House (Map 80)**.

Our favourite restaurant (Because we're skint!)

While every Londoner loves a good clean white table cloth, extensive tasting menus and a waiter at your every beck and call – let's face it: we're broke. It seems almost with the credit crunch in mind (although the cheery and energetic staff act all but oblivious to the outside world) that **Franco Manca (Map 144)** opened its doors in Brixton Market to very hungry punters. The pizza here is perfect, and worth every moment on the endless queue that moves along in famished anticipation of the sour dough crusts and organic, ethically-sourced chorizo toppings. While awaiting our table underneath the diffused light of the marketplace's arches, a passerby challenges the growing crowd of would-be dinners with: "All this, for pizza?" Only to be berated, almost in unison, by the dedicated many: "Yes, but this is pizza from the gods." If it were not enough that the pizzas here come as cheaply as £4 and the flowing red wine for £1.40 a glass, everything here – from the flour to the toppings, beer and cloudy lemonade – is made from only the best ingredients, all somehow good for the earth and our pockets at the same time. So why are some of our Brixtonian friends still oblivious to this place? It's hard not to get the feeling the crowds aren't wanted here - from the exasperating opening hours (closing at 5pm every day except Sunday, when they don't open at all) to their tucked-away location. We're sorry to say, upon tasting the chewy brick oven taste of the puffed-up crusts, combined with fresh tomato sauce and perfect mozzarella – this secret's far from safe with us.

Key: £ : Under £10 / ££ : £10–£20 / £££ : £20–£30 / ££££ : £30–£40 / £££££: £40+
** : Does not accept credit cards./ † : Accepts only American Express / †† : Accepts only Visa and Mastercard*
Time listed refers to kitchen closing time on weekend nights

Map 1 • Marylebone (West)

Beirut Express	112 Edgware Rd	020 7724 2700	££	2 am	Chaotic, rude and the best Lebanese in town.
Maroush IV	68 Edgware Rd	020 7224 9339	££	12 am	Wax philosophical while smoking a hookah out front.
Nippon Tuk	225 Edgware Rd	020 7616 6496	££££	11.15 pm	One to avoid for vertigo sufferers—astounding, 23rd floor views.

Map 2 • Marylebone (East)

Comptoir Libanais	65 Wigmore St	020 7935 1110	£	8 pm	Uncompromisingly cheap and cheerful mezes.
Diwan	31 Thayer St	020 7935 2445	££	11 pm	Lebanese gorge spot.
Eat and Two Veg	50 Marylebone High St	020 7258 8595	££	10.30 pm	Just like mama's home cookin'—only more soya. A lot more soya.
Galvin Bistrot de Luxe	66 Baker Street	020 7935 4007	£££	11 pm	Veloutés, ballatines, tartares and escargots. Delicieux? Mais oui.
The Golden Hind	73 Marylebone Ln	020 7486 3644	££	10 pm	Fish and chips from the top-drawer. Can do BYOB.
Gordon Ramsay at Claridge's	Brook St	020 7499 0099	£££££	11 pm	A rich perfectionist's culinary art deco dream.
Hush Brasserie	8 Lancashire Ct	020 7659 1500	££££	11 pm	European food al fresco. Go on a lunch hour holiday.
No. 5 Cavendish Square	5 Cavendish Square	087 1223 5000	£££	11 pm	A No. 5 desperately trying to be as opulent as Chanel's.
Patisserie Valerie	105 Marylebone High St	020 7935 6240	£	9 pm	Boho coffee and pastry.
The Providores	109 Marylebone High St	020 7935 6175	££	11 pm	Sip Rioja and gorge on tapas for the cognoscenti.
Sakura	9 Hanover St	020 7629 2961	££	10 pm	Authentic Japanese queue. Worth it for the food.

Key: £ : Under £10 / ££ : £10–£20 / £££ : £20–£30 / ££££ : £30–£40 / £££££: £40+
** : Does not accept credit cards. / † : Accepts only American Express / †† : Accepts only Visa and Mastercard*
Time listed refers to kitchen closing time on weekend nights

Map 3 • Fitzrovia

Archipelago	110 Whitfield St	020 7383 3346	££££	10.30 pm	London's best, alright only, chocolate-covered scorpions and crocodile steaks.
Busaba Eathai	110 Wardour St	020 7255 8686	£££	11 pm	Never mind the shared benches, the food's too yummy.
Carluccio's Caffe	8 Market Pl	020 7636 2228	£££	11 pm	Pretty good for a chain. Have the espresso and ice cream.
Crazy Bear	26 Whitfield St	020 7631 0088	££££	10.30 pm	Thai deluxe. Where the media world feeds its clients.
Eagle Bar Diner	3 Rathbone Pl	020 7637 1418	££	11 pm	Trendy modern American diner; two words: Crocodile Burger.
Elena's L'Etoile	30 Charlotte St	020 7636 7189	£££££	11 pm	Old school French sophistication, politicians and journos.
Govinda's	9 Soho St	020 7437 4928	£*	8 pm	Cheap Krishna food. You know the deal.
Icco Pizza	46 Goodge St	020 7580 9688	£	11 pm	Zen it is not—but who cares at £3.50 a pizza?
Latium	21 Berners St	020 7323 9123	£££	10.30 pm	Romantic (and pricey) first date place.
Market Place	11 Market Pl	020 7079 2020	£	1 am	Warm buzz all day/night. Hot clientele/tepid prices.
Navarro's	67 Charlotte St	020 7637 7713	£££	10 pm	Delicioso! Smells like Seville, tastes like Seville.
Neel Akash	93 Charlotte St	020 7637 0050	£££	11 pm	Eccentric staff, fantastic food.
Ragam	57 Cleveland St	020 7636 9098	££	10.45 pm	Can't dis these dosas (potato crepes) at very decent prices.
Rasa Express	5 Rathbone St	020 7637 0222	£	11 pm	Take-away-priced Indian lunch boxes, seating included.
Roka	37 Charlotte St	020 7580 6464	£££	11 pm	Dazzling Izakaya concept Japanese.
Salt Yard	54 Goodge St	020 7637 0657	£££	11 pm	Intimate and sexy. Take a date. Get laid. Possibly.
Sardo	45 Grafton Way	020 7387 2521	££	10 pm	Hit after hit. Try the crab pasta.
Squat & Gobble	69 Charlotte St	020 7580 5338	£	4.30 pm	Scrumptious, cheap, tiny. Just squat and, um, gobble.
Stef's	3 Berners St	020 3073 1041	££	11 pm	You can't knock the gnocchi.
Thai Metro	36 Charlotte St	020 7436 4201	££	11 pm	Thai food, cooked well, served well, job done.

Map 4 • Bloomsbury (West)

Alara	58 Marchmont St	020 7837 1172	£££	7 pm	Hardcore veggie/vegan mecca, surprisingly good.
Bi Won	24 Coptic St	020 7580 2660	£	10 pm	Manhandling staff but great food.
Savoir Faire	42 New Oxford St	020 7436 0707	££	10.30 pm	Sweet little rustic restaurant, a stroll from Soho.

Map 5 • Bloomsbury (East)

Acorn House	69 Swinton St	020 7812 1842	£££	10.30 pm	Eco-chic: the Gwyneth Paltrow of restaurants.
Aki Bistro	182 Gray's Inn Rd	020 7837 9281	££	11 pm	Almost too Japanese Japanese.
Beas of Bloomsbury	44 Theobald's Rd	020 7242 8330	£	6 pm	You can watch the chefs create artisan cupcake masterpieces here.
Bread and Butter Sandwich Bar	100 Judd St	020 7713 7767	£*	9 pm	Notable for its very cheap al fresco fry ups.
Ciao Bella	86 Lamb's Conduit St	020 7242 4119	££	11 pm	Authentic, rustic feel Italian complete with piano.
Cigala	54 Lamb's Conduit St	020 7405 1717	££	10.45pm	Great service and gorgeous salty Spanish bread.
The Food Bazaar	59 Gray's Inn Rd	020 7242 6578	£*	9 pm	Casual and friendly with great hot food selection.
Fryer's Delight	19 Theobald's Rd	020 7405 4114	£*	10 pm	No frills chippie; big portions of chunky, salty, greasy tastiness.
Konstam	2 Acton St	020 7833 5040	££	10 pm	All food sourced within London. Should be grim—actually delicious.
La Provence	63 Gray's Inn Rd	020 7404 4920	£	10 pm	Super-friendly staff and a generous hot food deal.
Mary Ward Centre	42 Queen Sq	020 7269 6000	£*	5 pm	Hippy educational centre with a great organic cafe.
Paolina Thai Snack Bar	181 King's Cross Rd	020 7278 8176	£*	10 pm	Grotty exterior disguises this diamond of cheerful authentic Thai.
Swintons	61 Swinton St	020 7837 3995	££	9:30 pm	If Heaven made fishfinger sandwiches, they'd use Swintons' recipe.
Thai Candle	38 Lamb's Conduit St	020 7430 2472	£££	10 pm	Cosy, cheerful with a nice lunchtime meal deal.

Map 6 • Clerkenwell

Bada Bing!	120 St John St	020 7253 3723	£	4 pm	Excellent lunch joint. The toasted ciabattas are divine.
Clarks Pie and Mash	46 Exmouth Market	020 7837 1974	£*	5.30 pm	A last bastion of a lost London.
Dans Le Noir	30 Clerkenwell Green	020 7253 1100	£££££	9 pm	Blind waiters serve in pitch darkness: don't wear white.
The Eagle	159 Farringdon Rd	020 7837 1353	££	10.30 pm	London's first gastro pub—just look what they started.
Little Bay	171 Farringdon Rd	020 7278 1234	££	12 am	Posh-people food at pikey-people prices.
Moro	34 Exmouth Market	020 7833 8336	££££	11 pm	DO believe the hype.
The Quality Chop House	94 Farringdon Rd	020 7837 5093	££	10.45pm	OMG it's so BRITISH. Meat and potatoes like nowhere else.
Sandwichman	23 Easton St	020 7833 9001	£*	2.30 pm	Office delivery returns. Gourmet—and just 65p. Best lunch in London.
Vic Naylor's	38 St John St	020 7608 2181	£££	10.30 pm	Sting's gaff in Lock, Stock And Two Smoking Barrels. Nice.

Map 7 • Barbican / City Road (South)

Bavarian Beerhouse	190 City Rd	0844 330 2005	££	11 pm	Unlace your lederhausen for some serious schnitzel madness.
Carnevale	135 Whitecross St	020 7250 3452	££	11.00 pm	Veggie on the cheap.
De Santis	Old St	020 7689 5577	££	9.30 pm	Like being in Milan; owner Enzo takes care of you
NUSA Kitchen	9 Old St	020 7253 3135	£*	5 pm	People queuing? For ages? For soup? Now I've seen everything.
Warrin Thai Kitchen Stall	77 Whitecross St	N/A	£*	N/A	Pad thai wokked while you wait.

Map 8 • Liverpool Street / Broadgate

Damascu Bite Kebab	21 Shoreditch High St	020 72470207	£*	1 am	It's the way they grill them from the outside.
Eyre Brothers	70 Leonard St	020 7613 5346	££	10.45 pm	Great place run by the Eyre brothers—Jane no relation.
Gaucho Grill	5 Finsbury Ave	020 7256 6877	££££	11 pm	Divine, ohmigod, melt-in-your-mouth steak. Oops, drooling!
Ponti's Caffe	176 Bishopsgate	020 7283 4889	£	24 hrs	24 hour cafe for the inebriated insomniac.

Map 9 • Mayfair / Green Park

Alain Ducasse at The Dorchester	Park Ln	020 7629 8866	££££	10 pm	Better known for its extortionate prices than michelin-starred food.
El Pirata of Mayfair	5 Down St	020 7491 3810	£££	11.30 pm	Don't be put off by stuffy location—these are f'ing good tapas.
The English Tea Room at Browns	Albemarle Street	020 7518 4155	££££	11 pm	Ah, so that's what a £48 cup of tea tastes like.
Galvin at Windows	28th Floor, Hilton Park Lane	020 7208 4021	£££££	11 pm	Art Deco French overlooking Buckingham Palace. We're not worthy!
L'Autre	5 Shepherd St	020 7499 4680	££££	11 pm	Polish meets Mexican. Surprisingly well.
Nobu	15 Berkeley St	020 7290 9222	£££££	12 am	Rob a bank on the way as it's bloody expensive!
The Ritz	150 Piccadilly	020 7493 8181	£££££	10 pm	High tea amidst ornaments and swank - resist temptation to swipe towels.
Theo Randall at the InterContinental	1 Hamilton Pl	020 7318 8747	£££££	11 pm	Sincere and stylish cuisine unfortunately hidden behind a hotel façade.
The Wolseley	161 Piccadilly	020 7499 6996	££££	12 am	Over-hyped. There. We said it.

Map 10 • Piccadilly / Soho (West)

Cecconi's	5 Burlington Gardens	020 7434 1500	££££	11.15 pm	All-day menu for the spoilt. Delicious breakfasts.
Cha Cha Moon	15 Ganton St	020 7297 9800	££	11 pm	Like Wagamamas but for Chinese.
Chowki	2 Denman St	020 7439 1330	£££	11.30 pm	Rotating regional cuisines of India; brilliant.
Dehesa	25 Ganton St	020 7494 4170	£££	11 pm	Faux-rustic protein-rich tapas, sweetie.
Fernandez and Wells Coffee Bar	73 Beak St	020 7287 8124	££	6 pm	Perfect pasteis de nata and locally made ice-cream. Delightfully friendly!
Kulu Kulu	76 Brewer St	0871 971 6452	£	10 pm	Great, fresh, fast sushi for people on the go. Sit down is 45 minutes only.
Mildred's	45 Lexington St	020 7494 1634	££	10.30 pm	Great food, sometimes crap service. Get the sweet potato curry to takeaway!
Mosaico	13 Albermale St	020 7409 1011	£££	11 pm	Stylish Italian. Prices more for the Mayfair Mamas.
Nordic Bakery	14 Golden Sq	020 3230 1077	£	7 pm	Authentic sticky cinnamon buns, Karelian pies and smoked Moomin.

Key: £ : Under £10 / ££ : £10–£20 / £££ : £20–£30 / ££££ : £30–£40 / £££££ : £40+
** : Does not accept credit cards / † : Accepts only American Express / †† : Accepts only Visa and Mastercard*
Time listed refers to kitchen closing time on weekend nights

Ping Pong	45 Great Marlborough St	020 7851 6969	££	11 pm	Don't leave without trying a char sui bun!
Pure California	39 Beak St	020 7287 3708	£	6 pm	As pure a salad/juice as you'd find in the Sunshine State all made to order.
Sartoria	20 Saville Row	020 7534 7000	£££££	11 pm	The pick of the Conran restaurants.
Sketch	9 Conduit St	020 6594 500	£££	1 am	Colossally trendy kitsch palace.
Taro	61 Brewer St	020 7734 5826	£££	10.30 pm	Where London's Japanese locals eat sushi.
Ten Ten Tei	56 Brewer St	020 7287 1738	£££££	10 pm	The Japanese restaurant Japanese people love.
Tentazioni Restaurant	2 Mill St	0207 237 1100	££	10.45 pm	Stunningly sophisticated for a neighbourhood eaterie.
Thanks for Franks	26 Fouberts Pl	020 7494 2434	£*	6 pm	Good sandwiches.
Toku @ The Japan Centre	212 Piccadilly	020 7255 8255	££	10 pm	The best gyoza outside of Tokyo.
Wagamama	10 Lexington St	020 7292 0990	£	11 pm	Reliable, speedy noodle chain.
Wild Honey	12 St George St	020 7758 9160	£££	10.30 pm	This Michelin star's got skillz (and a damn good tête-de-veau).
Yauatcha	15 Broadwick St	020 7494 8888	£££££	11.45 pm	Traditional Chinese tea-house meets star-spangled media haunt.
Yoshino	3 Piccadilly place	020 7287 6622	££	10 pm	Back alley bentos so good you'll pretend they were your discovery.

Map 11 • Soho (Central)

Balans	60 Old Compton St	020 7439 2183	££	3 am	Share a 4am breakfast with the likes of Amy Winehouse.
Bar Bruno	101 Wardour St	020 7734 3750	£*	10 pm	Hidden Italian café hidden gem. Authentically loud and friendly.
Beetroot	92 Berwick St	020 7437 8591	£	10 pm	Awesome veggie/vegan place.
Bocca di Lupo	12 Archer St	020 7734 2223	£££	12 am	Italian for 'break a leg'; authentic fare gets your bocca watering.
Cafe Espana	63 Old Compton St	020 7494 1271	££	11 pm	Highly recommended. 10% off for eating with castanets (possibly).
Hummus Bros	88 Wardour St	020 7734 1311	££	11 pm	Where hummus is the main dish.
Imli	167 Wardour St	020 7287 4243	£	11 pm	Tapas + curry. Fusion gone insane but somehow works.
Italian Graffiti	163 Wardour St	020 7439 4668	£££	11 pm	Less 'street' than the name suggest. Nice though.
Jerk City	189 Wardour St	020 7287 2878	£	10 pm	Jamaican fast food. In doubt? Go for ackee and saltfish.
Leong's Legends	4 Macclesfield St	020 7287 0288	££	11 pm	A Taiwanese Chinatown legend.
Malletti	26 Noel St	020 7439 4096	£*	3 pm	Amazing! Use your mobile and you won't get served.
Maoz	43 Old Compton St	020 7851 1586	£*	1 am	Falafeltastic!
Paul	49 Old Compton St	020 7287 6261	£	10 pm	French cafe/bakery chain. Amazing baguettes!
Pizza Express Jazz Club	10 Dean St	020 7439 8722	£	11 pm	Surprisingly, jazz takes the mediocre chain up a notch.
Randall & Aubin	16 Brewer St	020 7287 4447	£££	11 pm	Over-indulgently carnal seafood delights which only call for champagne.
Red Veg	95 Dean St	020 7437 3109	£*	10 pm	Veggie fast food joint.
Snog	9 Brewer St	020 7494 3301	£*	12 am	If they had yoghurt and not milk in Clockwork Orange.
Soho Thai	27 St. Annes Ct	020 7287 2000	££	11 pm	Thai with a good range. In set meals: go for starter NOT dessert.
St Moritz	161 Wardour St	020 7734 3324	££££	11.30 pm	Swiss cheese heaven.
Sugar Reef	42 Great Windmill St	020 7851 0800	££££	10.30 pm	Wannabe a WAG? Get in 'ere!
Won Kei	41 Wardour St	020 7437 8408	££	10 pm	AKA Wonky's: institutionally rude service, cheap fast Chinese.

Map 12 • Soho (East)

Abeno Too	17 Great Newport St	020 7379 1160	££	11 pm	Addictive Okonomiyaki (pancakes) flipped and fried on the table.
Arbutus	63 Frith St	020 7734 4545	£££	11 pm	Chocolate soup! Worth it for that alone.
Assa	53 St Giles High St	020 7240 8256	££	12 am	Cheerful eager-to-please Korean cafe
Bar Italia	22 Frith St	020 7437 4520	££	4.30 am	Soho institution; perfect for people watching at any hour.
Barrafina	54 Frith St	020 7813 8016	£££	11 pm	Seriously, the best (and hippest) place for tapas.
Bincho Soho	16 Old Compton St	020 7287 9111	££	11.30 pm	Save on skewers every Tuesday

Boheme Kitchen and Bar	19 Old Compton St	020 7734 5656	£££	11.45 pm	You want frites with that? Deliciously snobby comfort food.
Café Emm	17 Frith St	020 7437 0723	£££	10.30 pm	Double-take cheap prices and wholesome fare. Wins popular vote.
Chinese Experience	118 Shaftesbury Ave	0207 437 0377	£££	11 pm	Popular for a reason. Overwhelmed? Go for the always-great set menu.
Corean Chilli	51 Charing Cross Rd	020 7734 6737	££	12 am	Karaoke and stir-fries with the Korean cool kids.
Ed's Easy Diner	12 Moor St	020 7434 4439	££	11 pm	It's like, you know? Soooo, like, American? You know?
Friendly Inn	47 Gerrard St	020 7437 4170	£	1 am	Where Londoners go for Chinese in Soho.
Gaby's	30 Charing Cross Rd	020 7836 4233	££	10 pm	High on tradition, low on frills. Authentically spartan.
Garlic & Shots	14 Frith St	020 7734 9505	££££	1 am	Garlic, garlic and more garlic. No-go zone for vampires.
Gay Hussar	2 Greek St	020 7437 0973	££	10.45 pm	Everything from strudel to cherry soup at this old-school Hungarian.
Haozhan	8 Gerrard St	020 7434 3838	££££	11 pm	Can't pick? This is the one.
Kettners	29 Romilly St	020 7734 6112	£££££	12 am	Sit and sup with the champagne set.
La Porchetta Pollo Bar	20 Old Compton St	020 7494 9368	££££	12 am	Cheap and cheerful Italian. In the West End? Well, exactly.
Le Beaujolais	25 Litchfield St	020 7836 2955	££	10 pm	Get insulted by a Frenchman here in London—Mai oui!
Maison Bertaux	27 Greek St	056 0115 1584	££*	5 pm	Heavenly cakes, art gallery, boutique downstairs, what's not to like?
Malaysia Kopi Tiam	67 Charing Cross Rd	020 7287 1113	£	11 pm	A beef rendang-infused oasis away from the West End's clatter.
New World	1 Gerrard Pl	020 7734 0396	£	11.45 pm	Crispy duck, Dim Sum, custard dumplings... bring it on!
Stockpot	18 Old Compton St	020 7287 1066	££*	12 am	Fantastically cheap stodge.
Taro	10 Old Compton St	020 7439 2275	££	10.30 pm	Like Taro Brewer Street. But gayer, obviously.

Map 13 • Covent Garden

Café Mode	57 Endell St	020 7240 8085	££	11.30 pm	Pizza, pasta, salad. No fuss.
Candy Cakes	36 Monmouth St	020 7497 8979	£	8 pm	Cupcakes almost too beautiful to eat. But eat them anyway.
Food for Thought	31 Neal St	020 7836 9072	£	8.30 pm	Queues this long mean they've got cheap, veg food right.
Great Queen Street	32 Great Queen St	020 7242 0622	£££	11 pm	Affordable, and might be London's best gastropub.
Kulu Kulu	51 Shelton St	0871 971 3476	££	10 pm	Tiny conveyor belt sushi joint. Bang on the money.
Mon Plaisir	21 Monmouth St	020 7836 7243	£££	11.15 pm	Not up to typical Paris standards, but still tres bon!
The Photographers' Gallery	Great Newport St	020 7831 1772	£*	6 pm	Artsy coffee spot with photos on view.
The Punjab	80 Neal St	020 7836 9787	£££	11.30 pm	Relive the days of the Raj in this old-school curry house.
Rock & Sole Place	47 Endell St	020 7836 3785	£££	11 pm	London's oldest chippie. Est. 1871. On-street, fairy-lit picnic benches. Huge portions.
Sarastro	126 Drury Ln	020 7836 0101	££	11.30 pm	Hilarious over-the-top decor; includes fornicating cherubs.
Souk Medina	1 Shorts Gardens	020 7240 1796	££	11 pm	Atmospheric Morrocan joint. Free refills on mouthwatering £20 set menu.

Map 14 • Holborn / Temple

Asadal	227 High Holborn	020 7430 9005	£££	10.30 pm	Go on—venture down those stairs—it's worth it.
Indigo @ OneAldwych	1 Aldwych	020 7300 1000	£££	11 pm	Sunday brunch and a movie—all in the same place!

Map 15 • Blackfriars / Farringdon

Beppe's	23 West Smithfield	020 7236 7822	££	3 pm	As classically Italian as oversized sunglasses. Only much, much better.
The Bleeding Heart	Bleeding Heart Yard, off Greville St	020 7242 2056	£££	10.30 pm	Historic, hard to find, eccentric beauty.
Cafe du Marche	22 Charterhouse Sq	020 7608 1609	£££	11 pm	Wonderful French cuisine in delightful venue. Tucked away in Charterhouse Square.
Gaucho Smithfield	93 Charterhouse St	020 7490 1676	££	11 pm	Where cows would choose to be eaten.

Key: £ : Under £10 / ££ : £10–£20 / £££ : £20–£30 / ££££ : £30–£40 / £££££: £40+
** : Does not accept credit cards./ † : Accepts only American Express / †† : Accepts only Visa and Mastercard*
Time listed refers to kitchen closing time on weekend nights

Kurz + Lang	1 St John St	020 7993 2923	£	11.30 pm	Ze German Bratwurst sausage at its zizzling best.
The Larder	91 St John St	020 7608 1558	£££	10.30 pm	Fresh, seasonal food, good breakfast menu and takeaway sarnies.
Pho	86 St John St	020 7253 7624	£	10.30 pm	Steaming bowlfuls for hungry Clerkenwell workers. Specialises in street food.
Portal	88 St John St	020 7253 6950	££££	10.15 pm	Astoundingly good Portuguese. Swanky but not stuffy.
Smiths of Smithfield	67 Charterhouse St	020 7251 7950	£££	10.45 pm	Overflowing with yuppies and trendy types; pricey but tasty.
St Germain	89 Turnmill St	020 7336 0949.	£££	11 pm	Sleek, chic. Bon Appetit.
St John's Smithfield	26 St John St	020 7251 0848	£££	11 pm	This place is ALL about the offal.
Tinseltown	44 St. John St	020 7689 2424	£	24 hrs	Funky diner serving great late-night milkshakes.
Vivat Bacchus	47 Farringdon St	020 7353 2648	£££	9.30 pm	Three wine cellars and a cheeseroom. A ROOM of cheese.
Yo! Sushi	14 St Paul's	020 7248 8726	£	11 pm	Sushi in Paul's shadow.

Map 16 • Square Mile (West)

Bar Bourse	67 Queen Street	020 7248 2200	£££££	12 am	Known as the Rolls Royce of city bars. And rightly so.
Sweetings	39 Queen Victoria St	020 7248 3062	£££	4 pm	Old fashioned institution for nostalgia trips. Lunch only.

Map 17 • Square Mile (East)

Gaucho City	1 Bell Inn Yard	020 7626 5180	££££	11 pm	The best steakhouse in the city. Located in former gold vaults.
The Mercer	34 Threadneedle St	020 7628 0001	££	9.30 pm	Proper British grub in a light contemporary atmosphere.
Rhodes 24	25 Old Broad St	020 7877 7703	£££££	8.30 pm	Anyone for Gherkin (building) with your Michelin star?
Wasabi	52 Old Broad St	020 7374 8337	£*	10 pm	Delicious sushi and bento for those in a rush.

Map 18 • Tower Hill / Aldgate

Jeff's Café	14 Brune St	020 7375 2230	£*	10 pm	Cheap as chips (which they serve here, incidentally).
S & M Café	48 Brushfield St	020 7247 2252	££	10 pm	Not what you think it is, perverts. Sausages and mash!

Map 19 • Belgravia

Amaya	Halkin Arcade, Motcomb St	020 7823 1166	££££	11.30 pm	Where the trendies go for their curry fix.
Boisdale, Victoria	15 Eccleston St	020 7730 6922	£££££	11 pm	Posh Scottish nosh. No deep-fried Mars Bars, sadly.
Noura	12 William St	020 7235 5900	££	11 pm	Frequently orgiastic Lebanese pig-outs, habibi.
One-O-One	101 Knightsbridge	020 7290 7101	££££	10 pm	One man's fish is another man's pleasure.
Yo! Sushi	102 Knightsbridge	020 7201 8641	££	10 pm	A London institution—we dream in sashimi on conveyor belts.

Map 20 • Victoria / Pimlico (West)

Grumbles	35 Churton St	020 7834 0149	££	11 pm	Unfashionably unfussy Brit/French home-cooking. Gorgeous pies, no grumbles.

Map 21 • Pimlico (East)

The Regency Café	17 Regency St	020 7821 6596	£*	7 pm	Proper British fry-ups and atmosphere in this 1940's café.
Vincent Rooms	1 The Victoria Centre, Vincent Sq	020 7802 8391	£££	7 pm	Brilliant food served by awkward catering students.

Map 23 • St. James's

Inn The Park	St James' Park	020 7451 9999	££££	7.30 pm	Watch the ducks watching you as you eat.

Stockpot	38 Panton St	020 7839 5142	££*	10.45 pm	Treacle pud & custard. Bish bash bosh.

Map 24 • Trafalgar Square / The Strand

Bistro 1	33 Southampton St	020 7379 7585	££	11.30 pm	Posh kebabs etc at bargain prices.
Café in the Crypt	Trafalgar Sq	020 7766 1158	££	10 pm	Spooky sandwiches and fruit crumble.
Covent Garden Market Café	Covent Garden	020 7240 4844	£*	10 pm	Cheap egg 'n' chips in heart of tourist London.
Farmer Brown	4 New Row	020 7240 0230	££*	8 pm	Cheap and very cheerful. Great lunches.
Gourmet Burger Kitchen	13 Maiden Ln	020 7240 9617	££	11 pm	Go for the Kiwiburger. Don't question the ingredients. Trust us.
India Club	143 Strand (Second floor, Strand Continental Hotel)	020 7836 0650	£	11 pm	Quirky run-down BYOB eaterie; more character than Brick Lane equivalents.
J Sheekey	28 St Martin's Ct	020 7240 2565	££££	11 pm	Old-fashioned seafood haven that the celebs still love.
RS Hispaniola	Victoria Embankment	020 7839 3011	£££	10 pm	Feel the bloat, on a boat.
Rules	35 Maiden Ln	020 7836 5314	£££££	10.30 pm	London's oldest restaurant with old-fashioned comfort food to match.
Thai Pot	1 Bedfordbury	020 7379 4580	££	11 pm	Busy but fast with fresh and generous helpings. Delicious Massaman curry.
Wahaca	66 Chandos Pl	020 7240 1883	£££	11 pm	Tasty Mexican market food/tapas. Always busy.

Map 25 • Kensal Town

Santo	299 Portobello Rd	020 8968 4590	££	11.30 pm	Fresh, frisky Mexican. Too bad about the resentful waiters.
Thai Rice	303 Portobello Rd	020 8968 2001	££	10.30 pm	Jaw-dropping food in sterile, bland enviornment.

Map 29 • Notting Hill Gate

Beach Blanket Babylon	45 Ledbury Rd	020 7229 2907	££££	12 am	Maze of baroque nooks and crannies where celebs nibble discreetly.
Cafe Diana	5 Wellington Terrace	020 7792 9606	£	10.30 pm	Creepy, kitsch shrine to Princess Diana with so-so food.
Costas Fish Restaurant	18 Hillgate St	020 7727 4310	££	10.30 pm	Heavenly, Cypriot-run fish and chips. Hellish Notting Hill prices.
Crazy Homies	125 Westbourne Park Rd	020 7727 6771	££	10.15 pm	Avoid first date awkwardness over quality Mexican at this lively get-up.
The Electric Brasserie	191 Portobello Rd	020 7908 9696	££	10 pm	Uber-trendy, worth a visit for the eggs benedict alone.
Geales	2 Farmer St	020 7727 7528	£££	10.30 pm	Feels ever-so-slightly like a front to appease visiting Americans.
Lucky 7	127 Westbourne Park Rd	020 7727 6771	£££	10.30 pm	Atmospheric diner for wistful yuppies.
Manzara	24 Pembridge Road	020 7727 3062	£	10 pm	Burek Obama for president! Arf.
Taqueria	139 Westbourne Grove	020 7229 4734	££	11 pm	Wash down these fresh mini-tacos with a good tequila.

Map 30 • Bayswater

Berdees Coffee Shop	84 Bishop's Bridge Rd	020 7727 0033	£*	9 pm	Hubbly Bubbly Jubbly. Chubbly?
Kiasu	48 Queensway	020 7727 8810	£	11 pm	The best budget Indonesian/Malaysian cuisine. Mmmm.... Char Kway Teow...
Royal China	13 Queensway	020 7221 2535	£££	11.15 pm	Keep the Cantonese dim sum comin'!
Tiroler Hut	27 Westbourne Grove	020 7727 3981	££££	12 am	Dementedly kitsch Austrian madhouse with lederhosen-clad waiters.

Map 32 • Shepherd's Bush (West)

Abu Zaad	29 Uxbridge Rd	020 8749 5107	£	11 pm	A colourful Syrian welcome. Posh Kebabs.
Esarn Kheaw	314 Uxbridge Road	020 8743 8930	£	11.30 pm	Outstanding Thai. Transport your taste buds to Bangkok.
Vine Leaves Taverna	71 Uxbridge Rd	020 8749 0325	£	1 am	Friendly staff, traditional grub, huge portions.

Map 33 • Shepherd's Bush

Jasmine	16 Goldhawk Rd	020 8743 7886	££	11 pm	Awesome Thai.
Jumbucks	24 Shepherd's Bush Green	020 8811 8111	£	1 am	Proper Aussie pies and heaps of Cherry Ripes served by smily peeps.Streuth!
Popeseye	108 Blythe Rd	020 7610 4578	££££	10.30 pm	London's ONLY member of the Aberdeen Angus Society.

Key: £ : Under £10 / ££ : £10–£20 / £££ : £20–£30 / ££££ : £30–£40 / £££££: £40+
** : Does not accept credit cards./ † : Accepts only American Express / †† : Accepts only Visa and Mastercard*
Time listed refers to kitchen closing time on weekend nights

Map 34 • West Kensington / Olympia

The Belvedere Restaurant	Abbotsbury Road	020 7602 1238	£££	11 pm	Sublime setting—the same cannot always be said for the service.

Map 35 • Kensington

Byron	222 Kensington High St	020 7361 1717	££	10 pm	London's best burger? Locals in the know say so.
Clarke's	124 Kensington Church St	020 7221 9225	££	10 pm	Elegant, English fine dining. Perfect brunch spot if feeling refined.
Kensington Roof Gardens	99 Kensington High St	020 7937 7994	££££	1 am	Truly spectacular roof gardens and devine restaurant 100 foot above HS Ken.
Maggie Jones's	6 Old Court Pl	020 7937 6462	£££	10.30 pm	A British culinary time warp, but we like it anyway.
Zaika	1 Kensington High St	020 7795 6533	££	10.45 pm	If you can afford to treat yourself this is the place. Starters at £12.95!

Map 36 • South Kensington / Gloucester Rd

Cafe Forum	146 Gloucester Rd	N/A	£*	11 pm	Strange proverbs about cows on the wall and £3.75 pizza. Student digs.
Jacobs	20 Gloucester Rd	020 7581 9292	££	10 pm	Brave the slow service for delicious veggie dishes and fresh juices.
The Kensington Creperie	2 Exhibition Rd	020 7589 8947	£*	11 pm	The best sweet and savoury crepes in London.
Little Japan	32 Thurloe St	020 7591 0207	£*	11.30 pm	Wowzers: bento for a fiver? Suspicious and delicious.
Odonno's	14 Bute St	020 7052 0732	£	11 pm	Gelato fix for homesick Italians and ice-cream freaks alike.

Map 37 • Knightsbridge

Zuma	5 Raphael St	020 7584 1010	£££	12 am	If your gal likes sushi, ideal for a romantic night out.

Map 38 • Chiswick

Boys Authentic Thai	95 Chiswick High Rd	020 8995 7991	££	10.30 pm	The staff are as funky and fresh as the food.
Chez Gerard	163 Chiswck High Rd	020 8742 1942	££££	11 pm	"The best steak-frites this side of Paris". Ya wallet'll cry!
Chris' Fish and Chips	19 Turnham Green Terrace	020 8995 2367	£*	12 am	It's all British-ness wrapped in warm, greasy paper.
The Devonshire	126 Devonshire Rd	020 7592 7962	£££	11 pm	A more affordable version of Ramsay.
Fouberts	2 Turnham Green Terrace	020 8994 5202	£	11 pm	Little Italian owned cafe. Excellent ice gream and gelato.
High Road Brasserie	162 Chiswick High Rd	020 8742 7474	££	11 pm	As good as it looks. The continent comes to the High Road.
Kalamari	4 Chiswick High Rd	020 8994 4727	££	12 am	For those with a feta fetish.
Zizzi	231 Chiswick High Rd	020 8747 9400	££	11.30 pm	Skip the mains—cut straight to the heavenly Apple Crumble.

Map 39 • Stamford Brook

Carpenter's Arms	91 Black Lion Ln	020 8741 8386	£££	11 pm	As gastropub as it gets.
Tosa	332 King St	020 8748 0002	£	10 pm	Low-key authentic yakitori (fried skewered meat) joint. Easy on the wallet.

Map 40 • Goldhawk Rd / Ravenscourt Park

Blah Blah Blah	78 Goldhawk Rd	020 8746 1337	££*	10.30 pm	Eccentric, worldly vegetarian. Kinda like your ex, only cooler.
Lowiczanka Polish Cultural Centre	238 King Street	020 8741 3225	££	10 pm	Stodgy grub, hard drink, concrete block. So Polish you'll need a passport.
Sagar	157 King St	020 8741 8563	££	11 pm	Yummy South Indian veggie food at a great price.

Map 41 • Hammersmith

The Gate	51 Queen Caroline St	020 8748 6932	££££	10 pm	Light and airy by day, cosy at night. Lovely food.

Map 42 • Baron's Court

Best Mangal	104 N End Rd	020 7610 1050	££	1 am	Proper good kebabs with heeeeaps of nosh. Can sit in too - a rarity.
Ta Khai	100 North End Rd	020 7386 5375	££	10 pm	Decent, cheap food. Interior as tacky as its name suggests.

Map 43 • West Brompton / Fulham Broadway / Earls Court

The Blue Elephant	3 Fulham Broadway	020 7385 6595	££££	11.30 pm	Disney's version of Bangkok—grandiose, expensive, but oh, so good.
Bodean's	4 Broadway Chambers	020 7610 0440	£££	11 pm	Stuff yourself on BBQ pulled-pork sandwiches. Yee haw!
Chutney Mary	535 King's Rd	020 7351 3113	££££	11.30 pm	Get coddled over a curry (at a price).
Pizza@Home	350 Old Brompton Rd	020 7244 8080	£*	10 pm	Maybe London's most authentic Italian pizza. Fast and cheap as chips!!
Vingt Quatre	325 Fulham Rd	020 7376 7224	£	24 hrs	24 hour booze! Incidentally, the food is very good.
Yo! Sushi	Fulham Road	020 7385 6077		11 pm	Japanese conveyor belt sushi for beginners.

Map 44 • Chelsea

Aubergine	11 Park Walk	020 7352 3449	££££	11 pm	Foie gras, lobster and truffles. Need we say more?
Eight Over Eight	392 King's Rd	020 7349 9934	££££	11 pm	Exotic and dripping with celebs.

Map 45 • Chelsea (East)

Chelsea Kitchen	451 Fulham Rd	020 3055 0088	£	11 pm	New place, same affordable stodge. A Winner.
Four o nine	409 Clapham Rd	020 7737 0722	££££	10.30 pm	Inviting and intimate, it's nice.
Le Columbier	145 Dovehouse St	020 7351 1155	£££	11 pm	Vive le Bistro!
Made In Italy	243 King's Rd	020 7352 1880	££	11 pm	"Food Mama used to Make." Unless you're not Italian, obviously.
My Old Dutch Pancake House	221 King's Rd	020 7376 5650	£	11.30 pm	Sweet or savory pancakey goodness in the heart of Chelsea.
Tom's Kitchen	27 Cale St	020 7349 0202	££££	11 pm	Crush-worthy (maybe just us?) Tom Aiken's British brasserie masterpiece.
Tom's Place	1 Cale St	020 7351 1806	£££	11 pm	Posh chippie.

Map 46 • Sloane Square

The Admiral Codrington	17 Mossop St	020 7581 0005	£££	10.30 pm	Go for simplicity here. Even the chips they get exactly right.
Bibendum Restaurant & Oyster Bar	81 Fulham Rd	020 7581 5817	£££££	11 pm	French institution with a cool (literally) oyster bar.
Blushes Cafe	52 King's Rd	020 7589 6640	£	1.30 am	Always reliable, always packed. C'est La Vie.
Foxtrot Oscar	79 Royal Hospital Rd	020 7352 4448	££	10 pm	Tango Alpha Sierra Tango Yankee.
Gordon Ramsay	68 Royal Hospital Rd	020 7352 4441	£££££	11 pm	Mmmmmm... debt...
Le Cercle	1 Wilbraham Pl	020 7901 9999	££££	12 am	Tapas-sized French yumminess. Pears with caramel popcorn, anyone?
Tom Aikens	43 Elystan St	020 7584 2003	£££££	11 pm	Artistic approach to just about everything.

Map 47 • Fulham (West)

The River Café	Thames Wharf, Rainville Rd	020 7386 4200	£££	11 pm	Fine dining by the Thames for champagne socialists.

Map 48 • Fulham

Fisher's Chips	19 Fulham High St	020 7610 9808	£	10 pm	Quality chips AND quality punning. It's why Britain's Great.

Map 49 • Parson's Green

De Cecco	189 New King's Rd	020 7736 1145	££	11 pm	Belissimo! Spaghetti a'll Aragosta is the signature dish and it's gooood!
Ghillies	271 New King's Rd	020 76109675	££	10.30pm	Chic, relaxed continental eatery.

Key: £ : Under £10 / ££ : £10–£20 / £££ : £20–£30 / ££££ : £30–£40 / £££££: £40+
** : Does not accept credit cards./ † : Accepts only American Express / †† : Accepts only Visa and Mastercard*
Time listed refers to kitchen closing time on weekend nights

Kebab Kid	90 New Kings Road	020 7731 0427	£*	10 pm	Kebabs so impressive you could bring your gran here.
Mao Tai	58 New King's Rd	020 7731 2520	££	1 am	Modern, chic and pricey-but-delectable Pan-Asian menu in Parsons Green.

Map 50 • Sand's End

Deep	The Boulevard, Imperial Wharf	020 7736 3337	££££	11 pm	Set for Gordon Ramsay's F-word. F-ing good itself.

Map 51 • Highgate

The Bull	13 North Hill Ave	0845 456 5033	£££	12 am	Chic eatery with perfectly positioned front terrace.
Cafe Rouge	6 South Grove	020 8342 9797	££	11 pm	Decent French restaurant and cafe chain
Kiplings	100 North Rd	020 8340 1719	££	11.30 pm	Swanky curry joint boasts Raffles Hotel stylings including resident pianist.
Papa Del's	347 Archway Rd	020 8347 9797	££	11 pm	Nice place. Good cookies. £3 pizzas after 9pm!
Red Lion And Sun	25 N Rd	020 8340 1780	££££	10 pm	Excellent Sunday roasts.

Map 52 • Archway (North)

Bengal Berties	172 Archway Rd	020 8348 1648	££	11 pm	Spit and sawdust venue with excellent nosh.
Fahrenheit	230 Archway Rd	020 8347 0333	££	11 pm	Corking Caribbean food with a broad smile.
The Lighthouse	179 Archway Rd	020 8348 3121	££	11 pm	Outstanding fresh fish joint flies beneath radar.

Map 53 • Crouch End

Banners	21 Park Rd	020 8348 2930	££££	11.30 pm	Notoriously child-friendly but the breakfasts make up for that.
Hot Pepper Jelly	11 Broadway Parade	020 8340 4318	££*	5 pm	Pepperphobes probably shouldn't come to this culinary wonder.
Milou's on the Hill	83 Hazellville Rd	020 7272 1188	£*	9 pm	Go there for the hilltop terrace and homemade smoothies.
Piya Cafe	59 The Broadway	020 8347 8861	££	12 am	Great cheap and friendly Mediterranean grub.
Thaitanic	66 Crouch End Hill	020 8341 6100	£	11 pm	Groanworthy name, moanworthy food!

Map 56 • Hampstead Village

Bacchus Greek Taverna	37 Heath St	020 7435 1855	£	11 pm	Lovely little place that has been here an age.
La Creperie De Hampstead	77 Hampstead High St	020 7372 0081	£*	11 pm	No crap crepes at this sublime French street stall.
The Louis Patisserie	32 Heath St	020 7435 9908	£	6 pm	Tea and gorgeous cakes beloved of elderly Eastern European gentlemen.
Tinseltown	104 Heath St	020 7435 2396	£	3 am	Welcome to milkshake heaven!

Map 58 • Parliament Hill / Dartmouth Park

Al Parco	2 Highgate West Hill	020 8340 5900	£	10 pm	Probably the best pizza in London.
Cafe Mozart	17 Swain's Ln	020 8348 1384	££	10 pm	Great place for lunch on a sunny day.
Kalendar	15 Swains Lane	020 8348 8300	££	11 pm	Pre-Heath brekkie, mid-Heath lunch or post-Heath dinner. All good!
Stingray Cafe	135 Fortess Rd	020 7482 4855	£	11 pm	Another reason why Tufnell Park rocks: great place!

Map 59 • Tufnell Park

Charuwan	110 Junction Rd	020 7263 1410	£££	10 pm	Friendly, quiet, tasty, cheap. Yup, it's pretty awesome.
Rustique Cafe	142 Fortess Rd	020 7692 5590	££	8 pm	Damn those tasty tasty cookies for being so small.

Map 60 • Archway

Archgate Café	5 Junction Rd	020 7272 2575	£	10 pm	Lovely English breakfasts face-off against equally ace Turkish food.
Iceland Fish Bar	11 Archway Rd	020 7272 6606	£	10 pm	Proper old-school chippie.
Junction Café	61 Junction Rd	020 7263 2036	£*	10 pm	Greasy. Spoon.
Kingfisher	657 Holloway Rd	020 7263 2160	£*	10 pm	Holloway's top fish and chip outlet.
La Voute	10 Archway Rd	020 7281 7314	£	4.30 pm	Ace brekkies and lunches in this snazzy caff.
Mosaic Café	24 Junction Rd	020 7272 3509	££	10.30 pm	Head for the back garden sun-trap in Summer.
Nid Ting	533 Holloway Rd	020 7263 0506	£££	11.15 pm	Bigger, meatier portions than most Thai Restaurants.
RRC Thai Cafe	36 Highgate Hill	020 7561 0421	£	10.30 pm	Cheap, tasty and beautifully presented Thai food.
St Johns	91 Junction Rd	020 7272 1587	££££	11 pm	Gastro pub oasis stranded among the pound-shops of Archway.
The Toll Gate	6 Archway Close	020 7687 2066	££	11 pm	On with the pince-nez for slightly self-satisfied veggie venue.

Map 61 • Holloway (North)

The Landseer	37 Landseer Rd	020 7263 4658	££	9.30 pm	Gastropub extraordinaire.
Pasteleiro	22 Seven Sisters Rd	078 7159 9938	£*	6 pm	Brazilian street grub.

Map 62 • Finsbury Park

Fassika	152 Seven Sisters Rd	020 7272 7572	££	12 am	Intimate with lovely food. Distinctly flirty waitresses though...
Le Rif	172 Seven Sisters Rd	020 7263 1891	£*	10 pm	Essential for all your banter and microwaved Tagine needs.
Petek	96 Stroud Green Rd	020 7619 3933	£	10.45 pm	Classy but cheap Turkish.

Map 63 • Manor House

Il Bacio	178 Blackstock Rd	020 7226 3339	££	11 pm	Friendly, reliable and huge portions.
New River Cafe	271 Stoke Newington Church St	020 7923 9842	£	11 pm	Steamy windows and top hangover cure fry-ups.

Map 64 • Stoke Newington

56	56 Newington Green	020 7359 6377	££	11.30 pm	Bring a date.
Alistair's Brasserie	35 Church Walk	020 7249 2782	££££	10 pm	Luxurious food with gobshite, luddite customers. Mmmmm.
Anglo Asian	60 Stoke Newington Church St	020 7254 9298	££	11.30 pm	Classic curry house right down to the free sherry.
Blue Legume	101 Stoke Newington Church St	020 7923 1303	£	11 pm	Dreamy eggs benedict, served under a giant aubergine.
Rasa N16	55 Stoke Newington Church St	020 7249 0344	££	11.30 pm	Vegetarian-style Indian cooking at its mouth-watering best.
Three Crowns	175 Stoke Newington Church St	020 7241 5511	££	9.30 pm	Impressive Victorian pub that's undergone gastropubification.
Yum Yum	187 Stoke Newington High St	020 7254 6751	£££	11 pm	Tasty tasty, Thai Thai. Go for the Kang Massuman.

Map 65 • West Hampstead

The Green Room	182 Broadhurst Gardens	020 7372 8188	££	11 pm	West Hampstead's newest joint brimming with charm. Nice risotto.

Map 66 • Finchley Road / Swiss Cottage

Bradleys	25 Winchester Rd	020 7722 3457	£££	11 pm	Your friendly face in the neighbourhood that loves wine.
Camden Arts Centre	Arkwright Rd	020 7472 5516	£	6 pm	Excellent food in buzzing artistic setting.
Singapore Garden	83 Fairfax Rd	020 7328 5314	££	11 pm	Surprising flavours make a welcome alternative on a night out.

Map 68 • Kilburn High Road / Abbey Road

Little Bay	228 Belsize Rd	020 7372 4699	££*	11 pm	Crazy cheap. Crazy cute!

Map 69 • St. John's Wood

Tupelo Honey	27 Parkway, Camden	020 7284 2989	££	11 pm	A coffee-shop, wine bar and restaurant combined.

Key: £ : Under £10 / ££ : £10–£20 / £££ : £20–£30 / ££££ : £30–£40 / £££££: £40+
** : Does not accept credit cards / † : Accepts only American Express / †† : Accepts only Visa and Mastercard*
Time listed refers to kitchen closing time on weekend nights

Map 70 • Primrose Hill

Cafe Seventy Nine	79 Regents Park Rd	020 7586 8012	£	6 pm	Excellent veggie fare, though you might have to wait.
J restaurant	148 Regents Park Rd	020 7586 9100	££	11 pm	Excellent food, especially brunch. Tempestuous service.
Legal Cafe	81 Haverstock Hill	020 7586 7412	£	6 pm	Great coffee, good food and wifi: a pleasant working environment.
Lemonia	89 Regents Park Rd	020 7586 7454	£££	11.30 pm	Fancy a real Greek meal?
Manna	4 Erskine Rd	020 7722 8028	££	11.30 pm	Aesthetically gorgeous veggie restaurant, serving scrumptious food.
Melrose and Morgan	42 Gloucester Ave	020 7722 0011	£	8 pm	Scrumptious food and coffee. Good for solo snacks.
Odette's	130 Regents Park Rd	020 7586 8569	£££	1 am	Delectably dainty restaurant, high-class service.
Primrose Bakery	69 Gloucester Ave	020 7483 4222	£	6 pm	A delectably dinky bakery. These cakes can't be missed.
Trojka	101 Regents Park Rd	020 7483 3765	££	10 pm	Authentically spartan but colourful decor. Nice 'n' quirky.
Two Brothers	297 Regents Park Rd	020 8346 0469	££	10 pm	Middle class fish & chips.

Map 71 • Camden Town / Chalk Farm / Kentish Town (West)

Andy's Taverna	81 Bayham St	020 7485 9718	££	11 pm	Big Greek restaurant with a garden.
Bar Gansa	2 Inverness St	020 7267 8909	££	12 am	More buzzing and pleasurable than a rampant rabbit.
Bar Solo	20 Inverness St	020 7482 4611	££	1 am	Where'd they find the waitresses? On the set of Clueless?
Bento Café	9 Parkway	020 7482 3990	££	11pm	Exquisite Japanese food at very reasonable prices.
Camden Bar and Kitchen	102 Camden High St	020 7485 2744	££	11 pm	Great burgers at this bohemian gem; sorry, McDonalds!
Camden Kitchen	102 Camden High St	020 7284 2744	£	11pm	Funky eatery, great for a relaxed date.
Cotton's	55 Chalk Farm Rd	020 7485 8388	££	10 pm	No hustle and bustle, just chill Jamaican-style.
Gilgamesh	The Stables Market, Chalk Farm Rd	020 7428 4922	£££*	12 am	Awesome surroundings will confuse the hell out of future archaeologists.
Haché	24 Inverness St	020 7485 9100	££	10.30 pm	Burger heaven for both vegetarians and carnivores.
Kim's Vietnamese Food Hut some	Unit D, Camden Lock Palace	N/A	£*	11 pm	Once you pass the Spanish Inqusition, excellent slop.
Limani	154 Regents Park Rd	020 7483 4492	£££	11 pm	Greek-Cypriot fare in a sophisticated environment. Friendly service.
Marathon Cafe	87 Chalk Farm Rd	020 7485 3814	£*	4 am	Legendary late-night venue serving kebabs, chips and beer.
Marine Ices	8 Haverstock Hill	020 7482 9003	£	11 pm	Fantastic ice cream restaurant with '70s decor and autographed photos.
Market	438 Parkway	020 7267 9700	£££	11 pm	The only restaurant in Camden deserving of the name.
Muang Thai	71 Chalk Farm Rd	020 7916 0653	£	11 pm	Quiet vibe, tinkly music, reliably decent food.
My Village	37 Chalk Farm Rd	020 7485 4996	£	9pm	Cute ethnic organic shop serving food, tea and coffee.
Than Binh	14 Chalk Farm Rd	020 7267 9820	£	10 pm	Excellent Vietnamese with very friendly and chatty staff.
Viet-anh Cafe	41 Parkway	020 7284 4082	£	11 pm	Surly service, cheap plentiful food. Would it hurt to smile?
Woody Grill	1 Camden Rd	020 7485 7774	£*	12 am	Late night post-alcohol food without salmonella poisoning.
Yumchaa Tea Space	91 Upper Walkway, West Yard, Camden Lock Market	020 7209 9641	£*	6 pm	The carrot cake... oh mama!
Zorya Imperial Vodka Room	48 Chalk Farm Rd	020 7485 8484	££	12 am	Vodka, vodka and more vodka. Oh... and gorgeous food too.

Map 72 • Kentish Town

Bintang Cafe	93 Kentish Town Rd	020 7813 3393	££	11 pm	Good for eating copiously in a gaudy shack.
Café Euro Med	225 Kentish Town Rd	020 7267 7761	£	9 pm	Fry ups with feta. Possibly not OK.
Eat Zone	18 Fortess Rd	020 7485 0152	£*	11 pm	Quick and delicious, with roughly 1 gazillion choices. Addictive.

Le Petit Prince	5 Holmes Rd	020 7267 3789	££	11 pm	Adorable homage to French cartoon character with excellent merguez.
Mario's Cafe	6 Kelly St	020 7284 2066	£*	10 pm	Saint Etienne's local greasy spoon.
The Oxford	256 Kentish Town Rd	020 7485 3521	££	9.45 pm	Smug comfort eating.
Pane Vino	323 Kentish Town Rd	020 7267 3879	££	10.30 pm	Staff can be Italian. Food can be fantastic.
Phoenicia	186 Kentish Town Rd	020 7267 1267	£	10 pm	Coffee n' baclava, falafel, meze. All a steal.

Map 74 • Holloway Road / Arsenal

Dastarkhan	203 Holloway Rd	0754 521 1010	££	2 am	Frankly bizarre Khazak place. Entertaining, but so so nosh.
Morgan M	489 Liverpool Rd	020 7609 3560	£££££	11 pm	Divine Frenchie. Mais zut alors! £1200 bottles of wine!
Tbilisi	91 Holloway Rd	020 7607 2536	££££	11 pm	Get your Georgian on.

Map 75 • Highbury

San Daniele Del Friuli	72 Highbury Park	020 7226 1609	£££	12 am	Like mama used to make—well someone had to say it.
Sariyer Balik	56 Green Lanes	020 7275 7681	£££	12 am	Turkish Seafood.

Map 76 • Edgeware Road / Marylebone (North)

Mandalay	444 Edgware Rd	020 7258 3696	£	10.30 pm	Cheap treats await, despite the God awful situation.
Sea Shell Of Lisson Grove	49 Lisson Grove	020 7224 9000	££	10.30 pm	Pescatarians will love this place—sorry, carnivores!
Zen Spice Market	Melcombe Place	020 7723 8890	££*	11 pm	Station sushi.

Map 77 • Mornington Crescent / Regent's Park

Chutneys	124 Drummond St	020 7388 0604	££	11.30 pm	Flavoursome, no-frills, fill-yer-boots affair. Bargainous buffet colossal.
Diwana Bhel Poori	121 Drummond St	020 7387 5556	££	11 pm	South-Indian veggie with tasty dosai and puris.
The Green Note	106 Parkway	020 7485 9899	££	11 pm	Excellent veggie tapas with a side of bongo drums.
Mestizo	103 Hampstead Rd	020 7387 4064	£££	11 pm	Great. The margarita is made by the devil himself.

Map 78 • Euston

Asakusa	265 Eversholt St	020 7388 8399	£££	11.30 pm	Authentic Japanese.
Banger Bros.	Euston Station	020 7387 6958	£	7.30 pm	Sing it: It's a small world (of sausages) after all!
Camino	3 Varnisher's Yard	020 7841 7331	£££	12 am	Sophisticated Spanish restaurant in Kings Cross. Seems wrong, somehow.
Chop Chop Noodle Bar	1 Euston Rd	020 7833 1773	£	11 pm	Great for a quick and cheap meal. Massive portions.
El Parador	245 Eversholt St	020 7387 2789	££	11 pm	Great tapas. A little ray of sunshine in your mouth.
Great Nepalese	48 Eversholt St	020 7358 6737	££	11 pm	Really the only option in the area.
Kitchin	8 Caledonia St	020 7713 8777	££	11 pm	Round-the-world all-you-can-eat. Vile and great.
Last Word Cafe	96 Euston Rd, St. Pancras	020 7380 1933	£*	5 pm	Coffee, croissants with the bonhomous boffins at the British Library.
Rodon Live	7 Pratt St	020 7267 8088	££	11 pm	Friendly rotund owner masks just above average food.
The Somerstown Coffee House	60 Chalton St	020 7691 9136	££	10 pm	Bistro food in grade II listed pub. Excellent set menu.

Map 79 • King's Cross

Addis	42 Caledonian Rd	020 7278 0679	££	11 pm	Lovely food with convivial sloth-like service.
Dallas Burger Bar	257 Caledonian Rd	020 7278 4955	£*	9 pm	JR smiles down as you destroy your arteries. Hilarious.
Euro Café	299 Caledonian Rd	020 7607 5362	£	10 pm	Loveable caff with some unusual specials.
Marathon	196 Caledonian Rd	020 7837 4499	££	12 am	Raw meat, ritualistic coffee and crazed dancing.
Menelik	277 Caledonian Rd	020 7278 0679	££	12 am	If only more places let you eat with your hands.
The New Didar	347 Caledonian Rd	020 7700 3496	£	12 am	Friendly staff willing to strike deals. Haggling gets you everywhere.
Oz	53 Caledonian Rd	020 7278 9650	£*	10 pm	Unusually well-kempt greasy spoon.

Key: £ : Under £10 / ££ : £10–£20 / £££ : £20–£30 / ££££ : £30–£40 / £££££: £40+
** : Does not accept credit cards / † : Accepts only American Express / †† : Accepts only Visa and Mastercard*
Time listed refers to kitchen closing time on weekend nights

Tony's Natural Foods	10 Caledonian Rd	020 7837 5223	£	11 pm	Vegan salad bar with peaceout garden, man.
Yum Yum	48 Caledonian Rd	020 7278 4737	£	11 pm	Super-cheap Chinese that may even remain in your stomach.

Map 80 • Angel / Upper St

Afghan Kitchen	35 Islington Green	020 7359 8019	£££*	10.45 pm	Only a few tables; Islington's smallest—and biggest— Afghan place.
The Albion	10 Thornhill Rd	020 7607 7450	££	10 pm	How many places offer whole suckling pigs? Not enough.
Alpino	97 Chapel Market	020 7837 8330	£	4 pm	This, guv'nor, is a proper tea'n'two slices caff. Alright?
The Breakfast Club	31 Camden Passage	020 7226 5454	££	9.30 pm	Not just breakfast, not a club. But just so gooood.
Candid Café	3 Torrens St	020 7837 4237	£	10 pm	Laid-back, arty cafe for dreamy types. Candle-lit. Perfect for lingering.
Desperados	127 Upper St	020 7226 3222	££	11.30 pm	Garish. More like the Mexico of MTV than the real world.
Elk in the Woods	39 Camden Passage	020 7226 3535	££	10.30 pm	Laid-back, hunting-themed eatery.
Fig and Olive	151 Upper St	020 7354 2605	££	11 pm	Incredibly busy at weekends which can affect service and quality.
Fine Burger Co	330 Upper St	020 7359 3026	£	10 pm	For when you've grown out of McDonalds.
Gem	265 Upper St	020 7359 0405	£££	11 pm	A good vibe is precious.
House	63 Canonbury Rd	020 7704 7410	£££	10.30 pm	Gastro bar-restaurant where seasonal food's served with flair. For those feeling flush.
Indian Veg Bhelpoori House	93 Chapel Market	020 7833 1167	£	10 pm	Honest all-you-can-eat Indian. Veggie propaganda on walls.
Isarn	119 Upper St	020 7424 5153	££	11 pm	Pretty, flower-adorned food, green curry cooked to perfection. Candle-lit courtyard.
Itsuka	54 Islington Park St	020 7354 5717	£	12 am	Cheap set menus and heartfelt J-Pop.
La Forchetta	73 Upper St	020 7226 6879	££	11.30 pm	Unpretentious, cheap pizza. Eat fast, then leg it.
La Porchetta	141 Upper St	020 7288 2488	£££	11 pm	This little pig says yes to good cheap pizza.
Le Mercury	140 Upper St	020 7354 4088	££	1 am	This place will seduce you AND your mother.
Masala Zone	80 Upper St	020 7359 3399	££	11 pm	Cheap, good thalis served on metal trays.
Mem & Laz	8 Theberton St	020 7704 9089	££	11 pm	Mediterranean chaos by candlelight.
Metrogusto	13 Theberton St	020 7226 9400	££	10.30 pm	Try not to let the menacing art put you off the amazing pasta.
Olive Grill	61 Upper St	020 7226 9002	£*	10 pm	The falafels are so good you may quit kebabs. Forever.
Ottolenghi	287 Upper St	020 7288 1454	££	10 pm	Staff you'll want to take home to meet your mum.
Pizzeria Oregano	19 St Alban's Pl	020 7288 1123	££	11 pm	Great pizza and lentil soup. Delicious odd couple.
Pomegranate	139 Upper St	020 7704 1002	££	12 am	Bright. And not in a clever way.
Rodizo Rico	77 Upper St	020 7354 1076	£££	11 pm	Meat. And lots of it.
Tortilla	13 Islington High St	020 7833 3103	££	10 pm	Damn good burritos!
The Trawlerman Fish Shop	205 Upper St	020 7354 0276	£*	11 pm	Top-notch British stodge.
Vigata Ristorante	Liverpool Rd	020 7226 1475	££	10 pm	Sardonic about Sicilian? This lobster linguine will soon fix that.
Zaffrani	47 Cross St	020 7226 5522	££	11 pm	Thinking man's curry.

Map 81 • Canonbury

Angel Cafe	100 Essex Rd	020 7704 6866	£	11 pm	Blue collar fusion cuisine: Brit greasy spoon serving Turkish boreks.
People's Choice Cafe	236 Essex Rd	020 7253 1798	£*	10 pm	Who are these people? And why choose here?
Raab's Bakery	136 Essex Rd	020 7226 2830	£	6 pm	Use your loaf sunshine.
Sabor	108 Essex Rd	020 7226 5551	££££	11 pm	Latin American; even the tables are tropical.
Zigni House	330 Essex Rd	020 7226 7418	£	12 am	Hearty East African eatery with boho, raffish charm.

Map 82 • De Beauvoir Town / Kingsland

Casaba	162 Essex Rd	020 7288 1223	££	7 pm	Fresh spin on Turkish meze and shisha bar.
Huong Viet	12 Englefield Rd	020 7249 0877	££	11 pm	A crumbling old bath house? Look again.
Puji Puji	122 Balls Pond Rd	020 7923 1106	££	10 pm	Malaysian Malaysian.

Map 83 • Angel (East) / City Rd (North)

Fifteen	15 Westland Pl	0871 330 1515	£££££	10 pm	Lots of Jamie Oliver. Lots of great, expensive food.

Map 84 • Hoxton

The Bean	126 Curtain Rd	020 7739 7829	£*	8 pm	Decent coffee! It's hard to find, you know.
The Diner	128 Curtain Rd	020 7729 4452	£££	10.30 pm	Door-stopper burgers that should come with health warnings.
F.Cooke	150 Hoxton St	020 7729 7718	££	8 pm	Pies, Liquor, Eels... British cullinary retardation at it's finest.
Macondo	8 Hoxton Sq	020 7729 1119	£	10 pm	Pleasant blend of cocktail bar and European cafe society.
Rivington Bar and Grill	28 Rivington St	020 7729 7053	££	11 pm	Emin on the walls, meat in the buns.
Shish	313 Old Street	020 7749 0990	££	10 pm	Great kebabs in surroundings devoid of authenticity.
Yelo	8 Hoxton Sq	020 7729 4626	£	11 pm	Suspiciously quick service, but cheap and tasty so who cares?

Map 85 • Stoke Newington (East)

Bagel House	2 Stoke Newington High St queues.	020 7249 3908	£*	10 pm	Bagels to rival Brick Lane and without the queues.
Cafe Z Bar	58 Stoke Newington High St	020 7275 7523	£*	11 pm	Popular grease-shop/hangover center for Stokey Lefties.
Testi	38 Stoke Newington High St	020 7249 7151	£££	12 am	Yes, it's named after bollocks. No, it's really not bollocks.

Map 86 • Dalston / Kingsland

19 Numara Bos Cirrik	34 Stoke Newington Rd	020 7249 0400	££	10 pm	Meat, meat, meat—oh and onion, pomegranate and turnip salad.
The Best Turkish Kebab	125 Stoke Newington Rd	020 7254 7642	£*	12 am	Feed your soul. Always buzzing.
Evin Bar and Cafe	115 Kingsland High St	020 7254 5634	££	11 pm	Fantastic Turkish place without the grease factor. Speciality is gozleme.
Mangal 1	10 Arcola St	020 7275 8981	£*	12 am	May the grill's smoke guide you, meat-loving friends.
Mangal 2	4 Stoke Newington Rd	020 7254 7888	££	12 am	Gilbert & George aren't the only ones loving this one.
Peppers and Spice	20 Kingsland High St	020 7275 9818	£*	10.30 pm.	The real deal: jerk, oxtail, festival, plantain, ackee. Everyting irie.
Shanghai	41 Kingsland High St	020 7254 2878	££	10.30 pm	Tasty, good-value Chinese hiding behind the facade of a dingy old Kaff.
Somine	131 Kingsland High St	020 7254 7384	£*	24 hrs	Reanimating red lentil soup, Turkish style. Around the clock.
Stone Cave	111 Kingsland High St	020 7241 4911	££	12 am	Cave look and cave feel. Up-scale(ish) Turkish. And great.
The Tea Rooms	155 Stoke Newington Rd	020 7923 1870	£	10 pm	Stokey in a tea-cup. Pleasant...

Map 87 • Hackney Downs / Lower Clapton

India Gate	75 Lower Clapton Rd	020 8986 0505	£*	11 pm	Very, very cheap, pretty cheerful and a little rank.
Parioli	90 Lower Clapton Rd	020 7502 3288	£	9 pm	Best food of any kind in Clapton.
Pogo Cafe	76 Clarence Rd	020 8533 1214	£*	9 pm	Vegan co-op community caff. Real food for thought.

Map 88 • Haggerston / Queensbridge Rd

Faulkner's	424 Kingsland Rd	020 7254 6152	£££	10 pm	Famous fish and fries (oh OK—chips).
LMNT	316 Queensbridge Rd	020 7249 6727	£££	10.45 pm	Eat inside an urn or by a sphinx's paws.
That Vietnamese Place	134 Kingsland Rd	020 7729 4843	££	10 pm	Not as memorable as the name would have you believe.
Usha	428 Kingsland Rd	020 7241 0836	£	11 pm	One of few curry houses in the area. Consistently good.
Viet Hoa Café	70 Kingsland Rd	020 7729 8293	£	11.30 pm	Bland looking cafe hides gorgeous delicacies.

Map 89 • London Fields / Hackney Central

Buen Ayre	50 Broadway Market	020 7275 9900	££££	10.30 pm	Vegetarians take note—run for the hills.
Cafe Bohemia	2 Bohemia Pl	020 8986 4352	£	11 pm	Feeling Bohemian? Quirky cafe with live blues/jazz/world Saturday nights.

Key: £ : Under £10 / ££ : £10–£20 / £££ : £20–£30 / ££££ : £30–£40 / £££££: £40+
** : Does not accept credit cards./ † : Accepts only American Express / †† : Accepts only Visa and Mastercard*
Time listed refers to kitchen closing time on weekend nights

Cat and Mutton	76 Broadway Market	020 7254 5599	££	10 pm	Gastropub without the gastropub nastiness.
Corner Deli	121 Mare St	020 8986 0031	£	9 pm	Nice spot for brunch away from the bustle of Broadway Market.
F.Cooke	9 Broadway Market	020 7254 6458	££	8 pm	We built empires on this stuff: remarkably unchanged gem.
Hai Ha	206 Mare St	020 8985 5388	££*	11 pm	Brilliant BYO Vietnamese cafe.
R Cooke and Sons	9 Broadway Market	020 7254 6458	£*	8 pm	Lor' love a duck! Pie n' mash shop—liquor an' all!
The Spurstowe Arms	68 Greenwood Rd	020 7254 4316	££	11 pm	Suntrap beer garden, good wine selection and gamey menu. Marvelous.

Map 90 • Homerton / Victoria Park North

Blueberries	87 Lauriston Rd	020 8985 5888	£	11 pm	Smart, bright little bistro of the exposed brickwork school.
The Empress of India	130 Lauriston Rd	020 8533 5123	£££	10 pm	Spiffy menu from brekkie through to dinner in Hackney Village.
The Fish House	126 Lauriston Rd	020 8533 3327	££	9.45 pm	Not as cheap as chips but still very good.

Map 91 • Shoreditch / Brick Lane / Spitalfields

Beigel Bakery	159 Brick Lane	087 1332 8040	£*	24 hrs	For 3am cravings; salted beef bagel from the Beigel Bakery.
Brick Lane Clipper Restaurant	104 Brick Ln	020 7377 0022	££	12 am	For less spice-oriented connoisseurs, Bengali Clipper's exceptional lamb korma.
Cafe Bangla	128 Brick Lane	020 7247 7885	££	12 am	Popular Bangladeshi adorned with psychedelic and surreal fantasy art.
Drunken Monkey	222 Shoreditch High St	020 7392 9606	££	12 am	Debauched, dimly-lit dim-sum drinking hole. Chinese lanterns and lethal mojitos.
Ethiopian Food Stall	Sunday Upmarket, Truman's Brewery, Brick Lane	N/A	£*	N/A	One of many great food stalls, get Brazilian desert after!
Green and Red	51 Bethnal Green Rd	020 7749 9670	£	11 pm	Foot-tappin' Mexican cantina for fab tacos and proper guacamole. Ole!
Hackney City Farm	1 Goldsmiths Row	020 7729 6381	££	4.30 pm	Animals! In Hackney! And some overpriced fry-up.
Hanoi Cafe	98 Kingsland Rd	020 7729 5610	££	11 pm	Cosy Viet joint, where the whole family's around.
Hawksmoor	157 Commercial St	020 7247 7392	£££	10.30 pm	France and America forget their differences for some serious steakage.
Jones Dairy Café	23 Ezra St	020 7739 5372	£*	3 pm	Sit back and watch the world go by at Columbia Road.
Le Taj	96 Brick Ln	020 7247 0733	££	11 pm	Bengali AND Indian menus, BYO, curry house.
Les Trois Garcons	1 Club Row	020 7613 1924	££££	11 pm	Kitch décor/slick service/fantastic grub.
Noodle King	185 Bethnal Green Rd	020 7613 3131	£*	11.30 pm	Half the normal price; double the normal portions. Come hungry.
Ping Pong	3 Steward St	020 7422 7650	££	11 pm	Serviceable dim sum in a frantic shitstorm.
The Premises	201 Hackney Rd	020 7729 7593	££	11 pm	Bistro swarming with musicians thanks to next door's recording studio.
Que Viet	102 Kingsland Rd	020 7033 0588	££	11 pm	So du jour—even Marc Jacobs munches noodles here.
Rootmaster	Elys Yard	079 1238 9314	££	10 pm	Eat on a bus without looking homeless.
Song Que	134 Kingsland Rd	020 7613 3222	££	11 pm	Still Little Vietnam's queen. An authentic, no-nonsense affair.
St John Bread and Wine	94 Commercial St	020 7251 0848	£££	11 pm	Minimalist and meaty. Anyone for deep-fried pig's head?
Story Deli	91 Brick Ln	020 7247 3137	£	9 pm	Lo-tech pizza joint. Think hipster Pizza Express.
Tay Do	60 Kingsland Rd	020 7739 0966	£	11 pm	Squish 'em in, feed 'em quick variety of cheap & filling Vietnamese cuisine.
Tay Do Cafe	65 Kingsland Rd	020 7729 7223	£££	12 am	Hectic and noisy. Just like Vietnam, then.
Viet Grill	58 Kingsland Rd	020 7739 6686	££	11 pm	Eccentric but tasty. Non edible tropical fish as decor...

Map 92 • Bethnal Green

Bistrotheque	23 Wadeson St	020 8983 7900	££	11 pm	Brunch, burlesque and pianist playing Smells Like Teen Spirit. Fabulous.
E Pellicci	332 Bethnal Green Rd	020 7739 4873	£	4.30 pm	Challenge your hangover to survive their fry-ups.
Little Georgia	87 Goldsmiths Row	020 7739 8154	££	10 pm	Hearty fayre from the former Soviet State. No drinks licence.

Wild Cherry	241 Globe Rd	020 8980 6678	££	4 pm	Buddhist staff serve yummy breakfasts to hungover partiers. Instant karma.

Map 93 • Globe Town / Mile End (North)

L'Oasis	237 Mile End Rd	020 7702 7051	££	11 pm	Well-loved local eaterie.
Matsu	558 Mile End Rd	020 8983 3528	££	11 pm	Japanese food? In Mile End? You're 'avin a giraffe aintcha?
The Morgan Arms	43 Morgan St	020 8980 6389	£££	12 am	Which joker invented the term "gastropub"? This is one of them.
Winkles	238 Roman Rd	020 8880 7450	££	10.30 pm	Outstanding seafood. Fishmonger's and delivery service available too.

Map 94 • Bow

Chicchi	516 Roman Rd	020 8141 4190	£*	7 pm	The Italians reclaim Roman Road.
G.Kelly Pie & Mash shop	526 Roman Rd	020 8980 3165	£	7 pm	Servin' ot 'ome-made pies, jellied eels 'n mash since 1937.
The Roman Tandoori	432 Roman Road	020 8980 1390	££	10 pm	If you can't stand eels, 'ave a curry instead.

Map 95 • Whitechapel (West) / St Katharine's Dock

Cafe Spice Namaste	16 Prescot St	020 7488 9242	££	10.30 pm	Open-minded Indian that strays far from run of the mill.
The Empress	141 Leman St	020 7265 0745	£	11.45 pm	Forget Brick Lane. This is where it's at.
Tayyab's	83 Fieldgate St	020 7247 9543	££	10 pm	Beautiful chaos. Don't eat for days beforehand.

Map 96 • Whitechapel (East) / Shadwell (West) / Wapping

Il Bordello	81 Wapping High St	020 7481 9950	£££	10 pm	Upscale neighbourhood Italian.
Tayyabs	83 Fieldgate St	020 7247 6400	£	12 am	Lipsmacking seekh kebabs alone are worth the queues.

Map 97 • Stepney / Shadwell (East)

Wapping Food	Wapping Wall	020 7680 2080	£££	11 pm	Stunning dining in 100 year old powerstation/ art gallery. Go!

Map 98 • Mile End (South) / Limehouse

La Figa	45 Narrow St	020 7790 0077	££	11 pm	Tasty Italian in courtyard setting.
The Narrow	44 Narrow St	020 7592 7950	£££	11 pm	Gordon Ramsay's nod to gastropubs—cracking views.
Orange Room Cafe	63 Burdett Rd	020 8980 7336	£££	11.30 pm	Tasty, fresh Lebanese food in a wasteland of stodgy takeaways.

Map 100 • Poplar (West) / Canary Wharf (West)

1802 Bar	Hertsmere Rd	087 0444 3886	££	11 pm	Dine inside the warehouse built by Napoleonic prisoners.
Browns	Hertsmere Rd	020 7987 9777	£££	11 pm	Always reliable.
Nicolas	480 One Canada Sq	020 7512 9092	££	10.30 pm	Micro French restaurant and vintners in one.
Plateau	Canada Pl	020 7715 7100	££££	10.30 pm	Striking views and truffle gnocchi.
Tiffin Bites	22 Jubilee Place	020 7719 0333	££	10 pm	Eat curry, watch Bollywood films.

Map 101 • Poplar (East) / Canary Wharf (East)

Gun	27 Coldharbour	020 7515 5222	£££	11 pm	Enjoyed by 18th century dockers and city workers alike.

Map 104 • South Bank / Waterloo / Lambeth North

Anchor & Hope	32 The Cut	020 7928 9898	££££	10.30 pm	A British gastro-pub obsession, long waits though.
Canteen	Royal Festival Hall, Belvedere Rd	084 5686 1122	££	10.30 pm	A menu that sums up the best of British food with aplomb.
Concrete	Southbank Centre	020 7928 4123	£	1 am	Restaurant/bar features Russian beer, food, absinthe.
The Cut Bar	66 The Cut	020 7928 4400	£££	11 pm	Brilliant chips. A cut above the rest.
Enis's Cafe	79 Waterloo Rd	N/A	£	11 pm	You wouldn't believe me if I told you. Just go.
Giraffe	Riverside Level 1	020 7928 2004	££	10.45pm	Good crowd pleaser. Though too much world music and balloons.
Livebait	45 The Cut	020 7928 7211	£££	11 pm	Very fishy, in a very good way.

Key: £ : Under £10 / ££ : £10–£20 / £££ : £20–£30 / ££££ : £30–£40 / £££££: £40+
** : Does not accept credit cards./ † : Accepts only American Express / †† : Accepts only Visa and Mastercard*
Time listed refers to kitchen closing time on weekend nights

Marie's Café	90 Lower Marsh	020 7928 1050	£	10.30 pm	Greasy spoon by day, a no-frills, super-yum BYO thai by night.
Oxo Tower Wharf	Barge House St	020 7803 3888	££££	11 pm	You might have to rob a bank, but the view's amazing.
RSJ	33 Coin St	0207 928 4554	££	11 pm	Forget about those crappy South Bank chains. Go here.
Skylon	Belvedere Rd	020 7654 7800	££££	10.45 pm	Expensive, but staffs' uniforms and view make up for it.
Studio 6	56 Upper Ground	020 7928 6243	££	11 pm	Service with a reluctant grunt doesn't stop the crowds.
Tas Cafe	33 The Cut	020 7928 2111	££	11.30 pm	Blink and you'll miss it. Buzzing Turkish cafe—best hummous in London.

Map 105 • Southwark / Bankside (West)

Baltic	74 Blackfriars Rd	020 7928 1111	££££	10.30 pm	Try Polish Hunter's stew: made with real Polish Hunters. Probably.
Blackfriars Cafe	169 Blackfriars Rd	020 7928 4034	£*	10 pm	Old-school, family-run greasy spoon; amazing fry-ups.
Laughing Gravy	154 Blackfriars Rd	020 7721 7055	££	12 am	Ropey exterior. Sounds odd. Bugger to get to.
The Table	85 Southwark St	020 7401 2760	£*	10.30 pm	Go and find out why we're all obsessed.
Tapas Brindisa	18 Southwark St	020 7357 8880	££	11 pm	If you can bear the crowds, lovely market-bordering eaterie.
Tate Modern Restaurant	Bankside	020 7887 8888	££	6 pm	Stunning views, crap food, clueless staff.

Map 106 • Bankside (East) / Borough / Newington

Amano	Clink St	020 7234 0000	££	10 pm	Trust Amano for stone-baked pizza and freshly-made flatbreads. We do.
Boot and Flogger	10 Redcross Way	020 74071184	££	8 pm	Splendidly gentleman's club-esque—all savile row suits and chesterfield sofas.
Brew Wharf	Brew Wharf Yard, Stoney St	020 7378 6601	££	11 pm	Unusual comfort food and tasty home brews.
Cantina Vinopolis	1 Bank End	087 0899 8856	££££	10.30 pm	Gourmet food and wine at a bad museum? Believe it.
Champor-Champor	62 Weston St	020 7403 4600	£££	10.15pm	Jaw-droppingly inspired high-end Malaysian cuisine. Totally impressive.
El Vergel	8 Lant St	020 7357 0057	£*	10 pm	Its Latin breakfast: Oh. My. God. Soooooo good.
Feng Sushi	13 Stoney St	020 7407 8744	££	10 pm	The best sushi in London and available to takeaway. Dangerous!
Fish!	Cathedral St	020 7407 3803	££	10.30 pm	Great fish. Simple. Let it have its exclamation mark.
Fusebox	12 Stoney St	020 7407 9888	£*	5 pm	Quick fusion fare that's well worth the queue.
Hing Loon	159 Borough High St	020 7378 8100	£	11 am	Stupidly cheap. Very cheerful. The duck rocks.
Roast	The Floral Hall, Stoney St	084 5034 7300	££	9.30 pm	Meat, glorious meat. High-end food. Fab location.
Silka	Southwark St	020 7378 7777	£££	11.30 pm	Curry house that won't damage your arse in the morning.
Tas	72 Borough High St	020 7403 7200	£££	11 pm	Meze madness.
Tas EV	72 Borough High St	020 7620 6191	££	11 pm	Reduce your carbon Footprint: come here and feel 1000 miles away.
Wright Bros Oyster Bar	11 Stoney St	020 7403 9554	£££	10.30 pm	Tastebuds say no, but libido says YES.

Map 107 • Shad Thames

Butlers Wharf Chop House	36 Shad Thames	020 7403 3403	£££	11 pm	What better place for British best than under Tower Bridge?
Delfina	50 Bermondsey St	020 7357 2400	££££	11 pm	Gallery/restaurant offering works of art on your plate.
Le Pont de la Tour	36 Shad Thames	020 7403 8403	£££££	11 pm	Blair & Clinton's rendezvous. Posh but gosh!
M Manze Pie and Mash	87 Tower Bridge Rd	020 7407 2985	£	2.30 pm	As English as it gets. Try it once.
Magdalen	152 Tooley St	020 7403 1342	££££	10.30 pm	Forever fascinating Franco-Spanish cuisine.
Village East	171 Bermondsey St	020 7357 6082	£££	11 pm	Superior food. Slick surroundings.

Map 108 • Bermondsey

Arancia	52 Southwark Park Rd	020 7394 1751	££	11 pm	A very decent neighbourhood Italian. Try the pumpkin gnocchi.
PoppyHana	169 Jamaica Rd	020 7237 9416	£	11 pm	Cute as a button Japanese. Don't be put off by the food sculptures.

Map 109 • Southwark Park

Mayflower	117 Rotherhithe St	020 7237 4088	£££	9.30 pm	The pub Sunday Lunch was invented for.
Simplicity	1 Tunnel Rd	020 7232 5174	££	10.30 pm	Boldly goes where no restaurant has gone before: Rotherhithe.

Map 111 • Rotherhithe (East) Surrey Quays

Café Nabo	Surrey Docks Farm, Rotherhithe St	020 7231 1010	££	10 pm	Rid the toxins with a healthy farmyard lunch.

Map 112 • Kennington / Elephant and Castle

Dragon Castle	114 Walworth Rd	020 7277 3300	££	11 pm	Odd locale for such a curious pocket of culinary authenticity.
Lobster Pot	3 Kennington Ln	020 7582 5556	£££	10.30 pm	Dine to a soundtrack of seagull caws. We don't kid.

Map 113 • Walworth

La Luna	380 Walworth Rd	020 7277 1991	££	11 pm	Ignore exterior. It's the garlic bread inside that counts.

Map 115 • Old Kent Road (East)

Roma Café	21 Peckham Park Rd	020 7639 7730	£	10 pm	Escape Peckham and enjoy a good fry-up here.

Map 117 • Deptford (West)

Yellow House	37 Plough Way	020 7231 8777	£££	10.30 pm	The food stands out as much as the yellow building.

Map 119 • Deptford (East)

Kaya House	37 Deptford Broadway	020 8692 1749	££	10.45 pm	Tiny but excellent. Toilet is in the kitchen!
Manzes	204 Deptford High St	020 8692 2375	£	5 pm	Who ate all the pies? You'll certainly want to.

Map 120 • Greenwich

Inside	19 Greenwich South St	020 8265 5060	£££	11 pm	Surprisingly sophisticated worldly foods for a modest local.

Map 121 • Camberwell (West)

Kazakh Kyrgyz Restaurant	158 Camberwell Rd	020 7277 2228	££	1 am	Unsuspectingly tantalising Central Asian cuisine – belly dancer included.
New Dewaniam	225 Camberwell New Rd	087 1426 2594	£	12 am	Mouth-watering Indian takeaway for a tenner.
Su-Thai	16 Coldharbour Ln	020 7738 5585	££	10 pm	Reassuringly delicious Massaman curry & corn fritters.

Map 122 • Camberwell (East)

Caravaggio	47 Camberwell Church St	020 7207 1612	£	11 pm	Cheap Italian with impressive fare. Stands out from the rest.

Map 124 • Peckham East (Queen's Road)

805 Bar Restaurant	805 Old Kent Rd	020 7639 0808	£££	12 am	West African oasis. In Peckham.

Map 127 • Coldharbour Lane / Herne Hill (West)

Café Prov	2 Half Moon Ln	020 7978 9228	£££	10 pm	Local art (for sale) decorates this relaxed restaurant/bar/ cafe.
Ichiban Sushi	58 Atlantic Rd	020 77387 006		11 pm	The bee's knees.
The Lounge	56 Atlantic Rd	020 7733 5229	£	10 pm	A local favourite for breakfast, recovery and hanging on weekends.
New Fujiyama	5 Vining St	020 7737 6583	£	10.30 pm	This place blows Wagamama's out of the water.

Map 128 • Denmark Hill / Herne Hill (East)

Lombok	17 Half Moon Ln	020 7733 7131	£££	10.30 pm	From Stir-fries to curries, a no-fuss pan-Asian standby.

Number 22	22 Half Moon Ln	020 7095 9922	£££££	10.30 pm	Gorge yourself on Spanish wine, sherry and loads of brilliant tapas.
Olley's Fish And Chips	65 Norwood Rd	020 8671 8259	££	10:30 pm	Try the "Jeffery Archer," cod and chips, no tart.

Map 129 • East Dulwich

The Palmerston	91 Lordship Ln	020 8693 1629	£££££	10 pm	Gastropub that's a lot more gastro than pub.
Sea Cow	37 Lordship Ln	020 8693 3111	££	11 pm	Fishmonger meets chip shop with Billingsgate beauties.

Map 130 • Peckham Rye

The Rye	31 Peckham Rye	020 7639 5397	££	10 pm	A pocket of delicious East Dulwich swank Peckham side.
Thai Corner Cafe	44 Northcross Rd	020 8299 4041	££*	11 pm	Tiny, laidback neighbourhood cafe.

Map 131 • Vauxhall / Albert Embankment

Thai Pavillion East	78 Kennington Rd	020 7582 6333	££££	12 am	Thai food you will crave in retro round room.

Map 132 • Battersea (West)

La Tosca	31 Battersea Square	020 7978 5395	££		Get some Italian style al fresco action.
Ransom's Dock	35 Parkgate Rd	020 7223 1611	£££	11 pm	Friendly, stylish, likes wine and children.

Map 134 • South Lambeth

Bar Estrella	115 Old South Lambeth Rd	020 7793 1051	£	12 am	Football on telly, tapas in tummy. The heart of Little Portugal.
Hot Stuff	19 Wilcox Rd	020 7720 1480	£	10 pm	Hard to find. Slightly dinghy. Mental Staff. Amazing food.

Map 135 • Oval

Adulis	44 Brixton Rd	020 7587 0055	£	11 pm	C'mon, it's yummmy and cheap. And we can't cook Eritrean.
The Bonnington Café	11 Vauxhall Grove	check website for Chef's mobile	£*	10.30 pm	Wonderful vegetarian meals in a communified (ex-squat) environment.

Map 136 • Putney

Chakalaka	136 Upper Richmond Rd	020 8789 5696	££	10.30 pm	A truly zebra-fied exterior but fantastically authentic South African food.
Moomba Bar & Kitchen	5 Lacy Rd	020 8785 9151		12 am	Messiah of brunch.
Talad Thai	320 Upper Richmond Rd	020 8789 8084	££	10.30 pm	Thai-ny, family-run restaurant with Thai supermarket, cooking classes and Thai regulars.

Map 137 • Wandsworth (West)

Miraj	123 Putney Bridge Rd	020 8875 0799	£	10 pm	Curry in a hurry? Cheap, tasty take away joint.
Yia Mas	40 Upper Richmond Rd	020 8871 4671	££	11 pm	Cosy, welcoming Greek/Cypriot place. No plate smashing.

Map 138 • Wandsworth (Central)

Brady's	513 Old York Rd	020 8877 9599	££	11 pm	Up-market fish and chip cafe and take-away.
Kathmandu Valley	5 West Hill	020 8871 0240	££	11.45 pm	Nepalese is the new black (read: curry).

Map 139 • Wandsworth (East)

The Fish Club	189 St John's Hill	020 7978 7115	££	10 pm	The thinking man's chippie.
Spice of Life	147 St John's Hill	020 7924 2112	££	11.30 pm	Peerless curry restaurant on the hill.

Map 140 • Clapham Junction / Northcote Rd

I Sapori di Stefano Cavallini	146 Northcote Rd	020 7228 2017	££	11 pm	Totally authentic. Pasta made on site daily.

Map 142 • Clapham Old Town

Benny's	30 North St	020 7622 5868	£*	11.30pm	Marvel at Benny's chest hair, chat and fish and chips.
Mooli	36 Old Town	020 7627 1166	££	11 pm	Good twist on the Italian local.

Tom Ilic	123 Queenstown Rd	020 7622 0555	£££	10.30 pm	British fare that's the business—a result of hard-earned talent.
Trinity	4 The Polygon	020 7622 1199	£££	10.30 pm	How to do local dining really quite fantastically well.

Map 143 • Clapham High Street

Café Wanda	153 Clapham High St	020 7738 8760	££	10.30 pm	Back away from the fantastic dessert counter, real slow.
The Fish Club	57 Clapham High St	020 7720 5853	££	10 pm	Posh fish and chips, worth the extra clams.
The Pepper Tree	19 Clapham Common South Side	020 7622 1758	£*	11 pm	Speedy Thai with soul.
The Rapscallion	75 Venn St	020 7787 6555	££££	10 pm	Good fall-back. Wee bit dear.
San Marco Pizzeria	126 Clapham High St	020 7622 0452	££†	11.30 pm	Arguably the best pizza outside Italy—take that New York!
Tsunami	5 Voltaire Rd	020 7978 1610	££££	10.30 pm	The new Nobu. Unbelievable. Unfortunate name.

Map 144 • Stockwell / Brixton (West)

Franco Manca	4 Electric Lane	020 7738 3021	££	5 pm	Organic pizza perfection for around a fiver. Worth any wait.
Speedy Noodle	506 Brixton Rd	020 7326 4888	£*	1 am	Prime location and the cheapest, worst food in Brixton.
SW9 Bar Cafe	11 Dorrell Pl	020 7738 3116	£	9 pm	Great hangover curing breakfasts (and hangover causing booze).

Map 146 • Earlsfield

Carluccio's	537 Garratt Ln	020 8947 4651	££	11:30 pm	Sensational pasta dishes and optional curbside setting.

Map 147 • Balham (West)

The Bombay Bicycle Club	95 Nightingale Lane	020 8673 6217	££	10 pm	Award winning curries.
Chez Bruce	2 Bellevue Rd	020 8672 0114	££££	10.30 pm	Worth its fancy-pants (read Michelin) star.

Map 148 • Balham (East)

Dish Dash	11 Bedford Hill	020 8673 5555	££	11 pm	Tasty food. Tiny portions. Laid back vibe.
Harrison's	15 Bedford Hill	020 8675 6900	££	10.30 pm	Great food if you can tolerate the 'look at me!' crowd.

Map 149 • Clapham Park

Dexter's	36 Abbeville Rd	020 8772 6646	££	3 pm	Perfect brunch spot for hungry hangovers
Grissini	31 Abbeville Rd	020 8675 6260	££		Cosy neighbourhood joint. Good midweek deals.

Map 150 • Brixton

Asmara	386 Coldharbour Ln	020 7737 4144	££	11.15 pm	Disconcerting but delicious curry with pancakes to mop it up.
Khan's	24 Brixton Water Lane	020 7326 4460	££	11 pm	Great curry, and BYO to boot. Have it!
Negril	132 Brixton Hill	020 8674 8798	£	10 pm	Tasty Carribean with veg options (which are joy).
Opus Café	89 Acre Ln	020 7737 3777	£	6 pm	Cakes and coffee. Niceness.
Upstairs Bar and Restaurant	89 Acre Ln	020 7733 8855	££££	10.30 pm	A real find. Getting discovered. Sshhh.

Map 151 • Tooting Bec

Masaledar Kitchen	121 Upper Tooting Rd	020 8767 7676	££	11 pm	Last word in top-notch Indian cuisine
Mirch Masala	213 Upper Tooting Rd	020 8672 7500	£	12 am	Cheap, no frills, award-winning curries. Sublime.

Map 152 • Tooting Broadway

Jaffna House	90 Tooting High St	020 8672 7786	££	12 am	Mediocre curry fare beneath flourescent bulbs.
Kebab and Hamburger Bar	64 Tooting High St	020 7820 8846	£*	10 pm	Fancy a doner kebab? Go nowhere else.
Radha Krishna Bhavan	86 Tooting High St	020 8682 0969	££	11.30 pm	Busy, buzzing, bhavan of South Indian curry.
Rick's Cafe	122 Mitcham Rd	020 8767 5219	£££	11 pm	Tooting's best kept culinary secret.
Sette Bello	8 Amen Corner	020 8767 5225	££	11 pm	A kiss on each cheek for every diner. Homely Italian.
Urban Coffee	74 Tooting High St	020 8682 9479	£*	10 pm	Nifty WiFi caff in the bowels of Tooting.

Whether you're buried under an avalanche of bills and chips in a student hovel or under a pile of crisply ironed £50 notes, you can't have failed to notice that us con-sumers are up shit creek without a paddle. There are now more shopping-sized holes on our high streets (goodbye Woolworths and good riddance Zavvi) and consumer spending is dropping at an alarming rate. While it's kind of fun to see the big boys struggle it's also depressing to see your favourite boutique slap on the 'Everything Must Go' sign. But perhaps, like in WW2 (or something), us Londoners will simply live on and even thrive under a new paradigm shift which stresses the home-grown, the hand made, the thrifty and the shifty. Fat chance, when you think about it. Now where did we put that Harvey Nics credit card?

All over the city there are folks who are trying desper-ately to hold on to their traditional roots in the face of gentrification, holding fast to old-fashioned shopkeeping where everyone knows everyone and every customer counts (such as Lamb's Conduit Street), and there are streets which have been gentrified but again, are doing their best to preserve (or in some cases, rejuvenate) a sense of community (such as Broadway Market). These places give a sense of locality even in the depths of London, but even when in the West End, amongst the multinational big boys, it's best to keep this idea of the city as a conurbation and plan which areas will best serve your needs—if only to save your feet. It's even possible to live and shop without lining the big boys' pockets. You really can find anything you want in Lon-don if you know where to go, and it's this feeling that you can unearth hidden treasure at any given moment that springs the step of shoppers local and visiting.

The Big Boys

When it comes to department stores, **Selfridges (Map 2)** is without a doubt the daddy—arguably, you can just get everything you need from here. If you happen to have inherited a small fortune that is. **Harvey Nics (Map 37)** and **Harrods (Map 37)** are very much for ladies who lunch, and the Knightsbridge set use them like corner shops—that's not to say they don't have their uses. For a more personal touch, **Fenwick (Map 2)** and **Liberty (Map 10)** are wonderful British institutions which take you far from the madding crowd. If all these close-quarters encounters get up your nose head to **Whiteleys (Map 30)** or the grander, newer **Westfield (Map 33)** Shopping Centres.

Haute et High Street

For flexing that plastic, Bond Street has always been the place to spend but Bruton Street, which branches off the main drag, is setting quite a precedent with **Matthew Williamson (Map 9)**, **Stella McCartney (Map 10)** and **Diane Von Furstenburg (Map 9)** all in residence. Al-ways one to mix things up and throw us off track, **Marc Jacobs' (Map 9)** London store is to be found on Mount Street—check out the Marc for Marc Jacobs range for affordable designer garb. If you want to feel like Alice down the rabbit hole, make a trip to **Dover Street Mar-ket (Map 9)**, owned by Rei Kawakubo of Comme Des Garçons—a real experience even if you're not buying. For those of us on a budget, **Topshop (Map 3)** is the grand kahuna of high street shopping—seventh heaven on three floors for fashionistas. For super-slick, sharp ready to wear you can't beat Spanish stores, **Zara (Map 2)** and **Mango (Map 3)** who both do high street with a little bit of dignity. New contenders for higher end high-street include **Cos (Map 10)** and **Hoss Intropia (Map 10)**, and let's not forget our stateside cousins who have sent ripples of excitement through the fash pack by opening flagship stores of **Banana Republic**, **American Apparel and Abercrombie & Fitch all (Map 10)** in the big smoke. There are also little shopping oases to be found in the capital. St Christopher's Place is hidden behind the hustle and bustle of Oxford Street and houses cool European brands like **Marimekko (Map 2)** and **Noa Noa (Map 2)** alongside more familiar fare. Kingly Court (behind Carnaby Street—itself a great shopping spot for trend-led labels) has some nice bou-tiques in **The Black Pearl (Map 10)** and **Twinkled (Map 10)**. The area around Seven Dials in Covent Garden which includes Neal's Yard is eclectic with high-end bou-tiques like **Orla Kiely (Map 13)** and **Koh Samui (Map**

13) on Monmouth and skatewear at **Slam City Skates (Map 13)** and **Superdry (Map 13)** on Earlham. Edgy fashion abounds in Hoxton: head to **Good Hood (Map 84)** to start your shopping crawl.

Back To The Future

Man, we invented vintage. Us lovers of the mothball have been burrowing through rags in the far reaches of the city for decades. Some of the best-known, best-loved shops include **Rellik (Map 25)** in Portobello (surely the number one destination for vintage now that Steinberg and Tolkein is sadly no more?), **Annie's (Map 80)** in Islington (a favourite of La Moss), and **Beyond Retro (Map 91)** and **Absolute Vintage (Map 91)** in Shoreditch (famous hunting ground for stylists). If you want to hear what the young, stylish and clueless get up to head to **Rokit (Map 71)** and eavesdrop on the staff's mindnumb-ing conversations. For genuine thrift, the turnover of goods in our charity shops is mind-boggling. **Oxfam Dalston (Map 86)** is renowned for being a good rum-mage: it's hit and miss but then that's the nature of the thrifting beast. The **Salvation Army (Map 80)** in Isling-ton is an extremely busy shop which can turn out some real gems from well-heeled N1 residents. Most hardy shoppers will happily tread the city twice over for good charity shop finds but if you want some certainty of find-ing designer threads you can't beat the British Red Cross in both **Victoria (Map 19)** and **Chelsea (Map 45)** where you will discover the likes of Ralph Lauren, Ar-mani and pairs of Manolos amongst the usual floatsam and jetsam. The **Notting Hill Housing Trust (Map 35)** is also a reliable source of local celebrities' cast-offs from like... yesterday. For all you true vintage fashion fiends who want to mingle with like-minded souls and find genuine vintage togs (i.e. pre-1980s) the **Frock Me! Vin-tage Fashion Fair (Map 45)** and **Anita's Vintage Fash-ion Fair (Map 140)** are unequalled for choice and vari-ety. Wake up and smell the mould.

Keep On Running, Cycling, Skating etc.

Lillywhite's (Map 10) is the obvious place to go for cheap sportswear—it has earned a bit of a bargain basement tag where once it was prestigious (the Lilly-whites were instrumental in the game of cricket during the 19th century) but it doesn't stop the shoppers pour-ing in, and tourists buying their favourite London team football shirts. **Sweatshop (Map 17)** is a chain of stores but the original Teddington shop is frequented by world-class athletes as well as Sunday joggers. The staff really know their stuff (why is this so rare!?) . If it's sweatshop-made stuff you're after head to **Niketown (Map 02)**, which is as scary as the name suggests. Though we're no Amsterdam, the economic shitstorm has inspired many Londoners to don skintight clothes and take to two wheels. **Bobbin Bicycles (Map 5)** in Clerkenwell embraces that fun with a range of beautiful vintage and special edition bikes. Their website proclaims "We're more like a boutique than a bikeshop,"—to keep over-heads down there is no store but an appointment only service at Bobbin's workshop, giving a real personal touch. If you're after a battered old charmer of a bike, **Recycling (Map 112)** does a fab job at selling second-hand wheels. If you've had your designer bike nicked, head down to Brick Lane at the weekend and buy it off some dodgy geezer. **Slam City Skates (Map 13)** is the only dedicated place for Southbank skaters to get their duds.

Home Sweet Home

John Lewis (Map 2) is a British standard (read: a tad old-fashinoned) and has been the store of choice for middle-class couples' wedding lists for decades. Their maxim is "never knowingly undersold", with fantastic staff (who all get a share of the profits) and MOR but well made stuff. **Twentytwentyone (Map 80)** is a de-signer's wet dream selling originals as well as new items. So impressive is their collection that

they often lend out furniture to film companies who want the au-thentic look of an era on set. The wonderfully named **Timorous Beasties (Map 6)** make wickedly amusing wallpapers—their most famous being a toile de jouy de-sign for modern days (spot the alcopop-drinking chavs and the Gherkin in the background). For a no-nonsense approach to home furnishing visit the old geezers on Mare Street at **Lazy Days (Map 89)** or the grimey **Sec-ond Time Around (Map 87)**. **Labour and Wait (Map 91)** does the retro home stuff better than most. If you want personable, "Where can I find one of these?" type of service try **Russell's Hardware and DIY (Map 151)** in Tooting.

Electricity For You And Me

Traditionally, Tottenham Court Road is the hideout for the anally retentive Hi-Fi nut and the nerdoid pirate radio enthusiast a-like. The area positively thrums with elec-tricity and in all cases it's best to shop around, play prices against each other and barter until you get the lowest price—often cash payment will get you well below the RRP. **Computer Exchange (Map 3)** is the one-stop shop for gaming, DVDs, computing and phones, which—as the name suggests—will part-exchange and knock money off for cash transactions. For audiovisual, **Richer Sounds (Map 106)** is a trusted chain, and if we're talk-ing electronics in the purist sense, **Maplin (Map 4)** is geek central. Whether you'll get anyone who knows what they're taking about is another matter. Photography en-thusiasts should check out the **London Camera Ex-change (Map 24)** for old-school SLRs and digital cam-eras. They specialise in Pentax, Nikon and of course, Leica.

Food Glorious Food

We're a piggish race, us Londoners. Whether it's forcing down jellied eels or overpriced mushroom sandwiches down **Broadway Market (Map 89)**, our bellies is never empty, guvna. While we're at it, we'll have an ostrich burger and some raclette down **Borough Market (Map 106)**. We have New York (and in particular, the Magnolia Bakery) to thank for the invasion of cupcake stores but the original and best is the **Hummingbird Bakery (Map 29)** which makes Red Velvet cupcakes that taste like little pieces of baked orgasm. Just try and restrain your-self from licking the last morsels of frosting from the pa-per. Ahem. Nostalgia for old style sweetie shops can be bought at **Mrs Kibble's Olde Sweet Shop (Map 10)** whether your fetish is for cola cubes, sherbet flying sau-cers or Wham bars. Shopping in the West End and need a sugar boost? For a bonne-bouche delicieuse, stop in at **Laduree's (Map 23)** Burlington Arcade shop and nab a caramel and salted butter macaroon and see what all the macaroon cult fuss is about. Numerous Italian delis can be found around the city selling cured meats, buffalo mozzarella, biscotti and everything else that Mama used to make—**I Camisa & Son (Map 11)** is small but crammed full of delicacies, while **Spiazzo (Map 53)** is bigger and spaklier. Organic freaks can by-pass the rather average Whole Foods chain and head to local independent places like **The Grocery (Map 91)** or **Mother Earth (Map 64)**. For the cheapest and best cof-fee-to-go in Soho try the Algerian Coffee Stores. Looking for Unicum? Look no further than **Gerry's Spirits Shop (Map 11)** where you can show off you knowledge of obscure liquors like Zubrowka Bison Grass Vodka and good quality Cachaça. Or you can just google 'obscure liquors' and save yourself the hassle. Up to you.

Art And Craft Supplies

Crafty types and closet Van Goghs can pick up supplies at **Cass Art (Map 80)** three-storey flagship store in Is-lington. There's everything here for aspiring Manga car-toonists and weekend watercolourists alike, and lots of fun bits and pieces for school holiday/rainy day projects in the basement. Much of the high quality stock can be found at cut-price throughout the year—stock up on Mo-leskine note and sketchbooks which are frequently marked down. **The London Graphic Centre (Map 13)** has more design-led stock as well as fine art material attracting architects and graphic designers. Known for its greeting cards and stationary, **Paperchase (Map 4)** on Tottenham Court Road also has—true to its name—an astonishing array of handmade papers on its top floor—from flocked designs

to fibrous papers made with dried flowers. You've got to love **Blade Rubber (Map 4)** just for its name, and for keeping sketches, photos, and memories intact. **Wyvern Bindery (Map 6)** is one of few of its kind to offer book-making services.

Axes, Saxes, Drums, Strums...

Traditionally, Tin Pan Alley (real name: Denmark Street) has always been the hub of musical creativity in the city. Back in the day when rents were affordable, a commu-nity grew up around this little side street which went on to see Jimi Hendrix and The Beatles record in the base-ments, and a young Elton John sitting on the rooftops penning "Your Song". Nowadays you may spot Jack White trying out a Digitech Whammy or Jonny Green-wood looking for some new toy to replace his Marshall Shred Master. If we had to chose a couple, we'd bug Macaris for cheapness and **Wumjos (both Map 12)** for friendliness. There are plenty of independent music stores to be found in London's boroughs, and often they are specialists, happy to have a natter about what ex-actly it is that you're looking for and what the weather's like. Try **Top Wind (Map 104)** for all your flute needs, **Duke of Uke (Map 91)** for banjo and ukulele-lovers, though the staff are a little arsey, and **Phil Parker (Map 1)** for all you jazz cats needing a hand with your brass. For the medieval troubadour in your life, **Hobgoblin (Map 3)** has its own luthier who makes lutes. Try **Ray Man (Map 71)** in Camden for unusual ethnic instruments and drone boxes. For the largest collection of sheet mu-sic in Europe, **Chappel of Bond Street (Map 11)** (now on Wardour Street but they've kept the name) is your destination. One thing though, will you instrument shop assistants please stop jamming while you're talking to us?

Music Non Stop

The slow, painful death of the CD can be seen in almost every indie music store in London, and it co-incides with the financial doom and gloom that has befallen Virgin Records, Zavvi and Sanctuary. Bizarrely, the death march of the traditional record shop has become a moonwalk: more and more boutique record shops are springing up selling new and used wax. The Berwick Street vinyl epicenter may have been drained of late, but other parts of London are become haunts for us of haunched posture and good taste. **Sister Ray (Map 11)** is for-ever teetering on the edge, but **Revival Records (Map 11)** is the long gone Reckless Records' offspring. If you find yourself on the Essex Road, have a gander at **Flashback (Map 83)** and **Haggle Vinyl (Map 83)**: you're sure to find something to please and appeal in the for-mer and appall in the latter. The **Music and Video Ex-change (Map 29)** in Notting Hill was way ahead of its time and has been the swapshop of choice for years, it's still the king as far as we're concerned. When south of the river, do as Camberwellians do and drop in at **Rat Records (Map 121)**. To guarantee a withering look from a record shop lifer go and discuss the use of niavity in Legowelt's output at **Phonica (Map 10)** in Soho. Catch some indie shmucks at **Pure Groove (Map 60)** in Hollo-way, and many a muso's all-round fave, Sounds of the **Universe (Map 11)** is owned by the Soul Jazz label.

Antiques And Bric-A-Brac, Flea Markets And Stalls

There may have been a time, dear reader, when Mar-kets sold fleas. And Brics and bracs. Perhaps we used to know what these elusive words meant. Frankly, we numbskulls at NFT don't care about etymology unless it's second hand and collectable. First stop on many shoppers' lists—both serious collectors and weekend browsers—are **Alfie's Antique Market (Map 76)** and **Gray's Antique Market (Map 2)**. Here you'll find art, antiques, jewellery, vintage clothing and rare books all housed under one roof.

Once the centre of the Britpop phenomenon in the '90s and a thriving mini-metropolis for vintage and antique stalls, Camden is going through something of an identity crisis with parts of the old Stables market and the Arches being shut down and redevelopment looming: what used to be a hotchpotch high street full

of character is fast becoming an identikit of any other shopping street in England. Much of the area was damaged by a fire in 2009, which thankfully gutted the Hawley Arms but not all the tat that has come to be sold in abundance round here. **Proud Gallery (Map 4)** has taken over the listed Horse Hospital building and packs of German and French kids on school trips puzzlingly rifle through the emo and goth gear that overfloweth. There is some gold to be found though in shops like **Episode (Map 71)** and **Rokit (Map 71)**, and certainly the place still has atmos-phere.

Well-known to scavengers, **Camden Passage (Map 80)** in Angel, rather confusingly, is a welcome retreat from the mallrat-filled N1 centre across the road in Islington. The Mall and also Pierrepoint Arcade (tucked away be-hind the passage) offer a cornucopia of clothing, jewel-lery, military paraphernalia, homewares, prints, and a host of other bits and bobs. On Saturdays, market stalls set up in the street and surprises like original Givenchy earrings from 1978 (4 quid!) can be salvaged from amongst the knick-knacks. This is another brilliant little vintage bazaar continually threatened by chains and re-devolpment. Go protest by buy any old crap.

Brick Lane (Map 91) also opens up on Sunday and in the summer there is a real carnival feel with fruit and veg, plumbing and DIY bits and pieces, electricals, toilet-ries, furniture (dentist's chair anyone?), clothes, DVDs lining the lane and spiling into Sclater Street. Watch your bags and all the silly haircuts. All manner of weirdness can be observed from performance art (a group dressed in bin bags, making intimidating penguin noises and hobbling on their knees after random punters en masse—really quite normal for Shoreditch) to people seemingly emptying out the contents of their bedrooms onto tarpaulins and sheets looking for enthusiastic buy-ers. Who wants to buy Teen Wolf on video? Somebody does. Brick Lane also has the added advantage of hav-ing many a watering hole and curry house where you can stop and people-watch if it all makes you want to go all 'Falling Down' on their asses. If that's not your thing, (Up)Market is held in the **Truman Brewery (Map 91)** every Sunday and showcases new designers as well as housing some vinyl, vintage and gourmet street food. It's got to be said that all this is superior than the now sani-tized **Spitalfields Market (Map 91)**.

Roman Road Market (Map 94) is proper gor-blimey, lor' love a duck cockney territory and there's lots to be had from fruit and veg, bed linen, and cute polka-dot sun-dresses for a tenner. In the summer, Saturdays are more of an occasion with stilt-walkers, jugglers and face paint-ers keeping the shoppers entertained. If Lady Luck is stroking your inner thigh you get some great bargains at **Deptford Market (Map 119)**.

Though certainly not as bountiful in treasure as the car boot sales of other parts of the country, London does have some. The best in Zone 2 is definitely the **Batter-sea Car Boot Sale (Map 141)**, a sprawling mess that kicks of around midday in a godsend to all us alcoholics and narcoleptics.

Map 1 • Marylebone (West)

Green Valley	36 Upper Berkeley St	020 7402 7385	Essential Lebanese supermarket: get the manoushe.
Marousch Deli	45 Edgware Rd	020 7723 0773	Lebanese food emporium—fresh coffee,ice-creams and best houmous in town.
Phil Parker	106 Crawford St	020 7486 8206	Brass-o-rama.
Spymaster	3 Portman Sq	020 7486 3885	Stab-proof vests, in house P.I., you know, the usual.
Totally Swedish	32 Crawford St	020 7224 9300	Salt liquorice and Plopp bars for scandiphiles.

Map 2 • Marylebone (East)

Browns South Molton Street	24 S Molton St	020 7514 0016	Sleep with someone rich, then bring them here.
The Button Queen	76 Marylebone Ln	020 7935 1505	Antique buttons galore for budding fashionistas.
Daunt Books	83 Marylebone High St	020 7224 2295	Almost intimidatingly beautiful book shop.
Divertimenti	33 Maryelbone High St	020 7935 0689	Go and pretend you need a £500 coffee machine.
Fenwick	63 New Bond St	020 7629 9161	A welcome escape from Oxford Street for those in the know.
Gray's Antique Market	58 Davies St	020 7629 7034	A world of bygone beauty a skip away from Bond Street.
John Lewis	278 Oxford St	020 7629 7711	Where John Betjeman would have gone if the world exploded.
La Fromagerie	2 Moxon St	020 7935 0341	Blow your inheritance on some Abbaye De Trois Vaux

Marimekko	16 St Christopher's Pl	020 7486 6454	Retro prints from Jackie Kennedy's favourite Finnish.
Niketown	236 Oxford St	020 7612 0800	Like a real town! Owned by Nike! But without sweatshops.
Noa Noa	14 Gees Ct	020 7495 8777	Desirable Boho Danish label.
Paul Smith Sale Shop	23 Avery Row	020 7493 1287	Cheap designer suits. Sweet.
Selfridges & Co	400 Oxford St	0800 123 400	A Mecca for the shopping elite who want everything.
The Widescreen Center	47 Dorset St	020 7935 2580	Telescopes, binoculars, projectors, screens, film cameras & virtual reality.
Zara	242 Oxford St	020 7318 2700	Spiffy suits and cute casualwear from the Balearic brand.

Map 3 • Fitzrovia

Computer Exchange	32 Rathbone Pl	0845 345 1664	Good selection of secondhand DVDs, games and gadgets.
Harmony	103 Oxford St	020 7734 5969	Also known as Butt Plugs R Us.
Hobgoblin Shop	24 Rathbone Pl	020 7323 9040	Folky paradise; impressive/amusing collection of alternative instruments.
Mango	225 Oxford St	020 7434 3694	Let's go Mango!
Maplin	218 Tottenham Ct Rd	020 7323 4411	A whole world of technical geeketry to immerse yourself in.
Paperchase	213 Tottenham Ct Rd	020 7467 6200	More than meets the eye to this high street card shop.
Scandinavian Kitchen	61 Great Titchfield St	020 7580 7161	Smorgasbord!
Stargreen Box Office	20 Argyll St	020 7734 8932	Try here for tickets to sold-out gigs.
Topshop	216 Oxford St	020 7636 7700	Kate Moss still loves it. We do too.

Map 4 • Bloomsbury (West)

Blade Rubber	12 Bury Pl	0845 873 7005	Scrapbooking materials plus traditional and made-to-order rubber stamps.
British Museum shop	Great Russell St	0800 218 2222	Have you lost your Elgin Marbles?
Cinema Bookshop	13 Great Russel St	020 7637 0206	Shrine to literary study of the moving image.
Gosh! Comics	39 Great Russell St	020 7636 1011	A Japanese school boy's wet dream. Comics galore!
London Review Bookshop	14 Bury Pl	020 7269 9030	Big books, big name personal appearances—and cake!
Maplin	218 Tottenham Ct Rd	020 7323 4411	A whole world of technical geeketry to immerse yourself in.
Paperchase	213 Tottenham Ct Rd	020 7467 6200	More than meets the eye to this high street card shop.
York Cameras	18 Bury Pl	020 7242 7182	New and second hand, specializing in Canon.

Map 5 • Bloomsbury (East)

Biba's Hair & Beauty	72 Marchmont St	020 7837 9555	Lovely, friendly hair salon, excellent prices, 15% student discount.
Bobbin Bicycles	19 Arlington Way	020 7837 3370	Making commuting fun - London's nicest cycling enthusiast.
Brunswick Center	Hunter St	020 7883 6066	Brutalist shopping centre pushing the utopian/dystopian envelope.
The Flash Centre	Marchmont St	020 7837 5649	Studio lighting specialists.
International Magic	89 Clerkenwell Rd	020 7405 7324	When you need some tricks up your sleeve.
Joy	The Brunswick	020 7833 3307	Funky Urban Outfitters type stuff, but cheaper.
Magma Concept Store	117 Clarkenwell Rd	020 7242 9503	Funky book & novelty shop.
Romanian Charity Shop	Lamb's Conduit St	020 8761 2277	Good quality clothes, good cause, warm feeling inside.

Map 6 • Clerkenwell

The Black Tulip	28 Exmouth Market	020 7689 0068	Think all florists are the same?
Brindisa Retail	32 Exmouth Market	020 7713 1600	Chorizo, salchichon, Serrano ham—famed importers Brindisa have it all.The Family Business.
London Tattoo	332 Goswell Rd	020 7833 5996	Was on the telly. Caused quite a buzz.
M and R Meats	399 St John St	020 7837 1781	So meat-savvy they'll even know the best cut on you.
Metro Imagining	32 Great Sutton St	020 7865 0000	Photo processing.
Tattoo Shop	58 Exmouth Market	020 7278 9526	Tatts for all the family.
Timorous Beasties	46 Amwell St	020 7833 5010	Outlandish prints for the daringly tasteless home.
Wyvern Bindery	56 Clerkenwell Rd	020 7490 7899	Book binding for theses, portfolios and presentations. Repairs and restoration.

Map 9 • Mayfair / Green Park

Diane Von Furstenberg	25 Bruton St	020 7499 0886	Forget the LBD, every girl needs a DVF.
Dover Street Market	17 Dover St	020 7518 0680	Serious designer wear for people with serious money.
Marc Jacobs	24 Mount St	020 7399 1690	Never out of fashion.
Matthew Williamson	28 Bruton St	020 7629 6200	The boy who knows how to dress real girls.

Map 10 • Piccadilly / Soho (West)

American Apparel	3 Carnaby St	020 7734 4477	25% off all sexual harrassment lawsuits.
Abercrombie & Fitch	7 Burlington Gardens	084 4412 5750	"Chinese food makes me sick..." Remember that song?
Me neither...Arigato	48 Brewer St	020 7287 1722	Japanese food store and sushi bar. Lychee jelly sweets, anyone?
b store	24 Savile Row	020 7734 6846	Tell the bank you'll look REALLY cool in these shoes.
Banana Republic	224 Regent St	020 7758 3550	Your Stateside buddies don't need to ship over your clothes anymore.
Behave	48 Lexington Sreet	020 7734 6876	Hipster clothes.

The Black Pearl	10 Kingly Ct	020 7439 0702	Because your earrings should rock as hard as you do.
Burlington Arcade	Burlington Arcade		Welcoming shoppers since 1819.
Cos	222 Regent St	020 7478 0400	COS you can. See what I did there?
Deal Real	3 Great Marlborough St	020 7287 7245	Hip-Hop mecca. Check out the open mic sessions.
The European Bookshop	5 Warwick St	020 7734 5259	For when you get sick of English.
Fortnum And Mason	181 Piccadilly	020 7734 8040	The world's poshest marmalades.
Georgina Goodman	44 Old Bond St	020 7493 7673	The only shoe worth having since that Mellon woman bought Jimmy Choo.
Hamley's	188 Regent St	0870 333 2455	World's biggest toy store. Terrifying just before Christmas.
Hatchard's	187 Piccadilly	020 7439 9921	Still musty, floors still creak, despite being owned by The Man.
Hoss Intropia	211 Regent St	020 7287 3569	High-end high street.
Liberty	214 Regent St	020 7734 1234	Splendid wood-panelled department store. Beautiful and obscure scents and perfumes.
Lillywhites	24-36 Lower Regent St	087 0333 9600	Good if you know exactly what you're looking for.
Mrs Kibble's Olde Sweet Shoppe	57 Brewer St	020 7734 6633	Tooth-rottingly good sweet shop. Who needs incisors, anyway?
Muji	41 Carnaby St	020 7287 7323	Japanese chain hits London—simple, minimalist goods but great quality.
Phonica	51 Poland St	020 7025 6070	Cutting edge vinyl/CD shop; alas, no Michael Bolton in stock.
Playlounge	19 Beak St	020 7287 7073	Toys for adults, no not those types of toys.
Richard James	29 Savile Row	020 7434 0605	Bespoke contemporary Savile Row tailoring.
Rigby & Peller	22 Conduit St	0845 076 5545	Furnishers of the Queen's basement.
SKK (Lighting)	34 Lexington St	020 7434 4095	Change your bedroom ambiance, light up your love life.
Stella McCartney	30 Bruton St	020 7518 3100	Stella's star keeps rising despite initial doubts in Fahionland.
Twinkled	1 Kingly Ct	020 7734 1978	Awesome selection of vintage clothes and accessories.
The Vintage Magazine Shop	39 Brewer St	020 7439 8525	Yellowing magazines and a million student classic posters.

Map 11 • Soho (Central)

Algerian Coffee Store	52 Old Compton St	020 7437 2480	Pick up some Blue Mountain beans and a 95p cappu-to-go.
American Retro	35 Old Compton St	020 7734 3477	Random hipster Americana junk. Recommended.
Bang Bang	9 Berwick St	020 7494 2042	Intimate secondhand clothes shop.
Calumet Trading	175 Wardour St	020 7434 1848	Cameras and accessories.
Chappel of Bond Street	152 Wardour St	020 7432 4410	...Which is actually on Wardour Street.
Cheapo Cheapo Records	53 Rupert St	020 7437 8272	The name's no lie - Cheapo records and DVDs.
Cowling & Wilcox	26 Broadwick St	020 7734 9556	Good arts supplies shop to spend your Monet in (groan!).
Gerry's	74 Old Compton St	020 7734 2053	A veritable alcoholic's Utopia.
I Camisa & Son	61 Old Compton St	020 7437 7610	The best Italian deli out of Italy.
Paradiso	60 Dean St	020 7287 2487	Sexier than most sex shops.
Revival Records	30 Berwick St	020 7437 4271	Sickly phoenix risen from the ashes of Reckless Records.
Sister Ray	34 Berwick St	020 7734 3297	Alternative vinyl, CDs and DVDs.
Sounds of the Universe	7 Broadwick St	020 7734 3430	Blow your friends' minds with obscure African vinyl.
Vinyl Junkies	94 Berwick St	020 7439 2923	Get your fix, you grubby vinyl fiend.

Map 12 • Soho (East)

Angels	119 Shaftesbury Ave	020 7836 5678	Chock full of fancy dress outfits.
Fopp	1 Earlham St	020 7845 9770	May Fopp never, ever die again. Long live the music bargain!
Forbidden Planet	179 Shaftesbury Ave	020 7420 3666	Cult/film/TV memorabilia shop that will leave Star Wars fans salivating.
Kokon to Zai	57 Greek St	020 7434 1316	Mad fashion laboratory providing competition for The Pineal Eye.
Macaris	92 Charing Cross Rd	020 7836 2856	Family run instrument shop with historic roots.
Magma	16 Earlham St	020 7240 7571	Super-cool housewares and knick-knacks from the Magma gods.
Magma	8 Earlham St	020 7240 8498	The high priest of f'ing cool books.
Maison Bertaux	27 Greek St	056 0115 1584	Secret basement boutique run by the girl-in-the-know, Pippa Brooks.
Porselli	9 West St	020 7836 2862	Before American Apparel...when only dancers wore dancewear...
Ray's Jazz	113 Charing Cross Rd	020 7437 5660	Convivial Shop/Cafe. Essential for Americana and, uh, jazz!
Rockers	Denmark St	020 7240 2610	Quiffs, picks, riffs and licks. Sick.
Turnkey	114 Charing Cross Rd	020 7419 9999	Every musical gadget you need for your next glitchtronica symphony.
Wunjo Guitars	20 Denmark St	020 7379 0737	Mind-bendingly friendly Scot selling lovely vintage gear...

Map 13 • Covent Garden

Blackout II	51 Endell St	020 7240 5006	Vintage heaven.
Cath Kidston	28 Shelton St	020 7836 4803	Kitsch at its most chic, and vice-versa.
Cybercandy	3 Garrick St	020 8801 8815	For when a plain old Mars bar just won't cut it.
David and Goliath	4 The Market Pl	020 7240 3640	Droll, funky t-shirts and other fun stuff.
Duffer of St George	34 Shorts Gardens	020 7836 3722	Rude tees.
Kiehls	29 Monmouth St	020 7240 2411	Kiehls UK Flagship store of New Yorks famous apothecarists.
Koh Samui	65 Monmouth St	020 7240 4280	Eclectic selection of labels like Chloe and Balenciaga amongst newer finds
Libidex	49 Shelton St	020 7836 5894	Caters for all your kinks. Yes, even that one.

The Loft	35 Monmouth St	020 7240 3807	Designer jumble sale.
London Graphic Centre	16 Shelton St	020 7759 4500	One stop shop for graphics geeks.
Neal's Yard Dairy	17 Shorts Gardens	020 7240 5700	Follow your nose to very fine cheeses.
Nigel Hall	18 Floral St	020 7379 3600	Where to get business casualed well.
Octopus	54 Neal St	020 7836 2911	Makes the everyday so much more fun.
Orla Kiely	31 Monmouth St	020 7240 4022	Trademark cutesy prints from the Irish designer.
Pop Boutique	6 Monmouth St	020 7497 5262	Retrotastic!
Scoop	40 Shorts Gardens	020 7240 7086	Queues out the door for freshly made gelato. Fragola rocks.
Screenface	48 Monmouth St	020 7836 3955	Professional theatre make-up which can withstand the sweat of clubbing.
Slam City Skates	16 Neal's Yard	020 7240 0928	Rambunctious skate shop.
Stanford's	Long Acre	020 7836 1321	Treasure trove of maps, travel books and accessories.
Superdry	35 Earlham St (Thomas Neal Centre)	0207 240 2140	Super funky pseudo-Japanese urban wear. Friendly staff.
Twosee	17 Monmouth St	020 7494 3813	Many exclusives at this quirky boutique, for those that care.
Urban Outfitters	42 Earlham St	020 7759 6390	Heaps of streetwear and crazy things for your house.

Map 15 • Blackfriars / Farringdon

Pure Groove Records	6 West Smithfield	020 7281 4877	Cool instore gigs/events and great selection of new indie releases.

Map 16 • Square Mile (West)

Church's Shoes	90 Cheapside	020 7606 1587	An English shoe institution.
Manucci	5 Cheapside	020 7248 1459	Feeling out of place? Get a suit here.
Space NK Apothecary	145 Cheapside	020 7726 2060	Skin care heaven.

Map 17 • Square Mile (East)

Sweatshop (City branch at Cannon's Gym)	Cousin Lane	020 7626 4324	Ickle version of the athletes' favourite frequented by suits.

Map 18 • Tower Hill / Aldgate

A. Gold	42 Brushfield St	020 7247 2487	Perfect for impressive picnic supplies. But smells like a sock.
Montezuma's	51 Brushfield St	020 7539 9208	Chocolate you'd leave your boyfriend for.
Petticoat Lane	Middlesex St	N/A	No petticoats here love, but look for the FCUK stall

Map 19 • Belgravia

British Red Cross Victoria	85 Ebury St	020 7730 2235	Green welly-brigade territory. Good range of mens' suits.
Moyses Flowers	Sloane Sq	020 7881 6425	Tastefully delicate posies to enchant your beloved.
Mungo & Maud	79 Elizabeth St	020 7952 4570	Real dogs don't wear clothes! Chihuahuas do though... and pugs...

Map 20 • Victoria / Pimlico (West)

Grays of Westminster	40 Churton St	020 7828 4925	Charming period shop specializing in Nikon.
La Bella Sicilia	33 Warwick Way	020 7630 5914	Old-skool deli with cheery old owners and pasta aplenty.
Rippon Cheese Stores	26 Upper Tachbrook St	020 7931 0628	A world of cheese.

Map 22 • Westminster

Haelen Centre	41 Broadway	020 8340 4258	All your hippy, wholemeal, organic needs under one roof.
National Map Centre	Caxton St	020 7222 2466	Nope, still can't find it.

Map 23 • St. Jame's

Patridges Deli	2 Duke of York St	020 7730 0651	Family run mega-deli to the queen.
Richard Caplan	25 Bury St	020 7807 9990	New and used equipment specializing in Leica.
Thai Smile	King St	020 8846 9960	Heaven for those who love Asian cooking. For the rest it's just intriguing.

Map 24 • Trafalgar Square / The Strand

Austin Kaye	425 The Strand	020 7240 1888	Vintage watches. Don't expect e-bay prices.
Australia Shop	27 Maiden Ln	020 7836 2292	Relive the holiday (minus the sun. Or Brad the dive-instructor).
The Italian Bookshop	5 Cecil Ct	020 7240 1634	"Of course, there is only one way to read Dante..."
London Camera Exchange	98 Strand	020 7379 0200	My lens is longer than yours.
Motor Books	13 Cecil Ct	020 7836 5376	The ultimate Dad shop.
Rohan	10 Henrietta St	020 7831 1059	Super-friendly fleece-clad staff wielding waterproofs.
Stanley Gibbons	399 Strand	020 7836 8444	World's leading stamp dealer attracts collectors, investors and the curious.

Map 25 • Kensal Town

Honest Jon's	278 Portobello Rd	020 8969 9822	Obscure and rare Jazz, Funk, Reggae and Hip-Hop.
Rellik	8 Golborne Rd	020 8962 0089	Opposite the Trellik Tower - geddit? Specialises in Queen Viv (Westwood).
Sol's Gents Hairdressing	87 Golborne Rd	020 8964 3949	Cut throat shaves at cut price in Little Morocco.
What Katie Did	281 Portobello Rd	0845 430 8743	Fabulous 1940s-inspired boudoir boutique for rib-crushing corsets, stockings and pointy bras.

Map 28 • Ladbroke Grove / Notting Hill (West)

Cowshed	119 Portland Rd	020 7078 1944	Express mani-pedis for women who have places to go etc.
The Cross	141 Portland Rd	020 7727 6760	The original London boutique...still going...
Virginia	98 Portland Road	020 7727 9908	If money is no object, what you want is here.

Map 29 • Notting Hill Gate

& Clarke's Bread	124 Kensington Church St	020 7221 7196	All-butter brioche and honey loaves for Harvey Nics, Selfridges - and you.
Bodas	38 Ledbury Rd	020 7229 4464	Everyday underwear that gives M&S a run for its money.
The Grocer on Elgin	6 Elgin Crescent	020 7221 3844	Restaurant standard ready meals for lazy people.
The Hummingbird Bakery	133 Portobello Rd	020 7229 6446	Takeaway cupcakes reminiscent of New York's Magnolia Bakery.
James Knight of Mayfair	67 Notting Hill Gate	020 7221 6177	The Queen's fish at the Queen's prices.
Melt	59 Ledbury Rd	020 7727 5030	Posh chocs made before your bulging eyes.
Music & Video Exchange	38 Notting Hill Gate	020 7243 8573	Invented second hand record shops. Best in London.
Negozio Classica	283 Westbourne Grove	020 7034 0005	Half bar, half store selling high-end Italian kitchen goods.
Portobello Road Market	Portobello Rd	n/a	Antiques, clothes, food, and more. A London institution.
R Garcia and Sons	248 Portobello Rd	020 7221 6119	Overwhelming selection of Spanish groceries.
Retro Man	34 Pembridge Rd	020 7792 1715	Vintage fixes for modern men. And men only.
Retro Woman	32 Pembridge Rd	020 7460 6525	Exclusive vintage ware that's worth it.
Rough Trade West	130 Talbot Rd	020 7229 8541	More character and better records than the soulless East Branch.
Travel Bookshop	13 Blenheim Cresent	020 7229 5260	I DARE you to ask them about Hugh Grant.

Map 30 • Bayswater

Planet Organic	42 Westbourne Grove	020 7727 2227	Organic heaven.
Porchester Gate Spa	Queensway & Porchester Rd	020 7793 3980	Proper old school art deco Turkish baths and spa for less than £25!
Whiteleys Shopping Centre	Queensway	020 7229 8844	Slightly more soulful than Smithfields.

Map 32 • Shepherd's Bush (West)

Nut Case	352 Uxbridge Rd	020 8743 0336	About time nuts got some respect.

Map 33 • Shepherd's Bush

Whole Foods Market	63 Kensington High St	020 7368 4500	Overwhelming selection of organic exotica.

Map 35 • Kensington

Ben's Cookies	12 Kensington High St	0207 376 0559	Chunky cookies in wonderous flavours. Hidden in High Street Ken Station.
Buttercup	16 St Albans Grove	020 7937 1473	No other pleasure on earth comes close to these cupcakes.
Notting Hill Housing Trust	57 Kensington Church St	020 7937 5274	There's gold in that 'Hill.
Trailfinders	194 Kensington High St	020 7938 3939	Personable one stop shop for travel bookings, advice and services.
Whole Foods Market	63 Kensington High St	020 7368 4500	Overshelming selection of organic exotica.

Map 36 • South Kensington/Gloucester Rd

Snog	32 Thurloe Pl	020 7584 4926	Crazy frozen yoghurt joint with interior mad enough to be in Tokyo.

Map 37 • Knightsbridge

Burberry	2 Brompton Road	020 7968 0000	Flagship store of the classic British brand.
Harrods	87 Brompton Rd	020 7730 1234	Arch conspiracy theorist Mr Al-Fayed's still classy department store.
Harvey Nichols	109 Knightsbridge	020 7235 5000	More 1999 than 2009, but still a great department store.
Skandium	247 Brompton Rd	020 7584 2066	For lottery winners who can't shake their love of Ikea.

Map 38 • Chiswick

As Nature Intended	201 Chiswick High Rd	020 8742 8838	Main store from orgainc food company. Pricey but worth the trek.

The Bread Shop	296 Chiswick High Rd	020 8747 8443	Bloomin' marvellous bread! Great selection and they even do spelt loaves.
Eco-Age	213 Chiswick High Rd	020 8995 7611	Colin Firth's eco-friendly homeware store with recycled chairs and eco-paint.
Oxfam Books	90 Turnham Green Terrace	020 8995 6059	Fantastic fiction selection - the rich read too!
Something Nice	40 Turnham Green Terrace	020 8742 7135	Gifts you didn't even know you wanted. Great if you're stumped for pressies.
Theobroma Cacao	43 Turnham Green Terrace	020 8996 0431	Which translates as "Chocolate Thrombosis". Choccy penises? Leave it out!

Map 39 • Stamford Brook

Mac's Cameras	262 King St	020 8846 9853	Used and hard-to-find gear. Heaven for photography nerds.

Map 42 • Baron's Court

Curious Science	319 Lillie Road	020 7610 1175	Stock up on stuffed mutant cow heads and cases of eyeballs.

Map 43 • West Brompton / Fulham Broadway / Earls Court

Fulham Broadway Centre	Fulham Road	020 7385 6965	Shopping, cinema, retaurants and tube station all in one place.

Map 44 • Chelsea

Furniture Cave	533 Kings Rd	020 7352 2046	Swanky. Huge. Quintessentially Kings Road.
The Shop At Bluebird	350 King's Rd	0207 351 3873	Spend a fortune here and become an "edgy" individual.

Map 45 • Chelsea (East)

British Red Cross Chelsea	67 Old Church St	0845 054 7101	Known locally as La Croix Rouge Boutique.
Frock Me! Vintage Fashion Fair	Chelsea Town Hall, Kings Rd	020 7254 4054	Held every couple of months, "pre-war" tearoom refreshes shopping casualties.
The Hummingbird Bakery	47 Old Brompton Rd	020 7584 0055	Notting Hill's big brother with seating to devour Red Velvets and lattes.
Kate Kuba	24 Duke of York Sq	020 7259 0011	What more could a woman want?! Shoes, shoes, shoes...
Nomad Books	243 Fulham Rd	020 7736 4000	Glorious little place with added coffee shop.

Map 46 • Sloane Square

Fresh Line	55 King's Rd	020 7348 7995	Home made cosmetics—fresh!
Peter Jones	Sloan Sq	020 7730 3434	Upmarket department store. Argos of the 'daharlings' with cash to splash.
Space NK Apothecary	307 King's Rd	020 7351 7209	The Superdrug for the Sloane Square ladies who lunch.

Map 48 • Fulham

Hurlingham Books	91 Fulham High St	020 7736 4363	More stacked than Arnie was in the 70s.

Map 49 • Parson's Green

Calumet Trading	10 Heathman's Rd	020 7384 3270	Cameras and accessories.

Map 51 • Highgate

The Corner Shop	88 Highgate High St	020 8340 1118	Locals' favourite fending off the advance of Tesco's.
Dragonfly Wholefoods	24 Highgate High St	020 8347 6087	Great little organic food shop and juice bar.
Highgate Butchers	76 Highgate High St	020 8340 9817	Reassuringly expensive meat. Them cows m.ust have lived like kings.
Hop N Pops	389 Archway Rd	020 8348 0624	Great selection for all budgets.
Le Chocolatier	78 Highgate High St	020 8348 1110	Essential at Easter—not just eggs but whole chocolate chickens.
Oxfam Bookshop, Highgate	47 Highgate High St	020 8347 6704	Musty bookstore with some cracking titles.
Second Layer Records	323 Archway Rd	078 7805 1726	I was into Avant Rock before you were etc. etc.
Walter Castellazzo Design	84 Highgate High St	020 8340 3001	A lot of cool and ridiculously pricey things.
Wild Guitar	393 Archway Rd	020 8340 7766	Get your retro gear in this brilliant guitar shop.

Map 52 • Archway (North)

Archway Video	220 Archway Rd	020 8340 2986	Local favourite with videos/DVDs for sale and rent.
The Green Room	192 Archway Rd	020 8340 7759	Amazing selection of weird things you probably don't need.
Pax Guns	166 Archway Rd	020 8340 3039	Errm... "best" gun shop in the area?

Map 53 • Crouch End

Walter Purkis And Sons	17 The Broadway	020 8340 6281	Proof fish don't need their tasty batter skins.

Map 57 • Hampstead Heath

Daunt Books	51 S End Rd	020 7794 8206	A right daunty little shop.

Map 58 • Parliament Hill / Dartmouth Park

Corks	9 Swain's Ln	020 8340 4781	Superb selection of interesting wines and beers.

Map 59 • Tufnell Park

The Blue Carbuncle	130 Junction Rd	020 7272 6691	Uber-cool vintage clothes, cameras and collectibles.
North London Adoption Centre	135 Junction Rd	020 7272 6048	Need a cat? Of course you do! Miau!

Map 60 • Archway

Second Chance	79 St John's Way	020 7281 5449	Heaps of rubbish and the occasional incredible find.

Map 61 • Holloway (North)

Michael's Fruiterers	56 7 Sisters Rd	020 7700 1334	Fruit n veg fest. Nowhere's fresher.

Map 62 • Finsbury Park

The Happening Bagel Bakery	284 Seven Sisters Rd	020 8809 1519	Another Haringey gem, with some delicious pastries too!

Map 63 • Manor House

Trehantiri Music	365 Green Lanes	020 8800 3076	Giasou Marko me to kanonaki sou... All greek to me.

Map 64 • Stoke Newington

Ark	161 Stoke Newington High St	020 7275 9311	Cute little interiors and gift shop.
The Beaucatcher Salon	44 Stoke Newington Church St	020 7923 2522	Hairdressers and community hub.
Belle Epoque Boulangerie	37 Newington Green	020 7249 2222	Fancy schmancy, delicious pastries.
Bridgewood & Neitzert	146 Stoke Newington Church St	020 7249 9398	Renowned string section repair, exchange and sales.
Ocean Books	127 Church Walk	020 7502 6319	Great shack with out of print books and shite records.
Metal Crumble	13 Stoke Newington Church St	020 7249 0487	Affordable, flippin' gorgeous, jewellery made on site.
Ribbons and Taylor	157 Stoke Newington Church St	020 7254 4735	Long-standing vintage clothes shop—Stokey original.
Rosa Lingerie	3 Church Walk	020 7254 3467	The oldest knickers in Stokey.
Route 73 Kids	92 Stoke Newington Church St	020 7923 7873	Bus inspired toy shop.
S'graffiti	172 Stoke Newington Church St	020 7254 7961	You've been framed.
Sacred Art	148 Albion Rd	020 7254 2223	(Needles + Ink + Skin) x Pain = Art.
The Spence	161 Stoke Newington Church St	020 7249 4927	Bread elevated to an art form.
Stoke Newington Farmers Market	Stoke Newington Church St & Stoke Newington High St	020 7502 7588	Overpriced, organic, natural, Hea...Zzzzzzzzz.

Map 66 • Finchley Road / Swiss Cottage

Yeomans Grocers	152 Regent's Park Rd	020 7722 4281	Greengrocer that sells flowers and has a great juicebar.

Map 70 • Primrose Hill

J Michael & Daughter	73 Regents Park Rd	020 7722 9000	Georgous vintage to help you lighten your purse.
Miss Lala's Boudoir	148 Gloucester Ave	020 7483 1888	Dangerously hot underwear. Visit only if your purse is full.
Nicolas (off licence)	67 Regents Park Rd	020 7722 8576	A wide range of wines, including some cheap ones.
Press	3 Erskine Rd	020 7449 0082	Impressive array of brands for a boutique. Good sales.
Primerose Hill Books	134 Regents Park Rd	020 7586 2022	Fabulously curated selection of new books.
Primrose Newsagent	91 Regents Park Rd	020 7722 0402	Newsagent, stationers, post office, drycleaners and internet cafe.
Richard Dare	93 Regent's Park Rd	020 7722 9428	Quite lovely kitchen/cooking products.
Shepherd Foods	59 Regents Park Rd	020 7586 4592	Highly priced but quaint local deli.
Shikasuki	67 Gloucester Ave	020 7722 4442	Affordable vintage and modern design.
Tann Rokka	123 Regents Park Rd	020 7722 3999	Wildly expensive "lifestyle store" in old Primrose hill train station.

Map 71 • Camden Town / Chalk Farm / Kentish Town (West)

Acumedic	101 Camden High St	020 7388 6704	Chinese medicine centre offering acupuncture AKA polite masochism.

Black Rose	The Stables Market, Chalk Farm Rd	020 8279 2014	Gothic. Very, very gothic.
Cyberdog	The Stables Market, Chalk Farm Rd	020 7474 3737	Enormous sci-fi set displaying PVC, neon, and leather clubbing gear.
Episode	26 Chalk Farm Rd	020 7485 9927	Unusual vintage store with comparatively low ringworm risk.
Escapade	45 Chalk Farm Rd	020 7485 7384	Dress up as Wonder Woman! Also caters for females.
Eye Contacts	10 Chalk Farm Rd	020 7482 1701	Opticians that sells uber-trendy spectacles.
Graham and Green	164 Regents Park Rd	020 7586 2960	Wonderfully dinky yet scarily pricey shop.
Know How Records	3 Buck St	020 7267 1526	Pounding dance music and continuous party. Grates after a while.
Metal Militia	259 Camden High St	020 7734 5720	Screeeeeammm for me Camden High Street!!
Music & Video Exchange	208 Camden High St	020 7267 1898	Great secondhand music shop, seemingly staffed by grouches on Mogadon.
Ray Man Music	54 Chalk Farm Rd	020 7692 6261	Wonderful shop full of exotic instruments. Bavarian noseflute, anyone?
Rokit	225 Camden High St	020 7267 3046	Second hand, sorry, vintage clothing store to the stars.
Sounds That Swing	46 Inverness St	020 7267 4682	"It ain't worth a thing..." rockabilly, psych and doo-wop.
Up The Video Junction	Middle Yard, Camden Lock Pl	079 266 1294	Rare, out-of-print, cult DVD's.
Village Games	65 The West Yard	020 7485 0653	Huge selection of boardgames.

Map 72 • Kentish Town

Dots	132 St Pancras Way	020 7482 5424	Friendly music shop with free hash cakes...OK, just cookies.
Fish	161 Kentish Town Rd	020 7267 0139	Gift shop run by actress Sophie Thompson.
Phoenicia	186 Kentish Town Rd	020 7267 1267	Olives, just-roasted nuts, baclava, ice-cream bar. Meze heaven. Ditch Sainsburys.

Map 73 • Holloway

Bumblebee Natural Foods	33 Brecknock Rd	020 7284 1314	Hot veggie lunches, lush cakes. Organic fruitopia over the road.
DOC Records	5 Cardwell Terrace, Cardwell Rd	020 7700 0081	Probably full of contagious diseases. Worth a rummage.

Map 74 • Holloway Road / Arsenal

21st Century Retro	162 Holloway Rd	020 7700 2354	Mothballs and tweed in this retro paradise.
Fettered Pleasures	90 Holloway Rd	020 7619 9333	Treat your nan to something nice.
House of Harlot	90 Holloway Rd	020 7700 1441	Funky fetish fashion.

Map 75 • Highbury

Cabbies Delight Auto Parts	9 Green Lanes	020 7226 1692	21,000 car parts and 21 years experience.
Mother Earth	282 St Paul's Rd	020 7275 9099	Unfortunate New Age name, decent little shop.

Map 76 • Edgeware Road / Marylebone (North)

Alfie's Antiques Market	25 Church St	020 7723 6066	Kitsch oddball sanctuary for vintage treats.
Archive Secondhand Books & Music	83 Bell St	020 7402 8212	Old and unusual books.
Beatles London Store	231 Baker St	020 7935 4464	All you need is love, and no taste.
Elvisly Yours	233 Baker St	020 7486 2005	With stalkers like these, it's no wonder Elvis is hiding.
Lord's Cricket Shop	Lord's Cricket Ground, Lisson Grove	020 7616 8570	They won't even ask why you want a cricket bat.

Map 77 • Mornington Crescent / Regent's Park

Calumet Trading	93 Drummond St	020 7380 1144	Cameras and accessories.
Chess & Bridge	369 Euston Rd	020 7388 2404	Chess fetishists won't be able to control themselves here.
Greens and Beans	131 Drummond St	020 7380 0857	Wheat grass, supplements and tofu.

Map 78 • Euston

All Ages Records	27 Pratt St	020 7267 0303	Truly independent punk & hardcore record shop. F*** the system!
Housmans	5 Caledonian Rd	020 7837 4473	Bookshop for progressive peaceniks and radical revolutionaries.
Rock'n'roll Jumble Sale	15 Phoenix Rd	020 7419 6891	Monthly indie-themed bric-a-brac. Cool moustaches everywhere.
Transformation	52 Eversholt St	020 7388 0627	The world's largest shop for transvestites and transexuals. Seriously.

Map 79 • King's Cross

Continental Stores	26 Caledonian Rd	020 7837 0201	1960s Italian deli still run by original italian owners. Fab.
Cosmo Cornelio	182 Caledonian Rd	020 7278 3947	Old-skool, moustache trimming Italian barbers.

Map 80 • Angel / Upper St

A Ferrari Deli	48 Cross St	020 7226 1951	Yes, Mr Ferrari's grumpy. But he is 102.
After Noah	121 Upper St	020 7359 4281	Stuff your Nintendo Wiis—these are proper toys, retro-style.
Annie's	12 Camden Passage	020 7359 0796	Proper vintage—1900s to 1940s.
Camden Passage	Camden Passage	020 7359 0190	Thingamebobs, whatsits and doodahs aplenty.
Cass Art	66 Colebrooke Row	020 7354 2999	Large, neat-as-a-pin, extremely pleasing art supply shop.
Gill Wing Kitchen Shop	194 Upper St	020 7226 5392	Splendid array of kitchen gadgetry to keep foodies amused.
Monte's Deli	23 Canonbury Ln	020 7354 4335	Tasty, but look elsewhere if you need a hearty meal.
Palette London	21 Canonbury Ln	020 7288 7428	Islington's eclectic vintage shop—clothes, books, homeware.
Paul A Young chocolate shop	33 Camden Passage	020 7424 5750	"Everytime you go away..." you take a piece of chocolate.
Raymond Roe Fishmonger	Chapel Market	020 7833 8656	Market stall with a sea's worth of fish.
Salvation Army Islington	284 Upper St	020 7359 9865	Ramshackle charity shop. In a well-off area, meaning quality clobber.
Twentytwentyone	274 Upper St	020 7288 1996	Bauhaus to Boontje and beyond.

Map 81 • Canonbury

Get Stuffed	105 Essex Rd	020 7226 1364	Polar bear for the living room, anyone? Taxidermy emporium.
HG Lockey & Sons	8 Halton Cross St	020 7226 7044	For all your, er, coal and smokeless fuel needs.
Handmade and Found	109 Essex Rd	020 7359 3898	For something totally unique.
James Elliot Master Butcher	96 Essex Rd	020 7226 3658	So much choice they'd probably stock human if they could.
Raab's The Baker's	136 Essex Rd	020 7226 2830	Crusty white bloomers, chelsea buns. No paninis.
Sew Fantastic	107 Essex Rd	020 7226 2725	If you'd thought it up, you'd have opened it too.

Map 82 • De Beauvoir Town / Kingsland

North One Garden Centre	25 Englefield Rd	020 7923 3553	Dinky little garden centre catering for dinky little London gardens.

Map 83 • Angel (East) / City Rd (North)

Flashback	50 Essex Rd	020 7354 9356	Don't come in whistling Barbie Girl.
Haggle Vinyl	114 Essex Rd	020 7704 3101	Record shop that reminds you how little you know about music.
Past Caring	76 Essex Rd	N/A	Oddball collection of furniture, pictures and, if you're lucky, mannequins.

Map 84 • Hoxton

Good Hood	41 Coronet St	020 7729 3600	Like American Apparel before it got shit.
Sh!	57 Hoxton Sq	0845 868 9599	Dildo-tastic! Guys must come (ahem) accompanied by a galpal.

Map 85 • Stoke Newington (East)

Hamdys	167 Stoke Newington High St	020 7254 0681	Porn-free newsagents run by stubborn maverick.
Stoke Newington Bookshop	159 Stoke Newington High Street	020 7249 2808	Long-standing local stellar indie bookshop.

Map 86 • Dalston / Kingsland

Centre Supermarket	588 Kingsland Rd	N/A	Beers from all corners of the globe.
Dalston Mill Fabrics	69 Ridley Rd	020 7249 4129	Veritable treasure trove for budding Vivienne Westwoods and John Gallianos.
Oxfam Dalston	570 Kingsland Rd	020 7923 1532	Flagship charity shop. Go find treasures!
Party Party	9 Ridley Rd	020 7254 5168	Fancy dress and party supplies plus an outstanding cake decorating department.
Ridley Road Market	Ridley Rd	N/A	Giant (live!) snails, Nigerian DVDs, fresh fish, 'taters, "Pound a bowl!"
Sound 323 @ Cafe Oto	18 Ashwin St	077 0735 2638	Blisteringly avant record shack.
Turkish Food Centre	89 Ridley Rd	020 7254 6754	Olives and feta galore, bakery onsite, plus other fresh groceries.

Map 87 • Hackney Downs / Lower Clapton

The Pet Shop	40 Amhurst Rd	020 8986 6862	Brillant local pet shop.
Salvation Army Clapton	122-124 Lower Clapton Rd	020 8985 3902	Come all ye unfaithful...
Second Time Around	60 Lower Clapton Rd	020 985 5536	Buy back the old shit that got stolen last week.
Umit & Son	35 Lower Clapton Rd	na	Crazed film buff selling vintage porn, super 8 and crisps?!?

Map 89 • London Fields / Hackney Central

Artvinyl	13 Broadway Market	020 7241 4129	The best vinyl and CD covers, printed on canvas.

Broadway Market	Broadway Market	N/A	Yummy mummies and Guardian-reading couples peruse.
Burberry Factory Shop	29 Chatham Pl	020 8985 3344	Ever wondered how Burberry became associated with chavs?
Candle Factory	184 Mare St	020 8986 6356	Well-made, well-priced candles.
L'eau a la Bouche	49 Broadway Market	020 7923 0600	Cute French delicatessen shop.
Lazy Days	21 Mare St	078 1632 3848	Not far from Hackney Road where you'll find more furniture.

Map 90 • Homerton / Victoria Park North

Cheech Miller	227 Victoria Park Rd	020 8985 9900	Everything you need for the park: kites, frisbees, skateboards, unicycles.
The Ginger Pig	99 Lauriston Rd	020 8986 6911	Brilliant butcher bequeathing beef to the Borough.
Sublime	225 Victoria Park Rd	020 8986 7243	Boudoir-like boutique selling select and independent labels.
Work Shop	77 Lauriston Rd	020 8986 9585	Beautiful handmade pottery for home and kitchen by Caroline Bousfield Gregory.

Map 91 • Shoreditch / Brick Lane / Spitalfields

A Butcher of Distinction	91 Brick Ln	020 7770 6111	Distinct indeed, impeccable collection of preppy, fresh n' clean stylings.
Absolute Vintage	15 Hanbury St	020 7247 3883	If Imelda Marcos ran a misanthropic clothes shop.
Arckiv	37 Heneage St	07790 102 204	Those film kids get their vintage eyewear here.
Bangla City	86 Brick Ln	020 7456 1000	Breaks the rule saying you should avoid smelly supermarkets.
Bernstock Speirs	234 Brick Ln	020 7739 7385	Look no further if you're searching for a signature titfer.
Beyond Retro	112 Cheshire St	020 7613 3636	The Daddy of all jumble sales.
Blackman's Shoes	42 Cheshire St	078 5088 3505	Chaotic hole-in-the-wall selling £5 plimsolls.
Brick Lane	Brick Ln	N/A	Nathan Barleys still pissed off their face from the night before.
Caravan	3 Redchurch St	020 7739 9009	Quirky interiors shop with items new and old on offer.
Comfort Station	22 Cheshire St	020 7033 9099	Quirky and comforting collection of bags.
Columbia Road Market	Columbia Rd	N/A	Get there early, nab outside tables for brekkie then shop.
Columbia Road Flower Market	Columbia Rd	N/A	A Sunday morning hot spot for plant lovers. After 2pm is prime bargain time.
Duke of Uke	22 Hanbury St	020 7247 7924	For all your many ukelele and banjo needs.
FairyGothMother	15 Lamb St	020 7377 0370	Not entirely "Goth"- a Dita Von Teese of a shop...
The Grocery	54 Kingsland Rd	020 7729 6855	Selling the good life to lower Kingsland Road.
Hurwundeki	98 Commercial St	020 7392 9194	Boutique-y empire slowly creeping across London.
Labour And Wait	18 Cheshire St	020 7729 6253	Brilliant wee shop selling old and old looking goods.
The Laden Showrooms	103 Brick Ln	020 7247 2431	Eclectic bazaar of small labels scavenged by stylists and starlets.
Luna and Curious	198 Brick Ln	079 7744 0212	Curiouser and curiouser…lovely local artists' and designers' co-operative.
No One	1 Kingsland Rd	020 7613 5314	Sporty designer wear. Killer shades.
Nudge Records	20 Hanbury St	020 7655 4823	Notorious little shack owned by the Brothers Collishaw. Reggae/dub.
Rough Trade East	91 Brick Ln	020 7392 7788	East London outpost of the absurdly cool Rough Trade Records.
Scooter Emporium	10 Dray Walk, Brick Ln	020 7375 2277	Because it's much more fun to be a scooter commuter.
Second Tread	261 Hackney Rd	020 7033 9862	In every fashionista's little black book: seconds and ex-model shoes.
Taj Stores	112 Brick Ln	020 7377 0061	Weird and wonderful Eastern food.
Tatty Devine	236 Brick Ln	020 7739 9009	Bonkers jewellery loved by celebs, fashionistas and hipsters.
Taylor Taylor	137 Commercial St	020 7033 0330	French boudoir-style hairdressers with free cocktail bar. Feel like a princess.
Treacle	160 Columbia Rd	020 7729 0538	Dreamy cupcakes. Don't ask for coffee - this is a TEAshop!

Map 92 • Bethnal Green

AP Fitzpatrick	142 Cambridge Heath Rd	020 7790 0884	Art supplies and expert advice.

Map 93 • Globe Town / Mile End (North)

Massage Table Store	Bow Wharf, Grove Rd	020 8983 9800	For, you know, when you need a massage table.
Paul Mark Hatton	65 Roman Rd	020 8981 7110	Pocket ashtray anyone? Fans include Jack Nicholson and Liv Tyler.

Map 94 • Bow

Pure	430 Roman Rd	020 8983 2004	The place to spend your wedge in E3.
Roman Road Market	Roman Rd	020 7377 8963	Big, colourful, cheap as chips—bargain tat hawked by lively east-end traders.
Sew Amazing	80 St Stephens Rd	020 8980 8898	Long established sewing machine shop. Repairs and recycling service provided.
South Molton Drugstore	583 Roman Rd	020 8981 5040	Branded cosmetics and toiletries at knock-down prices.

Map 97 • Stepney / Shadwell (East)

East End Thrift Store	Assembly Passage	020 7423 9700	Come on Thursday nights for the in-store parties.
John Lester Wigmakers	32 Globe Rd	020 7790 2278	Need a syrup?

Map 104 • South Bank / Waterloo / Lambeth North

The Bookshop Theatre	51 The Cut	020 7633 0599	Thesp-oriented but charming, including a tiny stage for performances.
Calder Bookshop	51 The Cut	020 7620 2900	Enduringly fashionable hub for the unfashionably literate.
I Knit London	106 Lower Marsh	020 7261 1338	The UK's only knitting shop with a licensed bar. Wool is cool.
Konditor & Cook	22 Cornwall Rd	020 7261 0456	Yummy scrummy choccies and cake.
Oasis	84 Lower Marsh	020 7401 7074	Friendly independent salon for massages, waxing, facials and fab pedicures.
Radio Days	87 Lower Marsh	020 7928 0800	Cave of vintage wonders.
Scooterworks	132 Lower Marsh	020 7620 1421	Scooter shop has superb coffee. Word spreads. Becomes café too.
Silverprint	12 Valentine Pl	020 7620 0844	Specialist dealer in photographic consumables.
Southbank Book Market	Under Waterloo Bridge	0871 663 2501	Fun little scribe's market in brillant surroundings.
Top Wind	2 Lower Marsh	020 7401 8787	Serious flute worship.
Waterloo Camping	37 The Cut	020 79284110	Eccentric army surplus/camping store, run by two friendly brothers.
What The Butler Wore	131 Lower Marsh	020 7261 1353	'60s, '70s vintage boutique—retro-glam party garments plus resident moggy, Binky.

Map 105 • Southwark / Bankside (West)

Elephant & Castle Market	Elephant & Castle	N/A	An anti-Portobello Road Market...slightly dodgy but dirt-cheap.

Map 106 • Bankside (East) / Borough / Newington

German Deli	8 Southwark St	020 7250 1322	Sauerkraut and sausages if you like that kinda stuff.
Paul Smith	13 Park St	020 7403 1678	Kitsch and dolls from the fashion designer. Don't ask why.
Richer Sounds	2 London Bridge Walk	020 7403 1201	The original store of this small chain offering low prices.
Vinopolis	1 Bank End	020 7940 8300	Wine tasting and buying megastore. Spitting optional.

Map 107 • Shad Thames

The Design Museum Shop	Shad Thames	020 7940 8754	Stuff you wish you'd thought of.
Long Lane Deli	218 Long Ln	020 7403 7513	A popular Italian delicatessen.

Map 111 • Rotherhithe (East) Surrey Quays

Decathlon	Surrey Quays Rd	020 7394 2000	The Daddy of sports & outdoors shops.

Map 112 • Kennington / Elephant and Castle

Pricebusters Hardware	311 Elephant & Castle Shopping Centre	020 7703 8244	Impressively cheap, friendly staff and an amusing collection of bric-a-brac.
Recycling	110 Elephant Rd	020 7703 7001	They sell'em bikes, they fix'em bikes. Second hand.

Map 119 • Deptford (East)

Deptford Market	Deptford High St	N/A	Cheap, busy, eclectic: Proof that there IS life in Deptford.

Map 120 • Greenwich

Mr Humbug	Greenwich Market	020 7871 4944	Infinitissimal old-fashioned sweets to relive your childhood sugar buzzes.

Map 121 • Camberwell (West)

Butterfly Walk Shopping Centre	Denmark Hill	N/A	The usual attractions.
Rat Records	348 New Camberwell Rd	0779 542 4575	Ramshackle and friendly. There's bargains if you've got superhuman patience.

Map 123 • Peckham

Primark	51 Rye Ln	0207 639 9655	More of a chance of scoring that 'it' item at this branch.

Map 127 • Coldharbour Lane / Herne Hill (West)

Blackbird Bakery	208 Railton Rd	020 7095 8800	London needs more lovely independent bakeries (like this).

Map 129 • East Dulwich

The Cheeseblock	69 Lordship Ln	020 8299 3636	Best cheese south of the river.

Map 130 • Peckham Rye

Hope And Greenwood	20 North Cross Rd	020 8613 1777	Twee but tasty old-style sweets.

Map 133 • Battersea (East)

London Recumbents	Battersea Park	020 7498 6543	Much more fun in theory than in practice.

Map 134 • South Lambeth

Lassco House & Garden	30 Wandsworth Rd	020 7394 2100	Homebase for the unique, antique, or eccentric.
New Covent Garden Market	Nine Elms Ln	020 7720 2211	Known as London's Larder. Nowhere near Covent Garden

Map 140 • Clapham Junction / Northcote Rd

Anita's Vintage Fashion Fair	Battersea Arts Centre, Lavender Hill	020 8325 5789	Hardcore collectors, designers, and students find inspiration amongst the rails.
Huttons	29 Northcote Rd	020 7223 5523	Eclectic mix of unusual clothes, furniture and gifts.
QT Toys and Games	90 Northcote Rd	020 7223 8637	Toys for big and small kids. Cool gifts.
Russ	101 Battersea Rise	020 7228 6319	Model specialist—trains, boats, planes and more.
Sweaty Betty	136 Northcote Rd	020 7978 5444	Look like a total Betty, like, even when you're sweaty.

Map 141 • Battersea (South)

Battersea Car Boot Sale	401 Battersea Park Rd	07941 383 588	Yeah! A huge, tumultous boot sale that starts mid afternoon!

Map 142 • Clapham Old Town

M. Moen & Sons	24 The Pavement	020 7622 1624	Butcher for the bourgeoisie, incredibly good, massively expensive.

Map 143 • Clapham High Street

Apex Cycles	40 Clapham High St	020 7622 1334	Bikes fixed, bikes sold.
Paws	62 Clapham High St	020 7720 9962	Attendant, napping canines remind shoppers where the takings will go.
Today's Living	92 Clapham High St	020 7622 1772	Health foods, herbal remedies and other jiggery pokery.

Map 144 • Stockwell / Brixton (West)

A&C Co Grocers	3 Atlantic Rd	020 7733 3766	Portuguese-owned institution, famous for pestos, chorizo and mamma's tortilla.
Lisa Stickley London	74 Landor Rd	020 7737 8067	Dotty 1940s-inspired handbags to tea-towels. Cath Kidston but better.
The Old Post Office Bakery	76 Landor Rd	0207 326 4408	Disused P.O turned artisan baker's. Local loaf? The Brixton Rye.

Map 147 • Balham (West)

Bon Vivant	59 Nightingale Ln	020 8675 6314	Great local deli.

Map 148 • Balham (East)

Moxon's	Westbury Parade	020 8675 2468	Fresh fish for foodies with deep pockets. Knowledgeable staff.

Map 149 • Clapham Park

MacFarlanes	48 Abbeville Rd	020 8673 5373	Gourmet goodness galore.

Map 150 • Brixton

Traid	2 Acre Ln	020 7326 4330	Characterful recycled clothes. Touch of wank, but still we like.

Map 151 • Tooting Bec

Russell's Hardware & DIY	46 Upper Tooting Rd	020 8672 1576	DIY treasure chest. Friendly, helpful owners.
Wandsworth Oasis HIV/AIDs Charity Shop	40 Trinity Rd	020 8767 7555	Thrift store treasure trove.

Map 152 • Tooting Broadway

Tooting Market	21 Tooting High St	020 8672 4760	Quaint indoor labyrinth worth nosing about.

NFT
NFT
WHAT IS *THAT?!*
NFT
HUH? OH, IT'S WWW.NOTFORTOURISTS.COM
BUT WHY?! WHY WOULD YOU USE ANYTHING OTHER THAN ME?
NFT
WELL, THE WEBSITE JUST OFFERS A FEW THINGS THAT YOU DON'T: DAILY CONTENT, FUN PHOTOS, SEARCHABLE DATABASE... COOL STUFF LIKE THAT.
DEVASTATED
OH... I SEE...

NFT
BUT I FIT IN YOUR POCKET. YOU CAN TAKE ME ANYWHERE.
SWOOP!
NFT
OH!
TUCK TUCK
NFT
NFT
NFT
OH PLEASE. THE WEBSITE COULD NEVER REPLACE YOU. I NEED YOU BOTH TO GET THE MOST OUT OF MY CITY!

DISCOVER PALM.

BELGIUM'S AMBER BEER

In the early 1900's, PALM met the Belgian Brewing Guild challenge to create a new style of beer to uphold tradition, yet be refreshing like the newly popular pilsners and lagers. Now Belgium's leading amber beer is available in the London PALM Breweries, a 250 year old family-run, craft brewery, invites you to discover the magic of their well-balanced and approachable beer.

PLEASE ENJOY RESPONSIBLY
www.palmbreweries.com

Imported by Cave Direct. www.beermerchants.com

Quickmap
maps and mapmovies
the art of finding your way
www.quickmap.com
info@quickmap.com
Euston Tower London 2009

A

Abberley Mews	141	B2
Abbeville Mews	143	B1
Abbeville Road	143	B2
	149	A1/A2
Abbey Close	86	A2
	134	B1
Abbey Drive	152	A2
Abbey Gardens	42	B1
	68	B1
Abbey Orchard Street	22	A2
Abbey Road	65	B1
	68	A1/A2/B2
Abbey Street	107	A2/B1/B2
	108	A1
Abbeyfield Road	109	B1/B2
Abbot Street	86	B1
Abbot's Place	65	B1
Abbots Close	81	A1
Abbots Gardens	35	B2
Abbots Lane	107	A1
Abbots Terrace	53	A2
Abbotsbury Close	34	A1/A2
Abbotsbury Road	34	A1/A2
Abbotshade Road	110	A2
Abbotswood Road	129	A1/B1
Abchurch Lane	17	A2/B2
Abdale Road	32	A2
Aberavon Road	93	B2
Abercorn Close	68	B1
Abercorn Place	68	B1
Abercorn Walk	68	B1
Abercorn Way	115	A1
Abercrombie Street	132	B2
Aberdare Gardens	65	B2
Aberdeen Lane	75	B1
Aberdeen Park	75	A2/B1
Aberdeen Place	76	A1
Aberdeen Road	75	A2
Aberdour Street	107	B1
Abersham Road	86	B2
Abingdon Close	72	B2
Abingdon Road	35	B1
Abingdon Street	22	A2
Abingdon Villas	35	B1/B2
Abinger Grove	118	B2
Abinger Mews	26	A2
Abinger Road	39	A1
Ablett Street	116	B1
Abney Gardens	85	A1
Abyssinia Close	140	A1
Abyssinia Road	140	A1
Acacia Close	117	A2
Acacia Gardens	68	B2
Acacia Place	69	A1
Acacia Road	68	B2
	69	A1/B1
Acanthus Drive	115	A1
Acanthus Road	141	B1
Acfold Road	50	A1
Achilles Close	115	A2
Achilles Street	126	A1
Achilles Way	9	A1
Acklam Road	25	B1/B2
Ackmar Road	49	A1
Ackroyd Drive	99	A1
Acland Crescent	128	A2
Acol Road	65	B1
Acorn Walk	111	A2
Acre Drive	130	B1
Acre Lane	143	B2
	150	A1/A2
Acris Street	139	B1
Acton Mews	88	A1
Acton Street	5	A2
Ada Place	92	A2
Ada Road	122	A1/A2
Ada Street	89	B1
Adair Road	25	A1/A2
Adam & Eve Mews	35	B1/B2
Adam Street	24	A2
Adam Walk	47	A1
Adams Court	17	A2
Adams Mews	151	A1
Adams Place	74	B1
Adams Row	9	A1
Adamson Road	66	B2
Adderley Grove	140	B2
Addington Road	54	B1
	94	B2
Addington Square	121	A2
	122	A1
Addington Street	104	B1
Addison Avenue	28	B1
Addison Bridge Place	34	B1
Addison Crescent	34	A1
Addison Gardens	33	B2
Addison Place	28	B1
Addison Road	28	B1
	34	A1/B2
Addle Hill	15	B2
Addle Street	16	A2
Adelaide Close	127	A1
Adelaide Grove	32	A1
Adelaide Road	66	B1/B2
	69	A2
	70	A1/A2
	138	A1
Adelaide Street	24	A1
Adelina Grove	96	A2
	97	A1
Adelina Mews	149	B2
Adeline Place	4	B1
Adelphi Terrace	24	A2
Aden Grove	64	B1
Adeney Close	47	A2
Adie Road	40	A2
Adler Street	95	A1
Admiral Place	55	A2
	111	A2
Admiral Walk	26	B2
Admirals Gate	120	B1
Admirals Walk	56	A1/A2
Admirals Way	100	B2
Admiralty Close	119	B2
Adolphus Road	62	B2
	63	A1
Adolphus Street	118	B2
	126	A2
Adpar Street	31	A2
Adrian Mews	43	B2
Adys Road	129	A2
	130	A1
Affleck Street	79	B2
Afghan Road	132	B2
Agar Grove	71	B2
	72	B1/B2
	79	A1
Agar Place	72	B1
Agar Street	24	A1
Agate Road	40	A2
Agatha Close	96	B2
Agdon Street	6	B2
Agincourt Road	57	A1/B1/B2
Agnes Street	99	B1
Ainger Mews	70	A1
Ainger Road	70	A1
Ainsdale Drive	115	A1
Ainsley Street	92	B2
Ainsworth Close	122	B2
Ainsworth Road	89	B2
Ainsworth Way	68	A2
Aintree Street	42	B1
Air Street	10	B2
Airdrie Close	79	A2
Airedale Avenue	39	B1
Airedale Avenue South	39	B1
Airedale Road	147	B2
Airlie Gardens	35	A1
Aisgill Avenue	42	A2
Aiten Place	39	B2
Aitken Close	88	A2
Akenside Road	67	A1
Akerman Road	121	A1/B1
Alaska Street	104	A2
Alba Place	29	A1
Albany Courtyard	10	B1
Albany Mews	113	B1
Albany Road	54	B1
	113	B1/B2
	114	A1/B1
Albany Street	77	A1/B1
Albemarle Street	9	A2
Albemarle Way	6	B2
Albert Avenue	135	B1
Albert Bridge	45	B2
Albert Bridge Road	132	A1
	141	A1
Albert Close	89	B2
Albert Embankment	131	A1/B1
Albert Gardens	97	B2
Albert Gate	19	A1
Albert Mews	36	A1
	53	B2
Albert Place	35	A2
Albert Road	53	B2
	62	A1
Albert Square	135	B1
Albert Street	71	B1
	77	A2
Albert Terrace	70	B1
Albert Terrace Mews	70	B1
Albert Way	124	A1
Alberta Street	112	A2
Albion Avenue	143	A1
Albion Close	31	B2
Albion Drive	88	A1/A2
Albion Grove	64	B1/B2
Albion Mews	31	B2
	40	B2
	65	A1
	80	A1
Albion Place	15	A2
	40	B2

Street Index

Albion Road 64 A1/B1
Albion Square 88 A1
Albion Street 31 B2
110 B1
Albion Terrace 88 A1
Albion Way 15 A2
Albrighton Road 129 A1
Albury Street 119 A1
Alconbury Road 85 B2
Aldbridge Street 114 A1
Aldburgh Mews 2 B1
Aldebert Terrace 134 B2
135 B1
Aldenham Street 78 B1
Aldensley Road 40 A2
Alder Close 114 B2
Alder Mews 59 A2
Alderbrook Road 148 A1
Aldermanbury 16 A2
Aldermanbury Square 16 A2
Alderney Mews 106 B1
Alderney Road 93 B1
Alderney Street 20 B1/B2
Aldersgate Street 7 B1/B2
15 A2
16 A1
Alderson Street 25 A1
Alderton Road 128 A1
Alderville Road 49 B1
Aldford Street 9 A1
Aldgate 18 A2
Aldgate High Street 18 A2
95 A1
Aldine Place 33 A1
Aldine Street 33 A1
Aldis Street 152 A1
Aldred Road 65 A2
Aldrich Terrace 146 B1
Aldridge Road Villas 29 A2
Aldsworth Close 26 B2
Aldwych 14 B1/B2
Aldwych Underpass 14 B1
Alexander Mews 30 A1
Alexander Place 37 B1
Alexander Road 60 B2
61 B1
Alexander Square 37 B1
Alexander Street 30 A1
Alexandra Avenue 141 A2
Alexandra Close 118 B1
Alexandra Cottages 126 B2
Alexandra Grove 63 A1
Alexandra Place 66 B1
Alexandra Road 55 B2
66 B1
Alexandra Street 126 A1
Alexis Street 108 B1/B2
Alfearn Road 87 A2
Alford Place 83 B2
Alfoxton Avenue 55 A2
Alfred Mews 4 A1
Alfred Place 4 A1
Alfred Road 30 A1
Alfred Street 94 B2
Alfreda Street 141 A2
Alfriston Road 140 B2
Algarve Road 146 B1
Alice Court 137 A1
Alice Lane 94 A1
Alice Street 107 B1
Alice Walker Close 127 A2
Alie Street 95 A1
Aliwal Road 140 A1
Alkerden Road 38 A1
Alkham Road 85 A1
All Saints Close 134 B2
All Saints Passage 138 B1
All Saints Road 29 A1
All Saints Street 79 B1/B2
All Souls Place 3 B1
Allan Barclay Close 86 A1
Allard Gardens 149 A2
Allardyce Street 144 B1
Allcroft Road 71 A2
Allen Edwards Drive 134 B1/B2
Allen Road 64 B1/B2
94 A1
Allen Street 35 B1/B2
Allendale Close 122 B1
Allensbury Place 79 A1
Allerton Road 63 A2/B2
Allestree Road 48 A1
Allfarthing Lane 146 A1
Allgood Street 91 A2
Allhallows Lane 17 B1
Allingham Mews 83 A1
Allingham Street 83 A1
Allington Street 20 A1/A2
Allison Road 55 A1
Allitsen Road 69 B1
Allnutt Way 149 A1
Alloa Road 117 A2/B2
Alloway Road 93 B2
Allport Mews 97 A2
Allsop Place 2 A1
Alma Grove 108 B1
Alma Road 138 A2
139 B1
Alma Square 68 B1
Alma Street 71 A2
Alma Terrace 146 A2
Almeida Street 80 B2
Americ Road 140 A1
Almington Street 53 B2
61 A2
Almond Close 123 B2
Almond Road 109 B1
Almorah Road 82 B1
Alperton Street 25 A2
Alpha Close 76 B2
Alpha Grove 102 A1
Alpha Place 45 B2
Alpha Road 126 B2
Alpha Street 123 B2
Alpine Grove 90 B1
Alpine Road 116 A2
Alroy Road 55 B1
Alsace Road 114 A1
Alscot Road 107 B2
Alscot Way 107 B2
Altenburg Gardens 140 A1/A2
Althea Street 50 B1
Althorp Road 147 B1
Althorpe Grove 132 A1
Althorpe Mews 132 A1
Alton Street 99 B2
Alvanley Gardens 66 A1
Alverton Street 118 B1/B2
Alvey Street 114 A1
Alvington Crescent 86 B1
Alwyne Lane 81 A1
Alwyne Place 81 A1
Alwyne Road 81 A1
Alwyne Square 81 A1/A2
Alwyne Villas 81 A1/B1
Amazon Street 96 A1
Ambassador Square 102 B2
Ambassador's Court 23 B1
Amber Wharf 88 B1
Ambergate Street 112 A2/B2
Amberley Road 26 B2
Ambler Road 62 B2
Ambleside Close 90 A1/A2
Ambrosden Avenue 20 A2
Ambrose Street 108 B2
Amelia Street 112 A2
113 A1
Amen Corner 15 B2
America Square 18 B2
America Street 105 A2
Amerland Road 137 B2
Amersham Grove 126 A1
Amersham Road 126 A2/B2
Amersham Vale 118 B2
126 A2
Amhurst Park 86 A1
Amhurst Road 86 A1/A2/B2
87 B1/B2
89 A2
Amhurst Terrace 86 A2
Amiel Street 92 B2
Amies Street 140 A1
Amner Road 147 A2
Amor Road 40 A2
Amott Road 130 A1
Amoy Place 100 A1
Ampton Place 5 A2
Ampton Street 5 A2
Amsterdam Road 103 A2
Amwell Street 6 A1
Anatola Road 59 A2
Anchor Mews 82 A2
148 A2
Anchor Street 108 B2
Anchor Yard 7 A2
Ancill Close 47 A2
Andalus Road 144 B1
Anderson Road 90 A2
Anderson Street 46 A1
Anderton Close 129 A1
Andover Place 27 A2
Andover Road 61 A2
Andre Street 86 A2
87 B1
Andrew Borde Street 12 A2
Andrew Place 134 B1
Andrew's Road 89 B1
Anerley Street 141 A1
Anfield Close 148 B2
Angel Court 152 A1
Angel Mews 80 B1
96 B2
Angel Passage 17 B2
Angel Street 15 B2
Angel Walk 40 B2
Angell Park Gardens 145 B2
Angell Road 145 B2

Angler's Lane	71	A2
	72	B1
Anglo Road	94	A2
Angus Street	126	A1
Anhalt Road	132	A1
Anley Road	33	B1
Ann Lane	44	B2
Ann Moss Way	109	A2
Ann's Close	19	A1
Ann's Place	18	A2
Anna Close	88	A2
Annabel Close	100	A2
Annandale Road	38	A1
Annette Crescent	81	
Annette Road	61	B2
	74	A1
Annie Besant Close	94	A2
Anning Street	84	
Annis Road	90	B2
Ansdell Road	124	B2
Ansdell Street	35	A2/B2
Ansdell Terrace	35	B2
Ansell Road	151	B1
Anselm Road	42	B2
Ansleigh Place	28	B1
Anson Road	73	A1
Anstey Road	130	A1
Anstice Close	38	B1
Anthony Street	96	A2
Antill Road	93	B2
	94	B1
Antill Terrace	97	A2
Anton Street	86	B2
Antrim Grove	67	B2
Antrim Road	67	B2
Apollo Place	44	B2
Apothecary Street	15	B2
Apple Tree Yard	23	A2
Appleby Road	89	A1
Appleby Street	88	B1
Appledore Close	151	A1
Appleford Road	25	A1/A2
Applegarth Road	33	B2
	41	A2
Appold Street	8	B2
Apprentice Way	87	A2
Approach Road	92	A2
	93	A1
April Street	86	A2
Apsley Way	9	B1
Aquila Street	69	B1
Aquinas Street	104	A2
Arbery Road	93	B2
Arbour Square	97	A2/B2
Arbutus Street	88	A1
Arcadia Street	99	B2
Arch Street	106	B1
Archangel Street	110	A2
Archdale Road	130	A1/B1
Archel Road	42	A1/A2
Archer Square	125	A2
Archer Street	11	B1
Archery Close	31	B2
The Arches	48	B2
Archibald Mews	9	A1
Archibald Road	73	A1
Archibald Street	99	A2
Archie Street	107	A1
Archway Close	60	A1
Archway Mall	60	A1
Archway Mews	136	A2
Archway Road	51	A2
	52	A1/B1
	60	A1
Arcola Street	86	A1
Arctic Street	71	A2
Ardbeg Road	128	B2
Arden Crescent	102	A1/B1
Ardilaun Road	75	A2
Ardleigh Road	82	A1/A2
Ardshiel Close	136	A1
Argon Mews	43	B1
Argyle Place	40	B2
Argyle Road	93	B1
Argyle Square	5	A1
Argyle Street	5	A1
Argyle Way	115	A2
Argyll Close	144	A2
Argyll Road	35	A1
Argyll Street	10	A2
Ariel Road	65	A1
Ariel Way	33	A1/A2
Aristotle Road	143	B2
Arklow Road	118	B1/B2
Arkwright Road	66	A2
	67	A1
Arlesey Close	136	B2
Arlesford Road	144	A1
Arlingford Road	127	B1
Arlington Avenue	82	B1
	83	A2
Arlington Place	120	B2
Arlington Road	71	B1
	78	A1
Arlington Square	83	A2
Arlington Street	9	A2
	23	A1
Arlington Way	6	A2
Armadale Road	42	B2
Armagh Road	94	A2
Arminger Road	32	A1
Armour Close	74	B1
Armoury Way	138	B1/B2
Armstrong Road	36	B2
Arne Street	13	B2
Arneway Street	22	B2
Arnhem Place	102	A1
Arnold Circus	91	A1
Arnold Road	94	B2
	99	A2
Arnould Avenue	128	A2
	129	A1
Arnside Street	113	B1/B2
Arodene Road	150	A2
Arran Walk	81	A1
Artesian Road	29	A2/B2
Arthur Road	61	B2
Arthur Street	17	B2
Artichoke Hill	96	B1
Artichoke Place	122	B1
Artillery Lane	8	B2
	18	A1
Artillery Place	22	B1
Artillery Row	22	B1
Arundel Close	140	B1
Arundel Gardens	29	B1
Arundel Grove	64	B2
	82	A2
Arundel Place	80	A1
Arundel Square	74	B1/B2
	80	A1
Arundel Street	14	B2
Arundel Terrace	47	A1
Arvon Road	74	B2
Ascalon Street	133	A2
Ascham Street	72	A2
Ascot Road	55	B2
	152	B2
Ash Grove	89	B1
Ashanti Mews	87	B2
Ashbourne Grove	38	A2/B1
	129	B2
Ashbourne Road	152	B2
Ashbridge Street	76	B1
Ashbrook Road	60	A1/A2
Ashburn Gardens	36	B1
Ashburn Place	36	B1
	44	A1
Ashburnham Grove	120	B1
Ashburnham Place	120	B1
Ashburnham Retreat	120	B1
Ashburnham Road	44	B1
Ashbury Road	141	A2/B1
Ashby Grove	81	A2
Ashby Road	126	B2
Ashby Street	6	B2
Ashchurch Park Villas	40	A1
Ashcombe Street	49	B2
Ashcroft Road	93	B2
Ashdown Crescent	57	B2
Ashdown Walk	102	B2
Ashdown Way	151	A1
Ashenden Road	90	A2
Asher Way	95	B2
Ashfield Street	96	A2
	97	A1
Ashfield Yard	97	A1
Ashford Street	84	
Ashington Road	49	B1
Ashland Place	2	A1
Ashley Crescent	141	B2
Ashley Gardens	22	B1
Ashley Place	20	A2
Ashley Road	53	B1/B2
Ashlone Road	136	A1
Ashmere Grove	143	B2
Ashmill Street	76	B1
Ashmole Place	135	A2
Ashmole Street	135	A1
Ashmore Close	123	A1
Ashmore Road	25	A2
	26	A1
Ashmount Road	52	B2
Ashness Road	140	B2
Ashton Street	101	A2
Ashvale Road	152	A1
Ashwin Street	86	B1
Ashworth Close	122	B1
Ashworth Road	27	A2
Aske Street	84	
Askew Road	40	A1
Askill Drive	136	B2
Aslett Street	146	A1
Asolando Drive	113	A1
Aspen Close	59	A2
Aspen Gardens	40	B2

Street Index

Aspen Way	100	A2
	101	A2
Aspenlea Road	47	A1
Aspern Grove	57	B1
Aspinden Road	109	B1
Aspley Road	138	B2
Assam Street	95	A1
Assata Mews	75	B1
Assembly Passage	97	A2
Astbury Road	124	A2
Aste Street	103	A1
Astell Street	45	A2/B2
Astle Street	141	A2
Aston Street	98	A1
Astoria Walk	145	B1
Astrop Mews	40	A2
Astrop Terrace	40	A2
Astwood Mews	36	B1
Asylum Road	116	B1
	124	A1
Atalanta Street	47	A2
Atheldene Road	146	B1
Athelstane Grove	94	B1
Athelstane Mews	62	B1
Atherden Road	87	A2
Atherfold Road	143	A2
Atherstone Mews	36	B1
Atherton Street	132	B2
Athlone Close	87	B2
Athlone Street	71	A2
Atkins Road	148	A2
	149	B1/B2
	150	B1
Atlantic Road	127	A1/B1
	144	B2
Atlas Mews	74	B1
	86	B2
Atney Road	136	A2
Atterbury Road	55	B1
Atterbury Street	21	A2
Attneave Street	6	B1
Atwood Road	40	B2
Aubert Park	74	A2
	75	A1
Aubert Road	75	A1
Aubrey Place	68	B1
Aubrey Road	29	B1
	54	A1
Aubrey Walk	29	B1
Auburn Close	125	B2
Auckland Road	140	A1
Auckland Street	131	B1
Auden Place	70	B1
Audley Close	141	B2
Audley Square	9	A1
Audrey Street	88	B2
Augusta Street	99	B2
Augustine Road	33	B2
	41	A2
Augustus Close	40	A2
Augustus Street	77	B2
Auriga Mews	64	B1
Auriol Road	34	B1
Austin Friars	17	A2
Austin Friars Passage	17	A2
Austin Road	141	A2
Austin Street	91	A1
Austral Street	104	B2
Avalon Road	49	A2
Avarn Road	152	A2
Ave Maria Lane	15	B2
Avebury Street	84	A1
Aveline Street	131	B2
Avenell Road	62	B2
	74	A2
	75	A1
The Avenue	38	A2
	120	A2
	140	A2/B2
	141	B1
	147	A2
	148	A2
Avenue Close	69	B2
Avenue Road	52	A2
	53	A1
	66	B2
	69	A1/B1
Averill Street	47	A2
Avery Farm Row	19	B2
Avery Row	2	B2
Avis Square	97	B2
Avoca Road	151	A2/B2
Avocet Close	115	A1
Avondale Park Gardens	28	B1
Avondale Park Road	28	B1
Avondale Rise	129	A2
Avondale Square	115	A1
Avonley Road	125	A1/B1
Avonmore Place	34	B1
Avonmore Road	34	B1/B2
Avonmouth Street	106	B1
Axminster Road	61	B1/B2
Aybrook Street	2	A1
Aylesbury Road	113	B2
Aylesbury Street	6	B1/B2
Aylesford Street	21	B1/B2
Aylward Street	97	A1/A2
Aynhoe Road	41	A2
Ayres Street	106	A1
Ayrsome Road	64	A2
Ayrton Road	36	A2
Aytoun Place	145	A1
Aytoun Road	145	A1
Azania Mews	71	A2
Azenby Road	122	B2
Azof Street	103	B2

B

Baalbec Road	75	B1
Babmaes Street	23	A2
Baches Street	84	B1
Back Church Lane	95	A1/A2/B2
Back Hill	5	B2
Back Lane	53	A2
	56	B1
Backhouse Place	114	A1
Bacon Grove	107	B2
Bacon Street	91	A1/A2
Bacons Lane	51	B1
Bacton Street	93	A1
Baden Place	106	A2
Badminton Road	147	A2
Badsworth Road	121	A2
Baffin Way	101	A2
Bagley's Lane	49	A2
	50	A1
Bagshot Street	114	A1/B1
Baildon Street	119	B1
Bailey Mews	127	B1
Bainbridge Street	4	B1
Baird Street	7	A2
Baker Street	1	A2
	76	B2
Baker's Mews	2	B1
Baker's Rents	91	A1
Baker's Row	5	B2
	6	B1
Bakers Field	73	A2
Bakers Hall Court	18	B1
Bakery Close	135	B1
Bakery Place	140	A1
Balaclava Road	108	B1
Balcombe Street	76	B2
Balcorne Street	90	B1
Balderton Street	2	B1
Baldwin Crescent	121	A1
Baldwin Street	7	A2
Baldwin Terrace	83	B1
Baldwin's Gardens	14	A2
Bale Road	98	A1
Balfe Street	79	B1
Balfern Grove	38	B2
Balfern Street	132	B2
Balfour Mews	9	A1
Balfour Place	9	A1
Balfour Road	75	A2
Balfour Street	113	A1/A2
Balham Grove	148	A1/B1
Balham High Road	147	B2
	148	A2/B1
	151	A1/A2
Balham Hill	148	A2
Balham New Road	148	B1
Balham Park Road	147	B1/B2
Balham Station Road	148	B1
Balladier Walk	99	B2
Ballance Road	90	A2
Ballantine Street	138	A2
Ballast Quay	103	B2
Ballater Road	144	B1
Ballingdon Road	147	A2
Balls Pond Place	82	A1
Balls Pond Road	82	A1/A2
Balmer Road	94	B1
Balmes Road	82	B1/B2
Balmoral Grove	73	B2
Balmore Street	59	A1
Balniel Gate	21	B2
Baltic Court	110	A2
Baltic Place	82	B2
Baltic Street East	7	A2/B2
Baltic Street West	7	B1/B2
Balvaird Place	21	B2
Bamber Road	123	A1
Bamborough Gardens	33	B1
Banbury Road	90	B1/B2
Banbury Street	132	B2
Bancroft Road	92	B2
	93	B1
Banfield Road	130	A2
Banim Street	40	A2/B2
Banister Mews	65	B2
The Bank	51	B2
Bank End	106	A1
Bank Street	100	B2
Bankside	105	A2

Bankton Road 127 B1
Banner Street 7 A2/B2
Banning Street 103 B2
Bantry Street 122 A1
Banyard Road 109 A1
Baptist Gardens 71 A1
Barb Mews 33 B1
Barbara Castle Close 42 B2
Barbauld Road 64 B1/B2
Barbon Close 5 B1
Barchard Street 138 B2
Barchester Street 99 B2
Barclay Close 48 A2
Barclay Road 43 B1
Bard Road 28 B1
Bardolph Road 73 A2
Bardsey Place 97 A1
Bardsley Lane 120 A1
Barfett Street 25 A2
Barfleur Lane 118 A2
Barford Street 80 B1
Barforth Road 130 A2
Barge House Street 104 A2
Barge Lane 94 A1
Baring Street 82 B1
Bark Place 30 B1
Barker Drive 71 B2
78 A2
Barker Mews 142 B1
Barker Street 44 B1
Barkston Gardens 43 A2
Barkworth Road 116 B1
Barlborough Street 125 A1
Barlby Road 25 A1
Barleycorn Way 100 A1
Barlow Place 9 A2
Barlow Road 65 A1
Barlow Street 113 A2
Barmouth Road 146 A1
Barn Street 64 A1
Barnabas Road 90 A2
Barnaby Place 45 A1
Barnard Mews 140 A1
Barnard Road 140 A1
Barnard's Inn 14 B2
Barnardo Gardens 97 B2
Barnardo Street 97 B1/B2
Barnby Street 77 B2
78 B1
Barnes Street 98 A1/B1
Barnes Terrace 118 B2
Barnet Grove 91 A2
Barnett Street 96 A2
Barnfield Close 53 B2
Barnfield Place 102 B2
Barnham Street 107 A1
Barnsbury Grove 80 A1
Barnsbury Park 80 A1
Barnsbury Road 80 B1
Barnsbury Square 80 A1
Barnsbury Street 80 A1/A2
Barnsbury Terrace 80 A1
Barnsdale Avenue 102 A2/B2
Barnsdale Road 26 A1
Barnsley Street 92 B1/B2
Barnwell Road 127 B1
Barnwood Close 27 B1
Baron Street 80 B1
Baroness Road 91 A2
Barons Court Road 42 A1
Barons Keep 34 B1
Barons Place 104 A2
Barque Mews 119 A1
Barrett Street 2 B1
Barretts Grove 64 B2
Barriedale 126 B1
Barringer Square 151 B2
Barrington Close 57 B2
Barrington Road 53 A1
127 A1
145 B2
Barrow Hill Road 69 B1
Barrowgate Road 38 A1
Barry Avenue 86 A1
Barry Road 130 B1/B2
Barset Road 124 B2
Barter Street 4 B2
Bartholomew Close 7 B1
15 A2
139 B1
Bartholomew Lane 17 A1/A2
Bartholomew Place 7 B1
Bartholomew Road 71 B2
72 B1/B2
Bartholomew Square 7 A2
Bartholomew Street 106 B2
Bartholomew Villas 72 B1
Bartle Road 28 A1
Bartlett Close 99 B2
Bartlett Court 14 B2
Barton Close 90 A1
124 B1
Barton Road 42 A1
Barton Street 22 A2
Basevi Way 119 A2
Basil Street 37 A2/B2
Basin Approach 98 B1
Basing Court 123 A1
Basing House Yard 84
Basing Place 84
Basing Street 29 A1
Basingdon Way 128 A2
Basinghall Avenue 16 A2
Basinghall Street 16 A2
Basire Street 81 /B1
Baskerville Road 146 A2
Basnett Road 141 B2
Bassano Street 129 B2
Bassett Road 25 B1
28 A1
Bassett Street 71 A2
Bassingham Road 146 A1
Bastwick Street 7 A1
Basuto Road 49 A1
Batavia Mews 126 A1
Batavia Road 126 A1
Batchelor Street 80 B1
Bate Street 100 A1
Bateman Street 11 A2
12 A1
Bateman's Row 84
Bath Close 124 A1
Bath Court 5 B2
Bath Place 84
Bath Road 38 A2
39 A1
Bath Street 7 A2
Bath Terrace 106 B1
Bathurst Mews 31 B1
Bathurst Street 31 B1
Batley Place 85 B1
Batley Road 85 B1
Batman Close 32 A2
Batoum Gardens 33 B1
Batten Street 140 A1
Battersea Bridge 44 B2
Battersea Bridge Road 132 A1/B2
Battersea Church Road 132 A1
Battersea High Street 132 A1/B1
Battersea Market 132 B1
Battersea Park Road 132 B2
133 A1/A2/B1
141 A1/A2
Battersea Rise 139 B2
140 A1/A2/B1
Battishill Street 80 A2
Battle Bridge Lane 107 A1
Battle Bridge Road 78 B2
Battledean Road 74 B2
Batty Street 95 A2
Bavaria Road 61 A1
Bavent Road 121 B2
Bawdale Road 129 B2
Bawtree Road 125 A2
Baxendale Street 91 A2
Baxter Road 82 A1
Bayford Mews 89 B2
Bayford Street 89 B2
Bayham Place 78 A1
Bayham Street 71 B1
78 A1
Bayley Street 4 B1
Baylis Road 104 A2/B2
Baynes Mews 67 B1
Baynes Street 71 B2
Bayonne Road 47 A2
Bayston Road 85 B1
86 B1
Bayswater Road 29 B2
30 B1/B2
31 B1/B2
Baythorne Street 99 A1
Baytree Road 150 A2
Bazely Street 101 A2
Beachcroft Way 53 B1
Beacon Hill 73 B2
Beaconsfield Road 113 B2
114 B1
Beaconsfield Terrace Road 34 B1
Beadon Road 41 A1
Beak Street 10 B1/B2
Beale Place 94 A2
Beale Road 94 A1/A2
Bear Alley 15 B2
Bear Gardens 105 A2
Bear Lane 105 A1
Beaton Close 123 A1
Beatrice Place 35 B2
Beatrice Road 62 A2
108 B2
Beatty Road 64 B2
Beatty Street 78 A1
Beauchamp Place 37 B2
Beauchamp Road 140 A1
Beauchamp Street 14 A2
Beauclerc Road 40 A2
Beaufort Gardens 37 B2

Street Index

Beaufort Street 44 B2
Beaufoy Walk 131 B2
Beaulieu Close 128 A2
Beaumont Avenue 42 A1/A2
Beaumont Crescent 42 A2
Beaumont Grove 97 A2
Beaumont Mews 2 A1
Beaumont Place 4 A1
Beaumont Rise 53 B1
Beaumont Square 97 A2
Beaumont Street 2 A1/A2
Beauval Road 129 B2
Beavor Lane 39 B2
Beccles Street 100 A1
Beck Road 89 B1
Becket Street 106 B2
Beckford Place 113 B1
Beckway Street 113 A2
114 A1
Beckwith Road 128 B2
Bective Place 137 A1
Bective Road 137 A1
Bedale Street 106 A1/A2
Bedford Avenue 4 B1
Bedford Close 38 B1
Bedford Court 24 A1
Bedford Gardens 35 A1
Bedford Hill 148 B1/B2
Bedford Place 4 B2
Bedford Road 53 A1
143 A2/B2
Bedford Row 5 B1
14 A2
Bedford Square 4 B1
Bedford Street 13 B1
24 A1
Bedford Way 4 A2
Bedfordbury 24 A1
Bedlam Mews 131 A2
Bedser Close 135 A1
Beech Close 118 B2
Beech Street 7 B1/B2
Beech Tree Close 80 A1
Beechcroft Road 146 B2
151 A1
Beechdale Road 150 B2
Beechmore Road 141 A1
Beechwood Road 86 B1
Beehive Close 88 A1
Beehive Place 144 B2
Beeston Place 9 B1
19 A2
20 A1
Beira Street 148 A2
Bekesbourne Street 98 B1
Belfast Road 85 A1
Belfort Road 124 B2
Belfry Close 116 B1
Belgrade Road 64 B2
Belgrave Gardens 68 A1
Belgrave Mews North 19 A1/A2
Belgrave Mews South 19 A2
Belgrave Mews West 19 A1/A2
Belgrave Place 19 A2
Belgrave Road 20 A2/B2
Belgrave Square 19 A2
Belgrave Street 97 A2/B2
Belgrave Yard 19 A2
Belgrove Street 5 A1

Belinda Road 127 A2
Belitha Villas 80 A1
Bell Inn Yard 17 A2
Bell Lane 18 A2
Bell Lane (Pettycoat Lane) Market 18 A2
Bell Street 76 B1
Bell Street Market 76 B1
Bell Wharf Lane 16 B2
Bell Yard 14 B2
Bell Yard Mews 107 A1
Bellamy Close 42 A2
100 B1
Bellamy Street 148 A1
Bellefields Road 144 B2
145 B1
Bellenden Road 123 A1/B1
129 A2
Belleville Road 140 B1
Bellevue Road 147 B1
Bellgate Mews 58 B2
Bellina Mews 72 A2
Bellmaker Court 99 B1
Belmont Close 143 A1/B1
Belmont Road 143 B1
Belmont Street 71 A1
Belmore Lane 73 B1
Belmore Street 134 B1
Belsham Street 89 A2
Belsize Avenue 67 B1/B2
Belsize Court 67 A2
Belsize Crescent 67 B1
Belsize Grove 67 B2
Belsize Lane 66 B2
67 B1/B2
Belsize Mews 67 B1
Belsize Park 66 B2
67 B1
Belsize Park Gardens 67 B1/B2
Belsize Park Mews 67 B1
Belsize Place 67 B1
Belsize Road 66 B1
68 A1
Belsize Square 67 B1
Belsize Terrace 67 B1
Belthorn Crescent 149 B1
Belton Way 99 A2
Beltran Road 49 B2
Belvedere Buildings 105 B2
Belvedere Place 144 B1
Belvedere Road 104 A1
Bemerton Street 79 A2/B2
Bemish Road 136 A1
Ben Jonson Road 97 A2
98 A1/A2
Benbow Road 40 A2
Benbow Street 119 A1
Bendall Mews 76 B1
Bendemeer Road 136 A1
Benedict Road 145 B1
Bengeworth Road 128 A1
Benham Close 139 A2
Benhams Place 56 B1
Benhill Road 122 A1/B1
Benjamin Close 89 B1
Benjamin Mews 148 B2
Benjamin Street 15 A2
Bennerley Road 140 B1
Bennet Street 23 A1

Bennet's Hill 15 B2
Bennett Road 64 B2
145 A2
Bennett Street 38 B1
Benson Quay 96 B2
Benthal Road 85 B2
86 A2
Bentham Road 90 A2
Bentinck Mews 2 B1
Bentinck Street 2 B1
Bentley Road 82 A2
Benwell Road 74 A1/B2
Benwick Close 109 B1
Benworth Street 94 B2
Benyon Road 82 B1
Berber Place 100 A1
Berber Road 140 B2
Bere Street 97 B2
Beresford Road 55 A1
75 B2
Beresford Terrace 75 B2
Berestede Road 39 B1
Bergen Square 111 B2
Berger Road 90 A2
Berghem Mews 33 B2
Bergholt Mews 71 B2
Bering Square 102 B2
Berisford Mews 138 B2
Berkeley Gardens 35 A1
Berkeley Mews 1 A2
Berkeley Road 53 A1
Berkeley Square 9 A2
Berkeley Street 9 A2
Berkley Grove 70 A2
Berkley Road 70 A1/A2
Bermondsey Square 107 B1
Bermondsey Street 107 A1/B1
Bermondsey Wall East 108 A2
109 A1
Bermondsey Wall West 108 A1
Bernard Street 4 B2
5 B1
Bernays Grove 144 B2
Berners Mews 3 B2
Berners Place 3 B2
Berners Road 80 B1
Berners Street 3 B2
Bernhardt Crescent 76 A1/B1
Berriman Road 62 B1
Berry Place 6 B2
Berry Street 6 B2
Berryfield Road 112 A2
Berthon Street 119 A2
Bertram Street 59 A1
Berwick Mews 123 A2
Berwick Street 3 B1
11 A1/B1
Beryl Road 41 B1
Besant Place 129 A2
Bessborough Gardens 21 B2
Bessborough Place 21 B2
Bessborough Street 21 B2
Bessemer Road 121 B2
Besson Street 125 B1
Bessy Street 92 B2
Bestwood Street 117 A2
Beswick Mews 66 A1
Beta Place 144 B1

Bethnal Green Road 91 A1/A2
92 B1/B2
Bethwin Road 112 B2
121 A1/A2
Betterton Street 13 B1
Bettridge Road 49 B1
Betts Street 96 B1
Bev Callender Close 142 A1
Bevan Street 83 A2
Bevenden Street 84 B1
Beverley Close 139 A2
Beverley Road 38 A2
39 B1
Beversbrook Road 60 B1
Beverston Mews 1 A2
Beverstone Road 150 A2
Bevill Allen Close 152 A2
Bevin Close 110 A2
Bevin Way 6 A1
Bevington Road 25 B1
Bevington Street 108 A2
Bevis Marks 18 A1
Bewdley Street 80 A1
Bewick Street 142 A1
Bewley Street 96 B2
Bianca Road 115 B1
Bickenhall Street 1 A2
Bickersteth Road 152 A2/B2
Bickerton Road 59 A1/A2
Bickley Street 152 A1
Bicknell Road 128 A1
Bidborough Street 4 A2
5 A1
Bidbury Close 114 B1
Biddestone Road 74 A1
Biddulph Road 27 A2
Bidwell Street 124 A1
Biggerstaff Street 62 B1
Biggs Row 136 A1
Bigland Street 96 A1/A2
Billing Place 43 B2
Billing Road 43 B2
Billing Street 43 B2
Billington Road 125 B1/B2
Billiter Square 18 B1
Billiter Street 18 B1
Billson Street 103 B2
Bina Gardens 44 A1
Binfield Road 134 B2
Bingfield Street 79 A1/A2
Bingham Place 2 A1
Bingham Street 82 A1
Binney Street 2 B1
Binns Road 38 A1
Birch Close 59 A2
Birchfield Street 100 A1
Birchin Lane 17 A2
Birchington Road 53 A1
65 B1
Birchlands Avenue 147 B2
Birchmore Walk 63 B1/B2
Birchwood Drive 56 A1
Bird in Bush Road 114 B2
115 B1/B2
Bird Street 2 B1
Birdcage Walk 9 B2
22 A1
Birdhurst Road 139 B1
152 B1
Birdsfield Lane 94 A2
Birkbeck Mews 86 B1
Birkbeck Road 86 B1
Birkbeck Street 92 B2
Birkdale Close 115 A2
Birkenhead Street 5 A1
Birkwood Close 149 B2
Birley Street 141 A2
Birnam Road 61 A2
Biscay Road 41 B1
Bisham Gardens 51 B1
Bishop Kings Road 34 B1
Bishop Street 81 B1
Bishop Wilfred Wood Close 123 B2
Bishop's Avenue 48 B1
Bishop's Court 14 B2
15 B2
Bishop's Park Road 48 B1
Bishop's Road 132 A1
Bishops Bridge 31 A1
Bishops Bridge Road 30 B1/B2
31 A1
Bishops Road 42 B2
48 A1/A2
51 A2
Bishops Terrace 112 A1
Bishops Way 92 A2
93 A1
Bishopsgate 8 B2
17 A2
Bishopsgate Churchyard 8 B2
Bishopswood Road 51 A1
Bittern Street 106 A1/B1
Black Friars Lane 15 B2
Black Horse Court 106 B2
Black Lion Lane 39 B2
Black Prince Road 112 A1
131 B1/B2
Black Swan Yard 107 A1
Blackall Street 8 A1
Blackbird Yard 91 A2
Blackburn Road 65 A2
Blackburne's Mews 1 B2
Blackfriars Bridge 15 B1/B2
105 A1
Blackfriars Court 15 B2
Blackfriars Passage 15 B2
Blackfriars Road 105 A1/B1
Blackheath Hill 120 B2
Blackheath Road 119 B2
120 B1
Blackhorse Road 118 B1
Blacklands Terrace 46 A1/A2
Blackpool Road 123 B2
Blacks Road 40 B2
Blackshaw Road 152 B1
Blackstock Mews 62 B2
Blackstock Road 62 B2
63 B1
Blackthorn Street 99 A2
Blacktree Mews 145 B2
Blackwall Lane 103 A2/B2
Blackwall Tunnel 101 A2/B2
Blackwater Street 129 B2
Blackwood Street 113 B2
Blade Mews 137 A1
Blades Court 137 A1
Blagrove Road 25 B1
Blair Close 75 B2
Blake Gardens 49 A2
Blake Street 119 A1
Blakemore Gardens 40 B2
Blakeney Close 78 A2
Blakenham Road 151 B1
152 A1
Blakes Road 114 B1
122 A2
Blanch Close 124 A1
Blanchard Way 89 A1
Blanchedowne 128 A2
Blandfield Road 147 A2
Blandford Square 76 B2
Blandford Street 1 A2
2 A1/B1
Blantyre Street 44 B2
Blasker Walk 102 B2
Blechynden Street 28 A1
Bledlow Close 76 A1
Bleeding Heart Yard 15 A1
Blenheim Court 60 B2
Blenheim Crescent 28 A2
29 A1
Blenheim Gardens 150 B1/B2
Blenheim Grove 123 B1/B2
Blenheim Road 68 B2
Blenheim Street 2 B2
Blenheim Terrace 68 B1
Blenkarne Road 147 A1
Bletchley Street 83 B2
Bletsoe Walk 83 A2
Blissett Street 120 B2
Blithfield Street 35 B2
Bloemfontein Avenue 32 A1
Bloemfontein Road 32 A1/B1
Bloemfontein Way 32 A1
Blomfield Mews 31 A1
Blomfield Road 27 B1/B2
Blomfield Street 8 B2
Blomfield Villas 30 A2
Blondel Street 141 A1
Bloom Park Road 48 A1
Bloomburg Street 21 A1
Bloomfield Place 9 A2
Bloomfield Road 51 A2
Bloomfield Terrace 19 B2
Bloomsbury Place 4 B2
139 B1
Bloomsbury Square 4 B2
Bloomsbury Street 4 B1
13 A1
Bloomsbury Way 4 B1/B2
5 B1
Blore Close 134 B1
Blossom Street 91 B1
Blount Street 98 B1
Blucher Road 121 A2
Blue Anchor Lane 108 B2
Blue Anchor Yard 95 B1
Blue Ball Yard 23 A1
Bluebell Close 89 B2
Bluelion Place 107 A1
Blundell Close 86 A2
Blundell Street 79 A1/A2
Blyth Close 103 A2
Blythe Mews 33 B2

Street Index

Blythe Road	33	B1/B2
	34	B1
	41	A2
Blythe Street	92	A1
Blythwood Road	53	B2
Boadicea Street	79	B2
Boardwalk Place	101	A2
Boat Lifter Way	118	A1
Bob Marley Way	127	B1
Bobbin Close	142	A2
Bocking Street	89	B1
Bodney Road	87	B1
Bohemia Place	89	A2
Bohn Road	98	A1
Boleyn Road	64	B2
	82	A2
Bolina Road	116	A2
Bolingbroke Grove	140	A1/B1
	147	A1
Bolingbroke Road	33	B2
Bolingbroke Walk	132	A1
Bolney Street	135	B1
Bolsover Street	3	A1
Bolton Crescent	112	B1
Bolton Gardens	43	A2
Bolton Gardens Mews	43	A2
Bolton Road	68	A1
Bolton Street	9	B2
The Boltons	43	A2
Boltons Place	43	A2
Bombay Street	108	B2
Bomore Road	28	B1
Bonar Road	123	A1
Bonchurch Road	25	B1
Bond Street	38	A1
Bondway	134	A2
Bonham Road	150	A1
Bonhill Street	8	A1
Bonner Road	92	A2
	93	A1
Bonner Street	93	A1
Bonneville Gardens	149	A1
Bonnington Square	135	A1
Bonny Street	71	B2
Bonsor Street	122	A2
Booker Close	99	B1
Boot Street	84	
Booth Close	89	B2
Booth's Place	3	B1
Boothby Road	60	A1
Borough High Street	106	A1/A2/B1
Borough Road	105	B1/B2
	106	B1
Borrett Close	112	B2
Borrodaile Road	138	B2
Borthwick Street	119	A1
Boscastle Road	58	B2
Boscobel Place	19	A2
Boscobel Street	76	B1
Boscombe Road	32	B1
	152	B2
Boss Street	107	A2
Boston Gardens	38	B1
Boston Place	76	B2
Boston Street	88	B2
Bosun Close	100	B2
Boswell Street	5	B1
Bosworth Road	25	A1
Bothwell Street	47	A2
Botolph Lane	18	B1
Botts Mews	29	B2
Botts Passage	29	B2
Boulcott Street	97	B2
The Boulevard	50	A2
	147	B2
Boundaries Road	147	B1/B2
	148	B1
Boundary Lane	113	B1
Boundary Road	66	B1
	68	A1/A2
	69	A1
Boundary Row	104	A2
Boundary Street	91	A1
Bourchier Street	11	B2
Bourdon Place	9	A2
Bourdon Street	9	A2
Bourke Close	149	A2
	150	B1
Bourlet Close	3	B1
Bourne Place	38	A1
Bourne Road	54	A1/B1
Bourne Street	19	B2
Bourne Terrace	30	A1/A2
Bournemouth Close	123	B2
Bournemouth Road	123	B2
Boutflower Road	140	A1
Bouverie Mews	64	A2
Bouverie Place	31	B2
Bouverie Road	64	A1/A2
Bouverie Street	15	B1
Bovingdon Close	60	A1
Bovingdon Road	49	A2
	50	A1
Bow Common Lane	98	A2
	99	A1/A2/B2
Bow Road	94	B1/B2
Bow Street	13	B2
Bowater Close	150	B1
Bowden Street	112	A1
Bowditch	118	A1/A2
Bowen Street	99	B2
Bower Street	97	B2
Bowerdean Street	49	A2
Bowerman Avenue	118	B1
Bowfell Road	47	A1
Bowhill Close	135	A2/B2
Bowie Close	149	B2
Bowl Court	8	A2
Bowland Road	143	B2
Bowland Yard	19	A1
Bowling Green Lane	6	B1
Bowling Green Place	135	A2
Bowling Green Street	112	B1
	135	A2
Bowling Green Walk	84	
Bowmans Mews	61	B2
	95	B1
Bowmans Place	61	B1
Bowood Road	140	A2
Bowyer Place	121	A2
	122	A1
Bowyer Street	121	A2
Boxworth Grove	79	B2
Boyd Street	95	A1
Boyfield Street	105	B1
Boyle Street	10	B1
Boyne Terrace Mews	28	B2
Boyson Road	113	B1/B2
Boyton Close	92	B2
Brabant Court	18	B1
Brabazon Street	99	B2
Brabourn Grove	124	B2
Bracey Street	61	A1
Bracken Avenue	147	A2
Brackenbury Gardens	40	A2
Brackenbury Road	40	A2
Brackenfield Close	87	A1
Brackley Road	38	A2
Brackley Street	7	B2
Brackley Terrace	38	A2
Bracklyn Close	84	A1
Bracklyn Court	83	A2
Bracklyn Street	84	A1
Bracknell Gardens	66	A1
Brad Street	104	A2
Bradbourne Street	49	A1
Bradbury Mews	82	A2
Bradbury Street	82	A2
Braden Street	27	B1
Bradenham Close	113	B2
Brading Terrace	40	A1
Bradley Close	79	A2
	80	B1
Bradley Mews	147	B1
Bradmead	133	A1
Bradmore Park Road	40	A2/B2
Bradstock Road	90	A2/B2
Bradwell Street	93	B1
Brady Street	92	B1
Braemar Close	115	A2
Braes Street	81	B1
Braganza Street	112	A1/B2
Braham Street	95	A1
Braidwood Street	107	A1
Braintree Street	92	B2
Bramah Green	135	B2
Bramalea Close	51	A2
Bramber Road	42	B1/B2
Bramcote Grove	116	B1
Bramerton Street	45	B1
Bramfield Road	140	B1
Bramford Road	139	B1
Bramham Gardens	43	A2
Bramlands Close	140	A1
Bramley Crescent	134	A1
Bramley Road	28	A1
Brampton Road	55	B2
Bramshaw Road	90	B2
Bramshill Gardens	59	A1
Bramwell Mews	79	B2
Branch Hill	56	A1
Branch Place	84	A1
Branch Road	98	B1
Branch Street	122	A2
Brand Close	63	A1
Brand Street	120	B2
Brandlehow Road	137	A1
Brandon Road	79	A1
Brandon Street	113	A1/A2
Brandreth Road	151	A2
Brangton Road	131	B2
Branksea Street	47	A2
Branksome Road	150	A1
Bransdale Close	65	B1
Brantwood Road	128	B1
Brasenose Drive	47	A1
Brassey Road	65	A1

Brassey Square 141 B1
Bravington Place 25 A2
Bravington Road 25 A2
Bray Crescent 110 A2
Bray Place 46 A1
Brayards Road 123 B2
124 B1/B2
Brayburne Avenue 142 A2
143 A1
Brayfield Terrace 80 A1
Bread Street 16 B2
Bream's Buildings 14 B2
Brechin Place 44 A1
Brecknock Road 59 B1
72 A2
73 A1/B1
Brecon Mews 73 B1
Brecon Road 42 B1
Bredgar Road 59 A2
Breer Street 49 B2
Breezers Hill 95 B2
Bremner Road 36 A1
Brendon Street 1 A1
Brenthouse Road 89 A2
Brenton Street 98 B1
Bressenden Place 20 A2
Brett Close 64 A2
Brett Road 87 B1
Brettell Street 113 B2
Brewer Street 10 B2
11 B1
Brewery Road 73 B2
Brewhouse Lane 96 B1
136 A2
Brewhouse Walk 111 A2
Brewhouse Yard 6 B2
Briant Street 125 B1
Briarwood Road 143 B2
Briary Close 69 A2
Brick Court 14 B2
Brick Lane 91 A1/A2/B1
Brick Lane Street Market 91 A2/B1
Brick Street 9 B1/B2
Bride Lane 15 B1
Bride Street 74 B1
Brideale Close 114 B2
Bridel Mews 80 B2
Brides Place 82 B2
Bridewain Street 107 A2
Bridewell Place 15 B2
96 B1
Bridford Mews 3 A1
Bridge Approach 70 A2
Bridge Avenue 40 B2
Bridge Close 28 A1
Bridge Gardens 64 B1
Bridge House Quay 101 B2
Bridge Lane 132 A1/B2
Bridge Meadows 117 B1
Bridge Park 138 B1
Bridge Place 20 A2
Bridge Street 22 A2
Bridge View 40 B2
Bridge Yard 106 A2
Bridgefoot 131 B1
Bridgeman Road 79 A2
Bridgeman Street 69 B1
Bridgend Road 138 A2
Bridgeport Place 95 B2

Bridges Court 132 B1
Bridges Place 48 A2
Bridgewater Square 7 B2
Bridgewater Street 7 B2
Bridgeway Street 78 B1
Bridle Lane 10 B2
Bridport Place 82 B1
84 A1
Bridport Terrace 134 B1
Bridstow Place 29 A2
Brief Street 121 B1
Brierly Gardens 93 A1
Brig Mews 119 A1
Briggeford Close 85 A2
Brightlingsea Place 98 B1
Brightman Road 146 B1
Brighton Road 64 B2
Brighton Terrace 144 B2
Brightwell Crescent 152 A1/A2
Brill Place 78 B1/B2
Brindley Street 126 B1/B2
Brinsley Street 96 A2
Brisbane Street 122 A1
Briset Street 15 A2
Briset Way 61 A2
Bristol Gardens 27 B1
Bristol Mews 27 B1
Briston Grove 53 B2
Britannia Close 143 B2
Britannia Road 43 B2
49 A2
102 B2
Britannia Row 83 A1
Britannia Street 5 A2
Britannia Walk 84 B1
Britannia Way 49 A2
British Grove 39 B1
British Grove Passage 39 B1
British Grove South 39 B1
British Street 99 A1
Britten Street 45 B1/B2
Britton Street 6 B1
15 A2
Brixton Hill 150 A2/B1/B2
Brixton Hill Place 150 B1
Brixton Oval 150 A2
Brixton Road 112 B1
135 A2/B2
144 B2
145 A1/A2/B1
Brixton Station Road 144 B2
145 B1/B2
Brixton Station 144 B2
Road Street Market 145 B1
Brixton Water Lane 127 B1
150 A2
Broad Lane 8 B2
Broad Sanctuary 22 A2
Broad Street Avenue 8 B2
Broad Walk 70 B1
Broad Yard 15 A1
Broadbent Close 51 B2
Broadbent Street 9 A2
Broadfield Lane 79 A1
Broadhinton Road 142 A1
Broadhurst Close 66 B1
Broadhurst Gardens 65 B2
66 B1
Broadlands Close 51 A1/A2

Broadlands Road 51 A1/A2
Broadley Street 76 B1
Broadley Terrace 76 B1
Broadstone Place 2 A1
Broadwall 104 A2
Broadwater Road 152 A1
Broadway 22 A1
The Broadway 53 A2
Broadway Market 89 B1
Broadway Market Mews 89 B1
Broadway Mews 86 A1
Broadwick Street 10 A2/B2
11 A1
Brocas Close 69 A2
Brock Place 99 A2
Brock Street 124 B1
Brockham Street 106 B1
Brocklebank Road 146 A1
Brocklehurst Street 125 A2/B2
Brodia Road 64 A2
Brodie Street 115 A1
Brodlove Lane 97 B1
Brodrick Road 147 B1
Broken Wharf 16 B1
Brokesley Street 94 B1
99 A1
Bromar Road 129 A1/A2
Bromehead Street 96 A2
Bromell's Road 143 B1
Bromfelde Road 143 A2
Bromfield Street 80 B1
Bromley Place 3 A2
Bromley Street 97 A2/B2
Brompton Park Crescent 43 B1
Brompton Place 37 B2
Brompton Road 37 A2/B1/B2
Brompton Square 37 B1
Bromwich Avenue 58 A2
Brondesbury Road 65 B1
Brondesbury Villas 68 A1
Bronsart Road 42 B1
47 A2
48 A1
Bronti Close 113 B2
Bronze Street 119 A2
Brook Close 151 A2
Brook Drive 104 B2
112 A1/A2
Brook Gate 1 B2
Brook Green 41 A1/A2
Brook Mews North 30 B2
Brook Street 2 B1/B2
31 B1
Brook's Mews 2 B1
Brooke Road 85 B1/B2
87 A1/A2/B2
Brooke Street 14 A2
Brookes Market 14 A2
Brookfield 58 A1
Brookfield Park 58 A2
Brookmill Road 119 B2
Brooksbank Street 90 A1
Brooksby Street 80 A1
Brooksby's Walk 90 A2
Brookside Road 60 A1
Brookville Road 48 A1
Broome Way 122 A1
Broomfield Street 99 B2
Broomgrove Road 145 A1

Street Index

Broomhill Road 138 B1
Broomhouse Lane 49 B1
Broomhouse Road 49 B1
Broomsleigh Street 65 A1/A2
Broomwood Road 140 B1/B2
Brough Close 134 B2
Brougham Road 88 A2
89 B1
Broughton Drive 127 A1
Broughton Gardens 52 A2
Broughton Road 50 A1/B1
Broughton Road Approach 49 A2
Broughton Street 141 A2
142 A1
Brown Hart Gardens 2 B1
Brown Street 1 A1
Browning Close 27 B2
Browning Mews 2 A2
Browning Street 113 A1
Brownlow Mews 5 B2
Brownlow Road 88 A2
Brownlow Street 14 A2
Browns Lane 71 A2
Brownswood Road 63 B1
Broxash Road 147 A2
Broxwood Way 69 B2
Bruce Close 25 A1
Bruce Hall Mews 151 B2
Bruce Road 152 B2
Brudenell Road 151 A1/B2
Bruford Court 119 A2
Bruges Place 71 B2
Brune Street 18 A2
Brunel Road 109 A2
110 A1/B1
Brunswick Court 107 A1
Brunswick Gardens 29 B2
35 A1/A2
Brunswick Mews 1 A2
Brunswick Park 122 B1
Brunswick Place 2 A2
84 B1
Brunswick Quay 111 B1
Brunswick Road 101 A2
Brunswick Square 5 B1
Brunswick Villas 122 A1/A2
Brunton Place 98 B1
Brushfield Street 8 B2
18 A1/A2
Brussels Road 139 A2
Bruton Lane 9 A2
Bruton Place 9 A2
Bruton Street 9 A2
Bryan Road 111 A2
Bryanston Mews East 1 A2
Bryanston Mews West 1 A1
Bryanston Place 1 A1
Bryanston Square 1 A2
Bryanston Street 1 B1/B2
Bryanstone Road 53 A2
Bryantwood Road 74 B2
Bryett Road 61 B1
Brynmaer Road 141 A1
Bucharest Road 146 A1
Buck Street 71 B1
Buckfast Street 91 A2
Buckhold Road 138 B1
Buckhurst Street 92 B2
Buckingham Gate 9 B2
20 A2
22 A1
Buckingham Mews 9 B2
82 A2
Buckingham Palace Road 9 B2
20 A1/B1
Buckingham Place 9 B2
Buckingham Road 82 A1/A2
Buckingham Street 24 A1/A2
Buckland Crescent 66 B2
67 B1
Buckland Street 84 A1
Buckle Street 95 A1
Bucklersbury 16 B2
Buckley Road 65 B1
Buckmaster Close 145 B1
Buckmaster Road 140 A1
Bucknall Street 12 A2
Bucknell Close 144 B1
Buckner Road 150 A2
Buckters Rents 111 A2
Buer Road 48 B2
Bugsby's Way 103 B2
Bulinga Street 21 A2
Bull Yard 123 A2
Bullace Row 121 A2
Bullards Place 93 B1
Bullen Street 132 B2
Buller Close 123 A2
Bullied Way 20 A1
Bullivant Street 101 A2
Bulmer Mews 29 B1
Bulmer Place 29 B1
Bulstrode Place 2 B1
Bulstrode Street 2 B1
Bulwer Street 33 A1
Bunhill Row 7 A2/B2
Bunhouse Place 19 B2
Bunning Way 79 A2
Bunsen Street 93 A2
Burbage Close 106 B2
Burbage Road 128 B1
Burchell Road 124 A1
Burcote Road 146 A2
Burder Close 82 A2
Burder Road 82 A2
Burdett Mews 30 B1
67 B1
Burdett Road 93 B2
98 A2
99 A1/B1
100 A1
Burdett Street 104 B2
Burford Walk 50 A1
Burge Street 106 B2
Burgess Street 99 B1
Burgh Street 83 B1
Burghley Road 58 B2
72 A2
Burgos Grove 119 B2
Burgoyne Road 55 B2
144 A2
Burland Road 140 B2
Burleigh Place 136 B1
Burleigh Street 24 A2
Burlington Close 26 B1
Burlington Gardens 10 B1
Burlington Lane 38 B1/B2
Burlington Mews 137 B1
Burlington Place 48 B1
Burlington Road 48 B1/B2
Burma Road 64 B1
75 A2
Burnaby Street 44 B1
Burnbury Road 149 B1/B2
Burne Street 76 B1
Burnett Close 90 A1
Burney Street 120 A2
Burnfoot Avenue 48 A1
Burnham Close 115 A1
Burnham Street 92 B2
Burnhill Close 124 A1
Burnley Road 145 A1
Burns Road 141 A1
Burnsall Street 45 B2
Burnside Close 110 A2
Burnthwaite Road 42 B2
48 A2
Burntwood Close 146 B2
Burntwood Grange Road 146 B2
Burntwood Lane 146 B2
147 B1
Buross Street 96 A2
Burr Close 95 B1
Burrell Street 105 A1
Burrells Wharf Square 102 B2
Burrow Road 129 A1
Burrows Mews 105 A1
Burslem Street 95 A2
96 A1
Burstock Road 136 A2
Burston Road 136 B1
Burtley Close 63 A2
Burton Grove 113 B2
Burton Lane 145 A2
Burton Mews 19 B2
Burton Place 4 A2
Burton Road 65 B1
121 B1
Burton Street 4 A2
Burwell Close 96 A2
Burwood Place 1 A1
31 B2
Bury Close 110 A2
Bury Court 18 A1
Bury Place 4 B2
Bury Street 18 A1
23 A1
Bury Walk 45 A2
Busby Place 72 B2
Busby Street 91 A2
Bush Cottages 138 B1
Bush Lane 17 B1
Bush Road 89 B1
117 A1
Bushell Street 95 B2
Bushey Hill Road 122 B2
Bushnell Road 151 A2
Bushwood Drive 115 A1
Butcher Row 97 B2
Bute Gardens 41 A1/A2
Bute Street 36 B2
Butler Street 93 A1
Butterfield Close 108 A2
Butterfly Walk 121 B2
Buttermere Close 107 B2
Buttermere Drive 136 B2

Buttermere Walk 86 B2
Butterwick 41 A1/B1/B2
Buttesland Street 84 B1
Buxted Road 88 A1
129 A1
Buxton Mews 143 A2
Buxton Road 60 A2
Buxton Street 91 B1/B2
Byam Street 50 B2
Byfield Close 111 A2
Bygrove Street 99 B2
Bylands Close 110 A2
Byng Place 4 A1
Byng Street 100 B1/B2
Byrne Road 148 B2
Byron Close 88 A2
Byron Court 26 B2
Byron Mews 26 B2
57 A1
Bythorn Street 144 B1
Byton Road 152 B2
Byward Street 18 B1/B2
Bywater Place 111 A2
Bywater Street 46 A1
Bywell Place 3 B1

C

Cabbell Street 1 A1
Cable Place 120 B2
Cable Street 95 B1/B2
96 A1/B2
97 B1/B2
Cabot Square 100 B2
Cabul Road 132 B2
Cactus Close 122 B2
Cade Road 120 B2
Cadell Close 91 A2
Cader Road 146 A1
Cadet Drive 108 B1
115 A1
Cadet Place 103 B2
Cadiz Street 113 B1
Cadmus Close 143 B2
Cadogan Gardens 46 A2
Cadogan Gate 46 A2
Cadogan Lane 19 A1
Cadogan Place 19 A1/B1
Cadogan Square 37 B2
46 A2
Cadogan Street 46 A1/A2
Cadoxton Avenue 86 A1
Caedmon Road 74 A1
Cahill Street 7 B2
Cahir Street 102 B2
Caird Street 25 A2
Cairns Road 140 B1
Caistor Mews 148 B1
Caistor Road 148 B1
Caithness Road 33 B2
41 A2
Calabria Road 75 B1
Calais Gate 121 A1
Calais Street 121 A1
Calbourne Road 147 B2
Caldecot Road 121 B2
Caldervale Road 149 A1
Caldwell Street 135 B1/B2

Cale Street 45 A1/A2
46 A1
Caleb Street 106 A1
Caledonia Street 78 B2
Caledonian Road 74 A1/B1
78 B2
79 A2/B1/B2
Caledonian Square 72 B2
Caledonian Wharf 103 B2
Calico Row 139 A1
Callcott Street 29 B1
Callendar Road 36 A2
Callingham Close 99 B1
Callow Street 44 B1/B2
Calshot Street 79 B2
Calthorpe Street 5 B2
Calton Avenue 129 B1
Calverley Grove 60 A2
Calvert Avenue 91 A1
Calvert Street 70
Calvin Street 91 B1
Calypso Crescent 114 B1
Calypso Way 118 A1
Cambalt Road 136 B1
Camberwell Church Street 121 B2
122 B1
Camberwell Glebe 122 B1
Camberwell Green 121 A2
122 A1/B1
Camberwell Grove 122 B1/B2
129 A1
Camberwell New Road 112 B1/B2
121 A1/A2
Camberwell Road 113 B1
121 A2
Camberwell Station Road 121 A2
Camborne Mews 28 A2
Cambray Road 148 B2
Cambria Road 128 A1
Cambria Street 49 A2
50 A1
Cambridge Avenue 68 A1
Cambridge Crescent 92 A2
Cambridge Gardens 25 B1
28 A1
Cambridge Gate 77 B1
Cambridge Gate Mews 77 B1
Cambridge Grove 40 B2
Cambridge Heath Road 92 A2/B1/B2
96 A2
Cambridge Place 35 A2
Cambridge Road 26 A2
132 A1
Cambridge Square 31 B2
Cambridge Street 20 B1/B2
Cambridge Terrace 77 B1
Cambridge Terrace Mews 77 B1
Camden Gardens 71 B2
Camden High Street 71 B1
78 A1
Camden Lane 73 B1
Camden Lock Place 71 B1
Camden Mews 72 B1/B2
73 B1
Camden Park Road 73 B1
Camden Passage 80 B2

Camden Road 71 B1/B2
72 B1/B2
73 A2/B1/B2
74 A1
Camden Square 72 B2
Camden Street 71 B2
78 A1
Camden Terrace 72 B2
Camden Walk 80 B2
Camdenhurst Street 98 B1
Camellia Street 134 B2
Camelot Street 115 B2
Camera Place 44 B2
Camerton Close 86 B2
Camilla Road 108 B2
Camlet Street 91 A1
Camley Street 78 A2/B2
Camomile Street 8 B2
18 A1
Campana Road 49 A1
Campbell Road 94 B2
99 A2
Campdale Road 59 B2
Campden Grove 35 A1
Campden Hill 35 A1
Campden Hill Gardens 29 B1
Campden Hill Place 29 B1
Campden Hill Road 29 B1
35 A1
Campden Hill Square 29 B1
Campden House Close 35 A1
Campden Street 29 B1
Camperdown Street 95 A1
Camplin Street 125 A1/B1/B2
Canada Square 100 B2
Canada Street 111 A1/B1
Canal Approach 117 B2
Canal Boulevard 72 B2
Canal Close 98 A2
Canal Grove 115 B2
Canal Path 88 B1
Canal Street 113 B2
Canal Walk 82 B1
Cancell Road 121 A1
135 B2
Candahar Road 132 B2
Candover Street 3 B1
Candy Street 94 A2
Canfield Gardens 65 B2
66 B1
Canfield Place 66 B1
Canford Road 140 A2/B2
Canning Cross 122 B1
Canning Place 36 A1
Canning Place Mews 36 A1
Canning Road 63 B1
Cannon Drive 100 A1
Cannon Hill 66 A1
Cannon Lane 56 B2
Cannon Place 56 B2
Cannon Street 15 B2
16 B1/B2
17 B1/B2
Cannon Street Road 96 A1
Canon Beck Road 110 A1
Canon Row 24 B1
Canon Street 83 A1
Canonbury Crescent 81 /A2
Canonbury Grove 81 A1/B1

Street Index

Canonbury Lane 80 A2
Canonbury Park North 75 B2
81 A1
Canonbury Park South 75 B2
81 A1
Canonbury Place 81 A1
Canonbury Road 80 A2
81 B1
Canonbury Square 80 A2
Canonbury Street 81 /A1
Canonbury Villas 81 B1
Canonbury Yard 81
Canonbury Yard West 81 A1
Canrobert Street 92 A1/A2/B1
Cantelowes Road 72 B2
Canterbury Crescent 145 B1
Canton Street 99 B1
Cantrell Road 99 A1
Canute Gardens 109 B2
111 B1
Capel Court 17 A2
Capener's Close 19 A1
Capern Road 146 B1
Capland Street 76 A1
Capper Street 4 A1
Capstan Road 118 A1
Capstan Square 103 A2
Capstan Way 111 A2
Caradoc Close 29 A2
Caravel Mews 119 A1
Carbis Road 98 B2
Carburton Street 3 A1
Cardale Street 103 A1
Carden Road 130 A2
Cardigan Road 94 A2/B2
Cardigan Street 131 B2
Cardinal Bourne Street 106 B2
Cardinal Place 136 A1
Cardinals Way 52 B2
Cardine Mews 115 B2
Cardington Street 77 B2
Cardozo Road 73 B2
Cardross Street 40 A2
Cardwell Road 73 A2
Carew Close 62 B1
Carew Street 121 B1
Carey Gardens 133 B2
134 B1
Carey Lane 16 A1
Carey Street 14 B2
Carfax Place 143 B1
Carfree Close 80 A1
Cargill Road 146 B1
Carisbrooke Gardens 114 B2
Carker's Lane 72 A1
Carleton Road 60 B1
73 A1
Carlile Close 94 B2
Carlingford Road 56 B2
Carlisle Avenue 18 B2
Carlisle Lane 104 B1
131 A2
Carlisle Mews 76 B1
Carlisle Place 20 A2
Carlisle Road 62 A2
Carlisle Street 11 A2
Carlisle Way 152 A2
Carlos Place 9 A1
Carlow Street 78 A1
Carlton Drive 136 B1/B2
Carlton Gardens 23 A2
Carlton Grove 124 A1
Carlton Hill 68 A1/A2/B2
Carlton House Terrace 23 A2
Carlton Road 62 A1
Carlton Square 93 B1
Carlton Street 23 A2
Carlton Vale 27 A2
Carlwell Street 152 B1
Carlyle Mews 93 B1
Carlyle Place 136 A1
Carlyle Square 45 B1
Carmarthen Place 107 A1
Carmel Court 35 A2
Carmelite Street 15 B1
Carmen Street 99 B2
Carmichael Close 139 A2
Carmichael Mews 146 A2
Carminia Road 148 B2
Carnegie Street 79 B2
Carnie Lodge 151 A2
Carnoustie Drive 79 A2
Carnwath Road 49 B2
Carol Street 71 B2
Caroline Close 30 B1
Caroline Place 30 B1
141 A2
Caroline Place Mews 30 B1
Caroline Street 97 B2
Caroline Terrace 19 B2
Carpenter Street 9 A2
Carpenters Mews 73 B2
Carpenters Place 143 B1
Carr Street 98 A2/B1
Carrara Close 127 A1
Carrara Mews 86 B2
Carriage Drive East 133 A1
Carriage Drive North 132 A1
133 A1
Carriage Drive South 132 A1
133 A1
Carriage Drive West 132 A1
Carriage Place 64 B1
Carrick Mews 119 A1
Carrington Street 9 B2
Carrol Close 58 B1
Carron Close 99 B2
Carroun Road 135 A1
Carter Lane 15 B2
Carter Place 113 B1
Carter Street 112 B2
Carteret Street 22 A2
Carteret Way 118 A1
Carters Yard 138 B1
Carthew Road 40 A2
Carthew Villas 40 A2
Carthusian Street 7 B1
15 A2
Cartier Circle 101 B1
Carting Lane 24 A2
Carton Street 1 A2
Cartwright Gardens 4 A2
Cartwright Street 95 B1
Cartwright Way 47 A1
Carver Road 128 B1
Carysfort Road 63 B2
64 B1
Casella Road 125 B1
Casey Close 76 A2
Casimir Road 87 A2
Casino Avenue 128 B1/B2
Caspian Street 122 A1
Cassidy Road 48 A2
Cassilis Road 102 A2
Cassland Road 90 B1/B2
Casson Street 91 B2
Castellain Road 27 A1/B1
Castelnau 40 B2
41 B1
Castelnau Row 40 B2
Casterton Street 89 A2
Castle Baynard Street 15 B2
16 B1/B2
Castle Lane 20 A2
Castle Mews 71 A2
Castle Place 38 A1
Castle Road 71 A2/B2
Castle Yard 51 B2
105 A1
Castlebrook Close 112 A1/A2
Castlehaven Road 71 A2/B1/B2
Castlemain Street 91 B2
Castlereagh Street 1 A1
Castletown Road 42 A1
Castleview Close 63 A1
Castor Lane 100 A2
Catesby Street 113 A2
Cathay Street 109 A1
Cathcart Hill 59 B1
Cathcart Road 43 B2
44 B1
Cathcart Street 71 A2
Cathedral Street 106 A1
Catherall Road 63 B2
Catherine Griffiths Court 6 B1
Catherine Grove 120 B1
Catherine Place 9 B2
Catherine Street 13 B2
14 B1
Catherine Wheel Alley 18 A1
Catherine Wheel Yard 23 A1
Cathles Road 148 A2
Cathnor Road 32 B1
Catlin Street 115 A2
Cato Road 143 B2
Cato Street 1 A1
Cator Street 114 B2
123 A1
Catton Street 14 A1
Caulfield Road 124 B1
The Causeway 138 B1
Causton Road 52 B1
Causton Street 21 A2/B2
Cautley Avenue 148 A2
Cavalry Gardens 137 B1
Cavaye Place 44 B1
Cavell Street 96 A2
Cavendish Avenue 68 B2
Cavendish Close 76 A2
Cavendish Mews North 3 A1
Cavendish Mews South 3 B1
Cavendish Place 2 B2
Cavendish Road 55 B2
65 A1
148 A2/B2
149 A1/B1
Cavendish Square 2 B2

Cavendish Street	84	A1
Caversham Flats	46	B1
Caversham Road	72	B1/B2
Caversham Street	45	B2
Caxton Grove	94	B2
Caxton Road	33	A1/B1
Caxton Street	22	A1
Cayton Place	7	A2
Cayton Street	7	A2
	83	B2
Cazenove Road	85	A1/A2
	87	A2
Cecile Park	53	A2
	54	B1
Cecilia Road	86	A2/B2
Cedar Close	94	A2
Cedar Court	81	
Cedar Way	78	A2
Cedarne Road	43	B1
Cedars Mews	141	B2
	142	B1
Cedars Road	142	B1
Celandine Close	99	B1
Celandine Drive	88	A1
Celbridge Mews	30	A1
Celia Road	72	A2
Centaur Street	131	A2
Central Avenue	132	A1
	133	A1
	141	A1
Central Street	7	A1/A2
Centre Street	92	A2
Centric Close	71	B1
Centurion Close	79	A2
Centurion Lane	94	A2
Century Mews	87	B2
Cephas Avenue	92	B2
	97	A2
Cephas Street	92	B2
Cerise Road	123	A2
Cerney Mews	30	B2
Cervantes Court	30	B1
Cester Street	88	B2
Ceylon Road	33	B2
Chadwell Street	6	A2
Chadwick Road	122	B2
	123	B1
Chadwick Street	22	B1/B2
Chagford Street	76	B2
Chalcot Crescent	70	A1/B1
Chalcot Gardens	67	B2
Chalcot Road	70	/B1
Chalcot Square	70	A2
Chaldon Road	42	B1
Chale Road	150	B1
Chalk Farm Road	71	A1/B1
Chalk Hill Road	41	A2
Challoner Crescent	42	A2
Challoner Street	42	A1
Chaloner Court	106	A1
Chalton Street	78	B1
Chamber Street	95	B1
Chamberlain Street	70	A1
Chambers Road	73	A2
Chambers Street	108	A1/A2
Chambon Place	39	B2
Chambord Street	91	A2
Champion Grove	128	A2
Champion Hill	128	A2
	129	A1
Champion Park	128	A2
Chance Street	91	A1
Chancel Street	105	A1
Chancellors Road	41	B1
Chancellors Street	41	B1
Chancery Lane	14	A2/B2
Chandler Street	96	B1
Chandler Way	114	B1
	123	A1
Chandlers Mews	100	B1
Chandos Place	24	A1
Chandos Street	2	B2
Chantrey Road	144	B2
Chantry Close	26	B1
Chantry Street	83	A1
Chapel Court	106	A1
Chapel Gate Mews	143	A2
Chapel House Street	102	B2
	103	B1
Chapel Market	80	B1
Chapel Place	2	B2
	80	B1
	84	
Chapel Side	29	B2
Chapel Street	1	A1
	19	A2
Chapel Way	61	B2
Chapel Yard	138	B1
Chaplin Close	104	A2
Chapman Place	62	B2
Chapman Street	96	A1/A2
Chapone Place	11	A2
Chapter Road	112	B2
Chapter Street	21	A1
Chardin Road	38	A1
Chardmore Road	85	A2
	87	A2
Charecroft Way	33	B2
Chargrove Close	110	A2
Charing Cross	24	A1/B1
Charing Cross Road	4	B1
	12	A2/B2
	24	A1
Chariot Close	94	A2
Charlbert Street	69	B1
Charles Barry Close	142	A2
Charles Coveney Road	123	A1
Charles II Street	23	A2
Charles Lane	69	B1
Charles Place	77	B2
Charles Square	84	B1
Charles Street	9	A1/A2
Charleston Street	113	A1
Charleville Road	42	A1
Charlmont Road	152	A1/A2/B1
Charlotte Despard Avenue	141	A2
Charlotte Mews	3	B2
	28	A1
	34	B1
Charlotte Place	20	A2
Charlotte Road	84	
Charlotte Row	142	B2
Charlotte Street	3	A2/B2
Charlotte Terrace	79	B2
Charlow Close	50	B2
Charlton Kings Road	73	A1
Charlton Place	80	B2
Charlwood Place	20	B2
Charlwood Road	136	A1
Charlwood Street	20	B2
	21	A1
Charlwood Terrace	136	A1
Charnock Road	87	A1/A2
Charnwood Gardens	102	A1/B1
Charrington Street	78	B1
Chart Street	84	B1
Charterhouse Buildings	7	B1
Charterhouse Mews	15	A2
Charterhouse Road	86	A2
Charterhouse Square	7	B1
	15	A2
Charterhouse Street	14	A2
	15	A1/A2
Charteris Road	62	B1
Chartfield Avenue	136	B1
Chartfield Square	136	B1
The Chase	142	A1/B1
Chasefield Road	151	B1
Chaseley Street	98	B1
Chatfield Road	139	A1
Chatham Place	89	A2
Chatham Road	140	B1/B2
Chatham Street	113	A2
Chatsworth Road	90	A2
Chatterton Mews	63	B1
Chatterton Road	62	B2
	63	B1
Chatto Road	140	B2
Chaucer Drive	108	B1
	114	A2
Chaucer Road	127	B1
Cheam Street	124	B1
Cheapside	15	B2
	16	A1/B2
Cheesemans Terrace	42	A1/A2
Chelmer Road	90	A2
Chelmsford Close	41	B2
Chelsea Bridge	46	B2
Chelsea Bridge Road	46	B2
Chelsea Embankment	45	B1/B2
	46	B1/B2
Chelsea Harbour Drive	50	A2
Chelsea Manor Gardens	45	B2
Chelsea Manor Street	45	B2
Chelsea Park Gardens	44	B2
Chelsea Square	45	A1/B1
Chelsea Wharf	44	B2
Chelsham Road	143	A2
Cheltenham Terrace	46	A1
Chelverton Road	136	A1
Chenies Mews	4	A1
Chenies Place	78	B2
Chenies Street	4	A1
Cheniston Gardens	35	B2
Chepstow Close	136	B2
Chepstow Crescent	29	B2
Chepstow Place	29	B2
Chepstow Road	29	A2/B2
Chepstow Villas	29	B1/B2
Chequer Street	7	B2
Cherbury Street	84	A1
Cheriton Square	148	B1
Cherry Garden Street	109	A1
Cherry Tree Close	90	B1
Cherrywood Close	93	B2
Cherrywood Drive	136	B1

Street Index

Chertsey Street 151 B1
Cheryls Close 50 A1
Chesham Close 19 A2
Chesham Mews 19 A1
Chesham Place 19 A1/A2
Chesham Street 19 A2
Cheshire Close 126 B1/B2
Cheshire Street 91 A2/B2
Cheshire Street Market 91 A2/B2
Chesholm Road 64 B2
Chesilton Road 48 A1
Chesney Street 141 A1
Chesson Road 42 A2/B1
Chester Close 19 A2
Chester Close North 77 B1
Chester Close South 77 B1
Chester Cottages 19 B2
Chester Court 77 B1
Chester Crescent 86 B2
Chester Gate 77 B1
Chester Mews 19 A2
Chester Place 77 B1
Chester Road 59 A1
77 B1
Chester Row 19 B2
Chester Square 19 A2/B2
Chester Square Mews 19 A2
Chester Street 19 A2
91 B2
92 B1
Chester Terrace 77 B1
Chester Way 112 A1
Chesterfield Gardens 9 A1
55 B2
120 B2
Chesterfield Grove 129 B2
Chesterfield Hill 9 A1/A2
Chesterfield Mews 55 B2
Chesterfield Street 9 A1
Chesterfield Way 124 A2
Chesterford Gardens 66 A2
Chesterton Close 138 B1
Chesterton Road 25 B1
28 A1/A2
Chestnut Alley 42 B2
Chestnut Close 64 A1
126 B2
Chestnut Court 42 B2
Chestnut Grove 147 B2
148 B1
Chettle Court 54 B2
Chetwode Road 151 A1
Chetwynd Road 58 B1/B2
Cheval Place 37 B1/B2
Cheval Street 102 A1
Cheverton Road 52 B2
Cheyne Court 45 B2
Cheyne Gardens 45 B2
Cheyne Mews 45 B2
Cheyne Row 45 B1
Cheyne Walk 44 B2
45 B1/B2
Chicheley Street 104 A1
Chichester Road 30 A2
Chichester Street 20 B2
21 B1
Chichester Way 103 A2
Chicksand Street 91 B1/B2
Chiddingstone Street 49 A1
Chigwell Hill 96 B1
Chilcot Close 99 B2
Child's Place 43 A1
Child's Street 35 B2
Childebert Road 148 B1
Childeric Road 126 A1
Childerley Street 47 B2
Childers Street 118 B1/B2
Chillington Drive 139 A1
Chillingworth Road 74 B1
Chiltern Road 99 A2
Chiltern Street 2 A1
Chilton Grove 117 A2
Chilton Street 91 A2
Chilworth Mews 31 B1
Chilworth Street 30 B2
31 B1
China Hall Mews 110 B2
Ching Court 13 B1
Chipka Street 103 A1
Chipley Street 118 B1
Chippenham Gardens 26 A2
Chippenham Mews 26 B2
Chippenham Road 26 A2/B1/B2
Chipstead Street 49 A2
Chisenhale Road 93 A2
94 A1
Chiswell Street 7 B2
Chiswick Common Road 38 A1/A2
Chiswick High Road 38 A1/A2
39 B1
Chiswick Lane 38 A2/B2
Chiswick Lane South 38 B2
Chiswick Mall 38 B2
39 B1
Chiswick Square 38 B2
Chiswick Wharf 38 B2
Chitty Street 3 A2/B2
Chivalry Road 140 B1
Cholmeley Crescent 51 B2
Cholmeley Park 51 B2
52 A1/B1
Choppins Court 96 B1
Choumert Grove 123 B2
Choumert Mews 123 B1
Choumert Road 123 B1/B2
Chow Square 86 A1
Chrisp Street 99 B2
Christchurch Avenue 65 A1
Christchurch Hill 56 B2
Christchurch Road 53 A1
Christchurch Square 89 B2
Christchurch Street 45 B2
46 B1
Christchurch Terrace 46 B1
Christchurch Way 103 B2
Christian Street 95 A2/B2
Christie Road 90 B2
Christina Square 63 A1
Christina Street 8 A2
Christopher Close 110 A2
Christopher Place 78 B1
Christopher Street 8 B1/B2
Chryssell Road 135 B2
Chubworthy Street 125 A2
Chudleigh Street 97 A2/B2
Chumleigh Street 114 B1
Church Avenue 71 B2
Church Crescent 90 B1
Church Gate 48 B1
Church Lane 54 A2
151 B1/B2
152 A2
Church Road 51 A2
81 A2
Church Row 56 B1
Church Street 31 A2
38 B2
76 B1
Church Terrace 143 A2
Church Walk 64 B1
Churchcroft Close 147 B2
Churchfields 120 A2
Churchill Gardens Road 20 B2
Churchill Place 101 B1
Churchill Road 58 B2
Churchill Walk 90 A1
Churchway 78 B1
Churchwell Path 89 A2
Churchyard Row 112 A2
Churton Place 20 A2
Churton Street 20 A2/B2
Chusan Place 100 A1
Cicada Road 139 B1
146 A1
Cicely Road 123 A2/B2
Cinnamon Close 123 A1
Cinnamon Row 139 A1
Cinnamon Street 96 B1
Circus Mews 1 A2
Circus Place 8 B1
Circus Road 68 B1/B2
Circus Street 120 A1/B2
Cirencester Street 30 A1
Citadel Place 131 B1
Citizen Road 74 A1
City Garden Row 83 B1
City Road 7 A2
8 A1/B1
80 B1
83 B1/B2
84 B1
Clabon Mews 37 B2
Clack Street 110 B1
Claire Place 102 A1
Clancarty Road 49 B1/B2
Clanricarde Gardens 29 B2
Clapham Common North Side
140 A2
141 B1/B2
142 B1/B2
Clapham Common South Side
143 B1
148 A2
149 A1
Clapham Common West Side
140 A2/B2
147 A2
148 A1
Clapham Crescent 143 B1
Clapham High Street 143 A2/B1/B2
Clapham Manor Street 143 A1/B1
Clapham Park Road 143 B1/B2
Clapham Road 135 A2/B1/B2
143 A2
144 A1
Clapton Common 86 A1

Clapton Square 87 B2
Clapton Way 86 A2
Clare Gardens 29 A1
Clare Lane 81
Clare Market 14 B1
Clare Mews 49 A2
Clare Road 126 B1
Clare Street 92 A2
Claredale Street 92 A1/A2
Claremont Close 6 A2
Claremont Grove 38 B1
Claremont Road 52 A1
Claremont Square 6 A1/A2
Claremont Street 120 A1
Clarence Avenue 149 A2/B2
Clarence Crescent 149 A2
Clarence Gardens 77 B1
Clarence Mews 87 B2
110 A1
148 A1
Clarence Place 87 B2
Clarence Road 87 A2/B2
119 A2
Clarence Terrace 76 B2
Clarence Walk 143 A2
Clarence Way 71 B1/B2
Clarendon Close 31 B2
90 B1
Clarendon Cross 28 B2
Clarendon Drive 136 A1
Clarendon Gardens 27 B2
Clarendon Grove 78 B1
Clarendon Mews 31 B2
Clarendon Place 31 B2
Clarendon Road 28 A2/B2
Clarendon Street 20 B1/B2
Clarendon Terrace 27 B2
Clareville Grove 44 A1
Clareville Street 44 A1
45 A1
Clarewood Walk 127 A1
Clarges Mews 9 A2
Clarges Street 9 A2/B2
Claribel Road 121 B1
Clarissa Street 88 A1
Clark Street 96 A2
97 A1
Clarke's Mews 2 A2
Clarkson Row 77 A2
Clarkson Street 92 A2
Claude Road 123 B2
Claude Street 102 B1
Clave Street 96 B1
Clavell Street 120 A1/A2
Clavering Avenue 47 A1
Claverton Street 20 B2
Claxton Grove 41 B2
Clay Street 1 A2
Claybrook Road 41 B2
Claylands Place 135 A2
Claylands Road 135 A1/A2
Clayton Crescent 79 B2
Clayton Drive 118 A1
Clayton Mews 120 B2
Clayton Road 123 A2/B2
Clayton Street 112 B1
135 A2
Clearbrook Way 97 A1
Clearwell Drive 27 B1

Cleaver Square 112 B1
Cleaver Street 112 A1
Clegg Street 96 B1
Clemence Street 98 B2
Clement Avenue 143 B2
Clements Lane 17 B2
Clements Road 108 A2/B2
Clennam Street 106 A1
Clenston Mews 1 A1
Clephane Road 75 B2
81 A2
Clere Street 8 A1
Clerkenwell Close 6 B1
Clerkenwell Green 6 B1
Clerkenwell Road 5 B2
6 B1/B2
Clermont Road 89 B2
Cleve Road 65 B1
Cleveland Avenue 39 A1
Cleveland Gardens 30 B2
55 B2
Cleveland Grove 97 A1
Cleveland Mews 3 A2
Cleveland Place 23 A2
Cleveland Road 82 B1
Cleveland Row 23 A1/B1
Cleveland Square 30 B2
Cleveland Street 3 A1/A2/B2
Cleveland Terrace 30 B2
31 A1
Cleveland Way 92 B2
97 A1/A2
Cleveleys Road 87 A2
Clifden Mews 90 A2
Clifden Road 90 A1/A2
Cliff Road 73 B1
Cliff Villas 73 B1
Clifford Drive 127 A1
Clifford Street 10 B1
Clifton Court 76 A1
Clifton Crescent 124 A1
Clifton Gardens 27 B1/B2
38 A1
Clifton Grove 86 B2
Clifton Hill 68 A1/A2
Clifton Place 31 B1
110 A1
Clifton Rise 126 A1
Clifton Road 27 B2
53 A1
81 A2
Clifton Street 8 A2/B2
Clifton Terrace 62 B1
Clifton Villas 27 B1
Clifton Way 124 A1/A2
Clinger Court 84 A1
Clink Street 106 A1
Clinton Road 93 B2
Clipper Close 110 A1
Clipstone Mews 3 A1
Clipstone Street 3 A1
Clissold Crescent 63 B2
64 B1
Clissold Road 64 A1/B1
Clitheroe Road 143 A2
144 A1
Cliveden Place 19 B2
Cloak Lane 16 B2
Clock Tower Mews 83 A2

Clockhouse Place 136 B2
Clonbrock Road 64 B2
Cloncurry Street 47 B2
48 B1
Clonmel Road 48 A2
Cloth Fair 7 B1
Cloth Street 7 B1
Clothier Street 18 A1
Cloudesdale Road 148 B1
151 A2
Cloudesley Place 80 B1
Cloudesley Road 80 B1
Cloudesley Square 80 B1
Cloudesley Street 80 B1
Clover Mews 46 B1
Club Row 91 A1
Clunbury Street 84 A1
Cluny Mews 35 B1
Cluny Place 107 B1
Cluse Court 83 A1
Clyde Street 118 B2
Clydesdale Road 29 A1
Clyston Street 133 B2
Coach & Horses Yard 10 B1
Coach House Lane 74 A2
Coach House Yard 138 A2
Coach Yard Mews 53 B2
Coate Street 92 A1/A2
Coates Avenue 146 A2
Cobb Street 18 A2
Cobbett Street 135 B1
Cobble Lane 80 A2
Cobble Mews 63 B1
Cobham Close 140 B1
Cobham Mews 72 B2
Coborn Road 94 B1
Coborn Street 94 B1
Cobourg Road 114 A2/B2
Cobourg Street 77 B2
Coburg Close 20 A2
Cochrane Mews 68 B2
Cochrane Street 68 B2
Cock Lane 15 B2
Cockpit Yard 5 B1
Cockspur Court 23 A2
Cockspur Street 23 A2
24 A1
Code Street 91 B2
Codling Close 95 B2
Codrington Mews 29 A1
Coin Street 104 A2
Coity Road 71 A2
Coke Street 95 A1
Colas Mews 65 B1
Colbeck Mews 43 A2
Colberg Place 86 A1
Colchester Street 95 A1
Cold Blow Lane 125 A1/A2
Cold Harbour 101 B2
Coldbath Square 5 B2
Coldharbour Lane 121 B2
127 A1/A2
128 A1
150 A2
Coldharbour Place 121 B2
Coldstream Gardens 137 B1
Cole Street 106 B1
Colebeck Mews 80 A2
Colebert Avenue 92 B2

Colebrooke Place 80 B2
Colebrooke Row 80 B1/B2
Coleford Road 138 A2
Colegrove Road 114 B2
Coleherne Mews 43 A2
Coleherne Road 43 A2
Colehill Gardens 48 B1
Colehill Lane 48 A1/B1
Coleman Fields 81
83 A2
Coleman Road 114 B1
122 A2
Coleman Street 7 B2
16 A2
Coleridge Close 142 A2
Coleridge Gardens 43 B2
66 B1
Coleridge Lane 53 A2
Coleridge Road 53 A1/A2
62 B1
Colestown Street 132 B2
Colet Gardens 41 A2
Coley Street 5 B2
Colina Road 55 A2
Collamore Avenue 146 B2
Collard Place 71 B1
College Approach 120 A2
College Close 87 B2
College Crescent 66 B2
College Cross 80 A2
College Grove 78 A2
College Hill 16 B2
College Mews 22 A2
138 B2
College Place 44 B1
78 A1
College Street 16 B2
College Terrace 94 B1
College Yard 72 A1
Collent Street 90 A1
Collett Road 108 A2
Collier Street 79 B1/B2
Collin's Yard 80 B2
Collingbourne Road 32 A1
Collingham Gardens 43 A2
Collingham Place 35 B2
Collingham Road 35 B2
43 A2
Collingwood Street 92 B1
Collins Road 63 B2
75 A2
Collinson Street 105 B2
Collison Place 64 A2
Colls Road 124 A2
Collyer Place 123 A1
Colmar Close 93 B1
Colmore Mews 124 A1
Colnbrook Street 105 B1
Cologne Road 139 A2
Colombo Street 104 A2
Colonnade 4 B2
Colthurst Crescent 63 B1
Coltman Street 98 A1
Columbia Road 91 A1/A2
Colvestone Crescent 86 B1/B2
Colville Gardens 29 A1
Colville Houses 29 A1
Colville Mews 29 A1/A2
Colville Road 29 A1/B1
Colville Square 29 A1
Colville Terrace 29 A1/A2
Colwell Road 129 B2
Colwick Close 53 B1
Colwith Road 47 A1
Colworth Grove 113 A1
Comber Grove 121 A2
Combermere Road 144 A2/B1/B2
Comeragh Mews 42 A1
Comeragh Road 42 A1
Comet Place 119 B1
Comet Street 119 B1
Comfort Street 114 B1
Commercial Road 95 A1/A2
96 A1/A2
97 A1/B1/B2
98 B1/B2
100 A1
Commercial Street 91 B1
Commercial Way 115 B1/B2
122 A2
123 A1/A2
Commodity Quay 95 B1
Commodore Street 98 A1
Common Mile Close 149 A2
Community Lane 73 A1
Compayne Gardens 65 B2
66 B1
Compton Avenue 80 A2
Compton Close 99 A2
123 A1
Compton Place 5 A1
Compton Road 75 B1
81 A1
Compton Street 6 B2
Compton Terrace 80 A2
Comus Place 113 A2
114 A1
Comyn Road 140 A1
Conant Mews 95 B2
Concanon Road 144 B1
Concert Hall Approach 104 A1
Concorde Way 116 A2
117 A1
Condell Road 133 B2
Conder Street 98 B1
Condray Place 132 A1
Conduit Mews 31 B1
Conduit Passage 31 B1
Conduit Place 31 B1
Conduit Street 10 A1
Conewood Street 63 B1
Congreve Street 114 A1
Coniger Road 49 A1
Coninghan Road 32 B1
Coningsby Road 55 B1
Conistone Way 79 A2
Conlan Street 25 A1
Connaught Close 31 B2
Connaught Place 1 B1
31 B2
Connaught Road 62 A1
Connaught Square 31 B2
Connaught Street 1 A1
31 B2
Connor Street 90 B1
Cons Street 104 A2
Consort Road 123 A2/B2
124 B1
130 A2
Constantine Road 57 A1/A2
Constitution Hill 9 B2
Content Street 113 A1
Convent Gardens 29 A1
Conway Mews 3 A2
Conway Street 3 A1/A2
Conybeare 69 A2
Conyer Street 93 A2
Cookham Crescent 110 A2
Cooks Road 112 B1/B2
Coolhurst Road 53 A1
Coomassie Road 25 A2
Coombe Road 38 A1/A2
Coombs Street 83 B1
Coomer Mews 42 B2
Coomer Place 42 B2
Coomer Road 42 B2
Cooper Close 104 B2
Cooper's Row 18 B2
Coopers Close 92 B2
97 A2
Coopers Lane 78 B2
Coopers Road 114 A2
115 A1
Coopersale Road 90 A2
Cope Place 35 B1
Cope Street 111 B1
Copeland Drive 102 B2
Copeland Road 123 B2
Copenhagen Place 98 B2
99 B1
Copenhagen Street 79 B1/B2
80 B1
Copleston Mews 129 A2
Copleston Road 129 A2
Copley Close 112 B2
Copley Street 97 A2
Copperas Street 119 A2
Copperfield Road 98 A2
Copperfield Street 105 A2
Coppock Close 132 B1/B2
Copthall Avenue 8 B1
17 A1
Copthorne Avenue 149 B2
Coptic Street 4 B1
Coral Row 139 A1
Coral Street 104 B2
Coram Street 4 A2
Corbden Close 123 A1
Corbet Court 17 A2
Corbet Place 91 B1
Corbetts Lane 109 B2
Corbetts Passage 116 A2
Corbridge Crescent 92 A2
Corby Way 99 A2
Corbyn Street 53 B2
61 A1
Cordelia Close 127 A2
Cordelia Street 99 B2
Cording Street 99 B2
Corfield Street 92 B2
Corinne Road 59 B2
72 A2
73 A1
Cork Square 95 B2

Cork Street 10 B1
Cork Street Mews 10 B1
Corlett Street 76 B1
Cormont Road 121 A1/B1
Cornelia Street 80 A1
Corner House Street 24 A1
Corney Reach Way 38 B1
Corney Road 38 B1
Cornford Grove 148 B2
Cornhill 17 A1/A2
Cornwall Avenue 92 B2
Cornwall Crescent 28 A2
Cornwall Gardens 35 B2
36 B1
Cornwall Gardens Walk 35 B2
Cornwall Grove 38 B2
Cornwall Mews South 36 B1
Cornwall Mews West 35 B2
Cornwall Road 62 A1
104 A2
Cornwall Street 96 B2
Cornwall Terrace 2 A1
Cornwall Terrace Mews 2 A1
Cornwallis Road 60 A2/B2
61 A1/B1
Cornwallis Square 60 B2
Cornwood Drive 97 A1
Coronation Avenue 64 B2
Coronet Street 84
Corporation Row 6 B1/B2
Corporation Street 73 B2
Corrance Road 144 B1
Corry Drive 127 A1/B1
Corsham Street 84 B1
Corsica Street 75 B1
Cortayne Road 49 B1
Corunna Road 133 A2
Corunna Terrace 133 B2
Cosbycote Avenue 128 B1
Cosmo Place 4 B2
Cossall Walk 124 A1
Cosser Street 104 B2
131 A2
Costa Street 123 B2
Cosway Street 76 B1
Cotall Street 99 B1
Coteford Street 151 B1/B2
Cotham Street 113 A1
Cotleigh Road 65 B1
Cotswold Mews 132 A1
Cottage Green 122 A1
Cottage Grove 143 A2/B2
Cottage Place 37 B1
Cottage Road 74 B1
Cottage Street 101 A1
Cottesbrook Street 125 A2
Cottesloe Mews 104 B2
Cottesmore Gardens 35 B2
Cottingham Road 135 A1
Cottington Street 112 A1
Cotton Row 139 A1
Cotton Street 101 A2
Cottons Gardens 91 A1
Cottons Lane 106 A2
Cottrill Gardens 87 B1
Coulson Street 46 A1
Coulter Road 40 A2
Councillor Street 121 A2
Counter Street 106 A2
Countess Road 72 A2
County Grove 121 A2
County Street 106 B1
Courland Grove 134 B1
Courland Street 134 B1
Court Gardens 74 B2
80 A1
Court Street 96 A2
Courtauld Road 53 B1
Courtenay Square 131 B2
Courtenay Street 131 B2
Courtfield Gardens 35 B2
43 A2
Courtfield Mews 36 B1
Courtfield Road 36 B1
Courthope Road 57 B2
Courtnell Street 29 A2
Courtney Road 74 B2
Courtside 53 A1
The Courtyard 80 A1
Cousin Lane 17 B1
Coventry Close 68 A1
Coventry Road 92 B2
Coventry Street 11 B1/B2
Coverdale Road 32 B2
Coverley Close 91 B2
Coverton Road 152 A1
Cowcross Street 15 A2
Cowick Road 151 B1/B2
Cowley Road 135 B2
Cowley Street 22 B2
Cowling Close 28 B1
Cowper Road 64 B2
Cowper Street 8 A1
Cowthorpe Road 134 B1
Coxson Way 107 A2
Crabtree Close 88 B1
Crabtree Lane 47 A1
Craddock Street 71 A1
Craigs Court 24 B1
Crail Row 113 A2
Cramer Street 2 A1
Crammond Close 47 A2
Crampton Street 112 A2
Cranbourn Street 12 B2
Cranbrook Road 38 A2
Cranbrook Street 93 A1
Cranbury Road 50 B1
Crane Grove 74 B2
Crane Street 123 A1
Cranford Street 97 B2
Cranford Way 54 A2
Cranleigh Mews 132 B2
Cranleigh Street 78 B1
Cranley Gardens 44 A1/A2
Cranley Mews 44 A1
Cranley Place 45 A1
Cranmer Court 143 A2
Cranmer Road 121 A1
135 A2
Cranswick Road 116 B1
Cranwell Close 99 A2
Cranwood Street 84 B1
Cranworth Gardens 135 B2
Craven Hill 30 B2
Craven Hill Gardens 30 B1/B2
Craven Hill Mews 30 B2
Craven Mews 141 B2
Craven Park Road 86 A1
Craven Road 30 B2
31 B1
Craven Street 24 A1/B1/B2
Craven Terrace 30 B2
Crawford Mews 1 A2
Crawford Passage 6 B1
Crawford Place 1 A1
Crawford Road 121 B2
Crawford Street 1 A1/A2
Crawthew Grove 129 A2
130 A1/B1
Crayford Road 73 A2
Crediton Hill 66 A1
Credon Road 116 B1
Creechurch Lane 18 A1
Creechurch Place 18 A1
Creed Lane 15 B2
Creek Road 119 A1/A2
120 A1/A2
Creekside 119 A2/B2
Crefeld Close 47 A2
Cremer Street 91 A1/A2
Cremorne Road 44 B1/B2
Crescent 18 B2
Crescent Grove 143 B1
Crescent Lane 143 B1
149 A2
Crescent Place 37 B1
Crescent Road 53 A1/B1
Crescent Row 7 A1/B1
Crescent Stables 136 B1
Crescent Street 79 A2
Cresford Road 49 A2
50 A1
Cresset Road 90 A1
Cresset Street 143 B1
Cressfield Close 57 B2
Cressida Road 52 B2
Cressington Close 64 B2
Cresswell Gardens 44 A1
Cresswell Place 44 A1
Cressy Court 40 A1
97 A2
Cressy Place 97 A2
Cressy Road 57 A1/B1
Crestfield Street 5 A1
Crewdson Road 135 B2
Crews Street 102 B1
Crewys Road 124 B1
Crichton Street 142 A2
Cricketfield Road 87 A2/B1
Crieff Road 146 A1
Crimscott Street 107 B2
Crimsworth Road 134 B1
Crinan Street 79 B1
Cringle Street 133 A2
Cripplegate Street 7 B2
Crisp Road 41 B1
Crispin Street 18 A2
Cristowe Road 48 B2
Criterion Mews 60 A1
Crockerton Road 151 A1
Croft Street 117 A2
Croftdown Road 58 B1/B2
59 A1
Crofters Way 78 A2
Crofton Road 122 B2
Crofts Street 95 B1
Crogsland Road 71 A1

Street Index

Cromartie Road 53 B1
Cromer Road 152 B2
Cromer Street 5 A1
Cromford Road 137 A2
Crompton Street 31 A2
Cromwell Avenue 40 B2
51 B2
52 B1
Cromwell Crescent 35 B1
Cromwell Gardens 36 B2
37 B1
Cromwell Grove 33 B1
Cromwell Mews 36 B2
Cromwell Place 36 B2
52 B1
Cromwell Road 35 B1/B2
36 B1/B2
121 A1
Crondace Road 49 A1/A2
Crondall Street 84 /A2/B1
Cronin Street 123 A1
Crooke Road 117 B2
Crookham Road 48 A2
Crooms Hill 120 A2/B2
Crooms Hill Grove 120 A2
Cropley Street 83 A2
84 A1
Crosby Court 106 A2
Crosby Row 106 A2
Crosby Walk 86 B1
Crosland Place 141 B2
Cross Close 124 B1
Cross Keys Close 2 B1
Cross Road 122 B2
Cross Street 80 B2
81 B1
Crossfield Road 67 B1
Crossfield Street 119 B2
Crossford Street 144 A1/A2
Crosslet Street 113 A2
Crosslet Vale 120 B1
Crossley Street 74 B1
Crossthwaite Avenue 128 A2/B2
Crosswall 18 B2
Crossway 64 B2
82 A2
Croston Street 89 B1
Crouch End Hill 53 A1/A2/B1
Crouch Hall Road 53 A1/A2
Crouch Hill 53 A2/B2
Crowborough Road 152 A2
Crowder Street 96 A1
Crowhurst Close 145 A2
Crowland Terrace 82 B1
Crown Close 66 A1
Crown Mews 39 B2
Crown Office Row 14 B2
Crown Place 72 A1
Crown Street 121 A2
Crown Works 92 A2
Crowndale Road 78 A1
Crownstone Road 150 A2
Crowther Close 42 B2
Crowthorne Road 28 A1
Croxley Road 26 A1
Crozier Terrace 90 A2
Crucifix Lane 107 A1
Cruden Street 83 A1
Cruikshank Street 6 A1
Crusoe Mews 64 A1
Crutched Friars 18 B2
Crystal Palace Road 130 A1/B1
Cuba Street 100 B1/B2
Cubitt Street 5 A2/B2
6 A1
Cubitt Terrace 142 A2
143 A1
Cubitts Yard 13 B1
Cudworth Street 92 B1/B2
Culford Gardens 46 A2
Culford Grove 82 A2
Culford Mews 82 A1
Culford Road 82 A2/B2
Culling Road 109 A2
Culloden Close 115 A2
Cullum Street 18 B1
Culmore Road 124 A1/A2
Culmstock Road 140 B2
Culross Street 1 B2
Culvert Place 141 A1
Culvert Road 141 A1
Culworth Street 69 B1
Cumberland Close 86 B1
Cumberland Crescent 34 B1
Cumberland Gardens 6 A1
Cumberland Gate 1 B1/B2
31 B2
Cumberland Market 77 B1
Cumberland Mills Square 103 B2
Cumberland Place 77 B1
Cumberland Street 20 B1/B2
Cumberland Terrace 77 B1
Cumberland Terrace Mews 77 A1/B1
Cumming Street 79 B2
Cundy Street 19 B2
Cunningham Place 76 A1
Cupar Road 141 A2
Cureton Street 21 A2
Curlew Street 107 A2
Cursitor Street 14 B2
Curtain Road 8 A2
84
Curtis Street 107 B2
Curtis Way 107 B2
Curzon Gate 9 A1
Curzon Street 9 A1/A2
The Cut 104 A2
105 A1
Cutcombe Road 121 B2
Cuthbert Street 31 A2
Cutler Street 18 A1
Cutlers Square 102 B1
Cutlers Terrace 82 A2
Cyclops Mews 102 B1
Cygnet Street 91 A1
Cygnet Street Street Market 91 A1
Cynthia Street 79 B2
Cyntra Place 89 A2
Cypress Place 3 A2
Cyprus Close 55 B1
Cyprus Place 93 A1
Cyprus Street 92 A2
93 A1
Cyrena Road 130 B1
Cyril Mansions 141 A1
Cyrus Street 6 B2
Czar Street 119 A1

D

D'Arblay Street 10 A2
11 A1
D'Eynsford Road 122 A1
D'Oyley Street 19 B2
Dabin Crescent 120 B1/B2
Dacca Street 118 B2
Dacre Street 22 A1
Dafforne Road 151 A1
Dagmar Road 62 A1/A2
122 B1/B2
Dagmar Terrace 80 B2
Dagnall Street 141 A1/A2
Dagnan Road 148 A2
Dairy Farm Place 124 A2
Dairy Mews 144 B1
Daisy Lane 49 B1/B2
Dakin Place 98 A1
Dalberg Road 127 B1
Dalby Road 138 A2
Dalby Street 71 A2
Dale Road 57 B2
112 B2
Dale Row 28 A2
Dale Street 38 A1
Dalebury Road 151 A1
Daleham Gardens 66 B2
67 A1
Daleham Mews 67 B1
Daley Street 90 A2
Daley Thompson Way 142 A1
Dalgleish Street 98 B1
Daling Way 94 A1
Dalling Road 40 —
Dallington Street 6 B2
Dalmeny Avenue 73 A1
Dalmeny Road 59 B2
60 B1
73 A1
Dalston Lane 86 B1/B2
87 B1
Dalwood Street 122 A2
Dalyell Road 144 A2/B2
Dame Street 83 A1
Damer Terrace 44 B1
Damien Street 96 A2
Dan Leno Walk 43 B2
Danbury Street 83 B1
Danby Street 129 A2
Dancer Road 48 A2
Dane Place 94 A1
Dane Street 14 A1
Danecroft Road 128 B1
Danehurst Street 48 A1
Daneville Road 121 B2
122 B1
Daniel Close 152 B1
Daniel Gardens 114 B2
Dansey Place 11 B2
Dante Place 112 A2
Dante Road 112 A2
Danube Street 45 A2/B2
Danvers Road 53 A1
Danvers Street 44 B2
Daphne Street 146 A1
Daplyn Street 91 B2
Darenth Road 86 A1
Darfield Way 28 A1

Darien Road 139 A2
Darlan Road 48 A2
Darley Road 140 B1
Darling Row 92 B1
Darnley Road 89 A2
90 A1
Darnley Terrace 28 B1
Darrell Road 130 B1
Darren Close 54 B1
Darsley Drive 134 B1
Dartford Street 113 B1
Dartmouth Close 29 A2
Dartmouth Hill 120 B2
Dartmouth Park Avenue 59 A1
Dartmouth Park Hill 51 B2
59 A1/A2/B1
Dartmouth Park Road 58 B1/B2
59 B1
Dartmouth Place 38 B1
Dartmouth Row 120 B2
Dartmouth Street 22 A2
Dartmouth Terrace 120 B2
Darville Road 86 B1
Darwen Place 92 A2
Darwin Street 113 A2
Dashwood Road 54 B1
Datchelor Place 122 B1
Date Street 113 B2
Dault Road 146 A1
Davenant Road 60 B2
Davenant Street 91 B2
Daventry Street 76 B1
Davey Close 74 B1
Davey Street 114 B2
David Mews 2 A1
Davidge Street 105 B1
Davidson Gardens 134 A2
Davies Mews 2 B1
Davies Street 2 B1
9 A2
Dawes Road 42 B1/B2
43 B1
Dawes Street 113 A2/B2
Dawson Place 29 B2
Dawson Street 88 B2
Dayton Grove 124 A2
De Barowe Mews 75 A1
De Beauvoir Crescent 82 B2
De Beauvoir Road 82 A2/B2
De Beauvoir Square 82 B2
De Crespigny Park 121 B2
122 B1
De Laune Street 112 B1
De Morgan Road 50 B1
De Vere Gardens 36 A1
De Vere Mews 36 A1
De Walden Street 2 A1
Deacon Mews 82 B1
Deacon Way 113 A1
Deal Porters Way 110 B1
Deal Road 152 B2
Deal Street 91 B2
Deals Gateway 119 B2
Dean Bradley Street 22 B2
Dean Close 90 A1
110 A2
Dean Farrar Street 22 A2
Dean Ryle Street 21 A2
Dean Stanley Street 22 B2
Dean Street 3 B2
11 A2/B2
Dean Trench Street 22 B2
Dean's Yard 22 A2
Deancross Street 96 A2
Deanery Mews 9 A1
Deanery Street 9 A1
Deans Buildings 113 A2
Deans Court 15 B2
Deans Mews 2 B2
Debnams Road 109 B2
Decima Street 107 B1
Deck Close 110 A2
Deeley Road 133 B2
134 B1
Deepdene Road 128 A2
Deerdale Road 128 A1
Defoe Close 111 B2
152 B1
Defoe Place 151 B1
Defoe Road 64 A2
Delaford Road 116 B1
Delaford Street 42 B1
Delamere Terrace 30 A2
Delancey Street 77 A1/A2
78 A1
Delaware Road 27 A1
Delawyk Crescent 128 B1
Delhi Street 79 B1
Dell's Mews 20 A2
Della Path 87 A1
Dellow Street 96 B2
Delmare Close 144 B2
Delorme Street 47 A2
Delta Street 91 A2
Delverton Road 112 B2
Delvino Road 49 A1
Dempster Road 139 B1
Denbigh Close 29 B1
Denbigh Mews 20 A2
Denbigh Place 20 B2
Denbigh Road 29 B1
Denbigh Street 20 A2/B2
Denbigh Terrace 29 B1
Denewood Road 51 A1
Denholme Road 26 A1
Denis Way 143 A2
Denman Place 10 B2
Denman Road 123 A1
Denman Street 10 B2
Denmark Grove 80 B1
Denmark Hill 121 B2
128 A2
Denmark Place 94 B2
Denmark Road 121 A1/B2
Denmark Street 12 A2
Denne Terrace 88 B1/B2
Denning Close 68 B1
Denning Road 56 B2
Dennington Park Road 65 A2
Denny Crescent 112 A1
Denny Street 112 A1
Denton Road 54 A2
Denton Street 138 B2
Dents Road 147 A1
Denyer Street 46 A1
Deodar Road 136 A2
137 A1
Deptford Bridge 119 B2
Deptford Broadway 119 B2
Deptford Church Street 119 A1/B2
Deptford Ferry Road 102 B2
Deptford Green 119 A1
Deptford High Street 119 A1/B1/B2
Deptford High Street Street Market 119 B1/B2
Deptford Strand 118 A2
Deptford Wharf 118 A2
Derby Gate 24 B1
Derby Road 90 B1
Derby Street 9 A1
Derbyshire Street 91 A2
92 B1
Dereham Place 84
Derek Walcott Close 127 B2
Dericote Street 89 B1
Dering Street 2 B2
Derinton Road 151 B1/B2
Derry Street 35 A2
Derwent Grove 129 A2
Desborough Close 30 A2
Desborough Street 30 A1
Desmond Street 118 B1
126 A1
Despard Road 60 A1
Deverell Street 106 B2
Devereux Road 140 B2
Devizes Street 84 A1
Devon Gardens 55 B2
Devon Street 116 B1
Devonia Road 83 B1
Devonport Mews 32 B1
Devonport Road 32 B1
Devonport Street 97 B1
Devons Road 99 A2
Devonshire Close 2 A2
Devonshire Drive 120 B1
Devonshire Grove 116 B1
Devonshire Mews 38 A1
Devonshire Mews North 2 A2
Devonshire Mews South 2 A2
Devonshire Mews West 2 A2
Devonshire Place 2 A2
35 B2
Devonshire Place Mews 2 A2
Devonshire Road 38 A1/B1
152 B1
Devonshire Row 8 B2
Devonshire Row Mews 3 A1
Devonshire Square 18 A1
Devonshire Street 2 A1/A2
3 A1
38 B1
Devonshire Terrace 30 B2
Dewar Street 130 A1
Dewey Road 80 B1
Dewey Street 152 A2
Dewhurst Road 33 B1/B2
Dewsbury Terrace 71 B1
Diamond Street 122 A2
Diamond Terrace 120 B2
Diana Close 118 B2
Dibden Street 81 B1
Dickens Square 106 B1
Dickens Street 142 A1/A2
Dickenson Road 53 B2
Dieppe Close 42 A2
Digby Crescent 63 B1

Street Index

Digby Road 90 A2
Digby Street 92 B2
93 B1
Diggon Street 97 A2
Dighton Court 112 B2
113 B1
Dighton Road 138 A2
139 B1
Dignum Street 80 B1
Digswell Street 74 B2
Dilke Street 46 B1
Dimes Place 40 B2
Dimson Crescent 99 A2
Dingle Gardens 100 A2
Dingley Place 7 A2
Dingley Road 7 A1/A2
Dingwall Road 146 B1
Dinmont Street 92 A2
Dinsmore Road 148 A2
Disbrowe Road 42 B1
Disney Mews 55 B2
Disney Place 106 A1
Disney Street 106 A1
Disraeli Road 136 B1/B2
Diss Street 91 A2
Distaff Lane 15 B2
Distillery Lane 41 B1
Distillery Road 41 B1
Distin Street 131 B2
Ditchburn Street 101 A2
Dixon Road 126 A1
Dobson Close 66 B1
Dock Hill Avenue 110 A2
Dock Street 95 B1
Dockers Tanner Road 102 B1
Dockhead 108 A1
Dockley Road 108 A1
Docwra's Buildings 82 A1
Dod Street 99 B1
Doddington Grove 112 B2
Doddington Place 112 B2
Dodson Street 104 B2
Dog Kennel Hill 129 A1/A2
Dolben Street 105 A1
Dolby Road 48 B2
Dolland Street 131 B2
Dolman Road 38 A1
Dolman Street 144 B1
Dolphin Close 110 A1
Dolphin Lane 100 A2
Dombey Street 5 B1
Domett Close 128 A2
Domingo Street 7 A1/B2
Dominion Street 8 B1
Don Phelan Close 122 A1
Donato Drive 114 B1
Doncaster Gardens 55 B2
Donegal Street 79 B2
Doneraile Street 47 B2
48 B1
Dongola Road 98 A1
Donne Place 37 B1
Doon Street 104 A1
Dora Street 98 B2
Dora Way 145 A2
Dorchester Court 128 B1
Dorchester Drive 128 B1
Dorchester Grove 38 B2
Doria Road 49 A1
Doric Way 78 B1
Dorking Close 118 B2
Dorlcote Road 146 A2
Dorman Way 66 B1
Dormay Street 138 B1
Dorncliffe Road 48 B1
Dorothy Road 140 A1
Dorrell Place 144 B2
Dorrington Street 14 A2
Dorrit Street 106 A1
Dorset Buildings 15 B1
Dorset Close 76 B2
Dorset Rise 15 B1
Dorset Road 134 A2
135 A1/B1
Dorset Square 76 B2
Dorset Street 1 A2
2 A1
Dorton Close 122 A2
Dorville Crescent 40 A1
Doughty Mews 5 B1
Doughty Street 5 B2
Douglas Road 81 A1
Douglas Street 21 A1
Douglas Way 119 B1
126 A2
Douglas Way Street Market 119 B1/B2
Doulton Mews 66 A1
Douro Place 35 B2
Douthwaite Square 95 B2
Dove Court 16 A2
Dove Mews 44 A1
Dove Road 82 A1
Dove Row 88 B2
92 A1
Dove Walk 19 B2
Dovehouse Street 45 A1/B1
Dover Street 9 A2
Dover Yard 9 A2
Dovercourt Road 129 B2
Doverfield Road 150 B1
Doves Yard 80 B1
Doveton Street 92 B2
Dowdney Close 72 B2
Dowgate Hill 17 B1
Dowlas Street 122 A1/A2
Down Place 40 B2
Down Street 9 A1/B1
Down Street Mews 9 B1
Downers Cottages 142 B2
Downfield Close 26 B2
Downham Road 82 B1/B2
Downhills Park Road 55 A2
Downing Street 24 B1
Downs Park Road 86 A2/B2
87 B1
Downs Road 86 A2
87 A1/A2
Downsbury Mews 138 B1
Downshire Hill 56 B2
Downside Crescent 57 B1
Downtown Road 111 A2
Dowrey Street 80 B1
Dowson Close 128 A2
Doyce Street 105 A2
Doynton Street 59 A1
Draco Street 113 B1
Dragon Road 114 B1
Dragoon Road 118 A2/B1
Drake Close 110 A2
Drake Street 5 B1
14 A1
Drakefield Road 151 A1
Drakeley Court 74 A2
Drakes Courtyard 65 A1
Drappers Way 108 B2
Dray Gardens 150 A2
Draycott Avenue 37 B1
46 A1
Draycott Close 122 A1
Draycott Mews 48 B2
Draycott Place 46 A1/A2
Draycott Terrace 46 A2
Drayford Close 26 A1
Draymans Mews 122 B2
Drayson Mews 35 A1
Drayton Gardens 44 A1
Drayton Park 74 A2/B2
Drayton Park Mews 74 B2
Dresden Close 66 A1
Dresden Road 52 B2
Driffield Road 94 A1
The Drive 48 B1
Droop Street 25 A2
Drovers Place 124 A1
Druid Street 107 A1/A2
Drum Street 95 A1
Drummond Crescent 78 B1
Drummond Gate 21 B2
Drummond Road 108 A2
Drummond Street 77 B1/B2
Drury Lane 13 A1/A2/B2
14 B1
Dryden Street 13 B2
Drylands Road 54 A1
Drysdale Place 84
Drysdale Street 84
Dublin Avenue 89 B1
Ducal Street 91 A2
Duchess Mews 2 B2
Duchess of Bedford's Walk 34 A2
35 A1
Duchess Street 2 B2
3 B1
Duchy Street 104 A2
Ducie Street 144 B1
Duck Lane 11 A1
Duckett Mews 55 B2
Duckett Road 55 B2
Duckett Street 98 A1
Dudley Street 31 A1
Dudmaston Mews 45 A1
Dudrich Mews 129 B2
Duff Street 99 B2
100 A2
Dufferin Avenue 7 B2
Dufferin Street 7 B2
Dufour's Place 10 A2
Dugard Way 112 A1/A2
Duke of Wellington Place 9 B1
Duke of York Square 46 A2
Duke of York Street 23 A2
Duke Road 38 A1/B1
Duke Shore Place 100 A1
Duke Street 2 B1
10 B1
23 A1

Duke Street Hill 106 A2
Duke's Mews 2 B1
Duke's Road 4 A2
Duke's Yard 2 B1
Dukes Avenue 38 A1
Dukes Lane 35 A2
Dukes Place 18 A1/A2
Dulas Street 62 B1
Dulford Street 28 A1
Dulka Road 140 B2
Dulwich Lawn Close 129 B2
Dulwich Road 127 B1/B2
Dulwich Village 129 B1
Dumbarton Road 150 B1
Dumont Road 64 A2
Dumpton Place 70
Dunboyne Road 57 B1
Dunbridge Street 91 B2
92 B1
Duncan Road 89 B1
Duncan Street 80 B1/B2
Duncan Terrace 80 B1/B2
Duncannon Street 24 A1
Dunch Street 96 A2
Duncombe Road 52 B2
Dundas Road 124 B2
Dundee Street 96 B1
Dunelm Street 97 A2
Dunford Road 74 A1
Dunloe Street 88 B1/B2
Dunlop Place 108 A1
Dunn Street 86 A1
Dunnage Crescent 118 A1
Dunollie Place 72 A2
Dunollie Road 72 A2
Dunraven Street 1 B2
Dunsany Road 33 B2
41 A1
Dunsmure Road 86 A1
Dunstable Mews 2 A2
Dunster Court 18 B1
Dunsterville Way 106 A2
Dunston Road 88 A1/B1
141 A2/B2
Dunston Street 88 A1
Dunton Road 108 B1
114 A1
Dunworth Mews 29 A1
Duplex Ride 19 A1
Durand Gardens 135 B1/B2
Durant Street 91 A2
Durfey Place 122 A1
Durham House Street 24 A2
Durham Place 46 B1
Durham Road 61 A2
62 B1
Durham Row 98 A1
Durham Street 131 B1
Durham Terrace 30 A1
Durham Yard 92 A1
Durlston Road 87 A2
Durnford Street 120 A2
Durrell Road 48 B1
Durward Street 91 B2
Durweston Mews 1 A2
Durweston Street 1 A2
Dutch Yard 138 B1
Dutton Street 120 B2
Dwight Court 48 B1
Dylan Road 127 A2
Dylways 128 A2
129 B1
Dymock Street 49 B2
Dyne Road 65 A1
Dynevor Road 64 A2/B2
Dynham Road 65 B1
Dyott Street 4 B1
12 A2
Dysart Street 8 B2

E

Eade Road 55 B2
Eagle Close 116 B1
Eagle Court 15 A2
Eagle House Mews 148 A2
Eagle Mews 82 A2
Eagle Place 44 A1
Eagle Street 14 A1
Eagle Wharf Road 83 A2
84 A1
Eagling Close 99 A2
Eamont Street 69 B1
Eardley Crescent 43 A1
Earl Street 8 B2
Earlham Street 12 A2
13 B1
Earls Court Gardens 35 B2
43 A1
Earls Court Road 35 B1/B2
43 A1/A2
Earls Court Square 43 A1/A2
Earls Terrace 34 B2
Earls Walk 35 B1
Earlsferry Way 79 A2
Earlsfield Road 146 A1/B1
Earlsthorpe Mews 147 A2
Earlstoke Street 6 B2
Earlston Grove 89 B2
Early Mews 71 B1
Earnshaw Street 4 B1
12 A2
Earsby Street 34 B1
Easley's Mews 2 B1
East Arbour Street 97 A2
East Dulwich Grove 129 A2/B1
East Dulwich Road 129 A2
130 A1/A2
East Ferry Road 101 B2
103 A1/B1
East Gardens 152 B1
East Harding Street 15 B1
East Heath Road 56 A2/B2
57 A1
East Hill 138 B2
139 B1
East India Dock Road 100 A1/A2
101 A1/A2
East Lane 108 A1
East Mount Street 96 A2
East Parkside 103 A2
East Pier 96 B1
East Poultry Avenue 15 A2
East Road 46 B2
84 B1
East Row 25 A1
East Smithfield 95 B1/B2
East Street 113 A2/B1/B2
114 A1
East Surrey Grove 123 A1
East Tenter Street 95 A1
Eastbourne Mews 31 A1
Eastbourne Road 152 B2
Eastbourne Terrace 31 A1/B1
Eastbury Grove 38 B2
Eastbury Terrace 97 A2
Eastcastle Street 3 B1/B2
Eastcheap 17 B2
18 B1
Eastcote Street 144 A2
Eastfield Street 98 A2
Eastfields Avenue 137 A2
Eastlake Road 121 B1
Easton Street 6 B1
Eastwood Close 74 B1
Eaton Close 19 B2
Eaton Drive 127 A1/B1
Eaton Gate 19 B2
Eaton Lane 20 A1
Eaton Mews North 19 A2
Eaton Mews South 19 A2
Eaton Mews West 19 B2
Eaton Place 19 A2/B2
Eaton Row 19 A2
Eaton Square 19 A2/B2
Eaton Terrace 19 B2
Eaton Terrace Mews 19 B2
Eatonville Road 151 A1
Eatonville Villas 151 A1
Ebbisham Drive 135 A1
Ebenezer Street 83 B2
84 B1
Ebley Close 114 B2
Ebner Street 138 A2
Ebor Street 91 A1
Eburne Road 61 B1
Ebury Bridge 20 B1
Ebury Bridge Road 20 B1
Ebury Mews 19 A2
Ebury Mews East 19 A2
Ebury Square 19 B2
Ebury Street 19 A2/B2
Eccles Road 140 A1/A2
Ecclesbourne Road 81
Eccleston Bridge 20 A1/A2
Eccleston Mews 19 A2
Eccleston Place 19 A2
Eccleston Square 20 B1/B2
Eccleston Square Mews 20 A2/B2
Eccleston Street 19 A2
Eckford Street 79 B2
Eckstein Road 140 A1
Edbrooke Road 26 B2
Eddiscombe Road 49 A1
Eden Close 35 B1
Eden Grove 74 B1
Edenbridge Close 115 A2
Edenbridge Road 90 B2
Edenham Way 25 B2
Edenhurst Avenue 48 B2
Edensor Gardens 38 B1
Edensor Road 38 B1
Edenvale Street 50 B2
Edgar Kail Way 129 A1
Edgarley Terrace 48 A1/B1
Edge Street 29 B2

Street Index

Edgel Street 138 A2
Edgeley Lane 143 B2
Edgeley Road 143 A1/B2
Edgware Road 1 A1/B1
76 A1/B1
Edinburgh Close 92 A2
Edinburgh Gate 37 A2
Edis Street 70
Edison Road 53 A1
Edith Grove 44 B1
Edith Road 34 B1
Edith Row 49 A2
Edith Terrace 44 B1
Edith Villas 34 B2
Edith Yard 44 B1
Edithna Street 144 A1
Edmund Street 122 A1
Edna Street 132 A1
Edric Road 125 A1
Edward Mews 77 B1
Edward Place 118 B2
Edward Square 111 A2
Edward Street 118 B2
119 A1
126 A1
Edwardes Square 34 B2
35 B1
Edwards Cottages 80 A2
Edwards Lane 64 A1
Edwards Mews 1 B2
80 A2
Edwin Street 92 B2
Eel Brook Close 49 A2
Eel Brook Studios 49 A2
Effie Place 43 B1
Effie Road 43 B1
Effingham Road 55 A1
Effra Parade 127 B1
Effra Road 150 A2
Egbert Street 70
Egerton Crescent 37 B1
Egerton Drive 120 B1
Egerton Gardens 37 B1
Egerton Gardens Mews 37 B1
Egerton Place 37 B1
Egerton Road 86 A1
Egerton Terrace 37 B1/B2
Eglantine Road 138 B2
139 B1
Eglington Court 112 B2
Eglon Mews 70 A1
Egmont Street 125 B2
Elaine Grove 57 B2
Elam Close 121 B1
Elam Street 121 B1
Eland Road 141 B1
Elba Place 113 A1
Elbe Street 50 A1
Elcho Street 132 A1
Elcot Avenue 115 B2
Elder Avenue 53 A2
Elder Street 91 B1
Elder Walk 81 B1
Elderfield Place 151 B2
Elderfield Road 90 A2
Eldon Grove 67 A2
Eldon Road 35 B2
Eldon Street 8 B2
Eleanor Close 110 A2
Eleanor Road 89 A1
Eleanor Street 99 A2
Electric Avenue 144 B2
Electric Avenue Street Market 144 B2
Electric Lane 144 B2
150 A2
Elephant & Castle 105 B2
112 A2
Elephant Lane 109 A2
Elephant Road 112 A2
Elf Row 97 B1
Elfindale Road 128 B1
Elfort Road 74 A2
Elgar Close 119 B1
Elgar Street 111 B2
Elgin Avenue 25 A2
26 B1/B2
27 A1/A2
40 A1
Elgin Crescent 28 A2/B2
29 A1
Elgin Mews 29 A1
Elgin Mews North 27 A2
Elgin Mews South 27 A2
Elgood Close 28 B1
Elia Mews 80 B2
Elia Street 80 B2
83 B1
Elias Place 135 A2
Eliot Mews 68 B1
Elizabeth Avenue 81
82 B1
Elizabeth Bridge 20 A1
Elizabeth Close 27 B2
99 B2
Elizabeth Court 22 B2
Elizabeth Fry Road 89 B2
Elizabeth Mews 67 B2
Elizabeth Square 110 A2
Elizabeth Street 19 A2/B2
20 A1
Elkstone Road 25 B2
Ella Mews 57 A1
Ella Road 53 B2
Ellaline Road 47 A1
Ellen Street 95 A2
Ellerby Street 47 B2
Ellerdale Close 67 A1
Ellerdale Road 56 B1
67 A1
Ellerslie Road 32 A1/A2
Ellerton Road 146 B1/B2
Ellery Street 124 B1
Ellesmere Road 38 B1
94 A1
Ellesmere Street 99 B2
Ellingfort Road 89 A2
Ellington Street 74 B1/B2
Elliott Road 38 A1
121 A1
Elliott Square 69 A2
Elliott's Place 80 B2
Elliotts Row 105 B1
112 A2
Ellis Street 19 B1
Ellsworth Street 92 A2
Elm Close 59 A2
Elm Court 14 B2
Elm Grove 53 B2
123 B1
Elm Park 150 B2
Elm Park Gardens 44 A2/B2
45 A1/B1
Elm Park Lane 44 B2
Elm Park Mansions 44 B1/B2
Elm Park Road 44 B2
45 B1
Elm Place 44 A2
Elm Row 56 A2
Elm Street 5 B2
Elm Tree Close 68 B2
Elm Tree Road 68 B1/B2
Elmbourne Road 151 A2
Elmcroft 54 A1
Elmfield Avenue 54 A1
Elmfield Road 148 B1/B2
Elmfield Way 26 B1/B2
Elmhurst Street 143 A1
Elmington Road 122 A1
Elmore Street 81
82 B1
Elms Crescent 149 A1/A2
Elms Mews 30 B2
Elms Road 149 A1
Elmstone Road 48 A2
Elmwood Court 141 A2
Elmwood Road 128 B2
Elnathan Mews 27 B1
Elphinstone Street 74 A2
Elrington Road 86 B2
Elsa Street 98 A1
Elsdale Street 90 A1/B1
Elsden Mews 93 A1
Elsham Road 33 B2
Elsie Road 129 A2
Elsley Road 141 B1
Elspeth Road 140 A2
Elsted Street 113 A2
114 A1
Elswick Street 50 A1
Elsworthy Rise 69 A2
Elsworthy Road 69 A1/A2
Elsworthy Terrace 69 A2
Elsynge Road 139 B2
Elthiron Road 49 A1
Elthorne Road 60 A1/A2
Elton Place 64 B2
Eltringham Street 139 A1
Elvaston Mews 36 B1
Elvaston Place 36 B1
Elverton Street 21 A1
22 B1
Elwin Street 91 A2
Elwood Street 63 B1
74 A2
Ely Place 15 A1
Elyne Road 54 B2
Elysium Place 48 B2
Elysium Street 48 B2
Elystan Place 46 A1
Elystan Street 46 A1
Elystan Walk 80 B1
Emba Street 108 A2
Embankment 47 B2
136 A1
Embankment Gardens 46 B1
Embankment Place 24 B2

Emden Street	50	A1
Emerald Street	5	B1
Emerson Street	105	A2
Emery Hill Street	20	A2
	21	A1
	22	B1
Emery Street	104	B2
Emlyn Road	39	A1
Emma Street	92	A2
Emmanuel Road	148	B2
	149	B2
Emmott Close	98	A2
Emperor's Gate	35	B2
	36	B1
Empire Square	61	B1
Empire Wharf Road	103	B2
Empress Approach	43	A1
Empress Mews	121	B2
Empress Place	43	A1
Empress Street	113	B1
Emu Road	141	A2
Endell Street	13	A1/B1
Endlesham Road	147	A2/B2
Endsleigh Gardens	4	A1/A2
Endsleigh Place	4	A2
Endsleigh Street	4	A2
Endwell Road	126	B1
Endymion Road	55	B1/B2
	150	B2
Enfield Road	82	B2
Enford Street	1	A2
	76	B1
Englands Lane	67	B2
Englefield Road	81	A2
	82	B1/B2
	88	A1
Englewood Road	148	A2
English Grounds	107	A1
English Street	99	A1
Enid Street	108	A1
Ennis Road	62	B1
Ennismore Avenue	39	A1
Ennismore Gardens	37	A1
Ennismore Gardens Mews	37	A1
Ennismore Mews	37	A1
Ennismore Street	37	B1
Ensign Street	95	B2
Ensor Mews	44	A1
Enterprise Way	138	A1
Enterprize Way	118	A1/A2
Epirus Mews	42	B2
Epirus Road	42	B2
Epping Close	102	B1
Epping Place	80	A1
Epple Road	48	A2
Epworth Street	8	A1
Equity Square	91	A2
Erasmus Street	21	A2
Eric Street	93	B2
	98	A2
Ericcson Close	138	B1
Erlanger Road	125	B1
Ernest Street	97	A2
	98	A1
Ernshaw Place	136	B2
Errington Road	26	B1
Errol Street	7	B2
Erskine Mews	70	A1
Erskine Road	70	A1
Esmeralda Road	108	B2
Esmond Street	136	A2
Essendine Road	27	A1
Essex Court	14	B2
Essex Gardens	55	B2
Essex Road	80	B2
	81	A2/B1
	82	A1
	83	A1
Essex Street	14	B2
Essex Villas	35	A1
Essian Street	98	A1
Estcourt Road	42	B1
Este Road	132	B2
	140	A1
Estelle Road	57	B2
Esterbrooke Street	21	A1
Eswyn Road	152	A2
Eternit Walk	47	B1
Ethel Street	113	A1
Ethelbert Street	148	B2
Ethelburga Street	132	A1
Ethelden Road	32	A1
Ethnard Road	115	B2
Eton Avenue	66	B2
	67	B1
Eton College Road	70	A2
Eton Garages	67	B1
Eton Road	70	A1/A2
Eton Villas	70	A2
Etta Street	118	B1
Eugenia Road	116	A2
Europa Place	7	A2
Eustace Road	42	B2
	43	B1
Euston Grove	78	B1
Euston Road	77	B1/B2
	78	B1/B2
Euston Square	78	B1
Euston Street	77	B2
Evandale Road	121	B1
	145	A2
Evangelist Road	72	A2
Evelina Road	124	B1/B2
Evelyn Court	84	A1
Evelyn Gardens	44	A1/A2
Evelyn Street	117	A2
	118	A1/B1/B2
	119	A1
Evelyn Walk	84	A1
Evelyn Yard	3	B2
Evenwood Close	136	B2
Everatt Close	137	B2
Evergreen Square	88	A1
Everilda Street	79	B2
Evering Road	86	A1/A2
	87	A2
Everington Street	47	A2
Everleigh Street	62	B1
Eversholt Street	78	A1/B1
Evershot Road	53	B2
	61	A2
Eversleigh Road	141	A1/A2/B1
Everthorpe Road	129	A2
Everton Buildings	77	B2
Evesham Street	33	A2
Evesham Walk	122	B1
	135	B2
Evesham Way	141	B2
Ewald Road	48	B2
Ewart Place	94	A2
Ewe Close	73	B2
Ewer Street	105	A2
Ewhurst Close	97	A2
Exeter Mews	43	B1
	65	B2
Exeter Road	65	A1
Exeter Street	14	B1
	24	A2
Exeter Way	126	A1
Exhibition Road	36	A2/B2
Exmouth Market	6	B1
Exmouth Mews	77	B2
Exmouth Place	89	B1
Exmouth Street	97	A1
Exon Street	114	A1
Exton Street	104	A2
Eyot Gardens	39	B1
Eyot Green	39	B1
Eyre Court	68	B2
Eyre Street Hill	5	B2
Eythorne Road	121	A1
	135	B2
Ezra Street	91	A2

F

Fabian Road	42	B2
Fair Street	107	A1/A2
Fairbairn Green	121	A1
Fairbridge Road	60	A1/A2
Fairburn Court	136	B2
Fairchild Close	132	B1
Fairchild Place	8	A2
Fairchild Street	84	
Fairclough Street	95	A1/A2
Fairfax Place	34	B1
	66	B1
Fairfax Road	55	A1
	66	B1
Fairfield Drive	138	B2
Fairfield Gardens	53	A2
Fairfield Road	53	A2
	54	A1
Fairfield Street	138	A2/B2
Fairfoot Road	99	A2
Fairhazel Gardens	65	B2
	66	B1
Fairholme Road	42	A1
Fairholt Road	63	A2
Fairholt Street	37	B1
Fairmead Road	60	B1/B2
Fairmount Road	150	B2
Fakruddin Street	91	B2
Falcon Grove	140	A1
Falcon Lane	140	A1
Falcon Road	132	B2
	140	A1
Falcon Terrace	140	A1
Falconberg Court	12	A2
Falconberg Mews	12	A1/A2
Falkirk Street	84	
Falkland Place	72	A2
Falkland Road	55	A1
	72	A2
Fallow Court	115	A2
Falmouth Road	106	B1/B2
Fane Street	42	A2

Street Index

Fann Street 7 B2
Fanshaw Street 84
Faraday Close 74 B1
Faraday Road 25 B1
Fareham Street 11 A2
Farleigh Place 86 A1
Farleigh Road 86 A1/A2
Farm Close 43 B1
Farm Lane 43 B1
Farm Place 29 B1
Farm Street 9 A1
Farmer Street 29 B2
Farmers Road 121 A1
Farncombe Street 108 A2
Farnell Mews 43 A2
Farnham Place 105 A2
Farnham Royal 131 B2
Faroe Road 33 B2
Farrance Street 99 B1
Farrer Road 53 A1
Farrier Street 71 B2
Farrier Walk 44 B1
Farringdon Lane 6 B1
Farringdon Road 6 B1
15 A1
Farringdon Street 15 A1/B1/B2
Farrins Rents 111 A2
Farrow Lane 124 A2
125 A1
Farrow Place 111 B2
Farthing Fields 96 B1
Fashion Street 91 B1
Fassett Road 86 B2
Fassett Square 86 B2
Faulkner Street 125 B1
Faunce Street 112 B2
Favart Road 49 A1
Fawcett Close 132 B1
Fawcett Street 43 B2
44 B1
Fawe Park Road 137 A1/A2
Fawe Street 99 B2
Fawley Road 65 A2
66 A1
Fawnbrake Avenue 127 B2
128 A1/B1
Featherstone Street 7 A2
Featley Road 145 B2
Felden Street 48 A1
Felgate Mews 40 B2
Felix Avenue 53 A2
Felix Place 127 B1
Fellbrigg Road 130 B1
Fellbrigg Street 92 B1
Fellows Court 88 B1
Fellows Road 66 B2
67 B1
69 A2
70 A1
Felmersham Close 143 B2
Felsberg Road 150 B1
Felsham Road 136 A1/A2
Felstead Gardens 103 B1
Felton Street 84 A1
Fenchurch Avenue 18 B1
Fenchurch Buildings 18 B1
Fenchurch Place 18 B2
Fenchurch Street 17 B2
18 B1/B2
Fendall Street 107 B2
Fenelon Place 34 B2
Fenham Road 123 A2
Fenn Street 90 A2
Fenner Close 109 B1
Fenner Square 139 A2
Fenning Street 106 A2
Fentiman Road 134 A2
135 A1/A2
Fenton Close 86 B2
145 A1
Fenwick Grove 130 A1
Fenwick Place 143 A2
Fenwick Road 130 A1
Ferdinand Place 71 A1
Ferdinand Street 71 A1/B1
Fergus Road 75 B1
Ferguson Close 102 B1
Ferme Park Road 54 A1/B1
Fermoy Road 25 A2
Fern Close 84 A2
Fern Street 99 A2
Fernbank Mews 148 A2
Ferncliff Road 86 A2/B2
Ferndale Road 143 B2
144 B1/B2
Ferndene Road 128 A1/A2
Fernhead Road 26 A1/B1
Fernhurst Road 48 A1
Fernlea Road 148 B1/B2
Fernsbury Street 6 A1
Fernshaw Road 44 B1
Fernside Road 147 B2
Ferntower Road 64 B1
Ferrey Mews 145 A2
Ferriby Close 80 A1
Ferrier Street 138 A2
Ferris Road 130 B1
Ferron Road 87 A1
Ferry Lane 38 B2
Ferry Street 103 B1/B2
Festing Road 47 B2
Fetter Lane 14 A2/B2
Ffinch Street 119 B1
Field Road 42 A1
Field Street 5 A2
Fieldgate Street 95 A1/A2
96 A1
Fieldhouse Road 149 B1
Fielding Road 33 B2
Fielding Street 113 B1
Fieldview 146 B1/B2
Fieldway Crescent 74 B2
Fife Terrace 79 B2
Filey Avenue 85 A2
87 A2
Filmer Road 42 B1
48 A1
Finborough Road 43 A2/B2
152 B2
Finch Lane 17 A2
Finch Mews 123 A1
Finchley Place 68 B2
Finchley Road 66 —
68 B2
Findon Road 32 B1
Finland Street 111 B2
Finlay Street 47 B2
Finnis Street 92 B1
Finsbury Avenue 8 B2
Finsbury Circus 8 B1/B2
Finsbury Market 8 B2
Finsbury Park Avenue 55 B2
Finsbury Park Road 62 B2
63 B1
Finsbury Pavement 8 B1
Finsbury Square 8 B1
Finsbury Street 7 B2
Finsen Road 128 A1
Fir Grove Road 145 A2
Fir Trees Close 111 A2
Firbank Road 124 B1
Fircroft Road 151 A1
Firecrest Drive 56 A1
First Avenue 25 A2
First Street 37 B2
Firth Gardens 48 B1
Fish Street Hill 18 B1
Fisher Close 90 A2
Fisher Street 14 A1
Fishermans Drive 110 A2
Fishers Court 125 B1
Fishers Lane 38 A1
Fisherton Street 76 A1
Fitzalan Street 112 A1
Fitzgeorge Avenue 34 B1
Fitzhardinge Street 1 A2
Fitzhugh Grove 146 A2
Fitzjames Avenue 34 B1
Fitzjohn's Avenue 56 B1
66 B2
67 A1
Fitzmaurice Place 9 A2
Fitzroy Mews 3 A1
Fitzroy Park 51 B1
Fitzroy Road 70 /B1
Fitzroy Square 3 A2
Fitzroy Street 3 A2
Fitzroy Yard 70 B1
Fitzwarren Gardens 52 B1
Fitzwilliam Road 142 B2
143 A1
Five Bell Alley 100 A1
Fives Court 112 A2
Fiveways Road 121 B1
145 B2
Flamborough Street 98 B1
Flamborough Walk 98 B1
Flanchford Road 39 A2
Flanders Crescent 152 B2
Flanders Road 38 A2
39 A1
Flanders Way 90 A1
Flank Street 95 B1
Flask Walk 56 B1/B2
Flaxman Court 11 A1
Flaxman Road 121 B1/B2
127 A2
Flaxman Terrace 4 A2
Fleece Walk 73 B2
Fleet Road 57 A1/B1
Fleet Square 5 A2
Fleet Street 14 B2
15 B1/B2
Fleet Street Hill 91 B2
Fleetwood Street 64 A2
Fleming Close 26 B1
Fleming Court 31 A2

Fleming Road 112 B2
Fletcher Street 95 B2
Fleur de Lis Street 91 B1
Flint Street 113 A2
Flinton Street 114 A1
Flitcroft Street 12 A2
Flockton Street 108 A1
Flodden Road 121 A1
Flood Street 45 B2
Flood Walk 45 B2
Flora Close 99 B2
Flora Gardens 40 B1
Floral Street 13 B1
Florence Road 62 A1
119 B1
126 B2
Florence Street 80 A2
Florence Terrace 126 B2
Florence Way 147 B2
Florfield Road 89 A2
Florian Road 136 A2
Florida Street 91 A2
92 A1
Floris Place 142 A2
Flowers Mews 60 A1
Flowersmead 151 A1
Foley Street 3 B1
Folgate Street 8 B2
91 B1
Folly Mews 29 A1
Folly Wall 103 A2
Fontarabia Road 141 B2
Fonthill Mews 62 B1
Fonthill Road 62 B1
Forbes Street 95 A2
Forburg Road 87 A2
Ford Close 94 A1
Ford Road 94 A1
Ford Square 96 A2
Ford Street 94 A1
Fordham Street 95 A2
96 A1
Fordingley Road 26 A1
Fordwych Road 65 A1
Fore Street 7 B2
Fore Street Avenue 7 B2
Foreign Street 121 B1
Foreshore 118 A2
Forest Grove 86 B1
Forest Road 86 B1/B2
89 A1
Forest Way 59 A2
Forfar Road 141 A2
Forge Place 71 A1
Forman Place 86 A2
Formosa Street 27 B1
Forset Street 1 A1
Forster Road 150 B1
Forston Street 83 A2
Forsyth Gardens 112 B2
Fort Road 108 B1
Fort Street 18 A1
Fortescue Avenue 89 A2
Fortess Grove 72 A2
Fortess Road 58 B2
72 A2
Fortess Walk 72 A2
Fortess Yard 72 A2
Forthbridge Road 141 B2
Fortnam Road 60 B2
Fortuna Close 74 B1
Fortune Green Road 65 A2
Fortune Place 115 A1
Fortune Street 7 B2
Forum Close 94 A2
Fosbury Mews 30 B1
Foscote Mews 26 B2
Foskett Road 48 B2
Foster Lane 16 A1
Foubert's Place 10 A2
Foulden Road 86 A1/A2
Foulden Terrace 86 A1
Foulis Terrace 45 A1
Foulser Road 151 A1
Foundry Close 110 A2
Foundry Mews 77 B2
Fount Street 134 B1
Fountain Court 14 B2
Fountain Green Square 108 A2
Fountain Mews 57 B1
Fountain Place 121 A1
135 B2
Fountayne Road 85 A2
Four Seasons Close 94 B2
Fournier Street 91 B1
Fowey Close 95 B2
Fowler Close 139 A2
Fowler Road 81 B1
Fownes Street 140 A1
Fox Close 92 B2
Fox & Knot Street 15 A2
Foxbourne Road 151 A2
Foxham Road 60 B1
Foxley Close 86 B2
Foxley Road 112 B1
121 A1
Foxley Square 121 A1
Foxmore Street 132 A1/B2
Framfield Road 74 B2
Frampton Park Road 89 A2
Frampton Street 76 A1
Francis Chichester Way 141 A2
Francis Close 103 B2
Francis Street 20 A2
22 B1
Francis Terrace 59 B2
Francis Terrace Mews 59 B2
Franciscan Road 151 A2/B1/B2
152 A2
Franconia Road 149 A1
Frankfurt Road 128 B1
Frankham Street 119 B1/B2
Frankland Close 109 B1
Frankland Road 36 B2
Franklin Square 42 A2
Franklin's Row 46 B2
Fraser Street 38 A1/B1
Frazier Street 104 B2
Frean Street 108 A1
Fred White Walk 73 B2
Freda Corbett Close 114 B2
Frederic Mews 19 A1
Frederica Street 79 A2
Frederick Close 31 B2
Frederick Crescent 121 A1
Frederick Road 112 B2
Frederick Square 110 A2
Frederick Street 5 A2
Frederick Terrace 88 A1
Frederick's Place 16 A2
Frederick's Row 6 A2
Freedom Street 141 A1
Freegrove Road 73 B2
Freeling Street 79 A2
Freemantle Street 114 A1
Freke Road 141 B2
Fremont Street 89 B2
French Place 84
Frensham Street 115 B1
Frere Street 132 B2
Freshfield Avenue 88 A1
Freshwater Close 152 B2
Freshwater Road 152 B2
Freston Road 28 A1/B1
33 A2
Frewin Road 146 B2
Friars Mead 103 A2
Friary Court 23 B1
Friary Road 115 B2
123 A2
Friday Street 16 B1
Frideswide Place 72 A1
Friend Street 6 A2
Friendly Place 120 B1
Friendly Street 126 B2
Frigate Mews 119 A1
Frimley Way 93 B1
Frinton Road 152 B2
Friston Street 49 B2
Frith Street 12 A1
Frithville Gardens 32 A2
Frobisher Road 55 A1/A2
Frogley Road 129 A2
Frogmore 138 B1
Frognal 56 A1/B1
66 A2
Frognal Close 66 A2
Frognal Court 66 A2
Frognal Gardens 56 A1
Frognal Lane 66 A1/A2
Frognal Rise 56 A1
Frognal Way 66 A2
Frome Street 83 B1
Froude Street 142 A1
Fryday Grove Mews 149 B1
Fulbourne Street 91 B2
Fulbrook Road 59 B1
Fulford Street 109 A1
Fulham Broadway 43 B1
Fulham High Street 48 B1/B2
Fulham Palace Road 41 B1/B2
47 A1/A2/B2
48 A1/B1
Fulham Park Gardens 48 B2
Fulham Park Road 48 B2
Fulham Road 37 B1
43 B1/B2
44 A2/B1
45 A1/A2
46 A1
48 A2/B1/B2
Fuller Close 91 A2
Fullerton Road 138 A2/B2
139 B1
Fullwoods Mews 84 B1
Fulmead Street 50 A1
Fulton Mews 30 B1

Furber Street 40 A1
Furley Road 115 B2
123 A2
Furlong Road 74 B2
Furness Road 50 B1
Furnival Street 14 A2/B2
Furrow Lane 90 A1
Furze Street 99 A2
Furzedown Road 151 B2
Fyfield Road 145 B2
Fynes Street 21 A1

G

Gables Close 122 A2
Gage Street 5 B1
Gainford Street 80 B1
Gainsborough Court 32 B2
Gainsborough Gardens 56 B2
Gainsborough Road 39 A1
Gainsford Street 107 A2
Gairloch Road 122 B2
Gaisford Street 72 B1
Galatea Square 130 A2
Galbraith Street 103 A1
Gale Street 99 A2
Galen Place 4 B2
Galena Road 40 B2
Gales Gardens 92 B2
Galesbury Road 146 A1
Galleon Close 110 A1
Galleywall Road 109 B1
Gallia Road 75 B1
Galsworthy Avenue 98 A1
Galsworthy Terrace 64 A1/B1
Galveston Road 137 A2
Galway Close 116 B1
Galway Street 7 A2
Gambetta Street 142 A1
Gambia Street 105 A1
Gandolfi Street 114 B1
Garbutt Place 2 A1
Gard Street 7 A1
Garden Court 14 B2
Garden Mews 29 B2
Garden Place 88 A1
Garden Road 68 B1
Garden Row 105 B1
Garden Street 97 A2
Garden Terrace 21 B1
Garden Walk 84
The Gardens 130 A1/A2
Gardners Lane 16 B1
Gardnor Road 56 B2
Garfield Mews 141 B2
Garfield Road 141 B2
Garford Street 100 A1
Garlick Hill 16 B2
Garlinge Road 65 A1
Garnault Mews 6 B1
Garnault Place 6 B1
Garner Street 92 A1
Garnet Street 96 B2
Garnett Road 57 B1
Garnham Street 85 B1
Garnies Close 114 B2
Garratt Lane 138 B2
146 B1
152 A1
Garratt Terrace 152 A1
Garrett Street 7 A2
Garrick Close 139 B1
Garrick Street 12 B2
13 B1
Garrison Road 94 A2
Garter Way 110 A2/B2
Gartons Way 139 A1
Garway Road 30 B1
Gascoigne Place 91 A1
Gascony Avenue 65 B1
Gascoyne Road 90 B2
Gaskarth Road 148 A2
Gaskell Street 143 A2
Gaskin Street 80 B2
Gaspar Close 35 B2
Gaspar Mews 35 B2
Gassiot Road 151 B1
152 A2
Gastein Road 41 B2
Gataker Street 109 A1
Gatcombe Road 60 B1
Gate Mews 37 A1
Gate Street 14 A1
Gateforth Street 76 B1
Gateley Road 144 B2
Gatesborough Street 8 A2
Gateway 113 B1
Gateway Mews 86 A1
Gathorne Street 93 A1
Gatliff Road 20 B1
Gatonby Street 123 A1
Gatton Road 152 A1
Gauden Close 143 A1
Gauden Road 143 A1/A2
Gaunt Street 105 B2
Gautrey Road 124 B2
Gavel Street 113 A2
Gaverick Mews 102 B1
Gaviller Place 87 A2
Gawber Street 92 B2
Gayfere Street 22 B2
Gayhurst Road 88 A2
89 A1
Gayton Crescent 56 B2
Gayton Road 56 B2
Gayville Road 140 B2
Gaywood Street 105 B1
Gaza Street 112 B2
Gearing Close 151 B2
Geary Street 74 B1
Gedling Place 107 A2
Gee Street 7 A1
Geffrye Street 88 B1
Geldart Road 123 A2
Geldeston Road 85 A2/B2
87 A2
Gellatly Road 124 B2
Geneva Drive 127 A1
Geoffrey Close 121 B2
George Beard Road 118 A2
George Inn Yard 106 A2
George Lowe Court 30 A1
George Mathers Road 112 A2
George Mews 77 B2
George Row 108 A1
George Street 1 A1/A2
2 B1
George Yard 2 B1
17 A2
George's Road 74 B1
Georges Square 42 B2
Georgette Place 120 B2
Georgiana Street 71 B2
Georgina Gardens 91 A2
Gerald Mews 19 B2
Gerald Road 19 B2
Geraldine Road 139 B1
146 A1
Geraldine Street 104 B2
Gerard Place 90 B1
Gerards Close 116 B1
Gernon Road 93 A2
Gerrard Place 12 B1
Gerrard Road 80 B2
83 B1
Gerrard Street 12 B1
Gerridge Street 104 B2
Gertrude Street 44 B1/B2
Gervase Street 124 A1
Ghent Way 86 B1
Gibbon Road 124 B2
Gibbs Green 42 A2
Gibraltar Walk 91 A2
Gibson Close 92 B2
Gibson Gardens 85 A1
Gibson Road 131 A2/B2
Gibson Square 80 B1/B2
Gideon Road 141 B1/B2
Giesbach Road 60 A1
Giffin Street 119 B1/B2
Gifford Street 79 A2
Gilbert Place 4 B2
Gilbert Road 112 A1
Gilbert Street 2 B1
Gilbey Road 152 A1
Gilbeys Yard 71 B1
Gildea Street 3 B1
Gilden Crescent 57 B2
Gilkes Crescent 129 B1
Gill Street 100 A1
Gillespie Road 62 B2
63 B1
74 A2
Gillett Street 82 A2
Gillies Street 71 A2
Gillingham Mews 20 A2
Gillingham Row 20 A2
Gillingham Street 20 A2
Gilpin Close 31 A1
Gilstead Road 50 A1
Gilston Road 44 A1/B1
Giltspur Street 15 A2/B2
Giraud Street 99 B2
Girdlers Road 41 A2
Gironde Road 42 B2
48 A2
Glading Terrace 86 A1
Gladsmuir Road 52 B1
60 A1
Gladstone Place 94 A2
Gladstone Street 104 B2
105 B1
Gladwell Road 54 B1
Gladwyn Road 136 A1
Gladys Road 65 A1
Glaisher Street 119 A1/A2

Glamis Place 97 B1
Glamis Road 97 B1
Glanville Road 150 A1
Glasford Street 152 B2
Glasgow Terrace 20 B2
Glass Street 92 B2
Glasshill Street 105 A1
Glasshouse Fields 97 B2
Glasshouse Street 10 B1/B2
Glasshouse Walk 131 B1
Glasshouse Yard 7 B1
Glasslyn Road 53 A1
Glastonbury Place 97 B1
Glastonbury Street 65 A1
Glaucus Street 99 A2
Glazbury Road 34 B1
Glebe Close 38 A1
Glebe Place 45 B1
Glebe Road 88 A1
Glebe Street 38 A1
Gledhow Gardens 44 A1
Gledstanes Road 42 A1
Glegg Place 136 A1
Glen Terrace 101 B2
Glenaffric Avenue 103 B2
Glenarm Road 87 B2
Glenbrook Road 65 A2
Glenburnie Road 151 A1
Glendall Street 144 B1
Glendarvon Street 136 A1
Glendower Place 36 B2
Gleneagles Close 115 A2
Glenelg Road 150 A1
Glenfield Road 149 B1
Glenfinlas Way 121 A1
Glengall Causeway 102 A1
Glengall Grove 103 A1
Glengall Road 65 B1
114 B2
Glengall Terrace 114 B2
Glengarnock Avenue 103 B2
Glengarry Road 129 B2
Glenhurst Avenue 58 B1
Glenilla Road 67 B2
Glenloch Road 67 B2
Glenmore Road 67 B2
Glenrosa Street 50 B2
Glentham Gardens 40 B2
Glentham Road 39 B2
40 B2
41 B1
Glenthorne Mews 40 B2
Glenthorne Road 40 B2
41 A1
Glentworth Street 76 B2
Glenville Grove 126 A2
Glenwood Road 55 A2
Glenworth Avenue 103 B2
Gliddon Drive 87 A1
Gliddon Road 34 B1
42 A1
Globe Pond Road 110 A2
111 A2
Globe Road 92 A2/B2
97 A2
Globe Street 106 B1
Globe Terrace 92 B2
Globe Yard 2 B1
Gloucester Avenue 70 /A2
Gloucester Circus 120 A2
Gloucester Crescent 71 B1
Gloucester Drive 62 B2
63 A1
Gloucester Gardens 30 B2
Gloucester Gate 77 A1
Gloucester Gate Mews 77 A1
Gloucester Mews 30 B2
Gloucester Mews West 30 B2
Gloucester Place 1 A2
76 B2
Gloucester Place Mews 1 A2
Gloucester Road 36 A1/B1
44 A1
Gloucester Square 31 B2
88 B2
Gloucester Street 20 B2
Gloucester Terrace 30 A1/A2/B2
Gloucester Walk 35 A1
Gloucester Way 6 B2
Glycena Road 141 B1
Glyn Road 90 A2
Glyn Street 131 B1
Glynde Mews 37 B2
Godalming Road 99 B2
Goddard Place 59 B2
Godfrey Street 45 B2
Goding Street 131 B1
Godley Close 125 B1
Godley Road 146 B1/B2
Godliman Street 15 B2
Godman Road 123 B2
Godolphin Road 32 B1
Godwin Close 83 A2/B2
Golborne Gardens 25 A2
Golborne Mews 25 B1
Golborne Road 25 A2/B1
Golborne Road Street Market 25 B1
Golden Cross Mews 29 A1
Golden Lane 7 A2/B2
Golden Square 10 B2
Goldhawk Mews 32 B1
Goldhawk Road 33 B1
39 A2/B1
40 A1/A2
Goldhurst Terrace 65 B2
66 B1
Golding Street 96 A1
Goldington Crescent 78 A1/B1/B2
Goldington Street 78 B2
Goldman Close 91 A2
Goldney Road 26 B2
Goldsboro Road 134 B1
Goldsmith Road 123 A2
Goldsmith Street 16 A1
Goldsmith's Row 89 B1
91 A2
92 A1/A2
Goldsmith's Square 92 A1
Goldsworthy Gardens 116 A2
Goldwin Close 124 A2
Gomm Road 109 A2/B2
Gonson Street 119 A2
Gonville Street 48 B2
Goodge Place 3 B2
Goodge Street 3 B2
Goodhart Place 98 B1
Goodinge Close 73 B1
Goodman's Stile 95 A1
Goodmans Court 18 B2
Goodmans Yard 18 B2
Goods Way 78 B2
Goodwin Close 108 B1
Goodwin Road 32 B1
Goodwin Street 62 B1
Goodwood Road 125 A2
126 A1
Gophir Lane 17 B1
Gopsall Street 84 A1
Gordon Close 60 A1
Gordon Grove 121 B1
Gordon House Road 58 B1
Gordon Place 35 A1/A2
Gordon Road 123 B2
124 B1
Gordon Square 4 A2
Gordon Street 4 A1
Gore Road 89 B2
90 B1
Gore Street 36 A1/B1
Gorham Place 28 B1
Goring Street 18 A1
Gorleston Road 55 B2
Gorleston Street 34 B1
Gorst Road 147 A1
Gorsuch Place 91 A1
Gorsuch Street 91 A1
Gosberton Road 147 B2
Gosfield Street 3 A1
Goslett Yard 12 A2
Gosling Way 135 B2
Gosset Street 91 A2
Gosterwood Street 118 B1
Goswell Road 6 A2
7 A1/B1
Gottfried Mews 58 B2
Gough Square 15 B1
Gough Street 5 B2
Gould Terrace 87 B2
Goulden House Approach 132 B2
Goulston Street 18 A2
Goulston Street (Pettycoat Lane) Market 18 A2
Goulton Road 87 B2
Govan Street 92 A2
Gowan Avenue 48 A1
Gower Close 149 A1
Gower Court 4 A1
Gower Mews 4 B1
Gower Place 4 A1
Gower Street 4 A1/B1
77 B2
Gower's Walk 95 A1
Gowlett Road 130 A1
Gowrie Road 141 B2
Grace Jones Close 86 B2
Gracechurch Street 17 A2/B2
Graces Mews 122 B1
Graces Road 122 B1/B2
Grafton Crescent 71 A2
Grafton Gardens 55 B2
Grafton Mews 3 A2
Grafton Place 78 B1
Grafton Road 57 B2
71 A2
Grafton Square 142 B2
143 A1/B1

Street Index

Grafton Street 9 A2
Grafton Terrace 57 B1
Grafton Way 3 A1/A2
4 A1
Grafton Yard 71 A2
Graham Road 86 B2
89 A1/A2
Graham Street 83 B1
Graham Terrace 19 B2
Granard Road 147 A1
Granary Road 91 B2
Granary Square 80 A1
Granary Street 78 B2
Granby Street 91 A2
Granby Terrace 77 B2
Grand Avenue 15 A2
Grand Junction Wharf 83 B1
Grand Parade Mews 136 B2
Grand Union Close 26 B1
Grand Union Crescent 89 B1
Grand Union Walk 71 B2
Grandison Road 140 B2
Granfield Street 132 A1
The Grange 107 B2
Grange Grove 75 B1
81 A1
Grange Road 51 A2
107 B1/B2
108 B1
Grange Street 84 A1
Grange Walk 107 B1/B2
Grange Walk Mews 107 B2
Grange Yard 107 B2
Grangeway 65 B1
Gransden Avenue 89 A2
Grant Road 139 A2
140 A1
Grant Street 80 B1
Grantbridge Street 83 B1
Grantham Place 9 B1
Grantham Road 38 B1
144 A1
Grantley Street 93 B1
Grantully Road 27 A1/A2
Granville Place 1 B2
43 B2
Granville Road 54 B1
Granville Square 6 A1
Granville Street 6 A1
Grape Street 13 A1
Gratton Road 33 B2
Gravel Lane 18 A2
Gray Street 104 A2
Gray's Inn Road 5 A1/A2/B2
14 A2
Gray's Inn Square 14 A2
Gray's Yard 2 B1
Grayling Road 64 A1
Grayshott Road 141 A1/B1
Grazebrook Road 64 A1
Great Castle Street 2 B2
3 B1
Great Central Street 76 B2
Great Chapel Street 3 B2
11 A2
Great Chart Street 139 A1
Great Church Lane 41 B2
Great College Street 22 A2
Great Cumberland Mews 1 A1/B1
Great Cumberland Place 1 A2/B2
Great Dover Street 106 A1/B1/B2
Great Eastern Street 84 /B1
Great George Street 22 A2
Great Guildford Street 105 A2
106 A1
Great James Street 5 B1
Great Marlborough Street 10 A1/A2
Great Maze Pond 106 A2
Great New Street 15 B1
Great Newport Street 12 B2
Great Ormond Street 5 B1
Great Percy Street 6 A1
Great Peter Street 22 B1/B2
Great Portland Street 3 A1/B1
77 B1
Great Pulteney Street 10 B2
Great Queen Street 13 A2/B2
Great Russell Street 4 B1/B2
Great Scotland Yard 24 B1
Great Smith Street 22 A2/B2
Great Spilmans 129 B1
Great St. Thomas Apostle 16 B2
Great Suffolk Street 105 A1/A2/B2
106 B1
Great Sutton Street 6 B2
Great Swan Alley 17 A1
Great Titchfield Street 3 A1/B1
Great Tower Street 18 B1
Great Trinity Lane 16 B2
Great West Road 38 B2
39 B1/B2
40 B1/B2
41 B1
Great Western Road 25 A2/B2
29 A2
Great Winchester Street 8 B2
Great Windmill Street 10 B2
11 B1
Greatfield Close 59 B1
Greatorex Street 91 B2
Greek Street 12 A1
Greek Yard 24 A1
Green Arbour Court 15 B2
Green Bank 96 B1
Green Dale 129 B1
Green Dale Close 129 B1
Green Dragon Court 106 A1/A2
Green Dragon Yard 91 B1
Green Hundred Road 115 B2
Green Lanes 55 A2/B1/B2
63 A1/B2
64 B1
75 A2
Green Street 1 B2
Green Terrace 6 B2
Green Walk 107 B1
Greenacre Square 110 A2
Greenaway Gardens 66 A2
Greenberry Street 69 B1
Greencoat Place 20 A2
21 A1
22 B1
Greencoat Row 22 B1
Greencroft Gardens 65 B2
66 B1
Greenfield Road 95 A1/A2
Greenham Close 104 B2
Greenhill 56 B1
Greenhill's Rents 15 A2
Greenland Mews 117 B2
Greenland Place 71 B1
Greenland Quay 111 B1
Greenland Road 71 B1/B2
Greenland Street 71 B1
Greenman Street 81 B1
Greenroof Way 103 A2
Greenside Road 40 A1
Greenway Close 63 B2
Greenwell Street 3 A1
Greenwich Church Street 120 A2
Greenwich High Road 119 B2
120 A1/A2/B1
Greenwich Quay 119 A2
Greenwich South Street 120 A1/B1
Greenwich View Place 102 A2
Greenwood Place 72 A1
Greenwood Road 86 B2
89 A1
Greet Street 104 A2
Gregory Place 35 A2
Greig Terrace 112 B2
Grenade Street 100 A1
Grenard Close 123 A1
Grendon Street 76 B2
Grenfell Road 28 A1/B1
152 B2
Grenville Mews 36 B1
53 B2
Grenville Place 36 B1
Grenville Road 53 B1/B2
Grenville Street 5 B1
Gresham Place 60 A1
Gresham Road 127 A1
145 B1/B2
Gresham Street 16 A1/A2
Gresley Road 52 B2
Gresse Street 3 B2
Greswell Street 47 B1
Greville Mews 68 A1
Greville Place 68 A1
Greville Road 68 A1
Greville Street 14 A2
15 A1
Grey Eagle Street 91 B1
Greycoat Place 22 B1
Greycoat Street 21 A1
22 B1
Greyhound Road 41 B2
42 A1/B1
47 A1/A2
Griggs Place 107 B1
Grimsby Street 91 B2
Grimshaw Close 51 A2
Grimston Road 48 B2
Grimwade Close 124 B1
Grindal Street 104 B1
Grinling Place 118 B2
Grinstead Road 117 B2
118 A1
Grittleton Road 26 B2
Grocer's Hall Court 16 B2
Groom Crescent 146 A1
Groom Place 19 A2
Groombridge Road 90 B1/B2
Groomfield Close 151 B1
Grosvenor Avenue 75 B2
Grosvenor Cottages 19 B2

Grosvenor Crescent 19 A2
Grosvenor Crescent Mews 19 A1/A2
Grosvenor Gardens 19 A2
Grosvenor Gardens Mews
East 9 B1
North 19 A2
South 19 A2
Grosvenor Gate 9 A1
Grosvenor Hill 9 A2
Grosvenor Park 113 B1
121 A2
Grosvenor Place 19 A2
Grosvenor Road 20 B1/B2
21 B1/B2
Grosvenor Square 1 B2
2 B1
9 A1
Grosvenor Street 9 A1/A2
Grosvenor Terrace 113 B1
121 A1
Grosvenor Wharf Road 103 B2
Grotto Passage 2 A1
The Grove 51 B1
53 B2
Grove Cottages 45 B2
Grove End Road 68 B1/B2
76 A1
Grove Gardens 76 A2
Grove Hall Court 68 B1
Grove Hill Road 129 A1
Grove Lane 122 B1
128 A2
129 A1
Grove Mews 29 A1
33 B1
Grove Park 122 B2
Grove Place 56 B2
148 A2
Grove Road 90 B1
93 A2/B2
Grove Street 118 A1/A2/B2
Grove Terrace 58 B1/B2
Grove Terrace Mews 58 B2
Grove Vale 129 A2
Grove Villas 101 A1
Grovedale Road 60 A1
Grovelands Close 122 B1
Groveway 135 B2
Grummant Road 123 A1
Grundy Street 99 B2
Gubyon Avenue 127 B2
128 B1
Guildford Grove 120 B1
Guildford Road 134 B2
Guildhouse Street 20 A2
Guilford Place 5 B1
Guilford Street 4 B2
5 B1/B2
Guinness Close 90 B2
Guinness Square 107 B1
Guion Road 49 A1
Gulliver Street 111 B2
Gun Street 18 A1
Gunmakers Lane 94 A1
Gunners Road 146 B2
Gunstor Road 64 B2
Gunter Grove 44 B1
Gunterstone Road 34 B1
Gunthorpe Street 91 B1
Gunton Road 87 A2
Gunwhale Close 110 A2
Gurney Road 50 B2
Guthrie Street 45 A2
Gutter Lane 16 A1
Guy Street 106 A2
Gwalior Road 136 A1
Gwendolen Avenue 136 A1/B1
Gwendolen Close 136 B1
Gwendwr Road 34 B1
Gwyn Close 50 A1
Gwynne Close 38 B2
Gwynne Place 6 A1
Gwynne Road 132 B1
Gylcote Close 128 B2

H

Haarlem Road 41 A2
Haberdasher Street 84 B1
Habitat Close 124 B1
Hackford Road 135 B2
Hackford Walk 135 B2
Hackney Road 91 A1/A2
92 A1/A2
Haddo Street 120 A1
Haddonfield 117 A1
Hadleigh Close 92 B2
Hadleigh Street 92 B2
Hadley Gardens 38 A1
Hadley Street 71 A2/B2
Hadrian Close 94 A2
Hadrian Mews 80 A1
Hafer Road 140 A1
Haggerston Road 88 A1/B1
Hague Street 92 B1
Hainton Close 96 A2
Halcomb Street 84 A2
Halcrow Street 96 A2
Haldane Road 42 B2
Haldon Road 137 B2
Hale Street 100 A2
Hales Street 119 B1
Half Moon Court 7 B1
Half Moon Crescent 79 B2
Half Moon Lane 127 B2
128 B1/B2
Half Moon Street 9 B2
Halford Road 42 B2
43 B1
Haliday Walk 82 A1
Halidon Close 87 B2
Halkin Mews 19 A1
Halkin Place 19 A1
Halkin Street 19 A2
Hall Gate 68 B1
Hall Place 31 A2
Hall Road 68 B1
Hall Street 7 A1
Hallam Mews 3 A1
Hallam Street 3 A1/B1
Halley Street 98 A1/A2
Halliford Street 81
82 B1
Halliwell Road 150 A1
Halpin Place 113 A2
Halsbury Road 32 A1
Halsey Mews 46 A1
Halsey Street 37 B2
46 A1
Halsmere Road 121 A1
Halstead Court 84 B1
Halton Cross Street 81 B1
Halton Place 81 B1
Halton Road 80 A2
81 B1
Hambalt Road 148 A2
149 A1
Hamble Street 50 B1
Hamilton Close 76 A1
111 A2
Hamilton Gardens 68 B1
Hamilton Lane 75 A1
Hamilton Mews 9 B1
Hamilton Park 75 A1
Hamilton Park West 74 A2
Hamilton Place 9 A1/B1
60 B2
Hamilton Square 106 A2
Hamilton Street 118 B2
119 B1
Hamilton Terrace 68 A1/B1
The Hamlet 128 A2
Hamlet Gardens 39 B2
Hamlet Way 106 A2
Hamlets Way 98 A2
99 A1
Hammersmith Bridge 40 B2
Hammersmith Bridge Road 40 B2
41 B1
Hammersmith Broadway 41 A1
Hammersmith Flyover 40 B2
41 B1
Hammersmith Grove 40 A2
41 A1
Hammersmith Road 34 B1
41 A1/A2
Hammond Street 72 B1
Hamond Street 84 A2
Hampden Close 78 B2
Hampden Gurney Street 1 A1
Hampden Road 60 B1
Hampshire Hog Lane 40 B1
Hampshire Street 73 B1
Hampson Way 135 B1
Hampstead Grove 56 A1/A2
Hampstead High Street 56 B1
Hampstead Hill Gardens 57 A1
Hampstead Lane 51 A1/B1
Hampstead Road 77 A2/B2
78 A1
Hampstead Square 56 A2
Hampton Close 26 A2
Hampton Court 80 A2
Hampton Street 112 A2
Hana Mews 87 B2
Hanbury Mews 83 A2
Hanbury Street 91 B1/B2
Handel Street 5 A1
Handforth Road 135 A2
Handley Road 90 B1
Hankey Place 106 B2
Hanley Gardens 53 B2
Hanley Road 53 B2
Hannay Lane 53 B1
Hannell Road 42 B1
Hannibal Road 97 A2

Street Index

Hannington Road 142 B1
Hanover Gardens 135 A2
Hanover Gate 76 A2
Hanover Park 123 A2
Hanover Place 99 A1
Hanover Square 2 B2
Hanover Street 2 B2
Hanover Terrace 76 B2
Hanover Terrace Mews 76 B2
Hans Crescent 37 A2/B2
Hans Place 37 B2
Hans Road 37 B2
Hans Street 37 B2
Hansard Mews 33 B2
Hanscomb Mews 143 B1
Hansler Road 129 B2
Hanson Close 148 A2
Hanson Street 3 A1
Hanway Place 3 B2
Hanway Street 3 B2
Harben Road 66 B1
Harberson Road 148 B1
Harberton Road 52 B2
Harbet Road 31 A2
Harbinger Road 102 B2
Harbledown Road 49 A1
Harbord Close 122 B1
Harbord Street 47 B1/B2
Harbour Avenue 50 A2
Harbour Exchange Square 103 A1
Harbour Road 128 A1
Harbut Road 139 A2
Harcombe Road 64 B2
Harcourt Street 1 A1
Harcourt Terrace 43 A2
Harders Road 123 B2
Hardess Street 128 A1
Harding Close 113 B1
Hardinge Street 97 B1
Hardwick Street 6 A1/B1
Hardwicke Mews 6 A1
Hardwicks Way 138 B1
Hardwidge Street 107 A1
Hardy Close 110 A2
Hare & Billet Road 120 B2
Hare Court 14 B2
Hare Marsh 91 B2
Hare Row 92 A2
Hare Walk 84 A2
Harecourt Road 75 B2
Haredale Road 128 A1
Harewood Avenue 76 B1/B2
Harewood Place 2 B2
Harewood Row 76 B1
Harford Mews 60 B2
Harford Street 93 B2
98 A1
Hargrave Park 59 A2
Hargrave Place 73 B1
Hargrave Road 60 A1
Hargwyne Street 144 A1/B1
Haringey Park 53 A2
Harley Gardens 44 A1
Harley Grove 94 B2
Harley Place 2 B2
Harley Road 69 A2
Harley Street 2 A2/B2
Harleyford Road 135 A1
Harleyford Street 135 A2

Harmony Place 115 A1
Harmood Grove 71 B1
Harmood Place 71 A1
Harmood Street 71 A1/A2/B1
Harmsworth Mews 104 B2
Harmsworth Street 112 B1/B2
Harold Road 54 A1
Harp Lane 18 B1
Harper Road 106 B1
Harpley Square 93 B1
Harpsden Street 141 A2
Harpur Mews 5 B1
Harpur Street 5 B1
Harriet Close 88 A2
Harriet Street 19 A1
Harriet Walk 19 A1
Harringay Gardens 55 A2
Harringay Road 55 A2
Harrington Gardens 43 A2
44 A1
Harrington Road 36 B2
Harrington Square 77 A2
78 B1
Harrington Street 77 B2
Harris Street 122 A1
Harrison Street 5 A1
Harrow Lane 101 A1
Harrow Place 18 A1
Harrow Road 25 A1/A2
26 B1/B2
30 A1/A2
31 A1/A2
Harroway Road 132 B1
Harrowby Street 1 A1
Harrowgate Road 90 B2
Hart Street 18 B2
Hartham Close 73 B2
Hartham Road 73 B2
Hartington Road 134 A2/B2
Hartismere Road 42 B2
Hartlake Road 90 A2
Hartland Road 71 B1/B2
Hartley Street 93 A1
Hartnoll Street 74 B1
Harton Street 119 B2
Harts Lane 125 B2
Hartswood Road 39 A2
Hartwell Street 86 B1
Harvey Road 54 A2
122 A1
Harvey Street 84 A1
Harwood Road 43 B1
49 A2
Harwood Terrace 50 A1
Haselrigge Road 143 B2
Hasker Street 37 B2
Haslam Close 80 A2
Haslam Street 123 A1
Haslemere Road 53 B1/B2
Hassard Street 91 A2
Hassett Road 90 A2
Hastings Close 123 A2
Hastings Street 4 A2
5 A1
Hatcham Park Mews 125 B1
Hatcham Park Road 125 B1/B2
Hatcham Road 116 B2
Hatchard Road 60 A2/B2
Hatchers Mews 107 A1

Hatfield Close 125 B1
Hatfields 104 A2
Hatherley Gardens 53 A2
Hatherley Grove 30 B1
Hatherley Street 20 A2
21 A1
Hathorne Close 124 B1
Hatley Road 62 B1
Hatteraick Street 110 B1
Hatton Garden 5 B2
14 A2
Hatton Place 15 A1
Hatton Row 76 A1
Hatton Street 76 A1/B1
Hatton Wall 14 A2
15 A1
Haul Road 78 B2
Haunch of Venison Yard 2 B2
Havannah Street 102 A1
Havelock Street 79 A2/B1
Havelock Terrace 133 A1
Haven Mews 80 A2
98 A2
Haven Street 71 B1
Haverfield Road 93 B2
Haverhill Road 148 B2
149 B1
Havering Street 97 B1
Haverstock Hill 67 A2/B2
70 A2
71 A1
Haverstock Road 57 B2
Haverstock Street 83 B1
Havil Street 122 A2
Hawes Street 80 A2
Hawgood Street 99 B2
Hawke Place 110 A2
Hawks Mews 120 B2
Hawksley Road 64 A1
Hawksmoor Mews 96 A1
Hawksmoor Street 47 A2
Hawkstone Road 109 B2
Hawley Crescent 71 B1
Hawley Mews 71 B1
Hawley Road 71 B1/B2
Hawley Street 71 B1
Hawthorn Avenue 94 A2
Hawthorn Crescent 151 B1
152 A2
Hawthorne Close 82 A2
Hawtrey Road 69 A2
Hay Hill 9 A2
Hay Street 92 A1
Hay's Lane 106 A2
Hay's Mews 9 A1/A2
Haycroft Road 150 A1
Haydens Place 29 A1
Haydon Street 18 B2
Haydon Way 139 B1
Hayes Grove 129 A2
Hayes Place 76 B1
Hayfield Passage 97 A2
Hayfield Yard 97 A2
Hayles Street 105 B1
112 A2
Hayman Street 80 B2
Haymarket 11 B1
23 A2
Haymerle Road 115 B1

Hayne Street 15 A2
Hayter Road 150 A1/A2
Hayward's Place 6 B2
Hazel Close 59 A2
123 B2
Hazelbourne Road 148 A2
Hazellville Road 53 B1
Hazlebury Road 49 A2
50 B1
Hazlewell Road 136 B1
Hazlewood Crescent 25 A1/A2
Hazlitt Mews 34 B1
Hazlitt Road 34 B1
Head Street 97 A2/B2
Head's Mews 29 B2
Headfort Place 19 A2
Headington Road 146 B1
Headlam Road 149 A2/B2
Headlam Street 92 B1/B2
Heald Street 126 A2
Healey Street 71 A2
Hearn Street 8 A2
Hearn's Buildings 113 A2
Hearnshaw Street 98 A1
Hearnville Road 147 B2
Heath Hurst Road 57 A1
Heath Road 142 A1/A2
Heath Side 56 B2
Heath Street 56 A2/B1/B2
Heathcote Street 5 A1
Heather Close 62 B1
142 A1
Heather Walk 25 A1
Heathfield Avenue 146 A2
Heathfield Gardens 146 A1
Heathfield Road 146 A1/A2
Heathfield Square 146 A1/A2
Heathfield Street 28 B2
Heathmans Road 49 A1
Heathville Road 53 B2
Heathwall Street 140 A2
141 B1
Heaton Road 123 B2
152 B2
Heaven Tree Close 75 B2
Heaver Road 132 B1
Hebdon Road 151 B1
Heber Road 129 B2
130 B1
Hebron Road 40 A2
Heckfield Place 42 B2
Heckford Street 97 B2
Heddington Grove 74 B1
Heddon Street 10 B1
Hedger Street 112 A2
Hedgers Grove 90 A2
Hedingham Close 81
Hedley Row 64 B1
Heiron Street 112 B2
Helby Road 149 A2
Helen's Place 92 B2
Helena Place 89 B2
Helena Square 110 A2
Hellings Street 95 B2
Helmet Row 7 A2
Helmsley Place 89 B1
Helsinki Square 111 B2
Hemans Street 134 A1
Hemberton Road 143 A2
Hemingford Road 79 A2/B2
80 A1
Hemingway Close 58 B1
Hemming Street 91 B2
Hemstal Road 65 B1
Hemsworth Court 84 A2
Hemsworth Street 84 A1/A2
Hemus Place 45 B2
Henderson Drive 76 A1
Henderson Road 146 A2
Hendham Road 151 A1
Hendre Road 114 A1
Hendrick Avenue 147 A1/A2
Heneage Street 91 B1
Heneagle Lane 18 A1
Henfield Close 60 A1
Henley Drive 108 B1
Henley Street 141 A2
Henniker Mews 44 B1
Henning Street 132 B2
Henrietta Close 119 A1
Henrietta Mews 5 A1
Henrietta Place 2 B1/B2
Henrietta Street 24 A1
Henriques Street 95 A2
Henry Dent Close 128 A2
Henry Doulton Drive 151 B2
Henry Jackson Road 136 A1
Henry Road 63 A1
Henshall Street 82 A1
Henshaw Street 113 A2
Henstridge Place 69 B1
Henty Close 132 A1
Hepburn Mews 140 B2
Hepworth Walk 57 B1
Herald Street 92 B2
Herald's Place 112 A1
Herbal Hill 6 B1
Herbert Crescent 37 B2
Herbert Street 57 B1
Herbrand Street 4 A2/B2
Hercules Place 61 B1
Hercules Road 104 B2
131 A2
Hercules Street 61 B1
Hereford Mews 29 B2
Hereford Place 126 A2
Hereford Retreat 115 B1
Hereford Road 29 B2
94 B2
Hereford Square 44 A1
Hereford Street 91 A2
Hereward Road 151 B1
Heritage Close 127 A2
Heritage Place 146 B1
Hermes Close 26 B1
Hermes Street 79 B2
Hermit Place 68 A1
Hermit Street 6 A2
Hermitage Road 55 B2
Hermitage Row 86 B2
Hermitage Street 31 A1
Hermitage Wall 95 B2
Herndon Road 138 B2
139 B1
Herne Hill 127 B2
128 B1
Herne Hill Road 127 A2
128 A1
Herne Place 127 B2
Heron Drive 63 B1
Heron Place 111 A2
Heron Quay 100 B1/B2
Heron Road 127 A2
Herondale Avenue 146 B2
Herrick Road 63 B1
Herrick Street 21 A2
Hertford Place 3 A2
Hertford Road 82 A2/B2
Hertford Street 9 A1
Hertslet Road 61 B2
74 A1
Hertsmere Road 100 A1/A2
Hesewall Close 143 A1
Hesketh Place 28 B1
Heslop Road 147 B2
Hesper Mews 43 A2
Hesperus Crescent 102 B2
Hessel Street 96 A1
Hestercombe Avenue 48 A2/B1
Heston Street 126 B2
Hetherington Road 143 B2
Hetley Road 32 B1
Hewett Street 8 A2
Hewison Street 94 A2/B2
Hewitt Road 55 A1
Hewlett Road 94 A1
Heyford Avenue 134 A2
Heygate Street 113 A1
Heysham Lane 56 A1
Heyworth Road 87 A2
Hibbert Street 139 A1
Hickin Street 103 A1
Hicks Close 139 A2
Hicks Street 117 B2
Hide Place 21 A1
High Holborn 4 B2
13 A1
14 A1/A2
High Road 86 A1
High Street Colliers Wood 152 B1
High Timber Street 16 B1/B2
Higham Road 55 A2
Highbank Way 54 B2
Highbury Corner 74 B2
Highbury Crescent 75 B1
Highbury Grange 75 A1/A2
Highbury Grove 75 A1/B1
Highbury Hill 74 A2
75 A1
Highbury New Park 63 B2
75 A2/B1/B2
Highbury Park 63 B1
75 A1
Highbury Place 74 B2
75 B1
Highbury Quadrant 63 B1/B2
Highbury Station Road 80 A2
Highbury Terrace 75 B1
Highbury Terrace Mews 74 B2
Highcroft Road 53 B1/B2
Highfields Grove 51 B1
Highgate Avenue 51 A2/B2
Highgate Close 51 A1
Highgate High Street 51 B1/B2
Highgate Hill 51 B2
60 A1

Street Index

Highgate Road 58 A1/B1
72 A1/A2
Highgate West Hill 51 B1
58 A1/A2
Highlands Close 53 B2
Highshore Road 123 B1/B2
The Highway 95 B2
96 B1/B2
97 B1/B2
Highwood Road 60 B2
Hilary Close 43 B2
Hilda Locket Walk 145 A2
Hildreth Street Market 148 B1
Hildyard Road 43 B1
Hilgrove Road 66 B1
Hill Gate Walk 53 A1
Hill Road 68 B1
Hill Street 9 A1/A2
Hillbeck Close 116 B1
Hillbrook Road 151 A1/B1
Hillbury Road 151 A2
Hillcrest 51 A2
Hilldrop Crescent 73 A1/B1
Hilldrop Lane 73 A1/B1
Hilldrop Road 73 A1
Hillery Close 113 A2
Hillfield Court 67 B2
Hillgate Place 29 B1/B2
148 A1
Hillgate Street 29 B1
Hilliards Court 96 B1/B2
Hillier Road 140 B2
Hillingdon Street 112 B2
113 B1
Hillman Street 89 A2
Hillmarton Road 73 A2/B2
74 B1
Hillmead Drive 127 A1
Hillrise Road 53 B1
Hills Place 3 B1
Hillsboro Road 129 B1
Hillside Close 68 A1
Hillside Gardens 51 A2
Hillside Road 86 A1
Hillsleigh Road 29 B1
Hilltop Road 65 B1
Hillway 51 B1
58 A2
Hillyard Street 135 B2
Himley Road 152 A1/B2
Hinckley Road 130 A1
Hind Grove 99 B1
Hinde Mews 2 B1
Hinde Street 2 B1
Hindmans Road 130 B1
Hindmarsh Close 95 B2
Hindrey Road 87 B1
Hinton Road 127 A2
128 A1
Hippodrome Mews 28 B2
Hippodrome Place 28 B2
Hitchin Square 94 A1
Hithe Grove 110 B1
Hobart Place 19 A2
Hobday Street 99 B2
Hobury Street 44 B1/B2
Hocker Street 91 A1
Hockett Close 118 A1
Hodes Row 57 B2
Hodister Close 121 A2
Hodnet Grove 109 B2
Hofland Road 33 B2
Hogan Mews 31 A1
Hogan Way 85 A2
Hogarth Lane 38 B1
Hogarth Road 35 B2
Hogarth Roundabout Flyover 38 B1/B2
Holbeach Mews 148 B1
Holbeck Row 123 A2
Holbein Mews 19 B2
Holbein Place 19 B2
Holborn 14 A2
Holborn Place 14 A1
Holborn Viaduct 14 A2
15 B1/B2
Holbrook Close 59 A2
Holcombe Street 40 B2
Holcroft Road 90 B1
Holden Street 141 A1
Holdernesse Road 151 A1
Holford Mews 6 A1
Holford Place 6 A1
Holford Road 56 A2
Holford Street 6 A1
Holgate Avenue 139 A2
Holland Gardens 34 A1
Holland Grove 121 A1
135 B2
Holland Park 28 B2
34 A1
Holland Park Avenue 28 B1/B2
29 B1
33 B2
Holland Park Gardens 28 B1
34 A1
Holland Park Mews 28 B2
Holland Park Road 34 B2
Holland Place 35 A2
Holland Road 33 B2
34 A1/B1/B2
Holland Street 35 A1/A2
105 A1
Holland Villas Road 34 A1
Hollar Road 85 B1
Hollen Street 11 A1
Holles Street 2 B2
Holliday Square 139 A2
Hollingbourne Road 128 B1
Holloway Road 60 A1/B2
61 B1/B2
74 A1/B1/B2
Holly Bush Hill 56 A1
Holly Bush Vale 56 B1
Holly Grove 123 B1
Holly Hill 56 A1
Holly Lodge Gardens 51 B1
Holly Mews 44 A1
Holly Mount 56 A1
Holly Park 53 B2
Holly Road 38 A1
Holly Street 86 B1
88 A1
Holly Walk 56 A1/B1
Hollybush Gardens 92 A2
Hollybush Place 92 B2
Hollydale Road 124 A1/B2
Hollydene 123 A2
Hollymount Close 120 B2
Hollywood Mews 44 B1
Hollywood Road 43 A2
44 B1
Holm Oak Close 137 B1/B2
Holm Oak Mews 149 A2
Holman Road 132 B1
Holmbury Court 151 A1
Holmcote Gardens 75 B2
Holmdale Road 65 A2
Holmdene Avenue 128 B1
Holmead Road 43 B2
Holmes Close 130 A1
Holmes Place 44 B1
Holmes Road 71 A2
72 A1
Holmes Terrace 104 A2
Holmesdale Road 52 A1
Holmleigh Road 86 A1
Holmside Road 147 A2
Holsworthy Square 5 B2
Holton Street 93 B1
Holwood Place 143 B1
Holyhead Close 99 A2
Holyoak Road 112 A2
Holyoake Court 111 A2
Holyport Road 47 A1
Holyrood Street 107 A1
Holywell Close 116 B1
Holywell Lane 8 A2
84
Holywell Row 8 A2
Home Road 132 B2
Homefield Road 39 B1
Homefield Street 84 A2
Homer Drive 102 B1
Homer Row 1 A1
Homer Street 1 A1
Homerton Grove 90 A2
Homerton High Street 87 B2
90 A1/A2
Homerton Row 90 A1/A2
Homerton Terrace 90 A1
Homestead Road 42 B2
48 A2
Honduras Street 7 A2
Honeybourne Road 66 A1
Honeybrook Road 149 A1/B1
Honeywell Road 140 B1/B2
Hooper Street 95 A1/B1
Hooper's Court 37 A2
Hope Close 75 B2
Hope Street 139 A1/A2
Hopetown Street 91 B1
Hopewell Street 122 A1
Hopewell Yard 122 A1
Hopgood Street 33 A1
Hopkins Street 11 A1/B1
Hopkinsons Place 70 B1
Hopping Lane 81 A1
Hopton Street 105 A1
Hopwood Road 113 B2
Horatio Place 101 B2
Horatio Street 91 A2
Horbury Crescent 29 B1
Horbury Mews 29 B1
Horder Road 48 A1
Hormead Road 25 A2
Hornbeam Close 131 A2

Hornbeam Square 94 A2
Hornblower Close 111 B1
Hornby Close 66 B2
Hornsey Lane 51 B2
52 B1/B2
53 B1
Hornsey Lane Gardens 52 B1/B2
Hornsey Rise 53 B1
Hornsey Rise Gardens 53 B1
Hornsey Road 53 B1
61 A1/A2/B2
74 A1/B1
Hornsey Street 74 B1
Hornshay Street 116 B2
Hornton Place 35 A2
Hornton Street 35 A1/A2
Horse & Dolphin Yard 11 B2
Horse Guards Avenue 24 B1
Horse Guards Road 23 B2
24 B1
Horse Yard 80 B2
Horseferry Place 120 A1
Horseferry Road 21 A1/A2
22 B1/B2
98 B1
Horsell Road 74 B2
Horseldown Lane 107 A2
Horsemongers Mews 106 B1
Horseshoe Close 103 B2
Horseshoe Mews 150 A1
Horsford Road 150 A1/A2
Horsley Street 113 B2
Hortensia Road 43 B2
44 B1
Horton Road 89 A1
Hosack Road 147 B2
Hosier Lane 15 A2
Hospital Road 90 A2
Hotham Road 136 A1
Hothfield Place 110 B1
Hotspur Street 131 B2
Houghton Close 86 B2
Houghton Street 14 B1
Houndsditch 8 B2
18 A1/A2
Houseman Way 122 A1
Howard Mews 75 A1
Howard Road 64 B1/B2
Howards Lane 136 B1
Howbury Road 124 B2
Howden Street 130 A1
Howell Walk 112 A2
Howick Place 20 A2
22 B1
Howie Street 132 A1
Howitt Close 64 B2
Howitt Road 67 B2
Howland Mews East 3 A2
Howland Street 3 A2
Howland Way 111 A2/B2
Howletts Road 128 B2
Howley Place 31 A1
Hows Street 88 B1
Hoxton Market 84
Hoxton Square 84
Hoxton Street 84 /A1/A2
Hoyland Close 115 B2
Hoyle Road 152 A1
Hubert Grove 144 A1
Huddart Street 99 A1
Huddleston Close 92 A2
Huddleston Road 59 B2
73 A1
Hudson's Place 20 A2
Huggin Court 16 B2
Hugh Dalton Avenue 42 B2
Hugh Gaitskell Close 42 B2
Hugh Mews 20 A2
Hugh Street 20 A1/A2/B1
Hugo Road 59 B1
Hugon Road 49 B2
Huguenot Place 91 B1
139 B1
Huguenot Square 130 A2
Hull Close 110 A2
Hull Street 7 A2
Hullbridge Mews 82 B1
Hulme Place 106 B1
Humbolt Road 42 B1
Humphrey Street 114 A2
Hungerford Lane 24 A1/B1
Hungerford Road 73 B1/B2
Hungerford Street 96 A2
Hunsdon Road 125 A1
Hunslett Street 93 A1
Hunt Close 33 A2
Hunter Close 106 B2
147 B2
Hunter Street 5 A1
Huntingdon Street 79 A2
Huntley Street 4 A1
Hunton Street 91 B2
Huntsman Street 113 A2
Huntsworth Mews 76 B2
Hurley Crescent 110 A2
Hurlingham Gardens 48 B2
Hurlingham Road 48 B2
49 B1
Hurlingham Square 49 B2
Hurlock Street 63 B1
Huron Road 151 A2
Hurst Avenue 52 A2
Hurst Street 127 B2
Huson Close 69 A2
Hutchings Street 102 A1
Hutton Street 15 B1
Hyde Lane 132 A1
Hyde Park Corner 9 B1
Hyde Park Crescent 31 B2
Hyde Park Gardens 31 B1/B2
Hyde Park Gardens Mews 31 B1/B2
Hyde Park Gate 36 A1
Hyde Park Gate Mews 36 A1
Hyde Park Square 31 B2
Hyde Park Square Mews 31 B2
Hyde Park Street 31 B2
Hyde Road 84 A1
Hyde Street 119 A1
Hyde Vale 120 B2
Hydes Place 80 A2
Hydethorpe Road 148 B2
149 B2
Hyndman Street 115 B2
Hyson Road 109 B1

I

Ibbott Street 92 B2
Ickburgh Road 87 A1/A2
Ida Street 101 A2
Idlecombe Road 152 A2
Idol Lane 18 B1
Idonia Street 126 A2
Iffley Road 40 A2/B2
Ifield Road 43 A2/B2
Ifor Evans Place 93 B1
Ilchester Gardens 30 B1
Ilchester Place 34 A2
Ilderton Road 116 A1/B1/B2
124 A2
Iliffe Street 112 A2
Iliffe Yard 112 A2
Ilminster Gardens 140 A1
Imber Street 84 A1
Imperial Avenue 64 B2
Imperial College Road 36 B2
Imperial Crescent 50 B2
Imperial Road 50 A1
Imperial Square 50 A1
Imre Close 32 A1
Independent Place 86 A2
Inderwick Road 54 A1
Indescon Court 102 A2
India Street 18 B2
Indigo Mews 63 B2
101 A2
Industry Terrace 145 B1
Ingate Place 133 B1
Ingelow Road 142 A1
Ingersoll Road 32 A1
Ingestre Place 10 A2
Ingestre Road 58 B2
Inglebert Street 6 A1
Ingleborough Street 145 A1
Ingleby Road 61 B1
Inglemere Road 152 B2
Inglethorpe Street 47 B1/B2
Ingleton Street 145 A2
Inglewood Close 102 B2
Inglewood Road 65 A2
Inglis Street 121 B1
Ingram Close 131 A2
Ingrave Street 139 A2
Ingress Street 38 A1
Inkerman Road 71 A2
Inman Road 146 B1
Inner Circle 2 A1
Inner Temple Lane 14 B2
Innes Street 114 B1
Institute Place 87 B1
Inver Court 30 B1
Invermead Close 39 A2
Inverness Gardens 35 A2
Inverness Mews 30 B1
Inverness Place 30 B1
Inverness Street 71 B1
Inverness Terrace 30 B1
Invicta Close 99 B2
Invicta Plaza 105 A1
Inville Road 113 B2
Inworth Street 132 B2
Ion Square 91 A2
Irene Road 49 A1
Ireton Street 99 A2

Street Index

Iron Mill Road 138 B2
Ironmonger Lane 16 B2
Ironmonger Row 7 A2
Ironmongers Place 102 B1/B2
Ironside Close 110 A1
Irving Grove 144 A2
Irving Mews 81 A2
Irving Road 33 B2
Irving Street 24 A1
Isabel Street 135 B2
Isabella Mews 82 A2
Isabella Road 90 A1
Isabella Street 104 A2
Isambard Mews 103 A2
Isambard Place 110 A1
Island Road 116 A2
117 A1
Island Row 98 B1/B2
Isledon Road 62 B1
Islington Green 80 B2
Islington High Street 80 B1/B2
Islington Park Mews 80 A2
Islington Park Street 80 A2
Islip Street 72 A1/B2
Ivanhoe Road 129 A2
Ivatt Place 42 A2
Iveagh Close 90 B2
Iveley Road 142 A2
Iverna Court 35 B2
Iverna Gardens 35 B2
Iverson Road 65 A1/A2
Ives Street 46 A1
Ivimey Street 91 A2
Ivor Place 76 B2
Ivor Street 71 B2
Ivory Square 139 A1
Ivy Court 115 A2
Ivy Gardens 53 A2
Ivy Road 152 A1
Ivy Street 84 A1/A2
Ivybridge Lane 24 A2
Ivychurch Lane 114 A1
Ixworth Place 45 A2
46 A1

J

Jacaranda Grove 88 A1
Jack Walker Court 75 A1
Jackman Street 89 B1
Jackson Close 90 B1
Jackson Road 74 A1
Jacksons Lane 51 A2
Jacob Street 108 A1
Jacob's Well Mews 2 B1
Jaggard Way 147 B1
Jago Walk 122 A1
Jamaica Road 107 A2
108 A1/A2
109 A1/A2
Jamaica Street 97 A1/A2
James Collins Close 25 A2
James Court 81
James Joyce Walk 127 A2
James Street 2 B1
Jameson Street 29 B2
Jamestown Road 71 B1
Jamuna Close 98 A2
Jane Street 96 A2
Janet Street 102 A1
Janeway Place 108 A2
Janeway Street 108 A2
Jansen Walk 139 A2
Japan Crescent 53 B2
Jardine Road 97 B2
Jarrow Road 109 B1
Jarvis Road 129 A2
Jay Mews 36 A2
Jebb Avenue 150 B1/B2
Jedburgh Street 141 B2
Jeffreys Place 71 B2
Jeffreys Road 143 A2
Jeffreys Street 71 B2
Jeger Avenue 88 B1
Jelf Road 127 B1
Jenner Road 85 B1
86 A2
Jennings Road 129 B2
Jephson Street 122 B1
Jerdan Place 43 B1
Jeremiah Street 100 A2
Jermyn Street 23 A1
Jerningham Road 125 B2
Jerome Crescent 76 A1
Jerome Street 91 B1
Jerrard Street 84
Jersey Street 92 B2
Jervis Court 2 B2
Jervis Road 42 B2
Jessica Road 139 B1
Jessop Road 127 A2
Jessop Square 100 B2
Jew's Row 138 A2
Jewry Street 18 B2
Jeypore Road 146 A1
Joan Street 104 A2
105 A1
Jocelyn Street 123 A1
Jockey's Fields 5 B1
Jodane Street 118 A1
Jodrell Road 94 A2
Johanna Street 104 B2
John Adam Street 24 A1/A2
John Archer Way 146 A2
John Ashby Close 150 B1
John Campbell Road 82 A2
John Carpenter Street 15 B1
John Felton Road 108 A1
John Fisher Street 95 B1
John Harrison Way 103 A2
John Islip Street 21 A2/B2
John Maurice Close 113 A2
John Parker Square 139 A2
John Princes Street 2 B2
John Roll Way 108 A2
John Ruskin Street 112 B2
113 B1
John Silkin Lane 117 A2
John Smith Avenue 42 B2
John Spencer Square 81 A1
John Street 5 B2
John Williams Close 125 A1
John's Mews 5 B1
Johnson Close 88 A2
Johnson Street 97 B1
Johnson's Place 20 B2
Johnston Close 135 B2
Joiner Street 106 A2
Joiner's Arms Yard 121 B2
Joiners Place 75 A2
Jonathan Street 131 B1
Joseph Hardcastle Close 125 A2
Joseph Powell Close 148 A2
Joseph Street 99 A1
Josephine Avenue 150 A2
Joubert Street 141 A1
Jowett Street 123 A1
Jubilee Crescent 103 A2
Jubilee Place 46 A1
Jubilee Street 97 A1
Judd Street 5 A1
Juer Street 132 A1
Julia Street 57 B2
Julian Place 103 B1
Julius Nyerere Close 79 B2
Junction Approach 140 A1
Junction Mews 31 B2
Junction Place 31 B2
Junction Road 59 A2/B1/B2
60 A1
Juniper Crescent 71 A1/B1
Juniper Drive 139 A1
Juniper Street 97 B1
Juno Way 117 B1
Jupiter Way 74 B1
Justice Walk 45 B1
Jutland Close 60 A2
Juxon Street 131 A2

K

Kambala Road 132 B1
Kassala Road 141 A1
Katherine Close 110 A2
Katherine Square 28 B1
Kathleen Road 140 A2
Kay Road 144 A1
Kay Street 92 A1
Kay Way 120 A1
Kean Street 13 B2
Keats Close 57 A1
114 A2
Keats Grove 56 B2
57 A1
Keble Place 47 A1
Keel Close 110 A2
Keeley Street 13 B2
Keens Yard 75 B1
Keetons Road 108 A2
Keighley Close 73 A2
Keildon Road 140 A1
Keith Connor Close 142 A1
Kell Street 105 B1
Kellett Road 127 B1
Kellino Street 151 B1
Kelly Avenue 123 A1
Kelly Mews 26 B1
Kelly Street 71 A2/B2
Kelman Close 143 A2
Kelmore Grove 130 A1
Kelmscott Road 140 B1
Kelross Road 75 A1/A2
Kelsey Street 92 B1
Kelso Place 35 B2
Kelvedon Road 48 A2
Kelvin Road 75 A2
Kember Street 79 A2

Kemble Street 13 B2
Kemerton Road 128 A1
Kemplay Road 56 B2
Kemps Drive 100 A2
Kempsford Gardens 43 A1
Kempsford Road 112 A1
Kempson Road 49 A2
Kempthorne Road 118 A1
Kenbury Street 121 B2
Kenchester Close 134 A2/B2
Kendal Close 121 A1
Kendal Place 137 B1
Kendal Street 1 A1
31 B2
Kendall Place 2 A1
Kender Street 125 B1
Kendoa Road 143 B2
Kendrick Mews 36 B2
Kendrick Place 45 A1
Kenilford Road 148 A2
Kenilworth Court 136 A1
Kenilworth Road 93 A2
Kenmure Road 87 B1/B2
Kenmure Yard 87 B1
Kennard Street 141 A2
Kennet Close 139 A2
Kennet Road 26 B1
Kennet Street 95 B2
Kennet Wharf Lane 16 B2
Kenning Street 110 A1
Kenninghall Road 86 A2
87 A1/A2
Kennings Way 112 A1
Kennington Green 112 B1
Kennington Lane 112 A1/A2
131 B1/B2
Kennington Oval 135 A1/A2
Kennington Park Gardens 112 B1
Kennington Park Place 112 B1
Kennington Park Road 112 A1/A2/B1
Kennington Road 104 B2
112 A1/B1
Kenrick Place 2 A1
Kensal Road 25 A1/A2
Kensington Church Court 35 A2
Kensington Church Street 29 B2
35 A1/A2
Kensington Church Walk 35 A2
Kensington Court 35 A2
Kensington Court Mews 35 A2
Kensington Court Place 35 A2
Kensington Gardens Square 30 B1
Kensington Gate 36 A1
Kensington Gore 36 A1/A2
Kensington High Street 34 B1/B2
35 A1/A2/B1
Kensington Mall 29 B2
Kensington Palace Gardens 29 B2
Kensington Park Gardens 29 B1
Kensington Park Mews 29 A1
Kensington Park Road 29 A1/B1/B2
Kensington Place 29 B1/B2
Kensington Road 35 A2
36 A1/A2
37 A1
Kensington Square 35 A2
Kent Street 88 B1/B2
Kent Terrace 76 B2
Kent Yard 37 A1
Kentish Buildings 106 A1
Kentish Town Road 71 A2/B1/B2
72 A1/A2/B1
Kenton Road 90 A1/A2/B2
Kenton Street 5 A1
Kenway Road 35 B2
43 A1
Kenwood Avenue 125 B1
Kenwyn Road 143 B2
Kenyon Street 47 A2/B1
Kepler Road 143 B2
144 B1
Keppel Street 4 B1
Kerbela Street 91 A2
Kerbey Street 99 B2
Kerfield Crescent 122 B1
Kerfield Place 122 B1
Kerrison Road 132 B2
Kerry Path 118 B1
Kerry Road 118 B2
Kershaw Close 146 A1
Kersley Mews 132 B2
Kersley Road 64 A2
Kersley Street 132 B2
141 A1
Kerwick Close 79 A2
Keston Road 55 A2/B2
130 A1
Kestrel Avenue 128 B1
Keswick Road 136 B2
Kett Gardens 150 A2
Key Close 92 B2
Keyse Road 107 B2
Keystone Crescent 79 B1
Keyworth Street 105 B1/B2
Kezia Mews 117 B2
Kezia Street 117 B2
Khyber Road 132 B2
Kibworth Street 135 B1
Kiffen Street 8 A1
Kilburn High Road 65 A1/B1
68 A1
Kilburn Park Road 27 A1/A2
68 A1
Kilburn Place 65 B1
Kilburn Priory 68 A1
Kilburn Vale 68 A1
Kildare Gardens 30 A1
Kildare Terrace 30 A1
Kildoran Road 150 A1
Kilkie Street 50 B1/B2
Killarney Road 146 A1
Killick Street 79 B1/B2
Killowen Road 90 A1
Killyon Road 143 A1
Kilmaine Road 48 A1
Kilmarsh Road 40 B2
Kilmington Road 39 B1
Kiln Place 57 B2
58 B1
Kilner Street 99 B1
Kimbell Gardens 48 A1
Kimberley Avenue 124 B2
Kimberley Gardens 55 B2
Kimberley Road 144 A1
Kimpton Road 122 A1
Kinburn Street 110 A1
Kincaid Road 123 A2
Kinder Street 96 A1/A2
King Arthur Close 124 A2
King Charles Street 24 B1
King David Lane 97 B1
King Edward III Mews 109 A1
King Edward Street 15 B2
King Edward Walk 104 B2
King Edwards Road 89 B2
King George Street 120 B2
King Henry Street 64 B2
King Henry's Reach 41 B1
King Henry's Road 69 A2
70 A1/A2
King Henry's Walk 82 A2
King Henrys Walk 82 A2
King James Court 105 B2
King James Street 105 B1/B2
King John Court 84
King John Street 97 A2
King & Queen Street 113 A1
King Square 7 A1
King Stairs Close 109 A2
King Street 13 B1
16 A2/B2
23 A1/A2
39 B1/B2
40 B1/B2
41 A1
King William Street 17 A1/A2/B2
King William Walk 120 A2
King's Avenue 143 B2
149 A2/B2
King's Cross Bridge 5 A2
King's Cross Road 5 A2
6 A1/B1
King's Mews 5 B2
King's Road 43 B2
44 B1/B2
45 B1/B2
46 A1/A2/B1
49 A2
King's Scholars' Passage 20 A2
King's Terrace 78 A1
Kingdon Road 65 A2
Kingfield Street 103 B2
Kingham Close 33 B2
146 A1
Kinghorn Street 7 B1
Kinglake Street 114 A1
Kingly Street 10 A2
Kings Arms Yard 16 A2
17 A1
Kings Bench Street 105 A1
Kings Bench Walk 14 B2
Kings College Road 67 B1
Kings Crescent 63 B1
Kings Gardens 65 B1
Kings Grove 124 A1
Kings Head Yard 106 A2
Kings Mews 149 A2
Kings Place 106 B1
Kingsbury Road 82 A2
Kingsbury Terrace 82 A2
Kingscote Street 15 B2
Kingsdale Gardens 33 A2
Kingsdown Close 28 A1
116 B1

Street Index

Kingsdown Road 60 B2
61 A1/B1
Kingsford Street 57 B1
Kingsgate Place 65 B1
Kingsgate Road 65 B1
Kingshold Road 90 B1
Kingsland Green 82 A2
Kingsland High Street 86 B1
Kingsland Passage 82 A2
Kingsland Road 86 B1
88 A1/B1
91 A1
Kingsland Road Street Market 86 B1
Kingsley Mews 35 B2
Kingsley Place 51 B2
Kingsley Street 141 B1
Kingsmere Close 136 A1
Kingsmere Place 63 A2
Kingsmill Terrace 68 B2
Kingstown Street 70 B1
Kingsway 14 A1/B1
Kingswear Road 59 A1
Kingswood Road 150 B1
Kingwood Road 47 B2
48 A1
Kinloch Street 74 A1
Kinnerton Place North 19 A1
Kinnerton Place South 19 A1
Kinnerton Street 19 A1
Kinnerton Yard 19 A1
Kinnoul Road 42 B1
Kinsale Road 130 A1
Kipling Street 106 A2
Kirby Grove 107 A1
Kirby Street 15 A1
Kirk Street 5 B1
Kirkstall Avenue 55 B2
Kirkwall Place 92 B2
93 A1
Kirkwood Road 124 B1
Kirtling Street 133 A2
Kitcat Terrace 94 B2
Kite Place 92 A1
Kite Yard 132 A1
Kitson Road 122 A1
Kiver Road 60 B2
Klea Avenue 149 A1
Knapp Road 99 A2
Knapton Mews 152 B2
Knaresborough Place 35 B2
Knatchbull Road 121 A1/A2/B1
Knebworth Road 64 B2
Knighten Street 95 B2
Knightrider Street 15 B2
Knights Walk 112 A1
Knightsbridge 9 B1
19 A1/A2
37 A1/A2
Knightsbridge Green 37 A2
Knivet Road 43 B1
Knoll Road 138 B2
Knottisford Street 93 A1
Knowle Close 145 B1
Knowsley Road 141 A1
Knox Street 1 A2
Knoyle Street 125 A2
Kotree Way 108 B2
Kramer Mews 43 A1
Kreedman Walk 86 B2
Kylemore Road 65 A1
Kynance Mews 35 B2
36 B1
Kynance Place 36 B1
Kynaston Road 64 A2
Kyrle Road 140 B2
147 A2
Kyverdale Road 85 A1/A2
87 A2

L

Laburnum Close 124 A2
Laburnum Street 88 B1
Lacey Walk 94 B2
Lackington Street 8 B1
Lacon Road 130 B1
Lacy Road 136 A1
Ladbroke Crescent 28 A2
Ladbroke Gardens 29 B1
Ladbroke Grove 25 A1/B1
29 A1/B1
Ladbroke Mews 28 B2
Ladbroke Road 28 B2
29 B1
Ladbroke Square 29 B1
Ladbroke Terrace 29 B1
Ladbroke Walk 29 B1
Lady Margaret Road 59 B1/B2
72 A2
Lady Somerset Road 58 B2
72 A1
Lafone Street 107 A2
Lagado Mews 110 A2
Lairs Close 73 B2
Laitwood Road 148 B2
Laker Place 137 B1
Lakeside Road 33 B1/B2
Lakis Close 56 B1
Lalor Street 48 B1
Lamb Lane 89 B1/B2
Lamb Street 91 B1
Lamb Walk 107 A1
Lamb's Buildings 7 B2
Lamb's Conduit Street 5 B1
Lamb's Passage 7 B2
Lambert Road 150 A1
Lambert Street 80 A1
Lambeth Bridge 21 A2
Lambeth High Street 131 A1/B1
Lambeth Hill 15 B2
Lambeth Palace Road 104 B1
131 A1
Lambeth Road 104 B2
105 B1
131 A1/A2
Lambeth Walk 131 A2
Lamble Street 57 B2
Lambolle Place 67 B1/B2
Lambolle Road 67 B1
Lambourn Road 142 A1/B1
Lambourne Grove 116 A2
Lambrook Terrace 48 A1
Lambs Mews 80 B2
Lambton Place 29 B1
Lambton Road 53 B1
Lamerton Street 119 A1
Lamington Street 40 B2
Lamlash Street 112 A2
Lammas Road 90 B2
Lammermoor Road 148 A2
Lamont Road 44 B1/B2
Lampard Grove 85 A1/A2
Lampern Square 92 A1
Lampeter Square 42 B1
Lamplighter Close 92 B2
Lanark Mews 27 B2
Lanark Place 27 B2
Lanark Road 27 A2/B2
Lanark Square 103 A1
Lancaster Close 82 B2
Lancaster Court 30 B2
42 B2
48 A2
Lancaster Drive 67 B1
101 B2
Lancaster Gate 30 B2
Lancaster Grove 67 B1
Lancaster Mews 30 B2
138 B2
Lancaster Place 14 B1
Lancaster Road 28 A1/A2
29 A1
54 B1
62 A1
Lancaster Street 105 B1
Lancaster Terrace 30 B2
31 B1
Lancefield Street 25 A2
Lancell Street 64 A2
Lancelot Place 37 A2
Lanchester Way 125 B1
Lancing Street 78 B1
Landcroft Road 129 B2
Landells Road 130 B1
Landmann Way 117 B1
Landon Place 37 B2
Landon Walk 101 A1
Landons Close 101 B2
Landor Road 143 A2
144 A1/A2
Landridge Road 48 B1/B2
Landrock Road 54 B1
Landseer Road 60 B2
61 B1
The Lane 68 B1
Lanesborough Place 19 A2
Lanfranc Road 93 A2
Lanfrey Place 42 A2
Lang Street 92 B2
Langbourne Avenue 58 A2
59 A1
Langbourne Place 102 B2
Langdale Close 113 B1
Langdale Road 120 A1/B1
Langdale Street 96 A1
Langdon Park Road 52 A1/B1
Langford Close 68 B2
86 A2
Langford Green 129 A1
Langford Mews 80 A1
Langford Place 68 B2
Langford Road 50 A1
Langham Place 2 B2
3 B1
38 B1
Langham Street 3 B1

Langholm Close 149 B2
Langland Gardens 66 A2
Langley Lane 134 A2
Langley Street 13 B1
Langston Hughes Close 127 A2
Langthorn Court 17 A1
Langthorne Street 47 A1/B1
Langton Close 5 B2
Langton Road 121 A1
Langton Street 44 B1
Langtry Place 43 A1
Langtry Road 68 A1
Lanhill Road 26 A2/B2
Lansdowne Crescent 28 B2
29 B1
Lansdowne Drive 89 A1/B1
Lansdowne Gardens 134 B2
Lansdowne Mews 28 B2
Lansdowne Place 106 B2
Lansdowne Rise 28 B2
Lansdowne Road 28 B2
Lansdowne Terrace 5 B1
Lansdowne Walk 28 B2
Lansdowne Way 134 B1/B2
135 B1
Lant Street 106 A1
Lanterns Court 102 A2
Lanvanor Road 124 B1/B2
Lapford Close 26 A1
Larch Close 59 A2
118 B2
148 B1
Larcom Street 113 A1
Larissa Street 113 A2
Lark Row 92 A2
Larkhall Lane 134 B2
143 A1/A2
Larkhall Rise 142 A2
143 A1
Larnach Road 47 A1
Latchmere Road 132 B2
140 A2
141 A1/B1
Latchmere Street 132 B2
Latona Road 115 B1
Lattimer Place 38 B1
Laud Street 131 B1
Lauderdale Road 27 A1/B2
Launcelot Street 104 A2
Launceston Place 36 A1/B1
Launch Street 103 A1
Laundress Lane 86 A2
Laundry Road 42 B1
Laura Place 87 B2
Laurel Bank Gardens 48 B2
Laurel Close 59 A2
152 A1
Laurel Street 86 B1/B2
Laurence Pountney Hill 17 B2
Laurence Pountney Lane 17 B2
Laurie Grove 126 A1
Laurier Road 58 B2
59 B1
Lauriston Road 90 B1
Lausanne Road 124 B2
Lavell Street 64 B1
Lavender Close 44 B2
Lavender Gardens 140 A2
Lavender Grove 88 A2
Lavender Hill 140 A1/A2
141 B1/B2
Lavender Road 111 A2
139 A2
Lavender Sweep 140 A1
Lavender Terrace 140 A1
Lavender Walk 140 A1
Lavers Road 64 B2
Laverton Mews 43 A2
Laverton Place 43 A2
Lavina Grove 79 B1
Lavington Street 105 A2
Law Street 106 B2
Lawford Road 72 B1
82 B2
Lawless Street 101 A1
Lawn House Close 101 B2
Lawn Lane 134 A2
Lawn Road 57 B1
Lawrence Buildings 85 B1
Lawrence Close 94 B2
Lawrence Lane 16 A2
Lawrence Street 45 B1
Lawton Road 93 B2
Laxley Close 121 A1
Laxton Place 77 B1
Layard Road 109 B1
Laycock Street 80 A2
Laystall Street 5 B2
Laytons Buildings 106 A1
Lea Bridge Road 87 A2
Lea Square 94 A2
Leacroft Avenue 147 A1
Leadenhall Place 18 B1
Leadenhall Street 17 A2
18 B1/B2
Leake Street 104 A1/B1
Leamington Road Villas 29 A2
Leamore Street 40 B2
Leather Lane 5 B2
14 A2
Leather Road 116 A2
Leatherdale Street 92 B2
93 B1
Leathermarket Court 107 A1
Leathermarket Street 106 A2
107 A1
Leathwaite Road 140 A2/B2
Lebanon Gardens 138 B1
Lebanon Road 137 B2
Leckford Road 146 B1
Lecky Street 44 A2
Leconfield Road 64 B1
75 A2
Ledbury Mews North 29 B2
Ledbury Mews West 29 B2
Ledbury Road 29 A2/B2
Ledbury Street 115 B2
Lee Street 88 A1
Leeds Place 61 A2
Leeke Street 5 A2
Leerdam Drive 103 A2
Lees Place 1 B2
Leeson Road 127 B1
Leeway 118 A2
Legard Road 63 B1
Legion Close 80 A1
Legion Terrace 94 A2
Leicester Street 11 B2
Leigh Hunt Street 106 A1
Leigh Road 75 A1
Leigh Street 4 A2
5 A1
Leighton Crescent 72 A2
Leighton Grove 72 A2
73 A1
Leighton Place 72 A2
Leighton Road 72 A1/A2/B2
73 B1
Leinster Gardens 30 B2
Leinster Mews 30 B2
Leinster Place 30 B1
Leinster Square 29 B2
Leinster Terrace 30 B1/B2
Leith Yard 65 B1
Lelitia Close 88 A2
Leman Street 95 A1/B1
Len Freeman Place 42 B2
Lena Gardens 33 B1
Lendal Terrace 143 B2
Lennox Gardens 37 B2
Lennox Gardens Mews 37 B2
Lennox Road 62 B1
Lenthall Road 88 A2
Leo Street 124 A1
Leonard Place 64 B2
Leonard Street 8 A1/A2
Leontine Close 115 B2
123 A2
Leopards Court 14 A2
Leopold Mews 89 B2
Leopold Street 99 A1
Leppoc Road 149 A2
Leroy Street 107 B1
Lerry Close 42 A2
Lessar Avenue 148 A2
Lessingham Avenue 151 B1/B2
Leswin Place 85 B1
Leswin Road 85 B1
86 A1
Letchworth Street 151 B1
Letterstone Road 42 B1
Lettice Street 48 A2
Lettsom Street 122 B1
Levehurst Way 143 A2
Lever Street 7 A1/A2
Leverett Street 46 A1
Leverton Place 72 A2
Leverton Street 72 A2
Leweston Place 86 A1
Lewis Street 71 B2
Lewisham Road 120 B1
Lewisham Way 126 A1/B2
Lexham Gardens 35 B1/B2
Lexham Gardens Mews 35 B2
Lexham Mews 35 B1
Lexington Street 10 A2/B2
Lexton Gardens 149 B2
Leybourne Road 71 B2
Leybourne Street 71 B1
Leyden Street 18 A2
Leydon Close 110 A2
Leylang Road 125 A2
Liardet Street 118 B1
Liberia Road 75 B1
Liberty Mews 148 A1
Liberty Street 135 B1
Libra Road 94 A2

Street Index

Library Place 96 B2
Library Street 105 B1
Lichfield Road 93 B2
94 B1
Lidcote Gardens 145 A1
Liddell Road 65 A1
Lidfield Road 64 B1
Lidgate Road 122 A2
Lidiard Road 146 B1
Lidlington Place 78 B1
Lidyard Road 60 A1
Lifford Street 136 A1
Lighter Close 118 A1
Lighterman Mews 97 B2
Lightermans Road 102 A2
Ligonier Street 91 A1
Lilac Place 131 B1
Lilestone Street 76 B1/B2
Lilford Road 121 B1/B2
Lilian Close 64 B1/B2
Lilley Close 95 B2
Lillian Road 39 B2
Lillie Road 42 A2/B1/B2
43 A1/B1
47 A2
Lillie Yard 43 B1
Lillieshall Road 142 A2/B1/B2
Lily Place 15 A1
Lilyville Road 48 A2
Limburg Road 140 A1
Lime Close 95 B2
Lime Grove 32 B2
Lime Street 18 B1
Limeburner Lane 15 B2
Limeharbour 101 B1
103 A1
Limehouse Causeway 100 A1
Limehouse Link 97 B2
98 B1
100 A1/A2
Limerick Close 148 A2
Limerston Street 44 B1/B2
The Limes 29 B2
Linacre Close 130 A2
Lincoln Street 46 A1
Lincoln's Inn Fields 14 A1/A2/B1
Linden Gardens 29 B2
38 A1
Linden Grove 124 B1
Linden Mews 29 B2
82 A1
Linden Passage 38 A1
Lindfield Gardens 66 A2
Lindfield Street 99 B1
Lindley Street 96 A2
Lindore Road 140 A1
Lindrop Street 50 B2
Lindsay Square 21 B2
Lindsell Street 120 B1
Lindsey Street 15 A2
Linford Street 133 B2
Lingham Street 144 A1
Linhope Street 76 B2
Link Street 90 A1
Links Road 152 B2
Links Yard 91 B1
Linkway 55 B2
Linnell Road 122 B2
Linnet Mews 147 A2
Linom Road 143 B2
Linscott Road 87 B2
Linsey Street 108 A2/B1
Linstead Street 65 A1
Lintaine Close 42 B1
Linthorpe Road 86 A1
Linton Street 81
83 A2
Linver Road 49 B1
Linwood Close 122 B2
Lion Yard 143 B2
Lionel Mews 25 A1
Lipton Road 97 B2
Lisburne Road 57 A2
Lisford Street 123 A1
Lisgar Terrace 34 B2
Lisle Close 151 B2
Lisle Street 11 B2
Lissenden Gardens 58 B1
Lisson Grove 76 A1/B1
Lisson Street 76 B1
Liston Road 142 B2
Listowel Close 135 A2
Listria Park 64 A2
Litchfield Street 12 B2
13 B1
Lithos Road 66 A1/A2
Little Albany Street 77 B1
Little Argyll Street 10 A1
The Little Boltons 43 A2
Little Britain 15 A2/B2
Little Chester Street 19 A2
Little College Street 22 B2
Little Dean's Yard 22 A2
Little Dimocks 148 B2
Little Dorrit Court 106 A1
Little Edward Street 77 B1
Little Essex Street 14 B2
Little George Street 22 A2
Little Green Street 58 B1
Little New Street 15 B1
Little Newport Street 12 B2
Little Portland Street 3 B1
Little Russell Street 4 B1/B2
Little Sanctuary 22 A2
Little Smith Street 22 A2
Little Somerset Street 18 A2
Little St. James's Street 23 A1/B1
Little Titchfield Street 3 B1
Little Trinity Lane 16 B2
Littlebury Road 143 A1
Littlefield Close 59 B1
Livermere Road 88 A1
Liverpool Grove 113 B2
Liverpool Road 74 B1/B2
80 A1/A2/B1
Liverpool Street 8 B2
Livesey Place 115 B2
Livingstone Place 103 B1
Livingstone Road 139 A2
Livonia Street 11 A1
Lizard Street 7 A2
Llewellyn Street 108 A1
Lloyd Baker Street 6 A1
Lloyd Square 6 A1
Lloyd Street 6 A1
Lloyd's Avenue 18 B2
Lloyd's Row 6 B2
Loanda Close 88 A1
Loats Road 150 B1
Lochaline Street 41 B1
Lochinvar Street 148 A1/B1
Lock Mews 72 B2
Lockesfield Place 103 B1
Lockhart Close 74 B1
Lockhart Street 99 A1
Lockington Road 133 A1
Locksley Street 98 A2
Lockton Street 28 A1
Lockwood Square 108 A2
Lockyer Street 106 A2
Loddiges Road 89 A2
Loder Street 124 A2
Lodge Road 76 A1/A2
Loftie Street 108 A2
Lofting Road 79 A2
80 A1
Loftus Road 32 A2
Logan Place 35 B1
Lolesworth Close 91 B1
Lollard Street 112 A1
131 A2/B2
Loman Street 105 A2
Lomas Drive 88 A2
Lomas Street 91 B2
Lombard Lane 15 B1
Lombard Road 132 B1
Lombard Street 17 A1/A2/B2
Lombardy Place 30 B1
Lomond Grove 122 A1
Loncroft Road 114 B1
Londesborough Road 64 B2
London Bridge 17 B2
London Bridge Street 106 A2
London Fields East Side 89 B1
London Fields West Side 89 A1
London Lane 89 A1/A2
London Mews 31 B1
London Road 105 B1/B2
152 B2
London Street 18 B1
31 A1/B1
London Wall 7 B2
8 B1/B2
Long Acre 12 B2
13 B1/B2
Long Lane 7 B1
15 A2
106 A1/A2/B2
107 A1/B1
Long Meadow 73 B1
Long Road 142 B1
143 B1
Long Street 91 A1
Long Walk 107 B1
Long Yard 5 B1
Longbeach Road 141 B1
Longfellow Way 114 A2
Longford Street 77 B1
Longhedge Street 141 A2
Longhope Close 114 B1
Longlands Court 29 B1
Longley Road 152 B1/B2
Longley Street 108 B1
Longmead Road 152 A1
Longmoore Street 20 A2
Longnor Road 93 B1
Longridge Road 35 B1

Longshore 118 A1/A2
Longville Road 112 A2
Lonsdale Mews 29 A1
Lonsdale Place 80 A1
Lonsdale Road 29 B1/B2
38 B1/B2
39 A1/B1/B2
40 B2
41 B1
Lonsdale Square 80 A1/B1
Loraine Road 74 A1
Lord Amory Way 101 B1
Lord Hills Bridge 30 A1
Lord Hills Road 30 A2
Lord Napier Place 39 B2
Lord North Street 22 B2
Lord Roberts Mews 43 B2
Lordship Grove 64 A1
Lordship Lane 129 A2/B2
Lordship Park 63 B2
Lordship Park Mews 63 B2
Lordship Place 45 B1
Lordship Road 63 A2
64 A1
Lordship Terrace 64 A1
Lorenzo Street 5 A2
Loring Road 126 B1
Loris Road 33 B1
Lorn Road 145 A1
Lorne Close 76 A2
Lorne Gardens 33 B2
Lorne Road 62 A1
Lorrimore Road 112 B2
113 B1
Lorrimore Square 112 B2
Lothair Road North 55 B1/B2
Lothair Road South 55 B1
Lothbury 17 A1
Lothian Road 121 A1
Lots Road 44 B1/B2
50 A2
Loubet Street 152 B2
Loudoun Road 66 B1
68 A2/B2
Lough Road 74 B1
Loughborough Park 127 A2/B1
Loughborough Road 121 B1
127 A1/A2
145 A2
Loughborough Street 131 B2
Louisa Close 90 B2
Louisa Gardens 97 A2
Louisa Street 97 A2
Louise Bennett Close 127 B2
Louisville Road 151 A1
Louvaine Road 139 A2/B2
Love Lane 16 A2
Love Walk 121 B2
122 B1
Lovegrove Street 115 A2
Lovegrove Walk 101 B2
Lovelinch Close 116 B2
Lovell Place 111 B2
Loveridge Mews 65 A1
Loveridge Road 65 A1
Lovett's Place 138 A2
Lowden Road 127 B2
128 A1
Lowell Street 98 B1
Lower Addison Gardens 33 B2
Lower Belgrave Street 19 A2
Lower Clapton Road 87 A2/B2
Lower Grosvenor Place 9 B1
Lower James Street 10 B2
Lower John Street 10 B2
Lower Marsh 104 A2/B1/B2
Lower Marsh Street Market 104 A2/B1
Lower Merton Rise 69 A2
Lower Richmond Road 136 A1/A2
Lower Road 104 A1/A2
110 B1/B2
111 B1
117 A1/A2
Lower Robert Street 24 A2
Lower Sloane Street 46 A2/B2
Lower Terrace 56 A1/A2
Lower Thames Street 17 B2
18 B1/B2
Lowfield Road 65 A1
Lowman Road 74 A1
Lowndes Close 19 A2
Lowndes Court 10 A2
Lowndes Place 19 A2
Lowndes Square 19 A1
Lowndes Street 19 A1
Lowood Street 96 B2
Lowth Road 121 B2
Lowther Gardens 36 A2
Lowther Road 74 B1
Loxham Street 5 A1
Loxley Road 146 B2
Lubbock Street 125 B1
Lucan Place 46 A1
Lucas Street 126 B2
Lucerne Mews 29 B2
Lucerne Road 75 A1
Lucey Road 108 B1
Lucey Way 108 B2
Lucien Road 151 B2
Ludgate Broadway 15 B2
Ludgate Circus 15 B2
Ludgate Hill 15 B2
Ludgate Square 15 B2
Ludlow Street 7 A1
Ludwick Mews 126 A1
Lugard Road 124 A1/B1
Luke Street 8 A1/A2
Lukin Street 97 A1/B1
Lulworth Road 124 B1
Lumley Street 2 B1
Lupton Street 58 B2
72 A2
Lupus Street 20 B2
21 B1
Luralda Gardens 103 B2
Lurgan Avenue 41 B2
Lurline Gardens 133 A1/B1
141 A2
Luscombe Way 134 A2
Lushington Terrace 86 B2
Luton Place 120 B2
Luton Street 76 A1
Lutton Terrace 56 B2
Luxborough Street 2 A1
Luxemburg Gardens 41 A1
Luxford Street 116 A2
Luxmore Street 126 B2
Luxor Street 121 B1
Lyal Road 94 A1/B1
Lyall Mews 19 A2
Lyall Mews West 19 A2
Lyall Street 19 A2
Lydford Road 26 A1
Lydon Road 142 B2
Lyford Road 146 A2/B2
Lygon Place 19 A2
Lyham Close 150 B1
Lyham Road 143 B2
150 A1/B1
Lyme Street 71 B2
Lyminge Gardens 146 B2
Lymington Road 65 A2
66 A1/A2
Lympstone Gardens 115 B2
Lyn Mews 64 B2
94 B1
Lynbrook Grove 114 B1
Lyncott Crescent 141 B2
Lyndhurst Gardens 67 A2/B1
Lyndhurst Grove 122 B2
123 B1
Lyndhurst Road 67 A1/A2
Lyndhurst Square 123 B1
Lyndhurst Terrace 67 A1
Lyndhurst Way 123 A1/B1
Lynette Avenue 148 A2
Lynmouth Road 85 A1/A2
Lynn Road 148 A2
Lynton Road 53 A2
108 B1/B2
109 B1
Lynwood Road 151 A1/B1
Lyon Street 79 A2
Lyons Place 76 A1
Lyons Walk 34 B1
Lysander Grove 60 A1
Lysander Mews 60 A1
Lysia Street 47 A1
Lysias Road 148 A1
Lytcott Grove 129 B2
Lyte Street 92 A2
Lytham Street 113 B2
Lyttelton Close 69 A2
Lytton Grove 136 B1/B2
Lyveden Road 152 B1/B2

M

Mabledon Place 4 A2
Mablethorpe Road 42 B1
Macaulay Road 142 B1/B2
Macbeth Street 40 B2
Macclesfield Bridge 69 B1
Macclesfield Road 7 A1/A2
Macclesfield Street 11 B2
Macdonald Road 60 A1
Macduff Road 141 A2
Mace Close 96 B1
Mace Street 93 A1
Macfarland Grove 114 B1
Macfarlane Road 33 A1
Macfarren Place 2 A2
Mackay Road 142 A1
Mackennal Street 69 B1
Mackenzie Road 74 B1
Mackeson Road 57 A2
Mackintosh Lane 90 A2

Street Index

Macklin Street 13 A2
Mackrow Walk 101 A2
Macks Road 108 B2
Mackworth Street 77 B2
Macleod Street 113 B1
Maclise Road 34 B1
Macmillan Way 151 B2
Maconochies Road 102 B2
Macquarie Way 103 B1
Macroom Road 26 A1
Maddams Street 99 A2
Maddox Street 10 A1
Madinah Road 86 B2
Madras Place 74 B2
Madrigal Lane 121 A1
Madron Street 114 A1
Magdala Avenue 59 A2
60 A1
Magdalen Mews 66 A2
Magdalen Road 146 A2/B1
Magdalen Street 107 A1
Magdalene Close 123 B2
Magee Street 112 B1
Magnin Close 88 A2
Magnolia Place 143 B2
Maguire Street 107 A2
Mahogany Close 111 A2
Maida Avenue 31 A1/A2
Maida Vale 68 A1/B1
76 A1
Maiden Lane 24 A1
79 A1
106 A1
Maiden Place 59 B1
Maidenstone Hill 120 B2
Maidstone Buildings Mews 106 A1
Maidstone Street 88 B2
Maismore Street 115 B1
Maitland Park Road 57 B1
71 A1
Maitland Park Villas 57 B1
Major Close 127 A1
Major Road 108 A2
Makepeace Avenue 58 A2
59 A1
Makins Street 46 A1
Malabar Street 102 A1
Malam Gardens 100 A2
Malcolm Place 92 B2
Malcolm Road 92 B2
Malden Crescent 71 A1
Malden Place 57 B1/B2
Malden Road 57 B1/B2
71 A1
Maldon Close 81
128 A2
Malet Place 4 A1
Malet Street 4 A1/B1
Malfort Road 129 A1
The Mall 9 B2
23 B1/B2
24 B1
Mall Road 40 B2
Mallams Mews 145 B2
Mallinson Road 140 B1
Mallord Street 44 B2
Mallory Street 76 B1/B2
Mallow Street 7 A2
Malmesbury Road 94 B1/B2
Malpas Road 87 B1
126 B1/B2
Malt Street 115 A1
Malta Street 6 B2
Maltby Street 107 A2
Malthouse Drive 38 B2
Maltings Place 50 A1
107 A1
Malton Mews 28 A2
Malton Road 28 A1
Maltravers Street 14 B2
Malva Close 138 B2
Malvern Close 25 B2
Malvern Mews 26 A2
Malvern Road 26 A2
88 A2
Malvern Terrace 80 B1
Malwood Road 148 A1
Managers Street 101 B2
Manaton Close 123 B2
Manbre Road 41 B1
Manchester Drive 25 A1
Manchester Grove 103 B1
Manchester Mews 2 B1
Manchester Road 101 B2
103 —
Manchester Square 2 B1
Manchester Street 2 A1/B1
Manchuria Road 147 A2
Manciple Street 106 B2
Mandalay Road 148 A2
Mandarin Street 100 A1
Mandela Street 78 A1
135 B2
Mandela Way 107 B1/B2
114 A1
Mandeville Mews 143 B2
Mandeville Place 2 B1
Mandrake Road 151 A1
Mandrell Road 150 A1
Manette Street 12 A1/A2
Manfred Road 137 A2/B1
Manger Road 73 B2
Manilla Street 100 B1/B2
Manley Court 64 A2
Manley Street 70 /B1
Manningford Close 6 A2
Manningtree Street 95 A1
Manor Avenue 126 B2
Manor Court 50 A1
Manor Gardens 61 B1
Manor Grove 116 B1/B2
Manor Place 112 A2/B2
113 A1
Manor Road 64 A2
86 A1
Manorfield Close 59 B1
Manresa Road 45 B1
Manse Road 86 A2
Mansell Street 95 A1/B1
Mansfield Mews 2 B2
Mansfield Road 57 B2
Mansfield Street 2 B2
Mansford Street 92 A1
Mansion Close 135 B2
Mansion House Place 17 A1
Mansion House Street 17 A1
Manson Mews 45 A1
Manson Place 45 A1
Mantilla Road 151 B2
Mantua Street 139 A2
Mantus Close 92 B2
Mantus Road 92 B2
Manville Gardens 151 A2
Manville Road 151 A2
Manygates 148 B2
Mape Street 92 B1
Maple Close 149 A2
Maple Leaf Square 110 A2
Maple Place 3 A2
Maple Street 3 A2
92 A1
Mapledene Road 88 A1/A2
Maples Place 96 A2
Mapleton Crescent 138 B2
Maplin Street 93 B2
98 A2
Marble Arch 1 B1/B2
Marble Quay 95 B1
Marcella Road 145 A2
Marchant Street 125 A2
Marchbank Road 42 A2
Marchmont Street 4 A2
Marchwood Close 122 A2
Marcia Road 114 A1
Marcilly Road 139 B1/B2
Marco Road 40 A2
Marcon Place 87 B1
Marcus Garvey Way 127 B1
Marcus Street 138 B2
Marcus Terrace 138 B2
Mare Street 87 B2
89 A2/B1/B2
Maresfield Gardens 66 A2/B2
Margaret Buildings 85 A1
Margaret Ingram Close 42 B2
Margaret Road 85 A1
Margaret Street 2 B2
3 B1
Margaretta Terrace 45 B2
Margate Road 150 A1
Margery Street 6 A1
Margravine Gardens 41 B2
42 A1
Margravine Road 41 B2
42 A1
Marham Gardens 146 B2
Maria Close 108 B2
Maria Terrace 97 A2
Marian Place 92 A2
Marian Square 92 A2
Marian Street 92 A2
Marigold Street 108 A2
Marine Street 108 A1
Marinefield Road 50 A1
Mariners Mews 103 A2
Maritime Quay 102 B1/B2
Maritime Street 99 A1
Marius Passage 151 A2
Marius Road 151 A1/A2
Marjorie Grove 141 B1
Marjorie Mews 97 B2
Mark Lane 18 B1
Mark Street 8 A1
Market Approach 32 B2
Market Lane 33 B1
Market Mews 9 A1

Market Place 3 B1
Market Road 73 B2
Market Yard Mews 107 A1
Markham Place 46 A1
Markham Square 46 A1
Markham Street 46 A1
Marl Road 138 A2
Marlborough Avenue 88 A2/B2
Marlborough Close 112 A2
Marlborough Court 10 A2
Marlborough Gate House 30 B2
Marlborough Grove 115 A1
Marlborough Hill 68 A2/B2
Marlborough Place 68 B1/B2
Marlborough Road 23 B1
60 A2/B2
Marlborough Street 45 A2
Marlborough Yard 60 B2
Marloes Road 35 B2
Marlow Way 110 A2
The Marlowes 69 A1
Marmion Mews 141 B2
Marmion Road 141 B2
Marmont Road 123 A2
Marney Road 141 B1
Maroon Street 98 A1/A2
Marquess Road 82 A1
Marquis Road 62 A1
73 B1
Marriott Road 53 B2
61 A2
Marryat Square 48 A1
Marsden Road 129 A2
Marsden Street 71 A1
Marsh Street 102 B2
Marsh Wall 100 B1/B2
101 B1/B2
Marshall Close 146 A1
Marshall Street 10 A2/B2
Marshalls Place 108 A1
Marshalsea Road 106 A1
Marsham Street 21 A2
22 B2
Marshfield Street 103 A2
Marsland Close 112 B2
Marston Close 66 B1
Martaban Road 64 A2
Martara Mews 113 B1
Martel Place 86 B2
Martello Street 89 A1/A2
Martello Terrace 89 A1
Martha Court 92 A2
Martha Street 96 B2
Martha's Buildings 7 A2
Martin Lane 17 B2
Martindale Road 148 A2
Martineau Mews 74 A2
Martineau Road 74 A2
Martineau Street 97 B1
Marton Road 64 A2
Martys Yard 56 B1
Marville Road 48 A1
Marvin Street 89 A2
Mary Ann Gardens 119 A1/B1
Mary Datchelor Close 122 A1
Mary Place 28 B1
Mary Seacole Close 88 A1
Mary Street 83 A2
Marylands Road 26 B2

Marylebone Flyover 31 A2
76 B1
Marylebone High Street 2 A1/A2
Marylebone Lane 2 B1
Marylebone Mews 2 B2
Marylebone Passage 3 B1
Marylebone Road 1 A1
2 A1/A2
31 A2
76 B1/B2
77 B1
Marylebone Street 2 A1
Marylee Way 131 B2
Maryon Mews 57 A1
Masbro Road 33 B2
Mascotte Road 136 A1
Maskelyne Close 132 A1
Mason Close 115 A2
Mason Street 113 A2
Mason's Yard 23 A1
Masons Arms Mews 2 B2
Masons Place 7 A1
Massie Road 86 B2
Massingberd Way 151 B2
Massinger Street 114 A1
Massingham Street 92 B2
93 B1
Masters Drive 115 A2
116 B1
Masters Street 98 A1
Masthouse Terrace 102 B1
Mastmaker Road 100 B2
Matham Grove 129 A2
Matheson Road 34 B2
Matilda Street 79 A2/B2
Matlock Close 128 B1
Matlock Street 98 A1
Matthew Parker Street 22 A2
Matthews Street 141 A1
Matthias Road 64 B1/B2
Mattingley Way 114 B1
Mattison Road 55 A1
Maud Chadburn Place 148 A2
Maud Wilkes Close 72 A2
Maude Road 122 B1/B2
Mauleverer Road 150 A1
Maunsel Street 21 A1
Mauritius Road 103 B2
Maury Road 85 B2
86 A2
Mawbey Place 115 A1
Mawbey Road 114 A2
Mawbey Street 134 B2
Mawson Lane 38 B2
Maxted Road 130 A1
Maxwell Road 43 B2
49 A2
May Street 42 A2
Maya Close 123 B2
Mayall Road 127 B1/B2
Maybury Mews 52 B2
Mayfair Mews 70 A1
Mayfair Place 9 A2
Mayfield Avenue 38 A2
Mayfield Close 86 B1
149 A2
Mayfield Road 54 A1
88 A1
Mayflower Close 111 B1

Mayflower Road 143 A2
Mayflower Street 109 A2
Mayford Close 147 B1
Mayford Road 147 B1/B2
Maygood Street 79 B2
Maygrove Road 65 A1/A2
Maynard Close 43 B2
Maynards Quay 96 B2
Maysoule Road 139 A1/A2
Mayton Street 61 B2
Mazenod Avenue 65 B1
McAuley Close 131 A2
McCall Close 143 A2
McCrone Mews 67 B1
McCullum Road 94 A2
McDermott Close 132 B1
McDermott Road 123 B2
130 A1
McDowall Road 121 A2
McGregor Road 29 A1
McKerrell Road 123 A2
McLeod's Mews 35 B2
McMillan Street 119 A1
McNeil Road 122 B1
Mead Place 90 A1
Mead Row 104 B2
Meadcroft Road 112 B1/B2
Meadow Mews 135 A1
Meadow Place 134 A2
Meadow Road 135 A1
Meadow Row 106 B1
Meadowbank 70 A1
Meadowbank Close 47 A1
Meard Street 11 B2
Meath Street 133 B1
Mecklenburgh Place 5 B1
Mecklenburgh Square 5 B1/B2
Mecklenburgh Street 5 B2
Medburn Street 78 B1
Median Road 87 B2
Medina Grove 62 B1
Medina Road 62 B1
Medlar Street 121 A2
Medley Road 65 A2
Medway Buildings 94 A1
Medway Mews 94 B1
Medway Road 94 A1/B1
Medway Street 22 B2
Medwin Street 144 B1
Meeting Fields Path 89 A2
Meeting House Alley 96 B1
Meeting House Lane 123 A2
124 A1
Mehetabel Road 89 A2
90 A1
Melbourne Grove 129 A2/B2
Melbourne Mews 135 B2
Melbourne Place 14 B1
Melbourne Square 135 B2
Melbray Mews 48 B2
Melbury Court 34 A2/B2
Melbury Drive 122 A2
Melbury Road 34 A2/B2
Melcombe Place 76 B2
Melcombe Street 76 B2
Meldon Close 50 A1
Melgund Road 74 B2
Melina Place 68 B1
Melina Road 32 B1

Street Index

Melior Place 107 A1
Melior Street 106 A2
Mellish Street 102 A1/A2
Mellison Road 152 A1
Melody Lane 75 B1
Melody Road 139 B1
146 A1
Melon Place 35 A2
Melon Road 123 A1
Melrose Gardens 33 B1
Melrose Terrace 33 B1
Melton Street 77 B2
Melville Place 81 B1
Melyn Close 73 A1
Memel Court 7 B1
Memel Street 7 B2
Mendip Road 139 A1
Mendora Road 42 B1
Menotti Street 91 B2
Mentmore Terrace 89 A2/B1
Mepham Street 104 A1/A2
Mercator Place 102 B2
Mercer Street 12 A2
13 B1
Merceron Street 92 B1
Mercers Mews 59 B2
Mercers Place 41 A1
Mercers Road 60 B1/B2
Merchant Street 94 B1
99 A1
Mercier Road 136 B2
Mercury Way 117 B1
125 A1
Meredith Street 6 B2
Meridian Place 101 B1
Merivale Road 136 A2
Merlin Street 6 A1
Mermaid Court 106 A1/A2
Merrick Square 106 B1
Merrington Road 43 B1
Merrow Street 113 B2
Merrow Walk 113 B2
Merthyr Terrace 41 B1
47 A1
Merton Avenue 39 A1
Merton Rise 67 B1
Merton Road 138 B1
Meru Close 58 B1
Mervan Road 127 B1
Messina Avenue 65 B1
Meteor Street 141 B2
Methley Street 112 B1
Metropolitan Close 99 B2
The Mews 81
Mews Street 95 B2
Mexfield Road 137 A2
Meymott Street 104 A2
Meynell Crescent 90 B1/B2
Meynell Gardens 90 B1
Meynell Road 90 B2
Meyrick Road 139 A2
Micawber Street 83 B2
Michael Road 50 A1
Micklethwaite Road 43 B1
Middle Field 69 A1
Middle Lane 53 A2
Middle Lane Mews 53 A2
Middle Row 25 A1
Middle Street 7 B1
Middle Temple Lane 14 B2
Middle Yard 106 A2
Middlesex Court 39 B1
Middlesex Street 8 B2
18 A1/A2
Middleton Drive 110 A2
Middleton Grove 73 B1/B2
Middleton Mews 73 B2
Middleton Road 88 A1/A2
Middleton Street 92 A2
Midford Place 3 A2
Midhope Street 5 A1
Midhurst Way 87 A1
Midland Place 103 B2
Midland Road 78 B2
Midlothian Road 98 A2
Midmoor Road 148 B2
Midship Close 110 A2
Milborne Grove 44 B1
Milborne Street 90 A1
Milcote Street 105 B1
Mildenhall Road 87 A2
Mildmay Avenue 82 A1
Mildmay Grove North 82 A1
Mildmay Grove South 82 A1
Mildmay Park 64 B1
82 A1
Mildmay Place 82 A2
Mildmay Road 64 B1
82 A1/A2
Mildmay Street 82 A1
Mile End Place 93 B1
Mile End Road 93 B1/B2
94 B1
96 A2
97 A1/A2
Miles Place 76 B1
Miles Street 134 A2
Milford Lane 14 B2
Milk Street 16 A2
Milk Yard 96 B2
Milkwell Yard 121 B2
Milkwood Road 127 A2/B2
Mill Lane 65 A2
Mill Place 98 B1
Mill Pond Close 134 B1
Mill Row 84 A2
Mill Street 10 A1
107 A2
108 A1
Mill Yard 95 B1
Millard Close 64 B2
Millbank 21 A2/B2
22 B2
Millbrook Road 145 B2
Millender Walk 116 A2
Millennium Drive 103 A2
Millennium Place 92 A2
Millennium Way 103 A2
Miller Street 78 A1
Miller's Avenue 86 A1
Miller's Terrace 86 A1
Millers Court 39 B1
Millers Way 33 B1
Millfield Lane 58 A1
Millfield Place 58 A1
Millfields Road 87 A2
Millgrove Street 141 A1
Millharbour 100 B2
102 A2
Milligan Street 100 A1
Millman Mews 5 B1
Millman Street 5 B1
Millmark Grove 126 B1
Mills Court 84
Millshott Close 47 B1
Millstream Road 107 A2
Millwall Dock Road 102 A1
Millwood Street 28 A2
Milman's Street 44 B2
Milner Place 80 B2
Milner Square 80 A2
Milner Street 37 B2
Milson Road 33 B2
34 B1
Milton Avenue 52 A1
Milton Close 114 A2
Milton Court 7 B2
Milton Court Road 118 B1
Milton Grove 64 B1
Milton Park 52 A1/B2
Milton Place 74 B1
Milton Road 52 B2
127 B2
Milton Street 7 B2
Milverton Street 112 B1
Milward Street 96 A2
Mimosa Street 48 A2
Mina Road 114 A1
Mincing Lane 18 B1
Minera Mews 19 B2
Minerva Close 135 A2
Minerva Street 92 A2
Minet Road 121 B1
127 A1
Minford Gardens 33 B1/B2
Ming Street 100 A2
Minories 18 A2/B2
Minshull Street 134 B1
Minson Road 90 B2
Mint Street 106 A1
Mintern Street 84 A1
Minton Mews 66 A1
Mirabel Road 42 B2
Miranda Close 96 A2
Miranda Road 60 A1
Mission Place 123 A2
Mitali Passage 95 A1
Mitcham Road 152 A1/A2/B2
Mitchell Street 7 A2
Mitchison Road 82 A1
Mitford Road 61 B1
The Mitre 100 A1
Mitre Court 14 B2
Mitre Road 104 A2
Mitre Square 18 A2
Mitre Street 18 A1/A2
Moat Place 145 A1
Moberly Road 149 A2/B2
mod29W-2006-451 56 B2
Modbury Gardens 71 A1
Moelwyn Hughes Court 73 B1
Moffat Road 151 B1
Molasses Row 139 A1
Molesford Road 49 A1
Molly Huggins Close 148 B2
Molyneux Drive 151 B2

Molyneux Street 1 A1
Mona Road 124 B2
Monck Street 22 B2
Monclar Road 129 A1
Moncorvo Close 37 A1
Moncrieff Place 123 B2
Moncrieff Street 123 B2
Monkton Street 112 A1
Monkwell Square 7 B2
Monmouth Place 30 B1
Monmouth Road 30 B1
Monmouth Street 13 A1/B1
Monnery Road 59 B2
Monnow Road 108 B2
Monro Way 87 A1
Monsell Court 62 B2
Monsell Road 62 B2
63 B1
Monson Road 125 A1/B1
Montagu Mansions 1 A2
Montagu Mews North 1 A2
Montagu Mews South 1 A2
Montagu Mews West 1 A2
Montagu Place 1 A2
Montagu Row 1 A2
Montagu Square 1 A2
Montagu Street 1 A2
Montague Close 106 A2
Montague Place 4 B1
Montague Road 54 A1
86 B2
Montague Square 124 A2
Montague Street 4 B2
15 A2
Montaigne Close 21 A2
Montana Road 151 A2
Montclare Street 91 A1
Monteagle Way 86 A2
130 A2
Montefiore Street 142 A1
Montego Close 127 B1
Montem Street 61 A2
Montenotte Road 53 A1
Montford Place 131 B2
Montgomery Street 101 B1
Montholme Road 140 B2
Monthope Road 91 B2
Montpelier Grove 72 A2
Montpelier Mews 37 A2
Montpelier Place 37 A1/A2
97 B1
Montpelier Road 124 A1
Montpelier Square 37 A1/A2
Montpelier Street 37 A2/B2
Montpelier Terrace 37 A1
Montpelier Walk 37 A1/B1
Montreal Place 14 B1
Montrose Court 36 A2
Montrose Place 19 A2
Montserrat Road 136 A2
Monument Street 17 B2
18 B1
Monza Street 97 B1
Moodkee Street 110 B1
Moody Road 123 A1
Moody Street 93 B1
Moon Street 80 B2
Moor Lane 7 B2
Moor Place 7 B2
Moor Street 12 A2
Moore Park Road 43 B2
49 A2
Moore Street 37 B2
Moorfields 7 B2
Moorgate 8 B1
17 A1
Moorgate Place 17 A1
Moorhouse Road 29 A2
Moorland Road 127 A1
Mora Street 7 A2
Morant Street 100 A2
Morat Street 135 B2
Moravian Place 44 B2
Moravian Street 92 A2
Moray Mews 62 B1
Moray Road 61 A2
62 B1
Mordaunt Street 144 B2
Morden Wharf Road 103 A2
More Close 34 B1
Morecambe Close 97 A2
Morecambe Street 113 A1
Moreland Street 7 A1
Morella Road 147 A1
Moreton Close 20 B2
Moreton Place 20 B2
Moreton Street 21 A1/B1
Moreton Terrace 20 B2
Moreton Terrace Mews
North 20 B2
South 20 B2
Morgan Road 25 B2
74 B1
Morgan Street 93 B2
94 B1
Morgans Lane 107 A1
Moriatry Close 73 A2
Morie Street 138 A2
Moring Road 151 B2
Morland Mews 80 A1
Morley Street 104 B2
Morna Road 121 B2
Morning Lane 89 A2
90 A1
Mornington Avenue 34 B2
Mornington Crescent 77 A2
78 A1
Mornington Grove 94 B2
99 A2
Mornington Mews 121 A2
Mornington Place 77 A2
Mornington Road 126 A2
Mornington Street 77 A2
Mornington Terrace 77 A1/A2
Morocco Street 107 A1
Morpeth Grove 90 B1
Morpeth Road 90 B1
Morpeth Street 93 A1/B1
Morpeth Terrace 20 A2
Morris Place 62 B1
Morris Road 99 B2
Morris Street 96 A2
Morrish Road 150 B1
Morrison Road 145 A2
Morrison Street 141 B1
Morshead Road 27 A1
Morten Close 149 A2
Mortimer Crescent 68 A1
Mortimer Market 4 A1
Mortimer Place 68 A1
Mortimer Road 82 B2
Mortimer Square 33 A2
Mortimer Street 3 B1/B2
Mortimer Terrace 58 B1
Morton Close 96 A2
Morton Mews 43 A2
Morton Place 131 A2
Morton Road 81
Morval Road 127 B1
Morville Street 94 B2
Morwell Street 4 B1
Moscow Place 30 B1
Moscow Road 29 B2
30 B1
Moseley Row 103 B2
Moss Close 91 B2
Mossbury Road 140 A1
Mossford Street 98 A2
Mossop Street 37 B2
46 A1
Mostyn Grove 94 B2
Mostyn Road 121 B1
135 B2
Motcomb Street 19 A1
Mothers' Square 87 B2
Motley Avenue 8 A2
Motley Street 142 A2
Moulins Road 89 B2
90 B1
The Mount 56 A1
Mount Court 136 A1
Mount Mills 7 A1
Mount Pleasant 5 B2
Mount Pleasant Crescent 53 B2
Mount Pleasant Villas 53 B2
Mount Row 9 A1/A2
The Mount Square 56 A2
Mount Street 9 A1/A2
Mount Street Mews 9 A2
Mount Terrace 96 A2
Mount Vernon 56 A1
Mount View Road 53 B2
54 B1/B2
Mountague Place 101 A1
Mountbatten Mews 146 B1
Mountfort Crescent 80 A1
Mountfort Terrace 80 A1
Mountgrove Road 63 B1
Mountview Court 55 A2
Mowatt Close 60 A2
Mowlem Street 92 A2
Mowll Street 135 B2
Moxon Street 2 A1
Moye Close 92 A1
Moylan Road 42 B1
Muir Drive 146 A2
Muir Road 86 A2
87 A1
Muirfield Close 116 B1
Muirfield Crescent 102 A2
Mulberry Close 56 B1
130 B1
Mulberry Mews 126 A2
Mulberry Place 39 B1
Mulberry Road 88 A1
Mulberry Street 95 A1
Mulberry Walk 44 B2

Street Index

Mulgrave Road 42 B2
Mulkern Road 53 B1
60 A2
Muller Road 149 A2
Mullet Gardens 92 A1
Mulready Street 76 B1
Multon Road 146 A2/B2
Mulvaney Way 106 A2
Mumford Court 16 A2
Mumford Mills 119 B2
Mumford Road 127 B2
Muncaster Road 140 A2/B2
Mund Street 42 A2
Munden Street 34 B1
Mundy Street 84
Munro Mews 25 B1
Munro Terrace 44 B2
Munster Road 42 B1
47 A2
48 A1/A2/B2
49 B1
Munster Square 77 B1
Munton Road 113 A1
Murdock Street 115 B2
Muriel Street 79 B2
Murphy Street 104 B2
Murray Grove 83 B2
84 B1
Murray Mews 72 B2
Murray Street 72 B2
Musard Road 42 B1
Musbury Street 97 A1
Muscatel Place 122 A2
Muschamp Road 129 A2
Muscovy Street 18 B2
Museum Lane 36 B2
Museum Street 4 B2
13 A1
Musgrave Crescent 49 A1/A2
Musjid Road 132 B1
Mustow Place 48 B2
Muswell Hill Road 51 A2
Mutrix Road 65 B1
Mutton Place 71 A2
Myatt Road 121 A1
Myddelton Passage 6 A2
Myddelton Square 6 A2
Myddelton Street 6 B1/B2
Myddleton Avenue 63 B1
Myers Lane 117 B1
Mylius Close 125 B1
Mylne Street 6 A2
Myrdle Street 96 A1
Mysore Road 140 A2

N

Nag's Head Court 7 B2
Nairne Grove 128 B2
Nankin Street 99 B1/B2
Nansen Road 141 B2
Nant Street 92 A2
Nantes Close 139 A1/B1
Naoroji Street 6 A1
Napier Avenue 48 B2
102 B2
Napier Close 34 B1
126 A2
Napier Grove 83 A2/B2
Napier Place 34 B2
Napier Road 34 B1/B2
Napier Terrace 80 A2
Napoleon Road 87 A1
Narbonne Avenue 148 A2
149 A1
Narborough Street 49 B2
Narcissus Road 65 A2
Narford Road 87 B2
Narrow Street 97 B2
98 B1
100 A1
Naseby Close 66 B1
Nash Street 77 B1
Nasmyth Street 40 A2
Nassau Street 3 B1
Nassington Road 57 A1/A2
Nathaniel Close 91 B1
Navarino Grove 89 A1
Navarino Road 86 B2
89 A1
Navarre Street 91 A1
Navy Street 143 A1
Naylor Road 115 B2
123 A2
124 A1
Nazareth Gardens 123 B2
Nazrul Street 91 A1
Neal Street 13 A1/B1
Neal's Yard 13 B1
Nealden Street 144 A1
Neate Street 114 B2
Neathouse Place 20 A2
Nebraska Street 106 B1
Neckinger 107 A2/B2
Neckinger Street 108 A1
Needham Road 29 B2
Needleman Street 110 A2/B2
Nella Road 47 A1
Nelldale Road 109 B1
Nelson Gardens 92 A1
Nelson Place 83 B1
Nelson Road 54 A1
120 A2
Nelson Square 105 A1
Nelson Street 96 A1/A2
Nelson Terrace 83 B1
Nelson's Row 143 B1/B2
Nelsons Yard 78 A1
Nepaul Road 132 B2
Neptune Street 110 B1
Nesham Street 95 B2
Ness Street 108 A1
Netheravon Road 39 B1
Netheravon Road South 38 B2
39 B1
Netherfield Road 151 A1
Netherford Road 142 A2
Netherhall Gardens 66 A2/B2
67 A1
Netherhall Way 66 A2
Netherleigh Close 52 B1
Netherton Grove 44 B1
Netherwood Place 33 B1
Netherwood Road 33 B1/B2
Netherwood Street 65 A1
Netley Street 77 B2
Nettleton Road 125 B2
Nevada Street 120 A2
Nevern Place 43 A1
Nevern Road 35 B1
Nevern Square 35 B1
43 A1
Nevill Road 64 B2
Neville Close 78 B2
123 A2
Neville Gill Close 138 B1
Neville Street 45 A1
Nevinson Close 139 B2
Nevis Road 147 B2
New Bond Street 2 B2
10 A1/B1
New Bridge Street 15 B1/B2
New Burlington Mews 10 B1
New Burlington Place 10 A1
New Burlington Street 10 B1
New Butt Lane 119 B2
New Butt Lane North 119 B2
New Cavendish Street 2 A1/B2
3 A1
New Change 16 A1
New Charles Street 7 A1
New Church Road 114 B1
121 A2
122 A1
New College Mews 80 A2
New Compton Street 12 A2
New Court 14 B2
New Crane Place 96 B2
New Cross Road 119 B1/B2
124 A2
125 B1/B2
126 A1/A2
New End 56 B2
New End Square 56 B2
New Fetter Lane 14 A2/B2
New Globe Walk 105 A2
New Goulston Street 18 A2
New Inn Broadway 84
New Inn Passage 14 B1
New Inn Square 84
New Inn Street 84
New Inn Yard 84
New Kent Road 105 B2
112 A2
113 A1/A2
114 A1
New King Street 119 A1
New Kings Road 48 B2
49 A1/A2/B1
New London Street 18 B1/B2
New North Place 8 A2
New North Road 81 B1
82 B1
84 A1/B1
New North Street 5 B1
New Oxford Street 4 B1/B2
New Park Road 150 B1
New Quebec Street 1 A2
New Road 53 A2
96 A1/A2
New Spring Gardens Walk 131 B1
New Square 14 B2
New Street 8 B2
New Street Square 15 B1
New Union Close 103 A2
New Union Street 7 B2
New Wharf Road 79 B1

Newark Street	96	A2
Newburgh Street	10	A2
Newburn Street	131	B2
Newbury Mews	71	A1
Newbury Street	7	B1
Newby Place	101	A1
Newby Street	142	A1
Newcastle Close	15	B1
Newcastle Place	31	A2
Newcastle Row	6	B1
Newcombe Street	29	B2
Newcomen Road	139	A2
Newcomen Street	106	A1/A2
Newcourt Street	69	B1
Newell Street	100	A1
Newent Close	114	B1
Newgate Street	15	B2
Newhams Row	107	A1
Newick Road	87	A2
Newington Barrow Way	61	B2
	62	B1
Newington Butts	112	A2
Newington Causeway	105	B2
	106	B1
Newington Green	64	B1
Newington Green Road	64	B1
	82	A1
Newlands Quay	96	B2
Newman Passage	3	B2
Newman Street	3	B2
Newman Yard	3	B2
Newman's Court	17	A2
Newman's Row	14	A2
Newnham Terrace	131	A2
Newnton Close	63	A2
Newport Place	12	B2
Newport Street	131	A2/B1
Newton Place	102	B1
Newton Road	30	B1
Newton Street	4	B2
	13	A2
Newtons Yard	138	B1
Newtown Street	133	B1
Nicholas Lane	17	B2
Nicholas Mews	38	B1
Nicholas Road	92	B2
Nicholay Road	60	A2
Nicholl Street	88	B2
Nichols Close	62	A1
Nicholson Street	105	A1
Nicosia Road	146	A2
Nigel Playfair Avenue	40	B2
Nigel Road	130	A1
Nightingale Lane	147	A1/A2/B1
	148	A1
Nightingale Mews	93	A2
	112	A1
Nightingale Place	44	B1
Nightingale Road	81	A2
	87	A1
Nightingale Square	147	B2
Nightingale Walk	148	A1
Nile Close	86	A2
Nile Street	83	B2
	84	B1
Nile Terrace	114	B2
Nimrod Passage	82	A2
Nine Elms Lane	133	A2
	134	A1
Niton Street	47	A1
Noble Street	7	B2
	16	A1
Noel Road	80	B2
	83	B1
Noel Street	10	A2
	11	A1
Nolan Way	87	A1
Norbiton Road	98	B2
Norburn Street	28	A2
Norcott Road	85	B2
	86	A2
Norfolk Avenue	86	A1
Norfolk Crescent	31	B2
Norfolk Mews	25	B1
Norfolk Place	31	B2
Norfolk Road	69	A1
	152	B1
Norfolk Row	131	A1
Norfolk Square	31	B1/B2
Norfolk Square Mews	31	B2
Norfolk Terrace	42	A1
Norgrove Street	148	B1
Norland Place	28	B2
Norland Road	33	A2
Norland Square	28	B1/B2
Norman Grove	94	A1
Norman Road	120	A1
Norman Street	7	A2
Normanby Close	137	B1
Normand Mews	42	A1
Normand Road	42	A1/B1
Normandy Road	135	B2
Norris Street	23	A2
Norroy Road	136	A1
North Audley Street	1	B2
North Bank	76	A1
The (North Carriage Drive) Ring	31	B1
The North Colonnade	100	B2
	101	A1/B1
North Crescent	4	A1
North Cross Road	129	B2
	130	B1
North End Crescent	34	B2
North End Road	34	B1/B2
	42	A1/A2/B2
	43	B1
North End Road Street Market	42	B2
	43	B1
North Eyot Gardens	39	B1
North Flockton Street	108	A1
North Gower Street	77	B2
North Grove	51	B1
North Hill	51	A2
North Lodge Close	136	B1
North Mews	5	B2
North Passage	138	A1
North Road	51	A2/B1/B2
	73	B1/B2
North Row	1	B2
North Side Wandsworth Common	139	B1/B2
North Street	142	A2/B2
North Tenter Street	95	A1
North Terrace	37	B1
North Verbena Gardens	39	B2
North Villas	72	B2
North Wharf Road	31	A2
Northampton Grove	75	B2
	82	A1
Northampton Park	75	B2
	82	A1
Northampton Road	6	B1
Northampton Square	6	B2
Northampton Street	81	B1
Northbourne Road	143	B2
Northburgh Street	6	B2
Northchurch	113	A2
Northchurch Road	81	
	82	B1
Northchurch Terrace	82	B2
Northcote Mews	140	A1
Northcote Road	140	A1/B1
Northcote Road Street Market	140	A1/B1
Northdown Street	79	B1
Northey Street	98	B1
Northfield Road	86	A1
Northfields	137	A2
Northiam Street	89	B1/B2
Northington Street	5	B1/B2
Northlands Street	121	B2
Northolme Road	75	A2
Northpoint Square	72	B2
Northport Street	84	A1
Northumberland Alley	18	B2
Northumberland Avenue	24	B1/B2
Northumberland Place	29	A2
Northumberland Street	24	A1/B1
Northumbria Street	99	B2
Northview	61	B1
Northway Road	128	A1
Northwest Place	80	B1
Northwick Close	76	A1
Northwick Terrace	76	A1
Northwold Road	85	A1/A2
	87	A2
Northwood Road	52	A1
Norton Folgate	8	A2/B2
Norway Gate	111	B2
Norway Place	98	B2
Norway Street	120	A1
Norwich Street	14	B2
Norwood Road	127	B2
Notley Street	122	A1
Notting Hill Gate	29	B1/B2
Nottingdale Square	28	B1
Nottingham Court	13	B1
Nottingham Place	2	A1
Nottingham Road	147	B1
Nottingham Street	2	A1
Nottingham Terrace	2	A1
Novello Street	49	A1
Noyna Road	151	A1
Nugent Road	53	B1
Nugent Terrace	68	B1
Nunhead Crescent	130	A2
Nunhead Green	124	B1
Nunhead Grove	124	B1
Nunhead Lane	124	B1
	130	A2
Nunhead Passage	130	A2
Nursery Close	126	B1
	136	B1
Nursery Lane	88	B1
Nursery Road	89	A2
	144	B2

Street Index

Nursery Row 113 A2
Nutbrook Street 130 A1
Nutcroft Road 115 B2
Nutfield Road 129 A2
Nutford Place 1 A1
Nutley Terrace 66 B2
Nutt Street 114 B2
Nuttall Street 84 A2
Nutwell Street 152 A1
Nynehead Street 118 B1
125 A2
Nyton Close 53 B1

O

O'Leary Square 97 A1
O'Meara Street 106 A1
Oak Hill Park 56 A1
Oak Hill Park Mews 56 A1
Oak Hill Way 56 A1
Oak Lane 100 A1
Oak Park Mews 85 B1
Oak Place 138 B2
Oak Tree Road 76 A2
Oak Village 57 B2
58 B1
Oakbank Grove 128 A1
Oakbury Road 49 B2
50 B1
Oakden Street 112 A1
Oakeshott Avenue 58 A2
59 A1
Oakfield Court 53 B2
Oakfield Road 54 B2
62 A1/A2
Oakfield Street 43 B2
Oakford Road 58 B2
Oakhill Place 137 A2
Oakhill Road 137 A1/A2/B1
138 A1
Oakhurst Grove 130 A1/B1
Oakington Road 26 B2
Oakington Way 53 B2
Oaklands Grove 32 A1
Oaklands Place 143 B1
Oakley Crescent 83 B1
Oakley Gardens 45 B2
54 A1
Oakley Place 114 A2
Oakley Road 82 B1
Oakley Square 78 A1/B1
Oakley Street 45 B1/B2
Oakley Yard 91 A2
Oakmead Road 148 B1
Oakwood Court 34 A1/A2
Oakwood Lane 34 A2
Oat Lane 16 A1
Oberstein Road 139 A2
Oborne Close 128 B1
Observatory Gardens 35 A1
Observatory Mews 103 B2
Occupation Road 113 A1
Ocean Street 98 A1
Ockendon Mews 82 A1
Ockendon Road 82 A1/B1
Octavia Mews 25 A2
Octavia Street 132 A1
Octavius Street 119 B1
Odessa Street 111 B2
Odger Street 141 A1
Offerton Road 143 A1
Offley Road 135 A2
Offord Road 79 A2
80 A1
Offord Street 79 A2
Oglander Road 129 A2
Ogle Street 3 A1
Oil Mill Lane 39 B2
Okeburn Road 151 B1/B2
Olaf Street 33 A2
Old Bailey 15 B2
Old Barrack Yard 19 A1
Old Bellgate Place 102 A1
Old Bethnal Green Road 91 A2
92 A1/A2
Old Bond Street 10 B1
Old Brewers Yard 13 B1
Old Brewery Mews 56 B2
Old Broad Street 8 B2
17 A2
Old Brompton Road 36 B2
43 A1/A2
44 A1
45 A1
Old Buildings 14 B2
Old Burlington Street 10 B1
Old Castle Street 18 A2
Old Castle Street 18 A2
(Pettycoat Lane) Market
Old Cavendish Street 2 B2
Old Chelsea Mews 44 B2
Old Church Road 97 B2
Old Church Street 45 A1/B1
Old Compton Street 11 B2
12 A1/A2
Old Court Place 35 A2
Old Dairy Mews 148 B1
Old Devonshire Road 148 B1
Old Fleet Lane 15 B2
Old Ford Road 92 A2
93 A1/A2
94 A1/A2
Old Forge Mews 32 B1
Old Forge Road 60 A1
Old Gloucester Street 5 B1
Old Hospital Close 147 B1
Old Jamaica Road 108 A1
Old James Street 130 A2
Old Jewry 16 A2/B2
Old Kent Road 106 B2
107 B1
113 A1/A2
114 A1/A2
115 A1/B1/B2
116 B1
124 A1/A2
Old Manor Yard 43 A1
Old Marylebone Road 1 A1
Old Montague Street 91 B1/B2
Old Nichol Street 91 A1
Old North Street 5 B1
The Old Orchard 57 A2
Old Palace Yard 22 A2
Old Paradise Street 131 A1/A2
Old Park Avenue 147 A2
Old Park Lane 9 A1/B1
Old Pye Street 22 A1/A2
Old Quebec Street 1 B2
Old Queen Street 22 A2
Old Royal Free Place 80 B1
Old Royal Free Square 80 B1
Old School Close 103 A2
Old School Square 99 B1
Old Seacoal Lane 15 B2
Old South Lambeth Road 134 A2
Old Square 14 A2/B2
Old Street 7 A1/A2/B1
8 A1
84 B1
Old Town 142 B2
Old York Road 138 A2
Oldbury Place 2 A1
Oldfield Grove 117 A1
Oldfield Mews 52 B2
Oldfield Road 64 A2/B2
Oldhill Street 85 A2
87 A2
Oldridge Road 147 B2
148 A1/B1
Olga Street 93 A2
Olinda Road 86 A1
Oliver Mews 123 B1
Olivers Yard 8 A1
Ollerton Green 94 A2
Olliffe Street 103 A2
Olmar Street 115 B1
Olney Road 112 B2
113 B1
Olympia Mews 30 B1
Olympia Way 34 B1
Omega Close 102 A2
Omega Place 78 B2
Omega Street 126 B2
Ondine Road 129 A2
130 A1
Onega Gate 111 B2
Ongar Road 43 B1
Onslow Crescent 45 A1
Onslow Gardens 44 A1/A2
45 A1
Onslow Mews East 45 A1
Onslow Mews West 45 A1
Onslow Square 36 B2
45 A1/A2
Onslow Street 15 A1
Ontario Street 105 B1/B2
Ontario Way 100 A1
Opal Street 112 A1/A2
Openview 146 B1
Ophir Terrace 123 A1
Oppidans Mews 70 A1
Oppidans Road 70 A1
Orange Place 109 B2
Orange Street 23 A2
Orange Yard 12 A2
Oransay Road 81 A2
Oratory Lane 45 A1
Orb Street 113 A2
Orbain Road 42 B1
Orbel Street 132 A1/B1
Orchard Close 25 B1
81
Orchard Mews 52 A1
82 B1
Orchard Place 87 B1
Orchard Road 52 A1
Orchard Street 1 B2

Orchardson Street 76 A1
Orde Hall Street 5 B1
Ordell Road 94 B2
Ordnance Hill 69 A1/B1
Ordnance Mews 69 B1
Oriel Court 56 B1
Oriel Drive 47 A1
Oriel Road 90 A2
Orient Street 105 B1
112 A2
Orkney Street 141 A1
Orlando Road 142 B2
Orleston Mews 74 B2
Orleston Road 74 B2
Orme Court 30 B1
Orme Court Mews 30 B1
Orme Lane 29 B2
30 B1
Orme Square 30 B1
Ormeley Road 148 B1/B2
Ormiston Grove 32 A1
Ormond Close 5 B1
Ormond Mews 5 B1
Ormond Road 53 B2
Ormond Yard 23 A2
Ormonde Gate 46 B1
Ormonde Place 19 B2
Ormonde Terrace 69 B2
Ormsby Place 64 B2
Ormsby Street 88 B1
Ormside Street 116 B1
Ornan Road 67 B2
Orpheus Street 121 B2
Orsett Street 131 B2
Orsett Terrace 30 B2
Orsman Road 84 A2
Orton Street 95 B2
Orville Road 132 B1
Osbaldeston Road 85 A2
87 A2
Osbert Street 21 A1
Osborn Close 88 A2
Osborn Street 91 B1
Osborne Grove 62 B1
Osborne Road 62 A1
Oscar Faber Place 82 B2
Oscar Street 126 B2
Oseney Crescent 72 B2
Osier Mews 38 B2
Osier Street 92 B2
Osiers Road 138 A1
Oslo Square 111 B2
Osman Road 33 B1
Osnaburgh Street 77 B1
Osnaburgh Terrace 77 B1
Ospringe Road 72 A2
Osram Court 33 B1
Ossian Mews 54 B1
Ossian Road 53 B2
54 B1
Ossington Buildings 2 A1
Ossington Close 29 B2
Ossington Street 29 B2
Ossory Road 115 A1
Ossulston Street 78 B1
Osten Mews 35 B2
Osterley Road 64 B2
Osward Road 147 B2
Oswin Street 105 B1
Oswyth Road 122 B2
Othello Close 112 A1
Otterburn Street 152 B2
Otto Street 112 B2
Ouseley Road 147 B2
Outer Circle 2 A1/A2
69 B1
70
76 A2/B2
77 A1/B1
Outram Place 79 B1
Outwich Street 18 A1
The Oval 92 A2
Oval Place 135 A1/B1
Oval Road 70
71 B1
Oval Way 131 B2
Overbury Road 55 B2
Overstone Road 40 A2/B2
Overton Road 145 A2/B2
Ovex Close 103 A2
Ovington Gardens 37 B1/B2
Ovington Mews 37 B2
Ovington Square 37 B2
Ovington Street 37 B2
Owen Street 6 A2
Owen's Row 6 A2
Owgan Close 122 A1
Oxberry Avenue 48 B1
Oxendon Street 11 B2
23 A2
Oxenford Street 129 A2
Oxestalls Road 118 A1
Oxford Court 17 B1
Oxford Drive 107 A1
Oxford Gardens 25 B1
28 A1
Oxford Gate 41 A2
Oxford Road 62 A1
68 A1
136 A2/B2
Oxford Square 31 B2
Oxford Street 1 B2
2 B1/B2
3 B1/B2
Oxley Close 115 A1
Oxonian Street 129 A2
Oyster Row 97 B1

P

Pablo Neruda Close 127 A2
Pace Place 96 A2
Packington Square 83 A1
Packington Street 83 A1
Padbury Court 91 A2
Paddenswick Road 40 A1/B1/B2
Paddington Green 31 A2
Paddington Street 1 A2
2 A1
Padfield Road 128 A1
Pagden Street 133 A1
Page Street 21 A2
Pageant Crescent 111 A2
Pageantmaster Court 15 B2
Pages Walk 107 B1/B2
Pages Yard 38 B2
Paget Street 6 A2
Pagnell Street 126 A1
Painsthorpe Road 64 A2
Pakeman Street 61 B2
Pakenham Close 147 B2
Pakenham Street 5 B2
Palace Avenue 35 A2
Palace Court 29 B2
Palace Gardens Mews 29 B2
Palace Gardens Terrace 29 B2
35 A2
Palace Gate 36 A1
Palace Green 35 A2
Palace Mews 19 B2
42 B2
Palace Place 9 B2
Palace Street 9 B2
20 A2
Palatine Avenue 64 B2
Palatine Road 64 B2
Palemead Close 47 B1
Palfrey Place 135 A1/A2/B1
Palgrave Gardens 76 B2
Palissy Street 91 A1
Pall Mall 23 A1/A2
Pall Mall East 23 A2
Palliser Road 42 A1
Palmer Place 74 B1
Palmer Street 22 A1
Palmers Road 93 A2
Palmerston Road 65 A1
Palmerston Way 133 A1
Pancras Lane 16 B2
Pancras Road 78 B2
Pandian Way 72 B2
Pandora Road 65 A2
Pankhurst Close 125 B1
Panmure Close 75 A1
Panton Street 23 A2
Papworth Gardens 74 B1
The Parade 46 B1
132 A1
Paradise Road 134 B2
144 A1
Paradise Row 92 A2
Paradise Street 109 A1
Paradise Walk 46 B1
Paragon Mews 113 A2
Paragon Road 89 A2
Pardon Street 6 B2
Pardoner Street 106 B2
Parfett Street 96 A1
Parfrey Street 41 B1
Paris Garden 104 A2
The Park 51 A2
Park Avenue South 53 A1
Park Close 34 A2
90 B1
Park Crescent 2 A2
3 A1
Park Crescent Mews East 3 A1
Park Crescent Mews West 2 A2
Park End 57 A1
Park Hill 143 B2
149 A2
Park Lane 1 B2
9 A1/B1
Park Place 23 A1
82 B1
100 B1
Park Place Villas 31 A1

Street Index

Park Road 53 A1/A2
55 A2
76 A2/B2
Park Road North 38 A1
Park Square East 77 B1
Park Square Mews 2 A2
Park Square West 2 A2
Park Street 1 B2
105 A2
106 A1
Park View Mews 145 A1
Park Village East 77 A1/A2/B2
Park Village West 77 A1
Park Walk 44 B1/B2
Park West 31 B2
Park West Place 31 B2
Parker Mews 13 A2
Parker Street 13 A2
Parkers Row 108 A1
Parkfield Road 126 A1
Parkfield Street 80 B1
Parkgate Road 132 A1
Parkham Street 132 A1
Parkhill Road 57 B1
Parkhill Walk 57 B1
Parkholme Road 86 B2
Parkhouse Street 114 B1
Parkhurst Road 61 B1
73 A2
Parklands 51 B2
Parkside Crescent 62 B1
Parkside Road 141 A1
Parkthorne Road 149 B2
Parkview Court 138 B1
Parkville Road 42 B2
Parkway 71 B1
77 A1
Parliament Court 18 A1
Parliament Hill 57 A1/A2
Parliament Square 22 A2
Parliament Street 24 B1
Parma Crescent 140 A1
Parmiter Street 92 A2
Parnell Road 94 A2/B2
Parnham Street 98 B1
Parolles Road 52 B2
Parr Street 83 A2
84 A1
Parry Street 134 A2
Parsonage Street 103 B2
Parsons Green 49 A1
Parsons Green Lane 48 A2
49 A1
Parthenia Road 49 A1
Partington Close 53 B1
Parvin Street 134 B1
Pascal Street 134 A1
Pasley Close 112 B2
Passmore Street 19 B2
Pastor Street 112 A2
Patcham Terrace 133 B1
Pater Street 35 B1
Patience Road 132 B2
Patio Close 149 A2
Patmore Street 133 B2
Patmos Road 121 A1
Patriot Square 92 A2
Patshull Place 72 B1
Patshull Road 72 B1
Patten Road 146 A2
Patterdale Road 124 A2
Paul Street 8 A1
Paulet Road 121 B1
Paultons Square 44 B2
45 B1
Paultons Street 44 B2
45 B1
Pauntley Street 60 A1
Paveley Drive 132 A1
Paveley Street 76 A2/B2
The Pavement 142 B2
143 B1
Pavilion Road 37 A2/B2
46 A2
Pavilion Street 37 B2
Paxton Road 38 B1
Paxton Terrace 20 B2
Payne Street 118 B2
Peabody Avenue 20 B1
Peabody Close 20 B2
120 B1
Peachwalk Mews 93 A2
Peacock Street 112 A2
Peacock Yard 112 A2
Pear Close 126 A1
Pear Place 104 A2
Pear Tree Close 88 B1
Pear Tree Court 6 B1
Pear Tree Street 7 A1
Peardon Street 142 A1
Pearl Street 96 B2
Pearman Street 104 B2
Pearscroft Court 50 A1
Pearscroft Road 50 A1
Pearse Street 114 B1
Pearson Close 121 A2
Pearson Mews 143 B2
Pearson Street 88 B1
Peartree Lane 97 B1
Peary Place 93 A1
Peckett Square 75 A1
Peckford Place 145 A1/B2
Peckham Grove 114 B1
122 A2
Peckham High Street 123 A1/A2
Peckham Hill Street 114 B2
123 A2
Peckham Park Road 115 B1/B2
Peckham Road 122 B1/B2
123 A1
Peckham Rye 130 A2/B2
Pecks Yard 91 B1
Peckwater Street 72 A2
Pedlars Walk 73 B2
Pedley Street 91 B2
Peel Grove 92 A2
Peel Passage 29 B1
Peel Street 29 B1
Peerless Street 7 A2
Pegasus Close 75 A2
Pegasus Place 135 A2
Pekin Close 99 B2
Pekin Street 99 B1/B2
Pelham Close 122 B2
Pelham Crescent 45 A2
Pelham Place 37 B1
Pelham Street 36 B2
37 B1
Pelier Street 113 B1
Pellant Road 42 B1
Pellatt Road 129 B2
130 B1
Pellerin Road 64 B2
Pelling Street 99 B1
Pelter Street 91 A1/A2
Pemberton Gardens 59 B2
60 B1
Pemberton Place 89 A2
Pemberton Road 55 A1
Pemberton Row 15 B1
Pemberton Terrace 59 B2
Pembridge Crescent 29 B1
Pembridge Gardens 29 B2
Pembridge Mews 29 B2
Pembridge Place 29 B2
138 B1
Pembridge Road 29 B2
Pembridge Square 29 B2
Pembridge Villas 29 B2
Pembroke Avenue 79 A2
Pembroke Close 19 A2
Pembroke Gardens 34 B2
Pembroke Gardens Close 34 B2
Pembroke Mews 35 B1
93 B2
Pembroke Place 35 B1
Pembroke Road 34 B2
35 B1
Pembroke Square 35 B1
Pembroke Street 79 A2
Pembroke Studios 34 B2
Pembroke Villas 35 B1
Pembroke Walk 35 B1
Pembry Close 135 B2
Pembury Place 87 B1
Pembury Road 87 B1
Pemell Close 92 B2
Penally Place 82 B1
Penang Street 96 B1
Penarth Street 116 B1/B2
Pencombe Mews 29 B1
Pencraig Way 115 B2
Pendennis Road 55 A2
Penderyn Way 73 A1
Pendulum Mews 86 B1
Penfold Place 76 B1
Penfold Street 76 A1/B1
Penford Street 121 B1
Penn Road 73 A2/B2
Penn Street 84 A1
Pennack Road 114 B2
Pennant Mews 35 B2
Pennard Road 33 B1
Pennethorne Close 89 B2
Pennethorne Road 123 A2
Pennington Street 95 B2
96 B1
Penny Mews 148 B1
Pennyfields 100 A2
Penpoll Road 89 A1/A2
Penrith Close 136 B2
Penrith Road 55 B2
Penrose Grove 113 B1
Penrose Street 113 B1
Penry Street 114 A1
Penryn Street 78 B1
Pensbury Place 133 B2

Pensbury Street 133 B2
Penshurst Road 90 B1/B2
Pentland Gardens 138 B2
Pentland Street 146 A1
Pentney Road 148 B2
Penton Grove 80 B1
Penton Place 112 A2
Penton Rise 6 A1
Penton Street 80 B1
Pentonville Road 78 B2
79 B1/B2
80 B1
Pentridge Street 123 A1
Penywern Road 43 A1
Penzance Place 28 B1/B2
Penzance Street 28 B1
Pepler Mews 114 B2
Pepper Street 102 A2
103 A1
105 A2
Pepys Road 125 B2
Pepys Street 18 B2
Perceval Avenue 67 B2
Perch Street 86 A2
Percival Street 6 B2
Percy Circus 6 A1
Percy Mews 3 B2
Percy Street 3 B2
Percy Yard 6 A1
Perham Road 42 A1
Perkin's Rents 22 B2
Perkins Square 106 A1
Perren Street 71 A2
Perrers Road 40 B1
Perrin's Walk 56 B1
Perrins Court 56 B1
Perrins Lane 56 B1
Perrymead Street 49 A2
Perryn Road 108 A2
Perrys Place 3 B2
Perseverance Place 135 B2
Perth Road 62 A1/B1
Peter Street 11 B1
Peterboat Close 103 A2/B2
Peterborough Mews 49 B1
Peterborough Road 49 A1/B1/B2
Peterborough Villas 49 A2
Petergate 139 A1
Petersham Lane 36 A1/B1
Petersham Mews 36 B1
Petersham Place 36 B1
Petherton Road 75 A2/B2
Petley Road 47 A1
Peto Place 77 B1
Petticoat Lane Street Market 18 A1/A2
Petty France 20 A2
22 A1
Petty Wales 18 B2
Petworth Street 132 A1
Petyt Place 45 B1
Petyward 46 A1
Peyton Place 120 A2
Phelp Street 113 B2
Phene Street 45 B2
Philbeach Gardens 35 B1
42 A2
Philchurch Place 95 A2
Philip Lane 55 B2
Philip Walk 130 A2
Phillimore Gardens 34 A2
35 A1/B1
Phillimore Gardens Close 35 B1
Phillimore Place 35 A1
Phillimore Walk 35 A1/B1
Phillipp Street 84 A2
Philpot Lane 18 B1
Philpot Square 49 B2
Philpot Street 96 A2
Phipp Street 8 A2
Phipp's Mews 19 A2
Phoenix Close 88 A1
Phoenix Place 5 B2
Phoenix Road 78 B1
Phoenix Street 12 A2
Phoenix Wharf Road 107 A2
Physic Place 46 B1
Piccadilly 9 A2/B1/B2
10 B1/B2
Piccadilly Circus 10 B2
Pickard Street 7 A1
Pickering Close 90 B1
Pickering Mews 30 B1
Pickering Street 81 B1
Pickets Street 148 A1
Pickfords Wharf 83 B1
Pickwick Street 106 B1
Pickworth Close 134 B2
Picton Place 2 B1
Picton Street 122 A1
Pier Head 96 B1
Pier Street 103 A2
Pier Terrace 138 A2
Pigott Street 99 B1
Pilgrim Street 15 B2
Pilgrim's Lane 56 B2
Pilgrimage Street 106 B1/B2
Pilgrims Place 56 B2
Pilgrims Way 52 B2
Pilkington Road 123 B2
Pilot Close 118 B1
Pilton Place 113 A1
Pimlico Road 19 B2
20 B1
Pinchin Street 95 B2
Pindar Street 8 B2
Pindock Mews 27 B1
Pine Close 59 A2
Pine Grove 61 A2
Pine Street 6 B1
Pineapple Court 20 A2
Pinefield Close 100 A1
Pioneer Street 123 A1
Piper Close 74 B1
Pirie Close 128 A2
Pitfield Street 84 /A1/B1
Pitman Street 121 A2
Pitsea Place 97 B2
Pitsea Street 97 B2
Pitt Street 35 A1
Pitt's Head Mews 9 A1
Pixley Street 99 B1
Plantain Place 106 A2
Platina Street 8 A1
Plato Road 144 B1
The Platt 136 A1
Platt Street 78 B1
Playfair Street 41 B1
Playfield Crescent 129 B2
Playford Road 62 B1
Playhouse Yard 15 B2
Pleasant Place 81 B1
Plender Street 78 A1
Plender Street Market 78 A1
Pleshey Road 73 A1
Plevna Street 103 A1
Pleydell Avenue 39 A1
Pleydell Street 15 B1
Plimsoll Close 99 B2
Plimsoll Road 62 B2
Plough Court 17 B2
Plough Place 14 B2
Plough Road 139 A2
Plough Street 95 A1
Plough Terrace 139 A2
Plough Way 117 A1/A2
118 A1
Plough Yard 8 A2
Ploughmans Close 78 A2
Plover Way 111 B2
Plumbers Row 95 A1
Plumbridge Street 120 B1
Plummer Road 149 B2
Plumtree Court 15 B1
Plymouth Wharf 103 B2
Plympton Place 76 B1
Plympton Street 76 B1
Pocock Street 105 A1/A2/B1
Podmore Road 138 A2
Poets Road 64 B1
Point Close 120 B2
Point Hill 120 B2
Point Pleasant 137 A2
138 A1
Pointers Close 102 B2
Poland Street 3 B1
10 A2
Pollard Close 74 A1
Pollard Row 92 A1
Pollard Street 92 A1
Pollen Street 2 B2
Pollitt Drive 76 A1
Polperro Mews 112 A1
The Polygon 142 B2
Polygon Road 78 B1
Pomell Way 18 A2
Pomeroy Street 124 A2
Pomfret Road 127 A2
Pomoja Lane 60 B2
Pond Mead 129 B1
Pond Place 45 A2
Pond Square 51 B1
Pond Street 57 A1
Ponler Street 96 A1
Ponsford Street 90 A1
Ponsonby Place 21 B2
Ponsonby Terrace 21 B2
Pont Street 19 A1
37 B2
Pont Street Mews 37 B2
Ponton Road 133 A2
134 A1
Pontypool Place 104 A2
Poole Road 90 A1
Poole Street 84 A1
Pooles Buildings 5 B2
Pooles Lane 44 B1

Street Index

Pooles Park 62 B1
Poolmans Street 110 A2
Poonah Street 97 B1
Pope Street 107 A2
Popes Road 144 B2
145 B1
Popes Road Street Market 144 B2
Popham Road 81 /B1
Popham Street 81 B1
Poplar Bath Street 101 A1
Poplar Grove 33 B1
Poplar High Street 100 A2
101 A1/A2
Poplar Place 30 B1
Poplar Road 127 A2
128 A1
Poplar Walk 128 A1/B1
Poppins Court 15 B1
Porchester Close 128 A2
Porchester Gardens 30 B1
Porchester Gardens Mews 30 B1
Porchester Place 31 B2
Porchester Road 30 A1/B1
Porchester Square 30 A1/A2
Porchester Terrace 30 B1
Porchester Terrace North 30 A2/B2
Porden Road 150 A2
Porlock Street 106 A2
Portbury Close 123 B2
Portelet Road 93 B1
Porten Road 33 B2
Porter Square 61 A1
Porter Street 1 A2
2 A1
106 A1
Porteus Road 31 A1/A2
Portgate Close 26 A1
Portia Way 98 A2
Portinscale Road 136 B2
137 B1
Portland Avenue 86 A1
Portland Gardens 55 B2
Portland Grove 135 B1
Portland Mews 11 A1
Portland Place 2 B2
3 A1/B1
Portland Rise 63 A1
Portland Road 28 B2
Portland Square 96 B1
Portland Street 113 A2/B2
Portman Close 1 A2
Portman Gate 76 B1
Portman Mews South 1 B2
Portman Place 92 B2
Portman Square 1 A2/B2
Portman Street 1 B2
Portnall Road 25 A2
26 A1
Portobello Mews 29 B1
Portobello Road 25 A1/B1
29 A1/B1/B2
Portobello Road Street Market 25 B1
29 A1/B1
Portpool Lane 14 A2
Portsea Mews 31 B2
Portsea Place 31 B2
Portslade Road 142 A2
Portsmouth Street 14 B1
Portsoken Street 18 B2
Portugal Street 14 B1/B2
Post Office Court 17 A2
Post Office Way 134 A1
Potier Street 106 B2
Pott Street 92 B2
Potters Close 122 A2
Potters Fields 107 A1
Potters Road 50 B2
Pottery Lane 28 B1/B2
Pottery Street 108 A2
Poulton Close 87 B1
Poultry 16 B2
Pountney Road 141 B1
Powell Road 87 A1/A2
Powerscroft Road 87 B2
Powis Gardens 29 A1
Powis Mews 29 A2
Powis Place 5 B1
Powis Square 29 A1/A2
Powis Terrace 29 A2
Powlett Place 71 A1
Pownall Road 88 B2
89 B1
Poynders Gardens 149 B1
Poynders Road 149
A1/A2/B1/B2
Poynings Road 59 B1
Poyntz Road 141 A1
Poyser Street 92 A2
Praed Mews 31 B2
Praed Street 1 A1
31 B1/B2
Prague Place 150 A1
Prah Road 62 B2
Prairie Street 141 A2
142 A1
Pratt Mews 78 A1
Pratt Street 78 A1
Pratt Walk 131 A2
Prebend Gardens 39 A1
Prebend Street 81
83 A1
Premiere Place 100 A1
Prescot Street 95 B1
Prescott Place 143 B1
President Drive 96 B1
President Street 7 A1
Prested Road 140 A1
Preston Close 114 A1
Prestons Road 101 A2/B2
Prestwood Street 83 B2
Price Close 151 A1
Price's Street 105 A1
Prices Mews 79 B2
Prideaux Place 6 A1
Prideaux Road 144 A1
Prima Road 135 A2
Primrose Close 94 B2
Primrose Gardens 67 B2
Primrose Hill 15 B1
Primrose Hill Road 67 B2
70 A1
Primrose Hill Studios 70 B1
Primrose Mews 70 A1
Primrose Square 90 B1
Primrose Street 8 B2
Primrose Walk 126 A1
Prince Albert Road 69 B1/B2
70 B1
Prince Arthur Mews 56 B1
Prince Arthur Road 56 B1
67 A1
Prince Consort Road 36 A1/A2
Prince George Road 64 B2
Prince of Orange Lane 120 A1
Prince of Wales Drive 132 A1
133 A1
141 A1/A2
Prince of Wales Gate 37 A1
Prince of Wales Passage 77 B2
Prince of Wales Road 71 A1/A2
Prince of Wales Terrace 35 A2
36 A1
38 A1
Prince Regents Mews 77 B2
Prince Street 118 B2
119 A1
Princedale Road 28 B1/B2
Princelet Street 91 B1
Princes Close 63 A1
142 B2
Princes Gardens 36 A2
37 A1
Princes Gate 36 A2
37 A1
Princes Gate Court 36 A2
Princes Gate Mews 36 B2
37 B1
Princes Mews 29 B2
Princes Place 23 A1
28 B1
Princes Riverside Road 110 A2
Princes Square 29 B2
30 B1
Princes Street 2 B2
17 A1
Princes Yard 28 B2
Princess Crescent 63 B1
Princess Louise Close 31 A2
Princess May Road 64 B2
Princess Mews 67 B1
Princess Road 70 /B1
Princess Street 105 B1
Princeton Court 136 A1
Princeton Street 14 A1/A2
Print Village 123 B1
Printer Street 15 B1
Printers Inn Court 14 B2
Printers Mews 94 A1
Printing House Yard 91 A1
Prior Bolton Street 81 A1
Prior Street 120 B2
Prioress Street 106 B2
Priory Court 134 B1
Priory Gardens 38 A2
51 A2
Priory Grove 134 B2
Priory Mews 134 B2
Priory Park Road 65 B1
Priory Road 53 A1
65 B1/B2
Priory Terrace 65 B1
Priory Walk 44 A1
Pritchard's Road 92 A2
Priter Road 108 A2
Probert Road 127 B1
Procter Street 14 A1

Promenade Approach Road 38 B1
Prospect Cottages 137 A2
Prospect Place 56 B1
96 B2
97 B1
Prospect Street 109 A1
Prospero Road 52 B2
60 A1
Prothero Road 42 B1
Prout Road 87 A2
Providence Close 90 B2
Providence Court 1 B2
Providence Yard 91 A2
Provost Road 70 A2
Provost Street 84 B1
Prowse Place 71 B2
Prusom Street 96 B1/B2
Pudding Lane 18 B1
Puddle Dock 15 B2
Pulross Road 144 B1/B2
Pulteney Close 94 A2
Pulteney Terrace 79 B2
Pulton Place 43 B1
Pump Court 14 B2
Pump House Close 110 B1
Pump House Mews 95 B1
Pump Lane 124 A2
Pumping Station Road 38 B1/B2
Pundersons Gardens 92 A2
Purbrook Street 107 A2
Purcell Crescent 47 A2
Purcell Street 84 A1/A2
Purchese Street 78 B2
Purley Place 80 A2
Purser's Cross Road 48 A2
49 A1
Putney Bridge 48 B1
Putney Bridge Approach 48 B1/B2
Putney Bridge Road 136 A2
137 A1/A2
138 A1/B1
Putney High Street 136 A1/A2/B1
Putney Hill 136 B1
Pynfolds 109 A1
Pyrland Road 75 B2
Pytchley Road 129 A1/A2

Q

The Quadrangle 31 B2
Quadrangle Close 107 B1
Quadrant Grove 57 B1
Quaker Court 91 B1
Quaker Street 91 B1
Quantock Mews 123 B2
Quarrendon Street 49 A1
Quarry Road 146 A1
The Quarterdeck 102 A1
Quebec Mews 1 A2
Quebec Way 111 A1/B1
Queen Anne Mews 2 B2
Queen Anne Road 90 A2/B2
Queen Anne Street 2 B1/B2
Queen Anne's Gate 22 A1/A2
Queen Caroline Street 40 B2
41 A1/B1
Queen Elizabeth Street 107 A1/A2
Queen Elizabeths Close 63 B2
Queen Elizabeths Walk 63 A2/B2
64 A1
Queen Margaret's Grove 82 A1
Queen Square 4 B2
5 B1
Queen Square Place 4 B2
Queen Street 9 A2
16 B2
Queen Street Place 16 B2
Queen Victoria Street 15 B2
16 B2
Queen's Circus 133 A1
Queen's Crescent 71 A1/A2
Queen's Elm Square 45 A1
Queen's Gate 36 A1/A2/B2
45 A1
Queen's Gate Gardens 36 B1
Queen's Gate Mews 36 A1
Queen's Gate Place 36 B1
Queen's Gate Place Mews 36 B1
Queen's Gate Terrace 36 A1
Queen's Grove 68 B2
69 A1
Queen's Grove Mews 68 B2
Queen's Head Street 83 A1
Queen's Row 113 B2
Queen's Terrace 68 B2
Queenhithe 16 B2
Queens Club Gardens 42 A1/B1
Queens Drive 62 B2
63 B1/B2
Queens Gardens 30 B2
Queens Head Yard 106 A1
Queens Mews 30 B1
Queens Road 123 A2
124 A1/A2
125 B1
Queens Yard 4 A1
Queensberry Mews West 36 B2
Queensberry Place 36 B2
Queensberry Way 36 B2
Queensborough Mews 30 B1
Queensborough Passage 30 B1
Queensborough Studios 30 B1
Queensborough Terrace 30 B1
Queensbridge Road 86 B2
88 A2/B2
Queensbury Street 81
Queensdale Crescent 33 A2
Queensdale Place 28 B1
Queensdale Road 28 B1/B2
33 A2
Queensdale Walk 28 B1
Queensdown Road 87 A1
Queensland Road 74 A1
Queensmead 69 A1
Queensmill Road 47 A1
Queenstown Mews 133 B1
Queenstown Road 133 A1/B1
142 A1
Queensville Road 149 B2
Queensway 30 B1
Quemerford Road 74 A1/B1
Quernmore Road 54 B1/B2
Querrin Street 50 B2
Quex Mews 65 B1
Quex Road 65 B1
Quick Road 38 A1
Quick Street 83 B1
Quick Street Mews 83 B1
Quickswood 69 A2
70 A1
Quill Street 62 B2
Quilp Street 106 A1
Quilter Street 91 A2
Quorn Road 129 A1

R

Rabbit Row 29 B2
Raby Street 98 B1
Racton Road 42 B2
Radbourne Road 149 B1/B2
Radcliffe Road 107 B2
Radcot Street 112 B1
Raddington Road 25 B1
Radipole Road 48 A1
Radlett Place 69 A1
Radley Court 110 A2
Radley Mews 35 B2
Radnor Mews 31 B2
Radnor Place 31 B2
Radnor Road 114 B2
115 B1
Radnor Street 7 A2
Radnor Terrace 34 B2
Radnor Walk 45 B2
46 B1
Radstock Street 132 A1
Raeburn Street 144 B1
Raft Road 138 A1
Raglan Street 72 A1
Railey Mews 72 A2
Railton Road 127 B1/B2
Railway Approach 54 B2
106 A2
Railway Avenue 110 A1/B1
Railway Mews 28 A2
94 B2
Railway Rise 129 A2
Railway Street 78 B2
Rainbow Avenue 102 B2
Rainbow Street 114 B1
122 A2
Raine Street 96 B1
Rainham Close 140 B1
Rainsborough Avenue 117 A2
118 A1
Rainsford Street 31 B2
Rainville Road 47 A1
Raleana Road 101 B2
Raleigh Gardens 150 B2
Raleigh Street 83 A1
Ralston Street 46 B1
Ram Place 89 A2
Ram Street 138 B2
Rame Close 152 A2
Ramilles Close 150 A1/B1
Ramillies Place 10 A2
Ramillies Street 3 B1
10 A2
Rampart Street 96 A1/A2
Rampayne Street 21 A2/B1/B2
Ramsay Mews 45 B1
Ramsdale Road 152 A2
Ramsden Road 147 A2/B2
148 B1
Ramsey Mews 63 B1

Ramsey Street 91 A2
Ramsey Walk 75 B2
81 A2
Ramsgate Street 86 B2
Randall Close 132 A1
Randall Place 120 A1
Randall Road 131 B1
Randall Row 131 B1
Randell's Road 79 A1
Randolph Avenue 27 A2/B2
Randolph Crescent 27 B2
Randolph Gardens 27 A2
Randolph Mews 27 B2
Randolph Road 27 B2
Randolph Street 71 B2
Ranelagh Avenue 48 B2
Ranelagh Bridge 30 A1
Ranelagh Gardens 39 A2
48 B2
Ranelagh Grove 19 B2
Ranelagh Road 20 B2
Rangers Square 120 B2
Rangoon Street 18 B2
Ranmere Street 148 B2
Rannoch Road 47 A1
Ranston Street 76 B1
Ranwell Close 94 A1
Ranwell Street 94 A1
Raphael Street 37 A2
Rashleigh Street 142 A1
Ratcliffe Cross Street 97 B2
Ratcliffe Lane 97 B2
98 B1
Rathbone Place 3 B2
Rathbone Street 3 B2
Rathcoole Avenue 54 A2
Rathcoole Gardens 54 A2
Rathgar Road 127 A2
Rathmell Drive 149 A2
Rattray Road 127 B1
Raul Road 123 B2
Raveley Street 72 A2
Raven Row 96 A2
Ravenet Street 133 B1
Ravenfield Road 151 A1
Ravenna Road 136 B1
Ravenscourt Avenue 39 B2
Ravenscourt Gardens 39 A2/B2
Ravenscourt Park 39 A2/B2
Ravenscourt Place 40 B1
Ravenscourt Road 40 A1/B1
Ravenscourt Square 39 A2
Ravenscroft Street 91 A2
Ravensdale Road 86 A1
Ravensdon Street 112 B1
Ravenshaw Street 65 A1
Ravenslea Road 147 B1/B2
Ravensmede Way 39 B1
Ravenstone Street 148 B1
Ravenswood Road 148 B1/B2
Ravent Road 131 A2
Ravey Street 8 A2
Rawlings Street 46 A1
Rawson Street 141 A2
Rawstorne Place 6 A2
Rawstorne Street 6 A2
Ray Street 6 B1
Ray Street Bridge 6 B1
Raydon Street 59 A1

Raymond Buildings 5 B1
Raymouth Road 109 B1
Rayners Road 136 B2
Raynham Road 40 B2
Raynor Place 81
Reachview Close 71 B2
Reading Lane 89 A1/A2
Reapers Close 78 A2
Reardon Path 96 B1
Reardon Street 96 B1
Reaston Street 125 A1/B1
Reckitt Road 38 A1
Record Street 116 B1/B2
Recovery Street 152 A1
Rector Street 83 A1
Rectory Grove 142 A2/B2
Rectory Lane 151 B2
152 A2/B2
Rectory Road 85 A1/B1
86 A2/B1
Rectory Square 97 A2
Reculver Road 116 A2
117 A1
Red Anchor Close 45 B1
Red House Square 81 A2
Red Lion Close 113 B2
Red Lion Row 113 B1
Red Lion Square 14 A1
Red Lion Street 5 B1
14 A2
Red Lion Yard 9 A1
Red Place 1 B2
Red Post Hill 128 B2
129 B1
Red Square 64 B1
Redan Place 30 B1
Redan Street 33 B2
Redan Terrace 121 B1
Redbridge Gardens 122 A2
Redburn Street 45 B2
46 B1
Redcar Street 121 A2
Redcastle Close 97 B1
Redchurch Street 91 A1
Redcliffe Gardens 43 A2/B2
44 B1
Redcliffe Mews 43 A2
Redcliffe Place 43 B2
Redcliffe Road 44 B1
Redcliffe Square 43 A2
Redcliffe Street 43 A2/B2
Redcross Way 106 A1
Reddins Road 115 B1
Rede Place 29 B2
Redesdale Street 45 B2
Redfield Lane 35 B1/B2
Redfield Mews 35 B2
Redgate Terrace 136 B2
Redgrave Road 136 A1
Redhill Street 77 B1
Redington Gardens 56 A1
Redington Road 56 A1
Redman's Road 97 A1/A2
Redmead Lane 95 B2
Redmore Road 40 B2
Redriff Road 111 B1/B2
Redruth Road 90 B1
Redstart Close 126 A1
Redston Road 53 A1

Redvers Street 91 A1
Redwing Mews 128 A1
Redwood Close 94 B2
111 A2
Redwood Mews 142 A1
Reece Mews 36 B2
Reed Place 143 B2
Reedham Street 123 B1
130 A1
Reedholm Villas 64 B1
Reedworth Street 112 A1
Rees Street 83 A2
Reeves Mews 9 A1
Reform Street 141 A1
Regal Close 91 B2
Regal Lane 70
Regal Place 49 A2
94 B1
Regal Row 124 A1
Regan Way 84 A2
Regency Mews 121 A1
Regency Street 21 A2/B2
Regeneration Road 117 A1
Regent Place 10 B1
Regent Road 127 B2
Regent Square 5 A1
Regent Street 3 B1
10 A1/B1/B2
23 A2
Regents Bridge Gardens 134 A2
Regents Mews 68 B2
Regents Park Road 70 /A1/A2/B1
Regents Park Terrace 71 B1
Regents Row 88 B2
89 B1
Regina Road 53 B2
Reginald Road 119 B2
Reginald Square 119 B2
Regis Place 144 B1
Regis Road 71 A2
72 A1
Regnart Buildings 77 B2
Reighton Road 87 B2
Reizel Close 86 A1
Relay Road 33 A1
Relf Road 130 A1
Reliance Square 84
Relton Mews 37 A2
Rembrandt Close 19 B2
103 A2
Remington Street 83 B1
Remnant Street 14 A1
Rendlesham Road 86 A2
87 A1
Renforth Street 110 B1
Renfrew Road 112 A1/A2
Renmuir Street 152 B2
Rennie Street 104 A2
Rephidim Street 106 B2
Reporton Road 48 A1
Repton Street 98 B1/B2
Reservoir Road 126 B1
Resolution Way 119 B2
Reston Place 36 A1
Restoration Square 132 A1
Retcar Close 59 A1
Retford Street 91 A1
Retreat Place 89 A2
90 A1

Reveley Square 111 A2
Reverdy Road 108 B1
Rex Place 9 A1
Rheidol Mews 83 A1
Rheidol Terrace 83 A1
Rhoda Street 91 A1
Rhodes Street 74 B1
Rhodesia Road 143 A2
144 A1
Rhodeswell Road 98 A2/B2
Rhondda Grove 93 B2
Rhyl Street 71 A1/A2
Ribbon Dance Mews 122 B1
Ricardo Street 99 B2
Rich Lane 43 A1
Rich Street 100 A1
Richard Street 96 A1/A2
Richards Place 37 B2
Richardson Close 88 A1
Richardson's Mews 3 A2
Richbell Place 5 B1
Richborne Terrace 135 A1/B1
Richford Street 40 A2
Richmond Avenue 79 B2
80 B1
Richmond Buildings 11 A2
Richmond Crescent 80 B1
Richmond Grove 80 A2
Richmond Mews 11 A2
Richmond Road 88 A1/A2
89 A1/A2
Richmond Terrace 24 B1
Richmond Way 33 B2
Rickett Street 43 B1
Rickman Street 92 B2
Rickthorne Road 61 B1
Ridge Road 54 B1/B2
Ridgeway Gardens 52 B2
Ridgeway Road 127 A2
Ridgewell Close 81
Ridgmount Gardens 4 A1
Ridgmount Place 4 B1
Ridgmount Road 138 B2
Ridgmount Street 4 A1/B1
Riding House Street 3 B1
Ridings Close 52 B2
Ridley Road 86 B1/B2
Rifle Street 99 B2
Rigault Road 48 B1/B2
Rigden Street 99 B2
Rigge Place 143 B2
Riley Road 107 A2
Riley Street 44 B2
Rinaldo Road 148 B1
Ring Road 33 A1
Ringcroft Street 74 B2
Ringford Road 137 B2
138 B1
Ringmer Avenue 48 A1
Ringmer Gardens 61 A1
Ringwood Gardens 102 A2/B2
Ripon Road 55 B2
Ripplevale Grove 79 A2
80 A1
Risborough Street 105 A2
Risdon Street 110 B1
Risinghill Street 79 B2
Rita Road 134 A2
Ritchie Street 80 B1
Ritherdon Road 151 A2
Ritson Road 86 B2
Rivaz Place 90 A1
River Barge Close 103 A2
River Place 81 B1
River Street 6 A1
River Terrace 41 B1
Rivercourt Road 40 B1
Riversdale Road 63 B1/B2
Riverside Drive 38 B1
Riverside Gardens 40 B2
Riverton Close 26 A1
Riverview Gardens 47 A1
Rivington Place 84
Rivington Street 84
Rixon Street 74 A1
RK 20 B2
Roads Place 61 A1
Roan Street 120 A1/A2
Robert Adam Street 1 A2
2 B1
Robert Burns Mews 127 B2
Robert Close 27 B2
Robert Dashwood Way 112 A2
Robert Keen Close 123 B2
Robert Lowe Close 125 A2
Robert Street 24 A2
77 B1/B2
Robert's Place 6 B1
Roberta Street 91 A2
Roberts Close 111 A1
Roberts Mews 19 A2
Robertson Street 142 A1/A2
Robeson Street 99 A1
Robin Court 108 B1
Robin Grove 58 A2
Robin Hood Lane 101 A2
Robinscroft Mews 120 B1
Robinson Road 92 A2
152 B1
Robinson Street 45 B2
Robsart Street 145 A1/A2
Rochelle Close 139 B1/B2
Rochelle Street 91 A1
Rochester Mews 72 B1
Rochester Place 72 B1
Rochester Road 71 B2
72 B1
Rochester Row 20 A2
21 A1
22 B1
Rochester Square 72 B1
Rochester Street 22 B1
Rochester Terrace 72 B1
Rochester Walk 106 A1
Rochford Street 57 B1
Rock Grove Way 108 B2
Rock Street 62 B2
Rockingham Street 105 B2
106 B1
Rockland Road 136 B2
Rockley Road 33 B2
Rocliffe Street 83 B1
Roden Court 52 B2
Roden Street 61 B2
Rodenhurst Road 149 A1/A2
Roderick Road 57 A2
Roding Mews 95 B2
Rodmarton Street 1 A2
Rodney Place 113 A1
Rodney Road 113 A1/A2
Rodney Street 79 B2
Rodwell Road 129 B2
130 B1
Roffey Street 103 A1
Roger Street 5 B1/B2
Rokeby Road 126 B2
Rokesly Avenue 54 A1
Roland Gardens 44 A1
Roland Mews 97 A2
Roland Way 44 A1
113 B2
Rollins Street 116 B2
Rollit Street 74 B1
Rolls Buildings 14 B2
Rolls Road 114 A2
115 A1
Rollscourt Avenue 128 B1
Rolt Street 118 B1
Roman Road 39 A1
92 B2
93 A1/A2
94 A1/A2
Roman Way 74 B1
80 A1
Romberg Road 151 A1/A2
Romero Close 144 A2
Romford Street 96 A1
Romilly Road 62 B2
Romilly Street 12 A1
Romney Close 124 A2
125 B1
Romney Mews 2 A1
Romney Road 120 A2
Romney Street 22 B2
Rona Road 57 B2
Rona Walk 81 A2
Ronald Street 97 B1
Ronalds Road 74 B2
Rood Lane 18 B1
Rookery Road 142 B2
143 B1
Rookstone Road 152 A1
Rope Street 111 B1/B2
Rope Walk Gardens 96 A1
Ropemaker Road 111 B2
Ropemaker Street 7 B2
Ropemakers Fields 98 B1
Roper Lane 107 A2
Ropery Street 98 A2
99 A1
Ropewalk Mews 88 A2
Ropley Street 91 A2
Rosa Alba Mews 75 A1
Rosaline Road 42 B1
Rosary Gardens 44 A1
Rosaville Road 42 B2
Roscoe Street 7 A2/B2
Rose Alley 105 A2
Rose & Crown Yard 23 A1/A2
Rose Street 13 B1
Rosebank Gardens 94 A1
Roseberry Gardens 55 B2
Roseberry Place 86 B1
Roseberry Street 108 B2
109 B1
Rosebery Avenue 5 B2
6 A2/B1/B2

Street Index

Rosebery Gardens 54 A1
Rosebery Mews 150 B1
Rosebery Road 149 A2
150 B1
Rosebury Road 49 B2
50 B1
Rosedale Court 75 A1
Rosedew Road 47 A1
Rosefield Gardens 100 A2
Rosehart Mews 29 B2
Rosehill Road 139 B1
Roseleigh Avenue 75 A1
Rosemary Road 114 B2
Rosemary Street 82 B1
Rosemont Road 66 A2
Rosemoor Street 46 A1
Rosenau Crescent 132 A1
Rosenau Road 132 A1
Roseneath Road 147 A2
Roserton Street 103 A1
Rosethorn Close 149 B2
Rosina Street 90 A2
Rosmead Road 28 B2
Rosoman Place 6 B1
Rosoman Street 6 B1
Rossendale Way 71 B2
78 A2
Rossetti Mews 69 A1
Rossetti Road 115 A2
Rossington Street 87 A2
Rossiter Road 148 B1/B2
Rosslyn Hill 56 B1
67 A2
Rosslyn Park Mews 67 A2
Rossmore Road 76 B1/B2
Rostrevor Avenue 86 A1
Rostrevor Road 48 A1
Rotary Street 105 B1
Rotherfield Street 81
82 B1
Rotherhithe New Road 109 B1/B2
115 A2
116 A2
117 A1
Rotherhithe Old Road 110 B2
111 B1
Rotherhithe Street 109 A1/A2
110 A1/A2
111 A2/B2
Rotherhithe Tunnel 97 B1/B2
110 A1/B1
Rotherhithe Tunnel Approach 98 B1
110 B1
Rotherwood Road 136 A1
Rothery Street 80 B2
Rothsay Street 107 B1
Rothwell Street 70 A1
Rotterdam Drive 103 A2
Rouel Road 108 A1/B1
Rounton Road 99 A2
Roupell Street 104 A2
Rousden Street 71 B2
Routh Road 146 A2
Routledge Close 60 A2
Rowallan Road 47 A2
Rowan Road 41 A2
Rowan Terrace 41 A2
Rowan Walk 59 A2
Rowberry Close 47 B1
Rowcross Street 114 A2
Rowditch Lane 141 A1
Rowe Lane 87 B2
Rowena Crescent 132 B2
Rowfant Road 147 B2
Rowhill Road 87 B2
Rowington Close 30 A2
Rowland Hill Street 57 A1
Rowlands Close 51 A2
Rowley Gardens 55 B2
Rowley Way 68 A1/A2
Rowntree Close 65 A2
Rowstock Gardens 73 B1
Roxby Place 43 B1
Royal Avenue 46 B1
Royal Close 118 B1
Royal College Street 71 B2
78 A1
Royal Crescent 28 B1
33 A2
Royal Crescent Mews 33 A2
Royal Duchess Mews 148 A2
Royal Exchange Avenue 17 A2
Royal Hill 120 A2/B2
Royal Hospital Road 45 B2
46 B1/B2
Royal Mint Street 95 B1
Royal Naval Place 126 A2
Royal Oak Road 89 A1
Royal Oak Yard 107 A1
Royal Place 120 B2
Royal Road 112 B1/B2
Royal Street 131 A2
Royal Victor Place 93 A1
Royalty Mews 11 A2
Roydon Street 133 B1
Royston Street 93 A1
Rozel Road 142 A2
Rubens Place 144 B1
Ruby Street 115 B2
Ruby Triangle 115 B2
Rudall Crescent 56 B2
Rudloe Road 149 A1
Rudolf Place 134 A2
Rufford Street 79 A1
Rufus Street 84
Rugby Street 5 B1
Rugg Street 100 A1
Ruislip Street 151 B1
Rum Close 96 B2
Rumbold Road 43 B2
Rumsey Road 144 A2
145 B1
Runcorn Place 28 B1
Rupack Street 109 A2
Rupert Gardens 127 A1
Rupert Road 39 A1
60 B1/B2
Rupert Street 11 B1/B2
Rupert Street Market 11 B2
Rusbridge Close 86 A2
Rush Hill Mews 141 B2
Rush Hill Road 141 B2
Rusham Road 147 A2
Rushcroft Road 150 A2
Rushmead 92 A1
Rushmore Road 87 A2
Rushton Street 84 A1
Rushworth Street 105 B1/B2
Ruskin Walk 128 B1
Russell Close 38 B2
Russell Court 23 A1
Russell Gardens 34 A1
Russell Gardens Mews 34 A1
Russell Grove 135 B2
Russell Place 111 B2
Russell Road 34 A1/B1
53 A1
Russell Square 4 B2
Russell Street 13 B2
Russia Court 16 A2
Russia Dock Road 111 A2
Russia Lane 92 A2
Russia Row 16 A2
Rust Square 122 A1
Ruston Mews 28 A2
Ruston Street 94 A2
Rutherford Street 21 A1
Ruthven Street 90 B1
Rutland Gardens 37 A1
55 B2
Rutland Gardens Mews 37 A1
Rutland Gate 37 A1
Rutland Gate Mews 37 A1
Rutland Grove 40 B2
Rutland Mews 68 A1
Rutland Mews East 37 B1
Rutland Mews South 37 B1
Rutland Place 7 B1
Rutland Road 90 B1
Rutland Street 37 B1
Rutley Close 112 B1
Ruvigny Gardens 136 A1
Ryde Vale Road 148 B2
Ryder Drive 115 A2
116 B1
Ryder Mews 90 A1
Ryder Street 23 A1
Ryder Yard 23 A1
Ryders Terrace 68 B1
Rydon Street 81
Rydston Close 79 A2
Rye Lane 123 A2/B2
Rye Walk 136 B1
Ryecroft Street 49 A2
Ryland Road 71 A2
Rylett Road 39 A2
Rylston Road 42 B1/B2
Rymer Street 127 B2
Rysbrack Street 37 A2

S

Sabine Road 141 B1
Sable Street 80 A2
Sackville Street 10 B1
Saddle Yard 9 A1
Saffron Hill 6 B1
15 A1
Saffron Street 15 A1
Sage Mews 129 B2
Sage Street 96 B2
Sage Way 5 A2
Sail Street 131 A2
Sainfoin Road 151 A2
Saint Paul's Mews 79 A1
Salamanca Place 131 B1
Salamanca Street 131 B1

Salcombe Road 64 B2
Salcott Road 140 B1/B2
Sale Place 31 B2
Sale Street 91 A2
Salem Road 30 B1
Salford Road 149 B2
Salisbury Close 113 A2
Salisbury Court 15 B1
Salisbury Mews 42 B2
Salisbury Place 1 A2
121 A1
Salisbury Road 55 A2
Salisbury Square 15 B1
Salisbury Street 76 B1
Salmon Lane 97 B2
98 B1/B2
Salmon Street 98 B2
Salter Road 110 A2
111 A2/B2
Salter Street 100 A1
Salterford Road 152 A2
Salters Hall Court 17 B1
Salterton Road 61 B2
Saltoun Road 127 B1
150 A2
Saltram Crescent 26 A2
Saltwell Street 100 A2
Salutation Road 103 B2
Samels Court 39 B2
Samford Street 76 B1
Sampson Street 95 B2
Samuel Close 88 A2
125 A1
Samuel Street 114 B2
Samuels Close 39 B2
Sancroft Street 112 A1
131 B2
The Sanctuary 22 A2
Sanctuary Mews 86 B2
Sanctuary Street 106 A1
Sand's End Lane 50 A1
Sandale Close 63 B2
Sandall Road 72 B2
Sandalwood Close 98 A1
Sandbourne Road 126 B1
Sandbrook Road 64 B2
Sandell Street 104 A2
Sanderson Close 58 B1
Sanderstead Close 149 B1
Sandgate Lane 147 B1
Sandgate Street 115 B2
Sandilands Road 49 A2
50 A1
Sandison Street 130 A1
Sandland Street 14 A2
Sandlings Close 123 B2
Sandmere Road 143 B2
144 B1
Sandpiper Close 111 A2
Sandridge Street 60 A1
Sandringham Gardens 53 A2
Sandringham Road 86 B1/B2
Sandwell Crescent 65 A2
Sandwich Street 5 A1
Sandy's Row 18 A1
Sanford Street 117 B2
125 A2
126 A1
Sanford Terrace 85 B1
Sanford Walk 125 A2
Sangora Road 139 B2
Sans Walk 6 B1/B2
Sansom Street 122 A1
Santley Street 144 B1
Santos Road 137 A2
Sapphire Road 118 A1
Saracen Street 99 B1
Sardinia Street 14 B1
Sarsfeld Road 147 B1/B2
Satchwell Road 91 A2
Sattar Mews 64 A1
Saunders Close 100 A1
Saunders Ness Road 103 A2/B2
Saunders Street 131 A2
Savage Gardens 18 B2
Savannah Close 123 A1
Savernake Road 57 A2/B2
Savile Row 10 A1/B1
Savona Street 133 A2
Savoy Court 24 A2
Savoy Hill 24 A2
Savoy Mews 143 A2
Savoy Place 24 A2
Savoy Row 24 A2
Savoy Steps 24 A2
Savoy Street 24 A2
Savoy Way 24 A2
Sawmill Yard 94 A1
Sawyer Street 105 A2
106 A1
Saxby Road 150 B1
Saxon Road 94 B1
Sayes Court Street 118 B2
Scala Street 3 B2
Scampston Mews 28 A1
Scandrett Street 96 B1
Scarborough Road 62 A1/A2
Scarborough Street 95 B1
Scarsdale Place 35 B2
Scarsdale Villas 35 B1/B2
Scawen Road 117 B2
118 A1
Scawfell Street 88 B2
Sceptre Road 92 B2
Scholars Road 148 B2
Scholefield Road 60 A2
Schonfeld Square 63 B2
Schoolbank Road 103 B2
Schoolbell Mews 93 A2
Schoolhouse Lane 97 B2
Schooner Close 103 A2
110 A1
Schubert Road 137 A2
Sclater Street 91 A1
Sclater Street Street Market 91 A1
Scoble Place 86 A2
Scolars Place 64 A2
Scoresby Street 105 A1
Scotland Place 24 B1
Scotswood Street 6 B1
Scott Ellis Gardens 76 A1
Scott Lidgett Crescent 108 A1/A2
Scott Russell Place 102 B2
Scott Street 92 B1
Scotts Road 32 B1/B2
Scout Lane 142 B2
Scovell Road 105 B2
Scriven Street 88 A1
Scrutton Close 149 B2
Scrutton Street 8 A1/A2
Scylla Road 124 B1
130 A2
Seabright Street 92 B1
Seaford Street 5 A1
Seaforth Crescent 75 B2
Seagrave Road 43 A1/B1
Seal Street 86 A2
Searle Place 53 B2
Searles Close 132 A1
Searles Road 113 A2
Sears Street 122 A1
Sebastian Street 6 B2
Sebbon Street 80 A2
Secker Street 104 A2
Second Avenue 25 A2
Sedan Way 114 A1
Sedding Street 19 B2
Seddon Street 5 B2
Sedgmoor Place 122 A2
Sedgwick Street 90 A2
Sedleigh Road 137 B2
Sedlescombe Road 42 B2
43 B1
Seely Road 152 B2
Seething Lane 18 B2
Sekforde Street 6 B2
Selborne Road 121 B2
Selby Street 91 B2
Selden Road 124 B2
Selkirk Road 152 A1
Sellincourt Road 152 A1/B2
Selsdon Way 103 A1
Selsea Place 64 B2
Selsey Street 99 B1
Selwood Place 44 A2
Selwyn Road 94 B1
Semley Place 19 B2
Senior Street 30 A1/A2
Senrab Street 97 A2
Serenaders Road 145 A2
Serjeants Inn 14 B2
Serle Street 14 B2
Serman Lane 15 B2
Serpentine Road 37 A1
Setchell Road 107 B2
Setchell Way 107 B2
Seth Street 110 B1
Settles Street 95 A2
Settrington Road 49 B2
Seven Sisters Road 61 B2
62 B1/B2
63 A1/A2
Seven Stars Yard 91 B1
Severnake Close 102 B1
Severus Road 140 A1
Seville Mews 82 B2
Seville Street 19 A1
Sevington Street 26 B2
Seward Street 7 A1
Sewardstone Road 93 A1
Sextant Avenue 103 A2
Seymour Mews 1 A2
2 B1
Seymour Place 1 A1
76 B1
Seymour Road 55 A1

Street Index

Seymour Street 1 B1/B2
Seymour Walk 44 B1
Seyssel Street 103 B2
Shacklewell Green 86 A2
Shacklewell Lane 86 A1/A2/B1
Shacklewell Road 86 A2
Shacklewell Row 86 A2
Shacklewell Street 91 A2
Shad Thames 107 A2
Shadwell Pierhead 97 B1
Shaftesbury Avenue 4 B1
10 B2
11 B1/B2
12 A1/A2/B1
13 A1
Shaftesbury Mews 35 B1
149 A1
Shaftesbury Road 53 B1/B2
Shaftesbury Street 83 B2
84 A1
Shafto Mews 37 B2
Shafton Road 90 B1
Shakespeare Road 127 A2/B2
Shakspeare Mews 64 B1
Shakspeare Walk 64 B1/B2
Shalcomb Street 44 B1
Shalfleet Drive 28 A1
Shamrock Street 143 A1
Shand Street 107 A1
Shandon Road 149 A1
Shandy Street 97 A2
98 A1
Shanklin Road 53 A1/A2
Shannon Grove 144 B2
Shannon Place 69 B1
Shardcroft Avenue 127 B2
128 B1
Shardeloes Road 126 B1/B2
Sharon Gardens 89 B2
Sharpleshall Street 70 A1
Sharratt Street 116 B2
Sharsted Street 112 B1/B2
Shaw Crescent 98 A2
Shaw Road 129 A1
Shawbury Road 129 B2
Shawfield Street 45 B2
Shearling Way 73 B2
Sheba Place 91 B1
Sheen Grove 80 B1
Sheep Lane 89 B1
Sheepcote Lane 141 A1
Sheffield Street 14 B1
Sheffield Terrace 35 A1
Shelburne Road 74 A1
Sheldon Place 92 A1
Sheldrake Place 34 A2
Shelford Place 63 B2
Shelgate Road 140 A2/B1
Shelley Close 124 B1
Shellness Road 87 B1
Shellwood Road 141 A1
Shelmerdine Close 99 A1
Shelton Street 13 B1
Shenfield Street 84 A2
88 B1
Shenley Road 122 B2
Shepherd Street 9 A1/A2
Shepherdess Place 83 B2
Shepherdess Walk 83 A2/B2
Shepherds Bush Green 33 B1/B2
Shepherds Bush Market 32 B2
Shepherds Bush Place 33 B2
Shepherds Bush Road 33 B1
41 A1
Shepherds Close 52 A1
Shepherds Hill 51 A2
52 A1/A2
53 A1
Shepherds Lane 90 A2
Shepherds Walk 56 B1
Sheppard Drive 115 A2
Shepperton Road 81
82 B1
Sheppey Walk 81 A2
Sheraton Street 11 A1
Sherborne Lane 17 B2
Sherborne Street 82 B1
Sherbrooke Road 42 B1/B2
Sheridan Street 96 A2
Sheringham Road 74 B1
Sherlock Mews 2 A1
Sherriff Road 65 A1/B2
Sherwood Gardens 102 B2
115 A2
Sherwood Street 10 B2
Shetland Road 94 B2
Shillibeer Place 1 A1
Shillingford Street 80 A2/B2
Ship & Mermaid Row 106 A2
Ship Yard 102 B2
Shipka Road 148 B1/B2
Shipton Street 91 A2
Shipwright Road 111 B2
Shipwright Yard 107 A1
Shirbutt Street 100 A2
Shirland Mews 26 A1
Shirland Road 26 A1/A2
27 A1/B1
Shirley Grove 141 B2
Shirlock Road 57 B2
Shoe Lane 15 A1/B1
Shoot Up Hill 65 A1
Shooters Hill Road 120 B2
Shore Place 89 B2
Shore Road 89 B2
Shoreditch High Street 8 A2
91 A1
Shoreham Close 138 B2
Shorncliffe Road 114 A1
Shorrolds Road 42 B2
Short Road 38 B1
Short Street 104 A2
Shorter Street 18 B2
Shortlands 41 A2/B2
Shorts Gardens 13 A1/B1
Shottendane Road 48 A2
Shoulder of Mutton Alley 98 B1
Shouldham Street 1 A1
Shrewsbury Mews 29 A2
Shrewsbury Road 29 A2
Shrewton Road 152 B2
Shropshire Place 4 A1
Shroton Street 76 B1
Shrubbery Close 83 A1
Shrubland Road 88 A2
89 B1
Shurland Gardens 114 B2
Shuttle Street 91 B2
Shuttleworth Road 132 B1/B2
Sibella Road 143 A1
Sidbury Street 48 A1
Siddons Lane 76 B2
Sidford Place 131 A2
Sidings Mews 74 A1
Sidmouth Street 5 A1/A2
Sidney Grove 6 A2
Sidney Road 145 A1
Sidney Square 96 A2
97 A1
Sidney Street 96 A2
Sidworth Street 89 B1/B2
Sigdon Passage 87 B1
Sigdon Road 86 B2
87 B1
Signmakers Yard 78 A1
Silbury Street 84 B1
Silchester Road 28 A1
Silesia Buildings 89 A2
Silex Street 105 B1
Silk Street 7 B2
Silver Close 125 A2
Silver Road 33 A2
Silver Walk 111 A2
Silverbirch Walk 71 A1
Silverthorne Road 133 B1
142 A1/A2
Silverton Road 47 A1
Silvester Road 129 B2
130 B1
Silvester Street 106 B1
Silwood Street 109 B2
116 A2
Simms Road 108 B1/B2
Simon Close 29 B1
Simpson Street 132 B1/B2
Simpsons Road 101 A1
Simrose Court 138 B1
Sinclair Gardens 33 B2
Sinclair Road 33 B2
34 A1/B1
Singer Street 8 A1
Singleton Close 152 B1
Sir John Kirk Close 121 A2
Sirdar Road 28 B1
152 B2
Sise Lane 16 B2
Sispara Gardens 137 B2
Sister Mabel's Way 114 B2
Sisters Avenue 141 B1
Sistova Road 148 B1/B2
Sisulu Place 145 B2
Skelgill Road 137 A1
Skelton Close 86 B1
Skelwith Road 47 A1
Sketchley Gardens 116 A2
Skinner Court 92 A2
Skinner Place 19 B2
Skinner Street 6 B1/B2
Skinners Lane 16 B2
Skipworth Road 90 B1
Slaidburn Street 44 B1
Slaney Place 74 B1
Slater Mews 142 B2
Sleaford Street 133 A2
Slievemore Close 143 B2
Slingsby Place 13 B1
Slippers Place 109 A1

Sloane Avenue 37 B1
46 A1
Sloane Court East 46 B2
Sloane Court West 46 B2
Sloane Gardens 19 B2
Sloane Square 19 B2
Sloane Street 37 A2/B2
46 A2
Sloane Terrace 19 B1/B2
Sly Street 96 A1
Smallbrook Mews 30 B2
Smalley Close 85 B1
Smardale Road 138 A2
Smart Street 93 A1
Smart's Place 13 A2
Smeaton Street 95 B2
Smedley Street 143 A1/A2
Smith Close 110 A2
Smith Square 22 B2
Smith Street 46 B1
Smith Terrace 46 B1
Smith's Court 10 B2
Smithfield Street 15 A2
Smiths Yard 146 B1
Smithy Street 97 A1/A2
Smokehouse Yard 15 A2
Smugglers Way 138 A2
Smyrks Road 114 A1
Smyrna Road 65 B1
Smythe Street 101 A1
Snow Hill 15 A1/B2
Snow Hill Court 15 B2
Snowbury Road 50 B1
Snowsfields 106 A2
107 A1
Soames Street 129 A2
Soho Square 12 A1
Soho Street 3 B2
Sojourner Truth Close 89 A2
Solander Gardens 96 B2
Solebay Street 98 A1/A2
Solent Road 65 A2
Soley Mews 6 A1
Solon New Road 143 B2
144 B1
Solon Road 144 B1
Solway Close 86 B1
Solway Road 130 A1
Somerfield Road 62 B2
Somerfield Street 117 A1
Somerford Grove 86 A1
Somerford Street 92 B1
Somerford Way 111 A2
Somerleyton Road 127 A1/B1
Somers Close 78 B1
Somers Crescent 31 B2
Somers Mews 31 B2
Somers Road 150 B2
Somerset Gardens 51 B2
Somerset Square 34 A1
Somerville Avenue 47 A1
Sonderburg Road 62 B1
Sondes Street 113 B2
Sophia Square 111 A2
Sopwith Way 133 A1
Sorrell Close 125 A2
Sotheby Road 75 A2
Sotheran Close 89 B1
Sotheron Road 49 A2

Soudan Road 141 A1
Souldern Road 41 A2
South Audley Street 9 A1
South Black Lion Lane 39 B2
South Bolton Gardens 43 A2
South Carriage Drive 9 B1
19 A1
36 A2
37 A1/A2
The South Colonnade 100 B2
101 B1
South Crescent 4 B1
South Eaton Place 19 B2
South Edwardes Square 34 B2
South End 35 B2
South End Close 57 A1
South End Green 57 A1
South End Road 57 A1
South End Row 35 B2
South Grove 51 B1
South Hill Park 57 A1/A2
South Island Place 135 B2
South Lambeth Place 134 A2
South Lambeth Road 131 B1
134 A2/B2
135 B1
South Molton Lane 2 B1
South Parade 45 A1
South Park Mews 49 B2
South Place 8 B1
South Place Mews 8 B1
South Sea Street 111 B2
South Side 39 A1
South Square 14 A2
South Street 9 A1
South Tenter Street 95 B1
South Terrace 37 B1
South Villas 72 B2
South Wharf Road 31 A1/B2
Southall Place 106 A2
Southam Street 25 A1
Southampton Buildings 14 A2
Southampton Place 4 B2
Southampton Road 57 B1
Southampton Row 4 B2
14 A1
Southampton Street 24 A2
Southampton Way 122 A1/A2
Southborough Road 90 B1/B2
Southcombe Street 34 B1
Southcote Road 59 B1
Southcott Mews 69 B1
Southcroft Road 152 B2
Southern Grove 94 B1
99 A1
Southern Row 25 A1
Southern Street 79 B2
Southerngate Way 125 A2
126 A1
Southerton Road 40 A2/B2
Southey Road 135 B2
Southfields Road 138 B1
Southgate Grove 82 B1
Southgate Road 82 A1/B1
Southill Street 99 B2
Southolm Street 133 B1
Southview Close 152 A2
Southville 134 B1

Southwark Bridge 16 B2
106 A1
Southwark Bridge Road 105 B2
106 A1
Southwark Park Road 108 B1/B2
109 A1/B1
Southwark Street 105 A1/A2
106 A1
Southwater Close 98 B2
Southway Close 32 B2
Southwell Gardens 36 B1
Southwell Road 128 A1
Southwick Mews 31 B2
Southwick Place 31 B2
Southwick Street 31 B2
Southwold Road 87 A2
Southwood Avenue 51 A2/B2
Southwood Lane 51 A2/B1/B2
Southwood Lawn Road 51 A2
Southwood Smith Street 80 B1/B2
Sovereign Close 96 B1/B2
Sovereign Crescent 110 A2
111 A2
Sovereign Mews 88 B1
Spa Road 107 B2
108 A1
Spafield Street 6 B1
Spanby Road 99 A2
Spanish Place 2 B1
Spanish Road 139 B1
Sparsholt Road 53 B2
Spear Mews 43 A1
Spears Road 53 B1
Spedan Close 56 A1
Speechly Mews 86 B1
Speedwell Street 119 B1
Speedy Place 5 A1
Speldhurst Road 90 B1
Spelman Street 91 B2
Spence Close 111 B2
Spencer Mews 42 B1
135 B1
Spencer Park 139 B2
Spencer Place 80 A2
Spencer Rise 58 B2
Spencer Road 54 A1
139 B2
Spencer Street 6 B2
Spencer Walk 56 B1
136 A1
Spenser Grove 64 B2
Spenser Road 127 B1
Spenser Street 22 A1
Spensley Walk 64 A1
Spert Street 98 B1
Spicer Close 121 B1
Spindrift Avenue 102 B2
103 B1
Spital Square 8 B2
91 B1
Spital Street 91 B2
Spital Yard 91 B1
Spode Walk 66 A1
Sportsman Mews 88 B2
Sprimont Place 46 A1
Spring Gardens 23 A2
24 B1
Spring Mews 1 A2
Spring Park Drive 63 A2

Street Index

Spring Passage 136 A1
Spring Place 71 A2
Spring Street 31 B1
Springall Street 124 A1
Springdale Mews 75 A2
Springdale Road 64 B1
75 A2
Springfield Lane 68 A1
Springfield Road 68 A1
Springfield Walk 68 A1
Springhill Close 128 A2
Springtide Close 123 A2
Springvale Terrace 33 B2
Springwood Close 94 B2
Spur Road 9 B2
104 A2
Spurgeon Street 106 B2
Spurling Road 129 A2
Spurstowe Road 87 B1
Spurstowe Terrace 87 B1
The Square 41 B1
Square Rigger Row 139 A1
Squires Mount 56 B2
Squirries Street 91 A2
SR East Cross Route 94 A2
St. Agnes Close 89 B2
St. Agnes Place 112 B1
St. Alban's Place 80 B2
St. Albans Grove 35 B2
St. Albans Road 58 A2
59 A1
St. Albans Street 23 A2
St. Albans Terrace 41 B2
St. Alphage Gardens 7 B2
St. Alphonsus Road 143 B1
St. Andrew Street 14 A2
15 B1
St. Andrew's Court 146 B1
St. Andrew's Hill 15 B2
St. Andrews Close 116 B1
St. Andrews Road 42 A1
St. Andrews Square 28 A1
St. Ann's Crescent 138 B2
146 A1
St. Ann's Gardens 71 A1
St. Ann's Hill 138 B2
146 A1
St. Ann's Park Road 146 A1
St. Ann's Road 55 A2/B2
86 A1
St. Ann's Street 22 A2/B2
St. Ann's Terrace 69 B1
St. Anne Street 100 A1
St. Anne's Close 58 A2
St. Anne's Row 100 A1
St. Annes Passage 100 A1
St. Anns Road 28 B1
33 A2
St. Anns Villas 33 A2
St. Anselm's Place 2 B1
St. Anthonys Close 95 B2
St. Augustines Road 72 B2
73 B1
St. Barnabas Close 129 B1
St. Barnabas Street 19 B2
St. Barnabas Terrace 90 A2
St. Barnabas Villas 134 B2
St. Benedict's Close 152 A2
St. Benet's Place 17 B2
St. Botolph Street 18 A2
St. Bride Street 15 B1
St. Catherine's Mews 37 B2
St. Chad's Place 5 A2
St. Chad's Street 5 A1
St. Charles Place 28 A2
St. Charles Square 25 A1/B1
28 A1/A2
St. Clare Street 18 B2
St. Clement's Lane 14 B1
St. Clements Street 80 A1
St. Clements Yard 129 B2
St. Crispins Close 57 A1
St. Cross Street 14 A2
15 A1
St. Cyprian's Street 151 B1
St. Davids Close 116 B1
St. Davids Square 103 B1
St. Dionis Road 48 B2
49 A1
St. Donatts Road 126 B1
St. Dunstan's Hill 18 B1
St. Dunstan's Lane 18 B1
St. Dunstans Road 41 B1/B2
St. Edmunds Close 69 B2
St. Edmunds Square 47 A1
St. Edmunds Terrace 69 B1/B2
St. Elmos Road 110 A2
St. Ermin's Hill 22 A1
St. Ervans Road 25 B1/B2
St. Francis Road 129 A1
St. Gabriel's Close 99 B2
St. George Street 2 B2
10 A1
St. George's Close 133 B2
St. George's Drive 20 B1/B2
St. George's Square 21 B1
St. George's Square Mews 21 B1/B2
St. Georges Avenue 59 B2
60 B1
St. Georges Circus 105 B1
St. Georges Court 15 B2
St. Georges Fields 31 B2
St. Georges Mews 70 A1
104 B2
118 A1
St. Georges Road 104 B2
105 B1
St. Georges Square 98 B1
118 A1
St. Georges Terrace 70 A1
St. Georges Way 114 B1/B2
St. Gerards Close 149 A1
St. Giles High Street 12 A2
St. Giles Passage 12 A2
St. Giles Road 122 A1/B2
St. Helena Road 116 A2
117 A1
St. Helena Street 6 A1
St. Helens Gardens 28 A1
St. Helens Place 17 A2
St. Hilda's Road 40 B2
St. James Grove 141 A1
St. James Mews 103 A2
St. James Street 41 B1
St. James's 126 A1
St. James's Avenue 93 A1
St. James's Close 151 A1
St. James's Court 20 A2
22 A1
St. James's Crescent 145 B2
St. James's Drive 147 B1
151 A1
St. James's Gardens 28 B1
St. James's Market 23 A2
St. James's Passage 18 A2
St. James's Place 23 A1
St. James's Road 108 A2/B2
115 A2/B2
St. James's Square 23 A2
St. James's Street 9 A2
St. James's Terrace 69 B2
St. James's Terrace Mews 69 B2
St. James's Walk 6 B2
St. John Street 6 A2/B2
15 A2
St. John's Avenue 136 B1/B2
St. John's Church Road 87 B2
St. John's Close 42 B2
St. John's Crescent 145 B2
St. John's Gardens 28 B2
St. John's Hill 139 A2/B1/B2
140 A1
St. John's Hill Grove 139 A2/B2
St. John's Lane 15 A2
St. John's Mews 29 B2
St. John's Place 15 A2
St. John's Road 140 A1
St. John's Square 6 B2
15 A2
St. John's Villas 35 B2
St. John's Wood Court 76 A1
St. John's Wood High Street 69 B1
St. John's Wood Park 66 B1
69 A1
St. John's Wood Road 76 A1/A2
St. John's Wood Terrace 69 B1
St. Johns Grove 60 A1
St. Johns Villas 60 A1
St. Johns Way 52 B2
53 B1
60 A1/A2
St. Josephs Close 25 B1
St. Josephs Street 133 B1
St. Jude Street 82 A2
St. Jude's Road 92 A2
St. Katharine's Way 95 B1
St. Katharines Precinct 77 A1
St. Lawrence Street 101 A2
St. Lawrence Terrace 25 B1
St. Lawrence Way 135 B2
145 A2
St. Leonard's Terrace 46 B1/B2
St. Leonards Road 101 A2
St. Leonards Square 71 A1
St. Loo Avenue 45 B2
St. Luke's Avenue 143 B2
St. Luke's Close 7 A2
St. Luke's Street 45 A2
St. Lukes Mews 29 A1
St. Lukes Road 29 A1/A2
St. Margaret's Court 106 A1
St. Margaret's Street 22 A2
St. Margarets Avenue 55 A2
St. Margarets Lane 35 B2
St. Mark Street 95 A1

St. Mark's Grove 43 B2
St. Marks Close 28 A2
49 A1
120 B1
St. Marks Crescent 70
St. Marks Place 28 A2
St. Marks Rise 86 B1/B2
St. Marks Road 28 A1/A2
St. Marks Square 70 B1
St. Martin's Lane 12 B2
24 A1
St. Martin's Place 24 A1
St. Martin's Road 145 A1
St. Martin's Street 23 A2
St. Martin's-le-Grand 15 B2
16 A1
St. Martins Close 78 A1
St. Mary Abbots Place 34 B2
St. Mary Abbots Terrace 34 B2
St. Mary at Hill 18 B1
St. Mary Axe 18 A1
St. Mary's Gardens 112 A1
St. Mary's Gate 35 B2
St. Mary's Grove 81 A1
St. Mary's Mews 65 B1
St. Mary's Place 35 B2
St. Mary's Road 124 B2
St. Mary's Walk 112 A1
St. Marychurch Street 109 A2
110 A1
St. Marys Mansions 31 A2
St. Marys Path 80 B2
St. Marys Square 31 A2
St. Marys Terrace 31 A2
St. Matthew Street 22 B1
St. Matthew's Road 150 A2
St. Matthew's Row 91 A2
St. Maur Road 48 A2
St. Michael's Mews 19 B2
St. Michael's Road 145 A1
St. Michaels Gardens 25 B1
St. Michaels Street 1 A1
31 B2
St. Mildred's Court 17 A1
St. Nicholas Glebe 152 A2
St. Olaf's Road 48 A1
St. Olav's Square 110 B1
St. Oswald's Place 131 B1
St. Oswulf Street 21 A2
St. Pancras Way 71 B2
72 B1
78 A2
St. Paul Street 81
83 A1/A2
St. Paul's Avenue 110 A2
St. Paul's Churchyard 15 B2
St. Paul's Crescent 72 B2
79 A1
St. Paul's Place 82 A1
St. Paul's Road 75 B1/B2
80 A2
82 A1
St. Paul's Terrace 112 B2
St. Pauls Way 98 A2
99 A2/B1
St. Peter's Avenue 92 A1
St. Peter's Close 91 A2
92 A1
St. Peter's Grove 39 B2
St. Peter's Place 26 B2
St. Peter's Road 39 B2
St. Peter's Square 39 B1/B2
92 A1
St. Peter's Villas 39 B2
St. Peter's Way 82 B2
St. Peters Mews 55 A2
St. Peters Street 80 B2
83 A1/B1
St. Peters Terrace 48 A1
St. Petersburgh Mews 30 B1
St. Petersburgh Place 29 B2
St. Philip Square 142 A1
St. Philip Street 142 A1
St. Philip's Road 86 B2
St. Philip's Way 81
St. Rule Street 142 A2
St. Saviour's Road 150 A1
St. Silas Place 71 A1
St. Stephen's Road 94 A1/B1
St. Stephens Avenue 32 B1
St. Stephens Close 69 B2
St. Stephens Crescent 30 A1
St. Stephens Gardens 29 A2
30 A1
137 B1
St. Stephens Mews 30 A1
St. Stephens Terrace 135 B1
St. Swithin's Lane 17 B1
St. Thomas Street 106 A2
107 A1
St. Thomas's Gardens 71 A1
St. Thomas's Place 89 A2
St. Thomas's Road 62 B2
St. Thomas's Square 89 A2
St. Thomas's Way 42 B2
St. Vincent Street 2 A1
Stable Yard 23 B1
145 A1
Stable Yard Road 23 B1
Stables Way 131 B2
Stacey Street 12 A2
74 A1
Stackhouse Street 37 A2
Stadium Street 44 B1/B2
Staff Street 84 B1
Stafford Close 26 A2
Stafford Place 9 B2
Stafford Road 26 A2
94 B1
Stafford Street 9 A2
Stafford Terrace 35 A1
Staffordshire Street 123 A2
Stag Place 9 B2
Stainer Street 106 A2
Staining Lane 16 A1
Stainsbury Street 93 A1
Stainsby Road 99 B1
Stalbridge Street 76 B1
Stalham Street 109 A1
Stamford Brook Avenue 39 A1/A2
Stamford Brook Gardens 39 A2
Stamford Brook Road 39 A1/A2
Stamford Court 39 A2
Stamford Hill 85 A1
86 A1
Stamford Road 82 A2/B2
Stamford Street 104 A1/A2
105 A1
Stamp Place 91 A2
Stanbury Road 124 A1/B1
Standard Place 84
Standish Road 39 B2
Stane Grove 143 A2
Stanfield Road 94 B1
Stanford Place 114 A1
Stanford Road 35 B2
Stanford Street 21 A1
Stanhope Close 110 A2
Stanhope Gardens 36 B1/B2
52 A1
55 B2
Stanhope Gate 9 A1
Stanhope Mews East 36 B1
Stanhope Mews South 44 A1
Stanhope Mews West 36 B1
Stanhope Place 31 B2
Stanhope Road 52 A2/B2
Stanhope Row 9 A1
Stanhope Street 77 B1/B2
Stanhope Terrace 30 B2
31 B1
Stanier Close 42 A2
Stanlake Mews 32 B2
Stanlake Road 32 A2/B2
Stanlake Villas 32 B2
Stanley Close 134 A2
Stanley Crescent 29 B1
Stanley Gardens 29 B1
152 B2
Stanley Gardens Mews 29 B1
Stanley Grove 141 A2
142 A1
Stanley Road 152 B2
Stanley Street 126 A2
Stanley Terrace 61 B1
Stanmer Street 132 B2
Stanmore Street 79 B2
Stannard Mews 86 B2
Stannard Road 86 B2
Stannary Street 112 B1
Stansfield Road 144 B2
Stanswood Gardens 122 A2
Stanway Street 84 A2
Stanwick Road 34 B2
Stanworth Street 107 A2
Staple Street 106 B2
Staples Close 111 A2
Stapleton Hall Road 53 B2
54 B1/B2
Stapleton Road 151 A1
Star Place 95 B1
Star Road 42 A1/A2
Star Street 1 A1
31 B2
Star Yard 14 B2
Starboard Way 102 A2
Starcross Street 77 B2
Statham Grove 63 B2
Station Approach 48 B2
85 A1
104 A1/A2/B1
Station Avenue 127 A2
Station Passage 124 A1
Station Path 89 A2
Station Place 62 B2
Station Road 59 B1
Station Terrace 121 A2

Street Index

Staunton Street 118 B2
Stave Yard Road 110 A2
Staveley Close 73 A2
90 A1
124 A1
Stavordale Road 74 A2
Stayner's Road 92 B2
Stead Street 113 A1/A2
Stean Street 88 A1
Stebondale Street 103 B2
Stedham Place 4 B1
Steedman Street 112 A2
Steel's Lane 97 B1
Steeles Mews North 70 A2
Steeles Mews South 70 A2
Steeles Road 70 A1/A2
Steeple Close 48 B1
Steers Way 111 A2
Stella Road 152 B2
Stellman Close 86 A2
Stephan Close 89 B1
Stephen Mews 3 B2
Stephen Place 142 A2
Stephen Street 3 B2
Stephendale Road 49 B2
50 A1/B1
Stephenson Way 77 B2
Stepney Causeway 97 B2
Stepney Green 97 A2
Stepney High Street 97 A2
Stepney Way 96 A2
97 A1/A2
Sterling Gardens 125 A2
Sterling Street 37 A1
Sterndale Road 33 B1/B2
Sterne Street 33 B1/B2
Sternhall Lane 123 B2
Sterry Street 106 B2
Steve Biko Road 62 B1
74 A2
Stevedore Street 96 B1
Stevenage Road 47 A1/B1/B2
Stevens Avenue 90 A1
Stevens Street 107 A2
Stevenson Crescent 115 A2
Stew Lane 16 B2
Steward Street 18 A1
Stewart Street 101 B2
103 A2
Stewart's Grove 45 A2
Stewart's Road 133 A1/A2/B2
Stillington Street 20 A2
21 A1
Stirling Road 143 A2
Stock Orchard Crescent 74 A1/B1
Stock Orchard Street 74 B1
Stockholm Road 116 B2
Stockholm Way 95 B2
Stockhurst Close 136 A1
Stocks Place 100 A1
Stockwell Avenue 144 B2
Stockwell Gardens 135 B1
145 A1
Stockwell Green 144 A2
Stockwell Lane 145 A1
Stockwell Mews 144 A2
Stockwell Park Crescent 135 B1
145 A1
Stockwell Park Road 135 B1
145 A1/B1
Stockwell Park Walk 145 B1
Stockwell Road 144 A2/B2
145 B1
Stockwell Street 120 A2
Stockwell Terrace 135 B1
Stoke Newington Church Street 63 B2
64 A1/A2
Stoke Newington Common 85 B1/B2
Stoke Newington High Street 85 A1/B1
86 A1
Stoke Newington Road 86 A1
Stokenchurch Street 49 A2
Stone Buildings 14 A2
Stone Close 142 A2
Stone Hall Gardens 35 B2
Stone Hall Place 35 B2
Stonecutter Street 15 B1
Stonefield Street 80 B1
Stoneleigh Mews 94 B1
Stoneleigh Place 28 B1
Stoneleigh Street 28 B1
Stonells Road 140 B2
Stonenest Street 61 A2
Stones End Street 106 B1
Stoney Lane 18 A2
Stoney Street 106 A1
Stoneyard Lane 100 A2
Stonhouse Street 143 B1
Stonor Road 34 B2
Stopes Street 123 A1
Stopford Road 112 B2
Store Street 4 B1
Storers Quay 103 B2
Storey's Gate 22 A2
Stories Mews 122 B1
Stories Road 129 A1
Storks Road 108 A2
Stormont Road 51 A1
141 B1/B2
Story Street 79 A2
Stothard Street 92 B2
Stott Close 146 A2
Stoughton Close 131 B1
Stourcliffe Street 1 A1
Stowage 119 A1/A2
Stowe Road 32 B1
Stradbroke Road 75 A2
Stradella Road 128 B1
Strafford Street 102 A1
Strahan Road 93 B2
Straightsmouth 120 A1/A2
Straker's Road 130 A2
Strand 14 B1/B2
24 A1/A2
Strangways Terrace 34 B2
Stranraer Way 79 A2
Strasburg Road 133 B1
141 A2
Stratford Avenue 35 B2
Stratford Grove 136 A1
Stratford Place 2 B1
Stratford Road 35 B1/B2
Stratford Villas 72 B1
Strath Terrace 139 A2
Strathblaine Road 139 A2/B2
Strathearn Place 31 B1/B2
Strathleven Road 150 A1
Strathmore Gardens 29 B2
Strathnairn Street 108 B2
Strathray Gardens 67 B1
Stratton Street 9 A2
Strattondale Street 103 A1
Streatham Place 150 B1
Streatham Street 4 B1
Streathbourne Road 151 A2
Streatley Place 56 B2
Street Market 91 A2
92 B2
113 A2/B2
134 A2
Strickland Row 146 A1/A2
Strode Road 47 A2
Stroud Green Road 53 B2
62 A1/B1/B2
Strouts Place 91 A1
Strutton Ground 22 A1/B1
Strype Street 18 A1
Stuart Road 26 A2
Stubbs Drive 115 A2
116 A1
Stucley Place 71 B1
Studd Street 80 B2
Studdridge Street 49 A2/B1/B2
Studholme Street 124 A1
Studio Place 19 A1
Studland Street 40 B2
Studley Road 134 B2
Stukeley Street 13 A2
Sturdy Road 123 B2
Sturge Street 105 B2
Sturgeon Road 112 B2
Sturmer Way 74 B1
Sturry Street 99 B2
Sturt Street 83 B2
Stuttfield Street 95 A2
Styles Gardens 127 A1
Sudbourne Road 150 A1/A2
Sudbrooke Road 147 A2
Sudeley Street 83 B1
Sudlow Road 138 B1
Sudrey Street 106 A1
Suffolk Lane 17 B1
Suffolk Place 23 A2
Suffolk Road 38 B1
Suffolk Street 23 A2
Sugden Road 141 B1
Sulgrave Gardens 33 B1
Sulgrave Road 33 B1
Sulina Road 150 B1
Sulivan Road 49 B1/B2
Sullivan Close 139 A2
Sullivan Road 112 A1
Sultan Street 121 A2
Sumatra Road 65 A2
Sumburgh Road 147 A2
Summercourt Road 97 A1
Summerhouse Road 64 A2
Summerley Street 146 B1
Summers Street 5 B2
Summerskill Close 130 A2
Sumner Avenue 123 A1
Sumner Place 45 A1
Sumner Place Mews 45 A1
Sumner Road 114 B2
123 A1

Sumner Street 105 A2
Sumpter Close 66 B2
Sun Court 17 A2
Sun Passage 108 A1
Sun Road 42 A2
Sun Street 8 B1/B2
Sun Walk 95 B1
Sunbury Lane 132 A1
Sunderland Terrace 30 A1
Sundra Walk 97 A2
Sunlight Square 92 B2
Sunningdale Close 115 A2
Sunnyside Road 53 B1
Sunray Avenue 128 A2/B2
Sunset Road 128 A1
Surma Close 91 B2
Surr Street 73 B2
Surrendale Place 26 B2
Surrey Canal Road 116 B2
117 B1/B2
Surrey Gardens 55 B2
Surrey Grove 114 A1
Surrey Lane 132 A1
Surrey Quays Road 110 B1/B2
111 B1
Surrey Row 105 A1
Surrey Square 114 A1
Surrey Street 14 B2
Surrey Terrace 114 A1
Surrey Water Road 110 A2
Susannah Street 99 B2
Sussex Close 61 A1
Sussex Gardens 1 A1
31 B1/B2
55 B2
Sussex Mews East 31 B1
Sussex Mews West 31 B1
Sussex Place 31 B1
41 B1
76 B2
Sussex Square 31 B1
Sussex Street 20 B2
Sussex Way 60 A2
61 A1/B1/B2
Sutherland Avenue 26 B2
27 B1/B2
Sutherland Place 29 A2
Sutherland Road 38 B1
Sutherland Row 20 B1
Sutherland Square 113 B1
Sutherland Street 20 B1/B2
Sutherland Walk 113 B1
Sutterton Street 79 A2
Sutton Lane 6 B2
Sutton Place 87 B2
Sutton Row 12 A1/A2
Sutton Square 87 B2
Sutton Street 97 A1/B1
Sutton's Way 7 B2
Swaby Road 146 B1
Swaffield Road 146 A1
Swain Street 76 A2
Swains Lane 51 B1
58 A2
Swains Road 152 B1
Swallow Place 2 B2
Swallow Street 10 B1
Swan Lane 17 B2
Swan Mead 107 B1
Swan Road 110 A1/B1
Swan Street 106 B1
Swan Walk 45 B2
46 B1
Swan Yard 80 A2
Swanage Road 146 A1
Swandon Way 138 A2
Swanfield Street 91 A1
Swanscombe Road 33 A2
38 A1/A2
Swaton Road 99 A2
Sweden Gate 111 B2
118 A1
Swedenborg Gardens 96 A1
Sweeney Crescent 107 A2
Swift Street 48 A1
Swinbrook Road 25 B1
Swindon Street 32 A2
Swinford Gardens 145 B2
Swinton Place 5 A2
Swinton Street 5 A2
Swiss Terrace 66 B1
Sybil Mews 55 B1
Sybil Phoenix Close 117 B2
Sycamore Avenue 94 A2
Sycamore Gardens 40 A2
Sycamore Mews 142 B2
Sycamore Street 7 B1
Sydner Mews 86 A2
Sydner Road 86 A2
Sydney Close 45 A1
Sydney Mews 45 A1/A2
Sydney Place 45 A2
Sydney Street 45 A2/B2
Sylvan Grove 116 B1
Sylvester Road 89 A2
Symes Mews 78 A1
Symington Mews 90 A2
Syminster Mews 84
Symons Street 46 A2

T

Tabard Street 106 A1/B1/B2
Tabernacle Street 8 A1
Tableer Avenue 143 B1
149 A1
Tabley Road 73 A2
Tabor Road 40 A2
Tachbrook Mews 20 A2
Tachbrook Street 20 A2/B2
21 B1
Tadema Road 44 B1
Tadmor Street 33 A1
Taeping Street 102 B2
Tailworth Street 91 B2
Takhar Mews 132 B2
Talacre Road 71 A2
Talbot Court 17 B2
Talbot Road 29 A1/A2
30 A1
51 A2
129 A1
Talbot Square 31 B1
Talbot Yard 106 A1
Talfourd Place 123 A1
Talfourd Road 122 B2
Talgarth Road 34 B1
41 B1/B2
Tallis Street 15 B1
Talma Road 127 B1
Tamar Close 94 A2
Tamworth Street 43 B1
Tancred Road 55 B1
Tankerton Street 5 A1
Tanner Street 107 A1/A2
Tanners Hill 119 B1/B2
126 B2
Tanners Mews 126 B2
Tannington Terrace 62 B2
Tansley Close 73 B1
Tanswell Street 104 A2
Tantallon Road 147 B2
Tanza Road 57 A2
Taplow Street 83 B2
Tapp Street 92 B1
Tara Mews 53 A1/A2
Tarbert Road 129 B1
Tariff Crescent 118 A1
Tarling Street 96 A2
Tarn Street 106 B1
Tarragon Close 125 A2
Tarver Road 112 A2
Tarves Way 120 A1
Tasker Road 57 B1
Tasman Road 144 A1/B1
Tasso Road 42 B1
Tatham Place 68 B2
Tatton Crescent 86 A1
Tatum Street 113 A2
114 A1
Tauheed Close 63 B1
Taunton Mews 76 B2
Taunton Place 76 B2
Tavern Lane 145 A2
Taverner Square 75 A1
Taverners Close 28 B1
Tavistock Close 64 B2
82 A2
Tavistock Crescent 29 A1/A2
Tavistock Place 4 A2
5 A1
Tavistock Road 29 A1/A2
Tavistock Square 4 A2
Tavistock Street 14 B1
24 A2
Tavistock Terrace 60 B1
Taviton Street 4 A2
Tawny Way 111 B1
117 A1
Taybridge Road 141 B2
Taylor Close 118 B2
Tayport Close 79 A2
Teak Close 111 A2
Teale Street 92 A2
Tedworth Gardens 46 B1
Tedworth Square 46 B1
Teesdale Close 92 A1
Teesdale Street 92 A1
Teignmouth Close 143 B1
Telegraph Place 102 B2
Telegraph Street 17 A1
Telephone Place 42 A2
Telferscot Road 149 B2
Telford Road 25 A1/B1
Telford Terrace 20 B2
Tell Grove 129 A2
Temeraire Street 110 B1

Street Index

Temperley Road 147 A2
148 A1
Templar Street 121 B1
Temple Avenue 15 B1
Temple Lane 15 B1
Temple Place 14 B1/B2
Temple Street 92 A2
Temple West Mews 105 B1
Temple Yard 92 A2
Templecombe Road 89 B2
Templeton Place 35 B1
43 A1
Templeton Road 55 B2
Templewood Avenue 56 A1
Templewood Gardens 56 A1
Tench Street 96 B1
Tenda Road 108 B2
Tenison Way 104 A1
Tenniel Close 30 B1
Tennis Street 106 A2
Tennyson Street 142 A1
Tent Street 92 B1
Tenter Ground 18 A2
Tenterden Street 2 B2
Teredo Street 111 B1
Terminus Place 20 A1/A2
The Terrace 65 B1
Terrace Road 90 A1/B1
Terrapin Road 151 A2
Tetcott Road 44 B1
Teversham Lane 134 B2
Thackeray Road 142 A1
Thackeray Street 35 A2
Thame Road 110 A2
Thames Avenue 50 A2
Thames Circle 102 B1
Thames Crescent 38 B1
Thames Place 136 A1
Thames Street 120 A1/A2
Thane Villas 62 B1
Thane Works 62 B1
Thanet Street 5 A1
Thavies Inn 15 B1
Thaxton Road 42 A2
Thayer Street 2 A1/B1
Theatre Street 140 A2
Theberton Street 80 B1/B2
Theed Street 104 A2
Theobald Street 106 B2
Theobald's Road 5 B1/B2
Theresa Road 39 B2
Thermopylae Gate 103 B1
Thessaly Road 133 A2/B2
134 B1
Third Avenue 25 A2
Thirleby Road 20 A2
Thirsk Road 141 B1
152 B2
Thistlewaite Road 87 A2
Thistlewood Close 61 A2
Thomas Baines Road 139 A2
Thomas Darby Court 28 A1
Thomas Doyle Street 105 B1
Thomas More Street 95 B1/B2
Thomas Place 35 B2
Thomas Road 99 B1
Thompsons Avenue 121 A2
Thorburn Square 108 B1
Thoresby Street 83 B2
Thornbury Road 149 A2
150 B1
Thornbury Square 52 B1
Thorncliffe Road 149 A2
Thorncombe Road 129 B1/B2
Thorncroft Street 134 B1/B2
Thorndike Close 44 B1
Thorndike Road 81 A2
Thorndike Street 21 A1
Thorne Road 134 B2
Thorney Crescent 132 A1
Thorney Street 21 A2
Thornfield Road 32 B1/B2
Thorngate Road 26 B2
Thornham Street 120 A1
Thornhaugh Street 4 A2/B2
Thornhill Bridge Wharf 79 B2
Thornhill Crescent 79 A2
Thornhill Grove 80 A1
Thornhill Road 80 A1/B1
Thornhill Square 79 A2
Thornton Avenue 38 A2
Thornton Gardens 149 B2
Thornton Place 1 A2
Thornton Road 149 B2
Thornton Street 145 A2
Thornville Street 126 B2
Thorparch Road 134 B1
Thorpe Close 25 B1
Thorpedale Road 53 B2
61 A1/A2
Thoydon Road 93 A2
Thrale Street 106 A1
Thrawl Street 91 B1
Threadneedle Street 17 A1/A2
Three Colt Street 100 A1
Three Colts Lane 92 B2
Three Cups Yard 14 A2
Three Kings Yard 2 B1
Three Oak Lane 107 A2
Threshers Place 28 B1
Throgmorton Avenue 8 B1
17 A2
Thurland Road 108 A1
Thurleigh Avenue 147 A2
Thurleigh Road 147 A1/A2
Thurloe Close 37 B1
Thurloe Place 36 B2
37 B1
Thurloe Place Mews 36 B2
Thurloe Square 37 B1
Thurloe Street 36 B2
Thurlow Road 67 A1/A2
Thurlow Street 113 A2
114 B1
Thurlow Terrace 57 B1
Thurtle Road 88 B1
Tibberton Square 81 B1
Tiber Close 94 A2
Tiber Gardens 79 B1
Tidey Street 99 A2
Tidworth Road 99 A2
Tiger Way 87 A1
Tilbury Close 114 B2
Tile Kiln Lane 52 B1
Tile Yard 100 A1
Tilehurst Road 146 B1/B2
Tileyard Road 79 A1
Tilia Road 87 B2
Tiller Road 102 A1/A2
Tillett Square 111 B2
Tillett Way 91 A2
Tillings Close 121 B2
Tillman Street 96 A2
Tilney Court 7 A2
Tilney Street 9 A1
Tilson Close 114 B1
Tilson Gardens 150 B1
Tilton Street 42 B1
Timber Mill Way 143 A1
Timber Pond Road 110 A2
Timber Street 7 B2
Timberland Close 123 A1
Timberland Road 96 A2
Time Square 86 B1
Timothy Close 149 A1
Tindal Street 121 A1
Tinsley Road 97 A2
Tintagel Crescent 129 A2
Tintern Close 136 B2
Tintern Street 144 B1
Tinworth Street 131 B1
Tipthorpe Road 141 B2
Tisdall Place 113 A2
Titchborne Row 31 B2
Titchfield Road 69 B2
Titchwell Road 146 B2
Tite Street 46 B1
Titmuss Street 32 B2
Tiverton Road 55 B2
Tiverton Street 105 B2
Tivoli Road 53 A1
Tobago Street 100 B1
Tobin Close 67 B1
70 A1
Toby Lane 98 A1
Token Yard 136 A2
Tokenhouse Yard 17 A1
Tollbridge Close 25 A2
Tollet Street 93 B1
Tollhouse Way 60 A1
Tollington Park 61 A2
62 B1
Tollington Place 61 A2
Tollington Road 74 A1
Tollington Way 61 B1/B2
Tolmers Square 77 B2
Tolpuddle Street 80 B1
Tolsford Road 87 B1
Tomlins Grove 94 B2
Tomlins Terrace 98 A2
Tomlinson Close 91 A2
Tompion Street 6 B2
Tonbridge Street 5 A1
Tonsley Hill 138 A2/B2
Tonsley Place 138 A2/B2
Tonsley Road 138 B2
Tonsley Street 138 A2
Tony Cannell Mews 98 A2
Took's Court 14 B2
Tooley Street 106 A2
107 A1/A2
Tooting Bec Road 151 A1/A2/B2
Tooting Grove 152 A1
Tooting High Street 152 A1/B1
Topham Street 6 B1
Topsfield Close 53 A1
Topsham Road 151 A1/B2

Tor Gardens 35 A1
Torbay Street 71 B2
Torquay Street 30 A1
Torrens Road 150 A2
Torrens Street 80 B1
Torrey Drive 145 A2
Torriano Avenue 73 A1/B1
Torriano Cottages 72 B2
Torriano Mews 73 A1
Torrington Place 4 A1
95 B2
Torrington Square 4 A1
Tothill Street 22 A1/A2
Tottenham Court Road 4 A1/B1
Tottenham Lane 53 A2
54 A1/A2
Tottenham Mews 3 B2
Tottenham Road 82 A1/A2
Tottenham Street 3 B2
Totterdown Street 152 A1/A2
Toulmin Street 106 A1/B1
Toulon Street 121 A2
Tournay Road 42 B2
Tower Bridge 107 A2
Tower Bridge Approach 95 B1
Tower Bridge Road 107 A2/B1
Tower Close 67 A2
Tower Court 12 A2
Tower Hill 18 B2
Tower Mill Road 114 B1
Tower Royal 16 B2
Tower Street 12 A2
Town Court Path 63 A2
Town Hall Road 140 A2
Townley Road 129 B1/B2
Townley Street 113 A1
Townmead Road 49 B2
50 A2/B1/B2
Townsend Mews 146 B1
Townsend Street 113 A2
114 A1
Townsend Yard 51 B2
Townshend Road 69 B1
Toynbee Street 18 A2
Toynbee Street Market 18 A2
Tradescant Road 134 A2/B2
Trafalgar Avenue 114 A2/B2
Trafalgar Close 111 B1
Trafalgar Gardens 35 B2
97 A2
Trafalgar Square 24 A1/B1
Trafalgar Street 113 B2
Trafalgar Way 101 A1/A2
Trahorn Close 91 B2
Tranby Place 90 A2
Tranley Mews 57 A1
Tranmere Road 146 B1
Transept Street 1 A1
76 B1
Transom Close 118 A1
Transom Square 102 B2
Tranton Road 108 A2
Travers Road 62 B1
Treadgold Street 28 B1
Treadway Street 92 A2
Treaty Street 79 B2
Trebeck Street 9 A2
Trebovir Road 43 A1
Treby Street 98 A2
Trecastle Way 73 A1
Tredegar Mews 94 B1
Tredegar Road 94 B1/B2
Tredegar Square 94 B1
Tredegar Terrace 94 B1
Trederwen Road 89 B1
Trefoil Road 139 B1
Tregaron Avenue 53 B2
Tregarvon Road 141 B2
Tregothnan Road 143 A2
144 A1
Tregunter Road 43 A2/B2
44 A1
Treherne Court 151 A2
Trelawn Road 127 B1
Tremadoc Road 143 B2
Tremlett Grove 59 A2/B2
Tremlett Mews 59 B2
Trenchold Street 134 A2
Trent Road 150 A1
Tresham Crescent 76 A2/B2
Tressell Close 80 A2
Trevanion Road 34 B1
Trevelyan Road 152 A1/B1/B2
Treveris Street 105 A1
Treverton Street 25 A1
Trevithick Street 119 A1
Trevor Place 37 A2
Trevor Square 37 A2
Trevor Street 37 A2
Triangle Place 143 B1
Triangle Road 89 B1
Trident Street 111 B1
Trig Lane 16 B1
Trigon Road 135 A1
Trim Street 118 B2
Trinder Gardens 53 B2
Trinder Road 53 B2
Trinidad Street 100 A1
Trinity Church Passage 41 B1
Trinity Church Road 47 A1
Trinity Church Square 106 B1
Trinity Close 56 B1
Trinity Court 82 B2
Trinity Crescent 151 A1
Trinity Gardens 144 B1/B2
Trinity Grove 120 B2
Trinity Mews 28 A1
Trinity Road 138 A2
139 B1/B2
146 A1/A2
147 B1
151 A1
Trinity Square 18 B2
Trinity Street 106 B1/B2
Trio Place 106 B1
Troon Close 116 B1
Troon Street 97 B2
Trossachs Road 129 B1
Trothy Road 108 B2
Trott Street 132 B1
Troutbeck Road 125 B2
Trouville Road 149 A1
Troy Town 130 A1
Truman's Road 64 B2
Trump Street 16 A2
Trundle Street 106 A1
Trundleys Road 117 A1/A2/B2
Trundleys Terrace 117 A1
Truro Street 71 A1
Trussley Road 33 B1
Tryon Crescent 89 B2
Tryon Street 46 A1
Tudor Close 52 B1
67 B2
Tudor Grove 89 B2
Tudor Road 89 B2
Tudor Street 14 B2
15 B1
Tufnell Park Road 59 B1/B2
60 B1
61 B1
Tufton Street 22 A2/B2
Tulse Hill 150 A2
Tunis Road 32 A2/B2
Tunley Road 147 B2
Tunnel Avenue 103 A2
Tunnel Road 109 A2
Tunstall Road 144 B2
Turenne Close 139 B1
Turin Street 91 A2
Turk's Head Yard 15 A1
Turks Row 46 B2
Turle Road 61 A2
Turlewray Close 61 A2
Turnagain Lane 15 B1
Turnberry Close 116 B1
Turnberry Quay 103 A1
Turnchapel Mews 142 B1
Turner Close 121 A1
Turner Place 140 B1
Turner Street 96 A2
Turners Road 98 A2
Turneville Road 42 A1/A2
Turnham Green Terrace 38 A1/A2
Turnham Green Terrace Mews 38 A2
Turnmill Street 6 B1
15 A1/A2
Turnpike Close 126 A2
Turpentine Lane 20 B1/B2
Turquand Street 113 A1
Turret Grove 142 A2
Turville Street 91 A1
Twig Folly Close 93 A2
Twine Court 96 B2
Twisden Road 58 B2
Twyford Street 79 B2
Tyburn Way 1 B1
Tyers Gate 107 A1
Tyers Street 131 B1
Tyers Terrace 131 B1
Tyler Close 88 B1
Tyndale Court 102 B2
Tyndale Lane 80 A2
Tyndale Terrace 80 A2
Tyneham Road 141 A2/B2
Tynemouth Road 152 B2
Tynemouth Street 50 A1
Type Street 93 A1
Tyrawley Road 49 A2
Tyrrell Road 130 B1/B2
Tysoe Street 6 B1
Tyssen Road 85 B1
Tyssen Street 84 A2
86 B1/B2
Tytherton Road 60 B1

Street Index

U

Udall Street 20 A2
Ufford Street 104 A2
105 A1
Ufton Grove 82 B1
Ufton Road 82 B2
Uhura Square 64 B2
Ulster Place 2 A2
Ulva Road 136 B1
Ulverscroft Road 130 B1
Umberston Street 96 A1
Umfreville Road 55 B1/B2
Underhill Road 130 B1
Underhill Street 71 B1
Undershaft 18 A1
Underwood Road 91 B2
Underwood Row 83 B2
Underwood Street 83 B2
Undine Road 103 A1/B1
Undine Street 152 A2
Union Court 17 A2
Union Drive 98 A2
Union Grove 134 B1
143 A1
Union Road 143 A1/A2
Union Square 83 A1
Union Street 105 A1/A2
106 A1
Union Walk 91 A1
University Street 4 A1
Unwin Close 115 B1
Unwin Road 36 A2
Upbrook Mews 30 B2
Upcerne Road 44 B1
Upham Park Road 39 A1
Upland Mews 130 B1
Upland Road 130 B1/B2
Uplands Road 54 A2
Upnor Way 114 A1
Upper Addison Gardens 33 B2
34 A1
Upper Bank Street 100 A2/B2
Upper Belgrave Street 19 A2
Upper Berkeley Street 1 A1/A2
Upper Brockley Road 126 B2
Upper Brook Street 1 B2
Upper Cheyne Row 45 B1
Upper Clapton Road 87 A2
Upper Grosvenor Street 9 A1
Upper Ground 104 A1/A2
Upper Hampstead Walk 56 B2
Upper James Street 10 B2
Upper John Street 10 B2
Upper Mall 39 B2
40 B1
Upper Marsh 104 B1
131 A2
Upper Montagu Street 1 A2
Upper North Street 99 B2
100 A2
Upper Park Road 57 B1
Upper Phillimore Gardens 35 A1
Upper Richmond Road 136 A1/B1/B2
137 B1/B2
Upper St. Martin's Lane 12 B2
13 B1
Upper Street 80 A2/B1/B2
Upper Tachbrook Street 20 A2
Upper Terrace 56 A1/A2
Upper Thames Street 15 B2
16 B2
17 B1/B2
Upper Tollington Park 62 A1/A2/B1
Upper Tooting Park 151 A1
Upper Tooting Road 151 A1/B1
152 A1
Upper Tulse Hill 150 B1
Upper Wimpole Street 2 A2
Upper Woburn Place 4 A2
Upstall Street 121 B1
Urban Mews 55 B2
Urlwin Street 113 B1
Ursula Mews 63 A1
Ursula Street 132 A1
Urswick Road 87 B2
Usborne Mews 135 A1
Usher Road 94 A2/B2
Usk Road 139 A1
Usk Street 93 A1
Utopia Village 70
Uverdale Road 44 B1
Uxbridge Road 32 A1/B1/B2
33 B1
Uxbridge Street 29 B1/B2

V

Val McKenzie Avenue 62 B1
The Vale 44 B2
Vale Close 68 B1
Vale End 129 A2
Vale Grove 55 B2
Vale of Health 56 A2
Vale Road 55 B2
Vale Row 63 B1
Vale Royal 79 A1
Vale Terrace 55 B2
Valentia Place 127 A1
Valentine Place 104 A2
Valentine Road 90 A1/A2
Valette Street 89 A2
Vallance Road 91 A2/B2
Valmar Road 121 B2
Valnay Street 152 A2
Valonia Gardens 137 B2
Vanderbilt Road 146 B1
Vandon Street 22 A1
Vandy Street 8 B2
Vane Close 56 B1
Vane Street 21 A1
Vansittart Street 118 B1
Vanston Place 43 B1
Vant Road 152 A2
Vantage Mews 101 B2
Vantage Place 35 B1
Varcoe Road 116 B1
Varden Street 96 A1/A2
Vardens Road 139 B2
Varna Road 42 B1
48 A1
Varndell Street 77 B1/B2
Vassall Road 121 A1
135 B2
Vauban Street 108 A1
Vaughan Avenue 39 A1
Vaughan Road 128 A1
Vaughan Street 111 B2
Vaughan Way 95 B2
Vaughan Williams Close 119 B1
Vauxhall Bridge 21 B2
Vauxhall Bridge Road 20 A2
21 B2
Vauxhall Grove 134 A2
135 A1
Vauxhall Street 131 B2
Vauxhall Walk 131 B1
Vawdrey Close 92 B2
Venables Street 76 B1
Vencourt Place 39 B2
Venetia Road 55 B1
Venetian Road 121 B2
Venn Street 143 B1
Ventnor Road 125 A2
Vera Road 48 A1
Verbena Gardens 39 B1
Verdun Road 38 B2
Vere Street 2 B2
Vereker Road 42 A1
Verity Close 28 A1
Vermont Road 138 B2
Verney Road 115 A2
116 B1/B2
Verney Way 115 A2
Vernon Mews 34 B1
Vernon Place 4 B2
Vernon Rise 6 A1
Vernon Road 94 B2
Vernon Square 6 A1
Vernon Street 34 B1
Vernon Yard 29 B1
Verona Court 38 A2
Veronica Road 151 A2
Verran Road 148 B1
Verulam Street 14 A2
Vesta Road 126 B1
Vestry Mews 122 B2
Vestry Road 122 B2
Vestry Street 84 B1
Viaduct Place 92 B1
Viaduct Street 92 B1
Vicarage Crescent 132 A1/B1
Vicarage Gardens 35 A2
Vicarage Gate 35 A2
Vicarage Grove 122 A1
Vicars Close 89 B2
Vicars Road 57 B2
Viceroy Road 134 B2
Victoria Avenue 8 B2
Victoria Embankment 14 B1/B2
15 B1/B2
22 A2
24 A2/B2
Victoria Gardens 29 B1
Victoria Grove 36 A1
Victoria Grove Mews 29 B2
Victoria Mews 86 B2
142 B1
146 B1
Victoria Park Road 89 B1/B2
90 B1/B2
Victoria Park Square 92 A2
Victoria Rise 142 A1/B1
Victoria Road 36 A1/B1
53 B2
62 A1
65 B1

Victoria Square 9 B1
20 A1
Victoria Street 9 B1
20 A1/A2
22 A1/A2
Victoria Terrace 62 A1
Victoria Yard 95 A2
Victorian Grove 64 B2
Victorian Road 64 B2
Victory Place 98 B1
113 A1
Victory Way 111 A2
View Close 51 A1
View Road 51 A1/A2
Vigo Street 10 B1
Viking Close 94 B1
Villa Road 145 B2
Villa Street 113 B2
Village Way 128 B2
129 B1
Villiers Street 24 A1
Vince Street 84 B1
Vincent Close 111 A2
Vincent Square 21 A1
Vincent Street 21 A1/A2
Vincent Terrace 80 B2
83 B1
Vine Court 96 A1
Vine Hill 5 B2
Vine Lane 107 A1
Vine Street 10 B1
18 B2
Vine Street Bridge 6 B1
Vine Yard 106 A1
Vinegar Street 96 B1
Vineyard Walk 6 B1
Vining Street 127 A1
Violet Close 118 B2
Violet Hill 68 B1
Violet Road 99 A2
Violet Street 92 B2
Virgil Street 131 A2
Virginia Road 91 A1/A2
Virginia Street 95 B2
Viscount Street 7 B2
Vivian Comma Close 62 B2
Vivian Road 93 A2
Vivian Square 130 A2
Voltaire Road 143 A2/B1/B2
Vorley Road 60 A1
Voss Street 91 A2
92 B1
Vulcan Road 126 B1
Vulcan Square 102 B2
Vulcan Terrace 126 B1
Vulcan Way 74 B1
Vyner Street 92 A2

W

Wadding Street 113 A1
Wades Place 100 A2
Wadeson Street 92 A2
Wadham Gardens 69 A2
Wadham Road 136 A2
Wadhurst Road 133 A2
Wager Street 99 A1
Waghorn Street 130 A1
Wagner Street 124 A2
Waite Street 114 B2
Wakefield Mews 5 A1
Wakefield Street 5 A1
Wakeford Close 149 A1
Wakeham Street 82 A1
Wakehurst Road 140 B1/B2
Wakeling Street 97 B2
Wakley Street 7 A1
Walberswick Street 134 B2
Walbrook 17 A1
Walburgh Street 96 A1
Walcorde Avenue 113 A1
Walcot Square 112 A1
Walcott Street 21 A1
Waldemar Avenue 48 B1
Walden Street 96 A2
Waldo Close 149 A1
Waldron Mews 45 B1
Wales Close 124 A1
Waley Street 98 A1
Walford Road 64 B2
Walham Grove 43 B1
Walham Yard 43 B1
Walkers Court 86 B2
Walkers Place 136 A1
Wall Street 82 A1
Wallace Road 75 B2
Waller Road 125 B1
Waller Way 120 A1
Wallgrave Road 35 B2
Wallis Close 139 A2
Wallwood Street 99 B1
Walmer Place 1 A1
Walmer Road 28 A1/B1
Walmer Street 76 B1
Walnut Close 118 B2
Walnut Tree Walk 112 A1
131 A2
Walpole Mews 68 B2
Walpole Street 46 A1
Walsingham Place 147 A2
Walsingham Road 87 A1
Walt Whitman Close 127 A2
Walter Street 93 B1
Walter Terrace 97 A2
Walters Close 113 A1
Walterton Road 25 A2
26 A1/B1
Walton Close 134 A2
Walton Place 37 B2
Walton Street 37 B2
Walworth Place 113 B1
Walworth Road 112 A2
113 A1/B1
Wandle Road 151 A1
Wandon Road 43 B2
Wandsworth Bridge 49 B2
Wandsworth Bridge Road 49 A2/B2
Wandsworth Common West Side 139 B1
146 A1
Wandsworth High Street 138 B1/B2
Wandsworth Plain 138 B1
Wandsworth Road 131 B1
134 A2/B1
142 A1/A2/B1
143 A1
Wanless Road 127 A2
128 A1
Wanley Road 128 A2
129 A1
Wansdown Place 43 B1
Wansey Street 113 A1
Wapping Dock Street 96 B1
Wapping High Street 95 B2
96 B1/B2
Wapping Lane 96 B1
Wapping Wall 96 B2
97 B1
Warbeck Road 32 B2
Warburton Close 82 A2
Warburton Road 89 B1
Warburton Street 89 B1
Ward Road 59 B1/B2
Wardalls Grove 125 A1
Warden Road 71 A2
Wardens Grove 105 A2
Wardle Street 90 A2
Wardo Avenue 48 A1
Wardour Mews 11 A1
Wardour Street 3 B2
11 A1/B2
Warham Road 55 A1
Warham Street 121 A1
Warley Street 93 B1
Warlock Road 26 A1/B1/B2
Warlters Close 73 A2
Warlters Road 73 A2
Warltersville Road 53 B1
Warmington Road 128 B1
Warndon Street 116 A2
Warneford Street 89 B2
Warner Place 91 A2
Warner Road 121 A2/B2
Warner Street 5 B2
Warner Yard 5 B2
Warren Mews 3 A1
Warren Street 3 A1/A2
Warrender Road 59 B2
Warriner Gardens 141 A1/A2
Warrington Crescent 27 B1/B2
Warrington Gardens 27 B1
Warwick Avenue 27 B1
31 A1
Warwick Court 123 B2
Warwick Crescent 31 A1
Warwick Gardens 34 B2
35 B1
55 B2
Warwick House Street 23 A2
Warwick Lane 15 B2
Warwick Place 27 B1
Warwick Place North 20 B2
Warwick Road 34 B2
35 B1
43 A1
Warwick Row 9 B2
20 A2
Warwick Square 15 B2
20 B2
Warwick Square Mews 20 B2
Warwick Street 10 B2
Warwick Way 20 A2/B1/B2
Warwick Yard 7 B2
Water Lane 18 B1
71 B2
124 A2
125 A1

Street Index

Water Street 14 B2
Water Tower Place 80 B2
Watercress Place 82 B2
Waterfall Terrace 152 B1
Waterford Road 43 B1/B2
49 A2
Watergate 15 B2
Watergate Street 119 A1
Waterhouse Close 41 B2
67 A2
Wateridge Close 102 A1
Waterloo Bridge 14 B1
104 A1
Waterloo Close 90 A1
Waterloo Gardens 93 A1
Waterloo Place 23 A2
Waterloo Road 104 A1/A2/B2
Waterloo Terrace 80 A2
Waterlow Road 52 B1
Waterman Street 136 A1
Waterman Way 96 B1
Watermeadow Lane 50 B2
Waterside Close 94 A2
108 A2
Waterside Place 70
Waterson Street 91 A1
Waterworks Road 150 B2
Watford Close 132 A1
Watkinson Road 74 B1
Watling Court 16 B2
Watling Street 16 B1/B2
114 B1
Watney Market 96 A2
Watney Street 96 A2/B2
Watson Close 64 B1
Watson's Street 119 B1
Watsons Mews 1 A1
Watts Grove 99 A2/B2
Watts Street 96 B1
123 A1
Watts Way 36 A2
Wavel Mews 65 B1
Wavendon Avenue 38 A1
Waveney Close 95 B2
Waverley Place 62 B2
68 B2
Waverley Road 53 A1
Waverley Walk 30 A1
Waverton Road 146 B1
Waverton Street 9 A1
Wayford Street 132 B2
Wayland Avenue 86 B2
Waynflete Square 28 A1
Waynflete Street 146 B1
Weald Close 115 A2
Wear Place 92 B1
Weatherley Close 99 A1
Weaver Street 91 B2
Weavers Way 78 A2
Webb Street 107 B1
Webber Row 104 B2
Webber Street 104 A2/B2
105 B1/B2
Webbs Road 140 A1/B1/B2
Webster Road 108 A2
Wedderburn Road 67 A1/B2
Wedlake Street 25 A2
Wedmore Gardens 60 B1
Wedmore Mews 60 B2
Wedmore Street 60 B1/B2
Weedington Road 57 B2
71 A2
Weekley Square 139 A2
Weighhouse Street 2 B1
Weimar Street 136 A2
Weir Road 148 B2
149 B1
Weir's Passage 78 B1
Weiss Road 136 A1
Welbeck Street 2 A1
Welbeck Way 2 B1/B2
Welby Street 121 B1
Welham Road 152 A2
Well Court 16 B2
Well Road 56 B2
Well Street 89 B2
90 A1/B1
Well Walk 56 B2
Welland Mews 95 B2
Welland Street 120 A2
Wellclose Square 95 B2
Wellclose Street 95 B2
Weller Street 106 A1
Wellesley Avenue 40 A1
Wellesley Place 78 B1
Wellesley Road 57 B2
Wellesley Street 97 A2
Wellesley Terrace 83 B2
Wellfit Street 127 A2
Wellington Buildings 20 B1
Wellington Close 29 B2
Wellington Court 68 B2
Wellington Grove 120 B2
Wellington Mews 130 A2
Wellington Place 69 B1
76 A2
Wellington Road 68 B2
76 A2
Wellington Row 91 A2
Wellington Square 46 B1
Wellington Street 13 B2
14 B1
Wellington Way 94 B2
99 A2
Wells Mews 3 B1/B2
Wells Place 146 A1
Wells Rise 69 B2
Wells Road 33 B1
Wells Square 5 A2
Wells Street 3 B1
Wells Terrace 62 B1
Wells Way 36 A2
114 B1
122 A1
Wells Yard South 74 B1
Welmar Mews 143 B2
Welsford Street 108 B1
Welshpool Street 89 B1
Welstead Way 39 A1
Weltje Road 40 B1
Welwyn Street 92 B2
Wembury Mews 52 B1
Wembury Road 52 B1
Wendle Court 134 A2
Wendle Square 132 A1
Wendon Street 94 A2
Wenlock Road 83 B2
Wenlock Street 83 B2
84 A1
Wennington Road 93 A2
Wentworth Crescent 123 A2
Wentworth Mews 98 A2
Wentworth Street 18 A2
91 B1
Wentworth Street (Pettycoat Lane) Market 18 A2
Werrington Street 78 B1
Werter Road 136 A1
Wesley Close 62 B1
Wesley Street 2 A1
Wesleyan Place 58 B1
Wessex Street 92 B2
West Arbour Street 97 A2
The (West Carriage Drive) Ring 31 B1
37 A1
West Central Street 4 B1
West Cottages 65 A2
West Cromwell Road 34 B2
35 B1
West Cross Route 33 A2/B2
West Eaton Place 19 B2
West Eaton Place Mews 19 B2
West End Lane 65 A2/B1/B2
66 A1
West Garden Place 31 B2
West Gardens 96 B2
West Green Road 55 B2
West Grove 120 B2
West Halkin Street 19 A1
West Hampstead Mews 65 B2
West Harding Street 14 B2
West Heath Road 56 A2
West Hill 137 B1/B2
138 B1
West Hill Court 58 A1
West Hill Road 137 B1
West India Avenue 100 B1
West India Dock Road 100 A1/A2
West Lane 109 A1
West Mall 29 B2
West Mews 20 B2
West Parkside 103 A2
West Pier 96 B1
West Poultry Avenue 15 A2
West Road 46 B1
143 B2
149 A2
West Smithfield 15 A2
West Square 104 B2
105 B1
West Street 12 A2/B2
92 A2
West Tenter Street 95 B1
West Warwick Place 20 B2
Westacott Close 53 B1
Westbourne Bridge 30 A2
31 A1
Westbourne Crescent 30 B2
Westbourne Crescent Mews 30 B2
Westbourne Gardens 30 A1
Westbourne Grove 29 B1/B2
30 B1
Westbourne Grove Mews 29 B2
Westbourne Grove Terrace 30 B1

Westbourne Park Road 29 A1/A2
30 A1
Westbourne Park Villas 30 A1
Westbourne Road 74 B1
80 A1
Westbourne Street 31 B1
Westbourne Terrace 31 A1/B1
Westbourne Terrace Mews 30 B2
Westbourne Terrace Road 27 B1
31 A1
Westbridge Road 132 A1
Westbury Street 142 A2
Westcott Road 112 B2
Westcroft Square 39 B2
Westdean Close 138 B2
Western Lane 147 A2
Western Mews 25 B2
Western Place 110 A1
Western Road 145 B2
Western Terrace 39 B1
Westferry Circus 100 B1
Westferry Road 100 A1/B1
102 A1/B1/B2
103 B1
Westfield Close 44 B1
Westfield Way 93 B2
Westgate Street 89 B1
Westgate Terrace 43 A2
Westgrove Lane 120 B2
Westland Place 83 B2
Westlands Terrace 148 A2
Westminster Bridge 22 A2
Westminster Bridge Road 104 B1/B2
Westminster Gardens 21 A2
Westmoreland Place 20 B1/B2
Westmoreland Road 113 B1/B2
Westmoreland Street 2 A2
Westmoreland Terrace 20 B1/B2
Weston Park 53 A2
54 A1/A2
Weston Rise 5 A2
Weston Street 106 A2/B2
Weston Walk 89 B2
Westover Road 146 A1
Westport Street 97 B2
Westway 28 A1
29 A1/A2
30 A1/A2
31 A1/A2
Westwick Gardens 33 B1/B2
Wetherby Gardens 43 A2
44 A1
Wetherby Mews 43 A2
Wetherby Place 44 A1
Wetherell Road 90 B2
Wexford Road 147 B1
Weybridge Court 115 A2
Weyhill Road 95 A1
Weymouth Mews 2 A2
Weymouth Street 2 A1/A2
3 A1
Weymouth Terrace 88 B1
Whadcote Street 62 B1
Wharf Place 92 A2
Wharf Road 78 B2
79 B1
83 B1/B2
Wharfdale Road 79 B1
Wharfedale Street 43 A2
Wharton Street 6 A1
Whateley Road 129 B2
130 B1
Wheat Sheaf Close 102 B2
Wheatlands Road 151 A1
Wheatley Street 2 A1
Wheatsheaf Lane 47 A1
134 A2
Wheatsheaf Terrace 48 A2
Wheatstone Road 25 B1
Wheelwright Street 79 A2
80 A1
Wheler Street 91 A1/B1
Whetstone Park 14 A1/A2
Whewell Road 61 B1
Whidborne Street 5 A1
Whiskin Street 6 B2
Whistler Mews 123 A1
Whistler Street 74 B2
Whistlers Avenue 132 A1
Whiston Road 88 B1/B2
92 A2
Whitacre Mews 112 B1
Whitby Street 91 A1
Whitcher Close 125 A2
Whitcher Place 72 B1
Whitchurch Road 28 B1
Whitcomb Street 11 B2
23 A2
White Bear Place 56 B2
White Church Lane 95 A1
White Church Passage 95 A1
White City Close 32 A2
White City Road 32 A2
33 A1
White Conduit Street 80 B1
White Hart Street 112 A1
White Hart Yard 106 A2
White Horse Lane 93 B1
97 A2
White Horse Mews 104 B2
White Horse Road 97 A2/B2
98 A1
White Horse Street 9 A2/B2
White Horse Yard 16 A2
White Kennett Street 18 A1/A2
White Lion Court 17 A2
White Lion Hill 15 B2
White Lion Street 80 B1
White Post Street 124 A2
White Swan Mews 38 B1
White's Row 18 A2
White's Square 143 B2
Whitechapel High Street 95 A1
Whitechapel Road 95 A1
96 A1/A2
Whitecross Street 7 A2/B2
Whitefriars Street 15 B1
Whitehall 24 B1
Whitehall Court 24 B1
Whitehall Gardens 24 B1
Whitehall Park 52 B1/B2
Whitehall Place 24 B1
Whitehaven Street 76 B1
Whitehead Close 146 A1
Whitehead's Grove 46 A1
Whites Grounds 107 A1
Whitethorn Street 99 A2
Whitfield Place 3 A2
Whitfield Street 3 A2/B2
Whitgift Street 131 A1
Whitman Road 93 B2
Whitmore Road 82 B2
84 A2
Whitnell Way 136 B1
Whittaker Street 19 B2
Whittingstall Road 48 A2
Whittlesey Street 104 A2
Whorlton Road 130 A2
Wick Road 90 A1/A2
Wickersley Road 141 A2
Wickford Street 92 B2
Wickham Close 97 A2
Wickham Road 126 B2
Wickham Street 131 B1
Wicklow Street 5 A2
Wickwood Street 121 B1
Widdenham Road 74 A1
Widegate Street 18 A1
Widley Road 27 A1
Wightman Road 55 A1/B1
Wigmore Place 2 B2
Wigmore Street 1 B2
2 B1/B2
Wigton Place 112 B1
Wilberforce Mews 143 B1
Wilberforce Road 62 B2
63 B1
Wilbraham Place 19 B1
Wilby Mews 29 B1
Wilcox Road 134 A2
Wilcox Road Market 134 A2
Wild Court 13 B2
Wild Goose Drive 124 A2
Wild Street 13 B2
Wild's Rents 106 B2
107 A1
Wilde Close 88 A2
Wilde Place 146 A2
Wilderness Mews 142 B1
Wilfred Street 9 B2
20 A2
Wilkes Street 91 B1
Wilkin Street 71 A2
Wilkin Street Mews 71 A2
Wilkinson Street 135 B1
Wilks Place 84 A2
Willard Street 142 A1
Willes Road 71 A2
Willesden Lane 65 B1
William Close 42 B1
William IV Street 24 A1
William Margrie Close 123 B2
William Mews 19 A1
William Morris Way 50 B2
William Road 77 B1
William Square 111 A2
William Street 19 A1
Williams Buildings 92 B2
Williams Close 53 A1
Williamson Street 73 A2
Willingham Close 72 A2
Willingham Terrace 72 A2
Willington Road 143 A2
144 B1

Street Index

Willis Street 99 B2
Willoughby Mews 141 B2
Willoughby Road 55 A2
56 B1/B2
Willoughby Street 4 B1
Willow Bank 48 B2
Willow Bridge Road 81 A1
Willow Court 8 A2
Willow Place 20 A2
Willow Road 56 B2
Willow Street 8 A1/A2
Willow Tree Close 94 A1
Willow Walk 107 B2
Willowbrook Road 114 B2
Willowdene 51 A1
Wilman Grove 89 A1
Wilmer Gardens 84 A2
Wilmer Place 64 A2
Wilmington Square 6 B1
Wilmington Street 6 A1
Wilmot Close 123 A2
Wilmot Place 71 B2
72 B1
Wilmot Road 55 A2
Wilmot Street 92 B1/B2
Wilna Road 146 A1/B1
Wilsham Street 28 B1
Wilshaw Street 119 B1
Wilson Grove 108 A2
Wilson Road 122 B1
Wilson Street 8 A2/B1/B2
Wilsons Place 98 B2
Wilsons Road 41 B2
Wilton Avenue 38 A2
Wilton Crescent 19 A1/A2
Wilton Mews 19 A2
Wilton Place 19 A1
Wilton Road 20 A2
Wilton Row 19 A1/A2
Wilton Square 82 B1
Wilton Street 19 A2
Wilton Terrace 19 A1
Wilton Villas 81
82 B1
Wilton Way 86 B2
89 A1/A2
Wiltshire Close 46 A1
Wiltshire Gardens 55 B2
Wiltshire Road 145 B1/B2
Wiltshire Row 84 A1
Wimbolt Street 91 A2
Wimbourne Street 83 A2
84 A1
Wimpole Mews 2 A2
Wimpole Street 2 A2/B2
Winans Walk 145 A1
Winchelsea Close 136 B1
Winchendon Road 48 A2
Winchester Mews 66 B2
Winchester Place 52 B1
86 B1
Winchester Road 52 B1
66 B2
Winchester Square 106 A1
Winchester Street 20 B1/B2
Winchester Walk 106 A1
Wincott Street 112 A1
Windermere Road 60 A1
Winders Road 132 B1/B2
Windlass Place 118 A1
Windmill Close 108 B2
Windmill Drive 149 A1
Windmill Hill 56 A1/A2
Windmill Mews 38 A1
Windmill Road 38 A1
139 B2
146 A1
Windmill Row 112 B1
Windmill Street 3 B2
Windmill Walk 104 A2
Windrose Close 110 A2
Windrush Close 139 A2
Windsock Close 118 A1
Windsor Gardens 26 B1
Windsor Road 61 B1/B2
Windsor Street 83 A1
Windsor Terrace 83 B2
Windsor Walk 122 B1
Windsor Way 34 B1
Windspoint Drive 115 B2
Windus Road 85 A1
Wine Close 96 B2
Winforton Street 120 B2
Winfrith Road 146 B1
Wingate Road 40 A1
Wingfield Mews 130 A1
Wingfield Street 130 A1
Wingford Road 150 B1
Wingmore Road 128 A1
Wingrave Road 47 A1
Winifred Grove 141 B1
Winkley Street 92 A2
Winnett Street 11 B1
Winscombe Street 59 A1
Winsham Grove 140 B2
Winslade Road 150 A1
Winsland Mews 31 B1
Winsland Street 31 B1
Winsley Street 3 B1
Winslow Road 41 B1
Winstanley Road 139 A2
Winston Road 64 B1
Winterton Place 44 B1
Winterwell Road 150 A1
Winthorpe Road 136 A2
Winthrop Street 91 B2
Wiseton Road 147 B1
Wisley Road 140 B2
Witan Street 92 B2
Witanhurst Lane 51 B1
Witherington Road 74 B2
Witley Road 60 A1
Wivenhoe Close 123 B2
Wixs Lane 141 B2
Woburn Place 4 A2
Woburn Square 4 A2
Woburn Walk 4 A2
Wodeham Gardens 91 B2
Wodehouse Avenue 122 A2
123 A1
Wolfe Crescent 110 B2
Wolftencroft Close 132 B1
Wollaston Close 112 A2
Wolseley Road 53 A1
Wolseley Street 108 A1
Wolsey Mews 72 A1/B1
Wolsey Road 82 A1
Wolsey Street 96 A2
Wolverley Street 92 B1
Wolverton Gardens 41 A1
Womersley Road 54 B1
Wontner Close 81 B1
Wontner Road 147 B2
Wood Close 91 A2
Wood Lane 33 A1/B1
51 A2
Wood Street 7 B2
16 A1/A2/B2
38 B1
Woodall Close 101 A1
Woodberry Down 63 A2
Woodberry Grove 55 B2
63 A2
Woodbine Terrace 90 A1
Woodbridge Close 62 B1
Woodbridge Street 6 B2
Woodbury Street 152 A1
Woodchester Square 30 A1
Woodchurch Road 65 B1
Woodcroft Mews 117 A2
Woodfall Road 62 B1
Woodfall Street 46 B1
Woodfarrs 128 A2
Woodfield Gardens 26 B1
Woodfield Place 26 B1
Woodfield Road 25 B2
26 B1
Woodger Road 33 B1
Woodhouse Close 130 A1
Woodland Crescent 110 B2
Woodland Street 86 B1
Woodland Walk 57 B1
Woodlands Park Road 55 A2
Woodlands Way 137 A1
Woodlawn Close 137 B1
Woodlawn Road 47 A1/B2
48 B1
Woodlea Road 64 A1
Woodley Close 152 B2
Woodmere Close 141 B2
Woodquest Avenue 128 B1
Woodrush Close 125 A2
Woods Mews 1 B2
Woods Place 107 B1
Woods Road 123 A2
124 A1
Woodseer Street 91 B1/B2
Woodsford Square 34 A1
Woodside Mews 129 B2
Woodsome Road 58 B1/B2
Woodstock Grove 33 B2
Woodstock Mews 2 A2
Woodstock Road 62 A1/B1
Woodstock Street 2 B1/B2
Woodstock Terrace 101 A1
Woodview Close 55 B2
Woodville Road 64 B2
82 A2
Woodwell Street 139 B1
Woodyard Close 71 A2
Wooler Street 113 B2
Woolf Mews 4 A2
Woollaston Road 55 B1
Woolmore Street 101 A2
Woolneigh Street 49 B2
Woolstaplers Way 108 B1
Wooster Place 113 A2

Wootton Street	104	A2
Worcester Mews	66	A1
Wordsworth Place	57	B1
Wordsworth Road	64	B2
	114	A2
Worfield Street	132	A1
Worgan Street	111	B1
	131	B1
World's End Passage	44	B2
Worlidge Street	41	B1
Worlingham Road	129	A2
Wormwood Street	8	B2
Wornington Road	25	A1/B1/B2
Woronzow Road	69	A1/B1
Worship Street	8	A1/A2
Worsley Grove	87	A1
Worsopp Drive	143	B1
	149	A1
Wotton Road	118	B2
Wray Crescent	61	A2
Wren Road	122	B1
Wren Street	5	B2
Wrigglesworth Street	125	A1
Wrights Lane	35	A2/B2
Wrights Road	94	A1/A2
Wrotham Road	71	B2
	78	A2
Wroughton Road	140	B2
	147	A2
Wroxton Road	124	B2
Wyatt Close	111	B2
Wyatt Road	63	B1
Wybert Street	77	B1
Wychwood End	52	B2
Wyclif Street	6	B2
Wycliffe Road	141	A2
Wycombe Place	146	A1
Wycombe Square	29	B1
Wye Street	132	B1
	139	A2
Wyfold Road	48	A1
Wyllen Close	92	B2
Wymering Road	27	A1
Wynan Road	102	B2
Wyndham Crescent	59	B1
Wyndham Mews	1	A2
Wyndham Place	1	A2
Wyndham Road	121	A1/A2
Wyndham Street	1	A2
Wyneham Road	128	B2
Wynford Road	79	B2
Wynne Road	145	A1
Wynnstay Gardens	35	B1
Wynter Street	139	A1
Wynyard Terrace	131	B2
Wynyatt Street	6	B2
Wythburn Place	1	A1
Wyvil Road	134	A2

Y

Yabsley Street	101	A2
Yalding Road	108	B1
Yardley Street	6	A1/B1
Yarmouth Place	9	B2
Yarnfield Square	123	A2
Yeate Street	82	B1
Yeldham Road	41	B1
Yelverton Road	132	B1
Yeo Street	99	A2/B2
Yeoman Street	117	A2
Yeoman's Row	37	B1/B2
Yeomans Yard	95	B1
Yerbury Road	60	B1
Yoakley Road	64	A1/A2
Yoke Close	73	B2
Yonge Park	62	B1
York Bridge	2	A1
York Buildings	24	A2
York Gate	2	A1
York Grove	124	A2
York House Place	35	A2
York Mews	72	A1
York Place	139	A1/A2
York Rise	58	B2
York Road	104	A1/B1
	132	B1
	138	A2
	139	A1/A2/B1
York Square	98	B1
York Street	1	A1/A2
York Terrace East	2	A1/A2
York Terrace West	2	A1
York Way	73	B1
	78	B2
	79	A1/B1
Yorkshire Close	64	B2
Yorkshire Grey Place	56	B1
Yorkshire Grey Yard	14	A1
Yorkshire Road	98	B1
Yorkton Street	88	B2
Young Street	35	A2
Young's Buildings	7	A2
Yukon Road	148	A2

Z

Zampa Road	116	B2
Zander Court	92	A1
Zealand Road	93	A2
Zennor Road	148	B2
Zenoria Street	129	A2
Zoar Street	105	A2
Zoffany Street	60	A2

NOT FOR TOURISTS™ Custom Mapping

We'll map your world.

Need a custom map?

FT will work with you to design a custom map that promotes your company or event. FT's team will come up with something new or put a fresh face on something you ready have. We provide custom map-making and information design services to fit our needs—whether simply showing where your organization is located on one of our isting maps, or creating a completely new visual context for the information you wish convey. NFT will help you—and your audience—make the most of the place you're in, hile you're in it.

For more information, call us at 212-965-8650 or visit
www.notfortourists.com/custommapping.aspx

Not For Tourists™
www.notfortourists.com
Miami • Boston • Chicago • London • Los Angeles • New York City • Philadelphia • San Francisco • Seattle • Washington DC

NOT FOR TOURISTS™ Custom Books

Customize your NFT.

We can put **your organization's logo or message** on NFT using custom foil stamps of your (or our) design. Not For Tourists Guidebooks make **great gifts** for employees, clients, and promotional events.

For more information, call us at 212-965-8650, or visit www.notfortourists.com/corporatesales.aspx